DATE DUE

DEMCO 38-296

DICTIONARY OF

TWENTIETH CENTURY CULTURE

French Culture
1900-1975

DICTIONARY OF

TWENTIETH CENTURY CULTURE

French Culture
1900-1975

Edited by
Catharine Savage Brosman

Associate Editors

Tom Conley   Alice Pascal Escher   Peter S. Hansen

John Hutton   James P. McNab   Roy Jay Nelson

David O'Connell

A MANLY, INC. BOOK

 Gale Research Inc.

DETROIT • WASHINGTON, D.C. • LONDON

Printed in the United States of America

Published simultaneously in the United Kingdom
by Gale Research International Limited
(An affiliated company of Gale Research Inc.)

The paper used in this publication meets the minimum requirements of American National Standard for
Information Sciences-Permanence Paper for Printed Library Materials, ANSI Z39.48-1984 ∞™

Library of Congress Catalog Card Number 94-44385
ISBN 0-8103-8482-5

The trademark I(T)P™ is used under license.

10 9 8 7 6 5 4 3 2 1

TABLE OF CONTENTS

TOPICAL TABLE OF CONTENTS vii

EDITORIAL PLAN xiii

ACKNOWLEDGMENTS...................................... xv

FOREWORD xvii

TIMELINE...xxiii

ENTRIES A-Z 3

CONTRIBUTORS.................................... 407

INDEX 411

TOPICAL TABLE OF CONTENTS

HISTORY AND POLITICS
Action Française
Agadir Crisis
Algerian war
Blum, Léon
Brasillach, Robert
Briand, Aristide
Cohn-Bendit, Daniel ("Danny the Red")
Combes, Emile
Darlan, François
The Debacle
The Dreyfus Affair
The Drôle de guerre
Dunkirk
The Epuration
The Evian Accords
The Fifth Republic
Foch, Ferdinand
The Fourth Republic
The Free Zone
French Communist Party
Gaulle, Charles de
Indochinese War
The Liberation
Maginot Line
Maison de la Culture (Popular Front)
Manifeste des 343
Marne
Maurras, Charles
May 1968 Demonstrations
The Milice
Mouvement de la Libération des Femmes (Women's Liberation Movement)
The Occupation
Pétain, Philippe
Popular Front
La Rafle du Vel' d'Hiver
Rassemblement pour la République
The Resistance
Riot of 6 February 1934
Socialist Party
Somme
Spanish Civil War

Stavisky Affair
The Third Republic
Thorez, Maurice
Union des Démocrates pour la République
Verdun
Versailles
Vichy government
Worker priests
World War I
World War II

ART AND ARCHITECTURE
Alechinsky, Pierre
Arman
Arp, Jean
Association des artistes et des écrivains révolutionnaires
Auric, Georges
Bernard, Emile
Bonnard, Pierre
Bourdelle, Emile-Antoine
Braque, Georges
Brauner, Victor
Buffet, Bernard
Centre Pompidou
Cézanne, Paul
Chagall, Marc
Claudel, Camille
Cubism
Dada
Debord, Guy
Delaunay, Robert
Delaunay-Terk, Sonia
Delville, Jean
Denis, Maurice
Derain, André
Dongen, Kees van
Dubuffet, Jean
Duchamp, Marcel
Duchamp-Villon, Raymond
Dufy, Raoul
Dunoyer de Segonzac, André
Faure, Elie

Fautrier, Jean
Fauves
Fédération internationale des artistes révolutionnaires indépendants
Fénéon, Félix
Fini, Léonor
Forain, Jean-Louis
Fougeron, André
Friesz, Othon
Garaudy, Roger
Garnier, Tony
Gauguin, Paul
Gleizes, Albert
Goncharova, Nathalia
Gris, Juan
Groupe de recherche de l'art visuel
Isou, Isidore
La Fresnaye, Roger de
Larionov, Mikhail
Laurencin, Marie
Laurens, Henri
Le Corbusier
Le Fauconnier, Henri
Léger, Fernand
Lettrism
Lhôte, André
Lipchitz, Jacques
Magritte, René
Maillol, Aristide
Manifestes du surréalisme
Marcoussis, Louis
Marquet, Albert
Masson, André
Matisse, Henri
Metzinger, Jean
Monet, Claude
Mucha, Alphonse
Nabis
Nouveau Réalisme
Oppenheim, Meret
Ozenfant, Amédée
Pelloutier, Fernand
Picabia, Francis
Picasso, Pablo

Prizes
Raysse, Martial
Redon, Odilon
Rodin, Auguste
Rouault, Georges
Rousseau, Henri
Salon d'automne
Salon des Indépendants
Section d'Or
Sérusier, Paul
Signac, Paul
Situationist International
Soutine, Chaim
Steinlen, Théophile-Alexandre
Surrealism
Surréalisme révolutionnaire
Tanguy, Yves
Taslitzky, Boris
Tinguely, Jean
Utrillo, Maurice
Valadon, Suzanne
Vallotton, Félix
Vaneigem, Raoul
Vasarely, Victor
Villon, Jacques
Vlaminck, Maurice de
Vollard, Ambroise
Vuillard, Edouard
Zadkine, Ossip

CINEMA
Allégret, Yves
Allio, René
Arletty
Astruc, Alexandre
Autant-Lara, Claude
Aznavour, Charles
Bardot, Brigitte
Bazin, André
Becker, Jacques
Belmondo, Jean-Paul
Boyer, Charles
Bresson, Robert
Buñuel, Luis
Cannes Film Festival
Carné, Marcel
Chabrol, Claude
Chevalier, Maurice
Clair, René
Clément, René
Clouzot, Henri-Georges
Cocteau, Jean
Dalio, Marcel
Darrieux, Danielle
Delannoy, Jean

Delluc, Louis
Delon, Alain
Demy, Jacques
Deneuve, Catherine
Depardieu, Gérard
Dulac, Germaine
Duras, Marguerite
Duvivier, Julien
Epstein, Jean
Fernandel
Feuillade, Louis
Feyder, Jacques
Film noir
Florey, Robert
Franju, Georges
Fresnay, Pierre
Gabin, Jean
Gance, Abel
Gaumont, Léon
Godard, Jean-Luc
Grémillion, Jean
Guy, Alice
Léaud, Jean-Pierre
Lelouch, Claude
L'Herbier, Marcel
Linder, Max
Lumière, Louis
Malle, Louis
Melville, Jean-Pierre
Metz, Christian
Modot, Gaston
Montand, Yves
Moreau, Jeanne
Morgan, Michelle
Noiret, Philippe
Nouvelle Vague
Ophuls, Marcel
Ophuls, Max
Pagnol, Marcel
Pathé, Charles
Philipe, Gérard
Piccoli, Michel
Poetic realism
Prévert, Jacques
Prizes
Renoir, Jean
Resnais, Alain
Rivette, Jacques
Robbe-Grillet, Alain
Rohmer, Eric
Rouch, Jean
Signoret, Simone
Tati, Jacques
Tradition de qualité
Truffaut, François
Vadim, Roger

Vanel, Charles
Varda, Agnès
Vigo, Jean

DANCE
Archives Internationales de la Danse
Baker, Josephine
Balanchine, George
Ballet Théâtre Contemporain
Ballets Russes
Ballets Russes de Monte Carlo
Béjart, Maurice
Charrat, Janine
Chauvire, Yvette
Cocteau, Jean
Diaghilev, Serge
Duncan, Isadora
Fokine, Michel
Fuller, Loie
Karsavina, Tamara
Levinson, André
Lifar, Serge
Maisons de la Culture
Massine, Léonide
Nijinska, Bronislava
Nijinsky, Vaslav
Nouvelle Danse
Parade
Paris Opera Ballet
Petit, Roland
Preobrajenska, Olga
Rubinstein, Ida
Le Sacre du Printemps
Zambelli, Carlotta

LITERATURE
Abellio, Raymond
Alain-Fournier
Apollinaire, Guillaume
Aragon, Louis
Arland, Marcel
Aymé, Marcel
Barbusse, Henri
Bardèche, Maurice
Barrès, Maurice
Barthes, Roland
Bataille, Georges
Bazin, Hervé
Beauvoir, Simone de
Beckett, Samuel
Benda, Julien
Bernanos, Georges
Blanchot, Maurice
Bonnefoy, Yves
Bosco, Henri

Brasillach, Robert
Breton, André
Butor, Michel
Camus, Albert
Cardinal, Marie
Cayrol, Jean
Céline, Louis-Ferdinand
Cendrars, Blaise
Césaire, Aimé
Cesbron, Gilbert
Char, René
Chardonne, Jacques
Cixous, Hélène
Claudel, Paul
Cocteau, Jean
Colette
Dabit, Eugéne
Dada
des Forêts, Louis-René
Desnos, Robert
Dorgelès, Roland
Doubrovsky, Serge
Drieu La Rochelle, Pierre
DuBos, Charles
Du Bouchet, André
Duhamel, Georges
Duras, Marguerite
Ecole Normale Supérieure
Editions de Minuit
Editions des Femmes
Eluard, Paul
Emmanuel, Pierre
Fargue, Léon-Paul
Follain, Jean
Fort, Paul
France, Anatole
Frénaud, André
Gallimard, Gaston
Gary, Romain
Genet, Jean
Genette, Gérard
Gide, André
Giono, Jean
Giraudoux, Jean
Goldmann, Lucien
Goncourt Academy
Gracq, Julien
Grasset, Bernard
Green, Julien
Guillevic, Eugène
Guilloux, Louis
Les Hussards
Jabès, Edmond
Jaccottet, Philippe
Jacob, Max
Jammes, Francis

Jouhandeau, Marcel
Jouve, Pierre Jean
Kessel, Joseph
Kristeva, Julia
Lanson, Gustave
Larbaud, Valery
La Tour du Pin, Patrice de
Léautaud, Paul
Le Clézio, J. M. G.
Leduc, Violette
Leiris, Michel
Maeterlinck, Maurice
Mallet-Joris, Françoise
Malraux, André
Mandiargues, André Pieyre de
Manifestes du surréalisme
Martin du Gard, Roger
Mauriac, Claude
Mauriac, François
Maurois, André
Michaux, Henri
Modiano, Patrick
Montherlant, Henry de
Morand, Paul
Nouveau Roman
Nouvelle Critique
Ollier, Claude
Paulhan, Jean
Péguy, Charles
Perec, Georges
Péret, Benjamin
Philippe, Charles-Louis
Pinget, Robert
Pleynet, Marcelin
Poirot-Delpech, Bertrand
Ponge, Francis
Poulet, Georges
Prévert, Jacques
Prizes
Proust, Marcel
Radiguet, Raymond
Renard, Jean-Claude
Reverdy, Pierre
Ricardou, Jean
Rivière, Jacques
Robbe-Grillet, Alain
Roblès, Emmanuel
Roche, Denis
Rochefort, Christiane
Rolland, Romain
Romains, Jules
Roy, Claude
Roy, Jules
Sagan, Françoise
Saint-Exupéry, Antoine de
Saint-John Perse

Saint Pierre, Michel de
Sarraute, Nathalie
Sarrazin, Albertine
Sartre, Jean-Paul
Schehadé, Georges
Schlumberger, Jean
Seghers, Pierre
Senghor, Léopold Sédar
Simenon, Georges
Simon, Claude
Sollers, Philippe
Sorel, Georges
Soupault, Philippe
Supervielle, Jules
Surrealism
Tardieu, Jean
Todorov, Tzvetan
Tournier, Michel
Triolet, Elsa
Troyat, Henri
Tzara, Tristan
Unanimism
Vailland, Roger
Valéry, Paul
Vercors
Vian, Boris
Vildrac, Charles
Vitrac, Roger
Vivien, Renée
Wiesel, Elie
Wittig, Monique
Yourcenar, Marguerite

MUSIC
Aznavour, Charles
Baker, Josephine
Boulanger, Nadia
Boulez, Pierre
Brassens, Georges
Brel, Jacques
Bruant, Aristide
Charpentier, Gustave
Chevalier, Maurice
Concrete Music
Debussy, Claude
Dukas, Paul
Encyclopédie de la musique et Dictionnaire du Conservatoire
Fauré, Gabriel
Ferré, Leo
Gréco, Juliette
Honegger, Arthur
Indy, Vincent d'
Institut de Recherche et de Coordination Acoustique/Musique

Koechlin, Charles
Landowska, Wanda
Messiaen, Olivier
Milhaud, Darius
Mistinguett
Montand, Yves
Monteux, Pierre
Organists
Parade
Piaf, Edith
Polignac, Winaretta
Poulenc, Francis
Ravel, Maurice
Roussel, Albert
Le Sacre du printemps
Saint-Saëns, Camille
Satie, Erik
Les Six
Stravinsky, Igor
Trenet, Charles

NEWSPAPERS AND MAGAZINES

L'Action Française
Annales d'Histoire Economique et Sociale
L'Arche
L'Assiette au Beurre
Clarté
Combat
Commune
Esprit
L'Express
Le Figaro
Fontaine
France-Soir
Gerbe
Gringoire
L'Humanité
Je Suis Partout
Légitime Défense
Le Grand Jeu
Les Lettres Françaises
Littérature
Marianne
Le Monde
Nord-Sud
La Nouvelle Revue Française
Les Nouvelles Littéraires
Le Nouvel Observateur
Révolution Surréaliste
La Revue Musicale
Sic
Tel Quel
Le Temps
Les Temps Modernes

VVV

PHILOSOPHY AND THE SOCIAL SCIENCES

Alain (Emile Chartier)
Althusser, Louis
Aron, Raymond
Bachelard, Gaston
Baudrillard, Jean
Beauvoir, Simone de
Bergson, Henri
Bourdieu, Pierre
Camus, Albert
Centre National de la Recherche Scientifique
Deleuze, Gilles
Derrida, Jacques
Ecole Normale Supérieure
Existentialism
Febvre, Lucien
Foucault, Michel
Irigaray, Luce
Lacan, Jacques
Lefebvre, Georges
Lefebvre, Henri
Levinas, Emmanuel
Lévi-Strauss, Claude
Lévy, Bernard-Henri
Lyotard, Jean-François
Marcel, Gabriel
Maritain, Jacques
Merleau-Ponty, Maurice
Mounier, Emmanuel
Nizan, Paul
Nouveaux Philosophes
Poulet, Georges
Revel, Jean-François
Ricœur, Paul
Sartre, Jean-Paul
Structuralism
Teilhard de Chardin, Pierre
Weil, Simone

PLACES

Le Bateau Lavoir
Cabaret du Lapin Agile
Cabaret Voltaire
Café de Flore
Café de la Rotonde
Café du Dome
La Coupole
Les Deux Magots
Dunkirk
Latin Quarter
Left Bank

Marne
Montmartre
Montparnasse
Paris
Saint-Germain-des-Prés
Somme
Verdun

POPULAR CULTURE

Astérix
Aznavour, Charles
Baker, Josephine
Brassens, Georges
Brel, Jacques
Le Café-Théâtre
Cerdan, Marcel
Chanel, Coco
Chevalier, Maurice
Ferré, Leo
Gréco, Juliette
Mistinguett
Montand, Yves
La Nouvelle Cuisine
Piaf, Edith
Tintin
Trenet, Charles

THEATER

Adamov, Arthur
Anouilh, Jean
Antoine, André
Appia, Adolphe
Arrabal, Fernando
Artaud, Antonin
Audiberti, Jacques
Avignon Festival
Barrault, Jean-Louis
Barsacq, André
Baty, Gaston
Beckett, Samuel
Benedetto, André
Bérard, Christian
Bernhardt, Sarah
Blin, Roger
Boulevard Theaters
Brook, Peter
Camus, Albert
Cartel des Quatre
Casarès, Maria
Comédie-Française
Compagnie des Quinze
Copeau, Jacques
Craig, Edward Gordon
Crommelynck, Fernand
Dullin, Charles

Gémier, Firmin
Genet, Jean
Ghelderode, Michel de
Giraudoux, Jean
Guitry, Sacha
Ionesco, Eugène
Jamois, Marguerite
Jarry, Alfred
Jouvet, Louis
Lugné-Poe, Aurélien
Maisons de la Culture
Marceau, Marcel
Mnouchkine, Ariane

Nancy Festival
Obaldia, René de
Pitoëff, Georges
Pitoëff, Ludmilla
Planchon, Roger
Renaud, Madeleine
Rouleau, Raymond
Salacrou, Armand
Sartre, Jean-Paul
Theater of the Absurd
Théâtre Antoine
Théâtre de la Cité, Villeurbanne
Théâtre de l'Atelier

Théâtre de l'Athénée
Théâtre de l'Odéon
Théâtre de l'Œuvre
Théâtre du Châtelet
Théâtre du Gymnase
Théâtre du Soleil
Théâtre du Vieux-Colombier
Théâtre Libre
Théâtre Montparnasse
Théâtre National Populaire
Vilar, Jean

EDITORIAL PLAN

Culture is a broad term that has different meanings for different people. It is a word that is used variously to describe how we are alike, how we are different, and what we should aspire to know and appreciate. Thus the title of this work was the subject of careful deliberation by the advisory board at the initial planning meeting in 1990. At issue were basic definitions that determined the fundamental elements of the editorial rationale.

The consensus was that the *Dictionary of Twentieth-Century Culture (TCC)* should undertake to provide a ready reference for the vocabulary of culture, which the board defined as the broad language drawing on shared knowledge used by people of similar backgrounds to communicate with one another. A standard dictionary of language records the definitions of words used in verbal discourse; the advisory board agreed that such dictionaries are inadequate to define more complicated structures of meaning that *TCC* addresses. Communication is frequently extraverbal, drawing on shared experiences, common concepts, communal notions about celebrities, and universally construed messages conveyed by certain images. Culture embraces all aspects of life, from the mundane to the sublime, from the knowledge of grocery-item brand names and the images they connote to a familiarity with classic works of literature, music, and art.

Culture broadly construed is an unmanageable topic for a dictionary-type reference work. Comprehensive coverage would fill a large library. For practical reasons, it was necessary to narrow the scope of *TCC*. The advisory board elected to restrict the series to entries on people, places, terms, art forms, and organizations associated with creative expression in the humanities, those forms of creativity that seek to describe and interpret the human condition. Certainly physicists, chemists, physicians, mathematicians, jurists, and legislators are as creative in their own ways as writers, artists, actors, dancers, and musicians. But as specialists, they view the world from different, though no less important, perspectives than creative artists in the humanities do. Because we cannot do justice to all these worldviews in a single series, we have limited ourselves to the rich world of art, music, literature, drama, radio and television performance, movies, and dance. The advisory board elected not to include entries on individual works because works are described in entries devoted to their creators. Both high and low art that meet the qualification of having made a lasting impression on society will be covered. Endurance is a matter of editorial judgment, and it will be left to volume editors and the editorial board to make the necessary decisions about inclusion.

Obviously it is a distortion to suggest that creative expression occurs in isolation. Most art is not about art but about people from all walks of life and the ways they act, individually and in the company of others. The people, events, and ideas outside the arena of creative expression that stimulated artistic responses have a special significance in culture, and entries are provided to describe certain specific social and historical forces and the creative responses they prompted.

The purpose of *TCC* is not to prescribe what people should know about modern culture; rather, *TCC* attempts to describe and define what people have collectively thought was significant. The purpose of *TCC* entries is definition rather than analysis. Entries are concise, in some cases as brief as a few sentences. In rare cases does an entry exceed one thousand words.

The decision to organize *TCC* volumes geographically was a difficult one, determined by practical considerations and by assumptions about the readership for the series. In fact, of course, there are several distinct cultural groups in most countries, defined sometimes by religion, sometimes by ethnicity, sometimes by socio-economics. Careful attention is due separate cultural groups around the world, but that responsibility must be left to another work. *TCC* is devoted to cultural commonality, not cultural diversity.

Related to the decision to take the broad view of distinct cultures is the advisory board's perception of the audience for *TCC:* American high-school and college students and the patrons of American public libraries. The board has assumed a certain ethnocentrism among the audience, and thus *TCC* will be disproportionately American in character. Other volumes will, in most cases, concentrate on the dominant cultures of a country. Unarguably, comprehensive coverage of the topic is the work of lifetimes.

Certainly many significant entries could be added to those included here. Almost as certainly, entries that should have been included are inadvertently omitted. Significance is a subjective judgment, determined in large part by the cultural background to which the editors themselves are bound. There is some comfort in the anticipation that *TCC* will be a living project that continues its evolution after publication of this volume.

Richard Layman
Columbia, South Carolina
18 April 1994

DICTIONARY OF TWENTIETH-CENTURY CULTURE PUBLISHING PLAN

American Culture After World War II
American Culture Before World War II
Russian Culture After World War II
Russian Culture Before World War II
German Culture
African-American Culture
Arab Culture in the Middle East
Arab Culture in Northern Africa
French Culture
Hispanic Culture of South America

Hispanic Culture of Mexico, Central America, and the Spanish Caribbean
Italian Culture
British Culture After World War II
British Culture Before World War II
Native American Culture
Japanese Culture
Chinese Culture
African Culture South of the Sahara
Eastern European Culture
South East Asian Culture

ACKNOWLEDGMENTS

This book was produced by Manly, Inc. Karen L. Rood, senior editor, and Darren Harris-Fain were the in-house editors. They were assisted by George P. Anderson, Sam Bruce, and Philip B. Dematteis.

Production coordinator is James W. Hipp. Photography editor is Bruce Andrew Bowlin. Photographic copy work was performed by Joseph M. Bruccoli. Layout and graphics supervisor is Penney L. Haughton. Copyediting supervisor is Denise W. Edwards. Typesetting supervisor is Kathleen M. Flanagan. Systems manager is George F. Dodge. Julie E. Frick and Laura S. Pleicones are editorial associates. The production staff includes Phyllis A. Avant, Ann M. Cheschi, Melody W. Clegg, Patricia Coate, Brigitte B. de Guzman, Joyce Fowler, Laurel M. Gladden, Mendy Gladden, Stephanie C. Hatchell, Kathy Lawler Merlette, Jeff Miller, Pamela D. Norton, Delores I. Plastow, Patricia F. Salisbury, and William L. Thomas, Jr.

Walter W. Ross and Robert S. McConnell did library research. They were assisted by the following librarians at the Thomas Cooper Library of the University of South Carolina: Linda Holderfield and the interlibrary-loan staff; reference-department head Virginia Weathers; reference librarians Marilee Birchfield, Stefanie Buck, Cathy Eckman, Rebecca Feind, Jill Holman, Karen Joseph, Jean Rhyne, Kwamine Washington, and Connie Widney; circulation-department head Caroline Taylor; and acquisitions-searching supervisor David Haggard.

FOREWORD

The period covered by this volume is one of unprecedented cultural richness in France, a nation that had already demonstrated a preeminent position in European culture through its impressive accomplishments in fiction, poetry, drama, architecture, painting, drawing, sculpture, landscape design, music, philosophy, and aesthetic criticism — especially during the High Middle Ages, the Renaissance, the Age of Louis XIV, the Enlightenment, and the Romantic period. The intellectual and artistic leadership exercised by the French, especially in Paris, was shared of course with other nations and occasionally eclipsed, but it was often without peer. Around 1900 France dominated world culture to an unprecedented degree. Between the early decades of the century and the 1990s, there has been some dispersal of the tremendous cultural energies centered in Paris, and perhaps some decline has taken place in the overall French achievement in fields such as art and music. Yet, for the first three quarters of the twentieth century, France was the principal crucible of much that can be termed high culture.

Cultural historians will no doubt identify more than one reason for this preeminence. Part of it surely must be laid to the chance through which cultural giants such as Pierre Boulez, André Breton, Paul Cézanne, Claude Debussy, Marcel Proust, and Paul Valéry all appeared in this period. Part of it can be ascribed to the strong French traditions that even as the twentieth century draws to a close have not entirely disappeared. In France, to be a student of the arts or the intellectual disciplines is still, in the eyes of many — and despite the student riots of May 1968 — an honorable calling, not merely a stage on life's practical way or a deplorable excursion into *la vie de bohème* (bohemian life). The artistic achievements of the past, some of which literally loom over Paris, are inscribed also in the names of streets, the statues and monuments, and, most of all, in the minds and hearts of the citizens, whose education in the state system has impressed on them pride in the grandeur of French civilization.

In particular one must stress the number of cultural institutions in place around 1900 — including theaters, magazines, museums, conservatories and art schools, and academies — all of which attracted practitioners of the arts and intellectual disciplines. In some cases these established entities served as antagonists to those crusading against dominant forms; yet in other cases they were sources, inspirations, and outlets for cultural expression. Some of the accumulated cultural wealth of late-nineteenth-century France can be traced to the Middle Ages, Renaissance, or Neo-Classical period, some to Napoleon's time (collections in museums, including objects brought back from Egypt; the system of university and lycée education; and the beginnings of a lay tradition). Other aspects date from the post-Napoleonic years of the nineteenth century, whose *relative* stability and freedom from censorship would appear to have been an influential factor in an intellectual and cultural life that flourished despite industrialization and the rise of what many saw as an oppressive, philistine bourgeoisie.

Added to these reasons for the great flourishing of the arts and intellectual pursuits in France after 1900 is another, major factor: the immigration to France of many artists who were among the most brilliant of their age. Paris was a magnetic force, offering a wealth of opportunities to aspiring artists and intellectuals. The long list of creative individuals who achieved greatness after settling in France includes Italian-born poet Guillaume Apollinaire and Spanish artists Juan Gris and Pablo Picasso — all of whose associations with France began just before or shortly after the turn of the century — and ballet impresario Serge Diaghilev, dancer-choreographer Vaslav Nijinsky, and musican Igor Stravinsky — all born in Russia and associated with the world-renowned Ballets Russes, which was in fact founded in Paris in 1909. Other immigrant artists who left their native lands for Paris include Russian Marc Chagall and Hungarian Victor Vasarely. Poets Jules Supervielle (Uruguay) and Renée Vivien (England), novelists Françoise Mallet-Joris (Belgium) and Elsa Triolet (Russia), and dramatists Arthur Adamov (Russia), Fernando Arrabal (Spain), Samuel Beckett (Ireland), and Eugene Ionesco (Romania) are among the many writers from abroad who settled in France for a considerable time and wrote their most important works in French.

In some cases reasons for staying in Paris were personal or political. For many others Paris was simply the place to be, the original home of the avant-garde, the locus classicus for artistic pursuits. Whether they already knew French — as was the case with Ionesco,

Supervielle, Beckett, and Belgian writers such as Henri Michaux and Mallet-Joris — or they learned the language there, France afforded them a cultural home, including inspiration, the fraternity of other artists, and an audience. Some — including Stravinsky and Russian-born choreographer George Balanchine — eventually migrated further west to New York, where French and other European-born artists contributed greatly to making that city another Western cultural capital. The reader will find in this volume a large number of foreign-born figures who worked in France for significant parts of their productive years. Not everyone who worked in France is included, however, since for some their stays — even if important for their production — was too brief for them to be considered French.

What is meant by *culture* in this volume is not what an anthropologist would ordinarily understand by the term. T. S. Eliot — a product of an elite intellectual tradition, who deliberately placed himself and his work in that same elite minority — wrote in *Notes Towards the Definition of Culture* (1948) that it includes "all the characteristic activities and interests of a people." To adopt such a broad definition for a single survey would be unwieldy, indeed prohibitive.

The chief purpose of the present volume is not to describe all the features of modern France that contribute to its identity as a national, linguistic, and cultural unit, but rather to identify those achievements that express or derive from what is ordinarily thought of as high culture — including art, architecture, poetry, fiction, essay, drama, chamber and orchestral music, opera, and dance. To these traditional pursuits must be added the distinctly modern art of the cinema. In addition this volume includes figures in areas of intellectual achievement such as philosophy, history, and criticism. Readers also will find information on French political and social events that relate to cultural phenomena, as well as individuals who participated in those events.

Moreover, the boundaries of culture have been extended somewhat in this volume to include elements of what can be termed *popular culture*. The distinction between "popular" and "high" culture has become blurred in the twentieth century. Since 1900 new or improved technologies — plus factors such as increased literacy — have brought more and more people in contact with the arts than ever before. Modern communications advances have fostered an increasing cultural homogeneity and produced a new cultural consumerism, while at the same time they have lent themselves to the creation of new artistic media. The resulting immense range of expressions for the popular taste often tend to crowd out those cultural products that

appeal to the few, which thereby become more expensive and more of a luxury. The effects are several, including suspicion of and hostility toward everything that suggests elitism.

Yet France has been somewhat less affected by these changes than some other countries by virtue of the high regard in which culture is held there. The notion of good taste is doubtless more highly developed, more traditionally honored, and more widely applied in France than in any other nation. While a distrust of high culture and the growth of popular culture may be discerned in France and has changed the cultural landscape, frontal attacks on the very idea of taste by writers such as Breton and Louis-Ferdinand Céline and artists such as Marcel Duchamp called attention first of all to its continued dominance in the twentieth century. One could argue even that the strong cultural tradition in France has served to elicit its antithesis — artistic and intellectual iconoclasm — and that the attraction of such idol-breaking has proved invigorating, as well as responsible for drawing many foreign artists to France. As Pierre Albert-Birot wrote in a manifesto of 1916:

> The French Tradition: is to break the shackles
> The French Tradition: is to see and understand everything
> The French Tradition: is to search, discover, create ...
> Therefore the French Tradition IS TO NEGATE TRADITION
> Let's follow the tradition ....

The French sense of balance, collectively at least, has rarely been lost. (As Jean Cocteau wrote, "Between TASTE and VULGARITY, both unpleasant, there remains an *élan* and a sense of proportion: THE TACT OF UNDERSTANDING JUST HOW FAR YOU CAN GO TOO FAR.") Yet it is true that taste and elitism have gradually eroded in the twentieth century and that alternate standards of judgment — for high culture as well as culture aimed at the masses — have appeared.

At least since the early nineteenth century, moreover, there has been in France something that could be called midculture — including high-fashion design, the decorative arts, light opera, the café-concert, cartoons and caricatures, political satire, serial novels, midlevel journalism, boulevard comedies, enduring revolutionary songs (such as "Le Temps des cerises," dating from the 1871 Commune), amateur painting, and the modern sound-and-light shows. These manifestations of creativity are not without taste, artisanship, and thought, and they have wide appeal and some lasting interest, often to more than one class.

Culture in the twentieth century can no longer be regarded as it might have been in the age of Louis XIV, when patrons, producers, and "consumers" — clustered mostly in Paris and at the Sun King's court — consciously followed standards that they took to be universal on the one hand and elite on the other, supporting, paradoxically, a well-defined body of culture both for the few and, by implication at least, for the many. Modern French culture as a whole has no such aspirations to rarefied canons or neat boundaries. It overflows generic categories and tends to be influenced by and to embrace, in one sense or another, various popular and midlevel elements. In this volume, consequently, the reader will find entries on many people and productions from midlevel and popular culture. Yet all such figures, even reasonably well known, are not included. Representative cinema actors, singers, and television personalities are covered, as are important newspapers, magazines, and publishers.

Twentieth-century culture in France is thus far from being uniform and monolithic. Within the three-quarters of a century covered here one can identify several periods that stand out for their cultural coherence: the Belle Epoque, sometimes considered a prolongation of the nineteenth century, stretching from 1900 to the outbreak of World War I (1914–1918); that war itself, which the French still call the Great War, with its tremendous demographic devastation (more than one million French troops and civilians were killed and wounded each year of the war); the 1920s, marked to a great extent by Surrealism; the 1930s, a tumultuous time of major cultural and social strife and the birth of *la littérature engagée* (committed literature); the German Occupation of France (1940 — 1944) during World War II; the post–1945 period; and finally the 1960s and post–1968 years. A French cultural historian writing in 1975 argued that his nation had changed more in the previous twenty years than in the seventy-five years between the Franco-Prussian War and the close of World War II. Momentous alterations took place in the 1950s and the 1960s, with the student riots of 1968 marking that year as a major cultural watershed. The 1970s were a time of rapid economic and cultural change in France, as in the rest of Europe. Many trends have continued since 1975, the cutoff point for this volume, and where appropriate entries follow their topics beyond 1975.

In the above sketch of cultural periods in twentieth-century France, one must be struck by the rapidity with which one has given way to another. Jean-Paul Sartre is one of several thinkers who have argued that the pace of history has accelerated in the modern era. This acceleration touches on, and is reflected in, culture at all levels. In France it is to a considerable de-gree the function of the two world wars, followed by two colonial wars, one halfway around the globe in Indochina and marginalized until the traumatic defeat at Dien Bien Phu in 1954, the other just across the Mediterranean Sea in Algeria and brought home to the French in crucial ways throughout its duration (1954–1962). Following the hundred years after Napoleon's defeat in 1815 — a period during which there were relatively few armed conflicts in Europe — the Great War brought not only tremendous loss of life (the total killed and wounded for all belligerents approached twenty-nine million) but also a sense of the bankruptcy of the culture on which Europe was founded. Those writers and artists who survived the war — especially those who had been young at its outbreak and whose coming of age coincided with its carnage — generally wished to dissociate themselves from the politics and thought that had led to the catastrophe and turned to new ideals and new aesthetics in an attempt to create a new culture. The 1920s saw an outburst of anger and bitterness that has rarely had its equal; it also witnessed tremendous cultural vitality, as the survivors of the cataclysm broke old idols and set themselves to creating new modes of seeing and thinking, partly motivated by the Russian Revolution of 1917 and inspired as well by Sigmund Freud and iconoclasts such as Arthur Rimbaud, the Italian Futurists, prewar Cubists, and the Dadaists.

Although the influence of Surrealism — the most important postwar artistic development — endured throughout the 1930s and, exported to North America, the 1940s, much of the artistic vigor of the years immediately following World War I was lost, or became sidetracked, in the decade starting in 1930, which saw economic crises on both sides of the Atlantic, the successful commandeering of the Weimar Republic in Germany by the National Socialists, the consequent rearmament of Germany, the triumph of Fascism in Italy, grave social disturbances in France, the Spanish Civil War, the annexation of Austria by Germany, the Munich agreement by which France and Britain hoped to appease Hitler by allowing him to take still more territory, the Nazi-Soviet pact, and the outbreak of a new global war. Both what survived of Belle Epoque culture — in its aristocratic, bourgeois, and avant-garde forms — and the militant anticulture of Dada, the Surrealists, and other rebels of the 1920s seemed out of place to many intellectuals confronting the political and economic situation of the 1930s. To be accepted then as a fully serious artist and intellectual, one was expected to join antifascist committees, that is, to politicize oneself in the direction of Moscow, whose formula for socialism was considered as the solution for the troubles of the West. Except for the small number who resolutely refused to become Communist fellow travelers and those few who favored a politics of the Right, artists, writers, thinkers, and others on the cultural forefront in France adopted a creed of leftist social commitment, which, happily, did not produce only literature on the model of Soviet social realism and indeed resulted in some notable achievements. Yet this historicization of culture brought to an end many of the aesthetic experiments of previous years.

Change was furthered by the brief French involvement in World War II and the fall of France to Germany in June 1940, followed by the Occupation and the Liberation of 1944–1945. Perhaps the fissures in French society, and consequently in French culture, had rarely before been so deep as in this second postwar period. Collaboration and resistance under German Occupation had pitted French against French and established or revealed deep differences in ways of relating to the cultural past and envisaging the future. After 1945 political (and often religious) conservatives made frantic efforts to hold onto social structures they had known while at the same time rebuilding French prestige. They met with equal determination on the part of radicals who sought to destroy the remainder of what they saw as a failed old order and to redesign French society. Exchanges between cultural spokesmen for each side — writers, historians, and other commentators — were often bitter; the pace of such polemic was rapid.

The role of Charles de Gaulle on the cultural scene after 1945 deserves special mention. At this remove, one must judge his choices with respect to France generally successful. To be sure the Left hated and feared him; partisans of European community and North Atlantic cooperation resented his determination to maintain a position of French neutrality — or rather, superiority. Algerian Frenchmen felt betrayed by him. Even his supporters recognized his arrogance. His insistence that France continue to occupy the position of a great power was unrealistic, at times even silly, but under his leadership, during the first decade of the Fifth Republic, French prestige was indeed enhanced by both political and cultural measures. The latter included the founding of new theaters and cultural centers, the reorganization and redecoration of major institutions and buildings such as the Louvre and the Paris Opéra, cleaning the facades of Paris buildings, and other measures that created a high public profile for the arts in France, somewhat comparable to that under Louis XIV (to whom cartoonists often compared de Gaulle).

The impressive vitality and striking variety of twentieth-century French culture is consonant in the eyes of some observers with the great democratic developments of the century. This idea is provocative though open to qualification. It is true that in the seventeenth century absolute monarchy was responsible for one of the greatest flowerings of French culture, and historians have often observed the correlation between certain types of despotism and the flourishing of the arts, as in the Italian city-states during the Renaissance. Yet Greek culture reached its highest point under Athenian democracy, and the development of thought is ordinarily more vigorous as it is freer. Moreover — despite restrictions on freedom of speech and the press — another period of great achievement in France was the eighteenth century, when the dominant genius was that of the middle class — as audiences (especially for printed books) expanded greatly. For the first time in French history writers were no longer subservient to Church or State or patrons but wrote rather for their general audience and made money by sales of books (becoming, that is, *professionals*). The Enlightenment decentralization in literature (less in the graphic and musical arts, for economic reasons) — away from court and authority, toward the people — was repeated on a vaster scale in France in the twentieth century, as the Third Republic — for all its parliamentary crises, its moral flaws, its scandals, and its priggishness — expanded educational opportunities, provided a reasonably free atmosphere for artistic and intellectual expression, nurtured the cultural image it had inherited from the past, and provided a vast and relatively stable field for the growth of participatory democracy. Popularization of the arts and erosion of boundaries in taste, styles, and genres accompanied the popularization of politics. Although Paris has continued throughout the century to occupy a central and crucial place, one has the impression of tremendous diversity, powerful individualism, and sometimes almost an atomization of culture.

This individualism can be contrasted with another phenomenon in the cultural landscape: the number and importance of collaborative efforts. It would be a mistake to attribute them all to the political trend that stands in opposition to Enlightenment individualism — namely, socialism and state collectivization — since some of the most important collaborative efforts, such as the *Nouvelle Revue Française,* were carried on by those to whom statism was inimical. Yet there is probably some connection between collectivist social thought and collaborative artistic enterprise. In some sense, of course, all culture is collaborative; all artists are conditioned by their time. In "Tradition and the Individual Talent" (1919) Eliot argued that the literature of the past was the necessary foundation and context for that of the present. The theories of dialogism and intertextuality proposed by Mikhail Bakhtin, Julia Kristeva, and their followers are in part a restatement of the importance of other voices in a literary fabric. Among the collaborative undertakings or partly collective cultural phenomena to be noted in twentieth-century France are Unanimism, centered around the community of the Abbaye; the Fauves and the early Cubist group; the Ballets Russes; Dada and Surrealism; the Théâtre du Vieux-Colombier; magazines such as the *Nouvelle Revue Française, Les Temps Modernes,* and *Tel Quel;* and the totally collective Théâtre du Soleil. It is impressive to see how many major figures were sometimes part of these enterprises and of such performances as *Parade* (1917), with a scenario by Cocteau, settings and costumes by Picasso, choreography by Léonide Massine, music by Erik Satie, and program notes by Apollinaire.

Whatever the diversity, the individualism, and the decentralization observable on the cultural scene from 1900 onward, people around the world understand what is meant by "French culture." Its image is fostered by private and governmental activity, such as the assigning of French cultural attachés to cities all over the globe; the promotion of lectures, films, and art exhibitions abroad; the support of French-language schools in foreign cities; and the publicizing of cultural treasures available to tourists in France. Moreover, the tremendous influence that various developments in the arts and thought in France have exercised abroad is recognized everywhere, taken as a matter of course. Cubism, Surrealism, committed literature, the Theater of the Absurd, the *Nouveau Roman* (New Novel), structuralism, and poststructuralism all came from France. While none of these manifestations is uniquely French — many are markedly international — the imprint of the French on them is so great in most cases that the American public thinks of them as emanating from France. The presence of many U.S. expatriates in France in each generation indicates the strong sense that has prevailed to the present of its vigorous and magnetic cultural tradition. (The 1920s — when Ernest Hemingway, F. Scott Fitzgerald, Allen Tate, and others joined earlier arrivals such as Gertrude Stein and Edith Wharton in Paris — are only the most striking illustration.)

In the pages that follow some particular emphasis is given to the cultural crosswinds that have blown, usually from east to west, between France and North America. Developments and works that have found popularity or exercised influence in the United States are frequently noted. The aim of the volume remains, nevertheless, to furnish as balanced a selection of French cultural references as possible, one that represents the entire spectrum; readers will therefore find many figures who are not well known in America.

—C.S.B.

TIMELINE: SELECTED WORKS AND EVENTS

1900

Historical Events
Paris Exposition Universelle (World's Fair); inauguration of service on the Porte-de-Vincennes/Porte-Maillot subway line, the first line of the Paris Métro subway system.

Art & Architecture
Maurice Denis, *Hommage à Cézanne* (*Homage to Cézanne*);
Henri Matisse, *Le Pont Saint-Michel* (*Saint-Michel Bridge*)
Claude Monet, first canvases of Giverny lily ponds (1899–1900) exhibited;
Auguste Rodin, *Le Bon Génie* (*The Good Fairy*)
Alexandre III Bridge finished in Paris
Grand Palais exhibition hall finished in Paris
Construction of the Petit Palais exhibition hall in Paris

Drama
Romain Rolland, *Danton*

Literature
Maurice Barrès, *L'Appel au soldat* (The Appeal to the Soldier)
Paul Claudel, *Connaissance de l'Est* (translated as *The East I Know*)
Colette, *Claudine à l'école* (translated as *Claudine at School*)

Music
Gustave Charpentier, *Louise*

Philosophy/Psychology
Henri Bergson, *Le Rire* (translated as *Laughter*)
Sigmund Freud, *The Interpretation of Dreams* (in German)

Popular Culture
Maxim's Restaurant in Paris, opened in 1893, redecorated to mark the Exposition Universelle
Publication of the first *Guide Michelin* tourists' guide to France

1901

Historical Events
Albert, Prince of Wales, becomes King Edward VII; Czar Alexander III visits France, Russia's ally.

Art & Architecture
Henri Rousseau (Le Douanier), *Vue du Bois de Vincennes* (*View of the Vincennes Wood*)

Drama
André Gide, *Le Roi Candaule* (King Candaules)

Literature
Charles-Louis Philippe, *Bubu de Montparnasse* (translated as *Bubu of Montparnasse*)

Music
Maurice Ravel, *Jeux d'eau* (*The Fountain*)

Popular Culture
Fourth Salon of Bicycles and Automobiles

1902

Historical Events
Resignation of René Waldeck-Rousseau as prime minister of France; Emile Combes is named to succeed him.

Art & Architecture
Camille Pissarro, *Le Louvre et le Pont-Neuf* (*The Louvre and the Pont-Neuf*)

Auguste Rodin, *La Création*

Literature
Maurice Barrès, *Scènes et doctrines du nationalisme* (Scenes and Doctrines of Nationalism)
André Gide, *L'Immoraliste* (translated as *The Immoralist*)

1903

Historical Events
Pius X, a conservative, becomes pope; Edward VII of England visits France.

Art & Architecture
Eugène Atget, *Bords de la Marne* (*Banks of the Marne*)
Edgar Degas, *Danseuses en jaune* (*Dancers in Yellow Skirts*)
Henri Matisse, *L'Esclave* (*The Slave*)
Auguste Rodin, *Tête de Balzac* (*Head of Balzac*)

Drama
Georges Courteline, *La Paix chez soi* (translated as *Peace at Home*)

Literature
Anatole France, *Histoire comique* (translated as *A Mummer's Tale*)
Francis Jammes, *Le Roman du lièvre* (The Novel of the Hare)
The Goncourt Academy begins to function

Music
Claude Debussy, *Estampes* (Prints)

Popular Culture
First Tour de France bicycle race

1904

Historical Events
Anglo-French Entente Cordiale concerning colonial rivalries in Egypt and Morocco; Pius X censures the French government for its regulation of church affairs; France recalls its ambassador to the Vatican; Amsterdam congress of Socialists; *L'Humanité* founded by Jean Jaurès.

Art & Architecture
Paul Cézanne, *La Montagne Sainte-Victoire* (*Sainte-Victoire Mountain*)
Pablo Picasso settles at the Bateau-Lavoir in Montmartre.

1905

Historical Events
The Combes Law separates church and state in France; the French Socialist Party is founded; a crisis occurs when Germany protests the agreement of France and Spain to divide Morocco.

Art & Architecture
Albert Marquet, *Notre-Dame*
Auguste Perret, garage, rue de Ponthieu, Paris, one of the first uses of reinforced concrete
Pablo Picasso, *Les Saltimbanques* (*The Jugglers*)
Georges Rouault, *Tête de Christ* (*Head of Christ*)

Henri Rousseau, *Le Lion ayant faim* (*The Hungry Lion*)
Les Fauves (The Wild Beasts) baptized by Louis Vauxcelles in his review of the Salon d'Automne (fall art exhibition)

Literature
Vers et Prose founded by Paul Fort

Music
Claude Debussy, *La Mer* (*The Sea*)
Maurice Ravel, *Miroirs* (*Mirrors*)

1906

Historical Events
Exposition Coloniale (Colonial Fair) in Marseilles; start of Anglo-French military and naval conversations; international conference at Algeciras, Spain, concerning Morocco; the British launch the HMS *Dreadnought,* the first battleship with ten twelve-inch guns; French officer Alfred Dreyfus exonerated on treason charges; Radicals and Socialists win additional seats in the French Assembly.

Art & Architecture
Georges Braque, *Le Canal Saint-Martin* (*The Saint-Martin Canal*)
Paul Cézanne, *Le Jardin des Lauves* (*Lauves Garden*)
André Derain, *Le Pont de Londres* (*London Bridge*)
Albert Marquet, *Le Pont-Neuf* and *Le Pont-Neuf au soleil* (*The Pont-Neuf in Sunshine*)

Georges Rouault, *Au salon* (*In the Salon*)
Maurice Utrillo, *Le Quai Malaquais*
Pont de Passy (Passy Bridge) constructed

Drama
André Antoine becomes artistic director of the Théâtre de l'Odéon.

Literature
Paul Claudel, *Partage de midi* (translated as *Break of Noon*)
Anatole France, *Vers les temps meilleurs* (translated as *The Unrisen Dawn*)
Groupe de l'Abbaye organized

1907

Historical Events
Electricians' strike in Paris

Art & Architecture
Georges Braque, *L'Estaque*
Large show of works by Paul Cézanne (fifty-six canvases) in Paris
Edouard Manet's *Olympia* transferred from the Museum of Contemporary Art at the Luxembourg to the Louvre (displayed finally in 1917)
Pablo Picasso, *Les Demoiselles d'Avignon*
Henri Rousseau, *Charmeuse de serpents* (*The Snake Charmer*)

Literature
André Gide, *Le Retour de l'enfant prodigue* (translated as *The Return of the Prodigal*)

Philosophy
Henri Bergson, *L'Evolution créatrice* (translated as *Creative Evolution*)

Popular Culture
The newspaper *Le Matin* and Albert, Marquis de Dion, organize the International Automobile Rally from Paris to Peking.

1908

Art & Architecture
Marie Laurencin, *Groupe d'artistes* (*Group of Artists*)
Claude Monet, series of water lily paintings
Auguste Rodin, *La Cathédrale* (*The Cathedral*)
Henri Rousseau, *Joueurs de football* (*The Football Players*) and *La Carriole du père Juniet* (*Old Juniet's Cart*)
Maurice Utrillo, *La rue Drevet, Montmartre* (*Drevet Street, Montmartre*)

Literature
Nouvelle Revue Française founded in November

Anatole France, *L'Ile des pingouins* (translated as *Penguin Island*)

Music
Maurice Ravel, *Gaspard de la nuit* (*Gaspard of the Night*) and *Rhapsodie espagnole* (*Spanish Rhapsody*)

Philosophy
Georges Sorel, *Réflexions sur la violence* (translated as *Reflections on Violence*)

1909

Historical Events
Louis Blériot crosses the English Channel by airplane; France and Germany agree on the territorial integrity of Morocco.

Art & Architecture
F. T. Marinetti, first Futurist Manifesto, published in *Le Figaro*
Henri Matisse, *La Serpentine* (*The Serpentine*)
Henri Rousseau, *La Muse inspirant le poète* (*The Muse Inspiring the Poet*)
Maurice Utrillo, *La Rue des Abbesses* (*Abbesses Street*)

Dance
Ballets Russes founded in Paris

Literature
Guillaume Apollinaire, *L'Enchanteur pourrissant* (The Rotting Magician)
Maurice Barrès, *Colette Baudoche*
André Gide, *La Porte étroite* (translated as *Strait Is the Gate*)

1910

Art & Architecture
Umberto Boccioni, Futurist Manifesto (on painting), published in Italy
Georges Braque, *Le Sacré-Cœur*
Henri Rousseau, *Le Rêve* (*The Dream*)
Maurice Vlaminck, *Nature morte – formes cubistes* (*Still Life – Cubistic Forms*)

Dance
Michel Fokine, *L'Oiseau de feu* (*The Firebird*)

Literature
Guillaume Apollinaire, *L'Hérésiarque et Cie* (translated as *The Heresiarch and Company*)
Paul Claudel, *Cinq grandes odes* (translated as *Five Great Odes*)
Colette, *La Vagabonde* (translated as *The Vagabond*)
Charles Péguy, *Le Mystère de la Charité de Jeanne d'Arc* (translated as *The Mystery of the Charity of Joan of Arc*)

Music
Claude Debussy, *La Cathédrale engloutie* (*The Submerged Cathedral*)
Igor Stravinsky, *L'Oiseau de feu* (*The Firebird*)

1911

Historical Events
A German battleship anchors in the Moroccan port of Agadir, an act precipitated by a French violation of the 1909 Franco-German accord; the dispute is settled after France gives Germany part of the French Congo in return for recognition of a French protectorate in Morocco.

Art & Architecture
Eugène Atget, *91, rue de Turenne* (*91, Turenne Street*)
Georges Braque, *L'Homme à la guitare* (*Man With a Guitar*)
Robert Delaunay, *La Tour Eiffel* (*The Eiffel Tower*)
Marcel Duchamp, *Nu descendant un escalier I* (*Nude Descending a Staircase I*)
The sculptor Lucienne Antoinette Heuvelmans is the first woman to win the Prix de Rome.
Fernand Léger, *Les Toits* (*The Roofs*)
Henri Matisse, *Poissons d'or* (*Still Life with Goldfish*)

Dance
Michel Fokine, *Petrouchka, Le Spectre de la rose* (*The Specter of the Rose*) and *Le Martyre de Saint-Sébastien* (The Martyrdom of Saint Sebastian)

Literature
Nobel Prize for Literature: Maurice Maeterlinck
Jules Romains, *Mort de quelqu'un* (translated as *Death of a Nobody*)
Saint-John Perse, *Eloges* (translated as *Praises*)

Music
Claude Debussy, *Le Martyre de Saint-Sébastien* (The Martyrdom of Saint Sebastian)
Maurice Ravel, *Valses nobles et sentimentales* (*Noble and Sentimental Waltzes*)

1912

Historical Events
Raymond Poincaré becomes premier of France; French naval agreements with Russia and Great Britain; Sultan of Morocco accepts the protection of France; General Louis Lyautey appointed Resident General; Roland Garros crosses the Mediterranean by plane; Socialist Congress in Basel

Art & Architecture
Umberto Boccioni, Manifesto on Futurist sculpture
Marcel Duchamp, *Nu descendant un escalier II* (*Nude Descending a Staircase II*) and *Le Passage de la vierge à la mariée* (*The Passage from Virgin to Bride*)
Albert Gleizes, *Les Ponts de Paris* (*The Bridges of Paris*)
Odilon Redon, *La Naissance de Vénus* (*The Birth of Venus*)
Auguste Rodin, *Nijinsky*
Maurice Utrillo, *La rue Chappe* (*Chappe Street*)

Dance
Vaslav Nijinsky, *L'Après-midi d'un faune* (*The Afternoon of a Faun*)

Drama
Paul Claudel, *L'Annonce faite à Marie* (translated as *The Tidings Brought to Mary*)

Literature
Blaise Cendrars, *Les Pâques* (Easter)
Léon-Paul Fargue, *Poèmes* (Poems)
Anatole France, *Les Dieux ont soif* (translated as *The Gods Are Athirst*)

Music
Maurice Ravel, *Daphnis et Chloé*

1913

Historical Events
Raymond Poincaré becomes president of France; law requiring three years' military service takes effect in France; the first Arab Congress held in Paris.

Art & Architecture
Jean Metzinger, *La Femme à l'éventail* (*Woman With Fan*)
Man Ray, *The Village*
Edouard Vuillard, *Vue d'Hambourg* (*View of Hamburg*)
The Armory Show in New York introduces European avant-garde art to Americans

Cinema
Louis Feuillade, first episodes of his *Fantômas* serial

Dance
Vaslav Nijinsky, *Le Sacre du printemps* (*The Rite of Spring*), with music by Igor Stravinsky

Drama
Founding of the Théâtre du Vieux-Colombier

Literature/Criticism
Alain-Fournier, *Le Grand Meaulnes* (translated as *The Wanderer*)
Guillaume Apollinaire, *Alcools*
Blaise Cendrars, *La Prose du Transsibérien et de la Petite Jehanne de France* (translated as *The Prose of the Trans-Siberian Railroad and of Little Jeanne of France*)
Roger Martin du Gard, *Jean Barois*
Marcel Proust, *Du côté de chez Swann* (translated as *Swann's Way*)
Jacques Rivière, "Le Roman d'aventure" (The Novel of Adventure)
Jules Romains, *Les Copains* (translated as *The Boys in the Back Room*)

1914

Historical Events
Archduke Franz Ferdinand, heir to the Austrian throne, is assassinated in Sarajevo; Socialist René Viviani becomes premier of France; Germany declares war on France; Great Britain and France declare war on Austria-Hungary; first Battle of the Marne.

Art & Architecture
André Derain, *Fenêtre* (*Still Life in the Window*)
Pablo Picasso's *Les Saltimbanques* sold for 11,500 francs
Auguste Rodin, *Main sortant de la tombe* (*Hand Coming from the Tomb*)
The Sacré-Cœur basilica finished in Montmartre

Dance
Jacques Rouché becomes director of the Paris Opéra Ballet

Drama
Paul Claudel, *L'Echange* (translated as *The Exchange*)
Roger Martin du Gard, *Le Testament du Père Leleu* (Old Man Leleu's Will)

Literature
Deaths of Alain-Fournier and Charles Péguy in battle
André Gide, *Les Caves du Vatican* (translated as *The Vatican Swindle*)

1915

Historical Events
Stalemate along the western front; Italy enters the war on the Allied side.

Art & Architecture
Pablo Picasso, *Arlequin* (*Harlequin*)

Literature
Nobel Prize for Literature: Romain Rolland (awarded in 1916 for the year 1915)

1916

Historical Events
Siege of Verdun; Battle of the Somme.

Art & Architecture
Founding of Dada movement in Zurich
391 (Dadaist periodical) founded by Francis Picabia

Reinforced concrete hangars built at Orly airport

Literature
Henri Barbusse, *Le Feu* (translated as *Under Fire*)

1917

Historical Events
Battle of Chemin des Dames; United States enters the war; Bolshevik Revolution in Russia; Modane troop train crash (worst railway disaster until 1989)

Art & Architecture
Claude Monet, *Portrait de l'artiste* (*Self-Portrait*)
Francis Picabia, *Parade amoureuse* (*Sideshow in Love*)

Dance
Jean Cocteau, *Parade* (Sideshow)

Drama
Guillaume Apollinaire, *Les Mamelles de Tirésias* (translated as *The Breasts of Tiresias*)

Literature
Guillaume Apollinaire, "L'Esprit nouveau" (translated as "The New Spirit and the Poets")
Nord-Sud founded
Paul Valéry, *La Jeune Parque* (translated as *The Young Fate*)

Music
Maurice Ravel, *Le Tombeau de Couperin* (Couperin's Tomb)

1918

Historical Events
French counteroffensive led by Ferdinand Foch; armistice of 11 November ends World War I.

Art & Architecture
Claude Monet gives his 1914–1918 water lily series to the French nation.
Pablo Picasso, *Pierrot*

Drama
Michel de Ghelderode, *La Mort regarde à la fenêtre* (Death Looks through the Window)

Max Jacob, *Le Cornet à dés: Poèmes en prose* (The Dice Cup: Prose Poems)

Literature
Guillaume Apollinaire, *Calligrammes*
André Maurois, *Les Silences du colonel Bramble* (translated as *The Silence of Colonel Bramble*)
Tristan Tzara, *Vingt-cinq poèmes* (Twenty-Five Poems)

Music
Death of Claude Debussy

1919

Historical Events
Treaty of Versailles; founding of Clarté movement.

Art & Architecture
Henri Laurens, *La Femme à la guitare* (Woman with Guitar)
Fernand Léger, *Ville* (City)
Pablo Picasso, *La Table* (The Table)

Cinema
Abel Gance, *J'accuse* (I Accuse)

Dance
Léonide Massine, *Le Tricorne* (The Three-Cornered Hat)

Drama
Charles Vildrac, *Le Paquebot Tenacity* (translated as *The Steamship Tenacity*)

Literature
Roland Dorgelès, *Les Croix de bois* (translated as *Wooden Crosses*)
André Gide, *La Symphonie pastorale* (translated as *The Pastoral Symphony*)
Paul Valéry, *La Soirée avec Monsieur Teste* (translated as *An Evening with Mr. Teste*)
Prix Goncourt: Marcel Proust for *A l'ombre des jeunes filles en fleur* (translated as *Within a Budding Grove*)
Nouvelle Revue Française resumes publication after a hiatus during World War I.

1920

Historical Events
The French Communist Party founded

Dance
Jean Cocteau, *Le Bœuf sur le Toit* (The Nothing Happens Bar)

Drama
Firmin Gémier establishes the Théâtre National Populaire at the Trocadéro in Paris

Literature
André Breton and Philippe Soupault, *Les Champs magnétiques* (translated as *Magnetic Fields*)

Georges Duhamel, *Confession de minuit* (translated as *Confession at Midnight*)
André Gide, *Si le grain ne meurt* (translated as *If It Die...*), volume 1
Dada festival in Paris

Music
Composers Georges Auric, Louis Durey, Arthur Honegger, Darius Milhaud, Francis Poulenc, and Germaine Tailleferre are labeled Les Six.
Darius Milhaud, *Le Bœuf sur le Toit*

1921

Historical Events
Benito Mussolini elected to parliament in Italy, where the National Fascist Party is organized; resumption of diplomatic relations between France and the Vatican.

Art & Architecture
Pablo Picasso, *Trois Musiciens* (Three Musicians)

Drama
Jean Cocteau, *Les Mariés de la Tour Eiffel* (translated as *The Wedding on the Eiffel Tower*)
Charles Dullin establishes the Théâtre de l'Atelier.
Firmin Gémier begins to direct plays at the Théâtre de l'Odéon.

Literature
Marcel Proust, *Le Côte de Guermantes II* (translated as *The Guermantes Way*); *Sodome et Gomorrhe I* (translated as *Cities of the Plain*)

Music
Robert Roussel, Second Symphony

Philosophy
Alain, *Mars ou la guerre jugée* (Mars, or War Judged)

Popular Culture
French soccer team beats an English team for the first time.

Radio/Television
Regular radio broadcasts begin from the Eiffel Tower.

1922

Historical Events
Fascists take power in Italy; Pius XI becomes pope.

Art & Architecture
Jean Fautrier, *Promenade du dimanche* (Sunday Walk)
Le Corbusier, Ozenfant House, Paris
Amédée Ozenfant, *Composition*

Drama
Sarah Bernhardt acts in *La Gloire* by Maurice Rostand, her last role.
André Gide, *Saül*

Literature
Roger Martin du Gard, *Le Cahier gris* (translated as *The Gray Notebook*) and *Le Pénitencier* (translated as *The Penitentiary*)

François Mauriac, *Le Baiser au lépreux* (translated as *The Kiss to the Leper*)
Paul Valéry, *Charmes*
Death of Marcel Proust

Popular Culture
Coco Chanel introduces Chanel No. 5 perfume.

1923

Historical Events
French and Belgian troups occupy the Ruhr, an industrial region of Germany, during a dispute over war reparations – they remain until 1930; Adolf Hitler stages the Beer Hall Putsch in Munich.

Art & Architecture
Auguste Perret, reinforced concrete church of Notre-Dame, Le Raincy (1922–1923)

Cinema
Abel Gance, *La Roue* (The Wheel)

Dance
Bronislava Nijinska, *Les Noces* (*The Wedding*)

Drama
Jules Romains, *Knock* (translated as *Doctor Knock*)

Literature
François Mauriac, *Génitrix*
Raymond Radiguet, *Le Diable au corps* (translated as *Devil in the Flesh*)

Music
Igor Stravinsky, *Les Noces* (*The Wedding*)

1924

Historical Events
Death of Vladimir Ilyich Lenin.

Dance
Bronislava Nijinska, *Les Biches* (*The Darlings*)

Literature
André Breton, *Manifeste du surréalisme* (Manifesto of Surrealism)

Saint-John Perse, *Anabase* (translated as *Anabasis*)
Pierre Reverdy, *Les Epaves du ciel* (The Wreckage of Heaven)
Death of Anatole France

Music
Francis Poulenc, *Les Biches* (*The Darlings*)

1925

Historical Events
French campaign against dissident tribes in the Rif area of Morocco; Treaty of Locarno guaranteeing the Franco-German border is signed by France, Germany, and Great Britain.

Art & Architecture
Exposition of Decorative Arts, Paris

Cinema
Marcel L'Herbier, *Feu Mathias Pascal* (*The Late Mathias Pascal*)

Literature
André Gide, *Les Faux-Monnayeurs* (translated as *The Counterfeiters*)
Pierre Jean Jouve, *Les Mystérieuses Noces* (The Mysterious Wedding)

Popular Culture
Shalimar perfume created by Jacques Guerlain

1926

Historical Events
Joseph Stalin establishes control in the Soviet Union; Pope Pius XI condemns the antirepublican Action Française movement, which has sought to strengthen the political role of the church in France.

Art & Architecture
Fernand Léger, *Trois figures* (*Three Faces*)

Cinema
Dimitri Kirsanoff, *Ménilmontant*

Drama
Antonin Artaud and Roger Vitrac found the Théâtre Alfred Jarry
Jean Cocteau, *Orphée* (translated as *Orpheus*)

Literature
Louis Aragon, *Le Paysan de Paris* (translated as *Nightwalker*)
Georges Bernanos, *Sous le soleil de Satan* (translated as *The Star of Satan*)
Paul Eluard, *Capitale de la douleur* (Capital of Grief)
Henry de Montherlant, *Les Bestiaires* (translated as *The Bullfighters*)
Francis Ponge, *Douze petits écrits* (Twelve Little Writings)

1927

Historical Events
Charles Lindberg makes the first solo airplane flight from New York to Paris; construction begins on the Maginot Line of defensive fortifications along the border between Germany and France.

Art & Architecture
Le Corbusier, Citrohan House on pilings, Stuttgart

Le Corbusier and Pierre Jenneret, modern-style house in Garches

Pablo Picasso, *Femme assise* (Seated Woman)

Cinema
René Clair, *Un Chapeau de paille d'Italie* (An Italian Straw Hat)
Abel Gance, *Napoléon*

Dance
Death of Isadora Duncan

Literature/Criticism
Louis Aragon joins the French Communist Party
Julien Benda, *La Trahison des clercs* (The Betrayal of the Intellectuals)

André Gide *Voyage au Congo* (translated as *Travels in the Congo*)
Julien Green, *Adrienne Mesurat* (translated as *The Closed Garden*)
Henri Michaux, *Qui je fus* (Who I Was)
Marcel Proust, *Le Temps retrouvé* (translated as *Time Regained*), last volume of *A la recherche du temps perdu* (translated as *Remembrance of Things Past*)

Philosophy
Gabriel Marcel, *Journal métaphysique* (translated as *Metaphysical Journal*)

Popular Culture
Opening of La Coupole restaurant in Montparnasse, Paris

1928

Historical Events
French military service reduced to one year; signing of Kellogg-Briand Pact outlawing war; stabilization of the French franc at approximately one-fifth of its prewar value.

Art & Architecture
Francis Picabia, *Hera*

Cinema
Luis Buñuel, *Un Chien andalou* (An Andalusian Dog)
May Ray, *L'Etoile de mer* (Starfish)

Dance
George Balanchine, *Apollon musagète* (Apollo, Leader of the Muses)

Drama
Jean Cocteau, *Roméo et Juliette*
Marcel Pagnol, *Topaze*
Jules Romains, *Volpone*

Literature
André Breton, *Nadja*
André Malraux, *Les Conquérants* (translated as *The Conquerors*)
Benjamin Péret, *Le Grand Jeu* (The Great Game)

Music
Maurice Ravel, *Boléro*

1929

Historical Events
Economic crisis begins; last Allied troops withdraw from Rhineland.

Dance
Serge Lifar becomes director and *premier danseur étoile* of the Paris Opéra Ballet

Drama
Paul Claudel, *Le Soulier de satin* (translated as *The Satin Slipper*)
Jean Giraudoux, *Amphitryon 38*
Roger Vitrac, *Victor, ou les enfants au pouvoir* (Victor, or The Children Take Over)

Historiography
Founding of *Les Annales d'Histoire Economique et Sociale*

Literature
Eugène Dabit, *L'Hôtel du Nord* (translated as *Hotel du Nord*)
Henri Michaux, *Ecuador* (translated as *Ecuador, A Travel Journal*) and *Mes propriétés* (My Properties)

Popular Culture
Hergé, *Tintin* comic strip

1930

Historical Events
Nazis win 107 seats in the German Reichstag; Maurice Thorez becomes leader of the French Communist Party.

Art & Architecture
Enlargement of Place de la Concorde begun (finished 1932)
Le Corbusier, Villa Savoie, in Poissy-sur-Seine (1929–1930)

Cinema
Luis Buñuel, *L'Age d'or* (The Golden Age)
Jean Vigo, *A propos de Nice* (On the Subject of Nice)

Drama
Jules Romains, *Donogoo, ou Les miracles de la science* (translated as *Donogoo*)

Literature
André Breton, *Second Manifeste du surréalisme* (Second Surrealist Manifesto)
René Char, *Ralentir travaux* (To Slow Down Work)
Robert Desnos, *Corps et biens* (Shipwreck)

1931

Historical Events
Colonial Exposition in Vincennes; opening of the American Center in Paris; Louis Aragon convicted of inciting soldiers to mutiny and of provocation to murder with his poem "Front rouge" (Red Front) in *Persécuté persécuteur* (Persecuted Persecutor).

Cinema
René Clair, *A nous la liberté* (Give Us Liberty)
Alexander Korda, *Marius*
Jean Renoir, *La Chienne* (The Bitch)

Dance
Rolf de Maré establishes Archives Internationales de la Danse in Paris.

Drama
André Gide, *Œdipe* (translated as *Oedipus*)

1932

Historical Events
Nazis win 230 seats in the Reichstag; founding of the Association des Ecrivains Révolutionnaires (later Association des Ecrivains et Artistes Révolutionnaires); French pacification of Morocco achieved.

Art & Architecture
Henri Laurens, *La Petite Maternité* and *La Grande Maternité* (Small and Large Maternity)
Le Corbusier, Swiss Residence, Cité Universitaire, Paris (1930–1932)

Cinema
Marc Allégret, *Fanny*
Jean Cocteau, *Le Sang d'un poète* (*The Blood of a Poet*)
Jacques Prévert, screenplay for *L'Affaire est dans le sac* (It's in the Bag)

Literature
Jean Giono, *Le Grand Troupeau* (translated as *To the Slaughterhouse*)
Antoine de Saint-Exupéry, *Vol de nuit* (translated as *Night Flight*)

Jean Renoir, *Boudu sauvé des eaux* (*Boudu Saved from Drowning*)

Drama
Jean Anouilh, *L'Hermine* (translated as *The Ermine*); *Le Bal des voleurs* (translated as *Thieves' Carnival*)

Literature
Louis-Ferdinand Céline, *Voyage au bout de la nuit* (translated as *Journey to the End of the Night*)
Paul Nizan, *Les Chiens de garde* (translated as *The Watchdogs*)

Philosophy
Gaston Bachelard, *La Psychanalyse du feu* (translated as *Psychoanalysis of Fire*)
Henri Bergson, *Les Deux Sources de la morale et de la religion* (translated as *The Two Sources of Morality and Religion*)

1933

Historical Events
Adolf Hitler becomes chancellor of the German Reich.

Cinema
Jean Vigo, *Zéro de conduite* (*Zero for Conduct*)

Drama
Jules Supervielle, *Adam*

Literature
André Malraux receives the Prix Goncourt for *La Condition humaine* (translated as *Man's Fate*)

Radio/Television
Radio Paris becomes a national radio station

1934

Historical Events
The Stavisky Affair, in which many bank investors were swindled, culminates in Serge-Alexander Stavisky's suicide; riot of 6 February, involving right-wing groups protesting the dismissal of the Paris police chief; André Gide and André Malraux visit Berlin in a vain attempt to intercede for Georgi Mikhailovich Dimitrov, accused of setting the Reichstag fire.

Art & Architecture
André Lhôte, *Léda et le cygne* (*Leda and the Swan*)

Cinema
Jean Vigo, *L'Atalante*

Dance
Ida Rubinstein, *Perséphone*

Drama
Jean Cocteau, *La Machine infernale* (translated as *The Infernal Machine*)
Louis Jouvet begins productions at the Théâtre de l'Athénée

Literature
Pierre Drieu La Rochelle, *La Comédie de Charleroi* (translated as *The Comedy of Charleroi and Other Stories*)

Philosophy
Alain, *Les Dieux* (translated as *The Gods*)

Sociology/Anthropology
Creation of *Annales Sociologiques,* the continuation of the *Année Sociologique,* founded in 1898 by Emile Durkheim

1935

Historical Events
Italy invades Ethiopia; plebiscite in the Saar returns the territory to Germany; Franco-Russian treaty; first World Congress of the International Association of Writers for the Defense of Culture.

Drama
Jean Giraudoux, *La Guerre de Troie n'aura pas lieu* (translated as *Tiger at the Gates*)

Literature
Louis Guilloux, *Le Sang noir* (translated as *Bitter Victory*)

Radio/Television
Broadcast of first television program

1936

Historical Events
Reoccupation and remilitarization of Rhineland by Germany; leftist Popular Front coalition formed in France; Radical Party joins Popular Front, creating a majority, and coalition leader Léon Blum becomes prime minister; Spanish Civil War breaks out; Second Congress of the International Association of Writers for the Defense of Culture.

Cinema
Marcel Pagnol, *César*

Literature
Georges Bernanos, *Journal d'un curé de campagne* (translated as *Diary of a Country Priest*)

André Gide visits the Soviet Union with Eugène Dabit (who dies there) and others

Philosophy
Jacques Maritain, *Humanisme intégral* (translated as *True Humanism*)

Jean-Paul Sartre, *L'Imagination* (translated as *Imagination: A Psychological Critique*)

Sociology
Henri Godin and Yvan Daniel, *France, pays de mission?* (France, A Country of Missions?)

1937

Historical Events
Fall of Blum's government; Paris Exposition Universelle (World's Fair).

Art & Architecture
Pablo Picasso, *Guernica*
Palais de Chaillot and Musée d'Art Moderne constructed

Cinema
Julien Duvivier, *Pépé le Moko*
Marcel Pagnol, *Regain* (*Harvest*)
Jean Renoir, *La Grande Illusion* (*Grand Illusion*)

Drama
Jean Anouilh, *Le Voyageur sans bagages* (translated as *Traveller without Luggage*)

François Mauriac, *Asmodée* (translated as *Asmodée; or The Intruder*)

Literature
Nobel Prize for Literature: Roger Martin du Gard
Georges Simenon, *L'Assassin* (translated as *The Murderer*); *Le Blanc à lunettes* (translated as *Talata*); *Faubourg* (translated as *Home Town*); *Le Testament Donadieu* (translated as *The Shadow Falls*)

Music
Death of Maurice Ravel

Radio/Television
Regular television broadcasting begins

1938

Historical Events
Edouard Daladier becomes prime minister of France; German *Anschluss* (annexation of Austria); Munich agreement, allowing Hitler to take Sudetenland, is signed by France and England.

Cinema
Marcel Carné, *Le Quai des brumes* (*Port of Shadows*)
Marcel Pagnol, *La Femme du boulanger* (*The Baker's Wife*)
Jean Renoir, *La Bête humaine* (*The Human Beast*)

Drama
Henry de Montherlant, *Pasiphaé*

Literature/Criticism
Antonin Artaud, *Le Théâtre et son double* (translated as *The Theater and Its Double*)
Georges Bernanos, *Les Grands Cimetières sous la lune* (translated as *A Diary of My Times*)
Julien Gracq, *Au château d'Argol* (translated as *The Castle of Argol*)
Jean-Paul Sartre, *La Nausée* (translated as *Nausea*)

Music
Arthur Honegger, *Jeanne d'Arc au bûcher* (Joan of Arc at the Stake)

1939

Historical Events
End of Spanish Civil War; Nazi-Soviet pact of nonaggression, which leads to German partition of Poland; World War II breaks out.

Cinema
Marcel Carné, *Le Jour se lève* (*Daybreak*)
Jean Renoir, *La Règle du jeu* (*The Rules of the Game*)

Drama
Jean Giraudoux, *Ondine*

Literature
André Gide, *Journal 1889–1939* (translated as *The Journals of André Gide*)

Antoine de Saint-Exupéry, *Terre des hommes* (translated as *Wind, Sand, and Stars*)
Nathalie Sarraute, *Tropismes* (translated as *Tropisms*)
Jean-Paul Sartre, *Le Mur* (translated as *The Wall*)

Philosophy
Jean-Paul Sartre, *Esquisse d'une théorie des émotions* (translated as *The Emotions: Outline of a Theory*)

Popular Culture
The Moulin de la Galette nightspot in Montmartre designated a historic monument

1940

Historical Events

Invasion of France by Germany; fall of France and end of Third Republic; Charles de Gaulle flees to London; Philippe Pétain chosen as head of Etat Français (French State); government moves to Bordeaux, then Vichy.

Drama

Jean Cocteau, *Les Monstres sacrés* (The Idols)

Philosophy

Jean-Paul Sartre, *L'Imaginaire* (translated as *The Psychology of the Imagination*)

1941

Historical Events

Terrorist attacks against Germans in Paris indicate the beginnings of a Resistance movement; Japanese attack on Pearl Harbor; Germany and Italy declare war on the United States.

Drama

Jean Cocteau, *La Machine à écrire* (translated as *The Typewriters*)
Charles Dullin becomes director of the Théâtre Sarah-Bernhardt.

Literature

Louis Aragon, *Le Crève-cœur* (Heartbreak)

Music

Olivier Messiaen, *Quatuor pour la fin du temps* (Quartet for the End of Time)

Philosophy

Maurice Merleau-Ponty, *La Structure du comportement* (translated as *The Structure of Behavior*)

1942

Historical Events

Allied invasions of North Africa; German occupation of so-called Free Zone.

Art & Architecture

André Masson, *Paysage iroquois* (Iroquois Landscape)

Cinema

Christian-Jacque, *La Symphonie fantastique* (The Fantastic Symphony)

Drama

Jean Giraudoux, *L'Apollon de Marsac* (Rio de Janeiro)
Henry de Montherlant, *La Reine morte* (translated as *Queen after Death*)

Literature

Louis Aragon, *Les Yeux d'Elsa* (Elsa's Eyes)
Albert Camus, *L'Etranger* (translated as *The Stranger*)
Francis Ponge, *Le Parti-pris des choses* (translated as *The Voice of Things*)
Antoine de Saint-Exupéry, *Pilote de guerre* (translated as *Flight to Arras*)

Music

Boris Vian begins playing jazz in Claude Abadie's amateur jazz orchestra.

Philosophy

Albert Camus, *Le Mythe de Sisyphe* (translated as *The Myth of Sisyphus*)

1943

Historical Events

Founding of Comité Français de Libération Nationale (French Committee of National Liberation) in Algiers; resolution to establish the United Nations passed in the U.S. House of Representatives.

Art and Architecture

Jean Fautrier, *Les Otages* (1943–1945; The Hostages)

Drama

Jean Giraudoux, *Sodome et Gomorrhe* (translated as *Sodom and Gomorrah*)
Jean-Paul Sartre, *Les Mouches* (translated as *The Flies*)

Literature

Georges Bernanos, *Monsieur Ouine* (translated as *The Open Mind*)
Simone de Beauvoir, *L'Invitée* (translated as *She Came to Stay*)
Robert Desnos, *Le Vin est tiré* (The Wine Is Drawn)
André Malraux, *Les Noyers de l'Altenburg* (translated as *The Walnut Trees of Altenburg*)
Antoine de Saint-Exupéry, *Le Petit Prince* (translated as *The Little Prince*)

Philosophy

Jean-Paul Sartre, *L'Etre et le néant* (translated as *Being and Nothingness*)

1944

Historical Events

Allied invasion of Normandy; Liberation of Paris; Allies recognize Committee of National Liberation as the Gouvernement Provisoire de la République Française (provisional government of France); beginning of *épuration* (trials and executions for collaboration with the Germans).

Art & Architecture

Fernand Léger, *Cyclistes* (Cyclists)

Drama

Jean Anouilh, *Antigone*
Albert Camus, *Le Malentendu* (translated as *Cross Purpose*) and *Caligula*
Jean-Paul Sartre, *Huis-clos* (translated as *No Exit*)

Literature

Romain Gary, *Education européenne* (translated as *Forest of Anger*)
Disappearance of Antoine de Saint-Exupéry

Popular Culture
Founding of women's magazine *Marie-France*

1945

Historical Events
Death of Franklin D. Roosevelt; deaths of Adolf Hitler and Benito Mussolini; end of World War II; atomic bombs dropped on Hiroshima and Nagasaki; execution of Robert Brasillach for collaboration with the Germans; trial of Philippe Pétain; French vote by referendum to end the Third Republic.

Cinema
Marcel Carné, *Les Enfants du paradis* (*Children of Paradise*)

Drama
Jean Giraudoux, *La Folle de Chaillot* (translated as *The Madwoman of Chaillot*)

Literature
Jean-Paul Sartre, *Le Sursis* (translated as *The Reprieve*)
Léopold Sédar Senghor, *Chants d'ombre* (Songs of Shadow)
Elsa Triolet, *Le Premier Accroc coûte deux cents francs* (translated as *A Fine of 200 Francs*)

Paper remains scarce, but publishing activity increases.
Founding of *Les Temps Modernes*
Suicide of Pierre Drieu La Rochelle
Death of Paul Valéry
Death of Robert Desnos after liberation from a concentration camp
Repatriation of Jean Cayrol from a concentration camp

Philosophy
Maurice Merleau-Ponty, *La Phénoménologie de la perception* (translated as *The Phenomenology of Perception*)

Popular Culture
Founding of women's magazine *Elle*

Radio/Television
All private radio stations banned in France; proliferation of stations broadcasting from Luxembourg, Monte Carlo, and elsewhere in Europe

1946

Historical Events
Establishment of Fourth Republic; Winston Churchill's "Iron Curtain" speech; Charles de Gaulle withdraws from active political roles; nationalist (anticolonial) agitation in Indochina and first major clashes; first meeting of the United Nations General Assembly.

Art & Architecture
Henri Laurens, *La Lune* (The Moon)
Henri Michaux, *Peintures et dessins* (Paintings and Drawings)

Cinema
Jean Cocteau, *La Belle et la bête* (Beauty and the Beast)
Jean Renoir, *Une Partie de campagne* (*A Day in the Country*)

Drama
Jacques Audiberti, *Quoat-Quoat*
Armand Salacrou, *Les Nuits de la colère* (The Nights of Anger)
Jean-Paul Sartre, *Morts sans sépulture* (translated as *The Victors*) and *La Putain respectueuse* (translated as *The Respectful Prostitute*)

Literature
André Gide, *Thésée* (translated as *Theseus*)
Jules Romains, *Le 7 octobre,* the last volume of *Les Hommes de bonne volonté* (translated as *Men of Good Will*)
Jules Roy, *La Vallée heureuse* (translated as *The Happy Valley*)

Philosophy
Jean-Paul Sartre, *L'Existentialisme est un humanisme* (translated as *Existentialism*)

1947

Historical Events
Communists leave French government; proposal of Marshall Plan to aid economic recovery in Europe; beginning of Cold War; first mass Gaullist movement, Rassemblement du Peuple Français, founded.

Art & Architecture
Le Corbusier begins building collective housing in Marseilles.

Cinema
Claude Autant-Lara, *Le Diable au corps* (Devil in the Flesh)

Drama
Jean Anouilh, *L'Invitation au château* (translated as *Ring Round the Moon*)
Jean Genet, *Les Bonnes* (translated as *The Maids*)
Henry de Montherlant, *Le Maître de Santiago* (translated as *The Master of Santiago*)

Armand Salacrou, *L'Archipel Lenoir* (The Lenoir Archipelago)
Avignon Festival organized by Jean Vilar

Literature
Nobel Prize for Literature: André Gide
Albert Camus, *La Peste* (translated as *The Plague*)
Boris Vian, *L'Ecume des jours* (translated as *Froth on the Daydream*)

Philosophy
Simone de Beauvoir, *Pour une morale de l'ambiguïté* (translated as *The Ethics of Ambiguity*)
Maurice Merleau-Ponty, *Humanisme et terreur* (translated as *Humanism and Terror*)
Simone Weil, *La Pesanteur et la grâce* (translated as *Gravity and Grace*)

1948

Historical Events
Beginning of Soviet blockade of Berlin; Allies airlift supplies to the city.

Art & Architecture
Henri Michaux, *Meidosems*

Auguste Perret, Place de l'Hôtel de Ville, Le Havre (1948–1954)
Pablo Picasso, *La Cuisine* (The Kitchen)

Drama
Albert Camus, *L'Etat de siège* (translated as *State of Siege*)
Jean-Paul Sartre, *Les Mains sales* (translated as *Dirty Hands*)

Literature/Criticism
Hervé Bazin, *Vipère au poing* (translated as *Grasping the Viper*)
Maurice Blanchot, *La Part du feu* (Fire's Share)
René Char, *Fureur et mystère* (Furor and Mystery)
Antoine de Saint-Exupéry, *Citadelle* (translated as *The Wisdom of the Sands*)
Jean-Paul Sartre, *Situations, II* (translated as *What Is Literature?*)

Music
Pierre Schaeffer experiments in concrete music.

Philosophy
Maurice Merleau-Ponty, *Sens et non-sens* (translated as *Sense and Non-Sense*)

1949

Historical Events
NATO treaty signed; French recognize the Bao Dai government of Vietnam.

Cinema
Georges Franju, *Le Sang des bêtes* (The Blood of the Beasts)

Dance
Janine Charrat, *Abraxas*

Drama
Albert Camus, *Les Justes* (translated as *The Just Assassins*)
Jean Genet, *Haute Surveillance* (translated as *Deathwatch*)
Michel de Ghelderode, *Fastes d'enfer* (published 1937; translated as *Chronicles of Hell*)

Literature
Jean-Paul Sartre, *La Mort dans l'âme* (translated as *Iron in the Soul*)

Music
Olivier Messiaen, *Turangalîla*

Philosophy
Georges Poulet, *Etudes sur le temps humain* (translated as *Studies in Human Time*)
Jean Wahl, *Petite histoire de l' "existentialisme"* (translated as *A Short History of Existentialism*)
Simone Weil, *L'Enracinement* (translated as *The Need for Roots*)

Radio/Television
Journal télévisé (televised news) begins.

Sociology/Anthropology
Simone de Beauvoir, *Le Deuxième Sexe* (translated as *The Second Sex*)
Claude Lévi-Strauss, *Les Structures élémentaires de la parenté* (translated as *Elementary Structures of Kinship*)

1950

Historical Events
Beginning of Korean War.

Art & Architecture
Jean Dubuffet, *Le Metafisyx (Corps de dame)* (The Metafisyx [Woman's Body])

Cinema
Jean Cocteau, *Orphée* (Orpheus)
Max Ophuls, *La Ronde* (Rondelay)

Drama
Arthur Adamov, *La grande et la petite manœuvre* (The Great and the Little Maneuver); *La Parodie* (The Parody)

Literature
Marguerite Duras, *Un Barrage contre le Pacifique* (translated as *The Sea Wall*)

Philosophy
Simone Weil, *L'Attente de Dieu* (translated as *Waiting on God*)

1951

Historical Events
Coal and steel agreement among France, Germany, Italy, and Benelux countries (Belgium, The Netherlands, and Luxembourg).

Cinema
Robert Bresson, *Journal d'un curé de campagne* (Diary of a Country Priest)

Drama
Arthur Adamov, *L'Invasion* (The Invasion); *Le Professeur Taranne* (translated as *Professor Taranne*); *Le Sens de la marche* (Facing Forward)

Eugène Ionesco, *La Leçon* (published 1954; translated as *The Lesson*)
Jean-Paul Sartre, *Le Diable et le Bon Dieu* (translated as *The Devil and the Good Lord*)
Georges Schehadé, *Monsieur Bob'le*

Literature
Death of André Gide
Françoise Mallet-Joris, *Le Rempart des béguines* (translated as *The Illusionist*)
Marguerite Yourcenar, *Mémoires d'Hadrien* (translated as *Memoirs of Hadrian*)

1952

Art & Architecture
Le Corbusier, Maison Jaoul, Neuilly
Nicolaes de Staël, *Les Toits de Paris* (The Roofs of Paris)

Cinema
René Clément, *Jeux interdits* (Forbidden Games)

Drama
Roger Planchon creates the Théâtre de la Comédie.
Armand Salacrou, *Poof*

Creation of the Théâtre National Populaire at the Palais de Chaillot; plays produced include Bertolt Brecht's *Mother Courage and Her Children*

Literature
Nobel Prize for Literature: François Mauriac
Marcel Proust, *Jean Santeuil*

Music
Pierre Boulez, *Structures,* part one

Philosophy
Albert Camus, *L'Homme révolté* (translated as *The Rebel*)

Jean-Paul Sartre, *Saint Genet, comédien et martyr* (translated as *Saint Genet, Actor and Martyr*)

Public quarrel between Jean-Paul Sartre and Albert Camus

1953

Historical Events
Death of Joseph Stalin; European Coal and Steel Community launched.

Art & Architecture
René Magritte, *Le Monde invisible* (The Invisible World)
Pablo Picasso, *Femme assise* (Seated Woman)

Cinema
Henri-Georges Clouzot, *Les Salaires de la peur* (*The Wages of Fear*)
Jacques Tati, *Les Vacances de Monsieur Hulot* (*Mr. Hulot's Holiday*)

Dance
Janine Charrat, *Les Algues* (Seaweed)

Drama
Jean Anouilh, *L'Alouette* (translated as *The Lark*)
Samuel Beckett's *En attendant Godot* (written 1952; translated as *Waiting for Godot*)
Paul Claudel, *Christophe Colomb* (Christopher Columbus)

Literature/Criticism
Roland Barthes, *Le Degré zéro de l'écriture* (translated as *Writing Degree Zero*) published in book form
Yves Bonnefoy, *Du mouvement et de l'immobilité de Douve* (translated as *On the Motion and Immobility of Douve*)
Alain Robbe-Grillet, *Les Gommes* (translated as *The Erasers*)

1954

Historical Events
Fall of fortress of Dien Bien Phu in Indochina; Pierre Mendès-France becomes prime minister of France; cease-fire agreement signed in Geneva; outbreak of insurrection in Algeria, leading to Algerian war.

Dance
Maurice Béjart and Jean Laurent form Les Ballets de l'Etoile.

Drama
Eugène Ionesco, *La Cantatrice chauve* (translated as *The Bald Soprano*); *Amédée ou comment s'en débarrasser* (translated as *Amedee*); *Les Chaises* (translated as *The Chairs*)
Henry de Montherlant, *Port-Royal*
Jules Roy, *Les Cyclones* (The Cyclones)
Georges Schehadé, *La Soirée des proverbes* (The Evening of Proverbs)

Berliner Ensemble produces plays by Bertolt Brecht in Paris (including *Mutter Courage* in German and others in French).

Literature/Criticism
Michel Butor, *Passage de Milan* (Milan Passage/Passing of a Kite)
Jean Cayrol, *L'Espace d'une nuit* (translated as *All in a Night*)
Paul Léautaud, *Journal littéraire* (translated as *Journal of a Man of Letters*), volume 1
Marcel Proust, *Contre Sainte-Beuve*
Jean-Pierre Richard, *Littérature et sensation* (Literature and Sensation)
Françoise Sagan, *Bonjour tristesse*
Simone de Beauvoir receives the Prix Goncourt for *Les Mandarins* (translated as *The Mandarins*).

1955

Art & Architecture
Jean Bazaine, *Marée basse* (Low Tide)
Le Corbusier, Notre-Dame du Haut, Ronchamp (1951–1955)
Nicolaes de Staël, *Le Fort d'Antibes* (Antibes Fort)

Cinema
Henri-Georges Clouzot, *Les Diaboliques*
Alain Resnais, *Nuit et brouillard* (Night and Fog)

Dance
Les Ballets Modernes de Paris founded

Drama
Arthur Adamov, *Le Ping-Pong*
Eugène Ionesco, *Jacques ou la soumission* (translated as *Jack*)

Jean Tardieu, *Six pièces en un acte* (includes *La Serrure* [translated as *The Keyhole*] and others)

Literature/Criticism
Maurice Blanchot, *L'Espace littéraire* (translated as *The Space of Literature*)
Marguerite Duras, *Le Square* (translated as *The Square*)

Philosophy
Maurice Merleau-Ponty, *Les Aventures de la dialectique* (translated as *Adventures of the Dialectic*)
Pierre Teilhard de Chardin, *Le Phénomène humain* (translated as *The Phenomenon of Man*)

Sociology
Claude Lévi-Strauss, *Tristes tropiques*

1956

Historical Events
France grants independence to Tunisia and Morocco; Britain and France reestablish control of the Suez Canal after an Egyptian attempt to nationalize it; Soviet invasion of Hungary.

Art & Architecture
André Beaudin, *Le Pont du Louvre* (The Louvre Bridge)

Cinema
Robert Bresson, *Un Condamné à mort s'est échappé* (*A Man Escaped*)
Jules Dassin, *Du rififi chez les hommes* (*Rififi*)

Roger Vadim, *Et Dieu créa la femme* (*And God Created Woman*)

Drama
Jean Anouilh, *Pauvre Bitos, ou Le dîner des têtes* (translated as *Poor Bitos*)
Eugène Ionesco, *L'Impromptu de l'Alma* (translated as *Improvisation*)

Literature
Michel Butor, *L'Emploi du temps* (translated as *Passing Time*)
Albert Camus, *La Chute* (translated as *The Fall*)

Romain Gary, *Les Racines du ciel* (translated as *The Roots of Heaven*)

Lucien Goldman, *Le Dieu caché* (translated as *The Hidden God*)

Nathalie Sarraute, *L'Ere du soupçon* (translated as *The Age of Suspicion*)

1957

Historical Events
Battle of Algiers; Treaty of Rome establishes the European Economic Community (Common Market).

Art & Architecture
Jean Fautrier, *Tête de partisan, Budapest* (Head of a Partisan, Budapest)

Drama
Arthur Adamov, *Paolo Paoli*

Samuel Beckett, *Fin de partie* (translated as *Endgame*); *Acte sans parole* (translated as *Act without Words*)

Théâtre de la Cité established in Villeurbanne

Literature/Criticism
Michel Butor, *La Modification* (translated as *A Change of Heart*)

Albert Camus, *L'Exil et le royaume* (translated as *Exile and the Kingdom*)

Alain Robbe-Grillet, *La Jalousie* (translated as *Jealousy*)

Nobel Prize for Literature: Albert Camus

Music
Francis Poulenc, *Les Dialogues des Carmélites* (Dialogues of the Carmelites)

Philosophy
Georges Bataille, *La Littérature et le mal* (Literature and Evil)

1958

Historical Events
Revolt by European-Algerian settlers in Algeria; fall of Fourth Republic and return to power of Charles de Gaulle; referendum on the constitution of the Fifth Republic.

Art & Architecture
Construction of the Palais de l'UNESCO

Cinema
Louis Malle, *Les Amants* (The Lovers); *Ascenseur pour l'échafaud* (*Frantic*)

Drama
Eugène Ionesco, *Le Nouveau Locataire* (translated as *The New Tenant*)

Literature
Louis Aragon, *La Semaine sainte* (translated as *Holy Week*)

Simone de Beauvoir, *Mémoires d'une jeune fille rangée* (translated as *Memoirs of a Dutiful Daughter*)

Marguerite Duras, *Moderato cantabile*

Joseph Kessel, *Le Lion* (translated as *The Lion*)

Claude Ollier, *La Mise en scène*

Christiane Rochefort, *Le Repos du guerrier* (translated as *Warrior's Rest*)

Claude Simon, *L'Herbe* (translated as *The Grass*)

Philippe Sollers, *Une Curieuse Solitude* (translated as *A Strange Solitude*)

Elie Wiesel, *La Nuit* (translated as *Night*)

Music
Olivier Messiaen, *Catalogue d'oiseaux* (Catalogue of Birds)

1959

Cinema
Robert Bresson, *Pickpocket*

Alain Resnais, *Hiroshima mon amour*

François Truffaut, *Les Quatre cents coups* (The 400 Blows)

Drama
Jean Anouilh, *Becket, ou L'Honneur de Dieu* (translated as *Becket, or The Honor of God*)

Fernando Arrabal, *Pique-nique en campagne* (translated as *Picnic on the Battlefield*)

Jean-Louis Barrault becomes director of the Théâtre de l'Odéon.

Eugène Ionesco, *Rhinocéros*

Jean-Paul Sartre, *Les Séquestrés d'Altona* (translated as *The Condemned of Altona*)

Boris Vian, *Les Bâtisseurs d'empire* (translated as *The Empire Builders*)

Association Théâtrale des Etudiants de Paris founded

Literature
Raymond Queneau, *Zazie dans le métro* (translated as *Zazie*)

Nathalie Sarraute, *Le Planétarium* (translated as *The Planetarium*)

Music
Olivier Messiaen, *Oiseaux exotiques* (Exotic Birds)

Philosophy
Louis Althusser, *Montesquieu, la politique et l'histoire* (translated as *Politics and History: Montesquieu, Rousseau, Hegel, and Marx*)

Popular Culture
René Goscinny and Albert Uderzo, *Astérix le Gaulois* (Asterix the Gaul) comic strip

1960

Historical Events
Independence of Belgian Congo; independence of French Black Africa and French West Africa and formation of new nations, including Chad, Congo, Dahomey, Gabon, the Ivory Coast, Niger, and others; controversy surrounding the Algerian war, including Manifeste des 121 urging conscripts to refuse to serve in Algeria; publication of Jules Roy's *La Guerre d'Algérie* (translated as *The War in Algeria*); France tests its first atomic bomb.

Art & Architecture
Le Corbusier, Monastery of La Tourette, Eveux (1956–1960)

Cinema
Jean-Luc Godard, *A bout de souffle* (Breathless)

Jacques Rivette, *Paris nous appartient* (Paris Belongs to Us)

François Truffaut, *Tirez sur le pianiste* (Shoot the Piano Player)

Dance
Maurice Béjart, Grand Prix du Théâtre des Nations, Paris

Drama
Samuel Beckett, *La Dernière Bande* (translated as *Krapp's Last Tape*)
René de Obaldia, *Génousie* (translated as *Jenusia*)
Robert Pinget, *Lettre morte* (translated as *Dead Letter*)

Literature
Simone de Beauvoir, *La Force de l'âge* (translated as *The Prime of Life*)
Michel Butor, *Degrés* (translated as *Degrees*); *Mobile: Etude pour une représentation des Etats-Unis* (translated as *Mobile: Study for a Representation of the United States*)

Claude Simon, *La Route des Flandres* (translated as *The Flanders Road*)
Saint-John Perse receives the Nobel Prize for Literature.
Death of Albert Camus
Founding of Oulipo (Ouvroir de Littérature Potentielle [Workshop for Potential Literature])

Philosophy
Jean-Paul Sartre, *Critique de la raison dialectique* (translated as *Critique of Dialectical Reason*), volume 1

1961

Historical Events
John F. Kennedy visits Paris.

Art & Architecture
André Masson, *22 dessins sur le thème du désir* (22 Designs on the Theme of Desire)

Cinema
Alain Resnais, *L'Année dernière à Marienbad* (Last Year at Marienbad)
François Truffaut, *Jules et Jim* (Jules and Jim)
Agnès Varda, *Cléo de 5 à 7* (Cleo from 5 to 7)

Drama
Arthur Adamov, *Le Printemps 71* (Spring '71)
Armand Salacrou, *Boulevard Durand*
Georges Schehadé, *Le Voyage*

Literature
Jean Ricardou, *L'Observatoire de Cannes* (The Cannes Observatory)

Philosophy
Michel Foucault, *Folie et raison: Histoire de la folie à l'âge classique* (translated as *Madness and Civilization*)

1962

Historical Events
Evian accords end the Algerian war; Algerian independence in July; Cuban missile crisis; referendum for direct election of the president of the republic.

Cinema
Georges Franju, *Thérèse Desqueyroux* (Therese)

Drama
Jacques Audiberti, *La Poupée* (The Doll)
Eugène Ionesco, *Le Roi se meurt* (translated as *Exit the King*)
Robert Pinget, *Architruc*
Roger Planchon, *La Remise* (The Shed/The Handing Over)

Literature
Founding of *Tel Quel*

1963

Historical Events
France vetoes the application of Great Britain to join the Common Market.

Art & Architecture
GRAV group show *Labyrinthe*

Cinema
Chris Marker, *Le Joli Mai* (Lovely May)
Alain Robbe-Grillet, *L'Immortelle* (The Immortal One)

Dance
Festival International de la Danse de Paris founded

Drama
Aimé Césaire, *La Tragédie du roi Christophe* (translated as *The Tragedy of King Christophe*)
Jean Genet, *Les Paravents* (translated as *The Screens*)

Eugène Ionesco, *Le Piéton de l'air* (translated as *A Stroll in the Air*)
René de Obaldia, *Le Satyre de la Villette* (The Satyr of La Villette)
Summer theater Nancy Festival begins.

Literature/Criticism
Simone de Beauvoir, *La Force des choses* (translated as *Force of Circumstance*)
Edmond Jabès, *Le Livre des questions* (translated as *The Book of Questions*)
J. M. G. Le Clézio, *Le Procès-verbal* (translated as *The Interrogation*)
Alain Robbe-Grillet, *Pour un nouveau roman* (translated as *For a New Novel*)
Denis Roche, *Récits complets* (Complete Narratives)

1964

Historical Events
U.S. Congress passes the Gulf of Tonkin resolution, leading to escalation of the war in Vietnam.

Cinema
Jacques Demy, *Les Parapluies de Cherbourg* (The Umbrellas of Cherbourg)

Drama
Founding of the Théâtre du Soleil

Literature
Violette Leduc, *La Bâtarde* (translated as *The Bastard*)
Jean-Paul Sartre, *Les Mots* (translated as *The Words*)
Jean-Paul Sartre refuses the Nobel Prize for Literature.
Monique Wittig, *L'Opoponax* (translated as *The Opoponax*)

Philosophy
Maurice Merleau-Ponty, *Le Visible et l'invisible* (translated as *The Visible and the Invisible*)

Sociology/Anthropology
Claude Lévi-Strauss, *Le Cru et le cuit* (translated as *The Raw and the Cooked*)

1965

Historical Events
Charles de Gaulle elected president over François Mitterrand.

Drama
Marguerite Duras, *Des journées entières dans les arbres* (translated as *Days in the Trees*)

Literature
Jean Ricardou, *La Prise de Constantinople* (The Taking of Constantinople)
Albertine Sarrazin, *La Cavale* (translated as *The Runaway*)

Philosophy
Louis Althusser, *Pour Marx* (translated as *For Marx*); *Lire le Capital* (translated as *Reading Capital*)

1966

Historical Events
France leaves NATO.

Drama
Fernando Arrabal, *Le Cimetière des voitures* (published 1957; translated as *The Car Cemetery*)
Fernando Arrabal receives the Grand Prix du Théâtre.
Aimé Césaire, *Une Saison au Congo* (translated as *A Season in the Congo*)
René de Obaldia, *Du vent dans les branches de sassafras* (translated as *Wind in the Branches of the Sassafras*)

Literature/Criticism
Serge Doubrovsky, *Pourquoi la nouvelle critique?* (translated as *The New Criticism in France*)
Marguerite Duras, *Le Vice-Consul* (translated as *The Vice-Consul*)
Gérard Genette, *Figures I*
Jean-Claude Renard, *La Terre du sacre* (Land of the Coronation)

Philosophy
Michel Foucault, *Les Mots et les choses: Un Archéologie des sciences humanes* (translated as *The Order of Things: An Archeology of the Human Sciences*)
Jacques Lacan, *Ecrits*

1967

Historical Events
The Suez Canal is closed as a result of the Arab-Israeli War.

Cinema
Alain Robbe-Grillet, *Trans-Europe Express*
Jacques Tati, *Playtime*

Drama
Fernando Arrabal, *L'Architecte et l'Empereur d'Assyrie* (published 1965; translated as *The Architect and the Emperor of Assyria*)

Literature
André Malraux, *Anti-mémoires* (translated as *Antimemoirs*)

Philosophy
Jacques Derrida, *De la grammatologie* (translated as *Of Grammatology*)

1968

Historical Events
"May 1968" (student and worker riots in Paris), with protests at the Sorbonne and student occupation of the Théâtre de l'Odéon; Soviet invasion of Czechoslovakia.

Cinema
Luis Buñuel, *Belle de jour* (Beauty of Day)
Claude Chabrol, *La Femme infidèle* (*The Unfaithful Wife*)
Constantin Costa-Gavras, *Z*

Dance
Ballet Théâtre Contemporain established
"Le Ballet pour Demain" competition established by Jacque Chauraud

Drama
André Benedetto, *Napalm*

Literature
Simone de Beauvoir, *La Femme rompue* (translated as *The Woman Destroyed*)

1969

Historical Events
Georges Pompidou elected president of the Fifth Republic; Jacques Chaban-Delmas appointed prime minister; Pompidou initiates construction of the Centre Pompidou (Beaubourg), opened in 1977.

Cinema
Eric Rohmer, *Ma Nuit chez Maud* (*My Night with Maud*)

Drama
Aimé Césaire, *Une Tempête* (The Tempest)

Roger Planchon, *La Contestation et la mise en pièces de la plus illustre des tragédies françaises . . .* (The Disputation and Dismemberment of the Most Illustrious of French Tragedies . . .)
Théâtre du Soleil, *Les Clowns* (The Clowns)

Literature/Criticism
Julia Kristeva, *Séméiotikè: Recherches pour une sémanalyse* (translated as *Desire in Language: A Semiotic Approach to Literature and Art*)
Georges Perec, *La Disparition* (The Disappearance)

Jean-Claude Renard, *La Braise et la rivière* (The Coals and the River)

Monique Wittig, *Les Guérillères* (translated as *The Guerrillas*)

Music
Olivier Messiaen, *La Transfiguration de notre Seigneur Jésus-Christ* (The Transfiguration of Our Lord Jesus Christ)

1970

Historical Events
Great Britain joins the Common Market; death of Charles de Gaulle; Mouvement de la Libération des Femmes (Women's Liberation Movement).

Art & Architecture
Paul Rebeyrolle, *Coexistences*

Drama
Théâtre du Soleil, *1789*

1971

Historical Events
French feminists issue the Manifeste des 343, demanding the legalization of abortion; creation of the new (reconstituted) Socialist Party, with François Mitterrand as first secretary; first French nuclear submarine launched.

Cinema
Louis Malle, *Le Souffle au cœur* (Murmur of the Heart)

1972

Historical Events
Pierre Messmer replaces Jacques Chaban-Delmas as prime minister; salaries for men and women are equalized.

Cinema
Jean-Luc Godard and Jean-Pierre Gorin, *Tout va bien* (All Is Well)

Drama
Robert Pinget, *Identité* (Identity)
Théâtre du Soleil, *1793*

1973

Historical Events
French government establishes a commission on terminology to coin French technical words.

Cinema
Louis Malle, *Lacombe Lucien*
Alain Robbe-Grillet, *Glissements progressifs du plaisir* (Progressive Slidings into Pleasure)
François Truffaut, *La Nuit américaine* (Day for Night)

1974

Historical Events
Death of Georges Pompidou; election of Valéry Giscard d'Estaing as president of France; a series of reform laws is passed in France, including the Veil law legalizing abortion; the voting age lowered to eighteen.

Drama
Georges Perec, *La Poche Parmentier* (The Parmentier Pocket)

Philosophy
Louis Althusser, *Lénine et la philosophie* (translated as *Lenin and Philosophy*)
Michel Foucault, *L'Archéologie du savoir* (translated as *The Archeology of Knowledge*)

Literature
Roland Barthes, *S/Z*
Alain Robbe-Grillet, *Projet pour une révolution à New-York* (translated as *Project for a Revolution in New York*)
Michel Tournier, *Le Roi des aulnes* (translated as *The Erlking* and *The Ogre*)

Sociology
Simone de Beauvoir, *La Vieillesse* (translated as *Old Age*)

Drama
Robert Pinget, *Abel et Bella*

Literature
Louis Aragon, *Henri Matisse, roman* (translated as *Henri Matisse: A Novel*)
Julien Green is the first American elected to the Académie Française.
Jean-Paul Sartre, *L'Idiot de la famille* (translated as *The Family Idiot*)

Théâtre de la Cité, Villeurbanne, receives the title of Théâtre National Populaire.

Literature
Colloquium on Antonin Artaud and Georges Bataille organized by *Tel Quel* at Cerisy-la-Salle
Simone de Beauvoir, *Tout compte fait* (translated as *All Said and Done*)
Suicide of Henry de Montherlant

Dance
Le Théâtre du Silence founded

Drama
Eugène Ionesco, *La Soif et la faim* (translated as *Hunger and Thirst*)
Roger Planchon, *Le Cochon noir* (The Black Pig)

Literature
Edmond Jabès, *El, ou le dernier livre* (El, or the Last Book)

Literature/Criticism
Louis Aragon, *Théâtre/Roman* (Theater/Novel)
Serge Doubrovsky, *La Place de la Madeleine* (translated as *Writing and Fantasy in Proust*)
Julia Kristeva, *Révolution du langage poétique* (translated as *Revolution in Poetic Language*)
André Malraux, *La Tête d'obsidienne* (translated as *Picasso's Mask*)
Claude Mauriac, *Le Temps immobile* (Immobile Time)

1975

Cinema
  Marguerite Duras, *India Song*

Drama
  Le Théâtre du Soleil, *L'Age d'or* (The Golden Age)

Literature
  Marie Cardinal, *Les Mots pour le dire* (translated as *The Words to Say It*)

Hélène Cixous and Catherine Clément, *La Jeune Née* (translated as *The Newly Born Woman*)

Philippe Jaccottet, *A travers un verger* (translated as *Through An Orchard*)

Claude Ollier, *Fuzzy Sets*

Georges Perec, *W ou le souvenir d'enfance* (translated as *W or The Memory of Childhood*)

DICTIONARY OF

TWENTIETH CENTURY CULTURE

French Culture
1900-1975

A

RAYMOND ABELLIO

Born Jean-Georges Soules, Raymond Abellio (1907–1986) was a paradoxical and esoteric novelist and philosopher. After graduating from the Ecole Polytechnique, he earned his living in the years prior to **World War II** as an engineer, while engaged in politics with the **Socialist Party.** After the **Liberation** of Paris in August 1944, he was suspected of having had pro-German sympathies during the **Occupation** and found it prudent to move to Switzerland. He became Raymond Abellio and turned to writing to make a living.

His first novel, *Heureux les pacifiques* (1946; Happy Are the Peacemakers), was a partly autobiographical study of French intellectuals on the eve of the war. It was followed by *Les Yeux d'Ezéchiel sont ouverts* (1949; Ezechiel's Eyes Are Open), which won the Prix Sainte-Beuve. These novels portray one man's political journey from the Left to the Right as seen against the background of the 1930s, the war, and the postwar era.

Abellio's nonfiction works deal with esoteric subjects such as Gnosticism, numerology, and phenomenology. His three-volume autobiography, *Ma Dernière Mémoire* (1971–1980; My Last Memory) is characterized by a lucid intelligence and an implacable honesty.

REFERENCE:

Jean-Pierre Lombard, "Raymond Abellio," *Nouvelle Revue Française,* no. 407 (December 1986): 78–79.

— D.O'C.

L'ACTION FRANÇAISE

The Action Française was a nationalistic and antirepublican political party, of which the principal leaders were **Charles Maurras** and Léon Daudet, son of Alphonse Daudet. An outgrowth of the Ligue de la Patrie Française, founded in 1898, the party became the Ligue de l'Action Française in 1905. After **World War I** it was known as the Action Française. Directed in part toward increasing the political role of the Catholic church, it supported the Orléanist monarchists and, in the 1930s, the Camelots du Roi, a Fascist youth organization. Condemned by the Vatican in 1926, the Action Française was dissolved as a party in 1935. The daily newspaper *L'Action Française* (1908–1944) — published under the direction of Maurras and Daudet, with significant contributions from historian Jacques Bainville — supported the **Vichy government** during **World War II.** The paper ceased publication with the **Liberation.**

REFERENCES:

Michael Sutton, *Nationalism, Positivism and Catholicism: The Politics of Charles Maurras and French Catholics 1890–1914* (Cambridge: Cambridge University Press, 1982);

David Thomson, *Democracy in France: The Third and Fourth Republics* (Oxford: Oxford University Press, 1946);

Eugen Weber, *Action Française: Royalism and Reaction in Twentieth-Century France* (Stanford: Stanford University Press, 1962).

— C.S.B.

ARTHUR ADAMOV

Arthur Adamov (1908–1970) was one of the playwrights of the early 1950s whose work was categorized as *Nouveau Théâtre* (New Theater) or **Theater of the Absurd. (Samuel Beckett, Eugène Ionesco, and Jean Genet** were among the other dramatists in this school.) The New Theater, established in reaction to the comfortable, realist, or poetic drama of playwrights such as **Paul Claudel,** produced plays that did not rely on elab-

Leaders of L'Action Française; at center, just to the right of the bust of Cardinal Richelieu is Charles Maurras; on his right is Léon Daudet; to his left are Maurice Pujo and Henri Massis (Albert Harlinque)

orate settings or costumes and were performed in small halls holding audiences of about fifty people. The sparseness of the decor was key to the representation, for the plays themselves were meant to stand alone as events. This *degré zéro,* or transparency, of the New Theater permeated the language of the plays as well, leading Adamov to coin the term *littéralité* (literality). That is, the play is not symbolic in language; rather, it expresses its theme through the action, which is a direct image of the horror of the modern world. Thus New Theater is also called Theater of Cruelty.

Adamov, who was born to Armenian parents in the northern Caucasus region of Russia, spent much of his childhood in Switzerland and Germany before he and his family settled in Paris in 1924. Adamov was influenced by the Russian theater, as well as German expressionism and the works of his close friend **Antonin Artaud.** Adamov's first plays, produced between 1950 and 1955, are admired for their intense portrayal of the anguish caused by the brutality and absurdity of the postmodern world and have drawn more critical attention than his later work. In *La Grande et la petite manœuvre* (1950; The Great and the Little Maneuver), the protagonist, The Mutilated Man, is subjected to

successive dismemberments throughout the play. Adamov's early plays also include *L'Invasion* (1951; The Invasion), whose theme is the impossibility of communication; *Le Ping-Pong* (1955; translated); and La Parodie (1950; The Parody).

Adamov denounced all of his early work except *Le Professeur Taranne* (1951; translated) and turned to writing political (primarily Marxist) plays. This radical break reflects the influence of Bertolt Brecht. The first play in this new style, *Paolo Paoli* (1957; translated), is set during "la belle époque" and ridicules the exploitive nature of capitalism through a humorous portrayal of dealers in butterflies and feathers. *Le Printemps 71* (1961; Spring '71) is an epic about the Commune of 1871. The theme of *La Politique des restes* (1966; The Politics of Waste) is racism against blacks.

Adamov died in 1970 after taking an overdose of barbiturates.

REFERENCES:

John Joseph McCann, *The Theatre of Arthur Adamov* (Chapel Hill: University of North Carolina Department of Romance Languages, 1975);

John H. Reilly, *Arthur Adamov* (New York: Twayne, 1974).

— J.L.B.

The Agadir Crisis

The Franco-German diplomatic crisis of 1911 known as the Agadir, or Second Moroccan, Crisis originated in the unresolved Franco-German disputes over Morocco in 1905 (the First Moroccan Crisis). Morocco, one of the few unclaimed territories on the African continent, promised rich mineral resources and a strategic military location to the country that could win control over it. For these reasons European interest in the area was growing.

The dispute between France and Germany came to a head in July 1911 when the German battleship *Panther* anchored in the Moroccan port of Agadir. The French considered this move an act of aggression. The Germans, however, believed their action was justified because the French, by declaring martial law in the Moroccan capital of Fez, had violated a 1909 Franco-German accord that had reaffirmed the independence and territorial integrity of Morocco.

The confrontation led to a new agreement in November, by which France would hand over certain areas of the French Congo to Germany in exchange for recognition of a French protectorate in Morocco. The Agadir Crisis contributed to already-mounting international tensions and a developing war mentality in the years prior to **World War I.**

REFERENCES:

Geoffrey Barraclough, *From Agadir to Armageddon* (London: Weidenfeld & Nicolson, 1982);

Norman Rich, *Great Power Diplomacy, 1814–1914* (New York: McGraw-Hill, 1992).

— M.G.

Alain

The philosopher and essayist Emile Chartier (1868–1951), who took the pen name Alain (after the medieval poet Alain Chartier), exerted a major formative influence on French thought through his teaching in the first third of the twentieth century. He taught for ten years in the provinces (1892–1902) and then in Paris, first at the Lycée Condorcet and the Lycée Michelet (1902–1909). From 1909 until his retirement in 1933 — with time out for service in **World War I** – he taught at the prestigious Parisian Lycée Henri IV. Among his pupils were **André Maurois** and **Simone Weil.**

Alain worked out no philosophical system — indeed, he was skeptical of systems — but he carefully presented to his students aspects of the best thought of the past, up through the nineteenth century, as it related to timeless philosophical questions. He was par-

ticularly interested in aesthetics. Roughly speaking, his position was liberal and humanistic; he distrusted power and excessive logic. His thinking does not reflect the contributions of phenomenology or other contemporary schools. He was a resolute pacifist even during **World War II.**

His first publications were short essays in newspapers, written while he was still in the provinces. He continued writing such essays, which he called *propos* (words or purposes), for the rest of his life and collected them in books (1906–1936), including *Propos de littérature* (1933). Other noteworthy works are his *Mars ou la guerre jugée* (1921; translated as *Mars, or the Truth about War*) and his *Commentaires* on *Charmes* and *La Jeune Parque* by **Paul Valéry** (1936). Alain's philosophical-anthropological study, *Les Dieux* (1934; translated as *The Gods*), and his intellectual autobiography, *Histoire de mes pensées* (1936; History of My Thoughts), also reveal much about his manner of thinking. He was awarded the Grand Prix National des Lettres in 1951.

REFERENCES:

Bernard Halda, *Alain* (Paris: Editions Universitaires, 1965);

John Weightman, "Alain: For and Against," *American Scholar,* 51 (Summer 1982): 381–389.

— C.S.B.

Alain-Fournier

Henri Fournier (1886–1914), who took the pen name Alain-Fournier, is known chiefly for a single novel, *Le Grand Meaulnes* (translated as *The Wanderer*), published in 1913. The following year he was killed in one of the early engagements of **World War I.** A few of his writings appeared after his death, as did his correspondence with his friend **Jacques Rivière,** who had become his brother-in-law in 1909.

Le Grand Meaulnes, which was made into a successful film, has appealed to several generations of readers. Marked by Romantic idealism and by many other features of Romantic, even Gothic, novels, it tells the story of an idealized love shared by Augustin Meaulnes, a student, and Yvonne, a young woman whom he meets by chance at a strange celebration at a manor house hidden in the woods, where he stays several days. Yvonne promises to wait for his return, but he is prevented by various circumstances from finding his way back. He tries to find Yvonne in Paris, where she used to spend part of her time, but he is unsuccessful. Meanwhile, Valentine, the fiancée of Yvonne's brother, has disappeared. Without knowing it is she,

REFERENCES:

Robert Champigny, *Portrait of a Symbolist Hero: An Existential Study Based on the Work of Alain-Fournier* (Bloomington: Indiana University Press, 1954);

Robert Gibson, *The Land Without a Name: Alain-Fournier and His World* (London: Elek, 1975);

Stephen Gurney, *Alain-Fournier* (Boston: Twayne, 1987).

— C.S.B.

PIERRE ALECHINSKY

Born in Brussels, artist Pierre Alechinsky (1927–) was an early member of the **Surréalisme révolutionnaire** group in Belgium. Together with many artists from that short-lived group, he affiliated in 1949 with COBRA, an international experimental movement. (Its name derives from the first letters of Copenhagen, Brussels, and Amsterdam.)

Alechinsky's roots were not in **Surrealism** proper but in abstraction. He was attracted to what French critics called "Abstraction lyrique," characterized by free play with abstract forms and an emphasis on color. Though he participated in several cooperative projects for COBRA, he also became a distinctive visual artist in his own right. During the 1950s his canvases were characterized by thick impasto, forming a mass of linked and sometimes overlapping tiny forms. Beginning in about 1958 these works were increasingly replaced by canvases occupied by large imaginary creatures, and he began to produce works on paper, which were then affixed to canvases. Using watercolors and ink, he created images suggestive of experimental comic strips in which imaginary beings interact and speak. The titles of these witty fantasies refer to historically prominent artists of the fantastic, including Hieronymus Bosch, Pieter Brueghel the Elder, and the nineteenth-century Belgian painter James Ensor.

REFERENCES:

COBRA 40 Jaar Later / 40 Years After, edited by Chris van der Heijden (Amsterdam: SDU, 1988);

H. Harnason, *History of Modern Art* (New York: Abrams, 1968);

Willemijn Stokvis, *COBRA: An International Movement in Art After the Second World War* (New York: Rizzoli, 1987).

— J.H.

Alain-Fournier in 1913 (photograph by Dornac)

Meaulnes meets Valentine and becomes involved with her.

In his efforts to locate Yvonne, Meaulnes has the help of his friend François Seurel, who eventually finds her and reunites the couple. Yet Meaulnes seems strangely reluctant to return to the lost domain and begin again his idyll. The reader learns later that his involvement with Valentine had made him feel less worthy, or perhaps he has simply discovered that the world of the ideal is not compatible with reality. Nevertheless he and Yvonne marry, but on the evening of their wedding Meaulnes leaves on another quest, to help his new brother-in-law find Valentine. Seurel acts as a surrogate, although entirely platonic, husband to Yvonne, who dies giving birth to a daughter. At the end of the novel Meaulnes returns and takes his child, to whom Seurel has been a surrogate father.

Many recent readers consider Seurel, the introspective narrator of the novel, a more interesting character than Meaulnes. Much of the story is set in the village school, where the boys are pupils, and the book re-creates nostalgically not only a lost youth but also the particular flavor of such schools.

THE ALGERIAN WAR

The events known as the Algerian war (1954–1962) had a profound effect on French life and culture, dividing the French nation and resulting in Algerian independence from France. During this conflict, measures taken by the governments of the **Fourth Republic**

French soldiers searching an Algerian man near the end of the conflict in Algeria

(1946–1958) and **Fifth Republic** (1958–) — including conscription and censorship, as well as various other sorts of repression — were a source of great discord. Some intellectuals sympathized with the rebels to the point of active participation in underground networks. Others protested against the conduct of the war through journalism, essays, or drama.

Conquered partially in 1830 and for the most part subdued by 1847, Algeria was declared part of France in 1848. Because of this legal fiction, the question of Algerian independence could not be treated on the same terms as the status of the French protectorates and colonies freed in the aftermath of **World War II.** While it was technically not a colony, Algeria was also not on an equal footing with the departments of European France. The nine million "indigenous" Algerians (mostly Arabs and Berbers) had few legal rights and virtually no political power. France determined the economic and political destiny of Algeria largely for the benefit of the roughly one million settlers of European descent (French, Spanish, Maltese). Called *colons* or *pieds-noirs* (black feet), many of them belonged to families who had lived on Algerian soil for several generations, and they wanted Algeria to remain French.

No exact date can be assigned to the beginning of the conflict between Algeria and France. War was never declared, and the events were viewed as an in-surrection. There had been sporadic anti-French uprisings in Algeria since 1945. The outbreak of the war is, however, usually identified as 1 November 1954, when Algerian insurgents launched simultaneous attacks against several police outposts and other government offices.

Protest activity was considerable by 1957. Francis Jeanson was one of the most active participants in what was called the Jeanson network or "porteurs de valise" (suitcase carriers), who volunteered to smuggle funds and arms to proindependence Algerian terrorists. **Jean-Paul Sartre** expressed publicly his support and willingness to join, but he almost surely did not participate actively. His 1959 play *Les Séquestrés d'Altona* (translated as *The Condemned of Altona*), while ostensibly referring to **World War II,** had the Algerian conflict as its real reference. Sartre also campaigned against the war in *Les Temps Modernes.*

Other writers who criticized the French position — or at least certain aspects of it, such as the use of torture (which the government denied) — include **François Mauriac** (although once **Charles de Gaulle** came to power in 1958 Mauriac defended him staunchly); critic and novelist Pierre-Henri Simon; and Jean-Jacques Servan-Schreiber, founder and editor of the magazine *L'Express*. In his *Lieutenant en Algérie* (1957; translated as *Lieuten-*

antin Algeria), Servan-Schreiber, speaking as an eyewitness, denounced the use of torture and other unacceptable methods of dealing with the rebels in Algeria (such as shooting so-called escapees). Another exposé was Henri Alleg's *La Question* (1958; translated as *The Question*), for which Sartre wrote a preface. The book was officially confiscated, but some 150,000 copies were reportedly sold. In 1960 Jules Roy published his exposé *La Guerre d'Algérie* (translated as *War in Algeria*), which barely escaped censorship and sold more than 100,000 copies in a few weeks. That year Gen. Jacques Paris de Bollardière resigned his commission in protest against army measures in Algeria, and many eminent figures signed a document called the "Manifeste des 121" (Manifesto of the 121), urging military conscripts to refuse to serve in Algeria.

In addition to *Les Temps Modernes,* periodicals such as *L'Observateur, L'Express,* and even the respectable *Le Monde* expressed opposition to France's Algerian policy, and issues were often seized by authorities.

The height of the insurgency, led by the National Liberation Front (FLN), came in 1957–1958, in the so-called Battle of Algiers. The French army was able to destroy the insurgents' terrorist network in the city. Yet its methods of obtaining this goal, including torture, cost the French much-needed public support for the war, especially among intellectuals. The last four years of the war were characterized by a military stalemate, as French forces pursued the insurgents in search-and-destroy missions, introducing the use of helicopters in the process, but without being able to eliminate them completely. At the same time, the rebels, although commandeering much support from the villages and countryside, were never able to capture and hold a significant military objective. Their internecine quarreling and less-than-unanimous backing from other nations in the Arab world contributed to frequent political and military disarray.

The war came to an end with the signing of the **Evian Accords** in 1962. Thousands of pieds-noirs, who believed themselves betrayed by the French government, emigrated, leaving the Algerian economy in ruins. Most of these Algerians of European descent settled in France, while others went to Israel.

REFERENCES:

Hervé Hamon and Patrick Rotman, *Les Porteurs de valise* (Paris: Albin Michel, 1979);

Alistair Horne, *A Savage War of Peace: Algeria 1954–1962* (New York: Viking, 1978);

Emmanuel Roblès, ed., *Les Pieds-Noirs* (Paris: Philippe Lebaud, 1982);

John Talbott, *War Without a Name* (New York: Knopf, 1980).
                                                — D.O'C. and C.S.B.

YVES ALLÉGRET

During the brief period between 1945 and 1950 director Yves Allégret (1907–1987) dominated French cinema. His work in **film noir** reflected life and social conditions of the early Cold War era.

Introduced to the film industry in 1929 by his older brother Marc, Allégret began shooting short films in 1932 and made his first feature film in 1941, having learned the craft under producer Pierre Braunberger and director **Jean Renoir.** Married to actress **Simone Signoret** in 1944 (and divorced five years later), Allégret directed Signoret and **Marcel Dalio** in *Dédée d'Anvers* (1948; *Dédée*), a movie whose psychological realism differed from the **poetic realism** of the prewar French cinema. A grim and sleazy film-noir vision permeates the petty underworld of Allégret's characters. Life and human values are viewed with dispassion, even cynicism, in his movies, including his best-known film, *Une si jolie petite plage* (1949; *Riptide*). Though he continued to direct after this film, Allégret never again achieved the acclaim he earned during the late 1940s.

REFERENCES:

Roy Armes, *French Cinema* (New York: Oxford University Press, 1985);

François Truffaut, "A Certain Tendency of French Cinema," in *Movies and Methods,* two volumes, edited by Bill Nichols (Berkeley & Los Angeles: University of California Press, 1976), I: 224–236.
                                                — T.C.

RENÉ ALLIO

A significant figure in French cinema since the early 1960s, film writer and director René Allio (1924–) has been a forceful spokesperson for regional film production in an industry dominated by Parisian cinema. He also champions a style of filmmaking that exposes social conflict.

Allio began making movies after success as a stage director. In the early part of his career he was associated with vanguard theater in Paris, with the **Comédie-Française,** and with playwright and dramaturge **Roger Planchon.** In 1960 Allio created an animated film for Planchon's production of Nikolay Gogol's *Dead Souls*. Allio's first feature film, *La Meule* (1962; *The Haystack*), launched an active writing and directing career in motion pictures that includes more than ten feature films. His *La Vieille Dame indigne* (1964; *The Shameless Old Lady*) adapted from a story by Bertolt Brecht, moves to the setting of Marseilles, where Allio was born. *L'Une et l'autre* (1967; *The*

Other One) is about an actress who seeks moral independence after discovering the futility of her life. In the historical movie *Les Camisards* (1970) Allio uses neorealism to depict a failed Protestant revolt against Louis XIV in the Cévennes at the end of the seventeenth century. Allio's regionalism, his attention to historical detail, and his reflections on the world of theater make him a significant figure in French cinema of the last three decades.

REFERENCES:

Roy Armes, *French Cinema* (New York: Oxford University Press, 1985);

Jean-Luc Godard and Michel Delahaye, "Two Arts in One: René Allio and Antoine Bourseiller," *Cahiers du Cinéma in English*, 6 (December 1966): 24–33.

—T.C.

LOUIS ALTHUSSER

Louis Althusser (1918–1990) exerted considerable influence as a neo-Marxist **structuralist** philosopher who rejected standard interpretations of Marxism and the working-class movement. Born in Birmandreïs, Algeria, Althusser studied at the **Ecole Normale Supérieure,** where he taught from 1945 until 1980. He was a member of the **French Communist Party.**

Althusser claimed that the intentions behind *Capital* (1867–1894) and other works by Karl Marx could not, and should not, be sought. Rather, one must seek the unconscious infrastructure, or "problematic," of the texts. In *Pour Marx* (1965; translated as *For Marx*) and *Lire Le Capital* (1965; translated as *Reading Capital*), Althusser denounced humanist and "bourgeois" tendencies in Marxian criticism, which interpreted Marx's philosophy as addressing the concerns of the individual worker. According to Althusser, Marx abandoned the humanism of his early works and developed a "science of history" through which to examine the structure of societal change. In Althusser's reading of Marx's revolutionary message, change is not caused by individuals but by large-scale economic, political, ideological, and theoretical factors. When contradictions exist among these factors, the structure of society changes to resolve them.

Althusser, whose works also include *Montesquieu, la politique et l'histoire* (1959; translated as *Politics and History: Montesquieu, Rousseau, Hegel, and Marx*) and *Lenine et la philosophie* (1969; translated as *Lenin and Philosophy*) suffered from manic depression and was periodically hospitalized as a result. After he murdered his wife by strangulation in 1980, a Paris court found him insane and sent him to a mental hospital, from which he was released in 1984. His autobiography, *L'Avenir dure longtemps* (1992; translated as *The Future Lasts Forever*), was published after his death in 1990.

REFERENCES:

Louis Althusser, *The Future Lasts Forever: A Memoir* (New York: New Press, 1993);

Yann Moulier Boutang, *Louis Althusser: Une biographie* (Paris: Grasset, 1992);

Alex Callinicos, *Althusser's Marxism* (London: Pluto Press, 1976);

William C. Dowling, *Jameson, Althusser, Marx* (Ithaca, N.Y.: Cornell University Press, 1984);

Steven B. Smith, *Reading Althusser: An Essay on Structural Marxism* (Ithaca, N.Y.: Cornell University Press, 1984).

—C.S.B.

LES ANNALES D'HISTOIRE ECONOMIQUE ET SOCIALE

Founded in 1929 by **Lucien Febvre,** a professor at the Collège de France, and Marc Bloch, a professor at the University of Strasbourg and after 1936 at the Sorbonne, *Les Annales d'Histoire Economique et Sociale* was inspired in part by the writings of the late-nineteenth-century sociologist Emile Durkheim. The contributors to this journal have turned to social sciences such as anthropology, economics, and demography to stretch the boundaries of history and make it more scientific. The adherents of the approach practice what has been called "pots-and-pans" history, examining the day-to-day lives of ordinary people, as in Jacques Le Goff's studies of medieval life, which include *Pour un autre Moyen Age* (1977; translated as *Time, Work, and Culture in the Middle Ages*).

After **World War II** Fernand Braudel, who assumed Febvre's chair at the Collège de France in 1950, and other scholars pursued this thinking, rejecting simple narrative accounts of the past as being misleading. Emphasizing quantitative methods, the role of technologies, and the importance of studying everyday life, they proposed different views of historical time: long duration or geological time (in which slow changes in climate and the earth's surface take place), mean duration or social time (in which social and political forces, groups, and modes of living evolve), and short or individual time (in which individual decisions and acts, such as those of rulers, transpire). Among Braudel's publications are the three volumes of *L'Identité de la France* (1986; translated as *The Identity of France*).

After Braudel's retirement in 1972, Emmanuel Le Roy Ladurie took his place at the Collège de France, remaining there until 1988, when he became director of the Bibliothèque Nationale. Le Roy

Ladurie favors biological explanations more than his predecessors, who were under the influence of Karl Marx; moreover, Le Roy Ladurie owes a large debt to **structuralism,** especially the work of **Claude Lévi-Strauss,** and to semiotics.

REFERENCE:

Hope H. Glidden, "La Poésie du chiffre: Le Roy Ladurie and the *Annales* School of Historiography," *Stanford French Review,* 1 (Winter 1981): 277–294.

— C.S.B.

JEAN ANOUILH

Considered one of the most brilliant dramatists of twentieth-century France, Jean Anouilh (1910–1987) possessed an unparalleled sense of stagecraft and a mastery of language, which he used in plays that range from tragedy through farce and social comedy; they have also been successful in English translation.

Born in Bordeaux, Anouilh studied in Paris. In the late 1920s and early 1930s he worked in advertising, acted, and wrote film scripts to make money. In 1931 and 1932 he served as secretary to **Louis Jouvet's troupe.**

The titles Anouilh gave the collections of his plays that he began publishing in 1942 — *Pièces roses* (Pink Plays), *Pièces noires* (Black Plays), *Pièces brillantes* (Brilliant Plays), *Pièces grinçantes* (Grating Plays), and *Pièces costumées* (Costumed Plays) — suggest their range of tone. His subjects include borrowings from Greek tragedy; historical topics — as in *Pauvre Bitos* (written in 1956; translated as *Poor Bitos*), which concerns the French Revolution; and contemporary society. In *Antigone* (written, 1942; translated) the language is sober and spare, fitting the confrontation between expediency and idealism. Anouilh seems to favor idealism for its purity, but of course it is crushed. *Médée* (written in 1946; translated as *Medea*), with its uncompromising, and somewhat rehabilitated, heroine, similarly adheres to many of the conventions of classical tragedy although it has a modern tone. *L'Alouette* (written circa 1952; translated as *The Lark*), the story of Joan of Arc, again presents the spirit of purity confronting compromise. A similar struggle marks *Becket, ou l'honneur de Dieu* (written in 1959; translated as *Beckett, or the Honour of God*), known to English-language theater patrons through the 1960 stage production with Laurence Olivier and Anthony Quinn and the 1964 film version starring Richard Burton and Peter O'Toole.

Among Anouilh's plays on contemporary themes are *Le Bal des voleurs* (written in 1932; translated as

Jean Anouilh

Thieves' Carnival), *La Répétition ou L'amour puni* (written in 1950; translated as *The Rehearsal*), and *La Valse des toréadors* (written in 1951; translated as *Waltz of the Toreadors*). All these works are marked by bitterness and by skepticism concerning the ability of modern men to be happy in society. *La Répétition,* in which a group of guests rehearses a play by Pierre Carlet de Marivaux, displays the twentieth-century dramatist's brilliant linguistic gifts, as he re-creates in a modern mode the *marivaudage,* or bantering, for which his eighteenth-century predecessor is renowned.

REFERENCES:

John E. Harvey, *Anouilh: A Study in Theatrics* (New Haven & London: Yale University Press, 1964);

Edward Owen Marsh, *Jean Anouilh, Poet of Pierrot and Pantaloon* (London: W. H. Allen, 1953);

Leonard Cabell Pronko, *The World of Jean Anouilh* (Berkeley: University of California Press, 1961).

— C.S.B.

ANDRÉ ANTOINE

André-Léonard Antoine (1858–1943), a turn-of-the-century stage director, revolutionized the conventions of French theater, giving new meaning to the notion of stage realism. After an impoverished childhood (he began earning his keep at age thirteen), he took up amateur acting in Paris, with a group called the Cercle gaulois (Gallic Circle). His desire to direct and his ideas for the transformation of staging led him to quit his paying job at the gas company and found his own professional theater, the **Théâtre Libre,** in 1887. There his experimental staging set new standards for theatrical realism.

Early in the nineteenth century directors had sought to deceive the eye with cleverly painted backdrops, but in combination with three-dimensional props the painted scenery never appeared fully real. Antoine built three-dimensional sets to replace the backdrops. He also worked with his actors to eliminate the flamboyant declamation traditional on the French stage and to reproduce the intonations of everyday speech, the gestures of ordinary conversation. Finally, he sought to subordinate the entire production — settings, costumes, lighting, and acting — to the playwright's text, so that every detail of the staging would work to reveal the author's characters and their underlying psychology, much as the interior of a dwelling gives insights about its occupants.

The Théâtre Libre thus became the earliest French example of a "fourth-wall" stage, where the setting was a room with one wall removed, allowing audiences to peek in unobserved, so it seemed, upon a slice of "real life." Théâtre Libre sets were at times overly elaborate, crammed with suggestive, even distasteful, objects (such as real sides of beef hanging in a butcher-shop set).

Antoine provided a superior forum for the production of plays by such foreign authors as Henrik Ibsen and Leo Tolstoy and for adaptations of realist novels by Honoré de Balzac, Emile Zola, and the Goncourt brothers. Unfortunately, however, Antoine's changes made him enemies among the theatrical old guard, and his productions at times created scandals both moral and political: his view of reality seems to have included "leftist" sympathies for the poor and oppressed. Because of such controversy, the system of season subscriptions he used to finance his enterprise could not keep the company afloat, and he lost his theater to bankruptcy in 1894.

Antoine directed briefly on the government-subsidized stage of the **Théâtre de l'Odéon** before continuing his theatrical experiment at the **Théâtre Antoine** (1897–1906). Here, his realism was refined and simplified, with settings reduced to relatively few suggestive details. These sets were no longer imitations of reality. Instead they were an artistically controlled and nearly symbolic reality. Antoine served as the artistic director

of the Odéon from 1906 until 1914; this post was his last major theatrical activity, although he left retirement from time to time for brief artistic ventures.

His ideas on the importance of realism to the theater and to the comprehension of playwrights' comments on life are expressed in his "manifesto," *Le Théâtre Libre* (1900; The Free Theater), and in *Souvenirs sur le Théâtre Libre* (1921; translated as *Memories of the Theatre-libre*), his theatrical memoir. He also wrote a theater history called *Le Théâtre* (1932).

REFERENCES:

Bettina Knapp, *The Reign of the Theatrical Director: French Theatre 1887–1924* (Troy, N.Y.: Whitston, 1988);

Francis Pruner, *Les Luttes d'Antoine au Théâtre Libre* (Paris: Lettres Modernes, 1964);

James Bernard Sanders, *André Antoine, directeur à l'Odéon: dernière étape d'une odyssée* (Paris: Minard, 1978).

— R.J.N.

GUILLAUME APOLLINAIRE

One of the most important post-Symbolist poets in France, Guillaume Apollinaire (1880–1918) was a major figure of the pre–**World War I** avant-garde and the chief orchestrator of a new aesthetic in poetry, which he called "l'esprit nouveau" (the new spirit). Endowed with an extraordinary lyrical gift, he wrote beautiful, tender verse with echoes of medieval poetry and late Romanticism. He also produced poems in a wide range of other tones, from bitterly ironic through humorous to blasé. He helped French poetry discard some of its heavy Romantic and Symbolist rhetoric and its rigid versification, and by his aesthetic of surprise he prepared the way for **Surrealism.**

Apollinaire was born Guillaume-Albert-Wladimir-Alexandre-Apollinaire Kostrowitzky in Rome to a Polish mother and a father who has not been absolutely identified but was, almost surely, a Roman officer. Apollinaire had an unsettled childhood, spent mostly in Monaco. As a young man in Paris after 1899, he wrote both prose and poetry, did art criticism and other journalism, and worked at various other jobs to support himself. He was well acquainted with the painters of the **Bateau Lavoir,** as well as other **Cubists** and **Fauves** and their developing aesthetic. His first major collection of verse, *Alcools* (1913; translated), in which he deleted all punctuation, is the first great modernist volume in French poetry. Its poems range from simple ballads, based in part on songs and legends he had learned while working as a tutor in Germany, through hermetic and powerfully visionary poems, to narratives, autobiographical pieces, and the fifty-nine stanza "La Chanson du mal aimé" (translated as "Song of the Poorly Loved"), which shows an amazing range of images and tones. The forms in *Alcools* vary from alexandrines and regular octosyllabic meter to free verse.

Apollinaire's other main collection is *Calligrammes* (1918; translated), which includes *idéogrammes* (concrete poems, or poems printed in the shape of objects they represent), as well as such important *poèmes-conversations* as "Lundi rue Christine" (translated as "Monday, Christine Street") There are also extraordinary poems about World War I, some of them written at the front, where the poet served in the artillery. The year before this collection appeared, his play, *Les Mamelles de Tirésias* (The Breasts of Tiresias) was produced; along with the work of **Alfred Jarry,** it is one of the most important influences on the theater of France after 1950.

Wounded in the head by shrapnel in 1916, Apollinaire died in 1918 of Spanish influenza. His important aesthetic manifesto, the lecture *L'Esprit nouveau et les poètes* (translated as *The New Spirit and the Poets*), was published posthumously in the 1 December 1918 issue of *Mercure de France*. A collection of stories, *L'Hérésiarque et Cie* (1910; translated as *Heresiarch and Company*), showed his originality and power as a prose writer.

Many critics have dwelt more on the poet's colorful life than on his achievements as a writer and critic. He has been well served, however, by American translators such as Roger Shattuck and Anne Hyde Greet.

REFERENCES:

Wallace Fowlie, *Age of Surrealism* (Bloomington: Indiana University Press, 1960);

Roger Shattuck, *The Banquet Years* (New York: Harcourt, Brace, 1958);

Francis Steegmuller, *Apollinaire, Poet Among the Painters* (London: Rupert Hart-Davis, 1963).

— C.S.B.

APOSTROPHES

Under the direction of Bernard Pivot, the television interview program *Apostrophes* (1975–1990) was enormously popular and exercised considerable influence over the literate public, affecting book sales in particular. Pivot interviewed prominent authors and other intellectuals, such as **Marguerite Yourcenar, Jules Roy, Claude Lévi-Strauss,** and **Marcel Jouhandeau,** engaging them in lengthy discussions, not simply brief introductions and pleasantries. Pivot later presided over

Bouillon de culture (Culture Soup), a sequel to *Apostrophes.*

REFERENCE:

Bernard Pivot, *Le Métier de lire: Réponses à Pierre Nora* (Paris: Gallimard, 1990).

— C.S.B.

ADOLPHE APPIA

Adolphe Appia (1862–1928), a Swiss theorist of stagecraft, exercised a major influence on French theater through the effects his opinions had on **Jacques Copeau** and other kindred spirits. Appia opposed "realistic" stage sets and commercialization of the theater. He argued that the ideas of each play should be conveyed through the general visual effects of simplified and stylized scenery, costumes, gestures, and lighting, as well as by the sound of music and the words of the script. His theoretical writings include *La Mise en scène du drame wagnérien* (1895; Staging Wagnerian Drama); "Comment réformer notre mise en scène" (How to Reform Our Stagecraft), *La Revue* (1 June 1904); and *L'Œuvre d'art vivant* (1921; The Living Artwork).

REFERENCE:

Richard C. Beacham, *Adolphe Appia, Theatre Artist* (Cambridge: Cambridge University Press, 1987).

— R.J.N.

LOUIS ARAGON

The poet and novelist Louis Aragon (1897–1982), born Louis Andrieux, was "Mr. Communist" of the French literary world for many decades. Perhaps because of his unqualified adherence to the party and its politics — a position reflected in his fiction — he is not well known in the United States, despite his eminent position in French letters and his large literary output.

Aragon, an illegitimate son who was brought up to believe that his mother was his sister, saw military service in 1917–1919, during **World War I.** Like most of his generation, he was profoundly affected by this experience, during which he met and became close friends with **André Breton**. After the Armistice he and Breton, along with others, founded the **Surrealist** movement. Aragon's early writings are among the finest works of Surrealism; they include poetry and especially *Le Paysan de Paris* (1926; translated as *Nightwalker*), a prose work that created an "urban marvelous."

Louis Aragon in front of a poster promoting the cause of Republican Spain at the time of the Spanish Civil War (Les Actualités photographiques internationales)

In 1927 Aragon and other Surrealists joined the **French Communist Party.** Henceforth, he was preoccupied with returning literature to what he called "le monde réel" (the real world); the phrase serves as a series title for four of his novels. In 1928 he met the Russian exile **Elsa Triolet,** with whom he fell deeply in love. Married in 1939, they are one of the two most famous French literary couples of the twentieth century (the other being **Jean-Paul Sartre** and **Simone de Beauvoir.**

In the 1930s and 1940s Aragon published novels whose aim was to chronicle French society after 1900, showing the flaws in the ruling classes. *Les Cloches de Bâle* (1934; translated as *The Bells of Basel*) initiated the series he called Le Monde réel (1934–1944). A series of six novels, *Les Communistes* (1949–1951) deals

with the period at the beginning of **World War II.** Aragon's literary gifts could not redeem these works, which are tedious and blatantly tendentious.

His best poetry, however, transcends its political and social context. Some of his finest work was published during the German **Occupation** of France, while he engaged actively in the **Resistance** and published patriotic poems that quickly became famous and remained so, among them "Les Lilas et les roses" (translated as "The Lilacs & the Roses") and "Richard II quarante" (translated as "Richard II Forty" — a reference to William Shakespeare's royal hero and to the year of the **Debacle,** the German invasion of France). *Les Yeux d'Elsa* (1942; Elsa's Eyes), published in Switzerland, includes beautiful love lyrics and patriotic poems such as "La Nuit de Dunkerque" (translated as "Night at Dunkirk"). *Le Musée Grévin* (1943; Grévin Museum) is another Resistance collection. While employing modern techniques such as surprising juxtapositions and absence of punctuation, Aragon eschewed hermeticism in his poetry and cultivated the simple, direct expression of feeling, using metaphor extensively and often regular rhymed verse.

Aragon remained active as a writer almost to his death, producing an astounding number of works of fiction, poetry, literary criticism (for instance, on Stendhal), and art criticism (notably a mixed-genre work called *Henri Matisse, roman* [1971; translated as *Henri Matisse, A Novel*]). He was awarded the Lenin Peace Prize in 1957; in 1967 he was elected to the Académie Goncourt, a fact that reveals his acceptance into the mainstream of French literary life despite his faithfulness to Communism, even after revelations about Stalinist death camps.

REFERENCES:

Aragon, Poet of the French Resistance, translated by Rolfe Humphries, Hannah Josephson, Malcolm Cowley, and others, edited by Josephson and Cowley (New York: Duell, Sloan & Pearce, 1945);

Catharine Savage [Brosman], *Malraux, Sartre, and Aragon as Political Novelists* (Gainesville: University of Florida Press, 1965), pp. 43–60;

Rima Drell Reck, "Marxism, History, and Fiction," in her *Literature and Responsibility: The French Novelist in the Twentieth Century* (Baton Rouge: Louisiana State University Press, 1969), pp. 216–256.

— C.S.B.

L'ARCHE

The modest magazine *L'Arche* was one of the most important literary publications in French during **World War II.** Founded and published by Jean Amrouche with the patronage of **André Gide,** *L'Arche* was edited by Edmond Charlot. The magazine began its existence in Algiers in 1944 and was moved to Paris after the Liberation in 1945. It ceased publication for financial reasons in April 1947.

L'Arche published writings in French by both European and North African authors. Among the significant works that appeared in the magazine was Amrouche's monumental piece "L'Eternel Jugurtha, propositions sur le génie africain" (February 1946; Eternal Jugurtha: Propositions on the African Genius), which movingly explores the identity crisis of the colonized North Africans.

REFERENCE:
Jean Déjeux, "La Revue algérienne *Soleil* (1950–1952) fondée par Jean Senac et les revues culturelles en Algérie de 1937–1962," *Présence Francophone,* 19 (Fall 1979): 8.

—J.L.B.

ARCHIVES INTERNATIONALES DE LA DANSE

Swedish art patron Rolf de Maré established the Archives Internationales de la Danse in 1931 in Paris as a tribute to his avant-garde Ballet Suédois (Swedish Ballet, 1920–1925). The collection included more than six thousand books, magazines, programs, designs for costumes and sets, engravings, scores, and mementos relating to Western dance. A valuable resource for dance research, the center also organized lectures and exhibitions and published a magazine, *Archives Internationales de la Danse* (1932–1936).

The Archives Internationales de la Danse may be best known for its first choreographic competition, held in Paris in 1932. Kurt Jooss of Germany won the competition and received international recognition for his antiwar ballet, *The Green Table.* The archives organized a similar competition in 1947 in Copenhagen.

In 1950 de Maré donated most of the collection to the Paris Musée de l'Opéra. The museum refused material on the Ballet Suédois and documents from de Maré's Indonesian expedition of 1936. The rejected material formed the core of the Stockholm Dansmuseet (dance museum), created by Bengt Häger. De Maré died in 1964, making the Stockholm Dansmuseet sole heir to his fortune.

—A.P.E.

MARCEL ARLAND

Marcel Arland (1899–1986) was a leading and highly respected figure on the French literary scene from the 1920s through the 1970s. A critic and a fiction writer, he was editor of the *Nouvelle Revue Française* from 1953 until 1977. In an influential article published in 1924, he identified "un nouveau mal du siècle," or new malaise (referring to the *mal du siècle,* named and described by the French Romantic writers at the beginning of the nineteenth century). Arland had in mind the spirit of the 1920s, especially the excesses of **Dada** (with which he had himself been associated briefly) and **Surrealism**, both of which, in his view, were a literary and moral cul-de-sac.

Arland's best-known novel is probably *L'Ordre* (1929; Order), which won the **Prix Goncourt.** It features a young hero in revolt against society. Another widely admired work is *A perdre haleine* (1960; Out of Breath). Among the figures on whom he published critical books are Blaise Pascal and Pierre Carlet de Marivaux.

In 1948 Arland was instrumental in organizing gatherings of intellectuals at Royaumont, reviving a tradition begun by Paul Desjardins at Pontigny, where every summer from around 1905 until 1939 intellectuals gathered to study and discuss spiritual, cultural, and intellectual topics. Arland won the Grand Prix de Littérature de l'Académie Française in 1952 and the Grand Prix National des Lettres in 1960. He was elected to the Académie in 1968.

REFERENCE:
Jean Duvignaud, *Arland* (Paris: Gallimard, 1962).

—C.S.B.

ARLETTY

Born Léonie Bathiat, Arletty (1898–1982) was one of the most beautiful and famous French actresses of the 1930s and 1940s. In the role of Garance in *Les Enfants du paradis* (1945; *Children of Paradise*), written especially for her, she created one of the greatest portraits of a woman in French cinema: intelligent, independent, and stoic.

Having begun her acting career in 1920 as a comic stage actress, she appeared in her first film in 1931 and pursued parallel careers in film and the theater until the 1960s. Her first important movie was *Pension Mimosas* (1935), directed by **Jacques Feyder.** Her appearance in **Marcel Carné**'s *Hôtel du Nord* (1938) established her as a major figure in film. In Carné's *Le Jour se lève* (1939; *Daybreak*), *Les Visiteurs du soir*

(1942; *The Devil's Envoys*), and *Les Enfants du paradis* she developed a character type ideally suited to the melancholic and nostalgic moods of these films.

In the aftermath of **World War II** Arletty's reputation was damaged when she was convicted of collaboration because she had a love affair with a German officer under the **Occupation.** She was jailed for two months. Returning to the screen in 1949, she appeared in several films, of which the most notable was *Huis clos* (1954; *No Exit*), based on the play by **Jean-Paul Sartre.** She continued her work in the theater in roles such as Blanche in a French version of Tennessee Williams's *A Streetcar Named Desire*. Her only appearance in an American film was a small part in *The Longest Day* (1962).

REFERENCES:

Arletty, with Michel Souvais, *"Je suis comme je suis..."* (Paris: Carrère/Vertiges du Nord, 1987);

Christian Gilles, *Arletty, ou, La liberté d'être* (Paris: Séguier, 1988);

Jacques Siclier, "The Great Arletty," in *Rediscovering French Film*, edited by Mary Lea Bandy (New York: Museum of Modern Art / Boston: Little, Brown, 1983), pp. 127–130.

—W.L.

ARMAN

Born Armand Fernandez, Arman (1928–) is one of the most prominent artists to emerge from the **Nouveau Réalisme** group of the 1960s. His experiments with "found objects" began in 1955, when he produced *Cachets (Stamps),* an abstraction made by repeated imprints and overprints with a commercial rubber stamp. In 1959 he shifted to what he termed "accumulations" (piles of mass-produced goods) and *poubelles* ("trashcans"), in which clear glass or plastic boxes were filled with trash. In answer to **Yves Klein's** 1958 exhibition *Le Vide (The Void),* in which a gallery was left totally empty, Arman unveiled *Le Plein (The Fullness)* at the same gallery in 1960: the space was so stuffed with debris that one could see it only through the gallery windows. The same idea was carried out on a smaller scale in the 1960 assemblage *Boum, boum, ça fait mal (Boom, Boom, That Hurts)*, in which a transparent container was filled with toy plastic guns, and in *The Gorgon's Shield* (1962), an accumulation of silver dog combs in a wooden box with a Plexiglas cover.

Arman gradually abandoned the idea of wedging found objects into glass boxes, producing a more permanent effect by covering his arrays of massed goods in quick-hardening transparent polyester. Most often there is no overt message in such works beyond the tongue-in-cheek impact of converting bottle caps, eye-glasses, or ball bearings into expensive art objects. In the same vein, he produced works in which crushed tubes of paint mixed with the hardening plastic to produce overlapping veils of color. Sometimes, however, as with *Boum, boum*, there is a more pointed — if still indirect — message. In his *Glove Torso* (1967) a clear female torso is filled with dozens of rubber gloves, creating a generalized sense of violation. In his *colères* ("angers" or "tantrums") everyday objects — especially musical instruments — are crushed and broken, then mounted and displayed in transparent Plexiglas. His later works have returned to the grand scale of *Le Plein*. In 1975–1982 Arman, who became a citizen of the United States in 1972, assembled for a French sculpture park a piece called *Long Term Parking,* made of sixty automobiles embedded in a concrete slab.

REFERENCES:

Henry Geldzahler, *Pop Art 1955–70* (Sydney: International Cultural Corporation of Australia, 1985);

Marco Livingston, *Pop Art: A Continuing History* (New York: Abrams, 1990);

Jan van der Marck, *Arman* (New York: Abbeville, 1984);

Daniel Wheeler, *Art Since Mid-Century: 1945 to the Present* (Englewood Cliffs, N. J.: Prentice-Hall, 1991).

—J.H.

RAYMOND ARON

Philosopher Raymond Aron (1905–1983) was one of the most eminent intellectual figures of his generation. A product of the **Ecole Normale Supérieure** (1924–1928), where he was a fellow student of **Jean-Paul Sartre** and **Paul Nizan,** Aron also studied in Germany (1930–1933).

Aron and Sartre were longtime friends, but they disagreed on national policy and ideological issues in the 1950s. Aron supported liberal positions (as opposed to the radical dogmatism of many in his generation). In particular, he was skeptical about the **French Communist Party** and the Soviet Union during the Cold War period, denouncing the Soviet labor camps, for instance. His *L'Opium des intellectuels* (1955; translated as *The Opium of the Intellectuals*) criticized the pretensions of writers and other self-proclaimed authorities who presumed to speak out on matters of policy for which they were not trained. His other works include *Introduction à la philosophie de l'histoire* (1938; translated as *Introduction to the Philosophy of History*) and *Paix et guerre entre les nations* (1962; translated as *Peace and War*).

Jean Arp in his studio at Meudon, circa 1953

REFERENCES:

Robert Colquhoun, *Raymond Aron* (London: Sage Publications, 1986);

Jeremy Jennings, ed., *Intellectuals in Twentieth-Century France: Mandarins and Samurais* (New York: St. Martin's Press, 1993).
                                                              — C.S.B.

JEAN ARP

Best known for his abstract sculptures based on biological forms, Jean Arp (1887–1966) was born Hans Arp, the son of a German father and an Alsatian mother (*Jean* is the French form of *Hans*). He was fluent in both French and German from early childhood.

In 1911 — after formal art training in Strasbourg, Weimar, and Paris — Arp helped to found Der Moderne Bund (The Modern Federation) in Lucerne, Switzerland. Involvement with this artists' group brought him into contact with several overlapping circles of avant-garde artists, including Paul Klee and Wassily Kandinsky. Through Kandinsky he became involved with the expressionist Blaue Reiter (Blue Rider) movement, exhibiting at their second show. In 1915 Arp met artist Sophie Taeuber, with whom he collab-

orated on a series of embroideries, tapestries, and collages. They married in 1922 and worked closely together until her accidental death in 1943.

In 1916 Arp joined the Zurich wing of the **Dada** movement, helping to found the **Cabaret Voltaire** in 1916 and the Galerie Dada in 1917. In his autobiography Arp wrote that his art from this period stemmed from disgust with **World War I:** through art the Dadaists sought to save humanity from the madness of the times. This search led Arp to Paris in 1925, where he associated with the **Surrealists** and participated in their first show.

Though most of the Surrealists preferred more openly representational art (though on fantasy subjects), Arp's paintings and sculptures remained heavily abstracted for his entire artistic career, dominated by a sinuous sense of flow and rhythm. His earliest sculptures are reliefs, usually composed of two sheets of wood or metal glued together, with the image either standing out in bold relief or incised away. While some are reminiscent of the synthetic **Cubist** collages of **Pablo Picasso** and **Georges Braque,** Arp's pieces — sometimes depicting a clock, or a shirt and tie, or forks — are not composed of "found" objects produced as part of commercial culture. Rather, they are carefully worked and shaped to suggest or echo everyday objects.

Arp's sculptures swell and curve like biological constructs. Some — such as *Croissance* (1938; *Growth*) or *Silent* (1949) — represent abstract concepts; more work directly from biological models, including numerous torsos and the *Vénus de Meudon* (1956; *Venus of Meudon*), a streamlined variation on paleolithic stone fertility symbols. Arp described these works as "concretions," a merging of natural shapes.

REFERENCES:
Arp, 1886–1966 (Cambridge & New York: Cambridge University Press, 1987);
Herbert Read, *The Art of Jean Arp* (New York: Abrams, 1968).
— J.H.

FERNANDO ARRABAL

Fernando Arrabal (1932–   ) is best known for the plays he wrote during the 1950s. Born in Spanish Morocco and raised for the most part in Spain, he arrived in Paris to study in 1955. His earliest plays, translated into French by his wife, Luce Moreau, and published in Paris in 1958, are a macabre mix of mystery, religious ritual, and sadomasochism. They typically focus on naive and apparently innocent adult-children who are revealed as capable of performing acts of instinctive cruelty and animalistic sexuality, or on an evil mother figure and the son she victimizes.

It is generally agreed that the drama of Arrabal's own childhood in Spain led to his treatment of such motifs. His father, an army officer with sympathies for the Spanish Republic overthrown by Fascist Gen. Francisco Franco in 1936–1939, was arrested in 1936 and sentenced to death. This sentence was later commuted to thirty years in prison. He was eventually confined to a psychiatric ward, from which he escaped in 1942, never to be seen again. Arrabal later discovered documents that suggested his mother, who came from a conservative bourgeois background, had denounced her husband. His shock was so profound that, in a sense, he never recovered. His youth was difficult in other ways too. He was treated cruelly by priests at one school and was often mocked by classmates for his large head and frail body.

Arrabal's early works include *Le Tricycle* (written in 1953; translated), *Fando et Lis* (written in 1955; translated), *Les Deux Bourreaux* (written in 1956; translated as *The Two Executioners*), *Le Labyrinthe* (written in 1956; translated as *The Labyrinth*), and *Le Cimetière des voitures* (written in 1957; translated as *The Car Cemetery*). In 1959 *Pique-nique en campagne*

(written in 1952; translated as *Picnic on the Battlefield*) became his first play to be staged in France.

In 1962 Arrabal, Alexandro Jodorowsky, Jacques Sternberg, and Roland Topor founded the Panic Movement, in large part a parody of organized literary movements. Arrabal's "Panic" plays reflect a way of life governed by confusion, terror, and chance, as well as humor and euphoria. The best-known and most disturbing of these plays is *L'Architecte et l'empereur de l'Assyrie* (written in 1965; translated as *The Architect and the Emperor of Assyria*). A shocking portrayal of a power struggle, the two-character play reaches its climax when the architect grants the emperor's request to be devoured. He then metamorphoses into the emperor and at the end of the play finds himself greeting the return of the architect. Like Arrabal's earlier plays, *L'Architecte et l'empereur* deals with private fantasy, desire, and evil, but this play also addresses the issue of political repression.

In 1967, the year this play was produced and published, Arrabal made a conscious decision to become engaged politically, a decision due in part to his arrest that July in Madrid for having insulted his homeland in an inscription he wrote in a copy of one of his books. Imprisoned for several weeks before his trial, he was finally found not guilty. That same year he won the Grand Prix du Théâtre.

Since the late 1970s Arrabal has also written many novels; he received the Prix Nadal for *La Tour prends garde* (1983; translated as *The Tower Struck by Lightning*). In 1990 he published a play, *La Nuit est aussi un soleil* (1990; Night Is Also Sunshine), and a novel, *L'Extravagante Croisade d'un castrat amoureux* (1990; The Extravagant Crusade of a Castrated Lover).

REFERENCES:
Luis Oscar Arata, *The Festive Play of Fernando Arrabal* (Lexington: University Press of Kentucky, 1982);
John Thomas Donahue, *The Theater of Fernando Arrabal* (New York: New York University Press, 1980);
Peter L. Podol, *Fernando Arrabal* (Boston: Twayne, 1978).
— J.L.B.

ANTONIN ARTAUD

Although he was also a noted stage and film actor and an iconoclastic theater director, Antonin Artaud (1896–1948) is remembered primarily as the most visionary theoretician of the theater in his century. His writings provided the primary inspiration to directors during the "revolutionary" era of the 1960s and 1970s in France and abroad, confirming their convictions about the need for change.

Antonin Artaud (center) in the 1931 war melodrama *Les Croix de bois*

A native of Marseilles, Artaud arrived in Paris in 1920 and quickly became involved in the theatrical world. He joined **Aurélien Lugné-Poe**'s company and first appeared onstage in 1921. The following year, on the recommendation of **Firmin Gémier,** Artaud went to work at **Charles Dullin's Théâtre de l'Atelier,** where he received disciplined training as an actor and experience as a set designer. He planned the decor for Dullin's celebrated 1922 production of Pedro Calderón de la Barca's *La Vida es sueño* (translated as *Such Stuff as Dreams Are Made Of*), in which he also acted.

For some time Artaud had harbored doubts about the value of literature and indeed of language itself. He had already experimented with drugs and shown signs of mental instability. Although he continued acting in traditional plays, he was increasingly committed to theater as a shocking visual experience. In 1924 this attitude drew him to **Surrealism.** Artaud wrote for *La Révolution Surréaliste,* editing the third issue of that periodical (1925) and composing most of it. Yet it was soon obvious to him that, despite a professed interest in staged "happenings," **André Breton,** the leader of the Surrealists, had no serious understanding of theater. So in 1926 Artaud left the Surrealist movement and, with the help of Robert Aron and Surrealist playwright **Roger Vitrac,** founded his own

theatrical troupe, which he called the Théâtre **Alfred Jarry,** after the well-known subversive playwright.

During his parallel career in silent films Artaud played roles in **Claude Autant-Lara**'s *Faits divers* (1924; News in Brief), Marcel Vandal's *Graziella* (1925), Luitz-Morat's *Le Juif errant* (1925; The Wandering Jew), and other films, including **Abel Gance**'s monumental *Napoléon*, in which Artaud played the role of Marat (1927). The same year Artaud published a film scenario, *La Coquille et le clergyman* (The Seashell and the Clergyman). He was to continue film acting in France and abroad into the 1930s.

Theater remained, however, his primary preoccupation. Because the Théâtre Alfred Jarry had no home building, Artaud was obliged to negotiate for stage time here and there to get his productions before the public. He had hoped to revolutionize staging, but that dream was impossible to fulfill in rented halls, where he could not reconstruct the stage. Still, his performances startled audiences of the period, for they included rhythmic mumbling and screams and employed unusual lighting and multimedia effects, including projected films. The troupe performed at the Théâtre de Grenelle in 1927, at the Comédie des Champs-Elysées in 1928, and later in the same year they mounted an eerie staging of August Strindberg's *The Dream Play* (hooted down by vengeful Surrealists) at the Théâtre de l'Avenue. They then returned to the Champs-Elysées for Vitrac's *Victor ou les enfants au pouvoir* (Victor, or The Children Take Over). Artaud began giving lectures and writing on theater during the late 1920s and early 1930s. His subjects — "Art and Death," "Mise-en-scène [Staging] and Metaphysics," "Theater and the Plague," "Theater of Cruelty" — suggest the direction his thought was taking. His theoretical essays of this period were collected and published in 1938 as *Le Théâtre et son double* (translated as *The Theater and Its Double*).

His theoretical writings have been variously interpreted. In general he believed that examination of the human condition leads to the conclusion that language itself is a lie, a mendacious convention producing the false belief that multiple and ever-changing reality can be classified and understood rationally. Thinking in language allows one to "live" in the abstract, alienated from all that is real, including one's fellow human beings — whom one can thus torment complacently — and one's own body. True living — which consists of regaining nonverbal, animal contact with one's own physical being — requires the destruction of all intellectual order, of which language is the primary locus; this destruction is what Artaud calls "cruelty." He hoped that from this rediscovery of men's bestial selves a new and natural order would be born.

The role of theater is to reveal their animal selves to audience members, uncivilizing them and thus imbuing them with a force as virulent as a disease, a "plague" that they will in turn transmit to society at large, liberating it from the rational, linguistic, civilizing, and false moral order. Among the corollaries of this principle are the convictions that actors must possess total awareness of their bodies, being able to accomplish all movements of which the body is capable and to dominate even their breathing; that theater, as **Gaston Baty** had proposed, is not a verbal medium, not literature but a visual and auditory experience; that theatrical utterances exist for sound value rather than meaning (in the absolute they attain the primal scream, the voice of existence itself); that visual expression and use of theatrical space communicate through creation of ineffable symbols and myths; that "spreading the plague" requires actors to make direct contact with the public, leaving the stage to interact with audience members (this technique became commonplace in theaters of the 1960s), thus destroying the "fourth wall" convention; and that the primary emotions theater must convey are shock and fear, leading audiences to prehuman, nonverbal awareness of physical reality, a liberating and reconstructive experience.

The realization of these theories eluded Artaud. The Théâtre Alfred Jarry went bankrupt after 1928; fund-raising to launch a "Théâtre de la Cruauté" (Theater of Cruelty) was difficult, and Artaud was able to produce only one play, in 1935, under that name. It was *Les Cenci* (his own treatment of the theme of Percy Bysshe Shelley's 1819 verse drama *The Cenci*), which he staged at the Folies Wagram. The play ran only seventeen days and constituted a serious failure, on theoretical as well as financial grounds.

Always interested in non-Western expression (his thought had already been inspired by his observation of Cambodian and Balinese dances), Artaud traveled in 1936 to Mexico, where he visited indigenous peoples.

Upon his return to France, he was treated for drug dependency and again showed signs of mental imbalance. During a trip to Ireland in 1937, he was arrested for disturbing the peace (and resisting arrest) and unceremoniously shipped back to France. On shipboard he allegedly engaged in brawling, and on arrival he was handed over to French authorities in a straitjacket. He spent most of the rest of his life in mental institutions. Released in 1946, he gave a lecture and poetry readings in 1947 at the **Théâtre du Vieux-Colombier,** where he appeared haggard and anguished; he had realized, he said, that neither words nor screams were enough; what was needed were bombs. He died of cancer in 1948.

Front cover of the May 1905 issue of the satirical weekly founded by the anarchist journalist Gustave Blanchot

Artaud's influence was carried to the postwar generation principally by directors such as **Roger Blin,** who had been his assistant; **Roger Planchon,** who read his works; and **Peter Brook,** who staged some of Artaud's texts in France. Playwrights such as **Fernando Arrabal** and **Jean Genet** caught Artaud's spirit. In 1973, when the student-dominated **Nancy** theater festival proclaimed the death of the playwright in general and declared that the scenic space itself was the site of creation, it spoke with Artaud's voice.

REFERENCES:

Stephen Barber, *Antonin Artaud: Blows and Bombs* (London & Boston: Faber & Faber, 1993);

Martin Esslin, *Antonin Artaud* (New York: Penguin, 1977);

Ronald Hayman, *Artaud and After* (Oxford & New York: Oxford University Press, 1978);

Bettina Knapp, *Antonin Artaud, Man of Vision* (New York: David Lewis, 1969);

Mary-Helen Kolisnyk, "Surrealism, Surreption: Artaud's Doubles," *October,* 64 (Spring 1993): 79–90;

Edouard Roditi, "The Madness of Antonin Artaud," *Anais,* 11 (1993): 39–45.

— R.J.N.

L'ASSIETTE AU BEURRE

L'Assiette au Beurre (1901–1912) was a prominent satiric weekly edited by an anarchist journalist, Gustave Blanchot, under the pseudonym Gus Bofa. The title, meaning literally "plate of butter," is a slang term for graft. A prospectus for the journal asked, "Is it not a duty of art to fight the possessors of the plate of butter and all social wrongs?" Among the eclectic mix of radical artists of both the Left and the Right associated with the weekly were **Félix Vallotton, Théophile-Alexandre Steinlen, Jean-Louis Forain**, François Kupka, **Kees van Dongen,** Adolphe Willette, Jules Hénaut, Abel Faivre, and Caran d'Ache.

The editorial policy of the weekly, set by Blanchot, prominent Socialists such as Jean Jaurès, and anarchists such as Elisée Reclus, was firmly on the Left. Its most common targets were capitalism (usually portrayed in the form of top-hatted bankers and factory owners), the greed of landlords, government corruption and hypocrisy, the police, war and the military, and colonialism. The official art world was satirized through references to its pomposity and ostentation as well as merciless caricatures of its painters and their work. Special issues included attacks on Christianity, lawyers, quack doctors, and homosexuals. From its inception the journal was the target of repeated police and legal actions aimed at censorship or complete repression.

REFERENCES:

Donald Drew Egbert, *Social Radicalism and the Arts: Western Europe* (New York: Knopf, 1970);

Theda Shapiro, *Painters and Politics: The European Avant-Garde and Society, 1900–1925* (New York: Elsevier, 1976);

Ralph E. Shikes, *The Indignant Eye: The Artist as Social Critic* (Boston: Beacon, 1969).

—J.H.

ASSOCIATION DES ECRIVAINS ET ARTISTES RÉVOLUTIONNAIRES

The Association des Ecrivains et Artistes Révolutionnaires (AEAR) was founded in 1932 as the Association des Ecrivains Révolutionnaires, under the leadership of **Henri Barbusse, André Gide, Romain Rolland,** and Paul Vaillant-Couturier. Through public forums, demonstrations, and its official journal, *Commune,* the group was intended to unite writers who were members of or sympathetic to the **French Communist Party** as part of the struggle for socialism and the establishment of proletarian culture. In 1934 visual artists joined the association, and the name of the group took its final form. Among the

most prominent artists affiliating with the AEAR were **Fernand Léger,** Jean Lurçat, **Paul Signac,** and the Belgian Frans Masereel.

The formation of the AEAR coincided with a turn toward a militant, avowedly insurrectionary strategy by the Communist Party. The AEAR suffered from internal conflicts, most notably the affiliation of the **Surrealists** with the association in 1933 and their subsequent expulsion the same year because of their opposition to Joseph Stalin. When the Communist Party began to move toward creating a broad alliance with other groups against Nazism and Fascism (culminating in the formation of the **Popular Front** in July 1934), the existence of the openly revolutionary AEAR became a hindrance. It was folded into broader coalitions, such as the Comité de Vigilance des Intellectuels Antifascistes (CVIA) and the **Maison de la Culture.** *Commune* continued as the journal of the Maison de la Culture, which reached a peak membership of some seventy thousand before the outbreak of **World War II.**

REFERENCES:

David Caute, *Communism and the French Intellectuals, 1914–1960* (New York: Macmillan, 1964);

Donald Drew Egbert, *Social Radicalism and the Arts: Western Europe* (New York: Knopf, 1970).

—J.H.

ASTÉRIX

In 1959 René Goscinny and Albert Uderzo created the comic strip *Astérix le Gaulois* (Asterix the Gaul) for the comic weekly *Pilote.* The hero, a funny-looking little man with a mustache, is supposedly a Gaul living in Brittany at the time of the ancient Romans. Having become invulnerable after drinking a magic potion, Astérix leads his fellow Gauls in holding off the invading Romans and other adventures designed to show the superiority of the French. Becoming widely popular during the 1960s, the strip was syndicated and translated into numerous languages.

REFERENCE:

Maurice Horn, *The World Encyclopedia of Comics,* 2 volumes (New York: Chelsea House, 1976).

—C.S.B.

ALEXANDRE ASTRUC

Alexandre Astruc (1923–) is as well known for his pioneering essay "Naissance d'une nouvelle avant-garde" (*L'Ecran Français,* 1948; translated as "The

Birth of the Avant-Garde: The Camera-Stylo," as for the twelve films he completed between 1948 and 1976. In "The Birth of the Avant-Garde" he advocated what he called "caméra-stylo," using the camera in a self-consciously artistic way as a creative agent in its own right. While he encouraged a free use of literary materials in scenarios, he argued that cinema need not follow narrative formulas of fiction.

Astruc began his career in the 1940s as a critic of literature and film and was influenced by German movies of the 1920s. A friend and disciple of **Jean-Paul Sartre,** he influenced critic André Bazin, who in turn influenced **Nouvelle Vague** (New Wave) filmmakers **Jean-Luc Godard** and **François Truffaut.** Astruc's first work in filmmaking was as assistant to Marc Allégret in 1947; he also worked with Marcel Achard. In 1953 Astruc directed a noteworthy medium-length version of Jules-Amédée Barbey d'Aurevilly's *Le Rideau cramoisi* (The Crimson Curtain), a film that uses disjunctions of images and sounds with night photography to capture an eerie aura. His first feature film was *Les Mauvaises Rencontres* (1955; Bad Encounters). Astruc completed more adaptations before turning to journalistic cinema, including *Sartre par lui-même* (1976; Sartre by Sartre), directed with Michel Contat, and to television programs treating ethical dilemmas.

REFERENCES:

Alexandre Astruc, *Sartre by Himself: A Film Directed by Alexandre Astruc and Michel Contat,* translated by Richard Seaver (New York: Outback Press, 1978);

Lotte H. Eisner, "Venice Film Festival (Part II)," *Film Culture,* 2, no. 1 (1956): 24, 31;

Peter Graham, *The New Wave* (London: Secker & Warburg, 1968).

—T.C.

JACQUES AUDIBERTI

Although Jacques Audiberti (1899–1965) was a prolific author in all literary genres, he is most noted for his drama. Between 1945 and 1955 Audiberti, a native of Antibes, on the Riviera, wrote several powerful plays; yet they were not widely known to the public until the early 1960s, when producer Marcel Maréchal began staging them.

Like many proponents of the New Theater, or **Theater of the Absurd** — from whom he stands apart because his work is neither political nor philosophical — Audiberti brought to the stage the horror of the modern world. Mostly psychological, his drama is based on the conflict between good and evil, as manifested in the relation between the surface of everyday life and deeply hidden forces. The relationships of Au-

diberti's characters are dominated by sexuality. They are animalistic and pantheistic, sometimes taking on mythic dimensions. Audiberti was impressed by the theories of **Antonin Artaud,** on whom he published an essay.

Audiberti has been likened to **Guillaume Apollinaire** in that he is at once classical and modernist, contradictorily embracing the twentieth century while remaining a cultural anachronism. His plays draw their power from his language, which can range from the poetic to a verbal delirium that approaches nonsense while still conveying Audiberti's essential message: only the spoken word separates man from beast.

Audiberti had his beginnings with the *Nouvelle Revue Française* in the 1930s, receiving the first Prix Mallarmé in 1935 and publishing novels with **Gallimard** from 1938 until his death. He was awarded the Grand Prix National des Lettres in 1964. His best-known plays include *Quoat-Quoat* (1946); *Le Mal court* (1947; Evil Is Running); *La Fête noire* (1948; The Black Feast); *Le Cavalier seul* (1955; The Lone Rider); *La Poupée* (1962; The Doll); and *Opéra parlé* (1956; Spoken Opera).

REFERENCES:

David Bradby, *Modern French Drama 1940–1990* (Cambridge: Cambridge University Press, 1991);

Constantin Touloudis, *Jacques Audiberti* (Boston: Twayne, 1980);

George Wellwarth, *The Theatre of Protest and Paradox* (New York: New York University Press, 1964).

—J.L.B.

GEORGES AURIC

While the other members of **Les Six** developed distinctive styles and pursued independent careers, the composer Georges Auric (1899–1983) remained a disciple of **Jean Cocteau** and continued to write relatively simple, melodic music. He is remembered primarily for film scores, including those for Cocteau's *La Belle et la bête* (1946; *Beauty and the Beast*), *Orphée* (1949; *Orpheus*), and *Le Sang d'un poète* (1930; *Blood of the Poet*), and **René Clair's** *A nous la liberté* (1931; *Give Us Liberty*). The waltz he wrote for the movie *Moulin rouge* (1952) brought him worldwide renown.

Auric was president of the French union of composers and authors from 1954 to 1977 and director of the Paris Opéra and of the Opéra Comique from 1962 until 1979.

REFERENCES:

Antoine Goléa, *Georges Auric* (Paris: Ventadour, 1958);

Rollo Myers, *Modern French Music from Fauré to Boulez* (New York: Praeger, 1971), pp. 117–121.

—P.S.H.

CLAUDE AUTANT-LARA

Claude Autant-Lara (1903–) directed many of the films in the **tradition de qualité** that flourished during the years 1932–1956. Autant-Lara fought to promote French film at a time when American exports were reaping huge profits on French soil. Although he was among those filmmakers whom **Novelle Vague** (New Wave) director **François Truffaut** charged with working in an "ossified" tradition (in "Une Certaine Tendance du cinéma français," 1954; translated as "A Certain Tendency of French Cinema"), Autant-Lara began to earn for French cinema the sort of recognition that was later solidified by Truffaut under the banner of the New Wave.

Autant-Lara learned his trade as art director from **Marcel L'Herbier** (1919–1927) and as assistant to **René Clair** and **Jean Renoir.** While in Hollywood (1930–1932) he worked on French versions of American features. Returning to France in 1933, he directed his first feature film, *Ciboulette,* beginning work with the scenarists Jean Aurenche and Pierre Bost, writers who insisted on careful scripting of literary adaptations for the screen. The result of their collaboration on this and subsequent films was a sober visual style that gave authority to the psychological realism of the written text. Autant-Lara is best known for his studied versions of **Raymond Radiguet's** *Le Diable au corps* (1947; Devil in the Flesh), a novel of an adolescent boy's sentimental education, and Stendhal's *Le Rouge et le noir* (1954; The Red and the Black), a work that conveys many of the same themes in the context of the post-Napoleonic era. Like many of his films, Le Diable au corps challenged conventional morality with its story of an adolescent's affair with a married woman.

Autant-Lara was at the height of his career in the 1940s. Like that of many other filmmakers of his generation, his work was overshadowed in the late 1950s and the 1960s by New Wave cinema. He made his last film in 1977.

REFERENCES:

Roy Armes, *French Cinema* (New York: Oxford University Press, 1985);

Claude Autant-Lara, *La Rage dans le cœur: Chronique cinématographique du 20ᵉ siècle* (Paris: Veyrier, 1985);

Freddy Buache, *Claude Autant-Lara* (Lausanne: L'Age d'Homme, 1982);

Stephen Harvey, "Autant-Lara's *Douce,*" in *Rediscovering French Film,* edited by Mary Lea Bandy (New York: Museum of Modern Art, 1983), pp. 151–153;

L'Institut Lumière présente Claude Autant-Lara en 35 films (Lyons, 1983).

—T.C.

THE AVIGNON FESTIVAL

Organized by director **Jean Vilar** in 1947, the Avignon Festival, or Festival d'Avignon, has grown into an international celebration of theater and other arts, lasting several weeks each summer. It attracted about 8,000 spectators when it began as a one-week program in 1947; about 80,000 attended the festival in 1965, and nearly 150,000 in 1967. This phenomenal expansion was due essentially to Vilar's theatrical skill and marketing genius.

He set his summer theater in Provence, a pleasant vacation area. He staged his plays outdoors, in the vast open courtyard of the ancient papal palace in Avignon. His actors performed on a broad sloping platform set against the medieval battlements of the palace. As they used no backdrops and few props, lighting, costumes, and in particular fine acting became the primary sources of his dramatic effects, which highlighted the inner tensions felt by the characters. Vilar also brought well-known actors to his summer stage, including **Maria Casarès** and **Gérard Philipe.** Beginning in 1951, when he undertook the direction of the **Théâtre National Populaire,** with a regular winter season in Paris, Vilar was able to move actors and plays back and forth, breaking in a play in Avignon before restaging it in the fall in Paris or vice versa. He was also able to develop an audience in Paris that would follow his company to Avignon.

The festival consistently presented works by the most esteemed playwrights, such as Pierre Corneille's *Le Cid* in 1949, with Philipe giving a memorable performance in the title role; Molière's *L'Avare* (translated as *The Miser*) in 1952, with Vilar himself playing the lead role; William Shakespeare's *Macbeth* in 1954, with Casarès as Lady Macbeth; Pierre-Augustin Caron de Beaumarchais's *Le Mariage de Figaro* (translated as *The Marriage of Figaro*) in 1956; and **Jean Giraudoux's** *La Guerre de Troie n'aura pas lieu* (translated as *Tiger at the Gates*) in 1962. In 1966 ballet performances with **Maurice Béjart's** dance company were added to the program. Screenings of art films and other cultural events were soon included as well. Vilar later invited other directors to stage plays for the Avignon audiences; Philipe directed there, as did Georges Wilson and **Roger Planchon,** before an international public.

The student riots and general upheaval of **May 1968** left French theater companies unable to participate in the festival that year. Ballets were staged, however, and at Vilar's invitation the Living Theater, an American Off-Broadway troupe, staged an ensemble performance called *Paradise Now.* The spectacle was shocking enough to earn censure from the Avignon management, and the troupe, joining forces with radical French students and little-theater participants, roundly condemned Vilar and the festival for retrograde policies and politics. Although the broadened definition of theater that this movement implied had some resonance elsewhere, the Avignon Festival continued unscathed and unchanged. When Vilar died in 1971, Paul Puaux took charge of the festival, which continues to grow; more than twenty-five plays were performed there in 1975. In 1980 Bernard Faivre d'Arcier was named general director. Alain Crombecque assumed control in 1985.

REFERENCES:

Jean Vilar, ed., *Avignon: 20 ans de festival, souvenirs et documents* (Paris: Dedalus, 1966);

Philippa Wehle, "A History of the Avignon Festival," *The Drama Review,* 28 (Spring 1984): 52–61.

— R.J.N.

Marcel Aymé

MARCEL AYMÉ

Marcel Aymé (1902–1967) is admired in France as the author of perspicacious, witty, well-crafted short stories, such as those collected in *Le Passe-muraille* (1943; translated as *The Walker Through Walls*). He also published novels, including *La Jument verte* (1933; translated as *The Green Mare*). Often considered his masterpiece, this farcical satire about a small town and its feuding families is sometimes characterized as Rabelaisian.

Aymé was a moralist in the best French literary tradition — a painter of mores and character. He could be merciless in identifying human foibles and dissecting the human heart. Many of his works focus on provincial life. He sometimes created animal fables and mock epics and used fantasy, as in *La Vouivre* (1943; translated as *The Fable and the Flesh*). In *Uranus* (1948; translated as *The Barkeep of Blémont*) he denounced in fictional form the abuses that marked the post–1945 period in France.

Aymé also had a distinguished career as a playwright, with dramas such as *Clérambard* (1950; translated), produced at the **Comédie-Française.**

REFERENCES:

Dorothy Brodin, *The Comic World of Marcel Aymé* (Paris: Debresse, 1964);

Graham Lord, *The Short Stories of Marcel Aymé* (Nedlands, Perth: University of Western Australia Press, 1980).

— C.S.B.

CHARLES AZNAVOUR

Charles Aznavour (1924–) has had a long career as a singer, songwriter, and actor. By the 1950s he had become one of the top performers in France, and he continues to appear before sellout crowds in France and abroad, especially in the United States. To a greater extent than most other well-known performers, he has been able to keep his private life out of the media spotlight.

Born Shahnour Varenagh Aznavourian in Paris to a poor Armenian family that had fled the Turkish massacres of Armenians in 1915, Aznavour started work as a stage dancer and actor at age nine. During the 1940s he began writing songs for performers such as **Mistinguett, Maurice Chevalier,** and **Edith Piaf,** who encouraged him to perform his compositions himself. Aznavour first considered himself too short and unattractive for a career in the movies, but a small part in *La Tête contre les murs* (1959; Head Against the Wall), based on a novel by **Hervé Bazin,** brought him to the attention of the French film community. He has acted in about thirty French, American, and British films, playing the lead role in **François Truffaut's** *Tirez sur le pianiste* (1960; *Shoot the Piano Player*) and roles in *Un Taxi pour Tobrouk* (1961; *Taxi for Tobrouk*), *The Adventurers* (1970), and *And Then There Were None* (1974).

Aznavour's gravelly, tremulous voice conveys an unusual sense of pathos, passion, and even suffering. In love-struck songs such as "Un Beau Matin" (One Fine Morning) and his sentimental paean to motherhood, "La Mamma," which topped the French charts for twelve weeks in 1963, Aznavour teeters on the brink of camp but pulls back just enough to avoid disaster. On records as in live performances he is almost as adept in English as in French. He has composed songs for many films and television series, including the single "She" for the British television series *The Seven Faces of Woman*. The song reached the number one spot in the United Kingdom in 1975.

Aznavour is a living bridge to a musical past that has all but disappeared. With the passing of **Georges Brassens, Jacques Brel,** and **Yves Montand,** Aznavour and Gilbert Bécaud are the last of a legendary music tradition of the twentieth century.

REFERENCES:

Charles Aznavour, *Aznavour by Aznavour* (Chicago: Cowles, 1972);

Aznavour, *Yesterday When I Was Young* (London: W. H. Allen, 1979);

Yves Salgues, *Charles Aznavour* (Paris: Seghers, 1978).

—J.P. McN.

B

GASTON BACHELARD

Gaston Bachelard (1884–1962) was an influential philosopher and critic of literature or, more precisely, of the literary imagination. Having studied mathematics, physics, and philosophy at the Lycée Saint-Louis in Paris, Bachelard taught physics and then took his *docteur-ès-lettres* (doctorate in letters) in 1927 at the Sorbonne. Starting from a basis in the history and philosophy of science he moved on to investigate the effects of scientific discoveries on the structure of thought and the workings of the imagination, which he called "a faculty of surhumanity," in its encounter with the material world. In particular he examined the four elements of Greek scientific thought — earth, air, fire, and water, which he considered the raw materials of affective experience — in reference to modern poets and prose writers. *La Psychanalyse du feu* (1932; translated as *Psychoanalysis of Fire*), *L'Eau et les rêves* (1942; translated as *Water and Dreams*), *L'Air et les songes* (1943; translated as *Air and Dreams*), and *La Terre et les rêveries de la volonté* (1948; Earth and Dreams of Will) are the result of these investigations, which, although he did not rely on Freudian or Jungian models, may be loosely classed as psychoanalytic studies of archetypes.

REFERENCES:
Dominique Lecourt, *Marxism and Epistemology: Bachelard, Canguilhem, Foucault,* translated by Ben Brewster (London: New Left Books, 1975);

Roch C. Smith, *Gaston Bachelard* (Boston: Twayne, 1982);

Mary Tiles, *Bachelard, Science, and Objectivity* (Cambridge & New York: Cambridge University Press, 1984).

— C.S.B.

JOSEPHINE BAKER

Josephine Baker (1906–1975) was queen of the Folies-Bergère in Paris for more than thirty years and widely considered a French national treasure, admired for both her talent and her beauty. Costumed in little more than feathers or bunches of bananas, she performed with abandonment as singer, dancer, actress, and comedienne. Her work was raw and sensual, but with her impeccable timing and her gift for comedy and improvisation she raised music-hall dancing to an art form.

Born in Saint Louis, Missouri, Baker was a chorus girl in a Negro revue in Philadelphia before going to Paris in 1925. Soon after her arrival she appeared with the Paris Revue Nègre and quickly conquered the Parisian music halls. Baker decided to make France her home because she felt freer from racism there than in the United States. When she performed in the 1936 Ziegfeld Follies in New York, her appearances were unsuccessful, possibly because the Broadway show format did not allow for her brilliant improvisations or because racial customs of the time restricted her interaction with the white male chorus.

Throughout her life Baker worked to combat prejudice of any sort. She was an undercover agent for the French Resistance during **World War II.** After the war, she adopted a dozen children from different racial and ethnic backgrounds. She hoped that her children, nicknamed the "Rainbow Tribe," would offer an example of racial harmony.

One of Baker's best-known dances was "Fatou" (Banana Dance) in *La Folie du jour* (1926; The Day's Folly). She wore a skirt of rubber bananas, which vibrated wildly as she shook her body. Her dancing in the 1934 performance of Jacques Offenbach's *La Créole* was also widely praised, and she is credited with starting the Charleston rage in Paris during the 1920s. Her signature song was "J'ai deux amours" (I Have Two Loves). She made two sound motion pictures, *Zou Zou* (1934) and *Princess Tam Tam* (1935), and published her *Mémoires* in 1927. Several films have been based on her life, including the 1986 British documentary *Chasing a Rainbow: The Life of Josephine Baker.*

REFERENCES:
Mindy Aloff, "Josephine Baker's Naughty Jiggle Makes a Comeback: Jazz Age Princess," *Dance Magazine,* 63 (July 1989): 32–34;

Jean-Claude Baker, *Josephine* (New York: Random House, 1993);

Kiosk poster promoting Josephine Baker's premiere in Paris with La Revue Nègre, 1925

Josephine Baker and Jo Bouillon, *Josephine*, translated by Mariana Fitzpatrick (New York: Harper & Row, 1977);

Lynn Haney, *Naked at the Feast: A Biography of Josephine Baker* (New York: Dodd, Mead, 1981);

Patrick O'Connor, *Josephine Baker* (Boston: Little, Brown, 1988);

Phyllis Rose, *Jazz Cleopatra: Josephine Baker in Her Time* (New York: Doubleday, 1989).

                                                                    — A.P.E.

GEORGE BALANCHINE

Russian-born choreographer George Balanchine (1904–1983) began his illustrious career in the West in 1924, when **Serge Diaghilev** engaged him as the last chief choreographer for the **Ballets Russes.** Of the ten ballets Balanchine choreographed for the company, only two survive: *Apollon Musagète* (1928), with music by **Igor Stravinsky,** and *Le Fils prodigue* (1929; *The Prodigal Son*), with music by Serge Prokofiev.

The premiere of *Apollo,* as *Apollon Musagète* is now called, indicated a new direction for ballet and inaugurated a lifelong partnership between Balanchine and

Stravinsky, which would be the source of many of the greatest ballets of the twentieth century. The story of the ballet is of the Greek god Apollo's encounter with the muses Calliope, Polyhymnia, and Terpsichore. The dance *Apollo* is the primary example of neoclassic ballet (classical vocabulary used in a contemporary fashion), and it has influenced all modern ballet choreography.

Beyond his neoclassic style, Balanchine profoundly influenced the art with his plotless ballets, his union of virtuosic technique and choreographic intent, and his image of the ideal dancer. A trained musician, he is remembered as the most musical of all choreographers.

After Diaghilev's death in 1929 and the subsequent folding of the Ballets Russes, Balanchine worked with several European dance companies and also organized a new company in Paris, Les Ballets 1933, for which he created six ballets.

In 1934, at the suggestion of and with the support of Lincoln Kirstein, Balanchine started the School of American Ballet in New York City, which led to the formation of the New York City Ballet, one of the finest companies in the world. He remained its artistic director until his death in 1983.

REFERENCES:

Choreography by George Balanchine: A Catalogue of Works, compiled by Leslie George Katz, Nancy Lassalle, and Harvey Simmonds (New York: Eakens Press Foundation, 1983);

Don McDonagh, *George Balanchine* (Boston: Twayne, 1983);

Bernard Taper, *Balanchine* (New York: Collier, 1974).

                                                                    — A.P.E.

BALLET THÉÂTRE CONTEMPORAIN

The French Ministry of Culture established the Ballet Théâtre Contemporain (1968–1978) as a national center for choreography. In an effort to decentralize the arts it was first located in Amiens (rather than Paris) and transferred to Angers in 1972. The forty-five-member company of the Ballet Théâtre Contemporain worked and performed at **Maisons de la Culture** — cultural centers including performance spaces, libraries, and galleries. Focusing on the collaboration of dance and the other arts, Jean-Albert Cartier, the director, and Françoise Adret, the chief choreographer, engaged painters, musicians, and other choreographers to create a varied repertory that reflected contemporary life. The company toured frequently and conducted many educational programs aimed at expanding the dance audience. In 1978, with financial support from the French government and the city of Nancy, Ballet Théâtre Contemporain relocated in Nancy and became Le Ballet Théâtre Français de Nancy.

REFERENCE:
Linda Doeser, "Ballet Théâtre Contemporain," in *Ballet and Dance* (New York: St. Martin's Press, 1977), pp. 111–113.
— A.P.E.

LES BALLETS RUSSES

Les Ballets Russes (Russian Ballet), founded in 1909 by **Serge Diaghilev** to present Russian ballet and opera in Paris, revitalized dance, making it a serious modern art form. Under Diaghilev's management and artistic vision, choreographers, designers, composers, and librettists became true partners in the creation of ballets that became archetypes for the twentieth century.

Favoring experimentation over tradition, the artists of the Ballets Russes rejected the nineteenth-century aesthetic of influential choreographer and ballet master Marius Petipa. Their ballets were generally one act in length rather than three. Although their choreography usually retained the classical ballet vocabulary, it was original and expressive. Earlier ballets were conceived by the choreographer, who later consulted the composer and designer. In the Ballets Russes the choreographer, composer, designer, and Diaghilev all played roles in the initial conceptions of the works.

The Ballets Russes included in its repertory several modernist styles, including primitivism in *Le Sacre du printemps* (1913; *Rite of Spring*), Symbolism in *L'Oiseau de feu* (1910; *The Firebird*), **Cubism** in *Parade* (1917), Constructivism in *Les Noces* (1923; The Wedding), and neoclassicism in *Apollon Musagète* (1928). The company's influence reached beyond art into the worlds of fashion and design.

Although the artists of the early productions were Russian, the company never performed in Russia; it made its home in Paris, Monte Carlo, and London and toured extensively. Theaters were usually crowded for its performances, but the company struggled financially and was dependent on Diaghilev to raise money for its survival. The company disbanded after his death in 1929.

Perhaps the most important ballet company of the twentieth century, the Ballets Russes transformed the art of dance and launched major careers in the arts through its masterpiece productions. Many later companies trace their roots to it.

REFERENCES:
Jack Anderson, "The Ballets Russes: Past and Future," *Proceedings of the Society of Dance Scholars, 12–14 February 1988*, compiled by Christena L. Schlundt (Riverside, Cal.: Society of Dance Scholars, 1975);

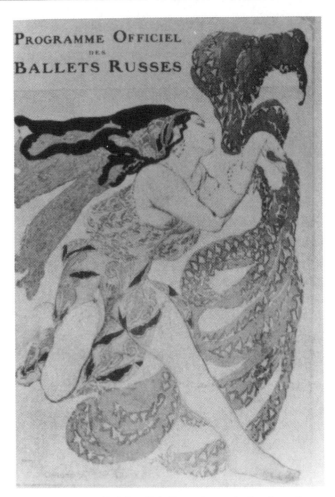

Program cover, with Léon Bakst's costume design for a Bacchante in the 1911 production of *Narcisse*

Nancy Van Norman Baer, ed., *The Art of Enchantment: Diaghilev's Ballets Russes, 1909–1929* (San Francisco: Fine Arts Museum of San Francisco, 1988);

Lynn Garafola, *Diaghilev's Ballets Russes* (New York & London: Oxford University Press, 1989);

Boris Kochno, *Diaghilev and the Ballets Russes,* translated by Adrienne Foulke (New York & Evanston, Ill.: Harper & Row, 1970);

Militsa Pozharskaya and Tatiana Volodina, *The Art of the Ballets Russes: The Russian Seasons in Paris 1908–1929* (New York: Abbeville Press, 1990).
— A.P.E.

LES BALLETS RUSSES DE MONTE CARLO

Following the demise of **Serge Diaghilev**'s **Ballets Russes** in 1929, several successive Ballet Russe companies were formed, hoping to capitalize on the success of the original company. None of the new companies had the monumental impact of Diaghilev, but they were important because they employed dancers and preserved many great ballets, performing them worldwide.

The Ballets Russes de Monte Carlo, formed by Col. Wassily de Basil and René Blum in 1932, featured Tamara Toumanova, Irina Boronova, and Tatiana Riabouchinska, remembered as the three "baby ballerinas" because of their extreme youth. By 1936, following disputes over legal rights to ballets from the Diaghilev company, de Basil had formed the Ballets Russes du Colonel de Basil, and Blum had organized the Ballets de Monte Carlo, with **Michel Fokine** as choreographer. The de Basil company performed under several different names, including Covent Garden Russian Ballet and finally Original Ballet Russe, before disbanding in 1951. Blum's company became the Ballet Russe de Monte Carlo in 1938, with **Léonide Massine** as choreographer and Serge Denham as managing director. This company relocated to the United States in 1939 and toured until 1962.

REFERENCES:

Jack Anderson, *The One and Only: The Ballet Russe de Monte Carlo* (New York: Dance Horizons, 1981);

Vicente García-Márquez, *The Ballets Russes: Colonel de Basil's Ballets Russes de Monte Carlo 1932–1952* (New York: Knopf, 1990);

Kathrine Sorley Walker, *De Basil's Ballets Russes* (New York: Atheneum, 1983).

— A.P.E.

HENRI BARBUSSE

Henri Barbusse (1873–1935) was known to his compatriots chiefly as the author of the most famous French novel of **World War I,** *Le Feu* (1916; translated as *Under Fire*).

Published in the middle of the conflict, when strident calls for *revanche* (revenge) against the German empire and patriotic rhetoric and iconography dominated journalism and the arts, the book was a near-total condemnation of war in general and the current conflict in particular. Glossing over nothing, *Le Feu* stressed the horrors of trench warfare and what Barbusse believed to be the pointlessness and criminality of the conflict. Also intended to show the need for social equality in France, the novel was banned by authorities in Germany, but the French did not dare censor it because of its widespread popularity, revealing the depth of antiwar feeling both at the front and among civilians.

After the publication of his second war novel, also called *Clarté* (1919; translated as *Light*), Barbusse turned mainly to writing political essays. In March 1919 he founded Clarté, a movement with a pacifist and internationalist program, as well as a journal of the same name. He joined the **French Communist Party** in 1923 and contributed to *L'Humanité.*

REFERENCES:

David Caute, *Communism and the French Intellectuals, 1914–1960* (London: Deutsch, 1964);

Frank Field, *Three French Writers and the Great War: Studies in the Rise of Communism and Fascism* (Cambridge: Cambridge University Press, 1975), pp. 21–78;

J. E. Flower, *Literature and the Left in France* (London: Macmillan, 1983), pp. 29–49.

— C.S.B.

MAURICE BARDÈCHE

Maurice Bardèche (1907–) is one of the most important right-wing intellectuals in twentieth-century France.

A graduate of the **Ecole Normale Supérieure**, he wrote *Histoire du cinéma* (1935; translated as *The History of Motion Pictures*) and *Histoire de la guerre d'Espagne* (1939; History of the War in Spain) with his brother-in-law **Robert Brasillach.** Unlike Brasillach, however, Bardèche, who was appointed to a chair in French literature at the University of Lille in 1942, did not collaborate with the Germans during the **Occupation** of France in World War II.

In 1945, after the execution of Brasillach for collaboration, Bardèche began to write in defense of his right-wing political views and was widely and vehemently attacked by the intellectual Establishment. In his *Lettre à François Mauriac* (1947; Letter to **François Mauriac**) and *Nuremberg ou la terre promise* (1948; Nuremberg, or the Promised Land), he attacked the **épuration,** questioned the legal rights and modus operandi of the Allies in the Nuremberg Trials, and denounced the Allied bombing of civilians in Germany during the war. These books caused a storm of controversy, and the second was banned. After a series of political trials on charges brought because of these books, Bardèche was sentenced to one year in jail. Although he was later pardoned, he remained under police surveillance until 1952 and was forbidden to leave France.

Denied access to the media, Bardèche founded his own publishing house, Les Sept Couleurs. Among his politically oriented studies of major French novelists are *Stendhal romancier* (1947; Stendhal the Novelist), *Louis-Ferdinand Céline* (1986), and *Léon Bloy* (1988).

REFERENCES:

Mary Jean Green, "Fascists on Film: The Brasillach and Bardèche *Histoire du cinéma*," *South Central Review*, 6 (Summer 1989): 32–47;

Alice Yaeger Kaplan, "The Late Show: Conversations with Maurice Bardèche," *SubStance*, 15, no.1 (1986): 44–68.
— D.O'C.

BRIGITTE BARDOT

The movie actress Brigitte Bardot (1934–) was the great French sex symbol of the late 1950s and the 1960s. In 1976, three years after her last film appearance and her retreat into isolation, she established the Foundation for the Protection of Distressed Animals, for which she received the French Légion d'Honneur in 1985.

Bardot was discovered at age fifteen by **Roger Vadim**, assistant to veteran director Marc Allégret; Vadim noticed her when her picture appeared on the cover of *Elle* magazine. She first appeared on the screen in 1952, the year she and Vadim married. She became famous after her appearance in *Et Dieu créa la femme* (1956; *And God Created Woman*), the first film Vadim directed on his own. Thenceforth she passed through a series of marriages and divorces. On screen her youthful, suntanned body, amply displayed in *Et Dieu créa la femme* and several otherwise unremarkable movies, projected a new image of women in postwar European film. Amoral, nonconformist, and indifferent, yet with a vein of childishness and innocence, Bardot's characters epitomized what **Simone de Beauvoir** called the "Lolita syndrome" — a juvenile sexuality without guilt.

Capitalizing on her fame, Bardot also worked for several well-known directors. She gained respect from critics for her appearances in **Jean-Luc Godard**'s *Le Mépris* (1963; *Contempt*) and **Henri-Georges Clouzot**'s *La Vérité* (1960; *The Truth*). She also had a cameo role in **Jean Cocteau**'s *Le Testament d'Orphée* (1960; *The Testament of Orpheus*).

REFERENCES:

Simone de Beauvoir, *Brigitte Bardot and the Lolita Syndrome*, translated by Bernard Frechtman (London: Deutsch, 1960);

Marjorie Rosen, *Popcorn Venus: Women, Movies and the American Dream* (New York: Coward, McCann & Geoghegan, 1973);

M. Sarne, "A Definition of Stardom," *Films and Filming* (October 1978);

J. Silke, "The Tragic Mask of Bardolatry," *Cinema*, 2 (1962).
— W.L.

Michel Piccoli and Brigitte Bardot in a scene from *Le Mépris* (1963)

JEAN-LOUIS BARRAULT

Since **World War II**, actor-director Jean-Louis Barrault (1910–) has been the most illustrious champion of modern and avant-garde theater in France. As the members of the **Cartel des Quatre** died during the war and the decade that followed, Barrault and **Jean Vilar** took their place as the mainstays of Parisian art theater. The acting company Barrault founded with his wife, **Madeleine Renaud,** has attained world renown.

Trained by **Charles Dullin**, Barrault acted at the **Théâtre de l'Atelier** from 1931 until 1935, when he directed his first production there, *Autour d'une mère* (About a Mother), based on William Faulkner's *As I Lay Dying*. The following year he directed and acted in *Le Tableau des merveilles*, freely adapted by **Jacques Prévert**, at Barrault's request, from Miguel de Cervantes's *El Retablo de las maravillas* (translated as *The Puppet Show of Wonders*). The cast included **Roger Blin**. Barrault's early accomplishments were praised by **Antonin Artaud** and admired by **Paul Claudel**, whose works Barrault would later stage.

Barrault also achieved some success as an actor in motion pictures such as **Marcel Carné**'s *Drôle de drame* (1937; *Bizarre, Bizarre*) and Christian-Jacque's *La Symphonie fantastique* (1942; The Fantastic Symphony). His greatest film role was that of the mime

Debureau in Carné's epic *Les Enfants du paradis* (1945; *Children of Paradise*), written by Prévert.

Barrault entered the **Comédie-Française** in 1940 and quickly became a member, or *sociétaire*. In that same year he married Renaud, who had already achieved fame in the national theater, made his Comédie-Française acting debut (as the title character in Pierre Corneille's play *Le Cid*), and directed Jean Racine's tragedy *Phèdre* (*Phaedra*) there. The next year he was artistic director for a grandiose spectacle at the Roland Garros stadium in Paris: André Obey's sports drama *800 mètres* (800 Meters) and Aeschylus's *The Suppliants* performed before an audience of thousands. In 1943, during the **Occupation,** his artistic staging of Claudel's *Le Soulier de satin* (*The Satin Slipper*) — which lasted about five hours and included an intermission for supper — was truly a national triumph. As an affirmation that God is at work in all human affairs, even in apparent evil, the play brought comfort to the French living under Nazi domination. The stellar cast included Barrault himself, as well as Renaud, Marie Bell, and Pierre Dux.

After the war Barrault and Renaud left the Comédie-Française to found their own troupe, the Compagnie Madeleine Renaud–Jean-Louis Barrault. During the late 1940s and the 1950s their most memorable performances included William Shakespeare's *Hamlet* in 1946, with Barrault in the title role; three more Claudel plays — *Partage de midi* (*Break of Noon*) in 1948, *L'Echange* (*The Exchange*) in 1951, and *Christophe Colomb* (*Christopher Columbus*) in 1953; and **Jean Giraudoux**'s *Pour Lucrèce* (*Duel of Angels*), also in 1953.

In 1959 Barrault was named director of the state-subsidized **Théâtre de l'Odéon.** He and Renaud renamed the hall "Théâtre de France" and presented a resolutely contemporary repertory, with acting and directing not only by their own troupe but also by young, avant-garde companies. Blin, **Roger Planchon,** and Jean-Marie Serreau directed avant-garde plays there before large Paris audiences. Playwrights such as **Samuel Beckett, Marguerite Duras, Jean Genet, Eugène Ionesco, Nathalie Sarraute,** and **Georges Schehadé** received the honors of the Odéon stage during Barrault's directorship. The triumphant 1960 performance of Ionesco's *Rhinocéros* by the Renaud-Barrault company is often credited with uniting the **Theater of the Absurd** with the theatrical mainstream. The staging of Genet's politically charged *Les Paravents* (*The Screens*) in 1966 brought on rioting at the theater by right-wing hooligans. In **May 1968** student rioters in the **Latin Quarter,** perhaps associating Barrault's Odéon with liberal causes such as freedom for youth and economic opportunity for the poor, took

refuge in the theater. Culture minister **André Malraux,** on the grounds that Barrault had not adequately resisted this invasion and vandalizing of state property, relieved the director of his post.

After 1968 the Renaud-Barrault company moved about in Paris, performing in various theaters, including a hall constructed in the abandoned Orsay railway station (which has since been transformed into a museum) and later at the Théâtre du Rond-Point. The company has made highly successful tours abroad, and Barrault furthered the cause of theater as intercultural communication by serving as director of a "Théâtre des Nations" in Paris and of an international house of theater, which helped attract **Peter Brook** to France.

Barrault's acting is remarkably stylized and physically disciplined; for his technique he appears to owe much to the French mime Etienne Decroux, with whom he worked in the 1930s. As a director he attains remarkable unity among all facets of performance, creating a kind of "total" theater by tightly integrating text, acting, lighting, music, and setting, to achieve a general "multimedia" effect. The extraordinary intensity of his own acting and of actors he directs leaves little doubt that the theatrical experience he strives to create for the public is akin to a religious communion.

Barrault's company sponsored *Cahiers de la Compagnie Madeleine Renaud–Jean-Louis Barrault* (1953–1988), an important theater periodical, and his books include *Souvenirs pour demain* (1972; translated as *Memories for Tomorrow*) and *Nouvelles réflexions sur le théâtre* (1959; translated as *The Theatre of Jean-Louis Barrault*).

REFERENCES:

Léon Chancerel, *Jean-Louis Barrault, ou l'ange noir du théâtre* (Paris: Presses Universitaires de France, 1953);

John K. Gillespie, "Interior Action: The Impact of Noh on Jean-Louis Barrault," *Comparative Drama,* 16 (Winter 1982–1983): 325–344;

Bettina Knapp, "Interview with Barrault," in *Off-Stage Voices: Interviews with Modern French Dramatists,* edited by Alba Amoia (Troy, N.Y.: Whitston, 1975), pp. 41–46.

— R.J.N.

MAURICE BARRÈS

Although writer and political figure Maurice Barrès (1862–1923) belongs in many ways to the nineteenth century, he was active for more than two decades in the twentieth, and many of his books, including some well-known ones, appeared after 1900. He is remembered mostly as a nationalistic, right-wing author who put his ideas into practice as a *député* (deputy, or legislator). His literary stock is no longer high, but at one time he was widely known and exercised considerable influence on slightly younger writers. Barrès may be considered a precursor of French literary fascism, as illustrated in **L'Action Française.**

Barrès began his literary career with three novels collectively called *Le Culte du moi* (1888–1891; The Cult of the Self) and marked by a decadent romanticism, but with *Les Déracinés* (1897; The Uprooted) he adopted a conservative morality and political outlook that stressed the need for fidelity to "the earth and the dead." He wanted to remain faithful to his birthplace, the province of Lorraine, part of which had been lost to Germany after the Franco-Prussian War (1870–1871); his voice was one of many that called for *revanche* (revenge) against the German empire and for seizure of the lost territory.

Barrès adopted anti-Semitic positions and was a staunch anti-Dreyfusard during the **Dreyfus Affair.** Although he had served as a leftist deputy at the outset of his political career (1889–1893), he was reelected as a rightist in 1906 and served until his death in 1923. His many nationalistic works include the novels *Colette Baudoche* (1909; translated), whose thesis is that French women should marry French men, not foreigners, and *La Colline inspirée* (1913; translated as *The Sacred Hill*), a fictionalized account of an early-nineteenth-century attempt to establish a mystical religious cult at the shrine at Sion-Vaudrémont in Lorraine. Both before and after **World War I,** Barrès was widely regarded as one of the principal spokesmen for French nationalism.

REFERENCES:

Denis W. Brogan, *French Personalities and Problems* (London: Hamilton, 1946);

Michel Curtis, *Three Against the Third Republic: Sorel, Barrès and Maurras* (Princeton: Princeton University Press, 1959);

Charles Stewart Doty, *From Cultural Rebellion to Counterrevolution: The Politics of Maurice Barrès* (Athens: Ohio University Press, 1976);

Philip Ouston, *The Imagination of Maurice Barrès* (Toronto: University of Toronto Press, 1974);

Robert Soucy, *Fascism in France: The Case of Maurice Barrès* (Berkeley, Los Angeles & London: University of California Press, 1972).

— C.S.B.

ANDRÉ BARSACQ

Theater director André Barsacq (1909–1973) was born in Russia and immigrated to France after the 1917 revolution. He rose to prominence in the Théâtre des Quatre Saisons (Four Seasons Theater) during the late 1930s and assumed control of the **Théâtre de l'Atelier** in 1940, after the departure of director **Charles Dullin.** Barsacq's approach to directing reflects the mood of much French theater during World War II: he kept a tight rein on his own company and often staged plays with traditional moral messages.

Barsacq appeared to take a cooperative stance toward the occupying Nazi regime, arguing in public for centralized control of French theaters. He did much to introduce the works of philosophically conservative playwright **Jean Anouilh,** staging a series of Anouilh plays from 1938 to 1951 — principally at the Atelier but also at the Théâtre des Arts and at the **Théâtre Montparnasse.** From time to time during and after the **Occupation,** he took the Quatre Saisons company on tour in the French provinces. A consummate man of the theater, he was one of the last directors to retain personal control of all phases of his productions.

REFERENCE:

Alfred Simon, *Dictionnaire du théâtre français contemporain* (Paris: Larousse, 1970).

— R.J.N.

ROLAND BARTHES

One of the most important French critics of the twentieth century, Roland Barthes (1915–1980) wrote extensively on sociology, semiotics, **structuralism,** and literary history, playing a major role among structuralist and poststructuralist critics. His theory of the importance of the reader's pleasure in literature assures him of a large following among students of literary and cultural criticism.

Barthes's article "Le Degré zéro de l'écriture," which appeared in the journal *Combat* in 1947, is an especially significant statement of his early work in sociology and literary theory. In this sociological approach to literary history Barthes selected 1848 as the date for a definitive break between classical literature and modern literature — a reading of nineteenth-century literary history that he shared with **Jean-Paul Sartre.** In the article Barthes also discussed "writerly" versus "readerly" texts in modern literature. For example, a writerly text would be a self-consciously experimental work such as James Joyce's *Ulysses* (1922); a readerly text would be a stylistically traditional novel by Stephen King. An expanded version of this article was included with other essays in *Le Degré zéro de l'écriture*; (1953; translated as *Writing Degree Zero*).

In 1949 Barthes met A. J. Greimas, who introduced him to structuralist linguistics, which became a powerful tool in Barthes's future study of culture and literature. He employed methods of structuralist linguistics in his work in sociology from 1952 to 1957, transforming himself from a Sartrean and a Marxist into a semiotician. Founded by Ferdinand de Saussure at the beginning of the twentieth century, the science of semiotics considers language as a system of signs in which discrete combinations of units create meaning. In 1957 Barthes published *Mythologies,* a series of essays that analyze various areas of popular culture — from food and wine to celebrities and wrestling — in terms of their component parts, which — like the parts of speech in language — combine to generate the meaning that they hold for the public. In the same year Barthes began work on his *Système de la mode* (1967; translated as *The Fashion System*), analyzing the codes of fashion.

By the mid 1960s, even though his professional appointments continued to reflect his work in sociology, Barthes had established himself as a literary critic in the structuralist school, with the article "L'Activité structuraliste" (Structuralist Activity) in 1963 and the book *Eléments de sémiologie* (1964; translated as *Elements of Semiology*). Most important was his book *Sur Racine* (1963; translated as *On Racine*), a controversial study that took an anthropological and psychoanalytical view of the world of Jean Racine's tragedy. This work provoked Raymond Picard to publish his *Nouvelle critique ou nouvelle imposture?* (1965; translated as *New Criticism or New Fraud?*). Picard used his disapproval of Barthes's approach to Racine to condemn the entire school that has come to be known as **La Nouvelle Critique** (New Criticism). Unlike traditional university criticism, which focused on the biographies of authors and their historical periods, the works of the new critics interpret the text apart from such contexts by applying twentieth-century methods and concepts, including psychoanalysis, Marxism, and structuralism. Barthes defended the new criticism in his response to Picard's attack, *Critique et vérité* (1966; Criticism and Truth). From his quarrel with Picard, Barthes emerged as the champion of structuralism, but he never completely subscribed to the movement's claims of scientific validity.

From 1970 until his death, Barthes's theories became increasingly radical. In this poststructuralist period of his career Barthes's focus on the role of the reader linked him to critics such as Mikhail Bakhtin and **Gérard Genette.** Barthes's personal sort of reader-response criticism focused on the pleasure experienced by the reader as the source of meaning in a literary work, a view he expressed in *Le Plaisir du texte* (1973; translated as *The Pleasure of the Text*). This emphasis on the role of the reader resulted in the belief that, as Barthes wrote, "the birth of the reader must be at the cost of the death of the author." Although not to be labeled a deconstructionist, Barthes certainly shared

with critics such as **Michel Foucault** and **Jacques Derrida** a belief in the importance of contradictions in the text and the conviction that there is a lack of closure, or indeed of any final meaning, in a literary work. This absence of closure is evident in Barthes's well-known *S/Z* (1970; translated), at once his most extensive literary analysis and his most radical exposition of literary theory. In this work Barthes analyzes Honoré de Balzac's story "Sarrasine" by breaking it into fragments. For Barthes the reader's reaction to the observance and rejection of literary codes, conditioned by knowledge of other texts, creates meaning in this story. Like Foucault, Barthes challenged the traditional understanding of the subject; *Roland Barthes par Roland Barthes* (1975; translated as *Roland Barthes by Roland Barthes*) is an autobiography that separates the subject from the author and challenges the notions of identity and self-knowledge at every turn.

Barthes's works are the musings of a "public experimenter" (as he once described the role of the writer) and not simply tools to be used easily by students of literature. After his death several of his critical essays were republished as *Le Bruissement de la langue* (1984; translated as *The Rustle of Language*). *Le Grain de la voix: Entretiens 1962–1980* (translated as *The Grain of the Voice: Interviews 1962–1980*) appeared in 1981.

REFERENCES:

Jonathan Culler, *Roland Barthes* (New York: Oxford University Press, 1983);

Annette Lavers, *Roland Barthes: Structuralism and After* (Cambridge, Mass.: Harvard University Press, 1982);

George R. Wasserman, *Roland Barthes* (Boston: Twayne, 1981).
— K.E.B.

GEORGES BATAILLE

The stature of Georges Bataille (1897–1962) has risen in the late twentieth century with the development of new approaches to the social sciences and a new wave of studies of eroticism. Classified variously as a novelist, a social scientist, a religious writer, and a philosopher, he is known for the obscurity of his writings. His subjects include economics, war, the sacred, and especially sexuality, for which he has been compared to the Marquis de Sade.

Trained at the Ecole des Chartes (1918–1920), Bataille, who had converted to Catholicism in 1914, went through an early period of conventional, if vibrant, mysticism. He renounced his faith in 1920 and adopted as a given the death of God, on which he built his subsequent search for transcendence, an anguished

Back of the Bateau Lavoir, a cluster of studios in the Montmartre district of Paris

search whose essence cannot be transmitted. In the 1920s he read G. W. F. Hegel, Friedrich Nietzsche, Karl Marx, and various gnostic writers, and he was influenced by the painter **André Masson** and the writer **André Malraux.** He was attracted and influenced by **Surrealism** but argued with **André Breton** over the Surrealists' claim to have found an alternative to Hegelian idealism.

Bataille's first narrative, *L'Histoire de l'œil* (1928; translated as *Story of the Eye*), an erotic tale, was published anonymously. In the 1930s he read widely in philosophy and sociology and became interested in yoga and other Eastern philosophies. These readings influenced the development of Bataille's idiosyncratic and mystical worldview, involving society, economics, eroticism, and religion. All his writings reveal an obsession with the sacred, which must be violated, through transgression of sexual and other social taboos, in order to be revitalized.

Bataille's important works started appearing in the 1940s; they include *L'Expérience intérieure* (1941; translated as *Inner Experience*), *Le Coupable* (1944; translated as *Guilty*), *La Part maudite* (1949; translated as *The Accursed Share*), and *La Littérature et le mal* (1957; translated as *Literature and Evil*). These works, like Bataille's writings generally, are deliberately synthetic, going beyond conventional classifications not only of genres but of bodies of knowledge in an effort

to create a new "human science." *Madame Edwarda* (1941), a story of "the divine prostitute," is less important in the author's own eyes but revealing about his concept of eroticism.

In 1946 Bataille founded the important critical review *Critique,* to which **Maurice Blanchot** contributed.

REFERENCES:

Nick Land, *The Thirst for Annihilation: Georges Bataille and Virulent Nihilism (An Essay in Atheistic Religion)* (London & New York: Routledge, 1991);

Michèle H. Richman, *Reading Georges Bataille: Beyond the Gift* (Baltimore & London: Johns Hopkins University Press, 1982).
— C.S.B.

LE BATEAU LAVOIR

The Bateau Lavoir (laundry boat) was the nickname given to a cluster of studios in an old factory building on rue Ravignan (now Place Emile-Goudeau) in **Montmartre.** During the first decade of the twentieth century, painters **Pablo Picasso, Kees van Dongen, Juan Gris,** and Amedeo Modigliani and poets André Salmon, Pierre MacOrlan, and **Max Jacob** were among the artists and writers who lived and worked there. Poet **Guillaume Apollinaire** was a frequent visitor.

Jacob said he named the long, ramshackle wooden building after the laundry boats moored in the Seine because of all the wash hanging outside on his first visit. Declared a historic landmark in December 1969, the Bateau Lavoir burned down five months later.

REFERENCES:

Cecily Mackworth, *Guillaume Apollinaire and the Cubist Life* (London: Murray, 1961);

John Richardson, with the collaboration of Marilyn McCully, *A Life of Picasso, Volume I: 1881–1906* (New York: Random House, 1991).

— C.S.B.

GASTON BATY

With lighting and choreography as his primary tools, Gaston Baty (1885–1952) earned a place as one of the most original theater directors in France during the period between the two world wars. He was a pure director, the only member of the **Cartel des Quatre** never to engage in acting, and he contested **Jacques Copeau**'s doctrine of the primacy of the playwright's text in all decisions about staging (generally upheld by the other Cartel members — **Charles Dullin, Louis Jouvet,** and **Georges Pitoëff**). For Baty, theater was at least as visual as it was verbal, and his was a pioneering venture in liberating the theater experience from "literature."

Growing up in Lyons, Baty was attracted early on to marionette theater, which became a lifelong fascination. Later, as a graduate student of art history in Munich, he delved into the theory of German stagecraft. Soon after his return to Lyons, he was studying theater history and jotting down his ideas on lighting and staging. He made the acquaintance of director **Firmin Gémier** in 1919, just as Gémier was producing his most spectacular Paris shows in the Cirque d'Hiver. Impressed by Baty's knowledge and ideas, Gémier hired him as lighting director — later making him general director — for the vast productions. Thus Baty began his active career at age thirty-four, directing spectacular pageants in the Gémier mode. Next, his mentor set Baty up as principal director at the short-lived Comédie Montaigne Gémier, where he fully established himself, most successfully directing Henri-René Lenormand's *Le Simoun* (The Simoom) in 1920 and **Paul Claudel**'s *L'Annonce faite à Marie* (translated as *The Tidings Brought to Mary*) in 1921 — on a theme Baty, as a committed Catholic, cherished.

In 1921 he put together his own company, the Compagnons de la Chimère, which operated for a month or so in a colorful shed near **Saint-Germain-des-Prés** before moving to the Studio des Champs-Elysées with the aid of impresario Jacques Hébertot. There,

Baty ran an experimental theater and honed the ideas he assembled in *Le Masque et l'encensoir* (1926; The Mask and the Censer). He attacked the uncontested dominance of language in the theater, mocking "Sire le mot" (Milord the Word); authors' scripts, although important as pretexts for theatrical events, were only one part of the art form, in which light and setting combine for a visual experience. Lighting, according to Baty, gave voice to the décor. In his productions he used highly stylized settings with spotlights, scrims, and backlighting as visual interpretations of the verbal text; the director shared responsibility with the playwright for the final product. Baty was apparently not averse to altering a script here and there for effect. Among his best-known presentations of the 1920s were Eugene O'Neill's *Emperor Jones* in 1923, Simon Gantillon's *Maya* in 1924, and in 1927 Shalom Anski's *The Dybbuk,* in which Baty's leading actress, **Marguerite Jamois,** triumphed as the woman possessed.

Each of these plays suggests spiritual or psychological realities beyond what the words can say, an expressive domain for Baty's *mise-en-scène.* Yet it was probably Baty's personal and subjective interpretation of Molière's *Le Malade imaginaire* (translated as *The Imaginary Invalid*), at the Théâtre de l'Avenue in 1929, that created the greatest scandal at the time. Tampering with the classical repertoire was taboo. Still, Baty's fresh interpretation showed how hidebound the **Comédie-Française** had become; that theater, seeking new directions, soon invited Baty and other Cartel members to direct there.

From 1930 until 1947 Baty occupied the **Théâtre Montparnasse.** He directed plays there until 1943, when Jamois succeeded him. During this period Baty and René Chavance wrote *La Vie de l'art théâtral des origines à nos jours* (1932; Life of Theater Art from the Beginnings to the Present). Among Baty's most memorable productions are Bertolt Brecht's *Three-Penny Opera* in 1930, his subjective adaptations of novels (Fyodor Dostoyevsky's *Crime and Punishment* in 1933 and Gustave Flaubert's *Madame Bovary* in 1936), and Jean Racine's *Phèdre* (translated as *Phaedra*) in 1940. At the Comédie-Française, he directed memorable productions of Eugène Labiche's *Un Chapeau de paille d'Italie* (translated as *An Italian Straw Hat*) in 1938, Racine's *Bérénice* in 1946, and **Armand Salacrou**'s *L'Inconnue d'Arras* (The Stranger of Arras) in 1949.

After leaving the Théâtre Montparnasse, Baty devoted his remaining years to marionette theater. Although at the end of his last published work, *Rideau baissé* (1949; Curtain Down), he recanted his attack on "Sire le mot" — affirming the central importance of the printed word to theater — his ideas and example inspired those directors who were to assert, in the 1960s, absolute control over the texts they staged.

REFERENCES:

Paul Blanchart, *Gaston Baty* (Paris: Nouvelle Revue Critique, 1939);

Raymond Cogniat, *Gaston Baty* (Paris: Presses Littéraires de France, 1953);

Jacques Guicharnaud, "Directors and Productions," in his *Modern French Theatre from Giraudoux to Beckett* (New Haven: Yale University Press, 1961), pp. 237–262;

Jacqueline de Jomaron, "Ils étaient quatre . . . ," in *Le Théâtre en France. 2: De la Révolution à nos jours,* edited by Jomaron (Paris: Armand Colin, 1989), pp. 227–270.

— R.J.N.

JEAN BAUDRILLARD

Jean Baudrillard (1929–) is one of the most visible and radical theorists of postmodernism. A product of the growing role played in society by the mass media, his work reflects the disenchantment and intellectual disarray that followed the political protests and rioting of **May 1968** and the demise of Communism in central Europe and the Soviet Union.

Baudrillard taught German at a lycée before beginning a twenty-year career as a sociologist at the University of Nanterre. In the 1980s, during the academic vogue of postmodernist theory, translations of Baudrillard's work made him well known in the English-speaking world. In 1987, when the opportunity arose to give up teaching, he seized it.

Baudrillard's interests have been wide-ranging, and his intellectual influences include Karl Marx, Sigmund Freud, Friedrich Nietzsche, Marshall McLuhan, **Jean-Paul Sartre, Roland Barthes**, and **Michel Foucault** — whom he turned against, however, in *Oublier Foucault* (1977; translated as *Forget Foucault*).

After first trying to reconcile it with semiotic theory, Baudrillard attacked Marxism, particularly in *Le Miroir de la production* (1973; translated as *The Mirror of Production*). He pointed to the inadequacy of Marxist theories of political economy for the analysis of both traditional and contemporary societies. In his view a fatal flaw at the heart of Marxism is its conception of the individual as defined by needs on the one hand and production on the other. Essentially, Baudrillard rejects any claim to privileged or absolute truth and any sense that long-term certainty is possible. In a turn that brings him close to deconstruction, he insists that all critical concepts are shaped by the fleeting historical circumstances in which they are formulated; thus Marxian self-certainty, like Cartesian or Enlightenment truths, is an ill-founded delusion.

In later works based on his personal journal, including *Amérique* (1986; translated as *America*), *Cool Memories, 1980–1985* (1987), and *Cool Memories II* (1990), Baudrillard employed a fragmentary, aphoristic style — a form that has become identified with postmodernism — to point to the state of confusion in contemporary society. He insists that any idea of progress must be abandoned, given the universal presence of the media, cybernetic control systems, and mass advertising. In a society flooded with proliferating objects and fashions — and especially signs — distinctions between reality and simulation become blurred and invalid. In a culture of what he calls *simulacra,* politics is packaged as entertainment; news — including reports of murder, mayhem, war, and famine — becomes spectacle; and the codes of social experience are determined in and through an atmosphere of simulation, an uncontrollable "hyperreality."

Baudrillard's interpretation of the contemporary scene is bleak. It includes the loss of the thinking subject in the vortex of mass culture, the loss of any possibility of authentic knowledge, and the loss of any reality that is meaningful. For example, in *America*, he says, Los Angeles and the rest of the country are just as much part of the play of hyperreality as is Disneyland.

REFERENCES:

Jean Baudrillard, *Baudrillard Live: Selected Interviews,* edited by Mike Gane (London & New York: Routledge, 1993);

Christopher Norris, "Lost in the Funhouse: Baudrillard and the Politics of Postmodernism," in his *What's Wrong with Postmodernism: Critical Theories and the Ends of Philosophy* (Baltimore: Johns Hopkins University Press, 1990), pp. 164–193.

— J.P.McN.

ANDRÉ BAZIN

André Bazin (1918–1958) was the most prominent and influential French film critic during the decade and a half immediately following **World War II.** At the magazine *Cahiers du Cinéma* he led a group of young writers and cineasts who coordinated their critical writing with filmmaking, including **Nouvelle Vague** (New Wave) directors **Claude Chabrol, Jean-Luc Godard, Jacques Rivette, Eric Rohmer,** and **François Truffaut.**

During the war Bazin inaugurated a cinema club in which he screened many films that were banned by the German occupational forces. After 1945 he became a film critic for several French journals. In 1947 he founded *La Revue du Cinéma,* and in 1951 he and Jacques Doniol-Valcroze launched *Cahiers du Cinéma,* a review that he directed until his untimely death at age forty in 1958.

Bazin believed that the montage technique, which juxtaposes images through extensive editing, manipulates the viewer and hampers the perception of reality. He thus preferred films that use deep-focus photography and long takes. He championed Orson Welles, **Jean Renoir,** and William Wyler as proponents of a "realist" cinema that refuses to fragment the film into montage. He promoted Italian neorealism of the late 1940s over the heavily edited French **tradition de qualité.** Bazin also subscribed to the "auteur theory," which argues that the style of great cinema depends on the central presence of the director's personal vision. According to this theory a director can make different kinds of films, but he or she will always leave an individualized imprint in framing and mise-en-scène. Bazin's writings were collected in the four-volume *Qu'est-ce que le cinéma?* (1958–1962; partially translated as *What Is Cinema?*). His aesthetic dominated French cinema until the early 1970s, when *Cahiers du Cinéma* abandoned auteur theory and moved to political and ideological readings of directors and styles.

REFERENCES:

Dudley Andrew, *André Bazin* (New York: Oxford University Press, 1978);

André Bazin, *What is Cinema?*, 2 volumes, translated and edited by Hugh Gray (Berkeley & Los Angeles: University of California Press, 1971);

Jim Hillier, ed., *Cahiers du cinéma: The 1950s* (Cambridge, Mass.: Harvard University Press, 1985).

— T.C.

HERVÉ BAZIN

The novels of Jean Pierre Marie Hervé-Bazin (1911–), who throughout his career has used the name Hervé Bazin, are concerned with the family and other human relationships. His work has been called devastating, for it spares nothing and no one, applying its scalpel particularly to relationships between parents and children.

Bazin, who is a member of the Académie Goncourt, published several books before *Vipère au poing* (1948; translated as *Grasping the Viper*) brought him literary success and notoriety. The novel portrays a mother in a most unfavorable light: "Folcoche" is so dreadful that her children first try to poison her and then attempt to drown her. The book is based somewhat on Bazin's own tormented childhood and hostility toward his mother (followed by unhappy experiences with women as an adult, including two failed marriages). *Vipère au poing* almost won the **Prix Goncourt;** but **Colette,** the author of eloquent portraits of maternal figures, could not vote for such a demolition of a mother.

Bazin's subsequent novels and collections of short stories are perhaps uneven, but the best have considerable literary merit, including *La Tête contre les murs* (1949; translated as *Head Against the Wall*); *Lève-toi et marche* (1952; translated as *Constance*); *Qui j'ose aimer* (1956; translated as *A Tribe of Women*); and *Au nom du fils* (1960; translated as *In the Name of the Son*). These works include some of the themes (and characters) of his first novel but go beyond them to consider other human problems. In all of them the time-honored subject of the pursuit of happiness receives close scrutiny.

Bazin has also written poems; one of his collections, *Jour* (1947; Day), won the Prix Guillaume Apollinaire, and in 1974 he was awarded the Grand Prix International de Poésie. A vigorous campaigner for the cause of peace, he was awarded the 1979 Lenin Peace Prize.

REFERENCES:

Michael Cardy, "Hervé Bazin's *L'Eglise verte*," *International Fiction Review,* 15 (Winter 1988): 27–29;

Philip A. Crant, "An Interview with Hervé Bazin," *Language Quarterly,* 31 (Winter–Spring 1993): 58–66;

Crant, "Some Thoughts on the Literary Development of Hervé Bazin," *Language Quarterly,* 10 (Spring–Summer 1972): 31–34.

— C.S.B.

SIMONE DE BEAUVOIR

Simone de Beauvoir (1908–1986) occupies an assured place as one of the two or three most important women writers of the twentieth century in France. Born in Paris, in **Montparnasse,** Beauvoir came from a conservative bourgeois family and studied philosophy at the Sorbonne, making an unusual career choice for a daughter of such a family. In 1929 she received the *agrégation* (the highest teaching certificate), graduating in second place, right after **Jean-Paul Sartre,** who shortly thereafter became her lover. Although by the mid 1930s each was having liaisons with others, they remained extremely close, both personally and professionally, until Sartre's death in 1980. Beauvoir taught at various lycées in the 1930s and early 1940s before devoting herself entirely to writing.

Her first work, *L'Invitée* (1943; translated as *She Came to Stay*), is a psychological novel based to a great degree on a love triangle formed earlier by Beauvoir, Sartre, and a student named Olga Kosakiewicz. It incorporates many insights that appear in Sartre's fiction of the 1930s and 1940s and especially in his *L'Etre et le néant* (translated as *Being and Nothingness*), also published in 1943; but Beauvoir's novel is not just a derivative work, since the two had worked

Dust jacket for the first American edition of Simone de Beauvoir's account of the ten years before the death of her long-time companion, Jean-Paul Sartre. First published in French as *La Ceremonie des Adieux,* the volume was translated in 1984.

out some of their views together, and Beauvoir doubtless contributed to the development of her friend's philosophical positions. She subsequently published other fiction. *Le Sang des autres* (1945; translated as *The Blood of Others*), *Tous les hommes sont mortels* (1946; translated as *All Men Are Mortal*), and *Les Mandarins* (1954; translated as *The Mandarins*), which earned her the prestigious **Prix Goncourt,** were followed by two novels in the 1960s: *Les Belles Images* (1966; translated) and *La Femme rompue* (1968; translated as *The Woman Destroyed*). *Les Mandarins* is a roman à clef, based in part on Beauvoir's love affair with American writer Nelson Algren; Sartre, **Albert Camus,** and Beauvoir herself served as models for the main characters.

In 1949 Beauvoir published a controversial two-volume study on women and women's condition, *Le Deuxième Sexe* (translated as *The Second Sex*), which immediately earned her the wrath of conservative critics. Some years later, the work became a central text for the new feminists, first in English-speaking countries and then in France, with the development of the **Mouvement de la Libération des Femmes** in 1970. Although many subsequent feminists have disagreed with her positions, finding her insufficiently radical and too prone to adopt male categories and points of view, Beauvoir is generally considered the most important founding figure of modern feminism. Among her most popular works are her four volumes of memoirs: *Mémoires d'une jeune fille rangée* (1958; translated as *Memoirs of a Dutiful Daughter*), *La Force de l'âge* (1960; translated as *The Prime of Life*), *La Force des choses* (1963; translated as *The Force of Circumstance*), and *Tout compte fait* (1972; translated as *All Said and Done*).

Beauvoir also wrote books on topics such as the United States, the Marquis de Sade, Communist China, and old age. Her philosophic essays, notably *Pyrrhus et Cinéas* (1944) and *Pour une morale de l'ambiguïté* (1947; translated as *The Ethics of Ambiguity*), are not among the major texts of French existentialism — Sartre's have that honor — but should not be neglected. They offer clear expositions of philosophic and political issues and occasionally outshine the writings of her colleague. In addition to publishing many books, Beauvoir was among the founders of the influential journal **Les Temps Modernes** and remained on the editorial board for years. She opposed the **Algerian war** vigorously and shared Sartre's political positions. They had a strong bias against the United States and anything smacking of bourgeois or capitalist politics while uncritically approving of the Soviet Union and, generally, the **French Communist Party.** Yet she was for the most part not active in political movements until the 1970s, when she marched in favor of abortion rights and various neo-Marxist causes. The last volume published during her lifetime was her homage to Sartre, including an account of his death and a record of conversations with him.

Beauvoir's stature comes less from a particular work or works than from her total production over her whole career. Feminists in particular prize the example of a woman who was successful in a literary and intellectual world dominated by men and who used her talents to challenge, in *Le Deuxième Sexe,* some of the most fundamental institutions and views of her society. While not a great stylist, Beauvoir used language to good effect, whether in the probing of emotion and other psychological feelings in her characters, the exposition of philosophical and political positions, the reporting of conversations, or the portrait of a time and a class (as in the first volume of her memoirs). Her words are direct and often persuasive, and the world she paints is a recognizable one in which the historical dilemmas of her time are depicted and probed — often with great acumen, though just as often with serious distortions.

REFERENCES:

Deirdre Bair, *Simone de Beauvoir: A Biography* (New York: Summit Books, 1990);

Catharine Savage Brosman, *Simone de Beauvoir Revisited* (Boston: Twayne, 1991);

Terry Keefe, *Simone de Beauvoir: A Study of Her Writings* (London: Harrap, 1983);

Elaine Marks, ed., *Critical Essays on Simone de Beauvoir* (Boston: G. K. Hall, 1987);

Renée Weingarten, *Simone de Beauvoir: A Critical View* (Oxford: Berg, 1988).

— C.S.B.

JACQUES BECKER

Jacques Becker (1906–1960), a major director overshadowed by the school of **poetic realism,** created a style that inspired **Nouvelle Vague** (New Wave) directors and received **André Bazin**'s incisive critical praise.

Becker developed his cinema of detail and visual breadth while working with **Jean Renoir** from 1931 to 1939; he was an assistant and player in Renoir's *Boudu sauvé des eaux* (1932; *Boudu Saved from Drowning*), *Madame Bovary* (1934), *Le Crime de Monsieur Lange* (1935; *The Crime of Mr. Lange*), *Une Partie de campagne* (1936; *A Day in the Country*), *La Grande Illusion* (1937; *Grand Illusion*), *La Règle du jeu* (1939; *The Rules of the Game*), and other features. He struck out on his own in 1939, directing, cowriting, or producing thirteen feature films by the time of his death in 1960.

Becker is best known for directing *Falbalas* (1945; *Paris Frills*), *Antoine et Antoinette* (1947; *Antoine and Antoinette*), *Casque d'or* (1952; *Golden Helmet*), *Touchez pas au grisbi* (1954; *Grisbi*), and *Montparnasse 19* (1957; *Modigliani of Montparnasse*). In all his films he fixed the camera on details and traits that define a social milieu. In the precision of his portraits, his staging, and his editing, he captured glimpses of the universals of the human condition in ways that the **tradition de qualité** directors, with their grander narrative visions, never matched.

REFERENCES:

Dudley Andrew, "*Casque d'or, casquettes,* a Cask of Aging Wine: Jacques Becker's *Casque d'or* (1952)," in *French Film: Texts and Contexts,* edited by Susan Hayward and Ginette Vincendeau (London: Routledge, 1990), pp. 157–172;

Roy Armes, *French Cinema since 1946,* second edition (London: Zwemmer / Cranbury, N.J.: Barnes, 1970), pp. 105–115;

Georges Sadoul, "Jacques Becker," in *Rediscovering French Film,* edited by Mary Lea Bandy (New York: Museum of Modern Art / Boston: Little, Brown, 1983), pp. 161–166.

— T.C.

SAMUEL BECKETT

The great Irish writer Samuel Beckett (1906–1989) is part of French as well as Anglo-Irish literature, since he settled permanently in France in 1937, composed a large number of his works in French, and translated others from English into French. (He also translated some of them from French into English.) While he no doubt belongs to the Irish literary tradition — one finds in his work Irish names and motifs and a distinctly Irish humor mixed with melancholy — he belongs also to the French, whose language he used brilliantly. His work is properly associated with the **Nouveau Roman** (New Novel) and the new drama, often called the **Theater of the Absurd.**

Beckett, who was born in Dublin, studied Romance languages at Trinity College there (B.A., 1927), taught briefly in Belfast, and in 1928 was awarded a fellowship to the **Ecole Normale Supérieure.** In Paris he published *Whoroscope* (1930), his poem inspired by the writings of French philosopher René Descartes, and began to translate part of James Joyce's *Work in Progress* into French. Beckett was one of the friends to whom Joyce, who had extremely poor eyesight, dictated passages of this work, which was later published in its entirety as *Finnegans Wake* (1939). Contrary to an often-repeated report, Beckett did not serve as Joyce's paid secretary. Returning to Dublin, he taught for four terms at Trinity and was granted a master's degree in 1931. That same year his book on **Marcel Proust** was published. Resigning in late 1931, Beckett spent several years traveling about with no fixed domicile, but by the late 1930s he had settled in Paris. After the fall of France to the Germans in 1940, he and his French companion, Suzanne Deschevaux-Dumesnil (whom he married in 1961), worked with the **Resistance** in gathering information for the Allies. During the **Occupation** of France he was an agricultural worker in a secluded village in southeastern France.

Beckett's first novels were *Murphy* (published in English in 1938, in Beckett's French in 1947) and *Watt* (written in English in the 1940s, published in 1953; translated, 1968). In these works the heroes and settings are fleshed out and somewhat conventional; yet much of the action takes place within the characters' minds, and the books include obvious archetypal motifs, such as the quest pattern. In Beckett's later novels the characters tend toward anonymity and im-

Scene from Samuel Beckett's *En attendant Godot* (1952) at the Théâtre Babylone (Bernand, Paris)

mobility, and speculation and linguistic play replace action.

Beckett's first French-language novel was *Molloy* (1951; translated), the initial volume of a trilogy that also includes *Malone meurt* (1951; translated as *Malone Dies*) and *L'Innommable* (1953; translated by Beckett as *The Unnamable*). Built, like *Murphy,* around a quest pattern, *Molloy* has the most action of the three novels; still, it is far from conventional. In the first part Molloy, lying in his mother's room, recalls his adventures, during which he has lost progressively most of his mobility, identity, and what one might call Cartesian certitudes. In some ways the second part seems logically to precede the first, thus creating a strange circular pattern as Jacques Moran is sent to find Molloy. One can easily read the bizarre transformations that Moran undergoes as the metamorphosis by which he becomes the object of his quest. In the second and third volumes of the trilogy, the hero and action tend even more toward dissolution than in *Molloy*.

In 1953 Beckett's play *En attendant Godot* (1952; translated by Beckett as *Waiting for Godot*) caused a sensation when it was produced in Paris. At first glance the two-act play seems static, although full of subtle dramatic moments, and it is generally described as a metaphysical drama: Godot, who sends word but never appears, represents God, and the two bums who await his arrival are, in this scheme, modern Everymen, abandoned in a meaningless universe. Two other characters, Pozzo and Lucky, form a model Hegelian master-slave relationship, suggesting the alienation

and enslavement of modern man, both metaphysically and politically. The play illustrates the metaphysical absurdity depicted by other dramatists of Beckett's generation. At the same time, however, it is filled with Irish humor. Sometimes called the most successful play of the century, it has been produced over and over in many countries; in 1988 Robin Williams and Steve Martin starred in a New York revival.

En attendant Godot was followed by other plays in French and some written originally in English. They include *Fin de partie* and *Acte sans parole* (1957; translated by Beckett as *Endgame* and *Act Without Words, I*). Like most of his work, they call into question the possibility of meaning. "Our existence is hopeless," Beckett was quoted as saying. Interspersed with these dramas were other prose works, such as *Nouvelles et textes pour rien* (1955; translated by Beckett as *Stories and Texts for Nothing*), and the novel *Comment c'est* (1961; translated as *How It Is*), whose French title is a pun on the verb *commencer* (to begin).

Beckett won the Nobel Prize for Literature in 1969. His French-language works, combining metaphysical questionings with earthy humor and a macabre melancholy, can be placed in the Rabelaisian tradition of French literature. Like François Rabelais, he wrote in a vigorous style that displays his fertile imagination. His works also have, however, a spareness, a pessimism, and a strong vein of antirealism that mark them as eminently modern. His voice is one of the most individual and yet universal among those writers who express the angst, horror, and hopelessness of the twentieth century.

REFERENCES:

Cathleen Culotta Andonian, *Samuel Beckett: A Reference Guide* (Boston: G. K. Hall, 1989);

Deirdre Bair, *Samuel Beckett: A Biography* (New York & London: Harcourt Brace Jovanovich, 1978; revised edition, New York: Summit, 1990);

John Fletcher, *The Novels of Samuel Beckett*, second edition (New York: Barnes & Noble, 1970);

Charles R. Lyons, *Samuel Beckett* (New York: Grove, 1984).

— C.S.B.

MAURICE BÉJART

A controversial choreographer and ballet director, Maurice Béjart (1927–) founded the internationally acclaimed Ballets du XXième Siècle (Ballet of the 20th Century) at the Théâtre de la Monnaie in Brussels in 1959. The company held regular seasons in Brussels, gave performances in Paris, and made frequent world tours, including appearances at Expo 67 in Montreal and the opening ceremonies at the 1968 Olympic Games in Mexico City.

Béjart's work is unconventional. He prefers to choreograph large theatrical spectacles suitable for arenas holding thousands of spectators, such as the Brussels Palais des Sports. These mixed-media productions blend poetry, singing, extravagant costumes, sound, and nontraditional uses of space to create unified works. Béjart is interested also in cinema and sport and how they relate to dance. His choreography — energetic and often highly erotic — requires dancers, predominantly male, with strong and dramatically expressive ballet technique. Béjart's critics say his work lacks subtlety, but all agree that it is provocative.

Born in Marseilles and trained at the Marseilles Opera Ballet School, Béjart toured with **Roland Petit**'s ballet company and several other European troupes before forming Les Ballets de l'Etoile in Paris with writer Jean Laurent in 1954. His innovative work with that company brought him the distinction of being called the greatest new talent of French ballet.

Béjart's first major work as a choreographer was a 1959 revival of *Le Sacre du printemps* (*The Rite of Spring*) in Brussels. Other notable ballets he created or revived are *Boléro* (1961), a version of *Roméo et Juliette* in which the star-crossed lovers are brought back to life (1966), and *Nijinsky, clown de Dieu* (1971; *Nijinsky, Clown of God*), a complex theatrical piece performed at the Brussels Palais des Sports and Madison Square Garden in New York City.

In 1970 Béjart founded in Brussels the Ecole Mudra — Centre européen de perfectionnement et de recherche des interprètes du spectacle (Mudra School — European Center for Perfecting and Research for Interpreters of Shows), a school and studio in which young people aged sixteen to twenty could experiment with total theater. (*Mudra* is the Indian word for gesture in sacred dance.)

Béjart has received the Grand Prix du Théâtre des Nations in Paris (1960 and 1962), the choreography award of the Paris Dance Festival (1965), the *Dance Magazine* Award (1974), and the Erasmus Prize (1974). In 1987, after disagreements with the director of the Théâtre de la Monnaie, Béjart moved to Lausanne, Switzerland, where he founded the Béjart Ballet Lausanne. In 1989 he choreographed *Révolution/Evolution* for the celebration of the bicentennial of the French Revolution at the Grand Palais in Paris. In 1992 Rudra Béjart Lausanne, a workshop school and ensemble of twenty-four professional dancers, replaced Béjart Ballet Lausanne. (*Rudra* is one of the names of the Hindu god Siva.)

REFERENCES:

Maurice Béjart, "Dynamic Tradition," in *Ballet and Modern Dance* (London: Octopus, 1974), pp. 100–104;

John Gruen, "Maurice Béjart," in *The Private World of Ballet* (New York: Viking, 1975), pp. 181–186;

Jean-Louis Rousseau, "From Wagner to Fellini," in *Béjart by Béjart* (New York: Congdon & Lattes, 1979), pp. 5–12;

Roger Stengele, *Who's Béjart* (Brussels: J. Verbeeck, 1972).

— A.P.E.

JEAN-PAUL BELMONDO

After some stage experience and supporting roles in nine films, actor Jean-Paul Belmondo (1933–) won worldwide fame with his starring role in **Jean-Luc Godard**'s *A Bout de souffle* (1960; *Breathless*), one of the chief works in the **Nouvelle Vague** (New Wave) in French cinema.

In this film Belmondo played a small-time hood, Michel, who fashions himself in the image of Humphrey Bogart. Belmondo's success and popularity led to a fashion trend known as "Belmondism." He played the same type of tough but comic character in successive movies by Godard, particularly *Pierrot le fou* (1964; *Crazy Pierrot*), and by such directors as Vittorio De Sica, Henri Verneuil, and **Jean-Pierre Melville,** for whom he made *Léon Morin, prêtre* (1961; Léon Morin, Priest), *Le Doulos* (1962; *Doulos the Finger Man*), and *L'Aîné des Ferchaux* (1962; *Magnet of Doom*).

After a lesser degree of success in several films he made during the 1960s, Belmondo made action films closer to the mainstream, in which he appeared in fast-paced, physically challenging, spectacular roles. While lacking the stylistic panache of his earlier work, these movies cemented Belmondo's status as an action-hero superstar. He continues to work regularly in French movies, though he no longer appears in the kind of vanguard films that made his early reputation.

REFERENCES:

Andrew Sarris, "Jean-Paul Belmondo," in *The National Society of Film Critics on the Movie Star,* edited by Elisabeth Weis (New York: Viking, 1981);

David Shipman, "Belmondo," *Films and Filming* (September 1964).

—W.L.

JULIEN BENDA

A critic and essayist, Julien Benda (1867–1956) attempted in his early books to defend reason against the counterclaims of sentiment, particularly in its many and persistent Romantic forms. One of the thinkers he criticized was **Henri Bergson**, in *Le Bergsonisme ou une philosophie de la mobilité* (1912; Bergsonism, or A Philosophy of Mobility). One of Benda's best-known works is *La Trahison des clercs* (1927; The Betrayal of the Intellectuals), in which he charged that writers who allow their political and social involvements to affect their work betray their vocation. Ironically, Benda, whose parents were nonpracticing Jews, began his career as an author with essays supporting the defense in the **Dreyfus Affair**, and after **World War II** he became strongly philo-Communist, devoting much of his writing to the defense of the Soviet Union. In *La France byzantine* (1945) he attacked **André Gide** and **Paul Valéry** for elevating the aesthetic over the intellectual and abandoning principles of identity, coherence, and fixity of thought.

REFERENCES:

Roy L. Nichols, *Treason, Tradition, and the Intellectual: Julien Benda and Political Discourse* (Lawrence: Regents' Press of Kansas, 1978);

Robert J. Niess, *Julien Benda* (Ann Arbor: University of Michigan Press, 1956);

Edward Timms, "Treason of Intellectuals? Benda, Benn, and Brecht," in *Vision and Blueprints: Avant-Garde Culture and Radical Politics in Early Twentieth-Century Europe,* by Timms, Peter Collier, and Raymond Williams (Manchester, U.K.: Manchester University Press, 1988), pp. 18–32.

—C.S.B.

ANDRÉ BENEDETTO

A playwright and producer of theatrical spectacles, André Benedetto (1934–) views drama as a political enterprise. Seeking to provoke the audience to revolutionary action, he has been quoted as saying, "Poetry and revolution are the same thing." His best-known play is *Napalm* (1968), an attack on American involvement in the Vietnam War. Among his other plays are *Rosa Lux* (1970), *Commune de Paris* (1971; Paris Commune), *La Madone des ordures* (1973; The Madonna of Filth), and *Geronimo* (1975). His plays are often ritualistic, employing symbols and allegories and featuring elevated language, sometimes verse. In his productions Benedetto blurs the distinction between amateur and professional performers, always playing the role of master of ceremonies himself.

In the 1960s Benedetto became associated with the Nouvelle Compagnie d'Avignon, a self-consciously regional theater company that combines a commitment to high quality with the political aim of revitalizing the region's Occitan language and culture for the purpose of rehabilitating a group that has been marginalized because it is a linguistic minority.

REFERENCE:

David Bradby, *Modern French Drama 1940–1990* (Cambridge: Cambridge University Press, 1991).

—C.S.B.

CHRISTIAN BÉRARD

Although he also designed fashions and sets for the ballet, the artist Christian Bérard (1902–1949) is best known as a theatrical set designer and scene painter. He created sets for many of the plays directed by **Louis Jouvet** at the **Théâtre de l'Athénée** in Paris.

Bérard, who first worked with Jouvet on the scenery for a 1934 production of **Jean Cocteau**'s *La Machine infernale* (*The Infernal Machine*), is particularly remembered for the set he created for Molière's *L'Ecole des femmes* (translated as *School for Wives*) at Jouvet's Athénée in 1936. The imprisoning walls around a house could be opened outward in certain scenes, revealing the garden. He is also known for his representation of faded elegance in the decor for Jouvet's 1945 production of **Jean Giraudoux**'s *La Folle de Chaillot* (translated as *The Madwoman of Chaillot*).

Bérard designed for other directors and theaters as well. He created sets for Cocteau's *La Voix humaine* (*The Human Voice*) at the **Comédie-Française** in 1930 and for André Brulé's staging of Cocteau's *Les Monstres sacrés* (The Idols) at the Théâtre Michel in

Georges Bernanos in 1929, the year he won the Prix Fémina for *La Joie*

1940. When Cocteau staged his *Renaud et Armide* (Renaud and Armide) at the Comédie-Française in 1943, he called on Bérard for the sets. In the same year Bérard was the set designer for a production of Giraudoux's *Sodome et Gomorrhe* (Sodom and Gomorrah) at the Théâtre Hébertot.

In 1947, when Jouvet chose him to create the scenery for **Jean Genet**'s avant-garde play *Les Bonnes* (translated as *The Maids*), Bérard acquitted himself well. Yet his sets themselves were never avant-garde. His approach seemed to have sprung from the realism of the Paris **boulevard theaters,** which — in collaboration with Jouvet — he refined and stylized for remarkable effects.

REFERENCES:

Jacqueline de Jomaron, "Louis Jouvet ou l'exigence," in *Le Théâtre en France. 2: De la Révolution à nos jours,* edited by Jomaron (Paris: Armand Colin, 1989), pp. 229–239;

Boris Kochno, *Christian Bérard* (New York: Panache Press, 1988).

— R.J.N.

HENRI BERGSON

Henri Bergson (1859–1941) is the most renowned French philosopher of the late nineteenth and early twentieth century, best known as the champion of the élan vital (vital spirit, or thrust — that is, the life force). He elaborated this metaphysical concept in reaction to a philosophical trend that had begun during the Enlightenment: the rejection of speculation about nonquantifiable, transcendent realities in favor of scientific investigation of what can be verified by experiment and observation.

Born in Paris to Jewish parents, Bergson, who was appointed to a chair at the Collège de France in 1900, was not a creative writer, but, like many other French philosophers, he was interested in topics — such as memory and the imagination — that also concern poets and novelists. Moreover, his style is highly poetic. The literary quality of his writings was recognized in 1927, when he was awarded the Nobel Prize for Literature.

Bergson established his reputation as a philosopher in 1889 with *Essai sur les données immédiates de la conscience* (translated as *Time and Free Will*). An important contribution to the discipline of psychology, it is — like much of his subsequent work — a study founded on his investigations of the human mind. His next book, *Matière et mémoire* (1896; translated as *Matter and Memory*), looks forward to Sigmund Freud's theory of the unconscious mind; according to Bergson, memory includes all one's past experiences, but the brain lets through to the immediate consciousness only recollections relevant to the moment.

Another important work, *Le Rire* (1900; translated as *Laughter*), presents Bergson's theory of comedy. In the influential *L'Evolution créatrice* (1907; translated as *Creative Evolution*) he argues against the mechanistic Darwinian understanding of evolution and stresses rather the creative and purposeful activity of the élan vital in shaping the direction of evolution. *Les Deux Sources de la morale et de la religion* (1932; translated as *The Two Sources of Morality and Religion*) takes a position that might be called spiritualist, although it reflects no orthodoxy.

Bergson emphasized what he called *la durée* (duration, or inner, human time) as opposed to rigid, chronological time; he similarly contrasted intuition, connected to the life force, with the intellect, which is a geometric, or measuring, faculty, the source of scientific thought. In each case Bergson preferred the inner, intuitive spirit to the exterior, mathematical one. Although he recognized that human freedom was difficult to demonstrate, he asserted that its existence was observed and felt by every human being.

Marcel Proust, who was acquainted with and distantly related to Bergson, was likewise interested in time and memory, and it is often supposed that Proust was influenced by the philosopher. Despite some resemblances in their views, however, there is no clear evidence to support this assumption. Although he was extremely influential in his own time, Bergson did not find favor with philosophers of the generations following his, who often denounced him as reactionary in his seeming to reject current philosophical trends in favor of an older, metaphysical approach.

REFERENCES:

Gilles Deleuze, *Bergsonism,* translated by Hugh Tomlinson and Barbara Habberjam (New York: Zone Books, 1988);

Robert C. Grogin, *The Bergsonian Controversy in France 1900–1914* (Calgary: University of Calgary Press, 1988);

A. R. Lacey, *Bergson* (London: Routledge, 1989).

— C.S.B.

GEORGES BERNANOS

Georges Bernanos (1888–1948) is recognized as the most important twentieth-century Catholic novelist in France, which after the turn of that century produced several important literary figures in what is sometimes known as the Catholic Renaissance. **André Malraux** called Bernanos "the greatest novelist of his time."

Born in Paris, Bernanos had a religious upbringing, and as a youth he participated in the antirepublican **Action Française** and Camelots du Roi movements. He was wounded in **World War I.** In 1917 he married Jehanne Pauline Marie Talbert d'Arc, a collateral descendant of Joan of Arc. The father of six children, he first struggled to earn a living as an insurance salesman. His first novel, *Sous le soleil de Satan* (1926; translated as *The Star of Satan*), displays his extraordinary talent for sounding the human soul, but it also reveals characteristic difficulties in composition. The novel has three story lines. In one a sixteen-year-old girl, Mouchette, kills the marquis who has made her pregnant. In the second a young priest, Donissan, overcomes spiritual temptation in an encounter with Satan himself and meets Mouchette, who refuses his compassion and takes her own life in an act of despair not unlike the emotion Donissan has undergone in his attempts to achieve sainthood. The final part is set on the last day in Donissan's life, revealing that he has become a saintly old priest who can read the secrets of souls. For Bernanos the demonic spirit present in this and other works is indicative of the twentieth century; he is particularly severe on physicians.

Sarah Bernhardt playing dead in a coffin at her home. Photos similar to this one were widely distributed during her lifetime.

After publication of *Sous le soleil de Satan,* Bernanos quit his job, henceforth eking out a living with his pen. His next novel, *L'Imposture* (1927), and a sequel, *La Joie* (1929; translated as *Joy*), are concerned with the intertwined stories of a nonbelieving priest and a saintly girl murdered by a drug-addicted Russian chauffeur. *La Joie* won the **Prix Fémina.** In 1936 Bernanos published *Journal d'un curé de campagne* (translated as *The Diary of a Country Priest*), generally considered his masterpiece and the basis for a successful film. Written in diary form, the novel is the story of a poor and humble, but idealistic and spiritual, young priest in his first parish, a village in the north. Beset with social, physical, and spiritual trials, he seems to fail on all sides; he is, however, successful in reviving the faith of a countess, who blames God for the death of her infant son but is reconciled just before her death. Himself stricken with cancer, the priest dies in a state of grace.

At first a partisan of General Francisco Franco during the **Spanish Civil War** (1936–1939), Bernanos, who was living in Majorca, changed positions when he realized the tactics Franquist forces were using, and he denounced them in *Les Grands Cimetières sous la lune* (1938; translated as *A Diary of My Times*). He spent most of **World War II** in South America. In the postwar

Serge Koussevitzky, Nadia Boulanger, and Aaron Copland in Boston, October 1945, shortly before Boulanger returned to France.

years he was one of the most vocal critics of prominent leftist political movements and their fascination with the Soviet Union. Among his last works are *Monsieur Ouine* (1943; translated as *The Open Mind*), a bitter denunciation of the secular values of the present, and *Dialogues des Carmélites* (1949; translated as *The Fearless Heart*), which **Francis Poulenc** turned into an opera.

REFERENCES:

Gerda Blumenthal, *The Poetic Imagination of Georges Bernanos* (Baltimore: Johns Hopkins University Press, 1966);

William Bush, *Georges Bernanos* (Boston: Twayne, 1969).

— C.S.B.

EMILE BERNARD

Artist and critic Emile Bernard (1868–1941) played an important role in the transitional period during and after the breakup of the original Impressionist circle. Trained as a painter by academic artist Fernand Cormon, Bernard was expelled for insubordination from Cormon's studio and then wandered across France, joining **Paul Gauguin** at Pont-Aven, Brittany, in 1888.

In the 1880s Bernard's style oscillated between a residual Impressionism and the pointillist technique of Georges Seurat and the Neo-Impressionists. Bernard eventually settled on what became known as cloisonnism, characterized by areas of flat, unadulterated color, heavily outlined in black or blue-black, reminiscent of both Japanese woodblock prints and stained-glass windows. Bernard's painting of iron bridges at Asnières (1887) typifies the new technique: though sec-

tions of the work (especially the grass) are loosely painted, the shadows of the pilings and the forms of the strolling man and woman are rendered simply as flat, black shapes. Bernard was probably the first artist to apply cloisonnism to studies of Pont-Aven; the simplicity and apparent naiveté of the style attracted Bernard, Gauguin, **Paul Sérusier**, and other Pont-Aven painters for its suggestions of a pre-industrial world. (Bernard wrote in 1886 that in Pont-Aven he "traveled back across the centuries, isolating myself increasingly from my contemporaries, whose preoccupations with the modern world inspired in me nothing but disgust. Bit by bit I became a man of the Middle Ages.") Bernard's view of Breton women in a green meadow, painted shortly after his arrival in Brittany in August 1888, uses cloisonnist techniques to suggest his notion of the essence of the province. In contrast (and perhaps in answer) to Seurat's better-known *Un Dimanche à la Grande Jatte* (1884–1886; *Sunday Afternoon on the Island of La Grande Jatte),* Bernard presents the viewer with a rural scene of harmony and peaceful interaction; the painting is dominated by the traditional peasant garb of Breton women. Both style and format were adapted by Gauguin for his own, more problematic studies of Breton peasant life, beginning with his *La Vision après le sermon* (1888; *Vision After the Sermon* (1888). Bernard and Gauguin exhibited together as part of the so-called Impressionists and Synthetists at the Café Volpini in 1889, but they eventually quarreled about who should take credit for the development of a new artistic movement.

After Gauguin departed for Tahiti in 1891, Bernard moved naturally to the Brotherhood of the **Nabis,** grouped around those artists remaining in Pont-Aven. After exhibiting with the Nabis in 1892 and 1893, he broke with them as well. From 1893 until 1900 he toured Egypt, Spain, and Italy, gradually moving toward an academic style and a fondness for sentimental religious themes. His major impact in his later career was as a critic, especially through his championing of the art of **Paul Cézanne** and Vincent van Gogh.

REFERENCES:

Wladyslawa Jaworska, *Gauguin and the Pont-Aven School,* translated by Patrick Evans (Greenwich, Conn.: New York Graphic Society, 1974);

Judy Le Paul, *Gauguin and the Impressionists at Pont-Aven* (New York: Abbeville, 1983);

Post-Impressionism: Cross-Currents in European Painting (London: Royal Academy of Arts, 1979).

— J.H.

SARAH BERNHARDT

Sarah-Henriette-Rosine Bernhardt (1845–1923) is known worldwide as one of the most famous stage actresses of all time. She belonged to a generation of charismatic actors who later became known as *monstres sacrés* (sacred monsters) because they were thought to be virtually superhuman in talent and inspiration and because they were adored by their public.

Possessing a speaking voice that was said to have an otherworldly beauty, the "divine Sarah" apparently depended heavily on the inspiration of the moment for the energy of her performance, so that the quality of her work varied enormously from night to night, even from act to act. Having studied with Joseph-Isadore Samson, a well-known actor of the preceding generation, she began acting at eighteen, on the stage of the **Comédie-Française** as the title character in an 1862 performance of Jean Racine's *Iphigénie*. Although she never became a member of the Comédie Française, she appeared there frequently during the second half of the nineteenth century, performing abroad as well. The range of her abilities suited her for both male and female roles; among her most famous parts were the title role in Racine's *Phèdre*, Doña Sol in Victor Hugo's *Hernani*, the title role in Alfred de Musset's *Lorenzaccio*, and Napoleon's son in *L'Aiglon* (The Eaglet), by Edmond Rostand. She also played Cordelia in *King Lear* and the title role in *Hamlet*.

In 1898 she became director of her own playhouse, the Théâtre Sarah-Bernhardt, where she also acted. Although she had to have a leg amputated in 1915, she continued to perform from time to time. Her last role, in *La Gloire* (1922), by Maurice Rostand, was written for her and allowed her to remain seated throughout. During the German **Occupation** of France (1940–1944), the Théâtre Sarah-Bernhardt was temporarily renamed Théâtre de la Cité; Sarah Bernhardt had been a Jew.

REFERENCE:

Ruth Brandon, *Being Divine: A Biography of Sarah Bernhardt* (London: Secker & Warburg, 1991).

— R.J.N.

MAURICE BLANCHOT

Maurice Blanchot (1907–) became known to North American readers during the final decades of the twentieth century because of the fashionable critical positions he set forth in works such as *Faux Pas* (1943; False Steps), *L'Espace littéraire* (1955; translated as *The Space of Literature*), and English-language collections of his essays, including *The Gaze of Orpheus, and*

Pierre Boulez with his teacher Olivier Messiaen at the Théâtre de l'Odeon in Paris, 1966

Other Literary Essays (1981) and *The Sirens' Song: Selected Essays of Maurice Blanchot* (1982). After the unsurpassed nineteenth-century model of Stéphane Mallarmé, Blanchot was one of the first authors writing in French to call into question the workings of language and hence of literature. He asked about the compatibility of language with consciousness and capacities for expression, and he explored its relationship with being and nonbeing (death) in a philosophical context influenced by philosopher Martin Heidegger as well as Mallarmé. Blanchot is also the author of complex and difficult fiction.

Blanchot, who subsequently evolved toward a so-called politics of philo-Semitism, began his career in the 1930s as a sympathizer of **Charles Maurras** and a contributor to nationalist right-wing journals. Anti-Semitic, he was attracted by terror as a political tactic; an early short story and the novel *Aminadab* (1942) present elements of a Kafkaesque, totalitarian universe characterized by estrangement and the absurd. He subsequently called the story "unfortunate" in its apparent foreshadowings of concentration camps, but his political positions remained ambiguous. The nightmarish atmosphere and absence of stable identity and conventional plot also mark Blanchot's subsequent novels, including *Le Très-Haut* (1948; The Most High), a retelling of the Orestes myth, and *L'Attente, l'oubli* (1962; Waiting, Forgetting). Blanchot's antirealism and questioning of fictional conventions are part of his program of contesting the function of literature, which depends on language, not only unreliable but a sign of nothingness. (The symbol is *not* the thing it symbolizes.) As the title of his 1942 book puts the question: *Comment la littérature est-elle possible?* (How Is Literature Possible?). Such positions have endeared Blanchot to Deconstructionists and critics such as **Jacques Derrida** and **Michel Foucault.**

REFERENCE:

Jeffrey Mehlman, *Legacies of Anti-Semitism in France* (Minneapolis: University of Minnesota Press, 1983).

— C.S.B.

ROGER BLIN

With skill, understanding, and enormous determination, theater director Roger Blin (1907–1984) brought the "new theater" or **Theater of the Absurd** of the 1950s to the attention of Parisian audiences and taught them to enjoy it. He played a major role in the establishment of the postwar avant-garde, and he is largely responsible for the success of **Samuel Beckett**'s plays on the French stage.

In the 1930s Blin made contact with Paris **Surrealists** and, through them, with **Antonin Artaud.** For a time Blin was Artaud's assistant and had a role in his play *Les Cenci* (translated as *The Cenci*) in 1935. After an initial interest in filmmaking, Blin moved definitively into the theater through the "October group," a leftist, non-Communist organization of the 1930s devoted to the use of theater as anti-Fascist propaganda and for promotion of social causes. There Blin met **Jacques Prévert,** who was working on *Le Tableau des merveilles,* a French adaptation of Miguel de Cervantes' *El Retablo de las maravillas* (translated as *The Puppet Show of Wonders*) for **Jean-Louis Barrault.** Barrault included Blin in the cast (1936) and employed him again in his stage adaptation of Knut Hamsun's novel *Hunger.* Blin was a stutterer, but — through personal discipline and working with Barrault on the techniques of mime — he surmounted his handicap.

It was not until after **World War II** that Blin began to direct. He was always a marginal director, usually working in so-called pocket theaters on the **Left Bank** along with directors such as Sylvain Dhomme, Jacques Mauclair, and Jean-Marie Serreau. Making the most of state aid programs for small theater companies, Blin participated in the expansion of the theater movement in and around Paris. His first successful production (1949) was of August Strindberg's *The Ghost Sonata,* translated into French by

Georges Braque in his studio

Arthur Adamov. Moving from theater to theater, and raising money however he could, Blin thereafter produced some thirty plays, most of them never before staged.

He staged two plays by Adamov — *La Petite et la Grande Manœuvre* (translated as *The Big and the Little Maneuver*) in 1950 and *La Parodie* (translated as *The Parody*) in 1952 — before Adamov's work had become known and appreciated. Then in 1953 at the Babylone he had a major success with Beckett's *En attendant Godot* (translated as *Waiting for Godot*) — a play in which nothing happens and which involves, for the most part, apparently pointless conversation between two bums. At the time, when nothing of the sort had ever been seen, staging the play involved high risk, but Blin carried it off, with scenery consisting of little except a fake tree. He was to stage three more Beckett plays: *Fin de partie* (translated as *Endgame*) in 1957, on the Right Bank at the Studio des Champs-Elysées; *La Dernière Bande* (translated as *Krapp's Last Tape*) in 1960, at the experimental wing (Salle Récamier) of the **Théâtre National Populaire;** and *Oh! les beaux jours* (translated as *Happy Days*), in which **Madeleine Renaud** triumphed as Winnie on the large stage and before a major audience at the **Théâtre de l'Odéon** in 1963.

Blin is also well known for having staged plays by the avant-garde dramatist and ex-convict **Jean Genet:**

Les Nègres (translated as *The Blacks*) in 1959 and *Les Paravents* (translated as *The Screens*) in 1966. He directed *Les Nègres* at the Théâtre de Lutèce with a troupe of black actors known as the "Griots," using a complicated set with a balcony on scaffolding, stairs, and overly lavish ceremonial costumes. For this nonmimetic theater he devised nonrealistic stagecraft, thus expanding possible readings of the texts: *Les Nègres* is not only about racism but also about the creation of stereotypes and their effects on the stereotyped. Blin's staging, which won high praise from Genet, renders both type and arbitrary judgment visible. *Les Paravents* is partly about colonialism, but, in his Odéon staging, Blin brought to life on the stage its larger reference to oppression in general. The performance brought out right-wing demonstrators, seeking to suppress it as unpatriotic. In 1960 Blin staged *The Caretaker,* the first Harold Pinter drama to be presented in France.

Whether he worked with a bare stage or a complicated set, Blin's nonrealistic settings and costumes, the seemingly choreographed movements he introduced, and his direction of actors created much of the visual style now considered inherent in the absurdist plays of the 1950s and 1960s.

REFERENCE:

Odette Aslan, *Roger Blin and Twentieth-Century Playwrights,* translated by Ruby Cohn (Cambridge: Cambridge University Press, 1988).

— R.J.N.

Georges Brassens (Roger-Viollet)

LÉON BLUM

Although he started out as a writer of literary and dramatic criticism, biography, and essays on social issues, Léon Blum (1872–1950) is chiefly remembered as a politician. Born in Paris of Jewish parentage, Blum as a young man contributed criticism to the *Revue Blanche.* His *Nouvelles Conversations de Goethe avec Eckermann* (1901; New Conversations Between Goethe and Eckermann) is a series of anonymously published, imaginary dialogues in which Johann Wolfgang von Goethe (1749–1832) and Johann Peter Eckermann (1792–1854) discuss social issues of Blum's time. In his controversial *Du mariage* (1907; On Marriage) Blum expresses the conviction that unsatisfactory sexual relations were the main cause of marital discord, and he defended premarital sex for women as well as men. *Stendhal et le beylisme* (1914; revised, 1930; Stendhal and Beylism), an important study of that Romantic novelist, followed.

In 1919 Blum was elected to the Chambre des Députés on the Socialist ticket, and in 1924 he became head of the French **Socialist Party.** In the same year he also helped to found the Cartel des Gauches, a coalition of non-Communist, left-wing political parties. As prime minister under the **Popular Front** (1936–1937), he presided over one of the most controversial governments of the **Third Republic.** He became prime minister again in 1938. In 1940 he was arrested by the **Vichy government.** Tried in 1942, he was released to the Germans in 1943 and deported to a German concentration camp. Freed by the Allies in 1945, he served again as prime minister in December 1946–January 1947.

REFERENCES:

Joel Colton, *Léon Blum: Humanist in Politics* (Durham, N.C.: Duke University Press, 1987);

Helmut Gruber, *Léon Blum, French Socialism, and the Popular Front: A Case of Internal Contradictions* (Ithaca, N.Y.: Cornell University Press, 1986);

Jean Lacouture, *Léon Blum,* translated by George Holoch (New York: Holmes & Meier, 1982);

William Logue, *Léon Blum: The Formative Years, 1872–1914* (De Kalb: Northern Illinois University Press, 1973).
                                                    — C.S.B.

PIERRE DE BOISDEFFRE

Critic, diplomat, novelist, and a generally conservative man of letters in the French tradition, Pierre de Boisdeffre (1924–) has been a voice of moderation during the second half of the twentieth century as a historian of modern French literature, including the most recent. Through the publication of his various histories and anthologies, which have gone through many editions, he has argued on behalf of tradition against innovation for its own sake.

Boisdeffre, who studied law and political science, later served as director of French radio from 1963 to 1968. His *Métamorphose de la littérature* (1950; Metamorphosis of Literature) won the Grand Prix de la Critique. Among the writers on whom he has published studies are **Maurice Barrès, Charles de Gaulle, André Gide,** and **Jean Giono.** His other books include *Les Ecrivains français d'aujourd'hui* (1963; French Writers of Today), *Les Poètes français d'aujourd'hui* (1973; French Poets of Today), and *Le Roman français depuis 1900* (1979; The French Novel Since 1900).

REFERENCE:

André Brincourt, "Pierre de Boisdeffre ou la passion des lettres," *Figaro,* 25 October 1985, p. 34.
                                                    — D.O'C.

PIERRE BONNARD

Together with **Edouard Vuillard** and **Félix Vallotton,** Pierre Bonnard (1867–1947) is one of the best-known artists in the urban wing of the **Nabi** brotherhood. Bonnard was a driving force behind Intimisme, the application of Impressionist techniques to interiors rather than landscapes. His use of color influenced many artists after him.

Bonnard's family expected him to pursue a career in law; he earned a law degree in 1888 and was called to the bar in November of the following year. His interest in painting was initially an avocation, pursued primarily on holidays. Yet he was accepted into the Ecole des Beaux-Arts in 1889, and his artistic interests gradually superseded any desire to be a lawyer.

Although Bonnard proclaimed, "I belong to no school; I am just trying to do something personal," **Paul**

André Breton with his second wife, Jacqueline Lamba Breton, at the 1936 Surrealist exposition in London

Gauguin and the Impressionists played major roles in shaping his work. Bonnard admired the Impressionists for their refusal to conform to rules of classical composition. He considered Gauguin's work more traditional, but he came to employ Gauguin's technique of using patches of flat color. An 1890 exhibition of Japanese woodblock prints convinced Bonnard, he noted later, that "color could express everything . . . with no need for relief or texture. I understood that it was possible to translate light, shapes, and character by color alone. . . ."

In the 1890s Bonnard's interest in a method approaching cloisonnism led him to the Nabis, where his love for Japanese prints caused him to be dubbed the "Nabi très japonnard" (very Japanese-loving Nabi). Unlike the Nabi painters in Pont-Aven, Brittany, led by **Paul Sérusier** and **Maurice Denis,** Bonnard had little interest in religious mysteries or Catholic symbols. Together with other Parisian Nabis (including Vuillard and Ker-Xavier Roussel), Bonnard was fascinated with interior spaces and the patterns of light and color that framed everyday life. Their work came to be called Intimisme. One portrait of a woman done around 1900 appears as an assemblage of patterns; the woman's neck, hands, and face emerge as relatively flat and stable patches in a riot of conflicting color patterns.

After 1900 his fascination with light and color led Bonnard back toward Impressionistic stylistic devices. His palette lightened, and the colors became more brilliant. In a 1908 painting showing a nude against the light, the forcefully modeled female figure stands in the midst of intense, mottled surfaces, all of whose colors are reflected by her wet skin.

REFERENCES:

André Fermigier, *Pierre Bonnard* (New York: Abrams, 1969);

Claire Frèches-Thory and Antoine Terrasse, *The Nabis: Bonnard, Vuillard, and Their Circle,* translated by Mary Pardoe (New York: Abrams, 1990);

Annette Vailland, *Bonnard* (Greenwich, Conn.: New York Graphic Society, 1965).

—J.H.

Yves Bonnefoy

Yves Bonnefoy (1923–) is one of the major poetic voices of his generation. His work has been admired by discriminating critics since the publication of his first collection, *Du mouvement et de l'immobilité de Douve* (1953; translated as *On the Motion and Immobility of Douve*). Yet his poetry is so hermetic that it has not earned him the sort of popularity accorded poets such as **Louis Aragon** and **Jacques Prévert.**

Bonnefoy, who studied mathematics and philosophy and later art history, began frequenting **Surrealist** circles in Paris in 1943, but he broke with that group in 1947. The wide range of his studies is reflected in his poetry, in which the influence of Stéphane Mallarmé is also discernible. In his poetry he is concerned with *présence* — tearing things away from their categories and descriptions and concentrating on their pure appearance to consciousness; in this manner he shows kinship with the phenomenologists, especially Edmund Husserl. Bonnefoy is also preoccupied with absences — as he puts it, the invisible bird or "bird in the ruins" and not the bird of the ornithologists. His poetry has thus a mysterious, even mystic, dimension and expresses what he calls the "will toward unity."

Among Bonnefoy's other collections of poetry are *Hier régnant désert* (1958; Yesterday Reigning Desert), *Pierre écrite* (1959; translated as *Words in Stone*), and *Ce qui fut sans lumière* (1987; translated as *In the Shadow's Light*). Bonnefoy has also translated works by William Shakespeare and published essays on literature, art, and architecture.

REFERENCES:

Mary Ann Caws, *Yves Bonnefoy* (Boston: Twayne, 1984);

John T. Naughton, *The Poetics of Yves Bonnefoy* (Chicago: University of Chicago Press, 1984).

—C.S.B.

Henri Bosco

Born in Avignon, in Provence, Henri Bosco (1888–1976) is known for novels that are marked by his southern origins. He did not strive for realism in his fiction and can be identified with no particular literary school or tendency.

Bosco's most widely read books include *L'Ane Culotte* (1937; translated as *Culotte the Donkey*) and *Le Mas Théotime* (1945; translated as *The Farm Théotime*), which won the Prix Renaudot, both set in Provence. His fiction is also shaped by his studies of Greek, Latin, and Italian — languages he taught at the lycée level — and his ten-year stay in Italy (1920–1930), where he became interested in the mystery cults of antiquity. The hermetic, somewhat strained novel *L'Antiquaire* (1954; The Antique Dealer) is based on the initiation-rite pattern of these cults. His fascination with the mysterious embraces the metaphysical, the magical — as in *L'Ane Culotte* — and the psychical — as in *Le Sanglier* (1932; The Wild Boar) and *Un Rameau de la nuit* (1950; translated as *The Dark Bough*), the story of a man who gradually changes identity, taking on the personality of a man who has been dead for several years. The role of nature and man's ambiguous relationship to it are central to several of Bosco's novels; they are often treated in semimythic terms.

Bosco lived and taught for twenty-four years in Morocco (1931–1955). *Des sables à la mer: Pages marocaines* (1950; Between Sand and Sea: Moroccan Pages) reflects his long residence there.

REFERENCES:

Henri Bosco: Mystère et spritualité (Paris: Corti, 1987);

Jacqueline Michel, *Une Mise en récit du silence* (Paris: Corti, 1986).

—C.S.B.

Nadia Boulanger

Nadia Boulanger (1887–1979) was an extraordinary musician who dedicated her life to teaching. Many of her students achieved worldwide recognition. A pupil of **Gabriel Fauré** in composition and Felix Guilmant in organ at the Paris Conservatory, she taught at the Ecole Normale de Musique and at the Conservatory, but most of her pupils were private, largely American at first and later from all over the world. She was the first woman to conduct the full New York Philharmonic Orchestra, the Boston Symphony Orchestra, and the Philadelphia Orchestra.

Hundreds of young Americans attended her courses at the American Conservatory in Fontainebleau or were her private pupils in Paris or the United States, where she resided during **World War II.** Among the first group of American students who worked with her in Paris in the 1920s were Aaron Copland, Walter Piston, Roy Harris, and Virgil Thomson, who all became prominent composers. Later David Diamond, Irving Fine, Elliott Carter, and Philip Glass became members of the "Boulangerie." Since some of these figures and other less famous students of Boulanger subsequently taught at prestigious American universities, her influence in the United States was extensive.

Called a "tender tyrant," Boulanger was a strict disciplinarian who demanded of her students a dedication equal to her own. She emphasized basic musicianship — solfège (sight reading), score reading, transposition, harmony, counterpoint, and orchestration — skills that many Americans lacked. Even her advanced students spent hours working on academic exercises, which she compared to dancers' exercises at the barre.

She did not impose a style upon her novice composers but counseled them on the proportions, clarity, and cohesion of their compositions in progress. She admired the economy of the neoclassical compositions of **Igor Stravinsky** and warned against the model of Arnold Schoenberg. At the famous "Wednesday afternoons" she held in her Paris apartment her students analyzed and played contemporary scores, or they sang Renaissance madrigals or cantatas of Johann Sebastian Bach. Attendance was by invitation; it was an honor to be on the guest list.

REFERENCES:

Bruno Monsaingeon, *Mademoiselle: Conversations with Nadia Boulanger,* translated by Robyn Marsack (Manchester: Carcanet, 1985);

Leonie Rosenstiel, *Nadia Boulanger: A Life in Music* (New York: Norton, 1982).

— P.S.H.

Boulevard Theaters

In the early years of the twentieth century, the boulevard theaters of Paris — located along the "grands boulevards" between the Opéra and the Place de la République and clustered in smaller streets around the Porte Saint-Martin — represented to that city what Broadway has meant to New York: dazzling entertainment, famous stars, and "hit" plays. They included halls such as the **Théâtre du Gymnase,** the Théâtre de la Porte Saint-Martin, the Théâtre de la Renaissance, the Variétés, and the Vaudeville. The Gymnase, the

Renaissance, and the Variétés are still in operation, but the heyday of boulevard shows is long past.

The boulevard playhouses, run by impresarios whose motivation is profit, attract audiences to their large halls by presenting star actors in entertaining but frivolous comedies or melodramas that involve scandalous situations, often including adultery. **Sacha Guitry** wrote and starred in many plays of this sort. Boulevard players perform farces and thrillers as well, and they generally offer numerous performances of the same play: for them, a long run is highly desirable. The modern origins of their staging techniques are in theatrical realism, as developed by **André Antoine.** Commercial boulevard houses strive to satisfy the tastes of the public rather than educate it. Indeed, the term *boulevard theater* stands for all those things that **Jacques Copeau** and the **Cartel des Quatre** opposed in their serious art theaters.

The boulevard has not always lacked social consciousness or poetic imagination; it has introduced its share of masterpieces. Among the noteworthy plays written for these theaters are Marcel Achard's *Voulez-vous jouer avec môa?* (1923; Wanna Play?) and *Turlututu* (1962); Tristan Bernard's *L'Anglais tel qu'on le parle* (1897; translated as *English as He Is Spoke*); Eugène Brieux's *Maternité* (1903; translated as *Maternity*), which called for less restrictive abortion laws and pointed to male guilt in the treatment of women; Georges Courteline's *La Paix chez soi* (1903; translated as *Peace at Home*); and François de Curel's *La Fille sauvage* (1902; The Wild Girl), which treats the interrelationship of civilization and barbarity in human beings. The boulevard theaters also fostered the talents of Georges Feydeau, a comic artist famous for drawing the logical conclusions from illogical plot situations, as in *Occupe-toi d'Amélie* (1908; translated as *Keep an Eye on Amélie*), and **Marcel Pagnol,** whose hit trilogy *Marius, Fanny,* and *César* (1929–1937) revealed his skill at comic caricature of "types" from the Marseilles docks. The best of all boulevard plays is Edmond Rostand's poetic drama *Cyrano de Bergerac* (1897; translated), one of the world's greatest melodramas.

While boulevard dramas often satirized bourgeois hypocrisy and greed, they tended to present women as inferior. Skillful caricature, the stock-in-trade of boulevard plays, is a technique of stereotyping. These theaters may well have contributed to the erroneous impression, taken home by some American soldiers after **World War I,** that the French were all sexually liberated and morally corrupt. As adultery, the idea of the "weaker sex," and stereotyping became less and less amusing to modern audiences, the fortunes of the boulevard theaters waned.

REFERENCES:

Michel Corvin, "Le Boulevard en question," in *Le Théâtre en France. 2: De la Révolution à nos jours,* edited by Jacqueline de Jomaron (Paris: Armand Colin, 1989), pp. 341–380;

Gabrielle Hyslop, "Pixerécourt and the French Melodrama Debate: Instructing Boulevard Theatre Audiences," in *Melodrama,* edited by James Redmon (Cambridge: Cambridge University Press, 1992), pp. 61–85;

René Lalou, "Le Miroir du théâtre," in his *Histoire de la littérature française contemporaine (de 1870 à nos jours)* (Paris: Presses Universitaires de France, 1947), I: 230–264.

— R.J.N.

Pierre Boulez

In 1945 a Paris concert devoted to **Igor Stravinsky**'s music was interrupted by a demonstration in the gallery. The hisses and whistles, coming from a group of **Olivier Messiaen**'s students at the Paris Conservatoire, expressed their disdain for neoclassical music, the prevailing "modern" style. Their leader was Pierre Boulez (1925–), who soon became the most important French musician of the post–World War II era. Convinced that the conventional resources for music are exhausted and that a new musical language must be created, Boulez has used his great skills as a composer, conductor, polemicist, and cultural politician to foster a new kind of music for the future.

In Messiaen's class Boulez's discovery of the compositions of Arnold Schoenberg, virtually unknown at that time in France, convinced him that the twelve-tone procedures gave a new basis and logic to music. Soon afterward he realized that the music of Anton von Webern went beyond Schoenberg's in its control of elements besides tones, such as rhythm, timbre, and dynamics. Boulez's two-part *Structures* (1952 and 1961) for two pianos is one of the first totally serial compositions. Extremely abstract and devoid of conventional expression, it is more often analyzed than performed, but it is an important landmark of postwar music.

Boulez's subsequent compositions employ other contemporary idioms, such as electronic sounds and aleatory elements. His Third Piano Sonata (1957), for instance, is printed in red and green ink and includes instructions for performing the parts in different orders. The performer can choose a "path" while playing the piece, with the result that each performance reveals a different aspect of the music, like a familiar view seen from a different position. This and subsequent compositions — *Le Marteau sans maître* (1954; The Hammer without a Master) for contralto and six instruments, which uses the poetry of **René Char,** and *Pli selon pli* (1964; Fold upon Fold), based on well-known texts by Stéphane Mallarmé — demand a complete reversal of traditional listening habits.

From 1946 to 1956 Boulez was the music director for the acting company of **Madeleine Renaud** and **Jean-Louis Barrault.** He composed music for their productions and in 1954 created a concert series called the Domaine Musical, which introduced little-known contemporary music to Paris audiences of fashionable society women, intellectuals, professional musicians, and students. Boulez conducted, chose the programs, wrote the program notes, and secured the necessary financial backing. Through these activities he became well known and acquired valuable conducting skills.

Boulez did not receive sufficient support and creative freedom in France, however, and he became receptive to foreign offers. A 1964 invitation to become guest conductor of the BBC Orchestra in London was followed by his appointment as guest conductor of the Cleveland Orchestra in 1965. He was principal conductor of the BBC Orchestra from 1971 to 1975 and music director of the New York Philharmonic from 1971 to 1977. During this period his extraordinary ear for orchestral balance and clarity of textures and his businesslike conducting greatly improved the quality of the playing, but his programs, which included much twentieth-century music, did not charm conventional audiences. Nonetheless, his work — along with his conducting of Richard Wagner's operas at the summer Bayreuth Festivals in Germany starting in 1966 — confirmed his position as one of the world's greatest conductors.

With the conception in the mid 1970s of the Centre National d'Art et de Culture (Beaubourg or **Centre Pompidou**), president Georges Pompidou felt that Boulez should head the music section. Boulez accepted the invitation in 1976 and returned to France, but on his own terms: that he be given the resources to create the Institut de Recherche et Coordination Acoustique/Musique (**IRCAM**). Boulez ended his war against the French musical establishment and determined to develop IRCAM into one of the principal achievements of his career. Much has been accomplished, including construction of vast underground headquarters adjacent to the main building and the expenditure of billions of francs to assemble a distinguished international staff of musicians and scientists, but the project has been surrounded by controversy.

REFERENCES:

Pierre Boulez, *Notes of an Apprenticeship,* translated by Herbert Weinstock (New York: Knopf, 1968);

Boulez, *Pierre Boulez on Music Today,* translated by Susan Bradshaw (Cambridge, Mass.: Harvard University Press, 1971);

Paul Griffiths, *Boulez* (London: Oxford University Press, 1978);

Dominique Jameux, *Pierre Boulez,* translated by Bradshaw (Cambridge, Mass.: Harvard University Press, 1991);

Joan Peyser, *Boulez* (New York: Schirmer Books, 1976).

— P.S.H.

EMILE-ANTOINE BOURDELLE

Emile-Antoine Bourdelle (1861–1929) was one of the few students of **Auguste Rodin** to escape from his teacher's shadow and emerge as a prominent artist in his own right.

Bourdelle grew up in an impoverished Montauban family, leaving school at age thirteen to work in his father's workshop. He studied art in Toulouse, winning admission to the Ecole des Beaux-Arts in Paris in 1884. He rebelled against the restrictions of the academic system, withdrawing from his classes in 1886 and beginning work as an independent artist. In 1893 he joined Rodin's studio, where he served as chief stone carver until the early 1900s. Bourdelle described and analyzed Rodin's contributions to art in his book *Rodin et la sculpture* (1908; Rodin and Sculpture).

Bourdelle's own work oscillated between a rather static and monumental classicism — typified by his equestrian statue of Gen. Carlos María de Alvear (produced between 1913 and 1915) — and a fluid elasticity reminiscent of Rodin. His statue of Heracles the Archer (1909) is striking in its attempt to bridge the gap: Heracles, kneeling on one foot with the other braced against a stone, draws back a huge bow, his face grimacing in concentration. The work is a study of intense, coiled power waiting to be unleashed. A similar search for a balance based on the interaction of contending forces can be found in his war memorial for his home city of Montauban produced between 1893 and 1902. It is dominated by a giant, distorted warrior brandishing a sword, his face contorted in agony. Arrayed around him are a dying soldier, a swirling banner, and an allegorical figure of France, urging on the defenders of the homeland. While earlier, traditional war memorials seem to convey either calm acceptance or a militant call to arms, Bourdelle's presents war as brutal and chaotic, resisting easy certainties. Bourdelle's sculptural group, dedicated to soldiers killed in the Franco-Prussian War (1870–1871), came under savage attack from conservative critics when a complete model was unveiled in 1897. The central figure, cast separately on bronze in 1898 and called the *Great War-*

rior of Montauban, is perhaps better known than the sculpture as a whole.

Some of Bourdelle's most ambitious projects were never completed. In 1888 he began work on a projected study of Ludwig van Beethoven that was never finished; at his death in 1919, Bourdelle had made around forty-five models and sculpted studies for it, together with a collection of drawings and watercolors. The first studies are careful and classically composed; after 1900, these studies became bolder and cruder, the mood more intense and ominous. He called one, done in 1901, the *Great Tragic Mask.*

REFERENCES:

Frederic V. Grunfeld, *Rodin: A Biography* (New York: Holt, 1987);

Ionel Jianou and Michel Duffet, *Bourdelle,* translated by Kathleen Muston (Paris: Arted, 1965).

— J.H.

PIERRE BOURDIEU

Pierre Bourdieu (1930–) is considered one of the most original thinkers among sociologists and cultural critics working in France. He became well known after the appearance of *Homo academicus* (1984; translated), a critical analysis of the French university system, but he has been publishing important works since the 1960s. In 1982 he was given a chair at the Collège de France.

Among Bourdieu's chief concepts are those of the field and the habitus. Fields — which include religion, education, science, journalism, and publishing — are distinguished by power relationships. The habitus is the system of strategies adopted by an actor in a field to deal with its power relationships. Bourdieu has sought to unmask the dominance of some fields; he has been especially concerned with the intellectual elite and its powerful role in France.

REFERENCES:

Richard Harker, Cheleen Mahar, and Chris Wilkes, eds., *An Introduction to the Work of Pierre Bourdieu: The Practice of Theory* (New York: St. Martin's Press, 1990);

Richard Jenkins, *Pierre Bourdieu* (London & New York: Routledge, 1992);

Jeremy Jennings, ed., *Intellectuals in Twentieth-Century France: Mandarins and Samurais* (New York: St. Martin's Press, 1993).

— C.S.B.

CHARLES BOYER

Charles Boyer (1897–1978) was the most commercially successful French actor in American movies. For more than thirty years he brought a suave charm, a distinctive accent, and a great versatility to a wide range of character and leading roles, both in America and Europe.

Boyer began his acting career in 1920, focusing most of his energies on the stage. He settled in Hollywood in 1934 and began a prosperous film career as one of the great screen lovers. He acted with Claudette Colbert in *Private Worlds* (1935), with Jean Arthur in *History Is Made at Night* (1937), with Irene Dunne in *Love Affair* (1939), and with Bette Davis in *All This and Heaven Too* (1940). In the early 1950s, while continuing to appear in American movies, he returned to making European films on a regular basis. His performance as the despairing husband of the unfaithful title character in **Max Ophuls**'s *Madame de . . .* (1953; *The Earrings of Madame De*), in which he displayed considerable range and screen presence, is one of his finest creations.

REFERENCES:

Charles Higham, "Charles Boyer: French Charmer," in *Close-Ups: Intimate Profiles of Movie Stars by Their Co-Stars, Directors, Screenwriters, and Friends,* edited by Danny Peary (New York: Workman, 1978), pp. 152–156;

Larry Swindell, *Charles Boyer: The Reluctant Lover* (Garden City, N.Y.: Doubleday, 1983).

— W.L.

GEORGES BRAQUE

Georges Braque (1882–1963) and **Pablo Picasso** were key figures in the development of Analytical and Synthetic **Cubism.** In the period of their collaboration — from 1908–1909 until **World War I** — the two played a crucial role in the development of the Cubist movement, which helped to shift the emphasis of modern art from the work of art as an imitation of nature to the work of art as an object on its own terms. "We were like two mountaineers roped together," Braque later wrote.

Braque, whose father owned a painting and decorating business in Le Havre, was apprenticed in that trade in 1899, earning a craftsman's diploma two years later. After a tour of military duty he determined to become an artist. Through friends, especially **Marie Laurencin,** he became acquainted with the work of **Henri Matisse** and the other **Fauves.** Braque's own painting quickly moved from a somber, dark style toward the brilliant colors and loose brushwork of the Fauves. Yet by 1906 his infatuation with Fauvism was already ebbing. ("You cannot remain forever in a state of paroxysm," he noted later.) The immediate result of this disillusionment was an interest in the work of **Paul**

Cézanne. In paintings such as his view from the Hotel Mistral in L'Estaque (1907) Braque began to explore landscape as an interlocking set of geometric shapes. In a painting of houses in L'Estaque, completed the following year, the trees are reduced to slightly tapered diagonals, with branches erupting as a set of V-shapes; the houses and hills alike are rendered as a series of slightly irregular prisms in shades of brown.

The two L'Estaque landscapes are separated by Braque's first meeting with Picasso and by Braque's first viewing of Picasso's famous *Les Demoiselles d'Avignon* (1907). Braque's monumental painting of a nude, dated December 1907, marks an immediate response to Picasso's painting. Braque's nude and his scene of houses at L'Estaque mark the beginning of his transition from painting in the vein of Cézanne to his first Cubist works.

The term *Cubist* was first used by critic Louis Vauxcelles in reference to Braque's landscapes. When Vauxcelles saw them in 1908, he wrote that Braque reduced everything — sites, figures, and houses — to geometric outlines, to cubes. From 1909 on Picasso and Braque did not so much collaborate as experiment and argue together. While other artists — notably **Jean Metzinger** and **Albert Gleizes** in their book *Du cubisme* (1912) — sought to define an ideological and theoretical basis for Cubism, both Picasso and Braque rejected the idea of Cubism as a defined movement. Braque said, "I was never aware of Cubism, for if I had been I would have exploited it. . . . As far as I was concerned, it had to be created." As Picasso noted later, "When we were doing Cubism, we were not trying to do Cubism, but just to express what was inside us."

Braque and Picasso developed Analytical Cubism (from approximately 1909 until 1912) and Synthetic Cubism (from roughly 1912 until the outbreak of World War I). In Analytical Cubism (a term coined by Cubist **Juan Gris**), the interest in simplified renditions of volumetric space was intensified by breaking up those volumes. Cézanne had often incorporated more than one vantage point at a time in his still lifes; in Analytical Cubism, multiple viewpoints were established simultaneously, as the object or subject depicted was broken apart and spread across the entire canvas. At the same time, colors became increasingly muted, eventually reduced to grays and black with occasional earth tones. In contrast, Synthetic Cubism radically redefined the whole idea of representation. This sort of Cubism began with a form of collage: if an analytical depiction of a café, for example, was still concerned with the means by which that café could be depicted on canvas, Synthetic Cubist works began by incorporating into the piece itself suggestive bits and pieces of that café — from wine labels to bits of napkins or tablecloths or fragments of newspapers read there. In Braque's painting of a fruit dish with glass (1912) the artist merged a charcoal sketch with strips of colored wallpaper.

After Braque's infantry service during World War I, in which he was seriously wounded, his work began to depart from Picasso's. While Picasso continued a process of experimentation marked by works on a heroic scale, Braque gradually settled into constrained studies of light, space, and pattern, increasingly involving a thick, flat rendition of an enclosed space — often still lifes — subdivided by intersecting rectangles and by silhouetted household objects.

REFERENCES:

Douglas Cooper, *The Cubist Epoch* (London: Phaidon, 1971);

Max Kozloff, *Cubism/Futurism* (New York: Harper & Row, 1973);

Edwin Mullins, *Braque* (London: Thames & Hudson, 1968).

— J.H.

ROBERT BRASILLACH

The gifted writer Robert Brasillach (1909–1945) earned a place in French literary and political history when he was tried and executed for collaboration with the Germans after the **Liberation** of France in 1945. He was one of the few literary figures put to death for political activities during **World War II.**

Educated at the **Ecole Normale Supérieure** and a member of the **Action Française,** Brasillach became dazzled by National Socialism on a visit to Nuremberg in 1937. He fought honorably for France in the war and was captured and held in a German prisoner-of-war camp, but when he returned to France in 1941 he began writing again for *Je Suis Partout,* a Fascist newspaper that had become openly collaborationist. After his arrest he spent time in the prison of Fresnes, where he wrote poetry. Recognizing Brasillach's gifts as a critic, celebrated authors such as **Jean Anouilh, Albert Camus,** and **François Mauriac** all pleaded for clemency for him, but it was not granted.

Among Brasillach's works are studies on Virgil and Pierre Corneille and an anthology of Greek poetry. He published two volumes of verse, *Poèmes* (1944; Poems) and *Poèmes de Fresnes* (1945; Poems from Fresnes), and seven novels, including *Comme le temps passe* (1937; translated as *Youth Goes Over*), none of which has proved popular. He also wrote *Histoire du cinéma* (1935; translated as *The History of Motion Pictures*) and *Histoire de la guerre d'Espagne* (1939; His-

tory of the War in Spain) with his brother-in-law **Maurice Bardèche.**

REFERENCES:

David Carroll, "Literary Fascism or the Aestheticizing of Politics: The Case of Robert Brasillach," *New Literary Theory,* 23 (Summer 1992): 691–726;

John Coombes, "Robert Brasillach: The Machismo of Impotence," in *Vichy France and the Resistance: Culture and Ideology* (Totowa, N.J.: Barnes & Noble, 1985), pp. 269–273;

Pol Vandromme, *Robert Brasillach, l'homme et l'œuvre* (Paris: Plon, 1956).

— C.S.B.

GEORGES BRASSENS

A solitary figure often seen standing on stage with a guitar, a microphone, and a chair on which to rest one foot, singer Georges Brassens (1921–1981) embodied in a modern form the long poetic and musical tradition of the Provençal troubadour. During his career he sold more than twenty million records.

Brassens's vocation came early, public recognition rather late. He began composing and writing in his native city of Sète, on the Mediterranean, in his mid teens and moved to Paris at eighteen. After some lean years there, his musical breakthrough occurred in 1952, with the help of the music-hall performer Patachou. Brassens went on to enjoy extraordinary success as a performer onstage, on radio, and on records, singing songs for which he wrote the music and usually the words. A 1954 recording for Philips won the Grand Prix du Disque (Grand Prize of Records), and in 1966 his appearances with **Juliette Gréco** at the **Théâtre National Populaire** were greeted with great critical acclaim. He received the Grand Prix de Poésie from the Académie Française in 1967.

The essence of Brassens's art was simplicity. He wrote many songs about death, including "Le Testament" (The Will), "Grand-père" (Grandfather), and "Pauvre Martin" (Poor Martin). Other songs, such as "La Chasse aux papillons" (The Butterfly Chase) and "La Première Fille" (The First Girl), feature the themes of love and desire. He had an anarchist's distaste for authority and love for nonconformity, illustrated in such songs as "La Mauvaise Réputation" (The Bad Reputation) and "Hécatombe." He made heroes of figures such as a compassionate vagrant and parents who marry well after their children are born.

Although Brassens's formal schooling was desultory and abridged, he had a connoisseur's knowledge of some of the major French poets, ranging from François Villon through Jean de la Fontaine, Charles Baudelaire, **Francis Jammes, Guillaume Apollinaire,** and **Louis Aragon.** The language of many of his ribald songs, such as "Le Gorille"

(The Gorilla), could have been taken from François Rabelais, whose works he knew well. The simplicity Brassens achieved in his lyrics, his music, and his stage presence was in fact a refinement of considerable artistic riches.

REFERENCES:

Martin Monestier, *Brassens, le livre du souvenir* (Paris: Tchon, 1982);

Christopher Pinet, "Astérix, Brassens, and Cabu: The ABC's of Popular Culture," in *Popular Traditions and Learned Culture in France: From the Sixteenth to the Twentieth Century,* edited by Marc Bertrand (Saratoga, Cal.: Anma Libri, 1985), pp. 275–286.
— J.P.McN.

Victor Brauner

Victor Brauner (1903–1966) typifies the artists of the international milieu that began to form in Paris in the 1920s around the **Surrealist** movement. His early paintings were influenced by **Paul Cézanne;** but his early stylistic experimentations grew increasingly fused with occult themes, spiritualism, and social protest, marked by techniques derived from German and French **Dada.**

Brauner identified his work with what he termed *surrationalisme,* a state beyond and superior to rationalism, embracing both the real and the symbolic. He described his evolving technique as *pictopoetry*; the term recalls the visual poetry of his fellow Romanian **Tristan Tzara,** but while Tzara literally arranged his poems on paper, Brauner's term refers somewhat ambiguously to using visual material in a manner analogous to poetry — evocative, metaphoric rather than literal, and working through suggestion rather than full description.

In 1925 — the year after he and poet Ilane Voronca founded the Dadaist review *75 HP* in Bucharest — Brauner emigrated from Romania to Paris, where he became acquainted with a growing circle of avant-garde artists. Although his work touched on issues and ideas current in Surrealist circles, he did not meet the Surrealist leader **André Breton** until 1933. Brauner's paintings and automatic drawings were noteworthy from the outset for their emphasis on the grim and the sinister. Breton praised Brauner's work for its intermingled themes of sexual desire and terror. In the early 1930s Brauner began to produce self-portraits showing himself as blinded; these works were seen as prophetic by the Surrealists when he was blinded in one eye in a 1938 fight. His formal affiliation with Breton's group ended in 1949, when he resigned following Breton's expulsion of the Chilean Roberto Matta.

The final years of Brauner's career were spent in a form of self-exile in the Swiss Alps, where he had taken refuge during **World War II.** His works of the 1950s and 1960s focus increasingly on private symbols and an exploration of death and finality.

REFERENCES:

Dawn Ades, *Dada and Surrealism Reviewed* (London: Arts Council of Great Britain, 1978);

André Breton, *Surrealism and Painting,* translated by Simon Watson Taylor (London: Macdonald, 1972), pp. 123–127;

René Passeron, *Phaidon Encyclopedia of Surrealism,* translated by John Griffiths (Oxford: Phaidon, 1978);

Sidra Stich, *Anxious Visions: Surrealist Art* (New York: Abbeville, 1990).
— J.H.

Jacques Brel

Jacques Brel (1929–1978) was a singer in the Parisian café tradition and a writer whose songs are still performed all over France and Belgium. His best-known song is surely "Le plat pays" (The Flat Country), a poetic tribute to Belgium, his native land.

Born in Brussels, Brel moved to Paris in 1953 to search for jobs singing and playing his guitar in cafés. He sang almost exclusively in French, with the notable exception of "Marieke," a song that includes both French and Flemish lyrics. After he had achieved success as a singer, he began acting and directing films. He also translated into French the 1965 American musical *Man of La Mancha,* by Mitch Leigh, Dale Wasserman, and Joe Darion, and starred in the Paris production; the musical appealed to his quixotic nature and invoked the themes of adventure, heroism, and failure that characterized his own work. The American public knows some of Brel's work from the American musical *Jacques Brel Is Alive and Well and Living in Paris,* which features translations of many of his songs by Mort Shuman. Brel died of cancer in 1978.

REFERENCES:

Eric Blau, *Jacques Brel Is Alive and Well and Living in Paris* (New York: Dutton, 1971);

Jean Clouzet, *Jacques Brel* (Paris: Seghers, 1964);

Carole Holdsworth, "Romantic Dualism in Jacques Brel's 'J'aimais,'" *Language Quarterly,* 20 (Spring–Summer 1982): 46–48, 52;

Bruno Hongre and Paul Lidsky, *Chansons Jacques Brel: Analyse critique* (Paris: Hatier, 1976).
— K.E.B.

Robert Bresson

One of the most individualistic and important film writers and directors of the post–**World War II** years, Robert Bresson (1907–) is a respected stylist whose work inspired directors of the **Nouvelle Vague** (New Wave). His films are at once austere and highly detailed, abstract and spiritual.

In 1934 Bresson directed a film, *Les Affaires publiques* (Public Doings; now lost), before going to work as an assistant director under **René Clair**. After Germany invaded France in 1940, Bresson spent a year as a prisoner of war. He directed and helped to write his first feature, *Les Anges du péché* (*Angels of the Streets*) in 1943. After 1945 he began an unusual career that lasted until 1983, with the completion of a screen adaptation of Emile Zola's *L'Argent*. Between 1945 and 1983 Bresson completed fewer than a dozen films, four of which have redefined the art of film narration.

All of his films depict ethical struggles, usually ending in failure or death. *Les Dames du Bois de Boulogne* (1945; *Ladies of the Park*), based on a tale by Denis Diderot, evokes an eerie, timeless setting. A similar play of light and darkness conveys metaphysical abstraction and Christian redemption in Bresson's adaptation of **Georges Bernanos**'s *Journal d'un curé de campagne* (1950; *Diary of a Country Priest*). In this film, winner of the International Film Prize at the Venice Film Festival in 1951, the spectator literally reads the words on the pages of the diary as they are being written and spoken by the protagonist until the writing dissolves into the images of the events described. When superimposed, the text, voice, and image give way to an urgent vision of light and darkness that captures dichotomous forces of good and evil transcending the frailty of human reality.

Un Condamné à mort s'est échappé (1956; *A Man Escaped*), written and directed by Bresson, is based on his own wartime experiences and a postwar memoir by André Devigny. The camera pinpoints objects that the hero eventually uses to escape from the darkness of the prison to the light of faith and redemption. In *Pickpocket* (1959) Bresson focused on the wages — and wagers — of sin and transgression among the underworld figures who frequent racetracks, public areas, and railways.

In most of Bresson's postwar films he cast unprofessional actors and actresses, whose performances create a flat aura free of conventional narrative psychology and causality. Language, both spoken and written, appears fragmented under the force of montage and the framing of sparse decors. The sound tracks are punctuated by offscreen noise, snatches of music, and carefully selected, almost random, utterances.

REFERENCES:

André Bazin, "*Le Journal d'un curé de campagne* and the Stylistics of Robert Bresson," in his *What is Cinema?*, volume 1, translated and edited by Hugh Gray (Berkeley & Los Angeles: University of California Press, 1971), pp. 125–143;

T. Jefferson Kline, "Picking Dostoevsky's Pocket: Bresson's Sl(e)ight of Screen," in his *Screening the Text: Intertextuality in New Wave French Cinema* (Baltimore: Johns Hopkins University Press, 1992), pp. 148–183;

Paul Schrader, *Transcendental Style in Film: Ozu, Bresson, Dryer* (Berkeley & Los Angeles: University of California Press, 1972);

Jane Sloan, *Robert Bresson: A Guide to References and Sources* (Boston: G. K. Hall, 1972).

—T.C.

ANDRÉ BRETON

More than anyone else, poet and prose writer André Breton (1896–1966) deserves to be called the "Father of **Surrealism**." In 1924 he and his friends **Louis Aragon** and **Philippe Soupault** founded the movement, and during his entire career Breton was faithful to its premises and remained its major driving force. His influence extends beyond France and the United States to include Latin American and black African writers as well.

Impressed by **Guillaume Apollinaire**'s play *Les Mamelles de Tirésias* (1917; The Breasts of Tiresias), Breton and Soupault wrote a presurrealist text, *Les Champs magnétiques* (1920; Magnetic Fields), applying what Breton had learned about psychic automatism as a medical student before **World War I**. In 1919 he founded the magazine *Littérature* with Aragon and **Paul Eluard.** By this time they had become acquainted with the radical movement called **Dada**, and in 1924 Breton published the first manifesto of their new movement, *Manifeste du surréalisme*. His credo was revolutionary: he called on individuals to discard all previous aesthetic principles — as well as the social structures they tended to reflect or reinforce — and to discover a new psychic and literary reality, using data derived from the unconscious, that would form the foundation for a new social order. He cited both Sigmund Freud and Karl Marx as models. Breton drew to his movement many gifted poets and painters, with whom he collaborated on several books, including *Ralentir travaux* (1928; Slow Down Work), with Eluard and **René Char,** and *L'Immaculée Conception* (1930; translated as *Immaculate Conception*), with Eluard. During the 1920s Breton also wrote the fictional work *Nadja* (1928; translated), which has been described as a forerunner of the **Nouveau Roman** (New Novel).

In 1927 Breton and some other Surrealists joined the **French Communist Party,** but he was quickly disillusioned. He continued producing poetry and prose, including his best-known poem, *L'Union libre* (Free Union), published anonymously in 1931; *Le Revolver à cheveux blancs* (1932; The White-haired Revolver); and *L'Amour fou* (1937; translated as *Mad Love*), inspired by Jacqueline Lamba, his second wife.

As with most of the other Surrealists, love played an enormous role in Breton's work.

Breton spent most of **World War II** in North America, principally New York, where he attracted a following among fellow French exiles and American surrealist writers and founded the magazine *VVV* (1942–1944); he also served as a speaker for the Voice of America. After the war he returned to France and published *Constellations* (1959), prose poems illustrated by Joan Miró, and his memoirs.

REFERENCES:

Anna Balakian, *André Breton, Magus of Surrealism* (New York: Oxford University Press, 1971);

Clifford Browder, *André Breton, Arbiter of Surrealism* (Geneva: Droz, 1967);

Wallace Fowlie, *Age of Surrealism* (Bloomington: Indiana University Press, 1960);

J. H. Matthews, *André Breton* (New York & London: Columbia University Press, 1967).

— C.S.B.

ARISTIDE BRIAND

In a long career as a politician and statesman of the **Third Republic,** Aristide Briand (1862–1932) served as prime minister of France eleven times and held ministerial positions in twenty-six different cabinets between 1906 and 1932. His range of interests was wide, but he had a special knowledge of law and foreign policy, serving as minister of foreign affairs seventeen times. For their efforts to achieve international cooperation he and German foreign minister Gustav Stresemann shared the Nobel Peace Prize in 1926.

An early convert to socialism, Briand was elected deputy for the working-class constituency of St.-Etienne in 1902. Known for his gifts as an orator, he spoke out vehemently on behalf of the right to strike. Briand and Jean Jaurès started the left-wing newspaper *L'Humanité* in 1904 and founded the **Socialist Party** of France in 1905. In that same year, in the wake of the **Dreyfus Affair,** Briand and **Emile Combes** were major authors of the so-called Combes law, separating Church and State.

By the time of his first term as prime minister (1909–1911), Briand had left socialism behind and angered his former political allies by his successful efforts to break the 1910 railway strike. In 1913 he was prime minister of a short-lived government and returned to that office again in October 1915, presiding over the French government during some of the worst defeats of **World War I.** In March 1917 he was forced out of office because of his lack of success in accelerating and intensifying the French war effort. Out of office from

1917 until 1921, he spoke out on behalf of the League of Nations.

Briand's successes in foreign affairs during the 1920s included helping to bring about the signing of the 1925 Locarno Pact, an attempt to normalize relations among France, Great Britain, and Germany, and the acceptance of the Kellogg-Briand Pact (1928), a sixty-nation agreement to renounce war as an instrument of policy. Briand, a "pèlerin de la paix" (pilgrim of peace), was one of the earliest advocates of a federal union of Europe.

REFERENCE:

Robert H. Ferrell, *Peace in Their Time: The Origins of the Kellogg-Briand Pact* (New Haven: Yale University Press, 1952).

— J.P.McN.

PETER BROOK

Peter Brook (1925–), a British theater and film director and writer who has worked primarily in France since 1970, represents the culmination of a century-old tradition in French theater of being open to foreign influence. He has contributed substantially to the popularization of experimental theater in France.

A prominent exponent of experimental theater, Brook had had a successful directing career on the London stage since 1945 and in British film since 1953. His connections with France date to early in his career. He directed a French version of Tennessee Williams's *Cat on a Hot Tin Roof* (1955), with **Jeanne Moreau** as Maggie, in Paris in 1956, and in England in 1964 he presented a workshop, the Theatre of Cruelty, based on texts by French theater theorist **Antonin Artaud.** That year he also produced scenes from **Jean Genet**'s *Les Paravents* (1961; translated as *The Screens*) on the London stage before its French premiere in 1966. In addition, he directed the film *Moderato Cantabile* (1960), based on a novel by **Marguerite Duras** and starring Moreau and **Jean-Paul Belmondo.**

As director of the Théâtre des Nations, **Jean-Louis Barrault** invited Brook in 1968 to give an extended theater workshop in Paris. Brook agreed and in 1970 assembled a company of multilingual actors from various countries under the auspices of his newly created Centre international de recherches théâtrales. Always concerned with the training of actors and their relationship to the audience, he taught them to explore new techniques and to work as a community. Their extensive tours included the Middle East and Africa.

In 1974 Brook moved his workshop, which had become an acting company, into a dilapidated former vaudeville house, Les Bouffes du Nord. With few props and no scenery on a "stage" consisting of the entire pit (with spectators occupying the balconies), his group presented a variety of plays ranging from William Shakespeare's *Timon of Athens* to a dramatization of an African tale, *L'Os* (The Bone), and Anton Chekhov's *The Cherry Orchard*. The creative work of Brook's community of actors has been highly acclaimed by critics and Paris audiences. Brook also staged a play based on the Indian epic *Mahabharata* at the **Festival d'Avignon** in 1985 and directed the film version in 1990. Performed in a quarry, the play lasted through the night. He also helped to write the screenplay for *Swann in Love* (1984), the English film version of "Un Amour de Swann," a section of **Marcel Proust**'s *Du côté de chez Swann* (1913).

For Brook, theater must not seek to mimic another reality in order to communicate experiences indirectly to an audience; instead, it must be its own true reality, in direct communion with the public. His ideas about theater are expressed primarily in three works: *The Influence of Gordon Craig in Theory and Practice* (1955), *The Empty Space* (1968), and *The Open Door: Thoughts on Acting and Theater* (1993).

REFERENCES:

Edward Trostle Jones, *Following Directions: A Study of Peter Brook* (New York, Bern & Frankfurt am Main: Peter Lang, 1985);

David Williams, ed., *Peter Brook: A Theatrical Casebook* (London: Methuen, 1988).

— R.J.N.

ARISTIDE BRUANT

Aristide Bruant (1851–1925), the most talented and productive of the Paris chansonniers (satirical singer-songwriters) at the end of the nineteenth century, was one of the pioneers of the *chanson réaliste*. Like Henri de Toulouse-Lautrec, who immortalized him in a painting, he contributed much to the image of a "naughty Paris," or what tourist literature advertises as "Paris by Night." Bruant filled his songs with references to quick-witted scamps and "gigolettes" — pert girls available for a price to gullible bourgeois merchants out for a night on the town.

Bruant's name will always be associated with **Montmartre,** especially Le Chat Noir (The Black Cat), the best-known cabaret of the district, and Le Mirliton (The Kazoo), which he established in 1885 and in which he performed until his retirement in 1924. On his many tours he carried the image of Montmartre into the provinces and abroad. He also signed his name to ghostwritten novels and plays.

A few of Bruant's songs, including "Les Canuts" (The Silk Workers) and "Nini peau de chien" (Nini Dog's Skin) have aged well and are still performed; **Yves Montand** is among the many performers who have included "Les Canuts" in their repertoires. Bruant's songs were collected in two books, *Dans la rue* (1889; On the Street) and *Sur la route* (1899; On the Road). In their extraordinary verbal inventiveness, their free flow of slang, and their bits of folklore and even church hymns, they anticipate the writings of authors such as **Boris Vian** and **Louis-Ferdinand Céline** and the work of modern comics such as Coluche.

REFERENCE:

Armond Fields, *Le Chat Noir: A Montmartre Cabaret and Its Artists in Turn-of-the-Century Paris* (Santa Barbara, Cal.: Santa Barbara Museum of Art, 1993).

— J.P.McN.

BERNARD BUFFET

Painter Bernard Buffet (1928–) enjoyed a remarkable, if brief, fame in the 1940s as an exponent of what was termed *misérabalisme* — intensely personal expressionist images of poverty and despair rendered by means of characteristically flattened and elongated figures. In his paintings Buffet, who had rejected social realism in his late teens, did not seek to spark revolt against injustice; rather he wanted only to depict a world of hopeless suffering.

As a person and artist, he was desperately shy and something of a recluse even at the height of his celebrity. Although he studied briefly at the Ecole des Beaux-Arts, he saw himself as largely self-taught (he began painting at age ten). While his work has sometimes been compared to the pre-**Cubist** work of **Pablo Picasso,** he denied any external influence on his style.

Buffet's painting is marked by a grim palette — a dark, flat background (often gray), with heavily outlined people and objects in gray, rose, lavender, and black. His human figures are typically gaunt and bony, their expressions ranging from mute despair to active suffering. Three images of Christ produced in 1952 — a flagellation, a crucifixion, and a resurrection — led one critic to write, "I defy any man not to be moved almost to sickness before these works."

Buffet's fame peaked in 1948, when he won the Critics' Prize at an annual exhibition in Paris; his first show in the United States (1950) was considered equally impressive and elicited great enthusiasm. By the time of a retrospective show of his work in Paris in 1958 his reputation was already on the wane; his work had begun to seem repetitive. Moreover, he was caught between opposing forces hostile to his work. In the 1940s several Communist artists and intellectuals, including painter Jean Bouret, had championed Buffet's work; but the expulsion of the Communists from the governing coalition of France in 1947 under the **Fourth Republic** had led the **French Communist Party** to adopt a harder line on cultural matters, and Buffet's work was increasingly denounced for expressing bourgeois pessimism. On the other hand, Buffet's lukewarm modernism and his vision of the modern world ran directly counter to the rising view, championed by the American critic Clement Greenberg, that the proper subject of art was art itself. By the end of the 1950s critical attention to Buffet's work had all but ceased.

REFERENCES:

Jean Giono, *Bernard Buffet* (Paris: Fernand Hazan, 1956);

Serge Guilbaut, *How New York Stole the Idea of Modern Art: Abstract Expressionism, Freedom, and the Cold War,* translated by Arthur Goldhammer (Chicago & London: University of Chicago Press, 1983).

—J.H.

LUIS BUÑUEL

Spanish-born filmmaker Luis Buñuel (1900–1983) began and ended his long career as a director of French films. He created masterpieces wherever he worked, often under difficult conditions.

Buñuel moved to Paris in the early 1920s. In 1924 he signed the original **Surrealist** manifesto (*Manifestes du surréalisme*), and in 1925 he became an assistant to director **Jean Epstein.** Buñuel wrote, directed, and produced his first film, *Un Chien andalou* (1928; *An Andalusian Dog*), with Spanish Surrealist artist Salvador Dalí. The techniques of the film medium are used to depict unconscious drives and desires, dreams, love, murder, and redemption. Almost three hundred shots are used in the seventeen-minute film, which begins with a scene of a razor (held by Buñuel) slitting a woman's eye just as clouds streak across a full moon, introducing the viewer to the story of a painful entry into a symbolic world. *Un Chien andalou* was immediately acclaimed as a great Surrealist work and was followed by its equal, *L'Age d'or* (1930; *The Golden Age*).

After reading Maurice Legendre's sociological study of the impoverished inhabitants of an area in southwestern Spain, Buñuel decided to collaborate with Elie Lotar and Pierre Unik on a regional documentary. The result, *Las Hurdes* (also titled *Tierra sin pan, Land without Bread,* and *Unpromised Land*), was completed in 1932 but not released until 1937. It created a furor in Paris and was banned in Republican Spain. *Las Hurdes* shows how the ethnographer's camera refuses to respect the Golden Rule, advocating sympathy for its subjects but undercutting its message with its experimental technique. In depicting their misery the movie presents a heroic view of the peasants, alluding to figures in Spanish and French baroque painting and using shocking images to enrage, and thus politicize, viewers.

After these early successes, Buñuel worked in Paris and Madrid as a dubber for Paramount and Warner Bros. and soon was hired to oversee productions at Filmofono Industries in Spain. After the fall of Spain to Francisco Franco and to fascism in 1939, Buñuel worked at the Museum of Modern Art in New York. During **World War II** he worked on foreign versions of Hollywood films. In 1947 he went to live in Mexico, where he made several brilliant low-budget films depicting social perversion and poverty. Between 1956 and 1977 Buñuel directed fourteen features, nine of which are French films. Among these movies are *Le Journal d'une femme de chambre* (1964; *Diary of a Chambermaid*), *Belle de jour* (1968; Beauty of Day), *Le Charme discret de la bourgeoisie* (1972; *The Discreet Charm of the Bourgeoisie*), *Le Fantôme de la liberté* (1974; The Phantom of Liberty), and *Cet obscur objet du désir* (1977; *That Obscure Object of Desire*).

In his later work Buñuel refused to use montage — manipulation of images through extensive editing — to control the viewer's attention, instead using Surrealism to mock repressive or effete social mores. In *Belle de jour* Catherine Deneuve plays an unsatisfied housewife who becomes a prostitute in a brothel where perversion reigns. *La Voie lactée* (1969; The Milky Way) is based on a pilgrimage that has been repeated annually since medieval times; in Buñuel's movie two travelers discover grotesque religious practices along the way between Paris and Saint-Jacques-de-Compostelle. *Le Charme discret de la bourgeoisie, Le Fantôme de la liberté,* and *Cet obscur objet du désir* are scathing satires of bourgeois ideology.

REFERENCES:

José Francesco Aranda, *Luis Buñuel: A Critical Biography,* translated by David Robinson (New York: Da Capo Press, 1976);

André Bazin, *The Cinema of Cruelty: From Buñuel to Hitchcock,* edited by François Truffaut, translated by Sabine D'Estré (New York: Seaver, 1982);

Luis Buñuel, *My Last Sigh* (New York: Knopf, 1983);

Paul Sandro, *Diversions of Pleasure: Luis Buñuel and the Cinema of Desire* (Columbus: Ohio State University Press, 1987);

Jenaro Talens, *The Branded Eye: Buñuel's "Un Chien andalou,"* translated by Giulia Colaizzi (Minneapolis: University of Minnesota Press, 1993).

—T.C.

MICHEL BUTOR

Perhaps the most talented and certainly one of the most productive writers of his generation, Michel Butor (1926–) is associated with the **Nouveau Roman** (New Novel), but much of his writing goes beyond what are usually considered its boundaries. **Surrealism, Marcel Proust,** and James Joyce have all exerted significant influences on his writing.

Born near Lille, Butor spent most of his youth in Paris, attended the lycée Louis-le-Grand, and attended the Sorbonne (1945–1949), where he studied philosophy under **Gaston Bachelard.** Butor's work has a strong philosophical bent, and much if not all of it can be considered a phenomenological quest. Since 1945, when he published an essay on painter Max Ernst, and 1948, when he published an article on Joyce, Butor has been writing art and literary criticism, establishing himself as one of the major critics of his generation. Much of his critical writing has been collected in three volumes titled *Répertoire* (1960, 1964, 1968).

Butor entered the teaching profession in 1950 and taught in Egypt, where he began his first novel, and England (1951–1953), where he completed it. *Passage de Milan* (1954), whose title may be translated as either Milan Passage or Passing of a Kite (a bird of prey), reveals an inventive author obsessed with an effort to render reality through an elaborate structure. In this case the structure of the work is furnished by a Parisian apartment house, the location for all sixty-six characters whose interior monologues are presented in the book. *L'Emploi du temps* (1956; translated as *Passing Time*) displays even more brilliantly Butor's preoccupation with reconstructing through words both the hero's experience and that of the English city where the action is set — a city whose reality extends backward through historical, biblical, and mythological periods of time. The structure is both temporal (a year spent in the city, five months spent in writing about it) and geographic (the urban landscape). Unlike Proust's masterpiece, however, *L'Emploi du temps* records a failure; time cannot be captured. The novel won the Prix Félix Fénéon and established Butor's reputation as a fiction writer.

His next novel, *La Modification* (1957; translated as *A Change of Heart*), a tour de force in which the narrator uses the second-person plural pronoun almost exclusively, recounts a man's agonizing attempt to choose between wife and mistress, presenting the crisis in terms of the mythology of Rome as Eternal City. The last of Butor's novels, *Degrés* (1960; translated as *Degrees*), attempts to describe the human relationships in a family (degrees of kinship) and in a lycée (degrees or levels of study) in terms of a poetic and historical geography (degrees of latitude and longitude) and in other meanings of the word *degré*. All four of Butor's novels reveal a mind obsessed with mathematical, historical, mythological, and poetic attempts to render reality, including the psychological and subjective dimension. Butor's art is the opposite of the *chosiste* (thing-directed), objective narration of **Alain Robbe-Grillet,** with whom he is nevertheless often associated as a *nouveau romancier* (new novelist).

Butor has spent much time in the United States, lecturing, teaching, and traveling. His interest in America is reflected in *Mobile: Etude pour une représentation des Etats-Unis* (1960; translated as *Mobile: Study for a Representation of the United States*), a work that conforms to no established genre or literary form in offering a series of seemingly discontinuous impressions of the United States both present and past, especially in regard to the racial question. Butor calls his second book about America, *6 819 000 litres d'eau par seconde* (1965; translated as *Niagara*), an "étude stéréophonique" (stereophonic study) and offers the reader as many as ten different routes by which to progress through the book.

Many of the roughly five dozen works Butor wrote after his four novels reveal in often poetic and imaginative ways his interest in painting, travel, dreams, music (Ludwig van Beethoven), and literature (William Shakespeare, Charles Baudelaire, **Henri Michaux,** and others). Like that of many other twentieth-century figures, his writing exemplifies the breakdown of literary genres and forms and attempts to borrow from the aesthetics of other art forms. Nearly everything he writes reveals a modern interest in disciplines such as ethnology, psychology, and mythography and his ingenuity in drawing on the insights and vocabularies afforded by these branches of knowledge. Despite the brilliance and inventiveness of his subsequent works, however, he will be best known, ultimately, for his fiction.

REFERENCES:

Mary Lydon, *Perpetuum Mobile: A Study of the Novels and Aesthetics of Michel Butor* (Edmonton: University of Alberta Press, 1980);

Dean McWilliams, *The Narratives of Michel Butor: The Writer as Janus* (Athens: Ohio University Press, 1978);

Lois Oppenheim, *Intentionality and Intersubjectivity: A Phenomenological Study of Butor's "La Modification"* (Lexington, Ky.: French Forum, 1980);

Michael Spencer, *Michel Butor* (New York: Twayne, 1974);

Jennifer Waelti-Walters, *Michel Butor: A Study of His View of the World and a Panorama of His Work, 1954–1974* (Victoria, B.C.: Sono Nis Press, 1977).

— C.S.B.

C

CABARET DU LAPIN AGILE

Also known as the Cabaret des Assassins, the Cabaret du Lapin Agile at 4, rue des Saules in Paris was one of several **Montmartre** cafés, bars, and bistros popular with avant-garde artists, militant anarchists, and assorted petty criminals in the late-nineteenth- and early-twentieth centuries.

Located on the nearly rural fringes of the Montmartre district, the bistro became a favorite gathering place for radical artists and various other bohemians after 1880, when it was bought by caricaturist and poet André Gill. He remodeled the bar in imitation of the Chat Noir, another popular Montmartre establishment, and named it the Cabaret des Assassins. It got its later, better-known name after Gill painted a sign depicting a rabbit leaping into a cooking pot. *Lapin à Gill* (Gill's rabbit) became the basis for the pun "lapin agile" (agile rabbit). The bistro still exists under the same name.

Other owners have included a former boulevard dancer known as Adèle and the radical poet **Aristide Bruant.** Bruant hired Frédéric Gérard, a former fishmonger, to run the bar; "Frédé" attracted a clientele of young artists and writers by offering food and drink in exchange for an occasional painting or poem. Under his management the bar began to attract militant anarchists and diverse intellectuals and artists, including, in the first decade of the twentieth century, a Spanish contingent grouped around **Pablo Picasso** and his friends. Picasso painted some of the decorations in the bar.

REFERENCES:

Theda Shapiro, *Painters and Politics: The European Avant-Garde and Society, 1900–1925* (New York: Elsevier, 1976);

Jerrold Seigel, *Bohemian Paris: Culture, Politics, and the Boundaries of Bourgeois Life, 1830–1930* (New York: Viking, 1986).
— J.H.

Interior of the Cabaret du Lapin Agile, circa 1905; Frédé is playing guitar

CABARET VOLTAIRE

The **Dada** movement began on 5 February 1916 at the Cabaret Voltaire, a nightclub in Zurich, Switzerland.

The manager and impresario of the Cabaret Voltaire, Hugo Ball, had invited the public to perform. Alongside the rather conventional entertainment most clients provided, a radical group — German Richard Huelsenbeck, Alsatian **Jean Arp,** and two Romanians, Marcel Janco and **Tristan Tzara** — put on an untraditional show, which included ringing bells, reciting poems in more than one language simultaneously, and beating out African-sounding rhythms on drums.

Over the next five and a half months the Cabaret Voltaire provided a testing ground for the experimental efforts that became known as Dadaism, from gymnastic or movement poems to noise poems. Tzara, who emerged as the leader of Dada and a major avantgarde figure of the decade, read his first Dada manifesto there and worked out Dadaist attacks on logic, reason, nationalism, convention, and tradition. The Cabaret Voltaire closed on 14 July 1916.

REFERENCE:
Gordon Frederick Browning, "The Cabaret Voltaire," in his *Tristan Tzara: The Genesis of the Dada Poem, or From Dada to Aa* (Stuttgart: Akademischer Verlag Hans-Dieter Heinz, 1979), pp. 9–36.

— J.P.McN.

CAFÉ DE FLORE

Associated primarily in the public mind with writers such as **Albert Camus** and **Jean-Paul Sartre,** who gathered there during and after **World War II,** the Café de Flore is located next door to **Les Deux Magots** in the **Saint-Germain-des-Prés** section on the **Left Bank** in Paris. The Flore was frequented by **Guillaume Apollinaire** and his circle before **World War I** and by members of the **Action Française** after the war. During the 1930s and 1940s **Pablo Picasso** was a regular at the Flore, which has been an extremely popular gathering place since the mid 1930s.

REFERENCES:
Arlen J. Hansen, *Expatriate Paris: A Cultural and Literary Guide to Paris in the 1920s* (New York: Arcade / Little, Brown, 1989);
Herbert R. Lottmann, *The Left Bank: Writers, Artists, and Politics from the Popular Front to the Cold War* (Boston: Houghton Mifflin, 1982).

— C.S.B.

CAFÉ DE LA ROTONDE

The Café de la Rotonde is one of the famous literary and artistic cafés of Paris. Located in **Montparnasse** at the intersection of the Boulevard Raspail and Boulevard Montparnasse, it has been somewhat less renowned than the **Café du Dôme** just opposite, but it has been popular with artists and writers since Victor Libion bought and enlarged it in 1911. He sold it in 1920, and it was considerably enlarged in 1924. Before **World War I** it, like the Dôme, was a gathering place for political exiles — from anarchists to socialists and communists. During the same period, and into the early 1920s, the Rotonde also attracted a large group of

artists and writers, including at various times artists Amedeo Modigliani, **Pablo Picasso, Francis Picabia, Chaim Soutine, André Derain,** and **Fernand Léger,** as well as writers **Guillaume Apollinaire, Max Jacob,** and **Blaise Cendrars.**

REFERENCES:
Billy Klüver and Julie Martin, *Kiki's Paris: Artists and Lovers 1900–1930* (New York: Abrams, 1989);
Kenneth E. Silver, *The Circle of Montparnasse: Jewish Artists in Paris 1905–1945* (New York: Universe Books, 1985).

— C.S.B.

CAFÉ DU DÔME

Located at 108 Boulevard du Montparnasse, where the Boulevard Raspail intersects it, the Dôme, which opened in 1898, is the oldest of the popular Parisian artists' cafés in **Montparnasse.** Among the early patrons were art students, particularly Americans, from the nearby art schools and studios. In 1903 it became a meeting place for a group of German artists led by Rudolf Levy. By 1908 German-speaking artists from Eastern Europe, the Balkan states, and Scandinavia had joined the group, which had become known as the Domiers. Expatriate political revolutionaries, including Vladimir Ilyich Lenin and Leon Trotsky, were also part of the clientele. After the outbreak of **World War I,** these groups no longer patronized the Dôme. During the interwar period the café served as one of the intellectual centers of Montparnasse, becoming more popular with artists than the **Café de la Rotonde** across the street. It also began to attract large numbers of Americans, especially tourists. **Surrealists Man Ray** and **Marcel Duchamp** often frequented the Dôme, as did **Jean-Paul Sartre** and **Simone de Beauvoir,** who continued to patronize the café after **World War II.**

REFERENCES:
Billy Klüver and Julie Martin, *Kiki's Paris: Artists and Lovers 1900–1930* (New York: Abrams, 1989);
Herbert R. Lottman, *The Left Bank: Writers, Artists, and Politics from the Popular Front to the Cold War* (Boston: Houghton Mifflin, 1982);
Kenneth E. Silver, *The Circle of Montparnasse: Jewish Artists in Paris 1905–1945* (New York: Universe Books, 1985).

— C.S.B.

LE CAFÉ-THÉÂTRE

Le café-théâtre is an important cultural phenomenon that has existed in Paris in its present form since 1966. In that year the young playwright Bernard Da Costa

Albert Camus in the typesetting room of *l'Express*

offered a theatrical show in a café called Le Royal in the **Montmartre** district. Because there are more plays and playwrights than the regular theaters can accommodate, the *café-théâtre* has become an important outlet for authors as well as for aspiring young actors and actresses.

The nineteenth-century cultural predecessor of the *café-théâtre*, the *café-concert* featured music, almost always including singing. The *café-théâtre*, in contrast, provides a purely dramatic experience, whether it be a one-man show (*un spectacle de solitaire*) or a succession of skits that constitute a play. Movie and television companies have found the *café-théâtre* a good source of actors for secondary roles, and some well-known figures got their start in this format, among them Coluche, **Gérard Depardieu**, Patrick Dewaere, and Miou-Miou. *Café-théâtre* productions are often collaborative efforts of companies, with the plot evolving as the rehearsals progress.

Since the *café-théâtre* does not benefit from the government subsidies given to state-owned and regular private theaters, the existence of each establishment is at best precarious. Nonetheless, there usually have been about twenty such establishments in operation at any one time.

REFERENCE:

Pierre Merle, *Le Café-Théâtre* (Paris: Presses Universitaires de France, 1985).

—D.O'C.

ALBERT CAMUS

Albert Camus (1913–1960) is one of the best-known modern French writers. His works, especially his novel *L'Etranger* (1942; translated as *The Stranger*) and his long essay *Le Mythe de Sisyphe* (1942; translated as *The Myth of Sisyphus*), have been widely read in literature and philosophy classes, perhaps even more than the works of his famous contemporary and sometime friend **Jean-Paul Sartre.** Camus was awarded the Nobel Prize for Literature in 1957.

Camus is generally associated with the philosophical notion of the absurd, which he treated explicitly in *Le Mythe de Sisyphe* and evoked in most of his fiction. Like Sartre, he is routinely considered an adherent of **existentialism.** Yet Camus considered existentialism an ontological philosophy built on a leap of faith; it is contradictory, he pointed out, because on the one hand it identifies the hopelessness of the human situation and the meaninglessness of life, which inspire dread, and yet, on the other hand it argues on the very basis of this lack of apparent meaning that human beings, in the midst of their dread, must "leap" by faith to assume a transcendent meaning. His position was a more psychological than philosophical response to the absurd. Debate on the value of his arguments and insights continues; to many critics in France his work stands out more for its classical, yet sensuous, style than for its substance.

Born in Algeria, Camus studied philosophy at the University of Algiers (1933–1936), finding an intellectual mentor in Professor Jean Grenier. Camus earned a *diplôme d'études supérieures,* but tuberculosis led him to abandon his teacher-preparation course. Philosophers who influenced his thought include Blaise Pascal, Søren Kierkegaard, and Friedrich Nietzsche. From 1935 to 1939 he was a member of the **French Communist Party,** writing his first plays for a Communist theater group, Théâtre du Travail (Labor Theater). He spent most of the war years in France, writing and participating in the **Resistance** movement Combat. He helped to found its newspaper, *Combat,* serving as a contributing editor until 1947.

The publication of *L'Etranger* and *Le Mythe de Sisyphe* in 1942, during the dark days of the **Occupation,** made Camus immediately famous as a spokesman for a generation that had seen their world crumble about them with the defeat of France and the bankruptcy of bourgeois idealism. *L'Etranger* features a protagonist who refuses to accept society's conventions because he realizes that they are based on a religion and traditional morality in which he no longer has faith. In both the end of the novel and *Le Mythe de Sisyphe,* however, Camus affirms humanistic values in the face of life's inherent meaninglessness. In succeeding years Camus's fame and prestige grew as his plays — especially the highly acclaimed *Caligula* (1944) — were staged, and other fiction appeared: the novels *La Peste* (1947; translated as *The Plague*) and *La Chute* (1956; translated as *The Fall*), as well as a collection of stories, *L'Exil et le royaume* (1957; translated as *Exile and the Kingdom*).

In 1952, the year after the publication of the long philosophical essay *L'Homme révolté* (translated as *The Rebel*), Camus had a falling-out with Sartre and his group, who disagreed with Camus's critique of revolutionary action. While Sartre and other French leftists at the time supported Stalinism as a means of achieving a Communist society, Camus rejected revolutionary oppression. In the same period Camus became embroiled, against his will, in the controversy surrounding the **Algerian war.** Unlike those clearly on the Left, who supported the rebels, Camus refused to condemn French attempts to suppress the rebellion while also declining to criticize rebel actions. Attempting to steer a middle course between partisans of "l'Algérie française" and proponents of independence for the territory, he was attacked by both sides. This political discomfort may have affected his writing; *La Chute,* for instance, treats with superb irony the logical and personal pitfalls awaiting those who presume to pronounce judgment, and some of the later stories are dark in tone.

Camus was killed in an automobile accident in 1960. While his literary stock remains high, he has in recent years been attacked on both sides of the Atlantic for his moral neutrality with respect to Algeria and the Arab question.

REFERENCES:

Raymond Gay-Crosier, *Albert Camus 1980* (Gainesville: University Presses of Florida, 1980);

Adele King, *Camus's "L'Etranger": Fifty Years On* (London: Macmillan, 1992);

Herbert R. Lottman, *Albert Camus: A Biography* (Garden City, N.Y.: Doubleday, 1979);

Patrick McCarthy, *Camus* (New York: Random House, 1982);

English Showalter, Jr., *Exiles and Strangers: A Reading of Camus's "Exile and the Kingdom"* (Columbus: Ohio State University Press, 1984);

Susan Tarrow, *Exile and the Kingdom: A Political Rereading of Albert Camus* (Birmingham: University of Alabama Press, 1985).

— C.S.B.

CANNES FILM FESTIVAL

The Cannes Film Festival, an annual two-week spectacular held in the spring on the French Riviera, has become internationally synonymous with excellence in the cinema. Although the festival struggled financially for its first few years and was canceled in 1948 for financial reasons, by 1951 it had become the prestigious international showcase to which its founders had aspired, attracting thousands of actors, actresses, and filmmakers from all over the world.

The idea of establishing a French film festival was proposed in 1938 by Philippe Erlanger, a public servant in the Association française d'action artistique. Erlanger's proposal was in reaction against the increasingly politicized Venice Film Festival, at which, that same year, Adolf Hitler intervened on behalf of the German entry — Leni Riefenstahl's film on the Berlin Olympics — just as the American entry was about to be named the winner. Although the French government approved Erlanger's proposal in 1939 and Cannes was chosen as the location, the festival could not take place because of the outbreak of **World War II.** After the **Liberation** Erlanger again submitted his idea to the government, and the first festival opened in spring 1946.

In its first year eleven prizes were awarded, one to each of the participating countries. **Jean Delannoy**'s *La Symphonie pastorale* (*The Pastoral Symphony*) won the award for best French film, and **Michèle Morgan,** who played the leading role in the film, was named overall best actress. After the first year, awards were given to best overall actor, actress, director, and film. There are also prizes exclusively for French movies, including the Prix **Louis Delluc** for the best French feature film, the Prix **Louis Lumière** for the best French short subject, the Prix **Jean Vigo** for the best French film on a social theme, and the Prix Emil Cohl for the best French cartoon.

REFERENCE:

Colin Crisp, *The Classic French Cinema 1930–1960* (Bloomington: Indiana University Press, 1993).

—M.G.

MARIE CARDINAL

Novelist Marie Cardinal (1929–) is one of the best-known feminist writers of the late twentieth century. Her novels *La Clé sur la porte* (1972; Open Door) and *Les Mots pour le dire* (1975; translated as *The Words to Say It*) each sold nearly four million copies in Europe, and *Les Mots pour le dire* has been translated into eighteen languages.

Not as radical as some of her contemporaries, Cardinal does not reject narrative conventions as being contaminated by patriarchy. She employs a somewhat-traditional, linear narrative style; yet she shares the concerns of feminist writers: the conditions of daughter, wife, and mother; the issue of female creativity; awareness of the body; and the struggle for liberation.

Cardinal's books are highly autobiographical. Beginning with her first novel, *Ecoutez la mer* (1962; Listen to the Sea), she has used writing as a means of self-discovery and of dealing with her problems as a woman. Some of these difficulties are typical — the demands of small children, for instance — but others suggest deep neurosis. In *La Souricière* (1965; The Mousetrap) the heroine has a pseudopregnancy parallel to the pregnancy of her husband's mistress, undergoes a mental breakdown, and commits suicide. *Les Mots pour le dire* is similarly concerned with mental illness and psychiatric methods for dealing with it, principally projection into language. In this book the heroine rebels against patriarchal standards of behavior for women.

Cardinal was born and raised in Algeria, and the experience of living under French colonialism is woven throughout her work. Her writing often displays a lyricism that has been associated with *pied-noir* (North African–born European) writers such as **Albert Camus.** But her treatment of the richly sensuous experience of living by the Mediterranean is necessarily shaded by historical realities: Algerian rebellion against French rule, the **Algerian war,** and, finally, independence in 1962. While deeply attached to her homeland and sharing some of the sense of uprootedness experienced by those who left during the rebellion or after 1962, Cardinal, who relocated to Paris in the 1960s, is sensitive to the parallelism between patriarchy and colonial domination. Reflections on Algeria occasioned by her first return visit to her homeland were published as *Au pays de mes racines* (1980; In the Country of My Roots). The Algerian war also lies in the background of *Les Grands Désordres* (1987; translated as *Devotion and Disorder*), in which the widow of a French soldier killed in that war attempts to help her deeply disturbed, drug-addicted grown daughter, and *Comme si rien n'était* (1991; As If Noticing Nothing), dominated by dialogues between two female cousins, one a married, nurturing grandmother and the other a divorced university professor who hides fears connected to her childhood in Algeria behind abstract ideas.

Cardinal has contributed to her reputation by participating in hundreds of conferences. She lives in Canada most of the year, teaching in Montreal, and travels widely in North America and Europe.

REFERENCES:

Carolyn A. Durham, *The Contexture of Feminism: Marie Cardinal and Multicultural Literacy* (Urbana: University of Illinois Press, 1992);

Françoise Lionnet, *Autobiographical Voices: Race, Gender, Self-Portraiture* (Ithaca, N.Y. & London: Cornell University Press, 1989).

—C.S.B.

MARCEL CARNÉ

A director who defined the fatalistic yet romantic style of **poetic realism** in French cinema from 1936 to 1939, Marcel Carné (1909–) is most often remembered for *Les Enfants du paradis* (1945; *Children of Paradise*), his epic study of theater and spectacle. He was influential in turning the focus of commercial movies from socialites to ordinary people.

In 1928 Carné quit a job in an insurance office to assist cameraman Georges Périnal. He worked under **René Clair** from 1928 to 1935, most notably on *Sous les*

Lobby poster for Marcel Carné's 1938 film about a cynical deserter from the army who falls in love

(1942; *The Devil's Envoys*) and with romantic illusion in *Les Enfants du paradis.* In both films he used historic settings and created a dreamy aura to mask from authorities the underlying theme of the human struggle for life against oppression. While *Le Jour se lève* stands as the finest cinematic embodiment of Sartrean **existentialism,** *Les Enfants du paradis* remains the most extensive and sustained view ever made of spectacle, drama, crime, and romance. A three-hour epic that stars **Arletty, Maria Casarès,** and **Jean-Louis Barrault,** the film pays homage to the Paris of Victor Hugo and Honoré de Balzac.

Yet Carné's greatest contributions are his prewar films. Although they are limited by the **tradition de qualité** of their screenplays or seem contrived next to those of Renoir, his films are marked by the wit of Prévert's writing, by the presence of two or three unrivaled stars, and by great painterly beauty. The quality of Carné's work declined after he broke with Prévert in 1948, and in the 1950s Carné's cinema became a foil for the new criticism and the films of the **Nouvelle Vague** (New Wave).

REFERENCES:

Roy Armes, *French Cinema* (New York: Oxford University Press, 1985);

Evelyn Ehrlich, *Cinema of Paradox: French Filmmaking under the German Occupation* (New York: Columbia University Press, 1985);

Maureen Turim, "Poetic Realism as Psychoanalytical and Ideological Operation: Marcel Carné's *Le Jour se lève,*" in *French Film: Texts and Contexts,* edited by Susan Hayward and Ginette Vincendeau (London: Routledge, 1990), pp. 103–116;

Edward Baron Turk, *Child of Paradise: Marcel Carné and the Golden Age of Cinema* (Cambridge, Mass.: Harvard University Press, 1989).

—T.C.

toits de Paris (1930; *Under the Roofs of Paris*). After gaining more experience with **Jean Renoir** and **Jacques Feyder** during the early 1930s, Carné began directing his own movies in 1936, producing four signature features by the end of the decade. *Drôle de drame* (1937; *Bizarre Bizarre*), *Quai des brumes* (1938; *Port of Shadows*), *Hôtel du Nord* (1938; North Hotel), and *Le Jour se lève* (1939; *Daybreak*) owe their success to Carné's collaboration with poet-screenwriter **Jacques Prévert,** set designer Alexandre Trauner, and composer Maurice Jaubert. The result was a realistic but controlled portrayal of tragedy in everyday life during the Great Depression, with destiny sealing the fates of characters who struggle against its machinations. Carné worked in a studio and used star performers — including **Jean Gabin,** Michel Simon, Jules Berry, and **Michèle Morgan** — endowing a world of gloom with a poetic aura.

After Germany invaded France in June 1940 Carné's prewar films were banned by the **Vichy Government** on so-called moral grounds as having contributed to the collapse of France with their harsh portrayal of French character. Carné responded to censorship with medieval allegory in *Les Visiteurs du soir*

LE CARTEL DES QUATRE

On 6 July 1927 the four foremost directors of serious Paris art theaters formed the Cartel des Quatre (Cartel of Four) for the purpose of lending each other moral and financial support against the exploitative, highly commercialized **boulevard theaters.** Two of these directors were alumni of **Jacques Copeau's** troupe: **Louis Jouvet,** then director at the Comédie des Champs-Elysées, and **Charles Dullin** at the **Théâtre de l'Atelier.** The other members of the Cartel were **Georges Pitoëff,** without a home theater at the time, and **Gaston Baty,** a protégé of **Firmin Gémier,** at the Studio des Champs-Elysées. This syndicate made possible the coordination of repertoires, advertising, tour schedules, and season-ticket policy. They usually worked in relatively small theaters, presenting plays for an educated, perhaps elite, public. At its height in the 1930s, the Cartel gradually came to an end as the four directors died between 1939 and 1952.

REFERENCES:

France Anders, *Jacques Copeau et le Cartel des Quatre* (Paris: Nizet, 1959);

Jean Hort, *Les Théâtres du Cartel et leurs animateurs: Pitoëff, Baty, Jouvet, Dullin* (Geneva: Skira, 1944);

Jacqueline de Jomaron, "Ils étaient quatre...," in *Le Théâtre en France. 2: De la Révolution à nos jours,* edited by de Jomaron (Paris: Armand Colin, 1989), pp. 227–270.

— R.J.N.

MARIA CASARÈS

Maria Casarès (1922–) gained renown in movies and on the stage, where she interpreted the major female roles in the dramas of **Albert Camus.** Her often-fiery physical style made her one of the best-known performers in France in the immediate postwar period. Frequently playing the lead in productions at the **Théâtre National Populaire** (T.N.P.) with **Jean Vilar,** she left her stamp on the theater of the 1950s, and she remained active into the 1980s in a broad range of roles.

Born in Spain, she took refuge in France with her republican father in 1936, at the time of the **Spanish Civil War.** She attended the Paris Conservatoire and won prizes for her acting in 1942 but did not graduate. Her first professional acting job was in a 1942 French production of John Millington Synge's *Deirdre of the Sorrows* at the Théâtre des Mathurins. She played in Camus's *Le Malentendu* (translated as *Cross Purpose*) in 1944, in his *L'Etat de siège* (translated as *State of Siege*) in 1948, and in his *Les Justes* (translated as *The Just Assassins*) in 1949.

Casarès's best-remembered film roles were in **Marcel Carné**'s *Les Enfants du paradis* (1945; *Children of Paradise*), **Robert Bresson**'s *Les Dames du Bois de Boulogne* (1945; *Ladies of the Park*), Christian-Jacque's version of Stendhal's *La Chartreuse de Parme* (1948; The Charterhouse of Parma), and **Jean Cocteau**'s *Orphée* (1950; *Orpheus*). In *Orphée* she gave a controlled, often-chilling, performance as Death. In **Alain Resnais**'s documentary *Guernica* (1950) she read the voice-over commentary, written by **Paul Eluard.** These performances won her stardom, but after the early 1950s she appeared in few films, devoting her energies to the theater.

In 1947 Casarès joined **Gérard Philipe** and **Roger Blin** in *Les Epiphanies* (Epiphanies), an avant-garde play by Henri Pichette that broke radically with mimetic and logical theatrical traditions. She acted at the

Comédie-Française in 1952 before moving in 1954 to the Théâtre National Populaire (T.N.P.), where her reputation helped increase ticket sales. Her performances for Vilar at the T.N.P. and at the **Avignon Festival** were often highly emotional, and she was accused by some critics of overacting. Her Lady Macbeth in William Shakespeare's *Macbeth* (Avignon, 1954) appeared frighteningly obsessed. Her Marie Tudor in Victor Hugo's drama of the same name (Avignon, 1955) epitomized Hugo's Romantic spirit. Her performance in Pierre Carlet de Chamblain de Marivaux's *Le Triomphe de l'amour* (translated as *The Triumph of Love*) at the T.N.P. in 1955 was especially popular with the public.

Casarès left the Vilar company in 1959 and toured South America, performing in Spanish. Then she participated in avant-garde theater in France, with some success. She acted, for example, in Blin's production of **Jean Genet**'s controversial *Les Paravents* (translated as *The Screens*) at the **Théâtre de l'Odéon** in 1966. She was also successful in **Jean-Louis Barrault**'s avant-garde staging of Seneca's *Medea* in 1967. In 1980 she published an autobiographical work, *Résidente privilégiée* (Privileged Resident).

REFERENCE:

Béatrix Dussane, *Maria Casarès* (Paris: Calmann-Lévy, 1953).

— R.J.N.

JEAN CAYROL

Jean Cayrol (1911–), who won the Grand Prix National des Lettres in 1984 and is a member of the Académie Goncourt, is a prolific author of novels, poetry, essays, and screenplays. His best-known film dialogues and scripts are those for *Nuit et brouillard* (1956; *Night and Fog*), about the concentration camps, and *Muriel* (1963), both directed by **Alain Resnais.** Although Cayrol is highly esteemed in France, very few of his books have been translated into English.

Cayrol, who began his literary career by publishing verse on religious themes, is a Catholic. His belief has influenced some of his work, but he is by no means dogmatic and is not a "Catholic writer" in the sense of someone who wishes to illustrate religion in his writings. The most important experience of his life is often expressed obliquely in his work: in 1942 he and his brother were arrested for working in the **Resistance,** sent to prison at Fresnes, and then deported to the concentration camp at Mauthausen, Austria, where his brother died. After the **Liberation** of France Cayrol returned home a haunted man. His experiences of imprisonment are reflected in the poems in *Miroir de la* *rédemption* (1944; Mirror of Redemption), written partly at Fresnes; his *Poèmes de la nuit et du brouillard* (1946; Poems of Night and Fog); and his first novel, *On vous parle* (1947; Someone Is Talking to You). Part of a trilogy titled *Je vivrai l'amour des autres* (I Shall Live Others' Love), *On vous parle* and its sequels deal with the difficulties of readaptation to the postwar world, but the strange, Lazaruslike hero who wanders through these books is a creature not only of the war but also of the modern world, with its alienation and absence of communication. With its hero's marginality in society and its minimal plot line, *On vous parle* foreshadowed some of the features of the **Nouveau Roman** (New Novel) of the 1950s.

Two of Cayrol's other successful novels are *L'Espace d'une nuit* (1954; translated as *All in a Night*) and *Les Corps étrangers* (1959; translated as *Foreign Bodies*). Like the trilogy and several other works by Cayrol, both books are concerned with memory. Much of his later fiction is highly fanciful and playful. The novels *Histoire d'une prairie* (1969; Story of a Prairie), *Histoire d'un désert* (1972; Story of a Desert), *Histoire de la mer* (1973; Story of the Sea), *Histoire de la forêt* (1975; Story of a Forest), *Histoire d'une maison* (1976; Story of a House), and *Histoire du ciel* (1979; Story of the Sky) propose to give the "histories" of various locations. Cayrol has also written short stories and several autobiographies, including *Il était une fois Jean Cayrol* (1982; Once Upon a Time There Was Jean Cayrol).

REFERENCES:

Catharine Savage [Brosman], "The Trilogy of Jean Cayrol," *Thought,* 44 (Winter 1969): 513–530;

Carlos Lynes, Jr., "Jean Cayrol," in *The Novelist as Philosopher: Studies in French Fiction 1935–1960,* edited by John Cruickshank (London: Oxford University Press, 1962), pp. 183–205;

Pierre Maury, "Jean Cayrol, la poésie au quotidien," *Magazine Littéraire,* 258 (1988): 114–121.

—C.S.B.

Louis-Ferdinand Céline

Novelist and playwright Louis-Ferdinand Céline (1894–1961) is one of the most controversial writers of the interwar and post-**World War II** periods for his harsh, direct style and his notorious political views.

Born Louis-Ferdinand Destouches, Céline was seriously wounded in **World War I,** nearly losing an arm. He trained as a physician after the war. He traveled widely in England, Africa, and the United States until 1928, when he began practicing medicine in a working-class suburb of Paris. He achieved immediate

Louis-Ferdinand Céline, circa 1934, about two years after the publication of his first novel (Albert Harlinque)

fame with his first novel, *Voyage au bout de la nuit* (1932; translated as *Journey to the End of the Night*), his finest work and one of the masterpieces of twentieth-century French fiction.

This autobiographical novel takes the protagonist, Bardamu, from the period of World War I— which Céline depicts as a senseless enterprise consisting mostly of suffering and butchery — to Africa, where he fails as a colonial representative, to New York and Detroit, and then back to France, where he barely survives as a doctor and falls increasingly into misery and failure. His existence is paralleled by that of a mysterious Robinson, his doppelgänger. *Voyage au bout de la nuit* is an indictment of all modern society, from the daily life of assembly-line workers in America to that of marginalized shopkeepers in the worst sections of Paris. Warmongering governments and industrial capitalism overpower the individual; life is a horrible joke from which there is no salvation, except a rare, brief love affair. Few characters in this long novel, which can be called a modern epic (or anti-epic), find favor with the novelist. The work caused an enormous critical stir and shocked readers with its crude realism and language. Céline was one of the first French authors to write in the spoken language of lower-class France, and in his pioneering book he went even further than nineteenth-century realists and their followers in portraying sordid reality and refusing to make it an objet d'art by stylizing it through literary language.

In 1936 Céline published his second novel, *Mort à crédit* (translated as *Death on the Installment Plan*), which recounts in an impressionistic fashion the childhood of the hero of *Voyage au bout de la nuit*. It was not as successful as his first book, but it remains an important document on the period. Céline followed *Mort à crédit* with controversial political works. *Mea culpa* (1936; translated) is an indictment of the Soviet Union, which he visited in 1936. The next year, in *Bagatelles pour un massacre* (Trifles for a Massacre), he attacked international Jewry, which he considered a danger to French society and European peace. His reputation as a dangerous anti-Semite was quickly established; he was not without an audience, however. In *L'Ecole des cadavres* (1938; School for Corpses) he proposed a Franco-German alliance against the Soviet Union and the Jews. These positions isolated him from both the left and the right. He remained throughout the remainder of his life in a sort of no-man's-land, an exile figuratively and often literally.

Under the German **Occupation** of France during World War II, Céline, who had served briefly on a French ship in the Mediterranean at the outbreak of the war, published a long essay, *Les Beaux Draps* (1941; A Fine Mess), blaming the French army for fleeing before the Germans and calling for radical changes in society. He also produced a novel, *Guignol's Band* (1944; translated), the second volume of which appeared in 1964 as *Le Pont de Londres* (London Bridge). After the Allied landings in Normandy in 1944, Céline left Paris for Germany, fearing that he would be accused of collaboration on the basis of his political sentiments. In March 1945 he moved to Denmark, where he was imprisoned for fourteen months of 1945–1946, after the French government demanded his extradition as a collaborator. He was granted amnesty in 1951 and returned to France to continue practicing medicine. A handful of books, some written during the Occupation, were published in the last ten years of his life. *D'un château l'autre* (1957; translated as *Castle to*

Castle), *Nord* (1960; translated as *North*), and *Rigodon* (1969; translated) are based mostly on his war experiences and abandon the guise of fiction.

Because of his anti-Semitism, his harsh judgments on French society, his momentary embracing of the Germans, and the accusation of collaboration, Céline was nearly persona non grata in the literary world for some time. Since critics began talking about him again in the mid 1960s his reputation has risen steadily. He is now recognized as a major voice of his generation whose influence was felt not only by French authors but also by American writers such as Henry Miller, William S. Burroughs, and Jack Kerouac.

REFERENCES:
J. H. Matthews, *The Inner Dream: Céline as Novelist* (Syracuse, N.Y.: Syracuse University Press, 1978);
David O'Connell, *Louis-Ferdinand Céline* (Boston: Twayne, 1976);
Merlin Thomas, *Louis-Ferdinand Céline* (New York: New Directions, 1979).
— C.S.B.

BLAISE CENDRARS

While he wrote many prose works, including what he loosely called novels, Blaise Cendrars (1887–1961) is known principally as a poet, one of the creators of literary modernism in France. His narrative poem *Les Pâques* (1912; Easter) — later called *Les Pâques à New York* — shares with poems by **Guillaume Apollinaire** the reputation of having introduced an entirely new tone into French verse, a tone that eschews the hyperbole and bathos of Romanticism and the disembodied reverie of Symbolism, partaking instead of the language of everyday conversation, especially the lexical and cultural vocabulary of the twentieth-century world, with its speed, its urbanism, and its inventions. Other important poems by Cendrars include *La Prose du Transsibérien et de la petite Jehanne de France* (1913; translated by John Dos Passos as *The Prose of the Trans-Siberian and of Little Jeanne of France*) and *Le Panama; ou, Les aventures de mes sept oncles* (1918: translated by Dos Passos as *Panama; or the Adventures of My Seven Uncles*).

Born Frédéric Sauser in Switzerland, Cendrars made Paris his home in 1912 and became a French citizen in 1916. Known for his adventurous, colorful life, he traveled widely — in Russia, the United States, and South America, as well as Europe — and fought with the Légion Etrangère (French Foreign Legion) during **World War I,** having his arm amputated after he was wounded in the Marne valley in 1915 and winning the Médaille Militaire and the Croix de Guerre. Much of what is recounted in his ostensibly autobiographical works, however, is misleading or false, so that his life appears in part as a self-created myth. His interests were wide; he worked in publishing with **Jean Cocteau** (1918–1924), was a supporter of avant-garde painting, participated in the filming of *J'accuse* (1919; *I Accuse*) and *La Roue* (1923; The Wheel) with **Abel Gance,** worked with **Darius Milhaud** and **Fernand Léger** on the ballet *La Création du Monde* (1923), and published a collection of African tales, *L'Anthologie nègre* (1921; translated as *African Saga*). One of Cendrars's admirers was Henry Miller, who wrote two perceptive essays on his friend.

REFERENCES:

Jay Bochner, *Blaise Cendrars: Discovery and Re-Creation* (Toronto: University of Toronto Press, 1978);

Monique Chefdor, *Blaise Cendrars* (Boston: Twayne, 1980);

Henry Miller, "Blaise Cendrars," in his *The Books in My Life* (Norfolk, Conn.: New Directions, 1952), pp. 58–80;

Miller, "Tribute to Blaise Cendrars," in his *The Wisdom of the Heart* (Norfolk, Conn.: New Directions, 1941), pp. 151–158.

— C.S.B.

Centre National de la Recherche Scientifique

France has a long tradition of government-sponsored aid to basic research through institutions such as the Collège de France and the Institut Pasteur. Created in 1930 the Centre National de la Recherche Scientifique (National Center for Scientific Research, or CNRS) is the largest national research establishment in France, with more than 1,300 laboratories that are either independent or associated with universities throughout France. The CNRS has a staff of almost 27,000, of whom about 11,500 are actual researchers; more than 15,000 are engineers, technicians, and administrators. Research is carried on in all fields of basic science, but the largest section of research at the CNRS is devoted to the "sciences de l'homme," which in the United States would be classified as the humanities or social sciences.

— J.P.McN.

Centre Pompidou

The Centre National d'Art et de Culture Georges Pompidou is the principal modern cultural center in Paris. Often referred to as the Centre Beaubourg after its location, it was the brainchild of Georges Pompidou, second president of the **Fifth Republic** and a staunch

advocate of modern art and architecture. The center includes several exhibit halls, a public library, **IRCAM** (Institut de Recherche et de Coordination Acoustique/Musique, devoted to developing electronic music), and one of the largest collections of modern art in the world. One exhibit space is given over to new architectural design and technology.

In 1971, two years after the idea of building such a center was approved, a design by Italian architect Renzo Piano and British architect Richard Rogers, with the collaboration of the Danish engineering firm Ove Arup, was selected from 681 submissions. The Pompidou Center opened to the public in 1977 amid a chorus of controversy. Located where Les Halles, the Paris central market, previously stood, the building makes no concession to tradition through architectural reference to the past. An imposing structure more than 500 feet wide and 138 feet high, it is all the more striking because of the relatively modest traditional structures that surround it and the high open square in front of it, which draws street performers. Most controversial is the way in which the design draws attention to its own contemporary technology: plexiglass escalators and brightly colored utility conduits and ventilation shafts are placed conspicuously on the outside rather than being concealed in the exterior.

The success of the center has far exceeded even the most optimistic expectations. Approximately eight million people visit the Pompidou Center each year, more than three times as many as were expected and rivaling the number of visitors to the Eiffel Tower. Given its extraordinary success, much of the controversy surrounding it has subsided, although anyone seeing it for the first time is still likely to be shocked by its unorthodox design.

REFERENCE:

Nathan Silver, *The Making of Beaubourg: A Building Biography of the Centre Pompidou, Paris* (Cambridge, Mass. & London: MIT Press, 1994).

— J.P.McN.

Marcel Cerdan

Marcel Cerdan (1916–1949) is one of two French boxers with international reputations. (The other is Georges Carpentier, who was world champion from 1920 to 1922.) Cerdan, who was born in Sidi-bel-Abbès, Algeria, began boxing early, and by age seventeen he was a well-known professional fighter throughout North Africa. In a career of 108 professional bouts, Cerdan lost only 4 fights, 2 outright and 2 through disqualifications. He was admired by fellow Algerian

Albert Camus and had a sentimental involvement with singer **Edith Piaf.**

Cerdan won the world middleweight title in September 1948, defeating American Tony Zale. In March 1949 he knocked out the British champion, Dick Turpin, but three months later he lost his world title to Jake LaMotta in Detroit, Michigan. In October 1949 Cerdan died in a plane crash in the Azores while en route to New York City for a return bout with LaMotta for the world championship.

REFERENCE:

Simone Berteaut, *Piaf: A Biography,* translated by June Guicharnaud (New York: Harper & Row, 1972).

—J.P.McN.

AIMÉ CÉSAIRE

Poet Aimé Césaire (1913–) is one of the principal advocates of *la négritude* — a term he proposed in 1934 to describe the consciousness of and pride in African heritage that was the basis for the movement he founded with **Léopold Senghor** and Léon-Gontran Damas.

Born in Martinique, Césaire went to Paris as a student in 1932. In 1934 Césaire, Damas, and Senghor founded *L'Etudiant Noir* (The Black Student), the journal in which Césaire introduced the concept of négritude. The short-lived journal, published from September 1934 until 1936, fostered interaction among blacks from Africa and the West Indies.

During the 1930s Césaire's positions on racial and cultural questions were considered radical. He emphasized the alienation felt by blacks, especially those in the West Indies, who are separated not only from Europeans and other whites by their skin color and culture but also from Africa, from which their forebears had been forcibly removed. He wanted to establish the value of blackness and recover the African values and culture taken from blacks by slave owners and colonizers; but he chose to do so in part through the literary forms and language of the French, instead of writing in the creole commonly spoken in Martinique. The influence of **Surrealism** is apparent in his influential long poem *Cahier de retour au pays natal* (1947; translated as *Memorandum on My Martinique* and *Return to My Native Land*), which expresses his anticolonialism and his anger at the oppression and poverty of blacks in Martinique — and throughout the world. First published in the journal *Volontés* in 1939, the poem was published as a book, with a preface by Surrealist **André Breton,** in 1947 and has been revised by Césaire several times. Other volumes of his poetry include *Les*

Armes miraculeuses (1946; translated as *The Miraculous Weapons*), *Soleil cou-coupé* (1948; Sun Cut at the Neck — a reference to a line by **Guillaume Apollinaire**), *Corps perdu* (1950; Lost Body), and *Ferrements* (1960; Irons).

Césaire returned to Martinique in September 1939 and began teaching school. (One of his pupils was the future anticolonialist revolutionary Frantz Fanon.) Césaire also took up politics, becoming mayor of Fort-de-France, the capital of Martinique, in 1945 and Communist deputy to the National Assembly of France in 1946. Some of his political views are expressed in *Discours sur le colonialisme* (1950; translated as *Discourse on Colonialism*). He resigned from the Communist Party in 1956 to protest the Soviet invasion of Hungary, and in 1958 he helped to found the socialist Parti Progressiste Martiniquais.

Césaire's views on the colonialist question are embodied in his best-known play, *La Tragédie du roi Christophe* (1963; translated as *The Tragedy of King Christophe*), based on the life of Haitian leader Henri Christophe, who served as an officer to Toussaint-Louverture and later declared himself king of Haiti. Another play, *Une Saison au Congo* (1966; translated as *A Season in the Congo*), deals with the 1961 assassination of Patrice Lumumba, first president of the Republic of Congo after its liberation from Belgium.

REFERENCES:

A. James Arnold, *Modernism and Negritude: The Poetry and Poetics of Aimé Césaire* (Cambridge, Mass.: Harvard University Press, 1981);

Aimé Césaire, *The Collected Poetry,* translated, with an introduction, by Clayton Eshleman and Annette Smith (Berkeley, Los Angeles & London: University of California Press, 1983);

Janis Pallister, *Aimé Césaire* (Boston: Twayne, 1991).

—C.S.B.

GILBERT CESBRON

Gilbert Cesbron (1913–1979) was one of the most popular and successful of the Roman Catholic novelists who emerged in France after **World War II.**

Born in Paris to a wealthy bourgeois family, Cesbron devoted most of his energies as a novelist to pleading the case of those less fortunate than himself. His best-known and most important novel, *Les Saints vont en enfer* (1954; translated as *Saints in Hell*), is about **worker priests,** members of the Catholic clergy who live among the working class and try to bring the gospel to those who have become alienated from the church. An overwhelming commercial success, the novel signaled the social agenda that the Catholic church would eventually adopt at the Second Vatican

Cézanne in his Lauves studio sitting in front of his *Large Bathers,* 1904 (photo by Emile Bernard)

Council (1962–1965). The work is superior in style and technique to Cesbron's later novels, written with similar good intentions but considerably less art.

In the mid 1960s Cesbron quarreled with **Michel de Saint Pierre,** whose best-selling novel *Les Nouveaux Prêtres* (1966; translated as *The New Priests*) attacked the "new priests" for practices that were at odds with church tradition, especially their use of Marxist rhetoric in their preaching and in their refusal of the sacraments to people deemed not to be true proletarians. Their disagreements, expressed openly in an exchange of newspaper columns, were a paradigm of the larger cultural clashes taking place within the church in the years immediately after the Second Vatican Council.

All of Cesbron's novels treat contemporary social problems from a compassionate point of view. For example, *Chiens perdus sans collier* (1954; Lost Dogs Without a Collar) deals with juvenile delinquency; *Avoir été* (1960; To Have Been) is about the neglect of the aged; and *Entre chiens et loups* (1962; Between Dogs and Wolves) treats the **Algerian war** and the problem of violence. *Mais moi je vous aimais* (1978; But I Loved You) is concerned with retarded children. Cesbron's novels were best-sellers, and he was widely respected because of the Catholic worldview that un-

derpins his works. Nonetheless he never received the critical acclaim that greeted Catholic novelists of an earlier generation such as **Georges Bernanos, Julien Green,** and **François Mauriac.**

REFERENCE:
Michel Barlow, "Gilbert Cesbron, Christian Writer," *Renascence,* 36 (Autumn–Winter 1983–1984): 67–76.

—D.O'C.

PAUL CÉZANNE

Painter Paul Cézanne (1839–1906) attempted to explore, redirect, and redefine the nature and means of representing reality. His experiments with capturing the essence of objects through shape rather than color, as the Impressionists had attempted, influenced many twentieth-century artists who took his ideas further into abstraction.

Cézanne was the son of a prosperous banker and businessman in the provincial town of Aix-en-Provence. Through an early friendship with Emile Zola, Cézanne was introduced into a milieu of discontented artists, notably the painter Camille Pissarro. In the early 1870s Cézanne worked closely with Pissarro, who was able to obtain an entry for the younger artist at the first Impressionist exhibition (1874), over the objections of others in the group.

Cézanne's early work earned him few supporters. He produced several canvases of rapes and murders that were blocky in form and murky in color. Edouard Manet termed them "foul." He was not won over by the two Cézanne paintings included in the 1874 show, one of which was intended as a homage to Manet's famous *Olympia* (1865). In his review of the exhibit Zola praised Cézanne's paintings, arguing that he "shows great originality" and "unquestionably has the temperament of a great painter." Yet even Zola had doubts about his younger friend's work, doubts that crystallized in Zola's 1886 novel, *L'Œuvre* (translated as *The Masterpiece?*). Cézanne took the novel's tortured protagonist, who commits suicide over his inability to reach his goals, to be a portrait of himself, and the two men never reconciled.

Cézanne's friendship with Pissarro had a major impact on his work. As part of the so-called School of Pontoise, which also included **Paul Gauguin,** Cézanne adopted the self-consciously rural imagery, warm colors, and flatly painted surfaces of the group. Even at the outset, however, there were clear differences between his work and that of Pissarro. For example, Cézanne did not share Pissarro's interests in hardworking peasants. Cézanne's *La Maison du pendu, à Auvers-sur-Oise* (1873; *The House of the Hanged Man at Auvers-sur-Oise*) and *Etude: Paysage à Auvers* (circa 1873; *Study: Landscape at Auvers*) share with Pissarro's landscapes of the same period a palette of strong reds and greens and a flat appearance produced by unified shades and brush strokes across the whole canvas. Unlike Pissarro, however, Cézanne also surrounded the objects he depicted with broad, usually dark, strokes so that shadows and outlines seemed almost like solid objects bound together in a kind of matrix. He told a colleague that his goal was to "make of Impressionism something solid, like the art in museums" — that is, to regain through new means the monumentality of academic painting.

After the death of his father in 1886, Cézanne made use of his ample inheritance to immerse himself in his painting with growing intensity. In still life and landscape paintings he explored the means by which an artist could represent depth and distance. He wrote to **Emile Bernard** that he should seek in nature "the cylinder, the sphere, the cone, putting everything in proper perspective, so that each side of an object or a plane is directed toward a central point." He suggested that the painter should begin by focusing on an illuminated area or object closest to the viewer: "In an orange, an apple, a ball, a head, there is a culminating

point and this point is always. . . . the closest to our eye. The edges of objects recede to a center placed on the horizon." To set off areas of brightness, Cézanne sometimes began by painting the shadows around those areas in order to focus on modulations of light, shadow, and gradations of color.

Cézanne's artistic experimentations represent part of a growing insistence in late-nineteenth- and early-twentieth-century art that the Impressionist goal of depicting nature in a direct and unmediated manner was not (or was no longer) tenable. He wrote, "I discovered that the sun, for instance, could not be *reproduced,* but that it must be *represented* by something else . . . by color." It was this aspect of Cézanne's work that intrigued not only the **Cubists** but also other twentieth-century avant-garde circles.

REFERENCES:

Andrea Belloli, ed., *A Day in the Country: Impressionism and the French Landscape* (Los Angeles: Los Angeles County Museum of Art, 1984);

Jean de Beucken, *Cézanne: A Pictorial Biography,* translated by Lothian Small (New York: Viking, 1962);

Stephen F. Eisenman and others, *Nineteenth-Century Art: A Critical History* (London: Thames & Hudson, 1994);

John Rewald, *Cézanne: A Biography* (New York: Abrams, 1986).

— J.H.

CLAUDE CHABROL

Of all the young critics for *Cahiers du Cinéma* who became **Nouvelle Vague** (New Wave) directors in the late 1950s, Claude Chabrol (1930–) remains the most difficult to categorize. His films bear the imprint of Alfred Hitchcock and **film noir,** but they also reach back to the great French tradition of literary and cinematic collaboration. He is perhaps the most commercial of the New Wave directors.

Like other members of the *Cahiers du Cinéma* group, Chabrol entered cinema through writing. After working as a film critic from 1953 to 1957, he became the head of a production company while directing his first feature, *Le Beau Serge* (1958; *Bitter Reunion*). He has since directed dozens of features, most of them understated psychological studies of crime and passion in the style of Hitchcock and Fritz Lang. Chabrol and **Eric Rohmer** are the authors of *Hitchcock* (1957; translated as *Hitchcock, The First Forty-Four Films*).

In *Les Cousins* (1959; *The Cousins*) Chabrol drew on the literary theme of Paris versus the provinces through the exchanges between Charles, a sober and rational bourgeois who comes to Paris from the provinces, and Paul, the Paris cousin who is Charles's libido or alter ego. The opposition at the heart of the dialogue between these two characters also informs *La Femme infidèle* (1968; *Unfaithful Wife*), *Le Boucher* (1970; The Butcher), and *La Rupture* (1970; *The Breakup*). These and other films — including the well-known *Les Bonnes Femmes* (1960; *The Good Women*) and *Les Biches* (1968; also released as *The Does* and *The Girlfriends*) — feature Chabrol's second wife, Stéphane Audran.

Chabrol's films are the result of a stable team of collaborators. A cool, reduced palette of colors and minimal forms lend a baroque starkness to settings that create a sensuous atmosphere. He has used narrative to question issues of sacrifice, religion, and myth in contemporary everyday settings. In his later movies he has developed an almost Balzacian vision, ordering the elements of a "human comedy" that moves between literature, as in *Madame Bovary* (1991), and ethnohistory, as in *Le Cheval d'orgueil* (1990; also released as *The Horse of Pride* and *The Proud Ones*).

REFERENCES:

Roy Armes, *French Cinema* (New York: Oxford University Press, 1985);

James Monaco, *The New Wave* (New York: Oxford University Press, 1976);

Robin Wood and Michael Walker, *Claude Chabrol* (New York: Praeger, 1970).

— T.C.

Marc Chagall in front of *The Praying Jew,* circa 1924, just after he returned to Paris from Moscow

MARC CHAGALL

Marc Chagall (1889–1985) is known for his fantastic, often whimsical paintings, which were equally influenced by Expressionism and **Cubism.** His paintings defy formal logic: his *I and the Village* (1911), for example, fuses human and animal motifs, abstract motifs, and a tiny Russian village. Superimposed over the cow's head is her dream (of being milked); two lovers stroll down the village street, but one is upside down.

Chagall was born to a poor Jewish family in Vitebsk, Russia. He studied art in Saint Petersburg from 1907 through 1910 under Léon Bakst; his first works mingle elements from the Impressionists and the **Fauves.** During a long stay in Paris (1910–1914) he became acquainted with avant-garde circles as a close friend of **Guillaume Apollinaire** and **Fernand Léger.**

With the outbreak of **World War I** Chagall returned to Russia. He was a supporter of both the February and the October Bolshevik revolutions of 1917. In 1918 he was appointed commissar for the fine arts in the Vitebsk region. He established an art school in the city and participated in the first Exhibition of Revolutionary Art (1919) in Petrograd (formerly Saint Petersburg). As a supporter of the Russian Futurists, Chagall came into conflict with the more abstract Suprematists, led by Casimir Malevich, who regarded Futurist painting as too traditional. Party leaders, on the other hand, were not always enthusiastic about any avant-garde trends. Chagall later recalled official challenges to his art: "Why is the cow green and why is the horse flying in the air? Why? What does that have to do with Marx and Lenin?" Chagall was removed from his commissar post in 1920, and for the next three years he worked in the Russian theater, especially the Jewish Kamerny Theater in Moscow. In 1923 he returned to Paris, devoting his energies to illustration as well as painting. He remained in Paris until 1941, when he fled the Nazi **Occupation** by accepting an invitation from the Museum of Modern Art in New York City. He returned to France in 1948, living there until his death.

Chagall's art draws from a wide variety of modernist themes and motifs; it is saved from a formless eclecticism, along with the common charge that it is uniformly lighthearted, by a continuing fascination with themes drawn from Russian folklore and Jewish mysticism. Russia remained for him a necessary starting point throughout his career: "I painted cows, dairies, roosters and the architecture of the Russian provinces as a source of forms because all these subjects are parts of the country I come from, and these things have without any doubt left in my visual memory a more profound impression than all the others that I may have received." In his 1913 *Self-Portrait with Seven Fingers,* for instance, a lighted Eiffel Tower can be seen prominently through an open window; yet Chagall himself is depicted painting a Russian peasant, a cow, and an onion-domed Orthodox church. After **World War II** Chagall often created sculptures, ceramics, and stained glass as well as paintings, and his works increasingly reflected religious themes and allusions to the Holocaust.

Chagall insisted that art had nothing to do with science, that paintings were intuitive works drawn from experience and the soul. "For me," he insisted, "a painting is a surface covered with representations of things ... within a certain framework in which logic and illustration have no importance. There may exist a mysterious fourth or fifth dimension — perhaps not only of the eye — that intuitively gives rise to a balance of plastic and psychical contrasts, piercing the eye of the spectator by new and unusual conceptions."

REFERENCES:

Sidney Alexander, *Marc Chagall: A Biography* (New York: Putnam, 1978);

Marc Chagall, *My Life,* translated by Elisabeth Abott (New York: Orion Press, 1960);

Charles Sorlier, ed., *Chagall by Chagall,* translated by John Shepley (New York: Abrams, 1979).

—J.H.

Coco Chanel

The world-renowned couturiere Coco Chanel (1883–1971) ruled the world of Paris fashion design for almost sixty years.

Born Gabrielle Chanel, she took the name Coco in 1905, after she made her stage debut at a music hall in Moulins, singing "Ko Ko Ri Ko" (Cockadoodle-do) and "Qui qu'a vu Coco dans l'Trocadéro?" (Who's Seen Coco at the Trocadero?) for a group of admiring cavalry officers who began calling for encores by chanting "Coco! Coco!" She soon abandoned her ambitions to have a career as a singer, and in 1909 she settled in Paris, where she began a millinery. By 1912 photographs of stylish women wearing Chanel hats were appearing in the influential magazine *Les Modes* (Fashions), and the next year Chanel opened a boutique in the fashionable resort of Deauville, where she began selling clothes she had designed herself the following summer, just before the outbreak of **World War I.** De-

spite the war, the house of fashion she opened in Biarritz in 1916 was so successful that she was able to open a second atelier in Paris a year later. Her simple clothing, which introduced the concept of sportswear to women, suited the mood of wartime France. In 1922 she introduced her famous perfume, Chanel No. 5, the success of which gave her a firm financial footing.

Chanel's designs inspired women to exchange complicated clothes for more-comfortable ones, such as jersey suits and dresses, short skirts, trench coats, and turtleneck sweaters; she also championed the wearing of costume jewelry and contributed to the popularity of bobbed hair. Although she retired in 1938, she returned to the world of haute couture in 1954. Never married, she was known in Parisian circles for her liaisons with the wealthy and famous, including Hugh Grosvenor, Duke of Westminster, reputedly the richest man in England and a member of the social set surrounding Edward, Prince of Wales.

REFERENCES:

Marcel Haedrich, *Coco Chanel* (Boston: Little, Brown, 1972);

Alice Mackrell, *Coco Chanel* (New York: Holmes & Meier, 1972);

Alex Madsen, *Coco Chanel: A Biography* (London: Bloomsbury, 1990).

—C.S.B.

René Char

Like many poets of his generation, René Char (1907–1988), whom **Albert Camus** called the "greatest living poet" in France, began his career as a **Surrealist;** and in retrospect he is considered one of the most talented of the poets associated with the movement. He wanted to eliminate all personal qualities from his work and rely on powerful, if discontinuous and obscure, images. *Artine* (1930), *Ralentir travaux* (1930; To Slow Down Work) — a collaboration with **André Breton** and **Paul Eluard** — and *Le Marteau sans maître* (1934; Hammer Without a Master) are considered classics of Surrealism. In 1934 Char began to distance himself from the Surrealists.

During the German **Occupation** of France in **World War II,** Char was a leader of the **Resistance** in his native Vaucluse, using the name Capitaine Alexandre. Char's *Feuillets d'Hypnos* (1946; translated as *Hypnos Waking,*) is a poetic reflection of these experiences.

Some of his best postwar poetry is in *Fureur et mystère* (1948; Furor and Mystery), which also includes *Feuillets d'Hypnos* and earlier works. Like his earlier Surrealist work, the postwar poems are mostly impersonal, dense, and aphoristic prose poems, with lightninglike images; but they also have a classical quality, tending even through their obscurity and suggestiveness toward universal concerns, expressed with a controlled lyricism. Char shared with his close friend Albert Camus a concern for humane values ("a humanism conscious of its duties"). This moral vision is apparent in *Fureur et mystère* as well as in later volumes such as *La Parole en archipel* (1962; The Word as an Archipelago), *Le Nu perdu* (1971; The Lost Nude), *La Nuit talismanique* (1972; The Talismanic Night), and *Aromates chasseurs* (1976; Hunter Perfumes).

REFERENCES:

Mechthild Cranston, *Orion Resurgent: René Char, Poet of Presence* (Madrid: Studia Humanitatas, 1979);

Virginia A. La Charité, *The Poetics and Poetry of René Char* (Chapel Hill: University of North Carolina Press, 1968);

James R. Lawler, *René Char: The Myth and the Poem* (Princeton: Princeton University Press, 1978).

—C.S.B.

Jacques Chardonne

Born Jacques Boutelleau, the son of a wealthy French father and an American mother, Jacques Chardonne (1884–1968) is one of the most undervalued French novelists of the twentieth century. His career underwent an eclipse after **World War II,** when he was accused by some of collaborating with the occupying Germans.

Chardonne's family left the region of Charente and settled in Paris when he was eighteen, after his father met with financial disaster. Chardonne went to work for a publishing firm in 1910. His novels deal especially with the theme of love within the context of marriage, a topic he considered eternally renewable, with universal significance. His successful first novel, *L'Epithalame* (1921; translated as *Epithalamion*), was followed by others, including *Les Varais* (1929), *Eva* (1930), and *Claire* (1931). In the 1930s, following the contemporary taste for the roman-fleuve or series novel, he produced the three-volume *Destinées sentimentales* (1934–1936; translated as *The House of Barnery*). In these works Chardonne favorably highlighted bourgeois traits such as hard work and the close-knit family, while criticizing the impersonal aspects of capitalism.

In the early years of World War II and the **Occupation** Chardonne made the mistake of publishing views that were held by many, perhaps most, French citizens but that most were prudent enough to keep to themselves. In *Chronique privée* (1939; Private Chronicle), *Chronique privée de l'an quarante* (1941; Private Chronicle of the Year 1940), and *Voir la figure* (1942;

To See the Face) he expressed his approval of the Vichy regime and the idea of a Europe united under German hegemony. Arrested in 1944, he spent three months in prison and was then released without trial, but his career was severely damaged.

Chardonne's postwar works include books that combine aspects of the novel with elements of autobiography in analyzing the quest for happiness. *Vivre à Madère* (1953; To Live in Madeira) is perhaps his best work in this mode.

REFERENCE:

William Kidd, "French Literature and World War II: Vercors and Chardonne," *Forum for Modern Language Studies*, 23 (January 1987): 38–47.

—D.O'C.

Gustave Charpentier

Gustave Charpentier (1860–1956), who began composing orchestral works in the 1880s, is remembered as the composer and librettist of *Louise,* a realistic opera with a contemporary setting that was an instant success when it opened at the Opéra Comique in 1900. It had been performed five hundred times by 1915 and one thousand times by 1935. The Zolaesque realism of *Louise* was a welcome change from the sumptuous productions usually presented at the Opéra during the early years of the twentieth century.

All the characters are working-class people from **Montmartre.** The plot evolves from the decision of Louise, a seamstress, to defy her parents by leaving home to live with her lover, Julien. The opera includes scenes in her simple apartment as well as in a square at night (where there are many touches of local color) and in the seamstresses' workroom. The depiction of lower-class characters, some of whom express socialistic ideas and condone free love, gives the work an immediacy and modernity rarely found in operas at the turn of the century. The best-known portion of *Louise* is the beautiful aria "Depuis le jour" (Since the Day), in which Louise rapturously sings of her first day of love.

In 1902 Charpentier founded the Conservatoire Populaire Mimi Pinson, which provided free musical training to shop girls. His opera *Julien* (1913), a sequel to *Louise,* was not as successful as its predecessor.

REFERENCES:

Kathleen Hoover, "Gustave Charpentier," *Musical Quarterly*, 25 (July 1939): 334–350;

Harvey E. Phillips, "Friend of the Working Girl," *Opera News*, 35 (19 April 1971): 28–30.

—P.S.H.

JANINE CHARRAT

French ballerina and choreographer Janine Charrat (1924–) is known for her dramatic performances and choreography. Two of her best-known ballets are *Abraxas* (1949) and *Les Algues* (1953; Seaweed). While a student at the **Paris Opéra Ballet** she had her first major role as the child dancer in the French film *La Mort du cygne* (1937; released in the United States as *Ballerina*).

Charrat showed an early interest in choreography and by age fifteen was choreographing duets for herself and **Roland Petit.** She spent much of her distinguished career performing and choreographing for companies in France and Europe. She appeared with **Serge Lifar's** Nouveau Ballet de Monte Carlo and the Grand Ballet du Marquis de Cuevas before joining Petit as choreographer for the Ballets des Champs-Elysées in 1945. In 1951 she founded and became chief choreographer for the Ballets Janine Charrat (called the Ballet de France from 1953 to 1958). While recovering from severe burns received in a Paris television-studio fire in 1961, she accepted the position of director of the Geneva Ballet, where she remained from 1962 until 1964. She was cochoreographer for the Ballet du Vingtième Siècle (Ballet of the Twentieth Century) in Brussels for one season. In 1970 she opened a studio in Paris. She continued to choreograph new works for Les Ballets Janine Charrat and other European companies through the 1980s. She was named to the Légion d'Honneur in 1973 and an Officier de la Légion d'Honneur in 1991.

—A.P.E.

YVETTE CHAUVIRÉ

Yvette Chauviré (1917–) was the epitome of the classical ballerina at the traditional **Paris Opera Ballet.** The height of her career came during the tenure of director **Serge Lifar,** who inspired her and created many brilliant roles for her, including L'Ombre (The Shadow) in *Mirages* (1947). She is best known for her interpretation of the title character in the classic French ballet of the Romantic period, *Giselle,* a role she danced for the first time in 1943.

Chauviré entered the Paris Opera Ballet school when she was ten and joined the company at the early age of thirteen. By age nineteen she was a *première danseuse* (principal dancer), and by twenty-eight she was a *première danseuse étoile* (star dancer). In addition to her work at the Paris Opera Ballet, she studied with Victor Gsovsky and Boris Kniaseff and was a guest artist with ballet companies worldwide. She re-tired from performing in 1972. She was named Chevalier de la Légion d'Honneur in 1964 and Officier de la Légion d'Honneur in 1974. She is the author of *Je suis ballerine* (1960; I Am a Ballerina).

REFERENCE:

Otis Stuart, "A Conversation with Yvette Chauviré," *Ballet International,* 7 (June–July 1984): 24–27.

—A.P.E.

MAURICE CHEVALIER

Maurice Chevalier (1888–1972) was the dominant male entertainer of Parisian music halls in the 1920s and went on to become one of the most famous showbusiness figures of the twentieth century. He made his debut as a café singer and comic in Paris in 1901, beginning a career that spanned more than sixty years. Passing easily from the stage to French and American movies, he came to epitomize the Parisian boulevardier — suave, urbane, and debonair.

Shortly after his service in **World War I,** under the influence of the music-hall star **Mistinguett,** Chevalier turned from comedy to playing the lead singer in musical revues. He began appearing in French films in 1908 and played his first role in a feature-length movie, *Le Mauvais Garçon* (The Bad Boy), in 1922. From 1928 to 1935 he lived in the United States, where he became a well-known screen actor, most notably in movies directed by Ernst Lubitsch. His first Hollywood performance was in *The Innocents of Paris* (1929). Starring opposite Jeanette MacDonald in films such as *The Love Parade* (1929), *Love Me Tonight* (1932), and *The Merry Widow* (1934), Chevalier assumed a defining role in popularizing lighthearted musical comedy, a genre that became hugely successful.

After his return to France in 1935 Chevalier reached the peak of his career. His renditions of songs such as "Prosper" (1935), "Ma Pomme" (1936; My Apple), and "Y a d'la joie" (1938; There Is Joy) confirmed his abilities as a singer and performer. During a period in which many artists took public positions on politics, especially on the Left, and politicized their work, he accepted the status quo. He played to the full the role of the jaunty *p'tit gars,* the "little guy" from the suburbs who makes it within the system and thereby validates it. During the **Occupation** of France by the Germans during **World War II,** Chevalier's willingness to perform for them hurt the good reputation he had enjoyed and almost cost him his life at the time of the **Liberation,** but eventually he was cleared of charges of active collaboration.

Cover for sheet music of a song popularized by Maurice Chevalier

Chevalier won over new cinema audiences after the war with performances in **René Clair**'s *Le Silence est d'or* (1947; *Man about Town*) and in American films that included *Gigi* (1958), *Can-Can* (1960), and *Fanny* (1961). He left the stage in 1968.

REFERENCES:

David Bret, *Maurice Chevalier: Up On Top of a Rainbow* (London: Robson, 1992);

Maurice Chevalier, *I Remember It Well,* translated by Cornelia Higginson (New York: Macmillan, 1970);

Michael Freedland, *Maurice Chevalier* (New York: Morrow, 1981).

— J.P.McN.

HÉLÈNE CIXOUS

Hélène Cixous (1937–) is one of the most radical, explicit, and outspoken feminist writers of the late twentieth century. With the development of radical feminism on both sides of the Atlantic, her works have achieved great notoriety and been the focus of critical studies that have labeled her one of the foremost feminist thinkers.

Born in Oran, Algeria, Cixous is a Sephardic Jew, the daughter of a French colonial doctor and an Austro-German mother; German was her first language. Extremely well read in both German and English literature, she has advanced degrees in English, which she has taught at the University of Paris VIII since 1968. She has published criticism on James Joyce, and in 1969 she participated in the founding of the important review *Poétique.* Cixous's concern for the marginalized and her interest in origins and myths are apparent in her first novel, *Dedans* (1969; translated as *Inside*), which is a product of self-psychoanalysis.

Cixous's ideas can be described as antithetical to patriarchal authority. Disclaiming the label of feminism as a patriarchal construction, she posits what she calls *écriture féminine* (feminine writing), which can, however, be practiced by both women and men. Such writing, influenced in theory by the work of **Jacques Derrida,** has as its general object to deconstruct the presuppositions of society and literature by which patriarchal thought, symbolized by the phallus, has been almost universally privileged. Cixous particularly believes that writing is a human construct that has been defined almost exclusively as masculine. Like truth, another human construct, writing should be refashioned to include women. Her concern over social repression is not limited to women's issues. For example, in 1975 she wrote a defense of Pierre Goldman, a Jewish immigrant, who in her eyes was wrongfully accused of homicide.

In 1974 Cixous's feminist concerns led to her founding of the Centre de Recherches en Etudes Féminines. The following year she published "Le Rire de la Méduse" (translated as "The Laugh of the Medusa"), an often-cited text on phallic sexuality and the symbolic system that, according to her, this sexuality establishes. She and Catherine Clément explored the same topics in *La Jeune Née* (1975; translated as *The Newly Born Woman*). These and other writings by Cixous, often explicitly concerned with language and with psychoanalytic topics, reveal the influence of and her reaction against the ideas of Sigmund Freud.

As a writer Cixous is known for her dense metaphorical style, which she employs in both her philosophical fiction and her personalized theoretical writings. Generic boundaries, like sexual ones, are often crossed or erased in her work. She has also published novelistic plays, two of which were produced by **Ariane Mnouchkine.** Her novels include *Le Troisième Corps* (1970; The Third Body) and *La Bataille d'Arcachon* (1987; The Battle of Arcachon); recent essays include *Entre l'écriture* (1986; Between/Enter Writing), about writing and painting.

REFERENCE:
Verena Andermatt Conley, *Hélène Cixous: Writing the Feminine* (Lincoln & London: University of Nebraska Press, 1984).
— C.S.B.

RENÉ CLAIR

Born René Chomette in Paris, director and screenwriter René Clair (1898–1981) stands among the great professional cineasts in the era that saw the shift from experimental and silent cinema to the sound industry. In the polemics that set the **Nouvelle Vague** (New Wave) in motion, **François Truffaut** accused Clair of representing the old guard. Yet the aspersions Truffaut cast on Clair will never diminish Clair's innovations in silent and early sound cinema — above all, his clever use of movement.

Trained at the Lycée Montaigne and the Lycée Louis-le-Grand from 1913 to 1917, Clair served in the French ambulance corps at the end of **World War I**. After living in a Dominican monastery for two years, he began an acting career in 1920 at the **Gaumont** studios. His first film as writer and director, *Paris qui dort* (1924; *The Crazy Ray*) inaugurated a career that included the **Surrealist** film *Entr'acte* (1924) before moving toward classical narrative, as in his meticulously edited 1927 version of Eugène Labiche and Marc Michel's boulevard play *Un Chapeau de paille d'Italie* (*An Italian Straw Hat*). Although Clair was at first opposed to the use of sound in movies, his early sound films became models of intricate construction, musical rhythm, and efficient montage.

Entr'acte and *Paris qui dort* are hilariously scathing views of reason and fascism. *Entr'acte* is a disjunctive record of impressions whose rhyme and reason resemble experiments in automatic writing. The film was a literal entr'acte in the performance of **Francis Picabia**'s *Relâche*, which was performed by the Swedish Ballet in Paris in November 1924 with music by **Erik Satie**. In *Paris qui dort* a doctor, Craze, invents a ray that, when emitted in Paris, freezes all movement. Only the guard at the top of the Eiffel Tower and a group of socialites landing in a private aircraft evade the ray. The guard and the socialites meet, and they wander through the photographically frozen city, eventually discovering the mad doctor. As a struggle ensues over his machine, the men move the handle, forcing Paris to move frenetically and then to freeze again. Craze sees that his ray can have deadening effects akin, it is implied, to narrative cinema. He is finally apprehended, and Paris returns to life.

During 1930–1933 Clair wrote and directed four important films: *Sous les toits de Paris* (1930; *Under the Roofs of Paris*), *Le Million* (1931; *The Million*), *A nous la liberté* (1931; *Give Us Liberty*), and *Quatorze juillet* (1933; *July 14th*). *A nous la liberté* criticizes Taylorism, a theory of scientific management, by taking up the dehumanizing conditions of factory labor and unemployment during the Depression. A film that inspired Charles Chaplin's *Modern Times* (1936), it is punctuated by clever sight gags and wondrous crowd sequences that reveal the collective chaos of the early 1930s.

After receiving hostile reviews over his failure to develop politically correct social themes, Clair directed movies for Alexander Korda in Great Britain from 1935 to 1938. In 1940 he immigrated to the United States and directed for Universal Studios. After **World War II** he returned to Paris and finished seven features — including *Les Grandes Manœuvres* (1955; *The Grand Maneuver*) and *Porte de Lilas* (1957; *Gates of Paris*). In general his postwar work is more serious than his earlier films, which inspired the Marx Brothers and American screwball comedies. Clair was elected to the Académie Française in 1960.

REFERENCES:
René Clair, *Cinema Yesterday and Today,* edited by R. C. Dale, translated by Stanley Appelbaum (New York: Dover, 1972);
R. C. Dale, *The Films of René Clair,* 2 volumes (Metuchen, N.J.: Scarecrow, 1986);
Celia McGerr, *René Clair* (Boston: Twayne, 1980).
—T.C.

CLARTÉ

The journal *Clarté* was established by the novelist **Henri Barbusse** in October 1919. With the goal of forming an international union of intellectuals in support of peace and socialism, it had a steering committee that included **Anatole France,** economist Charles Gide, **Romain Rolland,** American writer Upton Sinclair, painter **Théophile-Alexandre Steinlen,** Paul-Vaillant Couturier, and British novelist H. G. Wells. The *Clarté* movement drew support from a broad but diffuse intellectual milieu disgusted by the slaughters of **World War I** and hopeful that a new, just society would emerge from the shambles. Barbusse wrote that the *Clarté* movement would seek "to organize the struggle against ignorance and against those who direct it like an industry.... It is not born of any political or national influence. It is independent and international, it is sincerely and highly human."

Initially, the French membership of the movement was highly diverse; its chapter in Troyes even endorsed the conservative Bloc National in the 1924

N° 41 — 15 Août 1923   France : Le N

CLARTÉ

Bois gravé original de Serge Fotinsky

Woodcut by Serge Fotinsky on the cover of the 15 August 1923 issue of the journal founded in 1919 by Henri Barbusse

elections. Increasingly, however, the *Clarté* movement came to function as a cultural support group for the Bolsheviks. In January 1920 it organized the first French demonstration in support of the Third (Communist) International.

Actual membership in the *Clarté* group remained small — peaking at about five thousand members in France — but it played a major role in intellectual discourse. As the journal became increasingly focused on international support for Soviet Russia, the movement lost several of its founding members, including Gide (the uncle of **André Gide**) and (in 1923) Barbusse himself. From 1923 through 1925 *Clarté* gradually moved closer to the French **Surrealists,** owing to their common interest in avant-garde art and left-wing politics and their shared distaste for the sentimental radicalism of Anatole France. In 1925 *Clarté* and the Surrealists established a joint campaign against the French suppression of the Rif rebellion in Morocco. A complicated relationship developed, as *Clarté* and the Surrealists worked together on cultural and political pro-

jects while simultaneously seeking (sometimes in competition) to gain recognition from the **French Communist Party.**

In 1925 the Surrealists and the *Clarté* group announced their intent to dissolve their respective reviews and to launch a new joint publication, *La Guerre Civile.* Political and personality conflicts scuttled the project, however, and in June 1926 a new series of *Clarté* began to appear. The former Surrealist Pierre Naville, a Trotskyist activist, took charge of *Clarté* in 1927, and all ties with the Surrealists were severed. Under his direction *Clarté* pledged to abandon literary emphases and become a working-class organ. It ceased publication in 1928 and was replaced by an openly Trotskyist theoretical review, *La Lutte des Classes.*

REFERENCES:

David Caute, *Communism and the French Intellectuals, 1914–1960* (New York: Macmillan, 1964);

Donald Drew Egbert, *Social Radicalism and the Arts: Western Europe* (New York: Knopf, 1970);

Helena Lewis, *The Politics of Surrealism* (New York: Paragon House, 1988);

Maurice Nadeau, *History of Surrealism,* translated by Richard Howard (New York: Macmillan, 1965);

Nicole Racine, "The Clarté Movement in France, 1919–21," *Journal of Contemporary History,* 2 (April 1967): 195–208.

—J.H.

CAMILLE CLAUDEL

Sculptor Camille Claudel (1864–1943), the sister of poet **Paul Claudel,** has long remained overshadowed by **Auguste Rodin,** to whom she was an apprentice and later a colleague and lover for nearly fourteen years (1884–1898). During the 1980s, however, as a result of new studies, Claudel earned a reputation as an extraordinary artist with a distinct set of thematic concerns.

Claudel served as a model for many of Rodin's figures, including several in *La Porte de l'enfer* (1880–1917; *The Gates of Hell*) and actually sculpted an unknown number of works bearing Rodin's signature. Her figures are generally more naturalistic in execution and less given to expressionistic exaggerations than Rodin's. In comparison with Claudel's *Çacountala* (model, 1888; marble, 1895; bronze, 1905), for example, Rodin's superficially similar *L'Eternelle Idole* (1889; *The Eternal Idol*) is more abstracted thematically and emotively, less tied not only to specific myths and legends but also to concrete details of feeling and mood.

Boldly conceived and often strongly sensual, her sculptures sometimes sparked violent opposition from critics and patrons unwilling to accept such qualities in the work of a woman. *La Valse* (*The Waltz*), first exhibited in 1893 as a plaster maquette for a full-sized marble sculpture, depicts a nude man and woman in delicate balance, with bodies barely touching. An official from the French ministry of fine arts rejected it as "violent" in its realism and marked by a "surprising sensuality of expression." Given the norms of French official sculpture, the real reason for his objection seems to have been that a woman was the artist. The state rejected other important nudes by Claudel, including her *Çacountala* and *L'Age mûr* (plaster, 1899; bronze, 1903; *Maturity*). Even when Claudel added a flowing piece of drapery around the woman's lower body in *La Valse* (evident in the extant 1905 bronze version of the sculpture), it was still rejected on grounds that it violated propriety.

Most discussions of Claudel's works treat them autobiographically, in particular as reflections of her relationship with Rodin, but this approach denies her the intellectual ambition and reflection taken for granted in the work of men from the era. In her sculptures personal concerns are filtered through a broad range of myths, legends, and motifs. In her hands these narrative resources, reshaped by her experiences as a woman, took on radically new forms. It was common in the Symbolist period of the late nineteenth century, for instance, to depict a woman's long, unbound hair as a weapon or threat used to enslave men. In contrast Claudel's *Clotho* (1893) shows the old and withered subject (one of the Fates) as trapped under an endless mass of uncut hair.

In part because she had difficulty obtaining commissions for full-scale renderings of the works in question, Claudel repeated, reworked, and sometimes reinterpreted her favorite motifs and themes with slight revisions, giving them different titles. One couple, depicted variously in terra cotta and bronze from 1888 to 1905, is composed of a kneeling male nude embracing a nude female, who both rests on him and drapes over him while touching her own breast. As *L'Abandon* (model, 1888; marble, 1903; *Abandon*) the work is a generalized image of loss. As *Çacountala* it draws upon a classical Indian play by Kalidasa, in which a young king promises to return to a woman he has loved. As *Vertume et Pomone* (marble, 1905; *Vertumnus and Pomona*) the emphasis is shifted yet again: as the fruit nymph Pomona embraces the god Vertumnus, her dangling arm grows into his thigh. In place of love lost and regained, this final revision presents love as fusion, in which parting is impossible.

Lack of critical and commercial success — coupled with fears, perhaps partly justified, that Rodin was undermining her career — took a severe toll on Claudel. After an unsuccessful one-woman show in 1905, her depression intensified. She began to destroy many of her works; one week after her father died in 1913, her mother had her committed to a mental institution, with the apparent complicity of her brother Paul. Claudel blamed Rodin for her institutionalization and refused to sculpt. She remained in the Montdevergyes Asylum near Avignon until her death thirty years later. The revival of her reputation was largely due to the efforts of her great-niece Reine-Marie Paris and the playwright Anne Delbée, whose play *Une Femme* (1982; translated as *Camille Claudel: Une Femme*) focuses on Claudel's emotional struggles.

REFERENCES:

Claudine Mitchell, "Intellectuality and Sexuality: Camille Claudel, the Fin-de-Siècle Sculptress," *Art History,* 12 (December 1989): 419–447;

Reine-Marie Paris, *Camille: The Life of Camille Claudel, Rodin's Muse and Mistress,* translated by Liliane Emery Tuck (New York: Seaver Books, 1984);

Paris, *Camille Claudel* (Washington, D.C.: National Museum of Women in the Arts, 1988);

Paris and Arnaud de la Chapelle, *L'Œuvre de Camille Claudel: Catalogue raisonné* (Paris: A. Biro, 1991).

—J.H.

PAUL CLAUDEL

In the course of his long career Paul Claudel (1868–1955) became the foremost Catholic poet and playwright in France and one of the nation's most famous literary figures. His renown has not extended into Anglophone countries as much as that of some of his contemporaries. His works do not lend themselves well to translation, and his thinking runs counter to many contemporary trends and to much of the British and American philosophical tradition. A political conservative, Claudel also rejected modern science, including the theory of evolution.

Claudel, who was born of peasant stock in Champagne, moved to Paris as an adolescent, when his family relocated there so that his sister, **Camille Claudel,** could study sculpture. He attended the Lycée Louis-le-Grand (1883–1886). In about the same period he fell temporarily under the influence of materialist positivism, which undermined his Catholic beliefs and which he later judged to be a desperate, not to say depraved, philosophy. On Christmas Day of 1886, attending a service at Notre-Dame, he underwent an emotional and lasting conversion, inspired in part by the extremely un-Catholic poet Arthur Rimbaud, some of whose *Illuminations* Claudel had read. This religious experience brought about a radical change in his life and in the direction of his literary vocation, which he wished to put to the service of God.

In 1890 Claudel chose to enter the foreign service and spent all his active life as a diplomat, usually posted to distant countries — including China, Japan, Brazil, and the United States. His stays abroad contributed an important exotic element to his work. They also kept him apart from the literary circles in Paris and probably favored the development of his individual style. While his early writing (some of it published anonymously or under a pseudonym) shows the influence of Stéphane Mallarmé as well as Rimbaud, Claudel soon turned against the Symbolist aesthetic, as well as other nineteenth-century literary movements such as Romanticism and realism — the products of the Enlightenment and modern science — and turned rather to Aeschylus, Dante, Rimbaud, and the Bible for inspiration. Perhaps on the model of biblical verse or perhaps with William Shakespeare in mind, he developed a free-verse form called the *verset,* in which most of his work is written. It appears in his first verse play, *Tête d'or* (1890; revised, 1894; translated), and in what is probably his poetic masterpiece, *Cinq grandes odes* (1910; translated as *Five Great Odes*). The five poems in this collection, all lengthy and elaborately constructed, deal with spiritual and religious topics. "Les Muses" ("The Muses") and "La Muse qui est la grâce" ("The Muse Who Is Grace") do so in terms of the Greek tradition, while "L'Esprit et l'eau" ("Water and the Spirit"), "Magnificat," and "La Maison fermée" ("The Locked House") employ explicit biblical and Christian terms. In these odes Claudel proved himself a master of evocative beauty and emotion. Another work from the early part of his career, *Connaissance de l'Est* (1900; expanded, 1907; translated as *The East I Know*) is a group of beautiful prose poems on Oriental topics.

One of Claudel's best-known dramas is *L'Annonce faite à Marie* (1912; translated as *The Tidings Brought to Mary;* revised, 1948), based on his earlier *La Jeune Fille Violaine* (1901; The Girl Violaine), written in 1892–1893 and revised in 1898–1900. *L'Annonce faite à Marie* is set in the Middle Ages and dramatizes what some see as a moving affirmation of faith, even a miracle; to others the work is cumbersome and naive, even preposterous. *Partage de midi* (1906; translated as *Break of Noon*) is a psychological and spiritual drama involving a love triangle. The plot is based on an affair Claudel had before his marriage in 1906. *Le Soulier de satin* (1929; translated as *The Satin Slipper*), set at the time of Spanish settlement of the New World, is another drama of love and belief. Like the rest of Claudel's dramatic work, this elaborate play is difficult to produce; it was, however, successfully staged in

Paris in 1943 by **Jean-Louis Barrault** and followed by revivals of some of Claudel's earlier plays.

From his distant diplomatic posts Claudel maintained correspondence with many French literary figures, including **André Gide,** whom he tried in vain to convert to Catholicism. With other writers, including **Francis Jammes,** his proselytizing was more successful. In addition to dramatic and nondramatic poetry Claudel published literary criticism and biblical commentary. In his later decades he occupied a lofty position in conservative and Catholic circles. He was elected to the Académie Française in 1946.

REFERENCES:

Louis Chaigne, *Paul Claudel, The Man and the Mystic,* translated by Pierre de Fontnouvelle (New York: Appleton-Century-Crofts, 1961);

Joseph Chiari, *The Poetic Drama of Paul Claudel* (New York: Gordian Press, 1969);

Bettina L. Knapp, *Paul Claudel* (New York: Ungar, 1982);

John MacCombie, *The Prince and the Genie: A Study of Rimbaud's Influence on Claudel* (Amherst: University of Massachusetts Press, 1972);

Harold A. Waters, *Paul Claudel* (New York: Twayne, 1970).

— C.S.B.

RENÉ CLÉMENT

Best known for *La Bataille du rail* (1945; *Battle of the Rails*) and *Les Jeux interdits* (1952; *Forbidden Games*), two movies set in northern France during the 1940s, director-screenwriter René Clément (1913–) combined technical precision with keenly crafted scenarios in all his film work, setting a postwar standard not easily surpassed.

Clément studied architecture at the renowned Ecole des Beaux-Arts before trying animation and directing *Soigne ton gauche* (1936; Watch Out on the Left) with **Jacques Tati.** He worked on documentaries in Africa and the Middle East and collaborated with **Jean Cocteau** on *La Belle et la bête* (1946; *Beauty and the Beast*). Between 1945 and 1975 Clément wrote and directed a total of eighteen feature films.

La Bataille du rail was shot outside the studio with nonprofessional actors. A sketchy, unconnected series of episodes follows members of the **Resistance** during **World War II** as they bomb a German supply train, take hostages, and kill them without remorse. Sharing a great deal with **André Malraux's** perspective in *L'Espoir* (1937; *Man's Hope*), the film influenced many future French filmmakers.

Teamed with screenwriter Jean Aurenche, Clément revived the **tradition de qualité** in *Les Jeux interdits,* a delicate and probing study of children's reactions to the trauma of losing family in war. The movie focuses on their ritual compensations — their forbidden games — to mediate death and social misery. The somewhat-contrived script does not detract from the vigorous realism that depicts the gamut of the children's emotions. Close-ups and arresting points of view align the film with innovations that are otherwise associated with **François Truffaut** and **Jean-Luc Godard.** After the almost Italian neorealist style of *La Bataille du rail*, such an intensely psychological treatment of wartime trauma was unexpected. The film received the grand prize at the prestigious Venice Festival.

Clément's movies exhibit a clearly drawn signature that is at once literary and indebted to psychological realism. These characteristics are apparent even in his lesser films, such as his 1958 adaptation of **Marguerite Duras**'s early novel *Un Barrage contre le Pacifique* (*This Angry Age*), which was shot in Hollywood and Italy with Richard Conte, Silvana Mangano, and Anthony Perkins.

REFERENCES:

Roy Armes, *French Cinema Since 1946,* second edition, enlarged, volume 1: *The Great Tradition* (London: Zwemmer / Cranbury, N.J.: A. S. Barnes, 1970), pp. 94–104;

André Forwagi, *René Clément* (Paris: Seghers, 1967).

—T.C.

HENRI-GEORGES CLOUZOT

For nearly a decade and a half after **World War II,** Henri-Georges Clouzot (1907–1977) was among the most popular and critically acclaimed French directors. He is remembered for his carefully planned and edited films, especially his thrillers.

Like many of his generation, Clouzot came to cinema as a writer. While working for *Paris-Midi* in 1930 he was offered a position in the motion-picture industry that soon put him under the tutelage of E. A. Dupont and Anatole Litvak. After a bout with pleurisy that kept him in sanitoriums from 1934 to 1938, Clouzot took up screen writing and soon directed and helped to script his first feature, *L'Assassin habite au 21* (1942; *The Murderer Lives at 21*). In 1943 he completed *Le Corbeau* (*The Raven*) — a film that led to false charges of conspiracy with the Nazis because it was subsidized by a German company and was believed by some to impugn the French character. *Le Corbeau* was banned for two years after the **Liberation,** and Clouzot was prevented from directing for six months.

His 1947 *Quai des orfèvres* (*Jenny Lamour*) won him the best-director prize at the 1947 **Cannes Film Festival,** but the movie that made his popular reputation was *Le Salaire de la peur* (1953; *The Wages of Fear*), a remake of Raoul Walsh's *They Drive by Night* (1940), a taut tale of wildcat truckers. Clouzot's version includes breathtaking views of machinery on steep mountainsides. The vapid but eerie thriller *Les Diaboliques* (1955; *Diabolique*), starring **Simone Signoret,** follows the strategy behind a murder and was also popular. Strict adherence to contrived plotlines, plus a mechanical adaptation of the techniques of Alfred Hitchcock and Fritz Lang, assigns these and other films by Clouzot to a secure but derivative place in film history. He was also widely praised for his documentary *Le Mystère Picasso* (1956; *The Mystery of Picasso*), which the French government declared a national treasure in 1984.

REFERENCES:

Roy Armes, *French Cinema Since 1946,* second edition, enlarged, volume 1: *The Great Tradition* (London: Zwemmer / Cranbury, N.J.: A. S. Barnes, 1970), pp. 81–93.

—T.C.

JEAN COCTEAU

The immensely talented and prolific Jean Cocteau (1889–1963) may be best known to English-language audiences as the creator of the haunting films *Le Sang d'un poète* (1932; *The Blood of a Poet*), *La Belle et la bête* (1946; *Beauty and the Beast*), and *Orphée* (1950; *Orpheus*). He was also a playwright, a novelist, and a poet, and he worked with **Serge Diaghilev, Léonide Massine, Pablo Picasso,** and **Erik Satie** on the groundbreaking *Parade* (1917), often called the first truly modern ballet, as well as creating the innovative *Le Bœuf sur le toit* (1920), a spectacle with music by **Darius Milhaud.**

Cocteau's works demonstrate his commitment to modern aesthetics, particularly the principle of surprise in art. He held many of the same artistic principles as the **Surrealists,** though there was a mutual animosity between Cocteau and the members of that group. Cocteau's *Le Potomak* (1919), a work comprising poetry, prose, and drawings, probably had its source in automatic writing like that practiced by the Surrealists. Yet, paradoxically, Cocteau could also produce works, such as *Les Enfants terribles* (1929; translated as *Children of the Game*), that are in the best tradition of the French psychological novel, with a structured plot and a controlled, but sensitive, style. Indeed, he appreciated the classical tradition, which he praised in his essay *Le Secret professionnel* (1922; translated as *Professional Secrets*), and he could write prose rivaling that of the seventeenth-century masters.

Jean Cocteau and Pablo Picasso with a piano cover designed by Cocteau for the Anchorena family of Argentina in 1943 (Segalab)

His creations range in tone — sometimes within the same work — from the farcical and the melodramatic to the tragic and the ethereally poetic.

Such versatility and showmanship inevitably inspired criticism. Detractors claimed that Cocteau was shallow, too changeable, too willing to sacrifice quality in order to dazzle. This tendency was visible from his earliest appearance on the artistic scene — when actor Edward de Max gave a staged reading of the poems of his eighteen-year-old friend Cocteau — and it continued to the end of his life. He could always dash off a poem or a drawing or even a book with ease and was apparently at home in most artistic forms and genres.

His detractors notwithstanding, Cocteau's achievement is immense, in quality as well as quantity. He produced an eccentric and poetic war novel, *Thomas l'imposteur* (1923; *Thomas the Impostor*); he wrote an *Antigone* (1928) and two versions of the story of Oedipus, *Œdipe-roi* (1928; Oedipus the King) and *La Machine infernale* (1934; *The Infernal Machine*). Staged with modernist lighting, the second of these plays combines borrowings from William Shakespeare's *Hamlet* and the life of **Isadora Duncan** with

bits of farce and an eccentric fatalism to give new life to the myth. Cocteau also did his own *Roméo et Juliette* (1928) and adapted Tennessee Williams's *A Streetcar Named Desire* for the Paris stage in 1949. He wrote about homosexuality in *Le Livre blanc* (*The White Paper*), published anonymously in 1928, and about drugs in *Opium, journal d'une désintoxication* (1930; *Opium: The Diary of an Addict*) — after having taken opium in despair over the death of his lover and protégé **Raymond Radiguet** in 1923. Cocteau's play in the form of a monologue, *La Voix humaine* (1930; *The Human Voice*), is a perennial favorite.

Many of Cocteau's works center around the figure of the adolescent, as in *Thomas l'imposteur* and *Les Enfants terribles*. Others deal with the destiny of the poet and the creative process, and still others with human relationships. Many readers and audiences have felt transported into another world by Cocteau's creations, whether a pleasingly fanciful one or a somber, threatening one, in which neurosis and death are nearly perpetual threats.

While producing his many dazzling works of fiction, drama, and poetry, Cocteau lived the life of the aesthete and prominent member of the avant-garde. He knew and sometimes corresponded with such well-known writers and artists as **André Gide** and **Pablo Picasso;** he cultivated duchesses and pursued official honors — an effort crowned by his election to the Académie Française in 1955.

REFERENCES:

Frederick Brown, *An Impersonation of Angels: A Biography of Jean Cocteau* (New York: Viking, 1968);

Lydia Crowson, *The Esthetic of Jean Cocteau* (Hanover, N.H.: University Press of New England, 1978);

Wallace Fowlie, *Jean Cocteau: The History of a Poet's Age* (Bloomington: Indiana University Press, 1966);

Neal Oxenhandler, *Scandal and Parade: The Theatre of Jean Cocteau* (New Brunswick, N.J.: Rutgers University Press, 1973);

Francis Steegmuller, *Cocteau: A Biography* (Boston: Little, Brown, 1970).

— C.S.B.

DANIEL COHN-BENDIT

Daniel Cohn-Bendit (1945–), who became known as "Danny the Red" during the student riots of **May 1968,** is probably the best-known student leader from that period. The red-haired anarchist was born in France to German Jews who had fled the Nazis. He was registered as a stateless alien, formally adopting German citizenship in 1959 to avoid the French military draft. As a sociology student at the new Nanterre campus of the University of Paris, he was at the center of the student radical movement that began to emerge in France in late 1967. On 22 March 1968 he helped to organize a pivotal demonstration at Nanterre against the arrest of activists in the French campaign against the American military presence in Vietnam. The students who occupied the campus administration building in that demonstration became the nucleus of the "Mouvement du 22 mars" (March 22 Movement), which became an umbrella organization for rebellious students, repelled alike by the government of **Charles de Gaulle** and the conformism and conservatism of the **French Communist Party.**

Cohn-Bendit himself subscribed to a body of political and social theory firmly in the tradition of such nineteenth-century French anarchists as Jean Grave and Elisée Reclus. He codified these views in his *Le Gauchisme, remède à la maladie sénile du communisme* (1968; translated as *Obsolete Communism: The Left-Wing Alternative*). The title itself is a parody of *Left-Wing Communism: An Infantile Disorder* (1920), a famous manifesto by Vladimir Ilyich Lenin. In his introduction Cohn-Bendit described his book not as a historical account but as a polemic and part of an ongoing debate concerning the social and political events of May and June 1968, which for him proved that "revolution is possible in even a highly industrialized capitalist society." The issue for him, therefore, was not whether a social revolution was possible but what form it would take. A central issue was how to derail any attempt to guide spontaneous uprisings into a centralized, Leninized model. Cohn-Bendit counterpoised a somewhat-romanticized account of Nestor Makhno's rural anarchist guerrilla activity in 1918–1921 to the model of the Bolshevik uprising and concluded his manifesto with a call to arms.

Unlike many other participants in the 1968 upheaval, Cohn-Bendit remained true to his vision. Working for a time as an organizer of automobile workers, then as a preschool teacher, he was an active participant in a large 1986 reunion of militants in the German student radical movement; he was also a founding member of the German Green movement, and he edits an "alternative libertarian" review in Frankfurt am Main.

REFERENCES:

David Caute, *The Year of the Barricades: A Journey Through 1968* (New York: Harper & Row, 1988);

Daniel Cohn-Bendit and Gabriel Cohn-Bendit, *Obsolete Communism: The Left-Wing Alternative,* translated by Arnold Pomerans (New York: McGraw-Hill, 1969);

Alain Schnapp and Pierre Vidal-Naquet, *The French Student Uprising, November 1967–June 1968: An Analytical Documentary,* translated by Maria Jolas (Boston: Beacon, 1971).

— J.H.

COLETTE

Sidonie-Gabrielle Colette (1873–1954) was the most notable woman writer in France during the first half of the twentieth century, and her reputation remains well established. Some readers, especially in France, see her as a great stylist; and this evaluation is justified, for her writing combines felicitous, sometimes poetic, turns of phrase and pithy expressions of sharp psychological insights. Others consider her a connoisseur of domestic animals or a masterful painter of maternity and childhood as she experienced it in the provinces before the turn of the century. Still other readers value most her portraits of various social strata, especially a slightly shady artistic milieu in Paris before 1914 and the world of gigolos, cocottes (kept women), and actresses. Since the late 1960s Colette has been studied by scholars interested in the status and psychology of women.

Colette's life and the mores of many of her heroines suggest a woman unconcerned with conventional morality and determined to break out of the mold im-

Colette, 1907, in costume for the pantomime *Rêve d'Egypte*

posed on her sex. Colette grew up in the department of Yonne. In 1893, at age twenty, she married an older, established writer, Henry Gauthier-Villars, whose pen name was Willy. She began her career by ghostwriting *Claudine à l'école* (1900; translated as *Claudine at School*) for him. She published *Dialogues de bêtes* (Animal Dialogues) under the name Colette Willy in 1904 but continued ghostwriting for Willy through 1905. *Claudine à l'école,* based on her own experiences and written in a racy style, was followed by three others with the same heroine (1901–1903). After several years of unhappy marriage, Colette left Gauthier-Villars in 1906 and started a new, controversial career as a mime and actress, appearing onstage in provocative roles. During this period of her life she had several lesbian affairs, notably with the wealthy American expatriate Natalie Barney. In 1910 she published *La Vagabonde* (translated as *The Vagabond*), a novel in her mature manner, in which she investigates unhappy love and the temptations of sensualism.

In 1912 she married Henry de Jouvenel, a politician; the union lasted until 1923 and produced one daughter, on whom Colette doted. Colette's best-known novel, *Chéri* (1920; translated) concerns an affair between a woman in her forties and a much younger man. During the same period Colette was involved in a liaison with her stepson Bertrand de Jouvenel, her junior by more than thirty years. When this affair

ended, Colette became involved with Maurice Goudeket, whom she married in 1935.

The scandals so often attached to Colette were an asset to her career and probably remain responsible in some measure for her enduring fame. Yet it should not be thought that her works did not attract readers on their own merits. **Marcel Proust** was an early admirer, and **André Gide,** not an indulgent critic, praised the style of *Chéri*, which is characterized by concision and *le mot juste*. These qualities were also illustrated in the sequel, *La Fin de Chéri* (1926; translated as *The Last of Chéri*), and in other works from the decade, including *La Maison de Claudine* (1922; translated as *My Mother's House*), which memorializes her mother, and *Le Blé en herbe* (1923; translated as *The Ripening*), concerning two young lovers and an older woman.

In 1932 she published *Ces plaisirs* (translated as *The Pure and the Impure*), a novel expressing her views on homosexuality, and the following year she produced *La Chatte* (translated as *Saha the Cat*), about a triangular relationship in which a man prefers his cat to his wife. Among the books that followed, *Mes apprentissages* (1936; translated as *My Apprenticeships*), an explicitly autobiographical study, deserves attention for the light it sheds on her marriage to Willy. In 1944 she published *Gigi et autres nouvelles,* whose title story is one of her best-known works, made famous in the United States by the 1958 movie starring Leslie Caron and **Maurice Chevalier.** By 1945, when she became the first woman elected to the Académie Goncourt, Colette, despite her risqué past, had become a respectable and much-honored figure, a grande dame of French literature.

REFERENCES:

Margaret Davies, *Colette* (London: Oliver & Boyd, 1961);

Erica Mendelson Eisinger and Mari Ward McCarthy, *Colette: The Woman, The Writer* (University Park & London: University of Pennsylvania Press, 1981);

Elaine Marks, *Colette* (New Brunswick, N.J.: Rutgers University Press, 1960);

Joanne Richardson, *Colette* (London: Methuen, 1983);

Joan Stewart, *Colette* (Boston: Twayne, 1983).

— C.S.B.

COMBAT

Combat was an underground newspaper that gave its name to a **Resistance** group during the German **Occupation** of France during **World War II**. The newspaper was founded in November 1940 by Henri Frenay in Lyons, which was located in the **Free Zone** and thus not under direct German control until the zone was taken over in November 1942. First published as *Mouvement de Libération Nationale* (Movement for National Liberation), the paper represented the views of Frenay's underground political group. Renamed *Combat* in 1941, the paper was published clandestinely throughout the Occupation. The first issue to circulate openly appeared in Paris on 21 August 1944, four days before the **Liberation** of the city. After the Liberation, *Combat* became a Parisian daily, with a left-of-center but non-Communist orientation. Its best-known contributing editor was **Albert Camus.** His columns on the major issues of the day, which appeared regularly from 1944 to 1947, aroused a great deal of public controversy. *Combat* ceased publication in 1974.

The political movement whose views were expressed in *Combat* continued under Frenay's leadership and was active throughout the southeastern part of France. The organization had a strong Catholic component and recruited primarily among professional people and intellectuals, including civil servants, engineers, industrialists, and university professors.

Perhaps its most famous member was the now-legendary Jean Moulin, who was executed by the Germans in summer 1943; it is possible that he was denounced by rival Resistance members who felt he had an overly close relationship with the Communists and who feared that he was trying to transform the underground movement into a clandestine version of the **Popular Front.**

REFERENCES:

Marie Granet and Henri Michel, *Combat: Histoire d'un mouvement de Résistance de juillet 1940 à juillet 1943* (Paris: PUF, 1957);

Alan Morris, *Collaboration and Resistance Revisited* (London: Berg, 1992).

— D.O'C.

EMILE COMBES

Born in Roquecourbe (Tarn), Emile Combes (1835–1921) received his doctor of theology degree in 1860, then broke with the Catholic church and took up medicine. As a member of the Radical Party, he was elected a senator in 1885; he subsequently served as vice-president of the Senate (1894–1895), minister of public education (1895–1896), and premier (1902–1905). A staunch anticlerical, he supported measures restricting teaching by members of the religious orders and otherwise weakening clerical influence on the government and society of France. He proposed the legislation for separation of Church and State that became known as the Combes Law (1905).

REFERENCES:

R. D. Anderson, *France 1870–1914: Politics and Society* (London: Routledge & Kegan Paul, 1977);

Michael Sutton, *Nationalism, Positivism and Catholicism: The Politics of Charles Maurras and French Catholics, 1890–1914* (Cambridge: Cambridge University Press, 1982).

— C.S.B.

LA COMÉDIE-FRANÇAISE

Founded in 1680 under the edict of Louis XIV, the Comédie-Française in Paris (also known as the Théâtre Français) is the oldest government-subsidized national theater of France. It was created by the merging of three previously existing theater companies, including Molière's. Since 1812, under rules drawn up by Napoleon I, the Comédie-Française has been governed by its actor-members, known as *sociétaires,* who are responsible, under the direction of a general administrator, for artistic decisions. For most of the twentieth century, during which time it was housed at the Palais-Royal (Place André Malraux), it took as its principal mission the preservation of the French theatrical heritage, offering classic plays to generations of schoolchildren and interested adults for a reasonable price in an elegant, historical hall.

But tradition-centered organizations risk losing their public through failure to adapt to changing times. Under the administration of Emile Fabre (1918–1936), which was characterized by dwindling audiences and meager subsidies, the Comédie-Française sought to include new plays in the repertory, but the reading committees of *sociétaires* made some unfortunate choices, and the "Maison de Molière" maintained its reputation as boring and hidebound.

In 1936 the government search for a new administrator led first to playwright **Jean Giraudoux** and to director Louis Jouvet, who had been highly successful in his own theater. When they each refused the task, playwright Edouard Bourdet accepted it, but not without first demanding and obtaining greatly increased subsidies and a controlling voice in repertory selection and artistic decisions. He began by hiring **Jacques Copeau,** along with **Cartel des Quatre** members **Gaston Baty, Charles Dullin,** and Jouvet — then the best, most original directors in Paris — to direct plays at the national theater.

As this infusion of new blood was bringing the theater to life again, **World War II** abruptly interrupted. The Comédie-Française closed its doors when Nazi **Occupation** armies entered Paris in June 1940; after the expunging of all Jewish names from the list of *sociétaires,* the theater quickly reopened the same year. Copeau was named the new administrator, and the theater survived under Nazi censorship through the war years. The highlight was the 1943 presentation of **Paul Claudel**'s monumental work *Le Soulier de satin* (translated as *The Satin Slipper*), which concerns the Spanish conquest of Central America and could be read as having anti-Nazi overtones, although its public apparently included many German officers. French audiences seemed to have drawn strength from it, despite its length of about five hours. It was directed by the brilliant young **Jean-Louis Barrault,** who also acted in it, as did **Madeleine Renaud.**

After the war playwright André Obey administered the theater (1945–1947) and established a two-house system: the **Théâtre de l'Odéon** was combined with the Comédie-Française and baptized the Salle Luxembourg because of its proximity to the Luxembourg Gardens. There more modern and experimental plays were performed, while the "old" theater, now called the Salle Richelieu after a nearby street, retained the classical repertory. This system continued with varying success under several administrators until 1959, when the Odéon regained its autonomy. In 1955 actors from the Comédie-Française took plays on tour in the United States. Since then the artistic direction has changed with successive administrations, but some of the classical repertory is still performed. Late in the century the Comédie-Française began operating three halls, having taken under its wing the Théâtre Mogador and the **Théâtre du Vieux-Colombier.**

REFERENCES:

Pierre Dux, *La Comédie-Française racontée par Pierre Dux* (Paris: Perrin, 1982);

Anne Surgers, *La Comédie-Française: Un théâtre au-dessus de tout soupçon* (Paris: Hachette, 1982).

— R.J.N.

COMMUNE

While *Commune,* a revolutionary left-wing monthly, was relatively short-lived (July 1933–September 1939), it was the preeminent left-wing French journal of the 1930s. The official magazine of the militant **Association des écrivains et artistes révolutionnaires,** it was created to extend the work of the **French Communist Party** and international Communism into the cultural sphere and to forge an alliance between intellectuals and manual workers. The most important of the many left-wing writers of the 1930s — including **Louis Aragon, Henri Barbusse, André Gide,** and **Paul Nizan** — were involved with the magazine, either as contributors or members of the editorial staff.

The first issue of *Commune,* described as "une revue de combat" (a magazine of struggle), was largely written by Nizan, who put forth a platform of class war and proletarian revolution in opposition to the threat of fascism — not only in Germany, where Adolf Hitler had just become chancellor, but also in France, where some believed much of the bourgeoisie wanted a fascist government.

Commune was noteworthy for the importance it ascribed to intellectuals and artists, as opposed to scientists and social scientists, and for its acceptance of the avant-garde in the form of **Surrealism,** although the relationship between the Communists and the Surrealists was stormy. (For example, **Tristan Tzara** and René Crevel broke ranks with the Surrealists' leader, **André Breton,** in the early 1930s and proclaimed the vital importance of the collective in the transformation of society, as opposed to Surrealism's emphasis on the individual.)

A June 1935 writers' congress organized by *Commune* anticipated the victory of the **Popular Front** one year later. From September 1936 on, *Commune* took as its subtitle *Revue Littéraire Française pour la Défense de la Culture* (French Literary Review for the Defense of Culture). The association from which it had sprung had been dissolved a few months before, and the new version of the magazine — the journal of the **Maison de la Culture** — was less optimistic than the old and even less militant in advocating revolution. Faced in the late 1930s with the growing threat of war,

Scene from *Le Viol de Lucrèce*, performed by La Compagnie des Quinze

the magazine's writers saw alliance with the Soviet Union as the only hope for peace. The German-Soviet pact of August 1939 caused a schism among its editors; *Commune* was subsequently suppressed, along with all other journals that had expressed support for the Soviet Union.

REFERENCE:

Wolfgang Klein, *Commune: Revue pour la défense de la culture (1933–1939)* (Paris: Editions du CNRS, 1988).

— J.P.McN.

La Compagnie des Quinze

La Compagnie des Quinze, a "company of fifteen" former disciples of director **Jacques Copeau,** was active primarily from 1929 to 1934. With Michel Saint-Denis, Copeau's nephew, as their director and with André Obey as resident playwright, they performed at the **Théâtre du Vieux-Colombier** in Paris in 1931 and 1932. They also appeared regularly in England, spreading Copeau's ideas about revolutionizing the theater by thorough training for actors and by turning from naturalistic to ritualistic dramas similar to Bertolt Brecht's conception of "epic" theater. The ideas of the Compagnie des Quinze were not widely accepted by traditionalists, but their innovations were adopted by the avant-garde.

Some members of the company had been associated with Copeau during the early 1920s at the Théâtre

du Vieux-Colombier; they had all participated in Copeau's theater laboratory (1924–1929) in Burgundy, where the local farmers called the group "les Copiaus." After the breakup of the company due to financial problems and personal conflicts in 1934, Saint-Denis worked in England, Canada, and the United States, where he passed on Copeau's training to the rising generation of actors.

REFERENCES:

Denis Gontrand, ed., *Le Journal de bord des Copiaus* (Paris: Seghers, 1974);

Michel Saint-Denis, *Training for the Theatre: Premises and Promises,* edited by Suria Saint-Denis (New York: Theatre Arts Books / London: Heinemann, 1982).

— R.J.N.

Concrete Music

Concrete music, or *musique concrète,* is the name given to a type of experimental music developed by Pierre Schaeffer (1910–), a sound engineer at the Paris studios of the French National Radio in 1948. Working first with disc recordings but soon thereafter with tape, he recorded sounds, such as an automobile accelerating or a door slamming, and then altered them by playing the tape faster, or slower, or backward, to create a vocabulary of sounds from which a composition could be constructed. He called such works musique concrète because he worked di-

Jacques Copeau in the title role of *Les Fourberies de Scapin* at the Théâtre du Vieux-Colombier, 1920

rectly with sounds without the intervention of musical notation, instruments, or performers.

At first only short works were made, such as his *Etudes aux chemins de fer* (1948; Railroad Studies), which was not a recording of a train starting but an assemblage of train sounds. Another was his *Etude aux casseroles* (1948; Saucepan Study), based on the clatter of pans and dishes.

After Schaeffer was joined by composer Pierre Henry (1927–   ) they constructed more-serious compositions, such as their *Symphonie pour un homme seul* (1949–1950, revised 1966; Symphony for a Man Alone), based on modified vocal sounds (breathing, laughter, cries), and their *Le Voile d'Orphée* (1953; The Veil of Orpheus), which includes a reading of a Greek Orphic hymn.

In 1951 a Groupe de Musique Concrète was formed, and **Pierre Boulez, Olivier Messiaen,** and Edgard Varèse created compositions in the medium. Vladimir Ussachevsky and Otto Luening, professors at Columbia University, were among the first to use the idiom in the United States.

REFERENCE:

Bryan R. Simms, *Music of the Twentieth Century: Style and Structure* (New York: Schirmer, 1986), pp. 384–386.

— P.S.H.

JACQUES COPEAU

Although the directing career of Jacques Copeau (1879–1949) was short, the principles of staging and of training actors he developed at the **Théâtre du Vieux-Colombier** in Paris embody the spirit of the best French theater between the world wars and remained influential in many serious theaters in France and abroad well into the 1970s. Often authoritarian in his dealings with actors, he nonetheless left his mark on the theater.

Having worked as a theater critic for Paris periodicals and served from 1909 to 1913 as a director of the *Nouvelle Revue Française,* which he helped found with **André Gide, Jean Schlumberger**, and others, Copeau began directing plays in a theater he called the Vieux-Colombier in 1913. After a brilliant season his theater was closed for the duration of **World War I.** He managed to travel abroad, spending time with theater theorists such as **Edward Gordon Craig** and **Adolphe Appia** and corresponding with two of his best collaborators, **Charles Dullin** and **Louis Jouvet,** who were serving in the armed forces.

In 1917 the French government dispatched Copeau and most of his troupe, including Jouvet and Dullin, as goodwill ambassadors to New York while the United States considered entering the war. In two seasons the company staged more than forty plays and offered some three hundred performances at the old Garrick Theater. In 1919 Copeau reopened the Vieux-

Colombier and presented full seasons through 1924, when he "retired." That year he re-created the acting school he had developed in 1921 in conjunction with his Paris theater, establishing a sort of theater laboratory in the Burgundy countryside. After Copeau withdrew in 1929, the group continued as the **Compagnie des Quinze** (the Company of Fifteen) under the direction of Michel Saint-Denis. Copeau then traveled, giving lectures and play readings; he also directed periodically at the **Comédie-Française** from 1936 to 1940 and served as administrator there in 1940–1941, at the time of and after the fall of France.

Copeau's manifesto "Un Essai de rénovation dramatique: Le Théâtre du Vieux Colombier" (An Attempt at Renewing Drama: The Théâtre du Vieux-Colombier), published in the September 1913 issue of the *Nouvelle Revue Française,* proposed several goals for the theater. Referring to contemporary playwrights as "a handful of entertainers in the pay of shameless merchants," he attacked the profit motive and called for an independent theater capable of surviving on its receipts while offering the public reasonably priced seats. He also promoted repertory theater, disparaging long-running hits and decrying their stultifying effect on actors. Instead, he proposed a series of alternating plays, which would allow actors in the company to hone their skills on various roles within a single season. These plays, he wrote, should be of high artistic merit. Seeking to revive French classical theater and inspire the writing of poetically superior contemporary drama, Copeau berated the facile farces and exploitation pieces that enriched the **boulevard theaters** at the expense of true theater art. Theater, he thought, should educate the public taste rather than exploit it.

Further, the creation of "star" actors, according to Copeau, was simply a sales ploy of the commercial theater; it could only destroy the unity of a good troupe and make actors untrainable. Instead, Copeau sought to form a team of disciplined actors, each capable of a wide range of difficult roles and trained in all facets of their craft, including dancing, singing, improvisation, physical endurance, and breath control. For Copeau, everything — from stagecraft to setting to acting — was to be subordinate to the playwright's script; the director's duty became the accurate transmission of the text. Opposing both the overloaded realist sets of **André Antoine** and the Symbolist excesses of **Aurélien Lugné-Poe,** Copeau called for simplicity: "Let other gimmicks disappear, and for the new opus, leave us a bare stage."

Copeau's influence, pervasive until long after **World War II,** was spread by those he trained — notably his nephew and disciple Saint-Denis, who worked

in England, Canada, and the United States after 1934; and in France the **Cartel des Quatre.**

REFERENCES:

France Anders, *Jacques Copeau et le Cartel des Quatre* (Paris: Nizet, 1959);

Marcel Doisy, *Jacques Copeau ou l'Absolu dans l'art* (Paris: Le Cercle du Livre, 1954);

Maurice Kurtz, *Jacques Copeau: Biographie d'un théâtre* (Paris: Nagel, 1959);

Georges Lherminier, *Jacques Copeau* (Paris: Presses Littéraires de France, 1953);

John Rudlin, *Jacques Copeau* (Cambridge: Cambridge University Press, 1986).

— R.J.N.

La Coupole

Located at 102 Boulevard de Montparnasse in Paris, this popular **Left Bank** bar and restaurant was opened in 1927 by Ernest Fraux and René Lafon, not far from the well-known **Café du Dôme.** Decorated by thirty-two artists who resided in **Montparnasse** — including Moïse Kisling and **Fernand Léger** — the Coupole was an immediate success, attracting many of the same artists and writers who patronized the Dôme and the **Café de la Rotonde** across the street. During the 1920s the Coupole was also a regular meeting place for a group of Russian émigrés dominated by writer Ilya Ehrenburg. Another member of the group was **Elsa Triolet,** whom **Louis Aragon** met at the Coupole in 1928. Foreign and refugee artists and writers continued to frequent the Coupole throughout the 1930s and 1940s.

REFERENCES:

Billy Klüver and Julie Martin, *Kiki's Paris: Artists and Lovers 1900–1930* (New York: Abrams, 1989);

Kenneth E. Silver, *The Circle of Montparnasse: Jewish Artists in Paris 1905–1945* (New York: Universe Books, 1985).

— C.S.B.

Edward Gordon Craig

Edward Gordon Craig (1872–1966), a British director and theorist, exercised a major influence on the conception of theater in France, his primary country of residence after 1931. Expressing his views in *The Art of Theatre* (1905), *Towards a New Theatre* (1913), *The Theatre Advancing* (1921), and *Books and Theatres* (1925), he described the director as the free aesthetic interpreter of the script, indeed as artistic creator of the staged work, equal to or more important than the playwright. In this conception theater is no longer a branch of literature, but a visual art in its own right, dominated, disciplined, and styled by the director. French *metteurs-en-scène* (producer-directors), beginning with **André Antoine** and **Aurélien Lugné-Poe,** had been moving in the same direction as Craig. **Jacques Copeau,** who nonetheless insisted on the primacy of the written text, joined the **Cartel des Quatre** in pushing this conception of the director even further, taking strict charge of every phase of staged performance from acting, diction, and blocking to settings, costumes, and lighting.

REFERENCES:

Denis Bablet, *Edward Gordon Craig,* translated by Daphne Woodward (London: Heinemann, 1966);

Edward Craig, *Gordon Craig: The Story of His Life* (New York: Knopf, 1968);

Christopher Innes, *Edward Gordon Craig* (Cambridge: Cambridge University Press, 1983).

— R.J.N.

FERNAND CROMMELYNCK

Dramatist Fernand Crommelynck (1886–1970) wrote farces and carnivalesque plays that combine comic and tragic elements in bringing to bear a merciless and cruel analysis of human flaws. Filled with tense situations and grotesque moments, Crommelynck's plays plumb the depths of vice and expose human beings as funny yet monstrous.

Crommelynck was born in Paris to a French mother and a Belgian father. His father and uncle were actors, and he grew up in the theater world. During his teens the family settled in Brussels; it is possible to identify in his work, often described as baroque, something of the Belgian carnival spirit that can be seen in the work of Pieter Brueghel and other Flemish painters. Parallels also have been drawn between Crommelynck and such painters as James Ensor and Francisco Goya, whose grotesque world is a projection of psychological horrors.

Crommelynck began publishing plays shortly after the turn of the century. Produced in 1908, *Le Sculpteur des masques* (1911; translated as *The Sculptor of Masks*) is a successful mixture of farce and the macabre and one of his major plays. Set during Mardi Gras, it explores the position of the artist in society, the power and anguish of unlawful passion, and the violence that always threatens to break through human custom. Death is a powerful presence in the play. In *Le Sculpteur des masques* the dramatist uses masks to personify the disorderly inner world.

His *Le Cocu magnifique* (1921; translated as *The Magnificent Cuckold*) has been called the best farce

since those of Molière; yet questions of sexuality are raised more explicitly, and more disturbingly, than in Molière. A husband, erroneously accusing his wife of infidelity, forces her to sleep with another man to confirm that he has been cuckolded. The play thus explores the psychology of jealousy and the power of fantasy. It was successfully produced by **Aurélien Lugné-Poe** in Paris in 1920 and in Moscow in 1922 in a highly praised experimental staging.

Crommelynck's other major plays include *Les Amants puérils* (1921; The Childish Lovers), which unmasks personal illusions and was directed in Paris by **Gaston Baty,** and *Tripes d'or* (1930; Golden Intestines), a brilliant and ferocious study of avarice. About a miser who dies from eating gold, it was a commercial failure when it was produced by **Louis Jouvet** in 1925, but it remains a powerful study of human lust, combining elements featured in such Molière plays as *L'Avare* (translated as *The Miser*) and *Le Malade imaginaire* (translated as *The Hypochondriac*) with carnivalesque and crude scatological elements.

Crommelynck's theater is important for its introduction of resources of meaning other than speech. His innovations, including an emphasis on gesture and the use of masks, in some cases antedated or paralleled those of other important innovators of the modern theater, including **Alfred Jarry.** Crommelynck also stands out for the importance his work gives to collective psychology, as in the depiction of mass hysteria. In his dramas laughter is less a corrective to behavior than a terrible unmasking of the depths of human feeling.

REFERENCES:

David I. Grossvogel, *The Self-Conscious Stage in Modern French Drama* (New York: Columbia University Press, 1958);

Bettina L. Knapp, *Fernand Crommelynck* (Boston: Twayne, 1978).

— C.S.B.

CUBISM

Cubism was a relatively short-lived artistic movement that flourished in France in the decade before **World War I,** but its influence is unprecedented in modern art. Its emphasis on form and on capturing the essence of objects makes it the forerunner of later styles and movements in abstract art.

Historians of art and cultural historians are obliged to deal with more than one definition of the term *Cubism.* In the first decades of the twentieth century Cubism played such a pivotal role in avant-garde circles that it became common to use the term as a synonym for any vaguely abstract trend in art. In the late decades of the century some histories and analyses of Cubism have tended to apply the term broadly, including various contending (and partly overlapping) peripheral figures and trends that engaged, however briefly, with Cubist ideas, while other studies restrict discussion to the work of painters such as **Pablo Picasso, Georges Braque, Fernand Léger,** and **Juan Gris** and sculptors such as Picasso and **Jacques Lipchitz.**

The immediate origins of Cubism can be found in the works of the **Fauves** and of **Paul Cézanne.** Braque is the most prominent Cubist to have emerged from the Fauvist movement, although both Gris and Léger came from much the same milieu. The Cubists were also influenced by the attempts by **Henri Matisse** and his colleagues to simplify form and color, eliminating superfluous detail and residual traces of naturalism. But Cubism marked the beginning of still another search in art: an attempt not so much toward simplification as toward the breakdown and analysis of form. In that process Cézanne's insistence on underlying geometric forms in nature (notably the rod, cone, and cylinder) played a major role.

At the end of the nineteenth century artists had begun to go beyond domestic popular art as a source for their compositions, beginning with midcentury infatuations with Japanese woodblock prints. By the first decade of the twentieth century Picasso was looking for new ideas in two directions: pre-Roman Iberian sculpture, marked by blocky, massive figures with blunt, flat features, and more thoroughly abstracted and stylized African ceremonial masks, which were appearing on the Parisian market as a result of French colonial conquests. Picasso made no real effort to study the context, meaning, or purpose of these works; rather, he employed them primarily as a source for formal ideas and motifs and as a kind of format through which he could carry on his experiments with shape and color. Initiating what many critics call early Cubism, his *Les Demoiselles d'Avignon* (1907), a study of prostitutes in a brothel, acknowledges a debt to both sets of images: the somewhat geometricized, sharp-angled figures at left are clearly based on Iberian sculpture, while both figures at right — highly stylized, flattened, and situated ambiguously in space — derive from simplified adaptations of African masks. Equally important is the relation of the figures to the background: though they still stand out in color from the red, gray, and blue background, all five figures are embedded in that background, which is made up of ill-defined prismatic shapes.

The adjective *Cubist* was first used in 1908 by critic Louis Vauxcelles in reference to Braque's landscapes. The paintings produced by Picasso and Braque in 1908–1912 are devoted to the analysis and decomposition of volume in space and are conventionally termed Analytical Cubism. The development of this style was neither smooth nor continuous. The general direction can be identified, however, if one compares Picasso's 1910 portrait of **Ambroise Vollard** with his *L'Accordéoniste* (1911; *The Accordionist*). In the Vollard portrait the figure of the art dealer is relatively intact, though partly disassembled into overlapping flangelike shapes. Color is muted but largely naturalistic, grouped around the tans of Vollard's skin and the gray of his suit. In *L'Accordéoniste* all that remains of the musician is a kind of ridge or spine down the center of the painting; everything else has been dispersed across the canvas. Colors are limited to gray, brown, and a dark green, spread out in small patches across the surface.

Synthetic Cubism, which flourished from 1911 into the years of World War I, marked a radical redefinition of the whole nature of representation. Instead of re-creating the image of a place or milieu, artists undertook to build up a collage involving a variety of materials, including those set in or linked to the place itself. For example, in *Nature morte (Fantômas)* (1915; Still-Life: Fantômas) Gris assembled a variety of substances — from the cover of the potboiler thriller that gives the collage its name to part of the newspaper *Le Journal* to wood-grained paper and the image of a pipe — to suggest not a scene from *Fantômas* but a small café where it might have been read.

The efforts of Picasso and Braque were increasingly influential in a radical artistic circle. Among those drawn to Cubism were a handful of Parisian painters who seized a room at the 1911 **Salon des Indépendants** to proclaim their Cubist affiliation, most notably **Jean Metzinger, Albert Gleizes,** and **Henri Le Fauconnier.** Gleizes and Metzinger even took on the task, rejected by Picasso and Braque, of defining Cubism itself. Their *Du cubisme* (1912; translated as *Cubism*) treats the Cubist movement as the offspring of Cézanne and the culmination of decades of effort to reject a "superficial realism" (Impressionism) in favor of a "profound realism" aimed at realizing the essence, not merely the appearance, of reality. The art produced by Gleizes and Metzinger, however, is often condemned as a superficial borrowing of certain Cubist stylistic devices layered over otherwise traditional paintings. In part this condemnation stems from a tendency to see Picasso and Braque as the defining poles of Cubism and to classify projects different from theirs as misunderstandings or mislabelings. In any event, Gleizes used Cubism as a transition toward abstractions of flat, brightly colored geometric shapes. Metzinger's works, while perhaps not as superficial as usually claimed, are often awkward joinings of certain Cubist techniques or motifs (usually the partial disassemblage of forms) with a straightforward and traditional rendering of the scene. His *Danseuse au café* (1912; *Café Dancer*), for example, differs from Picasso works of 1910–1911 not only in its bright colors but in the fact that the figures and surrounding café scene are analyzed and disassembled only where they will not interfere with the easy interpretation of the picture by the viewer.

Cubism did not die with World War I, but Picasso and Braque began to move in other directions, and for those artists, such as Gris, who continued to work in the vein, Cubism became increasingly a personal style, part of an interacting continuum of avant-garde circles and movements. Cubism's descendants — Futurism, the Orphism or Simultanism of **Robert** and **Sonia Delaunay,** the De Stijl movement in the Netherlands —

flourished as Cubism proper became part of history, a set of ideas to be referred to and used as needed by experimental artists.

REFERENCES:

Douglas Cooper, *The Cubist Epoch* (London: Phaidon, 1971);

Cooper and Gary Tinterow, *The Essential Cubism: Braque, Picasso, and Their Friends, 1907–1920* (New York: Braziller, 1984);

Pierre Daix, *Cubists and Cubism* (Geneva: Skira, 1982);

John Golding, *Cubism: A History and an Analysis, 1907–1914* (Boston: Boston Book & Art Shop, 1959);

Christopher Green, *Cubism and Its Enemies* (New Haven: Yale University Press, 1987);

Robert Rosenblum, *Cubism and Twentieth-Century Art* (New York: Abrams, 1961).

—J.H.

D

EUGÈNE DABIT

Fiction writer Eugène Dabit (1898–1936) was a chronicler of the working classes from which he came. His left-wing sympathies and close acquaintance with anarchists and socialists contributed to his sensitive depictions of the proletariat, which were admired by **André Gide** and **Roger Martin du Gard,** both of whom advised Dabit on his writing.

Dabit's first novel, *L'Hôtel du Nord* (1929; translated as *Hotel du Nord*), which won the Prix Populiste, is largely based on his family's experiences during the 1920s, after his parents, who were of modest means, had managed to buy a small hotel. Their proletarian lodgers reappear in the loosely constructed book, which documents the loneliness and misery of city dwellers without means in France during the decade that followed **World War I.**

Petit-Louis (1930; Little Louis) draws on Dabit's experiences in the artillery during the war and documents the ways in which the conflict offered financial opportunity for many in the working classes. *Villa Oasis; ou les Faux-Bourgeois* (1932; Oasis Villa; or the Phony Bourgeois), which Gide considered Dabit's best book, concerns a brothel owner based on one of Dabit's uncles. The theme of this novel — as well as *Un Mort tout neuf* (1934; A Fresh Corpse) and *La Zone verte* (1935; The Countryside) — is the danger of worshiping the false god money. Dabit died in 1936, during a visit to the Soviet Union with a delegation of left-wing writers.

REFERENCE:

David O'Connell, "Eugène Dabit: A French Working-Class Novelist," *Research Studies,* 41 (December 1973): 217–233.

— C.S.B.

DADA

Dada was a short-lived but significant movement in literature and art that arose during **World War I** and continued into the 1920s. Although it began as an artistic expression, Dadaism soon came to embody rebellion against the war and the societies responsible for it. The anarchism and even nihilism of Dada expressed despair arising from wartime slaughter of human beings and the apparent death of human values inherent in it.

Dada was founded in February 1916 in Zurich by several artists who gathered at the **Cabaret Voltaire;** among them were **Tristan Tzara** (usually considered the leader), **Jean Arp,** Hugo Ball, and Richard Huelsenbeck. This cosmopolitan group claimed that the name *Dada* was meaningless and found by chance in a dictionary. (The word signifies a child's hobbyhorse.) After organizing some initial entertainments at the cabaret — which included untraditional music and simultaneous recitation of experimental poems in several languages — the group published a pamphlet, *Cabaret Voltaire* (May 1916), with contributions from Arp, **Pablo Picasso, Guillaume Apollinaire,** and others. The Cabaret Voltaire closed in July 1916, but the group continued to stage Dada entertainments and opened its "Galerie Dada" in Zurich in March 1917. In July they published the first issue of a magazine, *Dada,* which continued to appear, at irregular intervals, until 1921. The "literature" that appeared in *Dada* bore little resemblance to anything that had been considered literature before; much of it was cultivated nonsense.

The Dadaists, whose movement derived in part from Italian Futurism and its fascination with the modern, especially with the mechanical and technological, proposed to destroy all conventional notions of art in order to emancipate the literary and visual imagination. Their impulse was destructive and radical, turning easily to social protest. Their slogans were "Dada means nothing," and "Dada destroys and nothing more." They were particularly opposed to the bourgeoisie, whom they methodically set out to shock, just as the Romantics had done a hundred years before. Dada groups were organized in other cities — including Barcelona, New York, and Berlin — in addition to Zurich.

Around 1920 Dada artists **Marcel Duchamp, Francis Picabia,** and **Man Ray** took Dada from New York to Paris, where Tzara had also settled. They held festivals and other activities, often rowdy, and attracted **André Breton,** who had independently rebelled against conventional literature and was determined to seek a complete renewal in the arts and thought. With Breton as intermediary, Dada exercised considerable influence on **Surrealism,** but by 1924, when Dadaism had practically expired, Breton and his associates had distanced themselves from it, and Breton denied its importance as a movement.

REFERENCES:

Willard Bohn, ed. and trans., *The Dada Market: An Anthology of Poetry* (Carbondale & Edwardsville: Southern Illinois University Press, 1993);

Dada-Constructivism: The Janus Face of the Twenties (London: Annely Juda Fine Art, 1984);

John D. Erickson, *Dada: Performance, Poetry, and Art* (Boston: Twayne, 1984);

Manuel L. Grossman, *Dada: Paradox, Mystification, and Ambiguity in European Literature* (New York: Bobbs-Merrill, 1971).

— C.S.B.

Poster announcing François Darlan's talks with commissioners at Vichy on 19 February 1942

the war he returned to European films while continuing to make appearances in American movies such as *Gentlemen Prefer Blondes* (1953) and *Catch-22* (1970).

REFERENCE:

Marcel Dalio as told to Jean-Pierre Lucovich, *Mes Années folles* (Paris: J.-C. Lattès, 1976).

— W.L.

MARCEL DALIO

Marcel Dalio (1900–1983) was one of the leading character actors of pre–World War II French cinema. Though not physically impressive, he created memorable performances through his subtle characterizations.

In *La Grande Illusion* (1937; *Grand Illusion*), directed by **Jean Renoir,** Dalio played Rosenthal, a wealthy and amiable Jewish prisoner of war who supplies his fellow prisoners with food and wine. He created his greatest role, the nobleman Robert de Chesnaye, in Renoir's *La Règle du jeu* (1939; *The Rules of the Game*).

During the **Occupation** the Nazis displayed Dalio's face on posters in Paris as that of the "typical Jew." Dalio immigrated to the United States and made his first American film in 1941. He played the croupier in *Casablanca* (1943), but after that movie he did not find other parts that suited his distinctive talents. After

FRANÇOIS DARLAN

François Darlan (1881–1942), a career naval officer, was an important figure in the **Vichy government** during the German **Occupation** of France in **World War II.** Because he later cooperated with the Allies, his controversial wartime career has been interpreted from widely different perspectives in written accounts of the period.

Darlan commanded the Atlantic Squadron between 1934 and 1936. The title "Amiral de la Flotte" (Fleet Admiral) was created for him. He was commander-in-chief of French naval forces from 1939 to 1940. In the Vichy government he became navy minister in June 1940, and Premier **Philippe Pétain** chose Darlan as his successor. In February 1941 Darlan's responsibilities were increased after the dismissal of Vice-premier Pierre Laval, who was ousted under suspicion of trying to wrest power from Pétain. Following an interview with Adolf Hitler at Berchtesgaden in May 1941, Darlan signed the May Protocols, which gave the Germans valuable facilities in Syria and North Africa. The agreement was rejected by the Vichy government in June. The Germans returned Laval, a Nazi sympathizer, to power in April 1942, making him the real authority in the Vichy government, with Pétain remaining as a figurehead. Darlan resigned his governmental duties but retained his military command. In November 1942 he signed the armistice with the invading Anglo-American forces in Algiers. A month later he was assassinated by Fernand Bonnier de la Chapelle.

REFERENCES:
Peter Tompkins, *The Murder of Admiral Darlan: A Study in Conspiracy* (New York: Simon & Schuster, 1965);
Alexander Werth, *France 1940–1955* (Boston: Beacon, 1966).
— C.S.B.

DANIELLE DARRIEUX

Actress Danielle Darrieux (1917–) appeared in her first film in 1931 at age fourteen and has had a distinguished film career extending over more than six decades. She has particularly excelled in sophisticated comedies and romantic dramas where her wit, beauty, and aristocratic manner have been well displayed.

Darrieux's success as the beautiful and tragic Marie Vetsera in Anatole Litvak's *Mayerling* (1936) opened the international film world for her, but her major performances have been in the films of French directors Henri Decoin (her first husband), **Claude Autant-Lara,** and **Max Ophuls.**

During the early part of her career, Darrieux's performances were marked by elegance and sophistication. Later, in Ophuls's *La Ronde* (1950; *Rondelay*) and *Le Plaisir* (1952; *The House of Pleasure*), she used her considerable talents to create performances of great pathos: an understanding and sympathetic married woman who is confronted with her lover's impotence in *La Ronde* and a cynical prostitute in *Le Plaisir*. Perhaps her greatest performance was in Ophuls's *Madame de . . .* (1953; *The Earrings of Madame De*), where she played an aristocratic woman who is destroyed when a casual affair develops into a futile passion.

Darrieux possessed a fine singing voice, which she used on the stage and the screen. She played Marie Deverone, a French cabaret artist, in the 1951 M-G-M musical *Rich Young and Pretty* and worked often in a wide range of challenging character roles from the 1950s through the 1980s.

REFERENCE:
Richard Whitehall, "Danielle Darrieux," *Films and Filming* (December 1961).
— W.L.

THE DEBACLE

The French have often used the term *Debacle* to characterize the Battle of France, which opened hostilities between the German and French armies in **World War II,** lasting for six weeks (10 May–22 June 1940) and ending in ignominious defeat for the French army.

Although slightly outnumbered at the outbreak of hostilities (114 divisions to 94), the French were on the whole better armed and better equipped than the Germans. Moreover, if British and Dutch divisions are counted along with French troops, the Allies enjoyed virtual parity with the Germans. France made the mistake of relying on its defenses: having built the **Maginot Line** along the eastern border with Germany, the French waited for attack there and felt confident they could meet the challenge. The invasion came, however, through Belgium, which the Germans quickly overran before moving into France. Opposition was insufficient, and the Germans drove retreating forces to **Dunkirk** and poured over the roads leading south. Of the five million men under arms for France, some ninety thousand were killed; two hundred thousand were wounded; and 1.8 million were captured by the enemy.

REFERENCE:
Alistaire Horne, *To Lose a Battle: France 1940* (Boston & Toronto: Little, Brown, 1969).
— D.O'C.

GUY DEBORD

Writer and avant-garde filmmaker Guy-Ernest Debord (1931–1994) was perhaps the best-known and most influential figure in the **Situationist International** movement — largely because of his pamphlet *La Société du spectacle* (1967; translated as *The Society of the Spectacle*). His writings furnish the theoretical underpinnings for the work of a broad range of contemporary critics, from art historian T. H. Clark to critic of popular culture Greil Marcus. Debord especially influenced **Jean Baudrillard,** whose later work nonetheless diverges from Debord's Marxist-influenced critique of capitalist society.

Debord affiliated with the **Lettrist** movement of **Isidore Isou** in 1952, after the controversial screening of an Isou film at the **Cannes Film Festival.** (Lettrists created deliberately nonsensical art using letters or symbols without combining them into recognizable words.) Debord's own film debut came in the same year with *Hurlements en faveur de Sade* (Howls for de Sade), a fragmented arrangement of bits and pieces of Lettrist dialogue between four men and a woman; the screen was white when the characters spoke and black when they were silent, which was roughly sixty of the film's eighty minutes. Bits and pieces of film history were sandwiched between discussions of the suicide of the **Surrealist** Jacques Vaché and the fate of Jack the Ripper. The work sparked riots at showings in London and Paris. It also led to the formation of the Lettrist International (LI), a more militant, activist, and leftist faction of Lettrism. Later that year, when Isou distanced himself from an LI assault on a showing of Charlie Chaplin's 1931 movie *City Lights,* the breach between Debord and Isou became permanent.

In 1957 Debord led the LI into the new Situationist International. Within this new group he assumed a key role as theoretician and artist-activist. His 1959 film *Sur le passage de quelques personnes à travers une assez courte unité de temps* (On the Passage of a Few People through a Rather Brief Moment in Time) is a kind of postmortem for the Lettrists, in which reminiscences of Lettrist ideas and actions mingle with disconnected quotes appropriated from classical thinkers. Throughout the movie the goal is to emphasize the gulf between any documentary re-creation of events and real life.

Debord's international influence derives in large part from *La Société du spectacle.* An assemblage of theoretical musings and 221 numbered photographs, the book begins with the statement that "in societies where modern conditions of production prevail, all of life presents itself as an immense accumulation of *spectacles.* Everything that was directly lived has moved away into a representation." The spectacle — defined as "capital accumulated until it becomes an image" — plays the role of "the existing order's uninterrupted discourse about itself, its laudatory monologue." In this sense, the spectacular society is not simply an array of bread-and-circus events to divert attention or gain popularity for a given regime. On the contrary, it becomes the chief way in which people respond to and interpret the world, an all-embracing mediating framework encompassing and justifying the commodification

of leisure and private life. While individual initiative and autonomy are constantly praised in such a society, men and women are in practice reduced to passive participants in an oppressive social matrix.

Debord's response to the society of spectacle was to call for spontaneous resistance by the workers, who would thus "effect the dissolution of all classes by bringing power into the dealienating form of realized democracy, the Council . . ." He expressed the concern, however, that even the critique of spectacle might serve to retain it. Only when a critique is wedded to a practice of ongoing resistance, he believed, can it even hope to be effective. Debord's analysis of spectacular society, together with the deliberately provocative style of the Situationists, helped to frame not only the form but some of the demands of the French student movement in **May 1968.**

REFERENCES:

Guy Debord, *The Society of the Spectacle* (London: Rebel Press, 1987);

Greil Marcus, *Lipstick Traces: A Secret History of the Twentieth Century* (Cambridge, Mass.: Harvard University Press, 1989);

Sadie Plant, *The Most Radical Gesture: The Situationist International in a Postmodern Age* (London & New York: Routledge, 1992);

Elisabeth Sussman, ed., *On the Passage of a Few People through a Rather Brief Moment in Time: The Situationist International, 1957–1972* (Cambridge, Mass.: MIT Press, 1989).

— J.H.

CLAUDE DEBUSSY

Claude Debussy (1862–1918) was the most important and influential French composer of the twentieth century. His use of medieval modal scales and whole-tone scales instead of the modern major and minor scales, his free use of dissonance, and his unconventional harmonies opened up areas of music that have been explored ever since. In a real sense, twentieth-century Western music begins with Debussy.

The compositions he wrote before 1900 show his transition from a talented young composer of salon pieces to a mature artist with a highly personal and original style. In Debussy's early work Jules Massenet's influence is strong in his cantatas *L'Enfant prodigue* (1884; The Prodigal Son) and *La Demoiselle élue* (1888; The Blessed Demoiselle); that of **Gabriel Fauré** is visible in his *Suite bergamasque* (1890) for piano, which includes his most frequently performed composition, *Clair de lune* (Moonlight). As this familiar piece demonstrates, Debussy's early music was delicate, charming, and occasionally sentimental.

Cover of the catalogue for the Debussy Exposition, May 1942

his sensitive treatment of the instruments. The titles of many of his compositions, such as "Jardins sous la pluie" (1904; Gardens in the Rain), "Poissons d'or" (1907; Goldfish), and "Feux d'artifice" (1910–1913; Fireworks) suggest Impressionist paintings.

Debussy's major compositions include *Pelléas et Mélisande* (1892)—his only opera, which was based on the Symbolist drama by **Maurice Maeterlinck**—and his important piano pieces, in which he employed new sonorities, unusual timbres through unusual pedal techniques, and elaborate broken-chord figures dispersed over the keyboard. His principal works for orchestra, *La Mer* (1905; The Sea) and *Images* (1912), evoke colorful pictures of the sea and of Spain. He did not write lengthy, serious symphonies, believing that "Extreme complication is contrary to art."

Because of Debussy's failing health, his production declined in his last years. His principal works from this period are the ballet *Jeux* (1912), twelve etudes for piano (1915), and three sonatas: for cello and piano; flute, viola, and harp; and violin and piano (1915–1917). A definite change in style is found in these later compositions, in which the lush, evocative sounds of impressionism give way to a simpler, more austere ideal.

REFERENCES:

Stefan Jarocinski, *Debussy: Impressionism and Symbolism,* translated by Rollo Myers (London: Eulenberg Books, 1976);

Edward Lockspeiser, *Debussy: His Life and Mind,* 2 volumes (New York: Macmillan, 1965; revised edition, Cambridge: Cambridge University Press, 1978);

Arthur B. Wenk, *Claude Debussy and Twentieth-Century Music* (Boston: Twayne, 1983).

— P.S.H.

Prélude à L'Après-midi d'un faune (1894; Prelude to "The Afternoon of a Faun") is Debussy's most important early orchestral piece. The half-dreaming soliloquy of the faun in Stéphane Mallarmé's poem is well reflected in the sound of the orchestra, which features the flute and other woodwinds, the harp, and muted horns; it is reflected likewise in the relaxed tempo and sinuous melodies of the piece. The whole-tone scales and augmented chords, however, made its first performance controversial. The piece was later used in the well-known 1912 ballet choreographed by **Vaslav Nijinsky** for **Serge Diaghilev.**

Debussy's compositions between 1900 and 1910 include the masterpieces of Impressionist music that established him as a major composer. While the term *Impressionism* was first used to describe paintings by artists such as Auguste Renoir, **Claude Monet,** and Camille Pissarro, it has been applied with justice to the music Debussy composed during 1900–1910 because of similarities of aims and methods. The painters worked to achieve the effect of light on objects and landscapes by juxtaposing touches of pure color, while Debussy created new tone color through his orchestrations and

JEAN DELANNOY

Throughout his enormously productive career in film, Jean Delannoy (1908–) was a major proponent of the **tradition de qualité,** which based production on strict adherence to carefully wrought screenplays.

A director of and contributor to more than forty features, Delannoy won the 1946 **Cannes Film Festival** Prize for best film for *La Symphonie pastorale (The Pastoral Symphony)*, based on the book by **André Gide.** He also adapted **Jean-Paul Sartre**'s *Les Jeux sont faits* (1947; *The Chips are Down*), Victor Hugo's *Notre Dame de Paris* (1956; *The Hunchback of Notre Dame*), and Madame de Lafayette's *La Princesse de Clèves* (1960; *The Princess of Cleves*). Delannoy was the president of the Institut des Hautes Etudes Cinématographiques (IDHEC) in 1975.

Sonia and Robert Delaunay, 1923. His painting *Propeller* is behind them.

REFERENCES:

Evelyn Ehrlich, *Cinema of Paradox: French Filmmaking under the German Occupation* (New York: Columbia University Press, 1985);

C. D. E. Tolton, "D'André Gide à Jean Delannoy: L'optique de *La Symphonie pastorale*," *Texte et Médialité,* 7 (1987): 279–302.

—T.C.

ROBERT DELAUNAY

Robert Delaunay (1885–1941) and his wife, **Sonia Delaunay-Terk,** played pivotal roles in the development of the modernist art movement in Paris. His variations on **Cubism,** which stressed the importance of color over form, provided an important step in the transition to complete abstraction and influenced artists such as Paul Klee and the Italian Futurists.

Delaunay obtained most of his technical training in a studio producing backdrops for theaters. He began painting seriously in 1904. His early work was heavily influenced by the Impressionists and to a lesser extent by the **Fauves,** but by 1910 the influence of **Paul Cézanne** and friendships with **Jean Metzinger** and especially **Fernand Léger** brought Delaunay close to the first Cubist experiments. For Delaunay the importance of Cézanne and the Cubists lay above all in their ef-

forts to break apart objects, leaving them "existing as a collection of pieces." His painted studies of the Eiffel Tower in 1910 and 1911, which he later termed his "destructive" period, exemplify this newfound interest in the fragmentation of material objects. The tower is alternately wrenched apart and unfolded in a technique that opens up multiple, simultaneous views of the structure and its surroundings. Similar treatments of the cathedral at Laon and the Church of Saint-Séverin in Paris soon followed.

Delaunay's artistic collaboration with his wife, whom he married in 1910, coincided with the onset of his "constructive" period. In a series of views from his open window, large dots of color are assembled to produce a mosaic effect that is increasingly abstracted from any three-dimensional scene. By 1912 he had publicly repudiated any connection to Cubism, and the two Delaunays became engaged in what became known as Orphic or Simultanist paintings, consisting of overlapping, sometimes-segmented, circular forms of flat colors. (**Guillaume Apollinaire** invented the term *Orphisme,* which he described as "painting new structures out of elements that have not been borrowed from visual reality but entirely created by the artist.") Delaunay's paintings during this period sometimes included significant or vestigial representational imagery, as in *Hommage à Blériot* (1914; *Homage to Blériot*), in which circles are juxtaposed with images of airplane propellers, a flying bird, and even a small depiction of the Eiffel Tower in orange. More often, as in his 1912–1913 *Disques* (*Disks*) and *Formes circulaires cosmiques* (*Cosmic Circular Forms*), multicolored disks work as pure color and form without any overt or covert message.

The Delaunays lived in Spain and Portugal from 1914 to 1921. After **World War I** Robert Delaunay's work became more figurative than before. The couple collaborated in 1937 on huge murals for the Palais des Chemins de Fer and the Palais de l'Air for the Paris Exposition Universelle. Delaunay spent the last years of his life painting in rural southern France.

REFERENCES:
Sherry Buckleberrough, *Robert Delaunay: The Discovery of Simultaneity* (Ann Arbor, Mich.: UMI Press, 1992);

Robert Delaunay, *Robert Delaunay* (New York: Crown, 1976);

Gustav Vriesen, *Robert Delaunay: Light and Color* (New York: Abrams, 1969).

             — J.H.

SONIA DELAUNAY-TERK

Sonia Delaunay-Terk (1885–1979) was an influential artist in her promotion of abstraction. Many of her works successfully bridged the division between high art and commercial design.

After studying art in her native Russia, Sonia Terk moved to Paris for further study in 1905. Her first one-woman show was at the Paris gallery of German collector and critic Wilhelm Uhde in 1908. She was briefly married to Uhde before meeting and beginning her lengthy artistic collaboration with **Robert Delaunay,** whom she married in 1910.

From 1911 to 1914 the Delaunays developed the style that became known as Orphism or Simultanism. She credited the conception to a baby blanket she made for their son, Charles, in 1911; the assemblage of bits of flat, brightly colored fabric seemed reminiscent of **Cubist** experiments, although creating no sense of three-dimensional space and involving bold colors utterly alien to the contemporary work of **Pablo Picasso** and **Georges Braque.** Unlike her husband's Simultanist works, which at first reflected his background in conventional Cubism, hers were more throroughly abstract examinations of what she called "color rhythms." She employed the same style to create not only paintings but also collages, book bindings, clothing, and automobile finishes. Delaunay-Terk's oil painting *Prismes électriques* (1914; *Electric Prisms*) is characteristic of her work. Inspired by the bright

halos around the new electric lamps being installed on major Paris streets, it employs overlapping concentric circles, each divided into quadrants of different colors, to create a brilliant, pulsating pattern of complementary colors.

When the 1917 Russian Revolution ended her income from the Terk family fortunes in Russia, Delaunay-Terk responded by moving increasingly into commercial applications of her art, including costume and stage design, interior decorating, and fashion design. In 1924 she set up a studio to produce Simultanist fabrics and clothing. Selections from her patterned fabrics were exhibited at the **Salon d'Automne,** while her "Boutique simultanée," on which she collaborated with couturier Jacques Heim, was a major attraction at the 1925 Exposition Internationale des Arts Décoratifs in Paris. While her commercial enterprises are sometimes considered a retreat from the art world, she rejected the idea that abstract art was necessarily elitist and antidemocratic as well as the common conception that commercial production precluded real artistic quality. She insisted that her designs, mass-produced in ready-to-wear clothing, could play a role in the democratization of aesthetic values, helping to break down traditional barriers among high art, popular art, and commercial design. She consistently sought to unite disparate art forms: during the 1920s she produced a series of "dress-poems," in which dancing figures concealed and unveiled patterns of color and words through the motions of their bodies.

Delaunay-Terk refocused on painting during the 1930s, although she continued to work in commercial design in the following decades. In 1964 she donated several of her paintings to the Louvre, becoming the first living woman artist to have her work exhibited in the museum.

REFERENCES:
Whitney Chadwick, *Women, Art, and Society* (London: Thames & Hudson, 1990), pp. 249–257;

Arthur Cohen, *Sonia Delaunay* (New York: Abrams, 1975);

Sonia Delaunay, *Sonia Delaunay: Rhythms and Colors* (London: Thames & Hudson, 1972);

Axel Madsen, *Sonia Delaunay: Artist of the Lost Generation* (New York: McGraw-Hill, 1989);

Wendy Slatkin, *Women Artists in History*, second edition (Englewood Cliffs, N.J.: Prentice-Hall, 1990), pp. 136–138.

             — J.H.

GILLES DELEUZE

Gilles Deleuze (1925–) is a poststructuralist philosopher who has had a considerable impact on philosophers and literary theorists and critics since the early 1970s. His work, much of it done in collaboration with psychoanalyst Félix Guattari, offers a selective reinterpretation of Western metaphysical traditions in an effort to establish new philosophical bases for inquiry. It is part of a radical break in Continental thought from conventional philosophical modes. Deleuze is also concerned with praxis, which philosophers define as action in the world, and the social and political implications of ontology, the nature of being, as well as those of psychoanalysis.

Deleuze first attracted attention in France by editing a collection of philosophical essays, *Instincts et institutions* (1953; Instincts and Institutions), and writing a critical study, *Marcel Proust et les signes* (1964; translated as *Proust and Signs*). More influential, on both sides of the Atlantic, was his and Guattari's two-volume *Capitalisme et schizophrénie* (1972, 1980), especially the first volume, *L'Anti-Oedipe: Le capitalisme et la schizophrénie* (translated as *Anti-Oedipus: Capitalism and Schizophrenia*). In this work they explore desire and production and argue that the Oedipal triangle reflects the structure of capitalism; both, they claim, are associated with a syndrome of repression. Asserting that psychoanalysis and capitalism are intimately related, they argue that the role of labor in a political economy parallels that of the libido or desire in psychoanalysis. Desire itself is a machine driven toward production. Both capitalism and desire, they claim, involve alienation and are highly dependent upon images and myths, representations rather than realities. Thus the Oedipal myth appears to be especially significant because it features the father, the "agent of production." But Deleuze and Guattari reject the validity of the Oedipal myth and its "ridiculous claim to represent the unconscious." Their final argument is that psychiatry must be politicized, asserting that madness would no longer exist in a postcapitalist economy.

Deleuze's many other books, illustrating his difficult but acclaimed readings in the history of philosophy, include *Empirisme et subjectivité: Essai sur la Nature Humaine selon Hume* (1953; translated as *Empiricism and Subjectivity: An Essay on Hume's Theory of Human Nature*); *Nietzsche et la philosophie* (1962; Nietzsche and Philosophy); and *Foucault* (1986; translated).

REFERENCES:

Hazard Adams and Leroy Searle, eds., *Critical Theory Since 1965* (Tallahassee: Florida State University Press, 1986);

Michael Hardt, *Gilles Deleuze: An Apprenticeship in Philosophy* (Minneapolis: University of Minnesota Press, 1993).
                                                                    — C.S.B.

LOUIS DELLUC

The early death of Louis Delluc (1890–1924) did not reduce his enormous impact on French cinema, which continued through the 1950s. As the most prominent movie critic in post–**World War I** France, he successfully promoted cinema as an art form and formulated the concept of *photogénie,* the notion that movies stylize reality without altering it. He offered an extensive but largely uncodified theory of cinema fifty years before such writings became a recognized genre. His theories are worked out in his low-budget movies, whose constructive ideas exceed the quality of their realization.

In 1917 Delluc became the principal editor of the journal *Film,* a position he held until 1919. He also wrote on film for *Paris-Midi* (1918–1923). In 1920 he wrote the scripts for *Fumée noire* (Black Smoke), which he directed with René Coiffard, and *Le Silence* (The Silence), which he directed alone. Delluc also launched the *Journal du Ciné-club* and *Cinéma* (1921–1923). In the last three years of his life he wrote and directed five films, including *Fièvre* (1921; *Fever*).

Delluc almost single-handedly renewed interest in the French cinema industry after the collapse of its worldwide prestige after World War I. Like **Alexandre Astruc** and **André Bazin,** Delluc was a writer who turned to cinema as a means of transmitting his views to a large popular audience. He drew the attention of France to foreign cinema, such as the movies of Cecil B. deMille and Victor Sjöström, and he was the first person to extol the work of directors **Marcel L'Herbier, Abel Gance,** and **Germaine Dulac.**

In his writing Delluc asserted a need for conscious editing — what Bazin later called *découpage* — to underscore the qualities unique to the medium. He favored attention to all the details that create a mise-en-scène. A keen viewer of silent cinema, he noted how action must be controlled with more precision before a lens than on a stage. Delluc also called cinema a populist medium. Le Prix Delluc, named in his honor and granted for an exceptional French feature film, has been awarded annually (except during World War II) since 1937.

REFERENCES:

Richard Abel, *French Cinema: The First Wave, 1915–29* (Princeton: Princeton University Press, 1984);

Abel, *French Film Theory and Criticism, 1: 1907–1929* (Princeton: Princeton University Press, 1988);

Louis Delluc, *Ecrits cinématographiques,* 3 volumes, edited by Pierre Lherminier (Paris: Cinémathèque française, 1986–1990).
                                                                    — T.C.

ALAIN DELON

Alain Delon (1935–) is one of the most popular male stars in contemporary French film, despite a controversy in the 1960s concerning his ties with the underworld.

Delon made his debut in **Yves Allégret**'s *Quand la femme s'en mêle* (1957; *Send a Woman When the Devil Fails*). His first international recognition came with *Rocco e i suoi fratelli* (1960; *Rocco and His Brothers*), directed by Luchino Visconti. Delon played Rocco, a sensitive and thoughtful young man who moves with his hot-tempered brother Simon from Sicily to Milan, where Rocco's devotion to his brother undergoes severe trials.

After making several other pictures in Italy, Delon returned to France, where his roles in several gangster films established his popularity. He appeared with **Jean Gabin** in *Mélodie en sous-sol* (1963; *Any Number Can Win*) and in other distinguished films. In the mid 1960s he began producing some of his own movies. In 1984 he appeared in Volker Schlöndorff's *Un Amour de Swann* (*Swann in Love*), based on the novel by **Marcel Proust**.

REFERENCES:

R. Bean, "Reaching for the World," *Films and Filmmaking* (February 1965);

Olivier Dazat, *Alain Delon* (Paris: Seghers, 1988);

Alain Delon, "Creating with a Passion," *Films and Filmmaking* (June 1970).

—W.L.

JEAN DELVILLE

Artist Jean Delville (1867–1953) played a major role in Belgian Symbolism and in the Salons de la Rose+Croix organized by French Rosicrucian occultist Joséphin ("Sâr") Péladan in the 1890s. Delville led a schism from the Belgian avant-garde umbrella group Les XX in 1892. The same year he founded the Salon d'Art Idéaliste as a Belgian forum for Péladan's ideas. Following Péladan, Delville saw the universe as the emanation of a spiritual being. "Beauty," he wrote, "is one of the manifestations of the Absolute Being."

Delville's fascination with mystical religious ideas and the occult places him broadly within the Symbolist camp. His style, however, remained largely classical, even academic, in its insistence upon a literal, meticulously detailed rendering of his subjects. The goal was to make the mysterious concrete and corporeal: in his *Orphée* (1893; *Orpheus*), for example, the severed head of the musician, slain by Thracian women, floats on his lyre in a wash of blue-green water that reflects the lights of the stars.

The implication in *Orphée* that women are violent and dangerous was not coincidental. As laid down in 1893, Péladan's rules for the Salons de la Rose+Croix excluded women as participants. Auxiliary membership was possible for a woman only if she pledged to keep herself pure by abstaining from sexual love. In Delville's works women are repeatedly depicted as dangerous predators; in the graphite drawing *Idole de la perversité* (1891; *Idol of Perversity*) a Medusa figure, her skin apparently spotted with syphilitic sores, represents women in general. When not actively evil, Delville's female figures are at least alien and unknowable. An 1892 chalk portrait of the wife of Symbolist poet Stuart Merrill depicts her as a bodiless figure with glowing eyes and a mass of floating hair and clasping a book of magic.

Delville joined the faculty of the Glasgow School of Art in 1900. From 1907 until 1937 he taught at the Académie des Beaux-Arts in Brussels.

REFERENCES:

Robert L. Delevoy, *Symbolists and Symbolism* (New York: Rizzoli, 1978);

Robert Goldwater, *Symbolism* (New York: Harper & Row, 1979);

Edward Lucie-Smith, *Symbolist Art* (London: Thames & Hudson, 1972).

—J.H.

JACQUES DEMY

Jacques Demy (1931–1990) merits a place in film history for two of the many movies he wrote and directed, *Lola* (1961) and *Les Parapluies de Cherbourg* (1964; *The Umbrellas of Cherbourg*). His nostalgic works favor spectacle over story and include allusions to **New Wave** films.

Demy, who married film director **Agnès Varda** in 1962, paid homage in *Lola* to **Max Ophuls**'s *Lola Montès* (1955) and Josef von Sternberg's *Der blaue Engel* (1930; *The Blue Angel*). In Demy's *Lola* a confusion between an adult Lola (played by Anouk Aimée) and a daughter Lola makes human relations intertwine and interconnect as history eternally repeats itself in a movie reminiscent of Hollywood musicals. In *Les Parapluies de Cherbourg* Demy treated a subject worthy of Italian neorealism in sugary colors and in rhymed dialogue set to music. The unremitting implications of tragic destiny are conveyed through an almost-cloying mixture of sentimental music and bright colors. Most of Demy's films are marked by combinations of seemingly disparate elements — such as melodrama and realism — and allusions to film classics.

Catherine Deneuve and Jean Sorel in Luis Buñuel's 1967 movie *Belle de jour*

REFERENCE:

Richard Roud, "Rondo galant," *Sight and Sound,* 33 (Summer 1964): 136–139.

—T.C.

CATHERINE DENEUVE

Catherine Deneuve (1943–) was one of the two best-known French film actresses of the 1960s. (The other was **Jeanne Moreau.**) Both director **Luis Buñuel** and Chanel perfumes, for which she made print and television advertisements during the 1980s, drew successfully on Deneuve's aristocratic appearance and flawless, rather icy beauty.

Deneuve's specialty has been the portrayal of remote and aloof women, some of whom have darker sides. In Roman Polanski's *Repulsion* (1965) Deneuve played a woman who goes mad when left alone in an apartment for the weekend. In Buñuel's *Belle de jour* (1967; Beauty of the Day), based on a novel by **Joseph Kessel,** she played the role of Séverine, the beautiful but frigid doctor's wife who finds refuge from an unsatisfactory personal life by working in a brothel. In *Hustle* (1975) Deneuve portrayed a high-priced call

girl, and in **François Truffaut**'s *Le Dernier Métro* (1980; *The Last Métro*), she played a plotter against the Nazis. Deneuve's beauty was effectively employed in Tony Scott's *The Hunger* (1983), in which she played a vampire whose outward beauty masks ravages and decay within. In these various roles, her performances suggest an alluring promise that always seems to escape appropriation. She received an Academy Award nomination for her role in *Indochine* (1992).

REFERENCES:

Vincent Canby, "The Performer vs. the Role: Catherine Deneuve and James Mason," in *The National Society of Film Critics on the Movie Star,* edited by Elisabeth Weis (New York: Viking, 1981);

Roger Vadim, *Bardot, Deneuve, and Fonda,* translated by Melinda Camber Porter (New York: Simon & Schuster, 1986).

—W.L.

MAURICE DENIS

Maurice Denis (1870–1943) played a key artistic and theoretical role in the **Nabis** movement. He developed the concept of "Neo-Traditionism" as a means of depicting what he saw as traditional religious and social truths in an artistic language comprehensible to the modern world.

Denis is perhaps best known for a statement in his 1890 essay "Définition du néo-traditionnisme" (Definition of Neo-Traditionism): "Remember that a picture, before being a war horse, a nude or some sort of anecdote, is essentially a flat surface covered with colors assembled in a certain order." Often used to illustrate the development of European art toward abstraction, Denis's statement actually sought to differentiate what he saw as art's critical symbolic content from naturalistic attempts to capture material realities. For Denis a Byzantine Christ was a symbol, while a modern rendition of Christ was merely literary. In a world increasingly torn apart by conflicts, Denis saw the hermetic forms of ancient sacred art as a source of inspiration. The symbolic content of the supposedly "decorative" art of the Hindus, Assyrians, Egyptians, and Greeks, he believed, made it far superior to contemporary art, which he felt was concerned with depicting "vulgar sensations."

Nonetheless, while certain other artists close to the Nabis, notably Charles Filiger, modeled their work closely on Byzantine models, Denis insisted as well that modern art had to find a modern vocabulary with which to express itself. In a 1912 speech, for example, he noted that creative art is not a form of archaeology; a modern church gains its sacred character from its purpose and function, not from copying Romanesque or Gothic art — styles employed also, he pointed out, in train stations and casinos.

Denis's *Mystère catholique* (1890; *Catholic Mystery*) demonstrates his attempts to work out a balance between the new and the traditional. Employing a variation of the Neo-Impressionist technique of pointillism, the painting takes the form of a traditional Annunciation scene: Mary kneels as an angel greets her with "aspasmos" (hail). Yet the angel wears the vestments of a contemporary priest; in place of a Bible he holds an open missal; and he is attended by two altar boys. The message — as in repeated Annunciations, Visitations, and First Communions painted by Denis through the early 1900s — is that in the contemporary Roman Catholic church the miracles of the Bible are realized daily.

Later in the 1890s Denis abandoned the so-called scientific Neo-Impressionist dotted surface in favor of the "cloisonnist" style newly championed by **Emile Bernard** and **Paul Gauguin.** At Pont-Aven, Brittany, Denis found the balance he sought between the traditional and the new, considering Gauguin the "undisputed Master." At a time when many artists of Denis's immediate generation were adrift, Gauguin provided them with a few clear ideas. Denis's primary inheri-

tances from the older painter were a preoccupation with flat, heavily outlined forms and a quest for an underlying mystical essence beyond the everyday world. He refused, however, to participate in the Symbolist exhibitions of the 1890s, including the Salons de la Rose+Croix, because their mysticism mixed occult elements with Christian ones.

By the early 1900s Denis's search for ways to depict Catholic mysteries had led to a gradual retreat from forms and styles inherited from avant-garde circles. In 1919 he founded the Ateliers d'Art Sacré (Workshops for Sacred Art). His disgust with the modern world led him to the political far Right. He had been a violent anti-Dreyfusard at the time of the **Dreyfus Affair** in the 1890s, and he joined the reactionary **Action Française,** led by **Charles Maurras,** serving as the founder and honorary president of its chapter in Saint-Germain on the outskirts of Paris. He also illustrated Maurras's book *L'Avenir de l'intelligence* (1905; The Future of Intelligence), which described France as a captive of high finance and called for a return to the hereditary monarchy in alliance with the church.

REFERENCES:

Bernard Denvir, *Post-Impressionism* (London: Thames & Hudson, 1992);

Wladyslawa Jaworska, *Gauguin and the Pont-Aven School,* translated by Patrick Evans (Greenwich, Conn.: New York Graphic Society, 1972);

John Rewald, *Post-Impressionism from Van Gogh to Gauguin,* third edition (New York: Museum of Modern Art, 1978).

—J.H.

GÉRARD DEPARDIEU

Possibly one of the finest film actors in France since the 1970s and certainly one of the most prolific, Gérard Depardieu (1948–) is famous in Europe and well known in America.

Born into an impoverished family in Châteauroux in central France, Depardieu was a delinquent as a youth. In 1964 he and a friend, a drama student at the **Théâtre National Populaire** (TNP), left Châteauroux for Paris. The next day he accompanied his friend to the TNP and sat in on a lecture given by director **Charles Dullin.** He also met some of the leading drama coaches teaching at the TNP — Jean-Laurent Cocher, Jean-Pierre Darras, and Georges Riquier. Impressed by Depardieu's passion for the theater and his uncouth manner, they took him on as a student free of charge. His debut at the theater was in the role of Pyrrhus in **Albert Camus's** *Caligula*. The raw energy that he infused into this role mesmerized both the faculty and the students at the TNP, and he was soon considered their star pupil. He spent the remainder of the 1960s performing on stage and television.

By the early 1970s Depardieu had begun to appear in a few small film roles. His appearance in the outrageous *Les Valseuses* (1974; *Going Places*) brought him to public attention. Since then he has starred in an average of three to four films per year, winning international renown in movies such as *Le Dernier Métro* (1980; *The Last Metro*); *Le Retour de Martin Guerre* (1982; *The Return of Martin Guerre*); *Jean de Florette* (1986); *Camille Claudel* (1988), as **Auguste Rodin**; *Cyrano de Bergerac* (1990); *Green Card* (1990), his first American feature film; and *Germinal* (1994).

REFERENCES:

Robert Chazal, *Gérard Depardieu — l'autodidacte* (Paris: Hatier, 1982);

Marianne Gray, *Depardieu* (London: Sinclair-Stevens, 1991).

— M.G.

ANDRÉ DERAIN

Together with **Henri Matisse** and **Maurice Vlaminck**, André Derain (1880–1954) was a leader of the **Fauves** during the first two decades of the twentieth century. After interest in the movement had waned, he returned to a more traditional approach to art.

Derain's early art training, which began in the mid 1890s, was desultory and sporadic. In 1900 he met Matisse and Vlaminck at an exhibition of the works of Vincent van Gogh. The older Matisse talked Derain's parents into allowing him to pursue a career as a painter. Derain and Vlaminck grew especially close, sharing a studio in a decaying former restaurant on the Seine. While Vlaminck rejected the idea of "Great Art," Derain spent considerable time copying paintings in the Louvre. His style was less flamboyant and energetic than Vlaminck's and more tentative and eclectic than Matisse's. It was in 1905, while he was working closely with Matisse at Collioure, that Derain's painting most closely approximated that of his friend and colleague. That year works by Derain, Matisse, and other painters using bold colors were displayed together in the exhibit at the **Salons d'Automne** that earned them the name "les Fauves" (the wild beasts).

Derain was continually torn, however, between his simultaneous fascination with avant-garde art (from van Gogh and **Paul Cézanne** to **Pablo Picasso**) and his underlying academicism. After 1906 he came under the influence of Picasso for a time without ever becoming a **Cubist.** On the contrary, as Cubism began to take shape as a movement, Derain's art reversed direction. The style of his *Les Baigneuses* (1907; *The Bathers*), for example, is an awkward amalgamation of the styles of Picasso, Cézanne, and even Matisse. Derain's three figures are rounded in places, geometricized in others; in some segments of the painting there is a quasi-Cubist analysis of three-dimensional form, while in others there is a dominant flatness reminiscent of Matisse. By the late 1920s Derain's work began to approach a rather formal, sometimes stilted classicism, especially in his still lifes and female nudes. His writings increasingly invoked tradition, myth, and the need to communicate unambiguously with his viewers. Indeed, he came to reject the entire idea of art as experiment.

In 1940, during the German **Occupation** of France in **World War II,** Derain was interrogated by the Gestapo on suspicion of being a Jew; yet in 1941 he went to Nazi Germany as a member of a delegation of artists. Unlike some on the tour, he did not actively take part in German propaganda activities, and he later claimed he made the trip against his will. Nevertheless, the trip effectively terminated not only his influence but even his participation in major artistic exhibitions after the end of the war.

REFERENCES:

Jane Lee, *Derain* (Oxford: Phaidon / New York: Universe, 1990);

Denys Sutton, *André Derain* (London: Phaidon, 1959).

— J.H.

JACQUES DERRIDA

Jacques Derrida (1930–) is widely considered the most influential figure in the philosophical approach to language called deconstruction, which he introduced in a 1966 paper, "Structure, Sign and Play in the Discourse of the Human Sciences," delivered at Johns Hopkins University, where he claimed that **structuralism** was dead and one must go beyond it. Since the late 1960s Derrida has had a tremendous following among literary critics (particularly at Yale University in the 1970s) in the United States, where he has frequently lectured.

Born in Algeria of Jewish descent, Derrida studied in France and Germany and taught philosophy at the **Ecole Normale Supérieure** (1964–1984). Influenced by such thinkers as **Claude Lévi-Strauss,** Ferdinand de Saussure, Edmund Husserl, Martin Heidegger, and Friedrich Nietzsche, Derrida wanted to go beyond the structuralism of Lévi-Strauss and Saussure and beyond Husserl's notion of transcen-

Francis Ponge and Jacques Derrida at a conference in Cerisy-la-Salle devoted to Derrida's work, 1975 (Archives Pontigny-Cerisy)

dental consciousness to "deconstruct" much of the Western metaphysical tradition, which since Plato has seen a referent, or presence, existing behind words. Derrida's argument is that each word or symbol (signifier) in language refers only to another signifier, deferring any transcendent meaning into an endless play of language and undercutting the possibility of any definitive interpretation of a text. He denies even the possibility of defining his own enterprise, claiming that "all sentences of the type 'deconstruction is X' . . . miss the point." Among Derrida's best-known works are *De la grammatologie* (1967; translated as *Of Grammatology*) and *Glas* (1974; translated), which Christopher Norris describes as "a Joycean intertextual commentary on [G. W. F.] Hegel, [**Jean**] **Genet** and the problematic border-line between literature and philosophy."

While some literary critics have admired and emulated Derrida's playfully inventive readings of texts and his assertion that "there is nothing outside the text," other critics and many scholars in the Anglo-American philosophical community have dismissed his work as unintelligible or misguided. Detractors have called his ideas nihilistic, but supporters believe Derrida has opened positive new options within contemporary thought.

REFERENCES:

Geoffrey Hartman, *Saving the Text: Literature/Derrida/Philosophy* (Baltimore: Johns Hopkins University Press, 1981);

Christopher Johnson, *System and Writing in the Philosophy of Jacques Derrida* (New York: Cambridge University Press, 1993);

Christopher Norris, *Derrida* (Cambridge, Mass.: Harvard University Press, 1987);

John Sturrock, ed., *Structuralism and Since: From Lévi-Strauss to Derrida* (Oxford: Oxford University Press, 1979).

— C.S.B.

LOUIS-RENÉ DES FORÊTS

Louis-René des Forêts (1918–) is respected in France for his experiments in narration. Not as well known as the **Nouveaux Romanciers** (New Novelists), he shares their quest to transform traditional modes of narration in fiction; yet his work is less formulaic and more rigorous in its questions about the ability of language to communicate than that of some writers in that group.

Des Forêts's first novel, *Les Mendiants* (1943; translated as *The Beggars),* is decidedly his most conventional work, a novel of action and character, whereas his later fiction—especially the novel *Le Bavard* (1946) and the short-story collection *La Chambre des enfants* (1960; translated with *Le Bavard* as *The Children's Room*) — is concerned with writing itself, a meditation on the inadequacies of language and memory in the self's attempt to project its thoughts into words while hoping to express the value of existence. *Le Bavard,* narrated by a nameless figure fascinated with himself and his self-reflective monologue, may have influenced **Albert Camus**'s creation of the narrator figure in *La Chute* (1956; translated as *The Fall*). The stories in *La Chambre des enfants,* which won the Prix des Critiques, illustrate des Forêts's preoccupation with the relationship between the self and language, as well as with how narratives are constructed and how they attempt to preserve the past.

Des Forêts has also published a long poem, *Les Mégères de la mer* (1967; The Shrews of the Sea). In 1984, after seventeen years of literary silence, he began to publish extracts from a poetical autobiography, *Ostinato.*

REFERENCE:

John T. Naughton, *Louis-René des Forêts* (Amsterdam: Rodopi, 1993).

— C.S.B.

The terrace at Les Deux Magots

ROBERT DESNOS

One of the most talented poets of his immediate generation and one of the literary martyrs of **World War II,** Robert Desnos (1900–1945) started his literary career as a member of the **Surrealists.** He experimented with automatic writing and hypnotic trances and later published a novel on drugs, *Le Vin est tiré* (1943; The Wine Is Drawn). Written in forms varying from poetic prose to the traditional alexandrine, the collection *Corps et biens* (1930; Shipwreck) comprises his poetic work of the 1920s. In 1930, like many other Surrealists, he was expelled from the group by **André Breton,** in part because he found Breton's dogmatic Surrealism too restrictive and in part for his unwillingness to declare his allegiance to a Communist revolution. Yet Desnos did not abandon the Surrealist aesthetic, as is apparent in his experimental radio and film scripts of the 1930s.

As a member of a **Resistance** network during the German **Occupation** of France, Desnos continued to write. Arrested by the Gestapo in 1944, he was deported first to Buchenwald, then Auschwitz, and finally a ghetto/concentration camp in Terezin, Czechoslovakia. Desnos died of typhus shortly after being liberated by the Allies. Controversy over its authenticity surrounds what was long thought to be his last poem, a lyric supposedly written for his wife while he was interned by the Nazis.

REFERENCES:

Pierre Berger, *Robert Desnos* (Paris: Seghers, 1970);

Mary Ann Caws, *The Poetry of Dada and Surrealism* (Princeton: Princeton University Press, 1970);

Wallace Fowlie, *Mid-Century French Poets* (New York: Twayne, 1950);

Michel Murat, *Robert Desnos* (Paris: José Corti, 1988).

— C.S.B.

LES DEUX MAGOTS

This café in the Paris neighborhood of **Saint-Germain-des-Prés,** located on the Boulevard Saint-Germain, next door to the **Café de Flore** and facing the church of Saint-Germain-des-Prés, was popular with Americans, including Ernest Hemingway, and many of the **Surrealists** during the 1920s and 1930s. It became one of the favorite meeting places for **Jean-Paul Sartre, Simone de Beauvoir, Pablo Picasso,** and other intellectuals and artists during the 1930s and 1940s. After **World War II** it continued to be frequented by many other figures from the literary and art world, but it was never as consistently popular as the Flore.

REFERENCES:

Arlen J. Hansen, *Expatriate Paris: A Cultural and Literary Guide to Paris in the 1920s* (New York: Arcade/Little, Brown, 1989);

Herbert R. Lottman, *The Left Bank: Writers, Artists, and Politics from the Popular Front to the Cold War* (Boston: Houghton Mifflin, 1982).

— C.S.B.

Leonti Benois, Serge Grigoriev, Tamara Karsavina, Serge Diaghilev, Vaslav Nijinski, and Serge Lifar at a 1929 performance of the Paris Opera Ballet (Lipnitzki)

SERGE DIAGHILEV

Serge Diaghilev (1872–1929), the great impresario and founder of the **Ballets Russes,** assembled the most innovative and brilliant dance collaborations of the first half of the twentieth century. He transformed classical ballet into a vibrant modern art.

In his native Russia Diaghilev studied law and was a critic and art collector. With Alexandre Benois and Léon Bakst, he founded *Mir Iskusstva* (1898–1904; The World of Art), a controversial, progressive art magazine. After its demise Diaghilev organized art exhibits, operas, and ballets in Saint Petersburg and Paris. In 1908 he produced the successful all-Russian opera *Boris Godunov* in Paris, where on 19 May 1909 he staged a ballet performance that led to the formation of the Ballets Russes. Within the year the stunning premiere performances of *Le Pavillon d'Armide* (Armide's Pavillion), *Prince Igor*, *Le Festin* (The Banquet), and *Les Sylphides* introduced Paris to artists who would forever change the look of ballet. In the course of his career Diaghilev produced more than seventy ballets and eighteen operas.

Diaghilev was not an artist, but he had a flair for discovering and nurturing talent. For the Ballets Russes, he hired five of the century's most gifted choreographers: **Michel Fokine, Vaslav Nijinsky, Léonide Massine, Bronislava Nijinska,** and **George Balanchine.** With them — and with great composers, design-ers, and librettists — Diaghilev produced the first dance masterpieces of the twentieth century. Seventeen works survive, including *Petrouchka* (1911), with choreography by Fokine, music by **Igor Stravinsky,** and sets and costumes by Benois; *L'Après-midi d'un faune* (1912; The Afternoon of a Faun), with choreography by Nijinsky, music by **Claude Debussy,** and sets and costumes by Bakst; *Parade* (1917; Sideshow), with choreography by Massine, music by **Erik Satie,** sets, costumes, and curtain by **Pablo Picasso,** and libretto by **Jean Cocteau;** *Les Noces* (1923; The Wedding), with choreography by Nijinska, music by Stravinsky, and sets and costumes by **Natalia Goncharova;** and *Le Fils prodigue* (1929; The Prodigal Son), with choreography by Balanchine, music by Serge Prokofiev, sets and costumes by **Georges Rouault,** and libretto by Boris Kochno. Renowned dancers engaged by Diaghilev include Alexandra Danilova, **Tamara Karsavina, Serge Lifar,** Lydia Lopokova, Lydia Sokolova, and, briefly, Anna Pavlova.

The Ballets Russes disbanded after Diaghilev's death in 1929.

REFERENCES:

Nancy Van Norman Baer, ed., *The Art of Enchantment: Diaghilev's Ballets Russes, 1909–1929* (San Francisco: Fine Arts Museum of San Francisco, 1988);

Lynn Garafola, *Diaghilev's Ballets Russes* (New York & London: Oxford University Press, 1989);

Boris Kochno, *Diaghilev and the Ballets Russes,* translated by Adrienne Foulke (New York & Evanston: Harper & Row, 1970).

— A.P.E.

KEES VAN DONGEN

A prominent member of the **Fauves** group, artist Kees van Dongen (1877–1968) also supported himself through contributing biting caricatures to satirical reviews. Born in the Netherlands, he moved to Paris in 1899 and obtained French citizenship in 1929.

Van Dongen's first paintings were heavily influenced by the art of Rembrandt van Rijn. His initial attraction to artistic modernism came through politics. In Paris, where he lived in the self-consciously bohemian neighborhoods of **Montmartre,** van Dongen was introduced into the Paris art world by fellow anarchists, including the art critic **Félix Fénéon,** whose gallery held a one-man show for van Dongen in 1909.

Van Dongen's art demonstrates a continuing fascination with individuals on the margins of society, from prostitutes to street sweepers. In a 1908 review **Guillaume Apollinaire** characterized van Dongen as a preeminent social critic, but he used terms that suggest something less than full praise.

By the 1920s, as van Dongen's radicalism began to lessen, he increasingly took on the role of portraitist for the fashionable social and political elite. During **World War II** he was part of a delegation of French artists who toured Nazi Germany in 1941; as with the others, his reputation and career suffered after the war.

REFERENCES:

Joan Ungersman Halperin, *Félix Fénéon: Aesthete and Anarchist in Fin-de-siècle Paris* (New Haven: Yale University Press, 1988);

Theda Shapiro, *Painters and Politics: The European Avant-Garde and Society, 1900–1925* (Amsterdam: Elsevier, 1976).

— J.H.

ROLAND DORGELÈS

Roland Dorgelès (1886–1973) is known almost solely for one book: *Les Croix de bois* (1919; translated as *Wooden Crosses*), one of the best-known novels of **World War I.** Born Roland Lécavelé in Amiens, he went to Paris as an adolescent. Hoping to become a painter, he frequented **Montmartre,** about which he later wrote in *Montmartre, mon pays* (1925; Montmartre, My Homeland). There he met **Pablo Picasso** and other artists and was party to a famous hoax: a painting called *Le Soleil se couche sur l'Adriatique* (Sunset on the Adriatic), hailed by critics as a masterpiece when it was entered in the 1910 competition of the **Salon des Indépendants,** was in reality created by Dorgelès and his friends by tying a paintbrush to a donkey's tail.

Dorgelès, who volunteered as soon as war was declared in 1914, served in the infantry until combat wounds forced him into aviation duty in 1916. When his celebrated novel was published at the end of the war, it won the Prix Fémina. The work reflects his experiences at the front and shows the decency of the common man struggling to survive. Although Dorgelès does not gloss over the misery of life in the trenches, his idealism and love of country were not undermined as was the case with many other writers who served in World War I.

Dorgelès was a literary personality in Paris for more than fifty years and a longtime member of the Académie Goncourt. He wrote other war fiction — including the stories in *Le Cabaret de la belle femme* (1919; translated as *The Cabaret Up the Line*)—and after the war he wrote a series of travel books. In 1939, after **World War II** was declared but before the French army was attacked, he coined the phrase "**la drôle de guerre**" (the phony war).

REFERENCE:

Micheline Dupray, *Roland Dorgelès: Un siècle de vie littéraire française* (Paris: Presses de la Renaissance, 1986).

— C.S.B.

SERGE DOUBROVSKY

Serge Doubrovsky (1928–) is noted for his experimental autobiographical fiction and for his criticism, in which he presents distinctive psychoanalytic readings based on the work of **Jacques Lacan.** Of Jewish extraction, Doubrovsky, who received a *doctorat d'état* at the Sorbonne, settled in the United States in 1955 and has taught at New York University since 1966. Doubrovsky's fictional works include *Le Jour S* (1963; Day S), *Fils* (1977; Son), *Un Amour de soi* (1990; A Love of Self), and *Le Livre brisé* (1991; The Broken Book). He is best-known for critical books such as *Corneille et la dialectique du héros* (1964; Corneille and the Dialectic of the Hero) and *Pourquoi la nouvelle critique? Critique et objectivité* (1966; translated as *The New Criticism in France*). His book on **Marcel Proust,** *La Place de la Madeleine: Ecriture et fantasme chez Proust* (1974; translated as *Writing and Fantasy in Proust*), is one of the most controversial and extreme psychoanalytic studies of the novelist.

REFERENCES:

Hélène Jaccomard, *Lecteur et lecture dans l'autobiographie française contemporaine: Violette Leduc, Françoise d'Eaubonne, Serge Doubrovsky, Marguerite Yourcenar* (Geneva: Droz, 1993);

Marie Miguet, "Critique / autocritique / autofiction," *Les Lettres Romanes,* 43 (August 1989): 195–208.

                                                            — C.S.B.

Publication protesting the court-martial and imprisonment of Alfred Dreyfus

The Dreyfus Affair

The Dreyfus Affair, the most traumatic political event in France between the end of the Franco-Prussian War and the Commune in 1871 and the outbreak of **World War I** in 1914, erupted in 1891 when Alfred Dreyfus, an army captain of Jewish extraction, was accused of passing military secrets to German agents in Paris. In 1894 a military court found him guilty, and he was imprisoned on Devil's Island in French Guiana.

This event was catastrophic not only for Dreyfus and his family but also for French society as a whole, in the still somewhat shaky **Third Republic,** where opponents of democratic government were still numerous. In 1884 Pope Leo XIII had written *Nobilissima Gallorum Gens* (To the Most Noble French People), a papal letter exhorting the French bishops to urge the faithful to accept the legitimacy of the Third Republic. This letter, which called for the *ralliement* (winning over) of Catholics to the cause of democratic government, was intended to heal the open wounds afflicting French society since the French Revolution a century earlier. The Dreyfus Affair short-circuited this program. Catholics and republicans generally took opposing sides in the great national debate about Dreyfus's guilt, as evidence that came to light after the trial increasingly suggested that there had been a miscarriage of justice. On the Catholic side the Ligue de la Patrie Française (League for the French Fatherland) argued that the guilty verdict should not be overturned because the honor of the army was at stake, while on the republican side the Ligue des Droits de l'Homme (League for Human Rights) advocated dismissal of all charges.

The Catholic daily newspaper *La Croix* (The Cross) became the principal advocate of the anti-revisionist position, making many enemies in the process. To the *dreyfusards,* or supporters of Dreyfus, *La Croix,* published by the Assumptionist Order, symbolized the power of the clergy, which they took to be unenlightened and reactionary. After anticlerical political parties came to power in 1899, a series of reforms limiting the power of religious orders was enacted, culminating in the so-called **Combes** Law (1905), separating Church and State.

Not long after Dreyfus was convicted, evidence was discovered indicating that the real criminal in the Dreyfus case was Maj. Ferdinand Walsin-Esterhazy. Yet the army refused Dreyfus a new trial. In addition to pressures from various quarters to defend the army, anti-Semitism, which was widespread, was a factor in this decision. Esterhazy was tried, but he was acquitted in January 1898. Two days later Emile Zola published *J'accuse,* a letter to the president of the republic accusing the government of concealing the truth. After Col. Hubert Henry, one of the chief plotters, committed suicide and Esterhazy confessed, a new trial was ordered, resulting in the verdict of guilty with extenuating circumstances. Dreyfus was pardoned in 1899, and finally, in 1906, he was completely exonerated. The wounds created by the affair remained unhealed, however, through the first half of the twentieth century.

The Dreyfus Affair is reflected in countless literary works of the late nineteenth and the twentieth centuries. Among the major novelists who dealt with it were **Anatole France** and **Marcel Proust.**

REFERENCES:

Jean-Denis Bredin, *The Affair: The Case of Alfred Dreyfus,* translated by Jeffrey Mehlman (New York: Braziller, 1986);

Michael Burns, *Dreyfus: A Family Affair, 1789–1945* (New York: HarperCollins, 1991);

Douglas Johnson, *France and the Dreyfus Affair* (London: Blandford, 1966);

Géraldi Leroy, ed., *Les Ecrivains et l'Affaire Dreyfus* (Paris: Presses Universitaires de France, 1983);

Louis L. Snyder, *The Dreyfus Case: A Documentary History* (New Brunswick, N.J.: Rutgers University Press, 1973).

— C.S.B. & D.O'C.

PIERRE DRIEU LA ROCHELLE

Novelist, essayist, and critic Pierre Drieu La Rochelle (1893–1945) became notorious during **World War II,** when his right-wing politics led him to collaborate with the Germans during their **Occupation** of France. Drieu's politics cast a shadow upon his achievements as a writer. His contemporaries considered him one of the most brilliant writers of his generation. **André Malraux,** Drieu's executor, was an admirer, and Drieu's influence has been seen in the work of **Jean-Paul Sartre** and **Albert Camus.**

Wounded three times in **World War I,** with a deep wound leaving his left arm partially immobile, Drieu was awarded the Croix de Guerre in 1919. As with many other young veterans of that conflict, his wartime experiences left him utterly changed, disillusioned with the values at the heart of French society. In Paris after the war, he became friends with **Louis Aragon** and other **Surrealists,** contributed to their magazine, *Littérature,* and began publishing volumes of poetry and prose, including *Etat civil* (1921; Vital Statistics), a fictionalized autobiography; *Mesure de la France* (1922; The Measure of France), an analysis of his nation's physical and moral decline; and *Le Jeune Européen* (1927; The Young European), an expression of his literary alienation. During the 1920s he also began writing novels. His first, *L'Homme couvert de femmes* (1925; The Man Covered with Women), introduced Gille Gambier, a character who also appears in two of his later novels, *Drôle de voyage* (1933; Strange Journey) and *Gilles* (complete edition, 1942). Drieu's second novel, *Blèche* (1928) portrayed the figure of *le salaud,* the Sartrean man of bad faith.

Drieu's career as an esteemed, though not bestselling, novelist continued in the 1930s. *Le Feu follet* (1931; translated as *The Fire Within*), inspired by the 1929 suicide of Surrealist Jacques Rigaut, depicts the final three days in the life of a drug-addicted failed writer. The fine, painterly novel *Drôle de voyage* was followed by *La Comédie de Charleroi* (1934; translated

as *The Comedy of Charleroi and Other Stories*), a collection of short fiction concerning World War I. Drieu's severe judgments on French society paralleled his growing interest in National Socialism in Germany, and he announced his conversion to fascism with *Socialisme fasciste* (1934; Fascist Socialism). His visit in 1935 to the Nazi congress in Nuremberg convinced him of the promise of Adolf Hitler's vision of uniting Europe.

In 1939 an expurgated edition of *Gilles,* which may be Drieu's major novel, was published. Adding an *s* to the first name of Gille Gambier to indicate his multiple dimensions, Drieu portrayed the life of a man from 1917 to 1937. Drieu's quarrels with friends (he separated with Aragon over political issues), his reputation as a woman chaser (he had two wives and numerous liaisons), and his idiosyncratic judgments on culture and politics had already jeopardized his standing somewhat in the 1930s; but his collaboration sealed his disgrace. His political activities, particularly his editorship of the collaborationist version of the ***Nouvelle Revue Française*** for more than two years, branded him permanently. He published political essays and *Les Chiens de paille* (1944; Straw Dogs), a novel that depicts life in occupied France, and kept a diary that is valuable for its self-portrait and its assessment of France. Some months after the **Liberation** of Paris in August 1944, Drieu committed suicide, leaving an important unfinished work, *Mémoires de Dirk Raspe* (1966; Memoirs of Dirk Raspe), loosely based on the life of Vincent van Gogh. Although his work is currently undergoing some rehabilitation in the United States, his name remains anathema to many in France.

REFERENCES:

Frédéric Grover, *Drieu La Rochelle and the Fiction of Testimony* (Berkeley: University of California Press, 1958);

Rima Drell Reck, *Drieu La Rochelle and the Picture Gallery Novel* (Baton Rouge: Louisiana State University Press, 1990);

Robert Wohl, *The Generation of 1914* (Cambridge, Mass.: Harvard University Press, 1979).

— C.S.B.

LA DRÔLE DE GUERRE

A term coined by novelist and reporter **Roland Dorgelès,** the *drôle de guerre* refers to the nine-month period of **World War II** between the declaration of war and the actual outbreak of hostilities on the Western Front. Seized upon immediately by the British press, the term was translated as "the phony war."

France and Great Britain declared war on Germany on 3 September 1939 after the German armies had invaded Poland. The French army did not attack immediately, however, remaining in its defensive positions behind the **Maginot Line.** This situation lasted until the **Debacle** of May–June 1940, during which the Germans swept around the Maginot Line through Belgium and handily defeated the French.

REFERENCE:

François Fonvieille-Alquier, *The French and the Phony-War, 1939–1940,* translated by Edward Ashcroft (London: Stacey, 1973).

— D.O'C.

CHARLES DU BOS

Charles Du Bos (1882–1939) was an eminent literary critic between the two world wars. His criticism has its basis in aesthetics but also tends toward moral judgments, as in his *Le Dialogue avec André Gide* (1929; Dialogue with André Gide), whose burden is to show that his great contemporary and onetime friend was a demonic writer.

Du Bos wrote books about George Gordon, Lord Byron (1929), and **François Mauriac** (1933). Most of his essays on major nineteenth-century figures in English, German, and French literature are collected in his seven volumes of *Approximations* (1922–1937). Du Bos attempted to write his *approximations* in the manner of his subject, aiming to discover and share the poetic experience of the creative genius. Du Bos is also known as a diarist; the six volumes of his *Journal* were published posthumously.

REFERENCES:

Angelo Philip Bertocci, *Charles Du Bos and English Literature: A Critic and His Orientation* (New York: King's Crown Press, 1949);

Bertocci, "Charles Du Bos and the Critic of Genius," in *Modern French Criticism from Proust and Valéry to Structuralism,* edited by John K. Simon (Chicago: University of Chicago Press, 1972), pp. 61–83;

Charles Hill, "Walter Pater and the Gide-Charles Du Bos Dialogue," *Revue de Littérature Comparée,* 41 (July–September 1967): 367–384.

— C.S.B.

ANDRÉ DU BOUCHET

André du Bouchet (1924–) is a respected poet who won the Prix des Critiques in 1962. Born in Paris, he lived in the United States from 1941 to 1948 and studied in both France and the United States.

Du Bouchet's poetry appears simple but is not immediately accessible. He rejected the aesthetic of **Surrealism** and the rhetoric of Romanticism. Choosing

as his model **Pierre Reverdy,** du Bouchet followed him in writing a chastened poetry characterized by a plain vocabulary and short forms. Yet, like many of his contemporaries, du Bouchet's ambitions for his writing are far from simple. He is interested in the potentialities of language for going beyond the everyday, transforming reality so that the poet may identify and express the hidden and even create a state of epiphany. His verse is written in a variety of forms, including prose poems, *versets* (long, flexible free verse), and short unrhymed lines. Collections of du Bouchet's poetry include *Au deuxième étage* (1946; On the Second Floor), *Le Moteur blanc* (1946; White Motor), *Sol de la montagne* (1956; Mountain Soil), *Dans la chaleur vacante* (1959; In Vacant Heat), *Où le soleil* (1968; Where Is the Sun), *L'Incohérence* (1979; Incoherence), *Rapides* (1980; Rapids), *Le Surcroît* (1990; The Increase), and *Verses* (1990).

REFERENCE:

Serge Gavronsky, *Poems and Texts* (New York: October House, 1969).

— C.S.B.

JEAN DUBUFFET

Jean Dubuffet (1901–1985) emerged after **World War II** as one of the most prominent and influential French artists. Though his work shared some of the emphasis on pain and suffering that linked such disparate artists as **Bernard Buffet** and **Jean Fautrier** and tied them to the postwar period, Dubuffet's reputation and impact survived well after the end of that era, as he engaged in a series of experiments using new techniques.

Although Dubuffet began studying in 1918, his paintings and drawings were neither sold nor exhibited until 1942. In the meantime he supported himself as a wine merchant and then through a small puppet theater. His work was profoundly affected by his reading of Hans Prinzhorn's *Bildnerei der Geisteskranken* (1922; Pictures of the Insane), a study of paintings and drawings done by the mentally ill. To Dubuffet the works shown in Prinzhorn's book seemed far more direct and powerful than the paintings he had seen in art classes and museums. He developed the concept of *art brut* ("rough" or "raw" art), assembling artworks by naive and untrained artists as well as the insane. Art brut exhibitions were held in 1947 and 1951; in 1949 he published the catalogue *L'Art brut préféré aux arts culturels* (Rough Art Preferable to Cultural Art).

Dubuffet's own painting deliberately defies any concept of beauty or harmony. "I don't find the function of assembling colors in pleasing arrangements very

Jean Dubuffet

graffiti. By the late 1960s and early 1970s these shapes had become the basis for colored, three-dimensional abstract sculptures.

REFERENCES:

Jean Dubuffet, *Jean Dubuffet: A Retrospective* (New York: Guggenheim Foundation, 1973);

Andreas Franzke, *Dubuffet* (New York: Abrams, 1981);

Peter Selz, *The Work of Jean Dubuffet* (Garden City, N.Y.: Doubleday, 1962).

—J.H.

MARCEL DUCHAMP

One of the most influential figures in twentieth-century Western art, Marcel Duchamp (1887–1968) spent much of his career satirizing both the traditional and the avant-garde. A promising painter at the beginning of his career, he turned his attention to works that challenged artistic conventions and played on the relationship between the verbal and the visual. He pioneered found art and kinetic sculpture and provided a model for many artists after **World War II.**

The most famous sibling of an artistic family (his brothers **Raymond Duchamp-Villon** and **Jacques Villon** and his sister Suzanne Duchamp also became artists), Duchamp supported himself as a library worker and caricaturist until 1910. His early paintings exhibit a debt to the Impressionists and **Paul Cézanne,** a debt shared with many of his contemporaries. He experimented with **Cubist** ideas in the early 1910s before painting the two versions of what became his best-known work, *Nu descendant un escalier* (1911 and 1912; *Nude Descending a Staircase*). In a manner more closely linked to the Futurists than to Cubism, both versions show a fascination with motion. The first shows a clearly recognizable staircase, with the figure depicted much as in a series of stop-motion photographs. In the more famous second version, which created a scandal at the New York Armory Show in 1913, the multiple images of the descending figure have swollen to fill the entire painting as a series of partly fused, partly overlapping, and seemingly metallic shapes. The painting was so startling in its single-minded emphasis on unstoppable motion that it was rejected by the 1912 **Salon des Indépendants** — a body originally created, ironically, to offset precisely this form of censorship. It was exhibited at the October 1912 show of the **Section d'or** (Golden Section). For Duchamp the rejection he received confirmed his aversion to any organized group or tendency in art.

Duchamp quickly abandoned any interest in either Cubism or Futurism in favor of an "anti-art" fore-

noble," he wrote. Instead, painting is "a more immediate and direct vehicle than verbal language, much closer to a cry...." Beginning with *haute-pâte* (high-paste) works — in which the surface is covered with a thick, layered impasto, often of paint mixed with materials such as glue or sand, on which images are carved — Dubuffet created works drawing on children's art, comic-strip images, and graffiti. He incorporated materials as diverse as coal, asphalt, and mud into his works, pointing out their roles in everyday life and the sense of wonder that can be inspired by even the most commonplace substances. His subject matter is deliberately coarse, sometimes brutal: his painting *Volonté de puissance* (1946; *Will to Power*) is a harshly scrawled male figure in rough outline, with teeth and genitals emphasized, while *Le Métafisyx (Corps de dame)* (1950; *Metafisyx [Woman's Body]*) is a huge female form covered with incised, glyphlike shapes loosely suggesting prehistoric fertility images.

In his so-called *Hourloupe* works of the 1960s and beyond, Dubuffet composed free-form, flowing drawings and paintings, often with accompanying nonsense

Marcel Duchamp, Jacques Villon, and Raymond Duchamp-Villon in the garden of Villon's studio at Puteaux, 1914

shadowing **Dada,** in which he later participated. A few years later he stopped painting altogether. He repeatedly assaulted the whole notion of high art by lampooning its forms, its exhibitions, and above all its pomposity. His *L.H.O.O.Q.* (1919) is typical: a cheap reproduction of Leonardo da Vinci's *La Gioconda* (better known as *Mona Lisa*) with an inked-on mustache. Read aloud in French, the title sounds roughly like a phrase meaning "She has a hot ass." His *Fountain* (1917), rejected by an American independents' exhibition, was a urinal signed "R. Mutt."

Duchamp moved to the United States in 1915, leaving briefly to spend most of **World War I** in Argentina; he became a naturalized American citizen in 1954. In the United States he experimented with quasi-sculptural assemblages and "readymades" presented tongue-in-cheek from common household objects. Like the French **Nouveau Réaliste** artists and American Pop artists of the 1960s, he loved to play with the form and meaning of everyday objects, transforming them by removing them from their usual contexts and functions. Unlike his 1960s counterparts, however, he had no interest in proclaiming the monumentality or importance of his readymades; on the contrary, he argued that ideally he should be utterly disinterested in them.

By the 1920s Duchamp's assemblages had become larger and more complex. His *La Mariée mise à nu par ses célibataires, même* (1915–1923; *The Bride Stripped Bare by Her Bachelors, Even*) — also known as the *Large Glass* — is an ambitious but never-finished project, a wire and foil construction between two glass panels. It is a pseudomachine, involving the rotation of small objects dubbed "bachelors" around a constantly "undressing" bride. A mobile that does not in fact move, a machine that cannot function, it is simultaneously an expression of the modern fascination with machinery and a parody of it, using mechanical forms to replicate (and mock) a frustrated sexuality. When the glass was cracked in transit in 1926, Duchamp reportedly commented, "Now it is complete."

In the late 1950s and 1960s Duchamp became uneasy with the fact that more and more young artists referred to his work as their foundation or starting point. He even expressed some doubt about the renewal of art involving ready-made objects, arguing that the technique was becoming repetitive. Though he remained productive, he spent much of the second half of his life absorbed in his second passion, chess.

REFERENCES:

Sarane Alexandrian, *Marcel Duchamp,* translated by Alice Sachs (New York: Crown, 1977);

Pierre Cabanne, *The Brothers Duchamp: Jacques Villon, Raymond Duchamp-Villon, Marcel Duchamp,* translated by Helga and Dinah Harrison (Boston: New York Graphic Society, 1975);

Douglas Cooper, *The Cubist Epoch* (London: Phaidon, 1971);

John Golding, *Cubism: A History and an Analysis, 1907–1914* (Boston: Boston Book & Art Shop, 1959);

Arturo Schwarz, *The Complete Works of Marcel Duchamp* (New York: Abrams, 1969).

— J.H.

RAYMOND DUCHAMP-VILLON

Artist Raymond Duchamp-Villon (1876–1918) was distinguished from his artist brothers **Marcel Duchamp** and **Jacques Villon** by his attempts to translate and redefine certain ideas from **Cubist** painting in sculpture. He was also influenced by Futurism.

Duchamp-Villon's early work was partly inspired by that of **Auguste Rodin,** but by 1912–1913 his sculpture showed a clear interest in the Cubist analysis of form and volume. He gained notice at the 1912 **Salon d'Automne** as the primary designer of a model *Maison cubiste,* to be used to display paintings by several quasi- or near-Cubist painters. His *Reliefs* (1913), a bronze relief better known in English as *The Lovers,* avoids problems inherent in a three-dimensional Cubism by casting his figures as abstract curvilinear forms confined on a rectangular plate.

Throughout 1914 Duchamp-Villon worked on five successive versions of a bronze horse. The final version of *Le Cheval,* completed in August 1914, combines Futurist and Cubist elements. It is a quasi-mechanical object, an arrangement of shapes resembling gears and cylinders coiled as if to spring into action at any moment. In a 1913 letter to Walter Pach, Duchamp-Villon had spoken of the modern world as embodied in the form and idea of the machine: "The power of the machine imposes itself, and we can scarcely conceive living things any more without it."

With the outbreak of **World War I,** Duchamp-Villon enlisted in the French army as a medical aide. He contracted typhoid fever at the front in 1917, dying the following year.

REFERENCES:

Pierre Cabanne, *The Brothers Duchamp: Jacques Villon, Raymond Duchamp-Villon, Marcel Duchamp,* translated by Helga and Dinah Harrison (Boston: New York Graphic Society, 1975);

Douglas Cooper, *The Cubist Epoch* (London: Phaidon, 1971);

John Golding, *Cubism: A History and an Analysis, 1907–1914* (Boston: Boston Book & Art Shop, 1959).

— J.H.

RAOUL DUFY

Like some other early-twentieth-century artists, Raoul Dufy (1877–1953) was influenced by a sequence of avant-garde movements and practitioners, but he did not adhere to any one style. Prolific and versatile, Dufy is remembered for his work in decoration and design as well as for his paintings.

Leaving school at age fourteen to support his family by working as an apprentice in a coffee firm, Dufy studied art in night school. His first works were in an Impressionistic style. After viewing the **Fauves** at the first **Salon d'Automne** in 1905 and at the **Salon des Indépendants** of 1906, Dufy began to move toward the bright palette and simplified forms of **Henri Matisse** and his associates. He wrote later that the sight of Matisse's *Luxe, calme, et volupté* (1904; *Luxury, Calm, and Voluptuousness* — a quotation from poet Charles Baudelaire) ended any interest he had in the Impressionists. An equal fascination with the work of **Paul Cézanne** brought Dufy close to **Georges Braque** for a time, and by 1908 he was flirting with early **Cubist** ideas without ever quite being won over to them.

Beginning in the 1910s Dufy worked as a fabric designer and a woodcut artist; his experiences in both fields exerted a continuing influence over his painting, which was marked by clearly delineated and heavily outlined patches of color — often flat, sometimes patterned to suggest carpets, cloth, or vegetation. His colors varied from a somewhat naturalistic replication of natural shades, simplified to a single, uniform patch of color, to deliberate alterations, even reversals of perceived colors, as in his use of white patches to suggest shadows. In many of his later works, such as his *Hommage à Mozart* (1915; *Homage to Mozart*), the painting is essentially an assemblage of variegated lines and a few cross-hatched segments over broad, flat areas of bright color.

REFERENCES:

Raymond Cogniat, *Raoul Dufy,* translated by Thomas L. Callow (New York: Crown, 1962);

Georges Duthuit, *The Fauvist Painters,* translated by Ralph Manheim (New York: Wittenborn, Schultz, 1950);

Joseph-Emile Muller, *Fauvism* (New York: Praeger, 1967);

Dora Perez-Tibi, *Dufy,* translated by Shaun Whiteside (New York: Abrams, 1989);

Bryan Robertson and Sarah Wilson, *Raoul Dufy* (London: Arts Council of Great Britain, 1983).

— J.H.

GEORGES DUHAMEL

Once considered an important novelist and widely read in middle-class circles, Georges Duhamel (1884–1966) has fallen in standing as tastes have changed and younger generations of writers have replaced those who came to maturity before **World War I.** He is still remembered as the author of two cycles of realistic fiction, *Vie et aventures de Salavin* (1920–1932; Life and Adventures of Salavin), which comprises five novels and a short story, and the ten-volume *Chronique des Pasquier* (1933–1941; Pasquier Chronicle). These works are marked by the humanist values most prized during the years between the two world wars: social harmony, family loyalty, and the search for happiness.

Born in Paris, Duhamel began his literary career as an associate of the Groupe de l'Abbaye, or **Unanimists,** at about the same time that he was studying medicine (1903–1908). By 1914 he was a prolific author of poems, dramas, and fiction as well as a practicing physician. After medical service in World War I, during which he performed some two thousand operations, he published *Civilisation, 1914–1917* (1918), a protest against armed conflict; the book won the **Prix Goncourt** and a special award from the Académie Française, to which he was elected in 1935.

REFERENCES:

L. Clark Keating, *Critic of Civilization* (Lexington: University of Kentucky Press, 1965);

Bettina L. Knapp, *Georges Duhamel* (Boston: Twayne, 1972).
— C.S.B.

PAUL DUKAS

When Paul Dukas (1865–1935) graduated from the Paris Conservatoire he was regarded as a promising young composer because of his early Symphony in C Major (1896). The clever humor and imaginative orchestration of his next composition, *L'Apprenti sorcier* (1897; *The Sorcerer's Apprentice*), based on a poem by Johann Wolfgang von Goethe, brought him instant fame. The piece became known around the world and later reached millions more people when Walt Disney included it in the Mickey Mouse segment of his film *Fantasia* (1940).

Dukas's other compositions, which are also highly regarded by musicians, include an opera, *Ariane et Barbe-Bleue* (1907), based on **Maurice Maeterlinck**'s version of the Bluebeard story, and *La Péri* (1912), a ballet commissioned by **Serge Diaghilev.** Two important works for piano, a monumental sonata (1901) and his *Variations, interlude et final sur un thème de Rameau* (1903; Variations, Interlude, and Finale on a Theme by Rameau), are also greatly respected, but their length and technical demands are such that they attract few pianists.

From 1913 to the end of his life Dukas was professor of composition at the Paris Conservatoire. A perfectionist, he composed little after 1920 and destroyed his incomplete efforts. In 1934 he was elected to the Académie des Beaux-Arts. Dukas was also a distinguished commentator on music and contributed articles to various important journals. Many of these articles were later collected and published posthumously as *Les Ecrits de Paul Dukas sur la musique* (1948; Paul Dukas's Writings on Music).

REFERENCE:

Rollo Myers, *Modern French Music: Its Evolution and Cultural Background from 1900 to the Present Day* (Oxford: Blackwell, 1971), pp. 57–60.
— P.S.H.

GERMAINE DULAC

A gifted writer and poet, Germaine Dulac (1882–1942) is best known as a film critic who treated film as an art form and advocated an experimental "pure" cinema. The second woman director in France, she created several significant short films that put her theories into practice. She was also a pioneer of time-lapse photography, making movies that allow viewers to study the growth of plants.

Dulac displayed a feminist ethic in her first writings for *La Française,* a woman's magazine she edited from 1909 to 1913. She made her reputation as a director with *La Fête espagnole* (1919; The Spanish Fiesta), written by critic and director **Louis Delluc,** who supported her career. She studied movie production in Hollywood in 1921 and became a prominent administrator in the Cinéma-Club de France in 1922. Her best-known film, *La Souriante Madame Beudet* (1923; *The Smiling Miss Beudet*) is inspired by Gustave Flaubert's novel *Madame Bovary* (1856), with its theme of romantic isolation and the dreams of a small-town woman married to a greedy bumpkin. Dulac enhanced her reputation in filming **Antonin Artaud**'s screenplay for *La Coquille et le clergyman* (1927; The Seashell and the Clergyman), but the advent of sound ended her career as a director of creative films. She directed newsreels for the **Gaumont** studios during the 1930s.

REFERENCES:

Richard Abel, *French Cinema: The First Wave, 1915–29* (Princeton: Princeton University Press, 1984);

Abel, *French Film Theory and Criticism, 1: 1907–1939* (Princeton: Princeton University Press, 1988);

Sandy Flitterman-Lewis, *To Desire Differently: Feminism and the French Cinema* (Urbana: University of Illinois Press, 1990);

Louise Heck-Rabi, *Women Filmmakers: A Critical Reception* (Metuchen, N.J.: Scarecrow, 1984).

—T.C.

CHARLES DULLIN

A consummate actor and director, Charles Dullin (1885–1949) left his mark on twentieth-century French theater. He discovered and trained a whole generation of vibrant, energetic actors and theater workers, including **Antonin Artaud, Marguerite Jamois, Raymond Rouleau, André Barsacq,** the mime **Marcel Marceau, Jean Vilar,** and **Jean-Louis Barrault.**

Dullin acted first in Paris neighborhood clubs, then under **André Antoine**'s direction at the **Odéon. Jacques Copeau** later saw him act at the Théâtre des Arts and brought him to the **Théâtre du Vieux-Colombier** for its initial season in 1913. Despite his slight build, his unprepossessing appearance, and his hoarse nasal voice, Dullin became one of the most popular actors in Copeau's troupe and readily profited from Copeau's insistence on physical discipline and perfect diction. His most memorable roles are those of Harpagon, the lead in Molière's *L'Avare* (translated as *The Miser*), which he played on several occasions, and the title role in the Elizabethan drama *Volpone,* by Ben Jonson.

At the onset of **World War I** Dullin volunteered for military service; later he joined the Vieux-Colombier troupe in New York for the 1917 and 1918 seasons. He left Copeau there and returned to France, working for a time with **Firmin Gémier.** With the help of Copeau and others, he established his own theater in 1921. His **Théâtre de l'Atelier,** or "workshop theater," focused on experimental productions and the training of actors and owed a great deal to Copeau's ideals, except for set design. In contrast to Copeau's bare stage, Dullin preferred elaborate, artistic, and often expensive sets.

Dullin's repertoire emphasized classical plays, such as **Jean Cocteau**'s adaptation of Sophocles' *Antigone* and Calderón de la Barca's *La Vida es sueño* (translated as *Life Is a Dream*), both produced in 1922. He also produced Aristophanes' *The Birds* (1927) and *Peace* (1933) as well as plays by William Shakespeare, notably *Richard III* (1933) and *Julius Caesar* (1937). Old plays under his direction always revealed their modern relevance. For example, critics had no trouble seeing allusions to Benito Mussolini and Francisco Franco in his *Julius Caesar.* Often Dullin pointed to the current political and social pertinence of the classics by means of modern art. **Pablo Picasso,** whom he had met at the **Cabaret du Lapin Agile** during his early years in Paris, painted sets for the 1922 production of *Antigone,* and other modern artists also designed scenery for him. **Darius Milhaud** and **Arthur Honegger** composed music for some of Dullin's productions.

Dullin also worked well with contemporary playwrights, especially **Armand Salacrou,** whom he introduced to the public. After the failure of Salacrou's *Patchouli* in 1930, Dullin staged Salacrou's *Atlas Hôtel* in 1931 and finally was successful in 1938 with his *La Terre est ronde* (translated as *The World is Round*).

Dullin joined his fellow members of the **Cartel des Quatre** in directing for the **Comédie-Française** in the late 1930s, staging in 1937 Luigi Pirandello's *Cosi è se vi pare* (translated as *Right You Are! If You Think So*). In 1941 he accepted the position of director of the Théâtre **Sarah Bernhardt.** In wartime Paris, however, operating a theater was difficult, and Dullin, who was never good with money, experienced financial troubles. During this time he introduced **Jean-Paul Sartre**'s drama to the public, getting *Les Mouches* (translated as *The Flies*) past Nazi censors for its 1943 premiere despite its emphasis on freedom and what amounted to a message of recruitment for the **Resistance** movement. But his cash receipts continued to diminish, until the Paris municipal government in 1947 demanded he present a more popular repertoire or abandon his theater. He resigned and died two years later. He is the author of *Souvenirs et notes de travail d'un acteur* (1946; translated as *Recollections and Working Notes of an Actor*).

REFERENCES:

Benjamin Crémieux, "L'Art du metteur en scène et du comédien: Copeau, Jouvet, Dullin, Baty, Pitoëff," *Europe* (1947–1948): 130–150;

Jacqueline de Jomaron, "Ils étaient quatre . . .," in *Le Théâtre en France,* volume 2: *De la Révolution à nos jours,* edited by de Jomaron (Paris: Armand Colin, 1989), pp. 227–270;

Dorothy Knowles, "The Theatres and Producers," in her *French Drama of the Interwar Years, 1918–39* (London: Harrap, 1967), pp. 13–47.

—R.J.N.

ISADORA DUNCAN

Although Isadora Duncan (1877–1927) is called the mother of American modern dance, she lived much of her life in Paris and first experienced success in the salons and theaters of Europe. She broke with the technical and narrative restrictions of classical ballet to create a type of dance—inspired by the art of ancient Greece and her intuitions about nature—that would freely express one's deepest emotions. She inspired many modern French artists as well as **Michel Fokine** and other Russian dancers and choreographers.

Duncan was raised in San Francisco by a single mother who gave lessons in social dances and taught her children to appreciate ancient Greek art and literature. She began teaching dance and performing in her early teens, and at age eighteen, in 1895, she went to Chicago to work as a professional dancer in vaudeville. Three years later she was pursuing a solo career in New York, where she gained notoriety for her bare arms and unconventional dances, which were highly emotional and appeared spontaneous. In 1899, desiring to have her dance perceived as art rather than entertainment, Duncan moved to London. The following year she moved to Paris. During this period she made the controversial transition from ballet slippers to sandals and finally to bare feet and legs. Her movements began in the solar plexus, which she considered the spiritual and physical center of the body. They were simple, consisting of runs, skips, waltzes, and leaps. She dressed in Greek-inspired silk tunics and danced to the music of the great composers.

During the next two decades Duncan's reputation gradually reached greater and greater heights as she appeared throughout Europe and Russia. Her lecture *The Dance of the Future* (1902) was published as a pamphlet and became a manifesto for the new modern dance she and contemporaries such as Ruth St. Denis exemplified. Duncan also spent a great deal of time teaching girls and young women to express themselves through dance. She opened her first school in Grunewald, Germany, in 1904. She eventually adopted her six original pupils, the "Isadorables," who continued her teachings after her death.

Duncan attracted attention for her unconventional lifestyle. Her affair with **Edward Gordon Craig** resulted in the birth of a daughter in 1905. Five years later she had a son with another lover. Both children died in a 1913 accident when their car plunged into the Seine. In 1914 her third child, with yet another lover, died hours after birth. Her only marriage, to Russian poet Sergei Esenin in 1922, lasted little more than a year. Devastated by the deaths of her children, she expressed her suffering and anger in slower, more weighted dances often based on liturgical or revolutionary themes.

In addition to her artistic successes, Duncan was noteworthy during **World War I** for her dances to the "Marseillaise," which were aimed at encouraging patriotic fervor in the French and support for France among Americans.

Duncan's unexpected death was as dramatic as those of her children: the fringe of her long scarf, which

Isadora Duncan in a pose from one of her dances, circa 1903 (Elvira)

she tossed over her shoulder, caught in a wheel of a car in which she was riding, choking her to death.

REFERENCES:

Fredrika Blair, *Isadora: Portrait of the Artist as a Woman* (New York: McGraw-Hill, 1956);

Doree Duncan, Carol Pratt, and Cynthia Splatt, *Life into Art: Isadora Duncan and Her World* (New York & London: Norton, 1993);

Deborah Jowitt, "The Search for Motion: Images of Isadora," *Dance Research Journal,* 17, no. 2 / 18, no. 1 (1985–1986): 21–29.

—A.P.E.

DUNKIRK

The northernmost French port of Dunkirk (*Dunkerque* in French) was the site of a major evacuation of French and British troops at the time of the **Debacle,** the major German defeat of French and Allied troops in May and June 1940. The Germans encircled the French and British and drove them through Belgium to the sea. For the French the name *Dunkirk* often arouses considerable resentment. During the evacuation hundreds of British naval ships and civilian boats carried more than two hundred thousand English soldiers from Dunkirk across the English Channel, but only one hundred thousand French were evacuated, with many others left behind to become German prisoners. Although most of the British considered the evacuation a heroic and highly successful operation conducted under difficult circumstances, the number of French soldiers left behind contributed to strong anti-British feelings on the part of the French, which were heightened in July 1940, when most of the French fleet was bombarded and destroyed by the British at Mers-el-Kébir to keep the ships out of German hands. By the time Dunkirk was liberated by the U.S. Army in May 1945, more than three-quarters of its houses had been destroyed.

REFERENCES:

Norman Gelb, *Dunkirk* (New York: Morrow, 1989);

Walter Lord, *The Miracle of Dunkirk* (New York: Viking, 1982).
                                                    — C.S.B.

ANDRÉ DUNOYER DE SEGONZAC

Around any major artistic current there are one or more concentric circles of those intrigued by, but not wholly a part of, the movement proper. Some use the ideas of the movement as a springboard for their own conceptions; others, such as André Dunoyer de Segonzac (1884–1974) with regard to **Cubism,** seek to bridge the gap between the old and the new, employing bits and pieces of the new ideas and forms in combination with more traditional conceptions. He is also known for his many etchings created after **World War I.**

A former language student and unsuccessful applicant to the Ecole des Beaux-Arts, Dunoyer de Segonzac, who began his artistic career under the influence of Impressionism, first attracted notice as an artist with a 1910 album of drawings inspired by the dancing of **Isadora Duncan.** The following year he exhibited at the annual **Salon des Indépendants** in a room commandeered by those influenced by the Cubists, including **Roger de La Fresnaye** and **André Lhôte.** In 1912 Dunoyer de Segonzac was part of the first salon of the **Section d'or** (Golden Section), an independent showing of Cubist-influenced artists organized by the brothers **Marcel Duchamp** and **Jacques Villon.** The works exhibited were so eclectic that, according to the critic Maurice Raynal, it was proof that

the term *Cubist* was fast losing any specific meaning, instead being applied to any avant-garde art.

Dunoyer de Segonzac's painting displays a superficial interest in the early Cubist focus on the geometric; this technique was, however, little more than a surface over a more traditional representational art. In retrospect, except for the palette and a certain simplification of forms, little in Dunoyer's work is even reminiscent of Cubism.

REFERENCES:

Douglas Cooper, *The Cubist Epoch* (London: Phaidon, 1971);

Pierre Daix, *Cubists and Cubism,* translated by R. F. M. Dexter (New York: Rizzoli, 1982);

Christopher Green, *Cubism and Its Enemies: Modern Movements and Reaction in French Art, 1916–1928* (New Haven: Yale University Press, 1987);

Theda Shapiro, *Painters and Politics: The European Avant-Garde and Society, 1900–1925* (Amsterdam: Elsevier, 1976).
                                                    — J.H.

MARGUERITE DURAS

With a lengthy career and a long list of novels, plays, and films behind her, Marguerite Duras (1914–) is the best-known French woman writer at the end of the twentieth century. She and her admirers, many of them feminist critics, have succeeded in presenting her work to a wide public, not only in Europe but in North America. **Alain Resnais**'s 1959 film *Hiroshima mon amour,* for which she wrote the screenplay, was highly praised in artistic circles and was the first **Nouvelle Vague** (New Wave) film to achieve popularity with an international audience. Her novel *L'Amant* (1984; translated as *The Lover*) was widely publicized and made her almost a cult figure in France and abroad.

Duras's work is minimalist in approach: her dialogues are understated, intended to suggest much more than they reveal, and her style has a directness and simplicity, belying the psychological nuances that underlie it. She has created an extensive body of work from relatively few autobiographical experiences, repeatedly employing similar motifs, situations, and psychic uncertainties. Many critics have associated her with the **New Novelists;** like writers such as **Alain Robbe-Grillet,** she rejects fictional conventions such as full-length character portraits and authorial explanations. However, her work is more emotionally charged than much of his, often vibrating with lyricism and desire.

Duras was born Marguerite Donnadieu in Indochina, where her widowed mother tried with little success to run a plantation. Like *L'Amant,* several of her early works are set in a colonial world divided along lines of class, race, and language. Inspired perhaps by her mother's difficulties with the colonial administration, she began early to criticize colonial corruption and its exploitation of peoples and individuals.

After studies in Saigon, Duras moved to Paris in 1931 and took a degree in law and political science in 1935. In 1939 she married Robert Anthelme, a member of the **French Communist Party** (they were divorced in 1946), and was an active party member until she was ousted in 1950. She also participated in the **Resistance** against the German **Occupation** of France during **World War II** and completed her first novel, *Les Impudents* (The Impudent Ones), in 1943. Her works are usually not overtly political; rather than preaching about exploitation, as a social realist might, she suggests it from the inside, usually from a woman's point of view. For instance, her first play, *Le Square* (1955; translated as *The Square*), explores the mind of a young female domestic.

Much of Duras's work is marked by eroticism. Like her political views, though, this erotic element is understated. *Moderato cantabile* (1958; translated), a spare but lyrical novel, develops a highly eroticized relationship, without any physical lovemaking, between a working-class man and a married woman of the upper bourgeoisie who together have witnessed a crime of passion — the killing of a woman by her lover. Colored by class difference between the principal characters, the novel has been described by **Claude Roy** as "Madame Bovary rewritten by Béla Bartók." The same sort of tensions are visible in *Hiroshima mon amour,* where erotic attraction is played out against the double background of race differences and war experiences.

Alcohol also plays an important role in many works by Duras, a recovered alcoholic who was once hospitalized for treatment. Heavy drinking is crucial in her novel *Dix heures et demie du soir en été* (1960; translated as *Ten-Thirty on a Summer Night*) and in *Moderato cantabile.* In some cases alcohol is connected to the dual psychological process of forgetting and remembering, an important theme throughout her work.

Duras began directing films by working with Paul Seban on *La Musica* (1966; The Music) and has directed on her own several low-budget, avant-garde films, including *India Song,* which won a special prize at the 1975 **Cannes Film Festival,** and *Le Camion* (The Truck), made in four days in 1977. Her plays have been produced on several Parisian stages with some of the most prominent actors in France, and in 1983 she won the Grand Prix du Théâtre de l'Académie Française. She also has published journalism.

Among her later books are *La Douleur* (1985; translated as *The War: A Memoir*), which deals in an extremely personal vein with the emotional agonies of World War II, and *Les Yeux bleus cheveux noirs* (1988;

translated as *Blue Eyes, Black Hair*), a novel about a love affair between a homosexual and a prostitute. Here, as in many other works, Duras focuses on the question of sexual difference and identity. Feminist critics have appreciated this dimension of her work, and Duras has been sympathetic to the women's movement without espousing feminist orthodoxy.

REFERENCES:

Carol J. Murphy, *Alienation and Absence in the Novels of Marguerite Duras* (Lexington, Ky.: French Forum Monographs, 1982);

Trista Selous, *The Other Woman: Feminism and Femininity in the Work of Marguerite Duras* (New Haven: Yale University Press, 1988);

Sharon Willis, *Marguerite Duras: Writing on the Body* (Urbana & Chicago: University of Illinois Press, 1987).

— C.S.B.

JULIEN DUVIVIER

Julien Duvivier (1896–1967) was one of the best-known film directors of the 1930s and a key figure in the trend toward **poetic realism** during that decade. A prolific filmmaker, Duvivier was known for a technical and practical expertise that ensured completion of his movies on schedule.

Duvivier left his native Lille to train as an actor in Paris. He worked under **André Antoine,** then director of the well-known **Théâtre Libre,** who was turning toward cinema. Duvivier wrote and directed his first film, *Haceldama ou Le prix du sang* (Haceldama or The Cost of Blood), in 1919 and made twenty more silent films in the next decade. Duvivier then wrote and directed twenty sound features before the German invasion of France in 1940, when he immigrated to Hollywood and directed three features there.

Duvivier set the standard for the poetic realism of the 1930s with *La Belle Equipe* (1936; *They Were Five*), *Pépé le Moko* (1937), and *La Fin du jour* (1939; *The End of a Day*). In these films the hopes and illusions of the **Popular Front** are expressed through stories of intrigue and romance. *La Belle Equipe* depicts the aspirations and tribulations of a group representative of French workers confronting the Depression. Duvivier's most successful film, *Pépé le Moko,* appeals to nostalgia, exoticism, and the lost illusions of love among French exiles in Algiers. It inspired two American remakes and bears a strong resemblance to Michael Curtiz's classic *Casablanca* (1942). Banned by the French government in 1940 on the grounds of its supposed demoralizing effects, *Pépé le Moko* has since been recognized as a classic for its directorial style and its summation of conflicting ideologies.

In 1945 Duvivier returned to France, where he launched a return to poetic realism with *Panique* (1946; *Panic*), starring Michel Simon. Of the twenty features he produced after the war, Duvivier directed two truly memorable movies, both starring **Fernandel:** *Le Petit Monde de Don Camillo* (1951; *The Little World of Don Camillo*) and a sequel, *Le Retour de Don Camillo* (1953; *The Return of Don Camillo*).

Like Curtiz and Raoul Walsh in Hollywood, Duvivier was an all-purpose director who knew how to handle difficult actors and develop a flexible style. His narratives and stagings lack the wit and unpredictable turns of the works of **Jean Renoir,** but his movies compare well with those of other directors of the first order.

REFERENCES:

Raymond Chirat, *Julien Duvivier* (Lyons: Serdoc, 1968);

Jean Renoir, "Duvivier, le professionnel," *Figaro Littéraire* (4 December 1967);

Noel Simsolo, "A propos de Julien Duvivier," *Image et Son* (November 1981).

—T.C.

E

ECOLE NORMALE SUPÉRIEURE

Located in the **Latin Quarter,** on the **Left Bank** in Paris, the Ecole Normale Supérieure is the jewel institution among a group of French normal, or teacher-training schools. Its origins go back to 1794, when the Convention Nationale planned a system of state-run education. The school closed in May 1795 but was reestablished by Napoleon in 1810. Since that time, except for a few years in the 1820s, the school has been in continuous operation. In 1903 it became associated with the Sorbonne. Many, though not all, of the students at the Ecole Normale sit for the prestigious teacher-qualifying examination called the *agrégation*.

Those who are registered at the school and attend its lectures have traditionally been among the intellectual elite of France, and many famous figures have been associated with it as students or professors, including **Jean-Paul Sartre** and **Claude Lévi-Strauss.** Not all students who attend the Ecole Normale Supérieure intend to enter the teaching profession, although many do. *Normaliens* share a strong sense of pride and esprit de corps. In the late twentieth century some American students have enrolled there through exchange programs with universities in the United States. The school is featured in several twentieth-century French novels, including **Roger Martin du Gard**'s *Les Thibault* (1922–1940; translated as *The Thibaults*) and **Jules Romains**'s *Les Amours enfantines* (1932; Childhood Loves), the third volume of his *Les Hommes de bonne volonté* (1932–1946; translated as *Men of Good Will*).

REFERENCES:

Diane Rubenstein, *What's Left? The Ecole Normale Supérieure and the Right* (Madison: University of Wisconsin Press, 1990);

Robert J. Smith, *The Ecole Normale Supérieure and the Third Republic* (Albany: State University of New York Press, 1982).

— C.S.B.

EDITIONS DE MINUIT

The Editions de Minuit (Midnight Editions) began as a clandestine publishing operation in 1942, under the German **Occupation** of France during **World War II.** Founders Jacques Bedû-Bridel and Pierre de Lescure started out by publishing *Le Silence de la mer* (translated as *The Silence of the Sea*), an anti-Nazi novel by **Resistance** member Jean Bruller, who used the pen name **Vercors.** By the time of the **Liberation** in 1944 Editions de Minuit had published some forty volumes of Resistance literature — among them works by **Louis Aragon, François Mauriac, Jean Paulhan,** and **Elsa Triolet,** as well as Vercors

In the 1950s, under the leadership of Jérôme Lindon, the Editions de Minuit signed several of the **New Novelists — Michel Butor, Alain Robbe-Grillet,** and **Nathalie Sarraute.** The publishing house has continued to attract young, experimental authors.

REFERENCE:

Jacques Bedû-Bridel, *Les Editions de Minuit* (Paris: Editions de Minuit, 1945).

— C.S.B.

EDITIONS DES FEMMES

The founding of Editions des Femmes in 1974 marked the arrival of the women's movement on the publishing scene. Antoinette Fouque, the managing director of

Jean-Paul Sartre, sitting on the chimney, and other students on the rooftop of the Ecole Normale Supérieure, 1927

the publishing house, is one of the founders of the **Mouvement de la Libération des Femmes.**

Since the twelfth century France has had a strong tradition of women writers. In the twentieth-century — while **Colette, Simone de Beauvoir,** and many other women writers have written works treating the role of women in society — they have largely continued to have their books published by the same houses that put out men's works. Yet, as feminism has developed and increasingly become a separatist movement, some women writers have sought their own outlets, deliberately and sometimes provocatively distinguishing their work from their male colleagues'.

The writer most closely associated with Editions des Femmes is **Hélène Cixous,** who has had more than a dozen books published by the firm since 1975. In 1992 Editions des Femmes reported four hundred titles in print, ranging from fiction and poetry to history, art, and photography.

— C.S.B.

PAUL ELUARD

To many midcentury readers in France, poet Paul Eluard (1895–1952) was a literary hero. One of the principal exponents of **Surrealism** and author of some of its finest lyrics, Eluard, like fellow Surrealists **Louis Aragon** and **René Char,** became a poetic spokesman for French patriotism under the German **Occupation** of France during **World War II.** Eluard's lyrics, such as "Liberté," were printed and dropped by Royal Air Force planes into France, where they were memorized and passed on by word of mouth. While using some of the techniques of Surrealism, Eluard's poetry has a calculated simplicity and a controlled lyricism that have given his works a broader appeal than those of some other Surrealists.

Born Eugène Grindel in a middle-class quarter of suburban Paris, Eluard spent part of his childhood in a working-class neighborhood. Early on he showed his gift for poetry, and for a time he was influenced by **Unanimism** . In 1912–1914, while hospitalized in a Swiss sanatorium, he met Elena Diakanova (Gala), the subject of his first love poems, who became his wife in 1917. He reacted to **World War I** — in which he was gassed and suffered gangrene of the bronchi — with a violent hatred of war. After the war he was associated with **Dada** and then the Surrealist group. The principal collections of his poems from the mid 1920s are *Mourir de ne pas mourir* (1924; To Die from Not Dying) and *Capitale de la douleur* (1926; Capital of Grief).

Separation from Gala in 1930 was followed by a love affair with a woman known as Nusch (Maria Benz), whom he married in 1934, and Eluard was inspired to cultivate again the lyrical vein he demonstrated in his earlier love poems. *L'Amour la poésie* (1929; Love/Poetry) and *La Vie immédiate* (1932; The Immediate Life) illustrate his poetic mastery. As the

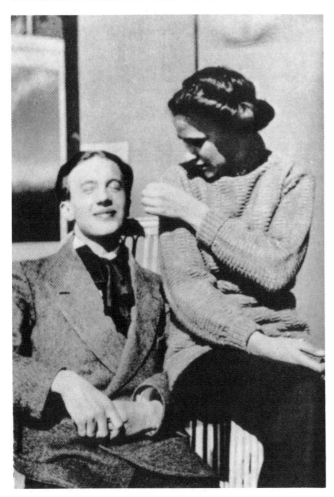

Paul Eluard in the Swiss sanitorium at Clavadel in 1913 with Elena Diakanova, whom he married in 1917

1930s wore on, his publications reflected his preoccupation with political matters. Early in the German Occupation of France he joined the **Resistance.** Having been a member of the **French Communist Party** briefly in the late 1920s, he rejoined the party in 1942, making a definitive break from **André Breton.** Eluard's political allegiance is reflected in *Poèmes politiques* (1947; Political Poems). After the death of Nusch in 1946, he met Dominique Lemor in 1949 and married her in 1951, again producing lyrics from personal inspiration.

REFERENCES:

Anna Balakian, *Surrealism: The Road to the Absolute* (New York: Noonday Press, 1959), pp. 165–187;

David Caute, *Communism and the French Intellectuals* (New York: Macmillan, 1954), pp. 371–388;

Robert Nugent, *Paul Eluard* (New York: Twayne, 1974).

— C.S.B.

PIERRE EMMANUEL

Pierre Emmanuel (1916–1984) established his reputation as a poet of the **Resistance** movement during the German **Occupation** of France during **World War II** and as a significant figure in the twentieth-century religious revival in French literature. He is considered one of the most impressive mid-century French poets. In his poetry Emmanuel, a Roman Catholic, has interpreted anew biblical and mythological epics, seeking to illuminate humanity's efforts to reconcile spiritual aspiration with carnal desire.

Born Noël Jean Mathieu, Emmanuel was greatly influenced by the visionary poetry of a fellow Catholic, **Pierre Jean Jouve.** Emmanuel's first book, *Elégies* (1940), was followed by *Tombeau d'Orphée* (1941; The Tomb of Orpheus), which reveals the influence of Jouve in its juxtaposition of the divine and erotic sides of human nature. During World War II Emmanuel actively supported the Resistance. He was briefly interested in Communism but repudiated it after traveling in Eastern Europe after 1945.

Emmanuel's early verse was highly rhetorical, even prolix, but he displayed a more sober style in *Cantos* (1944), one of his best-known collections, published in part as *XX Cantos* (1942) by the Resistance magazine *Fontaine. Versant de l'âge* (1958; The Downslope of Age), another major collection, demonstrates his mastery of a verse that is at once lucid and suggestive. All of his work is based on his belief that poetic language can seize and express the spiritual dimension of human life, but a pleasing sensory element in his poetry counteracts what might otherwise be too great an emphasis on the metaphysical.

Despite his effort to express spiritual values and his use of Christian material, Emmanuel is not an orthodox Catholic poet, and his work is not meant to proselytize. Lyrical and visionary, it invites the reader to share a spiritual adventure in which the ultimate stage is death and resurrection. Doubtless the most impressive illustration of this spiritual journey is *Le Grand Œuvre: Cosmogonie* (1984; The Great Work: Cosmogony), which treats the human drama from the time of Eden.

Emmanuel won the Grand Prix de Poésie de l'Académie Française in 1963 and was elected to the Académie in 1969. He served as president of the international writers' organization P.E.N. in 1969–1971 and of the French chapter of P.E.N. in 1972–1976.

REFERENCES:

Alain Bosquet, *Pierre Emmanuel: Une étude* (Paris: Seghers, 1959; revised, 1971);

Joseph Chiari, *Contemporary French Poetry* (New York: Philosophical Library, 1952), pp. 95–114;

Spire Pitou, "The Logos, the Mythos and Pierre Emmanuel," *Renascence,* 5 (Spring 1953): 104–110.

—C.S.B.

ENCYCLOPÉDIE DE LA MUSIQUE ET DICTIONNAIRE DU CONSERVATOIRE

The monumental *Encyclopédie de la musique et Dictionnaire du Conservatoire* is an eleven-volume work (1913–1926) designed by André Gédalge (1856–1926) as a universal repository of musical knowledge, in the tradition of the *Encyclopédie* of the eighteenth century. Although it is international in scope, most of the contributors were French. Distinguished scholars and musicians, including **Vincent d'Indy, Charles Koechlin,** and **Romain Rolland,** wrote many of the major articles, which still rank among the most important surveys of their fields.

Originally Gédalge planned an encyclopedia in three sections. The five-volume first section is devoted to the history of music, organized by countries and areas, and includes remarkable studies of non-Western music, particularly the music of the Far East and Africa. The second, six-volume section deals with subjects such as harmony, counterpoint, orchestration, and individual instruments, as well as musical forms, including opera. The third section, intended to include biographies, was never written.

—P.S.H.

JEAN EPSTEIN

Along with **Louis Delluc,** Jean Epstein (1897–1953) was one of the great early masters of film production and theory in the "second wave" of French cinema, which followed **World War I.** From 1922 until his death he wrote or directed more than forty movies, the best known of which are his impressionistic silent films. He was a transitional figure between silent experiments and both avant-garde and commercial sound films.

Born to Jewish parents in Warsaw, Epstein obtained a medical degree in 1916 in Lyons, where he met Auguste Lumière, brother of **Louis Lumière,** and in 1920 founded the cinema review *Le Promenoir.* Epstein became an enthusiastic and prolific writer on topics such as poetry, philosophy, photography, and cinema. He shot his first film, on Louis Pasteur, in 1922. Epstein was affiliated with vanguard cinema. Some of his movies, such as *Cœur fidèle* (1923; Faithful Heart), shuffle narrative continuity and temporal order in ways anticipating the **Nouvelle Vague** (New Wave). The

special effects of slow motion and superimposed images in *La Chute de la maison Usher* (1928), his adaptation of Edgar Allan Poe's story "The Fall of the House of Usher," foreshadow similar effects in Carl Theodor Dreyer's magnificent *Vampyr* (1932; *Vampire*).

Under the German **Occupation** of France during **World War II** Epstein was kept from working. He and his sister were arrested by the Gestapo, but friends and the International Red Cross prevented their deportation.

REFERENCES:

Richard Abel, *French Film Theory and Criticism, 1: 1907–1939* (Princeton: Princeton University Press, 1988);

Jean Epstein, *Ecrits sur le cinéma* (Paris: Seghers, 1975);

Pierre Leprohon, *Jean Epstein* (Paris: Seghers, 1964).

—T.C.

THE EPURATION

After the **Liberation** of Paris on 24–25 August 1944, a provisional government was gradually put in place as territory was progressively retaken from occupying German troops. The new government began purging the body politic of those who had aided or collaborated with the enemy. The many local tribunals that were empowered to render justice in this process of purification (épuration) — especially those presided over by Communists — often exceeded their mandates. Thousands of people who were apparently or clearly innocent were summarily executed, and their property was often confiscated by those who had accused them. The épuration became viewed as an excessive reaction to the circumstances and activities of the **Occupation.**

The precise number of executions is still hotly disputed, and many official documents remain classified. The leftists who conducted the purges claimed generally that some thirty-nine thousand people were sentenced to prison terms and forty thousand lost their civic rights, while fewer than a thousand were actually put to death. Opponents from the right wing charged that figures were much higher; some said there were as many as one hundred thousand executions, but these numbers cannot be substantiated.

REFERENCE:

Hilary Footitt and John Simmonds, *The Politics of Liberation: France 1943–1945* (New York: Holmes & Meier, 1988).

—D.O'C.

ESPRIT

The monthly *Esprit* (1932–   ), a magazine of Christian social thought, was the creation of **Emmanuel Mounier** (1905–1950), who shares with **Jacques Maritain** the distinction of being the leading Catholic intellectual of the twentieth century in France. Like so many other intellectuals of his generation, Mounier responded to the sense of historical crisis that marked the early 1930s.

From the outset refusing to be tied to any one political party, *Esprit* opened its pages to nonbelievers and Protestants as well as Catholics. The influence of **Charles Péguy** was visible in its blend of socialism and concern for social justice, nationalism, and religious mysticism — a mixture Mounier gave the name *le personnalisme* (personalism). Among the targets of its writers' wrath were the bourgeoisie and the established institutions, which Mounier called "le désordre établi" (the established disorder). He attributed many contemporary ills to unbridled individualism; but he also attacked the tyranny of collectivism, in the form of either Fascism or Communism, with their denial of spirituality and the needs of the individual.

At the start of **World War II,** publication of the magazine was interrupted briefly. It then appeared regularly until August 1941, when it was suppressed by **Vichy government** censors because of its attacks on totalitarianism. After the end of the war *Esprit* was the first magazine to resume publication, thanks to Mounier's extraordinary efforts. Its postwar positions, more clearly on the Left than had earlier been the case, called for support of workers against the power of capitalism and industry; dialogue with the **French Communist Party**; and a European alternative to American or Soviet hegemony. Mounier directed the magazine until his death in 1950.

REFERENCES:

Joseph Amato, *Mounier and Maritain: A French Catholic Understanding of the Modern World* (University: University of Alabama Press, 1975);

Eileen Cantin, C.S.J., *Mounier: A Personalist View of History* (New York: Paulist Press, 1973);

John Wright, "Emmanuel Mounier, *Esprit,* and Vichy, 1940–1944: Ideology and Anti-Ideology," in *Vichy France and the Resistance: Culture and Ideology,* edited by Roderick Kedward and Roger Austin (Totowa, N.J.: Barnes & Noble, 1985), pp. 171–189.

—J.P.McN.

THE EVIAN ACCORDS

The agreement known as the Evian Accords brought an end to the **Algerian war** on 18 March 1962. The provisions of the treaty were approved by the French people in a referendum on 8 April and by the Algerian people on 1 July.

Shortly after coming to power as the first president under the constitution of the **Fifth Republic, Charles de Gaulle** had delivered a speech on 16 September 1959 offering three options for the Algerians: (1) secession from France, that is, independence; (2) Francization, according to which the role and importance of French culture would be increased in the national mix; or (3) association with France, a loose federal political relationship. In the end the Algerian people fought for and won the first option.

While the Evian Accords were welcomed by many on both sides, many others in France believed that the agreements represented a betrayal by de Gaulle, who had earlier appeared sympathetic to those who wanted to maintain a French Algeria. In turning political power in Algeria over to the National Liberation Front, or FLN, de Gaulle was able to concentrate on building up the domestic economy of France.

REFERENCE:

Alistair Horne, *A Savage War of Peace: Algeria 1954–1962* (New York: Viking, 1978).

—D.O'C.

EXISTENTIALISM

The term *existentialism* often refers to the ideas of certain midcentury French writers and philosophers, especially **Jean-Paul Sartre** and **Simone de Beauvoir,** but it is not used thus exclusively. The adjective *existential* also may designate any philosopher or writer particularly concerned with human existence and individual experience in relation to a transcendent meaning of life or its absence.

The ancestors of modern French existentialism include Blaise Pascal and Søren Kierkegaard, who were both obsessed with the enormity of humanity's fallen condition and sin, which separate it from the divine and cause dread and anguish. Friedrich Nietzsche, who announced the death of God and urged a transvaluation of morality, is another forerunner, as is Fyodor Dostoevsky. In the early 1940s **Gabriel Marcel** applied the term *existentialism* to the philosophical positions of Sartre and Beauvoir, as well as his own. Sartre and Beauvoir, both atheists, were displeased by the label, doubtless because of its use by Christians such as Marcel, but it stuck. By the postwar period they and friends and colleagues such as **Albert Camus,** as well as many followers, were known as existentialists — first on the **Left Bank** of Paris and soon after throughout Europe and America. Sartre eventually accepted the term sufficiently to call a lecture *L'Existentialisme est un humanisme* (1946; translated as *Existentialism and Humanism*). In any case the term suits his work. Rejecting a philosophical tradition that posited a transcendent essence of human nature existing prior to actual human beings, Sartre asserted that existence precedes essence: each person is condemned to be free and is thus responsible for choosing his or her nature through a series of decisions. Camus, who is often labeled an existentialist, argued in his essay *Le Mythe de Sisyphe* (1942; translated as *The Myth of Sisyphus*) against what he considered existentialism to be — "philosophical suicide," a "leap of faith" that takes the believer across the abyss of absurdity from incomprehension and revolt at the meaninglessness of the universe to faith. Strictly speaking, therefore, the term should not be applied to Camus.

Sartre's existentialism had its roots principally in the phenomenology of Edmund Husserl and the investigations into the nature of being by Martin Heidegger. In *L'Etre et le néant: Essai d'ontologie phénoménologique* (1943; translated as *Being and Nothingness*) Sartre presents an elaborate philosophical exploration of human existence and its relationships with the world as experienced by the individual consciousness. He concluded that human beings have found themselves abandoned in a world without an overarching reason for the meaning of their existence; people have no absolute moral grounding for their actions. The emphasis in Sartre's seemingly nihilistic position upon nothingness and anxiety, which contrasts with but did not exclude a sometimes insouciant attitude toward existence, is probably the best-known side of French existentialism in Europe and abroad.

Beauvoir furnished the rudiments of an existentialist ethic in her *Pour une morale de l'ambiguïté* (1947; translated as *The Ethics of Ambiguity*). Sartre on occasion drew tentative ethical conclusions from his reflections but did not publish a coherent work on ethics during his lifetime. He repeatedly insisted, however, upon the total responsibility that derives from total freedom, encouraging people to live "authentically" rather than in "bad faith" through subjecting their wills to others or by following some preconceived notion of human nature. Further, he saw this responsibility in political terms, arguing that, because people are born free, it is the duty of everyone to bring about social and political conditions that allow for freedom to be practiced universally. He thus moved easily from an ethically indifferent philosophy of being to the defense of left-wing political positions. His massive *Critique de la raison dialectique* (1960; translated as *Critique of Dialectical Reason*) is an attempt to bridge the

gap between existentialism and Marxism. Elements of his existentialist thought are also featured, sometimes more comprehensibly, in his novels, stories, and plays.

While Sartre and Beauvoir had several disciples and the existentialist mentality was popular for some years, it produced few other figures of note. **Maurice Merleau-Ponty** is usually labeled a phenomenologist rather than an existentialist, but his thought has much in common with some of the strands that make up existentialism. While Marcel's Christian existentialism is acted out in his literary works, he is not generally considered a major literary figure and was not as influential a philosopher as Sartre. By the 1960s and 1970s **structuralism,** feminism, and other currents of thought had replaced existentialism as a fashionable intellectual position.

REFERENCES:

Hazel E. Barnes, *The Literature of Possibility* (Lincoln: University of Nebraska Press, 1959);

William Barrett, *Irrational Man: A Study in Existentialist Philosophy* (Garden City, N.Y.: Doubleday, 1958);

Joseph S. Catalano, *A Commentary on Jean-Paul Sartre's "Being and Nothingness"* (New York: Harper & Row, 1974);

Max Charlesworth, *The Existentialists and Jean-Paul Sartre* (New York: St. Martin's Press, 1976);

D. E. Cooper, *Existentialism: A Reconstruction* (Oxford: Blackwell, 1990);

Norman J. Greene, *Jean-Paul Sartre: The Existentialist Ethic* (Ann Arbor: University of Michigan Press, 1960);

Marjorie Grene, *Dreadful Freedom: A Critique of Existentialism* (Chicago: University of Chicago Press, 1948);

Frederick A. Olafson, *Principles and Persons: An Ethical Interpretation of Existentialism* (Baltimore: Johns Hopkins University Press, 1967);

George A. Schrader, *Existential Philosophers: Kierkegaard to Merleau-Ponty* (New York: McGraw-Hill, 1967).

— C.S.B.

L'EXPRESS

Founded by Jean-Jacques Servan-Schreiber and Françoise Giroud in May 1953, *L'Express* was the first French weekly newsmagazine in the general style of *Time* and *Newsweek* and has remained the most successful. While hostile to the **French Communist Party** throughout Servan-Schreiber's long tenure (1953–1977), *L'Express* consistently argued for state planning to aid in the industrialization of France and the modernization of social structures. The magazine advocated the creation of a new alliance of left-wing parties that would support policies leading to increased productivity rather than to the simple redistribution of wealth.

Front cover for the weekly newsmagazine that chose the
tiger as a symbol of its editorial policy

The first issue of *L'Express* included an interview
with the politician Pierre Mendès-France, to whom the
magazine would remain close. It shared his distrust of
colonial wars in general and in particular his views that
the **Indo-Chinese war** could not be won and that Tunisia and Morocco should be encouraged in their moves
toward independence, albeit while retaining strong ties
to France.

By the end of 1956, when France had been out of
Indochina for more than two years and the **Algerian war**
was two years old, *L'Express* argued that the war in Algeria was already lost — though it would not officially be
brought to a close until 1962. By 1957 the editorial writers
for *L'Express* took the highly controversial position that
independence for Algeria was inevitable.

With the creation of the **Fifth Republic** in 1958,
L'Express was unrelenting in its opposition not only to
any form of cooperation with the French Communists
but also to President **Charles de Gaulle,** although it did

open its pages to the fervent Gaullist **François
Mauriac.**

Starting in 1963 *L'Express* began increasingly to
appeal to a centrist public and especially a business-
minded audience. In September 1964 the format of
L'Express was changed to make it correspond more
closely to the newsmagazine models of *Time* and the
West German publication *Der Spiegel*. With seven
well-defined sections — France, the world, economics,
modern life, spectacles (that is, theater, music, dance,
and the cinema), books, and "Madame Express" — the
magazine increased in circulation from about 150,000
to more than 600,000 between 1964 and 1972. As the
magazine moved toward the political center, Jean
Daniel, who had been an important figure at
L'Express, left in 1964 to found a rival, leftist magazine, *Le Nouvel Observateur.* In its advocacy of a middle way between Gaullism and the left-wing platform
shared by the **Socialist Party** and the Communists,

L'Express supported the unsuccessful candidate Jean Lecanuet in the 1968 presidential elections.

As secretary general (1969–1971) and then president (1971–1975 and 1977) of the centrist Radical Party and as a deputy to the National Assembly (1970–1978), Servan-Schreiber divided his time between his magazine and a career in politics. This division of interests caused problems, and some members of the team at *L'Express* left in 1972 to create another newsmagazine, *Le Point.* Editor in chief Françoise Giroud left in 1974 to serve as secretary of the government ministry of women. Servan-Schreiber sold *L'Express* in 1977 to the Anglo-French financier James Goldsmith, and it changed hands again in 1987, when Bruno Rohmer took over as the publication director. *L'Express* is no longer a bold and innovative magazine, either in terms of editorial policies or format, but it continues to be the most widely read newsmagazine in France.

REFERENCES:

Jean-Jacques Servan-Schreiber, *The American Challenge,* translated by Ronald Steel (New York: Atheneum, 1968);

Servan-Schreiber and Michel Albert, *The Radical Alternative,* translated by H. A. Fields (New York: Norton, 1971).

—J.P.McN.

F

LÉON-PAUL FARGUE

Poet Léon-Paul Fargue (1876–1947) began his career as a member of the Symbolist circle whose poetry was published in the *Mercure de France* during the 1890s and the early years of the twentieth century. By the 1920s his work had evolved to reflect the new aesthetics associated with **Cubism** and **Surrealism** and assumed a modern, ironic tone.

Poems from Fargue's Symbolist period include *Tancrède* (1911), a sequence first published in the magazine *Pan* in 1895, and *Poèmes* (1912). *Espaces* (Spaces) and *Sous la lampe* (Under the Lamp), both published in 1929, collect poems in his later manner. Some critics consider Fargue more of a Surrealist than those who chose to be identified by that label. His poems are known for wit and verve, impressive wordplay and invention, as well as musicality. He particularly cultivated the prose poem.

Fargue's *Le Piéton de Paris* (1939; The Paris Pedestrian), a collection of articles on Paris between the world wars, also serves as an autobiography. Greatly admired and liked by many of his contemporaries, including **Saint-John Perse,** Fargue was awarded the Grand Prix Littéraire de la Ville de Paris in 1946. His important correspondence with **Valery Larbaud** is a useful source of information on his literary period.

REFERENCE:

André Beucler, *The Last of the Bohemians: Twenty Years with Léon-Paul Fargue,* translated by Geoffrey Sainsbury, with an introduction by Archibald MacLeish (New York: Sloane, 1954); republished as *Poet of Paris: Twenty Years with Léon-Paul Fargue* (London: Chatto & Windus, 1955).

— C.S.B.

ELIE FAURE

Elie Faure (1873–1937) was one of the most influential art historians of the twentieth century. His five-volume

Paul Valéry and Léon-Paul Fargue at Deauville, 1947

Histoire de l'art (1909–1921; translated as *The History of Art*), a landmark in art historiography, sets forth a view of art as not only an aesthetic creation but also as a mirror of civilization. *L'Esprit des formes* (1927; translated as *The Spirit of Forms*) adopts this same approach to art, emphasizing as well the importance of intuition. Because of their focus on the relationship of civilization to art, Faure's ideas greatly influenced novelist and art critic **André Malraux.**

131

Although visionary in some ways, Faure's work evinced a powerful nostalgia for the past, opposing the new avant-garde theories of artistic creation and favoring some traditional, even romantic, conceptions. He was convinced in particular that avant-garde art was inferior to traditional (including nineteenth-century) art because it followed intellectual formulas rather than relying for inspiration on artistic intuition and enthusiasm and because in the internationalist, avant-garde work of the mid 1920s and early 1930s artists often lost sight of their ethnic roots.

Faure's writings also include several studies of individual artists, including monographs on **Paul Cézanne** (1910), **Henri Matisse** (1920), and **André Derain** (1923). He also wrote works on history, sociology, and ethics, such as *La Conquête* (1917; The Conquest), *Napoléon* (1921), *Les Trois Gouttes de sang* (1929; The Three Drops of Blood), and *Les Désastres de la guerre* (1937; translated as *The Disasters of War*). His complete works were published in three volumes in 1964.

REFERENCE:

John Strand, "Polemics and Provocation in Paris: The Art Magazine Comes of Age," *Art International,* 5 (Winter 1988): 24–34.
—M.G.

GABRIEL FAURÉ

Although Gabriel Fauré (1845–1924) lived well into the twentieth century, his music remained in the nineteenth. The innovations of younger composers such as **Claude Debussy** and **Igor Stravinsky,** influential on many others, did not undermine the conventional tonality of his compositions. Within these nineteenth-century restrictions, he developed an original, recognizable style and wrote some of the masterpieces of fin de siècle French music.

Fauré's settings of poems by Paul Verlaine and other Parnassian and Symbolist poets of France reveal his melodic gifts. Modest in their resources and without climactic high notes, they illuminate the imagery and atmosphere of the poems. His piano music, influenced by Frédéric Chopin's, is also lyrical rather than dramatic, with graceful melodies surrounded by fanciful figurations. In these pieces Fauré's original and surprising modulations are noteworthy. His chamber music, particularly his sonatas for violin and piano, and his piano quartets and quintets are all beautifully constructed and frequently performed. In his setting of the requiem mass for soprano soloist, chorus, and orchestra, Fauré omitted the section describing the horrors of Judgment Day and enlarged those portions concerned

with the serenity of Paradise, creating a quiet and gentle work.

As professor of composition and director of the Paris Conservatory from 1905 until 1920, Fauré counted among his many students **Nadia Boulanger, Charles Koechlin, Maurice Ravel,** and Florent Schmitt. Fauré is considered to be a quintessential French composer because of the restraint, immaculate workmanship, feeling, and, above all, charm of his music.

REFERENCES:

Jean-Michel Nectoux, *Gabriel Fauré: A Musical Life,* translated by Roger Nichols (Cambridge: Cambridge University Press, 1991);

Robert Orledge, *Gabriel Fauré* (London: Eulenburg Books, 1979).

—P.S.H.

JEAN FAUTRIER

In the aftermath of **World War II,** French art was dominated by artists who attempted to capture some sense of the horror and misery of the war and the **Occupation** of France by German troops. One of the most prominent of such painters was Jean Fautrier (1898–1964). He is often classified as a *tachiste,* a term used to identify artists whose works are dominated by apparently random *taches,* or splashes, of color, but this classification contributes little to an understanding of Fautrier's style or subject matter.

A product of the Royal Academy and the Slade School in London, Fautrier had little success as an abstract artist before the war. Even then his subject matter often involved partial abstractions of grisly subject matter, as in *Les Peaux de lapins* (1927; *Rabbit Skins*), a still life of skinned rabbit carcasses.

Fautrier gradually evolved a painting technique he called *haute-pâte* (high paste), involving repeated layers of image on paper, compressed and glued to the canvas and covered with a thin wash of paint through which the darker underlying images are visible. His *Les Otages* (1943–1945; *The Hostages*), inspired by the mass Nazi deportations of French workers, is in many ways typical of his postwar work. In his preface to the exhibition catalogue for the series, **André Malraux** noted how the paintings gradually suppress both facial features and blood, so that in the end "nothing is left but lips, which are almost nerves, nothing but eyes which do not see. A hieroglyph of pain." Though Fautrier's output dropped off sharply in the 1950s, he produced a sequel of sorts to his hostage paintings, his

Partisans series (1956–1957), inspired by the Russian suppression of the Hungarian revolution of 1956.

REFERENCES:

Aftermath: France 1945–1954: New Images of Man (London: Barbican Centre, 1982);

Siegfried Gohr, "Fautrier: Through Paint, Alone," *Artforum*, 27 (September 1988): 111–116;

Daniel Wheeler, *Art Since Mid-Century: 1945 to the Present* (Englewood Cliffs, N.J.: Prentice-Hall, 1991).

— J.H.

FAUVES

As with many names assigned to experimental artistic circles, *Fauve* began as a derogatory epithet but was later embraced by the artists to whom it was applied and by their supporters. At the **Salon d'Automne** of 1905, room seven was taken over by a band of artists including **Henri Matisse, André Derain, Maurice Vlaminck,** Charles Camoin, Henri Manguin, and **Albert Marquet.** The conservative critic Louis Vauxcelles, noting in the room a small cupid (mistakenly identified as the work of Renaissance sculptor Donatello), exclaimed, "Ah Donatello! chez les Fauves!" (Ah, Donatello, among the wild beasts!).

The circle that later called itself the Fauves traced its origins to the first contacts between Matisse and Marquet at the studio of Gustave Moreau in 1895–1898. Moreau, best known as a sort of godfather to the Symbolist movement in painting, was noted for his relative tolerance for the experimental and unconventional in art. Asked to leave the Ecole des Beaux-Arts after Moreau's death in 1898, Matisse developed new ties over the next two years to Vlaminck and Derain.

Marcel Nicolle dismissed the works in room seven at the 1905 Salon d'Automne as "formless streaks of blue, red, yellow, and green, all mixed up, splashes of raw color juxtaposed without rhyme or reason, the naif and brutal efforts of a child playing with its paint-box." Yet amid his disapproval, Nicolle was able to select precisely the traits with which the Fauves sought to redefine painting: abandonment of superfluous detail, the "naive" simplification of forms, and especially the use of splashes of bold color (which Derain termed "color for color's sake"). Looking back on the movement from 1929, Matisse defined the Fauve effort as "construction by means of colored surfaces. A desire for a greater intensity of color...." Reacting against the diffuse representation of light through local colors in Impressionist art, the Fauves expressed light through a meeting of intensely colored surfaces. Form was to be defined not through drawing or shading, but by the direct juxtaposition of color.

Many of the Fauves were either militant anarchists or at least participants in a broadly defined anarchist, bohemian milieu. For them, their new art was not simply an aesthetic movement. They aimed at tearing down traditional rules and norms while seeking an absolute purity of form and color. Vlaminck spoke of his art as simultaneously an expression of his revolutionary views and a form of therapy. "What I could have achieved in social context by throwing a bomb ... I have tried to express in art."

The Fauves were not the first to attempt a socially oriented, anarchist-tinged art; some members of the group, most notably Matisse, had experimented briefly with the Pointillist style of the Neo-Impressionists. But whereas the Neo-Impressionists had sought to produce a "scientific" art, rooted in a close study of contemporary psychobiological theory (relating to optics), the libertarian instincts of the Fauves led them toward the demolition of rules and regulations, into an art based on intuition and empathy.

As a group the Fauves were both heterogeneous and short-lived. As early as 1908 the major figures were moving in distinct directions; some artists associated with Fauvist painting became intrigued first by **Paul Cézanne** (especially after a 1907 retrospective of his works) and then, through him, with the first stirrings of what became the **Cubist** movement. **Georges Braque** and **Fernand Léger** were among those who followed such a path. Others, including Vlaminck, pulled back from Cubism in favor of an eclectic, if eventually rather tepid, modernism. A few, such as Derain, returned to a rather traditional academic style.

REFERENCES:

Jean-Paul Crespelle, *The Fauves,* translated by Anita Brookner (Greenwich, Conn.: New York Graphic Society, 1962);

Georges Duthuit, *The Fauvist Painters* (New York: Wittenborn, Schultz, 1950);

Joseph-Emile Muller, *Fauvism* (New York & Washington, D.C.: Praeger, 1967);

John Russell, *The World of Matisse* (New York: Time-Life Books, 1974).

— J.H.

LUCIEN FEBVRE

The name of Lucien Febvre (1878–1956), one of the most important French historians in the twentieth century, is linked with that of the major journal of history the *Annales d'Histoire Economique et Sociale,* which he founded with Marc Bloch in 1929. Unlike conventional historians, who dealt with important political figures and events, Febvre focused on the history of societies, which he studied by relating economic, religious, geographic, and other factors.

Febvre began teaching in 1920 and from 1933 to the end of his life occupied the chair in the history of modern civilization at the Collège de France. His approach to history—combining history and the social sciences—drew especially on psychology, both individual and collective. His publications include *Un Destin: Martin Luther* (1928; translated as *Martin Luther, A Destiny*), *Le Problème de l'incroyance au XVIᵉ siècle* (1947; translated as *The Problem of Unbelief in the Sixteenth Century*), and *L'Apparition du livre* (1958; translated as *The Coming of the Book: The Impact of Printing, 1450–1800*), written in collaboration with Henri-Jean Martin.

REFERENCE:

Palmer A. Throop, "Lucien Febvre," in *Some Twentieth Century Historians: Essays on Eminent Europeans,* edited by S. William Halperin (Chicago: University of Chicago Press, 1961), pp. 277–298.

— C.S.B.

FÉDÉRATION INTERNATIONALE DES ARTISTES RÉVOLUTIONNAIRES INDÉPENDANTS

The formation of the Fédération Internationale des Artistes Révolutionnaires Indépendants (FIARI) was a direct — if belated — response to the Stalinization of both French and international associations of revolutionary-minded artists and intellectuals. The repeated purges of oppositional factions and leaders from the Soviet Communist Party were paralleled in France by purges of dissident individuals and groups from both the **French Communist Party** and the entire constellation of cultural and artistic associations linked to it. Similar purges occurred in other countries as well. A broad, if ill-defined, milieu of artists and intellectuals to the left of social-democrat reformers became unattached from any specific radical political movement. In January 1938 **André Breton** and Mexican painter Diego Rivera issued a "Manifesto for an Independent Revolutionary Art" (actually written by Breton and exiled Russian Communist Leon Trotsky) in an effort to organize what Breton termed "resistance against all the forces of domestication of the spirit." The manifesto was used to launch the FIARI, which set up usually short-lived committees in Paris, London, New York, Belgium, Mexico, Buenos Aires, and North Africa. **Surrealists** formed the core of its membership, especially in France. Its journal was *Clé* (Key).

Threatened with repression by Nazism, Fascism, and Stalinism in a world on the eve of a new global war, intellectual and artistic freedom was under attack everywhere. The manifesto called for "complete freedom for art" and "an anarchist regime of individual liberty" characterized by the slogan "No authority, no dictation, not the least trace of orders from above!" On that basis "thousands upon thousands of isolated thinkers and artists" scattered around the world were urged to unite in the new group, along with the "hundreds of small local magazines" dedicated to "seeking new paths and not subsidies."

The FIARI attracted many dissident radicals, including Marcel Martinet, **André Masson,** Maurice Nadeau, and Gérard Rosenthal in France and, internationally, Herbert Read, exiled Russian revolutionary Victor Serge, and Italian novelist Ignazio Silone. Two issues of *Clé* appeared in 1939, before the outbreak of **World War II** effectively dissolved the FIARI.

REFERENCES:

André Breton and Diego Rivera, "Manifesto for an Independent Revolutionary Art," in Breton's *What Is Surrealism? Selected Writings,* edited by Franklin Rosemont (New York: Monad Press, 1978), pp. 183–187;

Herbert S. Gershman, *The Surrealist Revolution in France* (Ann Arbor: University of Michigan Press, 1969), pp. 105–108;

Maurice Nadeau, *History of Surrealism,* translated by Richard Howard (New York: Macmillan, 1965), pp. 208–211.

—J.H.

FÉLIX FÉNÉON

Félix Fénéon (1861–1944) combined an active career as a critic of society and the arts with the life of a committed, militant anarchist. The range of his activities appears dizzying: he was equally at ease writing for the avant-garde *Revue Blanche,* the politico-artistic *La Vogue,* anarchist political journals such as *L'Emancipation Sociale,* and even the self-consciously vulgar "worker anarchist" periodical *Le Père Peinard,* which was published in the patois of the industrial working class. Painter Henri de Toulouse-Lautrec called Fénéon "Buddha," while to critic Rémy de Gourmont he was "Mephistopheles."

Fénéon's major impact on the art world came with his early championing of the Neo-Impressionist circle, especially in his *Les Impressionnistes en 1886* (1886; The Impressionists in 1886). For Fénéon the "scientific impressionism" of Georges Seurat and his colleagues — most vividly in Seurat's monumental *Un Dimanche à la Grande Jatte* (1884–1886; *A Sunday on La Grande Jatte*) — captured the spirit of his age: scientific, radical, and deeply involved in the depiction of the modern world. Fénéon's review of these Neo-Impressionists focuses on their optical theory and practice, especially their attempt to re-create precisely the light of the sun. Fénéon organized Seurat's first retrospective exhibition (1900) and edited the first *catalogue raisonné* of Seurat's work.

In 1894 Fénéon's political views and his unabashed proclamation of them provoked authorities to make him one of the defendants in a government show trial of anarchists that became known as the *Procès des trente* (Trial of the Thirty). Reacting to the assassination of President Sadi Carnot by an anarchist, the French government hoped to suppress anarchism by trying nineteen "militants" — including intellectuals, publishers, and theoreticians — and eleven "thieves" — a motley array of petty criminals who had proclaimed some sympathy for anarchism. Though most of the accused had never met, they were charged with forming an "association of evildoers." Fénéon ripped apart the prosecution's case in his testimony, to the apparent delight of much of the press. All but three burglars were acquitted.

In the early 1900s Fénéon used his contacts to help young (and often radical) artists get established in Paris and gave some of them their first one-man shows in his small studio. He also helped to introduce to the public **Claude Debussy** and, as editor of the *Revue Blanche*, **André Gide.**

REFERENCES:

Joan Ungersman Halperin, *Félix Fénéon: Aesthete and Anarchist in Fin-de-siècle Paris* (New Haven: Yale University Press, 1988);

John Hutton, *Neo-Impressionism and the Search for Solid Ground: Art, Science, and Anarchism in Fin-de-siècle France* (Baton Rouge: Louisiana State University Press, 1994);

Richard Whelan, "'Le Roi': Fénéon and the Neo-Impressionists," *Portfolio*, 3 (March–April 1981): 46–55.

— J.H.

FERNANDEL

Born Fernand Joseph Désiré Contandin, the actor Fernandel (1903–1971), one of the great comic performers of French cinema, came to the attention of an international public in the late 1940s. His performances were accented by his comic physical appearance, marked by a sad, enormous face set on a short, squat frame.

He began his career in vaudeville and made his first movie in 1930. Most of his early roles were serious, but he gradually became better known as a comic actor. **Marcel Pagnol**'s *La Fille du puisatier* (1940; *The Well-Digger's Daughter*), **Julien Duvivier**'s *Le Petit Monde*

Léo Ferré (Rapho)

de Don Camillo (1952; *The Little World of Don Camillo*), and Henri Verneuil's *Le Mouton à cinq pattes* (1954; *The Sheep Has Five Legs*) are among his best movies. In *Le Mouton à cinq pattes* Fernandel played six parts, displaying an immense range of characterization. In *Le Petit Monde de Don Camillo,* about the travails of a Communist mayor and the village priest, Fernandel brought a deft blend of comedy and seriousness to his role. His noncomedic roles included a part in **Sacha Guitry**'s *Tu m'as sauvé la vie* (1950; You Saved My Life).

REFERENCES:

Y. Gerald, "Fernandel's Comic Style," *Films in Review* (March 1960);

"I'm an Actor, Not a Comedian," *Films and Filmmaking* (October 1960).

— W.L.

LÉO FERRÉ

One of the most admired of figures in French popular music, Léo Ferré (1916–1993), who was born in Monte

Carlo, became known in the cabarets of the **Saint-Germain-des-Prés** section of Paris after **World War II.** He composed and wrote the lyrics for many of the songs that he performed and recorded. Others were his musical settings of poems by François Villon, Paul Verlaine, Charles Baudelaire, and **Louis Aragon.** Ferré also composed an oratorio on "La Chanson du mal aimé" ("Song of the Poorly Loved") by **Guillaume Apollinaire.** Among Ferré's best-known songs are "Paris-Canaille" and "Jolie Môme." His lyrics often include acerbic attacks on social institutions and conventional morality. Ferré also wrote two novels, *Benoît Misére* (1970; Benedict-Pauper) and *Testament phonographe* (1990; Phonograph-Will).

REFERENCES:

Léo Ferré: Les années Galaxie (Paris: Seghers, 1986);

Malcolm Reid, "Ferré," *Contemporary French Civilization*, 6 (Spring 1982): 259–270;

Françoise Travelet, *Dis donc, Ferré* (Paris: Hachette, 1976).

— C.S.B.

Louis Feuillade

Louis Feuillade (1873–1925) was a founding figure in French cinema. Between 1906 and 1925 he wrote and directed more than eight hundred short films, including the atmospheric serials for which he is best known. Although his work was championed by the **Surrealists** in the late 1910s and the 1920s, he was nonetheless a businessman who knew how to produce films cheaply and how to make a profit.

Feuillade entered the film industry in 1905, when **Alice Guy** hired him to write for **Gaumont** Productions. The following year he became a director and production chief for Gaumont. During **World War I** he helped to popularize the movie serial, producing films filled with comic and dramatic episodes centered on the battle between good and evil. The most successful and influential of these serials are *Fantômas* (1913–1914), *Les Vampires* (1915–1916; The Vampires), *Judex* (1916–1917), and *Barrabas* (1919–1920). Fantômas is a master criminal who outwits his enemy, police inspector Juve, through many disguises and stratagems. *Les Vampires,* also about clever criminals, was controversial for its supposed attack on middle-class mores. Among Feuillade's innovations in these and other serials are on-location photography, deep-focus shots, and moving shots. Feuillade's later works were less notable, and he came to be seen as part of a cinematic old guard. After a period of neglect following his death, his work was rediscovered in the 1940s.

REFERENCES:

Richard Abel, *French Cinema: The First Wave, 1915–29* (Princeton: Princeton University Press, 1984);

Noël Burch, *Life to Those Shadows* (Berkeley & Los Angeles: University of California Press, 1990);

Francis Lacassin, *Louis Feuillade* (Paris: Seghers, 1964);

Richard Roud, "Feuillade and the Serial," in *Rediscovering French Film,* edited by Mary Lean Bandy (New York: Museum of Modern Art, 1983), pp. 45–52.

— T.C.

Jacques Feyder

Jacques Feyder (1885–1948) was one of the best-known film directors in France during the 1920s and 1930s. He directed classic movies in the **poetic realist** style, most notably *Le Grand Jeu* (1934; *The Great Game*) and *Pension Mimosas* (1935).

Born Jacques Frédérix in Belgium, Feyder changed his name at the insistence of his father, who considered his son's theatrical career a disgrace to the family. Feyder acted in theater and film in Paris and Lyons from 1912 to 1914 and gained experience in cinema as an assistant to Gaston Ravel and as a director for **Léon Gaumont.** Feyder wrote and directed seventeen silent films during **World War I.** He made extraordinarily rich movie versions of French literary classics, including Emile Zola's *Thérèse Raquin* (1928; *Shadows of Fear*). After his *Les Nouveaux Messieurs* (1928; *The New Gentlemen*) was banned for its satire of the French Parliament, M-G-M studios lured Feyder to Hollywood. While in America he directed Greta Garbo's last silent feature, *The Kiss* (1929).

Feyder returned to France in 1931 and went back to Belgium in 1933, when he completed his best-known feature, *La Kermesse héroïque* (1935; *Carnival in Flanders*), a witty melodrama that brings to life the world of Frans Hals, Rembrandt van Rijn, and Peter Paul Rubens. The film was banned in France during the German **Occupation** in **World War II.** At that time Feyder immigrated to Switzerland with his wife, actress Françoise Rosay.

REFERENCES:

Richard Abel, *French Cinema: The First Wave, 1915–29* (Princeton: Princeton University Press, 1984);

Jacques Feyder and Françoise Rosay, *Le Cinéma, notre métier* (Paris: Cailler, 1946);

Charles Ford, *Jacques Feyder* (Paris: Seghers, 1973).

— T.C.

Michel Debré, keeper of the state seal (left), and Secretary of State Houphouët Boigny (behind the book press) examining the first copy of the Constitution of the Fifth Republic, 7 October 1958 (Edimedia)

THE FIFTH REPUBLIC

The Fifth Republic came into being in 1958 in large part as a result of the crisis caused by the **Algerian war.** Still in existence in 1994, it is the second longest French republic, ranking behind the **Third Republic** (1875–1940).

Essentially written by **Charles de Gaulle** and his advisers, the constitution of the Fifth Republic calls for a strong executive to counterbalance the preponderance of power held by the legislative branch under the constitutions of the Third Republic and the **Fourth Republic.**

The constitution seeks to establish a stable executive office in three ways. First, it mandates the direct election of the president, who holds office for seven years and may be reelected for an unlimited number of terms (although no president has yet served more than two). In the earlier republics executive power was invested in a prime minister elected by members of parliament. Second, the constitution calls for a two-round system of elections, with the two largest vote getters in the first round facing each other in the second round. This system not only has the merit of producing coali-

tions among parties, it also produces presidents who have the electoral support of a majority of the voters. Third, since the day-to-day running of the government is conducted by the prime minister, the president is insulated from attacks from the legislative branch and those resulting from shifts in public opinion. The prime minister is no longer elected by the parliament; he is named by the president and serves at his pleasure. Even if a prime minister resigns, the directly elected president remains in office.

De Gaulle was the first president elected under the constitution of the Fifth Republic. He was reelected to a second term in 1965. Owing in part to the student riots and general upheaval of **May 1968,** he resigned from office in 1969, after the French electorate had rejected a referendum that he had placed before them. It called for the administrative reorganization of France into "regions," which would replace in certain respects the traditional "departments" into which the country has been divided since the French Revolution. The French people are said to have generally been in favor of this new arrangement before it was placed on the ballot. According to some observers, voters may have turned down the proposal only because de Gaulle had threatened to resign if it was rejected. In this analysis the French had simply grown tired of de Gaulle and saw this referendum as a way to be rid of him.

Georges Pompidou, who had been de Gaulle's prime minister, became the second president of the Fifth Republic. He died in 1974 before completing his seven-year term. The third president was Valéry Giscard d'Estaing, leader of a party called the Républicains Indépendants (Independent Republicans). At the time this small right-of-center group was usually allied with the conservative Gaullists. He served one term (1974–1981).

An important constitutional test came when the 1981 presidential election was won by a non-Gaullist, François Mitterand, who had opposed de Gaulle and his constitution from the beginning. Representing the **Socialist Party,** he received 51.7 percent of the vote to Giscard's 48.3 percent in the second round. In the parliamentary elections that followed the combined parties of the left garnered 55.7 percent of the vote, with the Socialists alone obtaining an absolute majority of seats. This first transition of power from right to left went smoothly, demonstrating the institutional merits of the Fifth Republic in comparison to its predecessors.

REFERENCES:

Dorothy Pickles, *The Fifth French Republic* (New York: Praeger, 1960);

Frank Lee Wilson, *French Political Parties Under the Fifth Republic* (New York: Praeger, 1982).

— D.O'C.

LE FIGARO

The *Figaro,* which has the largest circulation of all French daily newspapers, has had a long history. Named after the disrespectful character in two plays by the eighteenth-century author Pierre-Augustin Caron de Beaumarchais, the paper first appeared as a weekly in 1826. After it was acquired by H. de Villemessant in 1854, it began to appear twice weekly. In 1867 it started to come out every day. Such well-known writers as Théodore de Banville and Jules-Amédée Barbey d'Aurevilly were then on its staff.

The *Figaro* has long been a conservative voice, and in recent decades it has been the leading conservative paper in France. It has, however, often published articles by writers who were not themselves conservatives. In the 1890s, while the right-wing anti-Semite Léon Daudet covered the aftermath of Captain Alfred **Dreyfus**'s first trial for the paper, other writers, including Emile Zola, used the columns of the paper to proclaim Dreyfus's innocence and to speak out against anti-Semitism. **Marcel Proust,** sympathetic to Dreyfus's cause, made his debut as a writer in the *Figaro.*

The 1930s were a particularly illustrious period for the *Figaro,* then under the directorship of Pierre Brisson. Among its contributors were **André Gide, François Mauriac,** and **Jean-Paul Sartre.** Under the German **Occupation** of France during **World War II,** Brisson kept the paper going for two years by moving it to Lyons, in the **Free Zone.** By keeping the paper apolitical, Brisson largely escaped the strict censorship of the **Vichy government.** He neither offered support to Vichy nor attacked those to whom it was opposed, such as the Allies, the Jews, and **Charles de Gaulle.** His honor intact, he closed down the paper in November 1942 when the Germans occupied the Free Zone.

At the end of the war Brisson resumed publishing the *Figaro* in Paris and, until his death in 1964, ran it successfully as an independent conservative newspaper. In the 1950s and early 1960s its vitality was remarkable, with large advertising revenues, a circulation twice that of the *Monde* — a rival in terms of quality and, to some degree, audience — and real diversity of opinion on major issues. Among its distinguished writers was **Raymond Aron,** who generally agreed with its conservative, nationalist leanings but did not hesitate to criticize President Charles de Gaulle or to call for an end to French colonialism.

Front page of *Le Figaro,* 23 October 1962

Under Brisson, a binding legal agreement kept the financial and editorial policies of the *Figaro* separate. This agreement came to an end in 1969, and the press magnates who had a controlling interest in the paper — first Jean Prouvost, then Robert Hersant — saw little reason to protect their writers' independence, especially in view of the unrest following the student riots of **May 1968.** When Hersant took over from the aging Prouvost in 1975, he was even less interested than his predecessor in tolerating divergence of opinion. Hersant appears to have enjoyed the support of Prime Minister Jacques Chirac, powerful right-wing industrialist Marcel Dassault, and others at the highest national level. By 1976 he had fired 30 staff journalists, and more than 160 of some 290 staff members had resigned. In 1977 others resigned, including Aron, who attacked Hersant in the newsmagazine the *Point.*

While Hersant's ruthless tactics have been controversial, his astuteness as a businessman cannot be doubted. His Groupe Hersant has grown into a press empire second in France only to Hachette Presse. His creation of the spin-offs *Figaro Magazine* and *Madame*

Figaro was a masterstroke, attracting many new readers and generating major advertising revenues. The circulation of *Le Figaro* in 1990 was about 4.2 million. Its actual influence as the near-official voice of the Right is even greater than these large circulation figures suggest.

REFERENCES:

J. W. Freiberg, *The French Press: Class, State, and Ideology* (New York: Praeger, 1981);

Jacques de Lacretelle, *Face à l'événement: "Le Figaro" 1826–1966* (Paris: Hachette, 1966).

—J.P. McN.

Film Noir

Named in 1955 by French critics Raymond Borde and Etienne Chaumeton, film noir usually refers to American movies of the 1940s and early 1950s, often based on American hard-boiled detective stories and using backlighting, unusual chiaroscuro effects, and expressionistic decors to depict a world of crime and deceit. Yet the French relationship to film noir is significant. First, the convention is named after the French "Série noire" translations of American hard-boiled crime stories. More important, film noir has some of its roots in France — particularly in the work of **Jean Renoir,** whose paradigmatic films *La Chienne* (1931; *The Bitch*) and *La Bête humaine* (1938; *The Human Beast*) inspired film-noir directors Fritz Lang and John Huston in America.

Most film-noir movies use flashbacks and elaborate narrative designs to reconstruct an inevitable course of events that lead to tragedy. The action takes place in vaguely defined settings that put the contemporary context — **World War II** and the beginning of the Cold War — into oblivion. Classic works of the genre include *Double Indemnity* (1944), *Murder My Sweet* (1945), and *The Lady from Shanghai* (1948).

French critics of the **Nouvelle Vague** (New Wave) looked both to American film noir and its literary origins as a source of inspiration for films that would move away from the stilted **tradition de qualité,** a reigning style of the 1930s and 1940s that in their estimation made boring and lifeless movies out of great literature. Renoir's films also helped to inspire a French revival of the genre in the work of **Jean-Pierre Melville** in the 1950s. Without the impact of Renoir or that of New Wave critics, film noir would not figure with such prominence in film history.

REFERENCES:

Raymond Borde and Etienne Chaumeton, *Panorama du film noir américain 1941–1953* (Paris: Editions de Minuit, 1955);

James Damico, "Film noir: A Modest Proposal," *Film Reader,* 3 (1978): 48–57.

—T.C.

Léonor Fini

Artist Léonor Fini (1918–) was born in Buenos Aires of an Argentine father and a German and Slovene mother and grew up in the city of Trieste after her parents' divorce. Without formal training in art, Fini experimented with a variety of techniques, and in 1935 she took up psychic automatism — the creation of art directly from the subconscious without intervention or editing by the conscious mind. This interest paralleled a focus on **Surrealism,** and in 1936 she moved to Paris, where she met Surrealists such as **Georges Bataille, Paul Eluard,** Salvador Dalí, and **Man Ray.**

Although Fini never formally affiliated with the Surrealists, she shares their interest in the mythic and the unconscious mind. Like Leonora Carrington and Remedios Varo, Fini's fascination with myth takes on explicit overtones of gender, marked in her case by a continuing attraction for the feline and the sphinx. Drawing upon these images of "feminine evil" in English Pre-Raphaelite and French Symbolist art, Fini reverses the symbols, making them positive (if deadly) images of feminine strength and power. In Jungian terms, Fini believes the soul and thus the unconscious are feminine (anima), while the waking world is the province of the masculine (animus). In her *Chthonian Deity Watching over the Sleep of a Young Man* (1947), the young man sleeps in a pose reminiscent of a classical female nude and is watched over by a powerful sphinx. In her later works Fini increasingly emphasized images of powerful women (or women-animal hybrids). Guardians with shaved heads were succeeded by sorceresses, who do battle against male power.

Fini spent the years of **World War II** in Rome; since 1946, she has lived in Paris.

REFERENCES:

Mary Ann Caws, Rudolf Kuenzli, and Gloria Gwen Raaberg, *Surrealism and Women* (Cambridge, Mass. & London: MIT Press, 1991);

Whitney Chadwick, *Women Artists and the Surrealist Movement* (London: Thames & Hudson, 1985);

Ann Sutherland Harris and Linda Nochlin, *Women Artists 1550–1950* (New York: Knopf, 1989), pp. 329–331.

—J.H.

ROBERT FLOREY

The varied career of director and screenwriter Robert Florey (1900–1979) demonstrates the international nature of French cinema. Between 1929 and 1950 he directed more than sixty features in America and Europe. His training in France gave an expressive signature to many films that would otherwise be the stuff of oblivion. After 1950, the year he received the Légion d'Honneur, he turned his attention to television.

In 1919 and 1920 Florey worked as an actor, screenwriter, and assistant director, first in Switzerland and then in France with **Louis Feuillade.** In 1921 Florey went to the United States, where he worked as a technical director, actor, and writer and became the foreign publicity director for stars such as Douglas Fairbanks, Mary Pickford, and Rudolph Valentino. Although he spent most of the 1920s as an assistant director, he directed his first American film, *Fifty-Fifty,* in 1923 and his first feature-length film, *One Hour of Love,* in 1927.

Florey and Joseph Santley directed the Marx Brothers' first feature, *The Cocoanuts* (1929), and Florey helped to write the scenario for James Whale's classic *Frankenstein* (1931). He also was associate director under Charles Chaplin for Chaplin's *Monsieur Verdoux* (1948), which was a failure in America but succeeded in France, where Florey was respected for his early work with Feuillade.

REFERENCE:

Brian Taves, *Robert Florey: The French Expressionist* (Metuchen, N.J.: Scarecrow Press, 1987).

—T.C.

FERDINAND FOCH

Ferdinand Foch (1851–1929) was perhaps the foremost military thinker in France during the **World War I** period. Early in the twentieth century he published two influential books on military tactics: *Des principes de la guerre* (1903; translated as *Principles of War*) and *De la conduite de la guerre* (1904; On the Conduct of War).

When World War I came in 1914, he commanded the 20th Army Corps. His doctrine of the offensive stipulated that it should be "not an infantry attack prepared by artillery, but an artillery attack to be exploited by infantry on as wide a front as possible." His great offensive planned for the Somme front in 1916 was only partially successful because of the large number of troops committed to the defense of **Verdun.**

Foch moved to the background for political reasons in late 1916 but came to the fore again when he was named commander of all Allied forces on 26 March 1918. Blunting the German offensive that spring and holding back his reserves until German troops had overextended themselves, he was able to launch a massive counteroffensive in late July and continue it into September. Benefiting from manpower made available by American entry into the war, he was able to dictate the terms of the armistice to the Germans in November. Foch received the marshal's baton in August of that year and became a member of the Académie Française on 11 November, the day of the armistice.

REFERENCES:

Thomas M. Hunter, *Marshal Foch: A Study in Leadership* (Ottawa: Directorate of Military Training, 1961);

James H. Marshall-Cornwall, *Foch as Military Commander* (London: Batsford, 1972).

—D.O'C.

MICHEL FOKINE

Michel Fokine (1880–1942), a ballet dancer with the Maryinsky Theater of Saint Petersburg starting in 1898, became the first chief choreographer of **Serge Diaghilev's Ballets Russes** in 1909. With the Ballets Russes Fokine instituted choreographic reforms that would profoundly affect the development of ballet choreography in the twentieth century.

Fokine's new ballet was a truly expressive art, based on reforms he outlined in a letter to the *Times* (London) on 6 July 1914. He eliminated preestablished movement phrases and allowed the theme of the ballet to determine style. He made the corps de ballet (the secondary dancers) part of the ballet rather than merely decoration, and he removed spectacle and frivolous pantomime. He advocated an alliance of all the arts in the creation of a work and endorsed using the music of the great composers, as did the legendary **Isadora Duncan.**

Except for *The Dying Swan* (1905), choreographed for Anna Pavlova in Saint Petersburg, Fokine created his most famous ballets for the Ballets Russes. *Les Sylphides* (1909), with music by Frédéric Chopin and sets and costumes by Alexandre Benois, was a new version of *Chopiniana,* first presented in 1907 at the Maryinsky Theater. A tribute to Romantic ballet, it was his primary example of abstract, plotless ballets. Later came *Schéhérazade* (1910), with music by Nicolay Andreyevich Rimsky-Korsakov and sets and costumes by Lev (Léon) Bakst, based on the first tale of *The Thousand and One Nights. L'Oiseau de feu* (1910; *The Firebird*), with music by **Igor Stravinsky,** sets by Aleksander Golovin, and costumes by Golovin with

Bakst, was based on several Russian legends about a magical bird. *Le Spectre de la rose* (1911; The Specter of the Rose), with music by Carl Maria von Weber and sets and costumes by Bakst, was a romantic pas de deux about a young girl and the spirit of a rose she brings home from her first dance. *Petrouchka* (1911), with music by Stravinsky and sets and costumes by Bakst, is set during a Saint Petersburg street carnival. The crowd scenes in this work exemplify Fokine's reforms.

While choreographer for the Ballets Russes, Fokine continued his association with the Maryinsky Theater and created ballets for the **Ida Rubenstein** and Pavlova companies. In 1914 Diaghilev replaced Fokine with **Vaslav Nijinsky** as chief choreographer. After working with later Ballet Russe companies, Fokine eventually settled in New York City, but he never again created works of great significance.

REFERENCES:

Lynn Garafola, "The Liberating Aesthetic of Michel Fokine," in her *Diaghilev's Ballets Russes* (New York & Oxford: Oxford University Press, 1989), pp. 3–49;

Dawn Lille Horwitz, *Michel Fokine* (Boston: Twayne, 1985).

— A.P.E.

JEAN FOLLAIN

A poet who eschewed rhetoric and what he called "discursiveness" to create instead a "poetry of concentration," a sort of "verbal incantation," Jean Follain (1903–1971) won the prestigious Prix Mallarmé in 1939. Among his principal themes is that of time. He has been called a poet of objects or of the quotidian, but his poems go beyond everyday words and things to fulfill his desire "to bring things together in an unexpected manner in order to describe a particular sentiment, a particular vision of the world and to use the simplest words in order to give them back their virtue, their profound value." Follain's books include *Paris* (1935), *Usage du temps* (1943; Use of Time), *Des heures* (1960; Hours), and *D'après tout* (1967; After All).

REFERENCE:

Serge Gavronsky, ed. and trans., *Poems and Texts* (New York: October House, 1969), pp. 65–79.

— C.S.B.

FONTAINE

Founded in 1939 in Algiers by Max-Pol Fouchet, *Fontaine* was one of the principal literary magazines of the French **Resistance** movement during **World War II.** Promoting patriotic literature opposing the **Vichy gov-** **ernment** of the so-called **Free Zone** of France, the magazine published works by poets such as **Louis Aragon** and **Paul Eluard,** including Eluard's famous poem "Liberté" (1942). In 1945 the magazine was moved to Paris, where it was edited by Edmond Charlot. The last issue of *Fontaine* appeared in 1947.

REFERENCE:

Pierre de Boisdeffre, *Histoire de la littérature de langue française des années 1930 aux années 1980,* 2 volumes (Paris: Perrin, 1985).

— C.S.B.

JEAN-LOUIS FORAIN

Jean-Louis Forain (1852–1931) typified in many ways the eclectic artist who came to the fore during and just after the Impressionist era. A close associate of Edgar Degas, Forain exhibited in four of the Impressionist exhibitions (1879, 1880, 1881, and 1886). Stylistically, his work drew from a variety of sources: some of his repeated themes and treatments (ballet dancers, operagoers and theatergoers) echo Degas, while his satires and the courtroom paintings he began in the early 1900s are reminiscent of Honoré Daumier's. Most of Forain's paintings are marked by a dark palette alien to Impressionist technique. He once commented, "The Impressionists have discovered the way to paint light, a magnificent discovery. But the cloud is also splendid, as are all the tones of a *grisaille.*"

Forain's work is marked by an interest in anecdotal incident that ties it more closely to nineteenth-century realist art than to Impressionism. His *Place de la Concorde* (1884) differs from Degas's painting of the same subject (1876) in its emphasis on an implied message of class distinction in the chance encounter of a top-hatted bourgeois and a street sweeper on the "plaza of concord." Similarly, Forain's pastels of ballet dancers differ from the equivalents by Degas in their relentless fascination with sexual encounters between the dancers and wealthy old men.

Forain's best-known works are his social and political caricatures of the 1880s and 1890s, in which he sought consciously to emulate Daumier's satirical depictions of the first half of the nineteenth century. Yet his politics quickly moved far to the right of Daumier's, a fact that became especially apparent during the social upheaval that accompanied the **Dreyfus affair.** Forain, who was associated with the conservative newspaper *Figaro* from 1893 until 1924, emerged as not only an anti-Dreyfusard but also a virulent anti-Semite. He and the print artist Caran d'Ache founded a review, *Psst...!* (1898–1899), which specialized in anti-Semitic slurs;

the same themes occur in his print collections of 1896, *Album Forain* and *Doux pays* (Sweet Country).

REFERENCES:

Lillian Browse, *Forain: The Painter, 1852–1931* (London: Elek, 1978);

Robert F. Byrnes, "Jean-Louis Forain: Antisemitism in French Art," *Jewish Social Studies,* 12 (January 1950): 247–256;

Campbell Dodgson, *Forain: Draughtsman, Lithographer, Etcher* (New York: M. Knoedler, 1936).

                                                              — J.H.

PAUL FORT

When he was eighteen, Paul Fort (1872–1960) founded the Théâtre d'Art, an important Paris theater that specialized in staging poetic, nonrealistic dramas. After it closed in 1893, Fort was associated with *Le Livre d'Art* and *La Plume* before founding and editing *Vers et Prose* (1905–1914). These magazines published important works by the Symbolists and by early modernists such as **Guillaume Apollinaire.** In his own poetry Fort employed the rhymes, rhythms, and assonance of traditional verse forms, but he printed these works as prose, calling them *Ballades françaises* (French Ballads) and publishing them in forty volumes beginning in 1897. Although his poetry has fallen into disfavor, Fort is remembered as an important editor and director.

REFERENCES:

Edmund Gosse, *French Profiles* (London: Heinemann, 1902);

Amy Lowell, *Six French Poets* (New York: Macmillan, 1916).

                                                              — C.S.B.

MICHEL FOUCAULT

Philosopher Michel Foucault (1926–1984) is widely considered a major French thinker of the second half of the twentieth century. While he has been dismissed by some critics for the radical nature of his thinking and the difficulty of his prose, his ideas have been adopted by many scholars in the humanities and social sciences. His interests were chiefly historical, cultural, and social, but his work also has implications for literary criticism and other disciplines.

Foucault began his career as a professor of psychology, but his multidisciplinary interests gradually led him toward philosophy. In 1970 he was appointed to a position at the prestigious Collège de France. Since the 1960s his fame has spread widely, including in the United States, where he lectured at various universities.

Michel Foucault and Yves Montand at Roissy, 22 September 1975, after they had been expelled from Spain for protesting the death sentences of Madrid militants (Pascal Lebrun)

Foucault classified much of his writing, dealing with institutional and discursive practices in their historical contexts, as "archeology," which he defined as "a task that consists of not — of no longer — treating discourses as groups of signs (signifying elements referring to contents or representations) but as practices that systematically form the objects of which they speak." Influenced by Friedrich Nietzsche, he called some of his other undertakings "genealogies." In these works he investigated the function of such discursive conventions interwoven with social practices and the relations of power they reinforce.

One of Foucault's principal theses is that authority and power in premodern societies were invested in a few authoritarian figures, but in the modern state organization they have been interiorized in collective ways of thinking more repressive than the loosely organized, ill-disciplined premodern order. In *Surveiller et punir: Naissance de la prison* (1975; translated as *Discipline and Punish: The Birth of the Prison*) he argued that institutions such as prisons, schools, the military, and factories make subjects of citizens by imposing complex codes of rules and habits that lead them to police themselves and others. In his view this freely accepted disciplinary society constitutes a type of fascism akin to that of twentieth-century totalitarian states. Foucault hoped to expose this network, in which so-called victims participate willingly, and thus to discredit modern democratic states, indirectly encouraging vast social and political revolution. Foucault believed that all knowledge and institutions are aspects of historical moments rather than of a transcendent nature.

Among the phenomena on which Foucault wrote are medicine, madness, prisons, and the history of knowledge. His major works include *Folie et déraison: Histoire de la folie à l'âge classique* (1961; translated as *Madness and Civilization: A History of Insanity in the Age of Reason*), *Les Mots et les choses: Une archéologie des sciences humaines* (1966; translated as *The Order of Things: An Archeology of the Human Sciences*); and *L'Archéologie du savoir* (1969; *The Archeology of Knowledge*). He published three volumes of a projected six-volume work, *Histoire de la sexualité* (1976–1984; translated as *The History of Sexuality*), before dying of complications from AIDS in 1984.

REFERENCES:

Michael Clark, *Michel Foucault: An Annotated Bibliography* (New York: Garland, 1983);

Hubert L. Dreyfus and Paul Rabinow, *Michel Foucault: Beyond Structuralism and Hermeneutics* (Chicago: University of Chicago Press, 1982);

Didier Eribon, *Michel Foucault,* translated by Betsy Wing (Cambridge, Mass.: Harvard University Press, 1991);

David Macey, *The Lives of Michel Foucault: A Biography* (New York: Pantheon, 1993);

John Rajchman, *Michel Foucault: The Freedom of Philosophy* (New York: Columbia University Press, 1985).

— C.S.B.

ANDRÉ FOUGERON

Of the artists favored by the **French Communist Party** during the 1940s and 1950s, André Fougeron (1913–) was preeminent. In contrast to more prominent painters affiliated with the party — most notably **Fernand Léger** and **Pablo Picasso** — Fougeron, a longtime party militant, was able to suit his style to the preferred aesthetic doctrine of Socialist Realism. So complete was this identity between party and painter, in fact, that in 1948 a Parisian party member was censured for indicating his dislike of Fougeron's work.

A former autoworker and the son of a mason, Fougeron first exhibited his work at the party's **Maison de la Culture** in 1936 as part of the artists' circle Les

Indélicats. In 1937 he exhibited with George Grosz, **André Masson,** and Picasso in a show titled Art Cruel. At the outbreak of **World War II** in 1939, he joined the army, becoming a Communist Party member the same year. After the fall of France in 1940 and the beginning of the German **Occupation,** Fougeron joined the **Resistance,** printing clandestine issues of underground periodicals, including **Les Lettres françaises,** in his studio. In 1942 he became general secretary of the underground Front National des Arts. One of the pamphlets he published for the Resistance was his *Vaincre,* an album of lithographs by nine artists.

For an artist identified with the doctrine of Socialist Realism, Fougeron's artistic career is marked by surprisingly abrupt shifts in both style and subject matter. Influenced early by Masson and Picasso, his **Spanish Civil War** paintings — including *Le Mort et la faim* (The Dead Man and Hunger) and *Espagne martyre* (Spain the Martyr) — represent a compromise between Picasso's free-ranging experiments and a more traditional realism. Fougeron's *Parisiennes au marché* (1948; Parisian Women at the Market), a depiction of shoppers staring at a counter filled with dead fish, marked a deliberate move back toward the nineteenth-century academic art of carefully posed models and pedantic literalism. In 1949 his new conservative style was fused with leftist didacticism in *L'Hommage à André Houiller* (Homage to André Houiller), showing a working-class family mourning a former Resistance hero killed by a policeman for posting Communist posters (one of which had been designed by Fougeron himself). In 1951–1952 Fougeron produced a series of canvases under the title *Le Pays des mines* (The Country of Mines), commissioned by the mine-workers' union. He followed this series with another of French peasants from the Loire Valley (1952).

Fougeron was not completely constrained by the dicta of Socialist Realism, however. In 1953 he was attacked by French Communist leaders, notably **Louis Aragon,** for his *Civilisation atlantique* (Atlantic Civilization), a huge canvas (roughly six by four meters) attacking the United States as a center of corruption and neofascism. Aragon objected not to the subject but to the style, which he labeled "coarse painting, hasty, scornful," an "anti-realist composition, without true perspective." Attempting to copy the vast, complex murals of Mexican artists such as Diego Rivera, David Alfaro Siqueiros, and José Clemente Orozco, Fougeron had created a dizzying montage of figures and symbols, juxtaposed in deliberately unsettling ways. In retrospect it can be seen that Fougeron was experimenting with techniques that were to become famous in the hands of such Pop artists as Richard Hamilton and

James Rosenquist. To Aragon and other Communist critics, however, the result was ugly and discordant.

With the Communist Party's gradual abandonment of Socialist Realism, Fougeron began to return to his cautious experiments with abstraction. He has painted many quasi-**Cubist** still lifes.

REFERENCES:

David Caute, *Communism and the French Intellectuals, 1914–1960* (New York: Macmillan, 1964);

Donald Drew Egbert, *Social Radicalism and the Arts: Western Europe* (New York: Knopf, 1970);

Sarah Wilson, "'La Beauté révolutionnaire'? Réalisme socialiste and French Painting, 1935–1954," *Oxford Art Journal*, 3 (October 1980): 61–69.

—J.H.

THE FOURTH REPUBLIC

In the aftermath of **World War II** the Fourth Republic was created in October 1946, when a majority of those voting in a referendum approved a new constitution. The extent to which the vote expressed the will of the French people was open to question because 32 percent of eligible voters abstained. (A typical voter turnout in a French election is more than 75 percent.) Moreover, the constitution was opposed by **Charles de Gaulle,** who — in the euphoria of victory over the Germans only a year earlier — had become a living symbol of French unity against a foreign enemy.

The new constitution was supposed to correct one of the chronic weaknesses of the **Third Republic,** its anemic executive power, but it failed to achieve this aim. The old pattern quickly reestablished itself: since most power was concentrated in the lower house of parliament, which elected the prime minister, a government could be toppled whenever it failed to win a vote of confidence in the National Assembly. Given that an abstention on such a vote was considered a vote of no confidence, governments came and went with frequency; the average life expectancy of a new government under the Fourth Republic was about six months. This institutional instability exerted a ripple effect on the French, many of whom were not sorry to see the system replaced by that of the **Fifth Republic** in 1958.

Nonetheless, during the Fourth Republic, France did achieve some important goals. It quietly continued social-welfare policies adopted under the **Vichy government** in an effort to ensure a dignified minimum standard of living for all, and it took steps to encourage an increase in the birth rate, which had been declining since the first half of the nineteenth century. It laid the groundwork for what would become the European Economic Community (EEC), or Common Market, and it embarked on the first five-year plan for France, attempting, quite successfully, to coordinate private and public investment for the benefit of the nation as a whole. This central planning was no small achievement in the Cold War period, when such government involvement was considered by some to have socialist or communist overtones.

The Fourth Republic is also credited with extricating France from colonial involvement in Indochina, Morocco, and Tunisia, although it can be argued that the end of the French presence in Indochina was more the result of governmental neglect than the outcome of reasoned policy and that this achievement came at a tremendous price in human lives and in national pride. Despite the qualified success it had with respect to former colonial possessions, the structural weaknesses of the Fourth Republic contributed to its inability to cope with the **Algerian war,** which ultimately led to its demise.

REFERENCE:

Philip M. Williams, *Crisis and Compromise: Politics in the Fourth Republic,* third edition, revised (Hamden, Conn.: Archon, 1964).

—D.O'C.

ANATOLE FRANCE

Generally considered a nineteenth-century writer, novelist and man of letters Anatole France (1844–1924) nevertheless lived well into the twentieth century and wrote some of his best-known books, such as *L'Ile des pingouins* (1908; translated as *Penguin Island*) and *Les Dieux ont soif* (1912; translated as *The Gods Are Athirst*), after 1900. Elected to the Académie Française in 1896, he won the Nobel Prize for Literature in 1921.

Born François-Anatole Thibault, France was greatly admired on both sides of the Atlantic for decades and was considered a modern master, a latter-day Voltaire who embodied an Epicurean wisdom based on skepticism. His style, characterized by grace, clarity, and wit, is illustrated particularly well in his well-known philosophical romance *La Rôtisserie de la reine Pédauque* (1893; translated as *The Queen Pédauque*). Much of his writing displays indulgence toward human foibles, but it also includes bitterly sarcastic attacks on institutions such as the Church and on evil and depravity. France belonged sufficiently to his age that his works began to

FRANCE-SOIR

The newspaper *France-Soir* began as a clandestine opposition publication called *Défense de la France* in summer 1941, during the German **Occupation** of the country in **World War II.** Following the **Liberation,** the paper was taken over and renamed by the advertising magnate Marcel Bleustein-Blanchet, who acted as a front for the publishing conglomerate Hachette. Under its longtime editor Pierre Lazareff *France-Soir* grew into the largest Parisian daily of the postwar period. At the time of **Charles de Gaulle**'s return to power in 1958, at the height of the **Algerian war** controversy, some of its issues sold more than two million copies.

By the mid 1970s, *France-Soir* was losing money and readers as a result of the erosion of its readership from the modest classes, many of whose members were moving out of Paris. In 1976 it was bought by the controversial press magnate Robert Hersant, who already had a controlling interest in eleven other daily newspapers, including the *Figaro.* By 1980, with the takeover of the *Aurore,* Hersant controlled nearly 50 percent of the Parisian daily press.

While steadfastly right-wing and vigorously anti-Communist throughout its history, *France-Soir* has, surprisingly, appealed generally to blue-collar readers. It offers relatively little serious news or in-depth analysis of major issues; more than 70 percent of its space is presently devoted to advertising, headlines, and photographs, in which anecdotal and human-interest elements are predominant. In 1991 it was the fifth most widely distributed newspaper in France.

REFERENCE:

J. W. Freiberg, *The French Press: Class, State, and Ideology* (New York: Praeger, 1981).

— J.P.McN.

Anatole France with his second wife, Emma Laprévotte, on their wedding day in 1920

fall into disfavor after **World War I,** but he should be considered not just a creature of his time but also a social critic and writer of enduring importance.

REFERENCES:

Carter Jefferson, *Anatole France: The Politics of Skepticism* (New Brunswick, N.J.: Rutgers University Press, 1965);

Reino Virtanen, *Anatole France* (New York: Twayne, 1968);

Loring Baker Walton, *Anatole France and the Greek World* (Durham, N.C.: Duke University Press, 1950).

— C.S.B.

GEORGES FRANJU

Georges Franju (1912–1987) is remembered for his promotion of film history and film preservation and for his documentaries, which betray a genius that captures in single images or in juxtaposed shots the beauty and ugliness of the human condition. A transitional figure bridging **poetic realism** and the **Nouvelle Vague** (New Wave), he inspired **Jean-Luc Godard** and other directors.

Franju became a set director for the Folies-Bergère and the Casino de Paris in 1932–1933. With Henri Langlois he inaugurated the Cercle du Cinéma film club in 1934, and in 1936 he helped to found the Cinémathèque Française, the institution that has made

Paris a center for the history of motion pictures. During his long career Franju directed twenty-one short and feature films, while also serving as secretary of the Fédération Internationale des Archives du Film (1938–1945) and of the Institut de Cinématographie (1945–1953).

Franju's first documentary, *Le Sang des bêtes* (1949; The Blood of Animals), is an unremitting look at the butchering of animals in a Parisian stockyard. The movie is so violent that it rivals — and even inspired — much of **Alain Resnais**'s concentration-camp movie *Nuit et brouillard* (1956; *Night and Fog*). *Hôtel des Invalides* (1951), commissioned to honor the French military hospital from the Napoleonic era to the present, records with grim irony the astonished gazes of shell-shocked "heroes" confined to wheelchairs. *Le Grand Méliès* (1952; Great Méliès) is a moving review of the works and ill fortunes of French cinema pioneer **Georges Méliès.** Franju turned to making feature films in the late 1950s, but since he is best at capturing the force of images, his narrative features, such as the prize-winning adaptation of **François Mauriac**'s *Thérèse Desqueyroux* (1962; *Therese*), tend to be somewhat flaccid. He directed for French television from 1965 until his death in 1987.

REFERENCES:

Raymond Durgnat, *Georges Franju* (Berkeley & Los Angeles: University of California Press, 1968);

Gabriel Vialle, *Georges Franju* (Paris: Seghers, 1968).

— T.C.

THE FREE ZONE

After the **Debacle,** or the fall of France, in 1940, an armistice was signed between France and Germany on 22 June as the war between Germany and England continued. A demarcation line was drawn through France from the northeast to the southwest. The territory north of the line, including the city of Paris and all of the Atlantic coastline, was placed in an Occupied Zone, while everything south of the line was declared to be in a Free Zone. A small area known as the Forbidden Zone was controlled by the German military commander in Brussels. Whereas in the Occupied Zone, the German army was present to maintain order, in the Free Zone the French themselves discharged this function, while also keeping the population from supporting the Allies. The **Third Republic** was replaced by the Etat Français (French State), popularly known as the **Vichy government** because of the location of its capital.

The city of **Vichy** was selected as the capital of the Free Zone because, as a popular watering spot, it had many hotels and other large buildings that could house a national government on short notice. The major cities of Lyons and Marseilles were also in the Free Zone, which constituted about two-fifths of the European territory of France.

When German troops occupied the southern half of the country on 11 November 1942, after the Anglo-American landings in North Africa, the Free Zone ceased to exist.

REFERENCE:

Gerhard Hirschfeld and Patrick Marsh, eds., *Collaboration in France: Politics and Culture during the Nazi Occupation 1940–1944* (Oxford & New York: Berg, 1989).

— D.O'C.

ANDRÉ FRÉNAUD

Recognized as an important voice in mid-twentieth-century poetry, André Frénaud (1907–) began writing poetry rather late, at age thirty-one. His first book, *Les Rois mages* (The Three Kings), appeared in 1943, the year after his return from captivity in a German prisoner-of-war camp. Like most poets of his generation, Frénaud was interested in and somewhat influenced by the **Surrealists** — as well as by their predecessors, major nineteenth-century poets such as Charles Baudelaire and Arthur Rimbaud. Yet Frénaud wished to go beyond the Surrealist aesthetic. Instead of seeking surreality, Frénaud begins with concrete reality while concerning himself with metaphysical questions, particularly the problem of being. His poetry, which often treats the theme of travel, is marked by tensions, contradictions, and close attention to language. Later collections of his poetry include *Il n'y a pas de paradis* (1962; There Is No Paradise) and *La Sainte Face* (1968; The Holy Face).

REFERENCES:

Serge Gavronsky, *Poems and Texts* (New York: October House, 1969);

C.A. Hackett, "André Frénaud and the Theme of the Quest," in *Modern Miscellany Presented to Eugène Vinaver by Pupils, Colleagues, and Friends,* edited by T. E. Lawrenson, F. E. Sutcliffe, and G. F. A. Gadoffre (Manchester: Manchester University Press, 1969), pp. 126–136.

— C.S.B.

FRENCH COMMUNIST PARTY

The French Communist Party (Parti Communiste Français) came into being in December 1920 as a result of a split in the **Socialist Party** at its congress in Tours; 130,000 originally joined the new party, leaving the Socialists with only 30,000 members. Planning to emulate the Bolshevik model of "democratic centralism," Marcel Cachin and other leaders of the exodus were opposed to the reliance on the democratic process within the Socialist Party, and they wanted closer ties to the Soviet Union. Throughout the 1920s and into the early 1930s the Communists were divided by internal bickering, and popular support for the party suffered accordingly. Membership dwindled from 52,000 in 1928 to 28,000 in 1933. This trend was reversed by the mid 1930s, after the party found a dynamic and articulate leader in **Maurice Thorez,** who guided the party along the Soviet line until his death in 1964. As the Communists grew in strength toward the end of the 1930s, Socialist leaders such as **Léon Blum** remained generally hostile to them because of their abrupt changes in political strategy dictated by Moscow and the ruthlessness of their methods.

The Nazi-Soviet nonaggression pact of 1939 caused great turmoil among the French Communists. Some party members, including **Paul Nizan,** could not approve a pact that would give the German aggressors a free hand in the East, at the expense of Poland and with considerable risk to France. The arguments for and against this pact and the conflicting loyalties it stirred are portrayed in "La Dernière Chance" (The Last Chance), a fragmentary novel by **Jean-Paul Sartre,** an excerpt of which was published in 1949 in *Les Temps Modernes.*

Except during the period from the beginning of the **Popular Front** government to the advent of the Cold War (1936–1947), the Communists refused until the mid 1960s to work within the framework of parliamentary democracy, which they rejected as a bourgeois tool to control the masses. Wedded to the idea of a revolution that would culminate in the dictatorship of the proletariat, the Communists were considered dangerous radicals by most French citizens, however much they might profess concern about social injustice.

By adopting a Programme Commun (Common Program) in June 1972, the Communists and Socialists attempted to overcome their longtime mutual animosity and suspicion. Seeking to establish a unified Left against the bourgeois Right, the French Communist Party and the Socialist Party pledged to support one another's candidates in run-off elections at various levels. Maintaining this unified front, they were finally able to elect a leftist government in the presidential and parliamentary elections of 1981, when François Mitterrand came to power.

Louis Aragon's six-volume novel *Les Communistes* (1949–1951) presents laboriously, and in a favorable light, the intellectual and personal adventures of French Communist Party leaders.

REFERENCE:

David S. Bell, ed., *Contemporary French Political Parties* (New York: St. Martin's Press, 1982).

—D.O'C.

PIERRE FRESNAY

Actor Pierre Fresnay (1897–1975) had a distinguished six-decade career in both motion pictures and the theater. He made his stage debut with the **Comédie-Française** and began his film career in 1915.

Fresnay established himself as a leading stage actor during the 1920s. His first important film role was the title role in *Marius* (1931), **Marcel Pagnol**'s screen adaptation of his 1928 play. Fresnay's best-known screen role was as an aristocratic French officer in *La Grande Illusion* (1937; *Grand Illusion*), directed by **Jean Renoir.** He also starred in the controversial film *Le Corbeau* (1943; *The Raven*), directed by **Henri-Georges Clouzot.** His many successful stage appearances include a role in **Jules Roy**'s play *Les Cyclones* (1954; *Cyclones*). Fresnay continued to work in film and television until his death, although the mannered, theatrical style of acting that he had perfected early in his career gradually fell out of fashion.

REFERENCE:

Charles Ford, "Pierre Fresnay," *Cinéma* (April 1975).

—W.L.

OTHON FRIESZ

Emile Othon Friesz (1879–1949), a participant in the **Fauve** movement, originally wanted to become a sea captain like his father. After an abortive attempt to run away to sea in 1896, Friesz was persuaded to follow his interest in art by enrolling in the academy in Le Havre, where he became friendly with **Raoul Dufy** and **Georges Braque.** He shared his new friends' interest in Impressionist art and was the first of the three to discover the paintings of **Henri Matisse** and his Fauve colleagues. A growing belief that color would be his "savior" from artistic mediocrity led Friesz toward Fauvist experiments, in which space is depicted through juxtaposed flat planes, distinguished only by color.

Even Friesz's early Fauve-style paintings are conspicuous, however, by their rather muted shades, unlike those of Matisse and **Maurice Vlaminck.** By 1908 Friesz's new interest in the art of **Paul Cézanne** was already leading him away from the Fauve use of defining color, toward a more-carefully drawn, linear style, which is quite evident in works painted in 1909, when he accompanied Dufy to Munich. Ironically, the interest in Cézanne that led Braque to **Cubism** gradually led Friesz back to the conventional landscapes he had learned to paint at the Le Havre academy. An artist of considerable ability, Friesz won the Carnegie Prize in 1924.

During the German **Occupation** of France during **World War II,** Friesz took a pro-German position, excluding works objectionable to the occupiers from the exhibitions he organized at the Salon des Tuileries. His political stance led to his 1941 tour of Germany at the invitation of the German sculptor Arno Breker. After the war Friesz's reputation suffered considerably because of cooperation with the Germans.

REFERENCES:

Jean-Paul Crespelle, *The Fauves,* translated by Anita Brookner (Greenwich, Conn.: New York Graphic Society, 1962);

Georges Duthuit, *The Fauvist Painters,* translated by Ralph Manheim (New York: Wittenborn, Schultz, 1950);

Joseph-Emile Muller, *Fauvism* (New York & Washington, D.C.: Praeger, 1967).

— J.H.

LOÏE FULLER

A dancer and a pioneer in the use of stage lighting, Loïe Fuller (1862–1928) combined light, color, fabric, and movement to produce effects that influenced the development of theatrical lighting and modern dance. An American, she made her Paris debut in 1892 at the Folies-Bergère. There and at the 1900 Paris Exposition "La Loïe" experimented with electric-powered carbon arc lights, colored gelatins, and large lanterns with painted slides — the forerunners of the modern system of projected stage lighting.

Fuller's stunning visual creations astounded audiences and inspired the leaders of the Symbolist and Art Nouveau movements, including the poet Stéphane Mallarmé and the artists Henri de Toulouse-Lautrec, Théodore Rivière, and Pierre Roche. She evoked natural images by projecting colored lights onto a stage draped in black velvet, where she would manipulate costumes made of hundreds of yards of silk gauze. Over her career her dances became more abstract and ambitious as she evolved from suggesting concrete images such as a lily to representing evocative landscapes such as the frozen north.

Fuller, who never formally studied dance technique, used natural or free-style movements. She developed her own, almost scientifically precise, technique for manipulating fabric in light through observation and experiment. She was best known for her serpentine and butterfly dances and *La Danse Feu* (The Fire Dance). In the *Danse Feu* she created the appearance of becoming engulfed in roaring flames by dancing on a plate of glass lit from below by a red spotlight.

Fuller also worked in cinema, making the first of at least four experimental films in 1904. Her innovations included the use of photographic negatives and slow motion to create special effects.

REFERENCES:

Loïe Fuller, *Fifteen Years of a Dancer's Life* (Boston: Small, Maynard, 1913);

Margaret Haile Harris, *Loïe Fuller: Magician of Light* (Richmond: Virginia Museum of Fine Arts, 1979);

Sally R. Sommer, "Loïe Fuller," *Drama Review,* 19 (March 1975): 53–67.

— A.P.E.

G

JEAN GABIN

Jean Gabin (1904–1976) was working as an auto mechanic when, through his father's friendship with an impresario, he found employment at the Folies-Bergère, a job that eventually led to an extremely successful film career. Gabin often played a heroic or suffering figure of modest, even proletarian, origin, sometimes at the end of his rope. Stoic, world-weary, and rarely smiling, he was the archetype of a certain sensibility of the 1930s: one in which the world seemed to grow increasingly threatening to individuals who felt powerless.

In **Julien Duvivier**'s *Pépé le Moko* (1937), one of the biggest hits in French film history, Gabin played a criminal hiding in the Casbah of Algiers. The picture was an international success and was later remade twice in Hollywood, most notably as *Algiers* (1938), with **Charles Boyer** in Gabin's role. In **Marcel Carné**'s *Quai des brumes* (1938; *Port of Shadows*) Gabin played a cynical army deserter who falls in love with a battered, romantic young woman. In *La Bête humaine* (1938; *The Human Beast*), directed by **Jean Renoir** and based on a novel by Emile Zola, Gabin brought to life Zola's drama of fate and heredity in his portrait of Lantier, the train engineer who kills himself after murdering his mistress. In Carné's *Le Jour se lève* (1939; *Daybreak*) Gabin again portrayed a character who takes his own life, this time after murdering the vile seducer of a flower girl. In all these films Gabin cultivated the image of an honest man of simple means who finds himself drawn to the wrong side of life or the law and is ultimately doomed.

After 1945 Gabin's proletarian image seemed passé, and it took some years for him to develop a new persona, that of a middle-class professional. Yet in *Touchez pas au grisbi* (1953; *Grisbi*), directed by **Jacques Becker**, Gabin was cast as a retired gangster

Jean Gabin and Michèle Morgan in *Quai des brumes* (1938), directed by Marcel Carné (Roger-Viollet)

who is lured back for one last job — a throwback to the sort of character he played in his earlier films. During the 1950s he also began to appear in comic roles and was active long enough to appear with some of the young stars of the late 1950s and the 1960s, including **Brigitte Bardot** and **Jean-Paul Belmondo**.

REFERENCES:

André Bazin, "The Destiny of Jean Gabin," in *What Is Cinema?*, 2 volumes, edited and translated by Hugh Gray (Berkeley: University of California Press, 1971), II: 176–178;

Andrew Sarris, "Jean Gabin," in *The National Society of Film Critics on the Movie Star,* edited by Elisabeth Weis (New York: Viking, 1981);

Ginette Vincendeau, "Community, Nostalgia, and the Spectacle of Masculinity," *Screen,* 26 (November–December 1985): 18–38.

— W.L.

GASTON GALLIMARD

Gaston Gallimard (1881–1975) played an important role in literary publishing in France. In 1911 he joined forces with **André Gide** and **Jean Schlumberger** to found the Editions de la *Nouvelle Revue Française.* The two novelists were expanding into book publishing after the success of the magazine *Nouvelle Revue Française* (*NRF*), which they and four other writers (briefly in association with Eugène Montfort) had founded in 1908. From the outset Gallimard had contacts with many important literary figures of the pre-1914 period, helping to draw public attention to the works of Gide, **Paul Claudel, Saint-John Perse,** and many other writers of quality. (The correspondence between Gallimard and **Marcel Proust** was published by the Gallimard publishing house in 1989.) By August 1914 when the outbreak of **World War I** interrupted the publication of the magazine and *NRF* books, Gallimard had brought out some sixty titles.

In 1919 Gallimard and the other shareholders set up the Librairie Gallimard to publish books and the *NRF,* as well as other magazines. With Gallimard in complete charge of operations, the house soon became the elite publisher of France. From 1919 to 1935 Gallimard authors won the prestigious Prix Goncourt eight of seventeen times. In 1933 Gallimard acquired the Bibliothèque de la Pléiade from Jacques Schiffrin, who had begun publishing it in 1931 and continued as its head. This new series became and remains the most prestigious literary collection in France. The number and range of books published by Gallimard grew through the 1930s, as the company quadrupled its original capital. One of the new young authors signed by Gallimard in the late 1930s was **Jean-Paul Sartre.**

Under the **Occupation** of France during **World War II,** Gallimard was able to get his confiscated business back from the Germans by agreeing to make right-wing author **Pierre Drieu La Rochelle** editor of the *Nouvelle Revue Française* and to allow him "extensive powers over the whole intellectual and political production" of the company. At the same time that he was cooperating with the occupiers' directives on what his firm should publish, Gallimard was providing support to the **Resistance.** After the war, although the magazine was banned because of the pro-Nazi material Drieu had published in it, Gallimard was cleared of

Gaston Gallimard (Roger-Viollet)

charges that he had collaborated with the enemy. The magazine was revived in January 1953 as the *Nouvelle Nouvelle Revue Française* (*NNRF*) and soon reverted to the original title.

During the 1960s Gallimard's son Claude, who had been affiliated with the firm since the late 1930s, gradually took over direction of the business, which remains the major literary publisher in France.

REFERENCE:

Pierre Assouline, *Gaston Gallimard: A Half-Century of French Publishing,* translated by Harold J. Salemson (San Diego, New York & London: Harcourt Brace Jovanovich, 1988).

— C.S.B.

ABEL GANCE

Abel Gance (1889–1981) is widely considered the greatest French director of the 1920s, a watershed decade in the history of cinema. A visionary and a mythomaniac in the tradition of Victor Hugo and like his contemporary **André Malraux,** Gance aimed at producing timeless and universal works of infinite breadth.

Born Eugène Alexandre Péréthon in Paris, Gance acted in his first film, *Molière,* in 1909, the year he began selling screenplays. Two years later he directed his first film, *La Digue* (The Dike), and created his own production company. Always concerned with expanding cinematic techniques, Gance enjoyed successes with *La Folie du Docteur Tube* (1916; The Madness of Doctor Tube), *Mater Dolorosa* (1917), and *La Dixième Symphonie* (1918; *The Tenth Symphony*). After military service at the end of **World War I,** he captured his negative reaction to the war in his *J'Accuse* (1919; *I Accuse*), which includes footage from actual battles.

In *La Roue* (1923; The Wheel) Gance launched an epic style that would dominate later silent films. A melodramatic story with a railroad setting, *La Roue* is filled with stunning shots that earned the admiration of figures such as **Jean Cocteau,** who proclaimed, "There is cinema before and after *La Roue* as there is painting before and after [**Pablo**] **Picasso.**" The movie was originally nine hours long and shown in three installments, but after visiting Hollywood and discovering how D. W. Griffith used montage, Gance cut it to five hours and later to two.

In 1926 Gance patented the pre-Cinemascope idea of Polyvision, which he used to great effect in his *Napoléon* (1927), now widely considered his masterpiece. A culmination of experiments in many of his earlier silent pictures, *Napoléon* features an unprecedented degree of camera movement, sudden shifts in perspective, and the prismatic effect of three screens side by side. While much of the film appears on a single screen, at times a separate image appears on each screen, or a single image is spread across all three. In terms of plot, Gance's tale of Napoleon depicts the confusion of events past and present, as well as dreams of the future, in a manner similar to **Marcel Proust**'s explorations of narrative time. Gance's film, shown in its original form in only eight European cities and shown in cut versions elsewhere, demonstrated that French cinema was not restricted to **Charles Pathé**'s and **Léon Gaumont**'s studio formulas, which had reigned since before World War I. For Gance film was an art, not merely a commercial commodity.

Gance lapsed into obscurity in the 1930s with the completion of the shift to sound film. Unable to achieve the effects he had created at the end of the silent era, he made a few commercial sound movies and directed screen adaptations of novels and stage plays. When, after two decades of research, Kevin Brownlow completed the restoration of *Napoléon* in 1979, he also revived interest in one of France's greatest directors.

REFERENCES:

Kevin Brownlow, *The Parade's Gone By* (Berkeley & Los Angeles: University of California Press, 1968);

Abel Gance, *Napoléon, as Seen by Abel Gance,* edited by Bambi Ballard (London: Faber & Faber, 1990);

Norman King, *Abel Gance: A Politics of Spectacle* (London: British Film Institute, 1984);

Steven Kramer and James Walsh, *Abel Gance* (Boston: Twayne, 1978).

—T.C.

ROGER GARAUDY

The career of Roger Garaudy (1913–) exemplifies in many ways the often-torturous path followed by Communist intellectuals in the twentieth century. From art critic, sometime novelist, philosopher, and official **French Communist Party** voice on the arts Garaudy moved to dissident and to outcast; from advocate of Communism to religious activist.

Garaudy joined the Communist Party in 1933 and was elected to the central committee in 1945. In the 1940s he began to serve as party spokesman on issues of aesthetics and philosophy. His doctoral thesis at the Sorbonne, "Contribution à la théorie marxiste de la connaissance" (Contribution to the Marxist Theory of Knowledge), was approved in 1953. His early interest in philosophy derived in large part from the influence of **Henri Lefebvre**; but he resolutely avoided the unorthodox ideas that led to Lefebvre's expulsion from the party in 1958. For the Garaudy of the 1940s no dissent from the party was possible; history, not people, had shaped its orientation. ("History exists," he wrote, "and we are at the end of its sharply defined trajectory.")

In 1956, however, Nikita Khrushchev's revelations made about repressive measures during the Stalinist era had a profound impact on Garaudy. Like other voices in the party, he criticized Stalinism; unlike the party leadership, he seemed increasingly to wrestle with what it meant to break with Stalinism in practice. Despite his election to the political bureau of the party in 1961, he began to take a cautiously independent line. His *D'un réalisme sans rivage* (1963; translated as *Realism Without Bounds*) paid lip service to the idea of socialist realism in art while redefining realism to include the patently unrealistic works of not only **Pablo Picasso** and **Fernand Léger** (who were, after all, party members) but even Franz Kafka.

In 1968 Garaudy defended the orientation of the Czechoslovak Communist Party during the "Prague Spring" but continued to denounce the Soviet invasion of Czechoslovakia long after the French party leadership decided to end discussion of the matter. He was expelled from the party in 1970, and in a series of works beginning with *Le Grand Tournant du socialisme* (1969; The Great Turning Point in Socialism) and *Toute la vérité* (1970; The Whole Truth), in which his position seemed to shift at random from social democrat to syndicalist, Garaudy attempted to work out a new political and philosophical stance, an undogmatic, or antidogmatic, Marxism.

At the same time Garaudy's growing interest in religion became evident. In *L'Eglise, le communisme, et les chrétiens* (1949; The Church, Communism, and Christians) he had insisted that a socialist society was not incompatible with religious belief, but in the 1960s he had begun to call for a Marxist-Christian dialogue, which would invigorate both systems of thought. After his expulsion from the party he began to speak of a "Christian Marxism," and he joined the Catholic church. His "Christian Marxism" became in turn linked with environmental concerns; he ran for president in 1981 on a "Green" ticket. Catholicism and environmentalism failed to satisfy him, however. Concerned that the doctrine of the Trinity undermined the essential unity of God, he announced his conversion to Islam in 1982.

REFERENCES:

David Caute, *Communism and the French Intellectuals* (New York: Macmillan, 1964);

Roger Garaudy, *From Anathema to Dialogue: A Marxist Challenge to the Christian Churches,* translated by Luke O'Neill (New York: Herder & Herder, 1966);

Garaudy, *Marxism in the Twentieth Century,* translated by René Haugue (New York: Scribners, 1970);

Sudhir Hazareesingh, *Intellectuals and the French Communist Party: Disillusion and Decline* (Oxford: Clarendon Press, 1991);

Martin Jay, *Marxism and Totality* (Berkeley: University of California Press, 1984);

Dale Vree, *On Synthesizing Marxism and Christianity* (New York & London: Wiley, 1976).

—J.H.

TONY GARNIER

Tony Garnier (1869–1948) is best known for *Une Cité industrielle* (1917; translated as *An Industrial City*), a portfolio of designs and sketches in which he intended to capture the form and essence of the city of the future. A utopian socialist by upbringing and personal conviction, Garnier gradually came to rebel against the classical architectural training he received at the Ecole des Beaux-Arts. As the winner of the Prix de Rome with a design for a state banking house in 1899, Garnier was sent to study at the French Academy in Rome. As a condition of his prize, he was to send back at regular intervals architectural drawings that demonstrated what he was learning. In 1901 he sent the first sketches of what was to become his *cité industrielle*; in addition to the drawings he enclosed a protomanifesto, in which he rejected the entire concept of learning architecture through the study of antiquity. His request to depart from the expected course of training was flatly turned down; instead he was ordered to execute a series of drawings based on the ancient Latin town of Tusculum. On his own time, however, he worked from 1901 through 1904 to complete his design for a city of the future. The drawings gradually became known, making a strong impact long before their compilation and publication.

As a utopia Garnier's *cité industrielle* is at first glance rather prosaic. He was meticulous in creating a precise geographical setting, as well as taking into account governmental, business, cultural, residential, and even agricultural needs. A hydroelectric dam provides power; there is even a cemetery. The absence of other features — churches, a jail, police stations, military barracks — is striking. Asked why he had omitted them, Garnier replied that in a just, socialist society there would be no need for churches and that the elimination of capitalism would in turn eliminate thieves and murderers.

In 1905 word of the preliminary sketches led to a commission from Edouard Herriot, the Radical Party mayor of Garnier's home city of Lyons, to rebuild part of the city. Completed structures for that project include abattoirs, a stadium, and a hospital, but the projected stock market and school of applied arts were never built.

Garnier's designs for the *cité industrielle,* together with his completed buildings, strongly influenced French architectural education and design. Their impact can be found in projects as diverse as those of the Italian Futurist Antonio Sant'Elia, whose *Città nuova* (New City) was published in 1914; the French architect **Le Corbusier,** who included three of Garnier's images in his *Vers une architecture* (1923; translated as *Towards a New Architecture*); and the German architect Walter Gropius.

REFERENCES:

Rayner Banham, *Theory and Design in the First Machine Age,* second edition (Cambridge, Mass.: MIT Press, 1981);

Donald Drew Egbert, *Social Radicalism and the Arts: Western Europe* (New York: Knopf, 1970);

Dora Wiebenson, *Tony Garnier: The Cité Industrielle* (New York: Braziller, 1969);

Wiebenson, "Utopian Aspects of Tony Garnier's Cité Industrielle," *Journal of the Society of Architectural Historians,* 19 (March 1960): 16–24.

—J.H.

ROMAIN GARY

Romain Gary (1914–1980) was a prolific and successful novelist whose books have been widely translated.

Born Romain Kacew in Moscow and reared in Russia and Poland by his Russian-Jewish mother, he learned French as a boy and chose it as his literary language. For his service in the French and British Air Forces during **World War II,** Gary received the Croix de Guerre and the Croix de la Libération and was made a Chevalier de la Légion d'Honneur. After the war he entered the French diplomatic service, spending part of his career in the United States as consul general in Los Angeles (1956–1960). During his twenty years as a diplomat, he wrote eleven of his more than thirty novels. His first, *Education européenne* (1944; translated as *Forest of Anger*), won the Prix des Critiques. It depicts the Poles' resistance to their German invaders during World War II and explores the contradictions of a European culture that could produce great cathedrals and music as well as the monstrous inhumanity of Nazism. Gary's 1956 novel *Les Racines du ciel* (translated as *The Roots of Heaven*) sold more than three hundred thousand copies in the United States and was awarded the Prix Goncourt. Considered by some to be the first novel on ecology, *Les Racines du ciel* treats the slaughter of African elephants in the context of larger social and philosophical issues.

In 1963 Gary divorced his first wife, English writer Lesley Blanch, to marry actress Jean Seberg and began participating with her in the American civil rights movement. Their activity, which created considerable controversy, is reflected in *Chien blanc* (1970; translated as *White Dog*), a nonfiction account of the couple's life set against the tense racial atmosphere of the 1960s. Gary and Seberg were divorced in 1970.

Gary wrote six novels under pseudonyms other than Romain Gary. He carried off a brilliant literary hoax in the 1970s by secretly publishing four novels under the pseudonym Emile Ajar (1974–1979), while continuing to write as Romain Gary. As Ajar he won a second Prix Goncourt, for *La Vie devant soi* (1975; translated as *Momo*), which was made into the successful movie *Madame Rosa* (1977), starring **Simone Signoret.** Gary contrived to have his cousin Paul Pavlowitch pose as Ajar in interviews, but the strain of continuing the complicated hoax eventually soured the cousins' relationship. Gary published his account of the elaborate scheme in *Vie et mort d'Emile Ajar* (1981; translated as *The Life and Death of Emile Ajar*).

Gary took his own life in 1980, a year after Seberg committed suicide. In his suicide note he referred to the last words of his last novel, *Les Cerfs-volants* (1980; The Kites): "I have finally explained myself fully."

REFERENCES:

Dominique Bona, *Romain Gary* (Paris: Mercure de France, 1987);

Leroy T. Day, "Gary-Ajar and the Rhetoric of Non-communication," *French Review,* 65 (October 1991): 75–83;

Bette H. Lustig, "Emile Ajar Demystified," *French Review,* 57 (December 1983): 203–212;

Ted Spivey, "Man's Divine Rootedness in the Earth: Romain Gary's Fiction," in his *The Journey Beyond Tragedy* (Gainesville: University Presses of Florida, 1980), pp. 126–138.

— C.S.B.

PAUL GAUGUIN

Paul Gauguin (1848–1903) is an important transitional figure in French painting. As a close friend and colleague of Camille Pissarro and **Paul Cézanne,** he participated in Impressionist exhibitions from 1881 through 1886. Then, as the Impressionist circle dissolved, he became the mentor for would-be successors, ranging from the "Impressionists and Synthetists" who held a group exhibition in 1889, to the **Nabis,** young artists whom he inspired to reject Impressionism at about the same time.

The grandson of the socialist and feminist Flora Tristan, Gauguin started work as a stockbroker in 1871. He soon became an amateur painter and an art collector, taking occasional art classes at the Académie Colarossi in Paris. By 1879 his artistic connections had led him to the Impressionists, and after the economic crash of 1882 he decided to switch careers, devoting himself full-time to painting. Unfortunately for the new artist, the Impressionists were breaking apart; their final show in 1886 marked the rise of Georges Seurat's "scientific" Neo-Impressionism. Pissarro and his sons affiliated with Seurat's circle, but Gauguin liked neither the new technique nor Seurat himself and chose to move to Pont-Aven, in Brittany — long the home of academic painters, who preferred what they saw as the conservative faith and piety of the Breton peasants to the modern world of the Impressionists.

In Brittany, Gauguin encountered **Emile Bernard**'s experiments with cloisonnism, which is characterized by flat patches of bright color heavily outlined in black. For Gauguin the new technique captured the sense of simplicity he sought in order to define an essentialist vision of the world. His adoption of the technique led to paintings such as his *La Vision après le sermon* (1888; *Vision After the Sermon*), a depiction of women in distinctive Breton garb, inspired by their priest's sermon to see a vision of Jacob wrestling with the angel. Gauguin attempted to donate the painting to a local church, which rejected it. This refusal is scarcely incomprehensible; unlike Bernard, who had wholeheartedly devoted himself to a quasi-medieval

Paul Gauguin in his studio, circa 1894 (Larousse Archives, Paris)

Atuana in the Marquesas Islands (1901–1903). Throughout his travels his goal was to find what he called the wild and the primitive — not necessarily, however, as it existed in reality. Gauguin freely invented at will and rarely exhibited a solid understanding of the myths or even the language of those around him; rather, he made Brittany or Tahiti the site or the occasion or even the excuse for his attempts to depict — or create — a world of mystery and faith.

Typical for his era, Gauguin sought to create what some termed "integral" painting, in which the imagery and meaning emerge from the totality of line and color, not from title or explicit reference to traditional iconography. Attempting to distinguish his work from that of the Symbolist Pierre Puvis de Chavannes, Gauguin wrote that "if Puvis called a painting *Purity* he would explain it by painting a young virgin with a lily in her hand — a well-known symbol; so everyone would understand." Gauguin, by contrast, would "paint a landscape with clear waters, without any stain from civilized man, perhaps without any people at all." (He added that "explanatory attributes — known symbols — would freeze the canvas in a sad reality and the question given would no longer be a poem.") This integrated imagery was not, however, to be produced "scientifically" and methodically, as with Seurat's Neo-Impressionists. On the contrary, he asserted that his paintings took shape "when the most intense emotions fuse in the depths of one's being, at the moment when they burst forth and issue like lava from a volcano. . . ."

Gauguin's art became the point of departure for a wide range of artists he left behind in France, centered around the young painters of the Nabi brotherhood. **Maurice Denis,** a theoretician for the Nabis, wrote in a 1909 essay that Vincent van Gogh and especially Gauguin represented a necessary period of "barbarism, revolution, and turmoil," critical for sweeping away the superficiality of Impressionist art. He added that "without the destructive and negative anarchism of Gauguin and Van Gogh, Cézanne's example, with all it comprised in the way of tradition, restraint, and order, would not have been understood." By making clear that painters should not attempt to re-create nature but rather try to "reproduce our emotions and our dreams by representing them with harmonious forms and colors," Gauguin set the stage for what Denis hoped would be an enduring art of essences and mystery.

Catholicism, Gauguin, though interested in spiritualism and the occult, was in practice skeptical and often sarcastic. In the painting a diagonal tree cuts the canvas in two; only the priest and a fraction of the women are on the side that includes the depiction of the vision, the others being on the side that features a portrait of a cow. The image of Jacob and the angel is apparently inspired by a Japanese woodblock print of sumo wrestlers by Katsushika Hokusai. In Gauguin's *Christ jaune* (1889; *Yellow Christ*) a commonplace Breton crucifix at a rural crossroads is depicted in the same yellow shade as the crops. This Christ is rooted in the Breton soil, where faith is part of their land — but is not necessarily Gauguin's. The adjectives he employed to describe the subjects of *La Vision après le sermon* reveal at least an ironic and detached attitude: "I think that in the figures I have achieved great simplicity — a rustic and superstitious reality."

Gauguin's search for a land unspoiled by modern progress and technology led him far afield — Brittany (variously from 1886 until 1890), Martinique (1887), Tahiti (1891–1893 and again 1895–1901), and finally

REFERENCES:

Richard Brettell, Françoise Cachin, Claire Frèches-Thory, and Charles F. Stuckey, with the assistance of Peter Zegers, *The Art of Paul Gauguin* (Washington, D.C.: National Gallery of Art / Chicago: Art Institute of Chicago, 1988);

Gen. Charles de Gaulle in Bayeux, 14 June 1944 (Imperial War Museum)

Robert Goldwater, *Symbolism* (New York: Harper & Row, 1979);

Fred Orton and Griselda Pollock, "Les Données bretonnantes: La prairie de représentation," *Art History,* 3 (September 1980): 314–344;

Belinda Thomson, *Gauguin* (London: Thames & Hudson, 1987).
                                                                    —J.H.

CHARLES DE GAULLE

Hero to many, traitor or dictator according to others, a great, yet often controversial, figure to much of the world, Charles de Gaulle (1890–1970) was the dominant political and military figure in France during the mid twentieth century. He was the leader of the Free French during **World War II** and provisional president after the **Liberation** (1945–1946). He became premier with special powers in 1958 and served as president of France (1959–1969) under the **Fifth Republic,** which he was instrumental in founding. Throughout his career he took as his mission the enhancement of French prestige in all areas — a cause that often made dealings between him and other leaders difficult.

Supremely confident in his abilities and judgment, he correctly assessed the threat of mechanized warfare from the Germans before their invasion of France in May 1940. Then a little-known brigadier general, de Gaulle burst upon the historical scene and the consciousness of many of his compatriots when, on 18 June, he broadcast from London over the BBC a short speech urging the French to resist and never abandon the struggle against the Nazi power that had just overrun their nation. He invited all those who could escape from the Continent to join him in England to work for the defeat of Germany.

De Gaulle's bold speech initiated an opposition movement with two faces. A small but significant **Resistance** movement in which the Communists were a major presence emerged in France a few months later and grew to become an important political and military force, and a London-based Free French movement worked with the British (whom de Gaulle nevertheless disliked and distrusted) and planned a provisional government for a liberated France. To many on the Continent the Free French movement abroad and de Gaulle's leadership in particular were beacons of hope. Even if its material impact was ultimately rather small in comparison to the Anglo-American contributions subsequent to the June 1944 Normandy landings, the Free French movement was of immense moral and psychological import. At the same time de Gaulle's call for active opposition against the **Vichy government** of **Philippe Pétain** — which in some senses was the legal French government — was a divisive influence that polarized French opinion. The argument has been made that de Gaulle's call to action was chiefly for the gallery and may even have been harmful. Journalism and literature of the war period were, of course, indelibly marked by his actions and their consequences.

De Gaulle, who dictated to Gen. Dwight D. Eisenhower some of the terms on which the battle to retake France would be fought (especially in regard to the liberation of Paris), was the most important voice in organizing the new government. De Gaulle's dominance in these proceedings greatly displeased the Communists, who had been instrumental in and took credit for much of the organized opposition to the Nazis in France. **Simone de Beauvoir**'s novel *Les Mandarins* (1954; translated as *The Mandarins*) is the best known of the many literary and journalistic works that reflect the virulent political quarrels of the post-Liberation period and de Gaulle's controversial role.

De Gaulle resigned as provisional president in 1946 when it became clear that the power of the **Fourth Republic** would flow from the parliament rather than the executive. He returned to power in May 1958 amid the crises created by the **Algerian war.** With supporters of French presence in the territory demonstrating in the streets of Algiers, de Gaulle cemented his popular support by telling the crowd, "I have understood you." In fact, de Gaulle, who had been cool toward the North African territories since they had shown Vichy sympathies in the early 1940s, was shortly to oversee the French withdrawal from Algeria and the granting of Algerian independence in 1962. As a result many French citizens, and especially the French in Algeria, felt betrayed and looked upon de Gaulle as a turncoat. De Gaulle's leadership of the Fifth Republic was decried by those on the Right as being soft on Algeria and by those on the Left as being repressive and despotic. Some of the worst years of French history since 1945 were doubtless those around 1960, when de Gaulle presided over a divided, embittered, increasingly violent nation. The crisis of **May 1968** nearly brought down his government, but de Gaulle held on to power. When voters rejected a 27 April 1969 referendum proposing the administrative reorganization of the country, despite de Gaulle's vigorous support, he resigned the presidency in the fourth year of his second seven-year term.

On the cultural scene, de Gaulle named **André Malraux** as his minister for culture (1959–1969), and thus could take indirect credit for some of the cultural accomplishments under his presidency. An author himself, he published various works on the military before

1940. His major literary work is *Mémoires de guerre* (1954–1959; translated as *War Memoirs*), painstakingly written during his years of political exile. Although often mentioned in writing of all sorts, he did not appear as a full-fledged character in fiction until **Jules Roy** put him into his novel *Le Tonnerre et les anges* (1975; Thunder and Angels).

REFERENCES:

Don Cook, *Charles de Gaulle: A Biography* (New York: Putnam, 1983);

Bernard Ledwidge, *De Gaulle* (New York: St. Martin's Press, 1982).

— C.S.B.

LÉON GAUMONT

Léon Gaumont (1864–1946) and his competitor **Charles Pathé** dominated the early years of French film. Gaumont began selling photographic equipment in 1895, the year the **Lumière** brothers exhibited their *cinématographe* in Paris. The following year Gaumont began to manufacture cinematic equipment, and soon he started to produce films. His first directors included **Louis Feuillade, Jacques Feyder,** and **Alice Guy,** who headed Gaumont's highly successful production company from 1896 to 1907.

In 1902 Gaumont invented the Chronophone, one of the first machines to synchronize movies and sound. He also was among the first to experiment with color photography, producing a short three-color film in 1918. In 1907 his company expanded its operations to include movie theaters and built regional offices and theaters in Great Britain, the United States, and Germany. When he retired in 1929 Gaumont ended an era that he had helped to fashion with energy and brilliance comparable to the talents of Thomas Edison. Most of his company was taken over by M-G-M, although Gaumont British survived into the 1930s before it was absorbed by another company.

REFERENCES:

Richard Abel, *French Cinema: The First Wave* (Princeton: Princeton University Press, 1984);

François Garçon, *Gaumont: A Century of French Cinema* (New York: Abrams, 1994);

Georges Sadoul, *French Film* (London: Falcon, 1953).

— T.C.

FIRMIN GÉMIER

A pioneer of the "people's theater" movement in France, director Firmin Gémier (1869–1933) was inspired early in his career by the success of Maurice Pottecher's people's theater in Bussang, a village in the

Vosges Mountains, during the 1890s. Gémier was also strongly influenced by *Le Théâtre du peuple* (1903; translated as *The People's Theater*), **Romain Rolland**'s powerful essay on the social role of theater. While he was to share **Jacques Copeau**'s disdain for money-conscious commercial theaters that pandered to audiences' lowest instincts, Gémier opposed Copeau's aesthetic elitism, seeking to build a theater financially and intellectually accessible to all, not only to wealthy Parisians. Thus he gave impetus both to the people's theater movement, which was often politically leftist, and to the dispersal of good theaters throughout France — two trends that were to strengthen after **World War II.**

Gémier got his start in the 1880s, acting in the blue-collar neighborhood theaters in Paris, and he mastered his craft first with **André Antoine** at the **Théâtre Libre** and later with **Aurélien Lugné-Poe** at the **Théâtre de l'Œuvre,** where he played the demanding title role in the premiere of **Alfred Jarry**'s *Ubu roi* (1896; translated). Gémier began directing in 1902, staging Rolland's revolutionary play *Le Quatorze Juillet* (translated as *The Fourteenth of July*) at the Théâtre de la Renaissance.

Gémier soon began developing his taste for the spectacular by producing epic pageants, one (in 1903) using twenty-four hundred actors on a Swiss hillside to portray the history of the Canton de Vaud before twenty thousand spectators, and another (in 1904) with some fifteen hundred actors and walk-ons on a stage built on pilings over a lake. He took up the reins of the **Théâtre Antoine** from its namesake in 1906 and directed there until 1914. In 1911 he created the Théâtre National Ambulant Gémier, a roving company that traveled with full sets and equipment, a tent show with 1,650 seats bringing Paris-style staging to the provinces behind a fleet of steam-powered tractors. During **World War I,** when Paris theaters were closed, Gémier founded a Shakespeare Society, for which he produced plays such as *The Merchant of Venice* (1917), in which he played Shylock.

In 1919 he took a fifty-year lease on the Cirque d'Hiver, a large Parisian circus hall near the Place de la République. There he produced vast pageants for the amusement of the working people, such as Saint-Georges de Bouhélier's *Œdipe, roi de Thèbes* (1919; Œdipus, King of Thebes), which included dance troupes, gymnasts, and parading animals working before immense, two-story sets. His assistant, **Gaston Baty,** was his lighting director and actually served as the *metteur-en-scène* (general director) for his later productions. In 1920 Gémier acquired a large, more traditional hall in the Trocadéro, where he established the **Théâtre National Populaire** (TNP) or National

People's Theater. It was indeed "national," for Gémier had managed to obtain a small government subsidy for his project. He was unable to produce many plays because of the insufficiency of the subsidy, but the TNP was to become, especially under **Jean Vilar,** a major force in the development of French theater.

In 1921 Gémier directed the short-lived Comédie Montaigne Gémier, a company in which both **Charles Dullin** and Baty worked with him. From 1921 until 1930 Gémier served as director of the **Théâtre de l' Odéon,** where he revitalized the French classics and staged brilliant Shakespeare productions, including *The Merry Wives of Windsor.* After 1930 he led a wandering existence. His dream of bringing entertaining theater to working-class and rural audiences would come close to fulfillment only in the decades after his death.

REFERENCES:

Paul Blanchart, *Firmin Gémier* (Paris: L'Arche, 1978);

Jacqueline de Jomaron, "Un Théâtre 'pour le peuple,' " in *Le Théâtre en France. 2: De la Révolution à nos jours,* edited by Jomaron (Paris: Armand Colin, 1989), pp. 305–322.

— R.J.N.

JEAN GENET

In France, a country that has produced many controversial writers, Jean Genet (1910–1986) is surely one of the most notorious. As a professed, repeatedly convicted, thief and an aggressive homosexual, he went farther than other radical writers in thumbing his nose at society. Ironically, society responded by adulation. Praise from some of the leading literary citizens of France was followed by official recognition. Although his supporters did not intend to do so, they reaffirmed for Genet the authority he needed to assert his own identity through defiance of that authority. When Genet died, the former minister of culture, Jack Lang, praised Genet and called those who opposed him hypocrites.

The entire relationship between Genet and his milieu is a textbook case of individual rebellion and societal recuperation. Whereas to some Genet was a literary genius, excelling at fiction and drama, to many his work constitutes a collection of filth unprecedented except perhaps by that of the Marquis de Sade. In these readers' minds it is questionable whether his literary standing would be so high had he not been such an enfant terrible, attracting the admiration of such important figures as **Simone de Beauvoir, Jean Cocteau,** and **Jean-Paul Sartre,** whose support played no small role in making Genet respectable in literature, by appealing to those of anarchist temperament who admire

Dolorès Vanetti, Jacques-Laurent Bost, Jean Cau, Jean Genet, and Jean-Paul Sartre at the Café Pont-Royal (Brinon-Gamma)

homosexual prostitution and crime. Both are deliberately structured around sacrilegious motifs. Genet's third novel, *Pompes funèbres* (1947; translated as *Funeral Rites*), explores the question of evil during the last days of the **Liberation** of France from the Germans in **World War II.** In his fourth novel, *Querelle de Brest* (1947; translated as *Querelle of Brest*), Genet for the first time presented an important female character.

These works, as well as the facts of his biography, made Genet notorious. But it is his dramas that have contributed the most to his reputation as a writer. *Haute Surveillance* (1949; translated as *Deathwatch*) and *Les Bonnes* (1954; translated as *The Maids*) were literary successes — the first won the Prix de la Pléiade, and the second was commissioned and staged by **Louis Jouvet** in 1947. Both plays involve game playing in hierarchical relationships of power and were made into films. Set in a bordello, *Le Balcon* (1956; translated as *The Balcony*) is more ambitious than Genet's earlier plays. By means of the fantasizing and playacting of the bordello's clients, Genet shows that his audience's policed world is no less a network of illusions. The play was successfully staged many times and became a film. His other major plays — *Les Nègres* (1958; translated as *The Blacks*) and *Les Paravents* (1961; translated as *The Screens*) — treat rebellious characters who are on the margins of society not owing to their sexuality or mores but because of their race and culture. Inspired by Genet's opposition to the **Algerian war** and concern for indigenous Africans, *Les Paravents* could not be presented in Paris until 1966.

During the last twenty years of his life, Genet was a political activist on behalf of the Palestinians, the Black Panthers, the students protesting in the United States against the Vietnam War, and the Baader-Meinhoff group of political terrorists in West Germany. In 1983 he received the Grand Prix National des Lettres. Shortly before his death, *Le Balcon* entered the repertory of the **Comédie-Française.**

REFERENCES:

Peter Brooks and Joseph Halpern, eds., *Genet, A Collection of Critical Essays* (Englewood Cliffs, N.J.: Prentice-Hall, 1979);

Joseph H. McMahon, *The Imagination of Jean Genet* (New Haven: Yale University Press, 1963);

Jeanette L. Savona, *Jean Genet* (London: Macmillan, 1983).
— C.S.B.

GÉRARD GENETTE

The reputation of Gérard Genette (1930–) as a literary theorist depends principally on his studies of the nature of fictional narrative. He uses **Structuralism** to explore the nature of literary texts and literary lan-

revolt but do not act it out themselves. Sartre made of him a hero, indeed a "saint," in his bulky study *Saint Genet comédien et martyr* (1952; translated as *Saint Genet Actor and Martyr*), which analyzed with dazzling ingenuity the dialectic between good and evil in Genet's life and work and made him out to be a literary genius.

Genet was born in Paris, an illegitimate child of an unidentified father and a mother who abandoned him almost immediately. He was in public institutions until the age of eight, when he was sent to live with a foster family. His petty thefts led him, he later asserted, to accept the identity of thief, granted him by others (for lack, presumably, of any other identity). He was put in a reformatory at age fifteen. There he adopted the homosexual practices that he subsequently made a foundation of his aesthetics as well as his own life. As a result of his many thefts, he was sentenced to prison for life in 1943 but released in 1944, thanks to Cocteau's intervention. In 1948, when Genet was again accused of theft and threatened with life imprisonment, Cocteau, Sartre, and others, claiming that Genet was a poet of genius, petitioned the president of France, who pardoned him.

In addition to his plays, Genet's works include *Le Condamné à mort* (1942; translated as *The Man Sentenced to Death*), a poem written in prison, and four novels. His first two novels, *Notre-Dame des Fleurs* (1944; translated as *Our Lady of the Flowers*) and *Miracle de la rose* (1946; translated as *Miracle of the Rose*), were written in prison and concern the sordid world of guage. His three-volume study *Figures* (1966, 1969, and 1972) furnishes extremely perceptive analyses of such aspects of fiction as voice, style, and time, drawing heavily for examples on the fiction of **Marcel Proust** and employing a vocabulary developed specifically to deal with his subject. Part of the third volume of *Figures* was translated as *Narrative Discourse: An Essay in Method* (1980), and selections from all three were translated as *Figures of Literary Discourse* (1982). Genette's other publications include *Introduction à l'architexte* (1979; translated as *The Architext: An Introduction*) and *Palimpsestes* (1982; Palimpsests).

REFERENCE:

Gérard Genette, *Figures of Literary Discourse,* translated by Alan Sheridan, with an introduction by Marie-Rose Logan (New York: Columbia University Press, 1982).

—C.S.B.

LA GERBE

La Gerbe (The Sheaf), a fascist political journal that claimed to be the "weekly of French will," was created during **World War II** by Alphonse de Chateaubriant (1887–1951), a bearded, prophetlike Breton who had come late in life to journalism and to fascism. The very title *Gerbe* calls to mind the fasces, the bundle of rods signifying authority in ancient Rome, from which the word *fascism* is derived.

The winner of a Prix Goncourt in 1911, Chateaubriant, who was nonetheless a rather unremarkable novelist, experienced a major spiritual crisis in the 1930s, as did many other writers and intellectuals of the period. He discovered in Adolf Hitler and the Nazis the charismatic leader and the chosen people for whom he longed. In his long tract *La Gerbe des forces* (1937; translated as *The Sheaf of Strength*) he described the führer as peace-loving and offered a dithyrambic portrait of him: "While Hitler has one hand raised in salute, outstretched towards the masses in the way we all know, his other hand, out of sight, never ceases to grasp devotedly the hand of the one who is called God." Chateaubriant, who built a chalet in the Black Forest in 1935, would eventually die in Austria.

During the German **Occupation** of France, Chateaubriant threw himself with apocalyptic fervor into his collaborationist enterprise. He was president of Collaboration, a group dedicated to spreading German National Socialism throughout Europe. In 1940 he founded *Gerbe,* molding it into the instrument of militant collaboration and the (often hysterical) voice of unbridled admiration for the Nazi cause. He claimed that the Germans knew better than the French themselves what was good for France. He applauded the

industrial and technological superiority of Germany, its racial purity, and the strength and beauty of its Aryan population. Inspired by Friedrich Nietzsche, Chateaubriant and his writers believed that the new superman was the Nordic type. In the words of M. Augier, writing in the 7 November 1940 issue of *Gerbe,* "The time has come to say that Apollo and Pallas Athena are images of the Nordic man and woman, a statement that could not be made in the days of the Jewish conspiracy." The magazine even expressed hope for a reconciliation of Catholic with fascist ceremonies.

Some well-known and acclaimed literary figures, including **Charles Dullin, Henry de Montherlant, Jean Cocteau, Marcel Aymé,** and **Jean Anouilh** allowed their creative work to be published in *Gerbe* alongside the fascist diatribes of Chateaubriant and other pro-Nazi journalists such as Henri Poulain and the former Communist Camille Fégy, who was editor for a time.

Inevitably, *Gerbe* ceased publication in 1944, with the Allied **Liberation** of France. Just as predictably, its writers took flight or were imprisoned. Fégy was sentenced to forced labor, while Poulain fled from a similar sentence. Chateaubriant escaped to Austria, avoiding a death sentence passed in his absence.

REFERENCES:

Alphonse de Chateaubriant, *La Gerbe des forces* (Paris: Grasset, 1937);

Pierre Milza, *Fascisme français, passé et présent* (Paris: Flammarion, 1987);

Pascal Ory, *Les Collaborateurs 1940–1945* (Paris: Seuil, 1976).

—J.P.McN.

MICHEL DE GHELDERODE

Michel de Ghelderode (1898–1962) began writing for the theater in 1919 and had plays performed in his native Belgium for more than twenty years before creating a literary sensation, indeed a scandal, in France in 1949, with the production of *Fastes d'enfer* (written in 1937; translated as *Chronicles of Hell*).

Born Adhémar-Adolphe-Louis-Michel Martens to Flemish parents in Ixelles, Belgium, Ghelderode had practically stopped writing plays in the late 1930s. By then he had served as the official author of the Popular Flemish Theater (1926–1932), had worked on a wide variety of theatrical spectacles, and had written some fifty plays. After the Parisian production of his anticlerical and scatological *Fastes d'enfer* — which followed the Paris performances of his *Hop Signor!* (written in 1936; translated) in 1947 and *Escurial* (1928; translated) in 1948 — his reputation was firmly established, at least among the avant-garde, in France, where he is now viewed as one of the most original and vigorous contemporary playwrights.

Ghelderode's theatrical work shows strong ties with the Belgian artistic tradition — puppet shows, paintings, popular theater, legends. It has been called a *kermis,* after the outdoor festivals of the Low Countries, and it has much in common with the weird paintings of his friend James Ensor. Ghelderode's theater is not one of the mind, not a psychological drama with few characters. Instead, he created enormous and rich spectacles, including masqueraders and grotesque figures, violence, death, obscenity, and an overflowing language. Some of his plays emphasize their own theatricality and that of life with characters such as actors, buffoons, and clowns. The theme of appearances versus reality is apparent throughout his work. Death is a constant presence. (Corpses play a role in *Fastes d'enfer.*)

Ghelderode's drama shows a certain affinity with the literature of the Renaissance and Baroque periods because of its vigor, its comprehensiveness, and its direct, Rabelaisian treatment of the body and death, as well as its defiance of categories. *Escurial* treats a Spanish Renaissance king and his jester, inspired in part by paintings by El Greco and Diego Rodríguez de Silva y Velázquez.

Other plays by Ghelderode include *La Mort du Docteur Faust* (1926; translated as *The Death of Doctor Faust*); *Christophe Colomb* (written in 1927; translated as *Christopher Columbus*); *Pantagleize* (written in 1929; translated); and *La Ballade du grand macabre* (written in 1934; Ballad of the Grand Macabre). These and other dramas and farces are often marked by buffoonery and absurdity mixed with grotesque and macabre elements, sometimes outright horror — not unlike Flemish Renaissance painting. Illustrating some of the views of **Antonin Artaud,** Ghelderode's drama is truly a theater of cruelty and tragedy, fitting, he believed, to his century.

REFERENCES:

David Grossvogel, *The Self-Conscious Stage in Modern French Drama* (New York: Columbia University Press, 1958), pp. 254–310;

Jacques Guicharnaud, *Modern French Theatre from Giraudoux to Beckett* (New Haven: Yale University Press, 1961), pp. 156–160;

David B. Parsell, *Michel de Ghelderode* (New York: Twayne, 1993).

— C.S.B.

ANDRÉ GIDE

On both sides of the Atlantic novelist and critic André Gide (1869–1951) is considered one of the most important literary figures of the first half of the twentieth

century. He has also been one of the most controversial. As an early disciple of Stéphane Mallarmé, he was devoted to aesthetic values and the independence of art from didactic concerns and other constraints; yet he was also keenly interested in moral and social questions. His pure, sober, but sensitive, style makes him one of the most classical of modern writers; at the same time he was a highly innovative fiction writer.

André-Paul-Guillaume Gide was born into a Protestant, upper-bourgeois family of Paris. Although he later abandoned the strict piety and morals of his childhood, becoming for all practical purposes an atheist, his upbringing influenced his lifelong concern with religion and morality — as did his homosexuality, which he acknowledged to himself for the first time in 1893, while traveling in North Africa. His first book, the romantic and highly autobiographical *Les Cahiers d'André Walter* (1891; translated as *The Notebooks of André Walter*), was intended to persuade his first cousin Madeleine, whom he had loved for some years, to marry him. The union finally took place in 1895, but remained unconsummated. Gide's other early works include *Paludes* (1895; translated as *Marshlands*) — a lively and original fiction about writing fiction, which may be looked upon as one of the first ancestors of the **Nouveau Roman** (New Novel) in France — and *Les Nourritures terrestres* (1897; translated as *Fruits of the Earth*), a lyrical meditation, interspersed with bits of narrative, on the beauties of North Africa, which he had visited for a second time in 1895, and the joys of emancipation. At its publication it sold almost no copies; yet in the 1920s it acquired a large following. Similarly unheralded by all but the most discerning critics was *L'Immoraliste* (1902; translated as *The Immoralist*), crafted like a traditional French psychological novel, with a balanced, harmonious style, but vibrating with modern concerns, including hedonistic individualism, the rejection of moral values, and — implied but unmentioned — pederasty. This narrative was followed in 1909 by *La Porte étroite* (translated as *Strait Is the Gate*), intended to show the opposite moral failing — exaggerated asceticism. In late 1908 the first issue of the **Nouvelle Revue Française** was published. Gide participated in the creation of the magazine, which became the most important French literary monthly of the first half of the twentieth century. Gide exerted considerable behind-the-scenes influence at the review and at the major publishing house that grew out of it in 1911 under the leadership of **Gaston Gallimard.**

In 1914 Gide published what he called a *sotie* (a type of farce), *Les Caves du Vatican* (translated as *The Vatican Swindle*), which has elements of the mock-epic. The book became the occasion for his definitive quarrel with his friend and longtime correspondent **Paul Claudel,** who had for some years been urging Gide to convert to Catholicism and objected to an oblique reference to a character's possible homosexuality, which Gide refused to remove. Many other readers were also offended. After **World War I** Gide published a widely admired narrative about self-deception, *La Symphonie pastorale* (1919; translated as *The Pastoral Symphony*), and a two-volume autobiography, *Si le grain ne meurt* (1920, 1921; translated as *If It Die*), in which he recounts how he discovered his homosexuality. He also published a parallel treatise on the same topic, *Corydon* (1920), an enlarged version of a work he had published anonymously, in a limited edition in 1911. To large numbers of readers and critics, Gide became persona non grata, and he was widely attacked in the conservative press. Yet he continued to exert an immense influence, through not only his fiction but also his personal contacts and his criticism, whose quality was at last recognized. André Rouveyre labeled him "le contemporain capital" (the great contemporary). In the same period, unknown even to most of the well-informed, Gide fathered the child of Elisabeth van Rysselberghe, the daughter of an old friend, Maria van Rysselberghe, known as "La Petite Dame." His longstanding interest in pedagogy was heightened as he helped to supervise his daughter's education and observed the processes through which she learned. His involvement was reported in the notebooks his old friend kept without his knowledge and published well after his death as *Les Cahiers de la Petite Dame.*

In Gide's fictional masterpiece, *Les Faux-Monnayeurs* (1925; translated as *The Counterfeiters*), he handled several plots, recounting them from different angles, including the perspective of a central character, the novelist Edouard, who is trying to write a novel called "Les Faux-Monnayeurs." Edouard, who keeps a journal (as Gide did throughout his life), writes drafts of episodes and becomes involved with most of the other characters. (While working on this novel, Gide kept, in addition to his regular diary, a special notebook that was published in 1926 as *Journal des Faux-Monnayeurs,* translated as *Logbook of the Coiners.*) In *Les Faux-Monnayeurs* the combination of several fictional techniques and the rejection of other, traditional ones; the multiplicity of characters and themes; and the central moral issues make this complex work a masterpiece of modernism. Nothing Gide published subsequently was of the same quality, although his final fictional work, *Thésée* (1946; translated as *Theseus*), is an expertly crafted rendering of the myth, with distinctly Gidean touches.

In the mid 1920s after travels in the Congo, Gide became interested in the colonial question. By 1930 he

André Gide

had become enthusiastic about Communism. A trip to the Soviet Union in 1936, however, led to disappointments and disagreements, which he recorded the same year in *Retour de l'U.R.S.S.* (translated as *Return from the U.S.S.R.*). At the end of the decade Gide published most of the journal he had kept for fifty years; it and its sequel are considered outstanding examples of the French *journal intime.*

Gide spent part of **World War II** in Nice and North Africa. He was awarded the Nobel Prize in 1947. His correspondence with Claudel was published before his death, which was followed by editions of his exchanges of letters with important literary figures such as **Jacques Copeau, Roger Martin du Gard,** and **Paul Valéry.** Various other posthumous publications and abundant critical studies have added to his stature.

REFERENCES:

Arthur E. Babcock, *Portraits of Artists: Reflexivity in Gidean Fiction 1902–1936* (Columbia, S.C.: French Literature Publications, 1982);

Germaine Brée, *André Gide* (New Brunswick, N.J.: Rutgers University Press, 1963);

Wallace Fowlie, *André Gide: His Life and Art* (New York: Macmillan, 1965);

Alain Goulet, *Fiction et vie sociale dans l'œuvre d'André Gide* (Paris: Minard, 1986);

G. W. Ireland, *Gide: A Study of His Creative Writings* (London: Oxford University Press, 1970);

Michael J. Tilby, *Gide, "Les Faux-Monnayeurs"* (London: Grant & Cutler, 1981);

David H. Walker, *Les Nourritures terrestres and La Symphonie pastorale* (London: Grant & Cutler, 1990).

— C.S.B.

JEAN GIONO

The novelist Jean Giono (1895–1970) is associated in the minds of French readers chiefly with two of his interests: pacifism and the region of Provence. These interests set him apart from many contemporaries, who preferred Paris, with its intense intellectual and literary activity, to the countryside and took positions on the question of war that were less extreme than Giono's.

Giono, whose antecedents were partly Italian, was born and lived most of his life in Manosque, a village in the Provençal department of the Basses-Alpes (the lower Alps). His parents were of peasant stock and uneducated; his father was an anarchist shoemaker. Giono was wounded in **World War I,** an experience that marked him indelibly.

His first major work, *Colline* (1919; translated as *Hill of Destiny*), has features that remained fundamental in the rest of his writings: a deep attachment to his region, a pastoral vision that found its antecedents in Virgil, and a vivid imagination. This early novel was followed by many more, as well as plays — including the popular *La Femme du boulanger* (1944; The Baker's Wife), poetry, translations, political essays such as *Refus d'obéissance* (1937; Refusal to Obey), travel books, and prefaces to works by authors such as Homer, Virgil, and Niccolò Machiavelli. Giono was also interested in painting, writing, for instance, on **Bernard Buffet,** and in cinema.

Colline is the first volume of a trilogy, which also includes *Un de Baumugnes* (1919; translated as *Lovers Are Never Losers*) and *Regain* (1930; translated as *Harvest*). Together the novels embody his pastoral vision, which seems timeless despite their modern setting. The aversion for war Giono had acquired in the trenches inspired his pacifist novel, *Le Grand Troupeau* (1931; translated as *To the Slaughterhouse*), which depicts war as the horrible disrupter of the age-old relationship by which men, animals, and nature are joined in an economy that provides the only harmonious, authentic existence.

Among the other well-known novels Giono published before 1940 are *Jean le bleu* (1932; translated as

Blue Boy), *Le Chant du monde* (1934; translated as *The Song of the World*), and *Que ma joie demeure* (1935; translated as *Joy of Man's Desiring*). With a title taken from the French words to one of Johann Sebastian Bach's most famous chorales, *Le Chant du monde* gives natural elements — particularly the seasons, the forest, and the river — the status of actors in the human drama. In this novel of epic proportions and archetypal features such as the search for the lost son and the taking of vengeance, a blind woman rescued from the forest by the hero seems to embody a vision that does not depend on sight and comprehends truly the fundamental verities of natural existence.

Giono's idiosyncratic political positions included condemnation of modern industrial society and concern for preserving the environment, as well as an interest in communal living, which he briefly pursued with a group called the Contadour movement. His resolute pacifism led him to support the Munich Pact of 1938. At the outset of **World War II** he consented to be mobilized, but he refused to participate in any military undertaking and was jailed for two months before being set free, partly on the urging of literary admirers. Near the end of the war he was jailed for five months on grounds of collaboration. Although he had not been an active collaborator and helped refugees escaping from the Nazis, Giono had contributed some apolitical fiction to the collaborationist journal **Gerbe,** a fact that came to the notice of prosecutors during the Communist-dominated **épuration.**

Giono's best postwar novel is *Le Hussard sur le toit* (1951; translated as *The Horseman on the Roof*), a tale of adventure and political intrigue set during the cholera epidemic of 1838. The hero, Angelo Pardi, may have been modeled in part on Giono's paternal grandfather, an Italian carbonaro. Displaying Giono's own vigor of mind and imagination, the book also reflects the influence of Stendhal, one of Giono's most cherished authors. Giono wrote three other books with the same hero: *Mort d'un personnage* (1949; Death of a Somebody), *Le Bonheur fou* (1957; translated as *The Straw Man*), and *Angelo* (1958; translated). Giono continued to write and publish until his death in 1970.

Like **François Mauriac,** Giono was a regionalist who created a fictional world closely tied to his provincial home; unlike Mauriac, however, he did not pursue his career in Paris, enter the arena of political journalism, or become a major figure of the bourgeois intelligentsia. In his regional isolation, however, as well as in his idiosyncrasies, he was a beacon for many readers, asserting the rights of the individual at the same time he celebrated collective action, and obstinately insisting on the moral and aesthetic value of life lived in harmony with nature. To many he remains a literary and political hero, a lyrical and seductive voice in the wilderness of industrial civilization, plotless experimental fiction, minimalist style, and moral cynicism.

REFERENCES:

Walter Redfern, *The Private World of Jean Giono* (Oxford: Blackwell, 1967);

Maxwell A. Smith, *Jean Giono* (New York: Twayne, 1966).
— C.S.B.

JEAN GIRAUDOUX

Best known as a playwright, Jean Giraudoux (1882–1944) was also a novelist of considerable stature, writing fiction and drama in a witty, fanciful style that tends to conceal disappointment with modern life. Born in Bellac, in what was formerly the province of Limousin, he retained great attachment to this area throughout his life. He studied German at the **Ecole Normale Supérieure** (1903–1904) and was an exchange student at Harvard University (1907–1908) before embarking on a career in the French foreign service in 1910.

After **World War I,** during which he served in the infantry and was wounded, he resumed his diplomatic position and also his budding literary career. Such novels as *Simon le pathétique* (1918; Simon the Pathetic), which draws heavily on Giraudoux's life before the war, and *Suzanne et le Pacifique* (1921; translated as *Suzanne and the Pacific*), an idiosyncratic version of the Robinson Crusoe experience, show an author whose irony is often directed toward himself. In *Siegfried et le Limousin* (1922; translated as *My Friend from Limousin*) Giraudoux dealt with a problem that occupied him throughout his adult life: the relationships between France and Germany and their two cultures. At the end of the decade Giraudoux turned this work into a play, *Siegfried* (1928; translated).

Throughout the rest of his life he wrote witty, intelligent dramas, mainly on subjects from the ancient world and most often produced by **Louis Jouvet.** These works rely greatly on the play of language, and their characters are, as **Jean-Paul Sartre** observed, manifestations of essences; Giraudoux's young women are particularly famous for displaying the quintessential traits of their sex. *Amphitryon 38* (1929; translated), a clever version of the myth of Amphitryon and Alcmene, is typical of many of his works in its witty embroidery on relationships between men and women. *Intermezzo* (1933; translated), an idealized fantasy, was followed by the somewhat bitter, though witty, *La Guerre de Troie n'aura pas lieu* (1935), a version of the outbreak of the Trojan War in which Greece and Troy clearly stand for Germany and France. Although Giraudoux's language does not lend itself well to translation, Christopher Fry's adaptation of this play, *Tiger at the Gates,* has been much admired. Among Giraudoux's last plays are *La Folle de Chaillot* (1945; translated as *The Madwoman of Chaillot*), in which common people take revenge against capitalist profiteers, and *Pour Lucrèce* (1953; adapted by Fry as *Duel of Angels*), a version of Livy's story of Lucretia, a woman famous for her virtue who commits suicide after she is raped. Giraudoux's somber play is the bleakest of the works in which he stressed the need for purity and innocence. Both these plays were produced after his death in 1944.

Giraudoux served his country as minister of wartime propaganda in 1939–1940, but his cultural interest in Germany and general conservatism led critics to misjudge his conduct during the German **Occupation** of France (1940–1944). Although he worked for a time as the **Vichy** regime's curator of public monuments, he was not sympathetic to Nazism and was angered by German atrocities.

REFERENCES:

Robert Cohen, *Giraudoux: Three Faces of Destiny* (Chicago: University of Chicago Press, 1968);

John H. Reilly, *Jean Giraudoux* (Boston: Twayne, 1979).
— C.S.B.

ALBERT GLEIZES

While histories of **Cubism** have always focused on **Pablo Picasso** and **Georges Braque,** other artists also made major contributions to the movement. Albert Gleizes (1881–1953) and **Jean Metzinger** played a key role in publicizing and defining Cubism as an artistic movement, especially through their book *Du cubisme* (1912; translated as *Cubism*).

The son of an industrial designer, Gleizes acquired most of his artistic training from working in his father's shop. His early work was primarily influenced by the Impressionists. His first public exhibitions were not at the radical **Salon des Indépendants** but at the Salon de la Nationale (the slightly more liberal of the two official salons).

In 1906 Gleizes became a founding member of the group that gathered at the Abbaye de Créteil, which several **Unanimists** helped organize, describing their venture as a "phalanstery, cooperative, and convent" designed to serve as a commune in which artists and writers could create, independent of the pressures of a capitalist society. Through the exhibitions and festivals organized there, Gleizes met Metzinger and **Henri Le Fauconnier,** who shared his interest in defining and working out a new art. Gleizes participated in the **Section d'Or** show in 1912.

Du cubisme was the first work to define Cubism in terms of modern paradigm shifts: there are references to the theory of relativity, simultaneity, and non-Euclidian space. The issues of simultaneity and the use of space recur frequently in the book; Gleizes and Metzinger argued, for example, that "today painting in oils allows us to express notions of depth, density, and duration supposed to be inexpressible, and incites us to represent, in terms of a complex rhythm, a veritable fusion of objects, within a limited space." In Gleizes's art such practice was wedded to a continuing empathy with the lives of working people, urban and rural. His *Les Moissonneurs* (1912; *The Harvesters*) focuses on the collective life of the peasantry on an epic scale, standing in sharp contrast to the portraits and still lifes that were the focus of Picasso's and Braque's studies in technique. At the level of form *Les Moissonneurs* departs from Picasso's Cubism not only in its brighter palette but in its most basic structure. Instead of decomposing the objects depicted into faceted, geometric forms, Gleizes employed both geometric divisions and sharp contrasts in color and tone to provide the entire painting with a choppy rhythm designed to echo the daily rhythm of village life.

When **World War I** erupted in 1914, Gleizes, a pacifist, was drafted although not as a combatant: he was set to organizing shows for the troops. His fiancée, Juliette Roche (daughter of a former cabinet minister), obtained his release in 1915. They married and left for New York City, where they remained until 1927, the year in which Gleizes, who had become a religious socialist, helped found an artists' commune on the model of the Abbaye de Créteil: the Moly-Sabata in Sablans, Isère, on the Rhône River. It lasted until 1951.

Actor Jean-Paul Belmondo with director Jean-Luc Godard on the set of *Pierrot le fou,* 1964 (Photofest)

REFERENCES:

Pierre Daix, *Cubists and Cubism* (New York: Rizzoli, 1982);

Donald Drew Egbert, *Social Radicalism and the Arts: Western Europe* (New York: Knopf, 1970);

John Golding, *Cubism: A History and an Analysis, 1907–1914* (Boston: Boston Book & Art Shop, 1959);

R. Stanley Johnson, *Cubism and La Section d'Or: Reflections on the Development of the Cubist Epoch, 1907–1922* (Chicago: Klee/Gustorf, 1991);

Daniel Robbins, *Albert Gleizes* (New York: Guggenheim Museum, 1964);

Robert Rosenblum, *Cubism and Twentieth-Century Art* (New York: Abrams, 1961).

—J.H.

JEAN-LUC GODARD

Jean-Luc Godard (1930–), one of the most respected living directors of French cinema, was a central figure in the **Nouvelle Vague** (New Wave) movement. A tire-less director of vanguard and intellectual films since 1957, he has addressed personal and political dilemmas in works that are artistic in their constantly innovative use of language and technique. Since 1959 Godard has directed and written more than thirty features and almost as many shorts or segments of other films, as well as movies for television.

Godard began his career in cinema as a critic — along with **André Bazin, François Truffaut,** and others — for the *Cahiers du Cinéma* from 1952 to 1959. He also wrote, produced, and directed a few short films before his first feature, *A bout de souffle* (*Breathless*), was released in early 1960. Written by Truffaut, the low-budget film employs a disjunctive style replete with jump cuts, hand-held-camera movement, and dolly shots taken from cars and pushcarts. Its style, its references to the heritage of French and Hollywood films, and its fragmented narrative all mark it as representative of the New Wave. The movie includes elements that Godard treated separately or with different emphasis in the 1960s, his most productive and influential decade, in films such as *Vivre sa vie* (1962; *My Life to Live*), *Le Mépris* (1962; *Contempt*), *Pierrot le fou* (1964;

Crazy Pierrot), and *Deux ou trois choses que je sais d'elle* (1966; *Two or Three Things I Know about Her*).

Following the social commentary of his futuristic *Alphaville* (1965), Godard turned to overtly political cinema. In *La Chinoise* (1967; *The Chinese*) he presents an analysis of political causes and effects that foreshadows the events surrounding the **May 1968** demonstrations staged by students in France, whereas *Weekend* (1968) deals with social breakdown and the moral failure of institutions. He also contributed a segment to the collaborative *Loin du Viet-nam* (1967; *Far from Vietnam*), which was critical of U.S. involvement in the war. During the 1970s Godard almost completely abandoned commercial films to devote himself to films promoting revolutionary causes.

Godard returned to artistic cinema in the late 1970s and released some of his greatest and most complex creations in the 1980s. *Passion* (1982) takes up colonization, art, and the politics of production. *Prénom: Carmen* (1983; *First Name: Carmen*) is a study of the Carmen story in opera, **film noir,** and the sociology of misogyny. The subject of mysticism and pantheism in the automobile age is explored in *Je vous salue, Marie* (1985; *Hail Mary*), which was condemned by the Roman Catholic church for its controversial updating of the Nativity story.

In all of his work Godard tests the limits of literature, cinema, and action through the lens of the camera. His films are both critical and sensual, comparable to personal and philosophical essays. When considered in their entirety, they form a rich artistic legacy.

REFERENCES:

Royal S. Brown, ed., *Focus on Godard* (Englewood Cliffs, N.J.: Prentice-Hall, 1972);

Gilles Deleuze, *Cinema 2: The Time-Image,* translated by Hugh Tomlinson and Robert Galeta (Minneapolis: University of Minnesota Press, 1989);

Julia Lesage, *Jean-Luc Godard: A Guide to References and Resources* (Boston: G. K. Hall, 1979);

Tom Milne, ed., *Godard on Godard: Critical Writings* (London: Secker & Warburg, 1972);

Richard Roud, *Jean-Luc Godard* (London: Secker & Warburg, 1967).

— T.C.

Lucien Goldmann

Born in Bucharest, Romania, Lucien Goldmann (1913–1970) settled in Paris in 1934, where he became known as a Marxist sociologist of literature, building on the principles and work of the critic György Lukács. Among his best-known works are *Le Dieu caché* (1956; translated as *The Hidden God*), a study of the playwright Jean Racine in the context of his seventeenth-century social group and his Jansenist ideology, and *Pour une sociologie du roman* (1964; translated as *Towards a Sociology of the Novel*), in which Goldmann discusses the novel in the twentieth century in the context of Communist ideology, focusing on the work of **André Malraux, Alain Robbe-Grillet,** and **Nathalie Sarraute.**

REFERENCES:

Mary Evans, *Lucien Goldmann: An Introduction* (Brighton, U.K.: Harvester Press / Atlantic Heights, N.J.: Humanities Press, 1981);

Jeremy Hawthorn, *Identity and Relationship: A Contribution to Marxist Theory of Literature* (London: Lawrence & Wishart, 1973);

William Mayrl, Introduction to Goldmann's *Cultural Creation in Modern Society* (Saint Louis: Telos Press, 1976);

Robert Sayre, "Lucien Goldmann and the Sociology of Literature," *Praxis,* 2 (Spring 1976): 129–148.

— C.S.B.

Natalia Goncharova

Together with colleagues such as **Sonia Delaunay-Terk** and Alexandra Exter, Natalia Sergeevna Goncharova (1881–1962) is part of a generation of Russian avant-garde women artists who emerged in the early 1900s, immigrating to France and other western European nations after the Russian Revolution of 1917 to have a powerful impact on the development of European modernism.

Goncharova, born in the region of Tula, went to Moscow as a student in 1892; in 1898 she enrolled in the Moscow Institute of Painting, Sculpture, and Architecture. An ongoing interest in Russian folk art and religious icons led her and **Mikhail Larionov** into a style that has been called Russian Neo-Primitivism. In 1910 the two used the third exhibition sponsored by *Zolotoe runo* (The Golden Fleece), a Russian magazine devoted to the **Fauves,** to launch their "primitive" style, drawing at will from Fauve-inspired bright colors and flat contours, as well as from traditional Russian embroidery, toys, and peasant woodcuts. Goncharova also exhibited several icons.

In 1912 Goncharova, Larionov, and others announced their adherence to what has become known as Cubo-Futurism, mingling the **Cubist** analysis of forms and volumes with some motifs from the Italian Futurists (especially "raylines," signifying motion). For Goncharova, this new allegiance did not mean a total break from the past. Conservative artists and government censors were not convinced. At an exhibition in 1912 her unconventional depictions of religious themes were denounced as blasphemous and removed.

By 1913 the Cubist-Futurist fusion in Goncharova's and Larionov's paintings had developed into what they called "Rayonism," defined by Larionov as a synthesis of Cubism, Futurism, and the Orphism of **Robert Delaunay** and his wife, Sonia Delaunay-Terk. Goncharova and Larionov defined Rayonism as a "style of painting independent of real forms, existing and developing according to the laws of painting." While Larionov's Rayonist paintings were intended as pure abstractions, Goncharova focused on depictions of mechanical and industrial themes — an engine, a cyclist, a factory — emphasizing speed and power. Her abstractions of industrial life are also related to her interest in fashion design and embroidery; they often feature attached ribbons, and once she even included an ostrich feather.

Goncharova and Larionov left Russia in 1915 to work on costumes and designs for **Serge Diaghilev's Ballets Russes.** The two settled permanently in Paris in 1918.

REFERENCES:

John Bowlt, ed. and trans., *Russian Art of the Avant-Garde: Theory and Criticism, 1902–1934* (New York: Viking, 1976);

Camilla Gray, *The Great Experiment in Art: Russian Art, 1863–1922* (New York: Abrams, 1962);

Ann Sutherland Harris and Linda Nochlin, *Women Artists, 1550–1950* (Los Angeles: Los Angeles County Museum of Art, 1976), pp. 60–64, 286–288;

Wendy Slatkin, *Women Artists in History,* second edition (Englewood Cliffs, N.J.: Prentice-Hall, 1990), pp. 133–135.

— J.H.

THE GONCOURT ACADEMY

The Goncourt Academy (Académie Goncourt) may be seen as the legacy of two literary brothers, Edmond (1822–1896) and Jules (1830–1870) de Goncourt, novelists and men of letters who lived and died in Paris. Founded by a bequest from Edmond de Goncourt, the academy, which began to function in 1903, is a literary institution with ten members (women are eligible as well as men) who traditionally meet at the Drouant Restaurant in Paris. The chief function of the academy is to award the Prix Goncourt (see **Prizes**) to the best imaginative prose work, usually a novel, published during the year. Although the prize is generally reserved for a young novelist, **Marcel Proust** was forty-eight when he won the Prix Goncourt for *A l'ombre des jeunes filles en fleurs* (1919; translated as *Within a Budding Grove*). Other distinguished recipients include **André Malraux,** for *La Condition humaine* (1933; translated as *Man's Fate*), and **Simone de Beauvoir,** for *Les Mandarins* (1954; translated as *The Mandarins*). Owing to the prestige of the Prix Goncourt, prizewinning authors can count on large sales figures and a wide readership.

REFERENCE:

Jacques Robichon, *Le Défi des Goncourt* (Paris: Denoël, 1975).

— C.S.B.

JULIEN GRACQ

If the novelist Julien Gracq (1910–) has never achieved popular success, it is in some measure because of his own attitude toward literature and the public. When he was awarded the Prix Goncourt for his novel *Le Rivage des Syrtes* (1951; translated as *The Opposing Shore*), he turned it down, believing the writer must remain untainted by commercialism and media exploitation. Yet his lack of popularity is due also to the highly metaphoric and surrealistic quality of his fiction. Indeed, **André Breton** called Gracq's first novel, *Au château d'Argol* (1938; translated as *The Castle of Argol*), the only true **Surrealist** novel.

Born Louis Poirier, Gracq studied at the **Ecole Normale Supérieure,** completing the *agrégation* in history in 1934. He taught history and geography for thirty-five years, until his retirement in 1970. His novels, however, reflect a penchant less for factual history than for symbol and myth. Influenced by Arthur Rimbaud and the German Romantic poets, as well as the Surrealists, his fiction also reveals his fascination with the Grail legend, which he first encountered as a youth when he attended a performance of Richard Wagner's *Parsifal.* The atmosphere of his fiction is often dreamy, and the text is heavy with symbolic figures and meanings. In some ways a version of the Grail quest, *Au château d'Argol* includes the seeds of all Gracq's later novels in its treatment of a search culminating at the threshold of an answer — a death that promises, at least implicitly, a redemption or rebirth. *Un Beau Ténébreux* (1945; translated as *A Dark Stranger*) is a complex, mystical allegory, filled with its characters' dreams. In *Le Rivage des Syrtes* Gracq magnifies and elaborates the Grail myth as a Surrealist principle, as his fictional world moves inevitably toward an imminent apocalypse. Even in *Un Balcon en forêt* (1958; translated as *Balcony in the Forest*), which is on the surface a novel of the **drôle de guerre,** symbolism and mythical elements turn the work into a psychological and metaphysical experience.

REFERENCES:

Carol J. Murphy, "Gracq's Fictional Historian: Textuality as History in *Le Rivage des Syrtes,*" *Romanic Review,* 80 (March 1989): 262–276;

Leon Riegel, "Waiting for War to Break Out: Jünger, Buzzati and Gracq," in *Literature and War,* edited by David Bevan (Amsterdam: Rodopi, 1990), pp. 97–108.

— C.S.B.

Bernard Grasset (center) with his lawyers during his 1948 trial for collaboration with the enemy during the German Occupation (Agence France-Presse)

LE GRAND JEU

Le Grand Jeu (1928–1930; The Great Game) was one of the most prominent intellectual reviews published by individuals at the edges of the **Surrealist** movement. Its editors — Roger Gilbert-Lecomte, René Daumal, Joseph Sima, and **Roger Vailland** — shared some of the Surrealists' ideas but were never fully allied with the movement. Like the Surrealists, they saw themselves as heirs to Arthur Rimbaud (described in the *Grand Jeu* as a "mystic, occultist, revolutionary poet").

While the Surrealists, however, became increasingly involved with revolutionary politics and aesthetics and began to define what they meant in practice by the term *Révolution Surréaliste* (Surrealist revolution), the *Grand Jeu* editors became equally absorbed with a mystical search for God. Relations between them and the Surrealists were effectively cut off in March 1929, at a conference set up by **André Breton** to discuss common revolutionary strategies and actions. In the course of this meeting Breton denounced the *Grand Jeu* for a variety of failings, including an article in which one of its editors defended the Paris police chief, and another calling a grisly child murderer and cannibal named Landru an inspiration and model

(rather than executed anarchists Nicola Sacco and Bartolomeo Vanzetti).

Vailland's halfhearted apology for calling the right-wing police chief the "purifier of our capital" and the refusal of the magazine to disavow the statement were used as an excuse for the Surrealists to disclaim any connection with the *Grand Jeu*. Much like the Surrealist expulsion of affiliates such as **Antonin Artaud** for being apolitical or Pierre Naville for being too political and the sharp repudiation of the so-called *surfascistes* (superfascists, a quasi-Surrealist current), the break with the *Grand Jeu* was a defining step in the development of the Surrealist movement.

REFERENCES:

Helena Lewis, *The Politics of Surrealism* (New York: Paragon House, 1988);

André Thirion, *Revolutionaries Without Revolution,* translated by Joachim Neugroschel (New York: Macmillan, 1975).

       — J.H.

BERNARD GRASSET

Bernard Grasset (1881–1955), an important figure in French literary publishing, launched his company in 1907. During the firm's early years he published books by young authors such as **Jean Giraudoux** and **François Mauriac.** In 1913, after other publishers had turned it down, Grasset published at the author's expense **Marcel Proust**'s *Du côté de chez Swann* (translated as *Swann's Way*), the first novel of his *A la recherche du temps perdu* (1913–1927; translated as *Remembrance of Things Past*). After **World War I** Grasset's business flourished, owing in part to the success of several sensational novels, including Louis Hémon's *Maria Chapdelaine* (1921; translated), first published in Canada in 1916, and Raymond Radiguet's *Le Diable au corps* (1923; translated as *The Devil in the Flesh*). During the same period Grasset also published books by promising young writers such as **André Malraux, Pierre Drieu La Rochelle, Paul Morand,** and **Henry de Montherlant.** In 1930 Grasset sold stock in his company for the first time, creating the Editions Bernard Grasset.

In 1948 Grasset was sentenced to a jail term for collaboration during the German **Occupation** of France in **World War II.** Suffering from mental and physical exhaustion, he was never imprisoned and spent the next several years in various psychiatric hospitals and rest homes. In 1953 he was granted amnesty and allowed once again to run his publishing house. Because of its history of service to French literature, the company was never shut down, but some of its best-known authors left for other publishers. By 1953 the company was in financial difficulty, and Grasset was able to save it only by allowing it to be absorbed by the fast-growing publishing empire of Louis Hachette. Editions Grasset remains an important literary imprint, with a large number of Prix Goncourt novels to its credit.

REFERENCE:

Gabriel Boillat, *La Librairie Bernard Grasset et les lettres françaises,* 3 volumes (Paris: Champion, 1974–1988).

— C.S.B.

Juliette Gréco (RAPHO)

JULIETTE GRÉCO

Actress and singer Juliette Gréco (1927–) captured the public imagination in France and abroad during the years following **World War II.** She remains closely identified with **Saint-Germain-des-Prés,** the Paris district that was home to many artists and writers loosely defined as **existentialists.**

At the **Café de Flore** Gréco was recruited for her first acting role by director Michel de Ré, and she performed in the local cellars that served as nightclubs, including the Tabou. The character of Saint-Germain-des-Prés was introduced to a larger public in a May 1947 article in the newspaper *Samedi Soir,* which included a photograph of Gréco and future filmmaker **Roger Vadim** standing pensively outside the Tabou.

Gréco became known not just for her real talents as a performer but also for her image. With her long, straight hair and her black clothes and loose-fitting raincoat, she created a fashion that seemed appropriate to the bohemian life of Saint-Germain-des-Prés.

Gréco was close to the principal artistic and intellectual personalities of the neighborhood, including **Jean-Paul Sartre, Jacques Prévert, Raymond Queneau,** and **Boris Vian.** Sartre was supposedly the first to encourage her to sing, presenting her with "La Rue des Blancs-Manteaux" (The Street of the White Cloaks), the only song lyrics he ever wrote. Gréco sang Sartre's lyrics to music by Joseph Kosma, who also wrote the music for many poems by Prévert, which Gréco performed and recorded, including "Barbara" and "Les Enfants qui s'aiment" (The Children Who Love One Another). She soon became known as one of the best chansonniers in Paris.

Gréco also enjoyed a successful acting career in both French and foreign movies, including *Au royaume des cieux* (1949; In the Kingdom of Heaven), *The Sun Also Rises* (1957), and *Whirlpool* (1959).

REFERENCE:

Michel Grisolia, *Juliette Gréco* (Paris: Seghers, 1975).

— J.P.McN.

JULIEN GREEN

Novelist Julien Green (1900–) secured his niche in French cultural history in 1971, when he became the first American citizen to be elected to the Académie Française, a body that has admitted few foreigners. Considered a master of French prose style, he also has a firm place in twentieth-century literary history as an important and prolific novelist, autobiographer, and diarist.

Although Green, whose first name was originally spelled *Julian,* was born and raised in Paris, his parents were from the American South. Their tales of the region and its history and myth gave their son a dual cultural heritage that has informed his career as a writer. He first lived in the United States in 1919–1922, as a student at the University of Virginia, where he wrote his first story, his only one in English. Since then Green has written almost exclusively in French; he has, however, often revealed his interest in the South. His first novel, *Mont-Cinère* (1926; translated as *Avarice House*), is set in Virginia, and he again drew on his Virginia undergraduate experiences for the novel many consider his masterpiece, *Moïra* (1950; translated), a Gothic-flavored tale of a university student who — torn between his religious fundamentalism and his sexuality — murders a temptress. Critics have seen in Green's fiction both the fascination with Puritanical moralism that characterizes the works of Nathaniel Hawthorne and the powerful sensuality often found in works by William Faulkner, Tennessee Williams, and other authors of the South. His novels have sold well in English translation.

Although Green's childhood had been outwardly happy and secure, the inner conflicts of his youth deeply influenced his work. His fiction and his diary include usually oblique references to his psychological torments from adolescence onward. At fourteen he experienced the tragedy of his mother's death, and during **World War I** he was further traumatized by the suffering of wounded soldiers stationed in his family's home. Green converted to Roman Catholicism in 1916 and resolved to enter the monastic life; but his con-

scious recognition of his long-repressed homosexuality led him to renounce a religious career in 1919. He was estranged from the church for nearly twenty years before becoming a practicing Catholic again.

Part of Green's literary success is due to his horrific psychological depictions of provincial life. In *Adrienne Mesurat* (1927; translated as *The Closed Garden*) he depicts a girl's attempts to escape from her unhappy life in the ironically named Villa des Charmes. *Léviathan* (1929; translated as *The Dark Journey*), whose title probably refers to the monster of fate, portrays a young man tormented by desire for a prostitute. Green's interest in Oriental mysticism is clear in the novels he published in the 1930s and 1940s. One of his best-known works, *Minuit* (1936; translated as *Midnight*), is a Gothic, but visionary, novel marked by mystical and erotic overtones. *Varouna* (1940; translated as *Then Shall the Dust Return*) depicts three characters from different historical periods who appear to be incarnations of the same soul.

Green spent the years from 1940 to 1945 in the United States, lecturing and writing. After **World War II** he wrote three plays that were stage successes in Paris, as well as novels, including *Le Malfaiteur* (1955; translated as *The Transgressor*), which treats explicitly the topic of homosexuality. *Chaque homme dans sa nuit* (1960; translated as *Each in His Darkness*) deals with homosexual desire against a background of other struggles between the spirit and the flesh. In 1963 Green began publishing his autobiography: *Partir avant le jour* (1963; translated as *To Leave Before Dawn*), *Mille chemins ouverts* (1964; translated as *The War at Sixteen*), and *Terre lointaine* (1966; translated as *Love in America*) speak frankly of his struggles with sexuality and religious belief. These three autobiographical volumes were followed by *L'Autre* (1971; translated as *The Other One*), a novel in which the mysterious workings of sexuality and religious faith are set against the disquieting historical background of Denmark during the Nazi Occupation.

In 1987 Green published his first novel in a decade, *Les Pays lointains* (translated as *The Distant Lands*), a nine-hundred-page chronicle of the Old South. He told interviewers that he began the book in the 1930s but abandoned it when he heard of Margaret Mitchell's *Gone With the Wind* (1936). He has continued to write into the 1990s.

REFERENCES:

Glenn S. Burne, *Julian Green* (New York: Twayne, 1972);

John M. Dunaway, *The Metamorphoses of the Self: The Mystic, the Sensualist, and the Artist in the Works of Julien Green* (Lexington: University Press of Kentucky, 1978).

— C.S.B.

JEAN GRÉMILLON

One of the great directors of the classical years of French cinema (1923–1958), Jean Grémillon (1901–1959) is better known in France than elsewhere, not only because his features are set on French soil but also because his personal style weds narrative to the atmosphere of the locations where his films were shot. Trained as a musician, he often wrote scores, as well as scripts, for his films.

Grémillon directed his first short in 1923 and his first feature in 1926. Finding little support for his work in France, he spent much of the 1930s directing in Spain and Germany. Returning to France after the outbreak of **World War II,** he wrote and filmed his most important movies — *Remorques* (1941; *Stormy Waters*), *Lumière d'été* (1943; Light in Summer), and *Le Ciel est à vous* (1944; *The Woman Who Dared*) — during the German **Occupation** of his native country. Subtly challenging the traditional French social values that were proclaimed throughout that period, these stylishly scripted movies are allusive and yield rich ambiguities that attest to a reflexive sense of cinema and ideology. In 1943 Grémillon was elected president of the Cinémathèque Française, a position he held until a year before his death.

REFERENCES:

Gilles Deleuze, *Cinema 1: The Movement-Image,* translated by Hugh Tomlinson and Robert Galeta (Minneapolis: University of Minnesota Press, 1987);

Richard Roud, "Jean Grémillon and *Gueule d'amour,*" in *Rediscovering French Film,* edited by Mary Lea Bandy (New York: Museum of Modern Art, 1983), pp. 121–123;

Geneviève Sellier, *Jean Grémillon: Le cinéma est à vous* (Paris: Méridiens Klincksieck, 1989).

—T.C.

GRINGOIRE

Gringoire, a right-wing literary and political weekly, was founded in November 1928 by publisher-politician Horace de Carbuccia. Growing quickly into one of the most successful journals of the 1930s and 1940s, the magazine published pieces by many right-wing writers, most notably the novelist and xenophobic polemicist Henri Béraud, who was the leading contributor from 1928 until the end of 1943, when he quarreled with Carbuccia.

The name *Gringoire* was derived from that of sixteenth-century satirical poet Pierre Gringore, on whom Théodore de Banville based a play (1866). By 1929 the circulation of *Gringoire* had reached 135,000. By the end of 1936 its virulent and single-minded opposition to the left-wing **Popular Front,** which came to power in that year, brought its circulation to the extraordinary number of 650,000.

Gringoire was consistent in its denunciation of England and the Soviet Union and in its attacks on Jews, democracy, the French Revolution, and the parliamentary system. It was predictably fulsome in its praise of Benito Mussolini's Italy and Spain under Francisco Franco. Unlike *Candide,* the right-wing journal on which it was modeled, *Gringoire* made no claim to appeal to an intellectual elite. Its political tactics had few limits. Its vicious, unfounded attacks on Roger Salengro, a minister in the Popular Front government, were said to have played a major part in his suicide in November 1936.

The extreme right-wing views expressed in *Gringoire* made it a natural ally of the **Vichy government** after the fall of France to the Germans during **World War II,** and it led the call for purging of "antinationalistic" elements, including Jews. During the war it maintained a circulation of more than half a million. The magazine ceased publication in 1944, as France was being liberated. During the **épuration,** Béraud was sentenced to death for collaboration, but his sentence was later commuted, and he was released from prison in 1950.

— J.P.McN.

JUAN GRIS

Next to **Pablo Picasso** and **Georges Braque,** Juan Gris (1887–1927) is the artist most closely linked to the origins and development of **Cubism** in the early twentieth century. Born José Victoriano González in Madrid, he studied art at the Escuela de Artes y Manufacturas, earning money by submitting his sketches to local newspapers. In 1906 he moved to Paris, settling in a studio next to Picasso's in the **Bateau Lavoir.** He continued to support himself as best he could as an illustrator (for the *Assiette au Beurre* and other satirical publications) until 1911, when he began to paint full-time.

Gris (José Victoriano González)'s identification with Cubist ideas was clear from the beginning of this period; he exhibited as a Cubist at the **Salon des Indépendants** of 1912, as well as the **Section d'Or** show the same year. Like Picasso and Braque, he preferred still lifes and portraits for his explorations of space and volume. In comparison to Picasso's, Gris's work is characterized by an emphatic precision and regularity, in which the object or subject is mapped out on a structural grid. (One critic complained that Gris structured his paintings with a triangle and a T-square.) His portrait of Picasso (1912), for example, plays off the relative irregularity of the face with the precise, triangular patterns of his jacket buttons. Though he adopted the name *Gris* (gray), his palette is more varied than the grays, blacks, and earth tones of Picasso and Braque, notably including muted shades of red, yellow, and blue.

By 1914 Gris (José Victoriano González) had followed Picasso and Braque into what became known as Synthetic Cubism — the use of collage and assemblage not only to suggest but also to reconstruct partly a time, place, or milieu. One of his 1914 still lifes, for example, uses varied materials layered and cut away to suggest a table in a café or winery — including part of a real newspaper. Often treated as examples of pure technique, Gris's Synthetic Cubist collages, much like Picasso's, actually used materials with a clear tie to social commentary: the scraps of newspaper he favored often featured articles on the spread of **World War I.**

In the 1920s Gris moved toward a greater simplification. Objects are suggested by flat surfaces of uniform color arranged to form a grid of triangular shapes. For example, his 1926 canvas showing a guitar with a sheet of music on a brown table can be viewed as sheet music on a red mat, with a bit of blue sky above and behind the guitar; in practice, though, the painting is composed of a set of acute and obtuse angles, the triangular points played off against the patches of color. The effect is stark, even barren.

For a time Gris worked for the **Ballets Russes** of **Serge Diaghilev** (1922–1923), designing a *fête merveilleuse* set in the Hall of Mirrors at Versailles in 1923. Conflicts with composers and fellow artists, including Braque, led him to give up the position. Hypertension and asthma combined to bring on an attack of bronchitis in 1926; his condition worsened, and he died in May 1927.

REFERENCES:

Juan Antonio Gaya Nuno, *Juan Gris,* translated by Kenneth Lyons (New York: Rizzoli, 1986);

Daniel-Henry Kahnweiler, *Juan Gris: His Life and Work* (New York: Abrams, 1969);

Patricia Leighten, *Re-Ordering the Universe: Picasso and Anarchism, 1897–1914* (Princeton: Princeton University Press, 1989);

Robert Rosenblum, *Cubism and Twentieth-Century Art* (New York: Abrams, 1961).

— J.H.

GROUPE DE RECHERCHE D'ART VISUEL

The Groupe de Recherche d'Art Visuel (GRAV) was one of several competing experimental art groups that were formed in Paris and then other European cities in the early 1960s. Their work is usually lumped together as the Nouvelle Tendance. GRAV was founded in 1960; its members included Horacio Garcia-Rossi, Julio Le Parc, François Morellet, Francisco Sobrino, Joel Stein, and Yvaral (son of Op artist Victor Vasarely). Their first group show, *Labyrinthe,* took place at the 1963 Paris Biennale.

Often categorized as what American critics generically term *Op Art,* the Nouvelle Tendance grew out of a fascination with modern science and technology and the manner in which light, sound, and kinetic motion could be employed to engage the spectator with the artwork. In the manifesto "Propositions sur le mouvement" (1961), the artists in GRAV asserted the need for a "new visual situation through experimentation with various relations between image, movement, and time within a single field of vision." GRAV favored group exhibitions with work displayed anonymously and rejected any notion of the static show. GRAV installations all involved the viewer as an active participant. (Le Parc insisted on viewer involvement to the point that spectators sometimes had to don special glasses to examine his work or even walk around the exhibit on shoes mounted on springs.) Since GRAV was dissolved in 1968, many of its affiliated artists have continued to work in the same vein.

Within the general framework of GRAV ideas, individual works actually cover a wide range of techniques and media. Morellet's *Sphere Screen* (1967), a 7 1/2' square containing a dense aluminum grid, is an example of what he called his *trames* (webs) of superimposed lines and wires. He wrote that "if you superimpose very simple forms . . . and vary the angle of superimposition, a whole series of structures appears." Powerful light sources in his assemblages produced multiple shadows and reflections. By contrast, Le Parc's works — such as his *Continuel-mobile, Continuel Lumière* (1963; Continual-Mobile, Continual [and] Light), a 5'3" motorized arrangement of lights — were the result of experiments with rotation, movement, and light. They were designed to swing and shift continually so as to pose constantly changing patterns of light, color, and darkness for the viewer. The works of both artists and their colleagues share an insistence on chance perspective, whether produced by the actions of the viewer (Morellet) or the installation itself (Le Parc). By 1968, when GRAV officially disbanded, its members had merged broader, more eclectic experiments with kinetic sculpture and light shows.

REFERENCES:

Cyril Barret, *Op Art* (New York: Viking, 1970);

Katherine Hoffman, *Explorations in the Visual Arts Since 1945* (New York: HarperCollins, 1991);

Frank Popper, *Origins and Development of Kinetic Art* (Greenwich, Conn.: New York Graphic Society, 1969);

Louis Guilloux with Albert Camus

Daniel Wheeler, *Art Since Mid-Century: 1945 to the Present* (Englewood Cliffs, N.J.: Prentice-Hall, 1991).

— J.H.

EUGÈNE GUILLEVIC

Eugène Guillevic (1907–) is considered in France to be one of the most important poets of his generation. His reputation was due in part to his political engagement. As a Communist he was associated with the **Resistance** during the German **Occupation** of France in **World War II,** and his poetry is sometimes overtly political. Yet his standing is based on more than respect for his political commitment.

Guillevic was born in Brittany, the son of a Breton sailor who became a policeman and moved his family to various barracks around France. Although French was spoken in his home, Guillevic experienced a type of linguistic alienation by living in areas where he heard mainly other languages — Breton, Walloon, Alsatian. The starkness of his verse and the world it evokes may reflect the harsh landscape he first knew and the impoverished circumstances of his youth.

Written in a sober, minimalist free verse that has been called lapidary, Guillevic's brief poems use ordinary language to describe the material world and man's place in it. (One of his poems, for example, is about earthenware dishes.) Although he is classified as a poetic "realist," Guillevic — like other poets of his time such as **André du Bouchet** and **Jean-Claude Renard** — believes that the material object points to a transcendent essence. The poet's role, he believes, is to attempt to go behind appearances to the elusive being of his object. Since the essence of the object resists words, however, Guillevic's aim, which has much in common with phenomenology, is tentative and precarious. The difficulty of the quest is suggested by the silences structured into the poem.

Guillevic's principal books include *Terraqué* (1942; Composed of Earth and Water), *Exécutoire* (1947; Executory), *Terre à bonheur* (1953; Earth for Happiness), *Trente et un sonnets* (1954; Thirty-One Sonnets), and *Euclidiennes* (1967; Euclidians).

REFERENCES:

Michael Bishop, *The Contemporary Poetry of France: Eight Studies* (Amsterdam: Rodopi, 1985);

Leonard Schwarz, "Guillevic/Levertov: The Poetics of Matter," *Twentieth Century Studies,* 38 (Fall 1992): 290–298.

— C.S.B.

LOUIS GUILLOUX

While only one novel by Louis Guilloux (1899–1980) — *Le Sang noir* (1935; translated as *Bitter Victory*) — has been translated into English, he was highly respected in France, championed by contemporaries such as **Albert Camus** and **André Malraux.** Literary historians associate him particularly with the 1930s, when he published *Le Sang noir* and other novels and was at the forefront of the antifascist activity that engaged so many writers at that time. Guilloux served as secretary to the Congrès Mondial des Ecrivains Antifascistes in 1934–1935 and visited the Soviet Union with **André Gide** and other literary figures in 1936.

Guilloux's work has sometimes been labeled populist. In his first novel, *La Maison du peuple* (1927; The People's House), he deals with the circumscribed world of respectable artisans and public servants of modest means, examining their social and political aspirations. The stress is on community, not Communism. Guilloux, who never joined the **French Communist Party** despite sharing its opposition to fascism, drew on his own modest Breton background, with its strong regional identification, for *La Maison du peuple. Le Sang noir,* which is centered on one day in 1917, highlights the lives of the socially oppressed, setting them in the context of the dreadful battles of that year. Its hero, Cripure, is a maladjusted, depressed lycée professor of philosophy, whose slide into paranoia and suicide suggests a generalized illness of civilization visible in the butchery of **World War I** and, more broadly speaking, the absurdity of existence.

Le Pain des rêves (1942; Bread of Dreams), which won the Prix Populiste, illustrates the necessity of dreams for dealing with harsh reality. In *Le Jeu de patience* (1949; The Jigsaw Puzzle), which was awarded the Prix Renaudot, Guilloux drew on his experiences during the two world wars and the **Popular Front** era of the 1930s, mixing historical moments with personal dramas that sometimes involve characters from previous novels.

Two of Guilloux's books were adapted for French television, and in 1967 *Cripure* (1962), Guilloux's play based on *Le Sang noir,* was successfully staged. He won the Grand Prix National des Lettres in 1967 and the Grand Prix de Littérature de l'Académie Française in 1973.

REFERENCE:

Mary Jean Matthews Green, *Louis Guilloux: An Artisan of Language* (York, S.C.: French Literature Publications, 1980).

— C.S.B.

SACHA GUITRY

Actor-playwright Sacha Guitry (1885–1957) typifies the spirit of much Parisian **boulevard theater** of the first half of the twentieth century. He wrote more than 120 plays, taking the male lead in virtually all of them. Although his plays entertained the bourgeoisie of his day, they seem dated and sexist to the modern taste, and few have stood the test of time. Guitry also wrote scenarios for thirty-five movies, directing thirty-one of them and starring in more than twenty.

Sacha Guitry was born in Saint Petersburg, Russia, the son of the celebrated actor Lucien Guitry, who played all the famous roles on the turn-of-the-century French stage and in 1902 became the director of the Théâtre de la Renaissance, a principal boulevard theater. The elder Guitry was one of the first actors to develop a constant persona for all his roles — indeed, to play himself, onstage and off. His son, who later wrote for him, adopted the same approach.

In the boulevard theaters Sacha Guitry most frequently played the gay deceiver, a devil-may-care seducer and lovable scoundrel who often suffered for his sins. As he wrote the plays in which he acted, he appeared to be playing out his real-life amorous indiscretions onstage, frequently opposite his latest wife (he married five times). His plays usually involve a scandalous situation and surprise. For instance, in *Le Veilleur de nuit* (1911; The Night Watchman) the husband uncovers his wife's adulterous schemes and, for his own purposes, encourages and abets them, to the consternation of his rival. While such plots may have been titillating to contemporary audiences, erotic action is absent. To attract his audience Guitry relied instead almost solely on improbable situations and on language, especially his skill with amorous dialogue. A notable example is *Faisons un rêve* (1916; Let's Dream a Dream). His memoirs of this period were published as *Si j'ai bonne mémoire* (1934; translated as *If Memory Serves*).

As a motion picture director Guitry often filmed his own plays. He is credited with innovation in voice-over narration in *Le Roman d'un tricheur* (1936; The Story of a Cheat). His other films include *Les Perles de la couronne* (1937; The Pearls of the Crown) and *Remontons les Champs-elysées* (1938; Let's Walk Up the Champs-Elysées).

REFERENCES:

Michel Corvin, "Le Boulevard en question," in *Le Théâtre en France. 2: De la Révolution à nos jours,* edited by Jacqueline de Jomaron (Paris: Armand Colin, 1989), pp. 342–380;

James Harding, *Sacha Guitry, the Last Boulevardier* (New York: Scribners, 1968);

Bettina Knapp, *Sacha Guitry* (Boston: Twayne, 1981);

Cover of *L'Illustration*, 30 May 1936, featuring Sacha Guitry's 1936 movie *Le Roman d'un tricheur*, in which he created six personas for himself

Alfred Simon, *Dictionnaire du théâtre français contemporain* (Paris: Larousse, 1970).

— R.J.N.

ALICE GUY

Alice Guy (1873–1968) was the first woman filmmaker, occupying a place in film history near Thomas Edison, **Louis Lumière,** and **Georges Méliès.**

In 1896 Guy became secretary to **Léon Gaumont,** for whom she began directing films. Some film historians believe her *La Fée aux choux* (1896; The Cabbage Fairy) to be the first film with a story. She was in charge of Gaumont's productions from 1897 to 1907, during which time she directed about four hundred short films, including some sound films synchronizing movie projection with voices recorded on a wax cylinder. Many of these movies were recordings of circus acts, opera performances, and dramatized folk and fairy tales.

In 1907 Guy left for the United States with her new husband, director Herbert Blaché, to establish the Gaumont subsidiary in New York. From that time forward she often used the names Alice Guy-Blaché and Alice Blaché in her film work. She created her own production company, Solax, in 1910 and settled in New Jersey. During this period she experimented with different recording speeds, double exposure, and backward film movement in addition to working with her husband on short narrative films. She left independent production in 1917 but continued to direct for other studios until 1922, when she divorced Blaché and returned to France. Unable to obtain any directing assignments, she sought to retrieve copies of her many one-reelers that had since disappeared. In 1955 she received the Légion d'Honneur for her contributions to cinema. Guy spent the last four years of her life in New Jersey.

REFERENCES:

Noël Burch, *Life to Those Shadows,* translated by Ben Brewster (Berkeley & Los Angeles: University of California Press, 1990);

Thomas Elsaesser and Adam Barker, eds., *Early Cinema: Space-Frame-Narrative* (London: British Film Institute, 1990);

Anthony Slide, ed., *The Memoirs of Alice Guy-Blaché* (Metuchen, N.J.: Scarecrow Press, 1986).

— T.C.

H

ARTHUR HONEGGER

Although identified as a member of **Les Six,** a group of composers who in the late 1910s and early 1920s denounced the seriousness of Romantic music, Arthur Honegger (1892–1955) saw no reason to reject traditional musical forms or to avoid making grand, serious statements in his music.

Born in Le Havre of Swiss parentage, Honegger received his early training in Zurich. When he enrolled at the Paris Conservatory in 1913 his favorite composers were Johann Sebastian Bach, Richard Wagner, Richard Strauss, and Max Reger — scarcely the idols of his friend **Darius Milhaud,** whose battle cry was "Down with Wagner!" After he and four other members of Les Six took part in **Jean Cocteau**'s ballet *Les Mariés de la Tour Eiffel* (1921; The Newlyweds of the Eiffel Tower), Honegger distanced himself musically from the group.

Honegger's first independent success was *Le Roi David* (1921; King David). The first of his large-scale choral works, the oratorio depicts events in the life of the biblical king in a mixture of Jewish-Oriental exoticism, pseudo folk songs, and rousing Bach-like choruses. It is still widely performed. His fame was confirmed with *Pacific 231* (1924), an orchestral tour de force suggesting the starting, acceleration, and stopping of a locomotive. This "symphonic movement" was followed by another called *Rugby* (1928), a tone poem written when such works were often considered hopelessly old-fashioned. The oratorio *Jeanne d'Arc au bûcher* (1938; Joan of Arc at the Stake), with a libretto by **Paul Claudel,** was another success for Honegger. He also wrote five symphonies (1930–1951), a great deal of piano music, chamber music, songs, and music for plays and films, including **Abel Gance**'s *La Roue* (1923; The Wheel) and *Napoléon* (1927).

Honegger's stated aim was to "write music that would be noticed by masses of listeners and at the same time be sufficiently devoid of banalities to interest music lovers," and he succeeded. During his lifetime he was recognized as one of the foremost composers of his generation.

Director Jean-Louis Barrault, composer Arthur Honegger, and Albert Camus with the company of *L'Etat de siège* at the Théâtre Marigny, 1948

REFERENCES:

Arthur Honegger, *I Am a Composer,* translated by Wilson O. Clough, with Arthur Willman (London: Faber & Faber, 1966);

Geoffrey K. Spratt, *The Music of Arthur Honegger* (Cork, Ireland: Cork University Press, 1987).

— P.S.H.

L'HUMANITÉ

L'Humanité, a daily newspaper founded in 1904 by **Socialist Party** leader Jean Jaurès, became the official organ of

175

the **French Communist Party** in 1920. Since then it has made all the party's causes its own, expressing unwavering support for the Soviet Union throughout its existence, opposing colonial wars, and continuing to call on the working classes to rise in revolution against the bourgeoisie.

As the fortunes of the Communist Party have fluctuated, so have those of *Humanité*. For example, the paper was unusually influential and widely read around 1936, when the left-wing **Popular Front** came to power. Its circulation was then more than three hundred thousand. During **World War II** it went underground after the Nazis occupied France. It reached new heights of influence in 1946 as the voice of a party that had played a major role in the French **Resistance** movement; its circulation climbed to four hundred thousand. Since then its prestige and circulation have declined steadily.

The militancy of *Humanité* has never been more in evidence than during the **Algerian war,** which it vehemently opposed. As the war spread, the sales of *Humanité* and another left-wing daily, *Libération,* were totally banned in Algeria, and since the formation of the **Fifth Republic** in 1958, the government has brought more than two hundred court cases against the paper in an attempt to soften its oppositionist stance or ruin it financially. Neither goal has been attained, but the paper has increasingly gained the reputation of being financed from abroad, by Communists of Eastern Europe.

With the breakup of the Soviet Union, reporters for *Humanité* — all members of the French Communist Party, one of the most inflexibly pro-Soviet parties in Europe — lost some sense of direction; yet the paper continues to appear.

REFERENCES:

Pierre Albert, *La Presse française* (Paris: La Documentation française, 1983);

Maurice Goldring and Yvonne Quilès, *Sous le marteau, la plume: La presse communiste en crise* (Paris: Megrelis, 1982).

—J.P.McN.

LES HUSSARDS

The Hussards were a loosely organized group of writers who emerged in the aftermath of **World War II.** Group member Roger Nimier (1925–1962) took the name from the title of his third novel, *Le Hussard bleu* (1950; translated as *The Blue Hussar*), about a young man who, like Nimier, fights with the Second Regiment of Hussards in Germany in the final phase of the war. Also included in the Hussards were Antoine Blondin (1922–), Jacques Laurent (1919–), and later Michel Déon (1919–). Nimier was probably the most original and talented writer of the group. By age twenty-eight he had written

A 1933 advertisement for the daily newspaper that had become the official organ of the French Communist Party

eleven novels, but after 1953 he fell silent. He died in an automobile accident in 1962.

Sharing neo-Romantic instincts, the spirited, sharp-tongued Hussards rebelled against the new world of conformity imposed by the Allied victory. In general, their political sympathies were right wing, a fact that helps to explain their disenchantment with the prevailing French desire for revenge against Germany and anyone who had shown the least sympathy for the idea of a Europe united under German hegemony. In 1953 the Hussards created their own literary review, the *Parisienne,* which proposed a *littérature de désengagement* (literature of disengagement) in place of the left-wing, purposefully political *littérature engagée* of **Jean-Paul Sartre** and his colleagues.

REFERENCE:

Jacques Brenner, "Hussards et mousquetaires," in his *Histoire de la littérature française* (Paris: Fayard, 1978), pp. 384–397.

—D.O'C.

I

THE INDOCHINESE WAR

The French colonial conflict in Indochina, an undeclared war in which France was involved from 1946 until 1954, can be best understood by contrasting the strong desire of the Vietnamese for independence with the equally strong determination of France to reassert its sovereignty in the region after **World War II.** The forces of social change unleashed in the aftermath of **World War I** had led Vietnamese nationalists, some of whom had aligned themselves with Communists in the 1920s and 1930s, to hope once again for independence. The rise of Japanese imperialism and Japan's military occupation of Indochina in 1940 created the necessary conditions for Ho Chi Minh, a longtime agent of Comintern (the Communist International movement controlled by the Soviet Union), and the Vietminh, Ho's broad-based coalition, to seek power as Japan's fortunes waned in 1945.

Indochina was considered a backwater of the Pacific theater of operations during the war, and President Franklin D. Roosevelt had indicated his opposition to France's return to the area as a colonial power. Yet Indochina started to take on strategic importance after American diplomats in Moscow during spring 1945 began to raise their concerns about Josef Stalin's postwar intentions, increasing the need for good relations between the United States and France. When Roosevelt died, President Harry S. Truman inherited a chaotic Indochina policy. State Department officials disagreed over whether the United States should cement relations with France by supporting its efforts to recolonize Indochina or keep its pledge to back independence for Vietnam. As **Charles de Gaulle** pushed the United States to support French plans to reoccupy Indochina, the Americans acceded to French demands, hoping that France would liberalize its rule. The nascent Cold War continued to chill Soviet-American re-

lations, as the fall of China to indigenous Communist forces in 1949 and the 1950 invasion of South Korea by Communist North Korea created the fear that backing the Vietminh would set off a domino effect whereby all Southeast Asia would go Communist.

In accordance with agreements reached by the Allied powers at Yalta and Potsdam in 1945, the French were allowed to return to Indochina. Although Indochina had been occupied by the Japanese in September 1940, a French administration, acting for the **Vichy government** put in power after the German **Occupation** of France, had remained in place until the Japanese imprisoned the French in March 1945 and turned Vietnam over to the Vietnamese emperor Bao Dai. When the French attempted to reestablish a full colonial presence in Vietnam, a conflict was set off between two powerful forces. Ho Chi Minh and his nationalist-Communist coalition in the north, with only lip-service support from the **French Communist Party,** wanted a measure of independence and self-determination; the French government, with its power base in the south, wanted to restore its colonial regime in all of Vietnam, not only to maintain its territories in Indochina but also to discourage other nationalist movements from breaking away from the French empire.

Negotiations aiming at a political settlement with Ho failed, owing in part to extremist elements on both sides and, critically, to French duplicity. As a result, hostilities broke out late in 1946, with several major clashes and six thousand Vietnamese civilian casualties resulting from a French naval bombardment of the city of Haiphong. By December 1946, when it became apparent that the two Vietnams would not be reconciled in a peaceful manner through negotiation, the Vietminh abandoned the cities and moved to jungle bases, beginning a protracted guerrilla struggle to evict the French.

The war dragged on for eight years. In 1949 the French recognized the Bao Dai government of Vietnam, but the insurgents of the north continued to make gains, linking up with Laotian and Cambodian Communist forces. The conflict culminated in the 1954 siege of the French garrison at Dien Bien Phu by Indochinese forces. The garrison, which could be resupplied only by air, held out for several weeks in April and May, falling on 7 May, after seven thousand French combatants had died and thousands more had been taken prisoner. France, under the premiership of Pierre Mendès-France, negotiated a settlement that eventually led to withdrawal.

The Geneva Accords were signed on 22 July 1954, bringing a formal end to the war. The accords divided Vietnam into two parts at the seventeenth parallel and provided independence for Cambodia and Laos. A controversial part of the agreement was a plan calling for Vietnamese elections that would be a preliminary step toward eventual reunification of the north and south. These elections never took place, in large part because the administration of President Dwight D. Eisenhower supported South Vietnam's claims that there could be no fair elections in areas under Communist control.

France's handling of the Indochinese situation in 1946 eliminated any possibility that Ho could maintain his leadership unless he accepted the military challenge thrown down by the French and forcing him into alliance with the most radical members of the Vietminh. France's insistence on regaining its colonial territory in Southeast Asia laid the groundwork for America's war in Vietnam and the eventual takeover of the whole country by the North Vietnamese Communists. The worst losers were, of course, the Vietnamese people.

Protest in France against the war was not widespread. The Communist newspaper *Humanité,* while opposing the presence of the French in Indochina, did not dare criticize the professional army. **Jean-Paul Sartre,** in the *Temps Modernes,* was one of the few eminent figures to raise his voice against the French colonial presence. **Jules Roy,** who resigned his colonel's commission in disagreement over the conduct of French operations in Indochina, published a detailed, critical report, *La Bataille dans la rizière* (1953; The Battle in the Rice Paddy), but he did not reveal all he knew about violations of the Geneva conventions until later. The battle of Dien Bien Phu was the topic of a 1992 film by Pierre Schoendorfer.

REFERENCES:

Lucien Bodard, *The Quicksand War: Prelude to Vietnam* (Boston: Little, Brown, 1967);

Joseph Buttinger, *A Dragon Embattled,* 2 volumes (London: Pall Mall Press, 1967);

Jacques Dalloz, *The War in Indochina 1945–1954* (Savage, Md.: Barnes & Noble, 1990);

Philip Davidson, *Vietnam at War: The History, 1946–1975* (New York: Oxford University Press, 1988);

Philippe Devillers and Jean Lacouture, *La Fin d'une guerre* (Paris: Seuil, 1960);

Bernard Fall, *Hell in a Very Small Place: The Siege of Dien Bien Phu* (New York: Lippincott, 1966);

Fall, *The Two Viet-nams: A Political and Military Analysis,* second revised edition (New York: Praeger, 1967);

Ronald E. M. Irving, *The First Indochina War* (London: Croom Helm, 1975);

Stanley Karnow, *Vietnam: A History* (New York: Viking, 1983).
                                                              —L.J.C.

VINCENT D'INDY

Although little of his music is still performed, Vincent d'Indy (1851–1931) was a respected composer and influential teacher during the first quarter of the twentieth century. Among his students who became important composers were **Erik Satie, Arthur Honegger,** and **Albert Roussel.**

A pupil and disciple of César Franck, d'Indy was a staunch champion of classicism and of Richard Wagner's operas. Taking a strict view of what music should be, he was not impressed by the highly colored scores of **Claude Debussy,** despite their friendship and his willingness to conduct Debussy's music, and he abominated the playfulness of Satie, **Igor Stravinsky,** and **Les Six.**

His high-minded Wagnerian-influenced operas were respectfully received and admired for their masterful workmanship, but they soon disappeared from the repertory. An orchestral piece with piano, the *Symphonie sur un chant montagnard français* (1886; Symphony on a French Mountain Air), is the only d'Indy composition that has not fallen into obscurity.

In addition to composing and conducting, in 1896 d'Indy helped to found (and later directed) the Schola Cantorum in Paris, a distinguished school of music with a curriculum that went far beyond the scope and aims of the typical conservatory of the time. Instead of focusing solely on producing virtuosic performers, it proposed to present the whole development of Western music from the Gregorian chant of the Middle Ages to the present. D'Indy's four-volume *Cours de composition musicale* (1903–1950; Course in Musical Composition), written with Auguste Sérieyx, is still admired for

Vincent d'Indy

its comprehensiveness. D'Indy also wrote biographies of Ludwig van Beethoven and César Franck and edited compositions by Claudio Monteverdi and Jean-Philippe Rameau.

REFERENCE:

Rollo Myers, *Modern French Music from Fauré to Boulez* (New York & Washington, D.C.: Praeger, 1971), pp. 34–40.

— P.S.H.

Institut de Recherche et de Coordination Acoustique/Musique

The Institut de Recherche et de Coordination Acoustique/Musique (IRCAM) in Paris is the music section of the grandiose Centre National d'Art et de Culture Georges Pompidou (**Centre Pompidou,** popularly called Centre Beaubourg). Opened in 1977, IRCAM promotes contemporary music, especially electronic music, through research and public programs. As large as a football field and entirely underground to be sheltered from city noises, the IRCAM facilities include studios, laboratories, offices, and an auditorium with movable walls and ceilings so that recording experiments can be done with controlled acoustics.

When **Pierre Boulez** was invited to head IRCAM in 1976, he accepted because it allowed him to continue working toward a solution of musical problems left unresolved since the 1950s, when many composers abandoned major-minor tonality and set off in several experimental directions that found little favor with the general public. Boulez firmly believed that a new musical language could be achieved only by the joint effort of musicians and scientists working with computers within an organization such as IRCAM.

Each department has its own director and staff. The instrument and voice department invents and disseminates innovations in traditional Western instrumental and vocal techniques and develops new instruments. Another department studies electronic sound production, while the computer department synthesizes sounds and explores the use of the computer in the creation and performance of music. The education department instructs visiting composers in the use of IRCAM resources, publishes findings, and sponsors public lectures. The institute also presents in France and abroad an ongoing concert series of contemporary and experimental music performed by the twenty-nine-member Ensemble InterContemporain.

Along with the accomplishments of IRCAM, there have been personality conflicts and disagreements over budgets. Boulez in particular has been a target of criticism as well as praise. The annual budget of more than five million dollars is envied by the directors of other state-subsidized cultural projects, and Boulez's choice of an international staff, his dictatorial manner, and his selection of programs have all been questioned. In 1993 he announced his retirement from IRCAM.

REFERENCES:

Dominique Jameux, *Pierre Boulez* (Cambridge, Mass.: Harvard University Press, 1991);

Roy McMullen, "Boulez' IRCAM: Amnesia in Nibelheim," *High Fidelity Magazine,* 27 (April 1977): 80–84.

— P.S.H.

Eugène Ionesco

Eugène Ionesco (1912–1994) is known worldwide for his contributions to the **Theater of the Absurd,** especially his first two plays, *La Cantatrice chauve* (published in 1954; translated as *The Bald Soprano*) and *La Leçon* (published in 1954; translated as *The Lesson*). These short dramas have been running on small Pari-

Eugène Ionesco (front) and the cast of his play *Jacques ou la soumission* (French Cultural Services)

sian stages almost continually since their initial performances in 1950 and 1951 respectively. Ionesco composed dozens of one-act and full-length plays and also wrote and lectured on the theater. In 1970 he was elected to the Académie Française.

Born in Romania to a French mother and a Romanian father, Ionesco spent most of his childhood in France, but he returned to his native country at age thirteen to join his father, who had won custody of his son in a divorce suit. In a household dominated by a hostile stepmother, Ionesco's adolescent years were turbulent. After graduation from the University of Bucharest, Ionesco returned to France in 1939, intending to pursue a degree at the Sorbonne. After spending part of **World War II** in Romania and part in France, he worked as a proofreader — an activity that may have focused his attention on the arbitrariness of language and its inadequacy to convey meaning. Inspired by the simpleminded practice dialogues he encountered when he was learning English in 1948, Ionesco wrote *La Cantatrice chauve,* in which two couples, the Smiths and the Martins, note that they have eaten an English dinner, discover that man and wife are married to one another, and utter other absurdities and non sequiturs. The soprano of the title is mentioned only in passing in a long, quasi-nonsensical monologue, delivered by a fire chief who arrives apropos of nothing.

La Cantatrice chauve is marked by two types of Ionescan absurdity — the nonsense that is latent in much conventional speech and the paralysis of routine. There are darker sides to Ionesco's theater as well — aspects that point to a fundamental metaphysical absurdity of the human condition. Like **Samuel Beckett,** Ionesco uses humor to reveal this absurdity. In his plays proliferating objects — chairs for invisible guests in *Les Chaises* (1954; translated as *The Chairs*), huge mushrooms (along with a giant, expanding corpse) in *Amédée ou comment s'en débarrasser* (1954; translated as *Amédée, or How to Get Rid of It*), furniture in *Le Nouveau Locataire* (1958; translated as *The New Tenant*) — suggest a threatening material environment, made worse perhaps by industrial society but signifying chiefly the metaphysical alienation between man and the world. Ionesco's plays also reveal great ferocity. When language gets out of control in *La Leçon,* the professor sadistically stabs his student with an invisible knife. In *Rhinocéros* (1959; translated) social conformity becomes vicious social oppression.

Ionesco answered variously the threats posed by absurdity and oppression. He envisioned a physical and ontological emancipation in *Amédée,* as the husband, free from earthly cares, floats away on the ballooning corpse. He made *Le Nouveau Locataire* end in entropy, as the new tenant, immobile and surrounded by barricades of furniture, chooses to remain in utter darkness and silence. In *Rhinocéros* he called for a political stand; only by refusing the oppressive conformity of "rhinoceritis" can the hero retain his freedom and identity. In nearly all of Ionesco's plays the audience experiences, even through the humor, a strong existential malaise. To the most disturbing threat of all — death — there can be no answer, as is shown in *Le Roi se meurt* (1963; translated as *Exit the King*). Although critics have connected the dark vision of Ionesco's plays to his unhappy childhood, in a deeper sense his voice is that of mid-twentieth-century malaise in a world gone mad.

REFERENCES:

Richard N. Coe, *Ionesco* (New York: Grove, 1961); revised as *Ionesco: A Study of His Plays* (London: Methuen, 1971);

Rosette C. Lamont, *Ionesco's Imperatives: The Politics of Culture* (Ann Arbor: University of Michigan Press, 1993);

Lamont and M. J. Friedman, eds., *The Two Faces of Ionesco* (Troy, N.Y.: Whitston, 1976);

Leonard C. Pronko, *Ionesco* (New York: Columbia University Press, 1965).

— C.S.B.

Luce Irigaray

Luce Irigaray (193?–), a student of **Jacques Lacan,** is one of the most important feminist theorists in the twentieth century. In her attempt to disrupt what she views as the phallocentric system of thought and language, one of Irigaray's main strategies is to attack phallocratic discourse, proposing instead a feminine alternative — a vision of language similar to **Hélène Cixous**'s *écriture féminine* (feminine writing), which Irigaray calls *le parler femme* (womanspeak). "Turn everything upside down," she writes, "inside out, back to front. . . . *Overthrow syntax* by suspending its eternally teleological order. . . . speak only in riddles, hints, allusions, parables. . . ."

Irigaray's dissertation, published as *Speculum de l'autre femme* (1974; translated as *Speculum of the Other Woman*), includes a feminist deconstruction of the work of Sigmund Freud. Her argument, which holds that Freud's system excludes women's sexuality, proved so controversial that it led to Irigaray's expulsion from the Ecole Freudienne at Vincennes. Her collection of essays *Ce sexe qui n'en est pas un* (1977; This Sex Which Is Not One) develops many of the central concerns introduced in her dissertation.

REFERENCES:

Raoul Mortley, *French Philosophers in Conversation: Levinas, Schneider, Serres, Irigaray, Le Doeff, Derrida* (London & New York: Routledge, 1991);

Joan Nordquist, *French Feminist Theory: Luce Irigaray and Hélène Cixous, A Bibliography,* Social Theory: A Bibliographic Series, no. 20 (Santa Cruz, Cal.: Reference and Research Services, 1991);

Margaret Whitford, *Luce Irigaray: Philosophy in the Feminine* (London & New York: Routledge, 1991).

— C.S.B.

Isidore Isou

Isidore Isou (1925–) was the founder of **Lettrism,** an avant-garde movement that appealed to young people in the decade after **World War II.** Through a reduction of poetry to letters and other symbols, as well as through puns, chance and deliberate juxtapositions of words and images, and complicated wordplay, Isou and the Lettrists sought to reinvent language and poetry.

Born Jean-Isidore Goldstein in Romania, Isou was able to escape from the Nazis with the help of the Jewish underground and found refuge in Paris in 1945. Together with Gabriel Pomerand (whom Isou expelled from the group in 1956), Isou launched Lettrism in 1946 with the one-issue review *La Dictature Lettriste* (1946; The Lettrist Dictatorship), which was designed to jolt a public all too familiar, after the events of World War II, with the implications of the word *dictatorship*. In 1947 the Lettrists covered Paris with handbills denouncing both social realism and **Surrealism** as reactionary and interrupted a lecture on **Dada** by demanding to know the speaker's stance on their new movement. The resulting publicity earned Isou a publishing contract for his first book, *Introduction à une nouvelle poésie et à une nouvelle musique, de Charles Baudelaire à Isidore Isou* (1947; Introduction to a New Poetry and Music, from Charles Baudelaire to Isidore Isou). This work was followed by his *La Mécanique des femmes* (1949; The Mechanism of Women) and Pomerand's *Saint Ghetto des prêts: Grimoire* (1950; Holy Ghetto of Loans: Book of Magic). The strategy of these volumes was to provoke reaction and even repression as a means of crystallizing support for Lettrism: *La Mécanique des femmes*, which was basically a sex manual, was briefly banned and earned Isou a short stay in a psychiatric hospital.

Isou's attempts to raise an insurgent youth movement in tune with his ideas were less than successful. In 1948 he showered Paris with leaflets promising that "12,000,000 youths will take to the streets to make the Lettrist revolution," but the results were almost twelve million short. His 1950 political manifesto, published in his review *Front de la Jeunesse* (Youth Front), argued that young people were the only major social sector outside a commodified culture. He called for the young to "cease to be a commodity." To put his ideas into action, in 1950 thirty members of his youth front broke into a Catholic orphanage to free the children, producing a small-scale riot. This event marked the end of Isou's political activism. He disavowed the invasion and disruption of the Easter mass at Notre-Dame Cathedral the same year although young Lettrists provided its leadership. An open break within Lettrism came with Isou's denunciation of Lettrist-led disruptions of Charles Chaplin's *City Lights* in 1952. One of his followers, **Guy Debord,** responded by creating the Lettrist International, which evolved into the **Situationist International.** Debord's group was far more revolutionary in intent than Isou's. Isou's original call for a youth revolt was scaled down and limited to minor reforms, including the right for superior students to skip grades, leave school early, and get government grants. Isou and his supporters were not in-volved in the student uprising of **May 1968,** unlike Debord's Situationists, who provided inspiration for many of the students. Referring to the events that spring, a former member of Isou's movement commented, "The disciples of the 'Youth Uprising' were not to be present when, finally, youth rose up." Isou thereafter limited himself largely to denunciations of various figures and long tracts seeking to prove who was the rightful heir to the Dadaists.

REFERENCE:

Greil Marcus, *Lipstick Traces: A Secret History of the Twentieth Century* (Cambridge, Mass.: Harvard University Press, 1989).

—J.H.

J

EDMOND JABÈS

The poetry of Edmond Jabès (1912–) is indebted to the Jewish tradition from which he came, in particular to the Cabala. It also reflects Arab influences and the exoticism of his native Egypt, as well as displaying parallels to **Surrealism.**

Born in Cairo in 1912, Jabès began publishing his poetry, which is written in French, in the late 1940s. He settled in France in 1957. A prolific poet, he was awarded the Prix des Critiques in 1970 for the entire body of his work. The title of one of Jabès's best-known books, *Le Livre des questions* (1963; translated as *The Book of Questions*), suggests the philosophic and linguistic interrogation that characterizes much of his writing. He often examines the question of identity. This prose volume was the first in a series of books with the same title but different, anagrammatic subtitles: *Yukel* (1964), *Yaël* (1967), *Elya* (1969), and *Aely* (1972) — all translated. These anagrams point to the way in which Jabès undermines language even as he explores the possibility of its meaning and how it symbolizes objects outside itself.

Other works by Jabès include *Chansons pour le repas de l'ogre* (1947; Songs for the Ogre's Meal); a collection of poems titled *Je bâtis ma demeure, 1943-1957* (1959; I Build My Dwelling, 1943-1957); *El, ou le dernier livre* (1973; El, or the Last Book); and a series of works bearing the title *Le Livre des ressemblances* (1976-1980; translated as *The Book of Resemblances*). Selections from *Je bâtis ma demeure* have been translated into English as *A Share of Ink* (1979).

REFERENCES:

Eric Gould, ed., *The Sin of the Book: Edmond Jabès* (Lincoln: University of Nebraska Press, 1985);

Studies in Twentieth Century Literature, special issue on Jabès, edited by Gould, 12 (Fall 1987).

— C.S.B.

PHILIPPE JACCOTTET

A translator of modern German and Italian authors as well as of Homer and Plato, Swiss author Philippe Jaccottet (1925–) is a highly regarded poet and has been a frequent contributor of critical pieces on poetry and other topics to the **Nouvelle Revue Française.** Jaccottet has also written widely respected fiction and critical essays.

The poems in Jaccottet's first collection, *Requiem* (1947), are composed in richly allusive, strict alexandrines, but over his career his verse has subsequently evolved to less rigid forms. His sensitive poetry, full of fine nuances, is often centered on nature. Jaccottet's major collections include *L'Effraie et autres poésies* (1953; The Owl and Other Poems), *L'Ignorant: poèmes 1952-1956* (1958), *Airs: poèmes 1961-1964* (1967; Airs: Poems), and *Leçons* (1969; Lessons). Some of his poetry has been translated into English as *Breathings* (1974) and *Selected Poems* (1984).

Jaccottet has also written prose meditations such as *La Promenade sous les arbres* (1957; The Walk Under the Trees) and the prose poem *A travers un verger* (1975; translated as *Through an Orchard*). Two volumes of passages from his notebooks for the years 1954-1967 have been published as *La Semaison: carnets* (1963 and 1971; translated as *Seedtime: Extracts from the Notebooks*).

REFERENCES:

Andrea Cady, *Measuring the Visible: The Verse and Prose of Philippe Jaccottet* (Amsterdam: Rodopi, 1992);

Alain Clerval, *Philippe Jaccottet* (Paris: Seghers, 1976).

— C.S.B.

MAX JACOB

Max Jacob (1876-1944), whose best-known work is *Le Cornet à dés* (1918; translated as *The Dice Cup: Selected Prose Poems*), has often been called a **Cubist** poet because of his aesthetic practice, which involves

Ortiz de Zaratte (front), Max Jacob, H. P. Roché, and Pablo Picasso in Montparnasse, 1916

changing tones and registers and varying viewpoints. He associated with the Cubists early in the twentieth century, meeting **Pablo Picasso** in 1901 and subsequently becoming friends with artist **Juan Gris,** avant-garde poet **Guillaume Apollinaire,** and art critic André Salmon — all of whom lived at or near the **Bateau Lavoir** after Picasso moved to a studio there in 1904. Jacob, who was a homosexual, also had connections with **Jean Cocteau** and **Raymond Radiguet.**

Jacob dedicated his first important book, *Saint Matorel* (1911), to Picasso, who did etchings for it. In his writing Jacob often included a harlequin figure, which was also a favorite subject for Cubist painters. (Jacob himself painted and constructed composite art objects.) Frequently characterized by flat tones of conversation and a morbid irony, his writing is filled with wordplay and fantasy.

Jewish by birth, Jacob was converted to Catholicism and baptized in 1915 with Picasso serving as his godfather. *La Défense de Tartufe* (1919; In Defense of Tartuffe), which he called "Ecstasy, remorse, visions, prayers, poems, and meditations of a converted Jew," describes Jacob's conversion. In 1921 he went to live next to the well-known Benedictine abbey at Saint-Benoît-sur-Loire, but he returned to Paris periodically. During the German **Occupation** of France in **World War II,** Jacob was arrested and interned by the Nazis because of his Judaic origins. He died in the concentration camp at Drancy, France.

REFERENCES:

Gerald Kamber, *Max Jacob and the Poetics of Cubism* (Baltimore & London: Johns Hopkins Press, 1971);

Annette Thau, *Poetry and Antipoetry: A Study of Selected Aspects of Max Jacob's Poetic Style* (Chapel Hill: University of North Carolina Department of Romance Languages, 1976).

— C.S.B.

FRANCIS JAMMES

Around 1900 Postsymbolist poet Francis Jammes (1868–1938) was considered one of the gifted writers of his generation by many of his contemporaries, but by the end of the twentieth century he was viewed as a minor figure associated with a minor movement called *le Naturisme*. His poetry is seldom read, but his correspondence with such important figures as **Paul Claudel, André Gide,** and Francis Vielé-Griffin is considered a valuable source of information on the literary history of his times.

Jammes, who lived most of his life in Orthez, a small town in the French Pyrenees, can be classified as a regional poet with a naive, sentimental bent. Having drifted away from the practice of Roman Catholicism, he returned to the church in 1905, through the influence of Claudel, and also became an explicitly Catholic writer. A poem such as "Prière pour aller au paradis avec les ânes" (Prayer to Go to Paradise with Donkeys), a touching portrait of humble beasts of burden, is characteristic of his simple faith and direct expression of feeling.

The most important collections of Jammes's poetry are *De l'angélus de l'aube à l'angélus du soir, 1888–1897* (1898; translated as *From the Angelus at Dawn to the Angelus at Dusk*) and *Clairières dans le ciel, 1902–1906* (1906; Clearings in Heaven, 1902–1906). He also wrote *Géorgiques chrétiennes* (1911–1912; Christian Georgics) and poetic novels and fables, including *Le Roman du lièvre* (1903; translated as *Romance of the Hare*). His poetic prose and his powers of description are still admired.

REFERENCES:

Amy Lowell, *Six French Poets: Studies in Contemporary Literature* (New York: Macmillan, 1915);

Robert Mallet, *Francis Jammes: Sa vie, son œuvre (1868–1938)* (Paris: Mercure de France, 1961).

— C.S.B.

Francis Jammes and François Mauriac in Paris, 1937

MARGUERITE JAMOIS

Among the best-known of twentieth-century French actresses, Marguerite Jamois (1901–1964) also achieved renown as a director. She got her start with **Firmin Gémier,** studied with **Charles Dullin,** and rose to stardom in the acting troupe of **Gaston Baty,** where she first performed in 1921, in a production of **Fernand Crommelynck**'s *Les Amants puérils* (The Childish Lovers). She remained with Baty's company at a succession of Paris theaters — La Chimère, the Studio des Champs-Elysées, the Théâtre de l'Avenue — until they found a more permanent home in 1930 at the **Théâtre Montparnasse.** There she acted female leads in a wide range of plays, including Alfred de Musset's *Les Caprices de Marianne* (translated as *The Caprices of Marianne*) in 1935, Baty's adaptation of Gustave Flaubert's novel *Madame Bovary* in 1936, Jean Racine's classic tragedy *Phèdre* (translated as *Phaedra*) in 1940, and William Shakespeare's *Macbeth* in 1943. For tragic heroines such as Phèdre she found a remarkably personal tragic tone, far different from the traditional, stylized accents taught in acting schools.

In 1943 Baty turned the theater and the company over to Jamois. She continued performing (for instance, in the title role of Robinson Jeffers's *Medea*) while directing the troupe's productions at the Montparnasse. In 1957 she won the Dominique Prize for her mise-en-scène of an adaptation of *The Diary of Anne Frank.*

REFERENCE:

Henri-René Lenormand, *Marguerite Jamois* (Paris: Calmann-Lévy, 1950).

— R.J.N.

ALFRED JARRY

Playwright Alfred Jarry (1873–1907) lived only a few years into the twentieth century. Yet his play *Ubu roi* (1896; translated) was one of the harbingers of a new, distinctively modern, twentieth-century theater that departs from both Symbolist drama and the realism of such nineteenth-century authors as Henri Becque.

185

Jarry derived the idea for *Ubu roi* from a schoolboy puppet show that he had helped to create. He developed the concept into a provocative farce featuring a grotesque, repulsive hero who becomes king of Poland. The first syllable the king speaks, *merdre,* announces the scatological quality of much of the dialogue and the deliberate distortion of reality through violation of language. (The word *merdre* is Jarry's fabrication, but it is close to a common obscenity.) The role of the absurd and the grotesque and the denial of ordinary reality make the play a precursor of both **Surrealism** and the **Theater of the Absurd.** The premiere of *Ubu roi* at the **Théâtre de l'Œuvre** created a scandal, and the play closed after the second performance.

Jarry also wrote eccentric novels and verse. His fictional work *Les Gestes et opinions du docteur Faustroll, pataphysicien* (1911; The Acts and Opinions of Doctor Faustroll, Pataphysician) introduced into French the term *pataphysics,* "the science of imaginary solutions"; the work displays Rabelaisian humor and tremendous inventiveness, which would later appeal to writers such as **Raymond Queneau** and other members of the Collège de Pataphysique. Among Jarry's other plays are *César-Antéchrist* (1895; translated as *Caesar Antichrist*); *Ubu enchaîné* (1900; translated as *Enslaved*); and *Ubu cocu* (1944; translated as *Ubu Cuckholded*).

Jarry died of meningeal tuberculosis, complicated by his longtime abuse of his health, particularly through the use of alcohol.

REFERENCE:

Roger Shattuck, *The Banquet Years: The Origins of the Avant-Garde in France 1885 to World War I* (New York: Harcourt, Brace, 1958; revised edition, New York: Vintage, 1968).

                             — C.S.B.

JE SUIS PARTOUT

During **World War II** *Je Suis Partout* (I Am Everywhere) became one of the leading collaborationist journals in Paris, with a circulation of close to three hundred thousand. Founded in 1930, the weekly was the creation of the publisher Arthème Fayard, who also owned the popular journal *Candide.* In the 1930s, a period of intense political polarization, *Je Suis Partout* moved from the center to the far right. By 1940 it counted among its writers many of the most virulent advocates of National Socialism, including **Robert Brasillach,** Alain Laubreaux, and Lucien Rebatet, who railed in its pages against Jews, democracy, and communism.

Under the direction of its longtime editor, historian Pierre Gaxotte (1895–1982), *Je Suis Partout* was at first moderately conservative and negative on many issues. It accurately forecast Adolf Hitler's rise to power in Germany. While it was unswerving in its opposition to the Soviet Communist regime, its point of view on other countries or ideologies could be less dogmatic. Gaxotte had a low opinion of Americans, "a jumble of poorly assimilated emigrants with little in common other than puerile vanity and the imperialism of suspender merchants" (31 March 1934). Yet he was sympathetic to Franklin D. Roosevelt and his willingness to take on Wall Street.

Gaxotte's conservatism, including distrust of democracy and opposition to universal suffrage, hardened into sympathy for fascism. He saw the election of **Léon Blum** and the left-wing **Popular Front** in 1936 as running counter to the true course of history, which was on the side of fascism. Gaxotte invited France to link up with the fascist powers and relentlessly attacked Blum's government, but he did not indulge in the gutter vulgarity of other right-wing journals, such as *Gringoire.*

In 1937 Gaxotte was succeeded as editor-in-chief by Brasillach, a well-known writer who was, like Gaxotte, a graduate of the highly competitive **Ecole Normale Supérieure.** Increasingly, *Je Suis Partout* called for a national (fascist) revolution, and its anti-Semitism grew more virulent. **Marcel Jouhandeau** and **Louis-Ferdinand Céline,** both vehement anti-Semites, were warmly welcomed, and issues devoted to attacking Jews were so popular that they were reprinted. Among other major writers who found favor with *Je Suis Partout* were **Jean Giraudoux** and **Henry de Montherlant.**

Throughout the German **Occupation** of France, *Je Suis Partout* was even more militantly anti-Semitic and profascist than before the war. Rebatet and Laubreaux called for the death of Jews, the victory of National Socialism, and the refusal of any form of compromise or concession. As the Allies advanced, they and their colleagues were forced to flee. The last issue of *Je Suis Partout* appeared on 16 August 1944, just before the **Liberation** of Paris. Laubreaux was condemned to death in absentia but escaped to Spain. Rebatet's death sentence was commuted to a prison term. Brasillach was condemned to death and executed in February 1945.

REFERENCE:

Pierre-Marie Dioudonnat, *'Je Suis Partout,' 1930–1944: Les Maurrassiens devant la tentation fasciste* (Paris: La Table Ronde, 1973).

                             — J.P.McN.

MARCEL JOUHANDEAU

The standing of the controversial novelist Marcel Jouhandeau (1888–1979) is disputed. To some he is a major author, to others an antipathetic pervert whose work has little literary value. Havelock Ellis considered him a genius, and **Claude Mauriac** praised him as a "mystic of hell." In his fiction and autobiographical writings Jouhandeau examined what he called the ecstasy of vice. As a homosexual who nevertheless married, he became the chronicler of a union based on disagreement — the anatomist of a domestic inferno.

Jouhandeau spent his childhood in a provincial town that he later portrayed, sometimes savagely, under the name Chaminadour. He had deeply ambivalent feelings toward his father, a butcher, but was devoted to his mother. As a boy, he was permanently marked by a homosexual experience. After settling in Paris and becoming a teacher, Jouhandeau published his first novel, *Les Pincengrain,* in 1924. His *Monsieur Godeau intime* (1926; Monsieur Godeau Portrayed Intimately) introduced an autobiographical character who would often reappear in his writings. In 1929 Jouhandeau married a dancer, Elisabeth Toulemon, who became the Elise of his books — his necessary adversary and negative pole.

The antagonisms that Jouhandeau acted out with his wife were integral to his artistic and religious identity. As an idiosyncratic mystic, he was convinced that his marital torment, like his sexual sins, constituted a theological drama that would bring about his salvation. "God is present in hell with me," he wrote. More than one hundred books sprang from his ceaseless analysis of his conjugal and sexual life and his provincial boyhood. They include *Algèbre des valeurs morales* (1935; Algebra of Moral Values); *De l'abjection* (1939; On Abjection), which reflects a deep psychological crisis of the 1930s; *Du pur amour* (1969; On Pure Love), a glorification of homosexuality; and volumes of the Monsieur Godeau cycle, including *Monsieur Godeau marié* (1933; Monsieur Godeau Married). His extensive series of autobiographical works and notebooks, published under the collective titles *Le Mémorial* (1948–1972) and *Journaliers* (1961–1978; Dailies), are held in great esteem by some readers for their vigor, style, and insight. Selections from his writings have been translated as *Marcel and Elise* (1953).

REFERENCE:

Jean Gaulmier, *L'Univers de Marcel Jouhandeau* (Paris: Nizet, 1959).

— C.S.B.

Pierre Jean Jouve

Pierre Jean Jouve (1887–1975) is one of the half-dozen major French poets of his generation. Highly respected by his fellow writers, he was utterly devoted to the literary life. At once a Catholic poet and a disciple of Sigmund Freud, he combined Freud's theories on death, sexuality, and the unconscious with elements of Christianity — especially from writings by great mystics such as Teresa of Avila and Saint John of the Cross — to create a highly visionary poetry that nonetheless offers a disturbing worldview marked by desire and guilt.

Jouve discovered poetry in the work of Stéphane Mallarmé. Other writers who eventually influenced him include Walt Whitman, Friedrich Hölderlin, William Blake, Arthur Rimbaud, Charles Baudelaire, and Gérard de Nerval. In the mid 1920s, under the influence of various mystical writers and a new love affair, he denounced everything that he had written before that date and burned all his papers and published writings. *Les Mystérieuses Noces* (1925; The Mysterious Wedding) announced the beginning of a new period of creativity; a later version, *Noces* (1928), is a poetic masterpiece in which the poet explores, often in dense, aphoristic, yet sensual language, the drama of sin and conversion, which he considered the essence of the spiritual life. A later collection, *Sueur de sang* (1933; Sweat of Blood), was even more powerful. Some of his verse has been translated into English as *An Idiom of Night* (1968).

Jouve's verse is characteristically short — including many four-line and even two-line poems, often untitled. He did occasionally write long poems, including "Songe" (Dream), which focuses on *vanitas vanitatum* and the guilt of sexual desire, and "Vrai corps" (True Body), on the Incarnation. Images such as the eye, the stain, the tree, and the stag are often repeated in his poetry.

Jouve published several novels in the 1920s, including *Paulina 1880* (1925; translated). In the 1930s Jouve, whose companion was a psychiatrist, added two books to his fictional works: *Histoires sanglantes* (1932; Bloody Stories) and *La Scène capitale* (1935; The Central Scene). Both are rich in symbolism and highly colored by Freudian notions. Poems he wrote during **World War II** were collected in *La Vierge de Paris* (1944; The Virgin of Paris). In 1954 he published an important autobiographical text, *En miroir* (In the Mirror). He is also the author of essays on Baudelaire and Wolfgang Amadeus Mozart, whose music plays a role in his poetry.

REFERENCES:

Catharine Savage Brosman, "Jouve's Spatial Dialectic in *Les Noces* and *Sueur de sang,*" *Australian Journal of French Studies,* 10, no. 2 (1974): 164–174;

Margaret Callander, *The Poetry of Pierre Jean Jouve* (Manchester: Manchester University Press, 1965).

— C.S.B.

LOUIS JOUVET

A major stage and film actor and an influential theater director, Louis Jouvet (1887–1951) worked at various times in all aspects of the theater, including lighting, set design, costuming, and prompting. As a youth, he applied repeatedly for admission to the Paris Conservatory, but he was never admitted. He was largely self-taught and widely read. (There is some irony in the fact that he was later invited to teach at the Paris Conservatory.)

In 1913 **Jacques Copeau,** who had seen Jouvet in a 1911 stage adaptation of Fyodor Dostoyevsky's *The Brothers Karamazov,* enlisted him for the new **Théâtre du Vieux-Colombier** troupe. Jouvet not only acted for Copeau in Paris and New York, but he soon became his stage manager, set designer, and primary assistant. In 1922 Jouvet went on to act and direct at the Comédie des Champs-Elysées, where his memorable productions included **Jules Romains**'s *Knock* (1923), Nikolay Gogol's *The Inspector General* (1927), **Jean Giraudoux**'s *Siegfried* (1928), *Amphitryon 38* (1929; translated), and *Intermezzo* (1933; translated), and **Jean Cocteau**'s *La Machine infernale* (1934; translated as *The Infernal Machine*).

Jouvet's virtually symbiotic relationship with the dramatist Giraudoux launched their careers and made both famous. Giraudoux's often lyrical scripts gave rise to the director's most sumptuous, yet elegant, sets, while Jouvet's characterizations as an actor inspired the playwright. In 1934, when Jouvet was called to teach at the Paris Conservatory, he was also named director at the **Théâtre de l'Athénée,** where he continued staging Giraudoux plays, including the premiere of *La Guerre de Troie n'aura pas lieu* (1935; adapted as *Tiger at the Gates*). He directed at the **Comédie-Française** in the late 1930s, when the management invited him and his fellow directors in the **Cartel des Quatre** to stage plays for the national theater.

During **World War II** Jouvet closed his Paris theater and went on tour. Giraudoux died in 1944, and when Jouvet, grief-stricken, returned to directing at the Athénée in 1945, he produced and acted in the premiere of Giraudoux's *La Folle de Chaillot* (translated as *The Madwoman of Chaillot*). Jouvet went on to stage Molière's *Dom Juan* in 1947 and *Tartuffe* in 1950, when he shocked audiences by playing the title character, who professes great piety, as a thin and sinister (rather than a fat and funny) hypocrite. He helped to launch **Jean Genet**'s career by staging *Les Bonnes*

Louis Jouvet in Paul Claudel's *L'Annonce faite à Marie* (French Cultural Services)

(translated as *The Maids*) in 1947, and he produced **Jean-Paul Sartre**'s grandiose *Le Diable et le Bon Dieu* (translated as *The Devil and the Good Lord*) in 1951.

Less revolutionary and more eclectic in his approach to theater than the other Cartel des Quatre directors, Jouvet was doubtless the most successful with the public; rather than following formulas, he strove for interpretations that worked. He is particularly remembered for his gaunt, aristocratic face and for his portrayals of famous characters, from the Contrôleur in Giraudoux's *Intermezzo* to Arnolphe in Molière's *L'Ecole des femmes* (translated as *The School for Wives*). He also appeared in some thirty films.

REFERENCES:

Jean Hort, *Les Théâtres du Cartel et leurs animateurs: Pitoëff, Baty, Jouvet, Dullin* (Geneva: Skira, 1944);

Bettina Knapp, *Louis Jouvet, Man of the Theatre* (New York: Columbia University Press, 1957).

— R.J.N.

K

TAMARA KARSAVINA

Russian ballerina Tamara Karsavina (1885–1978) is most often remembered for the roles she created for the **Ballets Russes,** where she was the great interpreter of **Michel Fokine**'s expressive choreography, the exquisite partner of **Vaslav Nijinsky,** and an intellectual match for **Serge Diaghilev.** She was the daughter of a dancer and teacher at the Maryinsky Theater in Saint Petersburg, where she debuted in 1902. Not until she joined Diaghilev's Ballets Russes in 1909 in Paris was she a great success and able to claim her place in dance history. Her beauty, grace, style, and dramatic expression enchanted audiences. Karsavina performed with both companies until 1918, when she permanently settled in the West. She continued as guest artist with the Ballets Russes until the company folded in 1929.

Karsavina created roles in many of Fokine's ballets, including *Les Sylphides* (1909), *L'Oiseau de feu* (1910; *The Firebird*), *Le Spectre de la rose* (1911; The Specter of the Rose), and *Petrouchka* (1911). She also created roles in works by Nijinsky and **Léonide Massine.**

Karsavina eventually settled in London, where she danced with Ballet Rambert in 1930–1931. She retired from performing in 1931 but continued to coach dancers and stage revivals of dances in the Ballets Russes repertory. She was vice-president of the Royal Academy of Dancing from 1946 until 1955. In addition to publishing an autobiography, *Theatre Street* (1931), she wrote *Ballet Technique* (1956) and *Classical Ballet: The Flow of Movement* (1962).

REFERENCE:

Gennady Smakov, "Tamara Karsavina," in his *The Great Russian Dancers* (New York: Knopf, 1984), pp. 189–199.

—A.P.E.

JOSEPH KESSEL

While he is not considered a writer of the first rank, and perhaps not even the second, Joseph Kessel (1898–1979) was a highly successful novelist and journalist. Sales figures for his novels outrank most of his contemporaries' earnings. *Le Lion* (1958; translated as *The Lion*), the story of a lion cub, sold more than 1,771,600 copies by 1980. Many of his books were translated into English and other languages and became best-sellers, and several were made into films, including *Belle de jour* (1928; translated), a novel about a married woman who works as a prostitute in the daytime. Directed by **Luis Buñuel** in 1968, the movie starred **Catherine Deneuve.**

Born in Argentina of Russian-Jewish parents, Kessel spent most of his early childhood in Russia before his family settled in France in 1908. He flew combat missions in **World War I** and was later awarded the Croix de Guerre and the Médaille Militaire. Immediately after the war he went with his squadron on an expedition through China, Indochina, India, and Ceylon. These early travels were followed by many others. Much of his work has an exotic flavor, and it frequently deals with action and adventure.

Based on his experience as a combat pilot, Kessel's second book, *L'Equipage* (1923; translated as *Pilot and Observer*), is one of the earliest French aviation novels. His interest in flying is also reflected in *Vent de sable* (1929; Wind of Sand), a nonfiction account of flights along the northwest coast of Africa with the great French aviator Jean Mermoz. When Mermoz disappeared with his plane in 1936, Kessel wrote a biography, *Mermoz,* which appeared later in the same year.

Kessel traveled to Spain in 1934 to cover the political drama that would culminate in the **Spanish Civil**

Models making one of the paintings in Yves Klein's
Anthropométries series, 9 March 1960 (Harry Shunk)

War. His short novel based on this experience, *Une Balle perdue* (1935; Stray Bullet), was admired by Ernest Hemingway. During the German **Occupation** of France in **World War II,** Kessel participated in the **Resistance** movement. After fleeing to England to escape the German gestapo, he wrote, at the request of **Charles de Gaulle,** *L'Armée des ombres* (1943; translated as *Army of Shadows*), an account of the Resistance movement. In 1944, at age forty-six, he joined a British air squadron and flew reconnaissance missions over occupied territory. For his exploits he was awarded a second Croix de Guerre. After the **Liberation** of France, Kessel began a long association with the newspaper *France-Soir.*

Much of Kessel's fiction is centered on individual and family dramas, such as love, infidelity, and alcoholism — themes that were reflections of his personal life. His most ambitious novel was the four-volume *Le Tour du malheur* (1950; Misfortune's Turn), one of the most revealing portrayals in French of society between the two world wars.

Kessel won the Grand Prix du Roman de l'Académie Française (1927) and many other awards. When he was elected to the Académie Française in 1962, he was one of the few members ever chosen who was not born in France.

REFERENCE:

Richard Cobb, *Promenades: A Historian's Appreciation of Modern French Literature* (Oxford: Oxford University Press, 1980).
— C.S.B.

YVES KLEIN

Yves Klein (1928–1962) is the most prominent of the artists called **Nouveaux Réalistes** (New Realists), who emerged in the 1950s. Though his career spanned less than a decade, his relentless exploration of the possibilities of monochrome art, coupled with his charismatic personality, gave him international influence, which had begun to spread to the United States by the time of his death from a heart attack in June 1962.

Klein's continuing fascination was with what he termed "le vide" (the void). His installation *Vide* (1958) consisted solely of emptying the Iris Clert Gallery in Paris and painting the interior walls white and the exterior walls blue. An intense blue — illustrative of the sky — was a dominant trait in Klein's art; in 1948 he "signed" the sky above the city of Nice, labeling it his first artwork. Describing his fascination with blue, he commented that "through color I experience a feeling of complete identification with space. I am truly free." Klein began to work his way through a complex exploration of the ways in which he could use blue monochromes to explore the relationship of space to body. In his *Anthropométries* series (begun in 1958), he covered female models in blue paint and then had them press their bodies against sheets of paper to produce imprints, emphasizing breasts, thighs, and torsos. (He patented the specific ultramarine shade he used as International Klein Blue [IKB].) In the follow-up *Cosmogénies* series (begun in 1960), he let rain splash onto freshly painted blue canvases.

As a New Realist, Klein is often lumped with American and English Pop artists, but his work has closer affinities to minimalism and to performance art, a tie emphasized by his *Symphonie monotone* (1960), in which three nudes imprinted their images on paper while a small orchestra performed a single-chord piece composed by Klein. The parallels between Klein's work and Pop art relate to some of the uses he made of traditional art; in 1962, for example, he made a plaster cast of the *Winged Victory of Samothrace,* coating it entirely with his patented blue. His *Portrait-relief d'Arman* (1962) is a bronze cast of his fellow New Realist **Arman,** painted blue and pressed against a panel covered in gold leaf.

REFERENCES:

Henry Geldzahler, *Pop Art, 1955–70* (Sydney: International Cultural Corporation of Australia, 1985);

Marco Livingstone, *Pop: A Continuing History* (New York: Abrams, 1990), pp. 47–55;

Pierre Restany, *Yves Klein* (New York: Abrams, 1982);

Daniel Wheeler, *Art Since Mid-Century: 1945 to the Present* (Englewood Cliffs, N.J.: Prentice-Hall, 1991);

Yves Klein, 1928–1962: A Retrospective (Houston: New York Arts Publisher, 1982).

— J.H.

CHARLES KOECHLIN

Although critics hold Charles Koechlin (1867–1950) in the highest esteem, and his pupils, including composers such as **Francis Poulenc** and Germaine Tailleferre (see **Les Six**), are warm in their praise, Koechlin's music is rarely performed, and indeed much of the prolific composer's work remains unpublished.

Perhaps this neglect can be attributed to his independence and originality. Koechlin belongs to no school or movement; he felt free to adopt any style appropriate to the piece he was composing, and there is hardly any type of music he neglected, from jingles to symphonies. He wrote hundreds of songs, many piano pieces, every variety of chamber music, large-scale orchestral and choral works, ballets, and music for films. Some of his songs have a simplicity similar to the works of **Erik Satie** and are close to music-hall chansons. Others are strongly dissonant and complicated. Much of his music employs conventional melody and harmony, but he was also a pioneer in the use of polytonality and even atonality.

Koechlin drew on many sources for inspiration. His favorite was Rudyard Kipling's *Jungle Book* stories, which provided the basis for seven works, including *Trois poèmes du Livre de la jungle* (1899–1910; Three Poems from *The Jungle Book*), *Les Bandar-Log*

(1939), and *La Loi de la jungle* (1939; The Law of the Jungle). Each of the movements of his *Seven Stars Symphony* (1933) is a sound "portrait" of famous film stars of the 1930s — Marlene Dietrich, Clara Bow, Lilian Harvey, Greta Garbo, Douglas Fairbanks, Charles Chaplin, and Emil Jannings.

Koechlin was also a respected writer on music. His textbooks on music theory, harmony, counterpoint, orchestration, and fugal composition were used by a generation of music students, and he wrote biographies of his teacher **Gabriel Fauré** and **Claude Debussy.** A Socialist with strong Communist leanings, he refused to accept membership in the Légion d'Honneur when it was offered in 1940.

REFERENCE:

Rollo Myers, *Modern French Music: From Fauré to Boulez* (New York & Washington, D.C.: Praeger, 1971).

— P.S.H.

JULIA KRISTEVA

One of the leading voices in theoretical feminism, Bulgarian-born critic Julia Kristeva (1941–) is widely known for creating the term *intertextuality.*

After earning her undergraduate degree in linguistics in Bulgaria, Kristeva immigrated to Paris in 1966. While pursuing a doctorate in linguistics, which she received in 1973, she worked and studied with **Lucien Goldmann, Claude Lévi-Strauss, Tzvetan Todorov,** and **Roland Barthes.** During this same period Kristeva allied herself with the critical group that established the journal *Tel Quel,* serving on its board and, in 1968, marrying its editor, critic and novelist **Philippe Sollers.** She was instrumental in acquainting fellow critics with the work of Russian formalist Mikhail Bakhtin and his compatriots. Since the mid 1970s Kristeva has taught at the University of Paris and maintained a psychoanalytic practice. Her theories draw on psychoanalysis, semantics, semiotics, and other social and linguistic sciences.

Building on the dialogic criticism of Bakhtin, Kristeva defined intertextuality in *Séméiotikè* (1969; translated as *Desire in Language: A Semiotic Approach to Literature and Art*). Now part of standard critical vocabulary, the term in its most basic meaning refers to the presence of one text in another, through quotation, allusion, or other sorts of echoes. Stressing its dependence on intertextuality, she defines European literature as an intersection of texts. This feature combines with the polysemy of language (multiple — sometimes contradictory — definitions of individual words) to produce texts that are essentially ambiguous.

Among her critical works are *Révolution du langage poétique* (1974; translated as *Revolution in Poetic Language*) and *Pouvoirs de l'horreur* (1980; translated as *Powers of Horror: An Essay on Abjection*).

Kristeva has also written fiction. Her novel *Les Samurai* (1990; translated as *The Samurai*) is a semi-autobiographical work that includes veiled characterizations of Barthes, **Jacques Lacan,** and **Michel Foucault.**

REFERENCES:

Alice Jardine, "Theories of the Feminine," *Enclitic,* 4 (Fall 1980): 5–16;

Oliver Kelly, *Reading Kristeva: Unraveling the Double-Bind* (Bloomington: Indiana University Press, 1993);

John Lechte, *Julia Kristeva* (London: Routledge, 1990);

Philip Lewis, "Revolutionary Semiotics," *Diacritics,* 4 (Fall 1974): 28–32.

— C.S.B.

L

JACQUES LACAN

A practicing psychoanalyst as well as a teacher and author, Jacques Lacan (1901–1981) has had tremendous influence on both sides of the Atlantic. Basing his theories on those of Sigmund Freud, which he interpreted idiosyncratically, Lacan was also influenced by Ferdinand de Saussure and **Claude Lévi-Strauss** and became the major champion of **structuralism** in psychoanalytic theory. One of his central ideas concerns the alienation of the child as he evolves from his original self (the subjective self, or self of the "mirror stage"), to the self of the imaginary order (in which he establishes a relation with this mirror image), and then to the symbolic self through the acquisition of language. Since language is associated with the male principle and the law, Lacan's views have had significant consequences for feminist theory, especially as it concerns literature. Many of his important writings are collected in *Ecrits* (1966; translated).

REFERENCES:

Robert Con Davis, ed., *Lacan and Narration: The Psychoanalytic Difference in Narrative Theory* (Baltimore: Johns Hopkins University Press, 1983);

Jacques Lacan, *The Language of the Self,* translated by Anthony Wilden (Baltimore: Johns Hopkins Press, 1968).

— C.S.B.

Jacques Lacan in the classroom (Pachkoff)

ROGER DE LA FRESNAYE

Roger de La Fresnaye (1885–1925) was among the young artists who were attracted to, but never quite melded into, the **Cubist** movement. The child of an aristocratic family, La Fresnaye studied at the Ecole des Beaux-Arts and at private art schools (1903–1908) and also with the sculptor **Aristide Maillol** (1910). Influenced initially by the **Nabis,** he met **Raymond Duchamp-Villon** in 1910 and began to experiment with ideas derived from **Paul Cézanne.** La Fresnaye partic-

193

ipated in the so-called *Maison cubiste* (Cubist House), designed by Duchamp-Villon for the 1912 **Salon d'Automne,** and also participated in the **Section d'Or** (1912).

When La Fresnaye's Le Cuirassier was shown at the **Salon des Indépendants** in 1911, it dominated the room allotted to those allied with the Cubists. La Fresnaye's painting of a mounted soldier in armor attempts to fuse a quasi-Cubist interest in simplified, sometimes faceted figures (and a Cubist palette of gray, brown, and dark red) with heroic subject matter directly related to Théodore Géricault's *Cuirassier* (1814). La Fresnaye's *La Conquête de l'air* (1913; *Conquest of the Air*) is an uneasy blend of intersecting Cubist planes of flat color, a floating tricolor flag and a balloon, circular clouds reminiscent of **Robert Delaunay**'s, and two partly abstract pilots talking over a table.

La Fresnaye's lungs were damaged during **World War I,** in which he won citations for bravery and was promoted to sergeant. After repeated hospital stays he died of pneumonia in 1925.

REFERENCES:

Douglas Cooper, *The Cubist Epoch* (London: Phaidon, 1971);

Pierre Daix, *Cubists and Cubism* (New York: Rizzoli, 1982);

John Golding, *Cubism: A History and an Analysis, 1907–1914* (Boston: Boston Book & Art Shop, 1959).

—J.H.

WANDA LANDOWSKA

Performer, teacher, and writer Wanda Landowska (1879–1959) spent much of her life in Paris, where she almost single-handedly encouraged a new interest in the harpsichord and early music.

After studying piano in her native Warsaw and in Berlin, Landowska moved to Paris in 1900. In 1903, when she first began performing on the harpsichord, most of the surviving eighteenth-century harpsichords were exhibited in museums but not played, having been superseded by the piano by the early nineteenth century. Her concerts (and later her recordings) of works by Johann Sebastian Bach, George Frideric Handel, François Couperin, and other Baroque composers revealed the beauty of their music when it was played on the instrument for which it had been written. She convinced the Pleyel piano manufacturers to construct a large two-manual harpsichord, on which she gave many recitals throughout Europe and the United States. Her recitals were warmly received, largely because of her lively playing and her charm.

Landowska attracted students from many European countries and the United States. Her house and studio in Saint-Leu-la-Forêt, a village fourteen miles north of Paris, attracted many music lovers, particularly for the Sunday-afternoon recitals she and her students gave there. With the outbreak of **World War II** Landowska immigrated to the United States, where she continued playing and teaching until her death.

During Landowska's lifetime a younger generation of musicians, including some of her former students, learned through research that not all of her ideas and performances were historically correct. The authenticity of her Pleyel harpsichord was also challenged as more historically accurate copies of eighteenth-century instruments began to be made. Nevertheless, the current strong interest in playing early music on period instruments can in large part be attributed to her influence.

REFERENCE:

Wanda Landowska, *Landowska on Music,* edited and translated by Denise Restout (New York: Stein & Day, 1964).

—P.S.H.

GUSTAVE LANSON

To generations of readers in Europe and North America, Gustave Lanson (1857–1934) was known as the most authoritative literary historian of France. His *Histoire de la littérature française* (1894), revised frequently after its initial publication, was long the vade mecum for students and professors, representing the full flowering of literary history as it developed from the early nineteenth century onward. By the late twentieth century Lanson's book had gone out of fashion, in part because of changing tastes in literature. For example, two poets whom he dismissed somewhat disparagingly, Christine de Pizan and Maurice Scève, were later reevaluated and became highly regarded. With challenges to the canon of French literature from feminists and minority groups — as well as the undermining of the validity of historical knowledge through the work of **Michel Foucault** and other philosophers and literary theorists — Lanson's conception of literary history has also been called into question.

Lanson, who was director of the **Ecole Normale Supérieure** from 1920 to 1927, published a major bibliography of French literature as well as books on Jacques-Bénigne Bossuet, Pierre Corneille, Voltaire, and other major figures.

Valery Larbaud, 1934

REFERENCES:

Michel Beaujour, "Rhetoric, Truth and Power," in *Writing in a Modern Temper: Essays on French Literature and Thought in Honor of Henri Peyre* (Saratoga, Cal.: Anma Libri, 1984), pp. 203–213;

Joseph N. Moody, *French Education Since Napoleon* (Syracuse: Syracuse University Press, 1978).

— C.S.B.

VALERY LARBAUD

Valery Larbaud (1881–1957) is one of the most cosmopolitan French writers of the first half of the twentieth century. Thanks to family wealth, Larbaud began to travel extensively in his youth. Proficient in several languages and literatures, particularly Spanish, Italian, and English, he became a translator and acted as a cultural link between France and other countries. In particular he was a champion of English-language literature, including the poetry of Walt Whitman. He translated works by Edgar Allan Poe, Nathaniel Hawthorne, John Milton, Arnold Bennett, Samuel Butler, and many other writers. An early partisan of James Joyce and the first to translate his work into French, Larbaud

was influenced by Joyce's stream-of-consciousness technique.

Larbaud's best-known original work, *A. O. Barnabooth: Ses œuvres complètes* (1913; partially translated as *A. O. Barnabooth: His Diary*), mixes fiction and poetry. Based partly on his own experiences, the book is about a wealthy young traveler from South America who wanders around Europe in search of experience. It was preceded by a novel about a young Peruvian girl, *Fermina Marquez* (1911), one of several works in which Larbaud sensitively explored childhood and adolescence.

Larbaud, who was a convert to Roman Catholicism, was closely associated with many other writers, including **André Gide** and **Paul Claudel,** and wrote for important periodicals such as the *Nouvelle Revue Française* and *Commerce*. He published criticism, travel writings, and a study on translation. His diary, *Journal inédit,* appeared in 1954 and 1955.

REFERENCES:

Cecily Mackworth, "Valery Larbaud and the Heart of England," in her *English Interludes* (London: Routledge & Kegan Paul, 1974), pp. 155–186;

Justin O'Brien, "Valery Larbaud: Complete Man of Letters," in his *The French Literary Horizon* (New Brunswick, N.J.: Rutgers University Press, 1967), pp. 193–208.

— C.S.B.

MIKHAIL LARIONOV

Mikhail Larionov (1881–1964) played a key role in the diffusion of Western European concepts of the avant-garde in Russia; after 1914, he played a similar role in encouraging the development of a wholly abstract art in France. Born in Teraspol, he was admitted to the Moscow Institute of Painting, Sculpture, and Architecture in 1898. He worked in a quasi-Impressionist style before experimenting with ideas and motifs he derived from Vincent Van Gogh, **Paul Cézanne,** and **Henri Matisse.**

In collaboration with **Natalia Goncharova,** Larionov began experimenting with so-called Neo-Primitive and Futurist (or Cubo-Futurist) ideas — creating an eclectic fusion of Russian folk art and religious icons mixed with **Fauve,** French **Cubist,** and Italian Futurist concepts. By 1911–1913 these experiments had culminated in what Larionov and Goncharova termed "Rayonism," in which the raylines used in Futurism to denote motion became axes along which the image could be dissected. Their Rayonist and Futurist manifesto of 1913 accused other modern artists of simply expressing "long-familiar artistic truths in their own words." By contrast, Rayonism was to be the basis for a truly modern art: "We've had enough of this manure. Now we need to sow. We have no modesty — we declare this bluntly and flatly — we consider ourselves to be the creators of modern art."

Larionov defined Rayonism as that art "concerned with spatial forms that can arise from the intersection of the reflected rays of different objects, forms chosen by the artist's will." While Goncharova continued to include representational elements in her paintings, Larionov insisted that "the objects that we see in life play no role" in art. His Rayonism was focused on "that which is the essence of painting itself . . . — the combination of colors, their saturation, the interrelation of colored masses, depth, texture. . . ." In his *Blue Rayonism* of 1912, for example, the canvas takes on something of the appearance of a shattered window, with colored lines breaking the surface into small geometric areas in which tans, rust brown, or blue predominate. Larionov's goal was to attain a "true feeling of art," with a "life which proceeds only according to the laws of painting as an independent entity, painting with its own forms, color, and timbre."

In 1915 Goncharova and Larionov left Russia to design sets and costumes for **Serge Diaghilev's Ballets Russes.** They became permanent residents of Paris in 1918.

REFERENCES:

John E. Bowlt, ed. and trans., *Russian Art of the Avant-Garde: Theory and Criticism, 1902–1934* (New York: Viking, 1976);

Camilla Gray, *The Great Experiment: Russian Art, 1863–1922* (New York: Abrams, 1962).

— J.H.

LATIN QUARTER

The Latin Quarter is a section of Paris on the **Left Bank** of the Seine (the south side of the river). Belonging to the fifth and sixth arrondissements of the city, the Latin Quarter was given its name because it is the site of the Sorbonne, a branch of the University of Paris founded in the thirteenth century for students of theology, and Latin is the traditional language of scholars. The Latin Quarter remains the quintessential student neighborhood, home to celebrated lycées — including Louis-le-Grand and Henri IV — and to many publishers, bookshops, cinemas, and small theaters. Other landmarks include the **Ecole Normale Supérieure,** the Collège de France, the Jardin du Luxembourg, and the Panthéon.

REFERENCES:

Herbert R. Lottman, *The Left Bank: Writers, Artist, and Politics from the Popular Front to the Cold War* (Boston: Houghton Mifflin, 1982);

Jerrold E. Seigel, *Bohemian Paris: Culture, Politics, and the Boundaries of Bourgeois Life* (New York: Viking, 1986).

— C.S.B.

PATRICE DE LA TOUR DU PIN

A major religious poet of the mid twentieth century, Patrice de la Tour du Pin (1911–1975) clearly expressed his antipathy to the modern, anarchic spirit in poetry.

Born Patrice de Champy de la Charce, of French and Scottish ancestry, the poet began his career by publishing verse in the *Nouvelle Revue Française.* His critically acclaimed *La Quête de joie* (1933; The Quest of Joy)—the product of a youthful romanticism, with Celtic overtones—was intended as the beginning of his long-term investigation of man's spirituality.

La Tour du Pin's work was interrupted when he was drafted for duty in the army at the onset of **World War II.** He was seriously wounded and held as a prisoner in Germany for more than two years, until his repatriation in 1942. This experience contributed to his *Une Somme de poésie* (1946; A Sum of Poetry), the first book of an impressive four-volume collection of poetic prose and verse. A philosophic mystic, the poet created a visible world that is progressively transfigured by "Mystery" and the divine spirit. The rich architecture of the volumes justifies comparison to a cathedral or to the polyphony of an orchestra. La Tour du Pin is also the author of *Psaumes de tous mes temps* (1974; Psalms of All My Times).

REFERENCES:

Yves-Alain Favre, "Patrice de La Tour du Pin: The Renaissance of a Liturgical Poetry," *Renascence,* 36 (Autumn–Winter 1983–1984): 1–2, 45–54;

J. C. Reid, "Poetry and Patrice de la Tour du Pin," *Renascence,* 7 (Autumn 1954): 17–29;

Derek Stanford, "First Thoughts on Patrice de la Tour du Pin," *Poetry Quarterly,* 9 (Winter 1947–1948): 225–231.

— C.S.B.

MARIE LAURENCIN

The fortunes and reputation of Marie Laurencin (1885–1956) have varied drastically since the 1920s. Both she and her critics saw her as a near-archetypal feminine voice in art. She asserted that "the genius of man intimidates me" but that "I feel perfectly at ease with everything feminine." For poet **Guillaume Apollinaire** — her colleague, critic, and lover — she was his complement: "C'est moi en femme!" (It's I as a woman), he declared. As the "feminine virtues" of the 1920s have become increasingly problematic, it has proven difficult to separate Laurencin's painting from the social stereotypes that surrounded it. At the same time her reputation has suffered because she is hard to classify. Apollinaire grouped her with the "scientific **Cubists**," but her painting bears virtually no resemblance to the art of **Pablo Picasso** or **Georges Braque.** It is only with the growing appreciation of the real diversity of early twentieth-century avant-garde painting that Laurencin's art can be judged apart from the overpowering shadow of her famous contemporaries.

Laurencin originally trained to be a painter of porcelain, studying art at the Académie Humbert, where she met Braque in 1905. He introduced her to Picasso and other circles of young experimental artists. In 1907 Picasso introduced her to Apollinaire, with whom she had a relationship — marked by collaboration, discussions, and frequent quarrels — that lasted until 1912. (Laurencin is the model for the cruel Tristouse Ballerinette of Apollinaire's *Le Poète assassiné*, 1916.)

In 1911 Laurencin exhibited two paintings in the "Cubist" room 41 at the **Salon des Indépendants**; in 1912 she participated in the so-called *Maison cubiste* (House of Cubism) at the **Salon d'Automne.** Yet there is little to connect her work with the Cubists'. Her portraits and fantasy images are simplified and flattened, with a relatively restricted palette, but there is no attempt to analyze or break up the forms of the figures, as there is in Cubist paintings. Her *Apollinaire et ses amis* (1908; *Apollinaire and His Friends*) resembles a **Nabi** painting blended with an ironic allusion to Picasso's *Les Demoiselles d'Avignon* (1907). Her *Jeunes Femmes* (1910–1911; *Young Women*) uses a Picasso-like palette of grays and browns; some of the background rocks have been faceted into geometric shapes, but the young women in the foreground (all of whom seem to bear Laurencin's face) are treated as rounded, flowing shapes in a distinctly non-Cubist fashion.

Laurencin entered into a disastrous marriage with a German painter, Otto von Waetjen, just as France and Germany became belligerents at the outbreak of **World War I.** She spent the war years in Barcelona, as did **Albert Gleizes** and **Francis Picabia,** and contributed to *391,* the **Dadaist** review edited by Picabia. Divorcing von Waetjen in 1920, she returned to Paris and worked primarily as a book illustrator. She designed costumes for the 1924 **Ballets Russes** produc-

tion of *Les Biches* (*The House Party*) and produced designs for wallpaper, textiles, and women's fashions. Beginning in the 1920s, her painting focused on brightly colored portraits in watercolors, crayon, or oil; she settled into a relatively set formula for them: nearly identical figures with huge eyes outlined in black, small, barely suggested noses, and brightly rouged lips.

REFERENCES:

Julia Fagan-King, "United on the Threshold of the 20th-Century Mystical Ideal: Marie Laurencin's Integral Involvement with Guillaume Apollinaire and the Inmates of the Bateau Lavoir," *Art History,* 11 (March 1988): 88–114;

Charlotte Gere, *Marie Laurencin* (New York: Rizzoli, 1977);

Ann Sutherland Harris and Linda Nochlin, *Women Artists, 1550–1950* (Los Angeles: Los Angeles County Museum of Art, 1976), pp. 295–296;

Douglas K. S. Hyland and Heather McPherson, *Marie Laurencin: Artist and Muse* (Seattle & London: University of Washington Press, 1989).

—J.H.

HENRI LAURENS

Henri Laurens (1885–1954) is unusual among **Cubist** sculptors. Most of those who sought to translate the basic concepts or forms of Cubist painting into three dimensions — from **Jacques Lipchitz** to **Raymond Duchamp-Villon** — took as their basis the analytical Cubist emphasis on geometric, faceted forms. Laurens's work is a direct extension of the collages of synthetic Cubism, so much that it has been denied that his works are sculptures at all.

Laurens was self-taught; his knowledge of sculpture came from his work as an apprentice stonemason. A friendship with **Georges Braque** led Laurens into the Cubist circle; he became close to **Pablo Picasso** and **Juan Gris** as well. Unlike many of his colleagues, he was declared unfit for military service in 1914, remaining free to develop and experiment with his work during **World War I.**

In mid 1915 Laurens began to take the synthetic Cubist collages of Picasso, Braque, and Gris as the basis for three-dimensional constructions, variously composed of stiff paper, wood, metal, or stone. His *Guitare* (1917–1918), for example, closely resembles Gris's collages from the same period, although in slightly greater relief. By 1918 these fragile paper or light-wood constructions were replaced by stone or plaster. The first of the new pieces mirror both the form and the color of his earlier constructions. Laurens gradually moved from works in this style to sculptures in the round, multiplanar shapes deriving from both analytical Cubism (especially in their faceted, geometric depictions of objects) and paintings of the synthetic period (in their verticality and sense of layered, overlapping planes). In comparison to his earlier *Guitare,* for instance, the *Guitare* of 1920, in terra-cotta, has a monumental quality in spite of its small size (14 1/4" by 4 3/4"); sculpted in the round, its multiple guitar necks jut upward from a massive, angular body.

Like many of his colleagues, Laurens gradually drifted away from Cubism. In the 1920s he turned to book illustration and more traditionally representational images derived from Greco-Roman mythology.

REFERENCES:

Douglas Cooper, *The Cubist Epoch* (London: Phaidon, 1971);

Pierre Daix, *Cubists and Cubism* (New York, Rizzoli, 1982);

Christopher Green, *Cubism and Its Enemies: Modern Movements and Reaction in French Art, 1916–1928* (New Haven & London: Yale University Press, 1987);

Robert Rosenblum, *Cubism and Twentieth-Century Art* (New York: Abrams, 1971).

— J.H.

Paul Léautaud (Izis)

JEAN-PIERRE LÉAUD

Actor Jean-Pierre Léaud (1944–) is best known for his work with director **François Truffaut,** who called Léaud the most interesting actor of his generation.

At age fourteen Léaud was chosen to play Antoine Doinel in Truffaut's *Les Quatre Cent Coups* (1959; *The 400 Blows*), one of the most memorable films of the postwar era. The experiences of Léaud's character are drawn from Truffaut's own tortured childhood. The freeze-frame of Doinel's haunting face that closes the film is one of the most memorable images of modern cinema.

Léaud acted in four more films in the same series, which chronicles Doinel's transformation from adolescence to adulthood: the "Antoine et Colette" episode of *L'Amour à vingt ans* (1962; *Love at Twenty*), *Baisers volés* (1968; *Stolen Kisses*), *Domicile conjugal* (1970; *Bed and Board*), and *L'Amour en fuite* (1979; *Love on the Run*). He also played a young lovestruck actor in Truffaut's Academy Award–winning *La Nuit américaine* (1973; *Day for Night*).

Léaud has also worked with other distinguished directors, including Bernardo Bertolucci, **Jean-Luc Godard,** and Pier Paolo Pasolini. In their films he traded on the image created in Truffaut's work, often bringing humor to an overtly political motion picture. He appeared in the tongue-in-cheek gangster send-up

I Hired a Contract Killer (1990) directed by Finnish director Aki Kaurismäki.

REFERENCE:

Jan Dawson, "Getting Beyond the Looking Glass" [interview], *Sight and Sound*, 43 (Winter 1973–1974), pp. 46–47.

— W.L.

PAUL LÉAUTAUD

Although he would appear to occupy a marginal place in modern French letters, Paul Léautaud (1872–1956) is known to all who study the literary history of France in the first half of the twentieth century, primarily for his nineteen-volume *Journal littéraire* (1954–1966; translated and abridged as *Journal of a Man of Letters, 1898–1907*), his memoirs of Paris literary life from 1893 to 1956. He is also known as a longtime contributor to the important *Mercure de France,* especially for the drama criticism he published under the name Maurice Boissard.

The illegitimate child of the prompter at the **Comédie-Française** and a minor actress, Léautaud had only the barest acquaintance with his mother, who left her lover and their child soon after his birth. Léautaud wrote about her in *Le Petit Ami* and about his father in *In Memoriam.* These two fictionalized autobiographies were followed by a third, *Amours,* about his early love affairs. All three works were serialized in the *Mercure de France* (1902–1906) and translated into English as *Child of Montmartre* (1959).

Léautaud's first publication in the *Mercure de France* had been poetry, but he had quickly realized that his true talent was for prose. He wrote his first drama criticism for the magazine in August 1907 and became a full-time staff member the following January, retiring in 1941. A reserved man on the margins of the literary world, he nonetheless came in contact with and was befriended by many of the greatest writers of his day and wrote about them and his own life in his *Journal littéraire.* His contemporaries were aware of its existence even before publication began during the last years of his life. The six-thousand-copy first edition of volume one, covering the years 1893–1906, was sold out in six weeks.

REFERENCE:

James Harding, *Lost Illusions: Paul Léautaud and His World* (Rutherford, N.J.: Fairleigh Dickinson University Press, 1974).

— C.S.B.

J. M. G. LE CLÉZIO

Jean Marie Gustave Le Clézio (1940–) became a literary celebrity at twenty-three when his first novel, *Le Procès-verbal* (1963; translated as *The Interrogation*), was awarded the Prix Théophraste Renaudot. This success was followed by other critically acclaimed novels, including *Le Déluge* (1966; translated as *The Flood*), *Le Livre des fuites* (1969; translated as *The Book of Flights*), and *Désert* (1980; Desert), selected by *Lire* as the best French book (fiction or nonfiction) of that year. Over the course of his career Le Clézio has published more than twenty-five books. He has also written prefaces for the poems of **Max Jacob** and for the 1965 French translation of Flannery O'Connor's *The Violent Bear It Away.*

Le Clézio belongs to the post-**Nouveau Roman** (New Novel) generation. Like the New Novelists, however, he is concerned with the problematics of writing, especially the problem of language, whose ultimate inability to express reality and truth is, ironically, one of the truths with which he struggles. In his novels Le Clézio explores the individual's relationship with na-

ture and society, and he especially focuses on the modern experience of alienation, which many of his characters feel strongly, to the point where they are unable to function. Much of his fiction has an unreal, sometimes allegorical quality and includes mythopoeic archetypes such as Everyman, the Fall, the Flood, and the double. Eschewing the verisimilitude of the conventional novel, Le Clézio combines genres (poetry, prose, graphics), employs wordplay, takes up philosophical questions directly, and calls attention to the fictiveness of his work by metafictional prologues and other devices.

Fascinated by anthropology, Le Clézio has traveled extensively in Mexico and the islands of the Indian Ocean, as well as in Canada and the United States. For four years he lived with Indian tribes in Panama. His experiences and studies have led to writings on Indian culture, including *Haï* (1971), devoted to American Indian art, and *Les Prophéties du Chilam Balam* (1976; The Prophecies of Chilam Balam), a translation of Mayan texts. Le Clézio's interest in nonoccidental societies may be related in part to his own exotic background, for though he was born in France, he identifies more closely with Mauritius (l'Ile de France), where the Le Clézio family settled after the French Revolution. He also spent part of his childhood in Nigeria.

Le Clézio, who holds a doctorate from the University of Perpignan, has taught at several institutions in the United States. His popularity as a subject of scholarly study attests to his standing as a novelist. At least three monographs on him have appeared in French, and many scholarly articles in French, English, and other languages have been devoted to his work.

REFERENCE:

Jennifer R. Waelti-Walters, *J. M. G. Le Clézio* (Boston: Twayne, 1977).

— C.S.B.

LE CORBUSIER

Architect and city planner Charles-Edouard Jeanneret (1887–1965), who used the professional name Le Corbusier (The Crowlike One), was Swiss-born and trained as an architect in Paris and Berlin; he settled in Paris in 1917. He first established himself as a painter, founding the Purist movement, built around the journal *Esprit Nouveau* (1920–1925; The New Spirit), with **Amédée Ozenfant.** In the magazine and in the essays collected as *La Peinture moderne* (1924; Modern Painting), the two analyzed and critiqued **Cubism** while defining themselves as part of a distinct and separate "post-Cubist" art. Whereas Cubism had been fragmented, intuitive, and individualistic, they wrote, Purism was built solidly on mathematics and the natural sciences, befitting an age of science and industry. As society became increasingly technological, art would inevitably respond to the issues and concerns of the machine age. Art should itself be machinelike, even interchangeable, based on prototypes derived directly from the mass-produced goods of industry: the *objet-type* or *objet-standard.* The two wrote that Purism selected such "elements from existing objects," preferring those "that serve the most direct of human uses; those which are like extensions of man's limbs, and thus of an extreme intimacy, a banality that makes them barely exist as subjects of interest in themselves...."

Le Corbusier's concepts of architecture derived from the same basic ideas; he called housing, for example, a machine for living. Making use of the durability and tensile strength of ferroconcrete, he designed and built houses as screen-wall constructions, self-consciously austere, stark, and functional. As an analogue to the *objet-type* of Purism, he proposed the *habitant-type,* "lightweight houses, supple and strong as car-bodies or airframes . . . ingenious in plan; they offer the comforts a wise man might demand."

In his *Vers une architecture* (1923; translated as *Towards a New Architecture*), Le Corbusier wrote that architecture and the "engineer's aesthetic" are inseparable; the engineer "puts us in accord with universal law" to achieve harmony; the architect "realizes an order which is a pure creation of his spirit; . . . he gives us the measure of an order which we feel to be in accordance with that of our world," to help one experience the sense of beauty. The goal was to use mass production to achieve both goals. The result would be the perfect "house-machine," "healthy (and morally so too) and beautiful in the same way that working tools and instruments which accompany our existence are beautiful." Only such machine housing could produce an amelioration of social dissonances; "architecture or revolution" were the alternatives Le Corbusier proposed. In pursuit of that restoration of harmony, his urban designs sometimes have an authoritarian tone. His Voisin Plan (1925) for Paris would have necessitated clearing away landmarks such as Les Halles (the central market), the Place de la Madeleine, the Rue de Rivoli, the Opéra, and the Faubourg Saint-Honoré, termed collectively "all this junk, which till now has lain spread over our soil like a dry crust...."

Le Corbusier's design for the Villa Savoye (Poissy, 1928–1930) is a two-story structure, with a large second story held on slender piers over a small ground floor (containing an entry hall and servants' rooms). Typically for Le Corbusier, the flat roof was configured for a roof garden; the rooms open onto a central terrace. The effect, to judge from photographs (the house was severely damaged in **World War II**), was stark and severe, but also open and spacious.

The apartments of the Unité d'Habitation (Marseilles, 1947–1952) remain controversial. Intended as an integrated community of duplex apartments for some sixteen hundred inhabitants — complete with a fifth-floor mall, a restaurant, and recreation areas — it never functioned as intended. The rooms, especially those for children, are painfully small; the shops and restaurant never thrived, as the residents continued to use street-level stores and enterprises.

Unlike the smooth ferroconcrete of his earlier buildings, the concrete of the Unité d'Habitation was left in a rough state, producing a "new brutalism." Typical of the new, crude style is Le Corbusier's design for the monastery of La Tourette (Eveux, 1957–1960), a large square of rough concrete, with spartan cells for the monks arranged around a central courtyard. Le Corbusier's crowning achievement was the new capital at Chandigarh for the Punjab state in India (1958–1962); he designed, among other structures, the secretariat, the high court, and the assembly.

REFERENCES:

Reyner Banham, *Theory and Design in the First Machine Age* (New York: Praeger, 1960), pp. 202–264;

Christopher Green, *Cubism and Its Enemies: Modern Movements and Reaction in French Art, 1916–1928* (New Haven & London: Yale University Press, 1987);

Jacques Guiton, ed., *The Ideas of Le Corbusier on Architecture and Urban Planning,* translated by Margaret Guiton (New York: Braziller, 1981);

Robert Hughes, *The Shock of the New* (New York: Knopf, 1980);

Le Corbusier, *Towards a New Architecture,* translated by Frederick Etchells (New York: Payson & Clark, 1927).

—J.H.

VIOLETTE LEDUC

With the increasing interest in literature written by women and in feminist theory, the writings of Violette Leduc (1907–1972) have attracted attention on both sides of the Atlantic. Before this development, however, she was already known and even lionized in select circles in France for her autobiographical works and her fiction, both of which candidly speak of her lesbianism.

Born illegitimate and disowned by her father, Leduc was reared by her grandmother. As she relates in her best-known autobiographical work, *La Bâtarde* (1964; translated as *The Bastard*), her difficult life was lived on the margins of society. Expelled from boarding school for illicit relationships, she failed at many jobs and at her one marriage. In 1944 Leduc shared a peasant cottage with the notorious homosexual writer Maurice Sachs, who informed on fellow Jews during the German **Occupation** of France and introduced her to black marketeering. Given to paranoia and other mental illnesses, Leduc was encouraged to write first by Sachs and then by **Simone de Beauvoir,** who critiqued her work and helped her to find a publisher. The result was Leduc's first book, *L'Asphyxie* (1946; Asphyxiation). A lesbian interlude was omitted from the first edition of her third work, *Ravages* (1955) by her publisher, **Gallimard.** Yet Gallimard later published the omitted episode as *Thérèse et Isabelle* (1966) and in the 1966 edition of *Ravages* (translated).

REFERENCES:

Isabelle de Courtivron, *Violette Leduc* (Boston: Twayne, 1985);

Colette Hall, "L'Ecriture feminine and the Search for the Mother in the Works of Violette Leduc and Marie Cardinal," in *Women in French Literature,* edited by Michel Guggenheim (Saratoga, Cal.: Anma Libri, 1988), pp. 231–238;

Shirley Neuman, "'An Appearance Walking in a Forest the Sexes Burn': Autobiography and the Construction of the Feminine Body," *Signature,* 2 (Winter 1989): 1–26.

— C.S.B.

HENRI LE FAUCONNIER

At the 1911 **Salon des Indépendants,** a group of young, self-proclaimed **Cubist** painters took over a gallery to exhibit their works jointly. Perhaps the most prominent of these works was the highly praised *L'Abondance (Abundance)*, by Henri Le Fauconnier (1881–1941). That such a role should be played by a painting with few, if any, discernible Cubist traits, by an artist whose connection to the Cubist movement was tenuous at best, speaks volumes about the nebulous definition of Cubism dominant at that time. To be sure, Le Fauconnier had played an important organizational role in pulling together Parisian artists with an interest in Cubist ideas. After works by **Albert Gleizes, Jean Metzinger,** and Le Fauconnier were hung together at the 1910 **Salon d'Automne,** the three began to meet regularly, inviting other like-minded artists to participate. Sessions at Le Fauconnier's studio at-

tracted many would-be Cubists, who watched *L'Abondance* gradually take form that year.

L'Abondance shares with Cubist art a muted palette (primarily of earth tones) and an interest in converting surface details into faceted, geometricized shapes. Apart from that, it is a rather traditional pastoral scene — a woman carries a plate of fruit, while her child gathers more in her arms — with a clear light source and a wholly commonplace use of perspective. The geometric shapes are not used, as they are in Cubist works, to analyze and break apart the figures and surrounding spaces but are simply *laid over* them to impose a superficial appearance of a "cubistic" work. Le Fauconnier's *Portrait de Jouve* (1909) is weaker than *L'Abondance* — a flat, heavily outlined image reminiscent of a **Nabi** painting but with the bright Nabi palette replaced by dark browns and grays.

Le Fauconnier's flirtation with Cubism, and with modernist art in general, was short-lived. Within two years he had returned to a more traditional representational painting, tepidly spiced with an occasional "modern" touch.

REFERENCES:

Douglas Cooper, *The Cubist Epoch* (London: Phaidon, 1971);

Pierre Daix, *Cubists and Cubism* (New York: Rizzoli, 1982);

John Golding, *Cubism: A History and an Analysis, 1907–1914* (Boston: Boston Book & Art Shop, 1968).

— J.H.

GEORGES LEFEBVRE

Georges Lefebvre (1874–1959) is known chiefly for his histories of the French Revolutionary period, including *Les Paysans du Nord pendant la Révolution française* (1924; Northern Peasants During the French Revolution), *La Révolution française* (1930; translated as *The French Revolution*), and *Napoléon* (1935; translated). From 1937 to 1945 he held the chair in revolutionary history at the Sorbonne. Although he was influenced by Marxism, he did not confine himself to economic history, as Marxists often do. Instead he saw history as a complex interaction of forces, examining aspects such as agrarian and social conditions and the peasantry. He is also known as a champion of quantitative methods. His work influenced **Jean-Paul Sartre.**

REFERENCE:

R. C. Cobb, "Georges Lefebvre," *Past and Present,* no. 18 (November 1960): 52–67.

— C.S.B.

Henri Lefebvre

HENRI LEFEBVRE

Philosopher Henri Lefebvre (1905–1991) was one of the most prominent intellectuals associated with the **French Communist Party.** Expelled from the party in 1958, after thirty years of membership, Lefebvre sought to develop an independent Marxist critique of modern consumer society and contributed to the emergence of **Situationism.**

Educated at the **Ecole Normale Supérieure,** where he was a friend of **Simone de Beauvoir,** Lefebvre became affiliated with the eclectic Marxist journal *Philosophies* (1924–1925), whose contributors included **Paul Nizan.** Lefebvre's interest in **Dadaism** and later **Surrealism** led him in 1928 to join the Communist Party along with other Surrealists. Like **Louis Aragon** and **Paul Eluard,** Lefebvre became increasingly involved in party politics.

Although Lefebvre was a loyal Communist, he was never an altogether orthodox one. In *Le Matérialisme dialectique* (1939; translated as *Dialectical Materialism*), he formally accepted the party's con-

cept of Marxism as a global system, but he undercut Stalinist dogmas. Instead of a "closed totality" (a definitive system), Lefebvre argued for an open totality, integrating a variety of conflicting ideas, "perpetually in the process of being transcended." Continuing to run afoul of Communist orthodoxy, Lefebvre was attacked by his former protégé **Roger Garaudy** for continued errors and was officially expelled from the party in June 1958. His *Problèmes actuels du marxisme* (1958) was a first attempt to come to grips with the nature of his dispute with the party leadership.

Even before his expulsion, Lefebvre's work had begun to bypass the often crude base/superstructure framework of Communist societal analyses to focus on the whole network of mediating structures which constituted what he termed "la vie quotidienne" (daily life). His analysis culminated in *La Vie quotidienne dans le monde moderne* (1968; translated as *Everyday Life in the Modern World*), where he advocated breaking away from the "bureaucratic society of controlled consumption." Lefebvre's criticisms of modern life were important to the development of Situationism in the 1960s, though he quarreled with movement leaders over strategy and tactics in the student demonstrations of **May 1968.**

REFERENCES:

David Caute, *Communism and the French Intellectuals, 1914–1960* (New York: Macmillan, 1964);

Martin Jay, *Marxism and Totality: The Adventures of a Concept from Lukacs to Habermas* (Berkeley & Los Angeles: University of California Press, 1984);

Henri Lefebvre, *Everyday Life in the Modern World,* translated by Sacha Rabinovitch (New York & Evanston: Harper & Row, 1971);

George Lichtheim, *Marxism in Modern France* (New York: Columbia University Press, 1966);

Greil Marcus, *Lipstick Traces: A Secret History of the 20th Century* (Cambridge, Mass.: Harvard University Press, 1989).
　　　　　　　　　　　　　　　　　　　　—J.H.

LEFT BANK

The Left Bank (south side) of the River Seine in Paris has been associated with intellectual and artistic life since the Middle Ages. The **Latin Quarter,** with the Sorbonne and other sections of the University of Paris, is located there, as is the Faubourg Saint-Germain, an aristocratic neighborhood featured in the works of Honoré de Balzac and mentioned by **Marcel Proust,** who uses the term with generic reference to aristocratic society. The area also includes **Montparnasse** and **Saint-Germain-des-Prés,** two neighborhoods frequented by writers and artists in the twentieth century.

Fernand Leger's *Les Disques dans la ville* (1918–1919, Musée national d'Art moderne, Paris)

The major monuments of the Left Bank are the Pantheon, the Eiffel Tower, and the Invalides, which contains Napoleon's tomb.

REFERENCE:

Herbert R. Lottman, *The Left Bank: Writers, Artists, and Politics from the Popular Front to the Cold War* (Boston: Houghton Mifflin, 1982).

— C.S.B.

FERNAND LÉGER

Fernand Léger (1881–1955), one of the most prominent avant-garde painters of the twentieth century, was by education and early training an architectural draftsman, working at that trade during the early years of the twentieth century. As was not uncommon among young artists of the **Left Bank,** his early art was heavily influenced by the Impressionists and then the **Fauves,** especially **Paul Cézanne.** Few of Léger's early paintings survive: in 1908 or 1909 he destroyed almost all of his early work. He wrote later that he had reacted against Impressionist art because "the period of the

Impressionists had been intrinsically melodious," whereas "my own was no longer so."

Cézanne's work led Léger directly to **Cubism.** His *Le Pont* (1909; *The Bridge*) closely resembles **Georges Braque**'s 1908 paintings of L'Estaque: multifaceted, simplified shapes in muted earth tones defined not by precise drawing but by juxtaposition of tones. Because the blunt-edged prisms that make up the trees and the bridges are simplified rather than analyzed, the work is not Cubist, but it demonstrates a growing interest in precisely the issues in painting that Braque, **Pablo Picasso,** and their colleagues were exploring.

Léger's encounter with the works of Picasso and Braque at the gallery of Daniel Henry Kahnweiler in 1910 marks his transition to a fully Cubist style of painting. His *Les Nus dans la forêt* (1901–1910; *Nudes in the Forest*) depicts three figures in an interconnected mass of cubes, cones, and rods representing the landscape. The palette is gray and forest green; the emphasis on simple geometric shapes makes the figures and background seem not so much analyzed into parts as mechanized into a world of robots and cogs.

This emphasis on mechanization as characteristic of the modern world became a staple of Léger's art. *La Partie de cartes* (1917; *The Cardplayers*), which draws on the painter's experience in the trenches near **Verdun** during **World War I,** treats the soldiers, who wear their medals and decorations, as mechanized weapons themselves, though remarkably cheerful ones. In this and similar works Léger is not so much criticizing the mechanization of the modern world as he is celebrating it. In a 1925 speech he even asserted, "I find a state of war more desirable than a state of peace.... This is nothing else than *life at an accelerated rhythm....*" Real life could be found only in struggle, in the street, "where the creative man must be. Life is revealed there, accelerated, deep, tragic."

After World War I, even as Léger's emphasis on machinery and technology deepened, his works took on none of the brutality or aggressiveness of the Italian Futurists, for example. Instead, Léger's paintings are filled with brilliant colors and forms derived from the industrial world, juxtaposed with segments of colored disks not unlike those of **Robert Delaunay** and **Sonia Delaunay-Terk.** Léger's *Les Disques dans la ville* (1918–1919; *The Disks of the Town*) is filled with images derived from urban driving, ranging from traffic signs to automobiles to a traffic policeman, all assembled in bits and pieces to suggest the crowding and dynamism of urban life. His animated films — most notably the fifteen-minute *Le Ballet mécanique* (1924; *The Mechanical Ballet*) — use stop-motion photographs of manufactured objects to produce the same effect.

Though seemingly concerned only with a joyous celebration of the technological world, Léger began in the 1920s to compose sympathetic, partly abstracted images of the workers who built and operated that technology. His monumental figures of the decade, beginning with *Le Mécanicien* (1920; *The Machinist*), represent both a growing desire to return to a greater degree of intelligibility and a manifestation of his social sensibilities. An anarchist before the war, Léger joined the **French Communist Party** in 1935 and supported the **Popular Front.** In 1936 and 1937 he spoke to groups of party workers, even debating the question of realism in social art. He rejected the Socialist Realism of Soviet painters and such French representatives of the style as **André Fougeron** and **Boris Taslitzky,** and he questioned the direct utility of art as an agitational weapon. He argued that art has to remain open and free if it is to play a positive role: "The work of art ought not to participate in the battle; it ought to be, on the contrary, a repose after the combat of daily struggles."

In 1940 Léger took refuge from the Nazis in the United States. Upon his return to France in 1945 he made public his membership in the Communist Party. Still opposed to a Soviet-style academic realism, he nevertheless began to create monumentalized images of the industrial working class, as in *Les Constructeurs* (1950; *The Builders*), a celebration of construction workers. His earlier technological themes took on a more openly political quality, as did poetry that he produced during this period. In his 1951 poem "Les Mains des constructeurs" (The Builders' Hands) he examines the heavy, blunted hands of builders, so unlike those of priests or supervisors. The poem ends with the prophecy that one day machines will work for the workers: "HIS MACHINE, HIS FACTORY, that time approaches / he's on the road to it. HIS LIFE IS BEGINNING TODAY!"

Léger's more open political stance coincided, however, with his collaboration with Jean Lurcat and **Georges Rouault** on a design for a facade mosaic at the church of Notre-Dame de Toute Grâce in Assy (1946–1949). Neither the Communist Party nor the Catholic church seems to have approved of his efforts. In 1952 he executed several murals for the United Nations building in New York City.

REFERENCES:

David Caute, *Communism and the French Intellectuals, 1914–1960* (New York: Macmillan, 1964);

Donald D. Egbert, *Social Radicalism and the Arts: Western Europe* (New York: Knopf, 1970);

Peter de Francia, *Fernand Léger* (New Haven & London: Yale University Press, 1983);

Christopher Green, *Léger and the Avant-Garde* (New Haven & London: Yale University Press, 1976);

Walter Schmalenbach, *Fernand Léger,* translated by Robert Allen and James Emmons (New York: Abrams, 1975).

—J.H.

LÉGITIME DÉFENSE

Légitime Défense (Legitimate Defense) was a **Surrealist** group founded in Paris in the early 1930s, bringing together writers, poets, and future politicians who became important in the cultural development of Martinique. The group took its name from a 1926 pamphlet in which Surrealist **André Breton** defended the movement against Communist attacks. The journal *Légitime Défense,* edited by group members Etienne Léro, René Ménil (both from Martinique), and others, was published for the Caribbean émigré population of Paris. It appeared only once, in 1932. Yet the writers of the group played a role in breaking down the rigid, often insipid, norms for poetry in their region — a self-consciously elevated style similar to that of the nineteenth-century Parnassian school in France. The models for Légitime Defense writers were the poets of the Harlem Renaissance in the United States, especially Langston Hughes and Claude McKay.

One prominent Caribbean émigré, **Aimé Césaire,** remained outside the group. Though he shared their Marxist politics and their Surrealist aesthetic orientation in general terms, he was suspicious of their lack of interest in shaping and defining an art and politics rooted in Caribbean, rather than Parisian, realities. He wrote later that the young members of the group were "Communists, and therefore we supported them. But very soon we had to reproach them ... for being *French* Communists. There was nothing to distinguish them from either the French Surrealists or the French Communists." The editorial-manifesto in the single issue of *Légitime Défense* listed the usual line of precursors to the Surrealists — the Marquis de Sade, Arthur Rimbaud, Sigmund Freud, Karl Marx, and others — but no figures at all from their own or any other non-European culture.

One of the group's founders, Léro, died in 1939; Ménil went on to collaborate with Césaire on *Tropiques,* a cultural and political journal published in Martinique in 1941–1945. After Césaire broke with Communism in favor of a Pan-African politics during the late 1950s, Ménil became a local functionary of the Communist Party.

REFERENCES:

A. James Arnold, *Modernism and Negritude* (Cambridge, Mass.: Harvard University Press, 1981).

—J.H.

MICHEL LEIRIS

Michel Leiris (1901–1991) is well known in France as a creative writer and an ethnologist. Born in Paris, he participated in the **Surrealist** movement, writing two Surrealist works — a collection of poems, *Simulacre* (1925; Simulacrum) and his only novel, *Aurora* (1934) — before he left the group in 1929. He began his career as an anthropologist by joining the Dakar-Djibouti expedition to Africa (1931–1933). His experiences during these travels resulted in his best-known ethnological work, *L'Afrique fantôme* (1934; Phantom Africa). In 1938 Leiris, **Maurice Blanchot,** and Roger Caillois founded the Collège de Sociologie.

Leiris pursued his literary career as well as his interest in ethnography and African art, on which he published essays. He is especially well known for his autobiographical works, *L'Age d'homme* (1939; translated as *Manhood*) and the four volumes of *La Règle du jeu* (Rules of the Game) — *Biffures* (1948; Erasures), *Fourbis* (1948; Odds and Ends), *Fibrilles* (1966; Fibrils), and *Frêle bruit* (1976; Frail Noise). He has also written on bullfighting in *Miroir de la tauromachie* (1938; Mirror of Bullfighting), and on artists such as **André Masson.** Leiris's interests in language and the sacred are apparent in all his writing.

REFERENCES:

Marc Blanchard, "Auteuil, le sacré, le banal, la zone," *MLN,* 105 (September 1990): 707–726;

Sean Hand, "The Sound and the Fury: Language in Leiris," *Paragraph: The Journal of the Modern Critical Theory Group,* 7 (March 1986): 102–120;

Jeffrey Mehlman, *A Structural Study of Autobiography* (Ithaca, N.Y.: Cornell University Press, 1974);

Anna Warby, "The Anthropological Self: Michel Leiris' 'Ethnopoetics,'" *Forum for Modern Language Studies,* 26 (July 1990): 250–258.

—C.S.B.

CLAUDE LELOUCH

Since the mid 1960s Claude Lelouch (1937–) has been one of the most popular filmmakers in France. Though sometimes criticized for dealing with superficial subjects, he is widely admired as a movie stylist and technician.

Born in Paris to a Jewish family, Lelouch spent **World War II** hiding with his mother from the Nazis. Soon after the war he became an avid moviegoer, spending hours each day watching genre films — westerns, adventure films, gangster pictures, and romantic movies — at the many theaters in the Strasbourg-Saint-Denis neighborhood of Paris. His greatest interest was in American movies, which had been banned during the German **Occupation** of France and made a triumphant return following the **Liberation.** As a young teenager Lelouch also began to frequent the Cinématèque Française, where he was introduced to the masterpieces of cinema history, but his primary interest remained the genre film.

Lelouch's first efforts at filmmaking took place at age thirteen, when his short movie *Le Mal du siècle* (Worldweariness) won the grand prize at the 1950 Cannes amateur film festival. After a brief career as a freelance news cameraman in 1956 and nearly four years in the military (1957–1960) directing instructional films for the army, he founded his own production company, Les Films 13. His first feature was *Le Propre de l'homme* (1960; *The Right of Man*), a low-budget movie that attracted no great interest. He soon got a lucky break: one of his creditors found him a job working on a new audiovisual project, the Scopitone, producing videolike films for France's leading pop singers. Through these videos Lelouch was able to develop the style that later characterized his work. His techniques included extravagant zooms, skillful melding of images and sounds, and inventive uses of color.

Lelouch continued directing feature films during the 1960s. His first major success — and the greatest of his career — came in 1966 with *Un Homme et une femme* (*A Man and a Woman*). The movie starred Jean-Louis Trintignant and Anouk Aimée, the first well-known actors to appear in his films. This romantic drama, which represented France at the **Cannes Film Festival** that year, shared the grand prize with Pietro Germi's *Signore e Signori* (*The Birds, the Bees, and the Italians*). Lelouch's picture became a commercial success in France and abroad. In the United States it played for extraordinary first runs of more than a year in several large cities and eventually won two Academy Awards, for best original screenplay and best foreign film.

Among other motion pictures produced and directed by Lelouch are *Vivre pour vivre* (1967; *Live for Life*), *La Vie, l'amour, la mort* (1968; *Life, Love, Death*), *Un Homme qui me plaît* (1969; *Love Is a Funny Thing*), *Le Voyou* (1970; *The Crook*), *L'Aventure c'est l'aventure* (1972; *Money, Money, Money*), *Le Chat et la souris* (1975; *Cat and Mouse*), and *Si c'était à refaire* (1976; *Second Chance*).

REFERENCE:

Peter Lev, *Claude Lelouch, Film Director* (Rutherford, N.J.: Fairleigh Dickinson University Press, 1983).

—M.G.

LES LETTRES FRANÇAISES

The Communist newspaper *Les Lettres Françaises* (French Letters) first appeared in 1941 in opposition to the **Vichy government** of the so-called **Free Zone** established after the German invasion of France during **World War II.** It ceased publication after protesting the Soviet invasion of Czechoslovakia of 1968 and reappeared in 1990. In the early 1990s it reached a small readership of about twenty-five thousand.

The name of **Louis Aragon** is inseparable from that of the *Lettres Françaises*. Aragon first joined the **French Communist Party** in 1927. Five years later, he broke with the **Surrealists** and committed himself fully to furthering the cause of communism. As one of the directors of the Communist newspaper *Ce Soir* (This Evening), for instance, he staunchly defended the German–Soviet pact of 1939.

During the German **Occupation,** Aragon became a symbol of the **Resistance.** By the time of the Allied **Liberation** of France in 1944, Aragon's prestige had greatly enhanced that of the Communist Party, which was viewed as the defender of freedom against the Nazis and the best hope for the future. In 1947 Aragon became director of the revived *Ce Soir,* and in 1949 he joined the staff of the *Lettres Françaises,* becoming its director when *Ce Soir* folded in 1953. He made it into a highly acclaimed periodical. Because of his reputation, he enjoyed greater freedom from party control than perhaps any other French Communist intellectual. As an advocate of Stalinist orthodoxy, he in turn exercised complete authority over the contributors to *Lettres Françaises*. Yet he himself came in for criticism for his deviations from Socialist Realism and for the "bourgeois" leanings of novels such as *Les Communistes* (1949–1951).

One of the more telling episodes occurred after Joseph Stalin died in 1953. Aragon commissioned from his friend **Pablo Picasso** a cover illustration to mark the occasion. Picasso's drawing of a lively young Stalin in a striped bathing suit lacked dignity in the eyes of the party faithful and led to a storm of protest. Aragon distanced himself from Picasso, agreeing that the artist was "incapable of doing a good but simple drawing of

the most beloved proletarian in the whole world" (*Lettres Françaises,* 18 April 1953).

Aragon's loyalty to the Communist Party was finally stretched beyond its breaking point by Soviet abuses of power. After he expressed his opposition to the Russian invasion of Czechoslovakia in 1968, it took the party just a few months to decide that, because of "financial difficulties," the *Lettres Françaises* had to cease publication.

REFERENCES:

David Caute, *Communism and the French Intellectuals* (New York: Macmillan, 1964);

Ariane Chebel d'Appollonia, *Histoire politique des intellectuels en France (1944–1954),* volume 2 (Paris: Editions Complexe, 1991).

—J.P.McN.

LETTRISM

Lettrism is one of the many splinter movements from, and would-be successors to, **Dada** and **Surrealism.** It was largely the creation of **Isidore Isou,** a Jewish refugee who arrived in Paris in 1945; with Gabriel Pomerand he launched Lettrism as a revolutionary movement in art and literature. Their method was provocation and denunciations through means such as leaflets and heckling of those they considered reactionary.

The Lettrists argued that human emancipation was bound inescapably to the liberation of the word itself: letters and words had to be freed from routine associations and meanings and then reshaped into the building blocks of a new and creative human existence. Seeking to undermine the apparent clarity or transparency of meaning in the written word, Lettrists incorporated alternate alphabets and glyphs (real or invented), Morse code, and braille into their poems. In painting, artists such as Maurice Lemaître incorporated words, letters, and pictograms into their work. For Isou creativity was the bedrock of human existence, offering anyone with the courage to grasp it the ability to be a god.

Prior to the construction of a new world, however, Lettrism took as its task the subversion of the existing one. For instance, Isou argued that cinema was entering a necessary *ciselant* (chiseling) phase in which the goal was to attack, disrupt, and generally tear apart the medium — both through deliberate disjunctures (including mismatched sound tracks) and scratching or mutilating the filmstrip itself. His 1951 *Traité de bave et d'éternité* (Treatise on Slime and Eternity) typifies this sort of filmmaking. In his

Un Soir au cinéma (1962; An Evening at the Movies) images were projected not for but rather on the moviegoers in their seats.

Isou's battle for a new human existence was energetic but not specific. His call for a youth revolt led to a Lettrist invasion of a Catholic orphanage in 1950; the attempt to set the children free was a debacle. In its aftermath Isou distanced himself from insurgent action. He denounced a subsequent episode in which four young men led by Michel Mourre took over an Easter high mass at Notre-Dame Cathedral in Paris to read a "sermon" accusing the Catholic church of "being the running sore on the decomposed body of the West." The "sermon" echoed Isou's ideas on the potential for human creativity in a world without God, but he backed away as controversy surrounded the action. Similarly, he denounced the attempt of four young Lettrists to disrupt a 1952 showing of Charles Chaplin's film *City Lights,* which they denounced as sentimental and reactionary. The language in their leaflets was as intemperate as Isou's had been, calling Chaplin a "fascist insect" and wishing him "a quick death." Isou's public denunciation of the attack led to the formation of a new faction, the Lettrist International (LI), whose leaders were **Guy Debord,** Gil Wolman, Serge Berna, and Jean-Louis Brau. This faction, which quickly became a separate group, set as its key task the "destruction of idols, especially when they claim to represent freedom."

The LI was largely inactive in the early 1950s. In its irregular magazine, *Potlatch,* the group began to work out some of the ideas that were to become central in Situationism. In January 1957 members of the LI met with like-minded artists and intellectuals, including Danish painter Asger Jorn and Italian artists Giuseppe Pinot-Gallizio and Piero Simondo, at what was proclaimed the First World Congress of Liberated Artists, in Alba, Italy. That congress led directly to the formation of the **Situationist International** later that year.

REFERENCES:

Stephen C. Foster, ed., *Lettrism: Into the Present* (Iowa City: University of Iowa Museum of Art, 1983);

Isidore Isou, "The Creations of Lettrism," *Times Literary Supplement,* 3 September 1964, pp. 796–797;

Martin Jay, *Downcast Eyes: The Denigration of Vision in Twentieth-Century Thought* (Berkeley & Los Angeles: University of California Press, 1993);

Greil Marcus, *Lipstick Traces: A Secret History of the Twentieth Century* (Cambridge, Mass.: Harvard University Press, 1989).

— J.H.

EMMANUEL LEVINAS

Philosopher Emmanuel Levinas (1906–) is an important figure in the fields of modern phenomenology and ethics. He was among the first to introduce the ideas of philosophers Edmund Husserl and Martin Heidegger in France. In doing so he laid the foundation for the phenomenological explorations of many French thinkers, including **Maurice Merleau-Ponty** and some of the **existentialists.**

Born in Kaunas, Lithuania, Levinas established himself as a philosopher and teacher in France. Two of his books, *La Théorie de l'intuition dans la phénoménologie de Husserl* (1930; translated as *Theory of Intuition in Husserl's Phenomenology*) and *En découvrant l'existence avec Husserl et Heidegger* (1949; Discovering Existence in Husserl and Heidegger), helped present these German thinkers to French intellectuals. The phenomenological method he introduced is the attempt to describe experience apart from its supposed relation to the outside world and thus to construct a philosophically defensible knowledge of the world.

Levinas's own philosophical inquiries, such as *De l'existence à l'existant* (1947; translated as *Existence and Existants*) and *Le Temps et l'autre* (1948; translated as *Time and the Other*), explore the limits of the phenomenological methods in their analyses of subjects such as time and death. In *Totalité et infini* (1961; translated as *Totality and Infinity*) he correlates phenomenology with ethical concerns, particularly the self's relationship with "the Other" (that is, its contact with other minds through language). Such investigations have led theorists to compare his work to that of other Jewish philosophers such as Martin Buber and Franz Rosenzweig. Similar concerns are also apparent in Levinas's *Humanisme de l'autre homme* (1972; Humanism of the Other Man) and his commentaries on Jewish texts, including *Quatre lectures talmudiques* (1968; translated in *Nine Talmudic Readings*). His thinking on the problem of the Other also influenced **Jacques Derrida.**

REFERENCES:

Richard A. Cohen, ed., *Face to Face with Levinas* (Albany, N.Y.: State University of New York Press, 1986);

Edith Wyschogrod, *Emmanuel Levinas: The Problem of Ethical Metaphysics* (The Hague: Nijhoff, 1974).

— C.S.B.

ANDRÉ LEVINSON

André Levinson (1887–1933) was the foremost European dance critic during the 1920s and 1930s. His career began in his native Russia, where he wrote for

Apollon, a Saint Petersburg art journal, and taught Romance languages at the university. He soon discovered his passion for dance and began reviewing ballet performances at Russian state theaters and traveling to Paris to review productions by the **Ballets Russes** of **Serge Diaghilev.** A staunch supporter of pure classical dance, he adamantly opposed the collaborative creations of the Ballets Russes — accusing Diaghilev of placing too much emphasis on music, costume, design, and novelty — and the choreographic reforms initiated by **Michel Fokine.** Many of Levinson's journalistic reviews were collected in *Staryi i novyi balet* (1918; translated as *Ballet Old and New),* which constitutes a defense of classicism in dance.

With his wife Levinson fled Russia during the revolution of 1917, eventually settling in Paris in 1921. He was immediately hired by the daily paper *Comoedia* to contribute a weekly dance column and also wrote for other French and Russian publications, including *Candide,* **Revue Musicale,** *Nouvelles Littéraires,* and *Temps.* He reviewed classical ballet, music-hall productions such as the acrobatic adagio acts of the Gertrude Hoffman Girls, performances by the Spanish dancer La Argentina, ethnic dances from the Far East and Africa, other black dance — particularly that of **Josephine Baker** — and early forms of modern dance in Germany.

Consistent throughout all his dance writings was his remarkable ability to capture the essence of dance in words, even if he disliked it. American critics Joan Acocella and Lynn Garafola say that Levinson was "the first to review dance consistently as choreography rather than merely performance, to argue from principle rather than merely from taste, and to draw those principles from within dance itself."

Among Levinson's books are *Ballet romantique* (1919; Romantic Ballet), *L'Œuvre de Léon Bakst* (1921; The Work of Leon Bakst), *La Danse au théâtre* (1924; Dance in the Theater), *La Vie de Noverre* (1925; Life of Noverre), *Marie Taglioni* (1929), *La Danse d'aujourd'hui* (1929; Dance Today), *Les Visages de la danse* (1933; Faces of Dance), and *Serge Lifar* (1934). He contributed to British and American publications, including *Theatre Arts Monthly* (New York), which, in an unsigned obituary, credits him with being the greatest influence on the establishment of dance criticism in the United States.

Levinson was also a literary and film critic and taught Russian literature at the Sorbonne. He received the Légion d'Honneur in 1927 and became a naturalized French citizen in 1932.

Claude Lévi-Strauss (Roger-Viollet)

REFERENCES:

André Levinson, *André Levinson on Dance: Writings from Paris in the Twenties,* edited by Joan Acocella and Lynn Garafola (Hanover & London: Wesleyan University Press / University Press of New England, 1991);

Levinson, *Ballet Old and New,* translated by Susan Cook Summer (New York: Dance Horizons, 1982).

—A.P.E.

CLAUDE LÉVI-STRAUSS

Anthropologist Claude Lévi-Strauss (1908–) is one of the most influential French intellectual figures of the period following **World War II.** Although he was not alone in the investigations that led to the formation of structural anthropology, he is its principal exponent.

Born in Brussels, Lévi-Strauss studied philosophy and law in France. In 1935–1939 he taught in Brazil, where he carried out field research among native tribes that influenced his later ideas. From 1942 to 1945 he taught at the New School for Social Research in New York and subsequently was French cultural attaché in the United States. In 1947 he returned to Paris, where he was named associate curator of the Musée de l'Homme. In 1959 he became professor of anthropology at the Collège de France.

The ideas of linguists Ferdinand de Saussure and Roman Jakobson, along with the work of Russian Formalists such as Vladimir Propp, contributed to the development of Lévi-Strauss's theories. His first major book, *Les Structures élémentaires de la parenté* (1949; translated as *The Elementary Structures of Kinship*), suggested from the start the **structuralist** approach that is his trademark. Comparing social phenomena to structural linguistics, Lévi-Strauss proposes that there are underlying structures in human society and history — systems not imposed by external factors but rather underlying society itself. His analysis of structures of kinship and myth allowed him to conclude that, in widely diverging places and times, there is a fundamental, universal code that actual social systems, both "primitive" and "civilized," reflect. This view represented a departure from the position of his eminent predecessor, the sociologist Lucien Lévy-Bruhl, who stressed differences among cultures.

The principles of structuralism as Lévi-Strauss elaborated them — in particular, his insistence that elements within systems derive their meaning from their relationships with each other rather than from their social expressions and his belief that thought is governed by binary oppositions — were applied in several other fields, including psychology, history, sociology, art, and especially literature. His best-selling autobiographical book, *Tristes tropiques* (1955; translated), was especially instrumental in gaining support for his ideas. During the 1960s and early 1970s structuralism was one of the dominant theories in Europe and the United States.

Other important works by Lévi-Strauss include his two-volume *Anthropologie structurale* (1958, 1973; translated as *Structural Anthropology*), *Le Totémisme aujourd'hui* (1962; translated as *Totemism*), *La Pensée sauvage* (1962; translated as *The Savage Mind*), and *Le Cru et le cuit* (1964; translated as *The Raw and the Cooked*). In 1973 he was elected to the Académie Française.

REFERENCES:

Roland A. Champagne, *Claude Lévi-Strauss* (Boston: Twayne, 1987);

Claude Lévi-Strauss, *Conversations with Claude Lévi-Strauss* (Chicago: University of Chicago Press, 1991);

Ino Rossi, ed., *The Unconscious in Culture: The Structuralism of Claude Lévi-Strauss* (New York: Dutton, 1974).
                                                        — C.S.B.

BERNARD-HENRI LÉVY

Bernard-Henri Lévy (1948–), who sometimes writes under the pseudonym Pierre Victor, is a member of the intellectual group known as the **Nouveaux Philosophes** (New Philosophers), which came to prominence in the 1970s. As a student Lévy studied under **Louis Althusser,** was associated with **Jean-Paul Sartre,** and participated in the leftist demonstrations of **May 1968.** His career, however, illustrates his generation's rejection of a philosophy of commitment and the sort of thoroughly left-wing politics epitomized by Sartre, in favor of a so-called postpolitical stance that seeks to revolutionize thinking about politics by rejecting old authorities and the accepted ideas they represent. In *La Barbarie à visage humain* (1977; translated as *Barbarism with a Human Face*), Lévy denounces Marxism as a monstrous totalitarian system that oppresses the mind and the body. Among his subsequent publications are *Testament de Dieu* (1979; translated as *Testament of God*), *Eloge des intellectuels* (1987; In Praise of Intellectuals), and *Les Aventures de la liberté* (1991; The Adventures of Freedom). In 1990 Lévy founded a magazine, *La Règle du Jeu* (Rules of the Game), and the following year he produced a television documentary devoted to the role of intellectuals in France. He has also published successful fiction.

REFERENCE:

Jeremy Jennings, ed., *Intellectuals in Twentieth-Century France: Mandarins and Samurais* (New York: St. Martin's Press, 1993).
                                                        — C.S.B.

MARCEL L'HERBIER

Marcel L'Herbier (1888–1979) was a driving force of vanguard cinema in France during its greatest years, the 1920s. Overshadowed by **Luis Buñuel** and **Abel Gance,** L'Herbier nevertheless was partially responsible for the growth of French film for more three decades, from the silent era to the beginnings of television.

Born in Paris, L'Herbier was educated at the Sorbonne, and in 1917–1918 he served in the photographic and cinematographic branch of the French army, where he was introduced to film. During these years he began an extensive career in scriptwriting. He directed a few films for **Léon Gaumont** in the years 1919–1922 and brought a new emphasis to the subjective visions of the characters through striking visual takes of landscapes and decor. **Filmmaker and critic Louis Delluc** praised one such film, the impressionistic *Eldorado* (1921), as "real cinema." When L'Herbier left Gaumont to obtain a greater freedom of expression, establishing his own production company in 1922, he worked with young directors such as **Claude Autant-Lara** and with veterans such as Delluc.

Paris on 26 August 1944, two days after French troops entered the city

One of L'Herbier's best-known films is *L'Inhumaine* (1924; *The New Enchantment*), which features decors created by artist **Fernand Léger** and music by **Darius Milhaud.** The following year L'Herbier directed his masterpiece, *Feu Mathias Pascal* (*The Late Matthew Pascal*). In that film he combined the angular lines of Léger's style with an equally prismatic narrative that foreshadows the experiments of **film noir** and the **Nouveau Roman** (New Novel). L'Herbier's adaptation of Emile Zola's *L'Argent* (1929; Money) extends the innovations of contemporary cinema.

L'Herbier continued to direct after the 1920s, but owing to commercial limitations his later films were more conventional. In 1936 he supported the Cinémathèque Française, founded by **Georges Franju** and Henri Langlois, and in 1943 he became founder and chief of the Institut des Hautes Etudes Cinématographiques (I.D.H.E.C.), the prestigious center for advanced film studies. He became a television producer in the 1950s.

REFERENCES:

Richard Abel, *French Film Theory and Criticism, 1: 1907–1939* (Princeton, N.J.: Princeton University Press, 1988);

Noël Burch, *Marcel L'Herbier* (Paris: Seghers, 1973).

— T.C.

ANDRÉ LHÔTE

André Lhôte (1885–1962) was among the near- or quasi-**Cubist** painters who emerged with the 1911 **Salon des Indépendants.** Hung not in the "Cubist" room 41, but with paintings by "allied" artists in room 43, Lhôte's work was heavily influenced by that of **Paul Cézanne.** By 1911 his paintings had begun to take on a rather timidly faceted "Cubist" appearance, though he used a brighter palette than his colleagues.

Lhôte set himself the task of formulating the "scientific laws of Cubism," leading one modern historian to call him the "academician of Cubism." It was he, for instance, who recorded the anecdote about insurance agent and amateur mathematician Maurice Princet instructing **Pablo Picasso** and **Georges Braque** on guidelines for handling objects. Beginning with a trapezoid, representing a table distorted by perspective, one should render it as *la table type* (the table as a kind of archetype) straightened up against the picture plane, as a tilted rectangle. The objects *on* the table should be revised in the same way: "Thus the oval of a glass would become a perfect circle. But this is not all: this glass and this table seen from another angle are nothing more than, the table a horizontal bar a few centimeters thick, the glass a profile whose base and rim are horizontal. Hence the need for another displacement...." Whether or not Princet actually delivered such a lecture, these instructions are not a bad working description of a Cubist decomposition of a traditional interior scene, but followed as an instruction booklet, they can produce stilted and lifeless results. For Lhôte the transition of Picasso and Braque from analytical to synthetic Cubism actually meant a split into two separate movements, the synthetic (a priori) Cubists, whose work was based on abstract construction, and the analytic (a posteriori) Cubists, whose work was based on the analysis of nature.

Lhôte's own work lacks both the rigor and the dynamic tension of Picasso's early work. Lhôte's *Rugby* (1920) is a prime example — a static image, without motion or internal tension, of partly disassembled rugby players confined in a series of flat geometric shapes.

REFERENCES:

Douglas Cooper, *The Cubist Epoch* (London: Phaidon, 1971);

John Golding, *Cubism: A History and an Analysis, 1907–1914* (Boston: Boston Book & Art Shop, 1968);

Christopher Green, *Cubism and Its Enemies* (New Haven: Yale University Press, 1987);

Robert Rosenblum, *Cubism and Twentieth-Century Art* (New York: Abrams, 1961).

— J.H.

THE LIBERATION

The Liberation of France during **World War II** began with the Allied landings in Normandy on 6 June 1944. All troops succeeded in establishing beachheads despite heavy resistance in some places, and by early July Allied forces in France had reached one million men. In late July troops succeeded in breaking through German defenses at Saint-Lô.

The liberation of Paris, which symbolized national liberation for many Frenchmen, began on 24 August, when Gen. Jacques Philippe Leclerc's Second Armored Division entered the city. Political as well as military issues were involved in this arrangement. The division had been flown hastily from Algeria to England so that French troops could participate in the campaign and be the first to enter Paris.

The French military played only a small role in the struggle against the Germans in northern France during this period, although 120,000 French fought in Italy in Operation Anvil during the same summer. Of the approximately 400,000 French military personnel outside Vichy France, only half were armed. An esti-

mated 150,000 were scattered around the world in garrison duty. **Charles de Gaulle** was so bitter about the minimal role that had been assigned to the French in the liberation of their own country that in 1964 he refused to attend the ceremonies commemorating the Normandy landings.

Once the national capital was freed, the **Vichy government** ceased to exist. In the midst of intense political dissension among **Resistance** groups, de Gaulle laid the groundwork for his provisional government. The post-Liberation period also witnessed the **épuration,** or settling of accounts with those suspected of sympathy with the German occupiers. The fighting continued in the east of France through the fall. Strasbourg was recaptured at the end of November, but German pockets of resistance held out in the east until February 1945.

REFERENCES:

Robert Aron, *France Reborn: The History of the Liberation, June 1944–May 1945,* translated by Humphrey Hare (New York: Scribners, 1964);

Antony Beevor and Artemis Cooper, *Paris After the Liberation* (London: Hamilton, 1994);

Hilary Footitt and John Simmons, *France, 1943–1945* (New York: Holmes & Meier, 1988).

— D.O'C.

SERGE LIFAR

Serge Lifar (1905–1986) is remembered chiefly as the premier danseur of the **Ballets Russes** from 1925 to 1929 and the ballet director and *premier danseur étoile* (principal dancer and star) at the **Paris Opéra Ballet** from 1929 to 1944 and again from 1947 to 1958. Before joining the Ballets Russes in 1923, he was a student of **Bronislava Nijinska** in his native city, Kiev. With the Ballets Russes in Paris he created roles in works by Nijinska, **Léonide Massine,** and **George Balanchine,** including the role of Borée in Massine's *Zéphire et Flore* (1925) and the title roles in Balanchine's *Apollon Musagète* (1928) and *Le Fils prodigue* (1929; *The Prodigal Son*). Called *le beau Serge,* he was one of the great dancers of the twentieth century, known for his passion, beautiful physique, neoclassic style, and strong technique.

More important than his contributions as a performer was Lifar's revitalization of the Paris Opera Ballet. Jacques Rouché, the Paris Opera director from 1914 to 1944, appointed Lifar as ballet director in 1929. During Lifar's tenure of nearly thirty years, the ballet company flourished. He maintained the great classical tradition while continuing Rouché's efforts to adopt innovations introduced by the Ballets Russes. The technical level of the dancers improved, and new French ballerinas replaced Italian *étoiles* (stars). New ballets were choreographed (many by Lifar, with him in the leading role), and classic ballets were revived. Most acclaimed was the 1932 revival of *Giselle,* with Olga Spessivtseva in the title role and Lifar as Albrecht.

Lifar was a prolific choreographer. His most discussed ballet is *Icare* (1935; *Icarus*), danced to percussion accompaniment. He also wrote more than twenty books, including his autobiography, *Ma Vie* (1965; translated).

Because of his efforts to keep the Paris Opera Ballet open during the German **Occupation** of France in **World War II,** Lifar was accused of collaboration and banned from the opera for the three years following the **Liberation.** During this period (1944–1947) he directed and danced in the Nouveau Ballet de Monte Carlo. He then returned to the Paris Opera Ballet for another ten years. Although he was still passionate about dance and a prominent presence in the company, his work as a dancer and choreographer declined.

Lifar founded the Paris Institut Choréographique (1947) and the Université de la danse (1957). He was made a member of the Académie des Beaux-Arts in 1968 and received the Carina Ari Medal (1974).

REFERENCE:

Serge Lifar, *Ma Vie: From Kiev to Kiev* (New York & Cleveland: World, 1965).

—A.P.E.

MAX LINDER

Max Linder (1882–1925) was among the first French stars of silent films and one of the great comedians working in that medium. In his hundreds of short movies, which he also wrote and directed after 1911, he created the first continuing comic movie character: a supposedly sophisticated dandy tripped up by circumstances.

Having started out as a stage actor, Linder entered motion pictures in 1905. He left the theater in 1908, and by 1910 he was a film star. His influence on silent film comedy was profound; Charles Chaplin considered himself Linder's "disciple." Linder made a few films in the United States in the late 1910s and early 1920s, including *The Three Must-Get-Theres* (1922), a parody of Douglas Fairbanks adventure movies. Plagued by poor health and depression after **World War I,** Linder died in a suicide pact with his wife, cutting short a remarkable career. Until copies of old films became more widely available in the late twenti-

eth century, his work was seen infrequently, and a re-evaluation of the scope and value of his work is just beginning.

REFERENCE:

Sheila Benson, "Max Linder Returns," *Film Comment,* 20 (September–October 1984): 4, 6.

—W.L.

JACQUES LIPCHITZ

Jacques Lipchitz (1891–1973) occupies a special place among those artists who attempted to translate **Cubist** concepts into the field of sculpture, both for the span of his Cubist period and for the determination with which he sought to work out a sculptural system less dependent on than analogous to Cubist painting.

Lipchitz was born in Lithuania and immigrated to Paris in 1909. He studied art at the Ecole des Beaux-Arts and then at the independent Académie Julien. He met **Pablo Picasso** and other Cubist artists, notably **Juan Gris,** in 1913. In the same year his sculptures, notably his bronze *Danseuse* (Dancing Woman), began to display a few, still rather timid, attempts to employ Cubist devices. In his *Marin avec guitare* (1914; *Sailor With Guitar*), a bronze, the cylindrical head of the figure and the machinelike arcs of the arms move somewhat farther in the same direction. Between 1915 and 1918 Lipchitz abandoned any residual naturalism and began to work with increasing confidence in the vocabulary of analytical Cubism. Most of his pieces from that period are columnar, vertically oriented constructions in stone, bronze, or wood. In some the total figure is formed from an aggregate of vertical shapes of different heights; in others ridges trace a diagonal across the figure; by 1916–1917 curvilinear shapes are sometimes played off against vertical or horizontal planes in Lipchitz's works.

It is impossible to trace a straightforward evolution in Lipchitz's art. Like Picasso, he sometimes switched directions abruptly, then doubled back again to play with forms or ideas discarded earlier. From 1917 through 1920 his forms became more representational; human subjects depicted are more or less intact and easily legible though faceted into a series of convex and concave curves played off against each other. In the 1920s, by contrast, he moved to a series of sometimes monumental forms deriving their dynamism from the interplay of intertwined curves (such as his *Joie de vivre,* an eleven-inch bronze designed in 1927).

In the 1930s and 1940s Lipchitz went on to flesh out these intertwined curves as struggling figures: Jacob wrestling with an angel, a bull battling a condor, Prometheus strangling the vulture. Most of these pieces depict Good in relentless combat with Evil.

Lipchitz fled the Nazis in 1941; in New York he participated in the work of Atelier 17, an experimental workshop transferred from Paris in 1940. His work and that of other European abstract artists had a major impact on American art in the 1940s.

REFERENCES:

Douglas Cooper, *The Cubist Epoch* (London: Phaidon, 1971);

Pierre Daix, *Cubists and Cubism* (New York: Rizzoli, 1982);

Christopher Green, *Cubism and Its Enemies: Modern Movements and Reaction in French Art, 1916–1928* (New Haven & London: Yale University Press, 1987).

—J.H.

LITTÉRATURE

The journal *Littérature* had a brief but brilliant existence in the years just after **World War I.** It was founded by three poets — **Louis Aragon, André Breton,** and **Philippe Soupault** — all of whom were influenced by the older writer **Guillaume Apollinaire.** Like him, the younger men were aware of living at a defining moment of history and of the need to chart new directions for literature and art. *Littérature* was a mirror and catalyst for artistic experimentation in a period of extraordinary creativity. The title was ironic, even derisory. Breton and his colleagues had no desire to adhere to established standards for what constituted "literature," nor did they want to cultivate or even please the public; they actually worried about how to avoid being accepted.

The first issue of *Littérature* appeared in 1919. Initially Breton, the future leader of the **Surrealists,** did not write much for the magazine, but his influence was preponderant. There was a seriousness of purpose about *Littérature* that echoed Breton's own, and one finds little of the playfulness of other avant-garde reviews of the period, such as *Sic.* In their defense of the new, writers for *Littérature* caustically attacked what was perceived as the old. For example, the leader of **Dada, Tristan Tzara,** described Rainer Maria Rilke as a "sentimental and rather stupid poet," while **Marcel Proust** was called a "laborious snob" — a true but inadequate description.

The magazine soon came to call for commitments for or against causes and individuals. At first it championed Dada, publishing in May 1920 three Dada man-ifestos advocating perpetual revolution, antiart, and free rein for instinct. It attacked all lucid, rational thinking in the Cartesian tradition, and Aragon denounced what he called the "clear French genius." But before long Breton grew tired of Dada's theatrics, and the break with the Dada circle was finalized in the April 1922 issue, with Breton's article "Drop Everything" advocating a clean break with family, friends, children, mistresses, and of course Dada.

Even before this break, Breton had sought to explore new possibilities beyond Dada. After a six-month interruption in publishing, *Littérature* reappeared in March 1922, with Soupault and Breton as codirectors. From September 1922 on, the only editor was Breton. In 1923 *Littérature* appeared irregularly. Yet Breton's dedication to charting new waters was as strong as ever, involving, for instance, hypnotic trances and spiritualist seances.

With the publication of his *Manifeste du surréalisme* (1924; translated as *Surrealist Manifesto*), Breton entered a new phase, in which his creative energies were channeled to a new, clearly defined goal; the era of wide-ranging aesthetic exploration represented by *Littérature* was over, and it ceased publication after the June 1924 issue.

REFERENCES:

Anna Balakian, *André Breton, Magus of Surrealism* (New York: Oxford University Press, 1971);

J. H. Matthews, *André Breton* (New York: Columbia University Press, 1967);

Michel Sanouillet, *Dada à Paris* (Paris: J. J. Pauvert, 1965).

—J.P.McN.

AURÉLIEN LUGNÉ-POE

Theater director Aurélien-Marie Lugné-Poe (1869–1940) resisted the realistic tendencies of the turn-of-the-century Paris stage and opened the theaters to Symbolist plays. Thus, in the vanguard of modernism he directed French theater down the road toward abstract portrayal of inner psychological and spiritual conflicts.

He began his theatrical career in high school, organizing an acting club called the Cercle des Escholiers at the Lycée Condorcet in Paris. The club staged several major productions, both under his directorship and after he left the school. Lugné-Poe directed and acted for a time in **André Antoine**'s **Théâtre Libre,** where realism was the dominant mode. He left in 1893, acquiring **Paul Fort**'s Théâtre d'Art, which he renamed the **Théâtre de l'Œuvre.** There he undertook to produce plays of lyrical beauty, in reaction against Antoine's naturalistic staging, which seemed to portray life as nothing more than a physical, materialistic enterprise lacking all spiritual dimensions. Rather than realistic constructions, Lugné-Poe chose suggestive painted backdrops and scrims, preferring props of symbolic value to mere utilitarian objects. Indeed, his sets were often created by notable painters, including **Pierre Bonnard, Odilon Redon,** and **Edouard Vuillard.** Lugné-Poe staged **Maurice Maeterlinck**'s *Pelléas et Mélisande* (translated) in 1893 at a theater called Les Bouffes-Parisiens, and then he brought a series of Henrik Ibsen's plays to the Théâtre de l'Œuvre, including *The Masterbuilder* in 1894 and *Little Eyolf* in 1895. With Lugné-Poe's symbolic staging and the mellifluously chanted stage diction he taught to his actors, these plays acquired a lyrical dimension quite different from Antoine's Ibsen productions. But Lugné-Poe's effort to inject a poetic soul into theater led to excesses that were just as egregious as those of deterministic realism.

In 1896 Lugné-Poe produced **Alfred Jarry**'s raucous, satiric farce *Ubu roi* (translated), usually considered the first truly modernist French play. While the play itself is antirealist in conception and tone, it attacks real bourgeois values and conservative political views. Lugné-Poe's symbolist staging of the play could thus reveal the union of the real and the imaginary.

Lugné-Poe's other successful productions of this period included Ibsen's *Peer Gynt* (1896), **Romain Rolland**'s *Les Loups* (1898; translated as *The Wolves*), and William Shakespeare's *Measure for Measure* (1898). But bad times came in 1899. Symbolism was temporarily out of favor in the public imagination, and Lugné-Poe's staunch defense of Capt. Alfred Dreyfus, falsely accused of treason in the **Dreyfus Affair,** did not sit well with wealthy, reactionary patrons. The Théâtre de l'Œuvre was near ruin, but Lugné-Poe was able to coax it back to life with a more eclectic repertory: he staged **André Gide**'s modernist *Roi Candaule* (translated as *King Candaules*) in 1901 and Maksim Gorky's somber *Lower Depths* in 1905.

It was doubtless **Paul Claudel**'s *L'Annonce faite à Marie* (translated as *The Tidings Brought to Mary*) that allowed Lugné-Poe to reveal his full genius for uniting the spiritual and the material worlds. This drama of the Incarnation, in which the theme of real human suffering symbolizes the spiritual principle of divine redemption, reached the stage of the Théâtre de l'Œuvre in 1912, and Claudel's *L'Otage* (translated as *The Hostage*) received a Lugné-Poe production in 1914.

1897 catalogue cover illustrating the Lumière Brothers' hand-cranked Cinématographe camera, the first commercial film projector

Like other Paris theaters, the Théâtre de l'Œuvre was closed during **World War I.** Lugné-Poe reopened it in 1918 and remained there as director until 1929, but the rejuvenated French theater movement of the postwar period soon left him behind, and he had few successes. When he left the Théâtre de l'Œuvre, it was to direct a few more productions on other stages; his last successful stagings were of **Jean Anouilh**'s *L'Hermine* (Ermine) in 1932 and of **Armand Salacrou**'s *L'Inconnue d'Arras* (translated as *The Unknown Woman of Arras*) in 1935. His reminiscences on the theater appeared, in 1930 and 1931, under the titles *La Parade* (The Sideshow) and *La Parade II;* one can also consult his *Dernière pirouette* (1946; Last Pirouette).

REFERENCES:

Gertrude R. Jasper, *Adventure in the Theater: Lugné-Poe and the Théâtre de L'Œuvre to 1899* (New Brunswick, N.J.: Rutgers University Press, 1947);

Bettina Knapp, *The Reign of the Theatrical Director: French Theatre 1887–1924* (Troy, N.Y.: Whitston, 1988);

Jacques Robichez, *Le Symbolisme au théâtre: Lugné-Poe et les débuts de l'Œuvre* (Paris: L'Arche, 1957).

— R.J.N.

LOUIS LUMIÈRE

Louis Lumière (1864–1948) is often called the father of French cinema, if not of world cinema. On 28 December 1895, using their new invention, the *cinématographe,* he and his brother Auguste (1862–1954) became the first to offer projected motion pictures to a paying audience. His movies are admired for their skillful use of framing and perspective and their depiction of events from real life.

The sons of an industrialist who ran a firm for developing chemical and photographic products, Louis and Auguste Lumière improved on existing film equipment in 1894 by perfecting a machine that pushed film over an aperture by means of a claw-and-sprocket mechanism. This machine, the *cinématographe,* could both record and project movies. They showed their first film, *La Sortie des usines Lumière* (Workers Leaving the Lumière Factory), in industrial exhibitions early in 1895. The first commercial showing, of ten shorts at the Grand Café on the Boulevard des Capucines in Paris, included *L'Arroseur arrosé* (The Sprinkler Sprinkled) and *Le Repas de bébé/Déjeuner de bébé* (Baby's Feeding Time). They soon showed many other movies, most less than a minute long, including *Déjeuner d'un chat* (1895; A Cat's Breakfast), *Charcuterie mécanique* (1895; Mechanical Sausage-Making), *Arrivée d'un train en gare de La Ciotat* (1895; Arrival of a Train at La Ciotat Railway Station), and *Démolition d'un mur* (1896?; Destruction of a Wall). When the last of these was shown backward, it became the first trick film.

These short movies are also significant in film history for their style and technique of composition. Each is carefully staged: despite the fixed camera and the single shot that defines the content of most of the films, narratives develop inside the frame. In *L'Arroseur arrosé,* for instance, viewers watch a man fall victim to his own prank with a garden hose. The frame of the shot that records the train arriving at La Ciotat station shows the locomotive moving from a distance and quickly filling the screen. According to historians, some of the first audiences thought the train would run over them and either fled the theater or hid under their chairs.

Despite such successes, the Lumières initially believed that cinema did not promise a lucrative future and turned down **Georges Méliès** when he offered to purchase the *cinématographe* in 1896. After directing around sixty films in 1895 and 1896, Lumière handed over the filmmaking to others, some of whom traveled the world recording events such as U.S. president William McKinley's inauguration in 1897. By 1898 Lumière's company had produced more than one thousand short films. By 1900, when he enjoyed successful showings at the Paris Exposition on a sixteen-by-twenty-one-meter screen, the number had risen to more than two thousand. The company abandoned filmmaking in 1905 in favor of manufacturing cameras and related items, and Lumière turned his attention to photography projects such as still projection and stereoscopic (3-D) films.

Both **Jean-Luc Godard** and **François Truffaut** allude to the work of Lumière in their **Nouvelle Vague** (New Wave) films. Truffaut reenacted *L'Arroseur arrosé* in one of his first movies, *Les Mistons* (1958; *The Mischief Makers*), and he reshot *Déjeuner d'un chat* in a stunning moment in *La Nuit américaine* (1973; *Day for Night*). Godard placed Lumière's statement to Méliès — "Cinema does not have a promising future" — in a sequence in *Le Mépris* (1963; *Contempt*). Both directors, and many others, have paid homage to the Lumières' contribution to the origins of a medium and art that has since played a major role in twentieth-century culture.

REFERENCES:

Noël Burch, *Life to Those Shadows* (Berkeley & Los Angeles: University of California Press, 1990);

Georges Sadoul, *Louis Lumière* (Paris: Seghers, 1964).

— T.C.

JEAN-FRANÇOIS LYOTARD

Jean-François Lyotard (1924–) is a leading writer on postmodernism, having given this concept common currency in France in many articles and in books such as *La Condition postmoderne* (1979; translated as *The Postmodern Condition*) and *Le Postmoderne expliqué aux enfants: Correspondance 1982–1985* (1986; translated as *The Postmodern Explained: Correspondence 1982–1985*).

From early in his career Lyotard combined an interest in philosophy with a commitment to political action. While teaching in Algeria just before the outbreak of the **Algerian war,** he became a supporter of the nationalist movement against French colonialism. On returning to France he participated in left-wing movements, and he was involved in the student revolt of **May 1968.**

While Lyotard does not use the term *postmodern* in his dissertation, which was published as *Discours, figure* (1971; Discourse, Figure), it anticipates some postmodern concerns. Far from sharing the confidence of adherents of **structuralism** or semiotics in the existence of underlying patterns that lend themselves to discovery and interpretation, he attacks reason, pattern, coherence, and any attempt to arrest the natural flow of desire. His ongoing interest in art and aesthetics is applied not to making sense of art but rather to celebrating the primacy of the raw figure or image.

In his mature work Lyotard celebrates desire over order and multiplicity over unity, even attacking the notion of a unified self, and he repudiates the binary opposition of subject and object. His enterprise is thus an attempt to subvert the Western philosophical tradition, with its belief in the existence of truth. Furthermore, Lyotard equates reason with capitalism, authority, and oppression, and he calls for the destruction of the apparatus of power. In his *Economie libidinale* (1974; translated as *Libidinal Economy*) he attacks systematic theory and advocates a Nietzschean liberation of libidinal energy and creative expression.

Since the mid 1970s Lyotard increasingly has applied himself to laying the foundations for a postmodern politics that would show a concern for justice and advocate multiple perspectives beyond the politics of consensus, which he believes disarms different points of view and silences marginalized voices. In *La Condition postmoderne* he expresses his suspicion and rejection of any totalizing system — whether social, political, or philosophical — that lays claim to lasting or universal validity. He views all such "narratives of power" as discredited dogmas to be dismantled and discarded. Lyotard thus appears to exclude any possibility of collective connection or shared understanding. Ultimately, therefore, his attacks on capitalism, patriarchy, and the reduction of the individual to a commodity appear to concede the inevitability of their own defeat.

REFERENCES:

Steven Best and Douglas Kellner, *Postmodern Theory, Critical Interrogations* (New York: Guilford, 1991);

Madan Sarup, *An Introductory Guide to Post-structuralism and Postmodermism* (Athens: University of Georgia Press, 1988).
— J.P.McN.

M

MAURICE MAETERLINCK

Although much of the poetry and drama of Maurice Maeterlinck (1862–1949) belongs to the nineteenth century, he lived and wrote well into the twentieth. One of his best-known works, *L'Oiseau bleu* (translated as *The Blue Bird*), an allegorical fairy play that denies the reality of death, was published in 1909.

Born in Ghent, Belgium, Maeterlinck was associated with Symbolist circles in both Belgium and France, where he settled in the 1890s. He began his literary career by publishing Symbolist verse, including *Serres chaudes* (1889; Hothouses). He is best known, however, as the author of dreamy, mysterious Symbolist dramas, including the famous *Pelléas et Mélisande* (1892; translated), a story of ill-fated love, on which **Claude Debussy** based an opera and for which **Gabriel Fauré** composed incidental music. Another notable Maeterlinck play is *L'Intruse* (1897; translated as *The Intruder*); the title refers to the unwelcome intrusion of death. Some of his plays were produced at the **Théâtre de l'Œuvre.**

Maeterlinck, whose interests included mysticism and insects, can be considered one of the theoreticians of Symbolist theater. He won the Nobel Prize for Literature in 1911.

REFERENCES:

Auguste Bailly, *Maeterlinck,* translated by Fred Rothwell (New York: Haskell House, 1974);

Linn Bratteteig Konrad, *Modern Drama as Crisis: The Case of Maurice Maeterlinck* (New York: Peter Lang, 1986).

— C.S.B.

THE MAGINOT LINE

The Maginot Line, the elaborate system of defensive fortifications built on France's eastern border between 1927 and 1936, took its name from André Maginot (1877–1932). As minister of war from 1922 to 1924 and

Tunnel on the Maginot Line

again from 1929 to 1932, Maginot played a decisive role in establishing the system, which was intended to protect Alsace and Lorraine against German attack. In the years between **World War I** and **World War II** these disputed border territories, which had been German from 1870 until 1918, took on a symbolic value that was incommensurate with their strategic importance. When the Battle of France began in May 1940 (see **Debacle**), the German advance came around to the north of the Maginot defenses, through the Ardennes Forest of Belgium and northwest France, instead of attacking the Maginot Line directly. Today it is a tourist attraction.

REFERENCE:

Judith M. Hughes, *To the Maginot Line: The Politics of French Military Preparations in the 1920s* (Cambridge, Mass.: Harvard University Press, 1971).

— D.O'C.

RENÉ MAGRITTE

René Magritte (1898–1967) is one of the best-known and most popular **Surrealist** painters. Even people who are unfamiliar with his name are likely to recognize some of his works; advertising has made wide use of his techniques and even some of his motifs.

As a student at the Brussels Académie des Beaux-Arts (1916–1918), Magritte, a Belgian, was less interested in avant-garde artistic movements than in Fantômas, the archcriminal whose exploits were detailed in the thirty-two novels by Pierre Souvestre and Marcel Allain that appeared monthly beginning in 1913. Magritte was especially taken with **Louis Feuillade**'s films on the same subject. Visual quotations and references to Fantômas dot Magritte's work throughout his career.

Magritte worked for a time for a wallpaper company and experimented tentatively with **Cubist** ideas, most notably in his *Trois femmes* (1922; *Three Women*), and with Futurist ones, as in *Jeunesse* (1922; *Youth*), a study of a nude young woman interlocked with that of a partially abstracted ship. These paintings are stiff and derivative, borrowing sometimes from several disparate (and not necessarily complementary) sources simultaneously.

In 1925 Magritte completed *Le Jockey perdu* (*The Lost Jockey*); though the original has been lost, a close copy made in 1940 gives a good sense of what was, in retrospect, his first foray into motifs that would become central to his work: ironic, seemingly random juxtapositions, in which human figures in particular travel in some bewilderment through crisply depicted but physically impossible landscapes. In this canvas, man and horse gallop through a sunlit world of huge banisters or balustrades, from which leafy branches sprout. The dislocated jockey and rider became a recurring motif in Magritte's work.

Magritte's interest in dreamlike landscapes can be traced in part to his growing interest in the art of the Italian Giorgio de Chirico; a fascination with dreams and Chirico in turn led him to the Surrealists. He made contact first with Belgian Surrealists in 1926. After moving to the outskirts of Paris the following year, he became close to **André Breton** and **Paul Eluard.** Magritte progressively refined what became his trademarks within the Surrealist movement: an insistence upon a seeming naturalism, with objects rendered in precise detail, and the use of jarring juxtapositions and unexpected details to overturn the way in which viewers see and interpret the scenes before them. In a 1940 essay he wrote that he sought to depict objects "with the appearance they have in reality, in a style sufficiently objective so that the subversive

effect . . . might exist again in the real world from which these objects had been borrowed." He became particularly adept at using juxtapositions and captions or titles to question the whole enterprise of art as a representation of external reality. An oil painting of a pipe (1928–1929) is prominently labeled *Ceci n'est pas une pipe* (This is not a pipe).

The idea that item and representation are not identical, that marvelous changes can come when one realizes that the two are, in fact, detached, was spelled out by Magritte in his picture essay, "Les Mots et les images" ("Words and Images"), published in *Révolution Surréaliste* in 1929. Opening with the statement that "an object is not so linked to its name that we cannot find a more suitable name for it," he illustrated the point with a drawing of a leaf, captioned "cannon." On the other hand, the line that "everything leads us to think that there is little relation between an object and what it represents" is illustrated by two identical drawings of a house, one labeled "real object," the other, "the represented object." Some of the images focus on levels of identity and differentiation: the statement "An object never performs the same function as its name or image" is accompanied by a drawing of a horse, a drawing of a painting of the same horse, and a man saying "horse."

From the outset Magritte stood apart from certain central Surrealist concerns; though Breton called for psychic automatism (automatic painting emerging uncensored from the unconscious), nothing could be more conscious or deliberate than Magritte's work. One of his most notorious pieces — *Le Viol* (*The Rape,* first sketched in 1934, redone as an oil painting in 1945) — depicts a woman's face as her body; in Magritte's words, "the breasts are eyes, the navel the nose, and the sexual organs replace the mouth." The displacement of the torso to the face jars the viewer; the result is a form of conceptual shift in which Magritte can suggest empathically the sense of violation that the gaze can convey. In his *La Philosophie dans le boudoir* (1947; *Philosophy in the Boudoir*), the title — taken from a pornographic novel by the Marquis de Sade — is appended to a negligee with prominent breasts and a pair of high-heeled shoes made from a woman's feet. Both are treated as part of her wardrobe, as even her body is forced into duty as part of a sexual persona.

Magritte noted that **World War II** and the German **Occupation** of France transformed his outlook and his art. Ironically, his decision was to move toward a more optimistic tone: "Before the war, my paintings expressed anxiety, but the experiences of war have taught me that what matters in art is to express charm. I live in a very disagreeable world, and my work is meant as a counter-offensive." The "counter-offensive" involved several experiments, from works modeled on those of Auguste Renoir to his well-known images of men in bowler hats who are confronted with everything from giant green apples to Sandro Botticelli's *Primavera* (circa 1477; *Spring*). Magritte's *La Grande Famille* (1947; *The Big Family*) is a morose, cloudy seascape; the gloom is broken by a patch of bright blue sky in the shape of a dove of peace borrowed from **Pablo Picasso.**

Magritte's newfound cheer, coupled with his decision to affiliate with the Belgian Communist Party in 1944, led to a full-scale breach with Breton and the official Surrealist movement. He complained that Breton had become stuffy and inflexible. Nor was he pleased to be cited as a forerunner by the Pop artists of the 1960s; he regarded their work as at best a "sugarcoated **Dadaism**" and as a celebration of all that was miserable in a society, a present that "reeks of mediocrity and the atom bomb."

REFERENCES:

Suzi Gablik, *Magritte* (Greenwich, Conn.: New York Graphic Society, 1976);

Pierre Gimferrer, *Magritte* (New York: Rizzoli, 1986);

Harry Torczyner, *Magritte: Ideas and Images,* translated by Richard Miller (New York: Abrams, 1977).

—J.H.

ARISTIDE MAILLOL

Focusing almost entirely on the female nude, Aristide Maillol (1861–1944) sought to reestablish classical sculpture, rejecting the innovations of his great predecessor **Auguste Rodin,** who had a powerful, but varied, impact on French and Belgian sculpture. Some artists sought to follow in Rodin's footsteps, and others sought to soften his art by fusing it with more traditional, classical forms, but Maillol was part of a third group that turned away from Rodin entirely.

Maillol began his artistic career as a painter, but progressive deterioration of his eyesight led him to switch to sculpture in 1895. Though he was a close friend of Rodin's student **Emile Bourdelle,** his artistic affiliations were with **Paul Gauguin** and the **Nabis,** especially **Maurice Denis.** Under their influence he came to reject the entire idea of invention or innovation in art: "I do not invent anything," he stated, "just as the apple tree cannot pretend to have invented its apples." Rodin's emotive, fragmented sculpture had little appeal for Maillol, who said that he did not understand it at all, judging it too contorted, too uneven, often too detailed. Even a later appreciation of the power of Rodin's work only intensified Maillol's efforts to dif-

ferentiate his art from Rodin's, saying, "I was trying to simplify, whereas he noted all the profiles, all the details."

Maillol's classicism, however, was a post-Rodin variant, a classicism stripped of its nineteenth-century anecdotalism, fetish for literal details, and sentimentality. Maillol once pointed out an ancient statue of Venus, smoothed and simplified by centuries under water, as the example of what he sought. At its worst Maillol's sculpture is static and rather listless; at their strongest his figures have an extraordinary fluidity. His bronze *La Méditerranée* (1902–1905; *The Mediterranean*), a nude woman resting one elbow on an upraised knee, is a study in balance with the body simplified into smooth arcs and angles. His lead statues *L'Air* (1938; *Air*) and *La Rue* (1939–1943; *The Street*) seem clichéd at first glance. Both are female nudes lying on their sides, one seemingly carried by a stiff current, the other seemingly buoyant and weightless. Yet the outward resemblance of classical bronzes is misleading; neither — especially *La Rue* — is concerned with classical balance or harmony. The human figure becomes the vessel, not the subject, for each piece, as the human form is edited and transformed to suggest the appropriate fluid medium personified in metal.

REFERENCES:

Aristide Maillol: 1861–1944 (New York: Guggenheim Museum, 1975);

Frederic V. Grunfeld, *Rodin: A Biography* (New York: Holt, 1987);

John Rewald, *Maillol* (London, Paris & New York: Hyperion Press, 1939);

Dina Vierny and Bernard Lorquin, *Maillol: La Méditerranée* (Paris: Editions de la Réunion des Musées Nationaux, 1986).

—J.H.

MAISON DE LA CULTURE (POPULAR FRONT)

The Maison de la Culture, established in connection with the **Popular Front** political movement in 1934, had its origins in the Maisons du Peuple established by Socialists in Belgium and France in the 1890s, marking a new stage in the orientation of socialist parties toward cultural concerns. The Maison du Peuple in Brussels, Belgium, was intended to serve as the center of the social, cultural, and educational life of Belgian workers. It included an assembly hall, a bakery and restaurant, and a library, and after the establishment of an art section in 1892, it offered an ambitious program of lectures, concerts, and tours of museums and galleries on free days.

The idea of a Maison du Peuple as a center of Socialist-oriented cultural enterprise proved contagious; centers were soon established in France, a small one in Paris as early as 1892. The Maisons du Peuple were to play the role of the medieval cathedrals — the focus of civic, social, educational, and artistic life. The idea inspired imitations also; in Lille the Christian Democrats set up their own *maisons des ouvriers* to keep their working-class supporters away from dangerous socialist ideas. The Syndicalist labor organizations called *bourses du travail* began to set up their own network of "workers' museums" and educational and cultural activities.

The Maison de la Culture was set up by the **French Communist Party** in 1934 as part of the groundwork for the **Popular Front,** effectively replacing the explicitly revolutionary **Association des écrivains et artistes révolutionnaires** (AEAR). A large maison was established in Paris with subsidiaries in other French cities. The first leaders were Paul Vaillant-Couturier and **Louis Aragon.** Whereas the Maisons du Peuple had been set up as party-led bodies, the Maison de la Culture, like the Popular Front itself, was officially a broad front of progressives coming together to oppose fascism. Among its most prominent members were Jean Lurcat, **Fernand Léger, André Lhôte,** and **Jacques Lipchitz.** The rhetoric surrounding the enterprise was nevertheless modeled directly on that of the Maisons du Peuple. In a 1937 appeal to artists published in *Commune,* the magazine that had become the official publication of the Maison de la Culture, the maisons were called the "new cathedrals" of the people.

REFERENCES:

David Caute, *Communism and the French Intellectuals, 1914–1960* (New York: Macmillan, 1964);

Donald Drew Egbert, *Social Radicalism in the Arts: Western Europe* (New York: Knopf, 1970);

Eugenia W. Herbert, *The Artist and Social Reform: France and Belgium, 1885–1898* (New Haven: Yale University Press, 1961);

John Hutton, *Neo-Impressionism and the Search for Solid Ground: Art, Science, and Anarchism in Fin-de-siècle France* (Baton Rouge: Louisiana State University Press, 1994).

— J.H.

MAISONS DE LA CULTURE (FIFTH REPUBLIC)

In 1961, at the urging of **André Malraux,** minister of culture under **Charles de Gaulle,** president of the **Fifth Republic,** the French government approved the creation of Maisons de la Culture (Houses of Culture) in ninety French cities. Only fifteen were eventually constructed. Among the provincial cities in which they are located are Grenoble, Rennes, Rheims, Le Havre, La Rochelle, Bourges, Nevers, and Amiens. These centers were conceived as part of the decentralization of culture, an attempt to improve the quality of life in the provinces by breaking up the monopoly on art, literature, and the performing arts that traditionally had been held by Paris.

The Maisons de la Culture are usually imposing buildings in or close to the centers of the cities. They offer support and provide space for local theater and dance productions (and sometimes opera), art exhibits, and film clubs. A library is usually included as well. Ironically, despite their founders' intentions, none of these provincial cultural centers can match the popularity of the **Centre Pompidou** in Paris. Not part of the network of Maisons de la Culture, it nonetheless offers, on a much grander scale and more successfully, many of the services provided in the provincial centers.

REFERENCE:

John Ardagh, "Culture in the Provinces: From Malraux's *Maisons* to the New Operatic Snobberies," in his *France in the 80s* (Harmondsworth, U.K.: Penguin, 1982), pp. 323–335.

— D.O'C.

LOUIS MALLE

Initially considered a **Nouvelle Vague** (New Wave) director of the late 1950s, Louis Malle (1932–) has developed a personal approach to filmmaking that covers a wide range of subjects and styles. Many of his films are character studies that treat personal and sexual dilemmas.

Born into a wealthy family, Malle studied political science at the Sorbonne before attending the Institut des Hautes Etudes Cinématographiques (1951–1953). His first involvement in a feature film was as codirector and one of the cameramen for Jacques-Yves Cousteau's successful first feature about his undersea adventures, *Le Monde du silence* (1956; *The Silent World*). Malle then assisted **Robert Bresson** on *Un Condamné à mort s'est échappé* (1956; *A Man Escaped*).

Malle's first feature-length movies, the thriller *Ascenseur pour l'échafaud* (1958; *Frantic*) and the controversial *Les Amants* (1958; *The Lovers*), are reminiscent of the **tradition de qualité** movies of the 1930s and 1940s. All Malle's films are charged with eroticism. As with much of Malle's work, critical opinion is split on his madcap adaptation of **Raymond Queneau**'s *Zazie dans le métro* (1960; *Zazie*) and his *Vie privée* (1962;

A Very Private Affair), starring **Brigitte Bardot** in a semi-autobiographical dramatization about the life of a movie star. One of his finest films, *Le Feu follet* (1963; *The Fire Within*), based on a novel by **Pierre Drieu La Rochelle,** is about an alcoholic who commits suicide. During the second half of the 1960s Malle experimented with several topics and styles, from the upbeat *Viva Maria* (1965) to *Le Voleur* (1967; *The Thief of Paris*), a period crime film. He also made two documentaries on India that the Indian government denounced as demeaning to their country. Malle combined lush color photography with a treatment of adolescence (including incest) in *Le Souffle au cœur* (1971; *Murmur of the Heart*). Male sadomasochism appears in *Lacombe Lucien* (1973), his retro-style movie about the German **Occupation** of France during **World War II,** while his *Black Moon* (1975) was inspired by Lewis Carroll.

Malle's first film made in the United States, *Pretty Baby* (1978), stars Brooke Shields as a twelve-year-old prostitute; the movie is still banned in some countries. In 1980, the year he married American actress Candice Bergen, Malle completed *Atlantic City,* an English-language film starring Burt Lancaster. (The movie was backed by French and Canadian companies.) *My Dinner with André* (1981) features a dinner conversation between two real people. Malle returned to France to direct *Au revoir les enfants* (1987; *Goodbye Children*), which is based on his childhood memories of a Catholic boarding school that took in Jewish children during the Occupation. *Damage* (1992) is an adaptation of a Josephine Hart novel. In 1994 Malle appeared as himself on the American television show *Murphy Brown,* which stars Candice Bergen.

REFERENCES:

T. Jefferson Kline, *Screening the Text: Intertextuality in New Wave French Cinema* (Baltimore: Johns Hopkins University Press, 1992), pp. 24–53;

Jacques Mallecot and Sarah Kant, eds., *Louis Malle par Louis Malle* (Paris: Athanor, 1978);

Richard Roud, "Malle x 4," *Sight and Sound,* 58 (Spring 1989): 125–127.

— T.C.

FRANÇOISE MALLET-JORIS

Françoise Mallet-Joris (1930–) is a popular and respected novelist. Her first novel, *Le Rempart des béguines* (1951; translated as *The Illusionist*), sold more than half a million copies and was turned into a movie in 1972. Several subsequent books have also sold well and lent themselves to film and televised adaptations. Mallet-Joris's *L'Empire céleste* (1958; translated as

Café Céleste) won the coveted Prix Fémina. She was elected to the jury of the Prix Fémina in 1969 and to the **Goncourt Academy** in 1970.

Born Françoise Lilar in Antwerp, Belgium, Mallet-Joris converted to Catholicism as an adult. Her religious faith is apparent in some of her fiction, which is primarily concerned with love and family. In her work few arrangements among human beings appear successful. Triangles and other tangled relationships abound, along with the Balzacian theme of money. Particularly interested in the portrayal of women characters, Mallet-Joris in 1960 collaborated in translating Shelagh Delaney's *A Taste of Honey,* a play in which two women boldly explore their limits. In a series of historical novels beginning with *Les Personnages* (1961; translated as *The Favourite*), Mallet-Joris explores the lives of historical figures such as Marie Mancini, an early mistress of Louis XIV, and Jeanne Guyon, a seventeenth-century mystic.

Mallet-Joris returned to a contemporary theme in *Les Signes et les prodiges* (1966; translated as *Signs and Wonders*), a novel dealing with the aftermath of the **Algerian war** and the repatriation of *pieds-noirs* (European settlers) from Algeria to mainland France. Her autobiographical best-seller, *La Maison de papier* (1970; translated as *The Paper House*) sold more than one million copies. Subsequently, she has published works for children and other novels that explore social issues in the context of daily life. Since 1983 Mallet-Joris has also served as a reader for the **Gallimard** publishing house.

REFERENCE:

Lucille Frackman Becker, *Françoise Mallet-Joris* (Boston: Twayne, 1985).

— C.S.B.

ANDRÉ MALRAUX

André Malraux (1901–1976) has deservedly been called a "Renaissance man." Not only a major novelist and art critic, he was also an important political figure and an adventurer — though his experiences are not as spectacular as those of T. E. Lawrence (Lawrence of Arabia), whom he admired.

A voracious reader, Malraux dropped out of school at seventeen and spent much of the 1920s and 1930s working for various publishers. His early tale anticipating the **Surrealist** vein, *Lunes en papier* (1921; Paper Moons), was admired by **André Breton.** In 1923 Malraux and his first wife, Clara, left for Indochina in search of adventure. Caught in possession of Cambodian archaeological treasures, Malraux was tried, con-

Minister of State for Cultural Affairs André Malraux with Marc Chagall, whom Malraux commissioned to paint the ceiling of the Opéra de Paris. Chagall's design is behind them. (Photo-Izis)

victed, and held under house arrest for violating laws on the protection of temples – an experience that opened his eyes to the corruption of the colonial administration. When freed, Malraux sought backing in France and then returned to Saigon to found a newspaper that championed the anticolonial movement. His interest in revolution, which is apparent in almost all his fiction, dates from this initial trip to Southeast Asia.

Although he and his wife returned to France in 1926 and did not observe the Chinese revolution of 1927 — the setting and background for *Les Conquérants* (1928; translated as *The Conquerors*) and *La Condition humaine* (1933; translated as *Man's Fate*) — his experiences in Indochina shaped these novels, as well as *La Voie royale* (1930; translated as *The Royal Way*). When Leon Trotsky criticized the portrayal of Chinese revolutionaries in *Les Conquérants,* Malraux remarked that his book was not an historical chronicle but "first of all an accusation against the human condition." In *La Condition humaine* Malraux's focus is

man's tragic solitude and search for transcendence in a universe without permanent values. Winner of the Prix Goncourt, the novel is one of the finest produced in France during the twentieth century.

In the 1930s Malraux became increasingly involved in politics and European peace movements. *Le Temps du mépris* (1935; translated as *Days of Wrath*), the first novel he set in Europe, is one of the earliest works of fiction to reveal the existence of Nazi concentration camps. When the **Spanish Civil War** broke out in 1936, Malraux immediately joined those fighting on the Republican side, organizing and commanding an international volunteer air force in 1936–1937. When it disbanded he spoke out for democracy in Europe and North America. Malraux also wrote *L'Espoir* (1937; translated as *Man's Hope*), a fictional rendering of this struggle, drawing on his own experience, and he directed a much-admired anti-Fascist film, *Sierra de Teruel* (1938; Teruel Mountain).

At the outbreak of **World War II,** Malraux volunteered for service in the French army. He was slightly wounded and was held briefly as a prisoner of war. After the fall of France he was active in the **Resistance** to the German **Occupation,** during which he was captured and would have been executed if he had not been freed through a clerical error. He also took part in military campaigns during the last months of the war, when French troops fought on the eastern front, and he was awarded the Légion d'Honneur and Croix de Guerre. Although written during the war and set in a prison camp in 1940, Malraux's final work of fiction, *Les Noyers de l'Altenburg* (1943; translated as *The Walnut Trees of Altenburg*) is not based principally on contemporary events. It is a meditation on historical action and the meaning of human existence in the face of death and the violence that marks the twentieth century. The novel again shows that for Malraux political involvement is always transcended by metaphysical questions — action (like art) being a way for mortal man to rebel against, and leave his mark on, an indifferent world. His crucial concept of metamorphosis — artistic transformation of experience and the world — evolved from his metaphysical interest.

In 1945 Malraux met **Charles de Gaulle,** beginning a friendship that would lead to Malraux's postwar involvement in government. Malraux served as minister of information in de Gaulle's post-**Liberation** provisional government (a few months in 1945–1946). When de Gaulle resigned Malraux turned to his longstanding interest in painting and sculpture. His concept of the "museum without walls" (that is, the juxtaposition of art objects from widely differing countries, periods, and collections, thanks to photography and printing) was central in his arguments concerning the development of styles and what they meant to the civilizations they expressed. Among his major publications in the field of art criticism are the three volumes of *Psychologie de l'art* (1947–1949; translated as *The Psychology of Art*), which were revised and enlarged as *Les Voix du silence* (1951; translated as *The Voices of Silence*), and *Saturne: Essai sur Goya* (1950; translated as *Saturn: An Essay on Goya*). When de Gaulle was elected president in 1958, he selected Malraux as minister of culture, a position he held in the **Fifth Republic** governments of de Gaulle and, briefly, Georges Pompidou, stepping down in 1969. His patronage of the arts fit well with his personal interest in art criticism. He commissioned **Marc Chagall** to execute the ceiling paintings of the Opéra de Paris and supported a flowering of cultural activities and institutions in the 1960s. He is also responsible for the cleaning of many Parisian buildings and monuments.

Malraux's *Antimémoires* (1967; translated) attracted international attention. Instead of employing a standard autobiographical approach, he emphasized the human condition as he and his contemporaries — including such figures as de Gaulle and Jawaharlal Nehru — had lived it. Malraux's other late books include *Les Chênes qu'on abat* (1971; translated as *Fallen Oaks*), a reconstruction of his conversations with de Gaulle, and *L'Homme précaire et la littérature* (1977; Precarious Man and Literature).

Over the course of his long career, Malraux had his detractors. Some criticized him for his versatility, and art critics in particular seem reluctant to acknowledge his achievements in a field they would like to protect against interlopers. Others attacked his politics, which moved along the spectrum from left to right, but which Malraux himself defended as being eminently reasonable, given the revelations in the 1930s about Stalinist purges in Russia and the obvious betrayal of the social revolution in the Soviet Union and elsewhere. His personal attitudes, including his reluctance to reveal much about himself, paired with a clear tendency toward self-mythologizing, irritated many. Even many of his critics acknowledge, however, that Malraux — a man who never graduated from a lycée — was the incarnation of "the intellectual as man of action."

REFERENCES:

Charles D. Blend, *André Malraux: Tragic Humanist* (Columbus: Ohio State University Press, 1963);

Gerda Blumenthal, *André Malraux: The Conquest of Dread* (Baltimore: Johns Hopkins University Press, 1960);

Thomas Jefferson Kline, *André Malraux and the Metamorphosis of Death* (New York & London: Columbia University Press, 1973);

Jean Lacouture, *André Malraux* (New York: Pantheon, 1975);

Walter G. Langlois, *André Malraux: The Indochina Adventure* (New York: Praeger, 1966).

— C.S.B.

ANDRÉ PIEYRE DE MANDIARGUES

André Pieyre de Mandiargues (1909–) is held in high regard by the French for his novels, poetry, and other writings. His books have appeared under the imprints of publishers such as **Gallimard** and **Grasset** in Paris and Grove Press in New York, but he is little known outside France, perhaps in part because he has not sought popularity and is a member of no important literary coterie.

Mandiargues's writing is characterized by its sadistic eroticism, fantasy, and strangeness, expressed often in a controlled, even classic, language. For some years after 1945 he was associated with **André Breton** and other **Surrealists.** Mandiargues identifies one of his early poems, *Hedera, ou la persistance de l'amour pendant une rêverie* (1945; Hedera, or The Persistence of Love During a Dream), as a Surrealistic work. Pagan and mythic elements, such as that of the quest, are featured in several of his works, such as *Le Lis de mer* (1956; translated as *The Girl Beneath the Lion*) and *La Motocyclette* (1963; translated as *The Motorcycle*). The book for which Mandiargues is best known, *La Marge* (1967; translated as *The Margin*), is a highly erotic work that earned him the Prix Goncourt.

Mandiargues has also written art criticism, some of which has been collected in *Le Belvédère* (1958; The Belvedere), *Deuxième Belvédère* (1962; Second Belvedere), *Troisième Belvédère* (1971; Third Belvedere), and *Le Cadran lunaire* (1958; The Moondial).

REFERENCE:

David J. Bond, *The Fiction of André Pieyre de Mandiargues* (Syracuse: Syracuse University Press, 1982).

— C.S.B.

MANIFESTE DES 343

A major event in the **Mouvement de la Libération des Femmes** was the appearance of "Un Appel de 343 femmes" (A Call from 343 Women), a public letter in the 5 April 1971 issue of the *Nouvel Observateur.* Each signatory to this letter, which became known as the *Manifeste des 343,* acknowledged that she had undergone an illegal abortion and demanded that French women be granted the right to terminate pregnancies legally if they so chose. This document had an enormous impact, leading to the enactment, on 17 January

1975, of the Veil Law (named for the well-known centrist liberal politician Simone Veil, who was then minister of health). This law, which legalized abortion within the first ten weeks of pregnancy, was followed by more liberal guidelines.

Among the signers of the letter were **Simone de Beauvoir, Catherine Deneuve,** lawyer Gisèle Halimi, **Violette Leduc, Jeanne Moreau, Christiane Rochefort, Françoise Sagan,** and actress Delphine Seyrig.

REFERENCE:

Elaine Marks and Isabelle de Courtivron, *New French Feminisms: An Anthology* (Amherst: University of Massachusetts Press, 1980).

— D.O'C.

Manifestes du surréalisme

The two manifestos that **André Breton** published under the titles *Manifeste du surréalisme* (1924) and *Second Manifeste du surréalisme* (1930) — translated together as *Manifestoes of Surrealism* — are the chief theoretical texts of the **Surrealist** movement. In *Qu'est-ce que le surréalisme?* (1934; *What Is Surrealism?*) Breton further defended and explained the movement.

The manifestos, especially the first, offer a scathing critique of previous literature (especially realism, as illustrated by Stendhal and Honoré de Balzac) and of some contemporary literary figures — among them **Maurice Barrès** and **Anatole France** — who embodied what Breton saw as the worst tendencies of the positivist, bourgeois culture dominant in France and the logic on which it was based. They praise the seminal work of thinkers such as Karl Marx and Sigmund Freud and of poets such as Arthur Rimbaud and Isidore Ducasse, and they set forth definitions and principles of the movement, which was to be a revolution in aesthetics, politics, and philosophy — a total remaking of human beings and their world.

REFERENCES:

Ferdinand Alquié, *The Philosophy of Surrealism,* translated by Bernard Waldrop (Ann Arbor: University of Michigan Press, 1965);

Anna Balakian, *André Breton, Magus of Surrealism* (New York: Oxford University Press, 1971).

— C.S.B.

Marcel Marceau

Marcel Marceau (1923–) revitalized the art of stylized pantomime. Having studied under **Charles Dullin**

and the mime Etienne Decroux, Marceau made his first public appearance in 1947 in a pantomime staged by **Jean-Louis Barrault** and his troupe. Marceau founded his own mime company shortly thereafter and developed for its productions a character called "Bip," a kind of alter ego for the mime himself, a modern-day Pierrot incarnating a blend of comedy and pathos. He sought to imbue pantomime with spiritual values, akin to those associated with the stylized gestures and facial expressions of Oriental theater. For a time Marceau's troupe staged full-fledged pantomime productions at the Théâtre de l'Ambigu. By the mid 1950s he was traveling widely outside France, giving highly successful solo performances. Beloved by audiences in North America and Asia, he has founded schools of mime in Europe, Japan, and the United States. He has made short films of his best Bip routines, and he has published *The Story of Bip* (1976). So far, however, he has brought no worthy disciples to public attention.

REFERENCE:

Ben Martin, *Marcel Marceau, Master of Mime* (New York: Penguin Books, 1979).

— R.J.N.

Gabriel Marcel

Philosopher and playwright Gabriel Marcel (1889–1973) was the first twentieth-century French thinker to whom the label of **existentialist** could appropriately be applied. Marcel gave currency to the term in a 1925 article introducing the ideas of Søren Kierkegaard. Although the thought of French intellectuals such as **Jean-Paul Sartre** and **Simone de Beauvoir** came to be described as existentialist, they did not like the label, at least in part because they differed from Marcel in their religious views. They were atheists, and Marcel converted to Roman Catholicism in 1929.

For the most part Marcel was not a systematic thinker. His *Journal métaphysique* (1927; translated as *Metaphysical Journal*), based on his diary, identifies the problem of thinking about "being" as an object and denounces philosophical abstraction in favor of more concrete approaches to the investigation of personal experience. Like many of his contemporaries, he emphasized the drama, even the anguish, of the human condition, but he refused to grant its absurdity and the finality of death. The terrible problem of freedom that so occupied Sartre became for Marcel a value by which people could reach out to others and recognize the transcendency that was for him the source of all being. Marcel explored freedom in what many philosophers consider his masterpiece, *Etre et avoir* (1935; translated as *Being and Having*), and in works such as the two-volume *Le Mystère de l'être* (1950; translated as *The Mystery of Being*) and *Homo viator* (1945; translated as *Introduction to a Metaphysic of Hope*).

Marcel's plays also explore his philosophical positions, which sometimes hurt their reception. The best known are *Un Homme de Dieu* (1925; translated as *A Man of God*), *Le Chemin de crête* (1936; translated as *Ariadne*), and *Le Signe de la croix* (1949; The Sign of the Cross). "My dramas," he wrote, "can be considered as the theater of the soul in exile. I have tried to show tragic alienation in all its forms."

REFERENCES:

William Cooney, ed., *Contributions of Gabriel Marcel to Philosophy: A Collection of Essays* (Lewiston, N.Y.: Edwin Mellen Press, 1989);

Kenneth T. Gallagher, *The Philosophy of Gabriel Marcel* (New York: Fordham University Press, 1962);

Paul Arthur Schilpp and Lewis Edwin Hahn, eds., *The Philosophy of Gabriel Marcel* (La Salle, Ill.: Open Court, 1984);

Thomas J. M. van Ewijk, *Gabriel Marcel: An Introduction,* translated by Matthew J. van Velzen (Glen Rock, N.J.: Deus Books, 1965).

—C.S.B.

LOUIS MARCOUSSIS

Louis Marcoussis (1878–1941) is best known for his **Cubist** paintings, produced for the most part between 1910 and 1913. Born Ludwig Casimir Ladislas Markous in Warsaw, Poland, he settled in Paris in 1903. Like other would-be painters at that time, he supported himself by doing caricatures for French satirical journals, especially the *Assiette au Beurre.* He worked primarily in a **Fauve** style and was unsatisfied with his efforts. In 1907 he abandoned painting altogether, until he met poet and critic **Guillaume Apollinaire** and painter **Georges Braque,** who introduced him to Cubism. (Apollinaire gave Markous his French name, after Marcoussis, a small village near Paris.)

In his Cubist works, some intended to decorate the Café Azon (a popular gathering place for the Cubists and their friends), Marcoussis approached closely the contemporary idiom of **Pablo Picasso.** In particular, his engraved portrait of Apollinaire (1912) exhibits a delicate balance between maintaining a clear likeness to the subject and a careful Cubist analysis of volumetric space. He followed Picasso and Braque through the collages of synthetic Cubism. Marcoussis's *Habitué* (1920) is a layered, textured (oil and sand) depiction of a café, with gambling and smoking. The painting is marked by large areas of solid color with fragmented details in contrasting shades.

As Marcoussis became quite popular as a painter and illustrator after **World War I,** his Cubism became increasingly attenuated, reduced to surface details.

REFERENCES:

Douglas Cooper, *The Cubist Epoch* (London: Phaidon, 1970);

John Golding, *Cubism: A History and an Analysis, 1907–1914* (Boston: Boston Book & Art Shop, 1959);

Theda Shapiro, *Painters and Politics: The European Avant-Garde and Society, 1900–1925* (New York & Amsterdam: Elsevier, 1976).

—J.H.

MARIANNE

The journal *Marianne: Grand hebdomadaire littéraire illustré* (Marianne: Large Illustrated Literary Weekly) was first published in October 1932 by **Gaston Gallimard,** whose publishing house owned several other journals, including the highly esteemed monthly *Nouvelle Revue Française.* By the time of the Second Republic (1848–1851) the name *Marianne* had been associated with republican or left-leaning values.

Emmanuel Berl (1892–1976), a prolific left-wing Jewish writer, accepted Gallimard's invitation to be the editor of *Marianne.* Encouraged by **André Malraux,** Berl made *Marianne* the leading left-wing weekly of the 1930s. While it continued to appear briefly after Berl's resignation in 1937, it was no longer the quality newspaper it had been under his stewardship.

According to Berl, Gallimard founded *Marianne* as a way to supplement the incomes of *Nouvelle Revue Française* writers and thus to keep them from abandoning his camp for better-paying and popular right-wing weeklies such as *Candide* or *Gringoire.* It also provided the publisher with another low-cost means of advertising his new books, as well as the *Nouvelle Revue Française.*

During the politically heated 1930s *Marianne* featured literature, cinema, and the arts alongside partisan editorials by Berl or Socialist deputy L. O. Frossard. Among the earliest contributors were **Antoine de Saint-Exupéry, André Maurois,** and **Jean Giono.** By 1934 the list included **Robert Desnos, Jean Cocteau,** Malraux, **Sacha Guitry, Pierre Drieu La Rochelle, Henry de Montherlant,** and even Walt Disney. *Marianne* was also the first to publish works by the well-known cartoonist Jean Effel.

Although *Marianne* never attained the circulation of its competition on the Right, it was influential. Berl supported the left-wing **Popular Front** government of France, which swept into power in 1936, but—having seen the horrors of trench warfare firsthand as

Jacques Maritain with Thomas Merton at Gethsemani Abbey in Kentucky, 1966 (John Howard Griffin)

a soldier during **World War I** — he was a lifelong pacifist and noninterventionist, even with the outbreak of the **Spanish Civil War** (1936–1939), when forces led by Gen. Francisco Franco and backed by the Fascist governments of Germany and Italy overthrew the elected Popular Front government of Spain.

Berl's avoidance of the gutter journalism of his right-wing competition contributed to the inability of *Marianne* to attract enough readers to cover its costs. Its losses became enormous, and in 1937 Gallimard sold the paper to the wealthy press magnate Raymond Patenôtre, who did not share Berl's political sympathies. Berl resigned and started his own magazine, *Pavé de Paris* (Paris Pavement). Because of his noninterventionist views, he was soon supporting the concessions made to Adolf Hitler in the Munich Pact (1938). After the Germans invaded France in 1940, he rallied to the cause of **Philippe Pétain**'s **Vichy government.**

REFERENCES:

Pierre Assouline, *Gaston Gallimard: A Half-Century of French Publishing,* translated by Harold J. Salemson (San Diego, New York & London: Harcourt Brace Jovanovich, 1988);

Emmanuel Berl, *Essais,* edited by Bernard Morlino and Bernard de Fallois (Paris: Julliard, 1985).

— J.P.McN.

JACQUES MARITAIN

Philosopher and theologian Jacques Maritain (1882–1973) was a well-known figure in France and abroad for much of the twentieth century. Associated with the religious revival that occurred in French thought after 1900, he was the best-known modern advocate of Thomism, based on the philosophy and theology of Saint Thomas Aquinas. He did not consider himself a Neo-Thomist, believing that those philosophers did not adhere closely enough to Aquinas's writings.

Maritain was reared as a Protestant but converted to Roman Catholicism in 1906 under the influence of Léon Bloy. He taught at the Institut Catholique de Paris from 1914 to 1940. In addition to defending and building on the thought of Aquinas, Maritain was concerned with combating the philosophy of **Henri Bergson,** whose religiously unorthodox ideas had earlier influenced him. He also stood in opposition to **Jean-Paul Sartre** and other atheist thinkers.

A Christian humanist who saw the religious and the secular as distinct but not separate, Maritain argued for the importance of Christian involvement in secular affairs. His thought is set forth in approximately seventy books, including *Eléments de philosophie* (1920, 1923; Elements of Philosophy); *Distinguer pour unir, ou Les degrés du savoir* (1932; translated as *The Degrees of Knowledge*), where he argues for the validity of scientific, philosophical, and religious knowledge; and *Humanisme intégral* (1936; translated as *True Humanism*). He was interested in aesthetics as well as metaphysics; for him poetry was a revelation of divine presence. Among his writings on aesthetics is *Creative Intuition in Art and Poetry* (1953), which grew out of the Mellon Lectures given at the National Gallery in Washington, D.C.

Maritain's wife, Raïssa, a converted Russian Jew, was his frequent collaborator and became an exponent of her husband's thought, as well as an author in her own right. They had several connections with literary circles in France. Maritain served as French ambassador to the Vatican (1945–1948) and taught at Princeton University (1948–1956) before retiring in 1960.

REFERENCES:

Joseph Amato, *Mounier and Maritain: A French Catholic Understanding of the Modern World* (Tuscaloosa: University of Alabama Press, 1975);

J. W. Evans, ed., *Jacques Maritain: The Man and His Achievement* (New York: Sheed & Ward, 1963);

John W. Hanke, *Maritain's Ontology of the Work of Art* (The Hague: Nijhoff, 1973);

William J. Nottingham, *Christian Faith and Secular Action: An Introduction to the Life and Thought of Jacques Maritain* (Saint Louis: Bethany Press, 1968).

— C.S.B.

THE MARNE

The first major battle of **World War I** took place on 9–12 September 1914 in and around the Marne River valley to the north of Paris. Since the German invasion of France by way of Belgium in August, the German and French armies had maneuvered in the open, with the French sustaining devastating losses. In the Battle of the Marne the French, under Marshal Joseph-Jacques Joffre, were able to stop the German advance. The turnabout restored French hopes for victory and caused them to assume the offensive in the following months. This battle was the focus of great patriotic feeling and is frequently alluded to in French literature.

A "race to the sea" followed, as the Germans tried to outflank the French, who continued to check them. The resulting stalemate, in which defensive weapons proved to be much more formidable than offensive ones, lasted for four years. In the second Battle of the Marne, on 15–18 July 1918, the last major German offensive was repulsed by the Allies.

REFERENCE:

David Stevenson, *French War Aims Against Germany: 1914–1919* (New York: Oxford University Press, 1981).

— D.O'C.

ALBERT MARQUET

Painter Albert Marquet (1875–1947) was unusual among the **Fauves** for his relatively restrained use of color, limiting the characteristic bright shades associated with the movement to small patches designed to stand out against a generally dark and muted canvas.

Marquet was among the first to experiment with what would become known as Fauvist techniques; he was always careful to give himself pride of place, alongside **Henri Matisse** and well ahead of such later Fauves as **André Derain** and **Maurice Vlaminck.** As Marquet later recalled, "Matisse and I were already working, before the 1900 Exhibition, in what was later to be called the Fauve style." Matisse and Marquet first met as students of the Symbolist painter Gustave Moreau. Marquet was something of a prodigy: he had been admitted to the Ecole des Arts Décoratifs at age fifteen. A loner with a caustic wit, he nonetheless became close to Matisse.

From the outset Marquet was interested in Matisse's bold colors more as an experiment than as an ongoing technique. He shared his friend's love for simplified forms, but he liked to contrast bright hues with shadowed areas, in a kind of modernized version of baroque *chiaroscuro* techniques. His most Fauve-like paintings were done as deliberate attempts to emulate Matisse (or, in 1906–1907, **Raoul Dufy**). Other works present an interplay of colors and patches of light and dark in a manner reminiscent of the urban **Nabis,** especially **Edouard Vuillard.** After the death of his mother in 1907, Marquet lived as something of a vagabond, touring Western Europe, North Africa, Russia, and the Middle East.

REFERENCES:

Jean-Paul Crespelle, *The Fauves,* translated by Anita Brookner (Greenwich, Conn.: New York Graphic Society, 1962);

Joseph-Emile Muller, *Fauvism* (New York & Washington, D.C.: Praeger, 1967);

John Russell, *The World of Matisse, 1869–1954* (New York: Time-Life Books, 1969).

— J.H.

Promotional card distributed by Roger Martin du Gard's publisher, Gallimard. The drawing is by Berthold Mahr.

ROGER MARTIN DU GARD

Novelist and playwright Roger Martin du Gard (1881–1958), who won the Nobel Prize for Literature in 1937, is known chiefly for *Les Thibault* (1922–1940; translated as *The Thibaults*), an eight-part series novel in the realistic mode. After **Marcel Proust**'s *A la recherche du temps perdu* (1913–1927; translated as *Remembrance of Things Past*), *Les Thibault* is probably the finest series novel in twentieth-century France. Other well-known works by Martin du Gard include *Jean Barois* (1913; translated), a novel in dialogue form, which transposes the **Dreyfus Affair** into fiction; *Confidence africaine* (1931; African Confession), a novella concerning incest; and *Un Tactiturne* (1932; A Taciturn Man), a play produced by **Louis Jouvet**. A lengthy posthumous novel, *Le Lieutenant-Colonel de Maumort*, appeared in 1983. A close friend of **André Gide,** Martin du Gard wrote *Notes sur André Gide* (1951; translated as *Recollections of André Gide*), and their correspondence has also been published. His massive journal was published in 1994.

Les *Thibault* is both a psychological study and a novel of manners. Built around the Thibault family, it portrays the differences in character between two brothers, Antoine and Jacques; their tender relationship with their foster sister, Gise; their difficulties with their overbearing father; and their sentimental adventures, against the background of upper-middle-class French society in the early years of the twentieth century. As a parallel and contrast to the Thibaults, the novelist created another family, the Fontanins, with a pious, Protestant mother, a philandering father, son Daniel (a friend of Jacques), and daughter Jenny. Martin du Gard excelled in depicting adolescents and their efforts to find themselves in a society that is rigid and moralistic. His interest in medicine is shown in his portrayal of Antoine, a doctor—among the most searching of such studies in French literature.

Les Thibault is also concerned with social and political forces and events, most strikingly **World War I.** Part seven, *L'Eté 1914* (1936; translated as *Summer 1914*), is a lengthy and historically faithful study of the weeks leading to the declaration of war that August. The author's background as a historian (he had studied at the Ecole des Chartes and taken a degree as a historiographer-paleographer in 1905) served him well in this meticulous, yet dramatic, reconstruction of events, during which he also follows the lives of the Thibaults and Fontanins. Jacques's vain efforts, as a young socialist, to rally workers throughout Europe against the war are portrayed sympathetically by Martin du Gard, who had been at the front and, in the 1930s, vigorously defended pacifism. Jacques's death as a result of his idealism in *L'Eté 1914* is paralleled by that of Antoine in part eight, *Epilogue* (1940; translation published in *Summer 1914*), where he dies sometime after having been exposed to poisonous gas at the front. *Les Thibault* may be seen as a commentary on French society and European politics of the early twentieth century, as well as a study of human behavior. It has been appreciated by Marxist critics, among them György Lukács.

REFERENCES:

Denis Boak, *Roger Martin du Gard* (Oxford: Clarendon Press, 1963);

Catharine Savage [Brosman], *Roger Martin du Gard* (New York: Twayne, 1968);

David Schalk, *Roger Martin du Gard: The Novelist and History* (Ithaca, N.Y.: Cornell University Press, 1967).

— C.S.B.

LÉONIDE MASSINE

Léonide Massine (1895–1979), a Russian dancer, joined **Serge Diaghilev**'s **Ballets Russes** in 1914, the year he created the role of Joseph in **Michel Fokine**'s *La Légende de Joseph* (*Legend of Joseph*). Already a splendid classical and character dancer, Massine developed his talents as a choreographer under Diaghilev.

His most famous ballets for the Ballets Russes were *Parade* (1917), *Le Tricorne* (1919; *The Three-Cornered Hat*), *La Boutique fantasque* (1919; The Fantastic Shop), and *Pulcinella* (1920). *Parade* is a particularly brilliant collaboration, combining the work of Massine; **Erik Satie,** the composer; **Jean Cocteau,** the librettist; and **Pablo Picasso,** the designer of sets, costumes, and curtain.

After the Diaghilev company folded in 1929, Massine worked with various Ballet Russe companies, ending up with the **Ballet Russe de Monte Carlo,** where he served as artistic director from 1938 to 1962. He choreographed *Gaîté parisienne* in 1938 and the film *The Red Shoes* in 1946. He spent his later years working in the United States.

REFERENCE:

Jack Anderson, *The One and Only: The Ballet Russe de Monte Carlo* (New York: Dance Horizons, 1981).

—A.P.E.

ANDRÉ MASSON

The best-known painters associated with **Surrealism,** most notably Salvador Dalí and **René Magritte** — have for the most part been associated with what might be termed the "naturalist" or "literalist" wing of the movement — those who produced dreamlike canvases, with an emphasis on illusionistic space and a traditional use of perspective. Other Surrealists, including André Masson (1896–1987) and the Chilean Roberto Matta, worked consistently in a visual language that is representational but highly abstracted. For Masson this approach was closely linked to the origins of Surrealism itself, particularly to the idea of psychic automatism: the attempt to paint directly from the subconscious via a Freudian free association. In the first five years of the Surrealist movement (1924–1929), the pioneers experimented with various tricks and games to elicit an art of free association, particularly the drawing game they called *Cadavre exquis* (Exquisite Corpse), in which each participant continued a drawing started by others, without being able to see what earlier players had done. As **André Breton** later wrote, "The pen that writes or the pencil that draws *spins* off an infinitely precious substance . . . charged with all the emotional potential contained within the poet or painter."

The form of Masson's early paintings was heavily influenced by **Cubism** — a form that was in many ways at war with the content. Paintings such as *Les Joueurs* (1923; *The Gamblers*) and *L'Aile* (1925; *The Wing*) have largely the appearance, and even the palette, of the analytical Cubist paintings of **Pablo Picasso.** The surface is divided into an interlocking grid of squares and triangles; the subject — gamblers at a card table, a bird in flight — is broken up and spread across the whole of the picture plane. At base, however, the Surrealist project (the direct expression of subconscious thoughts and desires) and that of the Cubists (the analysis of space and volume) are incompatible. Picasso's comment that Masson had "turned Cubism inside out" relates to the fact that Picasso's Cubism was an attempt at objective analysis of external forms, while Masson sought to express a subjective inner reality. It is not surprising that Masson moved quickly toward a qualitatively different medium, becoming increasingly preoccupied with automatic drawings. Then, in 1926–1927, he turned to sand paintings, applying glue in unplanned patches across the canvas, spreading it out with his fingers, and pouring sand onto the canvas. The uneven layers of sand and the glue-free patches of clean canvas provide not only a sense of depth to the near-random shapes but also a varied texture across the entire surface.

As with many others in Surrealist circles, Masson ran afoul of Breton and was among the prominent figures summarily purged in the second of Breton's *Manifestes du surréalisme* (1930; translation published in *Manifestoes of Surrealism*). This excommunication had little impact on Masson or the Surrealists. He drew closer to others who had been expelled along with him, especially **Antonin Artaud,** and he continued to participate in Surrealist exhibitions, though his art bore little resemblance to that of newer recruits to the movement.

Increasingly, Masson's painting was dominated by images of violence and sexuality — often both at once. His sand paintings had borne titles alluding to killing and devouring. His paintings from the late 1920s are filled with images of a violent eroticism, in which sexual imagery frequently mutates into images of death or mutilation. His experiences in **World War I,** during which he was severely wounded (in 1917), show up in sublimated images of skulls and bleak, shadowy woods. His abstracted nature scenes typically involve generalized slaughter. From the 1930s onward Masson experimented with several styles without ever settling comfortably into any one. Some works, including his *Labyrinthe* (1938), resemble Dalí's monstrous biomorphic shapes.

After his return to France from American exile during **World War II,** Masson published *Le Plaisir de peindre* (1950; *The Pleasure of Painting*), sections of which had appeared earlier in the magazine *Temps Modernes.* He began to emphasize a more relaxed sensuality, characterized by a loose, flowing style. He argued that the art of **Paul Cézanne** had led twentieth-century artists into a dead end: "A century of splendors and pictorial feasts (from [Eugène] Delacroix to [Auguste] Renoir) is succeeded by an ascetic era. Few artists, these fifty years, have escaped the linear imperative...." Drawing on arguments dating back to Delacroix and Théodore Géricault, Masson argued that a strong, linear style stifled any sense of motion. In the 1950s he began to seek an abstraction infused with Zen notions of spontaneity and intuitive flashes of enlightenment.

REFERENCES:

Michel Leiris, *André Masson and His Universe*, translated by Douglas Cooper (Geneva: Trois Collines, 1947);

Gaëtan Picon, *Surrealists and Surrealism, 1919–1939*, translated by James Emmans (New York: Rizzoli, 1977);

William S. Rubin, *André Masson* (New York: Museum of Modern Art, 1976).

—J.H.

Henri Matisse (Hélène Adant)

HENRI MATISSE

The career of Henri Matisse (1869–1954) marks the transition from the nineteenth-century avant-garde to that of the twentieth century. The product of an academic education and of affiliations (however brief) with rival modernist circles, Matisse and the other **Fauves** helped to delineate the emergence of new movements that transcended earlier artistic battles and posed a new set of issues and claims.

Matisse's early artistic training was in the studio of William Bouguereau (virtually the definitive academic artist), and he spent 1892–1897 working under Gustave Moreau. Moreau was a dreamy mystic, with eclectic tastes and a tolerance for individualism exceedingly rare in the ateliers around the Ecole des Beaux-Arts. At Moreau's studio Matisse met **Georges Rouault** and **Albert Marquet.**

Matisse's early works show a startling range of influences, from that of the seventeenth-century Dutch artist Jan de Heem to the Impressionists. Sometimes the influences merge in startling ways: his *La Desserte* (1897; *The Dinner Table*) is a de Heem reimagined by the Impressionists: a loosely painted rendering of a serving girl arranging flowers on a vast dinner table.

Precisely as Matisse was establishing friendships with artists who would later join him in the Fauve group (above all, **Maurice Vlaminck** and **André Derain**), he moved close to the Neo-Impressionists, led, after the death of Georges Seurat, by **Paul Signac.** The Neo-Impressionists sought to put Impressionism on a "scientific" basis, shaping their canvases in accord

with optical and psychological principles to produce an "integral canvas" in which each color and each line would contribute to a synthetic fusion of the real and the ideal. Matisse's *Luxe, calme, et volupté* (1904–1905; *Luxury, Calm, and Voluptuousness*) is modeled directly on works by the Neo-Impressionist Henri-Edmond Cross: scenes of nude women sunning themselves or brushing their hair on serene beaches. Matisse revises the models in ways that show clearly his differences with the Neo-Impressionists, however. While Cross's paintings have an underlying social-utopian reading (in which they represent the anarchist Golden Age of the future), Matisse's work is based on a poem — Charles Baudelaire's "L'Invitation au voyage" ("Invitation to Travel") — which promises only personal sanctuary and retreat from the world's cares. Stylistically, Matisse employs the pointillism of the Neo-Impressionists but strips that system of any scientific grounding. The small points of Cross and Signac are replaced by larger, oval lozenges of colors, selected intuitively with no emphasis on complementary colors or optical laws. Matisse absorbed the Neo-Impressionist idea of a harmonious, integral painting, but he rejected utterly the idea of a scientific painting: "When I choose a color," he wrote later, "it is not because of any scientific theory. It comes from observation, from feeling, from the innermost nature of the experience in question."

In 1905–1906 Matisse's art continued to evolve. The preliminary study for *Bonheur de vivre* (1905–1906; *Joy of Life*) keeps the lozengelike paint strokes of *Luxe, calme, et volupté* but combines them with long, ropelike outlines around certain figures and patches of loosely painted solid color. In the final version of the painting the surface is flatter while the nude figures have become sinuous, smoothly outlined shapes set off against brighter patches of color. In the portrait *Madame Matisse* (1905), dubbed *The Green Line* by Gertrude Stein, there are no longer any open areas; the canvas is filled with strongly outlined zones of a single color. Behind the figure of the painter's wife the canvas is divided between zones of red and green; her face is similarly divided, with the colors reversed. The "green line" refers to a broad, bold stripe of green down the middle of her face, which is divided (except for the mouth and eyes) into two distinct areas. Color has become arbitrary, but only with reference to the model. Within the painting the colors are chosen not to mirror reality but to make the painting itself work as an arrangement of pigments on a flat surface. (The green line, for example, helps to give the nose a distinct bridge it would otherwise lack.) Overall color and form are used to focus the artist's message; substitutions of different colors, simplifications, and exaggerations of form are acceptable precisely insofar as they impose the artist's vision on the viewer.

The exhibition of Matisse's works with those of colleagues such as Marquet and Vlaminck, in room seven of the 1905 **Salon d'Automne,** resulted in the derogatory epithet *fauve* (wild beast), by which the group became known. The name became a defiant affirmation of the demand for a radically new way of seeing and painting the subject. Matisse's *Danse,* a huge canvas painted in 1909 for a Russian connoisseur, captures his goal to subordinate everything in the work to a central rhythm. Everything not essential to the theme — all the details of background so essential in framing an academic work — is peeled away. A patch of green with an undulating edge stands in for the earth; the blue above is the sky. Bridging both are five nudes, their bodies impossibly elastic, dancing in a rough circle. The circle is deliberately broken: two hands in the foreground do not quite meet, and the efforts of the two dancers to grasp one another's hands gives to the whole dance a sense of unresolved tension.

Beginning in the second decade of the twentieth century, Matisse began to focus on domestic scenes in which areas of flat and patterned color are played off against each other. Forms became more simplified and

further abstracted, as in his *Danse* I (1931–1932) and II (1932–1933), in which abstracted, gray dancers are set off against smooth patches of pink, blue, and black. After a series of illnesses in the 1940s left him bedridden, he began to work on paper cutouts and collages; his 1947 book of images, *Jazz,* assembles bold, abstracted representations of jazz rhythms.

Apart from the specifics of his techniques and motifs, Matisse played a crucial role in making acceptable the idea that artistic truth is not a literal translation of the external world onto canvas. In the essay "L'Exactitude n'est pas la vérité" (1939; "Exactitude Is Not the Truth"), he insisted that "there is an inherent truth which must be disengaged from the outward appearance of the object to be represented. This is the only truth that matters."

REFERENCES:

Alfred H. Barr, Jr., *Matisse: His Art and His Public* (New York: Museum of Modern Art, 1951);

Jack Flam, *Matisse: The Man and His Art, 1869–1918* (Ithaca, N.Y.: Cornell University Press, 1986);

John Russell, *The World of Matisse, 1869–1954* (New York: Time-Life Books, 1969);

Nicholas Watkins, *Matisse* (Oxford: Phaidon, 1984).

— J.H.

CLAUDE MAURIAC

The son of the novelist **François Mauriac,** Claude Mauriac (1914–) has achieved his own considerable position in contemporary French letters through his fiction, criticism, and journalism. He is also known for his service as secretary to **Charles de Gaulle** (1944–1949).

Mauriac's career choice was influenced by childhood acquaintances with his father's famous literary friends, including **André Gide, André Malraux,** and **Jean Cocteau.** Among his early works were books on these authors, as well as Honoré de Balzac. In the 1950s he wrote two books on the cinema and *L'Alittérature contemporaine* (1958; translated as *The New Literature*), an influential essay on new trends in literature, especially the **Nouveau Roman** (New Novel). During the same decade he began to write innovative fiction of his own, starting with *Toutes les femmes sont fatales* (1957; translated as *All Women Are Fatal*) and *Le Dîner en ville* (1959; translated as *The Dinner Party*). These novels were followed by the splendid *La Marquise sortit à cinq heures* (1961; translated as *The Marquise Went Out at Five*), whose title was borrowed from a remark by **Paul Valéry,** and *L'Agrandissement* (1963; Enlargement). Unlike his father's novels, Mauriac's works undermine traditional fictional technique, chiefly by drawing on the mental processes of several characters at once in what he calls "interior dialogue" — a kind of collective stream of consciousness. Like **Marcel Proust,** whom he admires greatly, Mauriac devotes hundreds of pages to brief portions of time and follows the thought processes of his characters in great detail. Often classified with **Michel Butor, Alain Robbe-Grillet,** and other experimental writers as one of the New Novelists, Mauriac is different from them, especially Robbe-Grillet, in the depth of his psychological explorations.

Mauriac has also written a remarkable ten-volume series, *Le Temps immobile* (1974–1988; Immobile Time), combining elements of fiction, diary, and autobiography. Struggling with questions of identity, literary creation, politics, and aging, Mauriac meditates on time, his father, and himself in a world where the past and the present coexist. Portraits of the famous, including Malraux, de Gaulle, **Jean-Paul Sartre, Michel Foucault,** and of course his father are part of the rich fabric. In 1991 Mauriac published the first volume of *Le Temps accompli* (1991; Time Accomplished), a new series that treats Mauriac's life and familiar concerns beginning in 1983, without the frequent shifts to the past that characterize *Le Temps immobile. Le Pont du secret* (Bridge of Secrecy), the third volume of *Le Temps accompli,* was published in 1993.

REFERENCES:

Vivian Mercier, "Claude Mauriac: The Immobilization of Time," in his *The New Novel from Queneau to Pinget* (New York: Farrar, Straus & Giroux, 1971), pp. 315–362;

Leon Roudiez, "Claude Mauriac," in his *French Fiction Today* (New Brunswick: Rutgers University Press, 1972), pp. 132–151.

— C.S.B.

Charles de Gaulle awarding the Grand-Croix de la Légion d'Honneur to François Mauriac, 19 March 1960

FRANÇOIS MAURIAC

To many French readers from the 1920s until well past the middle of the twentieth century, François Mauriac (1885–1970) was the preeminent novelist of their country; his work was the exemplar of what fiction should be. His success was enormous, and honors were showered on him, including election to the Académie Française (1933), an honorary degree from Oxford University (1947), and the Nobel Prize for Literature (1952). His sensitive, vibrant prose has assured Mauriac a reputation as a great stylist. Although his major novels were translated into English, his fame was never as great in the United States as in Europe, in part because his world is essentially French, not to say provincial.

Mauriac's literary career was launched with a collection of poetry, *Les Mains jointes* (1909; Clasped Hands), which was praised by **Maurice Barrès.** Soon thereafter Mauriac began publishing soulful, usually short, novels that dwell on the psychological or family dramas of sensitive young men and women, often in the setting where he himself grew up — the city of Bordeaux and the surrounding region. Reflecting at least in part his own experience, his characters are influenced by society — particularly the institutions of the family and of religion — and nature — wind, pine trees, sun. Mauriac was the son of a pious Catholic mother, who was widowed when François was not quite two. The Roman Catholic faith, along with its social prescriptions, plays a major role in all his work. Another ever-present element in his novels is the passion of the flesh, suspect at best and condemned in most of its manifestations.

Mauriac's well-known novels of the 1920s include *Le Baiser au lépreux* (1922; translated as *The Kiss to the Leper*), *Le Désert de l'amour* (1925; translated as *The Desert of Love*), and *Thérèse Desqueyroux* (1927; translated as *Thérèse*). *Thérèse Desqueyroux* is probably the best known, but *Génitrix* (1923; translated in *The Family*) may well be Mauriac's finest novel of the decade. An account of the conflict involving a possessive mother, her sometimes rebellious middle-aged son, and the bride he takes fairly late in life, the novel illustrates better than any other of Mauriac's books the use of nature as a source of symbols and his evident conviction that passions rule human beings, possessing their bodies and spirits and turning life into a ferocious struggle.

At the end of the 1920s Mauriac underwent a religious crisis, which led him to question whether the artist's vocation was compatible with the Christian life. *Dieu et Mammon* (1929; translated as *God and Mammon*) is an outgrowth of this crisis. Its resolution, a transforming experience for Mauriac, led him to produce a more ambitious body of fiction, although not necessarily more impressive artistically and psychologically. These novels are often concerned with the phenomenon of conversion, as in *Le Nœud de vipères* (1932; translated as *Vipers' Tangle*) and *La Pharisienne* (1941; translated as *Woman of the Pharisees*).

In addition to fiction, Mauriac wrote criticism (including a book on **Marcel Proust**), a biography of Jean Racine, religious commentary, memoirs, and some successful and well-received plays, including *Asmodée* (1938; translated as *Asmodée; or, The Intruder*). His career as a journalist, which began in the 1930s, would alone have assured him a place in the cultural history of the twentieth century. Adopting rather conservative positions at first, he soon moved toward the Left, denouncing Francisco Franco, for example, during and after the **Spanish Civil War** (1936–1939). After the fall of France in 1940 and a brief enthusiasm for **Philippe Pétain**'s Vichy government, he rallied to the side of **Charles de Gaulle** and the Free French. Mauriac's pseudonymously published *Le Cahier noir* (1943; translated) is a denunciation of Nazi ideology. In the postwar period he criticized the excesses of political purges, and in the 1950s he entered the fray on colonialism, although he did not make public his opposition to the French presence in Algeria until de Gaulle, as president of the **Fifth Republic,** brought the **Algerian war** to a close. Some of his political positions, which he expressed in articles in the *Figaro* and later collected as *Bloc-Notes, 1951–1957* (1958; Notepad) and *Le Nou-*

veau Bloc-Notes, 1958–1960 (1961; New Notepad), enraged Catholic readers.

While many readers continued to admire Mauriac as a novelist, in the 1950s his work began to be overshadowed by changing literary trends, and he is no longer popular with young readers, who seem little interested in the nuances of his psychological studies and moral dramas. Ironically, he remains popular chiefly in the same sort of conservative circles that once considered his novels of passion scandalous. Mauriac remains, however, a major figure among French writers of the first half of the century. He was a consummate stylist, a painter of the eternal battle of good and evil for possession of the human soul, and a creator of a fictional world that can be situated at once among the pine trees of the Bordelais and everywhere that sensitive and passionate individuals face misunderstanding and unhappiness.

REFERENCES:

John E. Flower, *Intention and Achievement: An Essay on the Novels of François Mauriac* (Oxford: Clarendon Press, 1969);

Cecil Jenkins, *Mauriac* (New York: Barnes & Noble, 1965);

Malcolm Scott, *Mauriac: The Politics of a Novelist* (Edinburgh: Scottish Academic Press, 1980);

Maxwell A. Smith, *François Mauriac* (New York: Twayne, 1970).
                                                                    — C.S.B.

ANDRÉ MAUROIS

The prolific writer André Maurois (1885–1967) is best known in North America as the biographer of renowned literary and political figures such as Charles Dickens, Benjamin Disraeli, Victor Hugo, George Sand, Percy Bysshe Shelley, and George Gordon, Lord Byron. Maurois also wrote on François-René de Chateaubriand, Edward VII of England, Benjamin Franklin, **Marcel Proust,** Ivan Turgenev, and Voltaire, as well as publishing historical and social studies of France, England, and the United States. Most of his biographical and historical works have been translated into English.

Born Emile Herzog, Maurois was also a successful novelist. He began his career with *Les Silences du Colonel Bramble* (1918; translated as *The Silence of Colonel Bramble*), a fictionalized commentary on the sufferings of soldiers in **World War I,** based on what he had observed as a liaison officer assigned to the British army. This book and its sequel, *Les Discours du Docteur O'Grady* (1922; translated as *The Return of Doctor O'Grady*), had immediate success. He later produced a six-volume cycle of novels dealing with the problems of marriage: *Bernard Quesnay* (1926; translated), *Climats* (1928; translated as *Whatever Gods*

Jules Romains conferring the distinction of Grand Officier de la Légion d'Honneur on André Maurois, 1954 (Gerald Maurois)

May Be), *Le Cercle de famille* (1932; translated as *The Family Circle*), *L'Instinct du bonheur* (1934; translated as *A Time for Silence*), *Terre promise* (1945; translated as *Woman Without Love*), and *Les Roses de septembre* (1956; translated as *September Roses*). *Climats* is probably the best known of these books and is generally considered his fictional masterpiece.

Maurois, who had been a student of **Alain,** was elected to the Académie Française in 1938 and was awarded many prizes and honorary doctorates. He continues to be admired by the general reading public in France.

REFERENCES:

L. Clark Keating, *Andre Maurois* (New York: Twayne, 1969);

Jack Kolbert, *The Worlds of André Maurois* (Selinsgrove, Pa.: Susquehanna University Press, 1985).

— C.S.B.

CHARLES MAURRAS

The best-known monarchist among French literary figures of the twentieth century, Charles Maurras (1868–

1952) was a founder and the principal moving spirit of the **Action Française** movement, editing its newspaper with Léon Daudet. In the late nineteenth century Maurras achieved some renown for his verse and criticism. His critical studies, collected in books such as *Barbarie et poésie* (1925; Barbarity and Poetry), emphasize the classical values inherited from the ancient world and criticize the Romantic spirit, which he considered foreign to France. His literary achievements have fallen into obscurity, and not only because of his extremist political positions.

After the turn of the century Maurras devoted himself increasingly to politics, becoming a royalist after the **Dreyfus Affair** and having helped to found the Comité d'Action Française in 1899 as an outgrowth of the Ligue de la Patrie Française, which he considered too moderate. The group became known as the Ligue de l'Action Française in 1905, and on 21 March 1908 Maurras and Daudet published the first issue of the newspaper *Action Française*. Supporting the Orléanist monarchists, Maurras attempted to strengthen the political voice of the Catholic church as backing for his conservative agenda. Becoming known as the Action Française after **World War I,** the party

May 1968 demonstration (VIVA Dityvon)

was condemned by the Vatican in 1926 and dissolved in 1935, but Maurras and Daudet continued to publish the newspaper. During **World War II** they backed the **Vichy government** established after the German invasion of France in 1940. The paper ceased publication with the **Liberation** in 1944, and Maurras was arrested for collaboration with the Germans. In 1945 he was sentenced to life imprisonment at hard labor. In 1952 he was released for reasons of health but kept under a sort of house arrest in a clinic.

REFERENCES:

Pierre Boutang, *Maurras, la destinée et l'œuvre* (Paris: Plon, 1984);

Michael Sutton, *Nationalism, Positivism and Catholicism: The Politics of Charles Maurras and French Catholics 1890–1914* (Cambridge: Cambridge University Press, 1982).

— C.S.B.

MAY 1968 DEMONSTRATIONS

The so-called *événements* (events) of 1968, student protests culminating in rioting and a massive general strike during the month of May, precipitated a major governmental crisis. Coming as a surprise to President **Charles de Gaulle** and to the majority of the nation,

these dramatic events had an enduring psychological effect on French society and a considerable influence on French culture. They marked, or coincided with, changing tastes in literature and criticism, the eclipse of **Jean-Paul Sartre** and others as major spokesmen for youth, and the rise of new cultural stars, including some of the **Nouveaux Philosophes** (New Philosophers).

Ten years after the founding of the **Fifth Republic,** which had reestablished political and economic order in France and brought unprecedented prosperity, the crisis exposed the existence of unresolved conflicts. In retrospect the parliamentary elections of 1967 can be taken as a first warning that there was dissatisfaction with the regime. The right-of-center Gaullists narrowly won a majority in that election, and to have a comfortable working majority in the National Assembly they had to form a coalition with Valéry Giscard d'Estaing's right-wing Independent Republicans. De Gaulle was then in his tenth year of power, with four more years remaining in his second term. Whereas governments could be voted down and the political deck reshuffled under the constitutions of the **Third** and **Fourth Republics,** such flexibility was no longer possible.

The crisis developed on the new university campus at Nanterre, built in that working-class suburb of

Paris to help relieve the overcrowding at the original University of Paris. According to prevailing ideology in the late 1960s, the mission of the university system in France was to train young people to take their places in an increasingly technical society. Yet insufficient funds had been allocated to the universities, and they had been unable to hire enough capable faculty or to build enough new facilities. Dissatisfaction with the educational system was the primary factor behind the student unrest.

The Vietnam War also played an indirect role. After a Nanterre student was implicated in bombings at several American sites in Paris, including the American Express office, student militants protested his arrest. On 22 March they occupied the administration building to demonstrate against American "imperialism," giving rise to the "Mouvement du 22 mars" (March 22 Movement), which was led by **Daniel Cohn-Bendit** and other student activists and helped to coordinate the protests that followed. The campus was closed for a few days so that order might be restored. Yet protests continued at Nanterre, and all teaching was suspended there as of 3 May.

Student militants then took their campaign to the Sorbonne itself, in the heart of the **Latin Quarter** of Paris. When the university rector called in the dreaded CRS (Compagnies Républicaines de Sécurité), or riot police, pitched street battles occurred between students and police. Television amplified the repercussions of the events. The battles of 6 May resulted in the arrests of four hundred students and shocked the nation. The university was closed indefinitely, and students were ordered to abandon their barricades. But further melees, during which students hurled paving stones and Molotov cocktails, erupted on 10 May and continued into the night. By the next morning there had been another 460 arrests; 367 people had been injured, and more than 200 cars had been burned.

With television playing an important role in the events, claims of police brutality were heard. The trade unions began to support the students, although labor leaders were skeptical of the students' motives. Eventually some ten million workers went on strike, effectively paralyzing the country.

The drama reached a peak when de Gaulle vanished on 29 May, going to Germany to consult with French army officers there. By the time he returned the next day, he had resolved to stand firm. He dissolved the National Assembly and called for new elections. The result was a resounding pro–de Gaulle backlash, as citizens concerned about the breakdown in public order expressed their disapproval of the students' and unions' behavior. De Gaulle and his party won an overwhelming electoral victory.

For the workers the tangible result of May 1968 was, nevertheless, an immediate 7 percent pay raise, with another 3 percent coming later in the year. For the students a law was passed mandating a vast expansion of the national educational system: sixty-seven universities were created by 1972, thirteen of them in the vicinity of Paris.

In retrospect, some have seen the events of May 1968 as a symbol of a crisis in modern society, a form of revolt against the growing importance of the impersonal forces of technology. The Communists, whose leadership refused to endorse fully the actions of the striking workers, dismissed the students as mere upper-class children playing at revolution. Some commentators from other ideological backgrounds have also reached this conclusion.

REFERENCE:

Bernard E. Brown, *Protest in Paris: The Anatomy of a Revolt* (Morristown, N.J.: General Learning Press, 1974).

—D. O'C.

GEORGES MÉLIÈS

Georges Méliès (1861–1938) ranks with **Louis Lumière** and **Alice Guy** as a founding figure of French cinema. Méliès's works, which helped to establish movies with stories in commercial cinema, are still enchanting and wondrous creations.

Born in Paris, Méliès studied art and magic before purchasing the Théâtre Robert-Houdin in 1888 and beginning a successful career as an illusionist. He was inspired to try cinema when attending the premiere of the Lumière brothers' *cinématographe* screenings at the Grand Café on 28 December 1895. He offered to buy a *cinématographe* from the brothers, who turned him away, saying that cinema had no future. Méliès purchased a projector in England, and in April 1896 he began showing short films as part of his magic show. Later that year he began making his own films. At first he imitated Louis Lumière's documentation of everyday life, but he soon turned to fantasy and special effects. In 1897 he devoted his theater exclusively to showing movies. Success came quickly, owing in part to Méliès's innovations. After building the first studio in Europe, he was the first to film commercial movies indoors using artificial light and the first to experiment with multiple exposures, as well as time-lapse and stop-motion photography.

The films that have been preserved attest to Méliès's inventiveness. He re-created historical events, as in *Eruption volcanique à la Martinique* (1902; Volcanic Eruption in Martinique), and created imaginative films such as *L'Homme à la tête de caoutchouc* (1901; Man with a Rubber Head), a comic movie for which he constructed a pulley and ramp so that a camera could be moved to produce the illusion of a man's head expanding in a frame. Movies such as *Le Voyage dans la lune* (1902; *A Trip to the Moon*) have been compared to writings by Jules Verne and François Rabelais.

Méliès's emphasis on telling stories in his movies is even more significant for the history of cinema than his technical experiments. The success of his best-known work, *Le Voyage dans la lune,* established a public preference in France and abroad for fictional films over those taken from real life. In 1903 Méliès's brother, Gaston, opened an American production and distribution office for Méliès's films in New York, and a second branch was established in Montreal in 1905.

Méliès's films failed to evolve with the changing movie industry, and by 1910 audiences were familiar with his tricks, which other filmmakers imitated. His fortunes rapidly declined, and he made his last movie in 1913. Ten years later, even after selling his hundreds of films, he was bankrupt. By 1931 cineasts had rediscovered his work, and he was given the Légion d'Honneur for his contribution to cinema. **Georges Franju** paid homage to Méliès in his documentary *Le Grand Méliès* (1952; The Great Méliès).

REFERENCES:

Stan Brakhage, *Film Biographies* (Berkeley & Los Angeles: University of California Press, 1977);

Noël Burch, *Life to Those Shadows* (Berkeley & Los Angeles: University of California Press, 1990);

Paul Hammond, *Marvelous Méliès* (London: Gordon Fraser, 1974).

— T.C.

JEAN-PIERRE MELVILLE

Jean-Pierre Melville (1917–1973) was a respected and influential filmmaker whose early films were particularly influential among the directors of the **Nouvelle Vague** (New Wave).

Born Jean-Pierre Grumbach in Paris, he took his pseudonym from Herman Melville, his favorite writer. He became interested in film in his youth. After **World War II,** during which he served in the French military, he established his own production company. Between 1946 and 1972 he directed thirteen feature-length movies. Made independently on location with low budgets, these films often featured plots reminiscent of American crime thrillers.

Melville's reputation was launched with his first feature, *Le Silence de la mer* (1949; The Silence of the

Roger Duchesne (center) as the title character in Jean-Pierre Melville's 1955 movie, *Bob le flambeur*

Sea), based on a novel by **Vercors** and set during the German **Occupation** of France. Most of his works — including his best-known movie, *Bob le flambeur* (1955; Bob the Gambler) — draw on American **film noir,** a hard-boiled style that appeared in films such as Billy Wilder's *Double Indemnity* (1944), Robert Siodmak's *The Killers* (1946), and Rudolph Maté's *D.O.A.* (1950). Similar in tone to John Huston's film noir *The Asphalt Jungle* (1950), **Bob le flambeur** succeeded in breathing new life into what had become a tired convention.

Melville also appeared as an actor in his own films and others. **Jean-Luc Godard** paid him tribute in *A bout de souffle* (1959; *Breathless*) by casting him as a novelist interviewed by an eager American journalist (played by Jean Seberg).

REFERENCES:

Thomas M. Kavanagh, "The Narrative of Chance in Melville's *Bob le flambeur," Michigan Romance Studies,* 13 (1994): 139–158;

Colin McArthur, *Underworld USA* (London: British Film Institute, 1972);

Jean Wagner, *Jean-Pierre Melville* (Paris: Seghers, 1963).

— T.C.

MAURICE MERLEAU-PONTY

Philosopher Maurice Merleau-Ponty (1908–1961) is widely considered the greatest phenomenologist in France. Like other phenomenologists, Merleau-Ponty sought to gain a better understanding of the world — to explore the nature of experience without preconceived assumptions about it — but his ideas stand out in their emphasis on the importance of the body in human perception and his concession that any understanding of human existence is necessarily incomplete.

Merleau-Ponty's friend **Jean-Paul Sartre** introduced him to the phenomenology of Edmund Husserl. In 1945 Merleau-Ponty helped Sartre and **Simone de Beauvoir** establish the magazine *Temps modernes,* and he served as an editor for the journal for seven years. He also published his major work in 1945: *La Phénoménologie de la perception* (translated as *Phenomenology of Perception*). In this book Merleau-Ponty attempted to apply Husserl's ideas about experience to the physical world, stressing the primacy of perception as the mode of access to reality while affirming the reality of the world, which transcends human consciousness. Challenging Sartre's **existentialist** notion of complete freedom, he proposed that people simultaneously affect and are affected by the world. Merleau-Ponty was also interested in language, art, and the philosophy of history, and for some years he adopted a Marxist perspective, as in *Humanisme et terreur* (1947; translated as *Humanism and Terror*).

Though Merleau-Ponty was a classmate of Beauvoir and Sartre at the **Ecole Normale Supérieure** and for decades was closely associated with them and postwar existentialism, he broke with them after the Korean War began because he could no longer condone their hostility to the West and their adherence to Stalinist Communism, which he had earlier praised. Although he was also critical of capitalism, he came to believe that one was obliged to side with the Western democracies in the Cold War as long as the myth of a historical destiny for the Soviet Union was used to justify its extreme abuses of the ideal of socialist society. His important study *Les Aventures de la dialectique* (1955; translated as *Adventures of the Dialectic*) is a critique of Marxist ideology in the Cold War context.

REFERENCES:

Garth Gillan, ed., *The Horizons of the Flesh: Critical Perspectives on the Thought of Merleau-Ponty* (Carbondale & Edwardsville: Southern Illinois University Press, 1973);

Richard L. Lanigan, *Speaking and Semiology: Maurice Merleau-Ponty's Phenomenological Theory of Existential Communication* (The Hague: Mouton, 1972);

Kerry H. Whiteside, *Merleau-Ponty and the Foundation of an Existential Politics* (Princeton: Princeton University Press, 1988).

— C.S.B.

OLIVIER MESSIAEN

Olivier Messiaen (1908–1992) was the most important mid-twentieth-century French composer. At once emo-

tional and highly intellectual, his music celebrates love, nature, and especially his religious beliefs.

Beginning in the 1930s, Messiaen enlarged the resources of music in several ways, attempting to express the ineffable. Avoiding traditional major and minor scales, he invented new ones inspired by those of ancient Greece, India, Asia, and above all the songs of birds, which he began notating in his youth. He also avoided regular rhythmic patterns by altering the duration of his notes by fractional amounts. By using these nonmetrical rhythms he hoped to express the idea of timeless eternity, particularly in his *Quatuor pour la fin du temps* (1941; Quartet for the End of Time), written and first performed while he was a prisoner of war.

Beginning in 1931 Messiaen was organist at L'Eglise de la Trinité in Paris, where his improvisations proved him to be one of the great organists of the twentieth century. His compositions for organ are also noteworthy. He began teaching at the Ecole Normale de Musique and at the Schola Cantorum in 1936, and in 1942 he joined the faculty at his alma mater, the Paris Conservatory. There his course in musical analysis attracted and influenced a group of young composers reacting against the neoclassicism of **Igor Stravinsky** and others (the predominant style between the wars) and searching for new ideas. Among these students were **Pierre Boulez,** Karlheinz Stockhausen, and Iannis Xenakis. Messiaen's two-volume *Technique de mon langage musical* (1944; translated as *The Technique of My Musical Language*) also broadened their awareness of non-Western music.

Messiaen was particularly influential in his writing of total serial music, in which every musical element — pitch and duration of notes, dynamics, tempo, and timbre — is predetermined by formula and devoid of conventional expression. One such work, his piano composition *Mode de valeurs et d'intensité* (1949; Modes of Durations and Intensity), was one of the truly revolutionary pieces of its time. This technique dominated advanced musical thinking for some time.

In the 1950s Messiaen drew on bird songs for many of his compositions, including *Oiseaux exotiques* (1956; Exotic Birds) for piano and chamber orchestra and the lengthy piano piece *Catalogue d'oiseaux* (1958; Catalogue of Birds), which calls on the pianist to span the entire keyboard at vertiginous speeds. Like many of Messiaen's piano compositions, it is so difficult to play that it is beyond the capabilities of most pianists.

In his orchestral music Messiaen generally used huge groups of instruments. His ten-movement symphony *Turangalîla* (1949), one of his masterpieces, uses as many as one hundred, including several percussion instruments and the *ondes martenot,* an electronic instrument that makes voicelike sounds. His *La Transfiguration de notre Seigneur Jésus-Christ* (1969; The Transfiguration of Our Lord Jesus Christ), a ninety-minute piece for large orchestra, includes marimbas, vibraphones, many other percussion instruments, and a huge choir.

Messiaen said of his music, "All my works, either religious or not, are documents of faith glorifying the mystery of Christ. Through my poor stammerings about the Divine I have tried to find a music signifying a new epoch, a living and singing music." He also wrote, "I search for a sparkling music which would give voluptuously refined pleasure to the ear."

REFERENCES:

Carla Huston Bell, *Olivier Messiaen* (Boston: Twayne, 1984);

Paul Griffiths, *Olivier Messiaen and the Music of Time* (London: Faber & Faber, 1985).

— P.S.H.

CHRISTIAN METZ

During the 1960s and 1970s Christian Metz (1931–1992) helped to shift the orientation of French film theory away from the **New Wave** emphasis on the auteur to a semiotic analysis of films as texts; that is, as networks of autonomous codes independent of individuals such as directors, screenwriters, or stars. His work aided in the establishment of film theory as an accepted scholarly field and of semiotics as a major methodology for film theorists.

Trained in linguistics, Metz analyzed cinema as a **structuralist** might engage a problem in anthropology or history. Inspired by the work of **Roland Barthes,** Metz wrote essays exploring the features that made film resemble the elements of language. These writings were collected in *Essais sur la signification au cinéma* (1968; Essays on Signification in Cinema) and *Langage et cinéma* (1970; Language and Cinema). Metz later turned to psychoanalysis in *Le Signifiant imaginaire* (1977; translated as *The Imaginary Signifier*), which aligned film theory with the work of **Jacques Lacan** and other French psychoanalysts.

REFERENCE:

Marc Vernet and others, *Christian Metz et la théorie du cinéma* (Paris: Iris, 1990).

— T.C.

JEAN METZINGER

Jean Metzinger (1883–1956) and **Albert Gleizes** played an important role among those artists most concerned with defining **Cubism** as an artistic system, instead of a collection of ad hoc practices. Their book *Du cubisme* (1912; translated as *Cubism*) was a sustained effort to define and describe the nascent movement for viewers and artists.

Metzinger moved to Paris and settled in the **Montmartre** district in 1903. In 1909–1910 he became acquainted with the circle of artists grouped around **Pablo Picasso** and **Georges Braque,** becoming close friends with Gleizes and the artists of the so-called Puteaux circle (including **Marcel Duchamp** and **Raymond Duchamp-Villon**). Metzinger's first, tentative experiments with Cubist ideas date from this period.

In his essay "Note sur la peinture" (1910; translated as "A Note on Painting") Metzinger began his efforts to define Cubism, focusing on the idea of *simultaneity* — the replacement of traditional perspective so as to convey all aspects of the object at the same time. In *Du cubisme* Metzinger and Gleizes treated the new art as the definitive break with "superficial realism," which they identified with Impressionism. For them Cubism marked a genuine realism in its relentless attempt to analyze and define: "To compose, to construct, to design, reduces itself to this: to determine by our own activity the dynamism of form." At the same time the authors asserted, "Cubism, which has been accused of being a system, condemns all systems." They explained that Cubism was a *method* by which the artist could sweep away all limiting systems in search of "an indefinite liberty" to explore and reconstruct reality, with the aim of achieving beauty.

In regard to the so-called Cubist room at the 1911 **Salon des Indépendants, Guillaume Apollinaire** claimed that Metzinger was "the only adept of Cubism in the proper sense." Few critics since have agreed. Metzinger's art remained for the most part in the realm of pastiche: his *Paysage cubiste* (1911; *Cubist Landscape*) recalls Picasso's work of five years before, while his portrait of Gleizes (1912) is modeled on the works of **Juan Gris** (the resemblance is primarily superficial, however, with an underlying reliance on a rather traditional composition). Metzinger's *Danseuse au café* (1912; *Dancer in a Café*) is not an unattractive picture, but it is a somewhat deceptive one — a café scene like those of Henri de Toulouse-Lautrec, with a Cubist overlay. It is "Cubist" only where the fragmenting of the image interferes with an easy legibility of the major figures. By the 1920s, in paintings such as *L'Embarquement d'Arlequin* (1921; *Embarkation of Harlequin*), Metzinger had largely abandoned any specifically Cubist techniques. He claimed, however, that he had not abandoned Cubism. On the contrary, he said that he had so thoroughly realized it that it was no longer visible. In practice, however, his paintings remained in a partly abstracted, but largely traditional, vein of figurative art.

REFERENCES:

Douglas Cooper, *The Cubist Epoch* (London: Phaidon, 1971);

John Golding, *Cubism: A History and an Analysis, 1907–1914* (Boston: Boston Book & Art Shop, 1959);

Christopher Green, *Cubism and Its Enemies: Modern Movements and Reaction in French Art, 1916–1928* (New Haven & London: Yale University Press, 1987);

Robert Rosenblum, *Cubism and Twentieth-Century Art* (New York: Abrams, 1961).

— J.H.

Michaux guarded his private life carefully and never played the role of the literary man. He married during the German **Occupation** of France in **World War II;** his wife died in 1948. In 1956 he began experimenting with mescaline, which had a direct influence on his poetry and art during the ensuing years. In 1965 he rejected the Grand Prix National des Lettres.

REFERENCES:

Malcolm Bowie, *Henri Michaux: A Study of His Literary Works* (Oxford: Clarendon Press, 1973);

Laurie Edson, *Henri Michaux and the Poetics of Movement* (Stanford, Cal.: Anma Libri, 1985);

Virginia A. La Charité, *Henri Michaux* (Boston: Twayne, 1977);

Henri Michaux, *Selected Writings,* translated, with an introduction, by Richard Ellmann (New York: New Directions, 1951).

— C.S.B.

HENRI MICHAUX

Henri Michaux (1899–1984) was one of the most important poetic voices of his generation. Also an artist, he illustrated his volumes of poetry and exhibited his pen-and-ink drawings and watercolors at galleries in France and many other countries. Although his poetry, most of which is in free verse or poetic prose, seems straightforward and simply crafted, it is psychologically and verbally complex, difficult to translate because of its neologisms, puns, and other sorts of wordplay.

Born in Namur, Belgium, Michaux journeyed around the world as a sailor before settling in Paris in 1924, and he remained a great traveler for some decades. In Paris he was acquainted with members of the **Surrealist** movement. Always a maverick, he did not join the group, but in some ways his work constitutes the finest fulfillment of certain Surrealist premises, in particular by its use of dream material. The originality of his vision was revealed in his first collection, *Qui je fus* (1927; Who I Was), which was followed in 1929 by *Ecuador* (translated as *Ecuador, A Travel Journal*) and *Mes propriétés* (My Properties). In the 1930s and later, his many poems create a surreal world, drawn from the depths of the imagination, populated by strange beings, and characterized by an explosive violence. *La Nuit remue* (1935; The Night Moves) and *L'Espace du dedans* (1944; The Space Within) are two of his many impressive volumes. In Plume, a ne'er-do-well and strangely passive character who appears in many of Michaux's prose poems, Michaux incarnates the maladjustment he evidently sees as inevitable in the modern world. Translations of many of his poems were published in *Selected Writings* (1951).

DARIUS MILHAUD

Darius Milhaud (1892–1974) was the most versatile and prolific member of **Les Six.** He wrote more than five hundred compositions ranging from amusing short piano pieces to serious full-length operas, several ballets, film and theater music, symphonies, concertos, and chamber music.

After studying at the Paris Conservatory, Milhaud went to Brazil in 1917 as secretary to poet-diplomat **Paul Claudel,** who later wrote librettos for some of Milhaud's operas. In Brazil Milhaud became acquainted with the rhythms and orchestration of popular dances, such as the samba, which strongly colored his *Saudades do Brasil* (1921; Souvenirs of Brazil) for piano, as well as his ballet *Le Bœuf sur le toit* (1920; The Ox on the Roof). Soon after his return to France in 1919 he became a member of Les Six, the innovative group of young composers who carried out **Jean Cocteau**'s advice to avoid the rich aestheticism of the Romantic composers and to write "everyday" music instead. Milhaud's motto became "A bas Wagner!" (Down with Wagner!). With four members of Les Six, Milhaud wrote music for Cocteau's ballet *Les Mariés de la Tour Eiffel* (1921; The Newlyweds of the Eiffel Tower).

After a trip to New York, jazz became an important element of Milhaud's style, particularly in one of his best-known compositions, the ballet *La Création du monde* (1923; The Creation of the World). Later works reflected the folk music and dances of his native Provence and of other places he visited. In the years between the world wars much of Milhaud's music was polytonal (in more than one key simultaneously), making for sharp dissonances and often creating a raffish, out-of-focus effect that is sometimes compared to the **Cubism** of **Georges Braque** and **Pablo Picasso.**

In 1940 Milhaud went to the United States to teach at Mills College in California and during the summers at the Aspen Music School in Colorado. Many American composers studied with him, including several from the jazz world such as Dave Brubeck. After **World War II** Milhaud returned to Paris as professor of composition at the Paris Conservatory and divided his time among California, Colorado, and Paris until a few years before his death.

REFERENCES:

Paul Collaer, *Darius Milhaud* (San Francisco: S.F. Press, 1988);

James Harding, *The Ox on the Roof: Scenes from Musical Life in Paris in the Twenties* (New York: St. Martin's Press, 1972);

Darius Milhaud, *Notes Without Music,* translated by Donald Evans (London: Dobson, 1952).

— P.S.H.

LA MILICE FRANÇAISE

During the German **Occupation** of France in **World War II,** the notorious Milice Française (French Militia) helped to enforce **Vichy government** laws and fought alongside German military units against the guerrilla fighters of the French **Resistance.** The Milice was founded in 1942 by Joseph Darnand, a decorated hero of **World War I** and an admirer of **Philippe Pétain,** head of the **Vichy government** established to govern the so-called **Free Zone** after the German invasion of 1940. The group was originally called the Service d'Ordre Légionnaire (Legionnaires' Police Force) because it began as part of Xavier Vallat's Légion des Combattants (Combatants). Becoming an independent police force by January 1943, the Milice had about thirty thousand members by 1944 — mostly young men, who pledged themselves to what they called the crusade against Bolshevism. Their membership exempted them from the Service du Travail Obligatoire (Obligatory Work Service), or STO, program that the Germans had established, and many of the people the Milice hunted down were those who had refused to report for this service.

During the **épuration,** or purge trials, that took place after the **Liberation,** Darnand was convicted of treason and hanged. The Milice has since come to symbolize the extremes of perverted idealism that manifested themselves during the Occupation. The Milice's counterterror measures against Resistance supporters have been compared to certain aspects of the French army's behavior during the **Algerian war.**

Mistinguett singing for striking Frenchmen, June 1936

REFERENCE:

William D. Halls, *The Youth of Vichy France* (New York: Oxford University Press, 1981).

— D.O'C.

MISTINGUETT

Josephine Baker and Jeanne-Marie Bourgeois (1873–1956), who took the stage name Mistinguett, were the best-known women in French music halls between the world wars. Mistinguett's talents were well suited to an era of the musical revue, a form that had all but disappeared by the time she retired in 1951.

Early in her career Mistinguett became well known for her songs and sketches in musical revues at the Moulin Rouge, the Folies-Bergère (where she often performed with **Maurice Chevalier**), and especially the Casino de Paris. In 1908 at the Moulin Rouge she and Max Dearly created a new dance craze when they introduced the *valse chaloupée* (Apache dance), in which a macho male dancer throws around and "whips" his revealingly clad female partner. During **World War I** Mistinguett established her reputation with shows such as *Paris qui danse* (Paris Dances), *Paris qui jazz* (Paris Jazzes), and *En douce* (Easy Does It) at the Casino.

Like her vocal range, Mistinguett's repertory of songs was limited, but they helped create the image of a pert, saucy Parisienne with a ready reply on her lips.

Among her hit songs were "Mon homme" (1920; My Man), "Ça c'est Paris" (1926; That's Paris), and "C'est vrai" (1935; It's True). Fanny Brice performed an English version of "Mon homme" in the *Ziegfeld Follies* after Mistinguett visited the United States in 1924.

REFERENCE:
David Bret, *The Mistinguett Legend* (New York: St. Martin's Press, 1990).

—J.P.McN.

ARIANE MNOUCHKINE

Ariane Mnouchkine (1939–) has been the primary inspiration, facilitator, and guiding light of the theater cooperative known as the **Théâtre du Soleil** since its inception in 1964. A utopian commune, the company has no director, and each member contributes on an equal footing with all the others; but Mnouchkine, who shuns personal publicity, is first among equals, combining the contributions of others and organizing the major productions.

In 1959 Mnouchkine and Martine Franck brought together members of student theatrical societies in the Association Théâtrale des Etudiants de Paris, which they founded. Mnouchkine soon went beyond what was merely an independent student theater. In the early 1960s she took an extended trip to East Asia, where she observed ritual theater as well as Chinese theater of the Maoist period just prior to the Cultural Revolution. Then in summer 1963, at the first **Nancy Festival** of French student theater, leaders of the student movement discussed liberation from the cultural domination of the older generation. No longer content with standard staging of traditional plays, students began planning the total restructuring of theater. By 1964, when the Théâtre du Soleil was founded, the restructuring was under way.

With its roots in student theater the Théâtre du Soleil became a professional company, enrolling some fifty actors and technicians who lived together and collaborated on theatrical creations. Mnouchkine organized these shows, often providing the vision and the setting. After the events of **May 1968** she produced the troupe's best-known collective realizations: *Les Clowns* (1969; The Clowns), *1789* (1970), and *1793* (1972). The last two works are historical pageants about the French Revolution. Instead of having famous scenes acted out, Mnouchkine has period characters tell each other — and the audience — about the "news" of their time, performing (and reacting to) historical events as they understand them. For these plays Mnouchkine reinvented the concept of stage space. In an aging warehouse in Vincennes, a Paris suburb, the

company created a series of low stages connected by walkways, with standing room all around where the public milled about among the sets or sat in overhanging seating. This intermingling of stages and spectators brought the audience into the act, as it reacted to tales from history along with the actors.

Following in the footsteps of her father, Alexandre Mnouchkine, Ariane has directed two memorable films, which show the Théâtre du Soleil in action. In 1974 she made a film version of *1789;* she then wrote and directed *Molière*, a four-hour-long cinematic celebration of theater. In 1979 she and her company returned to the Vincennes warehouse to perform *Méphisto: Le roman d'une carrière* (Mephisto: The Novel of a Career), based on a Klaus Mann text.

In the 1980s Mnouchkine returned to the staging of William Shakespeare (the Théâtre du Soleil had performed *A Midsummer Night's Dream* in 1968). Using her own French translations of *Richard II* (1981) and *Twelfth Night* (1982), and a version of *Henry IV, Part I* (1984), she applied to Shakespeare the hieratic techniques of Oriental theater. In 1985 she directed the Théâtre du Soleil in **Hélène Cixous**'s *Norodom Sihanouk,* about Cambodia.

REFERENCES:
Thomas J. Donahue, "Mnouchkine, Vilar and Copeau: Popular Theater and Paradox," *Modern Language Studies,* 21 (Fall 1991): 31–42;
Bernard Dort, "L'Age de la représentation," in *Le Théâtre en France. 2: De la Révolution à nos jours,* edited by Jacqueline de Jomaron (Paris: Armand Colin, 1989), pp. 451–534;
Adrian Kiernander, *Ariane Mnouchkine and the Théâtre du Soleil* (New York: Cambridge University Press, 1993);
Kiernander, "The Orient, the Feminine: The Use of Interculturalism by the Théâtre du Soleil," in *Gender in Performance,* edited by Laurence Senelick (Hanover, N.H.: University Press of New England for Tufts University, 1992), pp. 183–192.

—R.J.N.

PATRICK MODIANO

Patrick Modiano (1945–) has established himself as a major French novelist of the latter half of the twentieth century. Like the **Nouveaux Romanciers** (New Novelists) of an earlier generation, Modiano creates a fictional world of narrative and moral uncertainty that strikes a familiar chord with many readers, describing this world of alienation and fear in his own transparently elegant style.

The son of a Flemish mother and a Middle Eastern Sephardic Jewish father, Modiano was born in Paris after the **Liberation** of the city from the German **Occupation.** Modiano has nevertheless often set his fiction in occupied France during **World War II.** He maintains that he is not fascinated by the period for itself; instead, he says, "the Occupation . . . supplies me with this ideal — somewhat turbid — climate, this somewhat bizarre light. But, in reality, it is a matter of the inordinately magnified image of what is happening today." The title of his first novel, *La Place de l'Etoile* (1968; The Place of the Star), is a pun on the name of a famous Paris plaza (now Place Charles de Gaulle) and the spot on the breast where Germans forced Jews to wear a yellow star. The alienated protagonist of *La Place de l'Etoile* lives out a phantasmagoric existence, imagining himself in various Jewish roles, from the Jew as martyr to the Jew as avenger. Yet whatever his fantasy, he remains an ostracized foreigner. Subsequent works concerned with German-occupied Paris include *La Ronde de nuit* (1971; translated as *Night Rounds*) and *Les Boulevards de ceinture* (1972; translated as *Ring Roads*), which won the Grand Prix du Roman. Modiano's screenplay for *Lacombe Lucien* (1974; translated), written with **Louis Malle,** also treats the Occupation.

Modiano won the prestigious Prix Goncourt for *Rue des Boutiques Obscures* (1980; translated as *Missing Person*), the story of an amnesiac detective whose search for his lost identity leads him back to the shadowy period of the Occupation. Since 1980 Modiano has written other fiction — including his fifteenth novel, *Un Cirque passe* (1992; A Circus Is Passing); children's books; a play, *La Polka* (produced in 1974); and an autobiographical work, *Remise de peine* (1988; Deferral of Punishment/Pain), which resembles his fiction in its concern with unexplained anguish and its hazy, discontinuous, fragmentary universe.

REFERENCES:

Alan Morris, "Patrick Modiano," in *Beyond the Nouveau Roman: Essays on the Contemporary French Novel,* edited by Michael Tilby (New York: Berg, 1990), pp. 177–200;

Gerald Prince, "Re-Membering Modiano, or Something Happened," *Sub-Stance,* no. 49 (1986): 35–43.

— C.S.B.

GASTON MODOT

Gaston Modot (1887–1970) was one of the most respected character actors in French motion pictures. During his lengthy career the cinema evolved enormously: he began in 1909 as an actor and screenwriter and made his last film appearance in 1962 at the height of the innovations of the **Nouvelle Vague** (New Wave).

Modot appeared in **Luis Buñuel's Surrealist** film *L'Age d'or* (1930; *The Golden Age*), which created a public scandal for its attacks on institutions and con-

ventional morality. Modot also starred in classic films such as **Julien Duvivier's** *Pépé le Moko* (1936), **Jean Renoir's** *La Grande Illusion* (1937; *Grand Illusion*) and *La Règle du jeu* (1939; *The Rules of the Game*), and **Marcel Carné's** *Les Enfants du paradis* (1945; *Children of Paradise*). Modot gave his best performances in Renoir's movies, bringing great sensitivity to his roles.

— W.L.

LE MONDE

Le Monde (The World), an employee-owned, independent daily Paris newspaper, has achieved a reputation of being comprehensive and almost scholarly in its coverage of French and international news, and it has many devoted readers at home and abroad. (Fourteen percent of its subscribers reside in countries other than France.) With its dense print, small headlines, and absence of photographs, *Le Monde* projects an image of seriousness. *Le Monde Diplomatique* (The Diplomatic World), *Le Monde de l'Education* (The World of Education), and *Le Monde Hebdomadaire* (The Weekly World) are successful spin-offs from the original daily.

Founded by Hubert Beuve-Méry in December 1944 — after the **Liberation** of most of France from German **Occupation** during **World War II** — *Le Monde* was modeled on the *Temps,* a Parisian daily, which had ceased publication in 1942, during the Occupation. Most of the journalists from the *Temps,* untainted by any suggestion of collaboration with the Nazis, joined the staff of the new paper. Beuve-Méry, a progressive Christian Democrat who had been active in the **Resistance,** remained director of the newspaper until 1969.

From the outset the *Monde* was attacked for its political positions, which were left of center but not radical. From the late 1940s Beuve-Méry advocated a strong, united Europe able to stand up to both the United States and the Soviet Union. With some justification, **Raymond Aron** denounced the paper's anti-Americanism, which he saw as being more virulent than its attacks on the Soviet Union. During the student riots and labor strikes of **May 1968,** both Gaullist and Communist critics attacked the *Monde* for its controversial support of the demonstrators. Some of the spirit of the student and worker uprisings infused the paper as Jacques Fauvet, Beuve-Méry's handpicked successor, hired several dozen new journalists, nearly all of whom had been deeply involved in and influenced by the student movement.

The *Monde* reached its highest circulation in the years just before the victory of François Mitterand and his left-wing coalition in 1981. In 1979 total circulation was about 445,000. Since 1981 circulation has slipped,

Offices of *Le Monde* on rue des Italiens, Paris

falling to three hundred thousand in 1990. To a considerable extent the paper's reputation for objectivity had been hurt by its close identification with the Socialist cause.

REFERENCES:

Jean-Noël Jeanneney and Jacques Julliard, *"Le Monde" de Beuve-Méry ou le métier d'Alceste* (Paris: Seuil, 1979);

Michel Legris, *"Le Monde" tel qu'il est* (Paris: Plon, 1976).

— J.P.McN.

CLAUDE MONET

It is commonplace to treat **Paul Cézanne** as a seminal figure in twentieth-century art, a forerunner of the **Cubists.** In contrast Claude Monet (1840–1926) is seen as a quintessentially nineteenth-century artist, bound to Impressionism. Nonetheless, Monet actually lived and worked for two decades longer in the twentieth century than Cézanne, and his influence and popularity began to grow just as the new century was dawning.

The son of a shopkeeper in Le Havre, Monet got his start as a caricaturist at local fairs. A major influence on his painting was the amateur Eugène Boudin, owner of a stationery and art supply shop, who encouraged him to paint out of doors, on the grounds that "everything that is painted on the spot always has a strength, a power, a vividness of touch that one doesn't find again in one's studio." In 1863 Monet moved to Paris to study under Charles Gleyre. In Gleyre's studio Monet met other artists who contributed to Impressionism, including Auguste Renoir and Alfred Sisley. During the Franco-Prussian War (1870–1871), Monet and Camille Pissarro fled to London, where they encountered for the first time the works of J. M. W. Turner.

Out of a diverse blend of influences, Monet's distinctive notion of the landscape began to take shape. He frequently invoked slogans involving spontaneity: "I don't paint landscapes," he once declared, "I paint moments." With a friend, Radical Party politician and future premier of France Georges Clemenceau, Monet adopted a stance of a naive and purely intuitive practice: "While you examine the world . . . philosophically, I simply exert myself toward a maximum of appearances, in direct correlation with unknown realities. . . . I have done nothing but observe what the universe has shown me, and then testified to that with my brush."

It was precisely this claim of a simple, unmediated reflection of reality that led hostile (or sometimes would-be successor) groups at the end of the century to denounce Impressionism as "superficial," concerned only with outward appearances. Diverse groups such as the Neo-Impressionists, the **Nabis,** the Symbolists, and later the **Fauves** all countered by expressing a need to capture the essence of the world, rather than its fleeting image.

To accept Monet's claim of spontaneity or the later attacks on that claim at face value is misleading, however. Monet's art is far from spontaneous, naive, or superficial. His coastal scenes from Etretat, painted repeatedly from the 1860s through the 1880s, are typical: while they capture the changing weather and light effects around the rocky cliffs, they also demonstrate a thorough absorption of Japanese wood-block prints by Hiroshige, especially his *Seashore at Izu.* Seemingly artless works by Monet such as the so-called haystack (actually grainstack) paintings (1891) omit traditional iconography (snoozing peasants, Biblical figures) and any comparative referent to establish size and distance. Yet they are intricately and carefully composed. The haystacks in the paintings are created from layers of dark paint over bright colors to convey the sense of light trickling through a huge but loosely arranged structure.

Monet's subject matter and style convey not so much a message as a broad attitude toward modern existence. In 1894 the Radical Party newspaper *Justice* devoted the front page of an issue to a long essay, "Révolution des cathédrales" (Revolution of the Cathedrals), in which Clemenceau called Monet's paintings of Rouen cathedral a convincing demonstration of the world, one which affirmed the "sovereignty of light." For Clemenceau, Monet swept away the idea of the world or nature as static or fixed, in favor of an image of eternal flux: "The wonder of Monet's sensing things is to see the stone vibrate and to have it given to us vibrating, bathed in luminous waves that collide and break into twinkling sparks. It is the end of the immutable canvas of death."

That notion of a direct, spontaneous depiction of a world in constant motion was already challenged when Clemenceau wrote his article. For the Neo-Impressionists around Georges Seurat and **Paul Signac,** evolving nature could be grasped only by rigorous study. For the Nabis such change was irrelevant, a shifting surface over an eternal, unchanging, and divine reality. For **Odilon Redon** any concern with the flux of the outside world was less interesting than what he saw when he looked into his own mind and fears. Cézanne and **Henri Matisse,** each in his own way, sought to capture an essential form beneath the shifting world of appearances. To all of these artists, Monet seemed a relic. Nonetheless, Monet's fascination with light and flux did not disappear. Some of the urban Nabis, particularly **Pierre Bonnard** and **Edouard Vuillard,** gradually moved back to a quasi-Impressionist focus on light and the spontaneity of modern existence.

REFERENCES:

Robert L. Herbert, "Method and Meaning in Monet," *Art in America,* 67 (1979), 98–108;

John House, *Monet: Nature into Art* (New Haven & London: Yale University Press, 1986);

John Rewald and Frances Weitzenhoffer, eds., *Aspects of Monet* (New York: Abrams, 1984);

Charles F. Stuckey, ed., *Monet: A Retrospective* (Hong Kong: Beaux Arts Editions, 1985);

Paul Hayes Tucker, *Monet at Argenteuil* (New Haven & London: Yale University Press, 1982).

—J.H.

Yves Montand

Yves Montand (1921–1991) was one of the most popular French singers and actors of the twentieth century.

Born Ivo Livi to a Jewish-Italian family that immigrated to Marseilles to escape Italian Fascism when he was two, Montand left school at age eleven, worked at odd jobs, and embarked on a career as a singer at age seventeen in Marseilles. By the end of **World War II** his lover **Edith Piaf** had helped him polish a style that he made his own: that of the urbane, worldly wise cabaret performer. His success came quickly. His rendition of the nostalgic song "Les Feuilles mortes" (1947; "Autumn Leaves") was an instant hit.

Montand's lengthy film career began with *Etoile sans lumière* (1946; *Star Without Light*), and **Henri-Georges Clouzot**'s *Le Salaire de la peur* (1953; *The Wages of Fear*) established Montand as a movie star. He starred opposite Marilyn Monroe in the Hollywood film *Let's Make Love* (1960). His marriage to **Simone Signoret,** whom he wed in 1951, withstood his well-publicized affairs with Monroe and others, lasting until Signoret's death in 1985. Both were active in left-wing and pacifist causes, but with the Soviet invasion of Czechoslovakia in 1968 Montand, like many French intellectuals, became disenchanted with Communism and grew politically conservative. He was given serious consideration in the 1980s as a center-right candidate for the French presidency.

After a decline in his film career during the 1970s, Montand made a comeback with acclaimed roles in *Jean de Florette* (1986) and *Manon des sources* (1986; *Manon of the Spring*). His only child, Valentin, was born to his lover Carole Amiel, some forty years his junior, in 1988. Montand died of a heart attack while making a film outside Paris in 1991.

REFERENCE:

Yves Montand, with Hervé Hamon and Patrick Rotman, *You See, I Haven't Forgotten* (New York: Knopf, 1992).

—J.P.McN.

Pierre Monteux

A conductor of world renown, Pierre Monteux (1875–1964) introduced a great deal of modern music to his audiences and played an important role in music in the United States. His manner before the orchestra was unemotional and even-tempered. **Igor Stravinsky** said that of all the conductors he had known, Monteux was "the least interested in calisthenic exhibitions for the entertainment of the audience and the most concerned to give clear signals to the orchestra."

After graduating from the Paris Conservatory as a violist and spending his apprentice years playing in orchestras, Monteux revealed his potential as a conductor when **Serge Diaghilev** invited him to conduct the **Ballets Russes** orchestra in 1911. During the next three years Monteux conducted the first performances of several modern works, including Stravinsky's

Petrouchka (1911) and the sensational *Le Sacre du printemps* (1913; translated as *The Rite of Spring*), in which the rhythmic complexities of the music were considered by some to make the work unplayable.

Monteux was later conductor for the New York Metropolitan Opera (1917–1919); the Boston Symphony Orchestra (1920–1924); the Amsterdam Concertebouw (1924–1929); the Orchestre Symphonique de Paris (1929–1938), which he founded; and the San Francisco Symphony Orchestra (1936–1952), which he developed into a first-class organization. He became a U.S. citizen in 1942. After his resignation from the San Francisco Symphony Orchestra, he resumed his career as a guest conductor. Among his other appearances was a series of performances at the Metropolitan Opera from 1953 to 1956. In 1961, at age eighty-six, he became director of the London Symphony Orchestra.

Monteux taught each summer at his conducting school in Hancock, Maine. Scores of young American conductors studied with him to learn his technique of achieving exciting, colorful performances with restrained and unemotional gestures.

REFERENCES:

John L. Holmes, *Conductors: A Record Collector's Guide* (London: Gollancz, 1988), pp. 198–201;

Harold C. Schonberg, *The Great Conductors* (New York: Simon & Schuster, 1967), pp. 328–330.

— P.S.H.

HENRY DE MONTHERLANT

Playwright and novelist Henry de Montherlant (1896–1972) is one of the most admired literary stylists of modern France. Because of the discipline and noble tone of his language, as well as his concern with moral dilemmas and psychological dramas like those of seventeenth-century French literature, his writing has been labeled *classic*. He brought to the French stage a superb sense of language and dramaturgy, and his plays will assuredly remain in the repertory.

Montherlant was not, however, widely admired as a man. Among major French writers of the twentieth century, he is surely the most thoroughly and most aggressively misogynistic. That this misogyny should be associated with his homosexuality — which he carefully disguised — is obvious; and yet his sexual tastes probably do not suffice to explain it. His scorn for women is echoed again and again in his work, especially in the tetralogy of novels that comprises *Les Jeunes Filles* (1936; translated as *The Girls*), *Pitié pour les femmes* (1937; translated as *Pity for Women*), *Le Démon du bien* (1937; translated as *The Demon of*

Good), and *Les Lépreuses* (1939; translated as *The Lepers*). As the second of these titles suggests, his misogyny is not unrelieved; indeed, it can be argued that he had an idealized idea of women and that he was irritated by their betrayal of their potentialities.

Montherlant created two sorts of female characters: the noble, virile ones whom he and his heroes could admire; and their opposites, clinging, sentimental, manipulative creatures who would destroy men and must therefore be cast off. Some of Montherlant's women, such as Soledad in *Les Bestiaires* (1926; translated as *The Bullfighters*), have elements of both types. In one of Montherlant's finest plays, *La Reine morte* (1942; translated as *Queen After Death*), the Spanish Infanta, a proud and self-controlled woman, is contrasted with Inès de Castro, a woman enslaved by love and maternity, who is secretly married to the prince and must be destroyed by the king for *raison d'état* (reasons of state). Even in her case, however, the imaginative poet in Montherlant portrays beautifully what he scorns: Inès's speech on pregnancy is unparalleled for its maternal tenderness.

Another reason for Montherlant's personal unpopularity is his aristocratic arrogance, which is apparent in most of his writing. Born into a noble family and baptized Henry Marie Joseph Frédéric Expedite Millon de Montherlant, he chose not only to acknowledge what separated him from others but to emphasize it, insisting that the values he inherited from the time when the aristocracy had not yet been dismantled — taste, style, courage, independence, disinterestedness — were supremely important, crucial to humanity as he wished it to be. He showed little but scorn for his own time. The heroes of his dramas, often borrowed from the past, have a noble disdain for the sort of self-interested calculations that, in Montherlant's view, are the ethic of the modern age. Often compared to the seventeenth-century playwright Pierre Corneille, whose dramas glorify duty and will, Montherlant was aware that Corneille's world and its belief in transcendent values had passed, and he consequently displayed an attitude of disabused superiority.

Montherlant also adopted political attitudes that enraged or scandalized his contemporaries. After having written about the value of war for developing virility in *Le Songe* (1922; translated as *The Dream*) and glorifying bullfighting in *Les Bestiaires,* he wrote *Le Solstice de juin* (1941; Summer Solstice), in which he blamed moral corruption in France for its rapid defeat by the Germans at the beginning of **World War II.** Moreover, similarities between his praise of sport and military virtues and certain Nazi tenets tended to reinforce the supposition that he was a Fascist at heart. It would, however, be erroneous to classify him as a militant collaborator or a fascist; he did not actively cooperate with the Germans during their **Occupation** of France and was only mildly punished at the end of the war for some statements he had made and for his failure to support the **Resistance.**

Among Montherlant's dramatic masterpieces is *Le Maître de Santiago* (1947; translated as *The Master of Santiago*), another work on a Hispanic theme. His novel *La Rose de sable* (1968; translated as *Desert Love*) is a critical treatment of French colonialism in North Africa. If it had been published in the 1930s, when it was written, Montherlant said, the book would have created intolerable international complications for France, and he waited more than thirty years to publish it.

In 1960 Montherlant was elected to the Académie Française. He committed suicide in 1972. His plays are regularly presented at the **Comédie-Française** and other Parisian theaters.

REFERENCES:

Lucille Becker, *Henry de Montherlant* (Carbondale: Southern Illinois University Press, 1970);

John Cruickshank, *Montherlant* (Edinburgh: Oliver & Boyd, 1964);

Richard J. Golsan, *Service Inutile: A Study of the Tragic in the Theatre of Henry de Montherlant* (University, Miss.: Romance Monographs, 1988).

— C.S.B.

MONTMARTRE

Located on a hill in the northern part of Paris, the area known as Montmartre became a center of artistic activity early in the twentieth century. Among the artists and poets who found lodgings and studios there are those who lived and worked at the **Bateau Lavoir** — including **Pablo Picasso, Juan Gris,** and **Max Jacob** — and frequented the famous **Cabaret du Lapin Agile** and the club known as the Chat Noir. At the center of Montmartre is the Byzantine-style basilica of the Sacré-Cœur (Sacred Heart), built in 1875–1914. Nearby, in the Place du Tertre, artists still exhibit and sell their paintings.

REFERENCES:

Charles Douglas, *Artist Quarter* (London: Faber & Faber, 1941);

Mariel Oberthur, *Cafés and Cabarets of Montmartre* (Salt Lake City: Gibbs M. Smith, 1984).

— C.S.B.

MONTPARNASSE

Montparnasse, a large district of Paris located on the south side of the Seine (that is, on the **Left Bank**), became an important center of artistic activity before the end of the nineteenth century. Later, especially in the 1920s and 1930s, the literary and artistic activity of Montparnasse was often mixed with politics, especially in popular meeting places such as the **Café de la Rotonde,** the **Café du Dôme,** and the **Coupole.** Several academies of art, including the Grande Chaumière, are also located in Montparnasse. Among the French authors who were particularly associated with the district are **Jean-Paul Sartre** and **Simone de Beauvoir.**

REFERENCES:

Charles Douglas, *Artist Quarter* (London: Faber & Faber, 1941);

Herbert R. Lottman, *The Left Bank: Writers, Artists, and Politics from the Popular Front to the Cold War* (Boston: Houghton Mifflin, 1982);

Kenneth E. Silver, *The Circle of Montparnasse: Jewish Artists in Paris 1905–1945* (New York: Universe Books, 1985).

— C.S.B.

PAUL MORAND

While he is not considered a major author, Paul Morand (1888–1976) nevertheless has a permanent place in the history of twentieth-century French writing as the inventor of a certain type of literary modernism, not the revolution in form created by other modernists, but an emphasis on the particular characteristics of modern life — its speed, glitter, mechanization, and immoralism.

Educated for a career in foreign affairs, Morand was one of several writers of his time who were also diplomats (among them **Paul Claudel, Jean Giraudoux,** and **Saint-John Perse**), a profession that in Morand's case sharpened his talent for cultural observation. His aim to describe modern life frankly is evident in his early book *Tendres stocks* (1921; first translated as *Green Shoots*). Published with a preface by **Marcel Proust,** it is a group of three stories centering on the lives of young women in London during **World War I.** Morand's second collection of stories, *Ouvert la nuit* (1922; translated as *Open All Night*), which sold well, portrays several women who are a part of the peculiar moral disintegration in post-1918 Europe. It was followed by a similar depiction of four colorful men, *Fermé la nuit* (1923; translated as *Closed All Night*). (Ezra Pound's translations of *Tendres stocks* and *Ouvert la nuit,* completed in 1922, were published as *Fancy Goods, Open All Night* in 1984.) Morand's account of his world travels, *Rien que la terre* (1926; translated as

Earth Girdled), reveals his belief that true exoticism is dead.

In the late 1920s and 1930s Morand turned his attention to matters of racial struggle, approaching the topic from a conservative, colonialist point of view in books such as *Magie noire* (1928; translated as *Black Magic*), which portrays the Negro race as unable to cope with the modern world. He also published books on the United States, including *U.S.A. 1927* (1928) and *New-York* (1930; translated).

Politically, Morand was decidedly right wing. After the German defeat of France in the **Debacle** at the beginning of **World War II,** he offered his services to the **Vichy government** in July 1940, serving as director of movie censorship in 1942 and as an ambassador (1943–1944). After the **Liberation** of France in 1944, Morand was exiled until 1953. He was elected to the Académie Française in 1968. For many readers Morand remains linked to Vichy and what they see as the errors of French conservatism.

REFERENCES:

Georges Lemaître, "Paul Morand," in his *Four French Novelists* (London & New York: Oxford University Press, 1938), pp. 303–392;

Bruno Thibault, *L'Allure de Morand: Du modernisme au pétainisme* (Birmingham, Ala.: Summa Publications, 1992).
                                                                    — C.S.B.

JEANNE MOREAU

Jeanne Moreau (1928–) has been internationally known as a leading French actress for decades; she even appeared on the cover of *Time* magazine in 1965. In addition to directing several films of her own, she has worked with such major directors as Michelangelo Antonioni, **Luis Buñuel,** Orson Welles, and **François Truffaut.**

Moreau began her stage and screen careers in 1948 and first gained critical recognition in two features directed by **Louis Malle:** *Ascenseur pour l'échafaud* (1958; *Frantic*) and *Les Amants* (1958; *The Lovers*). In *Les Amants* Moreau portrayed a frustrated housewife who seeks solace and sexual fulfillment by taking a lover. The frank, daring representation of sexuality in this film brought attention to her and Malle. In Antonioni's *La Notte* (1960; *The Night*), one of the most acclaimed French-Italian movies of the early 1960s, Moreau played the emotionally bankrupt wife of a novelist. In Truffaut's *Jules et Jim* (1961; *Jules and Jim*) Moreau played a woman in a thirty-year love triangle.

Jeanne Moreau as Catherine and Henri Serre as Jim in François Truffaut's 1961 movie *Jules et Jim*

Moreau worked with Buñuel in his *Le Journal d'une femme de chambre* (1964; *Diary of a Chambermaid*) and with Welles in his adaptations of Franz Kafka in *Le Procès* (1962; *The Trial*) and of William Shakespeare in *Campanadas a medianoche* (1966; *Chimes at Midnight*; *Falstaff*). She and **Brigitte Bardot** acted together in Malle's *Viva Maria* (1965). Moreau's allure, radically different from Bardot's, was based on a freethinking sensibility and a knowing sexuality. Her face, extremely moving in close-ups, had a grave, beautiful seriousness far different from Bardot's.

After the mid 1960s Moreau appeared in fewer films and began directing. In the early 1990s she played leading roles in *The Suspended Step of the Stork* (1991), directed by Theodoros Angelopoulos; Wim Wenders's *Bis ans Ende der Welt* (1991; *Jusqu'au bout du monde*; *Until the End of the World*); and Luc Besson's *La Femme Nikita* (1991).

REFERENCES:

Marguerite Duras, "The Affairs of Jeanne Moreau," *Show* (March 1963);

Penelope Gilliatt, "Jeanne Moreau," in *The National Society of Film Critics on the Movie Star,* edited by Elisabeth Weis (New York: Viking, 1981);

Molly Haskell, "La Lumière" [interview], *Film Comment,* 26 (March–April 1990): 20–21.
                                                                    —W.L.

MICHÈLE MORGAN

Screen actress Michèle Morgan (1920–) achieved stardom in the 1930s by playing variations on the character of the self-sacrificing, doomed heroine. In **Marcel Carné**'s film *Quai des brumes* (1938; *Port of Shadows*) she and **Jean Gabin** played romantic partners trapped in a corrupt society in which happiness is only fleeting.

After spending part of **World War II** in Hollywood, Morgan returned to France, where she once again proved herself to be an outstanding actress, excelling particularly at portraying beautiful and aloof heroines. She starred as the blind girl in **Jean Delannoy**'s *La Symphonie pastorale* (1946; The Pastoral Symphony), based on the book by **André Gide.** In the historical film *Destinées* (1953; *Daughters of Destiny*) she played Joan of Arc in the episode directed by Delannoy, and in *Napoléon* (1955), directed by **Sacha Guitry,** she portrayed Joséphine de Beauharnais. She was **Gérard Philipe's** medical assistant in **Yves Allégret**'s *Les Orgueilleux* (1953; *The Proud and the Beautiful*), and played a sophisticated divorcée desired by Philipe's character in **René Clair**'s *Les Grandes Manœuvres* (1955; *The Grand Maneuver*). She appeared in progressively fewer films after the 1960s.

REFERENCE:

Michèle Morgan with Marcelle Routier, *With Those Eyes,* translated by Oliver Coburn (London: W. H. Allen, 1978).

— W.L.

EMMANUEL MOUNIER

As the best-known advocate of the movement called Le Personnalisme, Catholic philosopher Emmanuel Mounier (1905–1950) has a permanent place in the intellectual history of the first half of the twentieth century. He is also known as the editor of the monthly *Esprit,* which he founded in 1932 and directed until his death.

Mounier was influenced by **Charles Péguy** and **Jacques Maritain,** among others. Personalism, which can be considered an intersection of Christianity, Marxism, and **existentialism,** grew out of his desire to reconcile Christian belief with progressive social thought and activism — a desire he shared especially with Nikolay Berdyayev, Denis de Rougemont, and Pierre-Henri Simon. Mounier was concerned with the individual human being as a person rather than as a philosophical or political abstraction. Attacking the emphasis on individualism in modern Western philosophy and society, he affirmed human community, which he considered the highest human goal, and the redemptive value of labor, warning of the dangers of capitalism and bourgeois society. Yet he also insisted upon the transcendent value of each person. He recognized human dependence upon circumstances but believed in the freedom to go beyond them; human beings should use the world for the advancement of human causes, he believed, rather than becoming subjected to the material world or attempting to master it. These positions were, he acknowledged, contradictory in some ways but were a natural consequence of trying to reconcile Christianity with the modern world.

Mounier exercised a wide influence over such writers and thinkers as **Jean Cayrol** and **Paul Ricœur.** He expressed his ideas in *Esprit* (which was banned by the **Vichy government** during **World War II**) and in books such as *Introduction aux existentialismes* (1946; translated as *Existentialist Philosophies: An Introduction*) and *Le Personnalisme* (1949; translated as *Personalism*).

REFERENCES:

Joseph Amato, *Mounier and Maritain: A French Catholic Understanding of the Modern World* (Tuscaloosa: University of Alabama Press, 1975);

John Wright, "Emmanuel Mounier, *Esprit,* and Vichy, 1940–1944: Ideology and Anti-Ideology," in *Vichy France and the Resistance: Culture and Ideology,* edited by Roderick Kedward and Roger Austin (Totowa, N.J.: Barnes & Noble, 1985), pp. 171–189.

— C.S.B.

MOUVEMENT DE LA LIBÉRATION DES FEMMES

The term *Mouvement de la Libération des Femmes* (Women's Liberation Movement) originated in the French press in August 1970, serving to underscore the progress that French women were then making in securing equal rights under the law. The immediate incident that provoked its formulation took place at the Tomb of the Unknown Soldier under the Arc de Triomphe in Paris. **Christiane Rochefort, Monique Wittig,** and several other feminists placed a wreath on the tomb and dedicated it to "the unknown wife of the soldier." Covering this event, the press created the term and applied it to the activities of the various women's groups that were coming into being at the time. Thus the expression does not refer to a particular party or organization but simply to the overall trend.

Prior to August 1970 militant women's groups, inspired by the demonstrations of **May 1968,** had already been formed in cities such as Paris, Lyons, and Toulouse.

REFERENCE:

Elaine Marks and Isabelle de Coutivron, *New French Feminisms* (Amherst: University of Massachusetts Press, 1980).

— D.O'C.

ALPHONSE MUCHA

Artist Alphonse Mucha (1860–1939) was born in his family's ancestral home, the Moravian town of Ivančice, in what is now the Czech Republic. Rejected by the Academy of Art in Prague (then the capital of Bohemia) in 1878, he earned a living decorating halls for dances until 1881, when he moved to Vienna, where he found favor with several influential patrons as a muralist. In 1885 he finally won admission to an art academy in Munich; in 1887 he moved to Paris, studying at the Académie Julien. It was there that he met several of the future **Nabis,** including **Pierre Bonnard, Paul Sérusier,** and **Edouard Vuillard.**

Mucha's career as a commercial artist began in earnest when a Prague publisher commissioned him to illustrate an epic poem, *The Adamites* (dealing with a medieval evangelical sect). Mucha did not complete the illustrations until 1895, but samples from the sequence produced new offers. By the 1890s his posters and illustrations had begun to exhibit a characteristic form and style: a central figure (almost always female) is in soft focus, and there is a suggestion of dreamlike solitude and quiet. A contemporary critic noted that, for Mucha, "the drawing must not be too realistic. A flat surface must be decorated with flat motives — none of that window effect which suggests that there is another dimension behind it. No plasticity, no presence of a frieze, but plenty of air. One must feel that there is a wall under the poster." Mucha's decorative posters resemble those of the Nabis, especially **Maurice Denis,** but he resolutely avoided the sense of sacramental mysticism that is typical in the Nabi works. Mucha's posters are decorative, sometimes coy, inevitably flattering. Those he did for **Sarah Bernhardt,** beginning in 1894, display both the strengths and the weaknesses of his art. Striking in their dramatic poses and sometimes bold coloring, they seldom evoke the energy and strength Mucha described in his written accounts of the actress.

Mucha's work as poster maker, illustrator, interior decorator, and designer of jewelry and furniture influenced the development of what became known as Art Nouveau. Tracing his forms and decorative patterns to Slavic antecedents, he insisted, however, that his own designs stood apart. At their best, his posters

Stained-glass window by Mucha

have a haunting, melancholy quality; as his production increased, that quality was all too often lost in a flood of quickly done, superficial, and clichéd subjects.

From 1906 through 1912 Mucha spent more time in the United States than in Europe, but he kept his commercial ties to Paris, while attempting to ground his art in the heritage of his birthplace. He returned to Bohemia in 1913. Mucha's *Slav Epic,* a series of historical works begun in 1910 and stretching over more than two decades, suffers from uneven production and a sometimes stilted straining for effect.

REFERENCE:

Jiri Mucha, *Alphonse Maria Mucha: His Life and Art* (New York: Rizzoli, 1989).

—J.H.

N

THE NABIS

The Nabis, or Nabi Brotherhood, were inspired by the Pont-Aven canvases of **Paul Gauguin** and **Emile Bernard** that were the main attraction at the eclectic Impressionists and Synthetists exhibition held at the Café des Arts in Paris in 1889. Over the next year avant-garde critics, including Albert Aurier and **Félix Fénéon,** hailed the show as the birthplace of a new art, a radical break from the Impressionist love for appearance and a move to a new emphasis on essence and the synthesis of the real and the ideal. As future Nabi **Maurice Denis** noted, "The appearance in an undistinguished setting, of an art then totally new, marked the beginning of the reaction against Impressionism."

By 1890 some of Gauguin's protégés were beginning (at first jokingly) to refer to themselves as the "Nabis" (from the Hebrew word for *prophet*). Denis and **Paul Sérusier** quickly emerged as the theoreticians of the new group, which also included painters Paul Ranson, **Pierre Bonnard, Edouard Vuillard,** and **Félix Vallotton,** and sculptor Georges Lacombe.

The Nabi protest against modern painting and the modern industrial world in general had several precedents, most notably the Nazarene Brotherhood, founded in Vienna in 1809, and the Pre-Raphaelite Brotherhood, established in Great Britain in 1849. Both of these earlier groups had taken as a starting point the idea that Western art went off track with the followers of Raphael, who allegedly valued style over content and material appearance over spiritual values. The Nazarenes consciously sought to emulate Netherlandish "primitives" of the fifteenth century; the Pre-Raphaelites incorporated a Netherlandish love for layered allegories into a love for hypernaturalistic, minute detail. The Nabis — most prominently Sérusier and Denis — echoed their predecessors in calling for a re-turn to a spiritual art. Many Nabis identified this art with medieval or Byzantine forms, while others (including Denis) sought to find a modern analogue or equivalent to the religious art of the past. The most detailed statements of Nabi beliefs can be found in Denis's essay "Définition du néo-traditionnisme" (1890; Definition of Neo-Traditionism) and Sérusier's *ABC de la peinture* (ABC of Painting), which was not published until 1921 but pulled together ideas he had promulgated for decades.

What would such art look like? For some close to the Nabis — most notably painter Charles Filiger — the answer was a direct return to a set of late-Byzantine forms. Denis called pre-Renaissance art sublime, noting that even the photograph of a work by the "primitives" was "enough to remind us what our soul is and that its gestures are sublime." He rejected, however, a facile identification of certain styles and periods as inherently sacred. The same Gothic style, he pointed out, could be used to construct a church or a railway station. The answer was to search out new ways to depict the sacred — and for him that meant a search through the works of Gauguin and, to a lesser extent, Vincent van Gogh. To Denis, those two artists were the aesthetic equivalent of barbarians, knocking down the traditions of art, so that new painters could infuse their raw ideas with faith and secure an art both sacred and modern.

The definitions of Nabi art developed by Sérusier and Denis bore little relation to the art of those called "urban Nabis," especially Bonnard and Vuillard. In 1899 Denis wrote that the work of Sérusier and Ranson, as well as his own, was "large" and "symbolic," painted in the studio and emphasizing the human figure, with "very plain and simple subjects, Latin style." By contrast, he charged, the painting of Vuillard, Bonnard, and Vallotton was "small" and "dark," done from life (that is, like the Impressionists' and therefore superficial). It would look better in a small, dim apartment than a studio or exhibition, he said; and it was marked by "complicated subjects," in a "Jewish style." Such terms reveal a darker side to his call for a Christian art and thus shed light on his later membership in the anti-Semitic **Action Française.** The urban Nabis lacked precisely the conservative political and religious philosophy of Denis and Sérusier; Vallotton was even an anarchist sympathizer. The art of Bonnard and Vuillard in particular came to focus mainly on interior, domestic scenes, treated not as religious statements but as complex interactions of colors and textures.

REFERENCES:

Catherine Boyle-Turner, *Paul Sérusier* (Ann Arbor: UMI Research Press, 1983);

Charles Chasse, *The Nabis and Their Period,* translated by Michael Bullock (New York: Praeger, 1969);

Robert Delevoy, *Symbolists and Symbolism* (New York: Rizzoli, 1978);

Wladyslawa Jaworska, *Gauguin and the Pont-Aven School,* translated by Patrick Evans (London: Thames & Hudson, 1972);

George Mauner, *The Nabis, Their History and Their Art, 1888–1896* (New York: Garland, 1978).

—J.H.

THE NANCY FESTIVAL

In summer 1963 the annual Nancy Festival was founded to encourage French student theater. Independent, student-directed acting clubs from all parts of France were invited to the city of Nancy to stage their best productions. As a seminal meeting ground for student actors and directors, the festival soon produced new concepts of theater in France.

Among the clubs participating from the outset were Martine Franck and **Ariane Mnouchkine**'s Association Théâtrale des Etudiants de Paris, which was soon to evolve into an avant-garde professional troupe called the **Théâtre du Soleil** (Sun Theater); the Théâtre 45, the acting club of the **Ecole Normale Supérieure,** which would later turn professional as the Théâtre de l'Aquarium; and the Groupe Théâtral du Lycée Louis-le-Grand.

Festival participants soon became aware that they shared a dissatisfaction with traditional theater. Seeking to develop the creative role of performers, they were following the theoretical line of **Antonin Artaud:** rather than mimicking some other supposed reality, performances were to be a reality unto themselves. Student dramatic groups were moving toward theater as ritual, with the stage as an "altar," on which a sacrificial rite was performed, or toward theater as a

sociopolitical phenomenon, in which the actors mingled with the audience, conjoining spectator and spectacle in such a way as to make audience members confront their social and political prejudices.

Under the direction of Jack Lang, who was to become minister of culture in the 1980s, the Nancy Festival was soon attracting student troupes from all over Europe, as well as from North and South America. A worldwide student movement was in formation, having as its principal tenets opposition to social injustice, to the Cold War, and specifically to the participation of the United States in the Vietnam War. Nancy was a meeting place for members of this generational movement. In 1967 the festival declared itself a Festival Mondial du Théâtre (World Theater Festival), eliminating the "student" label and accepting new-theater activists from around the world. When the social upheaval of **May 1968** occurred in France, it is perhaps not coincidental that a theater hall — the **Théâtre de l'Odéon** — was occupied by student protesters.

The Nancy Festival continued to encourage new theater after 1968. In 1971, for example, American Robert Wilson gained recognition in France for his spectacle titled *Le Regard du sourd* (translated as *Deafman Glance*), noted for the artistic expressiveness of its sets quite apart from the text.

REFERENCE:

Daniel Mortier, *Le Nouveau Théâtre* (Paris: Hachette, 1974).

—R.J.N.

BRONISLAVA NIJINSKA

Bronislava Nijinska (1891–1972), the younger sister of **Vaslav Nijinsky,** was a distinguished dancer, choreographer, and teacher. Like her brother, Nijinska graduated from the Imperial Ballet School in Saint Petersburg and joined the Maryinsky Theater. In 1909 she traveled to Paris to work with **Serge Diaghilev**'s **Ballets Russes,** dancing in ballets such as **Michel Fokine**'s *Carnaval* (1910) and *Petrouchka* (1911). Marriage and children took Nijinska back to Russia, where from 1915 to 1921 she performed at the Kiev Theater. In 1919 she opened her School of Movement, where **Serge Lifar** was her best-known student. She left Russia in 1921 with her mother and two children and accepted a position with the Ballets Russes as chief choreographer. There she created the acclaimed ballets *Les Noces* (1923; The Wedding), with music and text by **Igor Stravinsky** and costumes by **Natalia Goncharova,** and *Les Biches* (1924; The Darlings), with music by **Francis Poulenc** and costumes, sets, and curtain by **Marie Laurencin.**

United States, including the **Paris Opera Ballet** (1925–1926), Buenos Aires Teatro Colón (1926–1927, 1946), **Ida Rubinstein**'s company (1928–1929), her own Théâtre de la Danse (1932–1934), and the Polish Ballet (1937–1938). Charmed by California, she founded and directed the Bronislava Nijinska Hollywood Ballet School (1941–1950) and subsequently taught at her own studio in Hollywood. After 1945 Nijinska was ballet mistress for the Grand Ballet du Marquis de Cuevas. During her later years she reconstructed *Les Biches* (1964) and *Les Noces* (1966) for the Royal Ballet in London, confirming her place among the great twentieth-century choreographers.

REFERENCES:

Nancy Van Norman Baer, *Bronislava Nijinska: A Dancer's Legacy* (San Francisco: Fine Arts Museum of San Francisco, 1986);

Bronislava Nijinska, *Early Memoirs,* translated and edited by Irina Nijinska and Jean Rawlinson (Durham, N.C. & London: Duke University Press, 1992);

Roberta Reeder, "The Kireevsky Collection and the Neo-Russian Movement," *Dance Research Journal,* 18 (Winter 1986–1987): 32–36.

— A.P.E.

VASLAV NIJINSKY

The great dancer and choreographer Vaslav Nijinsky (1888–1950) established the prominent role of the male dancer in twentieth-century ballet, and with his choreographic innovations he brought dance into the modern era. The child of Polish circus performers, he grew up in Russia and had a successful career with the Maryinsky Theater in Saint Petersburg before he moved to Paris in 1909 to star in the **Ballets Russes.**

Nijinsky's technical virtuosity seemed physically impossible. Most admired and written about was his *entrechat dix* (a jump in which the dancer crosses the legs ten times). As an actor he was mesmerizing, appearing to transform himself into his characters. He created his most famous roles in the ballets of **Michel Fokine** — the Harlequin in *Carnaval* (1910), the Golden Slave in *Schéhérazade* (1910), Petrouchka in *Petrouchka* (1911), and Spectre in *Le Spectre de la Rose* (1911; The Specter of the Rose).

Nijinsky's choreography was the first example of modernism in dance. In 1912 he choreographed his first ballet, *L'Après-midi d'un faune* (*The Afternoon of a Faun*), followed in 1913 by *Jeux* and **Le Sacre du printemps** (*Rite of Spring*). Controversial in content and presentation, the dances shocked audiences of the time but have proven to be turning points in twentieth-century choreography.

Igor Stravinsky and Vaslav Nijinsky, dressed for his role in *Petrouchka*, 1912

Les Noces is known for its massive architectural human groupings and its sensitive treatment of the theme of an arranged wedding in a Russian peasant village. Nijinska was adamantly opposed to the original opulent costume designs for the ballet, believing that they conflicted with the disturbing rhythms and drama of Stravinsky's music and the seriousness of the wedding ritual. She eventually succeeded in changing the designs and acquired the distinction of being the only choreographer under Diaghilev to have complete control of a production. *Les Biches,* a satire on Parisian high society in which Nijinska created the role of the hostess, was a forerunner of neoclassic ballet (classic dance vocabulary used in a contemporary fashion).

Nijinska choreographed more than seventy works for companies in South America, Europe, and the

Nijinsky, who was nearly mute, went for long periods without speaking and appeared totally dependent on the director of the Ballets Russes, **Serge Diaghilev.** On Nijinsky's marriage to Romola de Pulszky during a South American tour, Diaghilev immediately dismissed him from the troupe, but he returned on a later occasion to choreograph *Till Eulenspiegel* (1916). Nijinsky's stage career ended in 1919, when he began to show signs of schizophrenia, and he spent the rest of his life in mental institutions. His wife edited and published *The Diary of Vaslav Nijinsky* in 1936.

REFERENCES:

Richard Buckle, *Nijinsky* (New York: Simon & Schuster, 1971);

Lynn Garafola, "The Vanguard Poetic of Vaslav Nijinsky," in her *Diaghilev's Ballets Russes* (New York & Oxford: Oxford University Press, 1989), pp. 50–75;

Lincoln Kirstein, *Nijinsky Dancing* (New York: Knopf, 1975);

Bronislava Nijinska, *Early Memoirs,* translated and edited by Irina Nijinska and Jean Rawlinson (Durham, N.C. & London: Duke University Press, 1992).

— A.P.E.

Paul Nizan

Considered one of the most brilliant writers and thinkers of his generation by contemporaries such as **Jean-Paul Sartre,** Paul Nizan (1905–1940) was killed in the evacuation of **Dunkirk** at the beginning of **World War II.** A Marxist, he devoted much of his relatively small body of work to scathing criticism of capitalistic society.

Nizan, whose father was a railway engineer, studied philosophy at the **Ecole Normale Supérieure,** passing his *agrégation* examinations in 1929, two years after he joined the **French Communist Party.** During the 1930s Nizan earned his living by teaching philosophy and by contributing to periodicals such as *Humanité,* a Communist Party organ.

Based partly on his experience in the Arabian peninsula as a tutor with an Anglo-French family in 1926–1927, Nizan's first book, *Aden, Arabie* (1931; translated), is a critique of capitalist imperialism and the French university system. In *Les Chiens de garde* (1932; translated as *The Watchdogs*) he again attacked the thinking of the French governing classes — especially their belief in immutable (Cartesian) reason and the sanctity of the "inner man" — which he regarded as pretexts for their holding onto power and ignoring social problems. In *Antoine Bloyé* (1933; translated) Nizan cast his father's life in fictional form as an illustration of class experience (the failure of those who do not understand the needs and destiny of the proletariat) and as an existential tragedy.

Paul Nizan, January 1926

A fervent Marxist and agitator, Nizan was nevertheless measured in his account of his 1934 visit to the Soviet Union, seeing it as an evolving society that, while still plagued with problems, embodied hope for the future. The following year he wrote one of the major French political novels of the 1930s, *Le Cheval de Troie* (translated as *The Trojan Horse*), which deals with social unrest and uprisings — such as those connected to the **Stavisky Affair** (1933–1934) — symptomatic of social ills in Europe. His best novel, *La Conspiration* (1938; The Conspiracy), winner of the Prix Interallié, focuses on a group of politically active students in their twenties whose diverging experiences, including betrayal and suicide, both idealize and mock political commitment.

Nizan could not approve the Nazi-Soviet Pact of 1939, and upon being mobilized for service in the French military at the outbreak of World War II, he resigned from the Communist Party. This act led to his denunciation by **Maurice Thorez** and other Communists, who attempted in the 1940s to destroy his intellectual and literary reputation, even accusing him of betraying party secrets to the French government. His reputation was defended by Sartre, **Maurice Merleau-Ponty, Albert Camus,** and other intellectuals. Sartre based the character Schneider in his "Drôle d'amitié" (1949; Strange Friendship) on Nizan.

REFERENCES:

Walter Redfern, *Paul Nizan: Committed Literature in a Conspiratorial World* (Princeton, N.J.: Princeton University Press, 1972);

Susan Rubin Suleiman, *Authoritarian Fictions* (New York: Columbia University Press, 1983).

— C.S.B.

PHILIPPE NOIRET

Philippe Noiret (1930–) is one of the most versatile and striking French screen actors of his generation.

Tall and heavy, Noiret had a long apprenticeship in small parts, gradually making a name for himself in comic and serious roles. One of his early triumphs was his portrayal of the impassive husband of the chain-smoking, rebellious heroine in **Georges Franju's** *Thérèse Desqueyroux* (1962; *Therese*), based on the novel by **François Mauriac.** Noiret subsequently appeared as a NATO economist in Alfred Hitchcock's *Topaz* (1969) and as a fearful engineer in *Murphy's War* (1971). During the 1970s he began working with Italian directors. His performance in Marco Ferreri's *La Grande Bouffe* (1973; The Great Feed) was highly acclaimed. As a judge who has an Oedipal relationship with his elderly mother, Noiret performed with calculated restraint as his character and two friends (played by Marcello Mastroianni and **Michel Piccoli**) eat themselves to death during a single weekend. In another Italian film, *Nuovo Cinema Paradiso* (1988; *Cinema Paradiso*), Noiret played an old projectionist who shares his love for the movies with a young man. Noiret has also worked with the French director Bertrand Tavernier.

REFERENCES:

Dominique Maillet, *Philippe Noiret* (Paris: Veyrier, 1989);

"Tavernier et Noiret: An Interview with France's Unique Director-Actor Collaboration," *Films in Review,* 34 (March 1983): 163–170; (April 1983): 230–237.

— W.L.

NORD-SUD

Nord-Sud (North-South) was one of many ephemeral avant-garde magazines that had a brief, but consequential, existence toward the end of **World War I.** Dom-

inating the literary avant-garde of the period until his death in 1918, the poet **Guillaume Apollinaire** encouraged the creation of the magazine, which first appeared in March 1917. Its editor, **Pierre Reverdy,** was a fervent admirer of Apollinaire, as were the editors of such other short-lived literary magazines as *Littérature, Sic,* and *391.* The last issue of *Nord-Sud* — number 16 — appeared in October 1918.

The title came from contemporary Paris. The Nord-Sud is a subway line, now number 12, which connects the two main artists' districts, **Montmartre** and **Montparnasse.** The main financial backer of the magazine was the wealthy couturier Jacques Doucet, a friend of many artists, including Reverdy, **André Breton,** and **Jean Cocteau.** Doucet's collections of manuscripts and editions now form the nucleus of the Bibliothèque littéraire Jacques-Doucet (Jacques Doucet library) in Paris.

Nord-Sud published articles on the visual arts and literature, reviews of poetry, and information about prominent literary figures. The magazine also published pieces by many of the leading writers of the period, including Apollinaire, Breton, **Louis Aragon,** and **Philippe Soupault.**

Although a resolute defender of the avant-garde, Reverdy fought against being labeled a **Cubist,** a Futurist, or a new-futurist and against any threat to his artistic independence. He sought to lay bare the common ground that underlay many diverse artistic movements of the period, especially their rejection of realism and naturalism. He was a thoughtful, eloquent advocate for the Cubist painters, insisting on the autonomy of the artistic or poetic work, freed from representation of the real. On the one hand Reverdy's austere insistence upon the artistic creation of a pure mental image, freed from anecdote or banal associations, brought him close to the classical Cubism of **Juan Gris.** On the other, his advocacy of the juxtaposition of radically disparate terms, destabilizing perception and causing surprise, would be picked up and developed by Breton in his *Manifeste du surréalisme* (1924).

REFERENCES:

Jean Schroeder, *Pierre Reverdy* (Boston: Twayne, 1981), pp. 56–64;

Francis Steegmuller, *Cocteau: A Biography* (Boston: Little, Brown, 1970), pp. 219–221.

— J.P.McN.

NOUVEAU RÉALISME

Nouveau Réalisme (New Realism) was a French art movement that flourished in France and some other

European countries during the early 1960s. Similar in intent to American Pop art, Nouveau Réalisme rejected the Abstract Expressionism of the 1950s in order to explore contemporary culture.

Nouveau Réalisme was launched in spring 1960 with a group exhibition in Milan and a manifesto by critic Pierre Restany. A second show, with a new manifesto, "A 40° au-dessus de dada" (40° Beyond **Dada**), was held in Paris in May 1961. Artists associated with Nouveau Réalisme from the beginning included **Yves Klein, Arman, Jean Tinguely,** and Daniel Spoerri; artists later affiliated with the group included **Martial Raysse,** Christo, Mimmo Rotella, and Niki de Saint-Phalle.

In its founding statement Restany argued that henceforth the "vision of things should be inspired by the feelings of modern nature which is that of the factory and city, publicity and mass media, science, and technology." The founders of the group, whose concerns and techniques varied widely, shared an interest in mass-produced goods employed in different ways as art objects. One obvious inspiration for such art was **Marcel Duchamp**'s use of "readymade" objects (including a urinal). While Duchamp had sought to question and parody the whole nature of art, the Nouveaux Réalistes — however tongue-in-cheek they seemed — sought to monumentalize the readymade object as part of a glorification of the world of mass commercial production. Restany insisted that "the new realism registers sociological reality without any controversial intention." The term *Nouveau Réalisme* itself derives from **Fernand Léger**'s writings of the 1920s in which he describes his own enthusiasm for the world of industry.

The art of the Nouveaux Réalistes varies dramatically in form, content, and execution. Some of these artists mounted and replicated exactly the mass-produced object. Others shattered and reconfigured it — sometimes to emphasize chaos, sometimes to recombine the fragments into aesthetically pleasing patterns. Some artists took industrial goods or images from the mass media and played with them by ripping them from their original contexts, juxtaposing them in startling ways, or blowing them up to monumental size. Within a few years the disparate aims and fortunes of its members had torn the group apart, though the term remained as a kind of catchphrase for French and other European Pop art.

REFERENCES:

Henry Geldzahler, *Pop Art, 1955–70* (Sydney: International Cultural Corporation for Australia, 1985);

Marco Livingstone, *Pop Art: A Continuing History* (New York: Abrams, 1990);

Daniel Wheeler, *Art Since Mid-Century: 1945 to the Present* (Englewood Cliffs, N.J.: Prentice-Hall, 1991).

— J.H.

LE NOUVEAU ROMAN

The term *Nouveau Roman* (New Novel) refers to a new departure in fiction that was introduced in the early 1950s by a small group of innovative writers and then carried further by these authors and a second generation of New Novelists. The term *Nouveau Nouveau Roman* (New New Novel) is even seen on occasion, but it is much less clearly defined than the original New Novel. While the New Novelists typically rejected conventional plots, characterization, and narrative techniques, they did so in different ways and thus do not constitute a formal school.

Among those who are generally considered New Novelists are, first and foremost, **Alain Robbe-Grillet,** whose novel *Les Gommes* (1953; translated as *The Erasers*) served as a call for a new fiction. Others include **Samuel Beckett, Michel Butor, Claude Ollier, Robert Pinget, Jean Ricardou, Claude Simon, Philippe Sollers,** and especially **Nathalie Sarraute.** Her innovative sketches called *Tropismes* (translated as *Tropisms*) appeared as early as 1939, but it was only in the mid 1950s that they attracted much attention. Similarly, some of **Marguerite Duras**'s works of the 1950s would justify classifying her with the New Novelists, although she is less concerned than they with radical departures in fictional form. Most of these experimental writers had the same publisher: **Editions de Minuit,** under the leadership of Jérôme Lindon. **Claude Mauriac** is sometimes called a New Novelist, but despite his concern with extending the province of fiction, his work is more akin to the psychological analysis practiced by **Marcel Proust** and other older figures than the radical experimentation of the New Novelists.

In *Pour un nouveau roman* (1963; translated as *Towards a New Novel*) Robbe-Grillet observed that fiction is always evolving and called for a literature free of anthropomorphic metaphors. His position is thus closer to that of the phenomenologists than to that of the Romantics. In practice, while Robbe-Grillet avoided metaphor and simile in the strict sense, in works such as *La Jalousie* (1957; translated as *Jealousy*) elements of the material world are constantly used as correlatives of disturbing psychological impulses; he simply has his characters refer to the world in a manner different from the conventional metaphoric one. He also called for eschewing traditional psychological analysis. His fiction generally remains faithful to this program although the human psyche, particularly in abnormal states, is still the basis for many of his works. Furthermore, Robbe-Grillet denounced the myth of realism or mimesis; he is more interested in mental space and time than their real equivalents. In his fiction the results of these and other programmatic positions include the absence of a coher-

Jérôme Lindon of Editions de Minuit (fourth from left) and the New Novelists, 1959: Alain Robbe-Grillet, Claude Simon, Claude Mauriac, Robert Pinget, Samuel Beckett, Nathalie Sarraute, and Claude Ollier

ent, chronologically organized plot; confusion between interior and exterior; and a declarative, seemingly flat style charged with psychological resonances. His work is often called objective; yet human subjectivity dominates, perhaps more strikingly even than in novels that analyze the subject.

Sarraute's essay collection *L'Ere du soupçon* (1956; translated as *The Age of Suspicion*) approaches fiction differently. Asserting that readers in this skeptical modern age cannot "believe" in fiction as they did in earlier times, she calls for a rejection of Balzacian formulas for creating detailed character portraits. Instead she asks for deeper insights into the individual psyche and for better dialogue in fiction. Mauriac's *L'Alittérature contemporaine* (1958; translated as *The New Literature*), which helped to publicize the work of the New Novelists, similarly calls for something that would be "nonliterary" (using *literary* in the pejorative sense). Other critical writings of the New Novelists include the essays in Butor's *Répertoire* (1960; translated in part in *Inventory*), in which he speaks of the novel as an investigation of reality, and Ricardou's various books about the New Novel.

These critical positions suggest how what appeared to be a general phenomenon with coherent aesthetics consisted of varied and sometimes contradictory tendencies. Yet New Novels do have features in common. Robbe-Grillet, Butor, and Simon share an obsession with inner, subjective time. Duras and Sarraute tend toward minimal explanation. Simon's expansive style includes a wide range of psychological and physical detail. As for Butor, no author, including Proust, has been so obsessed with attempting to wring layers of meaning from every moment and every perception.

For nearly all these writers the sense of the unknowability of existence, despite experience and examination, is central: experience flees from categories that would capture it, including language. This elusiveness is most evident in their undermining of the notion of plot. Either the plot is self-contradictory (as in some works by Robbe-Grillet) or it is nearly internalized (as in other fiction by Robbe-Grillet and the works of Duras and Sarraute). In the most extreme development the plot is the writing of the story. Also seen in the 1950s novels of Butor, Pinget, and Robbe-

Grillet, this tendency is most developed in the work of Ricardou, whose *La Prise de Constantinople* (1965; The Taking of Constantinople) — called on the back cover "La Prose de Constantinople" — is a novel about writing itself. The presence of internal references, repetitions, and self-reflexivity points to the inability of this literature to go beyond itself.

REFERENCES:

Stephen Heath, *The Nouveau Roman: A Study in the Practice of Writing* (London: Elek, 1972);

Ann Jefferson, *The Nouveau Roman and the Poetics of Fiction* (Cambridge: Cambridge University Press, 1981);

Vivian Mercier, *The New Novel from Queneau to Pinget* (New York: Farrar, Straus & Giroux, 1971);

John Sturrock, *The French New Novel* (London: Oxford University Press, 1969).

— C.S.B.

LES NOUVEAUX PHILOSOPHES

The term *Nouveaux Philosophes* (New Philosophers), used first by **Bernard-Henri Lévy,** refers to several anti-establishment writers and thinkers concerned with social and political issues, whose work began appearing in the late 1960s, after Marxism, **existentialism,** and **structuralism** had passed the height of their influence in France.

Lévy, Jean-Marie Benoist, and André Glucksmann are the most prominent New Philosophers; others include Maurice Clavel and Philippe Nemo, and there are many emerging thinkers who may be categorized as part of the group. There are also many contemporary philosophers and social critics — such as **Gilles Deleuze, Jean-François Lyotard,** and Michel Serres — who are not New Philosophers.

The appearance of the New Philosophers on the French intellectual scene coincided roughly with the student and worker protests of **May 1968.** Meant to bring to an end the institutional France of the **Fifth Republic,** these events also signaled the decline of the Marxist myth. In 1970 Benoist published *Marx est mort* (Marx Is Dead), and he and others denounced the murderous totalitarianism of Marxist societies, which older Communist sympathizers had often refused to acknowledge despite the evidence. Along with rejecting the dialectical thinking of Marxism, Benoist and his colleagues sought to discard other orthodoxies and ossified systems of thought, such as Freudianism and structuralism. They wanted to reassert the primacy of freedom and establish a groundwork for new thinking about humanity. **Jacques Derrida** and **Michel Foucault,** sometimes classed as New Philosophers themselves, had an influence on their thinking, as did **Louis Althusser,** a Marxist who challenged conven-

tional Marxism; **Jacques Lacan,** a psychoanalyst who questioned orthodox Freudianism; and **Claude Lévi-Strauss,** whose structuralism influenced Benoist.

Among the books published by the New Philosophers are Glucksmann's *Les Maîtres penseurs* (1977; translated as *The Master Thinkers*) and Lévy's *La Barbarie à visage humain* (1977; translated as *Barbarism with a Human Face*).

REFERENCES:

Pierre Bouretz, "Nouvelle philosophie," *Débat,* no. 50 (May-August 1988): 210–211;

John Rajchman, *Truth and Errors: Foucault, Lacan and the Question of Ethics* (New York: Routledge, 1991).

— C.S.B.

LE NOUVEL OBSERVATEUR

Along with the *Express* and the *Point,* the weekly *Nouvel Observateur* (New Observer) is one of the leading newsmagazines in France, with about 1.5 million regular readers.

The *Nouvel Obs,* as it is affectionately known, was founded in 1964 as a laboratory for progressive, chiefly socialist, ideas. Under the editorship of Jean Daniel, formerly with the *Express,* the magazine opposed the presidency of **Charles de Gaulle** and called for a new left-wing coalition of Communists and Socialists that would work to restructure society radically. The first issue featured an article by **Jean-Paul Sartre,** a champion of militant social action; the second included a commentary by Harold Wilson, the pragmatic Labour Party leader and newly elected prime minister of Great Britain.

Over the years writers for the magazine expressed an increasing distrust of Communism. Sympathetic to the student uprising of **May 1968,** the *Nouvel Observateur* blamed Communist inflexibility and lack of support for the failure of the student movement to achieve fundamental reform. In 1981 Daniel opposed the nationalizations advocated in the common program of the left-wing alliance led by François Mitterrand but still supported Mitterrand's bid for the presidency, urging Communist voters to abandon their party's candidate, Georges Marchais, even in the first round of voting. Mitterrand's election took some of the fire out of the *Nouvel Observateur.* No longer a journal of left-wing opinion with a daring bent, it has become a centrist newsmagazine much like its competitors.

REFERENCE:

Louis Pinto, *L'Intelligence en action: "Le Nouvel Observateur"* (Paris: Métailié/Presses Universitaires de France, 1984).

— J.P.McN.

LA NOUVELLE CRITIQUE

La Nouvelle Critique, or the French New Criticism, was a rejection of the French critical tradition preceding it. Unlike those critics who stressed extraliterary contexts such as biography and historical periods, those who offered impressionistic readings of literary works, or those who saw literature as a means toward political and social engagement, the critics associated with the Nouvelle Critique focused on understanding the literary work by using theories drawn from the social sciences. Since the 1960s the Nouvelle Critique has become an accepted method of analysis in universities in France and the United States.

In the nineteenth century French literary criticism developed in two strains, the "scientific" and the impressionistic. While scientific critics sought to practice objective analysis, impressionistic criticism was based on the personal opinions and judgments of the critic — or, in **Anatole France**'s celebrated formula, "les aventures de son âme au milieu des chefs-d'œuvre" (the adventures of one's soul amid masterpieces). Scientific literary criticism was adapted by **Gustave Lanson** and became the predominant method used in French universities. Through a descriptive technique based on biography and history, Lanson emphasized the verification of the text and its classification in the canon of literature.

Aggressively reacting against this university method in particular, the French New Critics emerged in the 1960s, at a time when the traditional intellectual foundations of the university and many assumptions of the intelligentsia were being challenged from within, as illustrated in the student demonstrations of **May 1968.** Pioneering changes were visible well before the Nouvelle Critique, however. Its two recognized forerunners are Marcel Raymond and Albert Béguin, two university professors. (Although the terminology used by the French New Critics opposes "new" to "university" criticism, the academic community remains a forum for such debate.) In *De Baudelaire au surréalisme* (1933; translated as *From Baudelaire to Surrealism*) Raymond studied the history of modern poetry based on inner affiliations rather than conscious intertextual borrowings. Béguin's *L'Ame romantique et le rêve* (1937; The Romantic Soul and the Dream) exemplifies one of the concerns of the Nouvelle Critique. Béguin wrote on the subconscious and its relation to artistic creation, claiming that the dream is the material of poetry. Thus he relied on psychoanalysis to determine the meaning of the work. A third precursor, **Gaston Bachelard,** was interested in the poetic act as manifested through the representation in the human mind of the four elements — fire, air, water, and earth. Jean-Pierre Richard, another important figure in the

critical revolution, called the characteristic patterns created by the artist's imagination "structures" or "themes." Thus the **structuralism** that is associated with the Nouvelle Critique relates to unconscious structures, not the formal structure of a work as described by the Anglo-American New Critics of the 1930s and 1940s.

The Nouvelle Critique achieved notoriety during the years 1964–1966 in the highly publicized debate between Sorbonne professor Raymond Picard and critic **Roland Barthes** occasioned by the 1963 publication of Barthes's study of Jean Racine. Picard attacked Barthes for his obscure critical language and his application of twentieth-century disciplines to the study of classical literature. For many Barthes's reply constituted the triumph of the Nouvelle Critique: he argued that language does not have a single meaning based in a specific historical era, that no critical position is entirely objective, and that the critic must be able to read and write symbolically. His assertion that the older criticism avoided subjects such as sexuality also undermined Picard's claims for its objectivity. While Barthes claimed that the clarity of traditional critical writing is based on class codes, one of the failings of the newer criticism, according to its adversaries, is that the language it uses relies on a personal vocabulary and obscure critical jargon that is often more elaborate or figurative than the poetry or prose under examination.

The Nouvelle Critique uses structuralism, psychoanalysis, Marxism, anthropology, **existentialism,** and other theories to explain a literary work. Owing to the idiosyncrasies of various New Critics, it is not a single school. Nonetheless, the French New Critics share the structural or thematic investigation of texts and a concern with the expressive potential of language. Jean-Paul Weber looked for the repetition of a theme in a literary work as evidence of a personal traumatic experience in an artist's childhood. Robert Champigny practiced literary psychoanalysis as well, while Charles Mauron, who focused on an obsession or fixation without considering it the exclusive source of literary creation, called his method "psychocriticism." Jean Starobinski also took a psychoanalytical approach, while Jean Rousset analyzed patterns of plot, and René Girard looked at the triangular organizational structure through which the hero is conditioned to approach the object of his desire. Barthes and Bachelard studied the archetypes present in literature. **Lucien Goldmann** took a Marxist structuralist approach, while **Maurice Blanchot**'s and **Georges Poulet**'s approaches were philosophical. Also part of the Nouvelle Critique is the French feminist critical movement, whose representatives include **Luce Irigaray** and **Julia Kristeva.**

REFERENCES:

Roland Barthes, *Criticism and Truth,* translated by Katrine Pilcher Keuneman (Minneapolis: University of Minnesota Press, 1987);

Serge Doubrovsky, *New Criticism in France,* translated by Derek Coltman (Chicago & London: University of Chicago Press, 1973);

Laurent LeSage, *The French New Criticism: An Introduction and a Sampler* (University Park & London: Pennsylvania State University Press, 1967);

Raymond Picard, *New Criticism or New Fraud?,* translated by Frank Towne (Pullman: Washington State University Press, 1969).

— J.L.B.

LA NOUVELLE CRITIQUE

In the years after **World War II** the **French Communist Party** founded or commandeered a series of intellectual journals in an effort to capture the intellectual high ground in domestic politics. *Nouvelle Critique* (New Criticism) was established in 1948 as the voice of the party in the arts.

Unlike such nominally independent publications as *Lettres Françaises* and *Pensée, Nouvelle Critique,* subtitled "Revue du marxisme militant," was intended from the start as an authoritative party organ. This fact was underscored by the choice of hard-line Stalinist Jean Kanapa as its editor. Its establishment coincided with a party campaign to impose on its affiliated artists and intellectuals support for a Soviet-style Socialist Realism, represented in France by **André Fougeron** and **Boris Taslitzky.**

Throughout the early 1950s *Nouvelle Critique* championed party orthodoxy in art and culture. A former student of **Jean-Paul Sartre,** Kanapa denounced both Sartre and **existentialism** as essentially fascist. In 1951 the review organized a conference of students and intellectuals to protest what it saw as the growing American dominance of Europe in the economic, political, and cultural spheres.

Nikita Khrushchev's denunciation of Joseph Stalin in 1956 and the Hungarian uprising the same year posed the same problems for the editors of *Nouvelle Critique* as they did for other groups close to the French Communists: timid first steps toward greater openness and flexibility were replaced by fresh attacks on opponents of Soviet intervention in Hungary. By the end of 1956 many members of the editorial board of the magazine had resigned or been removed by the party.

Throughout the 1960s and 1970s *Nouvelle Critique* alternated between attempts to discuss ideas originated by New Left forces outside the Communist Party and crude denunciations of them. Periods of greater openness alternated with new purges. The culmination came in the late 1970s, with rising calls inside the party for democratization and a renewal of left-wing unity. The response of the party leadership was to abolish both *Nouvelle Critique* and the often-critical journal *France-Nouvelle.* In March 1980 both were replaced by the review *Révolution;* editors of both previous publications who had been critical of the party leadership were missing from its masthead.

REFERENCES:

David Caute, *Communism and the French Intellectuals* (New York: Macmillan, 1964);

Donald Drew Egbert, *Social Radicalism in the Arts: Western Europe* (New York: Knopf, 1970);

Sudhir Hazareesingh, *Intellectuals and the French Communist Party* (Oxford: Clarendon Press, 1991).

— J.H.

LA NOUVELLE CUISINE

The term *nouvelle cuisine* (new cuisine) was coined in the 1960s to describe a movement away from the traditional French cuisine inspired by chefs such as Auguste Escoffier (1847–1935) and his friend Prosper Montagné (1865–1948), the author of the authoritative reference work *Larousse gastronomique* (1938). In rejecting heavy sauces rich in butter, cream, egg yolks, and flour — béchamel, hollandaise, and espagnole sauces, for example — the nouveaux cuisiniers sought to bring out the natural flavors of their market-fresh ingredients.

Culinary journalists Henri Gault and Christian Millau were the first to use the term *nouvelle cuisine.* In the 1960s and 1970s they described, advocated, and codified the methods of chefs such as Paul Bocuse, Michel Guérard, Jean Troisgros, Roger Vergé, Raymond Oliver, and others. Some of the younger chefs of the 1960s, including Bocuse, studied with the legendary Fernand Point at his renowned restaurant La Pyramide in Vienne, south of Lyons. Point has been called the godfather of nouvelle cuisine.

Whereas the older French cuisine was associated with an era of grand international hotels and belle-époque opulence, nouvelle cuisine may be found throughout France in restaurants owned by the chefs themselves, who make great use of produce from local markets as well as local wines. Beginning in 1964, the year of the Tokyo Olympics, Oliver and other younger chefs went to East Asia and borrowed several Chinese and Japanese culinary principles, including reduced cooking time for seafood, fowl, and vegetables, as well as a fondness for steaming. Their willingness to experiment included accepting new technologies — such as preparing foie gras in a microwave oven.

Although the new cuisine is lighter than the old and may appear simpler, it places just as many demands on chefs. For example, the apparent simplicity of Jean Troisgros's famous *saumon à l'oseille* (salmon with sorrel sauce), which has been copied throughout the world, is deceptive; it took him several years to perfect the sauce to his satisfaction, until it was light and transparent, without butter or cream. The dish was served at a luncheon in 1975, when President Valéry Giscard d'Estaing awarded Bocuse the Légion d'Honneur.

It has become common practice to belittle nouvelle cuisine, to claim, for example, that it is more pleasing to the eye than to the palate. The criticism is valid and inevitable to the extent that as the influence of the original nouvelle cuisine has spread throughout the world, chefs good, bad, and mediocre have applied the label to their cooking. Ultimately, however, in its emphasis on quality of produce and subtlety of flavor, it is an admirable contribution to world cuisine.

REFERENCES:

Paul Bocuse, *La Cuisine du marché* (Paris: Flammarion, 1976);

Gourmet's France (New York: Gourmet Books, 1978);

Michel Guérard, *La Grande Cuisine minceur* (Paris: Laffont, 1976).

— J.P.McN.

LA NOUVELLE DANSE

During the 1960s and 1970s there was tremendous growth in the popularity of modern dance, called "La Nouvelle Danse" (new dance) in France. For example, **Maurice Béjart**'s Ballet du Vingtième Siècle (Ballet of the Twentieth Century) attracted enthusiastic crowds totaling seventy thousand to the company's twenty performances in the Palace of the Popes at the 1968 **Avignon Festival.** Following Béjart's example at Avignon, dance moved from theaters into nontraditional performance spaces, becoming accessible to wider audiences. To further the democratization of dance, the French government established Centres chorégraphiques nationaux (national centers of choreography) in the provinces. The centers are home bases to dance companies that perform and hold educational programs. Companies such as those of Dominique Bagouet in Montpellier, Jean-Claude Gallotta in Grenoble, and Maguy Marin in Créteil have profoundly increased public interest in modern dance and raised the place of dance in the cultural lives of the French.

In 1968 the new Théâtre de la Ville, founded by Jean Mercure in the remodeled Théâtre Sarah Bern-

hardt, began to present modern dance. The number of modern-dance performances at the theater increased yearly, and by 1978 ten dance companies had presented eighty-three performances there. Also in 1968, Jacque Chauraud founded Le Ballet pour Demain (Ballet for Tomorrow) — the first French competition specifically designed to showcase young modern-dance choreographers — in the Paris suburb of Bagnolet. Some of the important French modern dancers who appeared in the Prix Bagnolet competition early in their careers are Gallotta, Bagouet, Régine Chopinot, Marin, François Verret, Joëlle Bouvier, and Régis Obadia. The competition is now held in Bobigny.

Since the creation of the Ballet pour Demain competition, other festivals and competitions highlighting modern dance have been started in Arles, Aix-en-Provence, Châteauvallon, Montpellier, and Lyons. Even the prestigious Festival international de la Danse de Paris (Paris International Dance Festival), founded in 1963, began to present modern dance when it allowed Merce Cunningham to participate in the fourth festival and awarded him the gold medal for best new choreography.

Three companies important to the development of modern dance in France are Les Ballets Modernes de Paris (1955–1975), founded by Françoise and Dominique Dupuy; the Théâtre du Silence, founded in 1973 in La Rochelle by Jacques Garnier and Brigitte Lefèvre; and the Groupe de recherche théâtrale de l'Opéra de Paris (Theater Research Group of the Paris Opera), or GRTOP, directed by American dancer Carolyn Carlson. GRTOP disbanded in 1980 when Carlson's contract expired. It was replaced by the Groupe de recherche chorégraphique de l'Opéra de Paris (GRCOP), under the direction of Garnier. This experimental group folded with the death of Garnier in 1989.

French modern dance can generally be classified as either abstract dance, influenced by American choreographers, or "danse-théâtre," with roots in German expressionism. Early French modern dance pioneers Jerome Andrews, Jaqueline Robinson, and Karin Waehner worked with Mary Wigman in Germany before opening schools in France. During the 1970s American dance companies — including those of Cunningham, Alwin Nikolais, Paul Taylor, and José Limon — as well as the German company of Pina Bausch were extremely influential when they performed at the Avignon Festivals, the international festivals in Paris, and the Théâtre de la Ville.

REFERENCES:

Bernadette Bonis, "The Shaping of French Dance — A Phenomenon and Its History," *Ballett International,* 11 (August–September 1988): 29–34;

Paul Bourcier, "100,000 Spectators Every Season for Contemporary Dance at the Théâtre de la Ville: An Interview with the Director, Gérard Violette," *Choreography and Dance,* 2, no. 1 (1992): 69–76;

Jacques Cottias, "The Sociological Evolution of the New Dance Public," *Choreography and Dance,* 2, no. 1 (1992): 39–53;

Jean-Claude Diénis, "1970: The Year of the Nouvelle Danse," *Choreography and Dance,* 2, no. 1 (1992): 35–37;

Joseline Le Bourhis, "The Spirit of the Time — French Impressions," *Ballett International,* 8 (December 1985): 54–59.
                                                                    — A.P.E.

LA NOUVELLE REVUE FRANÇAISE

The prestige of *La Nouvelle Revue Française* (The New French Review) is unequaled among French literary periodicals. A monthly, it was founded in 1908 as a politically independent review by **Jacques Copeau, Jean Schlumberger, André Gide,** André Ruyters, Henri Vangeon (who used the pen name Henri Ghéon), and Gide's brother-in-law Marcel Drouin (whose pen name was Michel Arnauld). In 1911, when the founders decided to expand into book publishing, they brought in **Gaston Gallimard** to handle that aspect of the business.

For the first few years of its existence the *NRF,* as it is often called, lost money and was helped out financially by Gide, Schlumberger, and Gallimard, who was in the process of turning the book-publishing aspect of the company into the most illustrious publisher of poetry and fiction in France. By 1913 the financial difficulties of the *NRF* were largely behind it, and it gained prestige and subscribers under Copeau's editorship. Aided by managing editor **Jacques Rivière,** Copeau identified and published work by the finest talents of the period, including **François Mauriac, Jules Romains,** and **Jean Giraudoux.** Gide, whose name did not appear on the masthead of the journal, played an influential advisory role.

Publication of the magazine was suspended during **World War I.** After the armistice Rivière succeeded Copeau as editor and the *NRF* continued to live up to its reputation as a showcase for the finest literary talent in France, publishing works by writers such as **Marcel Proust, Paul Valéry, Paul Claudel, Roger Martin du Gard,** and **Henry de Montherlant.**

Jean Paulhan — who became editor in 1925, after Rivière's death, and continued in that post until 1940 — was even more open to new European styles and literary directions than his predecessor. Among the younger writers he encouraged and published, with extraordinary prescience, were **Francis Ponge** in 1926, **Henri Michaux** and **Marcel Aymé** in 1927, and **Raymond Queneau** in 1936. André Malraux began contrib-

Marcel Arland, André Malraux, Jules Supervielle, Jean Paulhan, and in front of him, Paul Valéry. Beginning in January 1953 Arland and Paulhan were coeditors of *La Nouvelle Revue Française.*

uting to the *NRF* early in his career, and some of his novels were published serially in the magazine.

By the outbreak of **World War II** the reputation of the *NRF* was so great that Otto Abetz, the German ambassador to France, is said to have declared that there were three centers of power in France: the **French Communist Party,** the banking establishment, and the *Nouvelle Revue Française.* Paulhan published his last issue of the *NRF* in June 1940, as the Germans were attacking Paris.

During the **Occupation** the Germans allowed Gallimard to publish the journal under the editorship of **Pierre Drieu La Rochelle,** a gifted writer and regular contributor to the *NRF,* who was also a fascist sympathizer. His anti-Semitic and pro-Nazi beliefs represented a radical change of direction for a journal that he had earlier accused of being warmongering, leftist, and under the influence of Jews. Paulhan refused to be coeditor but remained on the editorial board of readers, and Gide published excerpts of his journal in the wartime *NRF*. After the war Mauriac claimed rather unconvincingly that the continuing appearance of the *NRF* gave voice to the French spirit during the dark days of the Occupation. Drieu committed suicide a few months after the **Liberation.** Gallimard and others associated with the journal were cleared of collaboration charges, but the magazine was banned because of the pro-Nazi views Drieu had published in it. It was revived in January 1953 as the *Nouvelle Nouvelle Revue Française,* with Paulhan and **Marcel Arland** as coeditors. It soon reverted to its original title, but it never regained the prestige and influence it had before the war.

REFERENCES:

Pierre Assouline, *Gaston Gallimard: A Half-Century of French Publishing,* translated by Harold J. Salemson (San Diego, New York & London: Harcourt Brace Jovanovich, 1988);

Justin O'Brien, ed., *From the "N.R.F."* (New York: Farrar, Straus & Cudahy, 1958);

Gilles Ragache and Jean-Robert Ragache, *La Vie quotidienne des écrivains et des artistes sous l'occupation, 1940–1944* (Paris: Hachette, 1988).

—J.P.McN.

NOUVELLE VAGUE

The term *Nouvelle Vague* (New Wave) refers to an influential style of cinema born in France in the late 1950s. While the New Wave directors each manifested a distinct personal style, they were united in their rejection of meticulously scripted commercial studio movies and their promotion of filmmaking that emphasized visual style over dialogue. The critical and commercial success of the New Wave in France and abroad led to an increased respect for French cinema.

During the early 1950s the best-known New Wave directors — **Claude Chabrol, Jean-Luc Godard, Jacques Rivette, Eric Rohmer,** and **François Truffaut** — wrote for *Cahiers du Cinéma,* a journal founded by **André Bazin.** A central tenet of the journal was the notion of the *auteur:* though films are collaborative ventures, these critics said, they should embody the personal ideas and style of the director. Through their writings the New Wave critics reconstructed a history of *auteurs* in most national traditions, especially from the United States. They also looked at film in terms of its form and eschewed the dominance in France of the

tradition de qualité, which discouraged improvisation and experiment.

Dozens of directors who were identified with the New Wave in a 1962 *Cahiers du Cinéma* article made their first feature films between 1958 and 1960. These movies include **Alain Resnais**'s *Hiroshima, mon amour,* Truffaut's *Les Quatre cent coups (The 400 Blows),* and Godard's *A bout de souffle (Breathless),* all released in 1959. In the early work of Truffaut, in all of Godard's films, and in most of Resnais's work a revolution indeed took place. While individual approaches varied, New Wave films were typically shot on minimal budgets and used unknown actors, location shooting, improvisation, and handheld cameras to optimal effect. New Wave works often mix elements of popular culture with the concerns of art films, and they frequently include allusions to other films. The New Wave had a significant international impact. Few national cinematic styles remained unchanged in its wake. The most prominent directors pursued different directions in the 1960s.

REFERENCES:

Peter Graham, *The New Wave* (London: Secker & Warburg, 1968);

James Monaco, *The New Wave* (New York: Oxford University Press, 1976).

—T.C.

LES NOUVELLES LITTÉRAIRES

The *Nouvelles Littéraires* (Literary News) first appeared in 1922, bearing as its full title *Les Nouvelles Littéraires, Artistiques et Scientifiques* (Literary, Artistic and Scientific News) and a subtitle indicating its identity as a weekly newspaper of information, criticism, and bibliography. It was created by Frédéric Lefèvre, who offered it for sale at a low price and in the format of a daily newspaper. This approach helped to assure its longevity as it went through many changes over its seventy years of existence. Its identity has not always been clear or well defined; it has changed hands frequently; and it has experienced major financial problems.

The first editors of the *Nouvelles Littéraires,* Jacques Guenne and Maurice Martin du Gard, placed a major emphasis on literary columns and book reviews, an emphasis continued through much of its history. From the beginning it failed to show a profit, and it would have folded without the backing of the publisher Larousse.

With the German **Occupation** of 1940, the *Nouvelles Littéraires* disappeared for the duration of **World**

War II. It was revived in 1945, though some of its columnists, including Martin du Gard and Edmond Jaloux, were not allowed to write for it because of their wartime collaboration with the Germans.

While the *Nouvelles Littéraires* could examine major issues of literature, philosophy, and the arts, its agreement with Larousse denied it the right to take partisan political positions. Given readers' avid interest in issues such as the **Algerian war** and later the student revolt of **May 1968,** this neutrality hurt circulation. Larousse withdrew its support in 1972, and the journal underwent some identity changes, as it went through several editors in the 1970s.

With Jean-François Kahn, who took over as editor in 1979, the *Nouvelles Littéraires* placed less emphasis upon literary criticism and more on politics, enjoying considerable success as a result. It found its niche not by imitating the general coverage of newsmagazines such as the *Express* or the *Point* but by providing in-depth coverage of one major current issue at a time.

With his balanced coverage of the political and the cultural arenas Kahn greatly increased circulation, which reached one hundred thousand in 1981. Circulation fell again after Kahn left in 1982, and since then the paper's fortunes have been mixed at best. The *Nouvelles Littéraires* disappeared in 1984 and was reborn briefly as the *Autre Journal* (The Other Journal). Then it was bought by FNAC, a highly successful chain of stores selling books and records, and reemerged in 1985 as the *Nouvelles.*

REFERENCE:

Michel Jamet, *La Presse périodique en France* (Paris: Colin, 1983), pp. 125–128.

—J.P.McN.

O

RENÉ DE OBALDIA

The dramatic and fictional works of René de Obaldia (1918–) are marked by humor and social criticism, combining whimsy and the absurd (employed in a manner similar to **Surrealism**) with clichés and poetic elements, often to pass severe judgments on the twentieth century, which he describes as an enormous prison.

Obaldia was the son of a French mother and a Panamanian father. The poet's cosmopolitan origins and experience may have contributed to the ease with which he moves from drama to poetry to fiction and combines disparate aesthetic elements. His service in **World War II,** particularly his experience as a prisoner of war in Poland, undoubtedly contributed to his dark vision. Obaldia's first dramatic success, *Genousie* (1960; translated as *Jenusia*), produced by **Jean Vilar,** concerns an eccentric woman and the snobs she entertains. As Jean-Louis Bory wrote, "One laughs at the expense of high society." Among Obaldia's other dramatic works is *Du vent dans les branches de sassafras* (1966; translated as *Wind in the Branches of the Sassafras*), which starred Michel Simon in the part of an accident-prone cowboy. Called a "delirious Western" by one critic, it includes speeches in alexandrines. *Et à la fin était le bang* (1974; And at the End was the Bang) is a piece of social criticism. Obaldia's novels include *Tamerlan des cœurs* (1955; Tamerlane of Hearts), in which a young writer's story, set in modern times, is fused with various events in world history, until history, in the form of the second world conflict, envelops him also. Another novel, *Le Centenaire* (1959; translated as *The Centenarian*), is narrated as the first-person memoir of an elderly man — a stream-of-consciousness meditation on time, memory, and the creative process. Obaldia has also made films and published more than five volumes of poems.

REFERENCES:
Martha O'Nan, "Names in René de Obaldia's *Du vent dans les branches de sassafras," Names,* 30, no. 2 (1982): 113–121;
Kamal Zein, "Entretien avec René de Obaldia," *Stanford French Review,* 2 (Spring 1978): 129–138.

— C.S.B.

THE OCCUPATION

After the **Debacle** of May–June 1940, in which Germany invaded and swiftly defeated France, an armistice was signed on 22 June. According to its terms, Germany annexed Alsace and Lorraine, which had been ceded to Germany at the end of the Franco-Prussian War (1871) and returned to France at the end of **World War I.** The rest of France was divided into three zones: the Forbidden Zone, the Occupied Zone, and the **Free Zone.** The small Forbidden Zone consisted of areas along the Atlantic coast and the Belgian border, which were placed under the authority of the German military commander in Brussels. The Occupied Zone, about three-fifths of French territory, consisted of the northern half of France and the Atlantic coast south of the Forbidden Zone. This area was occupied by the German army, which — as mandated by the armistice — was housed and fed by the French. The rest of France — that is, the southeastern part of the country and the Rhône Valley — remained a Free Zone, without German troops. Passage from one zone to another was forbidden.

The armistice agreement established Vichy, in the Free Zone, as the capital of all France. Led by **Philippe Pétain,** the **Vichy government** theoretically exercised its authority over all three zones except in military matters, but practically the government was subservient to the German Reich. Maintaining the fic-

German soldiers jeering at a column of French prisoners in 1940

tion of independence, Pétain in July 1940 spoke of his plans for a "révolution nationale" that would cleanse the nation of the parliamentary abuses of the **Third Republic.** After meeting personally with Adolf Hitler at Montoire in October 1940, however, Pétain became dedicated to the idea of "collaboration" with Germany in the construction of a new Europe under German hegemony.

Beginning in 1942, the Occupation forces encountered increasing difficulties in carrying out their policies. German military setbacks on the Eastern Front were accompanied by manifestations of political discontent in France. The Vichy authorities and their police force, the **Milice Française,** found themselves devoting much of their energy simply to repressing dissent. After the Anglo-American invasions of North Africa on 7 November 1942, German forces occupied the Free Zone on 11 November, and the division of the country into zones ceased to exist. By late 1942, as the **Resistance** passed into an armed phase, the government and the Germans found themselves involved in what has come to be seen as nothing less than a civil war.

During the 1980s the Occupation became the topic of considerable reexamination by historians.

Many came to the conclusion that after the **Liberation** there emerged in France a convenient national myth in which the country was cast as a nation of forty million resisters to the German presence. French politicians and others interested in restoring political harmony and in reorganizing France for the economic competition of postwar Europe had an interest in propagating this view of their nation. Now, however, historians generally agree that most of the French gave at least silent support to the collaborationist policies of the Vichy government. In some cases, certainly, leaders were more than willing to cooperate with the occupiers.

REFERENCES:

Gerhard Hirschfeld and Patrick Marsh, *Collaboration in France: Politics and Culture During the Nazi Occupation 1940–1944* (Oxford & New York: Berg, 1989);

John F. Sweets, *Choices in Vichy France: The French Under Nazi Occupation* (New York: Oxford University Press, 1986).

— D.O'C.

CLAUDE OLLIER

One of the creators of the **Nouveau Roman** (New Novel), Claude Ollier (1922–) was trained in law and commerce and held various positions in industry, banking, and colonial administration before turning to writing full-time in 1955. Like other experimental writers of his generation who once pursued nonliterary interests, Ollier brought an analytical mind to literature — a predilection that is evident in his work.

With his first novel, *La Mise en scène* (1958; translated), which received the Prix Médicis, he inaugurated what would become a complex series of eight novels, titled collectively *Le Jeu d'enfant* (Child's Play) and divided into two cycles of four volumes each. The first cycle is set on earth in locales such as North Africa and Mexico; the second is set in outer space. The complex tapestry of recurring characters, structures, situations, and passages in *Le Jeu d'enfant* has as its common theme a single protagonist's search for comprehension and identity in foreign settings. Among the novels in the series are the second, *Le Maintien de l'ordre* (1961; translated as *Law and Order*), the sixth, *Enigma* (1974), and the last, *Fuzzy Sets* (1975).

These titles are significant, for they suggest something of Ollier's approach to fiction. Like some other writers of the twentieth century — from **André Gide** in, for example, *Paludes* (1895; translated as *Marshlands*), through **Raymond Queneau** and **Michel Butor**, to **Georges Perec** with his complex verbal structures — Ollier treats literature as ludic — as an elaborate game that points to the artificial nature of "reality" as human beings construct it by means of the mind and language. Reality is a scenario or mise-en-scène. Although Ollier recognizes that order is crucial in any mental or linguistic representation, as in the social world, he challenges Western ideas of order, including political ones, particularly as opposed to non-Western (in this case Algerian) notions. The titles *Enigma* and *Fuzzy Sets* suggest Ollier's view of literature as a puzzle. (*Fuzzy set* is a mathematical term that suggests the impossibility of linear, integral reading, and the novel is presented as a sort of elliptical computer printout.)

Much like the fiction of **Jean Ricardou** and **Alain Robbe-Grillet**, the eight novels of *Le Jeu d'enfant* comprise a self-reflexive and self-critical project, an interrogation of fiction by fiction. Ollier calls into question such conventional aspects as identity of characters and coherence of plot, and he plays with fictional space and time.

In one sense the author of a project such as this should be in complete control of his constructs, since — like his fellow New Novelists — he has abandoned the mimetic pretense of mirroring reality and can manipulate his fictional materials as he wishes. Ollier's imaginary world, however, is far from lucid and does not seem entirely autonomous. Detective motifs abound, and the search — an old fictional organizing device borrowed from the epic — is crucial. Moreover, the reader frequently encounters disquieting criminal and sexual elements, such as rape. It is as if the linguistic construct of the novel were a projection — perhaps only semiconscious — of a set of mental complexes, the disturbing psyche of modern man, which language can express tentatively but not resolve.

As in the *Jeu d'enfant* series, travel motifs are frequent in Ollier's other works, including *Navettes* (1967; Shuttles) and *Marrakch Medine* (1979) — sketches concerned with that Moroccan city. *Souvenirs écran* (1981; Memory Screen) collects Ollier's discussions of films and filmmakers (1958–1968) during the rise of the ***Nouvelle Vague*** (New Wave) of French cinema. In *Déconnection* (1988; Disconnection) Ollier treats the disquieting past of Europe in the twentieth century. Reason and knowability, already called into question by the earlier novels, are qualified in this case by the terrible destruction of the twentieth century — a mad fictional world come true.

REFERENCES:
Cecile Lindsay, "Textual Intercourse: Reader Theory and the New Novel," *Structuralist Review*, 2 (Spring 1984): 99–115;
Review of Contemporary Fiction, special issue on Ollier and Carlos Fuentes, 8 (Summer 1988);
Sub-stance, special issue on Ollier, 13 (1976).

— C.S.B.

MARCEL OPHULS

Son of the celebrated film director **Max Ophuls**, Marcel Ophuls (1927–) is recognized in France for five films shot between 1960 and 1969 and, most recently, his Academy Award–winning documentary *Hôtel Terminus: Klaus Barbie — His Life and Times* (1988). Ophuls is best known for his documentary about France during **World War II**, *Le Chagrin et la pitié* (1969; *The Sorrow and the Pity*).

Born in Germany, Ophuls moved to France with his family in 1933 and became a French citizen in 1938. He became an American citizen after spending most of the 1940s in the United States. Returning to France in 1950, he studied philosophy at the Sorbonne before becoming a production assistant for John Huston on *Moulin Rouge* (1953) and for his father on *Lola Montès* (1955). Ophuls also worked with French ***Nouvelle Vague*** (New Wave) directors, directing one of the episodes of *L'Amour à vingt ans* (1962; *Love at Twenty*) in collaboration with **François Truffaut** and others. *Peau de banane* (1964; *Banana Skin*) and his *Feu à volonté* (1965; Fire at Will) were Ophuls's first features.

Scene from *Le Chagrin et la pitié* (1969), Marcel Ophuls's four-and-a-half-hour documentary about the Vichy regime and the German Occupation

In the mid 1960s Ophuls began making journalistic movies for television. Sponsored by German and Swiss producers, he spent three years making *Le Chagrin et la pitié*, a four-and-a-half-hour documentary culled from more than sixty hours of filmed interviews with French and German people who lived in the region around Clermont-Ferrand during the German **Occupation** of France in **World War II.** The accounts from both sides, interspersed with newsreels and archival footage, make apparent the contradictions between the received history of the actual events and the participants' reconstruction of them. While the film is not didactic, Ophuls's own stance is apparent. French television rejected the documentary for its negative portrait of **Vichy** collaborators, but it was a successful theater film in France and internationally.

Le Chagrin et la pitié established Ophuls as a nonfiction filmmaker and led to other subjective documentaries on such topics as American involvement in the Vietnam War and the struggle of Protestants and Catholics in Northern Ireland. He worked in American television from 1975 to 1979; since then he has been a director in France. His influence is particularly apparent in Claude Lanzmann's epic *Shoah* (1985), a nonfiction film about the Holocaust.

REFERENCES:

"Jean-Pierre Melville Talks to Rui Nogueira about *The Sorrow and the Pity*," *Sight and Sound* (Winter 1971–1972);

The Sorrow and the Pity: A Film by Marcel Ophuls, translated by Mireille Johnston, with an introduction by Stanley Hoffmann (New York: Dutton, 1972).

—T.C.

MAX OPHULS

Max Ophuls (1902–1957) ranks among the world's great movie directors. He worked in many countries, including Germany, France, and the United States. His movies are noteworthy for his fluid camera style, with the camera almost constantly in motion. Critics have found fault with his romantic themes and glittering spectacles, but in recent decades defenders have claimed that he was in fact examining false cultural values.

Born in Germany, Ophuls began directing plays in 1923 and directed his first film in 1930. After Adolf Hitler became chancellor of Germany in 1933 he moved his family to France and directed films in France, Italy, and the Netherlands. He became a

French citizen in 1938. With the **Debacle** and the fall of France in 1940 he fled to Switzerland and went to Hollywood the following year. Experiencing little success in America, Ophuls returned to France in 1949 and completed the four films on which his reputation largely rests: *La Ronde* (1950; *Rondelay*), *Le Plaisir* (1952; *House of Pleasure*), *Madame De . . .* (1953; *The Earrings of Madame De/The Loves of Madame De*), and *Lola Montès* (1955; *The Sins of Lola Montes*). All of these films deal with the difficult relationships among love, duty, and pleasure. Ophuls's vision is apparent in *Madame De . . .*, about a set of earrings passed around among a husband and wife and their lovers. The movie blends an elegant period setting with a continuously moving study of objects, producing an examination of established ideas about women's roles.

Some young French directors, such as **Jacques Demy,** were influenced by Ophuls's style and used it as a model during the height of the **Nouvelle Vague** (New Wave). Ironically, many New Wave critics, by attacking the **tradition de qualité,** to which Ophuls's work was related by content, contributed to the temporary neglect of his movies during the 1960s and early 1970s.

REFERENCES:

Andrew Sarris, ed., *Interviews with Film Directors* (New York: Bobbs-Merrill, 1967), pp. 350–356;

Paul Willemin, ed., *Ophuls* (London: British Film Institute, 1978);

Alan Williams, *Max Ophuls and the Cinema of Desire* (New York: Arno, 1980).

—T.C.

MERET OPPENHEIM

Meret Oppenheim (1913–) is among the most important women affiliated with the **Surrealist** movement. Born in Berlin, she is the daughter of a country doctor who was interested in Jungian psychoanalysis and granddaughter of a German feminist writer. Fascinated at age sixteen by the works of Paul Klee, Oppenheim began to experiment with small watercolor caricatures in a similar style. In 1932 she moved to Paris, where she met the Swiss sculptor Alberto Giacometti, through whom she became acquainted with **Jean Arp,** Sophie Taeuber Arp, Max Ernst, and **Man Ray.** She exhibited with the Surrealists from 1933 until 1937 and again occasionally from the end of **World War II** until 1960.

Oppenheim's work has typically involved playing with household objects, shifting colors, textures, and forms at will. Her best-known piece, for example, is *Fur Breakfast,* a fur-lined teacup with saucer and spoon, shown at the **Dada**/Surrealist Exhibition at the Museum of Modern Art in New York in 1937. Such

works — including a pair of high-heeled shoes served on a silver platter like a cooked goose or turkey — separate form from content, estranging the viewer from the everyday, and they also evoke new sensations by their unfamiliar textures and juxtapositions. Ironically, although several of Oppenheim's works became famous — the fur-lined teacup has become one of the most commonly reproduced Surrealist objects — she herself has remained relatively obscure. She is not mentioned in most standard accounts of the Surrealist movement.

REFERENCES:

Whitney Chadwick, *Women Artists and the Surrealist Movement* (London: Thames & Hudson, 1985);

Wendy Slatkin, *Women Artists in History from Antiquity to the 20th Century,* second edition (Englewood Cliffs, N.J.: Prentice-Hall, 1990);

Josephine Withers, "The Famous Fur-Lined Teacup and the Anonymous Meret Oppenheim," *Arts Magazine,* 52 (November 1977): 88–93.

—J.H.

ORGANISTS AND ORGAN MUSIC

For centuries organ music and organists have been an important facet of French music. From the late 1800s through most of the twentieth century, organists of other countries were likely to have been known only to their parishioners, but in France several of the most prominent composers played in the great churches and wrote music for the organ; some even made international concert tours.

César Franck (1822–1890), organist at the church of Sainte-Clotilde and professor of organ at the Paris Conservatory, was the founding father of the French organ school. He was well known for his improvisations and for compositions such as his *Grande Pièce symphonique* (1860; Grand Symphonic Piece) and *Pièce héroïque* (1878; Heroic Piece). Both works are brilliant, large-scale pieces that resemble his well-known Symphony in D Minor (1888). **Camille Saint-Saëns** (1835–1921) and his pupil **Gabriel Fauré** (1845–1924) held in turn the prestigious post of organist at the Church of the Madeleine in Paris. Saint-Saëns's Third Symphony (1886) includes an important part for the organ.

Charles-Marie Widor (1844–1937), for sixty-four years the organist at the imposing Church of Saint-Sulpice, succeeded Franck as professor of organ at the Paris Conservatory. He played an important role in acquainting the French public with Johann Sebastian Bach's organ works, hitherto neglected in France. He counted among his pupils many of the prominent organists of the next generation, including Louis Vierne (1870–1937), who, although blind, was organist at the Cathedral of Notre-Dame for many years, and Albert Schweitzer (1875–1965), the renowned missionary and Bach scholar whose research increased understanding of the sources of Bach's expressive language.

Félix Alexandre Guilmant (1837–1911), another distinguished teacher-virtuoso, succeeded Widor at the Paris Conservatory, where **Nadia Boulanger** and other well-known performers studied with him. His best-known pupil, Marcel Dupré (1886–1971), was called "the Horowitz of the organ" (a reference to pianist Vladimir Horowitz) because of his brilliant technique and astonishing improvisations. When he was in Paris Dupré played at Saint-Sulpice, but he toured widely, traveling to Australia, the Far East, and the United States.

Dupré's best-known pupil was **Olivier Messiaen,** whose playing at the Church of la Trinité made it a Mecca for all those interested in organ music. Messiaen's *Apparition de l'Eglise éternelle* (1931; Vision of the Eternal Church) and *La Nativité du Seigneur* (1935; The Birth of the Lord) are among the masterpieces of twentieth-century organ music.

All of these organists played on instruments designed and built by Aristide Cavaillé-Col (1811–1899), whose innovations greatly increased the variety of timbres, dynamics, and expressive potential of organs so that they approached the rich sound of symphony orchestras. The organists' compositions took full advantage of these resources and would not have been possible without them. Cavaillé-Col's imposing nineteenth-century-style instruments ultimately lost popularity as tastes later changed in favor of the baroque-style organ.

REFERENCES:

Norbert Dufourcq, *La Musique d'orgue française* (Paris: Floury, 1941);

Arthur Wills, *Organ* (London: Macdonald, 1984).

— P.S.H.

AMÉDÉE OZENFANT

Purism, one of the notable offsprings of **Cubism,** was launched with a small book, *Après le cubisme* (1918; After Cubism), by **Le Corbusier** and Amédée Ozenfant (1886–1966).

Ozenfant, who began using the term *le purisme* as early as 1916, had attempted to employ Cubist ideas in still lifes such as *Le Hasard* (1916; Chance), but had found his experiments unsatisfactory and Cubism itself problematic. In his essay "Notes sur le cubisme" (1916; Notes on Cubism) he insisted that Cubism was of critical importance because it had realized in part "its purist intentions of cleansing the plastic language of parasitic terms. . . ." Nonetheless, Cubism had halted before its tasks were complete, he charged; it had become elitist, shutting itself off from social upheavals, and — worse — had become decorative, ornamental, "charmingly pretty." In *Après le cubisme* Le Corbusier and Ozenfant intensified the attack, calling Cubism "a decorative art of romantic ornamentism." Purism was to seek out the essential, "the invariant," in its subjects, avoiding the "accidental, exceptional, impressionist, inorganic, protesting, picturesque. . . ." In pursuit of the "invariant," Purists allowed for distortion of the outward form: "All liberties are accepted in art except those which are not clear." Above all, the two wrote, a new, purified art had to deal with the machine age. Artists should follow the same rules of science and engineering as the inventors of machines because "the methods are the same: induction, analysis, conception, reconstruction."

The first Purist exhibition, held in 1918, revealed nothing of the new movement. Most of the paintings had been produced before the Purist idea had jelled. In later shows, and in the magazine *L'Esprit Nouveau* (1920–1925; The New Spirit), Ozenfant and Le Corbusier gradually elaborated a characteristic style. Purist art, they insisted, was not marked by a distortion of form in the Cubist sense; they spoke of "things arranged normally" as a starting point. One result was a tendency to treat forms as stacked or layered, two-dimensional cutouts, as in Ozenfant's *Accords* (1922), in which the flat shapes of a guitar, a pitcher, glasses, and bottles retain their outlined shapes but are sometimes interrupted or blocked by other, interposed forms. The focus on mass-produced goods is also characteristic of the movement.

As early as *Après le cubisme* Ozenfant had written that "there is a hierarchy in the arts: decorative art is at the base, the human figure is at the summit." By 1925 he had begun to reintroduce human figures into his works; he formally abandoned Purism as too restrictive. In *La Vie* (1931–1938; *Life*) he replaced the overlapping silhouettes of mass-produced goods with a tangled swarm of human figures, designed to evoke the intermingled elements of life: "love, tenderness, sleep, waking, pleasure, jealousy, pantheism, grace, brute force, health, weakness, strength, passion, melancholy, youth, age, etc."

REFERENCES:

Susan L. Ball, *Ozenfant and Purism: The Evolution of a Style, 1915–1930* (Ann Arbor: UMI Research Press, 1981);

Christopher Green, *Cubism and Its Enemies: Modern Movements and Reaction in French Art, 1916–1928* (New Haven & London: Yale University Press, 1987).

—J.H.

P

MARCEL PAGNOL

A highly successful dramatist by the time he was thirty, Marcel Pagnol (1895–1974) discovered his strongest calling in early sound films. In the late 1920s his plays about everyday life in southern France offered an alternative to the obscurities of **Surrealist** creations and to the refined but mechanical style of **boulevard theater.** His films achieved a similar success. He directed nearly twenty films between 1934 and 1967.

Born in Aubagne, in Provence, Pagnol served in the French army in both world wars. In 1925 *Marius,* one of his plays about life in the south of France, was performed in Paris and made him a national figure. Inspired by the advent of sound technology in movies and seeing them as a way to record and popularize plays, Pagnol wrote screen adaptations of *Marius* (1931) and *Fanny* (1932), and he wrote, produced, and directed *César* (1936) at the studio he founded in Marseilles in 1933. These three movies, named for members of one family, constitute Pagnol's Marseilles trilogy, his best-known work.

One of the first regional filmmakers, Pagnol bequeathed to viewers rich portraits of an almost timeless, archaic society set apart from the history of the 1930s and 1940s. His work inspired **Jean Renoir** to shoot *Toni* (1934), a precursor of Italian neorealism, in Martigues, a town not far from Pagnol's Aubagne and Marseilles; Pagnol produced the film. Pagnol's *Manon des sources* (1952; Manon of the Spring) was the basis for two of the most popular French films of the 1980s, Claude Berri's *Jean de Florette* (1986) and *Manon des sources* (1986; *Manon of the Spring*), which were influenced by the mood and setting of other Pagnol movies as well.

REFERENCES:

Claude Beylie, *Marcel Pagnol ou le cinéma en liberté* (Paris: Atlas, 1986);

Lobby poster for *Marius* (1931), adapted by Pagnol

C. E. J. Caldicott, *Marcel Pagnol* (Boston: Twayne, 1977);

Ginette Vincendeau, "In the Name of the Father: Marcel Pagnol's 'Trilogy' *Marius* (1931), *Fanny* (1932), *César* (1936)," in *French Film: Texts and Contexts,* by Susan Hayward and Vincendeau (London: Routledge, 1990), pp. 67–82.

—T.C.

PARADE

The ballet *Parade* (1917; Sideshow), presented by **Serge Diaghilev's Ballets Russes,** is best known not for the choreography by **Léonide Massine** but for the collaboration of three avant-garde artists: poet and playwright **Jean Cocteau,** painter **Pablo Picasso,** and composer **Erik Satie.** Although there is debate about the extent of the controversy provoked by the premiere of *Parade* on 18 May 1917, as a benefit for wounded soldiers, at the **Théâtre du Châtelet,** it certainly baffled an audience not prepared for experimental theater.

In the program for the ballet **Guillaume Apollinaire** wrote, "The innovating composer Erik Satie has turned this stage poem into astonishingly expressive music, so clear and simple that you can see in it the wonderfully lucid spirit of France itself. The Cubist painter Picasso and Massine, the most daring of choreographers, have brought it to the stage, consummating for the first time a union between painting and the dance — between plastic and mime — which heralds the arrival of a more complete art. From this new alliance there emerges in *Parade* a kind of surrealism." (This program note includes the first known use of the term *Surrealism* in the modern sense.)

Set on a street outside a circus tent, *Parade* has a simple plot. Performers — including a Chinese conjurer performing sleight-of-hand tricks, an American girl who is a takeoff on the heroine of *Perils of Pauline,* and two acrobats dressed in blue-and-white bodysuits — attempt to entice a crowd into paying to see a performance inside the tent. Angry managers from New York and Paris interrupt the circus acts. The spectators then disperse, thinking they have seen the show. The ballet ends with the collapsed circus performers alone on the stage.

Critics charged that Picasso's **Cubist** costume designs dominated the production and subordinated the choreography of the ballet. The striking costumes for the managers were so bulky and tall that they restricted the dancers' movements. The American manager's costume, for example, was a ten-foot-high collage incorporating skyscrapers, pipes, and a megaphone. Satie's music varied from irrelevant academic fugues to jazz and music-hall tunes. Cocteau initially insisted that the music include machine noises, but eventually these noises, except for the typewriter sounds, were transcribed for musical instruments.

Although the premiere of *Parade* was a failure, the revival four years later was the hit of the season. In 1973 the work was successfully revived by the Joffrey Ballet.

REFERENCES:

Jean Cocteau, *Cock and Harlequin: Notes Concerning Music,* translated by Rollo H. Myers (London: Egoist Press, 1921);

James Harding, *Erik Satie* (New York: Praeger, 1975);

Martha Schmoyer LoMonaco, "The Giant Jigsaw Puzzle: Robert Joffrey Reconstructs *Parade,*" *Drama Review,* 28 (Fall 1984): 31–45;

Frank W. D. Ries, *The Dance Theatre of Jean Cocteau* (Ann Arbor: UMI Research Press, 1986).

— A.P.E. and P.S.H.

PARIS

The position of Paris as literary, artistic, intellectual, and musical capital of France (as well as of Europe and the world for some decades of the twentieth century) can be contrasted with that of New York in the United States. While New York is often thought of as the artistic center of the United States, to some degree it has shared this position at various times with other cities. Moreover, American writers and artists have not felt obliged to live in New York, and many have chosen to preserve their regional identities by living elsewhere. In France even distinctly regional writers, such as **François Mauriac,** have usually settled in Paris and carried on their literary lives there. (**Jean Giono** is a striking exception.) Few publishing houses are located outside Paris, and the major French museums, art schools, conservatories, and orchestras are all in the capital. Moreover, the University of Paris and the **Ecole Normale Supérieure,** long the elite school of France for the liberal arts, have attracted some of the most talented French writers, philosophers, historians, and other intellectuals, who have generally remained in Paris for the rest of their careers.

While the roots of Paris — sometimes known familiarly as *Paname* — go back at least to the first century B.C., when Julius Caesar conquered Lutetia on the Ile de la Cité, the centralization of cultural activity in the city did not begin in earnest until the reign of Louis XIV (1643–1715), who successfully campaigned to establish cultural as well as political hegemony there, bringing to the court the finest writers, musicians, and artists. The tendency toward centralization was strengthened in the eighteenth century, when the philosophers all gathered in Paris, despite risks of persecution. Even Jean-Jacques Rousseau, who boasted of being a citizen of Geneva, felt obliged to go there. Napoleon Bonaparte's centralized administration (1804–1815) furthered the trend.

Whereas the Romantic poets of the first half of the nineteenth century preached a return to nature and often settled away from the capital, by the second half of the century Paris was the obligatory residence for poets, even those who cursed industrialization and urbanism. For painters the magnetism of the capital was even greater, and it remained so throughout the following century. Paris was the undisputed artistic capital of the world from the first decade of the twentieth century until the shattering events of **World War II.** After the German **Occupation** of France (1940–1944), many young French intellectuals and artists who had been separated from the capital gravitated there and contributed to a collective effort to restore French cultural prestige.

Under the cultural ministry of **André Malraux** (1958–1969) there was a considerable effort to decentralize certain areas of the arts, especially drama, by founding state-supported regional theaters, as well as fostering music and art in the provinces. Malraux proposed the creation of ninety **Maisons de la Culture** as regional cultural centers, though only fifteen were constructed. Although several cities have restored and enlarged their museums (and developed their old neighborhoods as historic attractions), this decentralization campaign has been judged only partly successful. In the 1980s and 1990s construction connected to the arts in Paris — the redoing of the Louvre and addition of its Pyramid, the new Opéra at the Place de la Bastille — has added to the city's artistic dominance. The preeminence of the city is, of course, reasonable in demographic terms, since the Parisian basin (city and suburbs) holds approximately one-sixth of the population of France.

In the twentieth century Paris has also served as a mecca for artists from abroad. Expatriates have swarmed over the bohemian neighborhoods of **Montmartre, Montparnasse,** and **Saint-Germain-des-Prés.** Some have come because their native countries were in turmoil; others because their homelands were on the cultural margin of Europe and offered them too little cultural intercourse and opportunity for proving themselves. American writers and artists have often profited from firsthand exposure to the European cultural milieu at its finest. Although the trend has been visible from the early years of the twentieth century, there were particularly large numbers of foreign artists and writers in Paris after **World War I.** The Russian Revolution and the social unrest that followed brought immigrants from the Soviet Union, Germany, and central European nations, especially in the 1930s. Others came from Spain after the **Spanish Civil War** broke out. Painters, sculptors, composers, performing musicians, dancers, theater directors, writers whose languages were English (Ernest Hemingway, Gertrude Stein, James Joyce, Samuel Beckett, Julien Green), Romanian (**Eugène Ionesco**), and Spanish (Fernando Arrabal, Jorge Semprún), and many others chose Paris

as their headquarters for a few years or the rest of their lives. Some — including Beckett, Green, Ionesco, and Arrabal — adopted French as their writing language. A second wave of displaced newcomers began after World War II. *The Paris Review,* a major English-language literary periodical, takes its name from the city where it was founded in 1952.

In the late twentieth century small separatist movements, or campaigns for cultural autonomy, have sprung up in areas such as the Basque country, Brittany, and Provence (where the Félibres in the nineteenth century had some success at re-creating literature in the Provençal tongue). A growing number of writers have been attracted away from the city and have begun to identify themselves with their regions. Yet Paris, as it has been for centuries, remains the cultural heart of France.

REFERENCES:

Charles Douglas, *Artist Quarter* (London: Faber & Faber, 1941);

Jerrold E. Seigel, *Bohemian Paris: Culture, Politics, and the Boundaries of Bourgeois Life* (New York: Viking, 1986).

— C.S.B.

THE PARIS OPÉRA BALLET

The Paris Opéra Ballet, the second-largest ballet company in the world by the late twentieth century, was established in 1669 by Louis XIV as the Académie Royale de l'Opéra. The oldest national ballet company, it has been in existence almost continually for more than three centuries, steadfastly representing traditional classical ballet.

Most of the great ballet performers of the eighteenth and nineteenth centuries danced at the Paris Opéra Ballet, including Gaétan Vestris, Marie Sallé, Marie-Anne Cupis de Camargo, Marie Faglioni, Fanny Elssler, and Emma Livry. During the middle of the nineteenth century, at the height of Romantic ballet, the Opéra was the thriving center of traditional dance and the site of the great, enduring ballets of the period, *La Sylphide* and *Giselle.* Unfortunately, during the second half of the nineteenth century the Opéra went into a decline and no longer produced important choreography or great French dancers. The center of ballet activity shifted to Saint Petersburg and Milan, and virtuosic Italian ballerinas replaced French dancers as the stars at the Opéra. The decline continued until the early twentieth century, when **Carlotta Zambelli,** the last of the Italian *étoiles* (stars), was the one extraordinary Opéra ballerina.

The stagnating repertory of the Paris Opéra Ballet became even more apparent after the arrival of

Serge Diaghilev's Ballets Russes in Paris in 1909. Sparked by the popularity of the new company, the Opéra slowly began to improve. Jacques Rouché, who was hired as director in 1914, endorsed the innovations of the Russians and encouraged expansion of the repertory. He hired the Russian ballerina Olga Spessivtseva as *première danseuse étoile* (principal dancer and star) and commissioned ballets from Russian choreographers Ida Rubinstein, Michel Fokine, and Bronislava Nijinska. He also hired Anna Pavlova to perform as a guest artist.

The most significant changes at the Opéra occurred when Rouché engaged the Ballets Russes star Serge Lifar as ballet director and premier danseur étoile in 1929. Lifar remained ballet director for most of the next thirty years and successfully revitalized dance at the Opéra. He created many new works in a neoclassic style, improved the technical level of the French dancers, and developed a new generation of French ballet stars such as Yvette Chauviré, Suzanne Lorca, Solange Schwartz, and Lycette Darsonval.

The years since Lifar left the Paris Opéra Ballet in 1958 have brought many changes. The Opéra has had eight directors: George Skibine (1958–1961), Michel Descombey (1961–1969), John Taras (1969–1971), Raymond Franchetti (1971–1977), Violette Verdy (1977–1981), Rosella Hightower (1981–1983), Rudolph Nureyev (1983–1989), and Patrick Dupond (1989–). Since the 1950s the Opéra has regularly welcomed guest performances of companies such as the New York City Ballet, Sadler's Wells Ballet of London, the Bolshoi Ballet, the Ballet de Marseille, and the Merce Cunningham Dance Company. Under the leadership of Rolf Liebermann, who was appointed general manager in 1973, the company became more eclectic, performing ballets and modern works by George Balanchine, Roland Petit, Cunningham, Glen Tetley, and Maurice Béjart. The Paris Opéra Ballet formed a junior company, the Compagnie Favart, and also founded a new modern dance ensemble, the Groupe de recherche théâtrale de l'Opéra de Paris (1974–1980; Theatrical Research Group of the Paris Opera), or GRTOP, directed by American dancer and Opéra étoile Carolyn Carlson. GRTOP was later replaced by the Groupe de recherche choréographique de l'Opera de Paris (1981–1984; Choreographic Research Group of the Paris Opera), or GRCOP, directed by Jacques Garnier. In addition to the formal performances in the Salle Garnier, the Opéra added performances at the Palais des Sports and the Palais des Congrès.

Although the repertory and dancing of the Paris Opéra Ballet have been modernized, it remains a center of great tradition. Most of the company's dancers are trained at its Ecole de Danse (School of Dance). As children the pupils are known as *petits rats* (little rats — a name that originated in the nineteenth century, when the young dancers were often so hungry that they would ravenously devour food given to them by male admirers after the performances). The Opéra places students entering the company at levels according to ability — *stagiaires* (a term referring to those undergoing a "stage," a sort of apprenticeship or testing period), *quadrilles, choryphées, sujets,* and *premiers danseurs,* with the term *étoile* reserved for the greatest stars. Some of the recent étoiles are Claire Motte, Wilfride Piollet, Noella Pontis, Jean Babilée, Ghisline Thesmar, Jean-Patrick Bonnefous, Georges Piletta, Michael Denard, and Patrick Dupond.

REFERENCES:

Linda Doeser, "France: The Paris Opéra," in *Ballet and Dance* (New York: St. Martin's Press, 1977), pp. 105–109;

Lynn Garafola, "Cradle of Classicism," *Dance Magazine,* 60 (July 1986): 52, 53;

Ivor Guest, *Le Ballet de l'Opéra de Paris: Trois siècles d'histoire et de tradition* (Paris: Théâtre National de l'Opéra, 1976).
                                                                    — A.P.E.

CHARLES PATHÉ

Charles Pathé (1863–1957), a pioneer motion-picture executive, controlled a vast network of cinema production and distribution facilities that dominated the world film market during the first years of the twentieth century. In 1896 Pathé and his brothers Emile (1860–1937), Jacques, and Théophile founded Pathé Frères, specializing in the importation of Edison phonographs from the United States. By 1901, when Charles left the phonograph side of the business to Emile, Théophile and Jacques had left the firm. Charles opened a film studio in Vincennes, just outside Paris, where he began experimenting with filmmaking. Using cameras developed by Louis Lumière and his brother Auguste, Pathé's company filmed many short subjects under the direction of Ferdinand Zecca (1864–1947), who had joined Pathé Frères in 1899.

By 1908 Pathé Frères was the largest motion-picture producer in the world, with branches in London, Moscow, New York, Kiev, Budapest, Calcutta, and Singapore. It is estimated that the firm controlled half the movie industry in the United States. In France its only serious rival was Léon Gaumont. In 1909 Pathé Frères produced its first "long" film, a four-reel version of Victor Hugo's *Les Misérables.* In that same year the firm made the first of the soon-to-be-world-famous *Pathé-Journal* newsreels, which began appearing in the United States the following year as *Pathé Gazette.* In

Jean Paulhan

1914 the firm produced the serial *The Perils of Pauline.* Pathé retired in 1929, but the company continued to operate under the direction of his former partner, Bernard Nathan, until its collapse in 1934.

REFERENCES:

Roy Armes, *French Cinema* (London: Secker & Warburg, 1985);

David Shipman, *The Story of Cinema: An Illustrated History,* volume 1 (London: Hodder & Stoughton, 1982).

— M.G.

JEAN PAULHAN

The critic and essayist Jean Paulhan (1884–1968) is known widely in French literary circles as a longtime editor of the *Nouvelle Revue Française* (*NRF*). Respected for his ability to identify and encourage talented new writers, Paulhan published early works by authors such as **Jean Giono, Julien Green, Jules Supervielle, André Malraux, Henri Michaux, Francis Ponge, Raymond Queneau,** and **Jean-Paul Sartre.**

Taking his degree in literature at the Sorbonne in 1905, Paulhan taught Latin and foreign languages and prospected for gold in Madagascar from 1907 until 1911. Returning to Paris, he taught the Malagasy language at the School for Oriental Languages and published his first book, on Malagasy poetics, in 1912. Mobilized at the start of **World War I,** Paulhan was wounded in battle. During his convalescence he wrote

his first major work, *Le Guerrier appliqué* (1917; The Applied Warrior), which deals with a soldier's attempts to find linguistic expression for his experiences. In 1920 Paulhan joined the staff of the *Nouvelle Revue Française,* becoming its editor in 1925 and remaining until 1940, with the German **Occupation** of France. Refusing to work with the fascist writer **Pierre Drieu La Rochelle,** who at the insistence of German authorities had been appointed editor of the collaborationist version of the *NRF,* Paulhan wrote for the underground newspaper *Résistance* and helped to found the Communist newspaper *Les Lettres Françaises* in 1941. When the *Nouvelle Revue Française* was revived as the *Nouvelle Nouvelle Revue Française* in January 1953, Paulhan agreed to serve with **Marcel Arland** as its coeditor, a post he held until his death.

Paulhan wrote the preface for *Histoire d'O* (1954; translated as *Story of O*), a notorious, best-selling erotic novel published under the name Pauline Réage. The identity of the author was long concealed, but ultimately she was identified as Dominique Aury, Paulhan's longtime lover, who was said to have written the novel to please him. (Some insisted Paulhan was the author.)

Paulhan's interest in language and his desire to replace old, inflated rhetoric with a new literary expression are evident in his best-known critical works, *Les Fleurs de Tarbes* (1941; The Flowers of Tarbes) and *Clef de la poésie* (1944; Key to Poetry). He gave particular value to paradox as a device of the rhetoric he proposed and in his own writing.

REFERENCES:

Alvin Eustis, "The Paradoxes of Language: Jean Paulhan," in *Modern French Criticism,* edited by John K. Simon (Chicago: University of Chicago Press, 1972), pp. 109–122;

John de St. Jorre, "The Unmasking of O," *New Yorker* (1 August 1994): 42–50.

— C.S.B.

CHARLES PÉGUY

Poet, dramatist, and journalist Charles Péguy (1873–1914) is not as well known in the Western Hemisphere as many other French writers of his generation; yet he is highly regarded in France. Of peasant origins, he was one of the least cosmopolitan French writers. Attached to traditions, devoted to the figure of Joan of Arc, and resolutely nationalist in politics (yet also leaning to socialism), he considered himself wholly and only French. In his crusading journalism, however, he took positions whose import goes well beyond the boundaries of France, becoming a spokesman for European humanism.

Author Charles Péguy in his bookshop at 8, rue de la Sorbonne, opened in 1898

Born to a poor provincial family in Orléans, Péguy was raised by his widowed mother, who made a meager living by caning chairs. Showing brilliance even as a boy, he attended schools on scholarship and moved to Paris to study at the **Ecole Normale Supérieure.** There he was deeply influenced by **Henri Bergson,** particularly the philosopher's belief that intuition is the only means of knowing the ultimate reality. He also became interested in socialism and was involved in the **Dreyfus Affair,** as a partisan of Alfred Dreyfus. Thus beginning his career as a crusader for justice, he opened a bookstore in 1898 and in 1900 started *Cahiers de la Quinzaine,* a review devoted to political and social questions.

In 1908 Péguy adopted an idiosyncratic form of the Catholic faith, which he had abandoned in his youth. Of a direct and unbending character, he made no attempt to win support for himself as a writer and fought single-mindedly for the causes and ideals that interested him, particularly the ideal of *la patrie.* He wrote and campaigned militantly for this almost mystical patriotic ideal, finally giving his life in support of it on the battlefield during the early stages of **World War I** (September 1914).

Péguy's creative works are not easily described, still less easily translated into English. Sometimes he used the classical alexandrine, either with other forms or alone, as in the beautiful lines from his long poem *Eve* (1913) that begins "Heureux ceux qui sont morts pour la terre charnelle" (Blessed are those who have died for the carnal earth). In his long lyric poems and some of his dramas he characteristically wrote in a free verse somewhat akin to the *verset* used by **Paul Claudel.** The most marked feature of his style in prose and verse is the repetition of words, phrases, and whole lines or sentences, building up to a verbal paroxysm. While such rhetorical excess is contrary to the French classical tradition, it is not without precedent, including the medieval mystery plays and the writings of Victor Hugo, to whom Péguy devoted a long critical work.

The best known of Péguy's plays is *Le Mystère de la charité de Jeanne d'Arc* (1910; translated as *The Mystery of the Charity of Joan of Arc*), based on a historical and polemical work he published in 1897. The play presents a patriotic peasant girl–saint in deliberately naive language that sometimes has modern echoes. This drama is the first of a trilogy that also includes *Le Porche du mystère de la deuxieme vertu* (1911; translated as *The Portico of the Mystery of the Second Virtue*) and *Le Mystère des saints innocents* (1912; translated as *The Mystery of the Holy Innocents*). The term *mystère* is a deliberate reference to medieval mystery plays but also alludes to the mysteries of the Christian religion and the three Pauline virtues (faith, hope, and charity). Péguy was likewise interested in the cathedral of Chartres and in the figure of Saint Geneviève, one of the patron saints of Paris, devoting moving lines to both.

REFERENCE:

Hans A. Schmitt, *Charles Péguy: The Decline of an Idealist* (Baton Rouge: Louisiana State University Press, 1967).

— C.S.B.

FERNAND PELLOUTIER

Although the rise of French syndicalism is often identified with the writings of **Georges Sorel,** the actual construction of syndicalist trade unions was largely the work of the anarchist militant Fernand Pelloutier (1867–1901). Little known outside France, his extensive writings on topics ranging from trade-union organizing to the social and political status of women to the nature of art have never been translated into English.

Pelloutier, who had been removed from his Catholic school for writing an anticlerical novel, began his adult life as a journalist and a supporter of the reformist Radical Party, but he quickly became disillusioned with reform politics and became an advocate of direct action and the general strike. In 1892 he helped to set up the anarchist Fédération des Bourses du Travail (a title that may be roughly translated as labor exchanges). He saw these exchanges not simply as union locals in the modern sense of the term but as "centers of study where the proletariat could reflect on their condition, unravel the elements of the economic problem so as to make themselves capable of the liberation to which they have the right." Each exchange was to offer job placement, assistance for travel related to employment, and insurance. In his *Histoire des bourses du travail* (1902; History of the Labor Exchanges), he insists that each *bourse* should have its own library and a labor museum dedicated to the accomplishments of the working class.

In 1896 Pelloutier spoke to the anarchist-oriented Groupe de l'art social in Paris on the social role of the arts. The speech, published that year as *L'Art et la révolte* (Art and Revolt), asserted that the arts played a crucial role in the process by which each child is taught what is allowed and what is not. Believing that in the modern world art — as the servant and accomplice of bourgeois society — was one of the forces holding back human emancipation, he called on artists to ally themselves with those in revolt against repression. The instrumentalist view of art presented in the speech became a model for syndicalist critiques of the role of art, and, less directly, it later influenced some **French Communist Party** views on the topic.

REFERENCES:

Anthony S. Baker, "Fernand Pelloutier and the Making of Revolutionary Syndicalism," in *Essays on Modern European Revolutionary History,* edited by Bede K. Lackner and Kenneth Roy Philip (Austin: University of Texas Press, 1977);

John Hutton, *Neo-Impressionism and the Search for Solid Ground: Art, Science, and Anarchism in Fin-de-siècle France* (Baton Rouge: Louisiana State University Press, 1994);

James Joll, *The Anarchists,* second edition (Cambridge, Mass.: Harvard University Press, 1980).

— J.H.

GEORGES PEREC

In a period when French literature reached the highest level of artifice it has known since the Renaissance, Georges Perec (1936–1982) was perhaps the greatest artificer. A linguistic genius attracted to mathematical thinking, he used words to create elaborate, self-conscious, but highly readable, intellectual puzzles. In this respect he may be classed with some writers of the **Nouveau Roman** (New Novel), although, younger than they, he bypassed more quickly the conventional novel and began exploring the possibilities of innovative form almost immediately.

Born to Polish-Jewish parents who were killed during **World War II,** Perec spent the war years in southern France. It is not surprising that loss and absence are among the themes running through his work. His training in social thought as a sociology student at the Sorbonne is reflected in his literary concern for what he called "the sociology of the quotidian."

Perec's first novel, *Les Choses: Histoire des années soixante* (1965; translated as *Les Choses: A Story of the Sixties*), exposes the compulsive, obsessive materialism of the decade. *Un Homme qui dort* (1967; A Sleeping Man) presents a man suffering from somnolence, clearly an existential malaise. Its second-person narration recalls **Michel Butor**'s *La Modification* (1957; translated as *A Change of Heart*). *La Boutique obscure: 124 rêves* (1973; The Dark Boutique: 124 Dreams) is based on Perec's dreams and their significance. In *W ou le souvenir d'enfance* (1975; translated as *W or The Memory of Childhood*), half autobiography and half fiction, the two types of narrative compose a critique of the dreadful experiences of World War II.

Even more striking than these books are Perec's linguistic tours de force, which were influenced by his involvement with the Ouvroir de Littérature Potentielle (Workshop of Potential Literature), or

Oulipo, a group that advocated formal structure as essential to the literary work (see **Raymond Queneau**). At three hundred pages, *La Disparition* (1969; The Disappearance) is the longest known lipogram (a composition omitting a letter or letters); the letter *e* does not appear in the novel, which deals with absences of other sorts as well. *Les Revenentes* (1972; The Ghosts) is also a lipogram — all vowels except *e* are excluded. *Ulcérations* (1974) is a heterogrammatic poem: each line is composed of the eleven letters in its title, with 399 anagrams in all. *Alphabets* (1976), a collection of heterogrammatic poems, is based on a mathematical formula that produces, among other effects, 1,936 lines of verse, corresponding to the year of Perec's birth.

Perec's most elaborate creation is *La Vie mode d'emploi* (1978; translated as *Life, A User's Manual*), which won the Prix Médicis. Rich in mathematical elements and explicitly concerned with puzzles, it is itself a seven-hundred-page puzzle chronicling the history of a Parisian apartment building ten stories high with ten units on each story. Into this architectural structure, which resembles a three-dimensional chessboard, Perec built a classic chess problem. The book includes the story of a cosmopolite who wants to devote his life to an elaborate project of puzzle solving and puzzle dissolving. Like the work of Jorge Luis Borges, Perec's brilliant achievements in fiction and poetry have much to say about twentieth-century social phenomena, the nature of reality, and human knowledge of the world.

REFERENCES:

Warren F. Motte, Jr., *The Poetics of Experiment: A Study of the Work of Georges Perec* (Lexington, Ky.: French Forum Monographs, 1984);

Paul Schwartz, *Georges Perec: Traces of His Passage* (Birmingham, Ala.: Summa, 1988).

— C.S.B.

BENJAMIN PÉRET

The closest disciple of **Surrealist André Breton,** poet Benjamin Péret (1899–1959) was codirector of the first issues of the magazine *Révolution Surréaliste.* Unlike most of the other Surrealists, Péret never renounced the principles and practices of the movement. The critic J. H. Matthews considered Péret's poetry to be first-rank Surrealist verse and superior to that of **Paul Eluard.**

Marked by strong Surrealist images and antiestablishment positions, Péret's collection *Le Grand Jeu* (1928; The Great Game) is among his most impressive achievements. *Je ne mange pas de ce pain-là* (1936; I Don't Swallow That), another collection of verse, shows the same rebellious temperament. Péret's hostil-

ity toward the pillars of society is also visible in his short stories, collected as *Le Gigot, sa vie et son œuvre* (1957; The Leg of Lamb, His Life and Work). Péret's anarchism was not confined to verbal expression; during the **Spanish Civil War** he went to Spain to work with anarchists. In *Le Déshonneur des poètes* (1945; The Dishonor of Poets) he attacked his former friend Eluard for his patriotic **Resistance** poetry, work that Péret found propagandistic.

REFERENCES:

Mary Ann Caws, "Benjamin Péret's Game and Gesture," in her *The Inner Theater of Recent French Poetry* (Princeton: Princeton University Press, 1972), pp. 75–105;

J. H. Matthews, *Benjamin Péret* (Boston: Twayne, 1975).

— C.S.B.

PHILIPPE PÉTAIN

A career military man, Philippe Pétain (1856–1951) was revered as a national hero for his service in **World War I.** His memory was disgraced, however, by his collaborationist policies as head of the **Vichy government** during **World War II.**

Pétain emerged into the national spotlight in 1916, when he led French forces to victory at **Verdun.** The following year he was credited with checking a mutiny in the ranks. He was named marshal of France in 1918 and remained a respected figure during the years between the two world wars. He was elected to the Académie Française in 1929, served as minister of war in 1934, and was named ambassador to Spain in 1939. After the German defeat of France in the **Debacle** of 1940 and the dissolution of the former French government, Pétain was given essentially dictatorial powers by the National Assembly. He almost immediately announced plans to rid the nation of parliamentary abuses that had existed under the **Third Republic** and later pledged to "collaborate" with Germany to unite all Europe as a new German empire.

Pétain's name was thenceforth associated throughout France with Vichy, whether one accepted collaboration with Germany as a necessary evil or favored a policy of resistance, following the lead of **Charles de Gaulle** and, later, Henri Giraud. During the **épuration,** or purge trials, that took place after the **Liberation** of France, Pétain was tried and condemned to death (1945). The sentence was later commuted to life in prison, and he died while incarcerated.

REFERENCE:

Richard Griffiths, *Marshal Pétain* (London: Constable, 1970).

— D.O'C.

ROLAND PETIT

A theatrical and witty French dancer and choreographer, Roland Petit (1924–) is a splendid performer whose choreography is sometimes criticized for being shallow, but he is extremely popular with audiences. Petit often uses literary themes for his ballets and has frequently collaborated with celebrated designers and writers, including **Jean Cocteau,** Max Ernst, Christian Dior, Yves Saint-Laurent, and David Hockney.

Petit was born in Paris and trained at the **Paris Opéra Ballet,** becoming a member of its company at age sixteen. Although he did not consider himself avant-garde, he thought that the troupe was not only traditional but stagnating, and he left it in 1944 to collaborate with disciples of **Serge Diaghilev.** With Boris Kochno, **Christian Bérard,** and Cocteau, he formed the first postwar French ballet company, Ballets des Champs-Elysées, in 1945. Petit and **Janine Charrat** were principal choreographers and dancers; Kochno, Bérard, and Cocteau were the artistic directors. The company encouraged experimental and unconventional work.

Petit's first choreographic success for the Ballets des Champs-Elysées was *Les Forains* (1945; The Sideshow Entertainers). In 1946 he choreographed *Le Jeune Homme et la mort* (The Young Man and Death), with libretto and costumes by Cocteau and with Jean Babilée and Nathalie Philippart in the main roles. In this startling and controversial dance drama a young man hangs himself in despair after being rejected by his lover. The choreography, a mixture of classical ballet, acrobatics, and gestures, was a harsh contrast to the music, the C-minor Passacaglia by Johann Sebastian Bach. Petit left the Ballets des Champs-Elysées in 1948, and the company folded in 1951.

In 1948 Petit formed the Ballets de Paris, which disbanded and reformed several times during the 1950s. For it he choreographed *Carmen* (1949), using excerpts from Georges Bizet's opera score. Dancing the title role in the first production of the ballet, the fiery, then-unknown Renée (Zizi) Jeanmarie was an overnight success. She became an international musical-comedy star while remaining a classical ballerina. She and Petit married in 1954.

The Ballet de Marseille, which Petit organized in 1972, is now the second largest company in France; it has regular seasons in Paris and tours to England, Russia, the Far East, and the United States.

Petit choreographed and danced with Jeanmarie in several movies, including *Hans Christian Andersen* (1951) and *Un-deux-trois* (1960; *Black Tights*). He was named Chevalier de l'Ordre des Arts et des Lettres (1962) and Chevalier de la Légion d'Honneur (1974).

REFERENCE:

Clement Crisp, "A Talent to Amuse," *Ballet News,* 2 (August 1980): 14–18.

—A.P.E.

GÉRARD PHILIPE

Gérard Philipe (1922–1959) had a brief but brilliant career as a stage and screen actor in France. Highly regarded and beloved by the public, he was honored by a French postage stamp two years after his death.

Philipe — who appeared on various Parisian stages, including the **Comédie-Française** — made his film debut in 1944. His first memorable role was in *Le Diable au corps* (1947; *Devil in the Flesh*), directed by **Claude Autant-Lara and based on the novel by Raymond Radiguet.** In this celebrated motion picture, which was banned in some European countries, Philipe played a precocious but awkward teenager who falls in love with a woman whose husband is at the front during **World War I.** Philipe's acting suggested a reflective, thoughtful passion different from the sort of instinctual drives suggested in the pre-1939 roles played by **Jean Gabin.**

Philipe's other romantic leads include the part of a suicidal adolescent in **Yves Allégret's** *Une si jolie petite plage* (1949; *Riptide*) and the alcoholic painter Amedeo Modigliani in **Jacques Becker's** *Montparnasse 19* (1958; *Modigliani of Montparnasse*). He starred in screen adaptations of well-known French novels such as Autant-Lara's version of Stendhal's *Le Rouge et le noir* (1954; The Red and the Black), **Julien Duvivier's** adaptation of Emile Zola's *Pot-Bouille* (1957), and, as Valmont, in an updated *Les Liaisons dangereuses* (1959; Dangerous Liaisons), directed by **Roger Vadim** and based on the novel by Pierre Choderlos de Laclos. Philipe also played the cynical count in *La Ronde* (1950; *Rondelay*), directed by **Max Ophuls.** One of the top romantic stars in French film after **World War II,** Philipe portrayed lovers in some period films by **René Clair** and **Sacha Guitry.**

REFERENCE:

R. F. Cousins, "Recasting Zola: Gérard Philipe's Influence on Duvivier's Adaptation of *Pot-Bouille*," *Literature/Film Quarterly,* 17 (July 1989): 142–148.

—W.L.

CHARLES-LOUIS PHILIPPE

Charles-Louis Philippe (1874–1909) is an important writer of French working-class fiction. This tradition

Jean Vilar and Gérard Philipe at a rehearsal of *Caprices de Marianne* during the 1958 Avignon Festival

originated with Romantics such as Victor Hugo and George Sand, as they glorified the common man and the soil, and it was developed further by Naturalists such as Emile Zola and by Jules Vallès, whose working-class novels were strident outcries against social injustice and calls to revolt. With his novel *Bubu de Montparnasse* (1901; translated as *Bubu of Montparnasse*) and other works, Philippe pursued this tradition without politicizing his narratives.

Philippe, whose father was a cobbler, began his career with a book published at his own expense, *Quatre histoires de pauvre amour* (1897; Four Stories of Poor Love). He clearly sympathized with his proletarian characters, whose errors he blames on society. *Bubu de Montparnasse,* his best-known novel, also holds social ills responsible for the situation in which his characters — a pimp and a prostitute — find themselves. His other novels include *Le Père Perdrix* (1903; translated as *A Simple Story*), based partly on his father's life, and *Marie Donadieu* (1904; translated), which draws on an affair he had with a friend's mistress.

REFERENCE:

J. E. Flower, "Sentimentality and Resignation: Charles-Louis Philippe," in his *Literature and the Left in France* (London: Macmillan, 1983), pp. 50–64.

— C.S.B.

EDITH PIAF

Singer Edith Piaf (1915–1963) was popular with audiences for almost thirty years, from the time she was discovered singing on a street corner in Paris in the 1930s until her death. It is some measure of her genius that writer and musician **Boris Vian** said she would have been successful if she had merely sung the telephone directory.

Born Edith Giovanna Gassion, she was spotted in the Pigalle section of Paris by a cabaret owner who called her "la môme Piaf" (the Piaf kid; *piaf* is a familiar French term for *sparrow*). It was an appropriate epithet for her, given her diminutive size, her seeming vulnerability, and her spirit. Her life, whose pathos fueled her singing, was one of childhood hardship, tragic love affairs (including one with **Yves Montand** and another with **Marcel Cerdan,** the world-champion boxer killed in a plane crash), and frequent life-threatening illnesses.

Piaf's songs possessed an emotional charge that gave new life to hackneyed themes, including trite situations involving big-hearted streetwalkers, inaccessible foreigners, and unhappy or hopeful lovers. Working with talented songwriters, she performed many songs that achieved huge success in France and abroad, including "L'Accordéoniste" (1938; The Accordionist),

"La Vie en rose" (1945), "Milord" (1952), and "Non, je ne regrette rien" (1960; No, I Regret Nothing).

For a time Piaf sang with a group called Les Compagnons de la Chanson (The Companions of Song). Their recording of "Les Trois Cloches" (performed in English as "The Three Bells") sold a million copies. Her tours of the United States in 1954 and 1957 were also successful.

REFERENCES:

Monique Lange, *Histoire de Piaf* (Paris: Ramsay, 1979);

Edith Piaf with Jean Noli, *My Life,* translated by Margaret Crosland (London & Chester Springs, Pa.: Peter Owen, 1990).

— J.P.McN.

FRANCIS PICABIA

The artistic career of Francis Picabia (1879–1953) demonstrates the difficulties of dividing the history of art into discrete, tidy movements and periods. An artist who claimed to have painted the first completely nonobjective painting, he also produced a series of wholly traditional nudes; he had ties at one point or another with **Cubism, Dada,** and **Surrealism.** For Picabia this sort of eclecticism was an essential attribute of his art: "You've got to be a nomad," he declared, "and pass through ideas as a man passes through towns and countries."

Named François Marie Martínez-Picabia y Davanne, Picabia was born in Paris to Spanish parents; he studied at the Ecole des Arts Décoratifs and in the studio of the academic painter Fernand Cormon. Until 1902 he produced primarily small landscapes and cityscapes in a resolutely traditional manner. In a 1902 letter the Impressionist Camille Pissarro noted that two of his sons had encountered a student of Cormon's (Picabia) who covered "endless quantities of canvas without taking into account the air or the light, and he paints everything a uniform brown!" Under the influence of Pissarro and his brother, Picabia began to experiment with Impressionist ideas, exemplified in his *Le Pont du chemin de fer, Moret* (1905; *Railroad Bridge, Moret*). His paintings in this style most closely resemble those of Alfred Sisley: the loose brush strokes and bright colors are combined with the sort of traditional perspective and drawing that **Claude Monet** had abandoned by the 1870s. In keeping with his new style, Picabia began to submit his works to the **Salon d'Automne** and the **Salon des Indépendants** instead of the older, more restrictive salons.

From 1908 until 1910 Picabia's work underwent a more dramatic transformation. After a brief flirtation with the pointillist style of the Neo-Impressionists gathered around **Paul Signac,** he began to zigzag through a variety of modernist movements, from the **Fauves,** to Cubism, to the Orphism of **Robert Delaunay** and **Sonia Delaunay-Terk.** Picabia's *Caoutchouc* (circa 1909; the word means "rubber") has been claimed as the first real abstraction, without link to any external subject or referent of any kind. For him this work was "pure painting": interlocking segments of flat color, centered on overlapping painted circles. (The painting has been interpreted as a bouncing ball or a still life of fruit on a table; it resembles closely Picabia's still lifes of a table with vase and flowers.) Over the next few years he oscillated from highly abstracted landscapes to rather conventional nudes. Friendship with **Marcel Duchamp** and **Raymond Duchamp-Villon** led him close to the Paris Cubists; he participated in the **Section d'Or** exhibition of 1912. His paintings from this period are broken into flat, geometric shapes, with a palette reduced to a narrow range of grays, blacks, and reddish browns; none of the canvases shows any interest in **Pablo Picasso**'s analysis of space.

Under the influence of the Dadaists, Picabia shifted again, this time to careful images of machine parts. As technical designs (which they resemble closely), they are meaningless; instead, they form complicated puns or resolve themselves into masks or body parts. This art of provocation — he titled an ink blot *Holy Virgin* — led him to the Surrealists, though not for long. By 1923 he had split with them and begun work on his *Transparences (Transparencies)*, layered pictures of overlapping contours, often parodying medieval and Renaissance painting.

During **World War II** Picabia produced a series of female nudes (1940–1942); some have seen these works as caricaturing the kitsch tastes of **Vichy** France, but others have noted the manner in which they seem to ape a clichéd eroticism of fascist aesthetics without the slightest sense of irony. His apparently good relations with the German occupiers led to his brief imprisonment at the end of the war. His postwar works are mostly dark abstractions in a thick impasto, dominated by enigmatic glyphs.

REFERENCES:

Maria Lluisa Borras, *Picabia,* translated by Kenneth Lyons (New York: Rizzoli, 1985);

William A. Camfield, *Francis Picabia: His Art, Life, and Times* (Princeton, N.J.: Princeton University Press, 1979);

Francis Picabia, *Picabia, 1879–1953,* edited by Richard Calvocoressi (Edinburgh: Scottish National Gallery of Modern Art, 1988).

— J.H.

PABLO PICASSO

Pablo Picasso (1881–1973) is the most prominent avant-garde artist of the twentieth century; for many his career is synonymous with the development of artistic modernism. That prominence both aids and hinders any summary analysis of his work: there is no dearth of information on the artist or his art; yet every assessment of a painting can be countered by a (vehemently) contradictory one.

Pablo Ruiz y Picasso was born in Málaga, Spain, where his father was a local artist and teacher of art. When Picasso was thirteen the family moved to Barcelona, where the father taught and the son took classes at La Llotja (The Exchange), the local art academy. The youth immersed himself increasingly in bohemian life, frequenting especially Els Quatre Gats (The Four Cats), set up in conscious celebration of the **Montmartre** cabarets of Paris as a center for radicals and the disillusioned. Like some of the bohemian clubs of Paris, Els Quatre Gats published its own journal, *Pèl & Ploma,* dedicated to winning a public for new trends in the arts.

Picasso moved to Madrid in 1901, collaborating with other young artists and writers in the publication of *Arte Joven* (Young Art), a mixture of anarchism and a purely artistic radicalism; but, frustrated by the climate of that city, he moved on to Paris the same year. There he found support from several influential critics and collectors, notably **Ambroise Vollard** and Gustave Coquiot.

With the move to Paris came a new style. Picasso's earlier work had been heavily influenced by Spanish masters, including Diego Velázquez and especially Francisco Goya. In France he deepened his interest in the lives of the poor, including studies of prostitutes incarcerated in the Saint-Lazare prison (whom he could paint for free). According to his friend Jaime Sabartès, Picasso insisted that "art emanates from Sadness and Pain. . . . Sadness lends itself to meditation . . . grief is at the basis of life. . . ." Some have seen Picasso's focus on the pain of the poor as an expression of his anarchist sympathies; others have noted its sometimes cruel and manipulative character. Whatever the source, the result was Picasso's "Blue Period," in which he created haunting, sometimes broken figures of the lost, the outcast, and the dying, saturated in deepest blue. Throughout his frequent moves over the next years — back to Barcelona, then back again to Paris — his mood of bleak misery intensified. Over time the relative clarity of the first paintings was replaced by scenes of private, sometimes layered meanings. *La Vie* (1903; *Life*) shows a nude man and woman confronting a second (clothed) woman with an infant;

Pablo Picasso, circa 1910, in his studio at 11, boulevard de Clichy

between them, a nude couple huddles together on a bed, while below them yet another nude figure huddles miserably. Scattered preliminary sketches made the implicit focus clear enough — a man charged with fathering an illegitimate child. The extent to which the picture is autobiographical (Picasso was the original model for the man in the picture, though he replaced his image with that of a friend in the final work), the precise relationship between the four figures or groups and the issue of whether Picasso employed figures from the Tarot have dominated discussion of this work. As with similar paintings — such as his *La Tragédie* (1903; *Tragedy*), in which a woman, a bearded man, and a child stand shivering on a beach — the specific resolution of figure and meaning is perhaps less important than the repeated mood of misery and loss.

Picasso was increasingly frustrated by his efforts to break from his academic training, to find new forms and concepts for his art. Rejecting the simplifications of **Henri Matisse** and the **Fauves,** he turned to the work of **Paul Cézanne** — especially his insistence on the underlying geometric shapes in nature. Two sources contributed to Picasso's attempts to rethink his work: pre-Roman Iberian sculpture (marked by massive, blunt-featured shapes) and African masks (highly stylized and abstracted). There is no evidence that Picasso studied either in depth; rather, they were important to him as raw material for his own experiments. *Les Demoiselles d'Avignon* (1907) marks his first attempt to synthesize all his new influences. The first sketches show a straightforward scene of a sailor surrounded by prostitutes in a brothel. The final work eliminates the sailor and, with him, all the open space of the room; the figures are bound together in a shallow, geometricized space. The figures at the left clearly show the influence of Iberian sculpture; the far more abstracted figures at the right are inspired by African masks. Though the picture is sometimes cited as the beginning of **Cubism,** it is more accurate to call it the beginning of the period of experimentation from which Cubism finally emerged. Together with **Georges Braque,** a former Fauvist equally inspired by Cézanne's work, Picasso began to work out a more systematized approach to the treatment of forms in space.

Many young artists inspired by Picasso — including **André Lhôte, Albert Gleizes, Jean Metzinger,** and eventually the Purists **Amédée Ozenfant** and **Le Corbusier** — sought to provide Cubism with a rigorous, precise, and scientific basis. Picasso rejected any such attempt, insisting that "when we were doing Cubism, we were not trying to do Cubism, but just to express what was inside us." He disavowed any talk of Cubism as a movement, and he and Braque did not participate in the *Maison cubiste* at the 1912 **Salon d'Automne** or the **Section d'Or** exhibition of that year. Instead, Picasso and Braque moved from what has been termed Analytical Cubism, in which the figure is broken apart and examined from all sides at once, to Synthetic Cubism, in which collage is used not so much to represent as to reconstruct the site or object depicted.

Picasso also rejected attempts by artists such as Gleizes and Metzinger to give Cubism an "epic" quality by examining the social life of the people; instead, he focused on still life and portraiture. This focus does not necessarily mean, however, that he totally avoided political subject matter or statements. His synthetic collages from 1912, for example, have been routinely treated as pure exercises in form: bits and pieces of newspapers, napkins, and labels from liquor bottles glued together to recapture the clubs and cabarets in which the artists drank and argued. A recent account of Picasso's anarchist affiliations has pointed out, however, that the newspaper articles were not chosen at random: many of them are accounts of mass slaughter in the Balkan War, the grim prelude to **World War I,** which broke apart the Cubist movement.

Many of the French Cubists were wounded or killed in the fighting (Picasso's Spain was neutral). Picasso retreated for a time to more classical compositions before venturing out again in new directions. Fluid, shifting shapes gradually coalesced into a series of images (inspired perhaps by Goya) of bulls and bullfights. With the outbreak of the **Spanish Civil War** in 1936 these motifs became, in turn, the basis for treatments of the agony of that conflict and the brutality of Francisco Franco and those who backed him. Picasso associated himself wholeheartedly with Republican Spain, agreeing to serve as curator of the Prado museum (in imitation of the actions of the anarchist Gustave Courbet during the Paris Commune of 1871). Picasso's *Guernica* (1937), a huge treatment of the annihilation of the Basque cultural center by bombers of the Germans' Nazi Condor Legion, harnessed Cubist forms to precisely the sort of "epic" topic he had rejected earlier. Though the final painting eliminated some of the stereotypically political motifs of the first sketch (including a huge clenched fist), the images themselves — largely derived from the account of the bombing in the newspaper *Humanité* — are a devastating indictment of the brutal attack. (By the terms of Picasso's will, the painting was not returned to Spain until the restoration of democracy there.)

After the war Picasso joined the **French Communist Party,** announcing that his painting was "an instrument of war for attack and defense against the enemy...." His 1953 murals at a deconsecrated chapel in Vallauris, *Guerre* (*War*) and *Paix* (*Peace*), contrasted the current world of war and oppression with a utopian future. His *Le Massacre en Corée* (1951; *Massacre in Korea*), deliberately adopting the format of Goya's *Third of May, 1808,* showed American troops slaughtering civilians in Korea. Like those of **Fernand Léger,** however, Picasso's attempts to create a politically engaged abstract art found little acceptance by either side during the Cold War. Western critics denounced him as a Communist (or, more subtly, argued that political subject matter was retrograde). Soviet writers denounced his art as "an aesthetic apology for capitalism," full of deformed and debased creatures. In the 1960s Picasso broke little new ground; some of his pieces rework famous paintings from French history, including Edouard Manet's *Déjeuner sur l'herbe.*

REFERENCES:

Alfred H. Barr, Jr., *Picasso: Fifty Years of His Art* (New York: Museum of Modern Art, 1946);

John Berger, *The Success and Failure of Picasso* (New York: Pantheon, 1965);

Pierre Cabanne, *Pablo Picasso: His Life and Times,* translated by Harold J. Salemson (New York: Morrow, 1977);

Patricia Leighton, *Re-Ordering the Universe: Picasso and Anarchism, 1897–1914* (Princeton: Princeton University Press, 1989);

Roland Penrose, *Picasso: His Life and Work* (London: Gollancz, 1958);

John Richardson, with Marilyn McCully, *A Life of Picasso, Volume 1: 1881–1906* (New York: Random House, 1991).

—J.H.

MICHEL PICCOLI

Michel Piccoli (1925–), one of the most recognized actors of French cinema, has appeared in more than one hundred major movie roles. His impressive film performances range from black comedy to quiet lyricism to savage sadism.

During the 1950s Piccoli was a familiar figure in crime thrillers, playing tough, sadistic characters, notably in a series of films directed by **Luis Buñuel.** In Buñuel's *La Mort en ce jardin* (1956; *Gina; Evil Eden; Death in the Garden*) Piccoli portrayed a priest who is compromised by a prostitute; in Buñuel's *Belle de jour* (1967; Beauty of Day) Piccoli played the dissolute Husson. In *Le Journal d'une femme de chambre* (1964; *Diary of a Chambermaid*) he was another frustrated libertine, pursuing his servants; and in *La Voie lactée* (1969; *The Milky Way*) he portrayed the Marquis de Sade. In **Jean-Luc Godard's** *Le Mépris* (1963; *Contempt*) Piccoli played an anxiety-ridden writer, and in *La Grande Bouffe* (1973; The Great Feed) he starred with **Philippe Noiret** and Marcello Mastroianni as a trio of distinguished citizens who eat themselves to death during one weekend. In recent years Piccoli has played several wizened father figures.

REFERENCES:

Robert Chazal, *Michel Piccoli, le provocateur* (Paris: France-Empire, 1989);

Michel Piccoli with Alain Lacombe, *Dialogues égoïstes* (Paris: Orban, 1976).

—W.L.

ROBERT PINGET

One of the creators of the **Nouveau Roman** (New Novel), Robert Pinget (1919–) is a highly inventive writer who puts his impressive verbal skills to imaginative use. Several of his more than two dozen novels and plays have been translated into English, including his novel *La Manivelle* (1960), translated by **Samuel Beckett** as *The Old Tune* (1961). More critically acclaimed than popular, Pinget has been praised on both sides of the Atlantic by authors such as **Alain Robbe-Grillet, Nathalie Sarraute,** and John Updike.

From the outset Pinget's work has been explicitly concerned with the nature of writing and thus deserves to be called metafiction. To expose the limiting conventions of traditional fiction and to suggest how fiction can break through these restrictions, he sometimes uses parody, as in his first book, the novel *Entre Fantoine et Agapa* (1951; translated as *Between Fantoine and Agapa*). Elsewhere, as in *Le Renard et la boussole* (1953; The Fox and the Compass), he writes fiction about the act of writing fiction, as his narrator tries to make a novel from elements of his own story. To destroy the imposed rationality of plot and to challenge language itself, Pinget stretches the novel form, suggesting that it is capable of accommodating reality as a mid-twentieth-century observer knows it, yet also pointing to the inability of mind and language to capture the world. In *Graal Flibuste* (1956), oblique references to the quest (*graal* or grail) and to pirate adventures (*flibustier* or buccaneer) perhaps suggest a journey to awareness, but the journey-novel form is undone as the narrative explodes in poetic fancy and incoherent plot.

Among Pinget's other novels are *Le Fiston* (1959; translated as *Monsieur Levert* and as *No Answer*), a revision of the epistolary form involving various levels of stories within stories, and *Clope au dossier* (1961), translated as *Clope* in his *Plays* (1966), although Pinget calls it a novel. *L'Inquisitoire* (1962; translated as *The Inquisitory*), written entirely in question-and-answer form, deals ostensibly with crimes and scandals, but it too refers ultimately to writing. It was followed by *Quelqu'un* (1965; translated as *Someone*), which won the Prix Fémina. *Passacaille* (1969; translated as *Passacaglia*) and *Fable* (1971; translated) are also metafictional. These novels and others can be said to form a cycle, since characters, events, and repeated motifs and preoccupations appear in more than one volume. Most of these books point to Pinget's concern with the use of language, the knowability of the world, and the search for meaning. His most recent novels are *L'Ennemi* (1987; translated as *The Enemy*) and *Théo ou le temps neuf* (1991; Theo or New Time).

Pinget has also written plays, produced in Paris and elsewhere, that are textually and thematically connected to his fiction. Two plays from 1961, *Architruc* (translated) and *L'Hypothèse* (translated as *The Hypothesis*), are among the best known.

REFERENCES:

Robert Henkels, *Robert Pinget: The Novel as Quest* (Tuscaloosa: University of Alabama Press, 1979);

Review of Contemporary Fiction, special Pinget issue, 3 (Summer 1983).

—C.S.B.

Ludmilla and Georges Pitoëff (left) in Henri René Lenormand's *Le Mangeur de rêves,* 1922

GEORGES PITOËFF

Georges Pitoëff (1886–1939), a theater actor, scenic designer, and director, broadened the horizons of the French theatergoing public between the world wars by staging important foreign plays in Paris. Along with **Gaston Baty** and **Antonin Artaud,** he helped to free French theater from the absolute dominance of the written text.

Pitoëff grew up and received his training in Russia, where he was nourished on the productions of Constantin Stanislavsky's Moscow art theater. He performed as an actor all over Russia (and even briefly had his own troupe) before 1914, when he immigrated to France, where he married Ludmilla de Smanov in 1915; she was to be the love of his life, his inspiration, and, as **Ludmilla Pitoëff,** the leading actress of his company. In the same year he launched a theater of his own in Geneva, neutral territory in the midst of **World War I.**

By 1921 this enterprise was thriving, and Jacques Hébertot, a French impresario, was sufficiently impressed to bring him back, along with members of his troupe, to perform at the Comédie des Champs-Elysées. In the 1922 season Pitoëff's Paris repertoire included Bernard Shaw's *Candida,* Henri René Lenormand's *Le Mangeur de rêves* (translated as *The Devourer of Dreams*), and Anton Chekhov's *The Sea Gull* — a truly international theater. Indeed, through his several Chekhov productions, Pitoëff gave the Russian dramatist his French voice. In 1923 Pitoëff brought Luigi Pirandello forcefully to the attention of Parisians with a French performance of *Sei personaggi in cerca d'autore* (translated as *Six Characters in Search of an Author*), and in 1924 he staged in Paris the musical *Histoire du soldat* (translated as *The Soldier's Tale*), by Charles-Ferdinand Ramuz and **Igor Stravinsky.** His productions revealed Pitoëff as a highly original set designer: he was always reluctant to perform in a decor he had not conceived himself.

Hébertot's financial situation made it necessary for Pitoëff to leave the Comédie des Champs-Elysées after 1924, and for ten years he led his company wherever theater space was available, often going on tour. Outstanding Paris productions of these years included Shaw's *Saint Joan* (1925; at the Théâtre des Arts), **Jean Cocteau**'s *Orphée* (1925; translated as *Orpheus;* Théâtre des Arts), and **André Gide**'s *Œdipe* (1932; translated as *Oedipus;* Théâtre de l'Avenue). Pitoëff participated in the creation of the **Cartel des Quatre** in 1927, but, as a foreigner, he was never asked, as were the other Cartel members, to direct at the **Comédie-Française.** Finally, in 1934, he found a home in the Théâtre des Mathurins, where his stellar 1937 season included William Shakespeare's *Romeo and Juliet,* **Paul Claudel**'s *L'Echange* (translated as *The Exchange*), and **Jean Anouilh**'s *Le Voyageur sans bagage* (translated as *Traveller without Luggage*). In 1939, though ill, he undertook the role of Dr. Stockmann in Henrik Ibsen's *An Enemy of the People,* but he was able to continue for only fifteen performances. Since his arrival in Paris some eighteen years earlier, he had worked hard, staging more than two hundred plays by 114 different authors.

His work as a scene designer derived from two principles: that the dramatist's responsibility ends when the play is published and that set design is an evolving art. From these notions springs the idea that actors, directors, and designers are free to build theatrical representations of which the script is but one element, albeit central. Furthermore, such constructions or reconstructions must evolve with the artistic temper of the times. Pitoëff was resolutely modernist, even expressionistic, in his scenery, often having recourse to compartmentalized settings (such as the virtual beehive he created for Ferdinand Bruckner's *The Criminals* in 1929) or abstract, geometric decors. In this sense he was the most innovative of the four Cartel des Quatre members. Actors were of predominant importance for him because it is they who animate the text. His own acting, although he never overcame his Russian accent, is remembered for the illuminating intelligence of his readings, for the Chaplinesque quality of his comedy, and for the warm sincerity of his love for Ludmilla, obvious to audiences whenever he played opposite her. His notes, lectures, and theoretical fragments were published in 1949 as *Notre Théâtre* (Our Theater), edited by Jean de Rigault.

REFERENCES:

Jean Hort, *La Vie héroïque des Pitoëff* (Geneva: Pierre Cailler, 1966);

Jacqueline de Jomaron, "Ils étaient quatre . . . ," in *Le Théâtre en France. 2: De la Révolution à nos jours,* edited by Jomaron (Paris: Armand Colin, 1989), pp. 227–270;

Rudolph Weiss, "Georges Pitoëff — His Shakespearean Productions in France," translated by Brian Keith-Smith, *Theatre Research,* 5 (1963): 72–84.

— R.J.N.

LUDMILLA PITOËFF

The renowned actress Ludmilla Pitoëff (1896–1951), born Ludmilla de Smanov in Tbilisi (in pre-Soviet Georgia), was the star and primary attraction of the theatrical productions staged by her husband, **Georges Pitoëff,** whom she married in 1915. Soft of voice and skillful in projection of intensity and conviction, she provided highly intelligent, captivating readings of roles ranging in scope from tragedy and pathos to whimsy and comedy.

For example, she starred in 1923 in Ferenc Molnár's whimsical *Liliom* (translated), and in 1925 she showed the breadth of her capabilities in the complex title role of Bernard Shaw's *Saint Joan.* For her 1932 performance in Arthur Schnitzler's *La Ronde* (translated from the original German as *Merry-Go-Round*) she changed costumes and characters quickly, handling all the female roles. Her superior diction and her intensity made her a powerfully tragic Juliet (at the age of forty-one) in the 1937 Pitoëff production of William Shakespeare's *Romeo and Juliet* and enhanced the lyric language of **Paul Claudel**'s *L'Echange* (translated as *The Exchange*), which the company reprised the same year: it was as Marthe in *L'Echange* that she doubtless reached the summit of her career. After her husband's death in 1939, she continued acting during **World War II,** performing in Claudel's *L'Annonce faite à Marie* (translated as *The Tidings Brought to Mary*) in New York, as well as in his *L'Echange,* in Henrik Ibsen's *A Doll's House,* and in other plays in Canada.

Those who knew the Pitoëffs unfailingly comment that Ludmilla was a constant inspiration to Georges, for he designed his sets around her vital presence and gave his strongest performances opposite her, as in *Liliom,* **Jules Supervielle**'s *La Belle au bois* (1932; Sleeping Beauty), *Romeo and Juliet,* and *L'Echange.* The couple had seven children, of whom only Sacha Pitoëff continued in the theater.

REFERENCES:

Henri-René Lenormand, *Les Pitoëff: Souvenirs* (Paris: Odette Lieutier, 1943);

Aniouta Pitoëff, *Ludmilla ma mère: Vie de Ludmilla et de Georges Pitoëff* (Paris: René Julliard, 1955).

— R.J.N.

ROGER PLANCHON

The theater director, playwright, and actor Roger Planchon (1931–) founded the **Théâtre de la Cité, Villeurbanne,** in a working-class suburb of Lyons in 1957. With skill and originality he made it the most distinguished regional theater in France and one of the nation's finest. His work set the standards for the decentralization of French theater in the second half of the twentieth century.

Of humble origins, Planchon grew up in the Lyons area, and, after a youthful fascination with cinema, he turned his fervent attention to the theater. Early influences were doubtless his own modest surroundings, the **Avignon Festival,** which took place not far away, and the writings of **Antonin Artaud.** By 1952 he had put together a company named the Théâtre de la Comédie to stage boisterous farces of its own collective devising. He soon moved the troupe into an abandoned paint shop in the center of Lyons. Scarcely 120 spectators could squeeze into the hall, but the troupe was nonetheless one of the rare independent companies outside Paris to have its own building. The group soon added classic comedies to its repertory, including William Shakespeare's *Twelfth Night* and *The Merry Wives of Windsor,* and in 1953 the actors undertook to perform **Arthur Adamov**'s avant-garde plays *Le Sens de la marche* (Facing Forward) and *Le Professeur Taranne* (translated as *Professor Taranne*).

Planchon next began exploring Bertolt Brecht's social realism, and in 1954 he arranged to stage Brecht's *The Good Woman of Setzuan.* Armed with photos of that production, he hastened to Paris to talk with Brecht, who had arrived there with his Berliner Ensemble. That discussion led Planchon to formulate a concept of the distinction between plays as scripts ("dramatic writing") and their staging ("scenic writing"); while the distinction may not have been new, the notion that the two forms of expression might clash in a single production, that the scenic writing might criticize the play, for example, led Planchon in original directions. A definite class consciousness, which has been termed Marxism, found expression in his early productions, although that tendency, never stridently militant, has been attenuated in later years. He staged other Brecht plays (*Fear and Misery of the Third Reich* in 1956, *Schweick in the Second World War* in 1961) and never scorned ideological comment on the stage.

Planchon's first Paris production was Adamov's *Paolo Paoli* (1957), which created something of a public sensation, although some critics found its ideology distasteful. While Planchon made a national name for himself, he could obtain no government money. Nationally subsidized theater was rare indeed outside of Paris. He accepted the offer of a larger theater hall from the municipality of Villeurbanne, a blue-collar suburb of Lyons, where he established his troupe in 1957 under the name Théâtre de la Cité. His success there finally brought the government to the realization that his troupe deserved financial encouragement. In 1959 the Théâtre de la Cité, Villeurbanne, was designated a "permanent company" (a title newly created for it) with government subsidy; it was promoted to "Centre Dramatique" in 1963. In 1972 the troupe re-

ceived the title of **Théâtre National Populaire** (TNP), which had formerly belonged to the company of **Jean Vilar** at the Palais de Chaillot in Paris. Planchon had developed not just an outstanding regional company but a fully recognized national theater outside Paris.

His stagings of the classics involved modern, dissonant settings (often designed by René Allio), which provided present-day commentaries on the plays. He created memorable productions of Shakespeare's *Henry IV,* parts 1 and 2 (1957) and Molière's *George Dandin* (1958) and *Tartuffe* (1962); he produced a second and perhaps still more shocking version of *Tartuffe* in 1973, with sets by Hubert Monloup. Other memorable creations were of Pierre Carlet de Marivaux's *La Seconde Surprise de l'amour* (translated as *The Second Surprise of Love*) in 1959, which created something of a scandal, and of Jean Racine's *Bérénice* (1966) and *Athalie* (1980). His stagings often evoke class conflict. For *George Dandin,* for example, he placed the protagonist's solid bourgeois mansion on one side of the set and on the other the humble peasant cottage where Dandin grew up. Dandin acted his role in the courtyard between them, in front of drying laundry, torn between two classes. The first *Tartuffe* played at the **Théâtre de l'Odéon** in Paris in 1964, at the invitation of **Jean-Louis Barrault,** and Planchon's troupe performed *George Dandin* at the Avignon Festival in 1966. He took other plays abroad, including a stage version of Alexandre Dumas *père*'s *Les Trois Mousquetaires* (translated as *The Three Musketeers*), which his troupe staged at the Edinburgh Festival in 1960.

Planchon has written several plays, often irreverent in tone, including *La Remise* (1962), *Bleus blancs rouges ou les libertins* (1967; Blues, Whites, Reds, or the Libertines), *L'Infâme* (1969; The Infamous One), *Le Cochon noir* (1973; The Black Pig), and *Gilles de Rais* (1976), concerning Bluebeard. A talented actor, he has played leading roles in his own plays and in plays by others, including Molière's Tartuffe and Shakespeare's Prince Hal in *Henry IV.*

The demonstrations of **May 1968** made Planchon's theater a center of political discussion, as some thirty directors met there to consider the role of the theater in the aftermath of the crisis. In reaction to the events, including the occupation of the Théâtre de l'Odéon by student activists and the demonstration at the Avignon Festival, Planchon composed a piece of "total theater," involving "quotations" from many sources, from Pierre Corneille to Vilar to the American musical *Hair;* its enormous title, which includes an untranslatable pun, is *La Contestation et la mise en pièces de la plus illustre des tragédies françaises, "Le Cid" de Pierre Corneille, suivie d'une "cruelle" mise à mort de l'auteur dramatique et d'une distribution gracieuse de* *diverses conserves culturelles* (1969; The Disputation and Dismemberment of the Most Illustrious of French Tragedies, Pierre Corneille's "The Cid," Followed by a "Cruel" Execution of the Playwright and a Free Distribution of Divers Cultural Canned Goods). Not really "total theater," it functions rather as a send-up of the genre.

Lacking Vilar's belief that theater can unite society, Planchon strives to attract and entertain blue-collar workers. Whether he has succeeded remains to be seen, but his productions obviously reach out to this audience, by their ideology and the location of his theater. Single-handedly he has developed the most successful French national theater outside Paris and spurred on the decentralization of theater in France.

REFERENCES:

Yvette Daoust, *Roger Planchon, Director and Playwright* (New York: Cambridge University Press, 1981);

Rosette C. Lamont, "Roger Planchon's *Gilles de Rais:* A Liturgy of Evil," *Modern Drama,* 25 (September 1982): 363–373.

— R.J.N.

MARCELIN PLEYNET

Poet and editor Marcelin Pleynet (1933–) is one of many twentieth-century writers who have called attention to the misunderstanding between poets and readers who expect poetry to be direct communication. His work is a reflection on poetry itself, its history and its possibilities for conveying meaning. As one poem puts it, he wonders "s'il est lisible" (if it is readable). He sometimes evokes great models such as Homer and Dante.

Pleynet, who became secretary of the influential literary journal *Tel Quel* in 1962, was later associated with the magazine *L'Infini.* He began publishing poetry in the early 1960s, writing in poetic prose or a spare free verse. His poetry is disciplined despite its frequent lack of punctuation, capitalization, and regular form. His first collection, *Provisoires amants des nègres* (1962; Temporary Lovers of Blacks), won the Prix Fénéon. Three of his early volumes of verse were collected in *Les Trois Livres* (1984; The Three Books). Others include *Stanze* (1973; Stanzas) and *Fragments du chœur* (1984; Fragments of the Choir), mixed verse and prose. He has also written fiction, including the novel *La Vie à deux ou trois* (1992; Life with Two or Three); literary criticism, including a book on the nineteenth-century French poet Isidore Ducasse, called Lautréamont; and art criticism, including *Système de la peinture* (1977; translated as *Painting and*

System), *Henri Matisse* (1986), and *Les Modernes et la tradition* (1990; Moderns and the Tradition).

REFERENCES:

Joan Brandt, "A Question of Privilege: Marcelin Pleynet and Lautréamont," *French Forum,* 15 (September 1990): 329–342;

Adelaide M. Russo, "Marcelin Pleynet: Mediating Surrealism — the Poet as Polemicist," *Dalhousie French Studies,* 21 (Fall-Winter 1991): 141–156.

— C.S.B.

POETIC REALISM

Poetic realism is a term used to describe a French film tradition of the 1930s. Featuring stories about ordinary people rather than the fantastically elegant figures of Depression-era Hollywood films, such movies were naturalistic and usually tragic in tone, while "poetic" in their scenic depiction of everyday life and the characters' noble struggles against destiny. Examples of the style include **Jean Vigo**'s *L'Atalante* (1934), **Marcel Pagnol**'s Marseilles trilogy (1931–1936), and especially **Marcel Carné**'s *Le Jour se lève* (1939; *Daybreak*). Some 1930s films by **Julien Duvivier** and **Jean Renoir** can also be considered examples of poetic realism.

REFERENCES:

Dudley Andrew, "Poetic Realism," in *Rediscovering French Cinema,* edited by Mary Lea Bandy (New York: Museum of Modern Art, 1983), pp. 115–119;

Marie-Claire Ropars and others, *Générique des années trente* (Paris: Presses de l'Université de Paris-VIII, 1987).

— T.C.

BERTRAND POIROT-DELPECH

Novelist, critic, and journalist Bertrand Poirot-Delpech (1929–) attracted the attention of the literary world when his first novel, *Le Grand Dadais* (1958; The Big Silly) won the Prix Interallié. This first novel was followed by *La Grasse Matinée* (1960; Staying in Bed Late); *La Folle de Lituanie* (1970; The Crazy Lithuanian Woman), which won the Grand Prix du Roman de l'Académie Française; and other works of fiction, some of which deal with the rather disabused mores and attitudes of this period and feature talented young men to whom failure seems more congenial than success. His novel *L'Eté 1936* (1984; Summer 1936) concerns the violent political events of the 1930s.

Poirot-Delpech became dramatic critic for *Monde* in 1959 and has been its chief literary critic since 1972. In these positions Poirot-Delpech has wielded considerable influence. Many of his columns have been collected as *Au soir le soir* (1969; From Evening to Evening) and *Feuilletons* (1982; Columns). He was elected to the Académie Française in 1986.

REFERENCE:

Yves Stalloni, "Bertrand Poirot-Delpech, *le Grand Dadais: Itinéraire d'un bachelier capricieux*," in *Le Roman de formation,* edited by François Rivière (Paris: L'Ecole des Loisirs, 1989), pp. 103–118.

— C.S.B.

WINARETTA POLIGNAC

Twentieth-century music, visual arts, and ballet — as well as the Institut Pasteur, the Collège de France, the Salvation Army, and many other worthy causes — have all profited greatly from the generous patronage of Winaretta Singer Polignac, Princesse Edmond de Polignac (1865–1944). Born in New York to a French woman and sewing-machine magnate Isaac Singer, she spent most of her life in France and in her palace in Venice. Passionately devoted to the arts, especially music, she helped many young composers by commissioning compositions and paying for their performances, many of which took place in her elegant neoclassical townhouse in Paris. Among the composers who dedicated compositions to her are **Darius Milhaud** and other members of **Les Six, Maurice Ravel,** and **Erik Satie.** In his autobiography **Igor Stravinsky,** one of her favorites and a frequent beneficiary of her largesse, described her as "an excellent musician, of wide culture, a painter endowed with undeniable talent [who] encouraged and was the patron of artists and the arts."

REFERENCE:

Michael de Cossart, *The Food of Love: Princesse Edmond de Polignac and Her Salon* (London: Hamilton, 1978).

— P.S.H.

FRANCIS PONGE

Francis Ponge (1899–1988) is one of the chief twentieth-century practitioners of the prose poem, known less for his considerable artistry with the form than for his "objective" approach to the world.

His first publication, *Douze petits écrits* (1926; Twelve Little Writings), a collection of satirical texts, was followed sixteen years later by *Le Parti pris des choses* (1942; translated as *The Voice of Things*), a collection of thirty-two pieces written in prose or free verse and concerned with natural beings such as pigeon, snail, and oyster or with man-made objects such as bread, pitcher, and door. Ponge, who found an enthusiastic supporter in **Jean-Paul Sartre,** attempted not to interject himself in his poems. Adopting a point of view that is as objective as possible (at least at the outset), he examines the various aspects of the object, trying to suggest its being by its appearances. As he wrote in "Déclaration: Condition et destin de l'artiste" (Declaration: The Artist's Condition and Destiny), "Consider the artist as an investigator . . . a worker . . . . Transcend classicism and romanticism by the primacy given to matter, the object." Only at the end, he believed, could one speak of an "essence" of the thing — the sum of all its aspects; the world seems autonomous and yet humanized by metaphor, and subjectivity finally wins out.

Ponge's use of language is careful and restrained; he eschews heavy-handed rhetoric and ornamentation for its own sake. Some of his sentences are simply *constats* (the stating of what is there and how things are). Yet in its simplicity this "being-there" takes on strong poetic overtones. Moreover, although he carefully avoided the explicit metaphysical questions that preoccupied many of his contemporaries, the question of the relationship of man to the world and their different sorts of realities is implicit in Ponge's poetry.

Ponge, who was a member of the **French Communist Party** for ten years (1937–1947), was engaged in **Resistance** journalism during **World War II.** His postwar works include *Le Grand Recueil* (three volumes, 1961; The Great Collection), *Le Savon* (1966; translated as *Soap*), and *pratiques d'écriture* (1984; Writing Practices). He received the Grand Prix National de Poésie in 1981 and the Grand Prix de Poésie de l'Académie Française in 1984.

REFERENCES:

Jean Cranmer, "Escargots and Oysters on the Half Shell: Francis Ponge à la carte," *Romanic Review,* 76 (November 1985): 429–443;

Robert W. Greene, "Francis Ponge, Metapoet," *Modern Language Notes,* 85 (May 1970): 572–592;

Virginia A. La Charité, *Twentieth-Century French Avant-Garde Poetry, 1907–1990* (Lexington, Ky.: French Forum Publishers, 1992);

Martin Sorrell, *Francis Ponge* (Boston: Twayne, 1981).

— C.S.B.

THE POPULAR FRONT

Associated with the antifascist strategy adopted by the Communist International in 1935, the Popular Front in France began as a mass movement and resulted in a political coalition that was able to form a short-lived government. Reacting to the right-wing demonstra-

Francis Ponge at Stanford University in 1965 (Karl-Heinz Bast)

tions of 6 February 1934, Communists and **Socialists** joined together in a counterdemonstration of 12 February 1934. This popular movement eventually led to a political coalition of three parties: the Radical Socialists; the Socialists led by **Léon Blum;** and the **French Communists.** Headed by Blum, the Popular Front government came to power on 6 June 1936, but the coalition was uneasy from the beginning because members of the Communist Party refused to take seats in his cabinet in case they should later decide to oppose his policies. The Popular Front government lasted 380 days, until 21 June 1937.

The chief goal of the Popular Front government was to bring about social change for the benefit of its working-class supporters, and it succeeded in imposing on French industry the principle of collective bargaining. During its first few days in power, the Popular Front secured an average increase of 12.5 percent in real wages for French workers, reduced the official workweek from forty-eight to forty hours without a corresponding drop in salaries, and instituted the policy of two weeks' paid vacation.

The election of the Popular Front in 1936, celebrated by a Bastille Day demonstration by one million people in Paris, ignited a cultural explosion. Seeking to democratize culture, the government and its supporters promoted various activities for the masses. Political plays were staged at the Théâtre du Peuple (People's Theater) by Socialist and Communist groups. A new association was set up to organize museum visits and classes for workers through the Communist Party **Maison de la Culture** (House of Culture). The journal *Commune* attempted to set up choral societies in every locality. Committees to promote literacy and reading were established, and public debates were held on the role of the arts in society. **Jean Renoir** produced new films to promote Popular Front ideology — *La Vie est à nous* (1936; *The People of France*), calling on the people to wrench control of France from the "200 families" of the rich and powerful, and *La Marseillaise* (1938), celebrating the revolutionary past and the unity of the nation.

Blum's Popular Front government was undermined by financial instability, exacerbated by its attempts to carry out massive reforms while the international economic environment was stagnant. Workers' euphoria led to continued massive strikes that weakened Blum's hold on power; shorter hours and more pay made French goods more expensive to manufacture and thus less competitive abroad; and the flight of capital to other countries led to a devaluation of the franc in September 1936. Blum's decision not to intervene militarily against fascist forces in the **Spanish Civil War** outraged his Communist supporters in particular, further weakening his coalition. Following the rejection by the Senate of a demand for emergency decree powers, Blum resigned.

REFERENCE:

Julian Jackson, *The Popular Front in France: Defending Democracy 1934–1938* (New York: Cambridge University Press, 1988);

Nicole Jordan, *The Popular Front and Central Europe: The Dilemmas of French Impotence* (Cambridge, U.K.: Cambridge University Press, 1993);

Charles Tilly, *The Contentious French: Four Centuries of Popular Struggle* (Cambridge, Mass.: Belknap Press of Harvard University Press, 1986).

— D.O'C. & J.H.

FRANCIS POULENC

Composer Francis Poulenc (1899–1963) was the member of **Les Six,** the controversial group of young composers in the early 1920s, most sympathetic to the ideals of **Jean Cocteau** and **Erik Satie.** Most of Poulenc's music is charming and amusing, occasionally including an intentional combination of playfulness and pathos. Though best known for his many piano pieces and various choral works, he wrote works in all the musical genres, including sonatas for individual wind instruments; a sextet for winds and piano; concertos for harpsichord, piano, and two pianos; and a ballet, *Les Biches* (1924; The Darlings), commissioned by **Serge Diaghilev.**

At a time when his colleagues were writing daring dissonances, Poulenc's melodies and harmonies were traditional, but he often slipped in a playful "wrong" note. He drew on both classical and popular music: *Les Biches,* for instance, includes elements of romanticism and jazz. In slow movements his melodies remind one of **Edith Piaf**'s nostalgic songs, in fast ones of the cancans of Jacques Offenbach. His songs are generally more serious than his other compositions. His many settings of poems by **Guillaume Apollinaire, Paul Eluard,** and **Max Jacob** are widely considered to be among the finest songs of the century. His religious works — including a *Mass* (1937), a *Stabat Mater* (1950), and a *Gloria* (1959) — are frequently performed, as is his *Dialogues des Carmélites* (1957; *Dialogues of the Carmelites*), an opera based on a play by **Georges Bernanos.**

REFERENCES:

Keith W. Daniel, *Francis Poulenc: His Artistic Development and Musical Style* (Ann Arbor, Mich.: UMI Research Press, 1982);

Francis Poulenc, *Diary of My Songs,* translated by Winifred Radford (London: Gollancz, 1985);

Poulenc, *My Friends and Myself: Conversations with Stéphane Audel* (London: Dobson, 1978).

— P.S.H.

GEORGES POULET

Literary critic Georges Poulet (1902–) — with Marcel Raymond, Jean Rousset, and Jean Starobinski — created the Geneva School of criticism. Extremely influential in the United States during the 1960s, Poulet was the first of many Continental thinkers adopted by American critics after **World War II.**

Practicing a somewhat erroneously labeled phenomenological method, Poulet searched in literature for "subjectivity without objectivity," for a pure, transcendental consciousness (the *cogito*) that would bridge the gap between author and critic. Such a revelation, he wrote, entails an intuitive openness to and identification with the work, which is considered with no reference to its historical or formal character.

Poulet is best known for *Etudes sur le temps humain* (1949; translated as *Studies in Human Time*), *La Distance intérieure* (1952; translated as *The Interior Distance*), *Le Point de départ* (1964; The Point of Departure), and *Mesure de l'instant* (1968; Measure of the Instant) — collectively titled *Etudes sur le temps humain*. His other books include *Les Métamorphoses du cercle* (1961; translated as *Metamorphoses of the Circle*), *L'Espace proustien* (1963; translated as *Proustian Space*), *Trois essais de mythologie romantique* (1966; Three Essays on Romantic Mythology), *La Conscience critique* (1971; The Critical Consciousness), and studies on Benjamin Constant, Charles Baudelaire, and Arthur Rimbaud.

Poulet taught at the University of Edinburgh (1927–1951), at Johns Hopkins University in the United States (1951–1957), and the University of Zurich (1957). With the prominence of **structuralism** in the late 1960s and of poststructuralism a decade later, Poulet's critical approach has fallen out of fashion.

REFERENCES:

Paul de Man, "The Literary Self as Origin: The Work of Georges Poulet," in his *Blindness and Insight: Essays in the Rhetoric of Contemporary Criticism* (Oxford: Oxford University Press, 1971), pp. 79–101;

Sarah N. Lawall, "Georges Poulet," in her *Critics of Consciousness: The Existential Structures of Literature* (Cambridge, Mass.: Harvard University Press, 1968), pp. 74–135;

J. Hillis Miller, "Georges Poulet's Criticism of Identification," in *The Quest for Imagination*, edited by O. B. Hardison (Cleveland: Case Western Reserve University Press, 1971), pp. 191–224.

— C.S.B.

OLGA PREOBRAJENSKA

Many of the greatest twentieth-century ballet stars in the West studied with Russian prima ballerina Olga Preobrajenska (1870–1962), who taught for almost forty years (1923–1960) at Studio Wacker in Paris. There "Madame Préo" trained Tamara Toumanova, Irina Baronova, and Igor Youskevitch, as well as British ballerina Margot Fonteyn, Yugoslavian dancer Mia Slavenska, and Americans Rosella Hightower and Marjorie Tallchief.

Preobrajenska's career began in her native Saint Petersburg, where she was a student at the Imperial Ballet School. After her graduation in 1889, she joined the Maryinsky Theater, where — with determination, impeccable technique, extraordinary musicality, and a radiant stage presence — she slowly climbed to the rank of prima ballerina by 1900. Some of her best-known roles were in *Coppélia, Esmeralda,* and *La Fille mal gardée* (*The Unchaperoned Daughter*). She remained with the Maryinsky as a performer and teacher until 1921, when she settled permanently in the West.

REFERENCES:

Laura Clandon, "Olga Preobrajenska at 86," *Dance Magazine*, 31 (February 1958): 48–51;

Elvira Roné, *Olga Preobrajenska: A Portrait,* translated and adapted, with an introduction, by Fernau Hall (New York: Dekker, 1978);

Gennady Smakov, "Olga Preobrajenska," in his *The Great Russian Dancers* (New York: Knopf, 1984), pp. 64–71.

— A.P.E.

JACQUES PRÉVERT

Jacques Prévert (1900–1977) was one of the finest screenwriters in France before **World War II** and one of the most accessible and popular French poets after the war. His delight in language and ordinary things and his gift for combining the two in playfully satiric ways contributed to his success in movies and poetry as well as his popular songs.

Prévert, who did not finish school, was associated with the **Surrealists** in the late 1920s. His first writings reflect the influence of their aesthetic practices, but his own verbal skills and imagination are apparent as well. In the 1930s he began writing

Jacques Prévert (Rapho)

screenplays that would help to define the lyrical, yet down-to-earth, style called **poetic realism.** He worked with several important directors, including **Jean Renoir** and most notably **Marcel Carné,** for whom he wrote the scripts for films such as *Le Quai des brumes* (1938; *Port of Shadows*), *Le Jour se lève* (1939; *Daybreak*), and *Les Enfants du paradis* (1945; *Children of Paradise*). Prévert also collaborated with Pierre Laroche on the script for Carné's *Les Visiteurs du soir* (1942; *The Devil's Envoys*).

Prévert's poems were first collected as *Paroles* (1945; partially translated as *Selections from Paroles*). A best-seller, the book was followed by other successful collections such as *La Pluie et le beau temps* (1955; *Rain and Good Weather*). His familiar style made his poems attractive to many readers, including students. Some of his lyrics were set to music in the late 1940s by Joseph Kosma and sung, with great success, in the nightclubs of **Saint-Germain-des-Prés** by singers such as **Juliette Gréco.** Among his best-known songs are "Barbara" and "Les Feuilles mortes" (performed in English as "Autumn Leaves"). "Familiale" (Family Scene) — in which the mother knits, the father carries on his business, and the son makes war — is a typical Prévertian satire.

REFERENCES:

William E. Baker, *Jacques Prévert* (New York: Twayne, 1967);

Anne Hyde Greet, *Jacques Prévert's Word Games* (Berkeley & Los Angeles: University of California Press, 1968).

— C.S.B.

The 1961 Prix Goncourt Jury. Standing, left to right: Gérard Bauer, Raymond Queneau, Philippe Hériat, Alexandre Arnoux, Pierre Mac Orlan; seated: Roland Dorgelès, André Billy (AFP)

PRIZES

In the twentieth century prizes have multiplied in all fields of the arts in France; there are well over a thousand listed in the *Guide des prix littéraires* (Guide to Literary Prizes), and there are many awards for artists, musicians, and filmmakers as well. Some prizes are obscure, but others confer considerable prestige on the winners and sometimes bring financial rewards through prize money or increased sales.

LITERARY PRIZES

The most prestigious prize given solely to French writers is doubtless the Prix Goncourt, created in 1903 and awarded each December by members of the **Goncourt Academy** for a work of fiction published during the year. Among the best-known laureates are **Marcel Proust** (1919), **André Malraux** (1933), **Simone de Beauvoir** (1954), **Romain Gary** (1956 and 1975, as Emile Ajar), and **Michel Tournier** (1970). Although the award is only for fifty francs, it assures tremendous sales.

Another important prize for fiction, dating from the early years of the twentieth century, is the Prix Fémina, established in 1904 by Mme C. de Broutelles with an original value of five thousand francs.

Awarded by a jury of twelve women writers, it can be given to a writer of either sex. **Julien Green** was awarded the Fémina in 1928, and **Robert Pinget** received it in 1965. This prize is now known as the Prix Fémina-Vacaresco.

The prestigious Prix Théophraste Renaudot — inaugurated in 1926 by a group of newspaper editors and named for the seventeenth-century founder of the first French newspaper, the *Gazette* — is awarded for a novel or short stories. It carries no monetary value but guarantees increased exposure and sales. It is awarded the same day as the Prix Goncourt and serves, in the eyes of some, to redress the errors of the Académie Goncourt. Among its laureates have been **Louis-Ferdinand Céline** (1932), **Jules Roy** (1946), **Jean Cayrol** (1947), **Julien Gracq** (1951), and **Michel Butor** (1957).

The Prix du Roman Populiste (or Prix Populiste) is awarded to a work that demonstrates sympathy for or interest in the modest classes of society. It was awarded for the first time in 1931, to **Eugène Dabit.** Other winners include **Jean-Paul Sartre** (for *La Nausée* [1938] — a choice that can be considered surprising), **Emmanuel Roblès** (1945), and **Christiane Rochefort** (1961).

293

The Grand Prix National des Lettres, created by the Ministry of National Education, is awarded at the end of each year to an author for the totality of his work, regardless of form or genre. It carries an award of twenty thousand francs. **Alain** (1951), **Saint-John Perse** (1959), **Jacques Audiberti** (1964), Jules Roy (1969), and **Marguerite Yourcenar** (1974) are among the writers who have received this award.

Other awards for fiction include the Prix de la Renaissance, established in 1921, and the Prix Médicis, whose recipients include **Claude Simon** (1967) and **Georges Perec** (1978). The Prix Interallié, given for fiction since 1930, includes no monetary award but brings considerable acclaim; among its winners have been **Roger Vailland** (1945) and **Claude Mauriac** (1963). Still another award for fiction is the Prix **Félix Fénéon,** which has been awarded to writers such as Michel Butor (1956) and **Patrick Modiano** (1969).

The Académie Française awards more than one hundred prizes. One of the most important is the Grand Prix du Roman, usually given to a young novelist; inaugurated in 1912, it is now worth thirty thousand francs. Two other major prizes given by the Académie are the Grand Prix de la Poésie, established in 1957 and awarded for the whole of a poet's work, and the Grand Prix de Littérature for a body of work, first awarded in 1912 and now worth fifty thousand francs. The Société des Gens de Lettres also gives many awards.

The Nobel Prize for Literature has been awarded to many French writers, including **Romain Rolland** (1915), **Anatole France** (1921), **Henri Bergson** (1925), **Roger Martin du Gard** (1937), **André Gide** (1947), **François Mauriac** (1952), **Albert Camus** (1957), Saint-John Perse (1960), and Claude Simon (1985).

MUSIC PRIZES

The most prestigious prize in music is the Grand Prix de Rome, awarded for composition by the Académie des Beaux-Arts from 1803 until 1968. It provided for a stay of four years at the Villa Medici in Rome and meant likely success for the recipient. The best-known winner is **Claude Debussy** (1884). The Société des Auteurs, Compositeurs et Editeurs de Musique (a composers' association) votes on prizes commissioned by the Ministry of Culture. There are also many smaller foundational prizes, most notably in areas of performance. Among them are the Concours International d'Orgue, Grand Prix de Chartres, for organ; the Concours International de Chant de Paris, for voice; the Concours International de Musique de Chambre, for chamber music; and the Concours International de Violoncelle Rostropovich, for cello. Winners are selected on the basis of their performances in

what are essentially contests, with entrance fees; awards range from ten thousand to one hundred twenty thousand francs, and receipt of the award heightens the performer's prestige.

MOTION PICTURE PRIZES

Among the prizes awarded at the internationally famous **Cannes Film Festival** are several reserved exclusively for French movies. The Prix **Louis Lumière,** named for the famous film pioneer, was the oldest film prize in France; it was awarded from 1934 until 1984. Some of the greatest names in French cinema have won this prize, including **Jacques Tati** (1950), **Louis Malle** (1965), and **François Truffaut** (1975). The Prix **Louis Delluc,** awarded between 1937 and 1989, was long considered the most prestigious prize. In addition to **René Clair, Jean-Luc Godard,** François Truffaut, **Henri-Georges Clouzot,** and Louis Malle, recipients include André Malraux (1945), **Jean Cocteau** (1946), Jacques Tati (1953), and **Eric Rohmer** (1970).

A prize called L'Etoile de Cristal (The Crystal Star), given by the Académie du Cinéma from 1955 until 1975, under the leadership of **Georges Auric,** was the forerunner of the present César awards (roughly the French equivalent of the Academy Awards in the United States). The Grand Prix is reserved for French films, but in other categories foreign films may compete. Among the winners of the Grand Prix are Truffaut (1962) and **Marguerite Duras** (1975).

ART AND ARCHITECTURE PRIZES

Prizes in the visual arts were modeled closely on those in literature and music. Most were awarded by and through the official Academie and Ecole des Beaux-Arts and the annual Salon. The apex of the system was the annual competition for the Grand Prix de Rome; the winner (typically an Ecole student) won a four-year scholarship to study at the branch Académie in Rome. Winning the prize typically assured a profitable career. Honors were also awarded for the competition to enter the Ecole; medals were awarded by the jury at the Salon.

The prizes and medals associated with the official art world were fiercely debated throughout the nineteenth century. (A debate over the proper nature of landscape painting led to the abolition of the Prix de Rome in landscape as early as 1863.) The disestablishment of the official Salon (1880) and the break-up of the Salon into rival institutions (1889) contributed to the decline in the importance of offical medals and prizes, as did the growing popularity of unofficial art schools. Both reform-minded rivals of the Salon — the **Salon des Independants** and the **Salon d'Automne** — rejected the idea of prizes and medals on principle. The growing importance of private dealers had largely eliminated the significance of official prizes by the early twentieth century.

The Société des Artistes français, as inheritor of the Salon tradition, continues to award the Prix Dulac (landscape painting), the Prix Gabriel Ferrier (history and figure painting), and the Prix Gustave Courtois (nudes and portraits). In architecture, apart from prizes awarded by private firms, the Académie d'Architecture awards annual gold and silver medals, as well as a vermeil medal of honor.

REFERENCES:

E. C. Bufkin, ed., *Foreign Literary Prizes: Romance and Germanic Languages* (New York: Bowker, 1980);

Guide des Prix littéraires (Paris: Cercle de la Librairie, annual);

Tad Bentley Hammer, *International Film Prizes: An Encyclopedia* (New York: Garland, 1991);

Musical America: International Directory of the Performing Arts (New York: Musical America Publishing, annual);

Gita Siegman, ed., *Awards, Honors & Prizes,* volume 2: *International and Foreign,* tenth edition (Detroit & London: Gale Research, 1994);

Harrison C. White and Cynthia A. White, *Canvases and Careers: Institutional Change in the French Painting World* (Chicago: University of Chicago Press, 1965).

— C.S.B.

MARCEL PROUST

In the view of most critics, Marcel Proust (1871–1922) was the greatest French novelist of the twentieth century. His piercing intelligence, his gifts as a satirist and verbal portrait painter, the wide scope of his interests, his originality of vision, and his masterful style that minutely examined phenomena and human beings all contribute to his monumental achievement. His long, seven-part masterpiece, *A la recherche du temps perdu* (1913–1927; translated as *Remembrance of Things Past*), offers a close and finely nuanced portrait of society in France from the late nineteenth century to the period of **World War I;** but it is also an intimate work, telling the story of an artistic vocation of which the hero is unaware until the end and exploring such subjective phenomena as sleep, memory, love, ambition, illusion, and disillusion.

Proust, who was born just outside Paris, was the son of a doctor who had come from the village of Illiers and a woman from the wealthy and respected Jewish bourgeoisie. He was, to all appearances, a somewhat sickly child, suffering from asthma. He attended the Lycée Cordorcet, where he excelled in the natural sciences and in philosophy, and he also studied at the Sorbonne. Except for a brief appointment as a librar-

Marcel Proust in Venice, circa 1904

ian, he never held a professional position. An early book, *Les Plaisirs et les jours* (1896; translated as *Pleasures and Regrets*), appeared with a preface by **Anatole France.** Proust also published translations of John Ruskin and articles in the **Figaro.** Yet he spent most of his youth in society — either in salons such as that of Mme Emile Strauss or with a group of young aristocratic friends, with whom he visited architectural monuments — and he was considered a dilettante at best. He kept his homosexuality secret from his adored mother; and in *A la recherche du temps perdu,* where homosexuality plays an important role, it is not attributed to the hero, but to the imposing but scarcely admirable Baron de Charlus, as well as to other characters.

An unfinished early novel, *Jean Santeuil* (translated), remained unpublished until 1952. In 1913, after the death of his parents and his near-total retreat from social activity, Proust submitted for publication a lengthy manuscript titled *Du côté de chez Swann* (translated as *Swann's Way*) — the first part of his masterpiece. Rejected by readers at several publishers — including **André Gide,** it finally appeared under the imprint of **Bernard Grasset,** who published it at Proust's expense. Its complex style — with its long, convoluted sentences — put off some readers, and the novel seemed to be lacking in action, even formless; rereadings and acquaintance with subsequent volumes showed it to be rigorously composed, with astonishing psychological richness and a poetic language that has no rival. Proust was prevented by World War I from immediately publishing the rest of *A la recherche du temps perdu;* he rewrote it, developing its internal possibilities but keeping most of the main structure. In 1919 *A l'ombre des jeunes filles en fleurs* (translated as *Within a Budding Grove*) won the Prix Goncourt; subsequent volumes followed. Proust's brother and publishers assembled the last volumes from manuscripts after the novelist's death.

By that time it was clear that — thanks to unparalleled gifts of observation and his personal experience — Proust had created one of the greatest French social novels. Yet his work is also modern, even modernist, in its aesthetics, its subjectivity, and its stretching of formal boundaries. Critics have often spoken of the *monologue intérieur,* or stream-of-consciousness technique, in connection with Proust's style, but his sentences are in some respects classical in structure, based on an entirely discernible, though greatly enriched, standard syntax. It can be argued, in fact, that Proust is one of the greatest heirs of the classical tradition since, like

his seventeeth-century predecessors, he dissects the human heart, draws general conclusions, and often puts his observations into pithy, balanced formulas. At the same time he is an heir to nineteenth-century realists in his portrayals of the mechanisms of society and of imposing social figures and to the symbolists in his search for the ideal reality behind phenomena.

REFERENCES:

Wallace Fowlie, *A Reading of Proust* (Garden City, N.Y.: Doubleday, 1964);

Gérard Genette, *Narrative Discourse: An Essay on Method,* translated by Jane E. Lewin (Ithaca, N.Y.: Cornell University Press, 1980);

Ronald Hayman, *Proust: A Biography* (New York: Harper & Row, 1990);

George D. Painter, *Marcel Proust: A Biography,* 2 volumes (London: Chatto & Windus, 1959, 1965);

Allison Winton, *Proust's Additions: The Making of "A la recherche du temps perdu"* (Cambridge: Cambridge University Press, 1977).

— C.S.B.

Q

RAYMOND QUENEAU

Raymond Queneau (1903–1976) is known to millions in France as the author of *Zazie dans le métro* (1959; translated as *Zazie*), which won the Prix de l'Humour Noir and was made into a film by **Louis Malle,** and of a charming poem on the carpe diem theme, "Si tu t'imagines" (If You Think), set to music and made popular as a song by **Juliette Gréco.** The fancifulness and ingenuity he demonstrates in these two works, along with his clear-sighted approach to life, created for him a well-deserved reputation as a witty, somewhat subversive commentator on mores.

Queneau is much more, however; he is an important link between **Surrealism,** with its verbal and formal experiments and its search for a reality above (or below) the daily one, and the midcentury experiments in fiction carried out in the **Nouveau Roman** (New Novel). In the 1920s he associated with the Surrealists, especially **André Breton** (whose sister-in-law he married and whom he satirized in the novel *Odile,* 1937). After publishing texts that show the influence of a Surrealist aesthetic, he turned to his own experiments. They included fiction — such as *Le Chiendent* (1933; translated as *The Bark Tree*), whose circular structure follows a rigorous mathematical formula, and *Chêne et chien* (1937; Oak and Dog), a "novel in verse" with a psychoanalytic dimension. In *Loin de Rueil* (1944; translated as *The Skin of Dreams*) — as in many other works by Queneau — dreams, fantasies, and supposed reality all intermingle. The theme of metamorphosis presented in this novel and *Zazie dans le métro* is important for Queneau, calling attention to the fluidity of past and present, the uncertain identity of the individual, and the instability of language.

Queneau also engaged in elaborate verbal games, for which he was especially gifted, in the context of

Raymond Queneau, circa 1959

Oulipo, a subgroup of the Collège de 'Pataphysique (a term coined by **Alfred Jarry**), which Queneau founded with a friend. Members of Oulipo (an abbreviation for Ouvroir de Littérature Potentielle, or Workshop for Potential Literature) set themselves complicated linguistic tasks and puzzles, some of which had mathematical foundations. Queneau's *Exercices de style* (1947; enlarged, 1963; translated as *Exercises in Style*), which recounts an unremarkable incident in ninety-nine ways, illustrates his aptitude for such undertakings; he even produced a learned paper on an aspect of number theory. These experiments, as well as some of his fiction, call attention to the arbitrary nature of language and the conventionality of literary genres. They show how close literature is to artifice and to games and how from the most insignificant elements of reality one can create elaborate verbal constructs. Queneau's work is thus allied to many experiments of the New Novelists.

REFERENCES:

Warren F. Motte, Jr., ed. and trans., *Oulipo: A Primer of Potential Literature* (Lincoln: University of Nebraska Press, 1986);

Christopher Shorley, *Queneau's Fiction: An Introductory Study* (Cambridge: Cambridge University Press, 1985);

Allen Thiher, *Raymond Queneau* (Boston: Twayne, 1985).

— C.S.B.

R

RAYMOND RADIGUET

The novelist Raymond Radiguet (1903–1923) is one of the enfants terribles of twentieth-century literature. His name has become almost synonymous with the image of a precocious genius who creates unrivaled masterpieces but burns himself out through physical abuse.

Before his short career ended, Radiguet produced journalism, experimental and traditional poetry, a play, and fiction. He also was acquainted with many well-known writers, artists, and musicians who recognized his genius. Chief among them was **Jean Cocteau,** who became Radiguet's mentor and companion and in whose company Radiguet indulged in an orgy of alcohol and drugs. Although his death was primarily the result of typhoid, his history of drug and alcohol abuse was a contributory factor.

Radiguet owes his literary renown to two short novels — *Le Diable au corps* (1923; translated as *Devil in the Flesh*), and *Le Bal du comte d'Orgel* (1924; translated as *The Count's Ball*) — brilliant psychological studies of love that fully deserve the epithet *classical* often assigned to them. The first, set during **World War I,** concerns a passionate affair between an adolescent and a young married woman; the second is also about illicit love, this time set in aristocratic circles. While such psychological studies have many models in French literature — going back to Mme de Lafayette in the seventeenth century and including Stendhal in the Romantic period and **Marcel Proust** in the early twentieth century — few authors have dealt with the affairs of the heart with such linguistic and psychological precision as Radiguet.

REFERENCES:

Margaret Crosland, *Raymond Radiguet: A Biographical Study with Selections from His Work* (London: Owen, 1976);

James P. McNab, *Raymond Radiguet* (Boston: Twayne, 1984).

— C.S.B.

LA RAFLE DU VEL' D'HIVER

During the Rafle du Vel' d'Hiver (The Roundup of the Winter Velodrome), which took place on 16–17 July 1942, French police — acting on orders from the occupying Germans — arrested more than twelve thousand Jews, many foreign born, and held them in the Winter Velodrome in Paris for deportation to Germany and other occupied countries. Most if not all were sent to Auschwitz. Now seen as a paradigm of the German **Occupation** of France during **World War II,** the *rafle* was not a unique event but part of a continuing process. During the month before the *rafle,* German Gestapo chief Heinrich Himmler set a quota of one hundred thousand Jews to be deported from France. It is estimated that about seventy-four thousand were deported by the end of the war.

The ideology of the **Vichy government** was in accord with that of the German occupiers. "Judeo-Bolshevism" was considered to be the principal enemy of the New Europe, and the Vichy French thus viewed Jews as security risks. By a Vichy decree of 3 October 1940, foreign-born Jews were placed in a special category, under the suspicion that many were part of a pro-Communist fifth column movement within France. By spring 1941 some forty thousand had already been arrested and detained in internment camps.

REFERENCE:

Alan Morris, *Collaboration and Resistance Reviewed* (London: Berg, 1992).

— D.O'C.

Jean Cocteau, Jean Hugo, Raymond Radiguet, and Pierre de Lacretelle in Lavandou, 1922

RASSEMBLEMENT POUR LA RÉPUBLIQUE

The Rassemblement pour la République (Assembly for the Republic), or RPR, is a designation for the latter-day followers of **Charles de Gaulle,** the founder of the **Fifth Republic.** It includes many members of the French middle classes and occupies a center-right position on the political spectrum. This name became official in December 1976 when Jacques Chirac set about uniting and reorganizing the various Gaullist groupings, some of which had existed since **World War II.**

Every few years the French are fond of renaming what is essentially the same political grouping because the leadership has changed or the party is out of power, thus creating confusion for those who observe French politics from the outside. After **World War II** the name Rassemblement du Peuple Français (Assembly of the French People) was applied to individuals in this center-right position. It was followed by the Union pour la Nouvelle République (Union for the New Republic) and the **Union des Démocrates pour la République** (Union of Democrats for the Republic), or the UDR, in 1969. Since the beginning of the Fifth Republic the Gaullists have changed their name five times.

During the 1970s, Valéry Giscard d'Estaing, who was president from 1974 until 1981, used the umbrella term Union pour la Démocratie Française (Union for French Democracy), or UDF, to refer to the moderate right political coalition that he led, which by 1978 had separated from the Gaullists.

REFERENCES:

J. R. Frears, *Political Parties and Elections in the French Fifth Republic* (New York: St. Martin's Press, 1977);

Frank Lee Wilson, *French Political Parties Under the Fifth Republic* (New York: Praeger, 1982);

Vincent Wright, *The Government and Politics of France,* third edition (New York: Holmes & Meier, 1989).

—D.O'C.

MAURICE RAVEL

Maurice Ravel (1875–1937), the composer of the well-known orchestral piece *Boléro* (1928), is sometimes considered a minor Impressionist in comparison with **Claude Debussy.** Yet his compositions — including songs, operas, ballets, orchestral works, chamber music, and piano pieces — are striking and original, drawing upon both classical and contemporary influences, and their continued popularity seems assured. He is also remembered for his orchestrations of some of his own piano pieces and of Modest Mussorgsky's *Pictures at an Exhibition* in 1922.

Ravel studied at the Paris Conservatory with **Gabriel Fauré,** and his early compositions, such as the *Pavane pour une infante défunte* (1899; *Pavane for a Dead Princess*) for piano and his String Quartet (1903), show the influence of his teacher in their modal harmonies and melodies. However, Ravel's *Jeux d'eau* (1901; Play of the Waters), which predates similar pieces by Debussy, employs a full-blown Impressionist style with its glittering figures and clashing, unresolved dissonances. Two other sets of piano pieces followed, *Miroirs* (1905; Mirrors) and *Gaspard de la nuit* (1908; Gaspard of the Night); because their technical demands are great, they are favored as showcase pieces by pianists who have the necessary skill. His music for the ballet *Daphnis et Chloé* (1912), commissioned by **Serge Diaghilev,** is his masterpiece of orchestral Impressionism.

The chromatic lushness of this work is not heard in his compositions of the 1920s, in which he returned to classical forms and dance rhythms, transparent textures, and acrid dissonances. One such work is his opera *L'Enfant et les sortilèges* (1925; The Child and Sorcery), written to a libretto by **Colette.**

Le Tombeau de Couperin (1917; In Homage to Couperin), for piano, is in the form of a baroque suite, including a prelude and fugue, several dances, and a toccata. The writing, as if for harpsichord, differs significantly from the Impressionistic style of Ravel's earlier piano pieces. His chamber music, much of which dates from this period, is similarly sparse. Like his two piano concertos (both 1931) — one of which is a well-known piece for the left hand only — the chamber music shows the influence of American jazz.

To Ravel's embarrassment, *Boléro,* originally ballet music that he dismissed as "wholly orchestral tissue without music," brought him worldwide fame and invitations to conduct abroad. (He made two visits to the United States.) In *Boléro* repetitions of a banal Spanish tune — each time differently orchestrated — gradually build to a huge climax. The composition has been used in American movies such as *Bolero* (1934), in which George Raft dances to its incessant rhythms, and *10* (1979), starring Bo Derek and Dudley Moore, in which the piece serves as an aphrodisiac. The Schwann music catalogue lists forty different recordings of *Boléro,* more than any other composition in any category.

REFERENCES:

Burnett James, *Ravel: His Life and Times* (New York: Hippocrene, 1983);

Arbie Orenstein, *Ravel: Man and Music* (New York: Columbia University Press, 1975);

Orenstein, ed., *A Ravel Reader: Correspondence, Articles, Interviews* (New York: Columbia University Press, 1990).

— P.S.H.

MAN RAY

American artist Man Ray (1890–1976) was a vital link between the artistic modernists in France and those in the United States. Born Emmanuel Radnitsky in Philadelphia, he came into contact with American experimental artists and photographers during the early 1910s at photographer Alfred Stieglitz's 291 Gallery in New York, where he attended anarchist Emma Goldman's Ferrer Modern Art School. He began to draw on the examples of Henry David Thoreau, Walt Whitman, artist Robert Henri, and the anarchist sculptor-poet Adolf Wolff in an effort to produce socially conscious, aesthetically experimental art.

The contemporary European paintings in the Armory Show in New York (1913) helped to direct Ray's work toward contemporary European avant-garde movements. Like most American experimental artists of his time, he was in the difficult position of being exposed simultaneously to a wide variety of these movements — many of which were based on contradictory principles — without having any real background in the origins and development of any of them. The result was an inevitable eclecticism and a tendency to copy forms of European modernism without thoroughly absorbing their theoretical or practical preconditions. His *War (A.D. MCMXIV)* (1913) is "**Cubist**" only in the blocky angularity of its figures; each is starkly drawn but surrounded with a dark halo, suggesting that it has been not so much painted as carved into the surface. Other works — most notably his *Promenades* (1915) — are flat, abstracted collages in bright colors.

Ray's encounters with **Francis Picabia** during Picabia's frequent visits to New York in 1913–1917 and especially with **Marcel Duchamp,** whom Ray met in 1916, drew him directly into European art movements. The three helped to establish the short-lived New York wing of the **Dada** movement. Man Ray became involved in the refashioning of readymade objects; his *Le Cadeau* (1920; *The Gift*) consists of a row of tacks glued to the flat side of an iron. In 1921 Man Ray moved to Paris, and, apart from a lengthy residence near Hollywood (1940–1951), he lived as a Parisian for the rest of his life.

During the 1920s Ray earned a living as a photographer for prominent society magazines, including *Vogue.* He also experimented with what he called "rayographs," a kind of photograph made by placing

Man Ray in his studio at 31 bis, rue Campagne Première, 1922 (Man Ray Trust)

REFERENCES:

Sarane Alexandrian, *Man Ray,* translated by Eleanor Levieux (Chicago: J. Philip O'Hara, 1973);

Neil Baldwin, *Man Ray: American Artist* (New York: Potter, 1988);

Merry Foresta and others, *Perpetual Motif: The Art of Man Ray* (New York: Abbeville Press, 1988);

Man Ray, *Self Portrait* (New York: McGraw-Hill, 1979);

Steven Watson, *Strange Bedfellows: The First American Avant-Garde* (New York & London: Abbeville Press, 1991).

—J.H.

MARTIAL RAYSSE

Although he was not a founding member of the **Nouveau Réalisme** (New Realism) group, artist Martial Raysse (1936–) quickly became one of its most prominent members. Trained as a child in his parents' pottery shop in Nice, he was influenced by the collages produced by **Henri Matisse** in his later years. Raysse himself was often called the "Matisse of neon and fluorescent painting." At a 1962 exhibition in Amsterdam, he put together an entire make-believe environment, *Raysse Beach,* taking as its point of departure the French Riviera. For his photographic acrylic and screen print canvas *Souviens-toi de Tahiti, France en 1961* (1963; *Remember Tahiti, France in 1961*) he used a photograph of a woman at the beach and attached a parasol and a beach ball to make the work more "real," but he deliberately undercut this realism by making the woman's face and left arm a bright, glowing red and her right arm and leg fluorescent green. This displacement of colors serves as a device for alienation; it confronts the spectator with the artificiality of the image (Raysse's as well as the original photograph). One series of paintings in the mid 1960s extended this practice: instead of repainting and modifying photographs of anonymous models, the *Made in Japan* series took neoclassical images by artists such as Jean Auguste Dominique Ingres and François Gérard and reworked them in harsh, almost electric, colors. "Beauty is bad taste," Raysse declared; his goal was to attack and subvert the whole notion of "tasteful" art in favor of the exuberance and open vulgarity of commercial imagery.

The demonstrations of **May 1968** had a major effect on Raysse's art. The repression of the student uprisings caused him to rethink his love for advertising and commercial art, which became for him a symptom of a commodified culture that repressed and co-opted any real dissent. Raysse turned increasingly to film to make his statements. From the 1970s on, his paintings have largely focused on pretechnological themes, especially the celebration of nature.

objects on photosensitive paper. His rayographs and photographs deal playfully with subject matter: *Noire et blanche* (1926; *Black and White*) juxtaposes the face of Kiki de Montparnasse (Alice Prin), his lover, with an African mask from the Ivory Coast. Both positive and negative images were printed, playing with issues of black and white as colors and as racial designations.

His earlier participation in Dada led him to the **Surrealists,** just as his interest in photography led him to film. *Emak Bakia* (1926) is a film collage incorporating naturalistic scenes, quick montages, and snippets of older movies in what he termed "a whole that still remained a fragment." During the same period he began to work with overexposed and underexposed film as a means of playing with the image.

Man Ray's post-1945 paintings range from seemingly "naturalistic" depictions of dreamlike, enigmatic scenes (reminiscent of the work of Salvador Dali) to abstractions that reject the flatness of his earliest paintings in favor of an illusionistic use of three-dimensional space.

REFERENCES:

Marco Livingstone, *Pop Art: A Continuing History* (New York: Abrams, 1990);

Martial Raysse, ou l'hygiène de la vision (Brussels: Palais des Beaux-Arts, 1967);

Daniel Wheeler, *Art Since Mid-Century* (Englewood Cliffs, N.J.: Prentice-Hall, 1991).

—J.H.

ODILON REDON

At the eighth (and final) Impressionist Exhibition in 1886, even the casual viewer would have noticed the deep ruptures that had split the group. It was especially evident when the works of the first wave of Impressionists were compared to those of the Neo-Impressionists grouped around Georges Seurat's *Un Dimanche à la Grande Jatte* (*Sunday at the Grande Jatte*). Nothing could have been less anticipated in an Impressionist show, however, than *Le Secret* (*The Secret*), a charcoal sketch by artist Odilon Redon (1840–1916). In an exhibition filled with light, Redon presented a dark and eerie scene of a tiny, gnomelike figure grasping the bars of a cell (or a window), tapping to be let out. Critic Henri Fèvre noted pensively that "the drawings of Odilon Redon strike a Baudelairean note à la Edgar Poe of nightmare grimaces where laughter is rictus, at once caricature and horrible."

Neither Redon's background nor his artistic training bound him to the Impressionists. After an early start studying architecture, he trained as an art student under the academic painter Jean Léon Gérôme (1864), until an emotional breakdown led him to return to his family home near Bordeaux. The major influences on Redon's later work were interests in Hinduism, the poetry of Poe and Charles Baudelaire, and especially the graphic work of the eccentric Rodolphe Bresdin (1822–1885), whose prints depict a despairing world filled with hidden nightmares.

Redon quickly concluded that the norms of traditional painting and drawing were unacceptable to him. In *A soi-même* (1922; *To Myself*), a hodgepodge of diary entries and remembrances, he noted his fundamental differences with Gérôme concerning the nature of drawing: "He exhorted me to enclose within a contour a form that I myself saw as quivering.... I have a feeling only for shadows, and apparent depths; all contours are without doubt abstractions...." For his academic teacher, nature was captured by clear, precise lines on a white field, but for Redon, everything was interconnected by shadows and shades of gray. He eventually reversed the commonplace lithographic technique of drawing a design on the lithographic stone (as one would an ink sketch). Instead he covered the entire stone with a greasy chalk, which he would then wipe in areas that were to appear lighter, or white, in the print.

As early as 1876, Redon noted his disagreements with Impressionism, terming it "a method of painting quite justified insofar as it concerns above all the representation of external things under the open sky..." but detecting a fundamental flaw: for him there was not much to be gained in "watching only what happens outside our dwelling.... The future, on the contrary, belongs to the subjective world." The goal of objectifying subjective fears and hopes was conceived as an ultimate act of human liberation. He insisted that "the art of suggestion is like an irradiation of the world by dreams from which thought has not been excluded.... [It] is a growth, an evolution of art toward the ultimate liberation of our lives, a development that will enable us to achieve our ultimate possibilities of expansion and open up to us the highest realms of moral being, providing us with that exaltation of spirit which is our deepest need."

The "art of suggestion" was not to be explained, defined, or limited by titles or explanatory captions. Insisting that it was useless to define anything, Redon rather focused on ways in which his art could inspire the viewer in the same way music inspires a listener — to create a mood of empathic understanding that transcends a textual comprehension. It is pointless to seek a direct equivalence between Redon's images and the artists to whom he paid homage in a series of prints inspired by Poe (1883), Francisco Goya (1885), and Gustave Flaubert (1889). The same is true of *Les Origines* (1883; *Origins*), inspired by Charles Darwin's theories of evolution, and *Les Fleurs du mal* (1890; *Flowers of Evil*), inspired by Baudelaire's famous work. Rather, the images are designed to replicate for the viewer the mood or emotional state brought about (in Redon, at least) by experiencing the originals. The images are deliberately cryptic, dominated by repeated motifs, including flowers and (sometimes detached) eyes.

After 1895 Redon began to shift from his bleak lithographs and charcoal sketches to watercolors, oils, and pastels saturated with rich color. By 1900 these bright canvases had become the near-exclusive focus of his work. He wrote that painting was like creating a new and beautiful substance: "To do as nature does, create diamonds, gold, sapphires, agates, precious metal, silk, flesh; it is a gift of delicious sensuality...." He abandoned his earlier social consciousness, including his insistence that his art was part of a general process of human liberation. His new emphasis was on sensual pleasures and on artists' struggles to resist any restrictions on their art. "To submit talent and even genius to concepts of justice or morality is a great error," he wrote in 1909.

REFERENCES:

Stephen Eisenman, *The Temptation of Saint Redon: Biography, Ideology, and Style in the Noirs of Odilon Redon* (Chicago: University of Chicago Press, 1992);

Philippe Jullian, *Dreamers of Decadence: Symbolist Painters of the 1890s,* translated by Robert Baldick (New York: Praeger, 1971);

The New Painting: Impressionism, 1874–1886 (San Francisco: Fine Arts Museums of San Francisco, 1986);

Odilon Redon, *To Myself* (New York: Braziller, 1986);

Michael Wilson, *Nature and Imagination: The Work of Odilon Redon* (New York: Dutton, 1978).

— J.H.

JEAN-CLAUDE RENARD

Jean-Claude Renard (1922–) is recognized as one of the most important French poets of the second half of the twentieth century. Some of his poetry has been translated into English, but a great deal remains unknown in English-speaking countries. A member of the Académie Mallarmé, Renard has won many prizes, including the Grand Prix de Poésie de l'Académie Française (1988). He has also lectured widely in Europe, Asia, and North America.

From his earliest poems, including *Juan* (1945), through his important midcareer books, such as *La Terre du sacre* (1966; Land of the Coronation) and *La Braise et la rivière* (1969; The Coals and the River), to works such as *Sous de grands vents obscurs* (1990; Below Great Dark Winds), Renard has been concerned with what he calls *mystery* — the interpenetration of the spiritual and the material in the world and in man. In his earliest work, which reflects to some degree the influence of **Paul Claudel,** the framework is orthodox Christianity (he was brought up in the Roman Catholic faith), but in later writings, including prose works dealing with poetry as a phenomenon, Renard widened his sense of how the spiritual manifests itself, insisting in particular on the power of language not just to evoke the invisible but to reveal it. Poetry is thus concerned with Being and the transcendental, which inhabit the immanent obscurely and which "a living language" can express.

Eschewing Romantic rhetoric and the excesses of **Surrealism,** Renard's poetry is often hermetic. He believes that the mystery at its heart cannot be seized directly but instead can be manifested only obliquely, through lightninglike touches, paradoxes, and images; yet he does not cultivate obscurity for its own sake.

Many of his works are concerned with travel and the exotic, where the framework of strangeness assists the poet in exploring the strangeness of language, perception, nature, and the spiritual life.

REFERENCES:

André Alter, *Le Sacre du silence* (Seyssel: Champ Vallon, 1990);

Jean Burgos and others, *Jean-Claude Renard ou les secrets de la chimère* (Fasano: Schena / Paris: Nizet, 1992);

Jean-Claude Renard, *Jean-Claude Renard: Selected Poems,* edited, with an introduction, by Graham Dustan Martin, translated by Elisabeth Deberdt-Martin and others (London: Oasis Books, 1978).

— C.S.B.

MADELEINE RENAUD

As a leading actress, first in the French national theater and then in her own troupe, which she founded with **Jean-Louis Barrault,** Madeleine Renaud (1903–1994) was instrumental in bringing the so-called **Theater of the Absurd** to the attention of the general public and in teaching traditional audiences to appreciate it.

With sound conservatory training, Renaud was admitted to the **Comédie-Française** at the age of twenty-one and received to full membership as a *sociétaire* in 1928. She played primarily stereotypical *ingénue* roles, the "sweet young thing," the "guileless girl" of classical French comedies, and later the occasional coquette in plays by Pierre-Augustin Caron de Beaumarchais and Pierre Carlet de Marivaux, all with elegance and aplomb.

During **World War II,** Renaud taught in state-sponsored theater schools. In 1940 she married Barrault, a new member of the Comédie-Française, who was also teaching theater. When Barrault organized the famous wartime production of **Paul Claudel's** epic **Le Soulier de satin** (translated as *The Satin Slipper*) in 1943, she played the innocent Doña Musique.

After the **Liberation** of France Renaud and Barrault left the Comédie-Française and formed the Compagnie Madeleine Renaud–Jean-Louis Barrault, housed for its first ten years at the Théâtre Marigny. Reputed to be a superior administrator, with her appreciation for simple elegance and sophistication, she is thought to have brought a bit of classical sobriety to the company's venturesome temperament. In any case she and Barrault were able to attract audiences for an eclectic repertory, ranging from Georges Feydeau's *Occupe-toi d'Amélie* (1948; translated as *Keep an Eye on Amélie*) to Anton Chekhov's *The Cherry Orchard* (1954), in both of which she played starring roles. Her

Scene from Jean Renoir's 1939 movie *La Règle du jeu*. Renoir, who played Octave, is second from left.

remarkable portrayal of Araminte in Marivaux's *Fausses confidences* (False Secrets) in 1946 changed the way Marivaux's plays were understood in France; she was to play the role often over the next two decades.

In 1959 Renaud and Barrault's company moved to the **Théâtre de l'Odéon,** a state-supported theater. The new codirectors renamed the hall Théâtre de France. There they staged works of the avant-garde, absurdist playwrights, often finding them in marginal pocket theaters and giving them the stamp of approval of a major, traditional company. Renaud triumphed as Winnie in **Samuel Beckett's** *Oh! les beaux jours* (translated as *Happy Days*) when **Roger Blin** directed it at the Théâtre de France in 1963. She played the role of a woman buried up to her neck in the earth, a prisoner of her human condition, with such simple dignity that she won great public understanding for the pathos of Beckett's aging character. She continued playing Winnie until she herself was past eighty.

After the Renaud-Barrault company was removed from their Théâtre de France for failure to stand up more staunchly against the student occupa-

tion of the state-owned building during the riots of **May 1968,** the troupe played in several other theaters. In her eightieth year Renaud played Madeleine in **Marguerite Duras's** *Savannah Bay,* revealing the classical, almost tragic, gravity underlying much modern and postmodern theater.

REFERENCES:

Pierre Chabert, "Madeleine Renaud," in *Women in Beckett: Performance and Critical Perspectives,* edited by Linda Ben Zvi (Urbana: University of Illinois Press, 1990);

Bernard Dort, "L'Age de la représentation," in *Le Théâtre en France. 2: De la Révolution à nos jours,* edited by Jacqueline de Jomaron (Paris: Armand Colin, 1989), pp. 451–534;

Noëlle Loriot, *Madeleine Renaud* (Paris: Presses de la Renaissance, 1993).

— R.J.N.

JEAN RENOIR

Jean Renoir (1894–1979) is widely regarded as the greatest of all French filmmakers. His work serves as a benchmark for cinema of any origin, be it silent or sound, old wave or **Nouvelle Vague** (New Wave). **Alain Resnais, François Truffaut, Jean-Luc Godard,** Bernardo Bertolucci, and many other directors have found in Renoir an important inspiration.

A son of the painter Auguste Renoir, Jean Renoir spent his childhood in his father's studios in Paris and southern France. In 1913 he completed a degree in philosophy and mathematics at the University of Aix-en-Provence. During **World War I** he suffered injuries while serving in the French cavalry, and he was injured again after transferring to the French air corps. In the early postwar years Renoir married his father's last model, Andrée Heuchling, who soon was known as Catherine Hessling when she starred in Renoir's first silent films. After she refused to play the role of the prostitute in Renoir's second sound film, *La Chienne* (1931; The Bitch), they separated. Renoir's silent movies, at first financed by his inheritance, include *La Fille de l'eau* (1925; The Water Girl), *Nana* (1926), *Tire-au-flanc* (1928; Get Out of It), and *La Petite Marchande d'allumettes* (1928; *The Little Match Girl*), which he directed with Jean Tedesco. In his silent films Renoir began to develop the visual style for which he is known, using long takes, deep-focus shots, and moving cameras. During this period and in the 1930s Renoir also acted occasionally, both in his own films and those of others.

Owing to the subtlety of his technique and his equally subtle attacks on middle-class hypocrisy, Renoir's achievement during the early sound era was little appreciated at the time. Yet he reached his maturity as a filmmaker during this period, directing thirteen important features between 1931 and 1939. Most deal with human relationships and class conflicts, including *La Chienne,* the comic *Boudu sauvé des eaux* (1932; *Boudu Saved from Drowning*), and *Toni* (1934), a movie in the **poetic realist** style filmed on location with nonprofessional actors. Some of these films — such as the fast-paced *Le Crime de M. Lange* (1936; *The Crime of Monsieur Lange*), about a man who works for an exploitative publisher — were made in collaboration with his leftist Groupe Octobre (October Group), which after 1935 was aligned with the **Popular Front.** He was also the main director of the collaborative Communist campaign film *La Vie est à nous* (1936; *The People of France*), which combines documentary and narrative techniques.

Renoir adapted works by Gustave Flaubert (*Madame Bovary* in 1934), Maksim Gorky (*Les Bas-Fonds* [*The Lower Depths*] in 1936), and Guy de Maupassant (*Une Partie de campagne* [*A Day in the Country*], also in 1936). The unfinished *Une Partie de campagne* was edited and released as a short film in 1946. *La Grande Illusion* (1937; *Grand Illusion*), Renoir's first international success, deals with conflicts between class and

nationality, while the subject of *La Marseillaise* (1938) is the French Revolution.

Following the success of his modern adaptation of Emile Zola's *La Bête humaine* (1938; *The Human Beast*) came Renoir's masterpiece, *La Règle du jeu* (1939; *The Rules of the Game*), a satire of modern French society that presents a convoluted story about upper-class characters and their servants. Long takes, fluid moving shots in corridors, and multilayered action in deep focus are used to convey interlocking narratives that cut across the French social spectrum. A commercial failure, the movie was cut and soon withdrawn. It was then banned by the French government as "demoralizing"; the ban was soon lifted but was reimposed during the **Occupation.** The only complete negative of the film was destroyed in 1942 in an Allied bombing, but in 1956, when Renoir's reputation was on the rise, fans restored it to its original form by piecing together film, negatives, and soundtracks from two hundred cans of film.

In 1940 Renoir shot *La Tosca* in Italy, and the following year he went to Hollywood on an invitation from director Robert Flaherty. Between 1941 and 1947 Renoir completed six films in Hollywood, most notably *The Southerner* (1945). For the rest of his life he divided his time between Beverly Hills and Paris. He completed eight more films — including his first color movie, *The River* (1951), shot in India; *Paris CanCan* (1955; *Only the French Can*); and *Eléna et les hommes* (1956; *Paris Does Strange Things*) — before his death in Los Angeles in 1979.

REFERENCES:

André Bazin, *Jean Renoir,* edited by François Truffaut, translated by W. W. Halsey II and William H. Simon (New York: Simon & Schuster, 1973);

Raymond Durgnat, *Jean Renoir* (Berkeley & Los Angeles: University of California Press, 1974);

Jean Renoir, *My Life and My Films,* translated by Norman Denny (New York: Atheneum, 1974);

Alexander Sesonske, *Jean Renoir: The French Films, 1924–39* (Cambridge, Mass.: Harvard University Press, 1980).
                                                                            — T.C.

THE RESISTANCE

The internal resistance to the German **Occupation** after the fall of France in June 1940 can be said to have begun later that year in both the **Free Zone** and the Occupied Zone as Frenchmen listened to the French-language BBC radio broadcasts from London. Maurice Schumann's *Les Français parlent aux Français* (Frenchmen Speak to Frenchmen), a radio segment that was

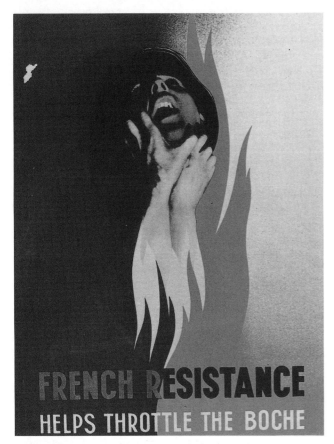

1944 poster by R. Louvat supporting the French Resistance

broadcast starting in 1943, is probably the most notable example of this form of Allied propaganda.

After Germany invaded the Soviet Union in June 1941, the **French Communist Party** (PCF), previously allied with the German Reich because of the Hitler-Stalin Pact of 1939, entered the internal resistance movement. On orders from Moscow the PCF built bridges to the non-Communist underground groups that already existed, and it soon played a dominant role in the overall resistance effort. The principal goal of the Resistance at this time was to sway public opinion to its side. The movement used sabotage and the assassination of German soldiers (the first was gunned down in the Paris subway in summer 1941) to force the enemy to take reprisals and thereby alienate the civilian population.

This strategy worked well. The occupying authorities soon inaugurated special judicial procedures for resisters, leading to the execution of hostages as reprisals for acts of terrorism. French opinion did shift as a result of these events: prior to June 1941 the population was generally opposed to acts of terrorism and sabotage committed by people in civilian clothes

against uniformed German army personnel; it was, on the whole, in favor of such actions by 1943.

Gen. **Charles de Gaulle,** based in London, tried to coordinate the various Resistance groups. His personal envoy, Jean Moulin, parachuted into France on 1 January 1942, and on 27 May 1943 the first meeting of the Conseil National de la Résistance (National Resistance Council), or CNR, took place in Paris.

After the Allied landings in Normandy in June 1944 the resisters continued for the most part to wage a war of terror and sabotage, but they also engaged in several pitched battles against the German Wehrmacht. Some units of Resistance fighters, particularly the guerrillas, were known as the Maquis (from a Corsican word meaning *thicket*). After the **Liberation** of Paris in August of that year the CNR, largely directed by Communists, organized the **épuration,** a series of purge trials to call to account those suspected of collaboration with the enemy.

One **Vichy government** measure that helped the Resistance recruit new members was the Service du Travail Obligatoire (Obligatory Work Service), or STO, program. The agreement for this program was signed with Germany on 16 February 1943 and implemented the following month. The purpose of the program was to increase the French labor force in German factories, where, by the end of 1942, 240,000 Frenchmen were working. According to the STO agreement, young men born in 1920, 1921, and 1922 could be drafted and sent to Germany as workers. By September 1944 there were some 700,000 French laborers in German industry, but several thousand escaped deportation by joining the Resistance.

REFERENCES:

Claude Chambard, *The Maquis: A History of the French Resistance Movement* (Indianapolis: Bobbs-Merrill, 1976);

Jean Lacouture, *De Gaulle,* translated by Patrick O'Brian, 2 volumes (New York: Norton, 1993);

Don Lawson, *The French Resistance* (New York: Wanderer Books, 1984);

David Schoenbrun, *Soldiers of the Night: The Story of the French Resistance* (New York: Dutton, 1980);

Pierre Seghers, *La Résistance et ses poètes* (Paris: Seghers, 1974).
                                                    — D.O'C.

ALAIN RESNAIS

Though not a prolific director, Alain Resnais (1922–) is one of the most significant French filmmakers since **World War II.** His work is at once profoundly disturbing and moving and highly intellectual.

Resnais was born in Vannes, Brittany, and studied cinema at the Institut des Hautes Etudes Cinématographiques for one year before being drafted in 1945 to serve in the Allied occupation forces in Germany and Austria. He also was a member of a traveling theater troupe. He began making short films, mostly documentaries, in 1946. Most are terse studies of art and artists such as Vincent van Gogh and **Pablo Picasso.** In the 1950s Resnais was influenced by novelist **Jean Cayrol**'s dedication to sustaining the memory of the Nazi death camps and the possibility of creating art in their shadow. The result was Resnais's best-known documentary, *Nuit et brouillard* (1955; *Night and Fog*). Written by Cayrol, the film combines color photography of contemporary Auschwitz with black-and-white documentary footage that details the butchery and horror of the camps. The moving camera suggests the instability of memory. Another documentary, *Toute la mémoire du monde* (1956; All the Memory of the World), which was subsidized by the French government to celebrate the Bibliothèque Nationale in Paris, turns the archive into a prison of the world's memory.

Resnais's first feature films employ a similarly unsettling style of camera movement, voiceover, and visual juxtaposition. Written by **Marguerite Duras,** *Hiroshima mon amour* (1959) deals with the repression of love and trauma in postwar Hiroshima, where the making of an antiwar film brings together a French woman and a Japanese man. Like *Hiroshima mon amour, L'Année dernière à Marienbad* (1961; *Last Year at Marienbad*), written by **Alain Robbe-Grillet,** is a complex, cryptic film that presents a nonlinear narrative concerned with time, memory, and perception. Though Resnais was older than the **Nouvelle Vague** (New Wave) directors, he was quickly associated with them, and these films contributed to a new international interest in French cinema.

Resnais's later films are largely variations on similar themes and techniques. They concern the **Algerian war** in *Muriel* (1963), the **Spanish Civil War** in *La Guerre est finie* (1966; *The War is Over*), and the Vietnam War in his segment of *Loin du Viet-nam* (1967; *Far from Vietnam*). *Stavisky* (1974) treats the **Stavisky Affair** of 1933–1934 and shows how facts cannot be disentangled from projections, images, and subjective memories. Resnais's first English-language film, *Providence* (1977), starring John Gielgud, also explores history, self, and identity. His more recent work includes *Mon oncle d'Amérique* (1980; My American Uncle), *La Vie est un roman* (1983; *Life Is a Bed of Roses*), and *L'Amour à mort* (1984; *Love unto Death*).

REFERENCES:

Roy Armes, *The Cinema of Alain Resnais* (London: Tantivy, 1968);

James Monaco, *Alain Resnais: The Role of Imagination* (London: Secker & Warburg, 1978);

Freddy Sweet, *The Film Narratives of Alain Resnais* (Ann Arbor: University of Michigan Press, 1981);

Maureen Turim, *Flashback in Film: Memory and History* (London: Routledge, 1989).

—T.C.

JEAN-FRANÇOIS REVEL

The anti-Marxist, pro-American philosopher Jean-François Revel (born Jean-François Ricard in 1924) served in the **Resistance** during **World War II.** He took his degree in philosophy at the Sorbonne in 1948 and taught in Algeria, Mexico, and Italy, returning to France to teach at lycées in Lille from 1956 to 1960 and in Paris from 1960 to 1963. His *Pourquoi des philosophes?* (1957; Why Philosophers?) was followed by the well-received *Sur Proust* (1960; translated as *On Proust*). He severely critiqued French politics in *En France* (1965; translated as *The French*), and in *Ni Marx ni Jésus: De la seconde révolution américaine à la seconde révolution mondiale* (1970; translated as *Without Marx or Jesus: The Second American Revolution Has Begun*) he outraged many of his fellow French intellectuals by criticizing Soviet and Chinese Communism and praising the United States — at the height of the Vietnam War. He elaborated his anti-Communist, prodemocratic position in *La Tentation totalitaire* (1976; translated as *The Totalitarian Temptation*). His pessimistic prediction in *Le Rejet de l'état* (1984; translated as *How Democracies Perish*) that the democratic countries would be overwhelmed by the spread of communism seems to have been falsified by the collapse of the Soviet empire.

REFERENCE:

Melinda Camber Porter, "The Sovereignty of the Writer: Françoise Sagan, J.-F. Revel, André Malraux, Régis Debray," in her *Through Parisian Eyes: Reflections on Contemporary French Arts and Culture* (Oxford: Oxford University Press, 1986), pp. 191–236.

—C.S.B.

PIERRE REVERDY

The poet Pierre Reverdy (1889–1960) is perhaps the closest French equivalent to the American poets called Imagists. Although he was acquainted with and less than a decade older than the major **Surrealists,** he was less interested in poetic revolution than in expressing the subtle experiences of the self and the unknown within the self, which he rendered in a well-crafted, impersonal free verse that relies somewhat on imaginative typography. Some of his apt images seem to arise from and express dreams and the unconscious, but his poems lack the excessive illogicism and the aggressive, explosive use of language that characterized most of the Surrealists' writing.

Reverdy, who came from a family of artisans with a peasant background, settled in Paris as a young man to write poetry, earning a meager living as a proofreader. He became acquainted with artists **Pablo Picasso** and **Georges Braque,** as well as poets **Guillaume Apollinaire** and **Max Jacob,** with whom he founded the magazine *Nord-Sud* (named for a Paris subway line) in 1917. During the 1920s the magazine began publishing work by the Surrealists, who called Reverdy "the greatest living poet." In the second half of the 1920s, however, he began to distance himself from Parisian literary life and turn toward religious meditation. *Plupart du temps* (1945; Most of the Time) and *Main d'œuvre* (1949; Labor) include most of his previous work.

REFERENCES:

Robert W. Greene, *The Poetic Theory of Pierre Reverdy* (Berkeley: University of California Press, 1967);

Virginia A. La Charité, *Twentieth-Century French Avant-Garde Poetry, 1907–1990* (Lexington, Ky.: French Forum Publishers, 1992).

— C.S.B.

LA RÉVOLUTION SURRÉALISTE

Published from 1924 to 1929, the journal *Révolution Surréaliste,* first edited by Pierre Naville and **Benjamin Péret,** served as a critical forum for the development of the cultural and political ideas of **Surrealism.** Early contributors, besides the editors, included **André Breton, Robert Desnos, Paul Eluard, Pierre Reverdy, Man Ray,** and many other Surrealists. Through its pages, the reader can trace the evolving Surrealist concept of *revolution.*

Initially the Surrealists tended to use the word *révolution* either in purely personal or psychological terms, or as a synonym for an individual war against the totality of modern existence; both uses had little in common with the revolutionary political upheavals around the world. The first issue of the *Révolution Surréaliste* featured an admiring essay on Germaine Berton, an anarchist assassin jailed for killing a leader of the **Action française.** This and other early issues of the periodical demonstrated an interest in an all-encompassing revolt against dominant culture, from demands to free all prisoners to descriptions of dreams and seances and expression of interest in Asian religions.

Pressures on *Révolution Surréaliste* to make its concept of revolution concrete came from within and from external forces, including the rival review *Clarté,* with which the Surrealists had a complicated relationship in the mid 1920s. In 1925 those involved in writing and publishing the *Révolution Surréaliste* met to determine whether Surrealist or revolutionary principles ought to rule their activities, but they failed to reach a consensus. After Breton assumed editorship with the fifth issue, the periodical began to exhibit a growing enthusiasm for the Russian Revolution and for Vladimir Ilyich Lenin and Leon Trotsky in particular. The Rif revolt against the French protectorate in Morocco, which peaked in 1925–1926, further intensified the politicization of the Surrealists, as the editors of *Révolution Surréaliste* and *Clarté* issued a joint proclamation, "La Révolution d'abord et toujours" (translated as "Revolution First and Forever"), in which they called for armed political revolution.

By 1928 many Surrealists had joined the **French Communist Party.** As part of their increasing political militancy, they rejected the idea of a specifically Surrealist revolution altogether in a letter to *Humanité,* and the logical outcome of this stand was to cease publishing the *Révolution Surréaliste.* Its successor, published from 1930 to 1933 (when the Surrealists' fondness for Trotsky resulted in their summary expulsion from the party), bore the significantly altered title *Le Surréalisme au service de la révolution* (Surrealism in the Service of the Revolution).

The *Révolution Surréaliste* was marked by an inventive, if sometimes bewildering, mix of graphics, dream descriptions, manifestos, press clippings, and parodies. Relatively straightforward political commentaries, such as Breton's review of Trotsky's book on Lenin (1925), jostled with essays designed to subvert the reader's complacent acceptance of what was written or depicted — such as, in the final issue, **René Magritte**'s "Les Mots et les images" (Words and Images), which was designed to break down any simple understanding of the relationship of words, pictures, and ideas.

REFERENCES:

Dawn Ades, *Dada and Surrealism Reviewed* (London: Arts Council of Great Britain, 1978);

Herbert S. Gershman, *The Surrealist Revolution in France* (Ann Arbor: University of Michigan Press, 1974);

Helena Lewis, *The Politics of Surrealism* (New York: Paragon House, 1988);

Maurice Nadeau, *The History of Surrealism,* translated by Richard Howard (New York: Macmillan, 1965).

— J.H.

LA REVUE MUSICALE

La Revue Musicale is the best-known and most influential French music journal. Established in 1920 and circulated worldwide, it has from the beginning included scholarly articles on a vast range of topics; some issues are devoted to a single composer.

The journal has always been a forum for contemporary music. In its early years it featured articles by and about composers such as Béla Bartók, **Arthur Honegger, Maurice Ravel,** and **Igor Stravinsky.** Reviews of new music and concert performances around the world made up much of each issue. Publication ceased with the onset of **World War II,** but a new *Revue Musicale* emerged in 1952. The news sections were discontinued, and in-depth articles and special issues became the rule.

— P.S.H.

JEAN RICARDOU

Jean Ricardou (1932–) is known as an experimental novelist and as a perceptive critic of the **Nouveau Roman** (New Novel). In both areas he expands on the formal possibilities of fiction.

Ricardou's *L'Observatoire de Cannes* (1961; The Cannes Observatory), his first book-length work of fiction, was followed by *La Prise de Constantinople* (1965; The Taking of Constantinople), an ingenious novel that plays on the similarity of the words *prise* and *prose* — indeed, the title appears as *La Prose de Constantinople* on the back cover. Ultimately, the novel makes fiction its own subject, thus deserving to be called *metafiction.* Both *L'Observatoire de Cannes* and *La Prise de Constantinople* are elaborate, highly self-conscious creations involving wordplay, allusions to mythology and history, the use of graphic symbols, repetition and variation, and other structuring devices — all of which constantly call attention to the form of the books and prevent the development of a conventional plot.

As a critic, Ricardou is best known for his four volumes on the principles of experimental fiction and the practices of his contemporaries, such as **Alain Robbe-Grillet:** *Problèmes du nouveau roman* (1967; Problems in the New Novel), *Pour une théorie du nouveau roman* (1971; For a Theory of the New Novel), *Le Nouveau Roman* (1973; The New Novel), and *Nouveaux problèmes du roman* (1978; New Problems in the Novel). In the 1980s he produced other creative works, including *Le Théâtre des métamorphoses* (1982; The Theater of Metamorphoses), which combines fiction and theory more explicitly than his previous works,

Jean Ricardou

and *La Cathédrale de Sens* (1988; The Cathedral of Sens), whose title plays on *Sens* and *sens* (sense or meaning).

REFERENCES:

Lynn A. Higgins, *Parables of Theory: Jean Ricardou's Metafiction* (Birmingham, Ala.: Summa, 1984);

Tobin H. Jones, "In Quest of a Newer New Novel: Ricardou's *La Prise de Constantinople*," *Contemporary Literature,* 14 (Summer 1973): 296–309;

Bruce A. Morrissette, "Generative Techniques in Robbe-Grillet and Ricardou," in *Generative Literature and Generative Art: New Essays,* by Alain Robbe-Grillet and others (Fredericton, N.B.: York Press, 1983).

— C.S.B.

PAUL RICŒUR

Paul Ricœur (1913–), one of the most important French philosophers of his generation, works in the difficult areas of **existentialism,** phenomenology, **structuralism,** and hermeneutics. Like several of his compatriots, such as **Raymond Aron** and **Jean-Paul Sartre,** he was influenced by the work of Edmund Husserl; other influences include Sigmund Freud, Martin Heidegger, and Karl Jaspers. He read works by Heidegger and Jaspers while a prisoner of war (1940–

1945) and published studies on Husserl and Jaspers after the war.

Ricœur is committed to a theological viewpoint; his work has been called (by Herbert Spiegelberg) "the philosophical buttressing of a Christian synthesis." Ricœur also situates his thought within the rationalist tradition. His writings on language, meaning, symbols and myths, narrative theory, and other aspects of the interpretation of texts have proven pertinent to literary studies.

A large number of Ricœur's many works have been translated into English. Among his best-known books are *Le Volontaire et l'involontaire* (1950; translated as *Freedom and Nature: The Voluntary and the Involuntary*), *Histoire et vérité* (1955; translated as *History and Truth*), *L'Homme faillible* (1960; translated as *Fallible Man*), *La Symbolique du mal* (1960; translated as *The Symbolism of Evil*), *De l'interprétation: Essai sur Freud* (1965; translated as *Freud and Philosophy*), *Le Conflit des interprétations: Essais d'herméneutique* (1969; translated as *The Conflict of Interpretations: Essays in Hermeneutics*). Ricœur has written about Sartre, **Albert Camus, Gabriel Marcel,** Søren Kierkegaard, Vladimir Ilyich Lenin, and Ludwig Wittgenstein. He has also been involved in polemical exchanges with **Roland Barthes** and **Jacques Lacan.**

Ricœur, who passed the *agrégation* in philosophy at the Sorbonne in Paris in 1935 and was granted the degree of *docteur ès lettres* from the University of Paris in 1950, was awarded the Croix de Guerre avec palme for his service in **World War II.** He joined the editorial board of the journal *Esprit* in 1947 and has taught at universities in France, the United States, and Canada.

REFERENCES:

S. H. Clark, *Paul Ricœur* (London & New York: Routledge, 1990);

David E. Klemm and William Schweiker, eds., *Meanings in Texts and Actions: Questioning Paul Ricœur* (Charlottesville & London: University Press of Virginia, 1993);

Mario J. Valdés, ed., *A Ricœur Reader: Reflection and Imagination* (Toronto & Buffalo: University of Toronto Press, 1991).
— C.S.B.

THE RIOT OF 6 FEBRUARY 1934

On 6 February 1934 members of various right-wing *ligues* (leagues), or paramilitary groups, demonstrated in various sections of Paris and marched to the National Assembly building, ostensibly to protest the dismissal of the Paris prefect of police, Jean Chiappe, by Prime Minister Edouard Daladier. Police fired into the crowd, killing fourteen demonstrators and wounding 236. The firing of Chiappe, who was suspected on the

Left of being unwilling to crack down on the flourishing *ligues,* was only the proximate cause of the rioting. The conviction that Daladier had concealed the truth about the **Stavisky Affair** of 1933–1934 had also contributed to the *ligues'* disgust with the parliamentary system.

Leftists have traditionally called the demonstrations an organized attempt by the extreme Right, often referred to as "fascists," to seize power at a time when the **Third Republic** was weak and held in disdain by a large cross section of the population. According to this view, the riot led to the formation of the left-wing **Popular Front** government of 1936. A more widely held view is that there was no plot, but that the rioting began as a spontaneous demonstration by right-wing groups that wanted to show their dissatisfaction with the status quo. This view is supported by the fact that the actions of the various groups were clearly disorganized. Moreover, the groups lacked a common program, sharing only their disgust with the repeated scandals of the Third Republic, and they also made no attempt to take over the parliament building.

REFERENCES:

Martin Blinkhorn, ed., *Fascists and Conservatives: The Radical Right and the Establishment in Twentieth Century Europe* (Boston: Unwin Hyman, 1990);

James Joll, ed., *The Decline of the Third Republic* (New York: Praeger, 1959).
— D. O'C.

JACQUES RIVETTE

Jacques Rivette (1928–) stands in the inner circle of French **Nouvelle Vague** (New Wave) directors, though his experimental films have received mixed critical responses and limited commercial success. He edited the prominent journal *Cahiers du Cinéma* from 1963 to 1965.

Born in Rouen, Rivette moved to Paris after **World War II** to write about film, first for the *Gazette du Cinéma* (1950) and then *Cahiers du Cinéma* (1952–1969). As a critic during the 1950s he promoted the work of American directors and supported what is known as the auteur theory. Starting in 1950, he also directed short films and worked as an assistant to directors such as **Jacques Becker** and **Jean Renoir.** From 1958 to 1960 Rivette worked on his first feature-length film, *Paris nous appartient* (1960; *Paris Belongs to Us*). (Though unreleased at the time, it was mentioned in **François Truffaut**'s *Les Quatre cent coups* [1959; *The 400 Blows*].) Like much of Rivette's work, *Paris nous appartient* deals with the relationship between reality and fiction.

Rivette has completed more than a dozen films (some of them delayed or unreleased) in an allusive, self-referential style. *Out One* (1971) is based on Honoré de Balzac's *Histoire des treize* (1839; translated as *The Thirteen* and *History of the Thirteen*), in which a character improvises a story about an event whose mystery is never solved; the film lasts almost thirteen hours and has never been shown in its entirety. Other significant efforts include *La Religieuse* (1965; *The Nun*) and *Céline et Julie vont en bateau* (1974; *Céline and Julie Go Boating*).

REFERENCES:

Roy Armes, *French Cinema* (New York: Oxford University Press, 1985);

Armes, *French Cinema Since 1946, 2: The Personal Style* (London: Zwemmer & Barnes, 1970);

James Monaco, *The New Wave* (New York: Oxford University Press, 1976);

David Rodowick, *The Difficulty of Difference* (London: Routledge, 1990);

Jonathan Rosenbaum, *Rivette — Texts and Interviews* (London: British Film Institute, 1977).

—T.C.

Andre Gide (seated) and, from left, Jean Schlumberger, Jacques Rivière, and Roger Martin du Gard, 1922

JACQUES RIVIÈRE

Critic and novelist Jacques Rivière (1886–1925) is best known for his association with the *Nouvelle Revue Française,* which he edited from 1919 to his premature death in 1925, and for his published correspondence with well-known authors, including **André Gide** and **Paul Claudel.**

Rivière was managing editor of the *Nouvelle Revue Française* in its early years. Before **World War I** he published an important essay, "Le Roman d'aventure" (The Novel of Adventure), calling for a renewal in French fiction. He was influenced first by Gide, then by Claudel. A later influence was **Marcel Proust,** about whom he published a 1924 critical study and with whom he exchanged letters. Rivière wrote other critical essays, collected in *Etudes* (1911; Studies) and *Nouvelles Etudes* (1947; New Studies), and a psychological novel, *Aimée* (1925). As editor of the *Nouvelle Revue Française* he maintained the policy of "quality above all" that had characterized the review before the war in the midst of controversies over what attitude to adopt toward German literature and on other subjects. He is also known as the correspondent and, later, brother-in-law of **Alain-Fournier;** their letters furnish valuable information on Alain-Fournier's development as a novelist and on prewar French literature.

REFERENCES:

Karen D. Levy, *Jacques Rivière* (Boston: Twayne, 1982);

Helen T. Naughton, *Jacques Rivière: The Development of a Man and Creed* (The Hague: Mouton, 1966).

—C.S.B.

ALAIN ROBBE-GRILLET

The best-known and most influential writer of the **Nouveau Roman** (New Novel), Alain Robbe-Grillet (1922–   ) is known worldwide for his novels and films. He has also published criticism and autobiographical works. Motion pictures such as *L'Année dernière à Marienbad* (1961; *Last Year at Marienbad*), which he wrote for **Alain Resnais** and which won the Golden Lion award at the Venice Film Festival, and *L'Immortelle* (1963; *The Immortal One*), which was awarded the Prix Louis Delluc, brought Robbe-Grillet's name before a large public. His novels have also become well known in Europe, North America (where he has a wide following), and South

America (where his influence is apparent in the works of some current writers).

Born in Brest, Robbe-Grillet had his study of agricultural science interrupted by a period of obligatory labor in Germany during the German **Occupation** of France in **World War II.** After the war he worked for a statistical institute, then went to Bulgaria, where he participated in the building of a railway, and from 1948 to 1951 he worked for the Institut des Fruits et Agrumes Coloniaux (Colonial Fruit Institute) in several tropical and subtropical countries. After returning to France for health reasons, Robbe-Grillet began writing and never returned to agriculture.

Robbe-Grillet's first published novel, *Les Gommes* (1953; translated as *The Erasers*), is a highly original creation that refers intertextually to mythology (Oedipus — the hero who kills his father) and the genre of the detective novel. The book reworks these models in startling ways. The treatment of time — centered on a period of twenty-four hours that, in a sense, never takes place — is especially original. In his next novel, *Le Voyeur* (1955; translated), the action also encompasses a period of twenty-four hours and involves a death (with a strong suggestion of murder), this time of a child; while the cause of her death is never fully resolved, evidence indicates that during that time the protagonist-voyeur may have assaulted and killed her during a gap left in the action of the novel.

This novel was followed by *La Jalousie* (1957; translated as *Jealousy*), perhaps the best-known example of Robbe-Grillet's fiction. The French title is a pun, denoting a type of window blind, as well as the sentiment. Even more rigorously than in his previous novels, Robbe-Grillet eschews all psychological analysis and commentary, achieving the tour de force of treating one of the most famous (and commonplace) literary themes without having recourse to traditional psychology. The unnamed hero does not speak directly about his feelings, nor does an authorial voice comment on them; rather, the text consists of an unbroken, almost monotonous series of observations of behavior from the main character's vantage point ("A ... [the woman] is now at the window.... A ... picks up her brush"). Since no psychological analysis is furnished, these observations alone convey affective impulses. Narrative time is principally psychological, not chronological: events are described repeatedly, in random order, as the narrator presumably revisualizes them in mental time, although there are also exterior reference points, such as the angle of the sun. Modifications take place in the different descriptions of the event, sometimes highly charged with emotion and symbolism, and there are several scenes that reach paroxysms of psy-

chotic feeling — perhaps alluding to a murder. But nothing can be demonstrated, any more than the narrator will ever have irrefutable proof of his wife's misconduct; and the novel ends on a gradual decrescendo, returning to the same motifs and scenes that recur throughout, although they are treated with less urgency than in early portions of the book.

Robbe-Grillet's subsequent novels include *Dans le labyrinthe* (1959; translated as *In the Labyrinth*), *La Maison de rendez-vous* (1965; translated as *Rendez-vous*); and *Projet pour une révolution à New-York* (1970; translated as *Project for a Revolution in New York*). The 1965 and 1970 novels are marked by a greater degree of violence and eroticism than had been present in Robbe-Grillet's earlier work. They also employ some of the same techniques, such as reversible chronology (events that undo themselves) and a rigorously objective narrative style. In the 1960s and 1970s Robbe-Grillet made several motion pictures, which feature the erotic plots and motifs visible in his fiction; *Glissements progressifs du plaisir* (1973; Progressive Slippages of Pleasure) is a good example of his cinematic work.

During the 1980s Robbe-Grillet stirred the reading public with two autobiographical books, *Le Miroir qui revient* (1984; translated as *Ghosts in the Mirror*) and *Angélique ou l'Enchantement* (1987; Angelica, or Enchantment). These works portray an author who is — in contrast to the presence that seemed to lurk behind Robbe-Grillet's fictional works — surprisingly humanized and willing to reveal much about his family and his development. A sequel to these volumes is *Les Derniers Jours de Corinthe* (1944; The Last Days of Corinthe). His volume of criticism on the novel, *Pour un nouveau roman* (1963; translated as *For a New Novel*), has become an essential text for students of fiction after 1950.

REFERENCES:

John Fletcher, *Alain Robbe-Grillet* (London & New York: Methuen, 1983);

Stephen Heath, *The Nouveau Roman: A Study in the Practice of Writing* (London: Elek, 1972);

Ann Jefferson, *The Nouveau Roman and the Poetics of Fiction* (Cambridge: Cambridge University Press, 1980);

Bruce Morrissette, *Intertextual Assemblage in Robbe-Grillet from Topology to the Golden Triangle* (Fredericton, N.B.: York Press, 1979).

— C.S.B.

EMMANUEL ROBLÈS

Although novelist and playwright Emmanuel Roblès (1914–) is not well known outside France, he is one of

Emmanuel Roblès sitting for sculptor Paul Belmondo, Paris, May 1981

the most important of the European writers to come out of Algeria. He and his famous friend **Albert Camus** are sometimes known as part of the Ecole d'Alger (Algiers School), which also included **Jules Roy,** Jean Pélégri, and Pascal Pia.

More interested in characters and story than in form, Roblès often writes about North Africa. Of mostly Spanish ancestry, he was born in Oran. His humble origins and what he observed around him inspired his sympathy with the working classes. His first novel, *L'Action* (1938), is the first French novel to feature an Arab revolutionary hero, and it depicts some of the social conditions that would lead to the **Algerian war** in 1954.

Roblès served in the French army in 1939 and 1940. After France surrendered to Germany in June 1940, he was demobilized in North Africa, where he spent the rest of **World War II** and occasionally helped escapees from occupied Europe pass into Morocco. He later worked for the Americans in Algeria and as a war correspondent. In 1943 his novel *Travail d'homme* (translated as *The Angry Mountain*), which deals with the struggles of workers, won the Grand Prix Littéraire de l'Algérie; in 1945 it also won the Prix Populiste.

After the war Roblès settled in Paris, though he periodically returned to Algeria. His play *Montserrat* (produced in 1948 and published in 1949; translated) is set in Venezuela in 1812. His novel *Les Hauteurs de la ville* (1948; The City Heights), which won the Prix Fémina, was also a critical and commercial success. Both works deal with the struggle for political and social freedom. From this point in his career Roblès published many plays and works of fiction, of which the best known is the novel *Cela s'appelle l'aurore* (1952; translated as *Dawn on Our Darkness*), about a doctor working among the poor. The play *Plaidoyer pour un rebelle* (published in 1965 and produced in 1966; translated as *Case for a Rebel*) deals with ethical problems posed by the Algerian insurrection. The novel *Norma ou l'exil infini* (1988; Norma or the Infinite Exile) is about a woman making a great sacrifice out of love.

Most of Roblès's work reveals his basic humanism, particularly his concern with the value of the individual and the importance of human solidarity in a brutal world to which only love gives meaning. In 1973 he was elected to the **Goncourt Academy.**

REFERENCES:
Folio, special Roblès issue, 15 (November 1983);

James A. Kilker, Preface to *Three Plays,* by Roblès, translated by Kilker (Carbondale: Southern Illinois University Press, 1978).
— C.S.B.

DENIS ROCHE

Denis Roche (1937–) is well known in France for his translations of Ezra Pound's *Cantos* (1917–1969). He is also admired as a poet in his own right and as a member in the 1960s of the editorial board of the authoritative critical journal *Tel Quel,* in the direction of which poets played a prominent role. As a poet, he acknowledges the legacy of Charles Baudelaire and Arthur Rimbaud, and the influence of **Surrealism** is visible in his work, particularly in his cultivation of surprise — by unusual images, strange juxtapositions, and bizarre syntax and line breaks. Yet he is much more concerned with formal qualities than were the Surrealists. This aesthetic is visible in his first collection, *Récits complets* (1963; Complete Narratives). Since then he has published several volumes of difficult, hermetic verse. Eschewing all rhetorical facility, he is concerned not only with form but in recording his *reflections* on form, suggesting a convergence with the **Nouveau Roman** (New Novel) and other sorts of avant-garde writing.

REFERENCES:
Serge Gavronsky, *Poems & Texts* (New York: October House, 1969);
Graham Dustan Martin, ed., *Anthology of Contemporary French Poetry* (Austin: University of Texas Press, 1971).
— C.S.B.

CHRISTIANE ROCHEFORT

When Christiane Rochefort (1917–) published her first novel, *Le Repos du guerrier* (1958; translated as *Warrior's Rest*), she immediately became one of the most controversial figures on the French literary scene. More than half a million copies of the book were sold over the next few years, and it was adapted for the screen and translated into fifteen languages.

The role of alcohol and the sexual daring in *Le Repos du guerrier,* reminiscent of the works of the Marquis de Sade and of **Louis-Ferdinand Céline,** scandalized both male and female readers. Predating the political feminism of the **Mouvement de la Libération des Femmes** (Women's Liberation Movement) by a dozen years, Rochefort's novel gave female sexuality an unprecedentedly prominent position that denied the limits often set on women's desires and autonomy.

Rochefort's next novel, *Les Petits Enfants du siècle* (1962; Little Children of the Century), which deals with life in the huge apartment complexes of the suburbs, won the Prix Populiste. *Les Stances à Sophie* (1963; Stanzas for Sophie) is a biting attack on the French bourgeoisie, always one of her targets — especially middle-class morality. She is similarly concerned with feminine psychology, as in her 1982 novel, *Si tu vas chez les femmes* (If You Go with Women), whose title is borrowed from a line in Friedrich Nietzsche's *Also sprach Zarathustra:* "If you go to women, remember to take your whip." Rochefort won the Prix Médicis for *La Porte du fond* (1988; The Back Door).

REFERENCES:
Micheline Herz, "Christiane Rochefort," in *French Women Writers: A Bio-Bibliographical Source Book,* edited by Eva Martin Sartori and Dorothy Wynne Zimmerman (New York: Greenwood Press, 1991), pp. 369–379;
Diana Holmes, "Realism, Fantasy, and Feminist Meaning: The Fiction of Christiane Rochefort," in *Contemporary French Fiction by Women: Feminist Perspectives,* edited by Margaret Atack and Phil Powrie (Manchester: Manchester University Press, 1990), pp. 26–40;
Carrie Noland, *Shifting Scenes: Interviews on Women, Writing, and Politics in Post-68 France* (New York: Columbia University Press, 1991), pp. 174–191.
— C.S.B.

AUGUSTE RODIN

By the mid nineteenth century, sculpture — especially monumental sculpture — had acquired a reputation for sterility and lifelessness. Though mid-nineteenth-century France was not without sculptors who fought to reverse this judgment — most notably François Rude and Jean-Baptiste Carpeaux — it was Auguste Rodin (1840–1917) whose work fundamentally changed modern sculpture. After Rodin, one could attempt to continue his work, to blend it with traditional elements, or to reject it (as did **Aristide Maillol**), but one could never ignore it. The Romanian artist Constantin Brancusi complained that to be close to Rodin was to copy him — that only distance would allow for an independent project.

Rodin's *Man with the Broken Nose,* submitted to the Salon of 1864, set a pattern for reception of his work. The bust was based on a man who did odd jobs in the neighborhood. At first Rodin was repulsed by his appearance, "But while I was working, I discovered that his head had a beautiful shape, that in his own way he was beautiful. . . ." Others disagreed; it did not help that, in Rodin's unheated studio, the plaster head had frozen and split, leaving only a mask. The sculpture

Rodin in his studio in Meudon with *The Thinker* (World's Graphic Press)

was rejected by the Salon jury as "an unfinished sketch," "hideous."

Man with the Broken Nose hinted at Rodin's fascination with subjects outside of classical canons of beauty and with apparently incomplete sculptures. His bronze of a shriveled old woman, *Celle qui fut la Belle Heaulmière* (1880–1883; *She Was Once the Helmet-Maker's Beautiful Wife*), provoked the accusation that he deliberately produced ugliness. Rodin insisted that in art only the false and artificial were truly ugly; that which was real, that which had character, had its own beauty.

Rodin's interest in "unfinished" sculpture had several sources. Like many of his contemporaries, Rodin was fascinated by classical fragments, such as the Barberini Torso, as well as by Michelangelo's uncompleted "slave" statues, in which the figures seem to emerge from the rough marble. He ridiculed the idea that a sculpture was finished only when it was composed of a complete body with all its limbs, arguing that an "uncompleted" work could be extraordinarily powerful. Other sculptors had made a similar argument, but Rodin went beyond sculptors such as

Medardo Rosso, who attempted to integrate sculpture and base or pedestal, creating a new iconography from the merger of the two. In Rodin's *The Wave Before* (1887, marble) a naiad flows upward from the water like a living wave; in his depictions of Andromeda or the Danaides the figures lie physically and emotionally collapsed, partly immersed in the sand around them.

Rodin's attempts to execute monumental commissions met with mixed success — scarcely surprising in view of his deliberate breach with sculptural traditions. Most ambitious was his work for bronze doors for a never-completed Musée des Arts Décoratifs in Paris. He conceived the doors as the embodiment of Dante's *Inferno,* dubbing them *La Porte de l'enfer* (*The Gates of Hell*). Though he never completed the project, life-size spinoffs from it include *Le Penseur* (1880; *The Thinker*) — originally intended as the figure of Dante, thinking the *Divine Comedy* into existence — and *Le Baiser* (1883; *The Kiss*), based on an early conception of the doomed lovers Paolo and Francesca.

In 1890 a literary committee commissioned Rodin to produce a monument to the novelist Honoré de Balzac. Attempting a heroic image of the rather unlovely novelist, Rodin was inspired by Balzac's dressing gown, hooded like a monk's. The completed *Balzac* (1898) shows the novelist, working at night, pulling the robe around him as he stares into the darkness. The committee flatly rejected the piece; hostile critics compared it to "a colossal foetus," a "bag of plaster," a "German larva . . . this beer-filled thing." Rodin's students had to defend the sculpture from a group of Ecole des Beaux-Arts students incited to destroy it by an editorial in a monarchist paper. (By contrast, a supporter called the work "a strident savage cry"; **Paul Signac** declared that next to it, surrounding sculptures looked like "hairdresser's dummies").

The controversy over the Balzac statue set the stage for the battle over Rodin's most important public commission, *Les Bourgeois de Calais* (*The Burghers of Calais*). The Calais city government had hired Rodin to make a sculpture of Eustache St. Pierre, one of five citizens who, to save their city, surrendered themselves in sackcloth and ashes and with nooses around their necks to the mercy of the English king Edward III in 1347. In 1884 Rodin produced a full complement of five sculpted figures atop a victory arch. His final design (1895) lacked the arch; the figures, set at ground level, presented a varied response to their fate, from utter despair to grim defiance. The Calais council members loathed the work, exiling it initially to a space adjacent to a public urinal. To them it was vulgar and unheroic; they would have preferred a more conventional scene of stereotypical courage, not an intense study of several men facing, in their own ways, the possibility of their deaths.

Much of Rodin's monumental sculpture was completed years after it was conceived; the first bronze of *Balzac* was not cast until 1939, while a planned memorial (1879) to the dead of the Franco-Prussian War proved so harsh that it was not cast until after **World War I** — under the new name *Défense de Verdun,* in reference to the battle of **Verdun,** which demonstrated the brutality and mass slaughter of modern war. Many of Rodin's projects, including a monument to Victor Hugo and a haunting image of Mary Magdalene passionately embracing a crucified Christ, were never completed. Left as sketches (on paper or in clay) are a multitude of flowing, shifting, often dancing figures, pared down to reveal the essence of motion and power, that break still further with academic norms.

REFERENCES:

Ruth Butler, *Rodin: The Shape of Genius* (New Haven: Yale University Press, 1993);

Frederic V. Grunfeld, *Rodin: A Biography* (New York: Holt, 1987);

William Harlan Hale, *The World of Rodin, 1840–1917* (New York: Time-Life Books, 1969);

Auguste Rodin, *Rodin: Eros and Creativity* (Munich: Prestel, 1992).

— J.H.

ERIC ROHMER

A decade older than his **Nouvelle Vague** (New Wave) comrades of the late 1950s, Eric Rohmer (1920–) has dedicated his career to making incisive films about human behavior. Neither as brash or flamboyant as the early **Jean-Luc Godard** and **François Truffaut,** Rohmer employs a minimalist style to narrate amusing dramas about everyday people.

Born Jean-Marie Maurice Scherer, Rohmer taught literature from 1942 to 1950, the year he founded, with Godard and **Jacques Rivette,** the *Gazette du Cinéma* and began directing short films. Better known as a critic during the 1950s, Rohmer had little success in making feature-length films. He was editor in chief of *Cahiers du Cinéma* between 1957 and 1963, and with **Claude Chabrol** he wrote a 1957 book on Alfred Hitchcock. Rohmer finished his first feature, *Le Signe du Lion* (*The Sign of Leo*) in 1959 before writing and directing a set of *six contes moraux* (Six Moral Tales) from 1962 to 1972. Rich in intimate conversations and locales that enhance the psychological dimensions of the situations, they deal with the moral decisions that people make when they decide to commit their affections to other people. Movies in this se-

ries include *Ma Nuit chez Maud* (1969; *My Night at Maud's*), his first international success; *Le Genou de Claire* (1970; *Claire's Knee*); and *L'Amour l'après-midi* (1972; *Chloë in the Afternoon*).

Since 1980 Rohmer has been crafting a series titled *comédies et proverbes* (Comedies and Proverbs). Similar in intent to the earlier series, these films — such as *Le Rayon vert* (1986; released as *The Green Ray* and as *Summer*) — deal with groups or society in general rather than individuals.

REFERENCES:

C. G. Crisp, *Eric Rohmer, Realist and Moralist* (Bloomington: Indiana University Press, 1988);

T. Jefferson Kline, *Screening the Text: Intertextuality in New Wave French Cinema* (Baltimore: Johns Hopkins University Press, 1992), pp. 119–147;

James Monaco, *The New Wave* (New York: Oxford University Press, 1976);

Martin Walsh, "Structured Ambiguity in the Films of Eric Rohmer," *Film Criticism,* 1 (Summer 1976): 30–36.

— T.C.

ROMAIN ROLLAND

During his lifetime writer Romain Rolland (1866–1944) was one of the best-known French figures worldwide. He has since fallen in popularity to such a degree that many readers would not recognize his name. His aesthetic and political idealism has fallen out of favor and seems out of touch with contemporary reality; moreover, his attitudes toward and answers to the social problems that concerned him now seem old-fashioned, as does his nineteenth-century tendency toward hero worship. Nonetheless he stands as an important reflection of his times.

Rolland began his prolific writing career as a novelist, playwright, biographer, and musicologist. His *Vie de Beethoven* (1907; translated as *Beethoven*), a biography of the composer, and other writings on music were considered masterful. He was particularly successful with his ten-volume roman-fleuve (series novel) *Jean-Christophe* (1905–1912; translated), which was long considered a fictional masterpiece by many readers and critics. It recounts the youth, development, love affairs, and final success of a gifted German-born musician and offers a critique of modern civilization.

Rolland was also widely known as a scholar of literature and of Indian religions, writing on figures such as Johann Wolfgang von Goethe, **Charles Péguy,** and Mohandas K. Gandhi. A well-known pacifist, Rolland fled to Switzerland at the beginning of **World War I** and conducted an antiwar campaign that included publication of *Au-dessus de la mêlée* (1915; translated

Romain Rolland with Mohandas Gandhi at Villeneuve, Switzerland, 1931

as *Above the Battle*). He received the Nobel Prize for Literature in 1915.

After the war his pacifism made Rolland persona non grata to many French, who resented what they considered his lack of patriotism; yet many Europeans continued to view him as a towering intellectual figure until years after his death. He published dozens of books on a wide range of topics, some of them multivolume works such as the lengthy social novel *L'Ame enchantée* (1922–1933; translated as *The Soul Enchanted*), and he wrote several plays dealing with the French Revolution. He was particularly appreciated in the Soviet Union, where his works sold millions of copies. His pacifism, to which he remained faithful throughout the 1930s and which he continually promoted through speeches and writings, found favor with the Soviets, as did his crusade against modern materialism, which the Soviets were happy to identify with capitalism. Moreover, he was long a fellow traveler of the Communists, believing in internationalism and hating social exploitation and oppression. History has since cast an ironic light on his visions of a utopian society in Russia; yet his commitment to international understanding and his concern for humane values insure his place in early twentieth-century thought. As the secretary of the Swedish Academy said when Rolland was honored with the Nobel Prize, Rolland stood out for "the lofty idealism of his literary production and . . . the sympathy and love of truth with which he has described different types of human beings."

REFERENCES:

Dushan Bresky, *Cathedral or Symphony: Essays on Jean-Christophe* (Bern, Switzerland: Lang, 1973);

Frederick John Harris, *André Gide and Romain Rolland: Two Men Divided* (New Brunswick, N.J.: Rutgers University Press, 1973);

Harold March, *Romain Rolland* (New York: Twayne, 1971);

William Thomas Starr, *Romain Rolland and a World at War* (Evanston, Ill.: Northwestern University Press, 1956);

Stefan Zweig, *Romain Rolland: The Man and His Work,* translated by Eden and Cedar Paul (New York: T. Seltzer, 1921).
— C.S.B.

JULES ROMAINS

Novelist, poet, and playwright Jules Romains (1885–1972) is now remembered chiefly for his association with **Unanimism,** a literary movement he helped found during the first decade of the twentieth century, and his twenty-seven-volume roman-fleuve (series novel), *Les Hommes de bonne volonté* (1932–1946; translated as *Men of Good Will*).

Born Louis Farigoule, Romains trained as a teacher at the **Ecole Normale Supérieure** in Paris and taught at several institutions at the outset of his career. As early as 1903 — when he had a vision of the collective soul of Paris — he had become interested in group dynamics and the psychology of the collectivity. He and his friend Georges Chennevière called this belief in collective wholes *Unanimisme.* The individual, Romains believed, was important only through unity with a group. In 1906 he became associated with the Groupe de l'Abbaye, the artists' community established that year in Créteil, near Paris. He developed his thinking on group psychology partly as a result of interaction with this group. Romains's later interest in Socialism is consistent with his Unanimist thinking. He contributed to the Socialist (later Communist) newspaper *Humanité,* and in the 1930s he was active in social and pacifist causes.

Early in his writing career Romains published poems and had a play produced by the well-known director **André Antoine.** His first Unanimist novel, *Mort de quelqu'un* (1911; translated as *The Death of a Nobody*), concerns a group of apartment-building residents who are united by the death of one of their fellow tenants. After **World War I,** which led him to see the negative side of group behavior, Romains wrote his first roman-fleuve under the collective title *Psyché* (1922–1929; translated as *The Body's Rapture*). His finest play, *Knock, ou Le Triomphe de la médecine* (1924; translated as *Doctor Knock*), about a charlatan who convinces the inhabitants of an entire town that he needs to heal them, was produced in 1923 with **Louis Jouvet** in the leading role. Romains and Stefan Zweig adapted Ben Jonson's *Volpone* in 1928.

T. S. Eliot and Jules Romains in London, 1949

Les Hommes de bonne volonté, a work nearly as ambitious as the series novels of Honoré de Balzac and Emile Zola and just as ambitious as those by **Georges Duhamel** and **Roger Martin du Gard,** was intended to give a panoramic view of French society between 1908 and 1933. Characters reappear from one volume to the next, but the focus is often on collective behavior, in accordance with Romains's Unanimist perspective. The first novel of the series, *Le 6 octobre,* covers only one day in 1908; similarly, in *Verdun* hundreds of pages are devoted to the famous 1916 battle there (see **Verdun**). This volume and its predecessor, *Prélude à Verdun,* deserve a permanent place among the best French novels about World War I. Although few novels in the series continue to be read widely, it remains one of the masterworks of twentieth-century social realism in France, and Romains's achievement in depicting crowds of civilians or soldiers should not be overlooked. After **World War II,** most of which he spent in the United States and Mexico, Romains's writing became less optimistic than his prewar works. He continued to produce novels and nonfiction until two years before his death.

REFERENCES:
Denis Boak, *Jules Romains* (New York: Twayne, 1974);
P. J. Norrish, *The Drama of the Group* (Cambridge: Cambridge University Press, 1958).

— C.S.B.

GEORGES ROUAULT

Though art critics often associate him with the **Fauves,** Georges Rouault (1871–1958) represents an art parallel to, rather than part of, that movement, which was led by **Henri Matisse.** His art is the product of a quite distinct mix of influences, including a deeply held Catholic faith and a strong pride in his working-class origins.

When Rouault met Matisse in the studio of Gustave Moreau (1892–1895), Rouault had already had a practical education as a commercial artist: from 1885 to 1890 he worked as an apprentice in a stained-glass shop. Some art historians consider that training a possible source for Rouault's use of color and his heavily outlined forms. While similar elements were appearing at that time in the art of the **Nabis** and the artists later called Fauves, those artists did not have Rouault's direct experience of medieval models. The impact of Moreau, who told students to imagine their colors rather than copy nature, was considerable on the young artist: he was to become the first curator of the Moreau museum after his teacher's death.

While his work shared with Matisse's an interest in simplified forms and strong colors, Rouault's colors are darker and moodier than Matisse's. (Rouault was a great admirer of Rembrandt van Rijn.) This distinction was apparent from the beginning of Rouault's career: *Le Chantier* (1897; *The Workplace*) shows a landscape soiled with soot from factory chimneys. In this murky scene two workers fight with sticks.

Through the early 1900s Rouault painted a series of dark, biblically inspired paintings, mixing elements from Rembrandt and Francisco Goya. From 1902 on he first augmented and later replaced such subjects with groups of canvases focusing on human misery and degradation: clowns and circuses, prostitutes, wicked and brutal judges. As Rouault wrote later, "If I have made the judges lamentable figures, it is no doubt because I was betraying the anguish that I feel at the sight of one human being having to judge another." Professing to be thoroughly apolitical, he nonetheless admitted his uneasiness with the legal proceedings he had witnessed; he refused to condemn the judges but declared that "if I have happened to confuse the head of the judge with that of the accused, this error only betrays my perplexity...." The works do not attack the legal system as such, in the manner of Honoré Daumier or **Jean-Louis Forain;** yet the inhumanity of the system is all the more appalling.

As a Catholic artist Rouault stands out in his era for his refusal to adopt the pseudomedievalism of **Maurice Denis, Paul Sérusier,** and other religious artists. His faith made him profoundly skeptical toward the modern world without leaving him nostalgic for the imagined joys of the Middle Ages. Like Daumier before him and **Pablo Picasso** afterward, Rouault was attracted to Don Quixote, the champion of lost causes. He wrote in a poem, "By all the most practical means. / Man destroys himself so well. / Chemistry and mechanics, sad idols, / Chemistry and mechanics, sinister idols. / ... will that which / Should serve to succor humanity / Serve to destroy it?" After **World War I** Rouault began work on a series of etchings designed to explore both his faith and his compassion for the suffering he had seen. The prints were completed by the mid 1920s but not published as a book until 1948, under the title *Miserere*. The series repeatedly juxtaposes the injustice of the world — one plate is titled "Homo homini lupus" (Man Is a Wolf to Man) — with

the salvation offered by Christ. A stark print of the Crucifixion is titled "Aimez-vous les uns les autres" (Love One Another). The same ideas are expressed in Rouault's oil paintings from the post-1918 period, especially in *Le Christ dans la banlieue* (1920; *Christ in the Suburbs*), in which two street children alone at night on a dark, sinister street in an industrial suburb are comforted by the appearance of Christ before them.

REFERENCES:

Jean-Paul Crespelle, *The Fauves,* translated by Anita Brookner (Greenwich, Conn.: New York Graphic Society, 1962);

Bernard Dorival, *Rouault,* translated by Gary Apgar (Naefels, Switzerland: Bonfini Press, 1983);

William A. Dyrness, *Rouault: A Vision of Suffering and Salvation* (Grand Rapids, Mich.: William E. Eerdmans, 1971).

—J.H.

JEAN ROUCH

As the central French proponent of cinéma vérité (film truth), Jean Rouch (1917–) is a powerful voice in ethnographic and documentary cinema. He earned degrees in literature and civil engineering before starting to make ethnographic films in Africa in 1947.

In the 1950s the development of improved technology, such as lightweight cameras and on-site sound-recording equipment, allowed Rouch to establish a new documentary style different from the traditionally "objective" approach Rouch himself used in such shorts as *Les Maîtres fous* (1955; *The Mad Masters*), about religious practices in colonial West Africa. Since Rouch and Edgar Morin directed *Chronique d'un été* (1961; *Chronicle of a Summer*) — a documentary about Parisians that Rouch described as *cinéma vérité* — Rouch's films have shown that the director cannot be a neutral agent in the representation of subjects, who are permitted to speak with their own voices free from narrative commentary. The director works with the material to show how the cinema affects both the viewers' and director's ideas.

In addition to directing several films since *Chronique d'un été*, Rouch has served as the director of the **Centre National de la Recherche Scientifique** and president of the Cinémathèque Française.

REFERENCES:

Roy Armes, *French Cinema Since 1946, 2: The Personal Style* (London: Zwemmer & Barnes, 1970);

Eric Barnouw, *Documentary: A History of the Non-Fiction Film* (New York: Oxford University Press, 1974);

M. Ali Issari and Doris A. Paul, *What Is Cinéma Vérité?* (Metuchen, N.J.: Scarecrow Press, 1979).

—T.C.

Henri Rousseau

RAYMOND ROULEAU

A major avant-garde theater director and actor, Raymond Rouleau (1904–) founded the Groupe Libre, a "**Surrealist**" theatrical troupe, in 1921 at the age of seventeen. From 1922 until his group disbanded in 1926, Rouleau was director of the Théâtre du Marais. In 1930 he took an acting job with **Charles Dullin**'s company at the **Théâtre de l'Atelier,** later joining **Antonin Artaud** at the Théâtre Alfred Jarry. Active in set design both in France and abroad, he is particularly known for his mise-en-scènes for **Jean-Paul Sartre**'s *Huis clos* (translated as *No Exit*) at the **Théâtre du Vieux-Colombier** in 1944, for Tennessee Williams's *A Streetcar Named Desire* in 1949 at the Théâtre Edouard VII, and for Georges Bizet's *Carmen* in 1959 at the Paris Opera.

— R.J.N.

HENRI ROUSSEAU

Henri Rousseau (1844–1910), known popularly as "Le Douanier" (the customs agent) because of his career as a toll collector, remains an almost unclassifiable figure in French art — a self-taught, naive artist whose work was nonetheless integrally related to trends and debates within the French fin de siècle art world. In a period when a self-conscious primitivism was espoused by artists from the Symbolists to the **Nabis,** he was the real thing — an artist whose work blended a surface naiveté with a deeply personal sense of style and purpose.

Rousseau followed up a lengthy term in the military, including service in Mexico (1861–1867) and in the Franco-Prussian War (1870–1871), with a job for the customs service of the municipality of Paris. He retired in 1885 and exhibited for the first time at the 1886 **Salon des Indépendants.** The exact date when he began to paint is uncertain; most estimates date his first, amateur works from about 1879–1880, though in a handwritten autobiographical sketch (1895) he insisted that it was not until 1885 that he made his "debut in Art after many disappointments and without any master but Nature...."

Rousseau described himself in 1894 as "in the process of becoming one of our best realist painters." Some of his works do, in fact, exhibit a stiff, literal attention to details of topography and foliage. *L'Octroi* (circa 1890–1900; *The Toll House*) is a meticulous reconstruction of a municipal tollgate, so careful in its linearity that it seems drawn with a T square. As is characteristic in his work, every detail, no matter how far away, is painted in crisp focus, though he does play off the hard, linear architecture against the soft, almost gauzy vegetation. These paintings coexist from the outset, however, with fantasy jungle scenes that help to indicate the path his work would take.

Rousseau's oil painting *La Guerre* (1894; *War*) suffers from his lack of training: the relationship between the bodies littering the ground and the scenery around them is awkward; the central image of war itself, personified as a woman with sword and torch riding a strangely elongated horse, is rigid and doll-like. Even so, the painting is strangely powerful. **Alfred Jarry,** who emerged as a champion of Rousseau, praised the work, as did the critic for the *Mercure de France,* L. Roy, who admitted that the painting was strange but found that very strangeness courageous and effective. He described the work as devastating, a landscape of death and desolation. "Shortly, the desolation will have become total, final. War gallops on over the scene, impassive, inexorable, like some implacable deity. . . ." He added that "only bad faith could lead one to believe that the man capable of suggesting such ideas to us is a bad artist."

The charge of "bad artist" was, in fact, the least of what was said of Rousseau. One critic stated that he "paints with his feet with his eyes closed." Another called him a "preprimitive." For some, he was the annual joke of the Salon des Indépendants — to the extent that some in the Salon were willing to break their central notion of a free, unjuried show to keep him out.

Rousseau's *La Bohémienne endormie* (1897; *The Sleeping Gypsy*) epitomizes his mature work. To Rousseau, as usual, it was a "realist" work, apparently intended in this case as homage to Jean Léon Gérôme, an academic painter whom Rousseau admired. Gérôme's *Les Deux Majestés* (*The Two Majesties*) showed a male lion seated in a desert landscape, admiring the setting sun. In Rousseau's work it is night, under a full moon, and in his words, "a wandering Negress, who plays the mandolin, with her jar next to her . . . is deeply asleep, worn out from fatigue. A lion happens to go by, sniffs at her, and does not devour her." Only the upraised tip of the animal's tail disturbs a frozen stillness; the painting has an eery, dreamlike quality in which the inexplicable is treated as ordinary.

Rousseau's final major work, completed shortly before his death from blood poisoning from a neglected cut, displays these qualities to a heightened degree. *Le Rêve* (1910; *The Dream*) is at once the most complex and the most enigmatic of his jungle paintings. Under a full moon, a nude woman reclines on a couch in the midst of a verdant jungle; at center two lionesses fan out, accompanied by a woman playing a flute. There is no explanation other than the title; as with *La Bohémienne endormie,* there is a clear tension between the crystal clarity with which the scene is depicted and the lack of any key by which it can be interpreted.

Rousseau's strongest impact on French art came after the 1905 **Salon d'Automne,** at which one of his paintings was exhibited with works by the **Fauves.** He shared the ridicule with which the work of **Henri**

Matisse and his colleagues was greeted by many but also the support they received from influential critics and artists. Beginning in 1907, he held repeated *soirées familiales et artistiques* — evening gatherings attended by friends, family, and a cross section of the French avant-garde, including **Guillaume Apollinaire, Georges Braque, Marie Laurencin,** and **Pablo Picasso.** In 1908 Picasso staged a huge "Rousseau Banquet" in Rousseau's honor. Picasso's art shows no evidence of Rousseau's influence; by the 1920s, however, the **Surrealists** included Rousseau in their pantheon of precursors. The art of **René Magritte** in particular demonstrates a clear debt to the older artist.

REFERENCES:

Yann Le Pichon, *The World of Henri Rousseau* (New York: Viking, 1982);

Roger Shattuck, *The Banquet Years: The Origins of the Avant-Garde in France, 1885 to World War I* (New York: Harcourt, Brace, 1958; revised, New York: Vintage, 1968);

Dora Vallier, *Rousseau* (New York: Crown, 1979).

—J.H.

ALBERT ROUSSEL

Albert Roussel (1869–1937) was not a prolific composer, and his music never enjoyed wide popularity, but he played an important role in twentieth-century French music. Although a contemporary of **Claude Debussy** and **Maurice Ravel,** he did not for the most part adopt the Impressionist style. Instead, while using contemporary musical techniques such as unusual harmonization, he composed in a more traditional style based on classical clarity of form and texture.

Roussel decided to devote his life to music only after serving as an officer in the French navy for seven years, during which he made several trips to the Far East. The music he heard there and on a later trip to India influenced his opera-ballet *Padmâvatî* (1923) and other works. After resigning from the navy in 1894, he enrolled at the Schola Cantorum, where he studied with the conservative composer **Vincent d'Indy** from 1898 to 1908 and where he taught counterpoint from 1909 to 1914. After serving in the army during **World War I,** Roussel devoted himself to composition.

His early compositions, such as the ballet *Le Festin de l'araignée* (1913; The Spider's Banquet), show traces of Debussy's style, but with Roussel's Second Symphony (1921) all signs of Impressionism disappear. In his later compositions — including his Third Symphony (1930) and Fourth Symphony (1934), written at a time when the symphonic form was widely considered out-of-date, and a neoclassical Suite in F (1926) — he achieved a highly individual style that was characteristically French in its fine balance between sentiment and intellect. The ballet *Bacchus et Ariane* (1931; Bacchus and Ariadne) is his best-known piece.

REFERENCE:

Rollo Myers, *Modern French Music: From Fauré to Boulez* (New York: Praeger, 1971), pp. 41–51.

— P.S.H.

CLAUDE ROY

Claude Roy (1915–) is one of the major Communist literary journalists and critics of contemporary France. Although he originally wrote for such right-wing newspapers as *Je Suis Partout* and the *Action Française,* at the end of the **Occupation** he joined the **French Communist Party.** He later distanced himself from the party, rejoined it, and finally was excluded from it; yet most of his critical writings reflect assumptions typical of Communist intellectuals of the mid twentieth century.

Roy's principal series of critical writings is *Descriptions critiques* (1949–1974; Critical Descriptions). His other works include his autobiography, *Somme toute* (1976; All in All); his novel *L'Ami lointain* (1987; translated as *Distant Friend*); and his journal, published as *La Fleur du temps* (1988; The Flower of Time).

REFERENCES:

David Coward, "Not Forgetting or Forgiving," *Times Literary Supplement,* 7–13 October 1988, pp. 209–210;

Coward, "Surrender to the Spoiling," *Times Literary Supplement,* 27 November–3 December 1987, p. 1333.

— C.S.B.

JULES ROY

Novelist, essayist, and playwright Jules Roy (1907–) is one of the most important writers of what is often called the Ecole d'Alger (Algiers School) — North African French writers of European extraction. He is also the outstanding French military writer of the twentieth century. During his long career his political positions — particularly on the **Indochinese War** and the **Algerian war** — earned him considerable notoriety, while the qualities of his writing have often been overlooked. He won the Grand Prix de l'Académie Française in 1958 and the Grand Prix National des Lettres in 1969.

Born of French parentage in Algeria, Roy entered the army after seminary studies and was a career officer from 1927 to 1953 — for much of that time in the air force. When France fell to Germany in the **Debacle** of 1940 he flew to Algeria with most of the other pilots. In 1942 he abandoned his loyalty to the **Vichy government** of Marshal **Philippe Pétain,** joined **Charles de Gaulle**'s Free French, and went to England. With the French branch of the Royal Air Force he flew thirty-seven missions over occupied territory. After **World War II** he was assigned to a desk job in Paris, but in 1953 he asked to be sent to Indochina. Upon returning from his assignment there he resigned his commission to mark his disagreement with French military policy.

Roy's earliest writings deal with flying (he is second only to **Antoine de Saint-Exupéry** as a writer on aviation) and with the early months of World War II, in which he lost several friends. After the war he published fiction based on his experiences, including *La Vallée heureuse* (1946; translated as *The Happy Valley*) and *Le Navigateur* (1954; translated as *The Navigator*). He also wrote three books about the problem in Indochina. These books created a following for him but attracted the wrath of many military authorities.

After the death of his close friend **Albert Camus** in 1960, Roy traveled to Algeria to observe the insurrection there. The result was *La Guerre d'Algérie* (1960; translated as *War in Algeria*), which barely escaped government censure and sold more than a hundred thousand copies in a few weeks, as well as many copies in translation. Roy was among the first writers to use the forbidden term *war* to describe the conflict; journalists and government spokesmen used *les événements* (the events). He was one of a handful of moderates who criticized government policy in Algeria and called for an accommodation with the rebels. As a former officer and the son of Algerian colonists, his positions seemed particularly scandalous to some in France.

The series of historical novels to which Roy gave the collective title *Les Chevaux du soleil* (1968–1975; The Horses of the Sun) deals with Algerian history and his own family, which settled there in the nineteenth century. The six novels cover the French conquest of 1830, the period of colonization, the scandalous story of his mother and father (Roy was the illegitimate son of a schoolteacher and a married woman), parts of his own early career, and, finally, what he considered the tragic failure of the French presence in Algeria and the war, which led to independence for Algeria in July 1962. In these novels Roy demonstrated great creative powers and an impressive range of stylistic mastery.

Roy has since published other novels and nonfiction and is widely honored in Algerian literary circles as a writer who has dared to speak against injustice. Other topics he has treated in his nonfiction include the battle of Dien Bien Phu, the basilica of Vézelay, and Lebanon. In the 1970s he returned to the subject of World War II, reexamining his experiences in autobiographical novels such as *Le Désert de Retz* (1978; The Retz Desert).

REFERENCE:

Catharine Savage Brosman, *Art as Testimony: The Work of Jules Roy* (Gainesville: University of Florida Press, 1989).

— C.S.B.

IDA RUBINSTEIN

Russian actress and dancer Ida Rubinstein (1885–1960) gave her most notable performances in Paris with the **Ballets Russes** of **Serge Diaghilev** and with the independent theatrical company she formed in France. A woman of extraordinary beauty, stage presence, and mystery — with a yearning for fame — she was extremely successful when the productions surrounding her were spectacular and required minimal movement and speech.

Rubinstein made her Western stage debut with the newly formed Ballets Russes. Diaghilev, encouraged by Rubinstein's devoted friends Léon Bakst and **Michel Fokine,** hired her after seeing her performances in *Antigone* and *Salomé* in Saint Petersburg. For the Ballets Russes she captivated audiences in the title role of *Cléopâtre* (1909) and as Zobéide in *Schéhérazade* (1910). Both roles required little dancing and mostly posing. Because Rubinstein was not a classically trained dancer, her participation in the Ballets Russes was limited and proved frustrating. As a result, she left the company to present her own productions. Because of her great wealth, she was able to hire away many of Diaghilev's artists, creating a rivalry with the great impresario.

Although she was a competent producer, she often misemployed great artists in order to highlight herself, as she did in the play *Le Martyre de Saint-Sébastien* (1911; The Martyrdom of Saint Sebastian) at the **Théâtre du Châtelet.** Written for Rubinstein by the Italian poet Gabriele d'Annunzio, the play had choreography by Fokine, sets and costumes by Bakst, and music by **Claude Debussy.** The audience walked out of the self-indulgent production, which lasted five hours; it had already been censored by the Catholic church because a woman dancer was to play a saint.

In 1928 Rubinstein formed a ballet company, Ballets Ida Rubinstein, hiring **Bronislava Nijinska** as ballet mistress and choreographer, **Léonide Massine** as choreographer, and Aleksandre Benois as artistic director. The company was marginally successful. Rubinstein retired from the stage in 1939 and spent the last years of her life in southern France out of the public eye. Eventually she and her works were largely forgotten; but many of the artists she hired achieved the stardom she desired for herself.

REFERENCES:

Michael de Cossart, "Ida Rubinstein and Diaghilev: A One-Sided Rivalry," *Dance Research: The Journal of the Society for Dance Research,* 1 (Autumn 1983): 3–31;

Charles S. Mayer, "Ida Rubinstein: A Twentieth Century Cleopatra," *Dance Research Journal,* 20 (Winter 1989): 33–51.

— A.P.E.

S

LE SACRE DU PRINTEMPS

Le Sacre du printemps (*The Rite of Spring*) was the first truly modern ballet. At its premiere on 29 May 1913 riots broke out in the Théâtre des Champs-Elysées in Paris. The music by **Igor Stravinsky** was harsh, loud, and full of uneven rhythms and harmonic tension, shocking and outraging the audience, as did **Vaslav Nijinsky**'s choreography and the libretto by Nicholas Roerich and Stravinsky. The audience at this **Ballets Russes** production was so unruly that the dancers could not hear the orchestra, and police were called to the theater.

The subject of *Le Sacre du printemps* is a primitive pagan ritual in pre-Christian Russia. The Chosen Maiden dances herself to death as a gift to the sun god, ensuring the arrival of spring. The dancers, costumed in hand-painted, shapeless smocks designed by Roerich, danced with feet turned in, arms and legs rigidly bent, and heads cocked to the side. Their movements consisted primarily of stamping, jumping, running, and trembling in complex syncopated rhythms. This version of the ballet was performed only nine times. The Ballets Russes successfully revived it in 1920 with new choreography by **Léonide Massine,** casting Lydia Sokolova as the Chosen Maiden. The original choreography was lost until 1987, when it was reconstructed by dance historian Millicent Hodson and Roerich scholar Kenneth Archer for the Joffrey Ballet. The music, which came to be judged a masterpiece, has continued to intrigue choreographers. New versions of the ballet were choreographed by **Maurice Béjart** in 1959, Kenneth MacMillan in 1962, and Glen Tetley in 1974.

REFERENCES:

Millicent Hodson, "Ritual Design in the New Dance: Nijinsky's *Le Sacre du printemps,*" *Dance Research: Journal of the Society for Dance Research,* 3 (Autumn 1985): 35–45;

Bronislava Nijinska, *Early Memoirs,* translated and edited by Irina Nijinska and Jean Rawlinson (Durham, N.C. & London: Duke University Press, 1992), pp. 448–471.

—A.P.E.

FRANÇOISE SAGAN

Françoise Sagan (1935–), a talented stylist and keen observer of human character and mores, has been one of the best-selling novelists in France since she exploded onto the literary scene at age nineteen with her first book, *Bonjour tristesse* (1954; translated).

Born Françoise Quoirez, Sagan became an international celebrity with *Bonjour tristesse,* which sold half a million copies in its first year and was translated into several languages. A short novel of manners in her characteristically spare style, it scandalized readers with its disabused attitude toward morality and surprised them with its maturity. The novel is about a young woman who is involved in her first love affair and who deliberately destroys the relationship between her widowed father and his new fiancée. With this work Sagan demonstrated her mastery of language as a tool to probe and lay bare the psyche.

Sagan followed *Bonjour tristesse* with three novels in quick succession: *Un Certain Sourire* (1956; translated as *A Certain Smile*), about an affair between a twenty-year-old woman and an older married man; *Dans un mois, dans un an* (1957; translated as *Those Without Shadows*), set in upper-class circles; and *Aimez-vous Brahms?* (1959; translated), about an affair between a young man and an older woman. These novels all deal in some way with solitude and disillusionment. Sagan's restrained, yet sensitive, style employs classical devices favored by masters of literary

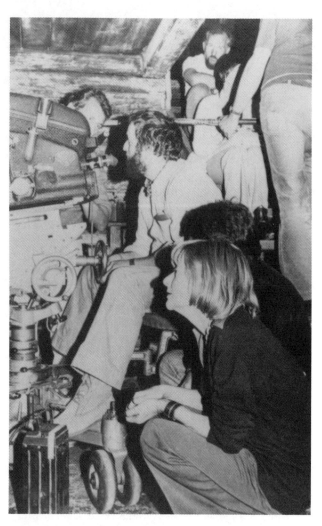

Françoise Sagan on the set of *The Blue Ferns*, the first film she directed, 1975 (Sygma)

psychology from Jean Racine and Madame de Lafayette through **André Gide.**

Sagan also had a noteworthy success in the theater with her first play, *Château en Suède* (1960; Castle in Sweden), a bitter comedy about exclusion and cruelty. She has since written other plays and novels, a screenplay, nonfiction books, and memoirs. *Réponses: 1954–1974* (1974; translated as *Réponses: The Autobiography of Françoise Sagan*) is a collection of excerpts from interviews. In 1985 she was awarded the Prix de Monaco for her work.

Sagan's fiction is generally not experimental, but her novel *Des Bleus à l'âme* (1972; translated as *Scars on the Soul*) is a hybrid of psychological narrative in her usual manner and self-conscious considerations on writing fiction. During the 1950s especially, her novels appealed to readers who were tired of the **existential-**

ist angst of **Jean-Paul Sartre** and other novelists of his generation, but her exposure of human conduct in an accessible, nonexperimental, but cultivated, style is chiefly responsible for her popularity.

REFERENCE:

Judith Graves Miller, *Françoise Sagan* (Boston: Twayne, 1988).

— C.S.B.

ANTOINE DE SAINT-EXUPÉRY

Writer and aviator Antoine de Saint-Exupéry (1900–1944) is widely known in English-speaking countries, where almost all of his writings have appeared in translation and where he is appreciated by children who have read his charming fable *Le Petit Prince* (1943; translated as *The Little Prince*). In France he is greatly admired as a classical stylist and as a pioneer of aviation literature — indeed, as the greatest practitioner of that genre.

Saint-Exupéry was a civilian aviator in the 1920s and 1930s and a military pilot during **World War II;** his experiences, including some spectacular crashes he survived, provided most of the material for his fiction and nonfiction, which is noteworthy for its richness of description and the author's reflections on moral concerns. Saint-Exupéry flew postal routes along the west coast of Africa during the 1920s and then helped to open the mail lines in the southern part of South America. His dangerous reconnaissance missions over northern France during the **Debacle** of 1940 form the basis for his autobiographical *Pilote de guerre* (1942; translated as *Flight to Arras*). In 1944, flying from Sardinia, he disappeared during a mission over Europe; the circumstances of his death remain unclear.

Other books by Saint-Exupéry include the short novels *Courrier sud* (1929; translated as *Southern Mail*) and *Vol de nuit* (1931; translated as *Night Flight*) and the nonfiction collection *Terre des hommes* (1939; translated as *Wind, Sand and Stars*) — all based on his flying experiences. There are also several posthumous publications. His popular books, *Le Petit Prince* included, constitute a thoughtful meditation on the nature of human life and the importance of values.

REFERENCES:

Curtis Cate, *Antoine de Saint-Exupéry* (New York: Putnam, 1970);

Brian Masters, *A Student's Guide to Saint-Exupéry* (London: Heinemann, 1972);

Joy D. Marie Robinson, *Antoine de Saint-Exupéry* (Boston: Twayne, 1984);

Maxwell Smith, *Knight of the Air* (New York: Pageant, 1956).

— C.S.B.

SAINT-GERMAIN-DES-PRÉS

The name Saint-Germain-des-Prés is given to the Paris neighborhood around the church of the same name, on boulevard Saint-Germain on the **Left Bank** (south side) of the Seine. It is the location of the **Café de Flore** and the **Deux Magots,** two famous cafés that served as headquarters for writers and other intellectuals. The neighborhood is close to many publishing houses, bookstores, and antique shops; it is within easy walking distance of the **Latin Quarter.**

After **World War II** the many small nightspots in Saint-Germain-des-Prés became popular with music lovers, who came to hear performers such as singer **Juliette Gréco** and jazz trumpeter-singer **Boris Vian.**

REFERENCE:

Herbert R. Lottman, *The Left Bank: Writers, Artists, and Politics from the Popular Front to the Cold War* (Boston: Houghton Mifflin, 1982).

— C.S.B.

SAINT-JOHN PERSE

Alexis Saint-Léger Léger (1887–1975), who wrote under the pen name Saint-John Perse, was a diplomat by profession, as well as one of the most admired, and most difficult, French poets of the twentieth century. In 1960 he was awarded the Nobel Prize for Literature. His long narrative poem *Anabase* (1924; translated as *Anabasis*) has been translated by such eminent writers as Hugo von Hoffmannsthal, Giuseppe Ungaretti, and T. S. Eliot.

Few French writers appear less Cartesian than Saint-John Perse. He eschewed standard French versification, preferring free verse — particularly the ample *verset,* a highly variable verse often several lines long — somewhat like that used by Arthur Rimbaud in his prose poems and by **Paul Claudel.** He employed few transitions and other logical devices, giving the privileged place to images or visions as opposed to rational thought processes. His metaphors are often lightninglike and explosive; they are almost always hermetic. He used a rich vocabulary, with many unusual place-names, botanical expressions, and recondite words.

The luxurious tropical setting of Guadeloupe, in the French West Indies — where Saint-John Perse was born and spent his childhood, as well as part of his adolescence — is apparent in his early work. His travels, especially his sojourns in China, where *Anabase* was composed, are visible in that poem, which dates from his middle period, called the "diplomatic" period. Several works of his third and final period reflect the many years he spent in the United States. The series "Images à Crusoé" (Crusoe's Images), published with other early work in *Eloges* (1911; translated as *Praises*), reveals — in the voice of an unhappy Robinson Crusoe back in London — the poet's nostalgia for the lost paradise. *Anabase,* which narrates in hermetic language a conquest in some vaguely oriental setting, has as its principal theme man's urge to push onward, seeking the new.

After the **Debacle,** or fall of France to Germany, in 1940, Léger settled in Washington, D.C., and worked for a time at the Library of Congress. Starting in 1942, he published one major poem after another, some of which were brought out in English by the Bollingen Foundation: these works include *Exil* (1942; translated), *Amers* (1957; translated as *Sea-marks*), and *Chronique* (1960; translated).

REFERENCES:

René Galand, *Saint-John Perse* (New York: Twayne, 1972);

Arthur Knodel, *Saint-John Perse: A Study of His Poetry* (Edinburgh: Edinburgh University Press, 1966);

Renato Poggioli, "The Poetry of Saint-John Perse," in his *The Spirit and the Letter* (Cambridge, Mass.: Harvard University Press, 1965), pp. 222–253;

Bernard Weinberg, "Saint-John Perse. *Anabase,*" in his *The Limits of Symbolism* (Chicago: University of Chicago Press, 1966), pp. 365–419.

— C.S.B.

MICHEL DE SAINT PIERRE

Michel de Saint Pierre (1916–1987) was one of the most popular Catholic novelists to appear in France after 1945.

Saint Pierre published his first novel, *Ce Monde ancien* (This Old World), in 1948. His first commercial success was *Les Aristocrates* (1956; translated as *The Aristocrats*), about an aristocratic family trying to adapt its centuries-old traditions to the new economic and social conditions of postwar France. He went on to write other popular novels in the Catholic tradition, including *Les Murmures de Satan* (1959; The Whisperings of Satan), a portrait of lay Catholics attempting to live a communal life, and *Les Nouveaux Aristocrates* (1960; translated as *The New Aristocrats*), about the transmission of religious values within a Jesuit secondary school.

Saint Pierre's best-known and most important novel is *Les Nouveaux Prêtres* (1964; translated as *The New Priests*), which deals with the cultural clash then occurring between traditional French priests and those emerging in the wake of the Second Vatican Council (1962–1965). During this period he engaged in a heated

CAMILLE SAINT-SAËNS

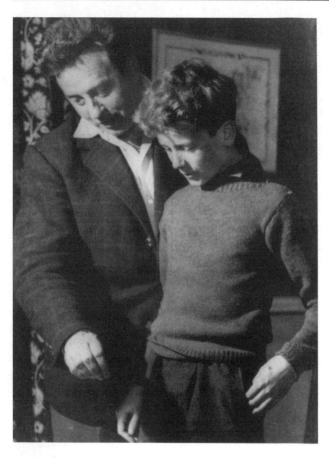

Michel de Saint-Pierre with his son Guillaume (Jean Mainburg)

public debate with another popular Catholic novelist, **Gilbert Cesbron,** who defended the new priests. *La Passion de l'abbé Delance* (1982; The Ordeal of Father Delance) is about the hero of *Les Nouveaux Prêtres,* who continues to fight the influence of Communism and materialism within the church.

Saint Pierre used fiction to tackle a variety of social issues as French life was rapidly modernized under the **Fifth Republic.** He examined the growing power of large corporations in *Le Milliardaire* (1970; The Billionaire), the place of lawyers in French society in *L'Accusée* (1972; The Accused), and the medical profession in *Docteur Erikson* (1982). He also published biographies and collections of essays.

REFERENCES:

David O'Connell, *Michel de Saint Pierre: A Catholic Novelist at the Crossroads* (Birmingham, Ala.: Summa, 1990);

O'Connell, "Michel de Saint Pierre and the Defense of Traditional Values," *Renascence,* 36 (Autumn–Winter 1983–1984): 88–106.

— D.O'C.

For nearly eighty years composer, pianist, and organist Camille Saint-Saëns (1835–1921) was an active force in French music. Except in his symphonic poems, where he was influenced by Franz Liszt, he remained true to classical harmonies and forms. In composing his twentieth-century works he was unaffected by the innovations of younger composers such as **Claude Debussy** and **Maurice Ravel.** In 1908, with his score for *L'Assassinat du duc de Guise* (*Assassination of the Duc de Guise*), Saint-Saëns became the first composer to write music specifically for a motion picture.

A child prodigy, Saint-Saëns gave concerts and wrote music before he was ten. He entered the Paris Conservatory in 1848 to study composition and organ. In 1852 he met Liszt, who later called him the greatest living organist. In 1853, at age seventeen, Saint-Saëns was appointed organist at the church of Saint Merry in Paris, and in 1857 he became the organist at La Madeleine, one of the most prestigious churches in the city. He held the post until 1875. As a pianist he was noted for his grace and speed in his performances of works by Wolfgang Amadeus Mozart and Ludwig van Beethoven as well as his own concertos, the first of which he completed in 1858.

Of his nearly two hundred published compositions, several are well known. His opera *Samson et Dalila* (1877) is still performed throughout the world. The symphonic poem *Danse macabre* (1874) and *Le Carnaval des animaux* (1886; *Carnival of the Animals*), for two pianos and orchestra, are perennial favorites at symphony concerts. (With the exception of "Le Cygne" [The Swan], one of the fourteen movements devoted to separate animals, including "Pianists," Saint-Saëns did not allow the lighthearted *Carnaval des animaux* to be performed publicly during his lifetime.) Among his more formal compositions are his five piano concertos (1858–1896), of which the second (1868) is most frequently played; his three concertos for violin and two for cello; and his Third Symphony (1886) in C minor with organ. He also wrote chamber music.

In the last decades of his life Saint-Saëns spent much time abroad, and in England he was considered the most important French composer of his day. At home he came to be viewed as a cantankerous, old-fashioned character. At age sixty-five he composed and conducted a cantata for the opening of the 1900 Paris Exposition; at eighty he was in San Francisco conducting another new cantata for the opening of the Panama-Pacific Exposition. Five years later, a year before his death, he played one of his concertos in Athens at a festival in his honor.

Armand Salacrou with producer Charles Dullin

REFERENCE:

James Harding, *Saint-Saëns and His Circle* (London: Chapman & Hall, 1965).

— P.S.H.

ARMAND SALACROU

The playwright Armand Salacrou (1899–1989) was prolific and versatile. His early dramas were produced mostly by **Aurélien Lugné-Poe; Charles Dullin** produced many of his later plays. He was also fortunate to collaborate with artists **André Masson** and **Raoul Dufy,** who designed stage sets for his plays.

Salacrou's early plays were chaotic and dreamlike, showing parallels with **Surrealism.** As his style evolved, it became more realistic and critical, even bitter, without wholly abandoning nonrealistic elements such as allegory and irrational time. He was often concerned with oppression and injustice.

Of modest antecedents, Salacrou was the son of a Radical Socialist politician who became powerful. Having an unhappy childhood and developing an awareness of social injustices as a young man, he was briefly a member of the **French Communist Party** in the early 1920s. In later years, even after success in the theater and in business, Salacrou continued to criticize bourgeois values.

In *Le Pont de l'Europe* (1929; The Bridge of Europe), first staged in 1927, a Frenchman who rules a distant land tries to find something more authentic in himself. The self is always unattainable; life offers only limitations instead of possibilities of a rich existence. *L'Inconnue d'Arras* (1936; translated as *The Unknown Woman of Arras*) is a tragedy of infidelity, in the form of a flashback. *La Terre est ronde* (1938; translated as *The World Is Round*) deals with Italian priest Girolamo Savonarola (1452–1498) and his Florentine dictatorship, clearly a representation of modern dictatorships. In *Un Homme comme les autres* (1937; A Man Like Others) and *Histoire de rire* (1940; translated as *No Laughing Matter*), Salacrou took up the old topic of the love triangle, with serious implications. *Les Nuits de la colère* (1946; translated as *Men of Darkness*) is concerned with the German **Occupation** of France during **World War II** and the questions of betrayal and moral responsibility in the face of the enemy. Salacrou considered *Boulevard Durand* (1960; translated), which deals with an unjust incident he had learned about as a boy, his finest dramatic achievement. The play displays the influence of some of Bertolt Brecht's dramatic theories, others of which Salacrou had earlier anticipated by breaking the dramatic illusion and having characters address the audience about the play. Because it seemed to present parallels with the **Algerian war,** the play was banned by **André Malraux,** then minister of culture.

There is also a metaphysical dimension to Salacrou's theater, an anguish that comes from the realization of human insignificance, as well as a pervasive determinism — elements that make his drama pessimistic. *Dieu le savait* (1951; God Knew So) illustrates both his interest in philosophical questions and his existential anguish.

REFERENCE:

Juris Silenieks, *Themes and Dramatic Forms in the Plays of Armand Salacrou* (Lincoln: University of Nebraska Press, 1967).

— C.S.B.

SALON D'AUTOMNE

By 1889 the term *salon* had come to apply to no fewer than three rival annual art exhibitions: the Salon des

Artistes Français, heir to the former state-sanctioned Salon (disestablished in 1880); the breakaway Salon de la Nationale, the product of an 1889 schism from the parent body; and the democratic **Salon des Indépendants,** created in 1884 as an exhibition space free of complicated rules, juries, and medals. The Salon d'Automne added one more rival to the mix: it was established in 1903 as a showplace for artists disenchanted with the two traditional, conservative salons but wary of the "radical" Independents' salon. Unlike the Salon des Indépendants, the Salon d'Automne had a jury, but it was selected by lot to prevent domination by cliques. The new salon was initiated by Yvanhoé Ramsbosson, a curator at the Petit Palais in Paris. Architect, art critic, and onetime anarchist sympathizer Francis Jourdain was selected to head the new body, whose members included Auguste Renoir, **Georges Rouault, Edouard Vuillard, Félix Vallotton,** and Symbolist poet Gustave Kahn.

As its name indicates, the Salon d'Automne was to be held every autumn (unlike its three rivals, which were held in the spring). After coping with limited space at the Petit Palais, the first Salon d'Automne was transferred to the Grand Palais, over the objections of the Salon de la Nationale, which regarded the space as its own. Beginning in 1905, the fall show was held regularly at that site.

The fame of the Salon d'Automne rests largely on the controversies surrounding the **Fauve** works exhibited at the 1905 show. The Salon d'Automne was never intended as an exclusively avant-garde exhibition; on the contrary it was seen as a bridge or meeting place, where diverse and contending trends could be observed, where works by established artists of the past could be viewed along with the most experimental contemporary work. An essay by **Elie Faure** in the catalogue for the 1905 salon points out the significance of exhibiting work by Jean-Auguste-Dominique Ingres and Edouard Manet in a show of modern work: "The Salon d'Automne has undertaken to demonstrate, by its retrospective exhibitions, the permanent right of revolutionary endeavor to rejoin tradition. . . . Ingres and Manet make us aware that the revolutionary of today is the classic of tomorrow." The effort to depict the salon as a solid middle ground between reaction and excess is apparent in a friendly review of the 1905 show by a critic for the *Times* of London, which serves as well to summarize the role of the Salon d'Automne thereafter: "The Salon d'Automne is made up . . . of revolutionary painters, but not of anarchists. There is no sensationalism here, but a quiet harmony of effort. . . ." (It should be noted that this critic neglected to mention the Fauves.)

REFERENCES:

Jean-Paul Crespelle, *The Fauves,* translated by Anita Brookner (Greenwich, Conn.: New York Graphic Society, 1962);

Bernard Denvir, *Post-Impressionism* (London: Thames & Hudson, 1992);

Ian Dunlop, "The Salon d'Automne," in his *The Shock of the New: Seven Historic Exhibitions of Modern Art* (New York: American Heritage Press, 1972), pp. 88–119.

—J.H.

SALON DES INDÉPENDANTS

Throughout most of the nineteenth century, the official, state-sponsored annual Salon remained the centerpiece of French artistic life. Each year the works exhibited numbered from three thousand to six thousand. (This number may seem large, but by the mid nineteenth century professional artists in France were producing perhaps two hundred thousand canvases per decade.) Protests against the number of works rejected (often avant-garde) resulted in two Salons des refusés — exhibitions of works turned away by juries — once in 1863 and again in 1874, but pressure continued for a democratically elected jury and a more inclusive policy. In 1880 the state officially disestablished the Salon, which from that point on was to be run by a semiprivate Société des Artistes français (Society of French Artists). (Final and total separation of the government and the official Salon did not come until 1912.) Jury selection was opened up somewhat, and the atmosphere slightly liberalized. The newly elected jurors, for example, overruled the remnants of the old guard in 1880 to award a gold medal to Edouard Manet. Nonetheless, the climate remained restrictive, and many artists objected on principle to the hierarchical organization, the very idea of a jury, and the awarding of medals.

In 1884 that opposition led to the institution of the first Salon des Indépendants. Two rival groups — the Groupe des Artistes Indépendants, led by Victor Sardey, and the Société des Artistes Indépendants (SAI), led by Albert Dubois-Pillet — fought for the right to organize the independent exhibitions. Sardey's group held the first Independents' salon in May 1884 but dissolved into warring factions. Dubois-Pillet's society stepped in to fill the gap, launching their efforts with a mass rally chaired by **Odilon Redon.** Over the following three years, Dubois-Pillet's SAI gradually won the upper hand and became the organizing force for the annual alternative salon.

The Salon des Indépendants modeled itself in key respects on the abortive Fédération des Artistes set up during the Paris Commune, under Gustave Courbet, in 1871: the Salon des Indépendants agreed to exhibit a set number of works by each affiliated artist. One objection to the official Salon was the way in which works were arranged: paintings were displayed ceiling to floor, with only favored artists hung "on the line" (at eye level). A democratically elected hanging committee took on those responsibilities for the Salon des Indépendants.

The rise of private dealers in the 1870s and 1880s had undermined the role of the salon as simultaneous exhibition place and art market. The Salon des Indépendants nevertheless retained an important role as a public showplace for new art; in the late nineteenth and twentieth centuries its openness to new artists and new ideas made it a central arena for avant-garde movements, from the Neo-Impressionists, who dominated the Salon in the 1890s, to the **Nabis, Fauves, Cubists,** and such Cubist offspring as the Purists and Orphists. It was the Salon des Indépendants, for example, that stepped in to organize a posthumous show for Vincent van Gogh in 1891, when the Impressionists' dealer Paul Durand-Ruel declined to do so.

REFERENCES:

Pierre Angrand, *Naissance des Artistes Indépendants* (Paris: Debresse, 1865);

Gustave Coquiot, *Les Indépendants, 1884–1920* (Paris: Ollendorff, 1920);

Jean Sutter, "The Société des Artistes Indépendants," in *The Neo-Impressionists,* edited by Sutter, translated by Chantal Deliss (Greenwich, Conn.: New York Graphic Society, 1970), pp. 213–215;

Harrison White and Cynthia White, *Canvases and Careers: Institutional Change in the French Painting World* (Chicago: University of Chicago Press, 1993).

—J.H.

NATHALIE SARRAUTE

The oldest of the writers associated with the **Nouveau Roman** (New Novel), Nathalie Sarraute (1900–) is one of the mid-twentieth-century pioneers of experimental fiction. Her first book, *Tropismes* (translated as *Tropisms*), attracted little attention when it appeared in 1939, but the expanded version, published by the **Editions de Minuit** in 1957, found an enthusiastic public prepared to appreciate her technical innovations. This preparation was owing to the work of novelists such as **Michel Butor** and **Alain Robbe-Grillet,** as well as Sarraute herself, who in the meantime had published other books — notably a novel, *Portrait d'un inconnu* (1948; translated as *Portrait of a Man Unknown*), with a laudatory preface by **Jean-Paul Sartre,** and her major

Actress Madeleine Renaud with Nathalie Sarraute (Bernand)

essay on principles and form of fiction, *L'Ere du soupçon* (1956; translated as *The Age of Suspicion*).

Sarraute was born in Russia and spent her early childhood there and in France and Switzerland. At age eight she settled in Paris with her father and stepmother. She took a degree in English (1920), studied law, and passed the bar in 1925, the same year she married a fellow law student. Her childhood uprootings and trilingual experience may have contributed to her sensitivity to the most delicate nuances of language and to the shades of feeling that words struggle to express.

Certainly her major concern is the individual's subliminal experience and the difficulties of communication and social adaptation that arise from the disparity between inner experience, on the one hand, and social structures and relationships, on the other. The latter are supposed to facilitate and reflect genuine social intercourse; but in Sarraute's world they barely cover over a seething inner life of discontent and maladjustment that the subjects themselves do not understand and that makes them fit badly into their society. The discontent springs in part from the sort of personal warfare that characterizes human relationships for Sartre and whose presence in Sarraute's work sheds light on his appreciative comments; conflict, not community, is the fundamental bond among human beings.

The results manifest themselves as obsessions, compulsions, paranoia, and manias of various sorts coexisting with the "sub-conversations" the characters carry on with themselves and others, which both conceal and reveal their truths. These manias often are fixed on objects — a tea cozy, a sofa — or social protocols. Sarraute gave the name *tropisms* to the mechanical movements by which compulsive personalities turn to or away from these objects or ceremonies — as well as from other human beings, whom they alternately dread and cultivate — in an effort to flee or impose themselves.

In addition to material objects, language plays an important role in Sarraute's world; as for Gustave Flaubert and **Marcel Proust,** language, even in its most ordinary form, marked by clichés of thought and expression, is a key to both social relationships and one's inner world. In contrast to most earlier novelists, however, particularly Honoré de Balzac, whom she discusses in *L'Ere du soupçon,* Sarraute eschews full-length portraits and the idea of fixed characters. Her personages are bundles of reactions rather than fully rounded, named people whose destinies the reader follows throughout the book and who move in a fleshed-out social world.

Sarraute's most popular novel, *Le Planétarium* (1959; translated as *The Planetarium*), deals both with a young couple hoping to take over an aunt's apartment and with the literary world, represented by an established novelist and an aspiring one. Among her other works are *Les Fruits d'or* (1963; translated as *The Golden Fruits*); *Entre la vie et la mort* (1968; translated as *Between Life and Death*), whose central consciousness is a writer; and *Vous les entendez?* (1972; translated as *Do You Hear Them?*). Some of her plays are collected in *Théâtre* (1978; translated as *Collected Plays of Nathalie Sarraute*). Her memoir, *Enfance;* (translated as *Childhood*), appeared in 1983.

REFERENCES:

Sarah Barbour, *Nathalie Sarraute and the Feminist Reader: Identities in Process* (Lewisburg, Pa.: Bucknell University Press, 1993);

Valerie Minogue, *Nathalie Sarraute and the War of the Words* (Edinburgh: University Press, 1981);

Helen Watson-Williams, *The Novels of Nathalie Sarraute: Towards an Aesthetic* (Amsterdam: Rodopi, 1981).

— C.S.B.

ALBERTINE SARRAZIN

Novelist and memoirist Albertine Sarrazin (1937–1967) has attracted readers on both sides of the Atlan-

tic for the rebelliousness she expressed in her life and her work and for the original treatment she gave to the experience of imprisonment.

Born in Algiers, the illegitimate child of a fifteen-year-old mother, Sarrazin led a troubled life. Adopted by a French couple when she was eighteen months old, Sarrazin was raped by an uncle when she was ten and sent to reform school by her parents in 1952. The next year she escaped and was arrested for armed robbery in December, serving half her seven-year sentence before escaping again in 1957. She was rearrested in September 1958 and sent back to prison until August 1964. Her writing career was cut short when she died during a kidney operation in 1967.

In her first autobiographical novel, *La Cavale* (1965; translated as *The Runaway*), Sarrazin used prison experiences to criticize social conventions, employing a strikingly individual first-person narrative voice. The nonfiction books *Journal de prison 1959* (1972; Prison Diary 1959) and *Le Passe-peine, 1949–1967* (1976; Doing Time, 1949–1967) also draw on her incarceration. Her second novel, *L'Astragale* (1965; translated as *Astragal*), depicts her protagonist's escape and life on the outside.

These works, and the punishments they reflect, are the product of her disturbed life, which also included experiences with lesbian and then heterosexual love. Gloria Steinem has called Sarrazin "a symbolic figure for the younger generation in France, a kind of James Dean for the intelligent girl rebel." Yet there is a conservative element in Sarrazin's outlook. She shows no concern with changing the social order and does not espouse the cause of prisoners' rights. Her work is rebellious, not revolutionary, and in this respect she fails to fit the expectations of many feminist and radical readers. She finds justification and happiness in romantic love, and the figure of the missing mother is at the heart of her work, through which she attempted to ground herself emotionally and to achieve social legitimacy.

REFERENCE:

Elissa Gelfand, "Albertine Sarrazin," in her *Imagination in Confinement: Women's Writings from French Prisons* (Ithaca, N.Y.: Cornell University Press, 1983), pp. 214–238.

— C.S.B.

JEAN-PAUL SARTRE

Jean-Paul Sartre (1905–1980) dominated the literary and intellectual scene of mid-century France and remains influential even though his reputation has fallen somewhat, following his death, in the wake of the inev-

Simone de Beauvoir and Jean-Paul Sartre during a weekly radio broadcast of *La Tribune des Temps Modernes*

itable reaction and revisionist assessments of his accomplishments. A novelist, playwright, critic of literature and art, philosopher, founder of a magazine (*Les Temps Modernes*), political writer, and activist, he put his hand to a wide variety of intellectual and literary undertakings and succeeded at them all — if success means enormous sales of books, long runs of one's plays, many disciples and admirers, and a high profile in one's own country and abroad. His chief contribution to his century may well be literary; he knew how to present the very feel of existence through words and to dramatize the personal, social, and philosophical conflicts of his time in memorable stories and plays. Critics of philosophy tend to minimize his original contributions to that field, pointing out the derivativeness of much of his thought and the greater originality of **Maurice Merleau-Ponty.**

When Sartre was an infant, his father died. Raised by his mother (the first cousin of Albert Schweitzer) and maternal grandparents, he later attributed some of his personality traits and life choices to an indulgent, somewhat idiosyncratic upbringing. He studied philosophy at the **Ecole Normale Supérieure** and the Sorbonne, passing the prestigious *agrégation* examination in 1929. Until **World War II** he made his living teaching philosophy. His first publication was a philosophical treatise, *L'Imagination* (1936; translated

as *Imagination: A Psychological Critique*), written in part under the influence of Edmund Husserl, with whose work he became well acquainted during a year spent in Berlin.

L'Imagination was followed by a novel, *La Nausée* (1938; translated as *Nausea*), generally considered his masterpiece, and a volume of short stories, *Le Mur* (1939; translated as *The Wall, and Other Stories*). It would be a mistake to suppose that these works are nothing but illustrations of **existentialism** in its Sartrean form, for he had not yet worked out his thought about being and existence, but they do show elements of his philosophy. "Le Mur," set during the **Spanish Civil War,** illustrates the utter absurdity of existence. "La Chambre" (translated as "The Room") deals with dementia — that is, extreme maladjustment to a meaningless world — and a failed effort to deny insanity. *La Nausée* recounts an ontological and epistemological adventure: what is being and what can one know about it? The hero, Roquentin, discovers that meaning does not adhere to objects but is a projection of himself — and that this self is, paradoxically, nothingness. The experience is nauseating; or rather, he is himself nausea. In a valueless world he has no recourse, with the exception of the art object (music, fiction) — something hard and coherent with its own internal logic, as opposed to the flaccidity of events and consciousness.

Sartre was not politically active in the 1930s, but he had leftist sentiments. He was mobilized at the outset of World War II and was taken prisoner by the Germans. Repatriated in 1941, he resolved to renounce all aestheticism and create what he called committed literature in support of radical thought. First, however, he finished his major philosophical work, *L'Etre et le néant* (1943; translated as *Being and Nothingness*), which identifies human consciousness with the nihilating faculty and denies to it, as in *La Nausée,* all essence. Having no predetermined "being," people are utterly free; this freedom, which puts all responsibility for themselves into their own hands, is both anguishing and enabling. This notion is the foundation of his existentialism; the philosophy is, however, better known in its more popular expressions, furnished by his literary works, than in its technical form.

During the war Sartre also wrote plays, two of which were produced under the German **Occupation** of France. *Les Mouches* (1943; translated as *The Flies*) is a retelling of the Orestes story, emphasizing freedom. *Huis clos* (produced 1944, published 1945; translated as *No Exit*) is a study of three characters in hell, whose *mauvaise foi* (bad faith) — their claim that they are not responsible for their actions, their refusal to admit their lack of essence — creates the dynamics of the play.

By the end of the war Sartre was a well-known figure in the **Saint-Germain-des-Prés** neighborhood of Paris and a hero to many young people, who saw in his rejection of middle-class morality, transcendent values, and the conventional novel of character the makings of a new literature and a new understanding of society and humankind. His famous postwar lecture on the responsibility of those who reject transcendent values to create their own was published as *L'Existentialisme est un humanisme* (1946; translated as *Existentialism and Humanism*). He published more plays and the three-volume fictional series *Les Chemins de la liberté* (The Roads to Freedom); the first, *L'Age de raison* (1945; translated as *The Age of Reason*), set in the 1930s and dealing with a disabused, disengaged philosophy professor, his mistress, and his disciples, is the best; but *Le Sursis* (1945; translated as *The Reprieve*), set at the time of the Munich agreements of 1938, is noteworthy for its technical feat in giving a sense of simultaneous action.

Sartre never joined the **French Communist Party,** but he was, for the remainder of his career, a strong supporter of Marxist socialism. He was sometimes thoroughly in agreement with the French party and the Soviet Union, sometimes critical of Soviet international conduct and thinking. He was adamantly against the policies of **Charles de Gaulle,** the capitalist system, the bourgeoisie, and the Western political alliances; his anti-Americanism grew steadily, especially when the French **Indochinese war** was succeeded by the American war in Vietnam. In the 1940s and 1950s he wrote dozens of articles on political questions. Some of his thinking culminated in the massive *Critique de la raison dialectique, Volume 1: Théorie des ensembles pratiques* (1960; translated as *Critique of Dialectical Reason: Theory of Practical Ensembles*), an attempt to reconcile his earlier existentialist positions with Marxism.

Sartre produced important psychocritical studies of Charles Baudelaire, **Jean Genet,** and Gustave Flaubert, and of himself in his autobiography *Les Mots* (1964; translated as *The Words*). In the 1950s he had two important plays successfully staged in Paris. *Le Diable et le Bon Dieu* (1951; translated as *Lucifer and the Lord*) is a study, set during the Reformation, of the dialectical confrontation between peasants and princes, Catholics and Protestants, good and evil. *Les Séquestrés d'Altona* (1959; translated as *Loser Wins* and as *The Condemned of Altona*), which concerns German responsibility for the horrors of World War II, also refers obliquely to the **Algerian war,** which Sartre denounced vigorously in other writings.

Sartre was never wholeheartedly embraced by the Communists, but to thousands of young people, from the late 1940s into the 1970s, he represented the quintessence of radical thought in Europe. His influence was wielded especially in the *Temps Modernes,* which pursued a radical policy on all issues. Only with the uprising of **May 1968** and the appearance on the scene of some young radicals who no longer saw the world in Cold War terms did it become clear that Sartre had lost some ground as a master. Even then, he continued to associate with young radicals, especially Maoists. In more conservative circles he was anathema and remains so to this day. His rejection of the Nobel Prize for Literature in 1964 — on grounds that accepting it would mean his appropriation by Western humanism and the middle classes — merely underlined the gulf between him and ordinary liberal thinking.

Sartre's relationship with **Simone de Beauvoir** has been lengthily, if not quite accurately, documented by her and others; their friendship and collaboration lasted from the late 1920s until his death. He had many other liaisons, some of them important in his experience; a late one ended in his legal adoption of Arlette El Kaïm.

REFERENCES:

Catharine Savage Brosman, *Jean-Paul Sartre* (Boston: Twayne, 1983);

Peter Caws, *Sartre* (London: Routledge & Kegan Paul, 1979);

Annie Cohen-Solal, *Sartre: A Life,* translated by Anna Cancogni (New York: Pantheon, 1987);

Thomas R. Flynn, *Sartre and Marxist Existentialism: The Test Case of Collective Responsibility* (Chicago: University of Chicago Press, 1984);

Christina Howells, *Sartre's Theory of Literature* (London: Modern Humanities Research Association, 1979);

Alex Madsen, *Hearts and Minds: The Common Journey of Jean-Paul Sartre and Simone de Beauvoir* (New York: Morrow, 1977).

— C.S.B.

ERIK SATIE

Erik Satie (1866–1925), an eccentric composer who rejected the seriousness, complexity, and subjectivity of Romanticism, had a lasting influence on twentieth-century music. Best known for his short piano pieces employing unornamented melodies with modal harmonies and unresolved dissonances, he was adopted as a model by the members of **Les Six** and other composers seeking a new direction for music. His innovations included dropping time signatures and bar lines from some of his compositions.

Born in Honfleur but raised in Paris, Satie dropped out of the Paris Conservatory in 1888 to become the pianist at the Chat Noir, a well-known cabaret in **Montmartre.** His first compositions were songs of little interest, but his three *Gymnopédies* (1888), for piano, are still his best-known and most frequently performed works. Their simple, melancholy melodies and sparse accompaniments are totally different from the sentimental, elaborate salon pieces of the time.

In 1898 Satie moved to Arcueil, a seedy working-class suburb. He composed little over the following years, supporting himself as a café pianist and later through commissions. Although largely self-taught and aware of his limitations, he studied harmony, counterpoint, and orchestration at the Schola Cantorum from 1905 to 1908. There he earned a well-deserved reputation for eccentricity. For instance, he called a 1903 piano duet *Trois morceaux en forme de poire* (Three Pieces in Pear Form) after someone criticized his music as formless. He was acquainted with a small group of musicians, including **Claude Debussy,** whom he had met in 1890.

After his studies Satie wrote several piano pieces, giving them ridiculous titles parodying the evocative titles Debussy and others gave their compositions. While Debussy called one of his pieces in Book I of *Préludes* (1910) "Les Sons et les parfums dans l'air du soir" (Sounds and Perfumes in the Night Air), taken from a line by Charles Baudelaire, Satie used such titles as *Préludes flasques (pour un chien)* (1913; Flabby

Erik Satie's whimsical sketch for a bust of himself

Preludes for a Dog) and *Embryons desséchés* (1913; Dried-up Embryos). Furthermore, Satie's scores are larded with instructions such as "Play like a nightingale with a toothache," "With astonishment," "Sheepishly," and "From the top of the teeth."

This playful rejection of "serious" music gave Satie a cult following among young composers of the 1910s and led in 1915 to his association with **Jean Cocteau.** Cocteau wrote the libretto and Satie the music for the ballet *Parade* (1917), one of the best-known theatrical events of the period — produced by **Serge Diaghilev**'s **Ballets Russes** and choreographed by **Léonide Massine,** with sets by **Pablo Picasso.** Satie's music for the ballet includes jazz elements and uses a typewriter, a whistle, and a siren. Satie also composed music for **Surrealist** and **Dada** theater pieces such as *Mercure* (1924; Mercury) and *Relâche* (1924; Intermission), which included a short film — *Entr'acte,* directed by **René Clair** , for which Satie wrote the music and in which he appeared. *Socrate* (1918; Socrates), a cantata based on passages from Plato, was unusual for Satie in its serious content.

As one of Satie's followers, the American composer John Cage, wrote years after Satie's death, "Satie is not only relevant but indispensable because he gave up illusions about ideas of order, expressions of sentiment, and all the rest of our inherited aesthetic claptrap."

REFERENCES:
Allan M. Gillmor, *Erik Satie* (Boston: Twayne, 1988);
James Harding, *Erik Satie* (New York: Praeger, 1975).
— P.S.H.

GEORGES SCHEHADÉ

Poet and dramatist Georges Schehadé (1910–1989) was, like several other modern French dramatists (including **Arthur Adamov, Fernando Arrabal, Samuel Beckett,** among others), a foreigner. Born in Alexandria, Egypt, he attended French schools in Lebanon and also studied in Paris. He was influenced by the **Surrealists,** sharing their interest in dreams and the relationship of dreams to truth, but his poetry is much more direct and displays lighter touches and more grace than much of theirs.

Schehadé's theater is a strange, poetic one, where ideals and visions are possible although always threatened. Critics have attributed some of his fancy to his Near Eastern origins. His best-known play, *Monsieur Bob'le,* produced in 1951 at the tiny Théâtre de la Huchette in Paris, concerns a sage and the villagers who admire him and his wisdom, which has wonderful effects. The play, in which Monsieur Bob'le leaves the village and dies before he can return, has mythic overtones. *La Soirée des proverbes* (produced in 1954; The Evening of Proverbs) is a fanciful play that emphasizes the purity and enthusiasm of youth, contrasted with the failures of age. *Histoire de Vasco* (Story of Vasco), staged in Paris in 1957, is a controversial play about a naive man who, despite himself, is implicated in war. (The reference is to the **Algerian war,** which was rag-

ing at the time.) The play suggests that innocence cannot long endure in the modern world. *Les Violettes* (1960; Violets) is a warning against the abuses of technology.

In 1986 Schehadé received the first Francophone Literature Prize of the Académie Française.

REFERENCES:
Leonard Pronko, "The Threshold of Eden: Georges Schehadé," in his *Avant-Garde: The Experimental Theater in France* (Berkeley: University of California Press, 1962), pp. 188–196;
Juris Silenieks, "Georges Schehadé: The Transfiguration of a Poetic Theater," *Modern Drama,* 10 (September 1967): 151–160;
Mona Takieddine Amyuni, "A Tribute to Georges Schehadé on Receiving the First Francophone Literature Prize of the Académie Française," *World Literature Today,* 63 (Winter 1989): 26–30.
— C.S.B.

JEAN SCHLUMBERGER

The author of novels, plays, poems, and nonfiction, Jean Schlumberger (1877–1968) is most often remembered as one of the founders and directors of the *Nouvelle Revue Française* and as a participator in the creation of the experimental **Théâtre du Vieux-Colombier.** He was a close friend of **André Gide** and remained within his literary circle for decades.

Schlumberger began writing fiction and poetry in the first years of the twentieth century and became influenced by Gide in the 1910s. One of Schlumberger's first important novels, *Le Camarade infidèle* (1922; The Unfaithful Comrade), is set in the aftermath of **World War I** and involves a returning soldier who lies about his comrade's heroism to his widow and falls in love with her. *Saint-Saturnin* (1931; translated as *The Seventh Age*) is a more complex and ambitious work, presenting the points of view of a large cast of diverse characters. The novel deals with aging, conflicts between generations, and marital conflicts in an upper-middle-class French family — the society Schlumberger knew best. For its structure and themes the work is sometimes compared to Gide's *Les Faux-Monnayeurs* (1925; translated as *The Counterfeiters*). Inspired by a Japanese No play, Schlumberger's last novel, *Stéphane le Glorieux* (1940; translated as *Stefan the Proud*), is a war story, set in a fictitious country, involving apparent heroism and guilt.

Schlumberger's nonfiction includes a book on the classical dramatist Pierre Corneille, *Plaisir à Corneille* (1936; Corneille with Pleasure), and a study of the trial of **Philippe Pétain** (1949). Schlumberger's correspondence with Gide was published in 1993.

REFERENCES:

Jean-Pierre Cap, "Jean Schlumberger et la *Nouvelle Revue Française* 1909–1914," *Esprit Créateur,* 14 (Summer 1974): 99–109;

Cap, *Techniques et thèmes dans l'œuvre romanesque de Jean Schlumberger* (Geneva: Perret-Gentil, 1971).

—C.S.B.

LA SECTION D'OR

The group known as the Section d'Or (Golden Section) is largely the product of meetings of **Jacques Villon** and his closest associates (including his brothers **Marcel Duchamp** and **Raymond Duchamp-Villon**) at Villon's studio in Puteaux in 1910. The group's name grew out of Villon's attempts to work out a systematic theory of **Cubist** representation. The concept of a "Golden Section," advanced in classical antiquity and again in the Renaissance, proposed an ideal ratio between the square and the diagonal through which the parts of the artwork may be given the most aesthetically pleasing relationship to each other and the whole. Interest in such mathematically derived ratios was reinforced by Duchamp's discussions with the amateur theorist and mathematician Maurice Princet.

Villon's theories bear little relation to the "scientific art" proposed by the Neo-Impressionists in the 1880s and 1890s and by the American Synchronists of the early twentieth century, and he minimized the debt to classical art as well, asserting later, "We knew nothing about the problem of the golden section of the ancient Greeks." Although he found Leonardo da Vinci's *Trattato della Pittura* (translated as *Treatise on Painting*) impressive, he claimed, "our ideas grew mainly out of discussion, and we didn't get too bogged down in science."

By 1911 a sizable group of artists were meeting regularly at the studios of Villon and **Albert Gleizes.** Among the participants were the Duchamp brothers, **Fernand Léger, André Lhôte, Roger de La Fresnaye, Juan Gris, Francis Picabia,** and **Jean Metzinger.** The ideas of the participating artists were in constant flux as the group drew upon contemporary scientific theory, varying ideas of abstraction, and a diffuse interest in social reform, tied in practice to anarchist or utopian beliefs. Through Gleizes in particular, the group inherited some of the **Unanimist** ideas and practices of the Abbaye de Créteil concerning social solidarity. (The name Section d'Or itself may well be a tongue-in-cheek reference to an earlier body of artists dedicated to social activism, the Section d'Art affiliated with the Brussels Maison du peuple [see **Maison de la Culture (Popular Front)**]).

The first and only Salon de la Section d'Or, held in Paris in October 1912, exhibited the works of thirty-two artists, with **Pablo Picasso** and **Georges Braque** noticeably absent. Public lectures by **Guillaume Apollinaire** and others were scheduled to build public interest, and a new magazine, *La Section d'Or,* was launched to coincide with the show. Criticism of the exhibition focused on its lack of any unifying style or motivating idea. The works ranged from relatively traditional representational works to the pure abstractions of Frank Kupka. Within two years the various artists of the Section d'Or had moved in so many contradictory directions that any sense of a common enterprise was impossible.

REFERENCES:

John Golding, *Cubism: A History and an Analysis, 1907–1914* (Boston: Boston Book & Art Shop, 1959);

R. Stanley Johnson, *Cubism and La Section d'Or: Reflections on the Development of the Cubist Epoch, 1907–1922* (Chicago & Düsseldorf: Klees/Gustorf Publishers, 1991);

Daniel Robbins, "From Symbolism to Cubism: The Abbaye of Créteil," *Art Journal,* 23 (Winter 1963–1964): 111–116.

—J.H.

PIERRE SEGHERS

Readers of modern French poetry owe an enormous debt to poet and publisher Pierre Seghers (1906–1987). A poet of stature, he received many poetry prizes, including the Prix Apollinaire (1958) and the Grand Prix de Poésie de la Ville de Paris (1979). Yet he is best known as an editor and publisher of other poets, such as **Louis Aragon, Paul Eluard,** and **Henri Michaux.** Seghers was an indefatigable friend to poets, especially those whose lyric gifts and tastes preserved them from coldly academic or cerebral writing. Under the German **Occupation** of France during **World War II,** he participated in clandestine publishing and founded the review that became *Poésie 40, Poésie 41* (through 1947), in which he published important verse from **Resistance** writers. In 1944 he and Eluard created Poètes d'aujourd'hui (Poets of Today), an ongoing series of short monographs on major and minor poets, which taken together provide an extensive and evolving profile of poetic practice in France.

Seghers also edited many anthologies and wrote critical works. *La Résistance et ses poètes* (1974; The Resistance and Its Poets) is not only an important anthology but also a significant historical document. Much of his own verse, published earlier in small volumes, was collected in *Le Temps des merveilles: Œuvres poétiques 1938–1978* (1978; Time of Marvels: Poetic

Works 1938–1978). His poems are characterized by lyricism and verbal richness.

REFERENCE:

Lucien Scheler, "Pierre Seghers," *Europe,* no. 705–706 (January–February 1988): 176–179.

— C.S.B.

LÉOPOLD SÉDAR SENGHOR

Poet and politician Léopold Sédar Senghor (1906–   ), who was president of his native country, Senegal, for two decades, is one of the most important African intellectuals and writers of the twentieth century — and a significant French poet. A product of two cultures, the Senegalese and the French, he has drawn on both in his artistic and political life. Although Senegal was not without turmoil during Senghor's presidency and although he was criticized for exercising undue authority, his achievements in the political arena are impressive.

Senghor was born south of Dakar, one of twenty-four children in a prosperous family. (His father was polygamous, though nominally Catholic.) Through his mother Senghor became familiar with animism. He studied in French Catholic schools in Dakar. In 1928 he won a scholarship to study in Paris, where he became a friend of Georges Pompidou and took a *licence* at the Sorbonne. In 1933 he became the first African to pass the competitive examination called *agrégation de grammaire.*

Senghor's sense of the value of African culture had already been awakened during his schooling in Senegal, but it was in Paris, where he joined the organization of student socialists and made friends with **Aimé Césaire** and Léon Damas, that he formulated his ideas. In 1934 they coined the term *négritude* to describe their consciousness of and pride in their African heritage and founded a magazine, *L'Etudiant Noir* (The Black Student), which they published until 1936.

Senghor became a citizen of France and remained there to teach, publish poems, and study African languages. While serving in the infantry during **World War II,** he was taken captive by the Germans and spent some eighteen months of 1940–1942 as a prisoner of war. Some of his war poems were smuggled out of the camp. After his release he went back to teaching in France and participated in the **Resistance.** His first collection of poems, *Chants d'ombre* (Songs of Shadow), which treats the loneliness of the black expatriate in Europe, was published in 1945, the same year in which **Charles de Gaulle** appointed him to a govern-

Léopold Sédar Senghor, president of Senegal, 1960 (A.F.P.)

ment commission studying colonial questions and he was elected to represent Senegal in the French Constituent Assembly.

In 1948 Senghor founded the Bloc Démocratique Sénégalais (BDS), which dominated Senegalese politics during the 1950s. He served as a French delegate to the 1949 Council of Europe and to the United Nations General Assembly (1950–1951) before he was elected to the French National Assembly in 1951. In 1955–1956 he was secretary of state for scientific research under French president Edgar Faure. With the collapse of the **Fourth Republic,** de Gaulle appointed Senghor to the group that formulated the constitution of the **Fifth Republic,** which ultimately led to independence for the French territories in West Africa, including Senegal. In September 1960 he was elected the first president of the new nation and continued to serve until stepping down in 1980.

During this period he continued to publish his poetry. A collection of Senghor war poems, *Hosties noires* (Black Hosts), appeared in 1948. Other collections of his verse include *Nocturnes* (1961; translated) and *Poèmes* (1964). Selected English-language translations of his poems have appeared, including three different volumes titled *Selected Poems* (1964, 1976, 1977) and another selection, *Poems of a Black Orpheus* (1981). As a poet Senghor has been influenced by writers such as **Paul Claudel** (on whom he published a critical study) and **Saint-John Perse,** but his topics are generally African ones. He has attempted to express in his poetry — and thus contribute to French literature — characteristically African qualities, such as reverence for nature and a dimension of mystery. He has acknowledged, in connection with his collection *Ethiopiques* (1956; Ethiopics), that African folklore and poetry were influential on both their form and content. He has generally wanted his verse to be accompanied by music, even suggesting appropriate instruments.

Senghor has also published many political books and essays on négritude, including *Nation et voie africaine du socialisme* (1961; translated as *Nationhood and the African Road to Socialism*); *Négritude et humanisme* (1964; translated as *Négritude and Humanism*); and *Pour une relecture africaine de Marx et d'Engels* (1976; Toward an African Rereading of Marx and Engels). He has won many prizes, including the Grand Prix International de la Poésie in 1970, and he was the first black African to be elected to the Académie Française (1983).

REFERENCES:

Sylvia Washington Bâ, *The Concept of Négritude in the Poetry of Léopold Sédar Senghor* (Princeton, N.J.: Princeton University Press, 1973);

Jacques Louis Hymans, *Senghor: An Intellectual Biography* (Edinburgh: Edinburgh University Press, 1971);

Irving Leonard Markovitz, *Senghor and the Politics of Negritude* (New York: Atheneum, 1969);

Janice Spleth, *Léopold Sédar Senghor* (Boston: Twayne, 1985).

— C.S.B.

PAUL SÉRUSIER

Paul Sérusier (1864–1927) was a founding member of the **Nabis,** a group that also included **Pierre Bonnard** and **Edouard Vuillard.** The paintings and theoretical writings of Sérusier and **Maurice Denis** helped to frame the group's key concepts and practices.

Like many of the Nabis, Sérusier came from a prosperous family and studied art at the Académie Julien. He met **Paul Gauguin** on a visit to Pont-Aven, in Brittany, in 1888. As reported by Denis, Gauguin told Sérusier the way to capture an image: "How does that tree look to you? It's a vivid green, isn't it? So take some green, the best green you've got on your palette. And that shadow's blue, really, isn't it? So don't be afraid — make it as blue as you can." The meeting inspired Sérusier to paint a small landscape on the lid of a cigar box he had with him. Depicting the Breton Bois d'Amour, *Le Talisman* (1888; *The Talisman*) is at first glance little more than a hodgepodge of bright patches of color, but it gradually coheres as a landscape. Denis argued that he and Sérusier had learned that "every work of art was a transposition, a caricature, the passionate equivalent of a sensation experienced." Though the painting differs markedly from Sérusier's mature work in its slapdash surface and in the lack of the heavy outlining he later used to define each object, *Le Talisman* began a process of experimentation as to how best to translate external reality into an essential idea conveyed in line and color.

Sérusier's lifelong interest in mysticism led him to study classical philosophers — especially Plotinus — and Christian theology. His paintings focused increasingly on the life of Breton peasants. "Deductive reasoning," he wrote, "led me to demand allegory, and Greek allegory I rejected; I was in Celtic territory.... Modern dress changes too often; for the figures in my pictures I adopted Breton costume, which belongs to no age." His *Triptyque Pont-Aven* (1892–1893; *Pont-Aven Triptych*) captures his notions of Celtic allegory. The form of the painting mimics simultaneously an altarpiece and a Japanese wall screen, fusing, in Sérusier's terms, the sacred and the decorative. In its depiction of women and one infant, the painting represents Pont-Aven life as tranquil, calm, and harmonious. Typically, it is utterly immobile. Later he denounced motion as "a destruction of equilibrium; to represent movement is absurd. A work of plastic art representing movement is intolerable to contemplate for any length of time."

Sérusier's *L'ABC de la peinture* (1921; translated as *The ABC of Painting*), published at the end of his career, summarized the ideas he had developed over a lifetime. Elaborating on the thought of a Catholic priest, Desiderius Lenz, he argued for a return to the conceptions (but not necessarily the specific forms) of pre-Renaissance art, in which the sacred idea was prized above naturalism and above technique generally. One central demand was that artists reject deliberately whatever artistic sophistication they had been taught, in order to rekindle a childlike naiveté. "Thoughts and moral qualities," he wrote, "can be represented only by formal equivalents. The faculty of perceiving these correspondences is what makes an artist. Everyone possesses that faculty at birth, in a state of potentiality; his personal work develops it; a bad education is capable of destroying it."

REFERENCES:

Caroline Boyle-Turner, *Paul Sérusier* (Ann Arbor, Mich.: UMI Research Press, 1983);

Charles Chassé, *The Nabis and Their Period,* translated by Michael Bullock (New York: Praeger, 1969);

Wladyslawa Jaworska, *Gauguin and the Pont-Aven School,* translated by Patrick Evans (Greenwich, Conn.: New York Graphic Society, 1972);

George Mauner, *The Nabis, Their History, and Their Art, 1888–1896* (New York: Garland, 1976).

— J.H.

Sic

The ephemeral journal *Sic,* subtitled *Sons Idées Couleurs Formes* (Sounds Ideas Colors Forms), had a short but significant life from January 1916 until the end of 1919. *Sic* was the creation of poet Pierre Albert-Birot, but much of its vitality came from the influence of poet **Guillaume Apollinaire,** who contributed many of his poems to the journal.

Sic expressed an optimism and openness to change that were more typical of the prewar years than the period of **World War I.** In the February 1916 issue Albert-Birot proclaimed his limitless faith in the Futurists: "You love the unknown, you love life, your ambitions are limitless, for all these reasons we must love you." Displaying none of the sectarian disdain and hostility toward others that would become characteristic of the **Dadaists** and later the Surrealists and eager to promote the new in all its artistic forms, Albert-Birot saw nothing wrong with supporting Futurism and then backing **Cubism** before welcoming **Tristan Tzara** and **Dada** to Paris.

While Albert-Birot and Apollinaire were the leading contributors to *Sic,* it published works by many writers who later became well known, including **Raymond Radiguet, Louis Aragon, Pierre Drieu La Rochelle, Jean Cocteau, André Breton,** and **Max Jacob.** Brilliant typographical experimentation, new poetry such as "Poems to be yelled and danced," and commitment to avant-garde movements such as "Nunisme" (Nowism) all found their place in *Sic.* Albert-Birot's high spirits were not able to withstand a mounting awareness of the horrors of war, and with the death of Apollinaire in late 1918, much of the creative energy behind the magazine was drained away. A memorial issue devoted to him (January–February 1919) was quite large but unimaginative and uncharacteristically maudlin. *Sic* lingered on until the end of 1919, but in losing Apollinaire it had lost its joie de vivre.

— J.P.McN.

Paul Signac

After the sudden death of Georges Seurat in 1891, Paul Signac (1863–1935) became leader of the Neo-Impressionists. He secured his position as main theoretician for the group with *D'Eugène Delacroix au néo-impressionnisme* (1899; translated as *From Eugène Delacroix to Neo-Impressionism*). Like Seurat and others, Signac contrasted the "Romantic Impressionism" of **Claude Monet** with the "Scientific Impressionism" of the new circle. The first, he argued, had been grounded in instinct and spontaneity, whereas the second was based on "reflection and permanence." For Signac only a scientific Impressionism could guarantee the "integrity of luminosity, of coloration, and of harmony."

The son of a prosperous businessman, Signac was interested in art from childhood. After his father's death in 1880, he studied for a time with artist Emile Bin, but they soon quarreled because Signac's interests in Impressionism and the lively illustrations in the magazine *Vie Moderne* were anathema to the older painter. His participation in bohemian circles (especially the Chat Noir cabaret in **Montmartre**) led him to an interest in anarchism, which in turn led to his boycott of the official artists' Salon. From the outset he exhibited his works in the **Salon des Indépendants,** first held in 1884. His first collaboration with Seurat dates from the same period, and by 1886 he had adopted Neo-Impressionism in full, from divided color (via a pointillist surface), to scientific optics, to Charles Henry's theories of the meanings inherent in lines and colors. While the emphasis on science as the basis for a modern art would set the Neo-Impressionists apart from rival movements such as the **Nabis** and the **Fauves,** all three groups shared — and passed on to their successors — a search for the essential rather than the transient or fleeting and an emphasis on depicting the meaning, rather than the appearance, of scenes or events.

As a committed anarchist, Signac, along with many other Neo-Impressionists, saw the quest for a scientific art as a necessary part of a broader search for a scientific, global theory of nature and society — to be found in the anarcho-communism of Peter Kropotkin and Jean Grave. In an 1891 essay published in Grave's paper *Révolte,* Signac wrote that the pressures of history were at work in the shaping of Neo-Impressionism as a revolutionary art. Even without consciously intending any social goal, just by breaking open outdated forms and rules, the artists had produced powerful images of modern life that "brought their testimony to the great social proceedings underway between workers and capital." While anarchist thinkers such as Pierre Joseph Proudhon had demanded that "works of art have a precise socialist thrust," Signac praised "pure aesthetes, revolutionaries by temperament, who leave the beaten path to paint what they see, as they feel it, and who very often unconsciously deal a solid blow of the pick to the old social edifice that, worm-eaten, cracks and crumbles like an old, deconsecrated cathedral."

Signac's political views found frequent expression in the satirical prints he produced for Grave's anarchist journals, but these ideas were seldom the direct focus for his paintings. One exception was *Au temps de l'harmonie* (1896; *In Times of Harmony*), a painting and a parallel multicolor lithograph depicting an anarchist Golden Age in the future. Signac later donated the painting to the **French Communist Party,** which hung it in the town hall of Montreuil in 1938. Beginning in 1892 Signac's paintings began to focus increasingly on the resort town of Saint-Tropez.

Signac broke with Grave and many other anarchist colleagues over their support for France in **World War I.** He later became a member of the French Communist Party and was active in the **Association des Ecrivains et Artistes Révolutionnaires** (AEAR) and the Comité de Vigilance des Intellectuels Anti-fascistes (Vigilance Committee of Anti-Fascist Intellectuals). Although his commitment to the Communist cause was intense, his attempts to relate that commitment to his own work were ambivalent. In an essay on art for *L'Encyclopédie française* (1935), he wrote that "true painting" required liberation from external nature, including even the idea of a subject; for the AEAR magazine **Commune,** however, he wrote that the spirit of the working class should suffuse every work of art.

REFERENCES:

Françoise Cachin, *Paul Signac,* translated by Michael Bullock (Greenwich, Conn.: New York Graphic Society, 1971);

John Hutton, *Neo-Impressionism and the Search for Solid Ground: Art, Science, and Anarchism in Fin-de-siècle France* (Baton Rouge: Louisiana State University Press, 1994);

Floyd Ratliff, *Paul Signac and Color in Neo-Impressionism* (New York: Rockefeller University Press, 1992);

Jean Sutter, ed., *The Neo-Impressionists,* translated by Chantal Deliss (Greenwich, Conn.: New York Graphic Society, 1970).
— J.H.

SIMONE SIGNORET

Actress Simone Signoret (1921–1985) was one of the most sensuous stars of French cinema during the 1940s and 1950s. She was often cast as a prostitute, most notably in *La Ronde* (1950; *Rondelay*), directed by **Max Ophuls.** Her appearance out of the shadows into the glow cast by a small lamp starts the merry-go-round of passion and despair that characterizes that movie. The pinnacles of her early career include *Casque d'or* (1952; *Golden Helmet*), directed by **Jacques Becker,** and **Henri-Georges Clouzot**'s *Les Diaboliques* (1955; *Diabolique*). The image of ripe sensuality Signoret conveyed in these pictures did much to define her screen image.

Signoret's marriage to director **Yves Allégret** in 1944 ended in divorce five years later. In 1958 she earned an Academy Award for her role as the older woman in the British film *Room at the Top*. She later received another nomination for her role in the American film *Ship of Fools* (1965). Despite these successes, she refused most Hollywood offers. Political interests and her 1951 marriage to actor **Yves Montand** drew much of her energy away from acting. Her extreme leftist positions caused her problems; she and Montand were banned from French media in the 1960s.

The actress's striking beauty was almost gone by the mid 1960s, replaced by a tired face and a heavy appearance. Yet she continued to act and gave some of her best performances. In Sydney Lumet's *The Deadly Affair* (1967) she played a survivor of a concentration camp; she also appeared in Lumet's 1968 film version of Henrik Ibsen's *The Sea Gull*. In Moshe Mizrahi's *La Vie devant soi* (1977; *Madame Rosa*) she played an old, dying Jewish prostitute who in her last days befriends an Arab youth.

REFERENCES:

Catherine David, *Simone Signoret,* translated by Sally Sampson (Woodstock, N.Y.: Overlook Press, 1993);

Simone Signoret, *Nostalgia Isn't What It Used to Be* (New York: Harper & Row, 1976).
— W.L.

GEORGES SIMENON

Known throughout the world as the creator of Commissioner Maigret, the superlative detective featured in many of his mystery novels, Georges Simenon (1903–1989) is a phenomenon in the world of literature for his immense production and his popularity — a popularity that did not exclude his appeal to discriminating readers such as **André Gide,** who called him perhaps the greatest novelist of the century. By one count he produced some 418 separate volumes (not including collections of short stories). They include the Maigret series of more than eighty novels; other detective novels; nondetective fiction, which he sometimes called *romans durs* (hard novels) and wished to have taken seriously as literature; memoirs; and pseudony-

Georges Simenon with Josephine Baker, 1925

mous works of various sorts. His works have been translated into fifty-five languages; a UNESCO survey of 1972 indicated that he was the most translated writer in the world after Lenin. His books have sold reportedly more than five hundred million copies.

Simenon, who was born in Liège, Belgium, went to Paris in 1922 to pursue a journalistic and literary career. Although he would live in many other places and would travel widely, Paris retained a special charm for him and serves as the locale of much of his fiction. He lived on a boat for two years, and ports and waterways are prominent in some of his work. He also resided in the United States for lengthy periods, and fifteen of his novels are set there.

Simenon's spare style is one of the reasons for his success. He uses the telling detail, the quick observa-

tion, making use of dialogue for exposition and conveying character. His handling of his characters' psychology is a major strength of his detective fiction. His thesis is that criminals are not monsters but ordinary human beings who fall into trouble through circumstances and have no other choice but to break the law. His Maigret stories are thus psychological and social novels as well as quest stories (the quester being Maigret but often other characters as well).

Pietr-le-Letton (1931; translated as *The Strange Case of Peter the Lett*) is the first work in which the name Maigret is given to the middle-aged police inspector who had been a figure in earlier detective novels by Simenon. *Le Chien jaune* (1931; translated as "A Face for a Clue") and *Les Caves du Majestic* (1942; translated as *Maigret and the Hotel Majestic*) are two of the most widely admired in the Maigret series. Simenon's nondetective fiction includes *Trois chambres à Manhattan* (1946; translated as *Three Beds in Manhattan*), the story of a passionate liaison in New York. His *Mémoires intimes* (1981; translated as *Intimate Memoirs*) — inspired at least in part by the suicide of his daughter — is a lengthy, self-serving yet self-accusatory account of his often tumultuous life.

REFERENCES:

Thomas Narcejac, *The Art of Simenon* (London: Routledge, 1952);

John Raymond, *Simenon in Court* (New York: Harcourt, Brace & World, 1968).

— C.S.B.

Claude Simon

Novelist Claude Simon (1913–) is one of the most important French writers since 1945; he received the Nobel Prize for Literature in 1985. Although several of his books have been translated into English and other languages and there is a considerable body of criticism on his work, he has not achieved wide popularity, probably because his writings are notorious for their difficulty.

Simon was born to French parents in Madagascar. The family returned to France while he was still an infant. After studies in Paris, including art lessons with **André Lhôte,** he participated as a volunteer in the **Spanish Civil War.** As a cavalryman in the May 1940 campaign of **World War II,** Simon barely escaped death in the **Debacle,** was captured and sent to prisoner-of-war camps, escaped, and participated in the **Resistance** during the remainder of the war. For a period he was confined to bed with tuberculosis; this period of idleness allowed him to concentrate his attention on sensory experience, which is central to his work. The phenomenologist **Maurice Merleau-Ponty** used some of Simon's writings to illustrate certain of his principles.

Simon began publishing his writings after the war. His early efforts are mostly psychological novels close in structure to conventional narratives. Beginning with *L'Herbe* (1958; translated as *The Grass*) he entered a more experimental phase. During this period Simon was linked with the writers of the **Nouveau Roman** (New Novel). Most of his works — like those of other New Novelists — have appeared under the imprint of the **Editions de Minuit,** and he has associated some with other members of the group. He differs from them, however, especially from **Alain Robbe-Grillet,** in some significant ways.

Influenced by the works of writers such as William Faulkner, James Joyce, and **Marcel Proust,** Simon during this part of his career was concerned with exploring the subjective dimensions of experience, including memory and imagination, and with continuing the search for a fictional form that fits the modern temper and modern ideas about reality. Like his modernist predecessors, he probed experiences that do not lend themselves to analysis but can be expressed through images, symbols, and occasionally myth; like them, he was obsessed with place, history, and the passage of time. He developed a nontraditional style, similar to stream of consciousness, intended to convey as much as possible of how the modern mind meets the world. It includes pages-long paragraphs, frequent elimination of punctuation and capitalization, run-on sentences, parenthetical passages within others, pronouns without antecedents, multiplication of perspectives, plays on words, striking visual images, and confusion of past and present. Simon's writing can also be qualified as postmodernist, since he pursues such deconstructive techniques as exploding plots, confusions of time and place and of narrators, and a refusal to conclude matters — all in a historical context in which the possibility of identifying and fostering human values is called into question.

Simon's experiences are reflected in many of his novels, including his finest work, *La Route des Flandres* (1960; translated as *The Flanders Road*), set during the May campaign, and *Le Palace* (1962; translated as *The Palace*), set during the Spanish Civil War. Family history adds another dimension to his work: *L'Herbe* and *La Route des Flandres* are Faulknerian explorations of the past. *Histoire* (1967; translated) is another effort to identify and come to terms with family history.

With *La Bataille de Pharsale* (1969; translated as *The Battle of Pharsalus*) — followed by *Orion aveugle* (1970; Orion Blinded) and *Les Corps conducteurs* (1971; translated as *Conducting Bodies*), an expansion of the text on Orion — Simon introduced a new direction in his work, focused less on the historical and psychological dimensions of experience than on the concrete and linguistic dimensions. Rather than pursuing a central narrative, each work includes multiple narrative strains, with transitions between them often accomplished through verbal or visual bridges. *Leçon de choses* (1975; translated as *The World about Us*) and *Les Géorgiques* (1981; translated as *Georgics*) also return to subjects such as the war in Spain and World War II. Simon's books also include *L'Acacia* (1989; translated as *Acacia*) and *Photographies* (1992).

REFERENCES:

Celia Britton, *Claude Simon: Writing the Visible* (Cambridge: Cambridge University Press, 1987);

Alistair B. Duncan, ed., *Claude Simon: New Directions* (Edinburgh: Scotland Academic Press, 1985);

Doris Y. Kadish, *Practices of the New Novel in Claude Simon's "L'Herbe" and "La Route des Flandres"* (Fredericton, N.B.: York Press, 1979);

J. A. E. Loubère, *The Novels of Claude Simon* (Ithaca, N.Y.: Cornell University Press, 1975);

Mary Orr, *Claude Simon: The Intertextual Dimension* (Glasgow: University of Glasgow French and German Publications, 1993);

Review of Contemporary Fiction, special Simon issue, 5, no. 1 (1985).

— C.S.B.

SITUATIONIST INTERNATIONAL

Beginning in the late 1950s, the radical movement designated as the Internationale situationniste, or Situationist International (SI), sought to enact a "revolution of everyday life." Though small and short-lived, it played a vital catalytic role in the development of intellectual rebellion in the 1960s, influencing many students and social analysts who had no direct contact with the group.

Critical of every aspect of modern society, the SI was formed in 1957 at a conference in Cosio d'Arroscia, Italy, as a fusion of several small splinter groups, most derived from the disintegration of **Surrealist** currents after **World War II.** Included at the conference were remnants of the artistic group COBRA (an abbreviation of "Copenhagen Brussels Amsterdam"), the **Lettrist International,** and the Movement for an Imaginist Bauhaus. Among the most prominent figures were writer **Guy Debord** and artists Asger Jorn and Constant Nieuwenhuys.

The Situationists took their name from the idea of the "constructed situation," in which events were framed in such a way as to break them from a mindless, conformist routine. For the SI modern society had become "spectacularized": the spectacle — defined by Debord as "capital accumulated until it becomes an image" — had come to dominate entertainment, education, and politics and combined them in a huge, interlocking network that permeated everyday life, converting it into the "existing order's uninterrupted discourse about itself, its laudatory monologue."

To prepare the way for an ultimate, and probably cataclysmic, emancipation from this alienated state, the SI sought to undermine the spectacle. Among the tools the Situationists advanced to assist in this process was *détournement* (diverting or embezzling) — the appropriation of images from mainstream culture turned against that culture by captions or context. The Situationists were also interested in what they termed "psychogeography," a study of the effects of a geographical environment upon individuals. To break open the imposed patterns and activities of daily urban life they advocated the *dérive* (drift), an aimless exploration of urban spaces advocated as a model for the playful re-creation of everyday existence as a whole.

The impact of the SI in France was limited until it played a role in sparking the student unrest of **May 1968,** and the initial uprising at the new University of Paris campus in Nanterre was preceded by a Situationist student revolt in Strasbourg in 1966 and 1967. The student union in Strasbourg had distributed an SI tract on the poverty of student life and similar materials; taken to court by the university administration, the student leaders admitted using funds illegally and promised to continue in the future. The scandal led to a widespread publicizing of SI ideas and publications. SI slogans were adopted by students in Nantes, Lyons, Nanterre, and especially the Sorbonne in Paris, where Situationists calling themselves the *enragés*, or enraged (after the committees of radicalized poor during the French Revolution), formed a committee to lead the student strike. With the gradual easing of tensions from the uprising, the Situationists quarreled bitterly among themselves. There were schisms and expulsions before the official dissolution of the movement in 1972, with individuals and smaller groups trying to preserve its ideals.

Situationist concepts continued to play a significant role in academic life, though usually emptied of their radical political content. For example, **Jean-François Lyotard,** who worked with the SI in 1968, based some of his theories on Situationist ideas but disagreed with their attempt to apply revolutionary theory — which they took seriously — by using it as a game. Lyotard argued that there can be no ultimate emancipation through revolution; all theories should be treated only as games. His *Economie libidinale* (1979; translated as *The Libidinal Economy*) similarly inverts the Situationist idea of a revolution in everyday life, asserting that there is no longer any distinction between the spectacle and reality and that any effort to subvert the spectacle invites the danger of totalitarianism.

REFERENCES:

Guy Debord, *Society of the Spectacle,* revised edition (Detroit: Red & Black, 1977);

Ken Knabb, ed. and trans., *Situationist International Anthology* (Berkeley, Cal.: Bureau of Public Secrets, 1981);

Greil Marcus, *Lipstick Traces: A Secret History of the Twentieth Century* (Cambridge, Mass.: Harvard University Press, 1989);

Sadie Plant, *The Most Radical Gesture: The Situationist International in a Postmodern Age* (London & New York: Routledge, 1992);

Elisabeth Sussman, ed., *On the Passage of a Few People through a Rather Brief Moment in Time: The Situationist International, 1957–1972* (Cambridge, Mass. & London: MIT Press, 1989);

Raoul Vaneigem, *The Revolution of Everyday Life,* translated by Donald Nicholson-Smith (London: Aldgate Press, 1983).

—J.H.

LES SIX

Les Six — **Georges Auric,** Louis Durey, **Arthur Honegger, Darius Milhaud, Francis Poulenc,** and Germaine Tailleferre — were French composers who in the late 1910s and early 1920s advanced modernist ideas and rejected Romanticism and Impressionism. Though each possessed a distinctive style even when they worked together, their music may in general be characterized as irreverent, employing unconventional harmonies and dissonance and drawing on popular influences such as jazz.

Although the six young composers had been friends since their days at the Paris Conservatory, they were united less by a program or any similarity in musical styles than by their admiration of **Erik Satie** and their desire to purge French music of German grandiloquence and Impressionist preciosity — the ideals that **Jean Cocteau** had expressed in his pamphlet *Le Coq et l'arlequin* (1918; translated as *Cock and Harlequin*). Encouraged by Cocteau, Les Six began presenting joint concerts in 1917. In 1920 critic Henri Collet wrote an article in which he called attention to "Les Six," these "Nouveaux Jeunes" (New Youth), as Satie dubbed them. The new term stuck, even though Durey abandoned the informal group in 1921.

SFIO antiwar poster, 1928

The remaining five collaborated on Cocteau's ballet *Les Mariés de la Tour Eiffel* (1924; The Newlyweds of the Eiffel Tower) and thereafter pursued different directions, but despite the increasing individuality of their music they were never allowed to forget their youthful association and name — sometimes to their annoyance.

REFERENCES:

James Harding, *The Ox on the Roof: Scenes from Musical Life in Paris in the Twenties* (New York: St. Martin's Press, 1972);

Darius Milhaud, *Notes Without Music,* translated by Donald Evans (London: Dobson, 1952).

— P.S.H.

THE SOCIALIST PARTY

The Socialist Party, or Parti Socialiste de France, originated in 1905 as the French branch of the Workers' International, or Section Française de l'Internationale Ouvrière (SFIO). Rapid change came after the Russian Revolution and the end of **World War I.** The SFIO retained only 30,000 members after 130,000 pro-Soviet members formally split from the organization in 1920 to form the **French Communist Party,** where young men of truly proletarian origin, such as **Maurice Thorez,** gained positions of importance. During the 1920s and 1930s, remaining independent of Moscow, the SFIO was able to recruit new members and develop able leaders, the most notable being **Léon Blum,** who led the party to victory in 1936 at the head of the **Popular Front** government.

After **World War II** the party was well represented in the legislative assembly, and its members held many cabinet positions in the revolving-door governments of the **Fourth Republic** (1946–1958). During the early years of the **Fifth Republic,** however, the SFIO remained relatively weak and was excluded from power.

In July 1969 the SFIO changed its name to Parti Socialiste, with Alain Savary as its first secretary. When François Mitterrand's political organization, the Convention des Institutions Républicaines, joined the Parti Socialiste in 1971, Mitterrand assumed the principal leadership position. Although unsuccessful in the election of 1974, the reorganized Socialists under Mitterrand did attain victory in 1981 and 1988.

REFERENCES:

David S. Bell, ed., *Contemporary French Political Parties* (New York: St. Martin's Press, 1982);

Bell and Byron Criddle, *The French Socialist Party: Resurgence and Victory* (New York: Oxford University Press, 1984).

— D.O'C.

PHILIPPE SOLLERS

Novelist and critic Philippe Sollers (1936–) is one of the major experimental writers of his generation. Although he began his career with a psychological novel, *Une Curieuse Solitude* (1958; translated as *A Strange Solitude*), which won the Prix Fénéon, he soon moved to a different kind of fiction, resembling the works of **Alain Robbe-Grillet** and the **Nouveau Roman** (New Novel), in which literature becomes self-conscious and interrogates its premises and its own language. *Le Parc* (1961; translated as *The Park*), for instance, includes a *mise en abyme* (interior self-reproduction) and deliberately confuses the boundaries between the narrative and the act of authorship.

Born Philippe Joyaux, Sollers moved to experimental fiction roughly at the beginning of his more than twenty-year association with the magazine *Tel Quel* (1960–1983), which he helped to found and edit.

Philippe Sollers (Seuil)

Inspired in part by **structuralism,** its program included examining language as an autonomous and opaque phenomenon, which meant that a literary object could be only an abstract invention, not a reflection of reality. An abstract invention is exactly what Sollers created in *Le Parc, Drame* (1965; translated as *Event*) and *Nombres* (1968; Numbers). Yet he remained concerned with the challenge of expressing inner and outer reality through language. *Nombres* has been praised by **Jacques Derrida** as the perfect deconstructive exercise, and it was called the "modern Bakhtinian novel" by **Julia Kristeva,** whom Sollers married in 1968.

After the student demonstrations of **May 1968** Sollers's program became politically as well as artistically radical, and for years he was a fervent Maoist, before converting to Catholicism in 1979. Works of his Maoist period include *Lois* (1972; Laws), an attempt to illustrate dialectical materialism, and *H* (1973), a hashish-inspired work without punctuation or other structural markers. Later novels include *Paradis* (1981; Paradise), a parody of Dante and a critique of modern civilization, and *Femmes* (1983; translated as *Women*), written in a less radical form. Sollers has published collections of his critical essays, including *L'Ecriture et l'expérience des limites* (1971; *Writing*

and the Experience of Limits), and he has written or edited books on **Roland Barthes, Antonin Artaud, Georges Bataille,** and **Auguste Rodin.**

REFERENCES:

Roland Barthes, *Writer Sollers,* translated by Philip Thody (Minneapolis: University of Minnesota Press, 1987);

Roland A. Champagne, *Beyond the Structuralist Myth of Ecriture* (The Hague: Mouton, 1977);

Stephen Heath, *The Nouveau Roman: A Study in the Practice of Writing* (London: Elek, 1972).

— C.S.B.

THE SOMME

In the face of the 1916 stalemate during **World War I,** the Allies undertook a great offensive in July along the Somme River in northern France. The battle of **Verdun,** which had lasted from February to June, had drastically depleted French forces, and the Germans had received advance warning of the attack and were able to plan accordingly. The battle of the Somme, fought in mud and with heavy artillery bombardments by both sides, was a disaster for the Allies. The British lost about four hundred thousand men, the French more than two hundred thousand.

REFERENCE:

Marc Ferro, *The Great War 1914–1918* (London: Routledge & Kegan Paul, 1973).

— D.O'C.

GEORGES SOREL

The social thinker Georges Sorel (1847–1922) would appear from his dates of birth and death to belong more to the nineteenth than to the twentieth century. Yet his principal work, *Réflexions sur la violence* (translated as *Reflections on Violence*), appeared in 1908, and it was chiefly in the interwar years that his ideas became influential, in France and Italy especially. His ideas belong to the strain of socialist thought that is called syndicalism because of its emphasis on the role of labor unions in social change.

Sorel, who was trained as an engineer, was influenced by both Karl Marx and Friedrich Nietzsche, adopting the dogma of class warfare from the former and borrowing from the latter theories of power and elitist views. He was also influenced by **Henri Bergson**'s theory of the élan vital (vital spirit). Struck by the mediocrity of the bourgeoisie, who oppressed others through their economic power, Sorel concluded that "audacious minorities" (exceptional men) should take charge and mobilize the masses. He viewed violence as a necessary and desirable means to reform society; the general strike would be the supreme weapon of class warfare.

Sorel was attracted to myth, rather than reason, as a motivating force for collectivities. He espoused, at various times, French monarchism and the Bolshevik Revolution in Russia. His advocacy of violent revolution put his thinking at odds with political rationalism and liberal democracy, and it can be considered a predecessor of the fascism that arose between the two world wars, as well as of Communist revolution. Among his other works are *Introduction à l'économie moderne* (1903; Introduction to Modern Economy), *Les Illusions du progrès* (1908; translated as *The Illusions of Progress*), and *Matériaux d'une théorie du prolétariat* (1919; Materials for a Theory of the Proletariat).

REFERENCES:

Jack J. Roth, *The Cult of Violence: Sorel and the Sorelians* (Berkeley: University of California Press, 1980);

John L. Stanley, *The Sociology of Virtue: The Political and Social Theories of Georges Sorel* (Berkeley: University of California Press, 1981).

— C.S.B.

PHILIPPE SOUPAULT

Associated with **Dada** before becoming a founder of the **Surrealist** movement, the writer Philippe Soupault (1897–1990) is best known for *Les Champs magnétiques* (1920; Magnetic Fields), one of the basic Surrealist texts, which he wrote in collaboration with **André Breton.** It was the result of automatic writing (uncorrected texts that spring from the uncontrolled imagination), to which Soupault was strongly committed.

Along with his fellow Surrealists, Soupault was a severe critic of **World War I** and the political and social system that had brought it about. He did not, however, follow Breton and others into the **French Communist Party,** and by the mid 1920s he and Breton had separated.

Soupault began his career by writing poetry, which was published in reviews such as *Sic* and in plaquettes such as *Aquarium* (1917) and *Rose des vents* (1920; Rose of the Winds). These early, free-verse poems were followed by *Georgia* (1926), a more controlled collection, in which irony and lyricism are juxtaposed. In the early 1920s he began to write novels, including *A la dérive* (1923; Adrift); *Les Dernières Nuits de Paris* (1928; translated by William Carlos Wil-

liams as *Last Nights of Paris*); and *Le Grand Homme* (1929; The Great Man), which includes a highly critical depiction of his uncle, automobile manufacturer Louis Renault. He continued to produce fiction in the 1930s, as well as writing essays and journalistic pieces that are often marked by the same lyricism that makes his poetic prose and verse so appealing. Some of these works reflect his cosmopolitan interests and his antifascism.

In the late 1930s Soupault began working for Radio Tunis. During **World War II** he was arrested in Tunis for engaging in antifascist propaganda; he was imprisoned for six months and tortured. After the war he worked for UNESCO. A half-dozen volumes of his verse appeared after 1945, including *Ode à Londres bombardée* (1946; translated as *Ode to Bombed London*).

REFERENCES:

J. H. Matthews, "Philippe Soupault," in his *Surrealist Poetry in France* (Syracuse: Syracuse University Press, 1969), pp. 17–30;

The Surrealists Look at Art: Eluard, Aragon, Soupault, Breton, Tzara (Venice, Cal.: Lapis Press, 1990).

— C.S.B.

CHAIM SOUTINE

The life and career of artist Chaim Soutine (1894–1943) paralleled in rough form those of his friend and colleague **Marc Chagall** but with a markedly self-destructive twist. Soutine was the tenth child born to a poor Jewish family in Lithuania. After some art training in Minsk and Vilnius, he managed to immigrate to France in 1912. In Paris he studied art in La Ruche (The Beehive), a ramshackle private studio run by Alfred Boucher, a conventional but socially conscious sculptor. For little or no rent La Ruche offered shelter, study, and an exhibition hall for penniless artists. There, Soutine met Chagall, **Jacques Lipchitz,** and Italian painter Amedeo Modigliani.

It is difficult to trace Soutine's early work since he was given to tearing up his paintings in a blind rage. Awkward, poor, and addicted to alcohol, he tended to ignore (or reject) both traditional and modernist movements in favor of a personal, somewhat violent, expressionism. The landscapes he painted at Céret, a town in the Pyrenees where he spent three years, demonstrate his expressive power. Painted in dark, somber colors, *Les Arbres, Céret* (1919; Trees at Céret) is dominated by a series of undulating tree trunks across the foreground. In *Paysage, Céret* (Landscape, Céret) the scene appears to lack structure completely, dissolving into a squirming mass of thickly applied paint in shades of

Chaim Soutine's *Le Pâtissier*, 1925 (private collection)

green and orange. By contrast, even **Fauve** landscapes appear as models of decorum.

Soutine is perhaps best known for his still lifes of fish, fowl, and especially beef carcasses. Inspired by Rembrandt van Rijn's *Slaughtered Ox*, Soutine's beef-carcass paintings are vivid and often gruesome. Soutine prevailed on a girl model to fetch fresh blood for him daily to pour over the decomposing flesh. While nauseated neighbors complained, he worked intensely until exhaustion forced him to stop.

By the 1930s Soutine had returned to painting landscapes as tangled and matted as his earlier ones but distanced from the viewer and markedly quieter in tone. With the defeat of France by the Germans in 1940 and the ensuing **Occupation,** he left Paris for Civry but refused invitations to immigrate to the United States. He suffered greatly from stomach ulcers and died after unsuccessful surgery to alleviate the condition.

REFERENCES:

Ernst-Gerhard Güse, ed., *C. Soutine, 1894–1943* (London: Arts Council of Great Britain, 1982);

Alfred Warner, *Chaim Soutine* (New York: Abrams, 1977; concise edition, 1985).

                    — J.H.

THE SPANISH CIVIL WAR

Civil war broke out in Spain in July 1936 when Gen. Francisco Franco led army forces under his command in an insurrection against the legally elected Frente popular (Popular Front) government of the Spanish Republic. Like the **Popular Front** government of France, it was a coalition of antifascist liberals, socialists, and communists. At this time the French Popular Front government of **Léon Blum** had only recently taken power and was under pressure from leftists within the governing coalition to intervene in Spain. Since Franco was supported by the fascist governments of Germany and Italy, the **French Communist Party** in particular was anxious to involve France in the conflict. The issue was one of the most controversial of the decade.

On 1 August 1936 Blum declared that he was against intervention, a policy that had the practical effect of preventing the Spanish Republicans from legally purchasing arms in France. This position alienated Blum from a large part of his political base and created yet another crisis for the beleaguered **Third Republic.**

The Spanish Civil War dragged on for three years. Among French writers who visited Spain during the conflict and in some cases played active roles were **André Malraux** and **Simone Weil.** After the fall of Barcelona and the defeat of Republican forces, Franco ended the war by marching into Madrid in 1939.

REFERENCE:

Julian Jackson, *The Popular Front in France: Defending Democracy, 1934–1938* (New York: Cambridge University Press, 1988).

                    — D.O'C.

THE STAVISKY AFFAIR

Serge-Alexander Stavisky, a confidence man with protectors among the politically well connected, provoked a scandal in late 1933 that led in turn to right-wing dissatisfaction and the **Riot of 6 February 1934.** The Stavisky Affair figures in many novels and political tracts that deal with the early 1930s, and it is the subject of **Alain Resnais**'s 1974 movie *Stavisky.*

Of Russian Jewish ancestry, Stavisky had been under investigation for fraud since 1927, with some eighty different allegations against him, but he had avoided trial in each case through the intervention of supporters. His last venture, the "Bayonne Affair," was a swindle of investors' funds that led to the arrest of a bank manager and a deputy mayor of Bayonne. When the scam was publicized, complaints from disenchanted investors in his schemes were echoed in the right-wing papers, creating a major national scandal.

The press campaign reached a crescendo after Stavisky was found dead, allegedly a suicide, on 8 January 1934. **Charles Maurras,** of the right-wing *Action Française,* urged that immigration laws be stiffened. On both Right and Left, the press was suspicious; it was widely suspected that the police had been ordered to arrange Stavisky's death to prevent him from implicating others by talking too much.

Since the ensuing riot discredited the extreme right wing and thus facilitated the election of **Léon Blum's Popular Front** government of 1936, many leftists considered the Stavisky Affair useful.

REFERENCES:

Julian Jackson, *The Politics of Depression in France, 1932–1936* (New York: Cambridge University Press, 1985);

Jackson, *The Popular Front in France: Defending Democracy, 1934–1938* (New York: Cambridge University Press, 1988).

— D.O'C.

Théophile-Alexandre Steinlen's *Poilu,* 1917 (Musee d'Orsay)

THÉOPHILE-ALEXANDRE STEINLEN

The art of Théophile-Alexandre Steinlen (1859–1923) exemplifies the contradictory pulls and pressures on a committed political artist of his era. He was a talented, if eclectic, painter, whose work ranges over most of the contending styles and ideas of the period. He is best known today for his caustic and didactic illustrations for some fifty-six magazines, mostly socialist and anarchist, including the *Chambard Socialiste,* the *Feuille, Gil Blas Illustré,* the *Petit Sou,* and the *Assiette au Beurre.* He is also known for his advertising posters, roughly in the style of Henri de Toulouse-Lautrec.

Steinlen was born in Lausanne, Switzerland, where a grandfather and uncle had achieved some local renown as commercial artists. After a brief stay at the university in Lausanne, Steinlen was sent to the mills in Mulhouse, France, to make designs for fabrics. He later moved to Paris, where he joined the bohemian circles of **Montmartre,** especially the group that gathered at Rodolphe Salis's Chat Noir (Black Cat) cabaret, and in 1883 he started contributing to the cabaret's weekly, *Le Chat Noir,* beginning a lengthy career as an illustrator.

Steinlen's art was closely matched to the journal for which it was intended. For radical political reviews his illustrations drew on staples of republican iconography that urged readers to rise up, to take a stand. To ensure a clear message he used stereotyped characters: the top-hatted businessman, the street urchin, the thief, the worker. His *18 mars* (18 March), published in the *Chambard Socialiste* in 1894, commemorates the revolutionary Paris Commune of 1871: Marianne, the traditional female symbol of the republic, marches in front of a phalanx of insurgent workers (with an artist prominently featured in the front row); the clasped hands of a farmworker and an urban artisan form a victory arch over Marianne's head. For less specifically partisan magazines, such as *Gil Blas Illustré* and the *Mirliton,* Steinlen's focus is less political than social; the illustrations run the gamut of daily life, depicting both rich and poor; the purely playful alternates with exposés of prostitution, poverty, oppression, and despair.

Igor Stravinsky

Steinlen's paintings have as their boundaries the works of Honoré Daumier, Edgar Degas, and Toulouse-Lautrec. A few focus explicitly on revolutionary icons, but more often the paintings and pastels are close studies of working-class figures, both men and women, whose impact depends not on stock types or explicit slogans but on the artist's strong empathy with the subjects.

In the early 1900s Steinlen opened up a shop for his prints in a working-class neighborhood. The move was more than a token gesture; Steinlen insisted that his work was for the poor. In the preface to the catalogue for Steinlen's 1903 one-man show in Paris, **Anatole France** wrote that Steinlen was the "master of the street," the voice of the urban poor: "Their life is his life, their joys his joy, their sadness his sadness. . . ." An independent supporter of anarchists and socialists in the 1890s, Steinlen became a founding member of the **French Communist Party** in 1920. His posters and paintings of the Parisian working class had a strong impact on the early art of **Pablo Picasso,** especially during Picasso's Blue Period, and Steinlen's mix of art and social activism also influenced the younger artist.

REFERENCES:

Phillip Dennis Cate and Susan Gill, *Théophile-Alexandre Steinlen* (Salt Lake City: Gibbs M. Smith, 1982);

Donald Drew Egbert, *Social Radicalism in the Arts: Western Europe* (New York: Knopf, 1970);

Susan Gill, "Steinlen's Prints: Social Imagery in Late 19th-Century Graphic Art," *Print Collector's Newsletter* (March 1979): 8–12;

Steinlen's Drawings: 121 Plates from "Gil Blas Illustré" (New York: Dover, 1980).

—J.H.

IGOR STRAVINSKY

Composer Igor Stravinsky (1882–1971) lived in France from 1920 until 1939, becoming a French citizen in 1934. His residence there helped to make Paris a world center of modern music, giving him a role similar to that of **Pablo Picasso** in painting.

Born in Russia, Stravinsky was already well known in Paris before **World War I** as the composer for the sensational ballets of **Serge Diaghilev,** including *L'Oiseau de feu* (1910; *The Firebird*), *Petroushka*

(1911), and — above all — *Le Sacre du printemps* (1913; *The Rite of Spring*). With their unorthodox harmonies and rhythms, these works — incorporating influences from Russian classical and folk music as well as French composers such as **Claude Debussy** and **Paul Dukas** — brought him instant fame as the most radical of living composers.

Stravinsky spent World War I in Switzerland and then settled in Paris. His compositions of the postwar years — called neoclassical because they draw on eighteenth-century models while using twentieth-century harmonies and rhythms — were entirely different from the prewar ballets that had made him famous. During this period he wrote primarily for small ensembles, as in his ballets *Pulcinella* (1920) and *Apollon musagète* (1928; Apollo, Leader of the Muses) and his octet for wind instruments (1923).

In 1925, while working with Diaghilev's **Ballets Russes,** Stravinsky first encountered the young choreographer **George Balanchine.** The two men became lifelong friends and together created twenty-seven ballets, most for Balanchine's New York City Ballet. Their partnership is one of the greatest in ballet history. Stravinsky also collaborated with **Jean Cocteau** on *Œdipe-roi* (1927) and with **André Gide** on *Perséphone* (1934), both neoclassical ballets.

In 1939 Stravinsky went to the United States to give a series of lectures at Harvard University. When the outbreak of **World War II** made his return impossible, he settled in Hollywood and became an American citizen in 1945. He changed his style again, exploring polytonality and serial techniques in a series of ballets, cantatas, and other works until the end of his life.

REFERENCES:

Boris Asaf'yev, *A Book About Stravinsky,* translated by Richard R. French, introduction by Robert Craft (Ann Arbor, Mich.: UMI Research Press, 1982);

Robert Craft, *Stravinsky* (New York: Knopf, 1972);

Olga Maynard, "Balanchine and Stravinsky: The Glorious Undertaking," *Dance Magazine,* 46 (June 1972): 44–58;

John Pasler, ed., *Confronting Stravinsky: Man, Musician, and Modernist* (Berkeley: University of California Press, 1986).
                                                                    — A.P.E. & P.S.H.

STRUCTURALISM

Much of what is original in French thought since **World War II** — including semiotics, poststructuralism, deconstruction, and postmodernism — has grown out of a response to or reaction against structuralism, a multidisciplinary approach to the humanities and social sciences that enjoyed its greatest vogue in the late 1950s and the 1960s, especially among anthropologists and literary critics in France and elsewhere. Many differences separate the thinkers identified during this period as structuralists. Nonetheless, **Claude Lévi-Strauss, Michel Foucault, Roland Barthes, Jacques Lacan,** and others shared a core of beliefs. Although they had a solid background in philosophy, the structuralists, influenced by Ferdinand de Saussure, Sigmund Freud, and Karl Marx, were grounded in the social sciences, including sociology, psychology, linguistics, and economics.

Many French intellectuals had grown disillusioned with Soviet Communism, to which they had earlier given allegiance, and with the **existentialism** of **Jean-Paul Sartre,** whose emphasis on heroic individualism seemed out of date and whose attempts to reconcile existentialism with Marxism many found unconvincing. The structuralists offered a critique of the idea of a free human subject existing outside social, economic, or ethnic structures. Instead, they underlined the primacy of such structures, attempting to expose universal mental patterns or "languages" that lay hidden and that, although of paramount importance within any system, were not immediately apparent. They also undermined the notion of a pattern to history, especially the Enlightenment idea of progress or Marxist faith in the inevitable triumph of the working class.

While in New York during World War II, anthropologist Lévi-Strauss was introduced to structural linguistics by Roman Jakobson. Through him Lévi-Strauss became familiar with the Swiss linguist Saussure's *Cours de linguistique générale* (1916; translated as *Course in General Linguistics*). Saussure came to exercise considerable influence on the structuralists. He had studied language as a self-sufficient system and underlined the arbitrary connection between the word or sign, the "signifier," and the concept or meaning, the "signified." He proposed a linguistic model in which neither the words in themselves nor the expression of thought was primary. Instead, he drew attention to language as a system of signs of similarity and difference and to the ways in which words are combined.

The structuralists applied Saussure's linguistic analysis to many areas of the human sciences. The publication of Lévi-Strauss's *Tristes tropiques* (1955; translated), the first volume of *L'Anthropologie structurale* (1958; translated as *Structural Anthropology*), and *La Pensée sauvage* (1962; translated as *The Savage Mind*) marks the beginning of the acceptance of structuralism. In his analysis of myths, especially those of Native Americans, he claimed he had found a universal pattern or basic system, of which each individual myth was a reworking or subset. Especially influential was his contention that the elements of myth in themselves were less important than the relations among them.

Whereas Lévi-Strauss undertook the structural analysis of traditional "primitive" myths, literary critic Barthes examined the workings of modern "myths" in *Mythologies* (1957; translated) and of fashion in *Système de la mode* (1967; translated as *The Fashion System*). The neo-Freudian psychoanalyst Lacan concluded that the unconscious was structured like a language, with its own grammar. While other major writers, including historian Foucault and the Marxist philosopher **Louis Althusser,** denied any debt to structuralism, Althusser's preoccupation with unconscious structures, like Foucault's concern to lay bare the linguistic structures of knowledge and power, reflected a concern with epistemological questions common to all the structuralists.

The optimism that underlay much structuralist thinking — its belief in a unified theory or fundamental systemwide coherence — has largely disappeared from the French intellectual scene since the 1970s. Lacan, Barthes, Foucault, and **Jacques Derrida** came to question any possibility of an objective understanding of language or structures and rejected the assumptions of coherence on which structural analysis was based. The resolute self-confidence of the structuralists has since been largely overtaken by a rejection of their firm beliefs in the form of poststructuralism, deconstruction, and postmodernism.

REFERENCES:

Art Berman, *From the New Criticism to Deconstruction: The Reception of Structuralism and Post-Structuralism* (Urbana: University of Illinois Press, 1988);

Roland A. Champagne, *French Structuralism* (Boston: Twayne, 1990);

Jonathan Culler, *Structuralist Poetics: Structuralism, Linguistics, and the Study of Literature* (Ithaca, N.Y.: Cornell University Press, 1975);

Edith Kurzweil, *The Age of Structuralism: Lévi-Strauss to Foucault* (New York: Columbia University Press, 1980);

Jean Piaget, *Structuralism* (New York: Basic Books, 1970).
                                                        —J.P.McN.

JULES SUPERVIELLE

The works of Jules Supervielle (1884–1960) have a secure place in the poetic canon of the twentieth century. He wrote in a modern voice, with a directness and lyricism that make his poems easily accessible and place him in the lineage of true poets. He has been called the poet of the daily miracle — the marvelous that inhabits ordinary life.

Supervielle was born in Montevideo, Uruguay, where his family, originally from the Pyrenees, was established in banking. When he was a few months old, he traveled to France with his parents, who both died the same year. After two years with his grandparents, he was taken back to South America by an uncle and aunt, who reared him. After believing for some years that he was one of their children, he discovered that his real parents were dead and was left with a lifelong sense of loss. Many of his poems — including "Le Portrait" (The Portrait) — deal with absence.

Supervielle's residence in Uruguay (until he was sent to study in Paris, and for lengthy periods later) is important for his poetry, which often features the pampas and a sense of freedom that may be particularly American. Still more important is the fact that he crossed the Atlantic by ship more than a score of times, spending whole months of his life on the ocean. The ocean is an important pole of his imaginary world; depth, breadth, height (in the form of sky), and rocking motion are evoked in a synthetic psychological and poetic experience. Finally, Supervielle's weak heart may also have contributed to the themes and tone of his verse; life and death, presence and absence, and the real and the unreal interpenetrate each other in a world that is nearly, but not quite, the quotidian, recognizable one.

Supervielle, whose ancestors included clockmakers, considered himself a fabricator, an artisan of words, whether in free verse or in regular forms. The fantasy of his verse seems much less studied than that of the **Surrealists.** Supervielle's poetry is the product of a mind that naturally works in metaphors rather than the result of an attempt to undo reason and disarticulate syntax. Yet the dimension of mystery — natural, psychological, metaphysical — is almost always present in his poems. The inner and outer worlds, moreover, are in constant dialogue, even confusion. Supervielle did not simply make poetry out of dreams. Images, rather than rhetoric, usually carry the weight of his poems — and thus he is modern — but the images operate within a coherent poetic system rather than remaining atomistic.

Supervielle's first collection of verse, *Brumes du passé* (Mists of the Past), appeared in 1900. His principal collections include *Débarcadères* (1922; Wharves); *Gravitations* (1925); *Le Forçat innocent* (1930; The Innocent Convict); and *La Fable du monde* (1938; The World's Fable). Some of his verse has been translated in *Selected Writings* (1967). Supervielle also published poetic fiction.

REFERENCES:

Jean R. Cranmer, "Jules Supervielle: Is *Le Forçat innocent?*," *French Review*, 55 (December 1981): 193–200;

Death of André Breton, 1922, Surrealist painting by Robert Desnos

Tatiana Greene, *Jules Supervielle* (Geneva: Droz, 1958).

— C.S.B.

SURREALISM

The movement called Surrealism was the outstanding feature on the French artistic landscape in the 1920s and one of the most important cultural manifestations of the century. Though it was principally a French creation, it was not confined to France. (There was an important Surrealist school in Belgium, for instance, as well as significant developments in other European countries and in the United States.) Surrealists sought a level of reality beyond that revealed by the dominant positivist worldview; they attempted to bypass the restrictions imposed by logic and conscious reason and to express instead the processes and insights of the subconscious. Surrealists believed that the dreamlike, irrational visions they created revealed the true nature of the human soul.

Surrealism was expressed in graphic and sculptural art, poetry, prose, theater, and cinema, as well as in various cultural happenings, when Surrealists gathered in private residences, small halls, or on the street

to act out some of their ideas. Its principal theoretical texts are collectively titled *Manifestes du surréalisme* (1924, 1930; translated as *Manifestoes of Surrealism*). Its influence has been far-reaching; **Michel Butor** claimed that virtually all writers of his generation had been affected by the movement, whether they wished to be or not. Even in the 1990s critics often speak of the surreal quality of a film or novel.

The founding figures of Surrealism include **André Breton, Louis Aragon,** and **Philippe Soupault.** Other literary figures associated with the movement were **René Char, Robert Desnos, Paul Eluard,** and **Benjamin Péret.** Graphic artists of the group include **Pablo Picasso,** Max Ernst, Giorgio de Chirico, Salvador Dalí, and **Man Ray.** The movement was the successor to **Dada,** a cosmopolitan cultural movement, but Surrealism had greater longevity and cohesiveness. An immediate predecessor of the Surrealists was poet **Guillaume Apollinaire,** whose call for a new aesthetics featuring surprise, in works such as "La Jolie Rousse" (1918; translated as "The Pretty Red-Head") and his 1917 lecture "L'Esprit nouveau" (translated as "The New Spirit and the Poets"), helped to crystallize the modernist movement. Apollinaire also coined the term *surréalisme.* Breton, the leader of the movement, remained faithful to its principles throughout his long career, but many other writers either defected or were excommunicated by Breton. Several of them, such as Aragon, Char, and Eluard, became associated with the **French Communist Party.**

The Surrealists proposed a radical revolution in the arts and literature — and in the Western view of reality. Thus the movement had an inherent political dimension that initially tended toward anarchism. Breton wrote that the simplest Surrealist act consisted of walking into the street and shooting a revolver at random. Born of the ruins of **World War I** — with its destructiveness and undermining of the humane, civilized principles that supposedly underlay European nations — Surrealism proclaimed the bankruptcy of Western society and culture, particularly the positivist view of reality on which it was founded and the hypocrisy of capitalism. The Surrealists looked to the works of Sigmund Freud, whose identification and analysis of the unconscious revealed the twin principles of eros (love) and thanatos (death) and pointed to a disruptive sexuality and a destructive death principle at the heart of supposedly enlightened civilization. They also employed the ideas of Karl Marx and other socialists to bolster their condemnation of society.

The Surrealists aimed at what they called "pure psychic automatism," which would convey "the true functioning of thought." As Breton wrote, in terms that recall the mystical tradition, they wished to reach the point at which rational contradictions would disappear, and death and life, the dreaming and the waking states, would converge. The principal faculty on which they hoped to draw was the unconscious. Two of the ways in which they exploited this hidden psychic world were automatic writing (unreflective, uncontrolled by reason) and the "cadavre exquis" (exquisite corpse), a text or drawing done piecemeal by various hands, with no one seeing what anyone else had produced. Surrealism was to be less an individual expression than a collective one. For the Surrealist true poetry would be, as Dalí put it, the "paranoid interpretation of reality."

REFERENCES:

Ferdinand Alquié, *The Philosophy of Surrealism,* translated by Bernard Waldrop (Ann Arbor: University of Michigan Press, 1965);

Alfred H. Barr, Jr., ed., *Fantastic Art, Dada, Surrealism* (New York: Museum of Modern Art, 1936; revised and enlarged, 1937);

Wallace Fowlie, *Age of Surrealism* (New York: Swallow Press, 1950);

J. H. Matthews, *Surrealism and Film* (Ann Arbor: University of Michigan Press, 1971);

Matthews, *Surrealism and the Novel* (Ann Arbor: University of Michigan Press, 1966);

Matthews, *Surrealist Poetry in France* (Syracuse: Syracuse University Press, 1969);

Matthews, *Theatre in Dada and Surrealism* (Syracuse: Syracuse University Press, 1974);

Maurice Nadeau, *The History of Surrealism,* translated by Richard Howard, with an introduction by Roger Shattuck (New York: Macmillan, 1965).

— C.S.B.

SURRÉALISME RÉVOLUTIONNAIRE

Surréalisme Révolutionnaire was the invention of a small group of **Surrealist** dissidents led by Belgian artist Christian Dotremont and French poet Noël Arnaud. Its origins lay in the French and Belgian **Resistance** to the Nazi **Occupation** during **World War II.** Dotremont in particular was active in the underground and had established ties with members of the **French Communist Party** during the war. In the absence of Surrealist leader **André Breton,** who spent the war years in the United States, several artists and writers affiliated with the Surrealists took steps to involve Surrealism in practical politics.

Beginning in 1946 Dotremont and his colleagues sought to reestablish ties between the Surrealists and Communists, ties that had been shattered with the expulsion of the Surrealists from Communist-led cultural groups in the 1930s. The precarious balance between Stalinist politics and avant-garde art proved impossible to sustain, however, especially after the onset of the Cold War. The only issue of the group's magazine, *Le Surréalisme Révolutionnaire,* was published in 1947. The French and Belgian sections of the group quarreled over specific political beliefs and attitudes toward abstract art. In an effort to resolve the debate and create a broader movement, both chapters sponsored an international conference, including Surrealist splinter groups from Denmark and the Netherlands. The offspring was the short-lived COBRA movement (1948–1951), built around an eclectic mix of experimental art and vaguely radical politics; its name derived from the first letters of Copenhagen, Brussels, and Amsterdam.

REFERENCES:

COBRA: 40 Jaar Later / 40 Years After, edited by Chris van der Heijden (Amsterdam: SDU, 1988);

Willemijn Stokvis, *COBRA: An International Movement in Art After the Second World War* (New York: Rizzoli, 1987).

— J.H.

T

YVES TANGUY

Best known for his fantastic landscapes, Yves Tanguy (1900–1955) was a major artist in the **Surrealist** movement. Some critics have suggested that the inspiration for his repeated depictions of flat plains occupied by cryptic, towering shapes was the landscape of Brittany, with its prehistoric menhirs and dolmens, where he spent part of his childhood.

Born in Paris Tanguy was the son of a sea captain and served as an apprentice officer on cargo ships (1918–1920), sailing to South America and Africa. Drafted into the army in 1920, he returned to Paris in 1922, met **André Breton** and **Jacques Prévert,** and became affiliated with the Surrealists.

Even within the tight-knit Surrealist camp, Tanguy remained a private figure. The year before his death he responded to a questionnaire about creativity with the statement, "I believe there is little to gain by exchanging opinions with other artists concerning either the ideology of art or technical methods." His first, rather stilted paintings from 1922–1926 do, however, show an effort to work through the styles and ideas of other artists, including Giorgio de Chirico. In 1927 his paintings began to take on the rough outline of his mature work. *Il faisait ce qu'il voulait* (1927; *He Did What He Wanted*) presents a bleak plain occupied with cryptic forms, from biomorphic pseudo-plants or animals to a huge inverted hexagonal cone. Recognizable figures (a man in the background, several letters of the alphabet) are jumbled with indecipherable ones. Intended as direct expressions of the unconscious mind, Tanguy's works deliberately defy any attempt at interpretation: "I expect nothing from my thinking mind," he proclaimed. "I am sure of my instincts."

By the late 1920s Tanguy's works came to occupy a unique space between those first-generation Surrealists who depicted dreamscapes in almost classically representational terms (such as **René Magritte** and Salvador Dalí) and the Surrealist abstract artists (including **André Masson** and Roberto Matta Echaurren). Tanguy's works are often structured around a traditional perspective, including a clear horizon line. Within that format small shapes crawl, creep, or fly among giant columns or pinnacles (some of which are also presented as living beings). All these elements come together in his *Mama, Papa est blessé!* (1927; *Mama, Papa Is Wounded!*).

With the outbreak of **World War II,** Tanguy took refuge in the United States, where he met and married American Surrealist Kay Sage. The two toured the Southwest (where the landscapes of flat desert plateaus and towering buttes reminded him of his paintings) before settling in Woodbury, Connecticut, in 1946. Tanguy, who became an American citizen, asserted that his new country had changed his art: "Perhaps it is due to the light," he mused, or to "a feeling of greater space here, more 'room.' " His late works have a much lower horizon line than earlier ones, devoting more space to vast, subtly colored skies. The foregrounds, by contrast, move even closer to the viewer. Biomorphic plant or animal shapes are replaced increasingly by razor-edged metallic towers.

REFERENCES:

Gaëtan Picon, *Surrealists and Surrealism, 1919–1939* (New York: Rizzoli, 1977);

James Thrall Soby, *Yves Tanguy* (New York: Museum of Modern Art, 1955);

Yves Tanguy (New York: Acquavella Galleries, 1974).

—J.H.

Jean Tardieu at his desk, 1944 (Robert Doisneau)

JEAN TARDIEU

Jean Tardieu (1903–) has had a successful career as a poet, critic, and playwright. While he is not always associated by critics with the **Theater of the Absurd,** some of his techniques and interests are similar to those of dramatists such as **Eugène Ionesco** and **Samuel Beckett.**

The dramas Tardieu wrote while working for Radio-Télévision Française between 1944 and 1974 — most of them one-act radio plays — draw on sound effects as well as language and make considerable use of monologues. He called one volume of his collected plays *Théâtre de chambre* (1955; Chamber Theater) and another *Poèmes à jouer* (1960; Poems for Performance). Some of his best plays have been translated and collected in *The Underground Lovers and Other Experimental Plays* (1968).

The subjects of Tardieu's plays are often social, combining various degrees of satire with lyrical and fantasy elements. He makes fun of social conventions and the deeper impulses visible below them. The multiplicity of the self is another of his concerns. He also makes fun of language in its function as a social instru-

ment and questions its powers to designate things. In *La Sonate et les trois messieurs* (1955; translated as *The Sonata and the Three Gentlemen*) language is used nonsensically, as if the play were a musical composition.

REFERENCES:

Martin Esslin, *The Theater of the Absurd,* third edition (Harmondsworth, U.K.: Penguin, 1980);

Jean Onimus, *Jean Tardieu, Un rire inquiet* (Seyssel: Champ Vallon, 1985);

Adelia V. Williams, *The Double Cipher: Encounter Between Word and Image in Bonnefoy, Tardieu, and Michaux* (New York: Peter Lang, 1990).

— C.S.B.

BORIS TASLITZKY

In many respects Boris Taslitzky (1911–) is the best example of the French Socialist Realist artist of the 1940s. Unlike **André Fougeron,** who was the premier realist championed by the **French Communist Party** from the end of **World War II** through the beginning of the Cold War, Taslitzky never flirted with avant-garde or abstract ideas. From its outset his career never devi-

Jacques Tati, as Hulot, attempting to clear a traffic jam in *Trafic*, 1971, which he directed

ated far from the needs and ideas of the Communist movement.

An immigrant to France from his native Russia, Taslitzky painted his first political work, depicting the killing of a young Communist by a policeman, when he was a student at the Ecole des Beaux-Arts in 1934. During the government of the **Popular Front** (1936–1937), he served as secretary of the painters and sculptors' section of the **Maison de la Culture.** He was arrested in 1941, during the German **Occupation** of France in World War II, and as a Jew he was deported to the Buchenwald concentration camp. After his liberation at the end of the war, he returned to France and played a prominent role in debates about the cultural and artistic line of the Communist Party.

For Taslitzky realism was "the sum of three conditions: the content of the work, the love of the content, technique used to express this content, these three being raised to the ideological level of the working class, which rises ceaselessly." He made a conscious attempt to ground his works in French traditions — some pay homage to Honoré Daumier, while his *Le Délégué* (*The Delegate*), a representation of a trade unionist shown at the 1948 **Salon d'Automne,** closely

resembles paintings of the Revolutionary sansculottes by Léopold Boilly.

Taslitzky's fortunes rose and fell with the fortunes of the French Communists. In 1946 he won the Prix Blumenthal for his sketches inspired by French **Resistance** to German Occupation and his Buchenwald experiences. In 1951, by contrast, two of Taslitzky's works were among seven paintings by Communist artists removed from the Salon d'Automne on orders of the government for allegedly "harming national sentiment": *Riposte, Port de Bouc* (Riposte, Port of Bouc), showing dockworkers in Marseilles under attack from police and their dogs, and a portrait (under the Stendhalesque pseudonym Julien Sorel) of Henri Martin, a naval officer who had distributed tracts against the **Indochinese War.** Both were reinstalled, under pressure of mass protests.

REFERENCES:

Julien Cain, *Boris Taslitzky: 111 dessins faits à Buchenwald, 1944–1945* (Paris: Bibliothèque Française, 1945);

David Caute, *Communism and the French Intellectuals, 1914–1960* (New York: Macmillan, 1964);

Donald Drew Egbert, *Social Radicalism and the Arts: Western Europe* (New York: Knopf, 1970);

Paris-Paris, 1937–1957: Créations en France (Paris: Centre Georges Pompidou, 1981), pp. 206–215.
—J.H.

JACQUES TATI

Director, screenwriter, and actor Jacques Tati (1908–1982) stands in a tradition of visual comedy that reaches back to **Max Linder,** Charles Chaplin, and Buster Keaton. In Tati's few films, which were popular and critical successes, the humor relies on subtle sight gags (there is almost no dialogue) and emerges from people at odds with modern society, the object of his satire.

Born Jacques Tatischeff in Le Pecq, Tati played professional rugby before finding success miming sports figures in cabarets and music halls in the 1930s. He carried his act into short films before serving in the French army during **World War II.** He directed and acted in his first feature film, *Jour de fête* (1949; The Big Day), about a village postman who comically attempts to emulate the high-speed delivery of American mailmen he observes in a movie.

A painstaking filmmaker, Tati spent four years on his next movie, *Les Vacances de Monsieur Hulot* (1953; *Mr. Hulot's Holiday*), which won the Prix Louis Delluc at the **Cannes Film Festival.** Here and in his next three films — *Mon oncle* (1958; My Uncle), *Playtime* (1967), and *Trafic* (1971; *Traffic*) — he plays a mild-mannered, somewhat bungling character who is befuddled by modern existence but remains sympathetic as gags happen at his own expense. His last film, *Parade* (1974), was made for television.

REFERENCES:

Lucy Fisher, *Jacques Tati: A Guide to References and Resources* (Boston: G. K. Hall, 1983);

Penelope Gilliatt, *Jacques Tati* (London: Woburn Press, 1973);

Brent Maddouk, *The Films of Jacques Tati* (Metuchen, N.J.: Scarecrow Press, 1977).
—T.C.

PIERRE TEILHARD DE CHARDIN

Jesuit Pierre Teilhard de Chardin (1881–1955) was a geologist, paleontologist, and philosopher. His beliefs about human life and the universe derive from Christian revelation and science, especially geology, paleontology, and from the theory of evolution.

Teilhard was ordained a Roman Catholic priest in 1911 and received a doctorate in paleontology at the

Pierre Teilhard de Chardin, 1951 (Archives de la Fondation Teilhard de Chardin)

Sorbonne in 1922. He first went to China on a paleontological expedition in 1923–1924; during a second stay there he was adviser to the National Geological Survey and collaborated on research that led to the discovery of Peking Man.

His synthesis of a broad evolutionary view of the universe with a mystical Christian outlook was regarded with disfavor by the Catholic church, which ordered him to restrict his publications to purely scientific reports. Alone or in collaboration he published more than twenty volumes on fossils and geology. Only in 1955, after his death, did his central philosophical work, *Le Phénomène humain* (translated as *The Phenomenon of Man*), appear. It argues that all forms of matter are connected and have spiritual meaning, each stage of development being a manifestation or incarnation of the divinity. He believed that humanity and the rest of the world are evolving toward the Omega Point — the end of the cosmic process, at which time individual consciousnesses will disappear and all life will be reunited with its source. He regarded this process as the "Christification" of humanity.

Teilhard's mysticism and anthropocentrism made his work suspect to many other scientists, but hundreds of thousands of copies of his books have been sold, and he is highly regarded as a thinker among those who want to accept the findings of modern science without renouncing their Christian beliefs. His highly imaginative view of a human destiny that escapes from religious damnation and geological destruction is particularly appealing. Among his other writings are *L'Energie humaine* (1939; translated as *Human Energy*), *Le Milieu divin: Essai de vie intérieure* (1957; translated as *The Divine Milieu: An Essay on the Inner Life*), and *L'Avenir de l'homme* (1959; translated as *The Future of Man*).

REFERENCES:

Claude Cuénot, *Teilhard de Chardin: A Biographical Study* (London: Burns & Oates, 1965);

Edward O. Dodson, *The Phenomenon of Man Revisited: A Biological Viewpoint on Teilhard de Chardin* (New York: Columbia University Press, 1984);

Thomas M. King, *Teilhard's Mysticism of Knowing* (New York: Seabury Press, 1981).

— C.S.B.

TEL QUEL

Whereas **Jean-Paul Sartre**'s *Les Temps Modernes,* with its advocacy of political commitment, was the preeminent journal of the 1950s, *Tel Quel,* founded in 1960 in opposition to it, became the leading intellectual review of the mid to late 1960s and early 1970s. Its commitment to literary theory has had a lasting effect on the direction of French intellectual life and letters.

The creation of writers **Philippe Sollers,** Jean-Edern Hallier, and four others, *Tel Quel* set as its goal the production of new literary forms evolving from **structuralism.** It reflected the influence of the critic **Roland Barthes** and, with its emphasis on avant-garde writing, including the **Nouveau Roman** (New Novel), pointed to the future — unlike Sartre's journal, which had been shaped by events of **World War II.**

In the mid 1960s writers **Marcelin Pleynet, Denis Roche,** and Jean-Pierre Faye gave *Tel Quel* a Marxist stance. Although it was notoriously difficult to read, it enjoyed wide circulation, helping to ensure the reputation of contributors such as the critics **Jacques Derrida, Gérard Genette,** and **Julia Kristeva.** In the late 1970s, a more conservative period than the years leading up to and immediately following the student demonstrations of **May 1968,** the appeal of *Tel Quel* waned. When it ceased publi-

cation in 1983, Sollers became editor of the journal *L'Infini,* which attempted to take the place of the defunct review.

REFERENCE:

Leslie Hill, "Philippe Sollers and *Tel Quel,*" in *Beyond the Nouveau Roman: Essays on the Contemporary French Novel,* edited by Michael Trilby (New York: Berg, 1990), pp. 100–122.

— J.P.McN.

LE TEMPS

Le Temps (Time), a respected daily newspaper that ceased publication during the German **Occupation** of France in **World War II,** is well known as the model for *Le Monde* (The World), which began appearing after the war. The seriousness of the *Temps,* its comprehensive coverage of news, its scholarly analysis of issues, its editorial independence, and its stark, unsensational format (with no photographs) are all features that were passed on to the *Monde.*

Founded as an opposition newspaper in the nineteenth century, the *Temps,* despite several changes in ownership over its history, largely kept its reputation of independence through its willingness to take positions against government policies when necessary. The perception of its editorial independence was undermined in the 1930s, however, when it was made public that a financial crisis had led its director, Louis Mill, to sell a controlling interest in the *Temps* secretly to the Comité des Forges, a powerful national steel trust.

Although the newspaper had been sympathetic to the Munich agreements, it refused to collaborate with German authorities during the Occupation and ceased publication in November 1942, when the Germans took control of the so-called **Free Zone,** the southern area of the country, from the collaborationist **Vichy government.** After the **Liberation** of France, the *Temps* was denied permission to resume publication — more as an effort to ensure independence from a controlling industrial trust than because of any claim of collaborationist sympathies. In fact, there was real continuity from the *Temps* to the *Monde,* which was printed on the same presses. Thirty of the thirty-one journalists who had worked for the *Temps* were hired by the *Monde,* including the director of the new paper, Hubert Beuve-Méry.

REFERENCE:

Jean-Noël Jeanneney and Jacques Julliard, *"Le Monde" de Beuve-Méry ou le métier d'Alceste* (Paris: Seuil, 1979).

— J.P.McN.

LES TEMPS MODERNES

Few figures have ever dominated the French intellectual scene as did **Jean-Paul Sartre** from the end of **World War II** until the 1960s. A cornerstone of his prominence was the periodical *Les Temps Modernes,* which he helped to found in 1945. Placing commitment to radical change in postwar France at the center of his efforts and repudiating the traditional role of the writer as mere *littérateur,* he took positions of anticolonialism and anticapitalism, advocating revolution and reconciliation of Marxism with his own brand of **existentialism.** An outgrowth of his commitment, the monthly *Temps Modernes* quickly became the leading French journal of opinion.

The first editorial board of *Temps Modernes* brought together much of the recognized intellectual elite of Paris. In addition to Sartre, its members included **Raymond Aron, Simone de Beauvoir, Michel Leiris,** and **Maurice Merleau-Ponty.** Aron left the staff in 1946 and remained alienated from Sartre for the next thirty years; Merleau-Ponty withdrew in 1953. Sartre's interests in political theory, philosophy, literature, and the social sciences — shared with his fellow staff members — became the concerns of a generation. A wide range of disciplines and contemporary topics was reflected in its pages. Although in the immediate postwar years Sartre was the target of violent attacks from the Communists, who labeled his existentialism a "sickness," the anti-American, pro-Soviet bias of the *Temps Modernes* constituted a sort of rapprochement with the **French Communist Party.**

While the circulation of the *Temps Modernes* was never great, its influence in the ten years following the war was considerable. During the 1960s, however, the end of the **Algerian war** in 1962, the failure of the student revolt of **May 1968,** and the development of new intellectual approaches such as **structuralism,** poststructuralism, and deconstruction weakened the younger generation's commitment to left-wing causes and sapped the vitality of the magazine, which is still published. After the deaths of Sartre in 1980 and Beauvoir in 1986, the circulation dropped to less than half its highest numbers.

REFERENCES:

Anna Boschetti, *The Intellectual Enterprise: Sartre and "Les Temps Modernes,"* translated by Richard C. McCleary (Evanston, Ill.: Northwestern University Press, 1988);

Howard Davies, *Sartre and "Les Temps Modernes"* (Cambridge: Cambridge University Press, 1987).

— J.P.McN.

THEATER OF THE ABSURD

Theater of the Absurd has served as a catchall phrase to designate the wave of nonverisimilar plays that began to appear on French stages directly after **World War II** — works by dramatists such as **Arthur Adamov, Samuel Beckett, Jean Genet, Eugène Ionesco,** and **Georges Schehadé.** Although plays by these authors vary widely in concept, structure, and tone, most have thematic connections to the philosophical concept of the absurd developed by **Albert Camus** in *Le Mythe de Sisyphe* (1942; translated as *The Myth of Sisyphus*).

In Camus's definition the absurd is based on the premise of a godless universe. If there is no god to validate morality, all choices are mere human decisions, none inherently preferable to any other. Nor is anything eternal: not only is death complete annihilation for the individual — there is no immortal soul — but everything that human beings have built, believed in, or fought for is destined for eventual disintegration. Although people may hope to communicate thoughts and feelings to their fellow human beings, language is unsuited to the expression of personal experience: a sentence such as "I'm in love" or "I'm in pain" can have only those meanings its hearer's experience can give it — not those with which its speaker tries to invest it. Thus in a valueless, impermanent world, people are essentially alone, separated by the barriers of language and subjective senses not only from other human beings but also from "reality" itself. This bleak universe is not, in itself, absurd. What is absurd is that such a meaningless cosmos should give birth to beings who desire precisely what they cannot have: human beings wish their lives to have unity and meaning, and they want their choices to have value; they long to be eternal; they seek true communication with others and objective contact with the world around them. "Absurdity" is the frustrating tension between what human life is in a godless universe and the strong human desires for nonexistent absolutes: permanence, meaningfulness, purpose, and communion. The so-called absurdist playwrights gave dramatic form to this tension in plays that, while not providing a conventional imitation of "reality," represent allegorically or symbolically the real state of mind "absurdity" can evoke.

The way in which language — through which human beings seek union with others — really functions as a barrier is exemplified in Ionesco's *La Cantatrice chauve* (1950; translated as *The Bald Soprano*). In this play the same noun designates a multitude of "realities," whose individual specificity is a matter of personal perception. For example, a character tells a story in which every person involved is named "Bobby Watson." (Language is scarcely more inadequate when it dictates the use of *tree* to designate every arboreal plant on earth.) The play also illustrates the failure of communication in ready-made, cliché-ridden, stereotypical conversations, the sort of linguistic structures often taught to language students. The suggestion is that linguistic structures generate thought, instead of thoughts producing language. Speech gives hearers the impression of comprehending, when in reality they are creating their own "meanings" in response to verbal stimuli.

Stereotyping is an example of language generating thought. The special terms used to designate others, through the stereotypical connotations they collect, tend to create both the others and the speaker and to determine the quality of human relationships. *La Cantatrice chauve* toys with the stereotypical identity attributed to the English. Genet's *Les Nègres* (1959; translated as *The Blacks*) represents the interaction of racial stereotypes, as whites judge blacks, and vice versa, on the basis of overdeveloped linguistic connotations and the linguistic dominance of generalities over specifics. Not only do racial groups believe in their own stereotypes of others but they also accept the identities that others' images create for them. Indeed, as Genet indicated in *Le Balcon* (1960; translated as *The Balcony*) stereotypically identified groups need each other: judges derive their identity and reason for being from criminals; likewise, police need rioters, and clerics need sinners.

Perhaps Beckett's plays most obviously create the mental climate of the absurd. *En attendant Godot* (1952; translated as *Waiting for Godot*), for example, portrays two hoboes, hanging around on a roadside, waiting for "Godot" to come to relieve them of their boredom and misery. In the meantime they can do as they please; but they cannot perceive any action, including suicide, as inherently worthwhile. The waiting itself seems to give some meaning to their lives, but since Godot never appears, that hope too is deceptive. In *Oh! les beaux jours* (1963; translated as *Happy Days*) Winnie is half buried in the earth, but at first she is still able to function; as the play progresses more and more of her disappears below ground, so that by the end she can do little more than talk. The absurdity of the human struggle against aging and death could scarcely be portrayed more poignantly. In these Beckett plays, as in many other absurdist dramas, the characters have clownlike, comical traits: their naive search for absolutes appears touchingly (or brutally) ridiculous.

Stage settings for absurdist dramas were most often manifestly fake — designers made sure that props and sets proclaimed their artificiality. Spectators were seldom expected to identify with characters, or even to believe in their reality, but audiences quickly perceived as familiar the situation the protagonists endured.

The plays were often staged in the tiny **Left Bank** "pocket theaters" of Paris, including the Babylone, Les Noctambules, and the Théâtre de la Huchette, the one-hundred-seat theater where Ionesco's *Cantatrice chauve* has played before sell out "crowds" since its opening in 1950. **Madeleine Renaud** and **Jean-Louis Barrault** brought the Theater of the Absurd into the Paris mainstream by presenting Ionesco's *Rhinocéros* in 1960, Beckett's *Oh! les beaux jours* in 1963, and Genet's *Les Paravents* (translated as *The Screens*) in 1966 at the **Théâtre de l'Odéon.** Works by the heterogeneous group of groundbreaking playwrights that changed French theater after World War II are now revered classics in France and are performed and appreciated worldwide.

REFERENCES:

Enoch Brater and Ruby Cohn, eds., *Around the Absurd: Essays on Modern and Postmodern Drama* (Ann Arbor: University of Michigan Press, 1990);

Cohn, *From Desire to Godot: Pocket Theater of Postwar Paris* (Berkeley: University of California Press, 1987);

Martin Esslin, *The Theater of the Absurd* (London: Methuen, 1974).

                       — R.J.N.

THÉÂTRE ANTOINE

After the collapse of his **Théâtre Libre, André Antoine** developed and refined his concept of scenic realism with his second major venture, the Théâtre Antoine, which he founded in 1896. Located on the boulevard de Strasbourg in Paris, the Théâtre Antoine has remained an important center for theatrical innovation.

As director of the theater from 1896 to 1906, Antoine took a simpler, realistic approach, with less elaborate staging, than he had employed earlier in his career. Significant works performed at the Théâtre Antoine included adaptations of Jules Renard's *Poil de Carotte* (1900; translated as *Carrot-Top*) and Emile Zola's *La Terre* (1902; translated as *The Earth*), as well as William Shakespeare's *King Lear* (1904).

Subsequent directors have maintained the innovative character of the Théâtre Antoine. Between 1906 and 1921 **Firmin Gémier** staged a broad spectrum of plays at the theater, often with an antiestablishment political message. Later notable productions at the Antoine include **Jean Cocteau**'s highly psychological adaptation of Sophocles' *Oedipus Rex,* which he directed himself in 1937; **Jean-Paul Sartre**'s **existentialist** plays,

Morts sans sépulture (translated as *The Victors*) and *La Putain respectueuse* (translated as *The Respectful Prostitute*), which headlined the Antoine's 1946–1947 season; and also Sartre's *Nekrassov,* which Jean Meyer directed in 1955.

REFERENCE:

Jean Chothia, *André Antoine* (Cambridge: Cambridge University Press, 1991).

—R.J.N.

THÉÂTRE DE LA CITÉ, VILLEURBANNE

Founded by **Roger Planchon** in 1957, when he moved the company he had begun in 1952 from Lyons into the municipal theater in Villeurbanne, the Théâtre de la Cité developed into the foremost regional theater of France. Since 1972 it has been designated as the **Théâtre National Populaire** (National People's Theater) of France.

Before **World War II,** theater in France was essentially Parisian. After the war French national governments became increasingly aware of their responsibility to provide cultural enrichment to the lives of all citizens, not just through museums, radio, and television, but through theater as well. To decentralize French theater, the government expanded national aid to include subsidies to non-Parisian companies, creating Centres Dramatiques (Dramatic Centers) outside Paris, in Toulouse, Strasbourg, Saint-Etienne, Rennes, Aix-en-Provence, and elsewhere. Companies were encouraged to perform in the working-class suburbs of Paris, as well as in **Maisons de la Culture** around the country. With its 1957 staging of **Arthur Adamov**'s *Paolo Paoli,* the Théâtre de la Cité was so quickly successful in Villeurbanne, a blue-collar suburb of Lyons that had provided the company the free use of a twelve-hundred-seat hall — as well as in Paris — that the group was designated a Troupe Permanente (Permanent Company) in 1959. This designation, invented for the group, provided entry-level funding in the national-theater system, an approach later used to aid theaters in Grenoble, Beaune, Rheims, Marseilles, Nantes, and other regional centers, as well as Lyons. Planchon's troupe was designated a Centre Dramatique in 1963, and in 1972 it became the only Théâtre National Populaire, a title previously held by **Jean Vilar** and his successors at the Palais de Chaillot in Paris. Under Planchon's consistent direction, a provincial company had set the standard for decentralized theater.

The Théâtre de la Cité performed a mixture of modern and classical drama for audiences in Villeurbanne. Works by Adamov; the social-realist plays of Bertolt Brecht, which sought not the empathy of the audience but an emotional distancing of the public from the protagonists; and the audacious dramas of Planchon himself were produced along with works by William Shakespeare, Molière, Jean Racine, and Pierre Carlet de Marivaux. Classical plays, however, were never staged in the traditional manner of the **Comédie-Française.** Settings, costumes, and stage movement — all of which Planchon called "scenic writing" — were usually at odds with standard readings of the plays, providing a present-day critique of their original premises. In 1980, for example, Planchon staged Racine's *Athalie* and Molière's *Dom Juan* as a double bill — both plays with the same set and the same actors — thus suggesting the cruel collusion between the seventeenth-century Church and State. This sort of staging has been successful in other regional theaters.

Planchon called special attention to his troupe's efforts by scheduling performances in Paris, at the **Avignon Festival,** and abroad — a tactic useful for other non-Parisian directors. He employed highly talented set designers, including René Allio, André Acquart, Hubert Monloup, and Ezio Frigerio. The troupe has developed superior actors, such as Jean Bouise, Colette Dompietrini, and Isabelle Sadoyan, not the least of whom is Planchon himself, who has starred in many productions.

REFERENCES:

Yvette Daoust, *Roger Planchon, Director and Playwright* (New York: Cambridge University Press, 1981);

Bernard Dort, "L'Age de la représentation," in *Le Théâtre en France. 2: De la Révolution à nos jours,* edited by Jacqueline de Jomaron (Paris: Armand Colin, 1989), pp. 451–534.

—R.J.N.

THÉÂTRE DE L'ATELIER

Founded in 1921 by **Charles Dullin,** the Théâtre de l'Atelier (Workshop Theater), located on the place Charles Dullin in the **Montmartre** section of Paris, is best known for Dullin's innovative stagings of plays from classical antiquity, Elizabethan England, Golden-Age Spain, and the French classical period. Among the moderns Dullin produced works such as Marcel Achard's *Voulez-vous jouer avec moâ?* (1923; Wanna Play?), Luigi Pirandello's *Cosi è se vi pare* (1924; translated as *Right You Are! [If You Think So]*), and **Armand Salacrou**'s *La Terre est ronde* (1938; translated as *The World is Round*).

André Barsacq, who succeeded Dullin as director of the Atelier in 1940, is well remembered for his staging and set design of a series of plays by **Jean Anouilh:** *Le Rendez-vous de Senlis* (1941; translated as *Dinner with the Family*), *Eurydice* (1942), *Antigone* (1944), *Roméo et Jeannette* (1946), *L'Invitation au château* (1947; translated as *Ring Round the Moon*), *Colombe* (1951), and *Médée* (1953; translated as *Medea*).

REFERENCES:

Antonin Artaud, "L'Atelier de Charles Dullin," in his *Œuvres complètes,* 13 volumes (Paris: Gallimard, 1961), II: 171–172;

Renée Saurel, "Dullin et l'Atelier," in *Encyclopédie du théâtre contemporain,* edited by Gilles Quéant (Paris: Olivier Perrin, 1959), pp. 47–53.

—R.J.N.

THÉÂTRE DE L'ATHÉNÉE

Constructed in the rue Baudreau in Paris in 1894, the four-hundred-seat Théâtre de l'Athénée first served as a strictly commercial venture, a so-called **boulevard theater,** but it became a serious art theater when **Louis Jouvet** established his troupe there in 1934. On its stage Jouvet mounted celebrated productions of **Jean Giraudoux**'s plays, including *Tessa* (1934), *La Guerre de Troie n'aura pas lieu* (1935; adapted as *Tiger at the Gates*), *Supplément au voyage de Cook* (1935; translated as *Supplement to Cook's Travels*), *Electre* (1937; translated as *Electra*), *L'Impromptu de Paris* (1937; Paris Impromptu), *Ondine* (1939), *La Folle de Chaillot* (1945; translated as *The Madwoman of Chaillot*), and *L'Apollon de Bellac* (1947; translated as *The Apollo of Bellac*). Jouvet also staged notable productions of Molière's plays *L'Ecole des femmes* (1936; translated as *The School for Wives*), *Dom Juan* (1947), and *Tartuffe* (1950).

After Jouvet's death in 1951, the stage of the Athénée reverted to the commercial formula of "hit" shows. In the 1960s, Françoise Spira established her "Théâtre vivant," or Living Theater, at the Athénée. **Jean-Paul Sartre**'s *Kean* was produced there in 1983, directed by Jean-Claude Drouot. The theater remains active under the name Théâtre de l'Athénée–Louis Jouvet.

REFERENCE:

Jacques Guicharnaud, "Directors and Productions," in his *Modern French Theatre from Giraudoux to Beckett* (New Haven: Yale University Press, 1961), pp. 237–262.

—R.J.N.

THÉÂTRE DE L'ODÉON

Constructed in 1782 by King Louis XVI near the Luxembourg Gardens to house performances of the **Comédie-Française,** the Théâtre de l'Odéon has played a central role in French theater history. Usually receiving a small government subsidy, the theater has remained active almost continually since its opening (except during the French Revolution and two or three fires), even after the Comédie-Française moved out in 1799 to occupy its present hall near the rue de Richelieu.

In modern times the Odéon building has housed companies under directors who had previously been successful in the private sector. **André Antoine** directed at the Odéon in 1894 and again from 1906 to 1914, refining his concept of naturalistic settings by severely limiting the array of "real" props. He brought noteworthy performances of William Shakespeare to the Odéon stage: *Julius Caesar* in 1907 and *Coriolanus* in 1910. **Firmin Gémier,** although better known for his efforts to develop a people's theater, also directed plays from the classical repertory at the Odéon from 1921 to 1930.

After **World War II** the Théâtre de l'Odéon was merged with the Comédie-Française and rebaptized the Salle Luxembourg, a name it kept from 1946 to 1959. Few performances of note took place in the theater during that period. In 1959 the theater regained its autonomy, under the direction of **Jean-Louis Barrault** (a disciple of **Charles Dullin**) and **Madeleine Renaud** (of the Comédie-Française), who had already achieved fame with their own company in other Paris theaters. They renamed the ancient hall "Odéon, Théâtre de France" and encouraged other directors to use it as well for their own best productions. Among the best-known Odéon offerings from this period are **Eugène Ionesco**'s *Rhinocéros* (1960) and Edward Albee's *A Delicate Balance* (1967), staged by Barrault and Renaud; **Samuel Beckett**'s *Oh! les beaux jours* (1963; translated as *Happy Days,*), directed by **Roger Blin;** and Molière's *Tartuffe* (1964), directed by **Roger Planchon.** In 1966 Blin's production of **Jean Genet**'s anticolonialist play *Les Paravents* (translated as *The Screens*) brought noisy protests and violent demonstrations by right-wing extremists to the Odéon. Despite smoke bombs inside and outside the theater, injured policemen, and many arrests, the performances continued.

The old theater was a focal point of another political firestorm two years later during the national crisis of **May 1968,** when militant students, demanding educational and other reforms, occupied the premises for several weeks. They prevented all performances from taking place and damaged or destroyed many of the elegant, traditional furnishings of the historic building. **André Malraux,** then minister of culture, chastised Barrault for failing to oppose more forcefully this destructive action of the radical Left and removed control of the theater from the Renaud-Barrault troupe.

Memorable performances in the restored Odéon after the Barrault era include Shakespeare's *Richard II* as staged by Pierre Chéreau in 1970 and Ionesco's *La Soif et la faim* (translated as *Hunger and Thirst*) in 1973.

REFERENCES:

Jean-Louis Barrault and Simone Benmusa, *Odéon, Théâtre de France* (Paris: Le Temps, 1965);

Christian Genty, *Histoire du Théâtre National de l'Odéon* (Paris: Fischbacher, 1982).

— R.J.N.

THÉÂTRE DE L'ŒUVRE

The Théâtre de l'Œuvre in Paris is best known for its association with director **Aurélien Lugné-Poe,** who guided its fortunes from 1893 until 1929, with a hiatus during **World War I.** He staged his Symbolist versions of Henrik Ibsen's plays: *Rommersholm* and *An Enemy of the People* in 1893, *The Master Builder* in 1894, *Brand* and *Little Eyolf* in 1895, and *Peer Gynt* in 1896. In that same year his staging of **Alfred Jarry**'s *Ubu roi* marked the true beginning of modernist theater in France. Also of historical importance was the first performance of **Paul Claudel**'s mystic, symbolic masterpiece, *L'Annonce faite à Marie* (translated as *The Tidings Brought to Mary*), on the stage of the Théâtre de l'Œuvre in 1912.

After Lugné-Poe's departure in 1929, a theater called Théâtre de l'Œuvre continued off and on in Paris into the 1980s, with various directors and troupes. Notable productions of this period include **Georges Pitoëff**'s production of Ibsen's *A Doll's House* in 1930, a staging of **Jean Cocteau**'s *Chevaliers de la Table Ronde* (translated as *Knights of the Round Table*) in 1937, Jean-Marie Serreau's introduction to the public of *Tous contre tous* (translated as *All Against All*) by avant-garde playwright **Arthur Adamov** in 1953, Jacques Mauclair's staging of Adamov's *Le Professeur Taranne* (translated as *Professor Taranne*) in 1954, and Serreau's presentation of Bertolt Brecht's *A Man's a Man* in 1955. The Théâtre de l'Œuvre still exists in the rue de Clichy.

REFERENCES:

Gertrude R. Jasper, *Adventure in the Theater: Lugné-Poe and the Théâtre de L'Œuvre to 1899* (New Brunswick, N.J.: Rutgers University Press, 1947);

Bettina Knapp, *The Reign of the Theatrical Director: French Theatre 1887–1924* (Troy, N.Y.: Whitston, 1988);

Jacques Robichez, *Le Symbolisme au théâtre: Lugné-Poe et les débuts de l'Œuvre* (Paris: L'Arche, 1957).

— R.J.N.

THÉÂTRE DU CHÂTELET

The most recent of a series of commercial theaters that have existed on the Place du Châtelet in Paris, the Théâtre du Châtelet has frequently served as a venue for ballet and opera that is not produced at the state-run Opéra and Opéra Comique. The modern heyday of the theater began in 1909, when **Serge Diaghilev** first brought the **Ballets Russes** (with dancers **Vaslav Nijinsky** and Anna Pavlova) and Russian opera there for a series of "Russian Seasons." In 1978 the Châtelet was designated a theater exclusively for musicals, and it has since become a concert hall, featuring classical music by orchestras and celebrated soloists.

REFERENCE:

Lynn Garafola, *Diaghilev's Ballets Russes* (New York & London: Oxford University Press, 1989).

— R.J.N.

THÉÂTRE DU GYMNASE

Located on the boulevard Bonne-Nouvelle in Paris, the Théâtre du Gymnase, a former vaudeville house transformed for the staging of plays, has long typified the French commercial or **boulevard theater.** Among the best-known actors to have appeared early in their careers on the stage of the Gymnase is **Charles Boyer,** who starred in Henri Bernstein's plays *La Galerie des Glaces* (1924; The Hall of Mirrors) and *Le Venin* (1927; Venom).

The Gymnase has on occasion escaped the standard boulevard fare of thrillers, farces, and comedies on the theme of adultery, with the production of a major avant-garde or literary play. The celebrated English director **Peter Brook** staged **Jean Genet**'s *Le Balcon* (translated as *The Balcony*) there in 1960, and **André Barsacq** directed a dramatic version of Fyodor Dostoyevsky's novel *The Idiot* on its stage in 1966. Marie Bell, a member of the **Comédie-Française,** directed at the Théâter du Gymnase from 1962 to 1985.

— R.J.N.

Setting at Théâtre du Soleil for *L'Age d'or*, 1975

THÉÂTRE DU SOLEIL

The Théâtre du Soleil (Sun Theater) was founded in 1964 as a utopian commune of about fifty actors and technicians, working together to produce shows of their own devising as well as traditional plays in innovative stagings. As a collectivity the company is not governed by a director, but **Ariane Mnouchkine** has served as primary theoretician, organizer, and set designer for the group. It sprang from the Paris student theater movement (the Sorbonne club for ancient theater dates back to the 1930s, for example) and specifically from the Association Théâtrale des Etudiants de Paris, founded in 1959 by Mnouchkine and Martine Franck, who was to become the official photographer of the Soleil company. As such the Théâtre du Soleil is a highly successful representative of the authorless, directorless new theater developed by the first post-1945 generation in France.

Like the young companies of the 1970s (Jérôme Savary's Grand Magic Circus, for example), the Théâtre du Soleil soon shed its amateur status, ceased putting on standard plays for the pleasure of it, and began seeking to create a different theater. The annual summer **Nancy Festival,** which after 1963 brought together student acting companies from all parts of

France and provided a forum for the ideas of the anti-establishment student movement of the 1960s, doubtless influenced the evolution of the Théâtre du Soleil.

In general terms the company worked to replace dominance with cooperation in the theatrical ethos. No playwright's script should completely dominate the company's efforts; no dominant director should circumscribe the creativity of actors and technicians; no performances should overwhelm audiences; but rather the actors and the public should create and appreciate a moment of celebration together. While this troupe worked toward these ends, its productions never exemplified theatrical anarchy: its work has been characterized by highly disciplined acting and thoughtful staging.

The company's major achievements include a 1964–1965 production of Maksim Gorky's *Les Petits-Bourgeois* (The Tradesmen), in a version by **Arthur Adamov;** a 1967 staging of *La Cuisine* (Cooking) by Arnold Wesker, in which precision in costume and gesture make up for the absence of props (actors chopped, kneaded, fried, and so forth so convincingly that they required no onstage food to prepare); a 1968 performance of William Shakespeare's *A Midsummer Night's Dream;* and *Les Clowns* (The Clowns), a 1969 collective creation, which — through bright lighting and

Théâtre du Vieux-Colombier

evocative gesture — became a general celebration for actors and audiences alike. The Théâtre du Soleil was invited to perform *Les Clowns* at the 1969 **Avignon Festival,** where it gained international recognition for the company.

In 1970 the troupe found a theatrical home in an old munitions warehouse called La Cartoucherie (cartridge shed) in the Paris suburb of Vincennes, where stages and seating can be rearranged for each show. There the company created two original and highly successful pageants based on French history. The first, *1789,* was performed on five acting spaces, or low stages, connected by bridges. The audience stood and moved about in the warehouse among these spaces, or sat on raised seats farther back. The action — provided by marionettes as well as live actors (some playing circus acrobats) — consisted of disconnected scenes united by a narrative voice; it showed people of the period reacting to the news of then-current events, such as the fall of the Bastille. Dialogue included excerpts from historical documents, such as records of debates in the Revolutionary Assembly, and culminated in a celebration of liberation that united actors and audience (although ominous indications of a repressive order to come are included in the pageant). *1789* drew more than 281,000 spectators to the Cartoucherie. In the 1972 season *1793,* a second historical creation, which evokes the

Reign of Terror, was also successful, but a 1975 production called *L'Age d'or* (The Golden Age), purporting to be a retrospective view of the present period, appears to have been less popular. The Théâtre du Soleil has continued its experiments into the 1990s.

REFERENCES:

Roland Amstutz and others, *Différent — Le Théâtre du Soleil: textes et entretiens* (Lausanne: La Cité, 1976);

Adrian Kiernander, *Ariane Mnouchkine and the Théâtre du Soleil* (New York: Cambridge University Press, 1993);

Kiernander, "The Role of Ariane Mnouchkine at the Théâtre du Soleil," *Modern Drama,* 33 (September 1990): 322–331;

Daniel Mortier, *Le Nouveau Théâtre* (Paris: Hatier, 1974).
                                                                — R.J.N.

THÉÂTRE DU VIEUX-COLOMBIER

In 1913 **Jacques Copeau** established his experimental repertory company in the Théâtre du Vieux-Colombier (Old Dovecote Theater) on the **Left Bank** in Paris, near the church of Saint-Sulpice. There he directed a high-quality repertoire staged with classical simplicity and veneration for the written script. In the process he created what was probably the most influential theater in Paris between the world wars.

The physical austerity of the Théâtre du Vieux-Colombier — onstage and in the hall — allowed for reasonably priced tickets for about 360 spectators, and the first season was a resounding success. The first production was Thomas Heywood's *A Woman Killed with Kindness,* and the 1913–1914 season included memorable stagings of Molière's *L'Amour médecin* (translated as *The Quacks, or Love's the Physician*) and *L'Avare* (translated as *The Miser*), as well as of **Paul Claudel**'s *L'Echange* (translated as *The Exchange*).

World War I interrupted all Parisian theater activity, and Copeau reopened the Vieux-Colombier in 1919 after spending two seasons in New York. His major productions included William Shakespeare's *A Winter's Tale* in 1920, Pierre-Augustin Caron de Beaumarchais's *Le Mariage de Figaro* (translated as *The Marriage of Figaro*) in 1921, and André Gide's *Saül* in 1922. Copeau's own play *La Maison natale* (translated as *The House into Which We Are Born*), performed in 1923, failed miserably. In addition to actor and stage manager **Louis Jouvet,** the troupe included Blanche Albane, Romain Bouquet, and **Charles Dullin.**

Beginning in 1921 Copeau also ran the Ecole du Vieux-Colombier, a school in which he provided rigorous training for his actors. In addition to elocution and oral interpretation, they studied singing and breath control, improvisation, mask making, costume sewing and design, and set painting. Copeau also hired the Fratellini clowns to teach his students gymnastics and mime.

Copeau's postwar productions were critical, but not commercial, successes. Obliged either to compromise his concept of theater as art or to lose his audience, he closed the Vieux-Colombier in 1924, continuing his acting school in the villages of Burgundy. He stopped teaching there in 1929.

Other directors used the stage and the Vieux-Colombier name into the 1950s. Noteworthy performances after the Copeau years include André Obey's *Noé* (translated as *Noah*) and *Le Viol de Lucrèce* (translated as *The Rape of Lucretia*), staged by Michel Saint-Denis and the **Compagnie des Quinze** in 1931; **Jean Anouilh**'s *L'Hermine* (Ermine) by the same company in 1932; Henrik Ibsen's *The Wild Duck,* directed by **Georges Pitoëff** in 1934; the premiere of **Jean-Paul Sartre**'s *Huis clos* (1944; translated as *No Exit*), directed by **Raymond Rouleau; Jean Vilar**'s staging of T. S. Eliot's *Murder in the Cathedral* in 1945; and Jacques Mauclair's 1953 production of **Eugène Ionesco**'s *Victimes du devoir* (Victims of Duty).

REFERENCES:

France Anders, *Jacques Copeau et le Cartel des Quatre* (Paris: Nizet, 1959);

Jacqueline de Jomaron, "Jacques Copeau: Le Tréteau nu," in *Le Théâtre en France. 2: De la Révolution à nos jours,* edited by Jomaron (Paris: Armand Colin, 1989), pp. 215–226;

John Rudlin, *Jacques Copeau* (Cambridge: Cambridge University Press, 1986).

— R.J.N.

THÉÂTRE LIBRE

The theatrical company called the Théâtre Libre, directed by **André Antoine,** began performing in March 1887 at 37, passage de l'Elysée-des-Beaux-Arts (now named rue Antoine). Under Antoine's domination the company helped end long-established Romantic and moralistic theatrical conventions by striving for detailed realism in staging and acting style while proclaiming its liberty to present reality at its most scandalous.

The troupe was financed in large part by season-ticket subscriptions, with the first two performances of each play open only to subscribers and the press. Among the important productions were Léon Hennique's *Jacques Damour* (1887; adapted from Emile Zola), Leo Tolstoy's *The Power of Darkness* (1888), *La Chance de Françoise* (translated as *Françoise's Luck*) by Georges de Porto-Riche (1888), *Ecole des veufs* (translated as *School for Widowers*) by Georges Ancey (1889), Henrik Ibsen's *Ghosts* (1890), *La Fille Elisa* (translated as *Elisa the Whore*) by Edmond de Goncourt (1890), *The Wild Duck* by Ibsen (1891), *Le Père Goriot,* adapted from Honoré de Balzac by A. Tarabant (1891), *Blanchette* by Eugène Brieux (1892), and *Eternal Lovers* (1893), a pantomime by Corneau and Gerbault, with music by André Messager. Antoine's enterprise piled up so many debts that in 1894 it went bankrupt. Antoine later founded and directed the **Théâtre Antoine.**

REFERENCE:

Samuel Waxman, *Antoine and the Théâtre-Libre* (Cambridge, Mass.: Harvard University Press, 1926).

— R.J.N.

THÉÂTRE MONTPARNASSE

The Théâtre Montparnasse in Paris is remembered primarily as the site of **Gaston Baty**'s greatest theatrical presentations. He directed there from 1930 until 1943, and his troupe remained there under the direction of his leading actress, **Marguerite Jamois,** until 1947.

Baty's first season at the Théâtre Montparnasse brought Bertolt Brecht's *Three-Penny Opera* to Paris. In 1935 he staged a highly successful performance of Alfred de Musset's *Les Caprices de Marianne* (translated as *The Caprices of Marianne*). For Baty a theatrical experience was always far more than the words of a script, and he attempted to demonstrate this concept by staging dramatic adaptations of novels with full visual effects, using lighting and stage settings to supplement verbal interpretation of the text. His version of Fyodor Dostoyevsky's *Crime and Punishment* appeared in 1933, and he produced an adaptation of Gustave Flaubert's *Madame Bovary* (with a redemptive conclusion for the heroine) in 1936. Under the German **Occupation** of France during **World War II,** the Montparnasse stage featured French-language versions of plays by William Shakespeare: *The Taming of the Shrew* in 1941 and *Macbeth* in 1942. Jamois performed the male title role of Musset's *Lorenzaccio,* a play with quasi-**existentialist** undertones, in 1945.

At Jamois's invitation **Charles Dullin** directed his last play in Paris (**Armand Salacrou**'s *L'Archipel Lenoir* [The Lenoir Archipelago]) at the Montparnasse in 1947. Other directors have followed Jamois at the Théâtre Montparnasse, but none has achieved particular acclaim. Located in the rue de la Gaîté, it now bears the name Théâtre Montparnasse–Gaston Baty, to distinguish it from its neighbor, the Théâtre de la Gaîté-Montparnasse.

REFERENCE:

Jacqueline de Jomaron, "Ils étaient quatre . . . ," in *Le Théâtre en France. 2: De la Révolution à nos jours,* edited by Jomaron (Paris: Armand Colin, 1989), pp. 227–270.

—R.J.N.

Poster promoting Théâtre National Populaire, circa 1950

THÉÂTRE NATIONAL POPULAIRE

The Théâtre National Populaire (National People's Theater), or TNP, is a French theater movement based on the principle that drama plays the essential social role of civilizing and unifying a nation. In general TNP has sought especially to make the insights of high culture available to members of the proletariat.

In 1920 theater director **Firmin Gémier** succeeded in obtaining a small government subsidy to launch a Théâtre National Populaire based on the principles set forth by **Romain Rolland** in *Le Théâtre du peuple* (1903; translated as *The People's Theater*). Although he succeeded in staging only one play — an epic spectacle on French history, at the Trocadéro in Paris — Gémier remained nominally in charge of the project until his death in 1933.

Gémier was succeeded by other directors (Alfred Fortier, Paul Abram, Pierre Adlebert), but the movement bore fruit only after 1950, when **Jean Vilar** — having been offered sufficient government funding — agreed to organize a company and produce a full season of plays each year for what he hoped would be largely a proletarian audience. He was already succeeding with his other theater project, the summer **Avignon Festival,** and with part of that company he launched a winter season in Paris, moving from theater to theater until he found a permanent home in spring 1952 in the Palais de Chaillot, which had been constructed in 1937 on the site of the Trocadéro.

Wanting a true people's theater, Vilar did away with the economic segregation that prevailed in other halls, where a few poor students crowded into a peanut gallery under the rafters while the elegantly attired wealthy filled the orchestra and boxes. His new hall seated two thousand, most on the same floor and with little difference in seating prices, all of which his subsidy kept low. Since the laborers he hoped to attract to the theater could scarcely afford in those days to own cars or use taxis, it was essential to start the performances early enough so that spectators could still catch the subway home before it shut down for the night. As that strategy severely reduced the dinner hour, Vilar arranged for inexpensive buffet suppers (often with wine and chamber music) to be available at the theater. He also eliminated the fee for coat checking and all tipping within the theater. This veritable revolution in French theatergoing traditions did bring in some less affluent people, but schoolteachers, clerical workers, and students were surely far more numerous than laborers. Vilar also worked with labor and student organizations, providing panel discussions and lectures by actors and directors for their meetings and selling tickets through their auspices.

Vilar offered consistently high-quality fare. His first season (1951–1952) included Bertolt Brecht's somber *Mother Courage and Her Children* and Heinrich von Kleist's *The Prince of Homburg*. During subsequent seasons, in which he often brought to Paris productions he had organized in Avignon the preceding summer, he presented Georg Büchner's historical drama *Danton's Death* in 1953, Pierre Carlet de Marivaux's seldom-staged *Le Triomphe de l'amour* (translated as *The Triumph of Love*) in 1955, and in 1958 **Alfred Jarry**'s metaphysical farce *Ubu roi* (translated) and Alfred de Musset's traditional comedy of manners *On ne badine pas avec l'amour* (translated as *No Trifling with Love*). In addition to his own considerable acting skill, Vilar brought star actors such as **Maria Casarès** and **Gérard Philipe** to the Palais de Chaillot stage at the heights of their careers. **Jeanne Moreau** and **Philippe Noiret,** later to star in movies, acted in Vilar's company.

Perhaps dissatisfied with his less-than-proletarian audience, Vilar left the TNP in 1963. By traditional measures his venture had been a success: he had filled his two-thousand-seat hall night after night, and by the end he was selling so many season tickets that few seats were left for individual performances. His troupe attracted about 430,000 spectators in his final year.

His disciple Georges Wilson took over the reins when Vilar left. Although Wilson sought to continue the policies of his predecessor with memorable stagings of Brecht, the TNP never regained its earlier luster. In a rare example of state censorship, Armand Gatti was refused authorization to stage his satirical play *La Passion du Général Franco* (The Passion of General Franco) at the TNP: it was deemed improper to criticize a foreign head of state from the stage of a national theater. In 1972, as Wilson stepped down, Jack Lang was given charge of the "Théâtre National de Chaillot," while the designation "Théâtre National Populaire" was awarded to **Roger Planchon**'s troupe at the **Théâtre de la Cité, Villeurbanne,** near Lyons. Thus for the first time a regional theater center became a national theater.

REFERENCES:

Thomas J. Donahue, "Mnouchkine, Vilar and Copeau: Popular Theater and Paradox," *Modern Language Studies,* 21 (Fall 1991): 31–42;

Bernard Dort, "L'Age de la représentation," in *Le Théâtre en France. 2: De la Révolution à nos jours,* edited by Jacqueline de Jomaron (Paris: Armand Colin, 1989), pp. 451–534;

Guy Leclerc, *Le T.N.P. de Jean Vilar* (Paris: Union Générale d'Editions, 1971).

— R.J.N.

THE THIRD REPUBLIC

The Third Republic of France was created in the wake of the German defeat of France in the Franco-Prussian War of 1870–1871 and lasted until the German invasion of France in May–June 1940, less than a year after the outbreak of **World War II.** During its existence the Third Republic was rocked by various crises. In the 1890s the **Dreyfus Affair** divided the country; much of **World War I** was fought on French soil; and during the interwar years the **Stavisky Affair** and the election of the **Popular Front** government of **Léon Blum** created tensions in the country. Nevertheless, the republic managed to survive until the **Debacle** of 1940, thus becoming the longest-lasting French republic to date.

In the confusion that followed the Franco-Prussian War — which ended the Second Empire of Napoléon III, nephew of Napoleon Bonaparte — the various French political parties and factions discussed several possible governmental arrangements, including a Bonapartist empire and the restoration of an Orleanist pretender to the French throne. In the end, after lengthy negotiations, the choice was made to create a republic, and a new constitution was adopted in 1875.

Despite repeated political crises under the Third Republic, France had a sound economy that showed solid growth in the years prior to World War I. Owing to the stability of the franc from 1875 to 1914, France became a nation of savers, and as such it loaned money to nations around the world. The period was also one of technological progress and belief in the values of science, as reflected in the

Maurice Thorez speaking at a French Communist Party function, with portraits of Lenin and Marx in the background. This scene is from the 1936 political film *La Vie est à nous.*

huge World's Fairs organized in Paris in 1878, 1895, and 1900.

Although the Third Republic survived World War I intact, the conflict exacted a severe toll. France lost two million men in the war, and in 1921 it had a population of only thirty-nine million, just one million more than it had had in 1866. A period of inflation during and after the war, followed by the worldwide economic depression that began in 1930, only exacerbated the strained political life of the nation. Ultimately, these problems played a role in the death of the Third Republic.

Perhaps the chief weakness of the constitution under the Third Republic was its vesting of an excessive amount of power in the legislative branch. The legislature was elected by the people, and in turn it elected the prime minister, or premier, who usually emerged victorious as a result of trade-offs among the various parties and coalitions. Thus the Third Republic had no strong and independent executive officeholder

who could be held directly accountable to the people.

After the June 1940 armistice with Germany divided most of France into the **Free Zone** and the Occupied Zone, the French National Assembly dismantled the Third Republic and created the Etat Français (French State), commonly known as the **Vichy government** because of the location of its capital.

REFERENCES:

R. D. Anderson, *France 1870–1914: Politics and Society* (London: Routledge & Kegan Paul, 1977);

Alexander Sedgwick, *The Third Republic: 1870–1914* (New York: Crowell, 1968).

— D.O'C.

MAURICE THOREZ

The son and grandson of miners, Maurice Thorez (1900–1964) was an extremely influential political figure, who led the Parti Communiste Français (PCF), or **French Communist Party,** for roughly three decades, keeping it close to the policies dictated by Moscow.

Born in Noyelle-Godault in the department of Pas-de-Calais, Thorez joined the Section Française de l'Internationale Ouvrière, or SFIO (see **Socialist Party**), in 1919. In December 1920, when the French Communist Party splintered off from the SFIO, Thorez followed and rose swiftly through the party hierarchy, becoming secretary-general, the highest-ranking party official, in 1930. Throughout the 1930s he closely followed the Stalinist party line, supporting the **Popular Front** government of **Léon Blum** in 1936.

After the Soviet–German nonaggression pact of 1939, the French government outlawed the PCF, forcing it underground. As proof of his loyalty to Moscow, Thorez deserted from the army in October. He continued to direct the PCF from Moscow, where he spent **World War II** as a guest of Nikita Khrushchev. The vast majority of the French considered his conduct to be less than patriotic. He was allowed to return to France after the **Liberation** in 1944, at which time he resumed control of the PCF. He was active in party affairs for the rest of his life.

REFERENCE:

David Caute, *Communism and the French Intellectuals, 1914–1960* (New York: Macmillan, 1964).

— D.O'C.

JEAN TINGUELY

Though originally affiliated with **Nouveau Réalisme** (New Realism) and a close collaborator of **Yves Klein,** Jean Tinguely (1925–) drew closer through his career to the artistic circles jointly termed *Nouvelle Tendance* (New Tendency), including Groupe Zéro and **Groupe de recherche de l'art visuel,** or GRAV, finally venturing into the loosely defined area of kinetic sculpture.

Born in Fribourg, Switzerland, Tinguely was a rebel from childhood. In 1939 he was arrested attempting to sneak into Albania to help fight the Italian Fascists. The same year, after his father found him a job in a department store, he was fired because he ripped the time clock from the wall. Interested in the **Dada** collages of Kurt Schwitters, Tinguely studied art for a time at the Kunstgewerbeschule in Basel (1941–1945), but his attendance was irregular. During **World War II** he participated in an anarchist-led study group of French and other Europeans who had fled to Switzerland to escape the Nazis.

After the war Tinguely began to fuse his interest in speed and motion with a Schwitters-like fascination

with found objects, including rubbish. Tinguely stated that "life is movement. Everything transforms itself, everything modifies itself ceaselessly. . . ." To attempt to freeze that motion was a "mockery of the intensity of life." Moving to Paris in 1953, he began to experiment with his ideas. He teamed up with Klein in 1958 to mount an exhibition of what they called "pure speed and monochrome stability." Tinguely's whirring, clicking, and rattling mechanisms whirled several of Klein's characteristic blue monochromes about at dizzying but purposeless speed. By 1959 Tinguely's creations had evolved into his "meta-matics," robotlike constructions that produced their own paintings. "Free yourself," his advertisements read, "and create your own abstract paintings with Tinguely's 'meta-matics.' " (A prize of fifty thousand francs was offered for the best work produced by the machines.)

Tinguely's *Hommage à New-York* (1960), set up on the grounds of the Museum of Modern Art in New York City, took his art a step further: once set in motion, the "homage" roared, beat drums, caught fire, and self-destructed within a half-hour — the incarnation of what he termed "total anarchy and freedom." More self-destructive assemblages followed, under the series name *Etudes pour une fin du monde* (*Studies for an End of the World*). Some machines parodied the world of industrial production — his *Rotozoa I* (1965) has to be fed with its own product to keep it running.

In addition to his machine constructs, Tinguely is known for his environmental sculptures. *Tête* (*Head*), a collaboration with Niki de Saint-Phalle, was first conceived in 1969 and finally completed in Milly-la-Forêt in 1987. Measuring 22.5 meters in height, it combines architecture, sculpture, and Tinguely's machine works. He has also collaborated with Saint-Phalle on gigantic, toylike sculptural groups and buildings, including the **Igor Stravinsky** Fountain constructed adjacent to the **Centre Pompidou** in Paris (1982–1983) and the fantasy buildings of the Tarot Garden in Garavicchio, Italy (1985–1986).

REFERENCES:

Pontus Hulten, *Jean Tinguely: A Magic Stronger Than Death* (New York: Abbeville Press, 1987);

Calvin Tomkins, *The Bride and the Bachelors: Five Masters of the Avant-Garde,* expanded edition (New York: Viking, 1965);

Daniel Wheeler, *Art Since Mid-Century: 1945 to the Present* (Englewood Cliffs, N.J.: Prentice Hall, 1991).

— J.H.

TINTIN

A popular comic strip drawn by Belgian cartoonist Georges Remi (1907–1983) under the pseudonym Hergé, *Tintin* was first published in the magazine *Petit*

Vingtième in 1929. The strip chronicles the adventures of the young reporter Tintin and his faithful dog Milou, who travel to foreign lands, help others, and unravel mysteries. Characters who appear frequently include Tintin's alcoholic companion Captain Haddock, the incompetent detectives Dupond and Dupont, and the absentminded inventor Professor Tournesol. *Tintin* was collected in twenty-three books over several decades. It is still popular, has been translated into many languages, and has generated an industry of T-shirts, figurines, and other licensed merchandise.

REFERENCES:

Jean-Marie Apostolidès, *Les Métamorphoses de Tintin* (Paris: Seghers, 1984);

Apostolidès, "Tintin and the Family Romance," *Children's Literature,* 13 (1985): 94–108;

Numa Sadoul, *Tintin et moi: Entretiens avec Hergé* (Paris: Casterman, 1975).

—K.E.B.

TZVETAN TODOROV

Tzvetan Todorov (1939–   ) played an important role in the development of narratology, or the poetics of narrative, especially because of his knowledge of the critics known as the Russian Formalists. Todorov's narratological project has had a lasting impact on critics such as Claude Bremond, **Gérard Genette,** Philippe Hamon, and Gerald Prince. Todorov studied under **Roland Barthes** and has taught at the **Centre National de la Recherche Scientifique** since 1968.

A Bulgarian by birth, Todorov writes in French and has lived in Paris for most of his career. He provided French literary critics with an entry into Russian Formalism when he translated works of the Formalists in his *Théorie de la littérature* (1965; Theory of Literature). Established forty years earlier but then unknown in France, Russian Formalism explored the internal order of the text and its linguistic elements. This approach immediately provided the French **structuralist** critics with a useful model for related projects. Another work in which Todorov presented Russian thought to the French-speaking world is *Mikhail Bakhtine: Le principe dialogique* (1981; translated as *Mikhail Bakhtin: The Dialogical Principle*).

Todorov elaborated his own poetics in the seminal work *Poétique* (1973; translated as *Introduction to Poetics*). According to him poetics seeks to establish "the general laws which govern the functioning of literature" by concentrating on the verbal structures present in the text. Influenced in his study of narratology by the work in linguistics of the Prague School, a circle of scholars that began in 1926 around the Rus-

sian Formalist Roman Jakobson, Todorov asserted that narratology consists of a universal grammar whose laws govern the structure of all stories, so that — as he writes in *Poétique de la prose* (1971; translated as *Poetics of Prose*) — "if the author could not quite understand what he was writing, the tale itself knew all along." In this universal grammar the plot of every story is structured around a series of transformations that result in a final equilibrium.

Todorov's work in the 1960s and 1970s included several general studies of narratology. He also described the narratological rules of particular works, as in his *Grammaire du "Décaméron"* (1969; Grammar of the Decameron). His belief that a literary genre has its own internal rules, creating a particular "horizon of expectations" for readers, led to his well-known *Introduction à la littérature fantastique* (1970; translated as *The Fantastic: A Structural Approach to a Literary Genre*).

During the 1980s Todorov took a comprehensive look at twentieth-century culture and history. His *Critique de la critique* (1984; translated as *Literature and Its Theorists: A Personal View of Twentieth-Century Criticism*) is an appraisal of the achievements and limitations of literary criticism. *La Conquête de l'Amérique: La question de l'autre* (1982; translated as *The Conquest of America: The Question of the Other*) and *Nous et les autres: Réflexions françaises sur la diversité humaine* (1989; translated as *On Human Diversity: Nationalism, Racism, and Exoticism in French Thought*) treat questions of colonialism and cultural perspectives.

REFERENCES:

Roland A. Champagne, *French Structuralism* (Boston: Twayne, 1990);

Victor Erlich, *Russian Formalism: History, Doctrine,* third edition (New Haven: Yale University Press, 1981).

—K.E.B.

MICHEL TOURNIER

Michel Tournier (1924–   ) is one of the major fiction writers of his generation in France. He is a member of the **Goncourt Academy** and has won such prestigious prizes as the Grand Prix du Roman de l'Académie Française and the Prix Goncourt.

Although Tournier was slightly too young to serve in **World War II,** he observed the **Occupation** firsthand while living in a suburb of Paris with his family, who respected German culture while feeling contempt for the Nazis. After the war he spent four years studying philosophy in Germany (1946–1950), adding to the acquaintance with German language and culture

Michel Tournier (Jerry Bauer)

he had acquired from his parents. After returning to Paris and failing the *agrégation* examination in philosophy, he abandoned the prospect of a university career and turned to editing, translating, and radio and television work before his writing career was solidly established.

Eschewing the aestheticism of the experiments of the **Nouveau Roman** (New Novel) writers, especially the rejection of narrative conventions such as plot and mimesis illustrated in works by **Alain Robbe-Grillet** and other New Novelists, Tournier writes stories recognizable as such. His topics, however, are not those of the conventional psychological novel or the novel of manners as practiced by writers since the seventeenth century and by modern authors as various as **Marcel Proust, Raymond Radiguet,** and **Françoise Sagan.** Tournier's underlying concern is to disturb, to be subversive. His books, often featuring bizarre characters and events, are perhaps better described as fables than as novels. In much of his writing he consciously makes use of myths and legends, notably the Cain and Abel story.

Tournier attracted widespread critical attention with his first novel, *Vendredi, ou les limbes du*

Pacifique (1967; translated as *Friday, or The Other Island*), a retelling of Daniel Defoe's *Robinson Crusoe.* His second, *Le Roi des aulnes* (1970; translated as *The Erlking* and *The Ogre*), is a disturbing novel whose self-important protagonist, Abel Tiffauges, is attracted to the Nazis and has a disquieting passion for carrying children on his shoulders. He ends up collaborating with the Nazis in Germany. Tournier's defenders have argued that the book condemns Abel's self-deception and blindness, but critics have labeled it as neo-Nazi.

Tournier's other novels include *Les Météores* (1975; translated as *Gemini*), which also deals with strange behavior, in this case the story of twin brothers and the perfect symbiotic relationship that one would like to cultivate with the other; *Gaspard, Melchior et Balthazar* (1980; translated as *The Four Wise Men*), based on the biblical story and legends of a fourth wise man who missed the Nativity; and *La Goutte d'or* (1985; translated as *The Golden Droplet*), about a North African boy's odyssey in France. Tournier has also published *Le Vent Paraclet* (1977; The Holy Spirit), an autobiographical work, and *Le Coq de bruyère* (1978; translated as *The Fetishist and Other Stories*), a collection of stories and a play.

REFERENCES:

William Cloonan, *Michel Tournier* (Boston: Twayne, 1985);

Colin Davis, *Michel Tournier: Philosophy and Fiction* (Oxford: Clarendon Press, 1988);

Susan Petit, *Michel Tournier's Metaphysical Fictions* (Amsterdam & Philadelphia: John Benjamins, 1991).

— C.S.B.

TRADITION DE QUALITÉ

The term *tradition de qualité* refers to French movies made between the early 1930s and 1960 in which a well-crafted screenplay based on a literary work is the heart of the film. The reputation of these films has suffered since the **Nouvelle Vague** (New Wave) critics and directors made them an object of attack.

François Truffaut spearheaded the attack on the tradition de qualité in "Une Certaine Tendance du cinéma français" (translated as "A Certain Tendency of the French Cinema"), published in the January 1954 issue of Cahiers du Cinéma. Truffaut and other Nouvelle Vague critics supported the auteur theory, which held that the director, not the screenwriter, should be the true author of a film, suffusing it with his or her own vision. Although films in the tradition may be elegantly written, they thought, as films they tended to be stilted, pretentious, and even condescending. Truffaut lashed out against older directors such as

Claude Autant-Lara, René Clément, and Jean Delannoy, claiming that their films and others in the *tradition de qualité* relied too heavily on dialogue and paid insufficient attention to the visual aspect of film. In contrast the Nouvelle Vague directors began their careers by making visually idiosyncratic films that were often inspired by popular fiction rather than "literature" and by drawing on less elegant models such as **film noir** and Hollywood B-pictures made between the two world wars. Critics and film historians have recently begun to rescue some films in the *tradition de qualité* from the neglect they suffered in the wake of the Nouvelle Vague.

REFERENCES:

Robert Sklar, *Film: An International History of the Medium* (New York: Abrams, 1993);

François Truffaut, "A Certain Tendency of the French Cinema," in *Movies and Methods: An Anthology,* edited by Bill Nichols (Berkeley & Los Angeles: University of California Press, 1976), pp. 224–237.

— T.C.

Charles Trenet, 1939

THE TREATY OF VERSAILLES

After **World War I** came to an end with the armistice of 11 November 1918, the Allies met at the Paris peace conference to consider the political shape of Europe. Their agreements were embodied in several treaties, including one signed in Versailles on 28 June 1919 — negotiated by French premier Georges Clemenceau, U.S. president Woodrow Wilson, British prime minister David Lloyd George, and Italian premier Vittorio Emanuele Orlando.

Having suffered enormous human losses and the destruction of much of its countryside, France wanted not only to punish Germany but to ensure that it would remain militarily weak. In the Treaty of Versailles Germany was obliged to acknowledge its guilt for the war and was assessed heavy reparations.

Other provisions of the Treaty of Versailles included the return to France of Alsace and Lorraine, ceded to Germany in the Franco-Prussian War (1870–1871), the division of German colonies among the Allies, and the establishment of the League of Nations. Because it opposed American participation in the League of Nations, the U.S. Congress refused to ratify the treaty.

Stripped of their colonies and forced to begin burdensome payments that strained their economy, the Germans soon rebelled against the provisions of the treaty and demanded revisions. The reparations were lifted in 1923, but the other terms remained until most were defied by Adolf Hitler in 1935. The harshness of the treaty's

terms is widely considered one of the seeds of **World War II.**

REFERENCE:

Sally Marks, *The Illusion of Peace: International Relations in Europe, 1919–1933* (New York: St. Martin's Press, 1976).

— D.O'C.

CHARLES TRENET

One of the most popular singers in France during the 1930s, Charles Trenet (1913–) was the author or interpreter of more than five hundred songs. After he appeared in the movie *La Route enchantée* (1938; The Enchanted Route), sales of sheet music and recordings of his songs skyrocketed. He remained a popular performer into the 1970s.

Trenet's youthful gaiety as a singer led to his nickname "Le Fou chantant" (The Singing Fool), a name borrowed from an Al Jolson character. Many of Trenet's songs, including "Fleur bleue" (1937; Blue Flower), display tenderness; others are marked by

Louis Aragon and his wife, Elsa Triolet, circa 1945 (IZIS)

sparkling humor, such as "Je chante" (1937; I Sing), which was also the title of one of several films in which he appeared in the late 1930s. Many of his songs became well known. "La Mer" (1945; The Sea), with its haunting rhythm and his precise intonation, captivated a worldwide audience. Translated into several languages, it was as popular in Asia, where it became the signature tune of Radio Tokyo, as in the West.

REFERENCE:

Geneviève Beauvallet, *Trenet* (Paris: Bréa, 1983).

— J.P.McN.

ELSA TRIOLET

Elsa Triolet (1896–1970) is known today chiefly as the wife of **Louis Aragon** and the inspiration of his love poems. They were one of the best-known literary couples of their generation. Yet she was also a novelist in her own right and would have a place in literary history even if she did not share Aragon's fame.

In Russia, where she was born Elsa Kagan, she was associated with literary figures; poet Vladimir Mayakovsky was her friend and her sister's lover, and she

knew Roman Jakobson and Viktor Shklovsky. In 1918 she married a Frenchman, André Triolet, from whom she was soon divorced. After some travels and the publication of three novels in Russian, she settled in Paris, met Aragon in 1928, and married him in 1939. The rumor that she was a Soviet agent in France has never been entirely put to rest. She did not join the **French Communist Party,** but she never denounced Soviet socialism, and, like her husband, she remained staunchly on the Left.

Her first French novel, *Bonsoir Thérèse* (Good Evening, Theresa), appeared in 1938, and during the German **Occupation** of France in **World War II** Triolet continued publishing for a time. *Le Cheval blanc* (1943; translated as *The White Charger*) is set during the interwar and war years. After she and Aragon had to go underground because of the **Resistance** activity in which they were involved, she published a story about the Resistance, *Les Amants d'Avignon* (1943; The Lovers of Avignon), under the pseudonym Laurent Daniel. It was collected in her 1945 book, *Le Premier Accroc coûte deux cents francs* (translated as *A Fine of 200 Francs*), which received the Prix Goncourt. The war is also the setting for *L'Inspecteur des ruines* (1948; translated as *The Inspector of Ruins*), a novel about a Frenchman who escapes from a concentration camp. During the war Trio-

François Truffaut on the set of *Les Quatre Cent Coups* (*The 400 Blows*), 1959

let participated in the founding of *Les Lettres Françaises,* a major Resistance publication, and was also associated with the leftist magazine *Europe.*

Her novels, though uneven, are noteworthy for their characterizations and their treatment of politics. They were republished with her husband's in *Œuvres romanesques croisées d'Elsa Triolet et Aragon* (1964–1974; Joint Fiction of Elsa Triolet and Aragon). Because of their longevity, his great productivity, and their unswerving commitment to leftist causes, Triolet and Aragon came to be a sort of literary and cultural monument of their own, an image of joint political commitment and a lifetime love affair.

REFERENCES:

Max Adereth, "French Resistance Literature: The Example of Elsa Triolet and Louis Aragon," in *Literature and War,* edited by David Bevan (Amsterdam: Rodopi, 1990), pp. 123–134;

Konrad Bieber, "Ups and Downs in Elsa Triolet's Prose," *Yale French Studies,* no. 27 (1961): 81–85.

—C.S.B.

HENRI TROYAT

The author of many best-selling novels, Henri Troyat (born Lev Tarassov in 1911) left his native Russia when his family immigrated to France after the 1917 revolution. His first novel, *Faux jour* (1934; False Light), won the Prix Populiste, and his third, *L'Araigne* (1938; The Spider), was awarded the Prix Goncourt. Troyat has proved a prolific author, and his many works, including six fiction cycles, have enjoyed enormous popular success. Writing in the tradition of the major nineteenth-century French and Russian novelists, such as Honoré de Balzac, Emile Zola, and Leo Tolstoy, Troyat presents sweeping historical narratives with large casts of characters. One of his cycles, the trilogy *Tant que la terre durera* (1947–1950; As Long as Earth Shall Last), takes its collective title from that of the first volume, translated as *My Father's House.* Another cycle, the five-volume *Les Semailles et les moissons* (1953–1958; The Seed and the Fruit), similarly takes its title from volume one (1953; translated as *Amelia in Love*); it also includes *Amélie* (1955; translated as *Amélie and Pierre*) and *La Rencontre* (1958; translated as *The Encounter*).

Troyat has also published travel studies and biographies of Russian figures, such as Tolstoy, Catherine the Great, Fyodor Dostoyevsky, and Aleksandr Pushkin. Although he was elected to the Académie Française in 1959, Troyat is valued more as a storyteller than as a stylist.

REFERENCE:

Nicholas Hewitt, *Henri Troyat* (Boston: Twayne, 1984).

— C.S.B.

FRANÇOIS TRUFFAUT

François Truffaut (1932–1984) was one of the most prominent directors to emerge from the **Nouvelle Vague** (New Wave), which revitalized French cinema in the late 1950s and early 1960s.

Truffaut's childhood in Paris was the basis for the miserable character portrayed in his first feature, *Les Quatre cent coups* (1959; *The 400 Blows*). He was virtually reared and protected by critic **André Bazin,** who once helped him pay debts incurred by the closing of a film club that Truffaut had founded on the **Left Bank** in 1949. Truffaut joined the French army in 1951 but deserted when his division was departing for Indochina (see **Indochinese War**). Dishonorably discharged, he took on odd film jobs before starting to write for Bazin's *Cahiers du Cinéma* and *Arts* in 1953. Truffaut's well-known polemical article "Une Certaine Tendance du cinéma français" (translated as "A Certain Tendency of the French Cinema"), which appeared in *Cahiers du Cinéma* in January 1954, furnished much of the doctrine of the Nouvelle Vague. Attacking the **tradition de qualité** for its focus on the screenplay rather than on visual elements, he instead advocated an auteur theory in which the film, though a collaborative effort, should embody the vision of the director. He pointed to certain Hollywood directors and to filmmakers such as **Jean Renoir** and **Robert Bresson** as examples of this view.

During the 1950s Truffaut worked with **Jacques Rivette** and Roberto Rossellini and directed three short films before the successful release of *Les Quatre cent coups*. He also collaborated with **Jean-Luc Godard** on the screenplay for Godard's first feature, *A bout de souffle* (1959; *Breathless*); both movies are seminal Nouvelle Vague works that led to the popularity of the movement. Truffaut followed these accomplishments with his two other masterpieces, the tragicomic thriller *Tirez sur le pianiste* (1960; *Shoot the Piano Player*) and *Jules et Jim* (1961; *Jules and Jim*), about a romantic triangle beginning before **World War I.** Though different in style, these three features are replete with allusions to the films and literary works that exercised a formative influence on Truffaut.

Truffaut directed nineteen more features before his death in 1984. They include three more films and a segment of another featuring Antoine Doinel, the autobiographical protagonist of *Les Quatre cent coups,* played by **Jean-Pierre Léaud;** the Academy Award–winning *La Nuit américaine* (1973; *Day for Night*), a film about filmmaking in which he played a director; *L'Homme qui aimait les femmes* (1977; *The Man Who Loved Women*); and *Le Dernier Métro* (1980; *The Last Metro*). He also played a scientist in Steven Spielberg's *Close Encounters of the Third Kind* (1977).

In addition to writing or collaborating on all his screenplays, Truffaut wrote much about cinema beyond his early critical work. His conversations with Alfred Hitchcock were published as *Hitchcock/Truffaut* (1966, revised 1985; translated as *Hitchcock*), his reviews were collected in *Les Films de ma vie* (1975; translated as *The Films of My Life*), and his voluminous correspondence was gathered in *François Truffaut Correspondance* (1990; translated as *François Truffaut: Letters*).

REFERENCES:

Don Allen, *François Truffaut* (London: Secker & Warburg, 1974);

Roy Armes, *French Cinema Since 1946. 2: The Personal Style* (London: Zwemmer & Barnes, 1970);

Jean Collet, *Le Cinéma de François Truffaut* (Paris: Lherminier, 1977);

Annette Insdorf, *François Truffaut* (Boston: Twayne, 1978);

T. Jefferson Kline, *Screening the Text: Intertextuality in New Wave French Cinema* (Baltimore: Johns Hopkins University Press, 1992), pp. 7–23;

James Monaco, *The New Wave* (New York: Oxford University Press, 1976).

—T.C.

TRISTAN TZARA

Tristan Tzara (1896–1963) was one of the founders of **Dada** and is usually considered its leader. Born Samuel Rosenstock in Romania, he settled in Zurich. He published one of the first Dada works, *La Première Aventure céleste de M. Antipyrine* (1916; The First Celestial Adventure of M. Antipyrine), and the important Dada manifestos (1916–1920) he collected in *Sept manifestes Dada* (1924; translated as *Seven Dada Manifestoes*), as well as experimental poetry, including *Vingt-cinq poèmes* (1918; Twenty-Five Poems). After moving to Paris in 1919, he exercised considerable influence among the Dadaists who gathered there, including for a brief time **André Breton,** who denounced Tzara in February 1922 and went on to found the **Surrealist** movement. During the 1930s Tzara produced several important prose poems and other works, including *L'Homme approximatif* (1930; translated as *Approximate Man*

377

and Other Writings), *L'Antitête* (1933; The Anti-Head), and *Midis gagnés* (1939; Noons Gained).

Tzara's aesthetic — like that of other Dadaists and later the Surrealists — was a radical rejection of literary precedents and standards and of Western culture, which he considered responsible for the cataclysm of **World War I.** Attacking rational language as an instrument of oppression, he sought to revitalize poetry through an explosive, anarchic language that would break through the straitjacket of bourgeois thought. Some of his early poetry is deliberately nonsensical, for he believed that sounds must be dissociated from the meanings to which they had been enslaved. "Thought is done in the mouth," he wrote, thereby giving a privileged place to unpremeditated verbalism as opposed to reflection and logic. His later work is characterized by a more controlled, though powerful, lyricism.

REFERENCES:

Mary Ann Caws, *The Poetry of Dada and Surrealism* (Princeton: Princeton University Press, 1970);

Robert Motherwell, *The Dada Painters and Poets: An Anthology,* second edition (Boston: G. K. Hall, 1981);

E. Peterson, *Tristan Tzara: Dada and Surrational Theorist* (New Brunswick, N.J.: Rutgers University Press, 1971).

— C.S.B.

U

UNANIMISM

Unanimism was an early-twentieth-century literary movement founded by **Jules Romains** (the writer most frequently identified with the movement), **Georges Duhamel, Charles Vildrac,** and others. These same young writers, along with painter **Albert Gleizes,** were associated with L'Abbaye, an artists' community created in 1906 in Créteil, near Paris. They are sometimes referred to as the Groupe de l'Abbaye, and Unanimism and the Abbaye experiment overlap considerably. The purpose of the community was to provide an escape from the dominant social order, and the group planned to support itself by printing books and literally cultivating their garden.

The principal concern of the Unanimists was with the relationship between the individual and society. Under the influence of Walt Whitman (whose work had been translated into French late in the nineteenth century), **Henri Bergson,** and Emile Durkheim and other sociologists, the Unanimists eschewed the idea of the representative individual human being and looked instead to collectivities as the source and expression of human experience, with the individual soul being part of a collective consciousness that both sums up and transcends separate minds. Romains's poems in *La Vie unanime* (1908; The Unanimist Life) and his novel *Mort de quelqu'un* (1911; translated as *The Death of a Nobody*) are among the best illustrations of this outlook, which has important implications for and connections with Urbanism, a major literary and social movement inherited from the nineteenth century.

The Unanimists, most of whom were poets, were also interested in versification. Discarding the artifices of Symbolist rhetoric and traditional prosody, they championed verse without rhymes or other formal markers, claiming that it was more suitable to the expression of modern experience.

Residents of the Abbaye de Créteil, the Unanimist communal living experiment, in 1907: (front row) Charles Vildrac, René Arcos, Albert Gleizes, Henri-Martin Barzun, Alexander Mercereau; (back row) Georges Duhamel, Berthold Mahn, Jacques d'Otémar

REFERENCES:

P. J. Norrish, "Unanimist Elements in the Works of Durkheim and Verhaeren," *French Studies,* 11 (1957): 38–49;

Ben F. Stoltzfus, "Unanimism Revisited," *Modern Language Quarterly,* 21 (1960): 239–245;

Leland Thielemann, "The Problem of Unity and Individualism in Romains' Social Philosophy," *Modern Language Quarterly,* 2 (1941): 249–262.

— C.S.B.

UNION DES DÉMOCRATES POUR LA RÉPUBLIQUE

The Union des Démocrates pour la République (Union of Democrats for the Republic), or UDR, is one of the labels applied to followers of **Charles de Gaulle.** The name came to be widely used in the campaigning preceding the referendum of 1969. It replaced the names of earlier Gaullist formations, such as Union pour la Nouvelle République (Union for the New Republic), or UNR. In 1976 the label UDR was taken over by one faction of Gaullists, led by Valéry Giscard d'Estaing, while other Gaullists, under the leadership of Jacques Chirac, assumed the label of **Rassemblement pour la République** (Assembly for the Republic), or RPR. Two years later the UDR was absorbed by the Union pour la Démocratie Française (UDF) as an anti-Gaullist, moderate-right party.

REFERENCES:

J. R. Frears, *Political Parties and Elections in the French Fifth Republic* (New York: St. Martin's Press, 1977);

Frank Lee Wilson, *French Political Parties Under the Fifth Republic* (New York: Praeger, 1982);

Vincent Wright, *The Government and Politics of France,* third edition (New York: Holmes & Meier, 1989).

—D.O'C.

Maurice Utrillo in the private chapel at his home in Le Vesinet

MAURICE UTRILLO

Painter Maurice Utrillo (1883–1955) was the illegitimate son of artist **Suzanne Valadon.** Although painter-journalist Miguel Utrillo signed papers accepting paternity in 1891, there is no evidence that he acted out of anything more than compassion for mother and child.

Utrillo left school at age sixteen and tried out at a series of jobs, failing badly at all of them. By eighteen he was an alcoholic, and for much of his life he suffered from alcohol and drug addiction. He was frequently arrested for public intoxication and was committed more than once to clinics and sanatoriums. Around 1902 Valadon suggested painting to her son as a means of therapy. He quickly became known for his depictions of the streets of **Montmartre.** Although they are reminiscent of Impressionist works in their loose brush strokes and apparent spontaneity, most of his scenes were derived from postcards (in part because street children tended to throw stones at him).

Around 1910 Utrillo entered his so-called white period, in which the palette gradually brightened and large patches of white pigment dominated the canvas. Over the next few years his work lost its Impressionist veneer; brush strokes became smaller, while the surfaces of the paintings are built up with plaster and glue to give them something of the texture of the scene depicted. In 1915–1919 he shifted his focus from panoramic street scenes to tighter views of single buildings or small clusters of structures. After 1920 the muted shades of his paintings were replaced by bolder colors, in street scenes filled with bustling people.

Unlike the works of Vincent van Gogh, Utrillo's careful, precise canvases give no sense of his tumultuous and often painful life. Writing that "for the indiscriminating, all artists are creatures with long hair, baroque ideas, and eccentric life styles. We are bizarre extraterrestrials, outlaws . . . ," he was well aware that his canvases were accepted in bourgeois homes where he himself would be turned away.

REFERENCES:

Jerrold Siegel, *Bohemian Paris: Culture, Politics, and the Boundaries of Bourgeois Life, 1830–1930* (New York: Viking, 1986);

Jeanine Warnod, *Maurice Utrillo,* translated by Ina Lee Selden (New York: Crown, 1983);

Alfred Werner, *Maurice Utrillo* (New York: Abrams, 1981).

—J.H.

V

ROGER VADIM

Born Roger Vadim Plémiannikov in Paris, Roger Vadim (1928–) is perhaps best known as the film director who has molded the careers of (and, in a few cases, married) some of the world's most beautiful women. Sexuality is a recurring motif of his movies, which critics have often characterized as lewd and dramatically unimpressive. He experienced great commercial success in the period 1956–1963, but by the mid 1960s his work had declined considerably in popularity.

Vadim began his career as an actor on the Paris stage. In 1949 he became assistant to director Marc Allégret, who directed **Brigitte Bardot** in her early pictures. Three years later Vadim and Bardot were married. In his first full-length film, *Et Dieu créa la femme* (1956; *And God Created Woman*), Vadim featured Bardot in a role that won her worldwide fame. During the shooting of the picture, however, she fell in love with her costar, Jean-Louis Trintignant. Vadim and Bardot were divorced the following year.

In 1958 Vadim married another woman who would later become one of his leading stars, Danish actress Annette Stroyberg. Her first role in a Vadim film was that of Madame de Tourvel in the controversial *Les Liaisons dangereuses* (1959), which set Pierre Choderlos de Laclos's well-known eighteenth-century erotic novel in the mid twentieth century. The marriage failed. Both Vadim and his wife were involved in extramarital affairs, Vadim with the young actress **Catherine Deneuve.**

Stroyberg and Vadim were divorced in 1963, the same year he met his third wife, American actress Jane Fonda. Vadim's producers had chosen her to star in a remake of **Jean Anouilh**'s *La Ronde* (1964; *Circle of Love*). They were married in 1965, and Fonda was featured in other Vadim films, including *La Curée* (1966;

The Game Is Over) and *Barbarella* (1968). They were divorced in 1973. Other Vadim films include *Sait-on jamais?* (1957; *No Sun in Venice*); *Le Repos du guerrier* (1962; *Love on a Pillow*), based on a novel by **Christiane Rochefort;** *Château en Suède* (1963; *Naughty, Nutty Chateau*), from the play by **Françoise Sagan;** and *Une Femme fidèle* (1976; *When a Woman in Love...*).

REFERENCE:

Roger Vadim, *Memoirs of the Devil*, translated by Peter Beglan (New York: Harcourt Brace Jovanovich, 1977).

—M.G.

ROGER VAILLAND

At its best the work of novelist and essayist Roger Vailland (1907–1965) is well crafted and thoughtful, portraying the turbulent times in which he lived. He was particularly adept at dialogue. Yet, taken as a whole, his writings reveal him to have been a talented but inconsistent writer with a taste for rebellion and libertinage.

As a student in Paris during the 1920s, Vailland associated with the fringe **Surrealist** group that published the magazine *Grand Jeu,* which was challenged in 1929 by **André Breton** for lack of political integrity. During the 1930s Vailland became increasingly dependent on drugs; later he underwent detoxification more than once. His rebellious side remained with him: his fiction often reflects disorderly behavior, a feature that has endeared him to the many French readers who appreciate iconoclasm.

During the German **Occupation** of France in **World War II,** Vailland became involved with the **Resistance** movement, perhaps mainly for the adventure. His personal experiences during this period were the

REFERENCES:

J. E. Flower, *Literature and the Left in France* (London: Macmillan, 1983);

Flower, *Roger Vailland: The Man and His Masks* (London: Hodder & Stoughton, 1975).

— C.S.B.

Roger Vailland, 1963, as he was writing *La Truite* (Garanger)

basis for his first novel, *Drôle de jeu* (1945; translated as *Playing with Fire* and *Playing for Keeps*). He became interested in Communism during the war and joined the **French Communist Party** as an enthusiastic Stalinist in 1952, but he left the party four years later.

After the war Vailland resumed his work as a journalist, as well as his drug use, and continued his literary career with novels such as *Les Mauvais Coups* (1948; translated as *Turn of the Wheel*) and *La Fête* (1960; translated as *The Sovereigns* and as *Fête*) and nonfiction books such as *Le Surréalisme contre la Révolution* (1948; Surrealism against the Revolution). Some of his novels deal with the failings of French society, while others illustrate social realism, both militant and propagandistic. Another major interest in his fiction is eroticism and the psychology of the libertine. His seventh novel — *La Loi* (1957; translated as *The Law*), set in southern Italy — was awarded the Prix Goncourt. He also co-authored the screenplay for *Les Liaisons dangereuses 1960* (1959; translated as *Roger Vadim's "Les Liaisons dangereuses"*).

SUZANNE VALADON

Artist Marie Clémentine Valadon (1867–1938) was the illegitimate daughter of a seamstress; she later changed her name to Suzanne because she thought it sounded more interesting than Marie. Her early years were spent at a variety of unsuccessful trades, including that of a trapeze artist in a circus. After injuring her back in a fall, she became an artist's model. She modeled for Pierre Puvis de Chavannes, Auguste Renoir, and Henri de Toulouse-Lautrec — in return not only for money but also for lessons in drawing and painting. Both Toulouse-Lautrec and Edgar Degas encouraged her to take up painting full time.

While opportunities for most nineteenth-century women were restricted, Valadon had the freedom that came with her lack of social standing. One way in which she exercised this freedom was painting the female nude, an occupation that had, ironically, become the exclusive preserve of male artists, just as the paintings themselves were viewed only by men. An intricate system of norms and codings had grown up to reinforce ideas of male power and female subordination. For example, the viewer most often looked down on the nude woman, who met his gaze with one of acquiescence or, more often, was asleep or otherwise unaware of being the object of stares. Those works that broke with or satirized these norms — including Edouard Manet's *Olympia* (1863) — were the subject of savage attack. Valadon used her own experiences to reshape and redefine the female nude. Her nudes are sometimes awkward and tense. While the traditional female nude seems unconscious of her nudity, the figure in *La Nue couchée* (Valadon's undated *Reclining Nude*) is aware of hers; she pulls herself inward, trying to cover herself, one leg crossing the other, her arm reaching across her body to shield her breasts. Other nude figures by Valadon focus on self-doubt and regret. Her 1921 canvas of a woman looking at herself in her mirror negates a standardized linkage between woman and mirror as symbols of vanity; Valadon's nude is pensive and troubled by what she sees in the mirror.

Valadon's male nudes, in contrast, are more traditional. Most are of her illegitimate son, future painter **Maurice Utrillo,** as a small child. *The Casting of the Net* (1914) shows her new husband, André Utter,

Suzanne Valadon in the mid 1930s

in three poses, impossibly muscular and angular, with strategically placed bits of net to ensure that his genitals are covered. Her *Adam et Eve* (1909) breaks from its classical model by making Adam and Eve grasp the fatal fruit simultaneously; again, Eve is frontally nude while Adam is covered by a bit of foliage.

REFERENCES:

Rosemary Betterton, "How Do Women Look? The Female Nude in the Work of Suzanne Valadon," in *Looking On: Images of Femininity in the Visual Arts and Media,* edited by Betterton (London: Thames & Hudson, 1990);

Therese Diamand Rosinsky, *Suzanne Valadon* (New York: Universe, 1994);

Jeanine Warnod, *Suzanne Valadon* (New York: Crown, 1981).

—J.H.

PAUL VALÉRY

Paul Valéry (1871–1945), whom the philosopher **Alain** called "Our Lucretius," is generally held to be the greatest poet of twentieth-century France, although partisans of **Guillaume Apollinaire** and **Paul Claudel** might claim the title for one of them. American poet James Dickey placed Valéry with T. S. Eliot, Rainer Maria Rilke, and William Butler Yeats in the pantheon of four great modern poets. Another American poet, Yvor Winters, called Valéry's "Le Cimetière marin" (translated as "The Graveyard by the Sea") and "Ebauche d'un serpent" (translated as "Silhouette of a Serpent") the two finest poems of the modern period. (Both poems were first collected in Valéry's *Charmes* [1922; translated].)

Valéry belongs to the post-Symbolist period, and throughout his work is visible the Symbolists' aesthetic of art for art's sake and exquisite craftsmanship — which he found in the work of Stéphane Mallarmé, who always remained his idol. (Valéry married a friend of Mallarmé's daughter.) There is nothing decadent about Valéry's work, however; indeed, he gave a classical form to the rather overbearing aestheticism and tardy Romanticism of the Symbolists at the same time that poets such as Apollinaire were carrying farther another potentiality of their predecessors, free verse and poetic experimentation. Valéry generally used the traditional alexandrine or other regular poetic forms and a refined, though sensual, diction. He polished his work in an effort to achieve poetic perfection, while realizing that perfection was unattainable. The blending of intellect and appeal to the senses is found in his shortest lyrics as well as his longer poems.

The influence of southern France, where Valéry was born and raised, is perceptible in such poems as "Le Cimetière marin" and, more generally, in his interest in classical Greek literature and architecture. His concern for the operations of the mind — that is, the mental, as opposed to the sentimental — is visible in his prose works, including *Introduction à la méthode de Léonard de Vinci* (1919; translated as *Introduction to the Method of Leonardo da Vinci*). At the outset of his career this concern led him to renounce poetry, after brilliant beginnings in the 1890s, when he published a few poems in little magazines. Not until 1912, when his friends **André Gide** and **Gaston Gallimard** persuaded him to look again at his youthful work, did Valéry return to writing verse. In 1917 he published *La Jeune Parque* (The Young Fate), a poem of 512 alexandrines built around a classical motif and dealing with the dawning of love and the awakening to consciousness and the knowledge of mortality. In 1920 he collected his early work in *Album de vers anciens* (Album of Early Verse).

Valéry is one of the most Cartesian of modern writers. There is also some kinship between him and the phenomenologists. When, in his treatise on dance, "L'Ame et la danse" (1920; translated as *Dance and the*

Soul), he defines knowing as "not being what one is," he posits the radical separation between self and the world with which phenomenology attempts to deal, as does poetry (which Valéry called "a language in a language"), in its way, through language, a physiological phenomenon that attempts to reach pure idea.

Valéry's interest in the potential of the mind as well as the challenge of poetry is the source of his *Cahiers* (1957–1961; Notebooks) and many other works. He published a treatise on architecture in the form of a Platonic dialogue (*Eupalinos, ou l'architecte,* 1923; translated as *Eupalinos, or the Architect*) and a modernized version of the Faust legend, *Mon Faust* (1941; My Faust). In 1925 he was elected to the Académie Française. His poetry has attracted many Anglophone readers, and he has been well served by critics in Great Britain and the United States, as well as by such translators as Richard Wilbur, Howard Moss, John Finlay, Malcolm Cowley, Denise Folliot, and James R. Lawler.

REFERENCES:

Christine Crow, *Paul Valéry: Consciousness and Nature* (Cambridge: Cambridge University Press, 1972);

W. N. Ince, *The Poetic Theory of Paul Valéry — Inspiration and Technique* (Leicester: Leicester University Press, 1961);

James R. Lawler, *The Poet as Analyst: Essays on Paul Valéry* (Berkeley: University of California Press, 1974);

Agnes E. Mackay, *The Universal Self: A Study of Paul Valéry* (London: Routledge & Kegan Paul, 1961);

Walter Putnam, *Paul Valéry Revisited* (New York: Twayne, 1995);

Alastair W. Thomson, *Valéry* (Edinburgh & London: Oliver & Boyd, 1965).

— C.S.B.

FÉLIX VALLOTTON

Beginning in the 1890s French art was torn by a variety of debates. Commercial and print artists vied with those wedded to a traditional idea of "high art"; anarchist and socialist artists warred with those who believed art should be based on social and aesthetic hierarchies. The factions were fluid, and several artists wound up in seemingly contradictory categories. Félix Vallotton (1865–1925) bridged several: a vigorous anarchist, he nonetheless affiliated with the **Nabis**, most of whom were religious conservatives; a powerful graphic artist, he nevertheless exhibited in Joséphin ("Sâr") Péladan's Salons de la Rose+Croix, dedicated to furthering a mystical, otherworldly art.

Vallotton was born in Lausanne, Switzerland. At age eighteen he moved to Paris to study art at the Ecole des Beaux-Arts and the Académie Julien. He broke from his academic training in 1890, after seeing

Woodcut self-portrait by Félix Vallotton, 1891 (Art Institute of Chicago)

a major showing of Japanese woodcut prints, and began to produce his own woodcuts, which characteristically play off large black patches against areas of stark white. In *La Manifestation* (1893; *The Demonstration*), the bottom of the print is white and empty; as one looks up at the picture, isolated figures in black gradually converge into a mass of quarreling, fleeing figures. In *La Charge* (1893; *The Charge*) the upper picture is empty except for a few dazed or wounded figures sprawled on the pavement. The lower half is filled with a mass of police (a flood of black uniforms, broken up only by the faces of the policemen); two victims are being choked and beaten in the foreground, their white clothes standing out against the unbroken black of the police charge.

Vallotton's attachment to the causes of anarchism and political protest was demonstrated by his prints for *L'Assiette au Beurre,* which devoted an entire issue to his work in 1902, and the anarchist *Temps Nouveaux* (New Times). He contributed to a print collection honoring the revolutionary Paris Commune of 1871 and was a prominent supporter of Alfred Dreyfus in the **Dreyfus Affair** in the 1890s.

Vallotton's affiliations with these causes would scarcely stand out in his era had he not simultaneously participated in the Nabis and the Salons de la Rose+Croix. The Rose+Croix exhibits had been launched in the name of theocracy, Mary, and "our suzerain Jesus." Vallotton's attraction to both the Rose+Croix shows and the Nabis seems to have derived from his interest in art as idea and symbol, to be invoked by the artist rather than mirrored from nature. His closest ties within the Nabi circle were with **Pierre Bonnard** and **Edouard Vuillard**, rather than the mystics **Maurice Denis** and **Paul Sérusier**. He shared with Bonnard and other Nabi *intimistes* a fascination with interior spaces and daily life, though his interest focused on small dramas between women and men. His series *Intimités* (1897–1898), published in the *Revue Blanche,* detailed confrontations in love and marriage; some of them were later used to shape full-scale paintings, such as *Intimité: Intérieur avec amants et paravent* (1898; *Intimacy: Interior, with Lovers and Screen*), in which a man and woman embrace in the center of a crowded apartment. Unlike Bonnard and Vuillard, Vallotton showed little interest in light or textured patterns; his woodcut training is evident in the linear drawing and the carefully contained, muted colors.

After 1901 Vallotton's interests in print art dwindled, in favor of oil paintings (primarily nudes and landscapes), in a style fusing the academic style in which he was trained with the hard, clear line of his woodcuts.

REFERENCES:

John House and Mary Anne Stevens, eds., *Post-Impressionism: Cross-Currents in European Painting* (London: Royal Academy of Arts, 1979);

Ralph E. Shikes, *The Indignant Eye: The Artist as Social Critic* (Boston: Beacon, 1969);

Mary Anne Stevens, *The Graphic Work of Félix Vallotton, 1865–1925* (London: Arts Council of Great Britain, 1976).
                                                                            — J.H.

RAOUL VANEIGEM

Raoul Vaneigem (1931–) played an important role in the theoretical development of the **Situationist International.** His *Traité de savoir-vivre à l'usage des jeunes générations* (1967; translated as *The Revolution of Everyday Life*) served as a handbook for the radical youth in the 1960s. Stripped of their radical optimism, many of its central ideas are reflected in the writings of **Jean-François Lyotard.**

Vaneigem became a leader among the Situationists in 1961. While **Guy Debord** traced the history of the movement and examined the characteristics of the all-encompassing "society of the spectacle," Vaneigem examined the meaning and possibility of re-

volt. He told listeners at a Situationist conference in 1961 that they were "warriors between two worlds, one which we do not recognize, another which does not yet exist," adding, "We must precipitate the crash, hasten the end of the world...." In a phrase that would become central to his work, the tract added that the insurgents of the 1871 Paris Commune had become masters "of their own history, not so much on the level of 'governmental' politics as on the level of their everyday life."

Vaneigem's focus on both the repressive, repetitive character and the explosive possibilities of daily life was a central characteristic of the Situationists' platform and partly inherited from the writings of the dissident Marxist **Henri Lefebvre.** Vaneigem's *Traité de savoir-vivre à l'usage des jeunes générations* is dominated by the theme of the need to escape from the oppression of everyday life, emphasizing the infinite possibilities of daily resistance, such as daydreaming, love and desire, and sympathy for others. "Everyone seeks spontaneously to extend such brief moments of real life," and unsatisfied desire is the basis for revolt. Vaneigem compared modern men and women to animated cartoon characters who "rush madly over the edge of a cliff without seeing it; the power of their imagination keeps them suspended ... but as soon as they look down and see where they are, they fall." The society of the spectacle was becoming saturated, he claimed; "the eruption of everyday reality" would inevitably follow.

Vaneigem's writings were a major underpinning of the **May 1968** uprising, especially among students. Ironically, that same eruption isolated him personally from the rebel students and his own colleagues when he was accused of leaving on vacation just as the revolt gained strength. Rumors of friction between Vaneigem and the other Situationist leaders persisted. In 1970 he resigned from the movement, following a cryptic communique from other leaders warning that they would not cover for "retired thinkers" or "unemployed revolutionaries." Since then Vaneigem has continued to write (usually pseudonymously) about the history of **Surrealism,** the idea of a revolutionary general strike, and other topics — all to investigate the nature of revolt and human freedom.

REFERENCES:

Greil Marcus, *Lipstick Traces: A Secret History of the Twentieth Century* (Cambridge, Mass.: Harvard University Press, 1989);

Sadie Plant, *The Most Radical Gesture: The Situationist International in a Postmodern Age* (London & New York: Routledge, 1992);

Elisabeth Sussman, ed., *On the Passage of a Few People through a Rather Brief Moment in Time: The Situationist International, 1957–1972* (Cambridge, Mass.: MIT Press, 1989);

Raoul Vaneigem, *The Revolution of Everyday Life,* translated by Donald Nicholson-Smith (London: Left Bank Books, 1983).

—J.H.

CHARLES VANEL

Actor Charles Vanel (1892–1989) was often described as the grand old man of French cinema. He began his film career in 1912 and appeared in nearly two hundred pictures during a career that lasted some seventy-five years.

Among the most noteworthy silent films in which he performed are *L'Âtre* (1922; The Hearth); *Pêcheur d'Islande* (1924; An Iceland Fisherman), based on the 1866 novel by Pierre Loti; **René Clair**'s *La Proie du vent* (1927; Prey of the Wind); and Karl Grune's *Waterloo* (1929), in which he played Napoleon.

Vanel made an easy transition to sound films, no doubt owing to his fine voice, and appeared in many movies during the 1930s and 1940s. He received a prize for best actor at the **Cannes Film Festival** for his portrayal of **Yves Montand**'s cowardly partner in *Le Salaire de la peur* (1952; The Wages of Fear), directed by **Henri-Georges Clouzot.** Vanel worked for Alfred Hitchcock in *To Catch a Thief* (1955), for **Luis Buñuel** in *La Mort en ce jardin* (1956; *Gina*; *Evil Eden*; *Death in the Garden*), and for **Jean-Pierre Melville** in *L'Aîné des Ferchaux* (1962; *Magnet of Doom*). He continued appearing in motion pictures until his death in 1989.

REFERENCE:

G. Sellier, "Charles Vanel, un 'non-séducteur' du cinéma français," *Cinéma* (October 1983).

—W.L.

AGNÈS VARDA

Though her first feature film, *La Pointe Courte* (1955), predated the movement by a few years, director Agnès Varda (1928–) is closely identified with **Nouvelle Vague** (New Wave) filmmaking.

Born in Brussels, Varda was trained in literature and psychology at the Sorbonne and in art history at the Ecole du Louvre. Married to director **Jacques Demy,** she worked as a stage photographer for the **Avignon Festival** and for the **Théâtre National Populaire** in Paris before moving into cinema. She won the Prix Méliès for her second feature, *Cléo de 5 à 7* (1961; *Cleo from 5 to 7*), and the Prix Louis Delluc for her third, *Le Bonheur* (1966; *Happiness*).

In ninety minutes *Cléo de 5 à 7* chronicles two hours in a singer's life as she awaits a doctor's diagno-

sis of her cancer symptoms. While the physical time in the film almost replicates that of Cleo's life, the hurried, disjunctive editing matches Cleo's state of mind as she wanders about Paris. The contemporary reference to the **Algerian war** in *Cléo de 5 à 7* demonstrates Varda's political interests, as does the feminist critique implicit in *Le Bonheur,* in which men's happiness comes at the expense of women, and her participation in the antiwar film *Loin du Viet-nam* (1967; *Far from Vietnam*). One of Varda's most significant movies is the pseudodocumentary *Sans toit ni loi* (1984; *Vagabond*), which follows a vagrant youth who passes through a southern French town in winter. The film begins with her death and, like Orson Welles's *Citizen Kane* (1941), reconstructs from interviews (which give way to flashbacks) her origins, life, and demise.

REFERENCES:

Sandy Flitterman-Lewis, *To Desire Differently: Feminism and the French Cinema* (Urbana: University of Illinois Press, 1990);

Susan Hayward, "Beyond the Gaze and into *femme-filmécriture*: Agnès Varda's *Sans toit ni loi* (1985)," in *French Film: Texts and Contexts,* edited by Hayward and Ginette Vincendeau (London: Routledge, 1990), pp. 285–296;

Louise Heck-Rabi, *Women Filmmakers* (Metuchen, N.J.: Scarecrow Press, 1984).

—T.C.

VICTOR VASARELY

Victor Vasarely (1908–) played a critical role in inspiring what became known as Op Art in the United States and *Nouvelle Tendance* (New Tendency) in France. Born in Hungary, he studied at the Budapest Bauhaus (1928) before moving to Paris in 1930. That same year marked his growing interest in mapping three-dimensional objects on two-dimensional grids. For a time the format for these oscillated between two different conceptions. In *L'Arlequin* (1935; *Harlequin*), a flat, black-and-white checkerboard is distorted, as though a clown were actually pressing through the flat surface from the other side. By contrast, his "material studies" from the 1930s are *trompe-l'œil* still lifes, with arrangements of the detritus of modern life, from string and rope to dice, combs — even a bone.

In the 1950s these illusionistic images were replaced by interlocking arrangements of flat, abstracted shapes with equally abstract names: *Chadar,* for example, and *Ortiz* (both from 1952). These resolutely flat, nonobjective canvases seemed to fit comfortably into the norms of contemporary abstraction. Yet his abstractions led him in a distinct direction; his 1951 exhibit *Naissances* (*Births*) consisted of black-and-white images of intricate linear patterns. He attributed their origins to his fascination as a child with a gauze bandage, whose intersecting threads shifted as he moved his arm. He called his images "photographismes," from his use of photographic equipment to enlarge them; the next step was to layer sheets of transparent Plexiglas, each with a drawing, so that the motion of the viewer's eye would make the images move and pulse.

Ultimately, Vasarely sought to play perceptual games with the viewer — to use optical illusions, seemingly similar but deceptive forms, and the interaction of colors to make the image convert from something passive and inert into something that would seem constantly to move, pulse, or shift in color or brightness. Vasarely argued that traditional subject matter had been "banished," along with the colors, shapes, and rules that had accompanied it. On a plane surface, he asserted, "a spatial phenomenon may appear one moment and vanish the next; as a result, the surface is constantly shifting." Art was no longer inspired by things seen but by the world of "chemistry, biochemistry, waves, fields...."

Vasarely's ideas were picked up and further elaborated (when not merely repeated) by the artists of the Nouvelle Tendance in the 1960s; among the groups of the so-called movement were Groupe Zéro and **Groupe de recherche de l'art visuel,** which included Vasarely's son Yvaral.

REFERENCES:

Cyril Barrett, *Op Art* (New York: Viking, 1970);

Gaston Diehl, *Vasarely,* translated by Eileen B. Hennessy (Naefels, Switzerland: Bonfini Press, 1973);

Werner Spies, *Victor Vasarely* (New York: Abrams, 1971);

Victor Vasarely, *Vasarely,* translated by I. Mark Paris (New York: Alpine Fine Arts Collection, 1979).

— J.H.

VERCORS

The novelist Jean Bruller (1902–) adopted the pseudonym Vercors after a mountain chain in southeastern France that was home to a **Resistance** network during the German **Occupation** of France in **World War II.** He is primarily known for one work, *Le Silence de la mer* (1942; translated as *The Silence of the Sea*), published by the clandestine press **Editions de Minuit,** which Bruller helped to found as a means of disseminating Resistance literature. *Le Silence de la mer* is about a German officer whose conduct in France is irreproachable and who eventually realizes the injustices of Nazism and asks for a transfer to the Russian front. Despite the sympathetic portrayal of the German officer,

the intent of the novel is not to support a Franco-German rapprochement; as an active member of the Resistance, Bruller was opposed to collaboration with the Nazis. Rather, the book was intended to show the French the danger of being swayed by German courtesy and culture.

REFERENCE:

William Kidd, *Vercors, "Le Silence de la mer" et autres récits: A Critical Introduction to the Wartime Writing* (Glasgow: University of Glasgow Press, 1991).

— C.S.B.

VERDUN

The Verdun River valley in northeast France was the site of the bloodiest battle of **World War I,** a German offensive against a fortified French position whose military importance was more symbolic than real. The French and the Germans each lost about three hundred thousand men. The heaviest fighting took place from February to June 1916.

The German command hoped that a military victory, especially with massive French casualties, would destroy the French desire to continue the war. Preferring to save resources for the planned battle of the **Somme** in July 1916, Marshal Joseph-Jacques Joffre did not want to fight at Verdun. In fact, by the time the Germans attacked, French weapons had been removed from Verdun. Yet Prime Minister **Aristide Briand** was convinced that the symbolic importance of Verdun was so great that it must be held. Despite great suffering, the French army — led by **Philippe Pétain,** who was henceforth known as the hero of Verdun — stopped the German advance. The battle retained enormous significance in France for decades thereafter. It appears in many literary works and is the focus in **Jules Romains**'s novel *Verdun,* one of the volumes in his series *Les Hommes de bonne volonté* (1932–1946; translated as *Men of Good Will*).

REFERENCE:

J. M. Winter, *The Experience of World War I* (New York: Oxford University Press, 1989).

— D.O'C.

BORIS VIAN

Boris Vian (1920–1959) achieved recognition as a novelist, playwright, jazz trumpeter, and singer. Themes of absurdity and nonconformity characterize all of his artistic undertakings. Although most of his novels met with only modest success during his lifetime, his bizarre

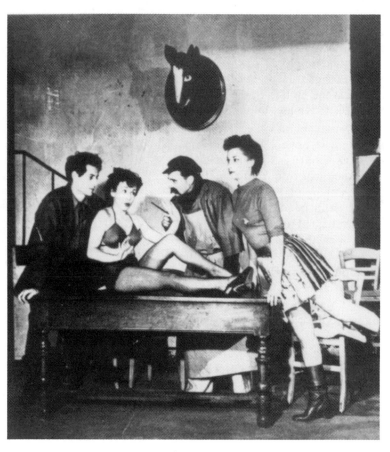

Scene from the 1950 production of Boris Vian's controversial play
L'Equarissage pour tous, mocking the French military

and often violent plots have subsequently lent themselves to psychoanalytical interpretations.

Hearing Duke Ellington play in 1938 sparked in Vian a vivid interest in jazz, and by 1942 he was playing the trumpet in a jazz orchestra. Through his participation in Parisian intellectual nightlife he met **Jean-Paul Sartre** in 1946, and Sartre published in his journal *Temps Modernes* some chapters of Vian's novel *L'Ecume des jours* (1947; translated as *Froth on the Daydream*). Vian's admiration for Sartre did not prevent him from mocking the philosopher's popularity in this novel, where he appears as "Jean-Sol Partre."

Early in his career Vian achieved notoriety because of a scandal involving one of his novels. In a conversation with an editor friend, Vian claimed that he could write an American-style detective novel, a genre which was popular in France. As proof, during a two-week vacation he wrote *J'irai cracher sur vos tombes* (1946; translated as *I Shall Spit on Your Graves*), published as Vian's French "translation" of

a novel by the fictitious American author Vernon Sullivan. Its sales soared in 1947, when a salesman named Edmond Rougé strangled his female companion in a Paris hotel room, leaving next to the body a copy of Vian's novel, open to a page describing the murder of a woman. Vian was identified as the author, accused of having offended public morality, and fined one hundred thousand francs. Despite this scandal, he wrote three more novels under the pseudonym Vernon Sullivan.

In the early 1950s Vian also wrote most of the poems published posthumously as *Je voudrais pas crever* (1962; I Don't Want to Die), and throughout the decade he wrote and performed songs, many of which have remained popular. Vian also enjoyed success as a playwright in the vein of the **Theater of the Absurd.** His plays *L'Equarissage pour tous* (1950; translated as *Knackery for All*) and *Le Goûter des généraux* (1962; translated as *The General's Tea Party*) mocked the French military. His most successful play was his last, *Les Bâtisseurs d'empire; ou, Le Schmürz* (1959; translated as *The Empire Builders*), an absurd saga of the disintegration of a family. Vian died of a heart attack on 23 June 1959, during a private showing of the film version of his *J'irai cracher sur vos tombes.*

REFERENCES:

Nicole Buffard-O'Shea, *Le Monde de Boris Vian et le grotesque littéraire* (New York: Peter Lang, 1993);

Alfred Cismaru, *Boris Vian* (New York: Twayne, 1974).

— K.E.B.

THE VICHY GOVERNMENT

The Etat Français (French State) that was established in collaboration with German occupying forces during **World War II** is better known as the Vichy government, for the central French spa town where its capital was located, after the government first sat briefly in Bordeaux.

After the defeat of the French military by German forces in the **Debacle** of May–June 1940, the armistice of 22 June divided France into a **Free Zone,** a Forbidden Zone, and an Occupied Zone. On 10 July the national assembly of the **Third Republic** voted overwhelmingly to revise the constitution of 1875. The resulting discussions culminated in the dismantling of the republic and the creation of the Etat Français. Under the new provisos an authoritarian parliament was established to control the Free Zone and the colonies. Labor unions were replaced by corporatist entities representing the various trades and professions. The Etat Français was headed by octogenarian **Philippe Pétain.** A military hero of **World War I** with a strongly antirepublican bias, Pétain had called for the French surrender well before it took place. Other key officials included **François Darlan,** who was assassinated in 1942, and vice-premier Pierre Laval.

Laval was dismissed from his position for plotting against Pétain, but he was reinstated and given leadership of the Vichy government in 1942, when Germany seized control of all of France. Pétain remained as a figurehead. The government became even more of a Nazi puppet regime during the next two years. The Vichy government fell as a result of the Allied invasion in 1944. A provisional government led by **Resistance** figure **Charles de Gaulle** was put in place until the establishment of the **Fourth Republic** (1946–1958). Laval was executed for treason in 1945; Pétain was also convicted of treason, but de Gaulle commuted his death sentence to life imprisonment.

REFERENCE:

Bertram M. Gordon, *Collaboration in Vichy France during the Second World War* (Ithaca, N.Y.: Cornell University Press, 1980).

— D.O'C.

JEAN VIGO

Jean Vigo (1905–1934) made only three short films and one feature-length movie during his brief career, but he is widely considered one of the most important and influential French filmmakers of the 1930s. He worked on all his films with noted cinematographer Boris Kaufman.

Born in Paris, Vigo was the son of the well-known anarchist Miguel Alemereyda, who was killed in prison in 1917; Vigo's mother was permanently hospitalized in 1925. Vigo's experiences in a boys' boarding school provided the background for his first fiction film, *Zéro de conduite* (1933; *Zero for Conduct*). He contracted tuberculosis a year before directing his first motion picture, *A propos de Nice* (1930; *On the Subject of Nice*), a **Surrealist** satire of the southern city and its tourism. His second was an eleven-minute short, *Taris* (1931), about a French swimming champion. *Zéro de conduite,* a forty-five-minute film about a revolution in a boys' boarding school, was quickly banned in France and was not released again until 1945. Vigo's only feature film was *L'Atalante* (1934), the story of the troubled marriage of a barge captain. Vigo died of leukemia days before its release, and the producers cut the film to make it more commercially viable. It was restored to its original length in 1990.

Zéro de conduite and *L'Atalante,* which rank among the great early sound movies, employ techniques of Surrealism and **poetic realism.** Both films experiment with the medium by using slow motion, unusual camera angles, underwater photography, back lighting, and aerial photography. Both have been seminal influences on directors, ranging from the Italian neorealists Roberto Rossellini and Federico Fellini to **François Truffaut** — especially in *Les Quatre cent coups* (1959; *The 400 Blows*) — to Bernardo Bertolucci in *Last Tango in Paris* (1973).

REFERENCES:

The Complete Jean Vigo (London: British Film Institute, 1983);

Tom Conley, "Vigo Van Gogh," *New York Literary Forum,* 5 (1983): 153–165;

P. E. Sales-Gomez, *Jean Vigo* (Berkeley & Los Angeles: University of California Press, 1972);

William G. Simon, *The Films of Jean Vigo* (Ann Arbor: University of Michigan Press, 1981).

— T.C.

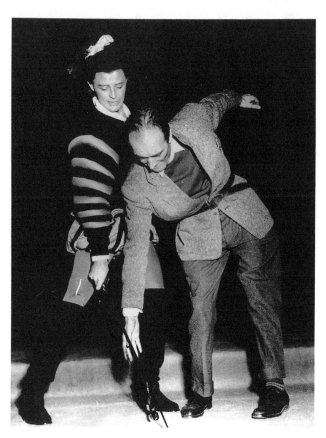

Rehearsal for Jean Vilar's production of *Le Cid* at the Théâtre National Populaire, 1951 (Studio Lipnitzki)

JEAN VILAR

Theater director and actor Jean Vilar (1912–1971) helped to bring about basic changes in French theater following **World War II,** opening it to a broader and more diversified audience. His innovations were not only techniques of staging but also ways of "marketing" theater and of obtaining government subsidies for play productions. His principal pioneering ventures were the **Avignon Festival** and the **Théâtre National Populaire.**

Having been trained under **Charles Dullin** at the **Théâtre de l'Atelier,** Vilar found employment during World War II as an actor and codirector with a road company called La Roulotte (The Covered Wagon). He later founded his own troupe in Paris, managing to stage plays by the Swedish dramatist August Strindberg in small theaters and finally attracting favorable attention with his production of T. S. Eliot's *Murder in the Cathedral* in 1945 at the **Théâtre du Vieux-Colombier.**

Vilar was already disillusioned, however, with French theater and the almost exclusively Parisian,

rather snobbish upper-middle-class audience it attracted. To establish high-quality theater outside Paris, he launched — with government aid — an Avignon Art Week in summer 1947. The next summer it became the Avignon Festival. With Léon Gischia, his set designer for the Eliot play, he laid out a vast outdoor stage in the Honor Courtyard of the Palace of the Popes in Avignon. The huge platform with no proscenium arch sloped toward the audience and was overhung with spotlights that could isolate a small corner of the stage or illuminate all of it. While the first season, which included a staging of William Shakespeare's *Richard III,* was not highly successful, the Avignon Festival soon expanded from one week to several each summer, packing in spectators from all over France and abroad to see such plays as Pierre Corneille's *Le Cid* and **André Gide**'s *Œdipe* (translated as *Oedipus*) in 1949, Molière's *L'Avare* (translated as *The Miser*) with Vilar in the title role in 1952, and **Jean Giraudoux**'s *La Guerre de Troie n'aura pas lieu* (adapted as *Tiger at the Gates*) in 1962. These plays were performed by brilliant actors, including **Gérard Philipe** and **Maria Casarès.** At first Vilar directed (or "organized," as he preferred to say) the performances himself; later he invited others to direct at Avignon.

In 1951 the national government saw the wisdom of Vilar's conviction that good theater was, after all, a public service, something owed to citizens of all classes. Offered a subsidy, Vilar elected to develop a project launched years earlier by **Firmin Gémier** but inadequately funded: a national people's theater. In 1952 he set up a large stage in the Palais de Chaillot in Paris, moving in as the headquarters of the North Atlantic Treaty Organization moved out. This stage had a proscenium fifty-five feet wide, a barely noticeable arch, and no curtain. Vilar used virtually no scenery — just a black backdrop and segmental lighting to move the action about the stage, from scene to scene and from place to place. Following the concept of the "bare stage" originally proposed by **Jacques Copeau,** Vilar kept props to a minimum to focus attention on characters' inner feelings. Vilar made no effort to produce the illusion of "reality," for he believed that the play itself was a reality created anew for the audience each night by the actors and that its purpose was to reveal the very nature of life and death to the audience. Vilar upheld most of Copeau's theory of theater, although he was not averse to hiring the occasional "star" actor. And so was born the Théâtre National Populaire, or TNP, as it was quickly baptized.

Although Vilar wanted a cross section of the Paris public to attend his plays, he never attained his goal. His tickets were reasonably priced because of his subsidy, his seating was more democratic than in other theaters, and he did away with tipping and other costly features of the traditional Paris "evening at the theater." Still, while he attracted students and teachers, he was unsuccessful in bringing in many laborers or other members of the proletariat.

The first season of the TNP (1951–1952) featured Bertolt Brecht's *Mother Courage and Her Children* and Heinrich von Kleist's *The Prince of Homburg*, both of which won high praise for Vilar. His staging of Henri Pichette's *Nucléa* in 1952 brought accusations that he was using his subsidy to produce propaganda against the French nuclear arsenal. Subsequent seasons featured plays that had stood the test of time, such as Victor Hugo's *Ruy Blas* in 1954 and Jean Racine's *Phèdre* (translated as *Phaedra*) in 1957. Vilar was determined to give working people a chance to appreciate drama of high quality, rather than the thrillers and sex farces with which many **boulevard theaters** sought to woo them. He also launched a short-lived attempt to bring more modern plays into the TNP repertory, opening a second theater, the Récamier, in 1959 to experiment with the best of contemporary drama. But none of Vilar's efforts to democratize theater was as successful as he wished. Disappointed with his failure to transform the laboring class through theater, Vilar did not request that his contract be renewed in 1963, and the TNP passed into other hands.

In 1968 Vilar invited an American Off-Broadway company, the Living Theater, to perform at Avignon. Their collectively created spectacle, *Paradise Now,* provoked enough scandal to convince Vilar to cancel their run. The actors then met with members of French little-theater groups and culture centers, including some Parisian extremists, and issued a pronouncement declaring that the proper role of theater was to transform the political and social landscape by radicalizing the population; Vilar and the Avignon Festival were condemned as retrograde.

Vilar's initiatives were nonetheless influential. The movement to decentralize French theater, to move it out of Paris and into every region in France, was under way. The principle of French government subsidies for theaters outside Paris was established, and the notion that high culture belonged to the masses as well as the upper classes had begun to take root.

REFERENCES:

Albert Bermel, "Jean Vilar: Unadorned Theatre for the Greatest Number," *Tulane Drama Review,* 5 (December 1960): 24–43;

Thomas J. Donahue, "Mnouchkine, Vilar and Copeau: Popular Theater and Paradox," *Modern Language Studies,* 21 (Fall 1991): 31–42;

Guy Leclerc, *Le T.N.P. de Jean Vilar* (Paris: Union Générale d'Editions, 1971).

— R.J.N.

Charles Vildrac

Charles Vildrac (1882–1971) is chiefly known for his work as a dramatist, though he also attracted notice for his poetry and his children's books. His reputation is based mainly on his play *Le Paquebot Tenacity* (1919; translated as *The Steamship Tenacity*), which was produced by **Jacques Copeau** in the same year it was published. A study in character contrasts, the play concerns two soldiers ready to leave France and immigrate to Canada; during a delay while their ship is being repaired they pay court to the same servant girl.

Born Charles Messager, Vildrac — along with his brother-in-law **Georges Duhamel** and **Jules Romains** — was a founder of **Unanimism,** an early-twentieth-century literary movement that emphasized the collective consciousness of human experience. Early in his career Vildrac published collections of his free-verse poetry, including *Poèmes 1905* (1906) and *Images et mirages* (1908; Images and Mirages). *Livre d'amour* (1910; translated as *A Book of Love*) is another notable collection. *Images et mirages* was printed at the artists' community of L'Abbaye, which Vildrac, Duhamel, and other Unanimists helped to form in 1906.

REFERENCES:

May Daniels, "Charles Vildrac," in her *The French Drama of the Unspoken* (Edinburgh: Edinburgh University Press, 1953), pp. 121–143;

Dorothy Knowles, "Studio Theater: The Unspoken," in her *French Drama of the Interwar Years 1918–1939* (London: Harrap, 1967), pp. 112–128.

— C.S.B.

Jacques Villon

The eldest of three brothers who made significant individual contributions to twentieth-century art, Jacques Villon (1875-1963) took a highly abstract, poetic approach to **Cubism** throughout his long career. Born Gaston Duchamp-Villon, he was the brother of **Marcel Duchamp** and **Raymond Duchamp-Villon.** While Marcel was eclectic, simultaneously experimenting with and satirizing avant-garde art, and

Raymond devoted his brief career to creating Cubist sculpture, Jacques Villon spent his early career in an attempt to establish a precise theoretical basis for Cubist art.

As a young man, Villon learned engraving from his grandfather. After studying law briefly at the Sorbonne (1894), Villon returned to his home in Rouen to study at the local art academy. He was back in Paris by 1895, beginning to establish himself as a commercial artist by producing satirical images for reviews such as the *Chat Noir* (Black Cat), *Gil Blas,* and the *Assiette au Beurre* (Plate of Butter). In 1902 his illustrations filled an entire issue of the *Assiette au Beurre.* By 1904 he was sufficiently established to serve on the organizing committee for the **Salon d'Automne,** a position he held until 1912, when he resigned in protest against his colleagues' hostility toward Cubist art.

Villon's interest in Cubism, which can be seen in his work from 1911 onward, differentiated him from **Georges Braque** and **Pablo Picasso** as much as it linked him to them. Villon attracted a circle of young artists — including **Albert Gleizes, Roger de La Fresnaye, Henri Le Fauconnier, Fernand Léger, Jean Metzinger,** and **Francis Picabia** — to his studio in Puteaux for theoretical and practical discussions on Cubist art. The result was the formation of the **Section d'Or** in 1912.

Villon's works differ from the analytical still lifes of Picasso and Braque and the quasi-symbolic depictions of the epic quality of modern life crafted by Gleizes. Villon's *Soldats en marche* (1913; *Soldiers on the March*) is at once more abstract and more figurative than Picasso's analytical works from 1907 to 1908. It is as though the soldiers were dimly seen through a varicolored, crystalline screen, for the surface geometric forms do not analyze or disassemble the soldiers so much as they form a prismatic layer between subject and viewer. Villon borrowed from Futurist painters the device of solid black diagonals, which he called "vol de mouche" lines (the flight of a fly).

In the 1920s Villon's work roughly paralleled the synthetic Cubist works of Picasso (from 1912 to 1914) with compositions resembling glued-together stacks of different-colored sheets of paper. Sometimes the result is static; elsewhere, as with his *Joie* (1921; *Joy*), the use of diagonal and intersecting lines creates a sense of dynamic motion.

With the German defeat of France in 1940 and the subsequent **Occupation** of the country, Villon moved from Paris south to safety in Tarn, in the **Free Zone.** His Tarn landscapes of the period represent a distinctive blend of abstraction and more traditional representational art — like pastel engineering sketches of outdoor scenes. By the 1950s these works had been supplemented by abstracted studies of speed and motion, focusing on airports and aircraft.

REFERENCES:

Pierre Cabanne, *The Brothers Duchamp: Jacques Villon, Raymond Duchamp-Villon, Marcel Duchamp,* translated by Helga and Dinah Harrison (Boston: New York Graphic Society, 1975);

Jacques Villon, Master of Graphic Art (1875–1963) (Boston: Museum of Fine Arts, 1964);

Daniel Robbins, ed., *Jacques Villon* (Cambridge, Mass.: Fogg Art Museum, 1976).

— J.H.

ROGER VITRAC

A participant in the **Surrealist** movement and a friend of dramatist **Antonin Artaud,** Roger Vitrac (1899–1952) wrote poetry and art criticism, as well as drama. His finest play is *Victor, ou les enfants au pouvoir* (1929; Victor, or The Children Take Over), an extremely funny farce that denounces the hypocrisy of middle-class adult values. The play not only shows its kinship with Surrealism but also anticipates the black humor and violence used later by dramatists of the **Theater of the Absurd.**

Before *Victor,* Vitrac composed several Surrealist sketches, including *Le Peintre* (1922; The Painter) and *Les Mystères de l'amour* (1924; The Mysteries of Love), a Surrealist play produced at the short-lived Théâtre **Alfred Jarry,** which he and Artaud founded in 1927. In the same year he brought out two collections of verse: *Humoristiques* (Humorous Verse) and *Cruautés de la nuit* (Night Cruelties). His later plays include *Le Loup garou* (1935; The Werewolf).

REFERENCES:

Derek F. Connon, "In the Gutter Looking at the Stars: Dualism in Vitrac's *Victor, ou Les enfants au pouvoir,*" *Modern Language Review,* 89 (July 1994): 595-605;

J. H. Matthews, "Vitrac," in his *Surrealist Poetry in France* (Syracuse: Syracuse University Press, 1969);

Matthews, "Vitrac" and "Antonin Artaud and the Théâtre Alfred Jarry," in his *Theatre in Dada and Surrealism* (Syracuse: Syracuse University Press, 1974), pp. 109–154.

— C.S.B.

RENÉE VIVIEN

A minor poet, Renée Vivien (1877–1909) was one of a group of lesbians writing in Paris during the early years of the twentieth century. She was a friend of **Colette,** who published a book on her in 1928, and American Natalie Clifford Barney, whose Paris salon was a meeting place for literary women. Born Pauline Mary Tarn in London, Vivien traveled extensively before settling in Paris. She translated into French the writings of Sappho and other poets of Lesbos as *Les Kitharèdes* (1904; The Cithara Players). Her infatuation with Greece and Hellenic traditions is also visible in her sensual, musical poetry. Among her collections of verse are *Cendres et poussières* (1902; Ashes and Dust), *Evocations* (1903), and *Les Flambeaux éteints* (1907; The Extinguished Torches). Her early death is attributed to self-imposed starvation.

REFERENCES:

Shari Benstock, *Women of the Left Bank: Paris, 1900–1914* (Austin: University of Texas Press, 1986);

Karla Jay, *The Amazon and the Page: Natalie Clifford Barney and Renée Vivien* (Bloomington: Indiana University Press, 1988).
                                                                              — C.S.B.

MAURICE DE VLAMINCK

A leader of the group of painters known as the **Fauves,** Maurice de Vlaminck (1876–1958) later claimed that he, not **Henri Matisse,** was the true founder of the movement.

Born in Paris to a Flemish family, Vlaminck came to art as a militant anarchist, having written for and even briefly edited the anarchist journal *Libertaire* (Libertarian). His approach to art, he later indicated, was equivalent to throwing bombs — an all-out assault on the world of existing art and the comfort of the propertied classes.

Largely self-taught, Vlaminck was disdainful of traditional art training, museums, and the influence of previous artistic movements. While his colleague **André Derain** found the basis for his work in classics of the past, studying them rigorously at the Louvre museum, Vlaminck argued that art should be intuitive, not systematic. "Our art," he proclaimed, "was not an invention, but an attitude. It was a way of being or acting, or thinking, of breathing...." Studying older works was useless, even pernicious, betraying a morbid fascination with dead objects. Vlaminck believed every generation had to start afresh, rethinking style and subject matter.

Vlaminck's anarchism initially led him close to the Neo-Impressionists, led in the 1890s by **Paul Signac.** Seeking a revolutionary "scientific" art, Neo-Impressionists composed their canvases of dots (points) carefully arranged according to optical theory. While Matisse experimented with Neo-Impressionist art briefly, Vlaminck incorporated an intuitive variation of the technique into a consistent personal style

that — along with the influence of Vincent van Gogh — is apparent in his Fauvist paintings. In his *Déjeuner* (1905; *Picnic*) he surrounds a working-class couple with a ferocious swirl of dots, splashes, and swirling lines of color. Like Matisse, Vlaminck chose his colors intuitively, but unlike Matisse's colors, Vlaminck's often exude menace. His *Danseuse du "Rat Mort"* (1906; *Dancer from the "Rat Mort"*) depicts a sickly bluish-gray dancer from the "Dead Rat" club surrounded by a chaotic field of refracted colors, out of which her hair and dress coalesce (or into which they dissolve).

The artist who proclaimed "I am Fauvism" was unable to remain comfortable within any movement for long. In 1906 Vlaminck began to work with **Pablo Picasso,** later claiming in his typical fashion that he had discovered African art — especially masks — "in all its primitive beauty and strength" and introduced Picasso and Derain to it. Although he painted a few still lifes in a quasi-**Cubist** manner, Vlaminck concluded ultimately that both the Fauves and the Cubists unduly restricted the artist with rules and theories.

In 1916–1917 Vlaminck began to focus on stormy landscapes, in dark colors, painted in a thick impasto. During the German **Occupation** of France in **World War II,** he was praised by collaborationist journals and participated with several other French artists in a 1941 tour of Germany. At the end of the war he was arrested for collaboration but quickly released. As with most participants in the German tour, his reputation and career suffered in the postwar period.

REFERENCES:

Jean-Paul Crespelle, *The Fauves,* translated by Anita Brookner (Greenwich, Conn.: New York Graphic Society, 1962);

Georges Duthuit, *The Fauvist Painters,* translated by Ralph Manheim (New York: Wittenborn, Schultz, 1950);

Pierre Mac Orlan, *Vlaminck,* translated by J. B. Sidgwick (New York: Universe Books, 1958);

Joseph–Emile Muller, *Fauvism,* translated by Shirley E. Jones (New York: Praeger, 1967);

Jean Selz, *Vlaminck,* translated by Graham Snell (New York: Crown, 1963).
                                                                              — J.H.

AMBROISE VOLLARD

As art dealer, author, and publisher, Ambroise Vollard (1869–1939) had a powerful impact on the development of modern art. He played a key role in the careers of artists such as **Aristide Maillol, Georges Rouault,** and **Pablo Picasso.** Yet not all artists and critics found Vollard congenial. Camille Pissarro found him grasping and greedy, and persuaded his son not to deal with

Pablo Picasso's *Portrait de Vollard, II,* circa 1937

him. Critic Edmond Jaloux wrote of Vollard's intelligence and generosity but also of his "starvation wages to his artists."

Vollard began his career as an art dealer by searching out valuable prints at stalls along the Seine in Paris and selling them for a profit. He went on to apprentice at the Union Artistique of Alphonse Dumas before opening his own gallery on the rue Laffitte (1893).

The art world into which Vollard plunged had already been transformed by private dealers. The annual Salon — huge, haphazardly organized — had never been an efficient mechanism for distributing art. Group shows, such as the Impressionist exhibitions of 1874–1886, helped provide a collective identity for the artists exhibiting at them, but they were marked by lack of continuity and internal rivalries. Private dealers such as Paul Durand-Ruel and Georges Petit had helped to launch and sustain the careers of several Impressionist painters and other young artists. Their shops were small; they organized their shows to maximize the impact of favorite artists; and they were able to attract a clientele interested in a specific style or

movement. Vollard launched his career as a champion of **Paul Cézanne** and Vincent van Gogh, both shunned by the larger dealers. His first exhibition of Cézanne's works helped Vollard establish contacts with an entire milieu of young artists and wealthy collectors, including Auguste Pellerin and Isaac de Camondo.

To encourage interest in contemporary artists, Vollard began in 1896 to publish albums of prints under the series title *Album d'estampes originales de la Galerie Vollard* (Gallery Vollard Album of Original Prints). These volumes were supplemented by the publication of thematic albums by specific artists, including **Maurice Denis**'s *Amour* (1898; translated as *Love*), **Edouard Vuillard**'s *Paysages et intérieurs* (1899; Landscapes and Interiors), and **Odilon Redon**'s *La Tentation de Saint-Antoine* (1898; translated as *The Temptation of Saint Anthony*). Vollard's next step was to publish volumes of poetry illustrated by artists he commissioned, including two works illustrated by **Pierre Bonnard:** Paul Verlaine's *Parallèlement* (1900; In a Parallel Fashion) and Longus's *Daphnis et Chloë* (1902).

Vollard also established himself as an author, primarily of reminiscences about the art world and biographies of his favorite artists. His *Souvenirs d'un marchand de tableaux,* published first in English translation as *Recollections of a Picture Dealer* (1936), traces his encounters with famous artists, critics, and the (sometimes hostile) public.

REFERENCE:

Una E. Johnson, *Ambroise Vollard Editeur: Prints, Books, Bronzes* (New York: Museum of Modern Art, 1977).

— J.H.

EDOUARD VUILLARD

Edouard Vuillard (1868–1940) and **Pierre Bonnard** represented the urban wing of the **Nabi** movement. Like Bonnard and **Félix Vallotton,** Vuillard is noted for his *intimiste* scenes of interior space and domestic life.

Vuillard's art would seem, at first glance, to have little in common with the mystical, devoutly religious works of Nabis such as **Maurice Denis** and **Paul Sérusier.** Strong ties bound him to them, however, at least initially. Vuillard shared their fascination with the fantasies of muralist Pierre Puvis de Chavannes (born in Vuillard's hometown of Cuiseaux, near the Jura Mountains). Like Denis and Sérusier, he came from a middle-class family and studied at the Académie Julien, where he met Sérusier, Bonnard, and Paul Ranson, another future Nabi.

Edouard Vuillard, K-X Roussel, and Claude Monet, 1923

Vuillard's first works were drawn eclectically from a broad range of ideas and styles. His *Déchargeurs* (1890; *Dockworkers*) uses the flat patches of heavily outlined colors associated with the cloisonnism of **Paul Gauguin** and **Emile Bernard,** but it covers them with a layer of dotted colors borrowed from **Paul Signac** and the other Neo-Impressionists. In the same year he created images composed of loosely painted zones of textured color (including a self-portrait of yellows, pinks, oranges, and greens). Vuillard complained in his diaries that his work was too haphazard, too lacking in method or theory: "It is . . . necessary to have a methodology in order to produce, without *knowing* in advance what will be the result."

The approach suggested by this statement became evident in the six panels Vuillard painted for the Desmarais family in 1892–1893. Focusing on the lives of women at home, in parks, and at work, these works were followed by a series of nine panels on the theme of public gardens, painted for the home of Alexandre Natanson. The two sets feature the characteristic Nabi depiction of exterior and interior alike via blocks of solid, flat color. Vuillard's contribution to the style is to cover some of these blocks with patterns of color, from the alternating browns and tans of paving stones to the play of solid-colored dresses against the repetitive patterns of wallpaper.

By the mid 1890s Vuillard had developed a dominant style. *La Table de toilette* (1895; *The Vanity Table*) is a dense interweaving of colors, shapes, and textures: a vase of flowers in left foreground; the face of a woman peeking from behind them (played off in

turn against the earth tones of the wallpaper); the interplay of striped dress, flowers, and tablecloth. For this style Vuillard typically preferred distemper to oil paint, making full use of its flat, chalky surface. To vary the surface and texture, he sometimes added sections of glue mixed with colored powder.

Vuillard's work continued on the same course in the twentieth century, though he employed his method more loosely and flexibly as he aged. With few exceptions his focus remained on the domestic — cheerful or soothing scenes of daily life.

REFERENCES:

Claire Frèches-Thory and Antoine Terrasse, *The Nabis: Bonnard, Vuillard, and Their Circle,* translated by Mary Pardoe (New York: Abrams, 1990);

Gloria Lynn Groom, *Edouard Vuillard: Painter-Decorator — Patrons and Projects, 1892–1912* (New Haven: Yale University Press, 1993);

John Russell, *Edouard Vuillard, 1868–1940* (London: Thames & Hudson, 1971);

Belinda Thomson, *Vuillard* (New York: Abbeville Press, 1988).

— J.H.

VVV

The magazine *VVV* (1942–1944) was founded by **André Breton** as an effort to reinvigorate **Surrealism.** Founded in New York, where Breton and other Surrealists spent much of **World War II,** the magazine had a staff that included French and other exiles from Nazi-occupied Europe, together with a few Americans. Its editorial directors were Breton, **Marcel Duchamp,** and Max Ernst; its publisher was American photographer and sculptor David Hare.

Although every effort was made to make *VVV* an international Surrealist journal, its emphases were French. Few American artists or writers were featured; though its first issues were primarily in English, with French and English texts for Breton's contribution, its last issues were almost entirely in French.

The first issue explained the title and aims of the journal: "V as a vow — and energy — to return to a habitable and conceivable world . . . VV of that double victory, V again over all that is opposed to the emancipation of the spirit . . . VVV towards the emancipation of the spirit, through these necessary stages." In the face of the **Occupation** of most of Europe by the Nazis and the unfolding of a brutal world war, Breton and his colleagues moved away from the explicitly po-litical stance of Surrealism in the 1930s toward one of individualism and opposition to schematized intellectual systems. He stressed the necessity of a quest for a "new myth" to liberate humanity by shattering and replacing those of capitalism and Christianity.

VVV published its last issue in February 1944. With the **Liberation** of France, French Surrealists began to return to their home country, where they established a new review, *Néon,* in 1948.

REFERENCES:

Dawn Ades, *Dada and Surrealism Reviewed* (London: Arts Council of Great Britain, 1978), pp. 375–405;

Franklin Rosemont, "Introduction: André Breton and the First Principles of Surrealism," in Breton's *What Is Surrealism? Selected Writings,* edited by Rosemont (New York: Monad Press, 1978), pp. 84–95.

—J.H.

SIMONE WEIL

Simone Weil (1909–1943) pursued a university career before moving toward political and social activism and a vocation of asceticism and mysticism. Although she published little in her lifetime, posthumous publications of her writings and the example of her life have established her reputation as a major figure in religious and moral thought.

Precocious as a child and a pupil of **Alain** in the late 1920s, Weil was a brilliant student of philosophy from 1928 to 1931 at the **Ecole Normale Supérieure,** where she passed the prestigious *agrégation* and was a classmate of **Jean-Paul Sartre, Claude Lévi-Strauss,** and **Maurice Merleau-Ponty** and an acquaintance of **Simone de Beauvoir.** She taught at five different schools between 1931 and 1938. During this period she became involved in social activism, advocating the formation of labor unions and taking a year off to work in Paris factories. These activities exemplified her concern for social justice. She routinely gave part of her meager salary to the poor, and during **World War II** she sent political prisoners half her ration tickets. She went to Spain at the outbreak of the **Spanish Civil War** in 1936 to support the Republican side, but she had to leave soon after her arrival because of a severe accidental burn.

Of Jewish extraction, Weil converted to Christianity during a period of intense religious experiences from 1936 to 1938 and turned her attentions from social involvement to spiritual searching. While she was drawn to the Roman Catholic church, she refused to be baptized and faulted the church for its rejection of other faiths and for deforming the Gospel. She also pronounced severe judgments on what she called "Jewish imperialism." Rarely orthodox in theology and rejecting the standard views of Western

history, her thought is unsystematic and syncretic, drawing from traditions such as Gnosticism and Greek philosophy; in the same passages she cites, for instance, the examples or teachings of the Upanishads, Prometheus, Plato, Christ, and Saint Paul. Along with her interest in the social gospel and its relationship to the modern world, she was drawn to metaphysical questions, to which she gave an idiosyncratic, mystical shaping. She has been compared to Blaise Pascal, the seventeenth-century philosopher with whom she shares the experience of religious anguish, and to such mystics as Saint Teresa of Avila and Saint John of the Cross.

In 1940 Weil moved with her parents from Paris to Marseilles, and the following year she worked as a farm laborer. In 1942 she and her family went to the United States, but she soon traveled to London, where she attempted to organize nurses for duty on the battlefields and worked for the Free French. Her health was not strong, and her death in a tuberculosis sanatorium in England is usually attributed to self-starvation.

Her books — which were assembled from passages in her letters, notebooks, and articles — include *La Pesanteur et la grâce* (1947; translated as *Gravity and Grace*), *L'Enracinement* (1949; translated as *The Need for Roots*), *La Connaissance surnaturelle* (1950; Supernatural Knowledge), and *L'Attente de Dieu* (1950; translated as *Waiting on God*). They were praised by prominent figures such as **Albert Camus, Julien Green,** and **Gabriel Marcel.** Her social thought is set forth in *La Condition ouvrière* (1951; The Workers' Condition). Her writings are vibrant and moving rather than abstract; they always have an **existential** dimension, whereby the individual in his or her concrete experience confronts the problems of being. She is held in high regard in France.

Simone Weil's war-time pass to London, 30 March 1943

REFERENCES:

John Hellman, *Simone Weil: An Introduction to Her Thought* (Waterloo, Ont.: Wilfrid Laurier University Press, 1982);

Thomas R. Nevin, *Simone Weil: Portrait of a Self-Exiled Jew* (Chapel Hill: University of North Carolina Press, 1991);

Simone Pétrement, *Simone Weil: A Life,* translated by Raymond Rosenthal (New York: Pantheon, 1977).

— C.S.B.

ELIE WIESEL

Romanian-born writer and lecturer Elie Wiesel (1928–) lived in France from 1945, when he was liberated from the Nazi concentration camp at Buchenwald, to 1956, when he moved to the United States. French has remained his chosen language even after he became an American citizen in 1963. He has been active as a journalist, professor, and activist in Jewish causes. Once called "the conscience of the Holocaust," he won the Nobel Peace Prize in 1986.

Wiesel and his family were deported from Romania in 1944, first to Auschwitz. His mother and three sisters remained there when Wiesel and his father were sent to Buchenwald. His father died of starvation, while his mother and one sister died in the gas chamber. After the war Wiesel learned French and studied at the Sorbonne. For years he did not want to write about his past, but when he finally concluded that he

could and should, he wrote on the subject with great effect.

Wiesel published his first book, a lengthy memoir about the concentration camps, in Yiddish. Encouraged by **François Mauriac,** he then condensed and translated it into French as *La Nuit* (1958; translated as *Night*). His best-known work, the book was written as a memorial to his deceased family members. Though this book is the only one of his works to deal directly with the imprisonment and deaths of Jews, the greater part of his other writings may be seen as a reaction to his experiences as a child of war and the camps. The autobiographical novels *L'Aube* (1960; translated as *Dawn*), *Le Jour* (1961; translated as *The Accident*), *La Ville de la chance* (1962; translated as *The Town Beyond the Wall*), and *Les Portes de la forêt* (1964; translated as *The Gates of the Forest*) are all infused with the sufferings of the interned.

Some of Wiesel's books are influenced by Hasidic traditions and deal with aspects of modern or traditional Jewish experience. *Le Testament d'un poète juif assassiné* (1980; translated as *The Testament*), for instance, is about a Jewish writer murdered by the KGB in the Soviet Union. *Le Crépuscule au loin* (1987; translated as *Twilight*) deals with questions of human behavior in the setting of a New York insane asylum. The general themes of good and evil and the particular destiny of the Jews, which he sees as one of unique suffering, run throughout his work.

Elie Wiesel

REFERENCES:

Harry James Cargas, ed., *Responses to Elie Wiesel: Critical Essays by Major Jewish and Christian Scholars* (New York: Persea Books, 1978);

Ellen S. Fine, *Legacy of Night: The Literary Universe of Elie Wiesel* (Albany: State University of New York Press, 1982);

Alvin H. Rosenfeld and Irving Greenberg, eds., *Confronting the Holocaust: The Impact of Elie Wiesel* (Bloomington: Indiana University Press, 1978).

— C.S.B.

Monique Wittig

The feminist writer Monique Wittig (1935–) is well known in militant women's circles of the United States and Europe. *Brouillon pour un dictionnaire des amantes* (1976; translated as *Lesbian Peoples: Material for a Dictionary*), which Wittig wrote with Sande Zeig, has been especially influential, and most of Wittig's other books have been translated into English and other languages. Although she uses literary forms, Wittig's interests are less aesthetic than cultural and anthropological. In her works she rewrites history to compensate for the obscuration of women in the past and to lay the foundations for a new social order.

Wittig's first book, *L'Opoponax* (1964; translated), which won the Prix Médicis, deals with childhood, ostensibly from a child's perspective rather than an adult's. Basic social questions of self-identity and the relationships between self and others are posed obliquely in the course of this work, which has a rather impressionistic presentation of reality. The novel also explores issues of dominant male language and culture — the tools and aims of education.

L'Opoponax, which merely suggests that cultural and sexual dominance by the male must be challenged, was followed by *Les Guérillères* (1969; translated), a group of prose pieces that describes a community of female warriors and explicitly attacks male hegemony, including the symbolism of the phallus. The book proposes instead a feminist cult and iconography based on the female anatomy. *Le Corps lesbien* (1973; translated as *The Lesbian Body*), which is in part a reworking of the Song of Solomon, carries still farther the themes of the female body and lesbian love.

Brouillon pour un dictionnaire des amantes attempts to redress supposed omissions in previous, male-dominated dictionaries — not by revealing suppressed words or cataloguing neologisms but by highlighting female myths and legendary figures and by giving new and idiosyncratic feminist meanings to selected words. Wittig and Zeig also wrote the play *Le Voyage sans fin* (1985; produced as *The Constant Journey*), which parodies Miguel de Cervantes's *Don Quixote* (1605). Wittig's *Virgile, non* (1985; translated as *Across the Acheron*), a feminist recasting of Dante's cosmography, proposes a utopian world of lesbian solidarity. Though she remains involved with the feminist movement in France, Wittig has resided in the United States since 1976.

REFERENCE:

Erika Ostrovsky, *A Constant Journey: The Fiction of Monique Wittig* (Carbondale & Edwardsville: Southern Illinois University Press, 1991).

— C.S.B.

Worker Priests

During the German **Occupation** of France in **World War II,** a program called Mission de France was organized to train priests to work among the lower classes, which had become estranged from the Church — as Henri Godin and Yvan Daniel pointed out in their book *France, pays de mission?* (1943; France, a Mission

Country?). After the program was put into action in the immediate postwar period, difficulties arose because the priests were accused of adopting Marxist ideology. By the early 1950s the movement was disbanded by papal order.

By the time of the Second Vatican Council (1962–1965) the fear that missionary priests would be contaminated by Marxism had receded, and the program was renewed. Called *prêtres au travail* (worker priests), the clerics work in teams rather than as individuals. Their hours are limited, and they are forbidden to hold office or perform official duties in labor unions. The movement continues into the present, although there is wide agreement that it has not realized the hopes held for it in its early days.

REFERENCE:

J. E. Flower, "The Church," in his *France Today,* fourth edition (London: Methuen, 1980), pp. 151–171.

— D.O'C.

WORLD WAR I

World War I, which the French still call La Grande Guerre (The Great War), was a devastating experience for the nation. Of the millions who were killed on both sides of the struggle, more than 1.25 million were French soldiers and civilians.

The war began in late July 1914 when Austria-Hungary declared war on Serbia. The next month German troops advanced through Belgium into France. This invasion led to the first battle of the **Marne** (9–12 September), in which the French succeeded in stopping the German offensive. Soon after this battle, which began with the two armies maneuvering in the open field, a military stalemate ensued, with the Germans and the Allies (mostly French and British troops) settling into trenches facing one another on a long front that reached from Belgium to Switzerland. Since defensive weapons, especially the machine gun, had the tactical advantage over offensive weapons, it was virtually impossible to displace well-entrenched and heavily armed defenders. Because large numbers of lives were lost in such attempts, commanders were hesitant to make the effort.

By 1916 both sides had resumed massive offensives. The Germans made **Verdun** a strategic objective, mainly for psychological reasons. The French were able to hold this fortress, but the cost in lives during the long battle (February–June 1916) was steep. So many resources were diverted to Verdun that the French offensive in the **Somme** that July did not meet with any real success.

After the United States entered the war in 1917, the Allies had the edge in manpower that they needed to launch the decisive operation of the war. Moreover, by this time the tank had been so much improved that it was an effective offensive weapon able to neutralize the defensive superiority of the machine gun. The last great Allied offensive was led by Marshal **Ferdinand Foch.** The German army faltered during autumn 1918, and an armistice was signed on 11 November. The war was formally brought to an end with the signing of the **Treaty of Versailles** and other treaties in 1919.

The effects of the war on French life — its demography, its politics, and its culture — were profound. While the French made a deliberate effort to maintain the impression that the Germans could not entirely succeed in eliminating the brilliant cultural life that had characterized Paris before the war, the number of cultural activities was in fact reduced, and many were discontinued. Several eminent writers were killed in the fighting, including **Alain-Fournier** and **Charles Péguy;** others, such as **Guillaume Apollinaire, Louis-Ferdinand Céline,** and **Jacques Rivière,** were captured or wounded. **Roger Martin du Gard** and **Jean Cocteau** served in the ambulance corps. Many young painters were also in the military, and some — including **Raymond Duchamp-Villon** — died; it was chiefly foreign artists, such as **Pablo Picasso,** who were still active in Paris. **Henri Barbusse** published his novel criticizing the conflict, *Le Feu: Journal d'une escouade* (1916; translated as *Under Fire: The Story of a Squad*), during the war. By the time it ended, many writers and artists shared his view, having become so repulsed by the slaughter that their understanding of what Western culture meant — and of their role as artists in it — was radically changed.

REFERENCE:

J. M. Winter, *The Experience of World War I* (New York: Oxford University Press, 1989).

— C.S.B. & D.O'C.

WORLD WAR II

World War II permanently changed the face of French life. As in **World War I,** much of the fighting occurred on French soil.

After France and Great Britain declared war on Germany in September 1939, following the German invasion of Poland, there was no action on the western front for the next few months, and the French began to call the conflict the **drôle de guerre** (the phony war). The situation changed on 10 May 1940, when German troops began a sweep through the Ardennes

French refugees during World War II

Forest region of Belgium, bypassing the **Maginot Line,** the massive French fortifications along the border between France and Germany. The French army was unable to stop the German offensive and capitulated after a few weeks; this campaign has come to be known as the **Debacle.** Approximately one hundred thousand French troops were evacuated to England from **Dunkirk;** many more were lost or captured. Retreating troops and tens of thousands of civilians swarmed over the roads to the north and west of Paris, which was occupied by the invaders on 14 June. **Jean-Paul Sartre**'s novel *La Mort dans l'âme* (1949; translated as *Troubled Sleep* and *Iron in the Soul*) and **Claude Simon**'s novel *La Route des Flandres* (1960; translated as *The Flanders Road*) are among the works that deal with the invasion and retreat.

By 16 June the French, in military and political disarray, asked for an armistice. Signed on 22 June, this agreement divided France into an Occupied Zone, including the northern half of the country plus the Atlantic coast; the Forbidden Zone, a small area controlled by the German military commander in Brussels; and a **Free Zone,** in the southern half of the country.

(The Free Zone ceased to exist after the German army occupied it as well in November 1942.) The **Third Republic** was replaced by the Etat Français (French State), popularly known as the **Vichy government,** with **Philippe Pétain,** one of the military heroes of World War I, as its premier. The period in French history from June 1940 through August 1944 is known as the **Occupation.**

Many eminent French cultural figures were abroad by chance or fled Paris before the armistice. Others managed to leave the country later. **André Breton** spent most of the war years in North America; **Roger Martin du Gard** was in the West Indies but returned to France; **Antoine de Saint-Exupéry** traveled to New York before returning to serve as a military pilot in 1944. Sartre and Simon were both taken prisoner. A **Resistance** movement against the Occupation began in 1941, with **Charles de Gaulle** emerging as its leader, although he was in England until 1944, and also including an important Communist element. Among the writers associated with it were **Louis Aragon, Albert Camus, René Char, Paul Eluard,** and **André Malraux.**

Allied troops invaded Normandy on 6 June 1944 (D-Day), and Paris was liberated by U.S. troops on 25 August 1944. The process of **Liberation** was lengthy, extending from D-Day until early 1945, when the last German troops were finally driven from French soil. Germany officially surrendered on 7 May 1945.

REFERENCES:

John Keegan, *The Second World War* (New York: Viking, 1990);

James Stokesbury, *A Short History of World War II* (New York: Morrow, 1980).

—C.S.B. & D.O'C.

Y

MARGUERITE YOURCENAR

Writer Marguerite Yourcenar (1903–1987) was widely known in France and abroad even before her election as the first woman member of the Académie Française in 1980. Best known as a historical novelist, she also published dozens of other works — plays, poems, essays, and translations — whose quality has assured her high literary standing. A naturalized U.S. citizen, who settled in the United States in 1939 and lived there until her death, she was also a member of the American Academy of Arts and Letters.

She was born Marguerite de Crayencour in Belgium, but as the child of a French father, she was a French citizen and grew up in France. She published her first books, collections of poetry, in the early 1920s

American poet Hortense Flexner and her translator, Marguerite Yourcenar, in Yourcenar's backyard

before writing her first novel, *Alexis; ou, Le Traité du vain combat* (1929; translated as *Alexis*). The book is a short psychological narrative in the manner of **André Gide,** whose work doubtless influenced the young writer, especially given their shared concern with homosexual love.

Over the two decades that followed her immigration to the United States, Yourcenar composed several works in various genres. With the best-selling *Mémoires d'Hadrien* (1951; translated as *Memoirs of Hadrian*), her imaginative portrait of the Roman emperor Hadrian written in the form of letters, she achieved widespread literary success. Its historical foundations, its concern with aesthetic and moral values, and its broad sweep appealed to many readers.

Another of Yourcenar's most admired novels is *L'Œuvre au noir* (1968; translated as *The Abyss*), a historical reconstruction of sixteenth-century Europe. While the work has been highly praised, some readers have found the dialogue stilted and the attempt to convey the minds of young men of the Renaissance — soldiers, scholars, alchemists — unsuccessful.

Yourcenar's personal interests included travel, environmentalism, and African-American spirituals and freedom songs. Captivated by myth, especially Eastern legends, she often included a mythic element in her works.

REFERENCES:

C. Frederick Farrell, Jr., and Edith R. Farrell, *Marguerite Yourcenar in Counterpoint* (Lanham, Md., New York & London: University Press of America, 1983);

Pierre Horn, *Marguerite Yourcenar* (Boston: Twayne, 1985).

— C.S.B.

Z

Ossip Zadkine

Ossip Zadkine (1890–1967) was among the first **Cubist** sculptors. Unlike his contemporaries **Henri Laurens** and **Jacques Lipchitz,** he quickly moved from Cubism to an idiosyncratic blend of modern and traditional forms.

Born in Smolensk, Russia, Zadkine immigrated in 1906 to England, where he took his first art classes. In 1909 he moved to Paris, studying briefly at the Ecole des Beaux-Arts. He began carving in wood and stone in 1911; his first Cubist experiments date from 1914.

Zadkine's Cubist works are built around simplified forms broken into broad, intersecting planes. *Femme à l'éventail* (stone, 1918; *Woman with a Fan*) is typical in its construction of a human figure around curved rods and rectangular blocks. *Musiciens* (bronze, 1936; *Musicians*) is reminiscent of **Pablo Picasso**'s *Trois musiciens* (1921; *Three Musicians*), though Zadkine's work is less abstract.

Zadkine would not be constrained by any single artistic movement or tradition. Like Picasso, he made use of African masks, as in his stone *La Belle Servante* (1920; *The Beautiful Servant*), but while Picasso used such masks as a jumping-off point for Cubism, for Zadkine they were simply one more source to be mined for his art, along with quasi-Polynesian carved deities and preclassical stone heads. His best-known monument is the war memorial he sculpted in 1951 for the city of Rotterdam, Netherlands, which the Germans had leveled in **World War II.** The stone sculpture depicts a bent, distorted human figure — with chest ripped open, arms raised as if to hold back the bombs, and head flung back — screaming in anguish or outrage.

REFERENCES:

John Berger, *Permanent Red: Essays in Seeing* (London: Writers & Readers, 1979), pp. 116–121;

Marevna Vorobiev, *Life in Two Worlds* (London & New York: Abelard-Schuman, 1962);

Ossip Zadkine, *Zadkine* (New York: Universe Books, 1959).

—J.H.

Carlotta Zambelli

The elegant Italian ballerina Carlotta Zambelli (1875–1968) upheld the great classical tradition of French ballet at a time when the **Paris Opera Ballet** was in decline and the **Ballets Russes** company was forging into modernism.

Born in Milan and trained at La Scala Ballet School, Zambelli debuted at the Paris Opera Ballet in 1894 and was quickly promoted to the principal position of *étoile* (star). Known for her brilliant technique, Zambelli was famous for performances such as her leading roles in *Coppélia, Giselle,* and *Sylvia.* Her most distinguished partner was the popular Paris Opera Ballet star Albert Aveline. Inseparable companions, they spent their lives dancing and teaching together.

In 1901 Zambelli was the last foreign ballerina to make a guest-star appearance at the Saint Petersburg Maryinsky Theater. In 1912 she was a guest artist with the Ballets Russes in London, performing the *Pas de trois* (dance for three) from *Le Pavillon d'Armide* with **Vaslav Nijinsky** and **Tamara Karsavina.** Zambelli had some artistic objections to the innovations of the Ballets Russes and would later heartily disapprove of the influence that **Serge Lifar,** a former member of the Ballets Russes, had on the Paris Opera Ballet during his long tenure as director (1929–1944, 1947–1958).

The French government awarded Zambelli the Médaille de la Reconnaissance Française in 1920 for her more than one hundred performances with the Théâtres des Armées and her appearances at charity galas during **World War I.** She replaced Rosita Mauri as principal teacher of the Paris Opera Ballet school in 1920 but continued to perform until 1934.

The first dancer to be elected to the Légion d' Honneur (1926), the *Grande Mademoiselle,* as she was called, was promoted to *officier* in 1956, the year after she retired from teaching. Her many celebrated students include Lycette Darsonval, Zizi Jeanmarie, and Claire Motte.

REFERENCE:

Ivor Guest, "Carlotta Zambelli," *Dance Magazine,* 48 (February 1974): 52–65; (March 1974): 43–58.

—A.P.E.

CONTRIBUTORS

C.S.B..Catharine Savage Brosman

J.L.B. ....Jennifer L. Brown

K.E.B..Katherine E. Brosman

L.J.C. ....Louis J. Campomenosi

T.C. ....Tom Conley

A.P.E. ....Alice Pascal Escher

M.G..Melanie Gordon

P.S.H..Peter S. Hansen

J.H..John Hutton

W.L. ....Warren Lubline

J.P.McN. ....James P. McNab

R.J.N..Roy Jay Nelson

D.O'C. ....David O'Connell

TWENTIETH
CENTURY
CULTURE

French Culture
1900-1975

INDEX

A

"A 40° au-dessus de dada," 256
A bout de souffle, 40, 164, 237, 263, 377
A la recherche du temps perdu (Proust), 168, 228, 295–296
A l'ombre des jeunes filles en fleurs (Proust), 166, 296
A nous la liberté, 21, 79
A perdre haleine (Arland), 14
A propos de Nice, 389
A Share of Ink (Jabès), 183
A soi-même (Redon), 303
A Taste of Honey, 221
A travers un verger (Jaccottet), 183
A. O. Barnabooth: Ses œuvres complètes (Larbaud), 195
L'Abandon (C. Claudel), 81
Abbaye de Créteil, 117, 163–164, 318, 337, 379, 391
ABC de la peinture (Sérusier), 251, 339
Abellio, Raymond (Jean-Georges Soulès), 3
Abetz, Otto, 262
L'Abondance (Le Fauconnier), 201
Abram, Paul, 368
Abraxas, 77
L'Acacia (Simon), 343
Académie Colarossi, 153
Académie d'Architecture, 295
Académie des Beaux-Arts, 103, 117, 212, 294
Académie du Cinéma, 294
L'Académie Française, 14, 54, 79, 82, 85, 117, 125, 140, 144, 169, 173, 180, 190, 209, 232, 234, 247–248, 278, 288–289, 294, 339, 372, 376, 384, 403
Académie Goncourt. *See* Goncourt Academy.
Académie Humbert, 197
Académie Julien, 212, 250, 339, 384, 394
Académie Mallarmé, 304
Académie Royale de l'Opéra. *See* Paris Opéra Ballet.
Academy Awards, 198, 205, 267, 294, 341, 377
Academy of Art, Prague, 250
L'Accordéoniste (Picasso), 93, 280
Accords (Ozenfant), 270
L'Accusée (Saint Pierre), 328
Achard, Marcel, 21, 50, 362
Ache, Caran d', 20, 141
Acocella, Joan, 208
Acquart, André, 362
Acte sans parole (Beckett), 39
L'Action (Roblès), 314
Action Française, 3, 31, 43, 54, 62, 105, 234, 252, 309, 323, 349
"L'Activité structuraliste" (Barthes), 32
Adam et Eve (Valadon), 383
The Adamites, 250
Adamov, Arthur, 3–4, 46, 287, 336, 360, 362, 364–365
Adèle, 61
Aden, Arabie (Nizan), 254
Adlebert, Pierre, 368
Adret, Françoise, 26
Adrienne Mesurat (Green), 169
The Adventurers, 23
AEAR. *See* Association des Ecrivains et Artistes Révolutionnaires.
Aely (Jabès), 183
Aeschylus, 30, 82
Les Affaires publiques, 56
L'Afrique fantôme (Leiris), 205
Agadir Crisis, 5
L'Age d'or, 59, 243, 366

L'Age de raison (Sartre), 334
L'Age d'homme (Leiris), 205
L'Age mûr (C. Claudel), 81
L'Agrandissement (C. Mauriac), 231
AIDS, 143
L'Aile (Masson), 229
Aimée, Anouk, 103, 205, 312
Aimez-vous Brahms? (Sagan), 325
"Aimez-vous les uns les autres" (Rouault), 320
L'Aîné des Ferchaux, 40, 386
L'Air (Maillol), 219
L'Air et les songes (Bachelard), 25
Airs: poèmes 1961–1964 (Jaccottet), 183
Ajar, Emile. *See* Gary, Romain.
Alain (Emile Chartier), 5, 234, 294, 383, 397
Alain-Fournier (Henri Fournier), 5, 312, 400
Albane, Blanche, 367
Albee, Edward, 363
Albert-Birot, Pierre, 340
Album d'estampes originales de la Galerie Vollard (Vollard), 394
Album de vers anciens (Valéry), 383
Album Forain (Forain), 142
Alcools (Apollinaire), 11–12
Alechinsky, Pierre, 6
Alemereyda, Miguel, 389
Alexis ou, Le Traité du vain combat, 404
Algèbre des valeurs morales (Jouhandeau), 187
Algerian war, 6–8, 37, 64–65, 72, 127, 129, 137, 144–145, 156, 158, 176, 215, 221, 233, 241, 264, 308, 314, 323, 334, 336, 360, 386
Algiers, 149
Algiers, Battle of, 8
Algren, Nelson, 37
Les Algues, 77
L'Alittérature contemporaine (C. Mauriac), 231, 257
All This and Heaven Too, 53
Allain, Marcel, 218
Allégret, Marc, 8, 21, 29
Allégret, Yves, 8, 103, 249, 279, 341, 381
Alleg, Henri, 8
Allies, 28, 38, 47, 306–308
Allio, René, 8–9, 287, 362
L'Alouette (Anouilh), 10
Alphabets (Perec), 278
Alphaville, 165
Also sprach Zarathustra (Nietzsche), 315
Althusser, Louis, 9, 209, 258, 352
Alvear, Carlos María de, 52
L'Amant (Duras), 120
Les Amants, 220, 248
Les Amants d'Avignon (Triolet), 375
Les Amants puérils (Crommelynck), 92, 185
L'Ame enchantée (Rolland), 318
"L'Ame et la danse" (Valéry), 383
L'Ame romantique et le rêve (Béguin), 259
Amédée ou comment s'en débarrasser (Ionesco), 180
Amélie (Troyat), 376
American Academy of Arts and Letters, 403
American Conservatory, Fontainebleau, 50
Amérique (Baudrillard), 35
Amers (Saint-John Perse), 327
L'Ami lointain (C. Roy), 323
Amiel, Carole, 245
Aminadab (Blanchot), 45
"Amiral de la Flotte," 96
Amour (Denis), 394
L'Amour à mort, 308

L'Amour à vingt ans, 198, 267
Un Amour de soi (Doubrovsky), 110
"Un Amour de Swann" (Proust), 58, 103
L'Amour en fuite, 198
L'Amour fou (Breton), 56
L'Amour l'après-midi, 317
L'Amour la poésie (Eluard), 124
L'Amour médecin (Molière), 367
Amours (Léautaud), 199
Les Amours enfantines (Romains), 123
Amphitryon 38 (Giraudoux), 163, 188
Amrouche, Jean, 13–14
Amsterdam Concertebouw, 246
Anabase (Saint-John Perse), 327
Anarchism, 95, 110, 133, 135, 340–341
Ancey, Georges, 367
And Then There Were None, 23
Andrews, Jerome, 261
L'Ane Culotte (Bosco), 49
Angélique ou l'Enchantement (Robbe-Grillet), 313
Angelo (Giono), 162
Angelopoulos, Theodoros, 248
De l'angélus de l'aube à l'angélus du soir, 1888–1897 (Jammes), 184
Les Anges du péché, 56
L'Anglais tel qu'on le parle (Bernard), 50
Animism, 338
Les Annales d'Histoire Economique et Sociale, 9, 133
L'Année dernière à Marienbad, 308, 312
L'Annonce faite à Marie (P. Claudel), 34, 82, 214, 286, 364
Annunzio, Gabriele d', 324
Anouilh, Jean, 10, 31, 54, 159, 214, 286, 363, 367, 381
Anski, Shalom, 34
L'Anthologie nègre (Cendrars), 70
Anthropologie structurale (Lévi-Strauss), 209, 351
Anthropométries (Klein), 190
L'Anti-Œdipe: Le capitalisme et la schizophrénie (Deleuze), 102
Antigone (Anouilh), 10, 363
Antigone (ballet), 324
Antigone (Cocteau), 84
Antigone (Sophocles), 118
Antimémoires (Malraux), 223
L'Antiquaire (Bosco), 49
L'Antitête (Tzara), 378
Antoine, André, 10–11, 50, 91–92, 118, 121, 213–214, 318, 361–363, 367
Antoine Bloyé (Nizan), 254
Antoine et Antoinette, 38
"Antoine et Colette," 198
Antonioni, Michelangelo, 248
Apollinaire et ses amis (Laurencin), 197
Apollinaire, Guillaume, 11–12, 21, 33, 54, 56, 62, 69, 71, 74, 95, 100, 110, 136, 142, 184, 197, 213, 225, 239, 255, 272, 291, 309, 322, 337, 340, 353, 383, 400
Apollo. See Apollon Musagète.
Apollon, 208
L'Apollon de Bellac (Giraudoux), 363
Apollon Musagète (ballet), 26–27, 211, 351
Apostrophes, 12
Apparition de l'Eglise éternelle (Messiaen), 270
L'Apparition du livre (Febvre), 134
Appia, Adolphe, 12, 90
L'Apprenti sorcier (Dukas), 117
Approximations (Du Bos), 113
Après le cubisme (Le Corbusier and Ozenfant), 270
L'Après-midi d'un faune (ballet), 109, 253

D'après tout (Follain), 141
Aquarium (Soupault), 347
Aragon, Louis, 12–13, 49, 54, 56, 88, 91, 112, 123–124, 136, 141, 143–144, 147, 202, 206, 213, 220, 255, 337, 340, 353–354, 375–376, 401
L'Araigne (Troyat), 376
Les Arbres, Céret (Soutine), 347
Arc de Triomphe, 249
L'Arche, 13–14
L'Archéologie du savoir (Foucault), 143
Archer, Kenneth, 325
L'Architecte et l'empereur de l'Assyrie (Arrabal), 17
L'Archipel Lenoir (Salacrou), 368
Architruc, 284
Archives Internationales de la Danse, 14
L'Argent (Zola), 56, 210
Ariane et Barbe-Bleue (Dukas), 117
Les Aristocrates (Saint-Pierre), 327
Aristophanes, 118
Arland, Marcel, 14, 263, 275
L'Arlequin (Vasarely), 386
Arletty, 14–15, 66
Arman (Armand Fernandez), 15, 191, 256
L'Armée des ombres (Kessel), 190
Les Armes miraculeuses (Césaire), 71
Armory Show, New York, 114, 301
Arnauld, Michel. *See* Drouin, Marcel.
Aromates chasseurs (Char), 76
Aron, Raymond, 15, 138, 243, 310, 360
Aron, Robert, 18
Arp, Hans. *See* Arp, Jean.
Arp, Jean, 16–17, 61, 95, 269
Arp, Sophie Taeuber, 16, 269
Arrabal, Fernando, 17, 19, 273, 336
Arrivée d'un train en gare de La Ciotat, 215
L'Arroseur arrosé, 215
L'Art brut préféré aux arts culturels, 113
Art Cruel, 143
L'Art et la révolte (Pelloutier), 277
Art Nouveau, 148
The Art of Theatre (Craig), 91
Artaud, Antonin, 4, 17–19, 21, 29, 46, 57, 117–118, 160, 167, 229, 252, 285, 287, 321, 346, 392
Arte Joven, 282
Arthur, Jean, 53
Artine (Char), 75
Arts, 377
As I Lay Dying (Faulkner), 29
Ascenseur pour l'échafaud, 220, 248
Asmodée (F. Mauriac), 233
Asnières, 44
Aspen Music School, 241
The Asphalt Jungle, 237
L'Asphyxie (Leduc), 201
L'Assassin habite au 21, 83
L'Assassinat du duc de Guise, 328
L'Assiette au Beurre, 20, 170, 225, 349, 384, 392
Association des Ecrivains Révolutionnaires. *See* Association des Ecrivains et Artistes Révolutionnaires.
Association des Ecrivains et Artistes Révolutionnaires (AEAR), 20, 88, 220, 341
Association française d'action artistique, 64
Association Théâtrale des Etudiants de Paris, 242, 252, 365
Astérix, 20
L'Astragale (Sarrazin), 332
Astruc, Alexandre, 20–21, 102

L'Atalante, 288
Atelier, Théâtre de l'. *See* Théâtre de l'Atelier.
Ateliers d'Art Sacré, 105
Athalie (Racine), 287, 362
Athénée, Théâtre de l'. *See* Théâtre de l'Athénée.
Atlantic City, 221
Atlas Hôtel (Salacrou), 118
L'Âtre, 386
L'Attente de Dieu (Weil), 397
L'Attente, l'oubli (Blanchot), 45
Au château d'Argol (Gracq), 166
Au deuxième étage (Du Bouchet), 113
Au nom du fils (Bazin), 36
Au pays de mes racines (Cardinal), 65
Au revoir les enfants, 221
Au soir le soir (Poirot-Delpech), 289
L'Aube (Wiesel), 398
Au-dessus de la mêlée (Rolland), 317
Audiberti, Jacques, 21, 294
Audran, Stéphane, 74
Augier, M., 159
Aurenche, Jean, 22, 82
Auric, Georges, 21, 294, 344
Aurier, Albert, 251
Aurora (Leiris), 205
Aurore, 145
Aury, Dominique, 275
Auschwitz, 299, 308
Autant-Lara, Claude, 18, 22, 97, 209, 279, 374
auteur theory, 36, 311, 373, 377
Autour d'une mère, 29
L'Autre (Green), 169
Autre Journal, 264
L'Avare (Molière), 22, 92, 118, 367, 390
Aveline, Albert, 405
L'Avenir de l'homme (Teilhard), 359
L'Avenir de l'intelligence (Maurras), 105
L'Avenir dure longtemps (Althusser), 9
L'Aventure c'est l'aventure, 205
Les Aventures de la dialectique (Merleau-Ponty), 238
Les Aventures de la liberté (Lévy), 209
Avignon Art Week. *See* Avignon Festival.
Avignon Festival, 22–23, 58, 67, 261, 287, 362, 366, 368, 386, 390–391
Avoir été (Cesbron), 72
Aymé, Marcel, 23, 159, 262
Aznavour, Charles, 23, 24

B

Baader-Meinhoff terrorists, 158
Babilée, Jean, 274, 279
Babylone, 46, 361
Bacchus et Ariane (Roussel), 323
Bach, Johann Sebastian, 50, 162, 175, 194, 269, 279
Bachelard, Gaston, 25, 60, 259
Bagatelles pour un massacre (Céline), 69
Bagouet, Dominique, 261
Les Baigneuses (Derain), 106
Bainville, Jacques, 3
Le Baiser (Rodin), 316
Le Baiser au lépreux (F. Mauriac), 233
Baisers volés, 198

Baker, Josephine, 25, 208, 241
Bakhtin, Mikhail, 32, 191
Bakst, Léon, 74, 109, 140–141, 324
Le Bal des voleurs (Anouilh), 10
Le Bal du comte d'Orgel (Radiguet), 299
Balanchine, George, 26, 109, 211, 274, 351
Le Balcon (Genet), 158, 361, 364
Un Balcon en forêt (Gracq), 166
Balkan War, 283
Ball, Hugo, 61, 95
La Ballade du grand macabre (Ghelderode), 160
Ballades françaises (Fort), 142
Une Balle perdue (Kessel), 190
Ballet de Marseille, 274, 279
Ballet du Vingtième Siècle, 77, 261
Le Ballet mécanique (Léger), 203
Ballet pour Demain, 261
Ballet Rambert, 189
Ballet romantique (Levinson), 208
Ballet Suédois, 14
Ballet Technique (Karsavina), 189
Ballet Théâtre Contemporain, 26
Ballet Théâtre Français de Nancy, 26
Ballets 1933, 26
Ballets de l'Etoile, 40
Ballets de Paris, 279
Ballets des Champs-Elysées, 77, 279
Ballets du XXième Siècle, 40
Ballets Ida Rubinstein, 324
Ballets Janine Charrat, 77
Ballets Modernes de Paris, 261
Ballets Russes, 26–28, 109, 140–141, 166, 171, 189, 196–197, 208, 211, 228–229, 245, 252–254, 272, 274, 324–325, 336, 351, 364, 405
Ballets Russes de Monte Carlo, 28, 229
Ballets Russes du Colonel de Basil, 28
Balzac, Honoré de, 11, 66, 74, 202, 221, 224, 231, 257, 312, 216–317, 319, 332, 367, 376
Les Bandar-Log (Koechlin), 191
Banville, Théodore de, 138, 170
Bao Dai, 177–178
"Barbara" (Gréco), 168, 292
Barbarella, 381
La Barbarie à visage humain (Lévy), 209, 258
Barbarie et poésie (Maurras), 234
Barberini Torso (Michelangelo), 316
Barbey d'Aurevilly, Jules-Amédée, 21, 138
Barbusse, Henri, 20, 28, 79–80, 88, 400
Bardèche, Maurice, 28, 54
Bardot, Brigitte, 29, 149, 221, 248, 381
Barney, Natalie Clifford, 86, 392
Baronova, Irina, 292
Barrabas, 136
Un Barrage contre le Pacifique (Duras), 83
Barrault, Jean-Louis, 29–30, 46, 51, 57, 66–67, 82, 88, 118, 224, 287, 304–305, 363–364
Barrès, Maurice, 30–31, 48, 224, 232
Barsacq, André, 31, 118, 362, 364
Barthes, Roland, 31–32, 35, 191–192, 239, 259, 311, 346, 351–352, 359, 372
Bartók, Béla, 121, 310
Les Bas-Fonds (Gorky), 306
Basil, Wassily de, 28
Bastille, 366
Bastille Day, 290
Bataille, Georges, 32–33, 139, 346

La Bataille dans la rizière (Roy), 178
La Bataille d'Arcachon (Cixous), 78
La Bataille de Pharsale (Simon), 343
La Bataille du rail, 82–83
La Bâtarde (Leduc), 201
Le Bateau Lavoir, 11, 33–34, 170, 184, 247
Les Bâtisseurs d'empire;ou, Le Schmürz (Vian), 388
Battle of France. *See* Debacle.
Baty, Gaston, 19, 34, 66, 88, 92, 157, 285, 367–368
Baudelaire, Charles, 54, 60, 116, 136, 146, 187, 230, 291, 303, 315,
    334–335
Baudrillard, Jean, 35, 98
Bausch, Pina, 261
Le Bavard (des Forêts), 107
Bayreuth Festivals, 51
Bazin, André, 21, 35–36, 38
Bazin, Hervé, 36
BBC Orchestra, 51
BBC Radio, 155, 306
"Un Beau Matin" (Aznavour), 24
Le Beau Serge, 73
Un Beau Ténébreux (Gracq), 166
Beauharnais, Josephine de, 249
Beaumarchais, Pierre-Augustin Caron de, 22, 138, 304, 367
Beauvoir, Simone de, 13, 29, 36–37, 62, 108, 124, 127–128, 156–
    157, 166, 201–202, 224, 238, 247, 293, 334, 360, 397
Les Beaux Draps (Céline), 69
Bécaud, Gilbert, 24
Becker, Jacques, 38, 149, 279, 311, 341
Becket, ou l'honneur de Dieu (Anouilh), 10
Beckett, Samuel, 3, 30, 38–39, 46, 180, 256, 273, 284, 305, 336, 356,
    360–361, 363
Becque, Henri, 185
Bedû-Bridel, Jacques, 123
Beethoven, Ludwig van, 52, 60, 179, 328
Béguin, Albert, 259
Béjart Ballet Lausanne, 40
Béjart, Maurice, 22, 40, 261, 274, 325
Belgian Communist Party, 219
Bell, Marie, 30, 364
La Belle au bois (Supervielle), 286
Belle de jour, 59, 104, 189, 284
La Belle Equipe, 121
La Belle et la bête, 21, 82–83
La Belle Servante (Picasso), 405
Les Belles Images (Beauvoir), 37
Belmondo, Jean-Paul, 40–41, 57, 149
Le Belvédère (Mandiargues), 223
Benda, Julien, 41
Benedetto, André, 41
Bennett, Arnold, 195
Benois, Alexandre, 109, 140, 324
Benoist, Jean-Marie, 258
Benoît Misére (Ferré), 136
Benz, Maria (Nusch), 124–125
Bérard, Christian, 41–42, 279
Béraud, Henri, 170
Berdyayev, Nikolay, 249
Bérénice (Racine), 34, 287
Bergen, Candice, 221
Bergson, Henri, 41–43, 226, 276, 294, 346, 379
Le Bergsonisme ou une philosophie de la mobilité (Benda), 41
Berl, Emmanuel, 225–226
Berlin Olympics, 64
Berliner Ensemble, 287
Berna, Serge, 207

Bernanos, Georges, 43, 56, 72, 291
Bernard, Emile, 44, 73, 105, 153, 251, 395
Bernard, Tristan, 50
Bernard Quesnay (Maurois), 233
Bernhardt, Sarah, 45, 250
Bernstein, Henri, 364
Berri, Claude, 271
Berry, Jules, 66
Bertolucci, Bernardo, 198, 306, 389
Berton, Germaine, 309
Besson, Luc, 248
Les Bestiaires (Montherlant), 246
La Bête humaine, 139, 149, 306
Beuve-Méry, Hubert, 243, 359
Bible, 82, 105, 165, 244, 373
Bibliothèque littéraire Jacques-Doucet, 255
Bibliothèque Nationale, 9, 308
Bibliothèque de la Pléiade, 150
Les Biches, 74
Les Biches (ballet), 197, 252–253, 291
Biffures (Leiris), 205
Bildnerei der Geisteskranken (Prinzhorn), 113
Bin, Emile, 340
The Birds (Aristophanes), 118
Bis ans Ende der Welt, 248
Bizarre Bizarre, 66
Bizet, Georges, 279, 321
Blaché, Herbert, 174
Black Moon, 221
Black Panthers, 158
Black Tights, 279
Blake, William, 187
Blanch, Lesley, 153
Blanchette (Brieux), 367
Blanchot, Gustave, 20
Blanchot, Maurice, 33, 45–46, 205, 259
Der blaue Engel, 103
Blaue Reiter movement, 16
Le Blé en herbe (Colette), 86
Blèche (Drieu La Rochelle), 112
Bleus blancs rouges ou les libertins, 287
Bleustein-Blanchet, Marcel, 145
Blin, Roger, 19, 29–30, 46–47, 67, 305, 363
Bloc Démocratique Sénégalais, 338
Bloc National, 79
Bloc-Notes, 1951–1957 (F. Mauriac), 233
Bloch, Marc, 9, 133
Blondin, Antoine, 176
Bloy, Léon, 226
Blue Rayonism (Larionov), 196
Blue Rider movement. *See* Blaue Reiter movement.
Blum, Léon, 47, 147, 186, 290–291, 345, 348–349, 369, 371
Blum, René, 28
Bob le flambeur, 237
Bocuse, Paul, 260–261
Le Bœuf sur le toit (ballet), 83, 240
Bogart, Humphrey, 40
La Bohémienne endormie (Rousseau), 322
Boilly, Léopold, 357
Bois d'Amour, Brittany, 339
Boisdeffre, Pierre de, 48
Boissard, Maurice, 198
Boléro (ballet), 40, 300–301
Bollingen Foundation, 327
Bolshevik Revolution, 74, 347
Bolsheviks, 80, 85

Bolshevism, 241
Bolshoi Ballet, 274
Bonaparte, Napoleon, 272, 369
Le Bonheur, 386
Bonheur de vivre (Matisse), 231
Le Bonheur fou (Giono), 162
Bonjour tristesse (Sagan), 325
Bonnard, Pierre, 48, 214, 245, 250–252, 339, 385, 394
Bonnefous, Jean-Patrick, 274
Bonnefoy, Yves, 49
Les Bonnes (Genet), 42, 158, 188
Les Bonnes Femmes, 74
Bonnier de la Chapelle, Fernand, 97
Bonsoir Thérèse (Triolet), 375
Books and Theatres (Craig), 91
Borde, Raymond, 139
Borges, Jorge Luis, 278
Boris Godunov (Opera), 109
Boronova, Irina, 28
Bory, Jean-Louis, 265
Bosch, Hieronymus, 6
Bosco, Henri, 49
Bossuet, Jacques-Bénigne, 194
Bost, Pierre, 22
Boston Symphony Orchestra, 49, 246
Botticelli, Sandro, 219
Le Boucher, 74, 347
Boudin, Eugéne, 244
Boudu sauvé des eaux, 38, 306
Les Bouffes du Nord, 58
Les Bouffes-Parisiens, 214
Bouguereau, William, 230
Bouhélier, Saint-Georges de, 157
Bouillon de culture, 12
Bouise, Jean, 362
Boulanger, Nadia, 49–50, 132, 270
Boulevard Saint-Germain, 327
boulevard theaters, 42, 50, 91, 173, 271, 363–364, 391
Les Boulevards de ceinture (Modiano), 243
Boulez, Pierre, 51, 90, 179, 238
Boum, boum, ça fait mal (Arman), 15
Bouquet, Romain, 367
Bourdelle, Emile-Antoine, 52, 219
Bourdet, Edouard, 88
Bourdieu, Pierre, 52
Bouret, Jean, 59
Les Bourgeois de Calais (Rodin), 316
La Boutique fantasque (ballet), 229
La Boutique obscure: 124 rêves (Perec), 277
"Boutique simultanée" (Delaunay-Terk & Heim), 101
Bouvier, Joëlle, 261
Bow, Clara, 191
Boyer, Charles, 52–53, 149, 364
La Braise et la rivière (Renard), 304
Brancusi, Constantin, 315
Brand (Ibsen), 364
Braque, Georges, 16, 53–54, 93–94, 101, 116, 133, 147, 163–164, 170–171, 197, 203, 210–211, 225, 239, 241, 283, 309, 322, 337, 392
Brasillach, Robert, 28, 54, 186
Brassens, Georges, 24, 54–55
Brau, Jean-Louis, 207
Braudel, Fernand, 9
Braunberger, Pierre, 8
Brauner, Victor, 55
Breathings (Jaccottet), 183

Brecht, Bertolt, 4, 8, 34, 89, 287, 362, 364, 368–369, 391
Breker, Arno, 148
Brel, Jacques, 24, 55
Bremond, Claude, 372
Bresdin, Rodolphe, 303
Bresson, Robert, 55–56, 67, 220, 377
Breton, André, 12, 18, 33, 55–57, 71, 75, 88, 96, 108, 125, 134, 167, 204, 213, 218–219, 221, 223–224, 229, 255, 278, 297, 309, 340, 347, 353–354, 355, 377, 381, 395–396, 401
Breton Bois d'Amour, 339
Briand, Aristide, 57, 387
Brice, Fanny, 242
Brieux, Eugène, 50, 367
Brisson, Pierre, 138
Broadway, 25, 50
Bronislava Nijinska Hollywood Ballet School, 253
Brook, Peter, 19, 30, 57–58, 364
The Brothers Karamazov (Dostoyevsky), 188
Brouillon pour un dictionnaire des amantes (Wittig), 399
Broutelles, Mme. C. de, 293
Brownlow, Kevin, 151
Bruant, Aristide, 58, 61
Brubeck, Dave, 241
Bruckner, Ferdinand, 286
Brueghel, Pieter the Elder, 6, 92
Le Bruissement de la langue (Barthes), 32
Brulé, André, 41
Bruller, Jean. *See* Vercors.
Brumes du passé (Supervielle), 352
Brussels Académie des Beaux-Arts, 218
Brussels Palais des Sports, 40
Buber, Martin, 207
Bubu de Montparnasse (Philippe), 280
Buchenwald, 357, 398
Büchner, Georg, 369
Budapest Bauhaus, 386
Buenos Aires Teatro Colón, 253
Buffet, Bernard, 58–59, 113, 162
Buñuel, Luis, 59, 104, 189, 209, 243, 248, 284, 386
Burroughs, William S., 69
Burton, Richard, 10
Butler, Samuel, 195
Butor, Michel, 60, 123, 232, 256–257, 267, 277, 293–294, 331, 353
Byron, George Gordon, Lord, 113, 233

C

Cabala, 183
Le Cabaret de la belle femme (Dorgelès), 110
Cabaret des Assassins. *See* Cabaret du Lapin Agile.
Cabaret du Lapin Agile, 61, 118, 247
Cabaret Voltaire, 16, 61–62, 95
"Ça c'est Paris" (Mistinguett), 242
Cachets (Arman), 15
Cachin, Marcel, 147
Çacountala (C. Claudel), 80–81
Cadavre exquis, 229
Le Cadeau (Ray), 301
Le Cadran lunaire (Mandiargues), 223
Caesar, Julius, 272
Café Azon, 225
Café de Flore, 62, 108, 168, 327
Café de la Rotonde, 62, 91, 247

Café des Arts, 251
Café du Dôme, 62, 91, 247
Café Volpini, 44
Cage, John, 336
Cahier de retour au pays natal (Césaire), 71
Le Cahier noir (F. Mauriac), 233
Cahiers (Valéry), 384
Les Cahiers d'André Walter (Gide), 160
Cahiers de la Compagnie Madeleine Renaud–Jean-Louis Barrault,
    30
Les Cahiers de la Petite Dame (Rysselberghe), 161
Cahiers de la Quinzaine, 276
Cahiers du Cinéma, 35–36, 73, 164, 263, 311, 317, 373, 377
Caillois, Roger, 205
Calderón de la Barca, Pedro, 18, 118
Caligula (Camus), 64, 105
Calligrammes (Apollinaire), 12
Le Camarade infidèle (Schlumberger), 336
Camelots du Roi, 3, 43
Camille Claudel, 106
Le Camion, 121
Les Camisards, 9
Camoin, Charles, 133
Camondo, Isaac de, 394
Campanadas a medianoche, 248
Camus, Albert, 37, 54, 62–65, 67, 71, 75–76, 87, 105, 108, 112,
    127–128, 173, 255, 294, 311, 314, 323, 360, 397, 401
Can-Can, 78
Candida (Shaw), 285
Candide, 170, 186, 208, 225
Cannes Film Festival, 64, 83, 98–99, 121, 205, 294, 358, 386
La Cantatrice chauve (Ionesco), 179–180, 360–361
Canton de Vaud, 157
Cantos (Emmanuel), 125
Cantos (Pound; trans. Roche), 315
"Les Canuts" (Bruant), 58
Caoutchouc (Picabia), 281
Capital (Marx), 9
Capitale de la douleur (Eluard), 124
Capitalisme et schizophrénie (Deleuze), 102
Les Caprices de Marianne (Musset), 185, 368
Carbuccia, Horace de, 170
Cardinal, Marie, 65
The Caretaker (Pinter), 47
Carina Ari Medal, 212
Carlson, Carolyn, 261, 274
Carmen (ballet), 279
Carnaval (ballet), 252–253
Le Carnaval des animaux (Saint-Saëns), 328
Carné, Marcel, 14, 29–30, 65–67, 149, 243, 248, 288, 292
Carnegie Prize, 148
Carnot, President Sadi, 135
Caron, Leslie, 86
Carpeaux, Jean-Baptiste, 315
Carpentier, Georges, 70
Carrington, Leonora, 139
Carroll, Lewis, 221
Cartel des Gauches, 47
Cartel des Quatre, 29, 34, 50, 66–67, 88, 91–92, 118, 188, 285–286
Carter, Elliott, 50
Cartier, Jean-Albert, 26
La Cartoucherie, Paris, 366
Casablanca, 96, 121
Casarès, Maria, 22, 66–67, 369, 390
Casino de Paris, 145, 241
Casque d'or, 38, 341

The Casting of the Net (Valadon), 382
Cat on a Hot Tin Roof (T. Williams), 57
Catalogue d'oiseaux (Messiaen), 238
Catch-22, 96
La Cathédrale de Sens (Ricardou), 310
Catherine the Great, 376
Catholicism, 32, 34, 43, 48, 67, 71–72, 81–82, 87, 105, 125, 127, 152,
    154, 159, 161, 165, 169, 181, 195, 204, 221, 224, 226, 232–234,
    249, 276–277, 304, 319–320, 324, 346, 358, 397
Cavaillé-Col, Aristide, 270
La Cavale (Sarrazin), 332
Le Cavalier seul (Audiberti), 21
Les Caves du Majestic (Simenon), 342
Les Caves du Vatican (Gide), 160
Cayrol, Jean, 67–68, 249, 293, 308
Ce Monde ancien (Saint Pierre), 327
Ce qui fut sans lumière (Bonnefoy), 49
Ce sexe qui n'en est pas un (Irigaray), 181
Ce Soir, 206
Ceci n'est pas une pipe (Magritte), 218
Cela s'appelle l'aurore (Roblès), 314
Céline et Julie vont en bateau, 312
Céline, Louis-Ferdinand, 58, 68–69, 293, 315, 400
Celle qui fut la Belle Heaulmière (Rodin), 316
Les Cenci (Artaud), 19, 46
The Cenci (Shelley), 19
Cendrars, Blaise, 62, 69–70
Cendres et poussières (Vivien), 393
Le Centenaire (Obaldia), 265
Centre de Recherches en Etudes Féminines, 78
Centre international de recherches théâtrales, 57
Centre National d'Art et de Culture Georges Pompidou. *See* Cen-
    tre Pompidou.
Centre National de la Recherche Scientifique (CNRS), 70, 320,
    372
Centre Pompidou, 51, 70, 179, 220, 371
Centres chorégraphiques nationaux, 261
Le Cercle de famille (Maurois), 234
Cercle des Escholiers, 213
Cercle du Cinéma, 145
Cercle Gaulois (Gallic Circle), 11
Cerdan, Marcel, 70–71, 280
Les Cerfs-volants (Gary), 153
Un Certain Sourire (Sagan), 325
"Une Certaine Tendance du cinéma français" (Truffaut), 22, 373,
    377
Cervantes, Miguel de, 29, 46, 399
Ces plaisirs (Colette), 86
Césaire, Aimé, 71, 204, 338
César (Pagnol), 50, 271
César awards, 294
César-Antéchrist (Jarry), 186
Cesbron, Gilbert, 71–72, 328
Cesbron, Michel, 72
"C'est vrai" (Mistinguett), 242
Cet obscur objet du désir, 59
Cézanne, Paul, 44, 53, 55, 72–73, 93, 100, 106, 114, 116, 132–133,
    148, 153–154, 193, 195, 203, 210, 230, 244–245, 282–283, 394
Chabrol, Claude, 35, 73–74, 263, 317
Chadar (Vasarely), 386
Chagall, Marc, 74–75, 223, 347
Le Chagrin et la pitié, 267–268
Les Chaises (Ionesco), 180
Chambard Socialiste, 349
"La Chambre" (Sartre), 333
La Chambre des enfants (des Forêts), 107–108

Champigny, Robert, 259
Les Champs magnétiques (Breton and Soupault), 56, 347
La Chance de Françoise, 367
Chanel perfumes, 5, 75, 104
Chanel, Coco, 75
Chanel, Gabrielle. *See* Chanel, Coco.
"La Chanson du mal aimé" (Apollinaire), 11, 136
Chansons pour le repas de l'ogre (Jabès), 183
Le Chant du monde (Giono), 162
Chants d'ombre (Senghor), 338
Un Chapeau de paille d'Italie (Labiche), 34, 79
Chaplin, Charles, 79, 140, 182, 191, 207, 212, 286, 358
Chaque homme dans sa nuit (Green), 169
Char, René, 51, 56, 75–76, 124, 353–354, 401
Charcuterie mécanique, 215
Chardonne, Jacques, 76
La Charge (Valloton), 384
Charlot, Edmond, 14, 141
Charlus, Baron de, 295
Le Charme discret de la bourgeoisie, 59
Charmes (Valéry), 5, 383
Charpentier, Gustave, 76
Charrat, Janine, 77, 279
Chartier, Alain, 5
La Chartreuse de Parme, 67
Chasing a Rainbow: The Life of Josephine Baker, 25
"La Chasse aux papillons" (Brassens), 54
Châtelet, Théâtre du. *See* Théâtre du Châtelet.
Le Chat et la souris, 205–206
Le Chat Noir, 58, 61, 247, 335, 340, 349, 392
Château en Suède (Sagan), 326, 381
Chateaubriand, François-René de, 233
Chateaubriant, Alphonse de, 159
Le Chantier (Rouault), 320
La Chatte (Colette), 86
Chaumeton, Etienne, 139
Chauraud, Jacque, 261
Chauviré, Yvette, 77, 274
Chavance, René, 34
Chekhov, Anton, 58, 285, 304
Le Chemin de crête (Marcel), 225
Les Chemins de la liberté (Sartre), 334
Chêne et chien (Queneau), 297
Les Chênes qu'on abat (Malraux), 223
Chennevière, Georges, 318
Chéreau, Pierre, 364
Chéri (Colette), 86
The Cherry Orchard (Chekhov), 58, 304
Chesnaye, Robert de, 96
Le Cheval (Duchamp-Villon), 116
Le Cheval blanc (Triolet), 375
Le Cheval de Troie (Nizan), 254
Le Cheval d'orgueil, 74
Chevalier, Maurice, 23, 77–78, 86, 241
Chevaliers de la Table Ronde (Cocteau), 364
Les Chevaux du soleil (J. Roy), 323
Chiappe, Jean, 311
Un Chien andalou, 59
Chien blanc (Gary), 153
Le Chien jaune (Simenon), 342
Le Chiendent (Queneau), 297
La Chienne, 139, 306
Les Chiens de garde (Nazin), 254
Les Chiens de paille (Drieu La Rochelle), 112
Chiens perdus sans collier (Cesbron), 72
La Chimère, Paris, 185

Chinese Revolution of 1927, 222
La Chinoise, 165
Chirac, Jacques, 138, 300, 380
Chirico, Giorgio de, 218, 353, 355
Chopin, Frédéric, 132, 140
Chopiniana (ballet), 140
Chopinot, Régine, 261
Les Choses: Histoire des années soixante (Perec), 277
Le Christ dans la banlieue (Rouault), 320
Christ jaune (Gauguin), 154
Christian Democrats, 220
Christian-Jacque, 29, 67
Christianity, 20, 82, 125, 127–128, 152, 154, 220, 226, 233, 239, 243, 249, 252, 276, 304, 311, 317, 320, 358–359, 396–397
Christo, 256
Christophe Colomb (P. Claudel), 30, 160
Christophe, Henri, 71
Chronique (Saint-John Perse), 327
Chronique d'un été, 320
Chronique des Pasquier (Duhamel), 117
Chronique privée (Chardonne), 76
Chronique privée de l'an quarante (Chardonne), 76
Chronophone, 156
Chthonian Deity Watching over the Sleep of a Young Man (Fini), 139
Church of la Trinité, 238, 270
Church of Saint-Germain-des-Prés, 108
Church of Saint Merry, 328
Church of Saint-Séverin, 100
Church of Saint-Sulpice, 269
Church of the Madeleine, 269
La Chute (Camus), 64, 108
La Chute de la maison Usher, 126
Ciboulette, 22
Le Cid (Corneille), 22, 30, 390
Le Ciel est à vous, 170
Le Cimetière des voitures (Arrabal), 17
"Le Cimetière marin" (Valéry), 383
cinéma vérité, 320
Cinéma-Club de France, 117
Cinemascope, 151
Cinémathèque Française, 145, 170, 205, 210, 320
cinématographe, 215
Cinq grandes odes (P. Claudel), 82
Cinquième République. *See* Fifth Republic.
Cirque d'Hiver, 34, 157
Un Cirque passe (Modiano), 243
Une Cité industrielle (Garnier), 152
Citizen Kane, 386
Città nuova (Sant'Elia), 152
City Lights, 182, 207
Civilisation atlantique (Fougeron), 143
Civilisation, 1914–1917 (Duhamel), 117
Cixous, Hélène, 78, 124, 181, 242
Clair de lune (Debussy), 98
Clair, René, 21–22, 56, 65, 78, 79, 249, 279, 294, 386
Claire (Chardonne), 76
Clairières dans le ciel, 1902–1906 (Jammes), 184
Clark, T. H., 97
Clarté, 28, 79–80, 309
Clarté (Barbusse), 28
Claudel, Camille, 80–81
Claudel, Paul, 29–30, 34, 80–82, 88, 150, 161, 184, 195, 214, 240, 247, 262, 276, 286, 304, 312, 327, 339, 364, 367, 383
Claudine à l'école (Colette), 86
Clavel, Maurice, 258

Clé, 134
La Clé sur la porte (Cardinal), 65
Clef de la poésie (Paulhan), 275
Clemenceau, Georges, 244–245, 374
Clément, Catherine, 78
Clément, René, 82–83, 374
Cléo de 5 à 7, 386
Cléopâtre (ballet), 324
Clérambard, 23
Clermont-Ferrand, 268
Cleveland Orchestra, 51
Climats (Maurois), 233–234
Les Cloches de Bâle (Aragon), 13
cloisonnism, 44, 48, 105
Clope au dossier (Pinget), 284
Close Encounters of the Third Kind, 377
Clotho (C. Claudel), 81
Clouzot, Henri-Georges, 29, 83, 147, 245, 294, 341, 386
Les Clowns (Mnouchkine), 242, 365–366
COBRA, 6, 343, 354
Cocher, Jean Laurent, 105
Le Cochon noir (Planchon), 287
The Cocoanuts, 140
Cocteau, Jean, 21, 29, 41–42, 67, 70, 82–84, 109, 118, 151, 157–159, 175, 184, 188, 225, 229, 231, 240, 255, 272, 279, 285, 291, 294, 299, 335, 340, 344–345, 351, 361, 364, 400
Le Cocu magnifique (Crommelynck), 92
Cœur fidèle, 126
Cohn-Bendit, Daniel, 85, 236
Coiffard, René, 102
Colbert, Claudette, 53
Cold War, 8, 15, 139, 144, 147, 177, 238, 252, 283, 334, 354, 356
colères (Arman), 15
Colette, 36, 85–87, 124, 301, 392
Colette, Sidonie-Gabrielle. *See* Colette.
Colette Baudoche (Barrès), 31
Collaboration, 159
Collège de France, 9, 42, 52, 70, 134, 142, 196, 208, 289
Collège de 'Pataphysique, 186, 297
Collège de Sociologie, 205
Collet, Henri, 344
Colline (Giono), 162
La Colline inspirée (Barrès), 31
Collioure, 106
Colombe, 363
Coluche, 58, 63
Columbia University, 90
Combat, 31, 64, 87
Combes Law, 57, 87, 111
Combes, Emile, 57, 87
La Comédie de Charleroi (Drieu La Rochelle), 112
Comédie des Champs-Elysées, 18, 66, 188, 285
Comédie-Française, 8, 23, 30, 34, 41–42, 45, 67, 87–88, 91, 118, 147, 158, 188, 199, 247, 279, 286, 304, 362–364
Comédie Montaigne Gémier, 34, 157
comédies et proverbes (Rohmer), 317
Comintern, 177
Comité d'action français. *See* Ligue de l'Action Français.
Comité de Vigilance des Intellectuels Antifascistes, 20, 341
Comité des Forges, 359
Comme le temps passe (Brasillach), 54
Comme si rien n'était (Cardinal), 65
Comment c'est (Beckett), 39
Comment la littérature est-elle possible? (Blanchot), 46
"Comment réformer notre mise en scène" (Appia), 12
Commentaires (Alain), 5

Commerce, 195
Common Market. *See* European Economic Community.
Commune, 20, 88–89, 111, 220, 290, 341
Commune de Paris (Benedetto), 41
Communism, 13, 20, 28, 35, 37, 41, 46–47, 56, 59, 64, 71, 87–88, 108, 125–127, 129, 135, 144, 151, 155–156, 161–162, 165, 172–173, 177–178, 191, 202, 204, 206, 236, 238, 243, 245, 254, 258, 275, 283, 289–291, 299, 306–309, 318, 323, 328, 334, 341, 351, 354, 357, 360, 382
Les Communistes (Aragon), 13, 206
Comoedia, 208
La Compagnie des Quinze, 89, 91, 367
Compagnie Favart, 274
Compagnie Madeleine Renaud–Jean-Louis Barrault, 30, 304–305
Compagnies Républicaines de Sécurité, 236
Les Compagnons de la Chanson, 281
Compagnons de la Chimère, 34
Concours International d'Orgue, 294
Concours International de Chant de Paris, 294
Concours International de Musique de Chambre, 294
Concours International de Violoncelle Rostropovich, 294
Concrete music (musique concrète), 89
Le Condamné à mort (Genet), 158
Un Condamné à mort s'est échappé, 56, 220
La Condition humaine (Malraux), 166, 222
La Condition ouvrière (Weil), 397
La Condition postmoderne (Lyotard), 215–216
Confidence africaine (Martin du Gard), 228
Le Conflit des interprétations: Essais d'herméneutique (Ricœur), 311
Congrès Mondial des Ecrivains Antifascistes, 173
Connaissance de l'Est (P. Claudel), 82
La Connaissance surnaturelle (Weil), 397
Les Conquérants (Malraux), 222
La Conquête (Faure), 132
La Conquête de l'air (La Fresnaye), 194
La Conquête de l'Amérique: La question de l'autre (Todorov), 372
La Conscience critique (Poulet), 291
Conseil National de la Résistance, 307
La Conspiration (Nizan), 254
Constant, Benjamin, 291
Constellations (Breton), 57
Les Constructeurs (Léger), 204
Constructivism, 27
Contadour movement, 162
Contandin, Joseph Désiré Fernand, 135
Contat, Michel, 21
Conte, Richard, 83
La Contestation et la mise en pièces de la plus illustre tragédes... (Planchon), 287
Continuel-mobile, Continuel Lumière (Le Parc), 171
"Contribution à la théorie marxiste de la connaissance" (Garaudy), 151
Convention des Institutions Républicaines, 345
Cool Memories, 1980–1985 (Baudrillard), 35
Cool Memories II (Baudrillard), 35
Copeau, Jacques, 12, 34, 50, 66, 88–92, 118, 157, 161, 188, 262, 366–367, 390–391
Copenhagen Brussels Amsterdam. *See* COBRA.
Copland, Aaron, 50
Coppélia, 292, 405
Le Coq de bruyère (Tournier), 373
Le Coq et l'arlequin (Cocteau), 344
La Coquille et le clergyman (Artaud), 18, 117
Coquiot, Gustave, 282

Le Corbeau, 83, 147
Coriolanus (Shakespeare), 363
Cormon, Fernand, 44, 281
Corneille et la dialectique du héros (Doubrovsky), 110
Corneille, Pierre, 22, 30, 54, 194, 246, 287, 336, 390
Le Cornet à dés (Jacob), 183
Les Corps conducteurs (Simon), 343
Corps et biens (Desnos), 108
Les Corps étrangers (Cayrol), 68
Le Corps lesbien (Wittig), 399
Corps perdu (Apollinaire), 71
Corydon (Gide), 161
Cosi è se vi pare (Pirandello), 118, 362
Cosmogénies (Klein), 190
Costa, Bernard Da, 62
Du côté de chez Swann (Proust), 58
Council of Europe, 338
Le Coupable (Bataille), 33
Couperin, François, 194
La Coupole, 91, 247
Courbet, Gustave, 283
Courrier sud (Saint-Exupéry), 326
Cours de composition musicale (d'Indy), 178
Cours de linguistique générale (Saussure), 351
Courteline, Georges, 50
Les Cousins, 73
Cousteau, Jacques-Yves, 220
Couturier, Paul-Vaillant, 79
Covent Garden Russian Ballet, 28
Cowley, Malcolm, 384
Craig, Edward Gordon, 90–92, 119
La Création du Monde, 70, 240
Creative Intuition in Art and Poetry (Maritain), 227
La Créole (musical), 25
Le Crépuscule au loin (Wiesel), 398
Crevel, René, 88
Crime and Punishment (Dostoyevsky), 34, 368
Le Crime de Monsieur Lange (Becker), 38, 306
The Criminals (Bruckner), 286
Cripure (Guilloux), 173
Critics' Prize, 58
Critique (Bataille), 33
Critique de la critique (Todorov), 372
Critique de la raison dialectique (Sartre), 128 334
Critique et vérité (Barthes), 32
Croissance (Arp), 17
La Croix, 111
Les Croix de bois (Dorgelès), 110
Croix de Guerre, 69, 112, 153, 189–190, 222, 311
Croix de la Libération, 153
Crombecque, Alain, 23
Crommelynck, Fernand, 92, 185
Cross, Henri-Edmond, 230
Le Cru et le cuit (Lévi-Strauss), 209
Cruautés de la nuit (Vitrac), 392
Cubism, 11, 16, 27, 53, 58, 73–74, 92–94, 100–101, 106, 114, 116, 120, 131, 133, 148, 163–166, 170, 171, 183–184, 193–195, 197–201, 203, 210–212, 218, 225, 229, 239–241, 244, 255, 270, 272, 281, 283, 301, 331, 337, 340, 391–393, 405
Cubo-Futurism, 165–166
Cuirassier (Géricault), 194
Le Cuirassier (La Fresnaye), 194
La Cuisine (Wesker), 365
Le Culte du moi (Barrès), 31
Cunningham, Merce, 261, 274
Cupis de Camargo, Marie-Anne, 273

La Curée, 381
Curel, François de, 50
Une Curieuse Solitude (Sollers), 345
Curtiz, Michael, 121–122
Les Cyclones (Roy), 147
"Le Cygne" (Saint-Saëns), 328
Cyrano de Bergerac (Rostand), 50, 106
Czechoslovak Communist Party, 151

D

D'Eugène Delacroix au néo-impressionnisme (Signac), 340
D-Day, 402
Da Costa, Bernard, 62
Dabit, Eugène, 95, 293
Dada, 14, 16, 55–56, 61–62, 95–96, 115, 124, 181–182, 197, 202, 206, 213, 219, 256, 269, 281, 301–302, 336, 340, 347, 353, 371, 377–378
Dada/Surrealist Exhibition, 269
Dakar-Djibouti expedition, 205
Daladier, Edouard, 311
Dalí, Salvador, 59, 139, 229, 302, 353–355
Dalio, Marcel, 8, 96
Damage, 221
Damas, Léon-Gontran, 71, 338
Les Dames du Bois de Boulogne, 56, 67
Dance Magazine, 40
Dance Magazine Award, 40
The Dance of the Future (Duncan), 119
Daniel, Jean, 129, 258
Daniel, Yvan, 399
Danilova, Alexandra, 109
Dans la chaleur vacante (Du Bouchet), 113
Dans la rue (Bruant), 58
Dans le labyrinthe (Robbe-Grillet), 313
Dans un mois, dans un an (Sagan), 325
Danse (Matisse), 231
La Danse au théâtre (Levinson), 208
La Danse d'aujourd'hui (Levinson), 208
La Danse Feu (Fuller), 148
Danse macabre (Saint-Saëns), 328
Danseuse (Lipchitz), 212
Danseuse au café (Metzinger), 94, 239
Danseuse du "Rat Mort" (Vlaminck), 393
Dante, 82, 288, 316, 346, 399
Danton's Death, 369
Daphnis et Chloé (ballet), 301, 394
Daprès tout (Follain), 141
Darion, Joe, 55
Darlan, François, 96–97, 389
Darnand, Joseph, 241
Darras, Jean-Pierre, 105
Darrieux, Danielle, 97
Darsonval, Lycette, 274, 406
Darwin, Charles, 303
Darwinian theory, 42
Dassault, Marcel, 138
Daudet, Alphonse, 3
Daudet, Léon, 3, 138, 234–235
Daumal, René, 167
Daumier, Honoré Daumier, 141, 320, 350, 357
Davis, Bette, 53
De l'abjection (Jouhandeau), 187

De l'existence à l'existant (Levinas), 207
De la conduite de la guerre (Foch), 140
De la grammatologie (Derrida), 107
De Stijl movement, 94
Dead Souls (Gogol), 8
The Deadly Affair, 341
Dean, James, 332
Dearly, Max, 241
Debacle, 13, 97, 113, 119, 146, 217, 248, 265, 268, 278, 323, 326–
    327, 342, 369, 389, 401
Débarcadères (Supervielle), 352
Debord, Guy, 97–98, 182, 207, 343, 385
Debureau, 30
Debussy, Claude, 98–99, 109, 132, 135, 178, 191, 217, 294, 300–301,
    322, 324, 328, 335, 351
Déchargeurs (Vuillard), 395
"Déclaration: Condition et destin de l'artiste" (Ponge), 289
Decoin, Henri, 97
Déconnection (Ollier), 267
deconstruction, 32, 35, 46, 351–352
Decroux, Etienne, 30, 224
Dedans (Cixous), 78
Dédée d'Anvers, 8
Défense de la France, 145
La Défense de Tartufe (Jacob), 184
Défense de Verdun (Rodin), 317
"Définition du néo-traditionnisme" (Denis), 105, 251
Defoe, Daniel, 373
Degas, Edgar, 141, 350, 382
"Le Degré zéro de l'écriture" (Barthes), 31
Le Degré zéro de l'écriture (Barthes), 31
Degrés (Butor), 60
Deirdre of the Sorrows (Synge), 67
Déjeuner (Vlaminck), 393
Déjeuner d'un chat, 215
Déjeuner sur l'herbe (Manet), 283
Delacroix, Eugène, 230
Delaney, Shelagh, 221
Delannoy, Jean, 65, 99, 249, 374
Delaunay, Robert, 94, 100–101, 166, 194, 203, 281
Delaunay-Terk, Sonia, 94, 100–101, 165–166, 203, 281
Delbée, Anne, 81
Le Délégué (Tazlitsky), 357
Deleuze, Gilles, 101–102, 258
A Delicate Balance (Albee), 363
Delluc, Louis, 65, 102, 117, 126, 209, 294
Delon, Alain, 103
Le Déluge (Le Clézio), 199
Delville, Jean, 103
deMille, Cecil B., 102
La Demoiselle élue (Debussy), 98
Les Demoiselles d'Avignon (Picasso), 53, 93, 197, 283
Démolition d'un mur, 215
Le Démon du bien (Montherlant), 246
Demy, Jacques, 103, 269, 386
Denard, Michael, 274
Deneuve, Catherine, 59, 104, 189, 224, 381
Denham, Serge, 28
Denis, Maurice, 48, 104–105, 154, 219, 250–252, 320, 339, 385, 394
Déon, Michel, 176
Depardieu, Gérard, 63, 105–106
"Depuis le jour" (Charpentier), 76
Les Déracinés (Barrès), 31
Derain, André, 62, 106, 132–133, 227, 230, 393
Derek, Bo, 301
A la dérive (Soupault), 347

El, ou le dernier livre (Jabès), 183
Le Dernier Métro, 104, 106, 377
La Dernière Bande (Beckett), 46
"La Dernière Chance" (Sartre), 147
Dernière pirouette (Lugné-Poe), 214
Les Dernières Nuits de Paris (Soupault), 347
Les Derniers Jours de Corinthe (Robbe-Grillet), 313
Derrida, Jacques, 32, 46, 78, 106–107, 258, 346, 352, 359
Des Bleus à l'âme (Sagan), 326
des Forêts, Louis-René, 107–108
Des heures (Follain), 141
Des principes de la guerre (Foch), 140
Des sables à la mer: Pages marocaines (Bosco), 49
Les Désastres de la guerre (Faure), 132
Descartes, René, 38
Deschevaux-Dumesnil, Suzanne, 38
Descombey, Michel, 274
Descriptions critiques (Roy), 323
Désert (Le Clézio), 199
Le Désert de l'amour (F. Mauriac), 233
Le Désert de Retz (Roy), 324
Le Déshonneur des poètes (Péret), 278
Desjardins, Paul, 14
Desmarais family, 395
Desnos, Robert, 108, 225, 309, 353
La Desserte (Matisse), 230
Un Destin: Martin Luther (Febvre), 134
Destinées, 249
Destinées sentimentales (Chardonne), 76
Les Deux Bourreaux (Arrabal), 17
Les Deux Magots, 62, 108, 327
Les Deux Majestés (Gérôme), 322
Deux ou trois choses que je sais d'elle, 165
Les Deux Sources de la morale et de la religion (Bergson), 42
Deuxième Belvédère (Mandiargues), 223
Le Deuxième Sexe (Beauvoir), 37
Deverone, Marie, 97
Devigny, André, 56
Devil's Island, 111
Dewaere, Patrick, 63
Dhomme, Sylvain, 46
Le Diable au corps (Radiguet), 22, 168, 279, 299
Le Diable et le Bon Dieu (Sartre), 188, 334
Les Diaboliques, 83, 341
Diaghilev, Serge, 26–28, 83, 99, 109, 117, 140, 166, 171, 189, 196,
    208, 228–229, 245, 252–254, 272, 274, 279, 291, 301, 324, 336,
    350–351, 364
Diakanova, Elena (Gala), 124
Le Dialogue avec André Gide (Du Bos), 113
Dialogues de bêtes (Colette), 86
Dialogues des Carmélites (Bernanos), 44, 291
Diamond, David, 50
The Diary of Anne Frank, 185
The Diary of Vaslav Nijinsky (Nijinsky), 254
Dickens, Charles, 233
Dickey, James, 383
La Dictature Lettriste, 181
Diderot, Denis, 56
Dien Bien Phu, Battle of, 178, 324
Dietrich, Marlene, 191
Le Dieu caché (Goldmann), 165
Dieu et Mammon (F. Mauriac), 233
Les Dieux (Alain), 5
Les Dieux ont soif (France), 144
La Digue, 151
Un Dimanche à la Grande Jatte (Seurat), 134, 303

Le Dîner en ville (C. Mauriac), 231
Dior, Christian, 279
Les Discours du Docteur O'Grady (Maurois), 233
Discours sur le colonialisme (Césaire), 71
Discours, figure (Lyotard), 216
Disney, Walt, 117, 225
La Disparition (Perec), 278
Disques (Delaunay), 101
Les Disques dans la ville (Léger), 203
Disraeli, Benjamin, 233
La Distance intérieure (Poulet), 291
Distinguer pour unir, ou Les degrés du savoir (Maritain), 226
Divine Comedy (Dante), 316
Dix heures et demie du soir en été (Duras), 121
18 mars (Steinlen), 349
La Dixième Symphonie, 151
D.O.A., 237
Docteur Erikson (Saint Pierre), 328
Doinel, Antoine, 198, 377
A Doll's House (Ibsen), 286, 364
Dom Juan (Molière), 188, 362–363
Domaine Musical, 51
Domicile conjugal, 198
Dominique Prize, 185
Dompietrini, Colette, 362
Don Quixote (Cervantes), 399
Donatello, 133
Dongen, Kees van, 20, 33, 110
Dorgelès, Roland, 110, 112
Dos Passos, John, 69
Dostoyevsky, Fyodor, 34, 127, 188, 364, 368, 376
Dotremont, Christian, 354
Double Indemnity, 139, 237
Doubrovsky, Serge, 110
Doucet, Jacques, 255
La Douleur (Duras), 121
Le Doulos, 40
Doux pays (Forain), 142
Douze petits écrits (Ponge), 289
Drame (Sollers), 346
The Dream Play (Strindberg), 18
Dreyer, Carl Theodor, 126
Dreyfus, Alfred, 111, 138, 214, 276, 384
Dreyfus Affair, 31, 41, 57, 105, 111, 141, 214, 228, 234, 276, 369, 384
Dreyfusard, 105
Drieu La Rochelle, Pierre, 112, 150, 168, 221, 225, 262–263, 275, 340
"Drôle d'amitié" (Sartre), 255
Drôle de drame, 29, 66
La Drôle de Guerre, 110, 112, 166, 400
Drôle de jeu (Vailland), 382
Drôle de voyage (Drieu La Rochelle), 112
"Drop Everything" (Breton), 213
Drouant Restaurant, 166
Drouin, Marcel (Michel Arnauld), 262
Drouot, Jean-Claude, 363
Du Bos, Charles, 113
du Bouchet, André, 113, 172
Du côté de chez Swann (Proust), 168, 295
Du cubisme (Metzinger and Gleizes), 53, 93, 163–164, 239
Du mariage (Blum), 47
Du mouvement et de l'immobilité de Douve (Bonnefoy), 49
Du pur amour (Jouhandeau), 187
Dubois-Pillet, Albert, 330
Dubuffet, Jean, 113–114

Ducasse, Isidore (Lautréamont), 224, 288
Duchamp, Marcel, 62, 96, 114–116, 120, 239, 256, 281, 301, 337, 391, 396
Duchamp-Villon, Raymond, 114, 116, 193–194, 197, 239, 281, 337, 391, 400
Duel of Angels, 163
Dufy, Raoul, 116, 147, 227
Duhamel, Georges, 116, 319, 379, 391
Dukas, Paul, 117
Dulac, Germaine, 102, 117
Dullin, Charles, 18, 29, 31, 34, 66, 88, 90, 105, 118, 157, 159, 185, 224, 321, 362–363, 367–368, 390
Dumas *père*, Alexandre, 287
D'un château l'autre (Céline), 69
D'un réalisme sans rivage (Garaudy), 151
Duncan, Isadora, 84, 118–120, 140
Dunkirk, 97, 119–120, 254, 401
Dunne, Irene, 53
Dunoyer de Segonzac, André, 120
Dupond, Patrick, 274
Dupont, E. A., 83
Dupré, Marcel, 270
Dupuy, Dominique, 261
Dupuy, François, 261
Durand-Ruel, Paul, 331, 394
Duras, Marguerite, 30, 57, 83, 120–121, 256–257, 294, 305, 308
Durey, Louis, 344
Durkheim, Emile, 9, 379
Duvivier, Julien, 121–122, 135, 149, 243, 279, 288
Dux, Pierre, 30
The Dybbuk (Anski), 34
The Dying Swan (ballet), 140

E

Earth Girdled (Morand), 248
L'Eau et les rêves (Bachelard), 25
"Ebauche d'un serpent" (Valéry), 383
L'Echange (P. Claudel), 30, 286, 367
Echaurren, Roberto Matta, 355
Eckermann, Johann Peter, 47
Ecole d'Alger, 314, 323
Ecole des Arts Décoratifs, 227, 281
Ecole des Beaux-Arts, 48, 52, 58, 82, 120, 133, 152, 193, 212, 230, 316, 357, 384, 405
L'Ecole des cadavres (Céline), 69
Ecole des Chartes, 32, 228
L'Ecole des femmes (Molière), 41, 188, 363
Ecole des veufs (Ancey), 367
Ecole du Louvre, 386
Ecole du Vieux-Colombier, 367
Ecole Freudienne, 181
Ecole Mudra — Centre européen de perfectionnement et de recherche des interprètes du spectacle, 40
Ecole Normale de Musique, 49, 238
Ecole Normale Supérieure, 15, 28, 38, 54, 106, 123, 163, 166, 186, 194, 196, 202, 238, 252, 254, 272, 276, 318, 333, 397
Ecole Polytechnique, 3
Economie libidinale (Lyotard), 216, 344
Ecoutez la mer (Cardinal), 65
L'Ecran Français, 20
Les Ecrits de Paul Dukas sur la musique (Dukas), 117
L'Ecriture et l'expérience des limites (Sollers), 346

Écriture féminine (Cixous), 181
Les Ecrivains français d'aujourd'hui (Boisdeffre), 48
Ecuador (Michaux), 240
L'Ecume des jours (Vian), 388
Edinburgh Festival, 287
Edison, Thomas, 156, 174
Editions Bernard Grasset, 168
Editions de la Nouvelle Revue Française, 150
Editions de Minuit, 123, 256, 331, 343, 387
Editions des Femmes, 123–124
Education européenne (Gary), 153
Edward III of England, 316
Edward VII of England, 233
Edward, Prince of Wales, 75
Effel, Jean, 225
L'Effraie et autres poésies (Jaccottet), 183
L'Eglise, le communisme, et les chrétiens (Garaudy), 152
Ehrenburg, Ilya, 91
Eiffel Tower, 70, 75, 79, 100–101, 203
Eisenhower, Dwight D., 156, 178
El Greco, 160
El Kaïm, Arlette, 334
Eldorado, 209
Electre (Giraudoux), 363
Eléments de philosophie (Maritain), 226
Eléments de sémiologie (Barthes), 32
Eléna et les hommes, 306
Elégies (Emmanuel), 125
Eliot, T. S., 327, 367, 383, 390
Elle, 29
Ellington, Duke, 388
Ellis, Havelock, 187
Eloge des intellectuels (Lévy), 209
Eloges (Saint-John Perse), 327
Elssler, Fanny, 273
Eluard, Paul, 56, 67, 75, 124–125, 139, 141, 202, 218, 278, 291, 309, 337, 353–354, 401
Elya (Jabès), 183
Emak Bakia (Ray), 302
L'Emancipation Sociale, 134
L'Embarquement d'Arlequin (Metzinger), 239
Embryons desséchés (Satie), 335
Emmanuel, Pierre, 125
The Emperor Jones (O'Neill), 34
L'Empire céleste (Mallet-Joris), 221
Empirisme et subjectivité: Essai sur la Nature Humaine selon Hume (Deleuze), 102
L'Emploi du temps (Butor), 60
The Empty Space (Brook), 58
En attendant Godot (Beckett), 39, 46, 361
En découvrant l'existence avec Husserl et Heidegger (Levinas), 207
En douce (musical), 241
En miroir (Jouve), 187
Encyclopédie de la musique et Dictionnaire du Conservatoire (ed. Gédalge), 126
L'Encyclopédie française, 341
An Enemy of the People (Ibsen), 286, 364
L'Energie humaine (Teilhard), 359
Enfance (Sarraute), 332
L'Enfant prodigue (Debussy), 98
L'Enfant et les sortilèges (Ravel), 301
Les Enfants du paradis, 14–15, 30, 65–67, 243, 292
"Les Enfants qui s'aiment" (Gréco), 168
Les Enfants terribles (Cocteau), 83–84, 299
English Channel, 120
Enigma (Ollier), 267

L'Ennemi (Pinget), 284
L'Enracinement (Weil), 397
Ensemble InterContemporain, 179
Enslaved (Jarry), 186
Ensor, James, 6, 92, 160
Entr'acte, 79, 336
Entre chiens et loups (Cesbron), 72
Entre Fantoine et Agapa (Pinget), 284
Entre la vie et la mort (Sarraute), 332
Entre l'écriture (Cixous), 78
Epilogue (Martin du Gard), 228
Les Epiphanies (Pichette), 67
L'Epithalame (Chardonne), 76
Epstein, Jean, 59, 126
épuration, 28, 126, 162, 170, 211, 241, 278, 307
L'Equarissage pour tous, 388
L'Equipage (Kessel), 189
L'Ere du soupçon (Sarraute), 257, 331–332
Erlanger, Philippe, 64–65
Ernst, Max, 60, 269, 279, 353, 396
Eruption volcanique à la Martinique, 236
Escoffier, Auguste, 260
Escuela de Artes y Manufacturas, 170
Escurial (Ghelderode), 159–160
Esenin, Sergei, 119
Esmeralda (ballet), 292
L'Espace du dedans (Michaux), 240
L'Espace d'une nuit (Cayrol), 68
L'Espace littéraire (Blanchot), 45
L'Espace proustien (Poulet), 291
Espaces (Fargue), 131
Espagne martyre (Fougeron), 143
L'Espoir, 82, 222
Esprit, 127, 249, 311
L'Esprit des formes (Faure), 131
"L'Esprit et l'eau" (P. Claudel), 82
Esprit Nouveau, 199, 270, 353
L'Esprit nouveau et les poètes (Apollinaire), 12
"Un Essai de rénovation dramatique: Le Théâtre du Vieux-Columbier" (Copeau), 91
Essai sur les données immédiates de la conscience (Bergson), 42
Essais sur la signification au cinéma (Metz), 239
L'Estaque, 203
Et à la fin était le bang (Obaldia), 265
Et Dieu créa la femme, 29, 381
Etat civil (Drieu La Rochelle), 112
L'Etat de siège (Camus), 67
Etat Français. See Vichy Government.
L'Eté 1914 (Martin du Gard), 228
L'Eté 1936 (Poirot-Delpech), 288
"L'Eternel Jugurtha, propositions sur le génie africain" (Amrouche), 14
Eternal Lovers (Corneau and Gerbault), 367
L'Eternelle Idole (Rodin), 80
Ethiopiques (Senghor), 339
L'Etoile de Cristal, 294
Etoile sans lumière, 245
L'Etranger (Camus), 63–64
Etre et avoir (Marcel), 224
L'Etre et le néant (Sartre), 36, 128, 334
Etude aux casseroles (Schaeffer), 90
Etude: Paysage à Auvers (Cézanne), 73
Etudes (Rivière), 312
Etudes aux chemins de fer (Schaeffer), 90
Etudes pour une fin du monde (Tinguely), 371
Etudes sur le temps humain (Poulet), 291

L'Etudiant Noir, 71, 338
Euclidiennes (Guillevic), 172
Eupalinos, ou l'architecte (Valéry), 384
Europe, 376
European Economic Community (EEC), 144
Eurydice (Anouilh), 363
Eva (Chardonne), 76
Eve (Péguy), 276
Evian Accords, 8, 127
Evil Eden, 386
Evocations (Vivien), 393
L'Evolution créatrice (Bergson), 42
"L'Exactitude n'est pas la vérité" (Matisse), 231
Exécutoire (Guillevic), 172
Exercices de style (Queneau), 297
Exhibition of Revolutionary Art, 74
Exil (Saint-John Perse), 327
L'Exil et le royaume (Camus), 64
existentialism, 37, 63, 66, 127–128, 168, 181, 207, 224, 238, 249,
    254, 258–260, 310, 326, 333, 351, 360–361, 368, 397
L'Existentialisme est un humanisme (Sartre), 128, 334
L'Expérience intérieure (Bataille), 33
Expo 67, 40
Exposition Internationale des Arts Décoratifs, 101
L'Express, 7–8, 128–130, 258, 264
Expressionism, 74, 80, 261
Exter, Alexandra, 165
L'Extravagante Croisade d'un castrat amoreux (Arrabal), 17

F

La Fable du monde (Supervielle), 352
Fabre, Emile, 87
Faglioni, Marie, 273
Fairbanks, Douglas, 140, 191, 212
Faisons un rêve, 173
Faits divers, 18
Faivre, Abel, 20
Faivre d'Arcier, Bernard, 23
Falbalas (Becker), 38
"The Fall of the House of Usher" (Poe), 126
Falstaff, 248
"Familiale" (Prévert), 292
Fancy Goods, Open All Night (Pound), 247
Fando et Lis (Arrabal), 17
Fanny (Pagnol), 50, 78, 271
Fanon, Frantz, 71
Fantasia, 117
Fantômas, 136
Le Fantôme de la liberté, 59
Fargue, Léon-Paul, 131
Fascism, 3, 17, 20, 31, 46, 54, 59, 79, 88, 127, 134, 159, 173, 186,
    220, 222, 226, 245, 247, 260, 262, 281, 311, 347, 348
Fastes d'enfer (Ghelderode), 159–160
"Fatou" (dance), 25
Faubourg Saint-Honoré, Paris, 200
Faulkner, William, 29, 169, 343
Faure, Elie, 131–132, 330, 338
Fauré, Gabriel, 49, 98, 132, 191, 217, 269, 301
Fausses confidences (Marivaux), 305
Fautrier, Jean, 113, 132
Fauves, 11, 53, 74, 93, 100, 106, 110, 116, 133, 147, 148, 165, 195,
    203, 225, 227, 230–231, 244, 281–283, 319–320, 322, 330–331,

340, 348, 393
Fauvet, Jacques, 243
Faux jour (Troyat), 376
Les Faux-Monnayeurs (Gide), 161, 336
Faux Pas (Blanchot), 45
Fayard, Artheme, 186
Faye, Jean-Pierre, 359
Fear and Misery of the Third Reich (Brecht), 287
Febvre, Lucien, 9, 133–134
Fédération des Artistes, 330
Fédération des Bourses du Travail, 277
Fédération Internationale des Archives du Film, 146
Fédération Internationale des Artistes Révolutionnaires
    Indépendants (FIARI), 134
La Fée aux choux, 174
Fégy, Camille, 159
Félibres, 273
Fellini, Federico, 389
feminism, 37, 117, 121
Une Femme (Delbée), 81
Femme à l'éventail (Zadkine), 405
La Femme du boulanger (Giono), 162
Une Femme fidèle, 381
La Femme infidèle, 74
La Femme Nikita, 248
La Femme rompue (Beauvoir), 37
Femmes (Sollers), 346
Fénéon, Félix, 110, 134–135, 251, 294
Fermé la nuit (Morand), 247
Fermina Marquez (Larbaud), 195
Fernandel, 122, 135
Ferré, Léo, 135–136
Ferrements (Césaire), 71
Ferrer Modern Art School, 301
Ferreri, Marco, 255
Le Festin (ballet), 109
Le Festin de l'araignée (Roussel), 322
Festival d'Avignon. *See* Avignon Festival.
Festival de Cannes. *See* Cannes Film Festival.
Festival international de la Danse de Paris, 261
La Fête (Vailland), 382
La Fête espagnole, 117
La Fête noire, 21
Le Feu (Barbusse), 28
Feu à volonté, 267
Le Feu follet (film), 221
Le Feu follet (Drieu La Rochelle), 112
Feu Mathias Pascal, 210
Feuillade, Louis, 136, 140, 156, 218
Feuille, 349
"Les Feuilles mortes" (song), 245, 292
Feuilletons (Poirot-Delpech), 289
Feuillets d'Hypnos (Char), 75
"Feux d'artifice" (Debussy), 99
Fèvre, Henri, 303
Feydeau, Georges, 50, 304
Feyder, Jacques, 14, 66, 136, 156
Fibrilles (Leiris), 205
Fièvre (Delluc), 102
Fifth Republic, 7, 70, 127, 129, 137, 144, 155–156, 176, 220, 223,
    233, 235, 258, 300, 328, 338, 345
Fifty-Fifty, 140
Figaro, 138–139, 141, 233, 295
Figures (Genette), 159
Filiger, Charles, 105, 251
La Fille de l'eau, 306

La Fille du puisatier, 135
La Fille Elisa (E. de Goncourt), 367
La Fille mal gardée (ballet), 292
La Fille sauvage (Curel), 50
Film, 102
Film noir, 8, 73, 139, 165, 210, 237, 374
Filmofono Industries, 59
Les Films de ma vie (Truffaut), 377
Fils (Doubrovsky), 110
Le Fils prodigue (ballet), 26, 109, 211
La Fin de Chéri (Colette), 86
Fin de partie (Beckett), 39, 46
La Fin du jour, 121
Fine, Irving, 50
Fini, Léonor, 139
Finlay, John, 384
Finnegans Wake (Joyce), 38
First Moroccan Crisis, 5
First World Congress of Liberated Artists, 207
Le Fiston (Pinget), 284
Flaherty, Robert, 306
Les Flambeaux éteints (Vivien), 393
Flaubert, Gustave, 34, 117, 185, 303, 306, 332, 334, 368
"Fleur bleue" (Trenet), 374
La Fleur du temps (C. Roy), 323
Les Fleurs de Tarbes (Paulhan), 275
Les Fleurs du mal (Redon), 303
Florey, Robert, 140
FNAC, 264
Foch, Ferdinand, 140, 400
Fokine, Michel, 28, 109, 119, 140–141, 189, 208, 228, 252–253, 274, 324
La Folie du Docteur Tube, 151
La Folie du jour (musical), 25
Folie et déraison: Histoire de la folie à l'âge classique (Foucault), 143
Folies-Bergère, 25, 145, 148–149, 241
Folies Wagram, 19
Follain, Jean, 141
La Folle de Chaillot (Giraudoux), 41, 163, 188, 363
La Folle de Lituanie (Poirot-Delpech), 288
Folliot, Denise, 384
Fonda, Jane, 381
Fontaine, 125, 141
Fontaine, Jean de la, 54
Fonteyn, Margot, 292
Forain, Jean-Louis, 20, 141, 320
Les Forains (ballet), 279
Forbidden Zone, 265, 389, 401
Le Forçat innocent (Supervielle), 352
La Force de l'âge (Beauvoir), 37
La Force des choses (Beauvoir), 37
Formes circulaires cosmiques (Delaunay), 101
Fort, Paul, 142, 213
Fortier, Alfred, 368
Foucault, Michel, 32, 35, 46, 192, 232, 258
Foucault (Deleuze), 102, 142–143, 194, 351–352
Fouchet, Max-Pol, 141
Fougeron, André, 143, 204, 260, 356
Foundation for the Protection of Distressed Animals, 29
Fountain (Duchamp), 115
Fouque, Antoinette, 123
Fourbis (Leiris), 205
Fourth Republic, 6, 59, 137, 144, 156, 235, 338, 345, 389
Fourth Symphony (Roussel), 322
Fragments du chœur (Pleynet), 288

Les Français parlent aux Français, 306
La Française, 117
France, Anatole, 79–80, 111, 144, 224, 259, 294–295, 308, 350
La France byzantine (Benda), 41
France-Nouvelle, 260
France, pays de mission? (Godin and Daniel), 399
France-Soir, 145, 190
Franchetti, Raymond, 274
Franck, César, 178–179, 269
Franck, Martine, 242, 252, 365
Franco, Francisco, 17, 43, 59, 118, 170, 226, 283, 348, 369
François Truffaut Correspondance (Truffaut), 377
Francophone Literature Prize of the Académie Française, 336
Franco-Prussian War, 31, 52, 111, 244, 265, 317, 321, 369, 374
Franju, Georges, 145–146, 210, 237, 255
Frankenstein, 140
Franklin, Benjamin, 233
Fratellini clowns, 367
Fraux, Ernest, 91
Frédérix, Jacques, 136
Free French, 155, 233, 323, 397
Free Zone, 87, 138, 141, 146, 206, 241, 265–266, 306, 359, 370, 389, 392, 401
Frêle bruit (Leiris), 205
Frénaud, André, 146
Frenay, Henri, 87
French Academy, Rome, 152
French Communist Party, 9, 13, 15, 20, 28, 37, 56, 59, 64, 80, 85, 88, 121, 125, 127–129, 134, 143, 147, 151–152, 173, 176–177, 202, 204, 206, 220, 254, 260, 262, 277, 283, 289–290, 307, 309, 323, 334, 341, 345, 347–348, 350, 354, 356–357, 360, 371, 375, 382
French Foreign Legion. *See* Légion Etrangère.
French Ministry of Culture, 26
French Ministry of Fine Arts, 81
French National Assembly, 338, 370
French National Radio, 89
French Parliament, 136
French republic, 137
French Resistance movement. *See* Resistance.
French Revolution, 40, 111, 137, 170, 199, 201, 242, 306, 318, 344, 363
Fresnay, Pierre, 147
Fresnes, 54
Freud, Sigmund, 25, 35, 42, 56, 78, 181, 187, 193, 204, 224, 229, 258, 310–311, 351, 354
Friesz, Emile Othon, 147–148
Frigerio, Ezio, 362
Front de la Jeunesse, 181
Front National des Arts, 143
Frossard, L. O., 225
Les Fruits d'or (Sarraute), 332
Fry, Christopher, 163
Fuller, Loïe, 148
Fumée noire, 102
Fur Breakfast (Oppenheim), 269
Fureur et mystère (Char), 75–76
Futurism, 74, 94–95, 100, 114, 116, 152, 165–166, 195, 203, 218, 255, 340, 392
Fuzzy Sets (Ollier), 267

G

Gabin, Jean, 66, 103, 149, 249, 279
Gaîté parisienne (ballet), 229
Galerie Dada, 16, 95
La Galerie des Glaces (Bernstein), 364
Gallimard, Claude, 150
Gallimard, Gaston, 150, 160, 225–226, 262–263
Gallimard (publishing house), 21, 150, 201, 221, 223
Gallotta, Jean-Claude, 261
Gambier, Gille, 112
Gance, Abel, 18, 70, 102, 150–151, 175, 209
Gandhi, Mohandas K., 317
Gantillon, Simon, 34
Garafola, Lynn, 208
Garaudy, Roger, 151–152, 202
Garbo, Greta, 136, 191
Garcia-Rossi, Horacio, 171
Garnier, Jacques, 261
Garnier, Tony, 152
Garrick Theater, 90
Gary, Romain, 153, 293
Gaspard de la nuit (Ravel), 301
Gaspard, Melchior et Balthazar (Tournier), 373
Gaston Baty, 185
Gatti, Armand, 369
Le Gauchisme, remède à la maladie sénile du communisme (Cohn-
    Bendit), 85
Gauguin, Paul, 44, 48, 73, 105, 153–154, 219, 251, 339, 395
Gaulle, Charles de, 7, 48, 85, 127, 129, 137–138, 144–145, 155–156,
    177, 190, 211, 220, 222–223, 231–233, 235–236, 243, 258, 278,
    300, 307, 323, 334, 338, 379, 389, 401
Gaullists, 300
Gault, Henri, 260
Gaumont, Léon, 136, 151, 156, 174, 209, 274
Gaumont Productions, 136
Gaumont Studios, 79, 117
Gauthier-Villars, Henry (Willy), 86
Gaxotte, Pierre, 186
The Gaze of Orpheus, and Other Literary Essays (Blanchot), 45
Gazette, 293
Gazette du Cinéma, 311, 317
Gédalge, André, 126
Gémier, Firmin, 18, 34, 66, 118, 156–157, 185, 361, 363, 368, 390
Genet, Jean, 3, 19, 30, 42, 46–47, 57, 67, 107, 157–158, 188, 334,
    360–361, 363–364
Genette, Gérard, 32, 158–159, 359, 372
Geneva Accords, 178
Geneva Ballet, 77
Geneva conventions, 178
Geneva School of criticism, 291
Genevieve, Saint, 277
Génitrix (F. Mauriac), 233
Le Genou de Claire, 317
Genousie (Obaldia), 265
Gentlemen Prefer Blondes, 96
George Dandin (Molière), 287
Georgia (Soupault), 347
Les Géorgiques (Simon), 343
Géorgiques chrétiennes (Jammes), 184
Gérard, François, 302
Gérard, Fréderic, 61
Gerbault, 367
La Gerbe, 159, 162
La Gerbe des forces (Chateaubriant), 159

Géricault, Théodore, 194, 230
Germi, Pietro, 205
Germinal, 106
Gérôme, Jean Léon, 303, 322
Geronimo (Benedetto), 41
Gestapo, 106, 108, 126
Les Gestes et opinions du docteur Faustroll, pataphysicien (Jarry),
    186
Ghelderode, Michel de, 159–160
The Ghost Sonata (Strindberg), 46
Ghosts (Ibsen), 367
Giacometti, Alberto, 269
Gide, André, 14, 20, 41, 48, 80, 82, 85–86, 88, 90, 99, 135, 150–151,
    156–157, 160–161, 164–167, 173, 184, 195, 214, 228, 231, 249,
    262–263, 267, 285, 294–295, 312, 326, 336, 341, 351, 367, 383,
    390, 404
Gide, Charles, 79
Gide, Madeleine, 160
Gielgud, John, 308
Gigi, 78
Gigi et autres nouvelles (Colette), 86
Le Gigot, sa vie et son œuvre (Péret), 278
Gil Blas, 392
Gil Blas Illustré, 349
Gilbert-Lecomte, Roger, 167
Gill, André, 61
Gilles (Drieu La Rochelle), 112
Gilles de Rais (Planchon), 287
Glissements progressifs du plaisir (Robbe-Grillet), 313
La Gioconda (Leonardo da Vinci), 115
Giono, Jean, 48, 162, 225, 272, 275
Girard, René, 259
Giraud, Henri, 278
Giraudoux, Jean, 22, 30, 41–42, 88, 163, 168, 186, 188, 247, 262,
    363, 390
The Girlfriends, 74
Giroud, Françoise, 128, 130
Giscard d'Estaing, Valéry, 137, 235, 261, 300
Gischia, Léon, 390
Giselle, 77, 212, 273, 405
Glas (Derrida), 107
Glasgow School of Art, 103
Glass, Philip, 50
Gleizes, Albert, 53, 93, 163–164, 197, 201, 239, 283, 337, 379, 392
Gleyre, Charles, 244
Glove Torso (Arman), 15
Glucksmann, André, 258
Gnosticism, 3, 397
Godard, Jean-Luc, 21, 29, 35, 40, 83, 145, 164–165, 198, 215, 237,
    263, 284, 294, 306, 317, 377
Godin, Henri, 399
Goethe, Johann Wolfgang von, 47, 117, 317
Gogh, Vincent van, 44, 106, 112, 154, 195, 251, 308, 331, 380, 393,
    394
Gogol, Nikolay, 8, 188
Golden Lion award, 312
Goldman, Emma, 301
Goldman, Pierre, 78
Goldmann, Lucien, 165, 191, 259
Goldsmith, James, 130
Golovin, Aleksander, 140
Les Gommes (Robbe-Grillet), 256, 313
Goncharova, Natalia, 109, 165–166, 195–196, 252
Goncourt Academy, 13, 36, 67, 87, 110, 166, 221, 293, 314, 372
Goncourt, Edmond de, 11, 367
Goncourt, Jules de, 11, 166

Gone With the Wind (Mitchell), 169
Gonzalez, Josée. *See* Gris, Juan.
The Good Woman of Setzuan (Brecht), 287
The Gorgon's Shield (Arman), 15
"Le Gorille" (Brassens), 54
Gorky, Maksim, 214, 306, 365
Goscinny, René, 20
Goudeket, Maurice, 86
Gourmont, Rémy de, 134
Le Goûter des généraux, 388
La Goutte d'or (Tournier), 373
Goya, Francisco, 92, 282–283, 303, 320
Graal Flibuste (Pinget), 284
Gracq, Julien, 166, 293
Le Grain de la voix: Entretiens 1962 (Barthes), 32
Grammaire du "Décaméron" (Todorov), 372
Grand Ballet du Marquis de Cuevas, 77, 253
Le Grand Dadais (Poirot-Delpech), 288
Le Grand Homme (Soupault), 347
Le Grand Jeu, 136, 167, 278, 381
Le Grand Meaulnes (Alain-Fournier), 5
Le Grand Méliès, 146, 237
Le Grand Œuvre: Cosmogonie (Emmanuel), 125
Grand Palais, Paris, 40
Grand Prix de Chartres, 294
Grand Prix de la Critique, 48
Grand Prix de la Poésie de l'Académie Française, 294
Grand Prix de Littérature de l'Académie Française, 14, 173, 294
Grand Prix de Poésie de l'Académie Française, 125, 289, 304
Grand Prix de Poésie de la Ville de Paris, 337
Grand Prix de Rome, 294
Grand Prix du Disque, 54
Grand Prix du Roman de l'Académie Française, 190, 243, 288, 294, 372
Grand Prix du Théâtre de l'Académie Française, 17, 121
Grand Prix du Théâtre des Nations, 40
Grand Prix International de la Poésie, 36, 339
Grand Prix Littéraire de l'Algérie, 314
Grand Prix Littéraire de la Ville de Paris, 131
Grand Prix National de Poésie, 289
Grand Prix National des Lettres, 5, 14, 21, 67, 158, 173, 240, 294, 323
Le Grand Recueil (Ponge), 289
Le Grand Tournant du socialisme (Garaudy), 152
Le Grand Troupeau (Giono), 162
La Grande Bouffe (Ferreri), 255, 284
Grande Chaumière, Montparnasse, 247
La Grande et la petite manœuvre (Adamov), 4
La Grande Famille (Magritte), 219
La Grande Illusion, 38, 96, 147, 243, 306
Grande Pièce symphonique (Franck), 269
Les Grandes Manœuvres, 79, 249
"Grand-père" (Brassens), 54
Les Grands Cimetières sous la lune (Bernanos), 43
Les Grands Désordres (Cardinal), 65
La Grasse Matinée (Poirot-Delpech), 288
Grasset, Bernard, 167–168, 295
Grasset (publishing house), 167–168, 223
Grave, Jean, 85, 340–341
Gravitations (Supervielle), 352
Graziella, 18
Great Depression, 66, 79, 288
Great Tragic Mask (Bourdelle), 52
Great Warrior of Montauban (Bourdelle), 52
Gréco, Juliette, 54, 168–169, 292, 297, 327
Green Card, 106

Green, Julien, 72, 169, 273, 275, 293, 397
Greenberg, Clement, 59
Greet, Anne Hyde, 12
Greimas, A. J., 31
Grémillon, Jean, 170
Grenier, Jean, 64
Griffith, D. W., 151
Gringoire, 170, 186, 225
Gringore, Pierre, 170
Gris, Juan, 33, 53, 93–94, 170–171, 184, 197, 212, 239, 247, 255, 337
Gropius, Walter, 152
Grosvenor, Hugh, 75
Grosz, George, 143
Groupe de l'art social, 277
Groupe de Musique Concrète, 90
Groupe de recherche chorégraphique de l'Opera de Paris (GRCOP), 261
Groupe de Recherche d'Art Visuel (GRAV), 171, 371, 387
Groupe de recherche théâtrale de l'Opera de Paris (GRTOP), 261, 274
Groupe des Artistes Indépendants, 330
Groupe Hersant, 138
Groupe Libre, 321
Groupe Octobre (October Group), 46, 306
Groupe Théâtral du Lycée Louis Grand, 252
Groupe Zéro, 371, 387
Grove Press, 223
Grune, Karl, 386
Gsovsky, Victor, 77
Guattari, Félix, 102
Guenne, Jacques, 263
Guérard, Michel, 260
Les Guérillères (Wittig), 399
Guernica, 67
Guernica (Picasso), 283
Guerre (Picasso), 283, 321
La Guerre Civile, 80
La Guerre d'Algérie (Roy), 8, 323
La Guerre de Troie n'aura pas lieu (Giraudoux), 22, 163, 188, 363, 390
La Guerre est finie, 308
Le Guerrier appliqué (Paulhan), 275
Guide des prix littéraires, 293
Guignol's Band (Céline), 69
Guillevic, Eugéne, 172
Guilloux, Louis, 173
Guilmant, Félix, 49, 270
Guitare (Laurens), 198
Guitry, Lucien, 173
Guitry, Sacha, 50, 135, 173, 225, 249, 279
Guy, Alice, 136, 156, 174, 236
Guyon, Jeanne, 221
Gymnopédies (Satie), 335

H

H (Sollers), 346
Habitué (Marcoussis), 225
Haceldama ou Le prix du sang, 121
Hachette (publishing house), 138, 145
Hachette, Louis, 168
Hadrian, 404
Häger, Bengt, 14

Haï (Clézio), 199
Hair (musical), 287
Halimi, Gisèle, 224
Les Halles, Paris, 200
Hallier, Jean-Edern, 359
Hals, Frans, 136
Hamilton, Richard, 143
Hamlet (Shakespeare), 30, 84
Hamon, Philippe, 372
Hamsun, Knut, 46
Handel, George Frideric, 194
Hans Christian Andersen, 279
Hare, David, 396
Harlem Renaissance, 204
Harpagon, 118
Harris, Roy, 50
Hart, Josephine, 221
Harvard University, 163
Harvey, Lilian, 191
Le Hasard (Ozenfant), 270
Haute Surveillance (Genet), 158
Les Hauteurs de la ville (Roblès), 314
Hawthorne, Nathaniel, 169, 195
Hébertot, Jacques, 34, 285
"Hécatombe" (Brassens), 54
Hedera, ou la persistance de l'amour pendant une rêverie
    (Mandiargues), 223
Heem, Jan de, 230
Hegel, G. W. F., 33, 39, 107
Heidegger, Martin, 45, 106, 128, 207, 310
Heim, Jacques, 101
Hemingway, Ernest, 108, 190, 273
Hémon, Louis, 168
Hénaut, Jules, 20
Hennique, Léon, 367
Henri IV, 196
Henri Matisse, roman (Aragon), 13
Henri, Robert, 301
Henry, Hubert Col., 111, 340
Henry IV, part 1 (Shakespeare), 287
Henry IV, part 2 (Shakespeare), 287
Henri Matisse (Pleynet), 288
Henry, Pierre, 90
Heracles the Archer (Bourdelle), 52
L'Herbe (Simon), 343
L'Hérésiarque et Cie (Apollinaire), 12
Hergé (Georges Remi), 371
L'Hermine (Anouilh), 214, 367
Herriot, Edouard, 152
Hersant, Robert, 138, 145
Hervé-Bazin, Jean Pierre Marie. *See* Bazin, Hervé.
Herzog, Emile. *See* Maurois, André.
Hessling, Catherine (Andrée Heuchling), 306
Heureux les pacifiques (Abellio), 3
Heywood, Thomas, 367
Hier régnant désert (Bonnefoy), 49
Hightower, Rosella, 274, 292
Himmler, Heinrich, 299
Hinduism, 303
Hiroshima mon amour, 120, 263, 308
Histoire (Simon), 343
Histoire de l'art (Faure), 131
L'Histoire de l'œil (Bataille), 33
Histoire de la forêt (Cayrol), 68
Histoire de la guerre d'Espagne (Brasillach and Bardeche), 28, 54
Histoire de la littérature française (Lanson), 194

Histoire de la mer (Cayrol), 68
Histoire de la sexualité (Foucault), 143
Histoire de mes pensées (Alain), 5
Histoire de Vasco (Schehadé), 336
Histoire des bourses du travail (Pelloutier), 277
Histoire des treize (Balzac), 312
Histoire d'O (Réage), 275
Histoire du ciel (Cayrol), 68
Histoire du cinéma (Bardèche), 28, 54
Histoire du soldat (Ramuz and Stravinsky), 285
Histoire d'un désert (Cayrol), 68
Histoire d'une maison (Cayrol), 68
Histoire d'une prairie (Cayrol), 68
Histoire et vérité (Ricœur), 311
Histoires sanglantes (Jouve), 187
History Is Made at Night, 53
Hitchcock, Alfred, 73, 83, 255, 317, 377, 386
Hitchcock (Chabrol and Rohmer), 73
Hitchcock/Truffaut (Hitchcock and Truffaut), 377
Hitler, Adolf, 64, 88, 97, 112, 159, 186, 226, 266, 268, 374
Hitler-Stalin Pact, 307
Ho Chi Minh, 177
Hockney, David, 279
Hodson, Millicent, 325
Hoffmannsthal, Hugo von, 327
Hokusai, Katsushika, 154
Hölderlin, Friedrich, 187
Hollywood, 53, 59, 268, 301, 306
Holocaust, 75, 268
Holy Virgin (Picabia), 281
Homer, 162, 288
L'Hommage à André Houiller (Fougeron), 143
Hommage à Blériot (Delaunay), 100
Hommage à Mozart (Dufy), 116
Hommage à New-York (Tinguely), 371
L'Homme à la tête de caoutchouc, 237
L'Homme approximatif (Tzara), 377
L'Homme couvert de femmes (Drieu La Rochelle), 112
Un Homme de Dieu (Marcel), 225
Un Homme et une femme, 205
L'Homme faillible (Ricœur), 311
L'Homme précaire et la littérature (Malraux), 223
L'Homme qui aimait les femmes, 377
Un Homme qui dort (Perec), 277
Un Homme qui me plaît, 205
L'Homme révolté (Camus), 64
Les Hommes de bonne volonté (Romains), 123, 318, 319, 387
Homo academicus (Bourdieu), 52
"Homo homini lupus" (Rouault), 320
Homo viator (Marcel), 225
Honegger, Arthur, 175, 178, 310, 344
Hop Signor!, 159
Horowitz, Vladimir, 270
Hosties noires (Senghor), 338
Hôtel des Invalides, 146
Hôtel du Nord (film), 14, 66
L'Hôtel du Nord (Dabit), 95
Hotel Mistral, L'Estaque, 53
Hôtel Terminus: Klaus Barbie — His Life and Times, 267
Hourloupe (Dubuffet), 114
Huelsenbeck, Richard, 61, 95
Hughes, Langston, 204
Hugo, Victor, 66–67, 99, 150, 233, 274, 276, 280, 317, 391
Huis clos (Sartre), 15, 321, 334, 367
800 mètres (Obey), 30
Humanisme de l'autre homme (Levinas), 207

Humanisme et terreur (Merleau-Ponty), 238
Humanisme intégral (Maritain), 227
L'Humanité, 28, 57, 175–176, 178, 254, 283, 309, 318
Humoristiques (Vitrac), 392
Hungarian revolution of 1956, 133
Hunger (Hamsun), 46, 104
Las Hurdes, 59
Hurlements en faveur de Sade (Debord), 98
Le Hussard bleu (Nimier), 176
Le Hussard sur le toit (Giono), 162
The Hussards, 176
Husserl, Edmund, 49, 106, 128, 207, 238, 310–311, 333
Hustle, 104
Huston, John, 237, 267
L'Hypothèse, 284

I

I and the Village (Chagall), 74
I Hired a Contract Killer, 198
Ibsen, Henrik, 11, 214, 286, 341, 364, 367
Icare (ballet), 212
L'Identité de la France (Braudel), 9
An Idiom of Night (Jouve), 187
The Idiot (Dostoyevsky), 364
Idole de la perversité (Delville), 103
L'Ignorant: poèmes 1952–1956 (Jaccottet), 183
Il était une fois Jean Cayrol (Cayrol), 68
Il faisait ce qu'il voulait (Tanguy), 355
Il n'y a pas de paradis (Frénaud), 146
L'Ile des pingouins (France), 144
Illuminations (Rimbaud), 81
Les Illusions du progrès (Sorel), 347
Images (Debussy), 99
"Images à Crusoé" (Saint-John Perse), 327
Images et mirages (Vildrac), 391
L'Imagination (Sartre), 333
Imaginist Bauhaus, 343
Imagism, 308
L'Immaculée Conception (Breton and Eluard), 56
L'Immoraliste (Gide), 160
L'Immortelle (Robbe-Grillet), 312
Imperial Ballet School, 252, 292
L'Imposture (Bernanos), 43
Impressionism, 44, 48, 73–74, 93, 99, 100, 114, 120, 126, 133, 141,
    153–154, 163, 203, 230, 244–245, 251–252, 259, 281, 300–301,
    303, 322, 340, 380, 394, 399
Les Impressionnistes en 1886 (Fénéon), 134
L'Impromptu de Paris (Giraudoux), 363
Les Impudents (Duras), 121
In Memoriam (Léautaud), 199
L'Incohérence (du Bouchet), 113
L'Inconnue d'Arras (Salacrou), 34, 214
Les Indélicats, 143
India Song, 121
Indochine, 104
Indochinese War, 129, 177–178, 323, 334, 357, 377
Indy, Vincent d', 126, 178–179, 322
L'Infâme (Planchon), 287
Inferno (Dante), 316
L'Infini, 288, 359
The Influence of Gordon Craig in Theory and Practice (Brook),
    58

Ingres, Jean-Auguste-Dominique, 302, 330
L'Inhumaine, 210
Intimité: Intérieur avec amants et paravent (Valloton), 385
The Innocents of Paris, 77
L'Innommable (Beckett), 39
L'Inquisitoire (Pinget), 284
L'Inspecteur des ruines (Triolet), 375
The Inspector General (Gogol), 188
L'Instinct du bonheur (Maurois), 234
Instincts et institutions (Deleuze), 102
Institut Catholique de Paris, 226
Institut de Cinématographie, 146
Institut de Recherche et de Coordination Acoustique/Musique
    (IRCAM), 51, 70, 179
Institut des Fruits et Agrumes Coloniaux, 313
Institut des Hautes Etudes Cinématographiques (IDHEC), 99,
    210, 220, 308
Institut Pasteur, 70, 289
Intermezzo, 163, 188
International Film Prize, Venice Film Festival, 56
International Klein Blue (IKB), 190
International Red Cross, 126
De l'interprétation: Essai sur Freud (Ricœur), 311
Intimisme, 48
Intimités (Valloton), 385
Introduction à la littérature fantastique (Todorov), 372
Introduction à la méthode de Léonard de Vinci (Valéry), 383
Introduction à la philosophie de l'histoire (Arman), 15
Introduction à l'architexte (Genette), 159
Introduction à l'économie moderne (Sorel), 347
*Introduction à une nouvelle poésie et à une nouvelle musique, de
    Charles Baudelaire à Isidore Isou* (Isou), 181
Introduction aux existentialismes (Mounier), 249
L'Intruse (Maeterlinck), 217
L'Invasion (Adamov), 4
L'Invitation au château (Anouilh), 363
"L'Invitation au voyage" (Baudelaire), 230
L'Invitée (Beauvoir), 36
Ionesco, Eugène, 3, 30, 179–181, 273, 356, 360–361, 363–364, 367
IRCAM. *See* Institut de Recherche et de Coordination
    Acoustique/Musique.
Irigaray, Luce, 181, 259
Iris Clert Gallery, 190
Islam, 152
Isou, Isidore, 182, 206–207

J

Jabès, Edmond, 183
Jaccottet, Philippe, 183
J'accuse, 70, 151
J'accuse (Zola), 111
Jack the Ripper, 98
Jacob, Max, 33–34, 62, 183–184, 199, 247, 291, 309, 340
Jacques Brel Is Alive and Well and Living in Paris (musical), 55
Jacques Damour (Hennique), 367
J'ai deux amours (Baker), 25
Jakobson, Roman, 208, 351, 372, 375
La Jalousie (Robbe-Grillet), 256, 313
Jaloux, Edmond, 264, 394
Jammes, Francis, 54, 82, 184
Jamois, Marguerite, 34, 118, 185, 367–368
Janco, Marcel, 61

Jannings, Emil, 191
Jardin du Luxembourg, Paris. *See* Luxembourg Gardens.
"Jardins sous la pluie" (Debussy), 99
Jarry, Alfred, 12, 18, 92, 157, 185–186, 214, 297, 322, 364, 369
Jaspers, Karl, 310–311
Jaubert, Maurice, 66
Jaurès, Jean, 20, 57, 175
Jazz (Matisse), 231
Je bâtis ma demeure, 1943–1957 (Jabès), 183
"Je chante" (Trenet), 375
Je ne mange pas de ce pain-là (Péret), 278
Je suis ballerine (Chauviré), 77
Je Suis Partout, 54, 186, 323
Je vivrai l'amour des autres (Cayrol), 68
Je voudrais pas crever (Vian), 388
Je vous salue, Marie, 165
Jean Barois (Martin du Gard), 228
Jean de Florette, 106, 245, 271
Jean le bleu (Giono), 162
Jean-Christophe (Rolland), 317
Jeanmarie, René (Zizi), 279, 406
Jeanne d'Arc au bûcher (Honegger), 175
Jeanneret, Charles-Edouard, 199
Jeanson, Francis, 7
Jeffers, Robinson, 185
Jesus Christ, 105, 317, 320
Le Jeu d'enfant (Ollier), 267
Le Jeu de patience (Guilloux), 173
Le Jeune Européen, 112
La Jeune Fille Violaine (P. Claudel), 82
Le Jeune Homme et la mort (ballet), 279
La Jeune Née (Cixous and Clément), 78
La Jeune Parque (Valéry), 5, 383
Jeunes Femmes (Laurencin), 197
Les Jeunes Filles (Montherlant), 246
Jeunesse (Magritte), 218
Jeux (Debussy), 99, 253
Jeux d'eau (Ravel), 301
Les Jeux interdits, 82
Les Jeux sont faits (Sartre), 99
J'irai cracher sur vos tombes (Vian), 388–389
Joan of Arc, 10, 43, 249, 275
Le Jockey perdu (Magritte), 218
Jodorowsky, Alexandro, 17
Joffre, Joseph-Jacques, 227, 387
Joffrey Ballet, 272, 325
John of the Cross, Saint, 187, 397
Johns Hopkins University, 106, 291
La Joie (Bernanos), 43, 392
Joie de vivre (Lipchitz), 212
"Jolie Môme" (Ferré), 136
"La Jolie Rousse" (Apollinaire), 353
Jolson, Al, 374
Jonson, Ben, 118, 318
Jooss, Kurt, 14
Jorn, Asger, 207, 343
Les Joueurs (Masson), 229
Jouhandeau, Marcel, 12, 186–187
Jour (H. Bazin), 36
Le Jour (Wiesel), 398
Jour de fête, 358
Le Jour S (Doubrovsky), 110
Le Jour se lève, 14, 66, 149, 288, 292
Jourdain, Francis, 330
Le Journal, 93, 113
Journal d'un curé de campagne, 56

Journal d'un curé de campagne (Bernanos), 43
Le Journal d'une femme de chambre, 59, 248, 284
Journal de prison 1959 (Sarrazin), 332
Journal des Faux-Monnayeurs (Gide), 161
Journal du Ciné-club, 102
Journal inédit (Larbaud), 195
Journal littéraire (Léautaud), 198–199
Journal métaphysique (Marcel), 224
Journaliers (Jouhandeau), 187
Jouve, Pierre Jean, 125, 187
Jouvenel, Bertrand de, 86
Jouvenel, Henry de, 86
Jouvet, Louis, 10, 34, 41–42, 66, 88, 90, 92, 158, 163, 188, 228, 318, 363, 367
Joyaux, Philippe, 345
Joyce, James, 31, 38, 60, 78, 195, 273, 343
Juan (Renard), 304
Judaism, 69, 74, 78, 85, 88, 126, 153, 159, 170, 181, 189, 221, 225, 227, 242–243, 245, 252, 263, 277, 357, 397–398
Judex, 136
Le Juif errant, 18
Jules et Jim, 248, 377
Julien (Charpentier), 76
Julius Caesar (Shakespeare), 118, 363
La Jument verte (Aymé), 23
Jung, Carl, 25, 269
The Jungle Book (Kipling), 191
Les Justes (Camus), 67
Justice, 245

K

Kafka, Franz, 151, 248
Kahn, Gustave, 330
Kahn, Jean-François, 264
Kahnweiler, Daniel Henry, 203
Kalidasa, 81
Kamerny Theater, Moscow, 74
Kanapa, Jean, 260
Kandinsky, Wassily, 16
Karsavina, Tamara, 109, 189, 405
Kaufman, Boris, 389
Kaurismäki, Aki, 198
Kean (Sartre), 363
Keaton, Buster, 358
Kellogg-Briand Pact, 57
La Kermesse héroïque, 136
Kerouac, Jack, 69
Kessel, Joseph, 104, 189–190
KGB, 398
Khrushchev, Nikita, 151, 260, 371
Kierkegaard, Søren, 64, 127, 224, 311
Kiev Theater, 252
Kiki de Montparnasse (Alice Prin), 109, 302
The Killers, 237
King Lear (Shakespeare), 361
King, Stephen, 31
Kipling, Rudyard, 191
Kirstein, Lincoln, 26
Kisling, Moïse, 91
The Kiss, 136
Les Kitharèdes (Vivien), 393
Klee, Paul, 16, 100, 269

Klein, Yves, 15, 190–191, 256, 371
Kleist, Heinrich von, 369, 391
Kniaseff, Boris, 77
Knock, ou Le Triomphe de la médecine (Romains), 188, 318
"Ko Ko Ri Ko" (song), 75
Kochno, Boris, 109, 279
Koechlin, Charles, 126, 132, 191
Korda, Alexander, 79
Korean War, 238
Kosakiewicz, Olga, 36
Kosma, Joseph, 168, 292
Kristeva, Julia, 191–192, 259, 346, 359
Kropotkin, Peter, 340
Kunstgewerbeschule, Basel, 371
Kupka, Frank, 20, 337

L

La Fontaine, Jean de, 54
La Fresnaye, Roger de, 120, 193–194, 337, 392
La Llotja, 282
La Scala Ballet School, 405
la Tour du Pin, Patrice de, 196
Labiche, Eugène, 34, 79
Labour Party (Great Britain), 258
Le Labyrinthe (Arrabal), 17, 171, 229
Lacan, Jacques, 110, 181, 192–193, 239, 258, 311, 351–352
Laclos, Pierre Choderlos de, 38, 279, 381
Lacombe, Georges, 251
Lacombe Lucien, 221, 243
Ladurie, Emmanuel Le Roy, 9–10
The Lady from Shanghai, 139
Lafayette, Madame de, 99, 299, 326
Lafon, René, 91
Lamba, Jacqueline, 56
LaMotta, Jake, 71
Lancaster, Burt, 221
Landowska, Wanda, 194
Lang, Fritz, 73, 83
Lang, Jack, 157, 252, 369
Langage et cinéma (Metz), 239
Langlois, Henri, 145, 210
Lanson, Gustave, 194, 259
Lanzmann, Claude, 268
Larbaud, Valery, 131, 195
Larionov, Mikhail, 165–166, 195–196
Laroche, Pierre, 292
Larousse (publishing house), 263–264
Larousse gastronomique (Montagné), 260
Last Tango in Paris, 389
Latin Quarter, Paris, 30, 123, 196, 202, 236, 327
Laubreaux, Alain, 186
Laurencin, Marie, 53, 196–197, 252, 322
Laurens, Henri, 197–198, 405
Laurent, Jacques, 176
Laurent, Jean, 40
Lautréamont (Pleynet), 288
Laval, Pierre, 97, 389
Lawler, James R., 384
Lawrence, T. E., 221
Lawrence of Arabia. *See* Lawrence, T. E.
Lazareff, Pierre, 145
Le Clézio, J. M. G., 199

Le Corbusier, 152, 199–200, 270, 283
Le Fauconnier, Henri, 93, 163, 201, 392
Le Goff, Jacques, 9
Le Parc, Julio, 171
League of Nations, 57, 374
Léaud, Jean-Pierre, 198, 377
Léautaud, Paul, 198–199
Lecanuet, Jean, 130
Lécavelé, Roland, 110
Leclerc, Jacques Philippe, 211
La Leçon (Ionesco) 179–180
Leçon de choses (Simon), 343
Leçons (Jaccottet), 183
Leduc, Violette, 200–201, 224
Lefebvre, Georges, 201
Lefebvre, Henri, 151, 202, 385
Lefèvre, Brigitte, 261
Lefèvre, Frédéric, 263
Left Bank, Paris, 46, 62, 91, 123, 127, 196, 202–203, 247, 327, 361, 366, 377
Left-Wing Communism: An Infantile Disorder (Lenin), 85
La Légende de Joseph (Fokine), 228
Legendre, Maurice, 59
Léger, Fernand, 20, 62, 70, 74, 91, 93, 100, 133, 143, 151, 203–204, 210, 220, 256, 283, 337, 392
Légion d'Honneur, 77, 140, 153, 174, 191, 222, 237, 261, 279, 406
Légion des Combattants, 241
Légion Etrangère, 69
Légitime Défense, 204
Leigh, Mitch, 55
Leiris, Michel, 205, 360
Lelouch, Claude, 205
Lemaître, Maurice, 206
Lemor, Dominique, 125
Lenin Peace Prize, 13, 36
Lenin, Vladimir Ilyich, 62, 74, 85, 309, 311, 342
Lénine et la philosophie (Althusser), 9
Lenormand, Henri-René, 34, 285
Lenz, Desiderius, 339
Leo XIII, pope of Rome, 111
Léon Bloy (Bardèche), 28
Léon Morin, prêtre, 40
Leonardo da Vinci, 115, 337
Les Lépreuses (Montherlant), 246
Léro, Etienne, 204
Lescure, Pierre de, 123
Let's Make Love, 245
Lettre à François Mauriac (Bardèche), 28
Les Lettres françaises, 143, 206, 260, 275, 376
Lettrism, 98, 181–182, 206–207
Lettrist International (LI), 98, 207, 343
Lève-toi et marche (H. Bazin), 36
Lévi-Strauss, Claude, 10, 12, 106, 123, 191, 193, 208–209, 258, 351–352, 397
Léviathan (Green), 169
Levinas, Emmanuel, 207
Levinson, André, 207–208
Lévy, Bernard-Henri, 209, 258
Levy, Rudolf, 62
Lévy-Bruhl, Lucien, 209
L'Herbier, Marcel, 22, 102, 209–210
L.H.O.O.Q. (Duchamp), 115
Lhôte, André, 120, 210–211, 220, 283, 342
Les Liaisons dangereuses, 279, 381–382
Liberation of France, 14, 54, 65, 67, 77, 83, 87, 112, 123, 126, 145, 155–156, 158–159, 176, 190, 205–206, 211–212, 222, 235,

241–243, 248, 263, 266, 278, 304, 307, 359, 371, 396, 402
Liberation of Paris, 3, 186
Libertaire, 393
"Liberté" (Eluard), 124
Libion, Victor, 62
Librairie Gallimard. *See* Gallimard.
Library of Congress, 327
Liebermann, Rolf, 274
Lieutenant en Algérie (Servan-Schreiber), 7
Le Lieutenant-Colonel de Maumort (Martin du Gard), 228
Lifar, Serge, 77, 109, 211–212, 252, 274, 405
Ligue de l'Action Française, 3, 234
Ligue de la Patrie Française, 3, 111, 234
Ligue des Droits de l'Homme, 111
Lilar, Françoise, 221
"Les Lilas et les roses" (Aragon), 13
Liliom (Molnár), 286
Limon, José, 261
Linder, Max, 212, 358
Lindon, Jérôme, 123, 256
Le Lion (Kessel), 189
Lipchitz, Jacques, 93, 197, 220, 212–213, 347, 405
Lire Le Capital (Althusser), 9
Le Lis de mer (Mandiargues), 223
Liszt, Franz, 328
Littérature, 56, 112, 213, 255
La Littérature et le mal (Bataille), 33
Little Eyolf (Ibsen), 214, 364
Litvak, Anatole, 83, 97
Living Theater, 22, 391
Le Livre blanc (Cocteau), 84
Le Livre brisé (Doubrovsky), 110
Livre d'amour (Vildrac), 391
Le Livre d'Art, 142
Le Livre des fuites (Le Clézio), 199
Le Livre des questions (Jabès), 183
Le Livre des ressemblances (Jabès), 183
Livry, Emma, 273
Livy, 163
Lloyd George, David, 374
Locarno Pact, 1925, 57
La Loi (Vailland), 382
La Loi de la jungle (Koechlin), 191
Loin de Rueil (Queneau), 297
Loin du Viet-nam, 165, 308, 386
Lois (Sollers), 346
Lola, 103
Lola Montès, 103, 267, 269
London Symphony Orchestra, 246
Long Term Parking (Arman), 15
The Longest Day, 15
Longus, 394
Lopokova, Lydia, 109
Lorca, Suzanne, 274
Lorenzaccio (Musset), 368
Lorraine, 31
Lotar, Elie, 59
Loti, Pierre, 386
Louis XIV, 9, 87, 221, 272–273
Louis XVI, 363
Louise (Charpentier), 76
Louis-Ferdinand Céline (Bardèche), 28
Le Loup garou (Vitrac), 392
Les Loups (Rolland), 214
Louvre, 101, 106, 273, 393
Love Affair, 53

Love Me Tonight, 77
The Love Parade, 77
Lower Depths (Gorky), 214
Lubitsch, Ernst, 77
Luening, Otto, 90
Lugné-Poe, Aurélien, 18, 91–92, 157, 213–214, 364
Luitz-Morat, 18
Lukács, György, 165, 228
Lumet, Sydney, 341
Lumière, Auguste, 126, 156, 274
Lumière, Louis, 65, 126, 156, 174, 215, 236, 274, 294
Lumière d'été, 170
Lumumba, Patrice, 71
"Lundi rue Christine" (Apollinaire), 12
Lunes en papier (Malraux), 221
Lurçat, Jean, 20, 204, 220
Lutetia, 272
La Lutte des Classes, 80
Luxe, calme, et volupté (Matisse), 116, 230–231
Luxembourg Gardens, Paris, 88, 196, 363
Lycée Cordorcet, 5, 213, 295
Lycée Henri IV, 5
Lycée Louis-le-Grand, 60, 79, 81, 196
Lycée Michelet, 5
Lycée Montaigne, 79
Lycée Saint-Louis, 25
Lyotard, Jean-François, 215–216, 258, 344, 385

M

M-G-M studios, 95, 136, 156
Ma Dernière Mémoire (Abellio), 3
Ma Nuit chez Maud, 317
"Ma Pomme" (Chevalier), 77
Ma Vie (Lifar), 212
Macbeth (Shakespeare), 22, 67, 185, 368
MacDonald, Jeanette, 77
Machiavelli, Niccolò, 162
La Machine infernale (Cocteau), 41, 84, 188
MacMillan, Kenneth, 325
Mac Orlan, Pierre, 33
Madame Bovary (Flaubert), 34, 117, 121, 185, 368
Madame Bovary 38, 74, 306
Madame de . . ., 53, 97, 269
Madame Edwarda (Bataille), 33
Madame Figaro, 138–139
Madame Matisse (Matisse), 231
Madame Rosa, 153
Made in Japan (Raysse), 302
La Madeleine, Paris, 328
Madison Square Garden, New York, 40
La Madone des ordures (Benedetto), 41
Maeterlinck, Maurice, 99, 117, 214, 217
Magie noire (Morand), 248
Maginot, André, 217
Maginot Line, 97, 113, 217, 401
"Magnificat" (P. Claudel), 82
Magritte, René, 218–219, 229, 309, 322, 355
Mahabharata, 58
Maillol, Aristide, 193, 219, 315, 393
Main d'œuvre (Reverdy), 309
"Les Mains des constructeurs" (Léger), 204
Les Mains jointes (F. Mauriac), 232

Le Maintien de l'ordre (Ollier), 267
Mais moi je vous aimais (Cesbron), 72
Maison cubiste (Duchamp-Villon and others), 116, 194, 197, 283
La Maison de Claudine (Colette), 86
Maison de la Culture, 20, 26, 88, 143, 219–220, 273, 290, 337, 357, 362
La Maison de papier (Mallet-Joris), 221
La Maison de rendez-vous (Robbe-Grillet), 313
La Maison du pendu à Auvers-sur-Oise (Cézanne), 73
La Maison du peuple (Guilloux), 173, 219–220
"La Maison fermée" (P. Claudel), 82
La Maison natale (Copeau), 367
Maisons du Peuple, 219–220
Le Maître de Santiago (Montherlant) 247
Les Maîtres fous, 320
Les Maîtres penseurs (Glucksmann), 258
Makhno, Nestor, 85
Le Mal court (Audiberti), 21
Le Mal du siècle, 205
Le Malade imaginaire (Molière), 34, 92
Le Malentendu (Camus), 67
Malevich, Casimir, 74
Le Malfaiteur (Green), 169
Mallarmé, Stéphane, 45, 49, 51, 82, 99, 148, 187, 160, 383
Malle, Louis, 220–221, 243, 248, 294, 297
Mallet-Joris, Françoise, 221
Malone meurt (Beckett), 39
Malraux, André, 30, 33, 43, 82, 112, 131–132, 220–223, 225, 231–232, 262, 273, 275, 293–294, 348, 364, 401
Malraux, Clara, 221
Mama, Papa est blessé! (Tanguy), 355
Les Mamelles de Tirésias (Apollinaire), 12, 56
"La Mamma" (Aznavour), 24
Man of La Mancha (Leigh, Wasserman, and Darion), 55
Man with the Broken Nose (Rodin), 315–316
Mancini, Marie, 221
Les Mandarins (Beauvoir), 37, 156, 166
Mandiargues, André Pieyre de, 223
Manet, Eduoard, 73, 283, 330, 382
Mangano, Silvana, 83
Le Mangeur de rêves, 285
Manguin, Henri, 133
La Manifestation (Valloton), 384
"Manifeste des 121," 8
Manifeste des 343, 223
Manifestes du surréalisme (Breton), 56, 59, 213, 224, 229, 255, 353
"Manifesto for an Independent Revolutionary Art" (Breton and Trotsky), 134
Mann, Klaus, 242
Manon des sources, 245, 271
A Man's a Man (Brecht), 364
La Manivelle (Pinget), 284
Maquis, 307
Marceau, Marcel, 118, 224
Marcel and Elise (Jouhandeau), 187
Marcel Proust et les signes (Deleuze), 102
Marcel, Gabriel, 127–128, 224–225, 311, 397
Marchais, Georges, 258
Marcoussis, Louis, 225
Marcus, Greil, 98
Mardi Gras, 92
Maré, Rolf de, 14
Maréchal, Marcel, 21
La Marge (Mandiargues), 223
Maria Chapdelaine (Hémon), 168
Le Mariage de Figaro (Beaumarchais), 22, 367

Marianne, 225–226
Marie Donadieu (Philippe), 280
Marie Taglioni (Levinson), 208
La Mariée mise à nu par ses celibataires, meme (Duchamp), 115
"Marieke" (Brel), 55
Les Mariés de la Tour Eiffel (Cocteau), 175, 240, 345
Marin avec guitare (Lipchitz), 212
Marin, Maguy, 261
Maritain, Jacques, 127, 226–227, 249
Maritain, Raïssa, 227
Marius (Pagnol), 50, 271
Marius, 147, 271
Marivaux, Pierre Carlet de, 10, 14, 67, 287, 304–305, 362, 369
The Marne, 140, 227, 400
Marquet, Albert, 133, 227, 230
Marquet, Gabriel, 231
Marquet, Gustave, 227
La Marquise sortit à cinq heures (C. Mauriac), 231
Marrakch Medine (Ollier), 267
Mars ou la guerre jugée (Alain), 5
"Marseillaise," 119, 290, 306
Marseilles, 50
Marseilles Opera Ballet School, 40
Le Marteau sans maître (Boulez), 51, 75
Martin, Henri-Jean, 134
Martin, Steve, 39
Martin du Gard, Maurice, 263–264
Martin du Gard, Roger, 95, 123, 161, 228, 262, 294, 319, 400–401
Martinet, Marcel, 134
Le Martyre de Saint-Sébastien (d'Annunzio), 324
Marx Brothers, 79, 140
Marx est mort (Benoist), 258
Marx, Karl, 9–10, 33, 35, 56, 74, 204, 224, 346, 351, 354
Marxism, 4, 9, 32, 35, 37, 72, 98, 128, 152, 165, 201–202, 204, 209, 228, 238, 249, 254, 258–259, 308, 334, 351– 352, 359, 385, 400
Mary Magdalene, 317
Maryinsky Theater, Saint Petersburg, 140–141, 189, 252–253, 292, 405
Le Mas Théotime (Bosco), 49
Masereel, Frans, 20
Le Masque et l'encensoir (Baty), 34
Le Massacre en Corée (Picasso), 283
Massenet, Jules, 98
Massine, Léonide, 28, 83, 109, 189, 211, 228–229, 272, 324–325, 336
Masson, André, 33, 134, 143, 205, 229–230, 355
The Master Builder (Ibsen), 214, 364
Mastroianni, Marcello, 255, 284
Maté, Rudolph, 237
Mater Dolorosa, 151
Le Matérialisme dialectique (Lefebvre), 202
Matériaux d'une théorie du prolétariat (Sorel), 347
Maternité (Brieux), 50
Matière et mémoire (Bergson), 42
Matisse, Henri, 53, 93, 106, 116, 132–133, 147–148, 195, 227, 230–231, 245, 282, 302, 319–320, 322, 393
Matta, Roberto, 55, 229
Matthews, J. H., 278
Mauclair, Jacques, 46, 364, 367
Maupassant, Guy de, 306
Mauri, Rosita, 406
Mauriac, Claude, 187, 231–232, 256–257, 263, 294
Mauriac, François, 7, 28, 54, 72, 113, 123, 129, 138, 146, 162, 168, 231–233, 255, 262, 272, 294, 398
Mauritius, 199

Maurois, André, 5, 225, 233–234
Mauron, Charles, 259
Maurras, Charles, 3, 45, 105, 234–235, 349
Les Mauvais Coups (Vailland), 382
Le Mauvais Garçon, 77
"La Mauvaise Réputation" (Brassens), 54
Les Mauvaises Rencontres, 21
Max, Edward de, 84
May 1968 Demonstrations, 22, 30, 35, 85, 137–138, 156, 165, 182,
    202, 209, 216, 236, 242–243, 252, 258, 264, 287, 302, 305, 344,
    346, 359–360, 363, 385
May Protocols, 97
Maya (Gantillon), 34
Mayakovsky, Vladimir, 375
Mayerling, 97
McKay, Claude, 204
McKinley, William, 215
McLuhan, Marshall, 35
Mea culpa (Céline), 69
Measure for Measure (Shakespeare), 214
Le Mécanicien (Léger), 204
La Mécanique des femmes (Isou), 181
Médaille de la Reconnaissance Française, 405
Médaille Militaire, 69, 189
Medea (Jeffers), 185
Medea (Seneca), 67
Médée (Anouilh), 10, 363
La Méditerranée (Maillol), 219
Les Mégères de la mer (des Forêts), 108
Méliès, Gaston, 237
Méliès, Georges, 146, 174, 215, 236–237
Mélodie en sous-sol, 103
Melville, Jean-Pierre, 40, 139, 237, 386
Mémoires (Baker), 25
Mémoires d'une jeune fille rangée (Beauvoir), 37
Mémoires de Dirk Raspe (Drieu La Rochelle), 112
Mémoires de guerre (de Gaulle), 156
Mémoires d'Hadrien (Yourcenar), 404
Mémoires intimes (Simenon), 342
Le Mémorial (Jouhandeau), 187
Mendès-France, Pierre, 129, 178
Les Mendiants (des Forêts), 107
Ménil, René, 204
Méphisto: Le roman d'une carrière (Théâtre du Soleil), 242
Le Mépris, 29, 164, 215, 284
La Mer (Debussy), 99, 375
Merce Cunningham Dance Company, 274
The Merchant of Venice (Shakespeare), 157
Mercure, Jean, 261
Mercure (Satie and others), 336
Mercure de France, 12, 131, 198–199, 322
Merleau-Ponty, Maurice, 128, 207, 237–238, 333, 343, 255, 360, 397
Mermoz, Jean, 189
Mermoz (Kessel), 189
Merrill, Stuart, 103
The Merry Widow, 77
The Merry Wives of Windsor (Shakespeare), 157, 287
Mers-el-Kébir, 120
Mes apprentissages (Colette), 86
Mes propriétés (Michaux), 240
Messager, André, 367
Messiaen, Olivier, 51, 90, 238–239, 270
Mesure de la France, 112
Mesure de l'instant (Poulet), 291
Le Métafisyx (Corps de dame) (Dubuffet), 114
Métamorphose de la littérature (Boisdeffre), 48

Les Métamorphoses du cercle (Poulet), 291
Les Météores (Tournier), 373
Metz, Christian, 239
Metzinger, Jean, 53, 93, 100, 163–164, 201, 239, 283, 337, 392
La Meule, 8
Meyer, Jean, 362
Michaux, Henri, 60, 240, 262, 275, 337
Michel, Marc, 79
Michelangelo, 316
Mickey Mouse, 117
Midis gagnés (Tzara), 378
A Midsummer Night's Dream (Shakespeare), 242, 365
Mikhail Bakhtine: Le principe dialogique (Todorov), 372
Milhaud, Darius, 70, 83, 175, 210, 240–241, 289, 344
Milice Française, 241, 266
Le Milieu divin: Essai de vie intérieure (Teilhard), 359
Mill, Louis, 359
Millau, Christian, 260
Mille chemins ouverts (Green), 169
1789 (Mnouchkine), 242, 366
1793 (Mnouchkine), 242, 366
Miller, Henry, 69–70
Le Milliardaire (Saint Pierre), 328
Le Million, 79
Mills College, 241
"Milord" (Piaf), 281
Milton, John, 195
Minuit (Green), 169
Miou-Miou, 63
Mir Iskusstva, 109
Miracle de la rose (Genet), 158
Mirages (ballet), 77
Le Mirliton, 58, 349
Miró, Joan, 57
Le Miroir de la production (Baudrillard), 35
Miroir de la rédemption (Cayrol), 68
Miroir de la tauromachie (Leiris), 205
Le Miroir qui revient (Robbe-Grillet), 313
Miroirs (Ravel), 301
La Mise en scène (Ollier), 267
La Mise en scène du drame wagnérien (Appia), 12
Les Misérables, 274
Miserere (Rouault), 320
Mission de France, 399
Mistinguett, 23, 77, 241–242
Les Mistons, 215
Mitchell, Margaret, 169
Mitterrand, François, 137, 147, 243, 258, 345
Mizrahi, Moshe, 341
Mnouchkine, Alexandre, 242
Mnouchkine, Ariane, 78, 242, 252, 365
Mobile: Etude pour une représentation des Etats-Unis (Butor), 60
Mode de valeurs et d'intensité (Messiaen), 238
Moderato cantabile (Duras), 57, 121
Moderato cantabile, 57
Modern Times, 79
Der Moderne Bund, 16
Les Modernes et la tradition (Pleynet), 288
Les Modes, 75
Modiano, Patrick, 242–243, 294
La Modification (Butor), 60, 277
Modigliani, Amedeo, 33, 38, 62, 279, 347
Modot, Gaston, 243
Moïra (Green), 169
Les Moissonneurs (Gleizes), 164
Molière, 22, 34, 41, 87, 92, 118, 151, 188, 242, 287, 362–363, 367,

390
Molloy (Beckett), 39
Molnár, Ferenc, 286
Moly-Sabata, 164
Mon Faust (Valéry), 384
"Mon homme" (Mistinguett), 242
Mon oncle, 358
Mon oncle d'Amérique, 308
Le Monde, 8, 138, 243, 359
Le Monde de l'Education, 243
Le Monde Diplomatique, 243
Le Monde du silence, 220
Le Monde Hebdomadaire, 243
Le Monde réel (Aragon), 13
Monet, Claude, 99, 244–245, 281, 340
Monloup, Hubert, 287, 362
Monroe, Marilyn, 245
Monsieur Bob'le (Schehadé), 336
Monsieur Godeau intime (Jouhandeau), 187
Monsieur Godeau marié (Jouhandeau), 187
Monsieur Ouine (Bernanos), 44
Monsieur Verdoux, 140
Les Monstres sacrés (Cocteau), 41, 45
Mont-Cinère (Green), 169
Montagné, Prosper, 260
Montand, Valentin, 245
Montand, Yves, 24, 58, 245, 280, 341, 386
Montdevergyes Asylum, 81
Montesquieu, la politique et l'histoire (Althusser), 9
Monteux, Pierre, 245–246
Monteverdi, Claudio, 179
Montfort, Eugène, 150
Montherlant, Henri de, 159, 168, 186, 225, 246–247, 262
Montmartre, 33, 58, 61, 63, 76, 239, 247, 255, 273, 282, 340, 349, 362, 380
Montmartre, mon pays (Dorgelès), 110
Montoire, 266
Montparnasse, 36, 62, 91, 202, 247, 255, 273, 368
Montparnasse 19 (Becker), 38, 279
Montserrat (Roblès), 314
Moore, Dudley, 301
Morand, Paul, 168, 247–248
Moreau, Gustave, 227, 230, 319–320
Moreau, Jeanne, 57, 104, 133, 224, 248, 369
Moreau, Luce, 17
Morellet, François, 171
Morgan, Michèle, 65–66, 248–249
Morin, Edgar, 320
Mort à crédit (Céline), 69
La Mort dans l'âme (Sartre), 401
Mort de quelqu'un (Romains), 318, 379
La Mort du cygne, 77
La Mort du Docteur Faust (Ghelderode), 160
Mort d'un personnage (Giono), 162
La Mort en ce jardin, 284, 386
Le Mort et la faim (Fougeron), 143
Un Mort tout neuf (Dabit), 95
Morts sans sépulture (Sartre), 362
Moscow Institute of Painting, Sculpture, and Architecture, 165, 195
Moss, Howard, 384
Le Moteur blanc (du Bouchet), 113
Mother Courage and Her Children (Brecht), 369, 391
La Motocyclette (Mandiargues), 223
Les Mots (Sartre), 334
Les Mots et les choses: Une archéologie des sciences humaines
(Foucault), 143
"Les Mots et les images" (Magritte), 218, 309
Les Mots pour le dire (Cardinal), 65
Motte, Claire, 274, 406
Les Mouches (Sartre), 118, 334
Moulin rouge, 21, 241, 267
Moulin, Jean, 87, 307
Mounier, Emmanuel, 127, 249
Mourir de ne pas mourir (Eluard), 124
Mourre, Michel, 207
Le Mouton à cinq pattes (Verneuil), 135
Mouvement de la Libération des Femmes, 37, 124, 223, 249, 315
Mouvement du 22 mars, 85, 236
Mozart, Wolfgang Amadeus, 187, 328
Mucha, Alphonse, 250
Mudra, 40
Munich Pact, 162, 226
Le Mur (Sartre), 333
Murder in the Cathedral (Eliot), 367, 390
Murder My Sweet, 139
Muriel, 67, 308
Les Murmures de Satan (Saint Pierre), 327
Murphy (Beckett), 38–39
Murphy Brown, 221
Murphy's War, 255
"La Muse qui est la grâce" (P. Claudel), 82
Musée de l'Homme, 208
Musée des Arts Décoratifs, 316
Le Musée Grévin (Aragon), 13
"Les Muses" (P. Claudel), 82
Museum of Modern Art, 59, 74, 269
La Musica, 121
Musiciens (Zadkine), 405
Musique concrète. *See* Concrete music.
Musset, Alfred de, 185, 368–369
Mussolini, Benito, 118, 170
Mussorgsky, Modest, 301
My Dinner with André, 221
My Father's House (Troyat), 376
Le Mystère de la charité de Jeanne d'arc (Péguy), 276
Le Mystère de l'être (Marcel), 225
Le Mystère des saints innocents (Péguy), 276
Le Mystère Picasso, 83
Les Mystères de l'amour (Vitrac), 392
Les Mystérieuses Noces (Jouve), 187
Le Mythe de Sisyphe (Camus), 63–64, 128, 360
Mythologies (Barthes), 32, 352

N

Nabis, 44, 48, 104, 153–154, 193, 197, 201, 219, 227, 244–245, 250–252, 320–321, 331, 339–340, 384–385, 394–395
Nadeau, Maurice, 134
Nadja (Breton), 56
"Naissance d'une nouvelle avant-garde" (Astruc), 20
Naissances (Vasarely), 386
Nana, 306
Nancy Festival, 19, 242, 252, 365
Napalm (Benedetto), 41
Napoleon I, 87
Napoléon III, 369
Napoléon, 18, 151, 175, 201, 203, 249
Napoléon (Faure), 132

Napoléon (G. Lefebvre), 201
Natanson, Alexandre, 395
Nathan, Bernard, 275
Nation et voie africaine du socialisme (Senghor), 339
National Liberation Front (FLN), 8, 127
National Socialism. *See* Nazism.
La Nativité du Seigneur (Messiaen), 270
NATO. *See* North Atlantic Treaty Organization.
Nature morte (Fantômas) (Gris), 93
La Nausée (Sartre), 293, 333–334
Navettes (Ollier), 267
Le Navigateur (Roy), 323
Naville, Pierre, 80, 167, 309
The Nazarene Brotherhood, 251
Nazi Condor Legion, 283
Nazism, 20, 54, 74, 83, 85, 88, 123, 134, 150, 153, 155–156, 159,
    162–163, 169, 181, 186, 222, 233, 243, 246, 263, 265, 307,
    371–373, 387, 389, 395–396, 398
Les Nègres (Genet), 47, 158, 361
Négritude et humanisme (Senghor), 339
Nehru, Jawaharlal, 223
Nekrassov (Sartre), 362
Nemo, Philippe, 258
Neo-Impressionism, 44, 105, 133–134, 153–154, 230, 244, 245, 303,
    331, 337, 340, 393, 395
Neon, 396
Nerval, Gérard de, 187
New Criticism. *See* La Nouvelle Critique.
New Novel. *See* Nouveau Roman.
New Philosophers. *See* Nouveaux Philosophes.
New Realism. *See* Nouveau Réalisme.
New School for Social Research, 208
New Theater. *See* Theater of the Absurd.
New Wave. *See* Nouvelle Vague.
New-York (Morand), 248
New York City Ballet, 26, 274, 351
New York Metropolitan Opera, 246
New York Philharmonic Orchestra, 49, 51
New York University, 110
Newsweek, 128
*Ni Marx ni Jésus: De la seconde révolution américaine à la seconde
    révolution mondiale* (Revel), 308
Nicolle, Marcel, 133
Nietzsche et la philosophie (Deleuze), 102, 106, 142, 346
Nietzsche, Friedrich, 33, 35, 64, 106, 127, 142, 159, 315, 346
Nieuwenhuys, Constant, 343
Nijinska, Bronislava, 109, 211, 252–253, 274, 324
Nijinsky, Vaslav, 99, 109, 141, 189, 252–254, 325, 364, 405
Nijinsky, clown de Dieu (Béjart), 40, 99, 109, 141, 325
Nikolais, Alwin, 261
Nimier, Roger, 176
"Nini peau de chien" (Bruant), 58
Nizan, Paul, 15, 88, 202, 254–255
Nobel Peace Prize, 57, 398
Nobel Prize for Literature, 39, 42, 63, 144, 161, 217, 228, 232, 294,
    318, 327, 334, 342, 398
Nobilissima Gallorum Gens (Pope Leo XIII), 111
Les Noces (ballet), 27, 109, 187, 252–253
Les Noctambules, Paris, 361
Nocturnes (Senghor), 338
Noé (Obey), 367
Le Nœud de vipères (F. Mauriac), 233
Noire et blanche (Ray), 302
Noiret, Philippe, 255, 284, 369
Nombres (Sollers), 346
"Non, je ne regrette rien" (Piaf), 281

Nord (Céline), 69
Norodom Sihanouk (Cixous), 242
Nord-Sud, 255, 309
Norma ou l'exil infini (Roblès), 314
Normandy, 307
Norris, Christopher, 107
North Atlantic Treaty Organization (NATO), 255, 390
"Note sur la peinture" (Metzinger), 239
Notes sur André Gide (Martin du Gard), 228
"Notes sur le cubisme" (Ozenfant), 270
Notre Dame de Paris (Hugo), 99
Notre-Dame des Fleurs (Genet), 158
Notre Théâtre (Pitoëff), 286
Notre-Dame Cathedral, 81, 182, 207, 269
Notre-Dame de Toute Grâce, 204
La Notte, 248
Les Nourritures terrestres (Gide), 160
Nous et les autres: Réflexions sur la diversité humaine (Todorov),
    372
A nous la liberté, 79
Nouveau Ballet de Monte Carlo, 77, 212
Le Nouveau Bloc-Notes, 1958–1960 (F. Mauriac), 233
Le Nouveau Locataire (Ionesco), 180
Nouveau Nouveau Roman, 256
Nouveau Réalisme, 15, 115, 255–256, 302, 371
Nouveau Roman (New Novel), 38, 56, 60, 68, 120, 123, 160, 199,
    210, 231–232, 242, 256–257, 266–267, 277, 284, 297–298, 310,
    312–313, 315, 331, 343, 345, 359, 373
Nouveau Théâtre. *See* Theater of the Absurd.
Les Nouveaux Aristocrates (Saint Pierre), 327
Les Nouveaux Messieurs, 136
Nouveaux Philosophes (New Philosophers), 209, 235, 258
Les Nouveaux Prêtres (Cesbron), 72, 327–328
Nouveaux problèmes du roman (Ricardou), 310
Nouveaux Réalistes, 190–191
Le Nouvel Observateur, 129, 223, 258
Nouvelle Compagnie d'Avignon, 41
La Nouvelle Critique, 32, 259–260
Nouvelle critique ou nouvelle imposture? (Picard), 32
nouvelle cuisine, 260–261
La Nouvelle Danse, 261
Nouvelle Nouvelle Revue Française (NNRF), 150, 263, 275
Nouvelle Revue Française, 14, 21, 90–91, 112, 150, 160, 183, 195–
    196, 225, 262–263, 275, 312, 336
Nouvelle Tendance, 171, 386–387
Nouvelle Vague (New Wave), 21–22, 35, 38, 40, 56, 66, 73, 79, 103,
    120, 126, 139, 145, 164, 215, 220, 237, 239, 240, 243, 263, 267,
    269, 306, 308, 311, 317, 373–374, 377, 386
Nouvelles Conversations de Goethe avec Eckermann (Blum), 47
Nouvelles et textes pour rien (Beckett), 39
Nouvelles Etudes (Rivière), 312
Nouvelles Littéraires, 208, 263–264
Nouvelles réflexions sur le théâtre (Barrault), 30
Les Noyers de l'Altenburg (Malraux), 222
Nu descendant un escalier (Duchamp), 114
Le Nu perdu (Char), 76
Nucléa (Pichette), 391
La Nue couchée (Valadon), 382
La Nuit (Wiesel), 398
La Nuit américaine, 198, 215, 377
"La Nuit de Dunkerque" (Aragon), 13
La Nuit est aussi un soleil (Arrabal), 17
Nuit et brouillard, 67, 146, 308
La Nuit remue (Michaux), 240
La Nuit talismanique (Char), 76
Nunisme, 340

Nuovo Cinema Paradiso, 255
Nuremberg ou la terre promise (Bardèche), 28
Nuremberg Trials, 28
Nureyev, Rudolph, 274
Les Nus dans la forêt (Léger), 203

O

O'Connor, Flannery, 199
O'Toole, Peter, 10
Obaldia, René de, 261, 265
Obey, André, 30, 88–89, 367
L'Observateur, 8
L'Observatoire de Cannes (Ricardou), 310
Occitan language, 41
occultist, 103
The Occupation (World War II), 3, 13, 15, 28, 30–31, 35, 38, 45, 64, 69, 74–77, 87–88, 96, 106, 112, 121, 123–126, 136, 138, 143, 145, 148, 150, 159, 163, 168–170, 172, 177, 190, 201, 205–206, 212, 218, 221–222, 237, 240–243, 247, 262–263, 266, 268, 273, 275, 299, 306, 313, 323, 334, 337, 348, 354, 357, 359, 368, 370, 372, 375, 381, 387, 392–393, 396, 399, 401
Occupe-toi d'Amélie (Feydeau), 50, 304
Occupied Zone, 146, 265, 306, 389, 401
October group. *See* Groupe Octobre.
L'Octroi (Rousseau), 321
Ode à Londres bombardée (Soupault), 347
Odéon, Théâtre de l'. *See* Théâtre de l'Odéon.
Odile (Queneau), 297
Œdipe (Gide), 285, 390
Œdipe-roi (Cocteau), 84
Œdipe, roi de Thèbes (Bouhélier), 157
Oedipus Rex (ballet), 351
Oedipus Rex (Sophocles), 361
Œuvre, Théâtre de l'. *See* Théâtre de l'Œuvre.
L'Œuvre (Zola), 73
L'Œuvre au noir (Yourcenar), 404
L'Œuvre d'art vivant (Appia), 12
L'Œuvre de Léon Bakst (Levinson), 208
Œuvres romanesques croisées d'Elsa Triolet et Aragon (Triolet and Aragon), 376
Off-Broadway, 22, 391
Offenbach, Jacques, 25, 291
Oh! les beaux jours (Beckett), 46, 305, 361, 363
L'Oiseau bleu (Maeterlinck), 217
L'Oiseau de feu (ballet), 27, 140, 189, 350
Oiseaux exotiques (Messiaen), 238
Oliver, Raymond, 260
Olivier, Lawrence, 10
Ollier, Claude, 256, 266–267
Olympia (Manet), 73, 382
Olympic Games, 1968, 40
On ne badine pas avec l'amour (Musset), 369
On vous parle (Cayrol), 68
Ondine (Giraudoux), 363
One Hour of Love, 140
O'Neill, Eugene, 34
Op Art. *See* Nouvelle Tendance.
The Open Door: Thoughts on Acting and Theater (Brook), 58
Opéra (Paris), 50, 200, 223, 321, 364
Opéra Comique, 76, 364
Opéra parlé (Audiberti), 21
Operation Anvil, 211

Ophuls, Marcel, 267–268
Ophuls, Max, 53, 97, 103, 267–269, 279, 341
L'Opium des intellectuels (Aron), 15
Opium, journal d'une désintoxication (Cocteau), 84
L'Opoponax (Wittig), 399
Oppenheim, Meret, 269
Orchestre Symphonique de Paris, 246
L'Ordre (Arland), 14
L'Ordre des Arts et des Lettres, 279
organists and organ music, 269–270
Les Orgueilleux, 249
Les Origines (Redon), 303
Orion aveugle (Simon), 343
Orlando, Vittorio Emanuele, 374
Orozco, José Clemente, 143
Orphée (ballet), 21
Orphée (Cocteau), 285
Orphée (Delville), 103
Orphée, 67, 83
Orphism, 100, 101, 166, 281, 331
Ortiz (Vasarely), 386
L'Os, 58
Ostinato (des Forêts), 108
L'Otage (Claudel), 214
Les Otages (Fautrier), 132
Où le soleil (du Bouchet), 113
Oublier Foucault (Baudrillard), 35
Oulipo (Ouvroir de Littérature Potentielle), 277, 297
Out One, 312
Ouvert la nuit (Morand), 247
Ouvroir de Littérature Potentielle. *See* Oulipo.
Ove Arup, 70
Oxford University, 232
Ozenfant, Amédée, 199, 270, 283

P

Pach, Walter, 116
Pacific 231 (Honegger), 175
Padmâvatî (Roussel), 322
Pagnol, Marcel, 50, 135, 147, 271, 288
Le Pain des rêves (Guilloux), 173
Paix (Picasso), 283
La Paix chez soi (Courteline), 50
Paix et guerre entre les nations (Arman), 15
Le Palace (Simon), 343
Palace of the Popes, Avignon, 261, 390
Palais de Chaillot, Paris, 287, 362, 368–369, 390
Palais des Congrès, Paris, 274
Palais des Sports, Paris, 274
Palais-Royal, Paris, 87
Palimpsestes (Genette), 159
Paludes (Gide), 160, 267
Pan, 131
Le Panama; ou, Les aventures de mes sept oncles (Cendrars), 69
Panama-Pacific Exposition, 328
Panic Movement, 17
Panique, 122
Pantagleize (Ghelderode), 160
Panthéon, Paris, 196
Paolo Paoli (Adamov), 4, 287, 362
Le Paquebot Tenacity (Vildrac), 391
Les Pâques à New York (Cendrars), 69

Parade (ballet), 27, 83, 109, 229, 272, 336, 358
Parade (Lugné-Poe), 214
La Parade II (Lugné-Poe) 214
Paradis (Sollers), 346
Paradise Now, 22, 391
Parallèlement (Verlaine), 394
Paramount, 59
Les Parapluies de Cherbourg, 103
Les Paravents (Genet), 30, 47, 57, 67, 158, 361, 363
Le Parc (Sollers), 345–346
Pardi, Angelo, 162
Paris (Follain), 141
Paris Biennale, 171
Paris CanCan, 306
Paris Commune of 1871, 4, 283, 330, 349, 384–385
Paris Conservatory, 49, 51, 67, 117, 132, 175, 188, 238, 240–241, 245, 269–270, 283, 301, 328, 330, 335, 349, 384–385
Paris Dance Festival, 40
Paris de Bollardière, Gen. Jacques, 8
Paris Exposition, 101, 148, 328
Paris Institut Choréographique, 212
Paris-Midi, 83
Paris Musée de l'Opéra, 14
Paris nous appartient, 311
Paris Opéra Ballet, 77, 211–212, 253, 273–274, 279, 405–406
Paris Opéra Ballet Ecole de Danse, 77, 274
Paris qui danse (revue), 241
Paris qui dort, 79
Paris qui jazz (revue), 241
The Paris Review, 273
Paris Revue Nègre, 25
Paris, Reine-Marie, 81
"Paris-Canaille" (Ferré), 136
Paris-Midi, 102
Parisienne, 176
Parisiennes au marché (Fougeron), 143
La Parodie (Adamov), 4, 46
La Parole en archipel (Char), 76
Paroles (Prévert), 292
Parsifal (Wagner), 166
La Part maudite (Bataille), 33
Partage de midi (P. Claudel), 30, 82
Parti Communiste Français (PCF). *See* French Communist Party.
Le Parti pris des choses (Ponge), 289
Parti Progressiste Martiniquais, 71
Parti Socialiste, 345
Une Partie de campagne, 38, 306
La Partie de cartes (Léger), 203
Partir avant le jour (Green), 169
Partisans (Fautrier), 133
Pas de trois (ballet), 405
Pascal, Blaise, 14, 64, 127, 397
Pasolini, Pier Paolo, 198
Passacaille (Pinget), 284
Passage de Milan (Butor), 60
Le Passe-muraille (Aymé), 23
Le Passe-peine, 1949–1967 (Sarrazin), 332
Passion, 165
La Passion de l'abbé Delance (Saint Pierre), 328
La Passion du Général Franco (Gatti), 369
Pasteur, Louis, 126
Patachou, 54
Patchouli (Salacrou), 118

Patenôtre, Raymond, 226
Pathé, Charles, 151, 156, 274–275
Pathé, Emile, 274
Pathé, Jacques, 274
Pathé, Théophile, 274
Pathé, Frères, 274
Pathé-Journal, 274
Paul, Saint, 397
Paulhan, Jean, 123, 262–263, 275
Paulina 1880 (Jouve), 187
Pauvre Bitos (Anouilh), 10
"Pauvre Martin" (Brassens), 54
Pavane pour une infante défunte (Ravel), 301
Pavé de Paris, 226
Le Pavillon d'Armide (ballet), 109, 405
Pavlova, Anna, 109, 140–141, 274, 364
Pavlowitch, Paul, 153
Le Pays des mines (Fougeron), 143
Les Pays lointains (Green), 169
Paysage cubiste (Metzinger), 239
Paysage, Céret (Soutine), 347
Paysages et intérieurs (Vuillard), 394
Le Paysan de Paris (Aragon), 12
Les Paysans du Nord pendant la Révolution française (Lefebvre), 201
Peace (Aristophanes), 118
Peau de banane, 267
Les Peaux de lapins (Fautrier), 132
Pêcheur d'Islande, 386
Peer Gynt (Ibsen), 214, 364
Péguy, Charles, 127, 249, 275–277, 317, 400
Le Peintre (Vitrac), 392
La Peinture moderne (Le Corbusier and Ozenfant), 199
Pèl & Ploma, 282
Péladan, Joséphin ("Sâr"), 103, 384
Pélégri, Jean, 314
Pelléas et Mélisande (Debussy), 99, 214, 217
Pellerin, Auguste, 394
Pelloutier, Fernand, 277
P.E.N., 125
Pensée, 260
La Pensée sauvage (Lévi-Strauss), 209, 351
Le Penseur (Rodin), 316
Pension Mimosas, 14
Pépé le Moko, 121, 149, 243
Le Père Goriot (Balzac), 367
Le Père Peinard, 134
Le Père Perdrix (Philippe), 280
Perec, Georges, 267, 277–278, 294
Péret, Benjamin, 278, 309, 353
La Péri (Dukas), 117
Perils of Pauline, 272, 275
Périnal, Georges, 65
Perkins, Anthony, 83
Les Perles de la couronne, 173
Perséphone (ballet), 351
Les Personnages (Mallet-Joris), 221
Le Personnalisme, 249
La Pesanteur et la grâce (Weil), 397
La Peste (Camus), 64
Pétain, Philippe, 97, 156, 226, 233, 241, 265–266, 278, 323, 336, 387, 389, 401
Petipa, Marius, 27
Petit, Georges, 394
Petit, Roland, 40, 77, 274, 279
Le Petit Ami (Léautaud), 199

Le Petit Monde de Don Camillo, 122, 135
Petit Palais, Paris, 330
Le Petit Prince (Saint-Exupéry), 326
Petit Vingtième, 371–372
Petit-Louis (Dabit), 95
La Petite et la Grande Manœuvre (Adamov), 46
La Petite Marchande d'allumettes, 306
Les Petits-Bourgeois (Gorky), 365
Les Petits Enfants du siècle (Rochefort), 315
Petrouchka (ballet), 109, 141, 189, 246, 252–253, 350
La Pharisienne (F. Mauriac), 233
Phèdre (Racine), 30, 34, 185, 391
Le Phénomène humain (Teilhard), 358
La Phénoménologie de la perception (Merleau-Ponty), 238
Phenomenology, 3, 5, 128, 237–238, 256, 291, 310, 383–384
Philadelphia Orchestra, 49
Philipe, Gérard, 22, 67, 249, 279, 369, 390
Philippart, Nathalie, 279
Philippe, Charles-Louis, 279–280
Philips, 54
La Philosophie dans le boudoir (Magritte), 218
Philosophies, 202
Photographies (Simon), 343
Pia, Pascal, 314
Piaf, Edith, 23, 71, 245, 280–281, 291
"Pianists" (Saint-Saëns), 328
Piano, Renzo, 70
Picabia, Francis, 62, 79, 96, 197, 281, 301, 337, 392
Picard, Raymond, 32, 259
Picasso, Pablo, 16, 33, 53–54, 58, 61–62, 83, 85, 93, 95, 101, 106,
    108–110, 118, 143, 151, 163–164, 170–171, 184, 197, 203, 206,
    210–212, 219, 225, 229, 239, 241, 247, 272, 281–283, 308–309,
    320, 322, 336–337, 350, 353, 392–393, 400, 405
Piccoli, Michel, 255, 284
Pichette, Henri, 67, 391
Pickford, Mary, 140
Pickpocket, 56
Pictures at an Exhibition (Mussorgsky), 301
Pièce héroïque (Franck), 269
Pièces brillantes (Anouilh), 10
Pièces costumées (Anouilh), 10
Pièces grinçantes (Anouilh), 10
Pièces noires (Anouilh), 10
Pièces roses (Anouilh), 10
pieds-noirs, 7–8, 65, 221
Pierre écrite (Bonnefoy), 49
Pierrot le fou (Godard), 40, 164
Le Piéton de Paris (Fargue), 131
Pietr-le-Letton (Simenon), 342
Piletta, Georges, 274
Pilote, 20
Pilote de guerre (Saint-Exupéry), 326
Les Pincengrain (Jouhandeau), 187
Le Ping-Pong (Adamov), 4
Pinget, Robert, 256–257, 284, 293
Pinot-Gallizio, Giuseppe, 207
Pinter, Harold, 47
Piollet, Wilfride, 274
Pique-nique en campagne (Arrabal), 17
Pirandello, Luigi, 118, 285, 362
Pissarro, Camille, 72–73, 99, 153, 244, 281, 393
Piston, Walter, 50
Pitié pour les femmes (Montherlant), 246
Pitoëff, Georges, 34, 66, 285–286, 364, 367
Pitoëff, Ludmilla, 285–286
Pitoëff, Sacha, 286

Pivot, Bernard, 12
Pizan, Christine de, 194
Place Charles de Gaulle, Paris, 243
Place de la Bastille, Paris, 273
Place de la Concorde (Forain), 141
Place de la Madeleine, Paris, 200
La Place de la Madeleine: Ecriture et fantasme chez Proust
    (Doubrovsky), 110
Place de la République, Paris, 50, 157
La Place de l'Etoile (Modiano), 243
Place du Tertre, Paris, 247
Place Emile-Goudeau, 33
Plaidoyer pour un rebelle (Roblès), 314
Le Plaisir, Paris, 97, 269
Plaisir à Corneille (Schlumberger), 336
Le Plaisir de peindre (Masson), 229
Le Plaisir du texte (Barthes), 32
Les Plaisirs et les jours (Proust), 295
Planchon, Roger, 8, 19, 22, 30, 286–288, 362, 363, 369
Le Planétarium (Sarraute), 332
"Le plat pays" (Brel), 55
Plato, 107, 336, 397
Plays (Pinget), 284
Playtime, 358
Le Plein (Arman), 15
Pleynet, Marcelin, 288, 359
Pli selon pli (Boulez), 51
Plotinus, 339
La Pluie et le beau temps (Prévert), 292
La Plume, 142
Plupart du temps (Reverdy), 309
Poe, Edgar Allan, 126, 195, 303
Poèmes (Brasillach), 54, 131, 338
Poèmes à jouer (Tardieu), 356
Poèmes de Fresnes (Brasillach), 54
Poèmes de la nuit et du brouillard (Cayrol), 68
Poèmes 1905 (Vildrac), 391
Poèmes politiques (Eluard), 125
Poems of a Black Orpheus (Senghor), 339
Poésie 40–41, 337
Le Poète assassiné (Apollinaire), 197
Poètes d'aujourd'hui, 337
Les Poètes français d'aujourd'hui (Boisdeffre), 48
Poetic realism, 8, 38, 65, 121–122, 136, 145, 288, 292, 306, 389
Poétique, 78, 372
Poétique (Todorov), 372
Poétique de la prose (Todorov), 372
Poil de Carotte (Renard), 361
Le Point, 130, 138, 258, 264
Le Point de départ (Poulet), 291
Point, Fernand, 260
La Pointe Courte, 386
pointillism, 44, 105, 133
Poirer, Louis. *See* Gracq, Julien.
Poirot-Delpech, Bertrand, 288
"Poissons d'or" (Debussy), 99
Polanski, Roman, 104
Polignac, Winaretta Singer (Princesse Edmond de Polignac), 289
Polish Ballet, 253
La Politique des restes (Adamov), 4
La Polka (Modiano), 243
Pomerand, Gabriel, 181, 206
Pompes funèbres (Genet), 158
Pompidou, Georges, 51, 70, 137, 223, 338
Ponge, Francis, 262, 275, 289
Le Pont (Léger), 203

Le Pont de Londres (Céline), 69
Le Pont du chemin de fer, Moret (Picabia), 281
Le Pont du secret (C. Mauriac), 232
Pont-Aven, Brittany, 44, 48, 339
Pontigny, 14
Pontis, Noella, 274
Pop art, 191, 219, 256
Popular Flemish Theater, 159
Popular Front, 20, 47, 87–88, 121, 147, 170, 173, 176, 186, 204, 219–220, 225–226, 289–290, 306, 311, 345, 348, 357, 369, 371
Le Porche du mystère de la deuxieme vertu (Péguy), 276
La Porte de l'enfer (Rodin), 80, 316
Porte de Lilas, 79
La Porte du fond (Rochefort), 315
La Porte étroite (Gide), 160
Porte Saint-Martin, Paris, 50
Les Portes de la forêt (Wiesel), 398
Porto-Riche, Georges de, 367
"Le Portrait" (Supervielle), 352
Portrait d'un inconnu (Sarraute), 331
Portrait de Jouve (Le Fauconnier), 201
Portrait-relief d'Arman (Klein), 191
Le Postmoderne expliqué aux enfants: Correspondance 1982–1985 (Lyotard), 215
Pot-Bouille, 279
Potlatch, 207
Le Potomak (Cocteau), 83
Pottecher, Maurice, 156
poubelles (Arman), 15
Poulain, Henri, 159
Poulenc, Francis, 44, 191, 252, 291, 344
Poulet, Georges, 259, 291
Pound, Ezra, 247, 315
La Poupée (Audiberti), 21
Pour Lucrèce (Giraudoux), 30, 163
Pour Marx (Althusser), 9
Pour un autre Moyen Age (Le Goff), 9
Pour un nouveau roman (Robbe-Grillet), 256, 313
Pour une morale de l'ambiguïté (Beauvoir), 37, 128
Pour une relecture africaine de Marx et d'Engels (Senghor), 339
Pour une sociologie du roman (Goldmann), 165
Pour une théorie du nouveau roman (Ricardou), 310
Pourquoi des philosophes? (Revel), 308
Pourquoi la nouvelle critique? (Doubrovsky), 110
Pouvoirs de l'horreur (Kristeva), 192
The Power of Darkness (Tolstoy), 367
Prado museum, Madrid, 283
Prague School, 372
Prague Spring, 151
Pratiques d'écriture (Ponge), 289
Prélude à L'Après-midi d'un faune (Debussy), 99
Prélude à Verdun (Romains), 319
Préludes (Satie), 335
Préludes flasques (pour un chien) (Satie), 335
Le Premier Accroc coûte deux cents francs (Triolet), 375
La Première Aventure céleste de M. Antipyrine (Tzara), 377
"La Première Fille" (Brassens), 54
Prénom: Carmen, 165
Preobrajenska, Olga, 292
Pre-Raphaelite Brotherhood, 251
Pretty Baby, 221
Prévert, Jacques, 29–30, 46, 49, 66, 168, 292, 355
"Prière pour aller au paradis avec les ânes" (Jammes), 184
Primavera (Boticelli), 219
Prin, Alice. *See* Kiki de Montparnasse.
Prince Igor (ballet), 109

The Prince of Homburg (Kleist), 369, 391
Prince, Gerald, 372
Princess Tam Tam, 25
La Princesse de Clèves (Lafayette), 99
Princet, Maurice, 210–211, 337
Princeton University, 227
Le Printemps 71 (Adamov), 4
Prinzhorn, Hans, 113
La Prise de Constantinople (Ricardou), 258, 310
Prismes électriques (Delaunay-Terk), 101
Private Worlds, 53
Prix Bagnolet, 261
Prix Blumenthal, 357
Prix de l'Humour Noir, 297
Prix de la Pléiade, 158
Prix de la Renaissance, 294
Prix de Monaco, 326
Prix de Rome, 152, 294
Prix des Critiques, 108, 113, 153, 183
Prix du Roman Populiste, 95, 173, 293, 314–315, 376
Prix Dulac, 295
Prix Emil Cohl, 65
Prix Félix Fénéon, 60, 281, 294, 345
Prix Fémina, 43, 110, 221, 284, 293, 314
Prix Fémina-Vacaresco, 293
Prix Gabriel Ferrier, 295
Prix Goncourt, 36–37, 117, 150, 153, 159, 166, 168, 222–223, 243, 293, 296, 372, 375–376, 382
Prix Guillaume Apollinaire, 36, 337
Prix Gustave Courtois, 295
Prix Interallié, 254, 288, 294
Prix Jean Vigo, 65
Prix Louis Delluc, 65, 294, 312, 358, 386
Prix Louis Lumière, 65, 294
Prix Mallarmé, 21, 141
Prix Médicis, 267, 278, 294, 315, 399
Prix Méliès, 386
Prix Nadal, 17
Prix Renaudot, 49, 173
Prix Sainte-Beuve, 3
Prix Théophraste Renaudot, 199, 293
Le Problème de l'incroyance au XVIe siecle (Febvre), 134
Problèmes actuels du marxisme (H. Lefebvre), 202
Problèmes du nouveau roman (Ricardou), 310
Le Procès, 248
Procès des trente, 135
Le Procès-verbal (Le Clézio), 199
Le Professeur Taranne (Adamov), 4, 287, 364
Programme Commun, 147
La Proie du vent, 386
Projet pour une révolution à New-York (Robbe-Grillet), 313
Prokofiev, Serge, 26, 109
La Promenade sous les arbres (Jaccottet), 183
Promenades (Ray), 301
Le Promenoir, 126
Les Prophéties du Chilam Balam (Clézio), 199
Propos (Alain), 5
Propos de littérature (Alain), 5
"Propositions sur le mouvement" (Groupe de Recherche d'Art Visuel), 171
Propp, Vladimir, 209
Le Propre de l'homme, 205
La Prose du Transsibérien et de la petite Jehanne de France (Cendrars), 69
"Prosper" (Chevalier), 77
Proudhon, Pierre Joseph, 340

Proust, Marcel, 38, 43, 58, 60, 86, 103, 110–111, 138, 150–151, 159, 166, 168, 202, 213, 228, 232–233, 247, 256–257, 262, 293, 295–296, 299, 308, 312, 332, 343, 373
Prouvost, Jean, 138
Providence, 308
Provisoires amants des nègres (Pleynet), 288
Psaumes de tous mes temps (la Tour du Pin), 196
Psst . . . l, 141
La Psychanalyse du feu (Bachelard), 25
Psyché (Romains), 318
Psychologie de l'art (Malraux), 223
Puaux, Paul, 23
Pulcinella (ballet), 229, 351
Pulszky, Romola de, 254
Purism, 199, 200, 270, 331
Pushkin, Aleksandr, 376
La Putain respectueuse (Sartre), 362
Puteaux circle, 239
Puvis de Chavannes, Pierre, 154, 382, 394
La Pyramide, 260
Pyrrhus et Cinéas (Beauvoir), 37

Q

Qu'est-ce que le cinéma? (A. Bazin), 36
Quai des brumes, 66, 149, 248, 292
Quai des orfèvres, 83
Quand la femme s'en mêle, 103
Quatorze juillet, 79
La Quatorze juillet (Rolland), 157
Les Quatre cent coups, 198, 263, 311, 377, 389
Els Quatre Gats, 282
Quatre histoires de pauvre amour (Philippe), 280
Quatre lectures talmudiques (Levinas), 207
Quatrième Républic. See Fourth Republic.
Quatuor pour la fin du temps (Messiaen), 238
Que ma joie demeure (Giono), 162
Quelqu'un (Pinget), 284
Queneau, Raymond, 168, 186, 220, 262, 267, 275, 278, 297–298
Querelle de Brest (Genet), 158
Qu'est-ce que le surréalisme? (Breton), 224
La Question (Alleg), 8
La Quête de joie (de la Tour du Pin), 196
Qui j'ose aimer (H. Bazin), 36
Qui je fus (Michaux), 240
"Qui qu'a vu Coco dans l'Trocadéro?" (Chanel), 75
Quinn, Anthony, 10
Quoat-Quoat (Audiberti), 21

R

Rabelais, François, 23, 39, 55, 160, 237
Racine, Jean, 30, 32, 34, 45, 165, 185, 233, 259, 287, 326, 362, 391
Les Racines du ciel (Gary), 153
Radical Party, 87, 130, 152, 244–245, 277
Radical Socialism, 290
Radiguet, Raymond, 22, 84, 168, 184, 279, 299, 340, 373
Radio-Télévision Française, 356
Radio Tokyo, 375

Radio Tunis, 347
Rafle du Vel' d'Hiver, 299
Raft, George, 301
Ralentir travaux (Breton, Eluard, and Char), 56, 75
Rameau, Jean-Philippe, 179
Ramsbosson, Yvanhoé, 330
Ramuz, Charles-Ferdinand, 285
Ranson, Paul, 251, 394
Raphael, 251
Rapides (du Bouchet), 113
Rassemblement du Peuple Français, 300
Rassemblement pour la République (RPR), 300, 380
Ravages (Leduc), 201
Ravel, Maurice, 132, 136, 289, 300–301, 310, 322, 328
Ray, Man, 62, 96, 139, 269, 301–302, 309, 353
Raymond, Marcel, 259, 291
Raynal, Maurice, 120
Le Rayon vert, 317
Rayonism, 166, 195–196
Raysse Beach (Raysse), 302
Raysse, Martial, 256, 302
Ré, Michel de, 168
Read, Herbert, 134
Réage, Pauline (Dominique Aury), 275
The Récamier, 391
Récits complets (Roche), 315
Reclus, Elisée, 20, 85
Redon, Odilon, 214, 245, 303, 330, 394
Réflexions sur la violence (Sorel), 346
Refus d'obéissance (Giono), 162
Regain (Giono), 162
Le Regard du sourd (Wilson), 252
Reger, Max, 175
La Règle du jeu (film), 38, 96, 205, 243, 306
La Règle du jeu (Leiris), 205
La Règle du Jeu (magazine), 209
Reign of Terror, 366
La Reine morte (Montherlant), 246
Le Rejet de l'état (Revel), 308
Relâche, 79, 336
Reliefs (Duchamp-Villon), 116
La Religieuse, 312
Rembrandt van Rijn, 110, 136, 320, 348
Remi, Georges. See Hergé.
La Remise (Planchon), 287
Remise de peine (Modiano), 243
Remontons les Champs-Elysées, 173
Remorques, 170
Le Rempart des béguines (Mallet-Joris), 221
Le Renard et la boussole (Pinget), 284
Renard, Jean-Claude, 172, 304
Renard, Jules, 361
Renaud et Armide (Cocteau), 42
Renaud, Madeleine, 29–30, 46, 51, 88, 304–305, 363–364
Renault, Louis, 347
La Rencontre (Troyat), 376
Le Rendez-vous de Senlis (Anouilh), 363
Renoir, Auguste, 99, 219, 230, 244, 306, 382
Renoir, Jean, 8, 22, 36, 38, 66, 96, 122, 139, 147, 149, 243, 271, 288, 290, 292, 305–306, 311, 377
Le Repas de bébé/Déjeuner de bébé, 215
Répertoire (Butor), 60, 257
La Répétition (Anouilh), 10
Réponses: 1954–1974 (Sagan), 326
Le Repos du guerrier (Rochefort), 315, 381

Républicains Indépendants, 137
Repulsion, 104
Requiem (Jaccottet), 183
Résidente privilégiée (Casarès), 67
Resistance, 13, 25, 38, 64, 67, 75, 82, 87, 108, 118, 121, 123, 125, 141, 143, 150, 155, 172, 176, 190, 206, 211, 222, 241, 243, 247, 266, 275, 278, 289, 306– 308, 337–338, 342, 354, 357, 375– 376, 381, 387, 389, 401
La Résistance et ses poètes (Seghers), 337
Resnais, Alain, 67, 120, 146, 263, 306–308, 312, 348
Restany, Pierre, 256
El Retablo de las maravillas (Cervantes), 29, 46
Le Retour de Don Camillo, 122
Le Retour de Martin Guerre, 106
Retour de l'U.R.S.S. (Gide), 161
Le Rêve (Rousseau), 322
Revel, Jean-François (Jean-François Ricard), 308
Les Revenentes (Perec), 278
Reverdy, Pierre, 255, 308–309
Révolution, 260
"La Révolution d'abord et toujours," 309
"Révolution des cathédrales" (Clemenceau), 245
Révolution du langage poétique (Kristeva), 192
Révolution/Evolution (Béjart), 40
La Révolution française (G. Lefebvre), 201
La Révolution Surréaliste, 18, 167, 218, 278, 309
Le Revolver à cheveux blancs (Breton), 56
La Revue (Appia), 12
Revue Blanche, 47, 134–135, 385
La Revue du Cinéma, 35
Revue Musicale, 208, 310
Rhinocéros (Ionesco), 30, 180, 361, 363
Riabouchinska, Tatiana, 28
Ricardou, Jean, 256–258, 267, 310
Rich Young and Pretty, 97
"Richard II quarante" (Aragon), 13
Richard III (Shakespeare), 118, 390
Richard II (Shakespeare), 242, 364
Richard, Jean-Pierre, 259
Ricœur, Paul, 249, 310–311
Rideau baissé (Baty), 34
Le Rideau cramoisi, 21
Riefenstahl, Leni, 64
Rien que la terre (Morand), 247
Rif revolt, 309
Rigault, Jean de, 286
Rigaut, Jacques, 112
Right Bank, Paris, 46
Rigodon (Céline), 69
Rilke, Rainer Maria, 213, 383
Rimbaud, Arthur, 81–82, 146, 166–167, 187, 204, 224, 291, 315, 327
Rimsky-Korsakov, Nicolay Andreyevich, 140
Riot of 6 February 1934, 311, 348
Riposte, Port de Bouc (Tazlitsky), 357
Riquier, Georges, 105
Le Rire (Bergson), 42
"Le Rire de la Méduse" (Cixous), 78
Le Rivage des Syrtes (Gracq), 166
The River, 306
Rivera, Diego, 134, 143
Rivette, Jacques, 35, 263, 311–312, 317, 377
Rivière, Jacques, 5, 262, 312, 400
Rivière, Théodore, 148
Robbe-Grillet, Alain, 60, 120, 123, 165, 232, 256–258, 267, 284, 308, 310, 312–313, 331, 343, 345, 373
Robinson Crusoe (Defoe), 373

Robinson, Jacqueline, 261
Roblès, Emmanuel, 293, 313–314
Rocco e i suoi fratelli, 103
Roche, Denis, 315, 359
Roche, Juliette, 164
Roche, Pierre, 148
Rochefort, Christiane, 224, 249, 293, 315, 381
Rodin, Auguste, 52, 80–81, 106, 116, 219, 315–317, 346
Rodin et la sculpture (Bourdelle), 52
Roerich, Nicholas, 325
Rogers, Richard, 70
Rohmer, Bruno, 130
Rohmer, Eric, 35, 73, 263, 294, 317
Roi Candaule (Gide), 214
Le Roi David (Honegger), 175
Le Roi des aulnes (Tournier), 373
Le Roi se meurt, 181
Les Rois mages (Frénaud), 146
Roland Barthes par Roland Barthe (Barthes), 32
Roland Garros stadium, 30
Rolland, Romain, 20, 79, 126, 157, 214, 294, 317–318, 368
Romains, Jules, 123, 188, 262, 318–319, 379, 387, 391
"Le Roman d'aventure" (Rivière), 312
Le Roman du lièvre (Jammes), 184
Le Roman d'un tricheur, 173
Le Roman français depuis 1900 (Boisdeffre), 48
Romeo and Juliet (Shakespeare), 286
Roméo et Jeannette (Anouilh), 363
Roméo et Juliette (ballet), 40, 84
Rommersholm (Ibsen), 364
La Ronde, 97, 269, 279, 341, 381
La Ronde (Schnitzler), 286
La Ronde de nuit (Modiano), 243
Room at the Top, 341
Roosevelt, Franklin D., 177, 186
Rosa Lux (Benedetto), 41
Rosay, Françoise, 136
La Rose de sable (Montherlant), 247
Rose des vents, 347
Rosenquist, James, 144
Rosenstock, Samuel. *See* Tzara, Tristan.
Rosenthal, Gérard, 134
Rosenzweig, Franz, 207
Les Roses de septembre (Maurois), 234
Rossellini, Roberto, 377, 389
Rosso, Medardo, 316
Rostand, Edmond, 50
Rotella, Mimmo, 256
La Rôtisserie de la reine Pédauque (France), 144
Rotozoa I (Tinguely), 371
Rouault, Georges, 109, 204, 230, 319–320, 330, 393
Rouch, Jean, 320
Rouché, Jacques, 211, 274
La Roue 70, 151, 175
Rouen Cathedral, 245
Le Rouge et le noir, 22, 279
Rougé, Edmond, 388
Rougemont, Denis de, 249
Rouleau, Raymond, 118, 321, 367
La Roulotte, 390
Rousseau, Henri, 321–322
Rousseau, Jean-Jacques, 272
"Rousseau Banquet," 322
Roussel, Albert, 178, 322
Roussel, Ker-Xavier, 48
Rousset, Jean, 259, 291

La Route des Flandres (Simon), 343, 401
La Route enchantée, 374
Roy, Claude, 121, 147, 323
Roy, Jules, 8, 12, 156, 178, 293–294, 314, 323
Le Royal, 63
Royal Academy, 132, 189
Royal Ballet, 253
Au royaume des cieux, 169
Rubens, Peter Paul, 136
Rubinstein, Ida, 141, 253, 274, 324
Rude, François, 315
Rudra Béjart Lausanne, 40
La Rue (Maillol), 219
Rue de Rivoli, Paris, 200
"La Rue des Blancs-Manteaux" (song), 168
Rue des Boutiques Obscures (Modiano), 243
Rugby (Honegger), 175
Rugby (Lhôte), 211
La Rupture, 74
Ruskin, John, 295
Russian Ballet. *See* Ballets Russes.
Russian Formalism, 372
Russian Neo-Primitivism, 165
Russian Revolution, 101, 273, 309, 345
Ruy Blas (Hugo), 391
Ruyters, André, 262
Rysselberghe, Elisabeth van, 161
Rysselberghe, Maria van, 161

S

Sabartès, Jaime, 282
Sacco, Nicola, 167
Sachs, Maurice, 201
Sacré-Cœur, Paris, 247
Le Sacre du printemps (ballet), 27, 40, 246, 253, 325, 351
Sade, Marquis de, 32, 37, 157, 204, 315
Sadoyan, Isabelle, 362
Sagan, Françoise, 224, 325–326, 373, 381
Sage, Kay, 355
Saint-Denis, Michel, 89, 91, 367
Saint-Exupéry, Antoine de, 225, 323, 326, 401
Saint Genet, comédien et martyr (Sartre), 158
Saint-Germain-des-Prés, Paris, 34, 62, 136, 168, 202, 273, 292, 327, 334
Saint Ghetto des prêts: Grimoire (Pomerand), 181
Saint Joan (Shaw), 285
Saint-John Perse, 131, 150, 247, 294, 327, 339
Saint-Laurent, Yves, 279
Saint-Lazare prison, 282
Saint-Léger Léger, Alexis. *See* Saint-John Perse.
Saint Matorel (Jacob), 184
Saint-Phalle, Niki de, 256, 371
St. Pierre, Eustache, 316
Saint Pierre, Michel de, 327–328
Saint-Saëns, Camille, 269, 328
Saint-Saturnin (Schlumberger), 336
Saint-Sulpice, 269
Sainte-Clotilde church, 269
La Sainte Face (Frénaud), 146
Les Saints vont en enfer (Cesbron), 71
Une Saison au Congo (Césaire), 71
Sait-on jamais?, 381

Salacrou, Armand, 34, 118, 214, 362, 368
Le Salaire de la peur, 83, 245, 386
Salengro, Roger, 170
Salis, Rodolphe, 349
Salle Garnier, 274
Salle Luxembourg, 88, 363
Salle Récamier, 46
Salle Richelieu, 88
Sallé, Marie, 273
Salmon, André, 33, 184
Salomé (ballet), 324
Salon, 294–295, 315–316, 329–330, 394
Salon d'Art Idéaliste, 103
Salon d'Automne, 101, 106, 116, 133, 194, 197, 201, 231, 281, 283, 294, 322, 330, 357, 392
Salon de la Nationale, 163, 330
Salon de la Section d'Or, 337
Salon des Artistes Français, 330
Salon des Indépendants, 93, 110, 114, 116, 120, 163, 170, 194, 197, 201, 239, 281, 294, 321–322, 330–331, 340
Salon des Tuileries, 148
Salons de la Rose+Croix, 103, 105, 384–385
Salons des refusés, 330
Salvation Army, 289
Samedi Soir, 168
Samson et Dalila (Saint-Saëns), 328
Les Samurai (Kristeva), 192
San Francisco Symphony Orchestra, 246
Sand, George, 233, 280
Le Sang des autres (Beauvoir), 37
Le Sang des bêtes, 146
Le Sang d'un poète, 21, 83
Le Sang noir (Guilloux), 173
Le Sanglier (Bosco), 49
Sans toit ni loi, 386
Sant'Elia, Antonio, 152
Santeuil, Jean, 295
Santley, Joseph, 140
Sappho, 393
Sardey, Victor, 330
"Sarrasine" (Balzac), 32
Sarraute, Nathalie, 30, 123, 165, 256–257, 284, 331–332
Sarrazin, Albertine, 332
Sartre par lui-même, 21
Sartre, Jean-Paul, 7–8, 13, 15, 21, 31–32, 35–37, 62–64, 66, 99, 108, 112, 118, 123, 127–128, 138, 147, 150, 157–158, 163, 168, 176, 178, 188, 201, 209, 224, 226, 232, 235, 238, 247, 254–255, 258, 260, 275, 289, 293, 310–311, 321, 326, 331–334, 351, 359–363, 367, 388, 397, 401
Satie, Erik, 79, 83, 109, 178, 191, 229, 272, 289, 291, 335–336, 344
Saturne: Essai sur Goya (Malraux), 223
Saudades do Brasil (Milhaud), 240
Saül (Gide), 367
Saussure, Ferdinand de, 32, 193, 208, 351
Savannah Bay (Duras), 305
Savary, Alain, 345
Savary, Jérôme, 365
Le Savon (Ponge), 289
La Scène capitale (Jouve), 187
Scève, Maurice, 194
Schaeffer, Pierre, 89–90
Schehadé, Georges, 30, 336, 360
Schéhérazade (ballet), 140, 253, 324
Schiffrin, Jacques, 150
Schlöndorff, Volker, 103
Schlumberger, Jean, 90, 150, 262, 336

Schmitt, Florent, 132
Schnitzler, Arthur, 286
Schoenberg, Arnold, 50–51
Schoendorfer, Pierre, 178
Schola Cantorum, 178, 238, 322, 335
School for Oriental Languages, 275
School of American Ballet, 26
School of Movement, 252
School of Pontoise, 73
Schumann, Maurice, 306
Schwann music catalogue, 301
Schwartz, Solange, 274
Schweick in the Second World War (Brecht), 287
Schweitzer, Albert, 269, 333
Schwitters, Kurt, 371
Scopitone, 205
Scott, Tony, 104
Le Sculpteur des masques (Crommelynck), 92
The Sea Gull (Chekhov), 285, 341
Seashore at Izu (Hiroshige), 244
Seban, Paul, 121
Seberg, Jean, 153, 237
Second Manifeste du surréalisme (Breton), 224
Second Moroccan Crisis. *See* Agadir Crisis.
Second Republic, 225
Second Symphony (Roussel), 322
Second Vatican Council, 72, 327, 400
La Seconde Surprise de l'amour (Marivaux), 287
Le Secret (Redon), 303
Le Secret professionnel (Cocteau), 83
Section d'Or, 114, 120, 163, 170, 194, 281, 283, 337, 392
Section Française de l'Internationale Ouvrière (SFIO), 345, 371
Seghers, Pierre, 337
Sei personaggi in cerca d'autore (Pirandello), 285
Selected Poems (Senghor), 339
Selected Writings (Michaux), 240, 352
Self-Portrait with Seven Fingers (Chagall), 75
Les Semailles et les moissons (Troyat), 376
La Semaison: Carnets (Jaccottet), 183
Séméiotikè (Kristeva), 191
semiotics, 31–32, 35, 351
Semprún, Jorge, 273
Seneca, 67
Senghor, Léopold Sédar, 71, 338–339
Le Sens de la marche (Adamov), 287
Les Sept Couleurs (publishing house), 28
Sept manifestes Dada (Tzara), 377
Les Séquestrés d'Altona (Sartre), 7, 334
Serge, Victor, 134
Serge Lifar (Levinson), 208
"Série noire," 139
Sérieyx, Auguste, 178
Serreau, Jean-Marie, 30, 46, 364
Serres chaudes (Maeterlinck), 217
Serres, Michel, 258
Sérusier, Paul, 44, 48, 250–252, 320, 339, 385, 394
Servan-Schreiber, Jean-Jacques, 7–8, 128, 130
Service d'Ordre Légionnaire, 241
Service du Travail Obligatoire (STO), 241, 307
Seurat, Georges, 44, 134–135, 153–154, 230, 245, 303, 340
The Seven Faces of Woman, 24
Seven Stars Symphony (Koechlin), 191
75 HP, 55
Seyrig, Delphine, 224
Shakespeare, William, 13, 22, 30, 49, 58, 60, 67, 82, 84, 118, 157, 185, 214, 242, 248, 286–287, 361–365, 367–368, 390

Shakespeare Society, 157
Shattuck, Roger, 12
Shaw, George Bernard, 285–286
"She" (Aznavour), 24
Shelley, Percy Bysshe, 19, 233
Shields, Brooke, 221
Ship of Fools, 341
Shklovsky, Viktor, 375
Shoah, 268
Shuman, Mort, 55
Si c'était à refaire, 206
Si j'ai bonne mémoire (Guitry), 173
Une si jolie petite plage, 8, 279
Si le grain ne meurt (Gide), 161
"Si tu t'imagines"(Gréco), 297
Si tu vas chez les femmes (Rochefort), 315
Sic, 213, 255, 340, 347
Sica, Vittorio de, 40
Siegfried (Giraudoux), 163, 188
Siegfried et le Limousin (Giraudoux), 163
Sierra de Teruel, 222
Signac, Paul, 20, 230, 245, 281, 316, 340–341, 393, 395
Le Signe de la croix (Marcel), 225
Le Signe du Lion, 317
Les Signes et les prodiges (Mallet-Joris), 221
Le Signifiant imaginaire (Metz), 239
Signore e Signori, 205
Signoret, Simone, 8, 83, 153, 245, 341
Le Silence, 102
Le Silence de la mer (Vercors), 123, 237, 387
Le Silence est d'or, 78
Les Silences du Colonel Bramble (Maurois), 233
Silone, Ignazio, 134
Sima, Joseph, 167
Simenon, Georges, 341–342
Simon, Claude, 256–257, 294, 342–343, 401
Simon, Michel, 66, 122, 265
Simon, Pierre-Henri, 7, 249
Simon le pathétique (Giraudoux), 163
Simondo, Piero, 207
Le Simoun (Lenormand), 34
Simulacre (Leiris), 205
Simultanism, 100–101
Sinclair, Upton, 79
Singer, Isaac, 289
Siodmak, Robert, 237
Sion-Vaudrémont, 31
Siqueiros, David Alfaro, 143
The Sirens' Song: Selected Essays of Maurice Blanchot (Blanchot), 45
Sisley, Alfred, 244, 281
Situationist International (SI), 97–98, 182, 202, 207, 343–344, 385
Siva, 40
Les Six, 21, 175, 178, 191, 240, 289, 291, 335, 344
six contes moraux (Rohmer), 317
6 819 000 litres d'eau par seconde (Butor), 60
Le 6 octobre (Romains), 319
Sjöström, Victor, 102
Skibine, George, 274
Slade School, London, 132
Slaughtered Ox (Rembrandt), 348
Slavenska, Mia, 292
Sobrino, Francisco, 171
Socialism, 20, 47, 54, 57, 71, 76, 137, 152–153, 164, 191, 219–220, 225, 238, 244, 258, 275, 290, 318, 371, 375
Socialisme fasciste (Drieu La Rochelle), 112

Socialist Party, 3, 47, 57, 129, 137, 147, 175, 345
Socialist Realism, 143, 204, 206, 260, 356
Société des Artistes français, 295, 330
Société des Artistes Indépendants, 330
Société des Auteurs, Compositeurs et Editeurs de Musique, 294
Société des Gens de Lettres, 294
La Société du spectacle (Debord), 97–98
Socrate (ballet), 336
Sodome et Gomorrhe (Giraudoux), 42
La Soif et la faim (Ionesco), 364
Soigne ton gauche, 82
Un Soir au cinéma (Isou), 207
La Soirée des proverbes (Schehadé), 336
Sokolova, Lydia, 109, 325
Sol de la montagne (du Bouchet), 113
Solax, 174
Soldats en marche (Villon), 392
Soleil cou-coupé (Césaire), 71
Le Soleil se couche sur l'Adriatique (Dorgelès), 110
Sollers, Philippe, 191, 256, 345–346, 359
Le Solstice de juin (Montherlant), 246
The Somme, 346, 387, 400
Une Somme de poésie (la Tour du Pin), 196
Somme toute (C. Roy), 323
La Sonate et les trois messieurs (Tardieu), 356
Song of Solomon, 399
"Songe" (Jouve), 187, 246
"Les Sons et les parfums dans l'air du soir" (Debussy), 335
Sophocles, 118, 361
Sorbonne, 9, 25, 36, 60, 110, 123, 151, 180, 196, 201–202, 208–209, 220, 236, 259, 267, 275, 277, 295, 308, 311, 333, 338, 344, 358, 365, 386, 392, 398
Sorel, Georges, 277, 346–347
La Sortie des usines Lumière, 215
Le Souffle au cœur, 221
Le Soulier de satin (P. Claudel), 30, 82, 88, 304
Soupault, Philippe, 56, 213, 255, 347, 353
La Souriante Madame Beudet, 117
La Souricière (Cardinal), 65
Sous de grands vents obscurs (Renard), 304
Sous la lampe (Fargue), 131
Sous le soleil de Satan (Bernanos), 43
Sous les toits de Paris, 66, 79
The Southerner, 306
Soutine, Chaim, 62, 347–348
Souvenirs d'un marchand de tableaux (Vollard), 394
Souvenirs écran (Ollier), 267
Souvenirs et notes de travail d'un acteur (Dullin), 118
Souvenirs pour demain (Barrault), 30
Souvenirs sur le Théâtre Libre (Antoine), 11
Souvestre, Pierre, 218
Souviens-toi de Tahiti, France en 1961 (Raysse), 302
Spanish Civil War, 43, 67, 143, 190, 222, 226, 233, 273, 278, 283, 291, 308, 333, 342–343, 348, 397
Le Spectre de la rose (Fokine), 141, 189, 253
Speculum de l'autre femme (Irigaray), 181
Spessivtseva, Olga, 212, 274
Sphere Screen (Morellet), 171
Der Spiegel, 129
Spiegelberg, Herbert, 311
Spielberg, Steven, 377
Spira, Françoise, 363
Spoerri, Daniel, 256
Le Square (Duras), 121
Stalin, Josef, 20, 151, 177, 206, 223, 260
Stalinism, 13, 64, 134, 151, 202, 238, 260, 371, 382

Les Stances à Sophie (Rochefort), 315
Stanislavsky, Constantin, 285
Stanze (Pleynet), 288
Starobinski, Jean, 259, 291
Staryi i novyi balet (Levinson), 208
Stavisky, 308, 348–349
Stavisky Affair, 254, 308, 311, 348–349, 369
Stein, Gertrude, 231, 273
Stein, Joel, 171
Steinem, Gloria, 332
Steinlen, Théophile-Alexandre, 20, 79, 349–350
Stendhal (Marie-Henry Beyle), 13, 22, 67, 162, 224, 279, 299, 357
Stendhal et le beylisme (Blum), 47
Stendhal romancier (Bardèche), 28
Stéphane le Glorieux (Schlumberger), 336
Sternberg, Josef von, 103
Sternberg, Jacques, 17
Stieglitz, Alfred, 301
Stockhausen, Karlheinz, 238
Stockholm Dansmuseet, 14
The Story of Bip (Marceau), 224
Strasbourg-Saint-Denis, Paris, 205
Strauss, Mme. Emile, 295
Strauss, Richard, 175
Stravinsky, Igor, 26, 50–51, 109, 132, 140–141, 178, 238, 245, 252–253, 285, 289, 310, 325, 350–351, 371
A Streetcar Named Desire (T. Williams), 15, 84, 321
Stresemann, Gustav, 57
Strindberg, August, 18, 46, 390
Stroyberg, Annette, 381
Structuralism, 9–10, 31–32, 106, 128, 158, 193, 209, 216, 239, 258–259, 291, 310, 346, 351–352, 359–360, 372
"Structure, Sign and Play in the Discourse of the Human Sciences" (Derrida), 106
Structures (Boulez), 51
Les Structures élémentaires de la parenté (Lévi-Strauss), 209
Studio des Champs-Elysées, 34, 46, 66, 185
Studio Wacker, 292
Sueur de sang (Jouve), 187
Suite bergamasque (Debussy), 98
Suite in F (Roussel), 322
The Sun Also Rises, 169
Supervielle, Jules, 275, 286, 352
Supplément au voyage de Cook (Giraudoux), 363
The Suppliants (Aeschylus), 30
Suprematism, 74
Sur la route (Bruant), 58
Sur le passage de quelques personnes à travers une assez courte unité de temps, 98
Sur Proust (Revel), 308
Sur Racine (Barthes), 32
Le Surcroît (du Bouchet), 113
Surrealism, 6, 11–14, 16, 18, 20, 33, 46, 49, 55–57, 59–60, 62, 71, 75, 79–80, 83, 88, 96, 98, 108, 112, 113, 124, 131, 134, 136, 139, 146, 166–167, 181, 183, 186, 202, 204, 206, 218–219, 221, 223–224, 229, 240, 243, 265, 269, 271–272, 278, 281, 292, 297, 302, 304, 308–309, 315, 321–322, 336, 340, 343, 347, 353–355, 377–378, 381, 385, 389, 392, 395–396
Le Surréalisme au service de la révolution, 309
Le Surréalisme contre la Révolution (Vailland), 382
Le Surréalisme Révolutionnaire, 354
Surréalisme Révolutionnaire, 354
Le Sursis (Sartre), 334
Surveiller et punir: Naissance de la prison (Foucault), 142
The Suspended Step of the Stork, 248

Suzanne et le Pacifique (Giraudoux), 163
Swann in Love, 58
Swedish Academy, 318
Swedish Ballet, 79
La Sylphide (ballet), 273
Les Sylphides (ballet), 109, 140, 189
Sylvia (ballet), 405
La Symbolique du mal (Ricœur), 311
Symbolist Movement, 27, 82, 91, 103, 105, 131–133, 139, 142, 148, 154, 185, 213, 214, 217, 227, 244, 296, 321, 330, 364, 379, 383, 399
La Symphonie fantastique, 29
Symphonie monotone (Klein), 191
La Symphonie ρastorale (Delannoy), 65, 99, 161, 249
Symphonie pour un homme seul (Schaeffer and Henry), 90
Symphonie sur un chant montagnard français (d'Indy), 178
Symphony in C Major (Dukas), 117
Symphony in D Minor (Franck), 269
Synge, John Millington, 67
Synthetism, 44, 153, 251
Système de la mode (Barthes), 32, 352
Système de la peinture (Pleynet), 288
S/Z (Barthes), 32

T

La Table de toilette (Vuillard), 395
Le Tableau des merveilles (Prévert), 29, 46
The Tabou, 168
tachism, 132
Un Tactiturne, 228
Tailleferre, Germaine, 191, 344
Talbert d'Arc, Jehanne Pauline Marie, 43
Le Talisman (Sérusier), 339
Tallchief, Marjorie, 292
Tamerlan des cœurs (Obaldia), 265
The Taming of the Shrew (Shakespeare), 368
Tancrède (Fargue), 131
Tanguy, Yves, 355
Tant que la terre durera (Troyat), 376
Tarabant, A., 367
Taras, John, 274
Tardieu, Jean, 356
Tarassov, Lev. *See* Troyat, Henri.
Taris, 389
The Tarot, 282
Tarot Garden, 371
Tartuffe (Molière), 188, 287, 363
Taslitzky, Boris, 204, 260, 356–357
Tati, Jacques, 82, 294, 358
Tavernier, Bertrand, 255
Un Taxi pour Tobrouk, 23
Taylor, Paul, 261
Technique de mon langage musical (Messiaen), 238
Tedesco, Jean, 306
Teilhard de Chardin, Pierre, 358–359
Tel Quel, 191, 288, 315, 345, 359
Temps, 208, 243, 359
Le Temps accompli (C. Mauriac), 232
Au temps de l'harmonie (Signac), 341
Le Temps des merveilles: Œuvres poétiques 1938–1978 (Seghers), 337
Le Temps du mépris (Malraux), 222

Le Temps et l'autre (Levinas), 207
Le Temps immobile (C. Mauriac), 232
Les Temps Modernes, 7–8, 37, 147, 178, 229, 238, 333–334, 359–360, 388
Temps Nouveaux, 384
10, 301
Tendres stocks (Morand), 247
La Tentation de Saint-Antoine (Redon), 394
La Tentation totalitaire (Revel), 308
Teresa of Avila, Saint, 187, 397
Terraqué (Guillevic), 172
La Terre (Zola), 361
Terre à bonheur (Guillevic), 172
Terre des hommes (Saint-Exupéry), 326
La Terre du sacre (Renard), 304
La Terre est ronde (Salacrou), 118, 362
La Terre et les rêveries de la volonté (Bachelard), 25
Terre lointaine (Green), 169
Terre promise (Maurois), 234
Tessa (Giraudoux), 363
"Le Testament" (Brassens), 54
Le Testament d'Orphée, 29
Testament de Dieu (Lévy), 209
Le Testament d'un poète juif assassiné (Wiesel), 398
Testament phonographe (Ferré), 136
Tête (Tinguely), 371
La Tête contre les murs, 23
La Tête contre les murs (H. Bazin), 36
Tête d'or (P. Claudel), 82
Tetley, Glen, 274, 325
Theater of the Absurd, 3–4, 18, 21, 30, 38, 46–47, 179, 186, 304, 356, 360–361, 388, 392
Theater of Cruelty. *See* Theater of the Absurd.
The Theatre Advancing (Craig), 91
Théâtre Alfred Jarry, 18–19, 321, 392
Théâtre Antoine, 11, 157, 332, 361, 367
Theatre Arts Monthly, 208
Théâtre d'Art, 142, 213
Théâtre de chambre (Tardieu), 356
Théâtre de France, 30, 305, 363
Théâtre de Grenelle, 18
Théâtre de la Cité, 45
Théâtre de la Cité, Villeurbanne, 286–287, 362, 369
Théâtre de la Comédie, 287
Théâtre de la Cruauté, 19
Théâtre de la Danse, 253
Théâtre de la Gaîté–Montparnasse, 368
Théâtre de la Huchette, 336, 361
Théâtre de la Monnaie, 40
Théâtre de la Porte Saint-Martin, 50
Théâtre de la Renaissance, 50, 157, 173
Théâtre de l'Ambigu, 224
Théâtre de l'Aquarium, 252
Théâtre de l'Atelier, 18, 29, 31, 66, 118, 321, 362, 390
Théâtre de l'Athénée, 41, 188, 363
Théâtre de l'Avenue, 18, 34, 185, 285
Théâtre de la Ville, 261
Théâtre de l'Odéon, 11, 30, 46–47, 67, 88, 157, 252, 287, 305, 361, 363
Théâtre de l'Œuvre, 157, 186, 213–214, 217, 364
Théâtre de Lutèce, 47
Théâtres des Armées, 405
Théâtre des Arts, 31, 118, 285
Théâtre des Champs-Elysées, 325
Théâtre des Mathurins, 67, 286
Le Théâtre des métamorphoses (Ricardou), 310

Théâtre des Nations, 30, 40, 57
Théâtre des Quatre Saisons, 31
Théâtre du Châtelet, 272, 324, 364
Théâtre du Gymnase, 50, 364
Théâtre du Marais, 321
Théâtre du peuple, 290
Le Théâtre du peuple (Rolland), 157, 368
Théâtre du Rond-Point, 30
Théâtre du Silence, 261
Théâtre du Soleil, 242, 252, 365–366
Théâtre du Travail, 64
Théâtre du Vieux-Colombier, 19, 88–91, 118, 188, 321, 336, 366–
        367, 390
Théâtre Edouard VII, 321
Le Théâtre et son double (Artaud), 18
Théâtre Français. See Comedie-Française.
Théâtre Hébertot, 42
Théâtre Libre, 11, 121, 157, 213, 361, 367
Théâtre Marigny, 304
Théâtre Michel, 41
Théâtre Mogador, 88
Théâtre Montparnasse, 31, 34, 185, 367–368
Théâtre National Ambulant Gémier, 157
Théâtre National de Chaillot, 369
Théâtre National Populaire (TNP), 22, 46, 54, 67, 105–106, 157,
        287, 362, 368–369, 386, 390
Théâtre Robert-Houdin, 236
Théâtre Sarah-Bernhardt, 45, 118, 261
Theatre Street (Karsavina), 189
Théâtre vivant, 363
Théo ou le temps neuf (Pinget), 284
Théorie de la littérature (Todorov), 372
La Théorie de l'intuition dans la phenomenologie de Husserl
        (Levinas), 207
Thérèse Desqueyroux (F. Mauriac), 146, 233, 255
Thérèse Desqueyroux, 146, 255
Thérèse et Isabelle (Leduc), 201
Thérèse Raquin, 136
Thésée (Gide), 161
Thesmar, Ghisline, 274
They Drive by Night, 83
Les Thibault (Martin du Gard), 123, 144, 228
Third (Communist) International, 80
Third of May, 1808 (Goya), 283
Third Piano Sonata (Boulez), 51
Third Republic, 47, 57, 111, 137, 144, 146, 235, 266, 278, 311, 348,
        369–370, 389, 401
Third Symphony (Roussel), 322
Third Symphony (Saint-Saëns) , 269
Thomas Aquinas, Saint, 226
Thomas l'imposteur (Cocteau), 84
Thomism, 226
Thomson, Virgil, 50
Thoreau, Henry David, 301
Thorez, Maurice, 147, 254, 345, 370–371
The Thousand and One Nights, 140
The Three Must-Get-Theres, 212
Three-Penny Opera (Brecht), 34, 368
Tierra sin pan, 59
Tiger at the Gates (Fry), 163
Till Eulenspiegel (ballet), 254
Time, 128–129, 248
Times (London), 140, 330
Timon of Athens (Shakespeare), 58
Tinguely, Jean, 256, 371
Tintin (Hergé), 371–372

Tire-au-flanc, 306
Tirez sur le pianiste, 23, 377
To Catch a Thief, 386
Todorov, Tzvetan, 191, 372
Tokyo Olympics, 260
Tolstoy, Leo, 11, 367, 376
Tomb of the Unknown Soldier, Paris, 249
Le Tombeau de Couperin (Ravel), 301
Tombeau d'Orphée (Emmanuel), 125
Toni, 271, 306
Le Tonnerre et les anges (Roy), 156
Topaz, 255
Topor, Roland, 17
La Tosca, 306
Totalité et infini (Levinas), 207
Le Totémisme aujourd'hui (Lévi-Strauss), 209
Touchez pas au grisbi, 38, 149
Toulemon, Elisabeth, 187
Toulouse-Lautrec, Henri de, 58, 134, 148, 239, 349–350, 382
Toumanova, Tamara, 28, 292
Le Tour du malheur (Kessel), 190
La Tour prends garde (Arrabal), 17
La Tourette monastery, 200
Tournier, Michel, 293, 372–373
Tous contre tous (Adamov), 364
Tous les hommes sont mortels (Beauvoir), 37
Toussaint-Louverture, 71
Tout compte fait (Beauvoir), 37
Toute la mémoire du monde, 308
Toute la vérité (Garaudy), 152
Toutes les femmes sont fatales (C. Mauriac), 231
tradition de qualité, 36, 38, 66, 139, 269, 373–374, 377
Trafic, 358
La Tragédie (Picasso), 282
La Tragédie du roi Christophe (Césaire), 71
La Trahison des clercs (Benda), 41
Traité de bave et d'éternité (Isou), 206
Traité de savoir-vivre à l'usage des jeunes générations (Vaneigem),
        385
La Transfiguration de notre Seigneur Jésus-Christ (Messiaen), 239
Transparences (Picabia), 281
Trattato della Pittura (Leonardo da Vinci), 337
Trauner, Alexandre, 66
Travail d'homme (Roblès), 314
Trenet, Charles, 374
Trente et un sonnets (Guillevic), 172
Le Très-Haut (Blanchot), 45
Le Tricorne (ballet), 229
Le Tricycle (Arrabal), 17
Trinity College, Dublin, 38
Trintignant, Jean-Louis, 205, 381
Triolet, André, 375
Triolet, Elsa, 13, 91, 123, 375–376
Le Triomphe de l'amour (Marivaux), 67, 369
Tripes d'or (Crommelynck), 92
Triptyque Pont-Aven (Sérusier), 339
Tristan, Flora, 153
Tristes tropiques (Lévi-Strauss), 209, 351
Trocadéro, Paris, 157, 368
391, 197, 255
Trois chambres à Manhattan (Simenon), 342
"Les Trois Cloches" (Les Compagnons de la Chanson), 281
Trois essais de mythologie romantique (Poulet), 291
Trois femmes (Magritte), 218
Les Trois Gouttes de sang (Faure), 132
Les Trois Livres (Pleynet), 288

Trois morceaux en forme de poire (Satie), 335
Les Trois Mousquetaires (Dumas *père*), 287
Trois musiciens (Zadkine), 405
Trois poèmes du Livre de la jungle (Koechlin), 191
Troisgros, Jean, 260–261
Troisième Belvédère (Mandiargues), 223
Le Troisième Corps (Cixous), 78
Troisième République. *See* Third Republic.
Trojan War, 163
Tropiques, 204
Tropismes (Sarraute), 256, 331–332
Trotsky, Leon, 62, 80, 134, 222, 309
Troyat, Henri, 376
Truffaut, François, 21–23, 35, 79, 83, 104, 164, 198, 215, 248, 263, 267, 294, 306, 311, 317, 373, 377, 389
Truman, Harry S, 177
Tu m'as sauvé la vie (Guitry), 135
Tudor, Marie, 67
Turangalîla (Messiaen), 238
Turgenev, Ivan, 233
Turlututu (Marcel), 50
Turner, J. M. W., 244
Turpin, Dick, 71
Twelfth Night (Shakespeare), 242, 287
291 Gallery, New York, 301
Tzara, Tristan, 55, 61–62, 88, 95, 213, 340, 377–378

U

Ubu cocu (Jarry), 186
Ubu enchaîné (Jarry), 186
Ubu roi (Jarry), 157, 185–186, 214, 364, 369
Uderzo, Albert, 20
Uhde, Wilhelm, 101
Ulcérations (Perec), 278
Ulysses (Joyce), 31
Un de Baumugnes (Giono), 162
Un-deux-trois, 279
Un Dimanche à la Grande Jatte (Seurat), 44
Un Rameau de la nuit (Bosco), 49
Unanimism, 117, 124, 163, 318–319, 337, 379, 391
The Underground Lovers and Other Experiments (Tardieu), 356
L'Une et l'autre, 8
Ungaretti, Giuseppe, 327
Unik, Pierre, 59
Union Artistique of Alphonse Dumas, 394
Union des Démocrates pour la République (UDR), 300, 379–380
L'Union libre (Breton), 56
Union pour la Démocratie Française (UDF), 300, 380
Union pour la Nouvelle République, 300, 379
Unité d'Habitation, 200
United Nations Educational, Scientific, and Cultural Organization (UNESCO), 342, 347
United Nations General Assembly, 338
United States Congress, 374
Universal Studios, 79
Université de la danse, 212
University of Aix-en-Provence, 306
University of Algiers, 64
University of Bucharest, 180
University of Edinburgh, 291
University of Lille, 28
University of Paris, 191, 196, 202, 272, 311, 344

University of Paris VIII, 78
University of Paris, Nanterre, 35, 85, 236
University of Perpignan, 199
University of Strasbourg, 9
University of Virginia, 169
University of Zurich, 291
Upanishads, 397
Updike, John, 284
Uranus (Aymé), 23
Urbanism, 379
U.S.A. 1927 (Morand), 248
l'usage des jeunes générations (Vaneigem), 385
Usage du temps (Follain), 141
Ussachevsky, Vladimir, 90
Utrillo, Maurice, 380, 382
Utter, André, 382

V

Les Vacances de Monsieur Hulot, 358
Vaché, Jacques, 98
Vadim, Roger, 29, 168, 279 , 381–382
La Vagabonde (Colette), 86
Vailland, Roger, 167, 294, 381–382
Vaillant-Couturier, Paul, 20, 220
Vaincre (Fougeron), 143
Valadon, Suzanne, 380, 382
Valentino, Rudolph, 140
Valéry, Paul, 41, 161, 231, 262, 383–384
Vallat, Xavier, 241
La Vallée heureuse (Roy), 323
Valéry, Paul, 5
Vallès, Jules, 280
Vallotton, Félix, 20, 48, 251–252, 330, 384–385, 394
La Valse (C. Claudel), 81
La Valse des toréadors (Anouilh), 10
Les Valseuses, 106
Les Vampires, 136
Vampyr, 126
Vandal, Marcel, 18
Vaneigem, Raoul, 385
Vanel, Charles, 386
Vangeon, Henri (Henri Ghéon), 262
Vanzetti, Bartolomeo, 167
Les Varais (Chardonne), 76
Varda, Agnès, 103, 386
Varèse, Edgar, 90
Variations, interlude et final sur un thème de Remeau (Dukas), 117
Varo, Remedios, 139
Varouna (Green), 169
Vasarely, Victor, 171, 386–387
Vasarely, Yvaral, 387
Vatican, 3, 227, 235
Vauxcelles, Louis, 53, 93, 133
Veil Law, 224
Veil, Simone, 224
Le Veilleur de nuit (Guitry), 173
Velázquez, Diego Rodriguez de Silva, 160, 282
Vendredi, ou les limbes du Pacifique (Tournier), 373
Venice Film Festival, 56, 64, 83, 312
Le Venin (Bernstein), 364
Du vent dans les branches de sassafras (Obaldia), 265
Vent de sable (Kessel), 189

Le Vent Paraclet (Tournier), 373
Vénus de Meudon (Arp), 17
Vercors, 123, 237, 387
Verdun, 140, 203, 278, 317, 319, 346, 387, 400
Verdy, Violette, 274
Vergé, Roger, 260
La Vérité, 29
Verlaine, Paul, 132, 136, 394
Verne, Jules, 237
Verneuil, Henri, 40, 135
Verret, François, 261
Vers et Prose, 142
Vers une architecture (Le Corbusier), 152, 200
Versailles, 171, 374, 400
Versant de l'âge (Emmanuel), 125
Verses (du Bouchet), 113
Vertume et Pomone (C. Claudel), 81
Vestris, Gaéton, 273
Vetsera, Marie, 97
Vézelay, basilica of, 324
Vian, Boris, 58, 168, 280, 327, 387–389
Vichy government, 3, 47, 66, 76, 96–97, 127, 138, 141, 144, 146,
     156, 163, 170, 177, 206, 211, 226, 233, 235, 241, 248–249,
     265–266, 268, 278, 281, 299, 307, 323, 359, 370, 389, 401
Victimes du devoir (Ionesco), 367
Victor ou les enfants au pouvoir (Vitrac), 18, 392
La Vida es sueño (Calderón de la Barca), 18, 118
Le Vide (Klein), 15, 190
La Vie (Ozenfant), 270, 282
La Vie à deux ou trois (Pleynet), 288
Vie de Beethoven (Rolland), 317
La Vie de l'art théâtral des origines à nos jours (Baty and Chav-
     ance), 34
La Vie de Noverre (Levinson), 208
La Vie devant soi (Ajar), 153, 341
"La Vie en rose" (Piaf), 281
La Vie est à nous, 290, 306
La Vie est un roman, 308
Vie et aventures de Salavin (Duhamel), 117
Vie et mort d'Emile Ajar (Gary), 153
La Vie immédiate (Eluard), 124
La Vie mode d'emploi (Perec), 278
Vie Moderne, 340
Vie privée, 220
La Vie quotidienne dans le monde moderne (H. Lefebvre), 202
La Vie unanime (Romains), 379
La Vie, l'amour, la mort, 205
La Vieille Dame indigne, 8
Vielé-Griffin, Francis, 184
La Vierge de Paris (Jouve), 187
Vierne, Louis, 269
Vietminh, 177–178
Vietnam War, 41, 158, 165, 236, 252, 268, 308
Vieux-Colombier, Théâtre du. See Théâtre du Vieux-Colombier.
Vigo, Boris, 389
Vigo, Jean, 65, 288, 389
Vilar, Jean, 22–23, 29, 67, 157, 265, 118, 287–288, 362, 367–369,
     390–391
Vildrac, Charles, 379, 391
Villa Medici, 294
Villa Oasis; ou, les Faux-Bourgeois (Dabit), 95
Villa Savoye, 200
La Ville de la chance (Wiesel), 398
Villemessant, H. de, 138
Villon, François, 54
Villon, Jacques, 114, 116, 120, 136, 337, 391–392

Le Vin est tiré (Desnos), 108
Les XX, 103
XX Cantos (Emmanuel), 125
Vingt-cinq Poèmes (Tzara), 377
Le Viol (Magritte), 218
Le Viol de Lucrèce (Obey), 367
The Violent Bear It Away (O'Connor), 199
Vipère au poing (Bazin), 36
Virgil, 54, 162
Virgile, non (Wittig), 399
Les Visages de la danse (Levinson), 208
Visconti, Luchino, 103
Vision After the Sermon (Bernard), 44
La Vision après le sermon (Gauguin), 153–154
Les Visiteurs du soir, 14, 66, 292
Vitrac, Roger, 18, 392
Viva Maria, 221, 248
Vivien, Renée, 392–393
Vivre à Madère (Chardonne), 76
Vivre pour vivre, 205
Vivre sa vie, 164
Vlaminck, Maurice, 106, 133, 148, 227, 230–231, 393
La Vogue, 134, 301
Voice of America, 57
La Voie lactée, 59, 284
La Voie royale (Malraux), 222
Le Voile d'Orphée (Schaeffer and Henry), 90
Voir la figure (Chardonne), 76
Les Voix du silence (Malraux), 223
La Voix humaine (Cocteau), 41, 84
Vol de nuit (Saint-Exupéry), 326
Le Voleur, 221
Vollard, Ambroise, 93, 282, 393–394
Le Volontaire et l'involontaire (Ricœur), 311
Volonté de puissance (Dubuffet), 114
Volontés, 71
Volpone (Jonson), 118, 318
Voltaire, 194, 233
Voronca, Ilane, 55
La Vouivre (Aymé), 23
Voulez-vous jouer avec môa? (Marcel), 50, 362
Vous les entendez? (Sarraute), 332
Voyage au bout de la nuit (Céline), 68–69
Le Voyage dans la lune, 237
Le Voyage sans fin (Wittig and Zeig), 399
Le Voyageur sans bagage (Anouilh), 286
Le Voyeur (Robbe-Grillet), 313
Le Voyou, 205
Vuillard, Edouard, 48, 214, 227, 245, 250–252, 330, 339, 385, 394–
     395
VVV, 57, 395–396

W

W ou le souvenir d'enfance (Perec), 277
Waehner, Karin, 261
Waetjen, Otto von, 197
Wagner, Richard, 51, 166, 175, 178
Walsh, Raoul, 83, 122
Walsin-Esterhazy, Ferdinand, 111
War (A.D. MCMXIV) (Ray), 301
Warner Bros., 59
Wasserman, Dale, 55

Waterloo, 386
Watson, Bobby, 361
Watt (Beckett), 38
The Wave Before (Rodin), 316
Weber, Carl Maria von, 141
Weber, Jean-Paul, 259
Webern, Anton von, 51
Weekend, 165
Weil, Simone, 5, 348, 397
Welles, Orson, 36, 248, 386
Wells, H. G., 79
Wells Ballet, 274
Wenders, Wim, 248
Wesker, Arnold, 365
Whale, James, 140
Whirlpool, 169
Whitman, Walt, 187, 301, 379
Whoroscope (Beckett), 38
Widor, Charles-Marie, 269–270
Wiesel, Elie, 398
Wigman, Mary, 261
Wilbur, Richard, 384
The Wild Duck (Ibsen), 367
Wilder, Billy, 237
Willette, Adolphe, 20
Williams, Robin, 39
Williams, Tennessee, 15, 57, 84, 169, 321
Williams, William Carlos, 347
Willy. *See* Gauthier-Villars, Henry.
Wilson, Georges, 22, 369
Wilson, Harold, 258
Wilson, Robert, 252
Wilson, Woodrow, 374
Winged Victory of Samothrace, 191
A Winter's Tale (Shakespeare), 367
Winters, Yvor, 383
Wittgenstein, Ludwig, 311
Wittig, Monique, 249, 399
Wolff, Adolf, 301
Wolman, Gil, 207
A Woman Killed with Kindness (Heywood), 367
Work in Progress (Joyce), 38
World War I, 3, 5, 11–12, 16, 28, 31, 43, 50, 53–54, 56–57, 62, 68–69,
    74–75, 77, 79, 90, 92–95, 101, 110, 112, 115–120, 124, 126,
    136, 140, 145, 150–151, 157, 161–164, 168–169, 171, 173, 177,
    189, 194, 197, 203, 212–214, 217, 225–229, 233–234, 241, 247,
    255, 262, 265, 273, 275–276, 278–279, 283, 285, 295–296, 299,
    306, 312, 317–320, 322, 336, 340–341, 345–347, 350–351, 354,
    364, 367, 369–370, 374, 377–378, 387, 389, 400–401, 406
World War II, 3, 5, 7, 9, 13, 15, 20, 25, 28–29, 31, 35, 41, 43, 46,
    50, 54–55, 57, 59, 62, 65, 68–69, 71, 75–77, 79, 82–83, 87–88,
    91, 96–97, 102, 106, 108, 110, 112–114, 121, 123–127, 134,
    136, 138–139, 141, 143–145, 148, 150, 153, 155, 157–159,
    161–162, 168–170, 172, 176–177, 180–181, 184, 186–188, 190,
    194, 196, 200, 205–206, 208, 211–212, 217–218, 221–222, 229,
    235, 237, 240–241, 243, 245–246, 248–249, 254, 260, 262,
    264–265, 267–269, 273, 277–279, 281, 286, 289, 291–292,
    299–300, 304, 307–308, 310–311, 313–314, 319, 323–324,
    326–327, 333–334, 337–338, 342–343, 345, 347, 351, 354–363,
    368–369, 371–372, 374–375, 381, 387, 389–390, 393, 395, 397,
    399–400, 405
World's Fairs (1878, 1895, 1900), 370
Wyler, William, 36

X

Xenakis, Iannis, 238

Y

"Y a d'la joie" (song), 77
Yaël (Jabès), 183
Yale University, 106
Yeats, William Butler, 383
Les Yeux bleus cheveux noirs (Duras), 121
Les Yeux d'Elsa (Aragon), 13
Les Yeux d'Ezéchiel sont ouverts (Abellio), 3
Yourcenar, Marguerite, 12, 294, 403–404
Youskevitch, Igor, 292
Yukel (Jabès), 183
Yvaral, 171

Z

Zadkine, Osip, 405
Zale, Tony, 71
Zambelli, Carlotta, 273, 405
Zazie dans le métro, 220, 297
Zecca, Ferdinand, 274
Zeig, Sande, 399
Zéro de conduite (Vigo), 389
Ziegfeld Follies, 25, 242
Zola, Emile, 11, 56, 72–73, 76, 111, 136, 138, 149, 210, 279–280,
    306, 319, 361, 367, 376
Zolotoe runo, 165
La Zone verte (Dabit), 95
Zou Zou, 25
Zweig, Stefan, 318

ISBN 0-8103-8482-5